Oxford Handbook of
Evolutionary
Psychology

Bob,

all best wishes,

Ian.

Oxford Handbook of
Evolutionary Psychology

Edited by

R.I.M. Dunbar

School of Biological Sciences, University of Liverpool

and

Louise Barrett

Department of Psychology, University of Lethbridge

OXFORD

UNIVERSITY PRESS

OXFORD
UNIVERSITY PRESS

Great Clarendon Street, Oxford OX2 6DP

Oxford University Press is a department of the University of Oxford.
It furthers the University's objective of excellence in research, scholarship,
and education by publishing worldwide in

Oxford New York

Auckland Cape Town Dar es Salaam Hong Kong Karachi
Kuala Lumpur Madrid Melbourne Mexico City Nairobi
New Delhi Shanghai Taipei Toronto

With offices in

Argentina Austria Brazil Chile Czech Republic France Greece
Guatemala Hungary Italy Japan Poland Portugal Singapore
South Korea Switzerland Thailand Turkey Ukraine Vietnam

Oxford is a registered trade mark of Oxford University Press
in the UK and in certain other countries

Published in the United States
by Oxford University Press Inc., New York

British Library Cataloguing in Publication Data

Data available

Library of Congress Cataloging in Publication Data

Data available

ISBN 978-0-19-856830-8

1 3 5 7 9 10 8 6 4 2

Typeset in Minion
by Cepha Imaging Pvt Ltd, Bangalore, India
Printed in Great Britain
on acid-free paper by
Biddles Ltd. King's Lynn, UK

Contents

Contributors

Dr Robert Aunger
Disease Control and Vector Biology Unit
Department of Infectious and Tropical Diseases
London School of Hygiene and Tropical
Medicine
London
UK

Professor Simon Baron-Cohen,
Autism Research Centre,
Psychiatry Department,
Cambridge University,
Cambridge,
UK

Dr Louise Barrett
Department of Psychology,
University of Lethbridge,
Lethbridge AL,
Canada

Professor Robert Barton
Department of Anthropology,
University of Durham,
Durham,
UK

Professor Jay Belsky
Institute for the Study of Children, Families
and Social Issues
Birkbeck University of London
London,
UK

Professor Tamas Bereczkei
Institute of Psychology
Janus Pannonius University,
Pécs,
Hungary

Dr Samuel Bowles
Behavioral Sciences program
Santa Fé Institute
Santa Fé, NM
USA

Professor Robert Boyd
Department of Anthropology
University of California
Los Angeles, CA
USA

Professor Redouan Bshary
Institut de Zoologie
Université de Neuchâtel
Neuchâtel
Switzerland

Dr Joseph Bulbulia
Department of Religious Studies,
Victoria University of Wellington,
Wellington,
New Zealand

Dr Josep Call
Max Planck Institute for Evolutionary
Anthropology
Leipzig
Germany

Professor Anne Campbell
Department of Psychology
Durham University
Durham
UK

Dr Joseph Carroll
English Department
University of Missouri – St. Louis
St. Louis, MO
USA

Dr Lee Cronk
Department of Anthropology
Rutgers University
New Brunswick, NJ
USA

Dr John Crook
Winterhead Hill Farm
Shipham,
Somerset
UK

Dr Ian Cross
Faculty of Music
University of Cambridge
Cambridge
UK

Professor Robin Dunbar
School of Biological Sciences
University of Liverpool
Liverpool
UK

Professor Ernst Fehr
Institute for Empirical Research
in Economics
University of Zurich
Zurich
Switzerland

Professor Mark Flinn
Departments of Anthropology and
Psychological Sciences
University of Missouri
Columbia, MO
USA

Dr Leonardo Fogassi
Dipartimento di Neuroscienze
Sezione di Fisiologia
Universita' di Parma
Parma
Italy

Professor Steve Gangestad
Department of Psychology
Logan Hall
University of New Mexico
Albuquerque, NM
USA

Mr Drew Gerkey
Department of Anthropology
Rutgers University
New Brunswick, NJ
USA

Professor Gerd Gigerenzer
Center for Adaptive Behavior and Cognition
Max Planck Institute for Human Development
Berlin
Germany

Professor Herbert Gintis
University of Massachusetts
Northampton, MA
USA

Ms Charlie Hardy
Centre for the Study of Group Processes
Department of Psychology
University of Kent
Kent
UK

Dr Joseph Henrich
Department of Anthropology
Emory University
Atlanta GA
USA
and
Department of Psychology
Department of Economics,
University of British Columbia
Vancouver B. C.
Canada

Dr Tjeerd Jellema
Department of Psychology
University of Hull
Hull
UK

Professor Douglas Kenrick
Department of Psychology
Arizona State University
Tempe, AZ
USA

Dr Simon Kirby
Language Evolution and Computation
Research Unit
School of Philosophy, Psychology
and Language Sciences,
University of Edinburgh
Edinburgh,
UK

Professor Kevin N. Laland
Centre for Social Learning and Cognitive
Evolution
School of Biology
University of St. Andrews
St. Andrews,
Fife
UK

Professor Bobbi Low
Evolutionary and Behavioural Biology,
School of Natural Resources and Environment,
University of Michigan,
Ann Arbor, MI
USA

Dr. Virpi Lummaa
Department of Animal and Plant Sciences
University of Sheffield
Sheffield
UK

Professor Ruth Mace
Department of Anthropology
University College London
London
UK

Dr Gianmatteo Mameli
King's College,
University of Cambridge,
Cambridge
UK

Dr Richard McElreath
Department of Anthropology
University of California,
Davis, CA
USA

Dr. Daniel Nettle
Psychology, Brain and Behaviour
University of Newcastle
Newcastle
UK

Dr Hugh Notman
Department of Psychology
University of Lethbridge,
Lethbridge, AL
Canada

Professor Jaak Panksepp
Department of VCAPP
College of Veterinary Medicine
Washington State University
Pullman, WA
USA

Dr Justin Park
Social and Organizational Psychology
University of Groningen
Groningen
The Netherlands

Professor David Perrett
School of Psychology,
University of St Andrews,
St Andrews,
Fife
UK

Professor Henry Plotkin
Department of Psychology,
University College London,
London
UK

Dr Drew Rendall
Department of Psychology,
University of Lethbridge,
Lethbridge, AL
Canada

Professor Gillian Rhodes
School of Psychology
University of Western Australia
Perth
Australia

Professor Giacomo Rizzolatti
Dipartimento di Neuroscienze
Sezione di Fisiologia
Universita' di Parma
Parma
Italy

Dr Gilbert Roberts
Psychology, Brain and Behaviour
University of Newcastle
Newcastle
UK

Dr Frank Salter,
Human Ethology Research Group
Max Planck Institute for Human Ethology
Andechs
Germany

Dr Lucie H. Salwiczek
Department of experimental psychology,
University of Cambridge
Cambridge
UK

Dr Mark Schaller
Department of Psychology
University of British Columbia
Vancouver
Canada

Professor Constantine Sedikides
School of Psychology
University of Southampton
Southampton
UK

Professor Stephen Shennan
Institute of Archaeology
University College London
London
UK

Professor Joan Silk
Department of Anthropology
University of California
Los Angeles, CA
USA

Professor Leigh Simmons
Centre for Evolutionary Biology
School of Animal Biology
University of Western Australia
Perth
Australia

Dr John Skowronski
Department of Psychology
Northern Illinois University
Dekalb, IL
USA

Professor David Sloan Wilson
Department of Biology and Anthropology
Binghamton University
Binghamton,
New York
USA

Dr Frank J. Sulloway
Institute of Personality and Social Research
University of California
Berkeley, CA
USA

Dr Peter M. Todd
Program in Cognitive Science,
University of Indiana,
Bloomington
IN
USA

Professor Michael Tomasello
Max Planck Institute for Evolutionary
Anthropology
Leipzig
Germany

Professor Carel van Schaik
Anthropological Institute and Museum
University of Zürich,
Zürich
Switzerland

Professor Mark van Vugt
Centre for the Study of Group Processes
Department of Psychology
University of Kent
Kent
UK

Professor John R. Vokey
Department of Psychology
University of Lethbridge
Lethbridge, AL
Canada

Professor Eckart Voland
Zentrum fuer Philosophie und Grundlagen der
Wissenschaft
Universitaet Giessen
Giessen
Germany

Professor Claus Wedekind
Department of Ecology and Evolution
University of Lausanne
Lausanne
Switzerland

Professor Wolfgang Wickler
Max Planck Institute for Ornithology
Seewiesen
Germany

Professor Bruce Winterhalder
Department of Anthropology
University of California
Davis, CA
USA

Dr Emily Wyman
Max Planck Institute for Evolutionary
Anthropology
Leipzig
Germany

SECTION I
Philosophical issues

Evolutionary psychology has its origins in the merging of two intellectual streams that have, in the past, largely been only tangentially related: evolutionary biology and psychology. We make a strong case here for maintaining the broadest possible remit for this nascent discipline, arguing that attempts to confine its interests to specific aspects of cognition or behaviour fail to appreciate both the lesson and the opportunity that Darwinian evolutionary theory offers us. The essence of the approach on which we have premised this volume is that the evolutionary approach is not a competing subdiscipline within psychology, but rather provides a framework for integrating psychology's diverse sub-disciplines and uniting them with those streams of organismic biology that concern themselves with behaviour—a programme that Celia Heyes (2000) has referred to as 'evolutionary psychology in the round'.

In the long run, the essence of any such development must focus on understanding the role of culture in the human condition. However spectacular and fascinating the cultural behaviour of animals like whales and primates may be, it is self-evidently not in the same league as that of humans. Equally, however, it is not enough simply to say that humans are different, and leave it at that. We need to understand *how* and *why* humans are so different from other animals. Plotkin reminds us that part of that difference lies in the capacity for shared knowledge, for recognizing socially constituted facts (what the philosopher John Searle refers to as 'institutional facts') and using these in the construction of our social relationships. A dollar bill is not just a unit of currency, it is also an agreement among a group of individuals to use it as the basis for trading relationships. However, the capacity for shared knowledge does not occur in a psychological vacuum: it depends on the prior existence of cognitive mechanisms capable of supporting such functions. We know almost nothing of what these cognitive mechanisms might be, though it is widely accepted that theory of mind and other facets of 'mentalizing' (see Baron-Cohen, Section IV) constitute the core.

The central importance of culture is also taken up by Mameli. One of the important issues he emphasizes is the fact that cultural transmission allows the transgenerational transmission of knowledge. In this way, humans shape the environment in which their children develop, thereby both speeding up the process of learning how to cope with the vagaries of the environment and structuring the social context in which the individual lives and makes its evolutionarily valent decisions. These, as Mameli reminds us, are all but unstudied aspects of human evolutionary psychology. In effect, humans niche-construct their environment. Laland explores this in more detail. Social learning, as Laland reminds us, is the core to cultural transmission, and the impact of cultural transmission can be so powerful that cultural knowledge can rachet up the impact of niche construction in an evolutionarily very powerful mix. We currently have almost no real understanding of how these processes work, or how they actually affect human reproductive and other decisions, though some initial modelling work confirms that these effects are likely to be very important.

At one level, multi-level selection forms an extension of niche construction theory: by creating higher-order structuring to populations of individuals (i.e. social groups), humans and other social species modify the environment of selection within which they live. Groups buffer individuals against certain selection pressures. Wilson reminds us that this is not naïve group selection, of the kind that bedevilled biology (and especially the study of animal behaviour and ecology) during the first half of the twentieth century. The important difference between naïve group selection and multi-level selection is that the latter emphasizes that it is genetic fitness at the level of individual (or more appropriately, of course, the individual allele) that provides the unit of cost-accounting, whereas the former assumes that it is the group itself. Wilson's point is essentially that selection can *act* at the level of the group but its consequences fall at the level of the individual. There has, to date, been no study that seeks to explore the consequences of group-level processes for individual fitness. It is a topic that urgently needs addressing.

Reference

Heyes, C. M. (2000) Evolutionary psychology in the round. In C. M. Heyes and L. Huber (eds) *Evolution of Cognition*, pp. 3–22. Cambridge University Press, Cambridge.

CHAPTER 1

Evolutionary psychology in the round

Robin Dunbar and Louise Barrett

1.1. Introduction

Although the closing decades of the nineteenth century witnessed a great deal of interchange between psychology and evolutionary biology, the hasty departure of James Baldwin from the American psychological scene in 1908 (thanks to the scandal of being caught in a brothel) triggered, for reasons that are more political than scientific, the virtual severance of contact between the two disciplines (Plotkin, 2004). Psychology became more heavily influenced by its alternate roots in physiology and the neurosciences, on the one hand, and the social sciences, on the other. Evolution played no significant role in psychology for the better part of a century. Indeed, the 1950s in particular witnessed a somewhat tetchy quarrel between the comparative psychologists (with their feet firmly planted in behaviourism and an experimental paradigm) and the ethologists (with their roots in evolutionary biology, and a focus on the observational study of an animal's behaviour in its natural environment).

In part, this drift away from biology reflected an increasing focus within academic psychology on questions of mechanism (with a broad focus on stimulus–response processes, motivation, cognition and, later, neuropsychology) and development. For the ethologists, these constituted just two of what eventually came to be known as 'Tinbergen's Four Why's'—the four kinds of questions that biologists can ask, the other two being questions about function (a teleonomic question that is, ultimately, about the genetic consequences of behaviour) and phylogeny (the evolutionary history of how a behaviour came to have its current form). Tinbergen (1963) pointed out that all four provide appropriate answers to the generic question '*Why* does an animal do *X*?'; all must in the end be answered for a full understanding, but each can be asked and answered independently. That is to say, our answer to one does not necessarily commit us to any particular answer for any of the others.

We want to make two general points in this chapter. First, the evolutionary approach necessarily enjoins us to take a broad disciplinary perspective to our subject matter (which, following Heyes (2000), we might refer to as 'evolutionary psychology in the round'). Second, an evolutionary view does not—and should not—commit us to any particular assumptions about the genetic determination of behaviour. Indeed, learning, and by extension cultural transmission, play an especially important role in the behaviour of humans, and we will never be able to understand human behaviour without understanding culture and the way it influences what humans do. These issues are explored in more detail elsewhere in this volume, but our main concern here is to provide a framework within which the chapters that follow can be understood.

1.2. **Asking the right questions**

The important consideration in the present context is that evolutionary (or Darwinian) theory provides a framework within which a diverse range of intellectual questions can be integrated. The significance of this is well illustrated by the role it has played within biology. A century ago, biology consisted of half a dozen or more quite separate disciplines (anatomy, zoology, botany, genetics, physiology, microbiology, biochemistry, etc.) that rarely interacted. The gradual acceptance of the theory of evolution as a central organizing principle has made it possible for these diverse interest groups to talk to each other in a common language in a way that had rarely been possible in the past.

Our claim here is that an evolutionary approach can and should do the same for psychology. Evolutionary psychology, we argue, is not a new and separate sub-discipline within psychology, but rather a framework theory that allows psychology's many diverse sub-disciplines to be integrated into a unitary whole. It is not our intention to demonstrate this claim here by showing how different psychological approaches could relate more effectively to each other. Rather, our aim is simply to make it clear that a developmental stance, for example, is not different from, or in intellectual opposition to, an evolutionary approach. Rather, an evolutionary perspective adds to a developmental approach by offering new ways of seeing development, prompting novel questions for empirical study, and, more broadly, allowing developmental psychologists to integrate their findings with those of neuropsychologists, cognitive psychologists and others. Life history theory, for example, is major feature of contemporary evolutionary ecology, with enormous relevance both to reproductive decision-making and to development. Yet, its implications have only recently begun to be explored. Several of the chapters in Section V draw on it in their explorations of different aspects of human reproductive behaviour.

In this context, it is particularly important to understand that an evolutionary approach does not commit us *ipso facto* to genetic determinism. To assume that it does is to commit a classic category mistake by failing to distinguish two of Tinbergen's Four Why's—functional questions versus ontogenetic (i.e. developmental) questions. Questions about genetic determinism belong to the realm of ontogeny (how the individual acquires its capacities during the course of development), but the core to an evolutionary approach lies in function (questions about the evolutionary goal-directedness of these capacities and the behaviour they make possible).

Of course, as an essentially biological question, the primary focus of functional questions lies in how an organism's behaviour maximizes its genetic fitness. But the fact that an individual acts so as to maximize its fitness does *not* mean that its behaviour is genetically determined, merely that it has a set of genetically inherited motivations (or goal states) that it seeks to satisfy. *How* it achieves those goal states will, at least in neurologically advanced species, depend on the individual's assessment of the costs and benefits of acting in one way rather than another, given its experience of the world. In evolutionary biology, every decision is a contingent one that depends on the details of the context. That context will obviously include many features of the physical environment, but in highly social species like humans it will also include the social environment. We return to this point again below. The issue here, however, is that the genes that are passed on from one generation to another need be not the genes for a particular behaviour, but may, rather, be the genes for a brain that is large enough, and complex enough, to make the decisions about how best to act in order to satisfy its motivations (thereby maximizing fitness). Questions about the roles of genes and the environment in the production of those brains, or any other aspect of the system, are of course interesting, but they remain quite separate, and are unaffected by the extent to which an individual can be shown to be maximizing its fitness.

The issue of ontogeny is, of course, an important one that has been the focus of yet another long-running debate within psychology in particular (the so-called nature/nurture debate). Biologists have largely accepted, since the 1960s, that this distinction is arbitrary and, worse still perhaps, misguided. We cannot separate genes from the environment in the simple-minded way implied by this dichotomy. Both nature and nurture are deeply implicated in the processes of development, even though it may be possible to discuss the magnitude of the relative contribution of genetic versus environmental effects to the differences between individuals. Nonetheless, no aspect of an organism's biology or psychology can be said to be wholly (or even mainly) due to its genes or the environment in which it grows up.

The distinction, nonetheless, is important in one key respect. If we recognize that questions about the mechanisms of inheritance are separate from questions about the evolutionary function of behaviour, then the way is opened up for the evolutionary study of culture as an important phenomenon in its own right. Self-evidently, culture depends on learning—specifically the social transmission of beliefs or rules of behaviour—but learning is simply another mechanism of inheritance in the grand evolutionary scheme. Biologists' perennial focus on genes (and, more recently, DNA) as the mechanism of inheritance is, perhaps, to be expected given their interest in the more hard-wired aspects of biology, such as anatomy. But it is crucial to remember that neither Darwin nor Mendel (widely considered to be the founding father of genetics) actually knew anything about genes or DNA. Both the Darwinian formula that underpins the theory of evolution by natural selection and Mendel's laws of inheritance that provide the *modus operandi* for Darwin's theory refer only to fidelity of copying (in other words, the similarity or correlation between parents and offspring). The evolutionary consequences work equally well whether the basis of that copying is genetic transmission or cultural learning. Of course, there are some differences in the details of how cultural and genetic evolutionary processes work, but their role in the bigger scheme of things is sufficiently similar to warrant them being treated as being equivalent [a point also emphasized by Mameli (Chapter 3) and Laland (Chapter 4); see also Barrett *et al.*, 2000; Dunbar *et al.*, 2005].

The fact that the nature/nurture debate has been so entrenched within psychology for so long perhaps provides us with an explanation for the recent history of evolutionary psychology. Our reading of the history of psychology suggests that, during the 1970s and 1980s, the environmentalists (the nurture-folk) began to win the nature/nurture debate, especially within developmental psychology—to the point, in fact, where the nature-folk were reduced to a minority

rump on the periphery where they continued to focus on somewhat arcane topics like intelligence and personality theory. The rise of evolutionary ideas in the study of animal behaviour during the 1970s (originally in the form of a sub-discipline that named itself sociobiology, but which later adopted the alternative name *behavioural ecology*) seems to have been viewed by the naturists as offering something of a bulwark against the nurturists, in part at least because it seemed to imply some form of genetic basis for cognition and behaviour.

This may, in turn, provide us with a way of articulating the equally fractionated sub-disciplines of evolutionary psychology. Since the mid-1990s, evolutionary psychologists have been embroiled in what might seem like an internecine war between those whose intellectual tradition lay within behavioural ecology (who sometimes refer to themselves as evolutionary anthropologists) and those whose intellectual tradition lay within psychology (who originally referred to themselves as Darwinian psychologists, but later co-opted the term 'evolutionary psychology'). In our view, this dispute is properly seen as being between two of Tinbergen's Four Why's, specifically between the functional approach (represented by the behavioural ecologists) and questions about proximate (mainly cognitive) mechanisms (represented by the evolutionary psychologists *sensu stricto*). Hence, we endorse the view advocated by Mameli (Chapter 3) that both together constitute the proper domain of evolutionary psychology *sensu latto* (which he signals with lower case initial letters).

It is equally important to appreciate in this respect that an evolutionary perspective does not of itself necessarily commit us to the claim that the mind is entirely organized on modular principles, even though some have argued trenchantly for such a case. Full-scale modularity is just one of a continuum of possibilities. Indeed, we do not doubt that the mind has *some* degree of modular structure, but it is a purely empirical question as to exactly what form this modularity takes, and how many modules there are. The issue cannot be resolved on *a priori* philosophical grounds, since evolution neither entails modularity nor requires it. It may well be that, in the adult, cognition behaves as though it were modular, but we have yet to establish whether that level of modularity is present at birth (or develops willy-nilly during childhood, irrespective of experience). More importantly, it may well be that many of the cognitive scripts that we see in adults behave like modules (may, indeed, even be hardwired in neural circuitry), but in fact arise by the switching of cognitive mechanisms from conscious thinking (where a lot of hard cognitive work has to be done 'up front') to more automated (subconscious?) processes once the phenomenon has been cognitively processed often enough during the course of development (there is, indeed, now neuroimaging evidence to support this suggestion).

Although this is an interesting issue in the developmental psychology of cognition, we do not see it as an *evolutionarily* interesting question: evolution is indifferent as to whether the mind is modular or not, since that is simply a matter of history (the stages through which the human mind evolved). We can, of course, ask questions about the efficiency of the mind's design, but there is equally no guarantee that evolution will always produce the most efficient design: there are too many examples of poor design in biology, of Heath-Robinson adaptations of existing components for new purposes for which they were not originally designed (a process biologists sometimes recognize by the term *exaptation*). Nor, on this point, do we find the concept of the environment of evolutionary adaptedness (EEA) especially convincing or helpful. It may be possible to explain, *ex post facto*, why modern humans and their minds have come to be the way they are by reference to past circumstances, but it is rarely possible to identify past circumstances with such precision as to be able to predict (prospectively) the outcome of any selection process (Strassman and Dunbar, 1998). Moreover, the historical process by which a particular behavioural or cognitive trait is acquired is often so complex and convoluted, it is often hard to know exactly what came when, or which particular time and circumstances played the seminal role. This is well illustrated by the evolution of speech and language. In addition to the need for fine motor control, the capacity for speech depends on anatomical capacities associated with bipedality (a flattened chest, the freeing of the chest wall muscles from the pressure of walking) which have a very ancient origin at the very root of the hominin tree some 6 MYA (Aiello, 1996). Without these preadaptations, it would be impossible for modern humans to sustain the long exhalations that are required for speech. Were these components of the story more or less important than the social or technological circumstances that created the functional demand for communication when language itself evolved in the late Pleistocene? The answer is not always as obvious as it might seem.

However, to take such a view does not, of itself, mean that we have to dismiss the evolutionary psychology *sensu stricto* approach in its entirety, a mistake that has frequently been made by its opponents (many of whom have not always taken the trouble to investigate its claims at first hand). There has been much empirical work of considerable worth carried out under this rubric, and its value should be recognized. The reality is that some aspects of our cognition and physiology do predispose us to behave in certain ways, or at least to have such behaviours as our default condition. For us, the more interesting issue is the fact that our brains allow us the luxury of being able to fine tune our behaviour more subtly in the light of circumstance: that, after all, is why large brains evolved. In all likelihood, we probably do come to the world with a set of default cognitive options, but our cognitive capacities—and the processes of cultural transmission that these make possible in addition to simple trial-and-error learning—allow us the option of fine tuning our behaviour to the circumstances in which we happen to find ourselves in what are often very subtle ways. Voland (Chapter 28) argues cogently, from a very detailed review of the evidence from historical demography, for exactly this interpretation. Rather, we take the view that these disputes are arcane and of the past. We should begin with a clear canvas and set about building a more integrated science that draws on all relevant perspectives.

1.3. **Taking the broad perspective**

Although the evolutionary approach was initially applied mainly to questions of cognition within psychology [prompting Cosmides and

Tooby's (1992) generic design-of-the-mind approach], recent years have witnessed a dramatic growth in areas traditionally associated with social psychology (for recent overviews, see Schaller *et al.*, 2006; Forgas *et al.*, in press). Indeed, there are good grounds for seeing the behavioural ecology approach as being traditional social psychology with an evolutionary backbone, and the evolutionary psychology *sensu stricto* approach as being conventional cognitive psychology with an evolutionary backbone.

Our view, and the one we have tried to promote here through our choice of contributions, is a more balanced one that takes a broader perspective. In selecting topics for inclusion in this volume, we have endeavoured to give weight to both the central importance of individual topics and the balance across the sub-disciplines that currently constitute evolutionary psychology. Our aim has been to work towards a synthesis of approaches, in the expectation that the range of topics which can be exposed to scrutiny from an evolutionary perspective will encourage a wider range of psychologists to take note of the evolutionary approach. Our message, more than anything else, is perhaps that the evolutionary approach enables us to ask questions that are both wide-ranging and interesting: more importantly, it prompts us to ask questions that are not conventionally asked. The fact that evolutionary theory provides a very powerful, well-articulated and thoroughly developed body of theory has enormous heuristic value because it allows us to make strong predictions about how individuals might be expected to behave if a particular hypothesis is true. The main benefit of evolutionary theory, therefore, is that it provides a fine scalpel for hypothesis-testing.

Despite our insistence on the importance of intellectual breadth, there is one area that has remained resolutely on the sidelines of evolutionary psychology, namely culture. Though a strong research programme developed in the study of gene–culture co-evolution during the 1990s, this has remained highly mathematical in focus, and rather peripheral to the main developments within the broader discipline. Its attention has been focused mainly on the mechanisms of learning and the dynamics of gene–culture co-evolutionary processes. Yet culture plays an important role in everyday human behaviour, both as a conduit through which we acquire knowledge about how to behave and as a framework that itself creates many of the costs and benefits of social life. Plotkin (Chapter 2) develops this theme in more detail, so we will not elaborate further on the broader question of the importance of culture. However, one point he makes is worth emphasizing in more explicit detail because it provides the basis for some major new developments in evolutionary psychology. And this is the fact that humans, like most primates, live in large, multilevel societies.

For the past four decades or so, evolutionary biologists and behavioural ecologists (and, following their lead, evolutionary psychologists *sensu stricto*) have tended to view the individual in isolation, making decisions about how to behave in his/her own best interests. The reality, of course, is that human (and, indeed, many mammal and bird) individuals are members of societies that exist for the individual's benefit. We ought not to view an individual as acting in isolation in quite the way we have done traditionally because every behavioural decision an individual makes has consequences for every other member of the community within which it is embedded, and those consequences will in due course feed back on the individual. In actuality, this is nothing new in behavioural ecology: it is, in effect, the lesson of Hamilton's Rule. Although Hamilton's Rule was originally proposed as an explanation for the evolution of altruism [Hamilton's (1964) famous theory of kin selection], it has since come to be seen, rightly, as the fundamental theorem of behavioural ecology. In a nutshell, Hamilton's Rule states that a gene for altruism will evolve to stability whenever the benefit to the recipient (in terms of number of additional future offspring born), when devalued by the coefficient of relatedness between recipient and altruist, exceeds the cost to the altruist (when measured as the number of future offspring lost). While strictly speaking just an approximation to Hamilton's original finding (Hamilton termed this 'neighbour-modulated fitness'), even so simple a formulation reminds us that the consequences of one's actions reverberate around the population, and feed back on one's own inclusive fitness (the composite fitness of a trait that results from summing one's personal fitness with the kinship-devalued fitnesses contributed by everyone else in the wider community). If I help you, I cannot so easily help someone else, and I have to balance the loss that I accrue as a direct result against all my other gains.

This becomes significant when individuals live in interdependent communities whose persistence and success is a product of the effectiveness with which individuals work together. In these cases, actions that destabilize the group's coherence—and the fragile social contract on which its existence is premised—ultimately risk adversely influencing the fitness of the individual decision-maker. Social (or even physical) ostracism inevitably has disastrous consequences for an individual, especially in small-scale societies. Cultural rules may provide particularly powerful mechanisms for enforcing social conformity, not least by creating a sense of group identity. From an evolutionary point of view, this may seem to result in individuals behaving in ways that are sub-optimal when seen from the individual's purely selfish point of view. But a wider perspective may reveal that the individual's *net* lifetime fitness is higher if he/she accepts some losses now in the expectation of receiving greater returns in the future.

The need to integrate culture into the story has been added extra impulse in recent years by two recent developments. One is the concept of multi-level selection, and the other niche construction theory. The principal issue behind both is that fitness may be influenced in a rather complex way by the fact that an individual's actions reverberate through the layers of the biological system. This has quite explicit implications in the case of niche construction theory, which argues that organisms can (and often do) alter the environment they live in by their own behaviour. Beavers and their dams are an obvious and familiar example. But social groups themselves are a form of niche construction—indeed, they are perhaps the most complex form of this phenomenon, especially when kinship is part of the process. In effect, the social groups of many monkeys and apes (and, by extension) humans are implicit social contracts: individuals collaborate to solve the problems of everyday survival and successful reproduction more effectively than they can do on their own. Ensuring that the group functions effectively *as* a group has crucial feedback consequences for the fitness of its individual members. It may also

create tensions within the group when individuals' preferred ecological, social or reproductive strategies differ.

The importance of multi-level selection, especially for understanding human behaviour, has been stressed for many years by Wilson (1975; this volume), but its implications have received very little attention. It has acquired particular significance in the light of the finding that human societies are themselves multi-level constructs. Seen from the individual's perspective, human social networks appear as a series of concentric circles (the so-called 'circles of acquaintanceship') whose sizes have a surprisingly constant scaling ratio of three (Zhou *et al.*, 2005). Although there is considerable individual variation in the size of these circles, nonetheless the typical sizes seem to be constant across a wide range of cultural and socio-economic circumstances (from hunter-gatherers to modern post-industrial societies). Each circle corresponds not only to quite discrete numbers of individuals, but also to particular frequencies of contact and feelings of intimacy (Hill and Dunbar, 2003). We do not, as yet, understand why human societies should have this form (though it may well be a trait characteristic of many mammals with complex social systems). Nonetheless, the different groupings seem to have social and ecological functions that are a critical component of our personal life-history strategies. Since group-living is costly, we benefit from living in communities of this kind only if they work effectively. Hence, ensuring that the group functions as a coherent unit and is not destabilized by individuals' actions becomes an essential component of our sociality. The tightly integrated nature of human social groupings means that each of us is deeply embedded in a complex network of relationships: as a result, the consequences of whatever we do inevitably reverberates through the layers of the system and has ramifications for everyone with whom we have to live.

The fact that societies exist as collaborative ventures itself raises an issue of considerable importance that has very much come to the fore within the past few years in evolutionary studies of human behaviour. This is the issue of social cooperation. If we are to maintain—and thus benefit from—socialities of this complexity, an intense form of prosociality is necessary since group members must compromise on at least some of their self-interest. But any such social contract is always at risk of being destabilized by freeriders (those who take the benefits of the social contract, but decline to pay all the costs). Social cooperation, and the behaviours that derive from it (freeriding, altruistic punishment, second-order public goods problems) have emerged as a particularly fruitful area of collaboration between evolutionary biologists, evolutionary anthropologists and those who now refer to themselves as evolutionary economists. Though most often investigated in isolation, these have to be seen within the broader picture of both the evolution of multi-level social systems and the role that culture plays in creating the environment within which cooperation games are played out in real life. Some of the chapters in Section VII will develop these themes in more detail.

1.4. Evolutionary psychology of the future

We end this introductory chapter with two brief observations about the future. The first is that evolutionary psychology is now clearly here to stay, notwithstanding the rather negative press it has received in recent years. (We are reminded somewhat wearily of the equally negative responses that greeted sociobiology in the later 1970s: contemporary forecasts of its imminent—indeed, actual—demise proved to premature.) However, its future, we are convinced, will depend on our capacity to integrate the various strands that have developed over the past decade or so. We hope this volume goes some way to initiating that process. The second point is, we believe, even more important, at least for the human end of evolutionary psychology. Embedding human behaviour into the cultural matrix within which humans live is, we believe, a particularly important and crucial challenge. In our view, some of

the current puzzles that bedevil the study of human behaviour may well evaporate when humans are seen as operating within a more complex multi-level social environment.

References

Aiello, L. C. (1996) Terrestriality, bipedalism and the origin of language. In W. G. Runciman, J. Maynard Smith and R. I. M. Dunbar (eds) *Evolution of Social Behaviour Patterns in Primates and Man*, pp. 269–290. Oxford University Press, Oxford.

Barrett, L., Dunbar, R. I. M. and Lycett, J. E. (2000) *Human Evolutionary Psychology*. Palgrave-Macmillan, Basingstoke and Princeton University Press, Princeton, NJ.

Cosmides, L. and Tooby, J. H. (1992) Cognitive adaptations for social exchange. In J. H. Barkow, L. Cosmides and J. H. Tooby (eds) *The Adapted Mind*, pp. 163–228. Oxford University Press, Oxford.

Dunbar, R. I. M., Barrett, L. and Lycett, J. E. (2005) *An Introduction to Evolutionary Psychology*. One World Books, Oxford.

Forgas, J., von Hippel, W. and Haselton, M. (eds) (in press) *Evolutionary Social Psychology*. Psychology Press, New York.

Hamilton, W. D. (1964) The genetical evolution of social behaviour. I, II. *Journal of Theoretical Biology* 7: 1–52.

Heyes, C. M. (2000) Evolutionary psychology in the round. In C. M. Heyes and L. Huber (eds) *Evolution of Cognition*, pp. 3–22. Cambridge University Press, Cambridge.

Hill, R. A. and Dunbar, R. I. M. (2003) Social network size in humans. *Human Nature* 14: 53–72.

Plotkin, H. (2004) Evolutionary Thought in Psychology: A Brief History. Blackwell, Oxford.

Schaller, M., Simpson, J. and Kenrick, D. (eds) (2006) *Evolution and Social Psychology*. Psychology Press, New York.

Strassman, B. I. and Dunbar, R. I. M. (1998) Human evolution and disease: putting the Stone Age in perspective. In S. C. Stearns (ed.) *Evolution in Health and Disease*, pp. 91–101. Oxford University Press, Oxford.

Tinbergen, N. (1963) On the aims and methods of ethology. *Zeitschrift für Tierpsychologie* 20: 410–433.

Wilson, D. S. (1975) A theory of group selection. *Proceedings of the National Academy of Sciences of the USA* 72: 143–146.

Zhou, W-X., Sornette, D., Hill, R. A. and Dunbar, R. I. M. (2005) Discrete hierarchical organization of social group sizes. *Proceedings of the Royal Society, London* 272B: 439–444.

CHAPTER 2

The power of culture

Henry Plotkin

2.1. Introduction

Mankind's natural place is in culture, and culture is a part of human biology because it is our biology that gives us the ability to enter into culture. For this reason any contrast or opposition that is made between biology and culture, or between genes and culture, or between evolution and culture, is an expression of a wholly wrong conception of the causal structure of the world. Culture is not an entity whose causal force can be placed in a different physical (or metaphysical) realm from the causal forces exerted by genes, or the concatenation of natural selection pressures that have moulded human evolution. The human capacity for culture is a product of evolution and as natural as having a bipedal gait or an opposable thumb. The causal differences between our thumbs and, say, a specific belief in justice lies in the length of the chains of causes that run from the different suites of genes that are the part-causes of both, in the numbers of genes making up those suites, almost certainly in the complexity of the proteomic pathways that lead to each—even though developmental biology yet knows little of how development into specific phenotypic features occurs—and to the significant involvement of neuronal networks in those parts of the human brain subserving cognitive functions that underly that belief in justice that are largely absent in the case of thumb use. But each is rooted in the evolved human genome. There is, creationism apart, only one other way of thinking about culture. This is to adopt a novel kind of Cartesian dualism which, because culture is a product of minds, asserts that the evolution which accounts for all other features of our species does not apply to our minds. No scientist of any worth could approve or sanction such a new form of dualism any more than can modern science tolerate Descartes' original notion of *res cogitans* as being different from *res extensa*.

None of this means that culture is simple. It is not just complex, but probably is the most complex thing on earth. And it is only in recognizing that complexity that we can hope to get any kind of scientifically acceptable biological hold on a phenomenon that generations of social scientists have feared, always correctly, would be conceptually destroyed by way of the oversimplification of a reductive biology. It is essential that culture be naturalized in the complex form that social scientists believe culture to take. This is not just because we need to carry the social scientists with us, though that is a good enough motive, but for two further reasons. The first is that human culture in its full majesty has characteristics that place it beyond the bounds of what we know of cultures in other species of animal, and so has to be placed within a specifically *human psychological* context. The second is that one of the most remarkable features of one of the most important forms of culture, social constructions, cannot be reduced beyond the common intentional states of the individuals making up any culture.

This underlies the difference between human and non-human culture. The former is not a more flamboyant instance of the latter; or the latter an etiolated variety of the former. They are different because humans have psychological mechanisms that are unique to our species.

2.2. **What culture is**

Most broadly defined, culture constitutes a sharing by way of some form of learning. Where human culture differs from the cultures of non-human species lies in what it is that is shared, and, as just stated, what can be shared is a product of the cognitive mechanisms that underlie culture (Plotkin, 2002). Forms of culture have been well documented in songbirds (Marler and Slabberkoorn, 2004), cetaceans (Rendell and Whitehead, 2001), chimpanzees (Whiten *et al.*, 1999) and orangutans (van Schaik *et al.*, 2003). In every case, what is shared by a process of learning is vocal signalling or acts relating to foraging, hunting and tool use. It is possible that similar forms of culture are present in other species, particularly carnivores. Such culture is certainly also present in humans. Human culture, however, also comprises the sharing of other things and it is in the range and nature of what is shared that human culture is unique.

Literally hundreds of definitions of human culture are on offer (Kroeber and Kluckhohn, 1952), and different schools of anthropology adhere to different theories of culture (Keesing, 1974). For the limited purposes of this chapter, culture will be defined in ideational terms, one advantage of which is that ideation falls squarely within the domain of, and so can make common conceptual cause with, psychology: "A society's culture consists of whatever it is one has to know or believe in order to operate in a manner acceptable to its members" (Goodenough, 1957, p. 167). Goodenough's definition also provides an important social psychological element: what is shared is knowledge, values, beliefs and customs, as well as the motor skills and actions alluded to above, that allow individuals to fit in to a social group. It is the variety of shared ideational forms, and the quantity of possible forms of knowledge within each category, that makes human culture so incomparably rich in comparison with the cultures of other species. However, a taxonomy

of the forms of knowledge that can be culturally transmitted is less likely to reap conceptual rewards within the confines of a brief analysis than explicit recognition of two of these forms. These are higher-order knowledge structures, and social constructions.

Social constructions are forms of social reality that exist by virtue of the agreement of the individuals making up a social group. Money is a social construction. So too is marriage, as is justice and patriotism. There are as many social constructions as there is agreement amongst members of a social group that they do exist, and take the form that they do. Justice in one culture may be based on shared resources, in another on revenge and equality of response between individuals, and in another on social rank. Social constructions may manifest a physical form. Religions give rise to temples. Money comes in the form of coins, pieces of paper, or even entries on a computer memory. But the real value of the piece of paper comprising a £50 note is miniscule and irrelevant. What matters is that the piece of paper is recognized as having a value equivalent to a moderate meal in a London restaurant by the restaurant owner to whom it is proffered. Without agreement social constructions cease to exist, and indeed at least twice in the twentieth century in different parts of the world such agreement has been withdrawn and money became worthless.

The necessity for agreement makes social constructions very strange entities. But it does not dematerialize them. Social constructions are interlocking neural network states in different individuals. The analysis of social constructions by Searle (1995) is magisterial. It rests on two features of the world. The one is the atomic theory of matter in which particles and aggregates of particles give rise to elements, compounds, forests and okapis. The second is the theory of evolution which explains how cellular and organ structures evolved, including the human brain which gives rise to consciousness and the capacity to represent objects and states of affairs of the world. Consciousness is a biological and hence physical state, and its intentionality, Searle argues, gives rise to a further distinction. On the one hand there are what he refers to as "brute facts", like the snow and ice at the summit of Mount Everest. The snow and ice exist independently of human existence, and independently of human intentional states. On the other hand, that the mountain straddles the border between Nepal and Tibet is an "institutional fact"—as is the identity of any nation state whose existence depends wholly on agreement. Institutional facts, unlike brute facts, are observer relative, the observer investing the institutional, cultural, world with three essential elements. One is the assignment of function, which Searle considers to be a specific aspect of human psychology, and hence functions are always observer-relative and not intrinsic to objects. One especially important form of agentive function is the construction of entities that stand for other things. That is, that represent other things. This includes language, symbols and maps.

The second element is what Searle refers to as collective intentionality, which social philosophers also refer to as "we-intentionality" (Tuomela and Miller, 1988) or shared cooperative activity (Bratman, 1992). Bratman's phrase captures precisely the circumstances under which we-intentionality arises—that of a group working together towards a shared goal and using shared knowledge to attain that end. Searle argues that we-intentionality is not simply the sum of individual intentional states because it is itself a source of individual intentionality. In other words "we" is a psychological state that stands apart from "I" or "you", is a powerful determinant of "I" and "you" intentional states, and links to emotions emanating from we-intentionality that give rise to the powerful motives for entering into group activities.

The third element of institutional facts and social reality is constitutive rules that regulate social activity and interaction. These range from rules for playing games for enjoyment, through instructions that regulate everyday social interactions, and on to rules of governance by which decisions are reached that affect the very creation of social reality itself. Legislation, in whatever form, is a set of constitutive rules by which further rules are established. Social reality that gives rise to other forms of social reality can be immensely complex and contentious. It may give rise to civil wars, and has done so; it is currently testing human ingenuity to its limit as European nation states, all social constructions, attempt the move towards a more integrated Europe, which is also a social construction.

At the heart of all social constructions is the structure "X counts as Y in C". Thus paper printed in a Royal Mint (X) counts as money (Y) in the United Kingdom (C). The X and Y terms can each in turn be linked by the iteration of the basic structure such that I can gain ownership with money of an entity, like land, in some distant place but not where I am standing at present; or it might allow me to gain possession of a book by purchase with money, but not have ownership of the contents of that book. There is no limit to such iteration, and hence no limit to the complexity of human culture. Yet there is a fragility to that complexity. "The central span on the bridge from physics to society is collective intentionality, and the decisive movement on that bridge in the creation of social reality is the collective intentional imposition of function on entities that cannot perform those functions without that imposition" (Searle, 1995, p. 41). Thus money as a physical entity has little value; only collective agreement imposes the function of value and hence the social fact of value that allows one to buy a meal, a book, or a piece of land. This is why brute facts like Everest's snow and ice do not lead to the kind of metaphysical giddiness to which contemplation of social facts may give rise. Snow and ice do not require that structure of "X counts as Y in C" embedded within a we-intentionality of agreed function deriving from specific constitutive rules. Money, however, does, and hence the form of human culture that has such massive causal force in determining human life and death, social reality, also has a fragility and a flexibility that cannot be accounted for simply in terms of rates of transmission of information. Fragility and flexibility are an intrinsic property of social constructions.

Now simple motor acts, like tying a shoe lace or wielding an implement, are low-order knowledge structures which impinge little, if at all, on social constructions. The latter, however, impel belief and action within a world of higher-order knowledge structures. Receiving an answer as to the identity of a good-value restaurant, for example, means that both the person posing the question and the one answering it share a great deal of knowledge in some form of semantic memory. They have to know what a restaurant is, as opposed to a temple or prison or school; and they each have to know what money is and share the knowledge that the same amount of money can be exchanged for a variable quality and quantity of food. So much of cultural exchange occurs within a world freighted with such knowledge (Sperber, 2000). A corner-stone of higher-order knowledge structures is Bartlett's (1932) notion of a schema, which is so at odds with the atomistic associationism of most research on memory. For Bartlett, memory was not a passive re-collection of stored information but a form of creative re-construction that occurs within the context of schemas, deep-lying generic knowledge structures that are products of particular cultures and which influence that re-constructive process. Waiters in restaurants in some cultures wear uniforms, but no person enculturated in that form of society would expect that the wearing of uniform dress means they are police officers with powers of arrest. So in recalling a disturbance in a restaurant, waiters will be remembered as playing one kind of role and police officers another.

Bartlett's ideas were revived in the 1970s and 1980s, first by Minsky (1975) who realized that artificial intelligence needed generic knowledge of the kind that Bartlett's notion of schemata addressed, and later by Schank and Abelson (1977) and Rummelhart and Norman (1985) who provided more detailed theoretical descriptions of schemata and introduced the notion of knowledge of actions appropriate to a specific cultural setting, like how to behave in a restaurant, within "scripts". There is much experimental evidence that non-human primates (Tomasello and Call, 1997) as well as some other mammalian and avian species (Pearce, 1987) are capable of acquiring limited forms of generic knowledge, though whether such knowledge plays any role in non-human cultures is, at least for the present, entirely speculative. What is unquestionable is that higher-order knowledge forms such as schemata and scripts are important components of human culture. Gaining knowledge of the dominant higher-order knowledge forms, as well as the prominent social constructions of a particular culture, are as important in the enculturation of any child into its own culture in the contemporary world, and probably has been so for thousands or tens of thousands of years, as is the acquisition of low-order knowledge forms comprising effective actions.

2.3. **Minimal psychological mechanisms**

Szathmary and Maynard Smith (1995) described eight major evolutionary transitions in the evolution of life on earth. The last of these was the transition between non-human primate and human societies with the appearance of language. The crucial role of language in human culture is not in doubt. But whether the evolution of language alone, however that might have occurred, is responsible for the difference between human and other cultures is debatable. What is increasingly accepted is that language on its own is insufficient for humans to enter fully into human culture (Donald, 1991; Tomasello, 1999). There are, however, differences of view as to what other processes and mechanisms of mind are necessary. Theory of mind, which is the ability to attribute intentional mental states to others and about which an increasing amount is understood in terms of its cognitive development and neurological basis (Baron-Cohen et al., 2000; Baron-Cohen, this volume, Chapter 16; Frith and Wolpert, 2004) is widely regarded as necessary for entering fully into human culture. This is especially the case if one accepts Sperber's argument about the significance and necessity of inference, and the weight and ubiquity of such inference, regarding both social and non-social entities, if one is successfully to enter into human culture. In addition to its role in drawing inferences, theory of mind might also be the psychological bridge between the intentional mental states of other individuals and the we-intentionality of cooperating groups invoked by the social scientists. If Searle and others are correct in pointing to the significance of collective intentionality, theory of mind might comprise at least a part of the psychological mechanisms causing we-intentionality.

There is an argument for at least one other characteristic of humans being necessary for entering into culture. This is the human responsiveness to social force which is manifested in so many social psychological studies of conformity and obediance. It is curious that social psychologists, responsible for most empirical studies of social force, some of a spectacular nature, have argued so little for its role in social constructions and social representations. In contrast, the biologists Boyd and Richerson (1985) developed a frequency-dependent bias model specifically to account for human group selection and the evolution of cooperation. They argued that humans are genetically predisposed to choose cultural variants, whatever form these might take, which are most frequent within the social group that they occupy. It should also be noted that this responsiveness to social force may provide the motive force for entering into we-intentionality—a kind of psychological glue that drives us to adopt the commonly held beliefs, values and knowledge of the social group of which we are a member.

Whether language, theory of mind, and responsiveness to social force are the only and necessary psychological traits that had to evolve before human culture appeared in anything like its present form, thus constituting Szathmary and Maynard Smith's eighth major evolutionary transition, is unknown. It is also not yet known whether these are traits present in other species, though Lloyd (2004) rightly warns about the difficulties involved in judging any trait to be uniquely human. But what has to be the case is that during the evolution of *Homo sapiens*, the minimal necessary psychological traits in some minimal state of function that support human culture had to have converged within the minds of a small number of humans to result in what might be termed "first culture". Whatever "first culture" comprised, it would not have taken the form of contemporary human culture. There is simply no basis for assuming that human culture sprang fully formed into the world 40 thousand or 80 thousand years ago in essentially the same form as human culture today. It has to be assumed that the advantages of first culture were such as to result in natural selection acting to sharpen up, perhaps alter substantially, these minimal psychological traits such that by 10–12 thousand years ago modern human cultures became possible.

Supporting this assumption is what we know about both language and theory of mind. This is that each employs component psychological mechanisms. Language requires working memory, a sensitivity to temporal order, the capacity to segment sensory input, discriminative mechanisms, and fine motor control to name but a few. Theory of mind is composed of a similar suite of separate mechanisms, some of them shared with language. It is unlikely that any cognitive processing is possible without working memory which therefore must be a mechanism operating in attributing intentional mental states to others. Theory of mind also requires specific attentional mechanisms sensitive to gaze direction, cognitive skills which allow the developmental switch from a dyadic to triadic interactions, as well as those leading to a capacity for pretence. The point is that just as human culture did not suddenly spring fully formed into the world, neither did the psychological mechanisms essential for it. As aggregate traits built from multiple psychological mechanisms were co-opted from previous functions to new functions, the necessary existing components would have provided a design space for selection to improve already complex mechanisms and functions to, perhaps, novel mechanisms with different functions. The general assumption of most evolutionary psychologists is that complex cognitive capacities like language are adaptations. The same must therefore characterize culture, but even more so. It is more a supertrait than a trait; an exaptation of exaptations. As Dennett (1995) argued, few functions remain constant and hence most adaptations are exaptations. Nonetheless, the complexity that culture and its constituent mechanisms presents to evolutionary biology is without precedent. As aggregates of exaptations built out of other exaptations, the psychological mechanisms that underpin culture, and culture itself, present evolutionary biology with a complexity unlike any other that it has ever had to explain.

2.4. The reach and power of culture

Despite the frailty of the most prominent feature of human culture, social constructions, they are also entities of significant causal power. The members of the International Committee of the Red Cross avow that the overwhelming majority of wars in recent human history have been driven by social constructions like ideologies, religion, ethnicity and concerns over gaining political and financial resource advantages for national states. All are social constructions;

and the wars they gave rise to resulted in the deaths of hundreds of millions of individuals and changed the lives of billions. Any claim that modern warfare, like that of the 20th century's world wars or the recent war in Iraq, is caused by increases in inclusive fitness of individuals because some participants will gain increased access to women (Pinker, 1997 for example) is simply rejected by most social scientists. It is considered to posit a causal chain explaining warfare to lengths beyond what is credible. It is also judged so crass and ignorant in its error as to warrant no serious rebuttal for many individual people in contemporary cultures touched by modern warfare.

Social constructions, for example in the form of religious or other moral injunctions on how to live one's life, also determine the daily behaviour of billions of people across the planet. Science too is a social construction, albeit a special one insofar as it deals with the nature of the universe. The application of science has brought material advantages in the form of light, warmth, food and protection against disease to most living humans. Social constructions may have strange qualities, but they are enormously powerful causes of human belief and behaviour, as well as the conditions in which we live our lives. But the power of culture does not stop there. Culture may also shape basic cognitive processes, as well as human evolution itself.

Lillard (1998) argues for significant variations in theories of mind across different cultures. The European–American (EA) theory of mind is a psychological mechanism for understanding the intentional states of others within a specific cultural setting in which the *individual mind*, with her or his individual needs or desires, is the central unit of understanding. This contrasts, Lillard argues, with many different cultural beliefs where the minds of others play little part in the kinds of causal attributions made by individuals. Whether it be the Illongot of the Philippines, the Tallensi of Africa, or Tibetan Buddhists, the individual has little relevance, the group is the dominant unit, and the mind is subsumed within complex concepts that include notions like heart, ancestry and the spirit world. Thus "although the mind is still behind the action, it is a different sort of mind than EAs think of" (Lillard, 1998, p. 15). Even the primacy of senses,

and our identification with them, varies across cultures. EA culture is dominated by sight and hearing; not so for the Ongee of the South Pacific, a people whose lives are centred upon odour and who greet others by asking, literally, "how is your nose?" Such ethnographical differences cannot be denied. Nonetheless, it can be claimed that what remains a human cultural universal is a psychological mechanism that attributes causal force to the social sphere, however different that sphere may be across different cultures, that is different from physical causation.

A more focused account of culturally induced psychological and neurological difference comes from a recent functional imaging study of dyslexic Chinese children (Siok *et al.*, 2004). Impaired reading of alphabetic script is associated with dysfunction of left temporoparietal regions of the brain where grapheme-to-phoneme conversion occurs. The Chinese language, however, is logographic and reading requires conversion from a graphic to a syllabic representation. What was observed in the Chinese children was dysfunction of the left middle frontal gyrus. This shows that "rather than having a universal origin, the biological abnormality of impaired reading is dependent on culture" (Siok *et al.*, 2004, p. 71). Whilst it is not surprising that writing systems of such fundamentally different designs as English and Chinese should impose different psychological and neurological requirements for reading, it remains the case that this is a clear-cut case of culturally driven causes of altered psychological mechanisms that are designed to achieve the same end of decoding written language.

There are many other studies on the effects of culture on cognitive and emotional development. Atran and his colleagues have reported how urban and rural children in North America categorize and generalize biological forms, the former doing so in terms of similarities to humans whilst the latter use more expert-based taxonomies which do not centre on humans (Medin and Atran, 2004). A recent study demonstrated how exposure to firearm crime alters the probability of adolescents perpetrating serious violence themselves (Bingenheimer *et al.*, 2005); these are findings that chime with the specialist training programmes that have to be instituted in order to ensure that soldiers will injure and kill other humans (Grossman, 1995). Many more such findings are given in Cole's extensive reviews (Cole, 1996; in press), many of which fit with either nativist or empiricist approaches to cognition because not even the most devout of nativists advances the view that the cognitive and emotional contents of the mind are fixed at birth. Culture is an intrinsic part of the developmental environment of all normal humans, and hence culture must have a causal role to play in all aspects of psychological development.

Finally, there is a reverse causality involving human culture. If, as argued earlier, culture is a product of evolution, culture must also have been a determining factor in human evolution. The most prominent instance has been the fixation within specific human populations of the mutant gene that allows for tolerance to lactose beyond weaning (Durham, 1991). This occurred in just those populations where the effects of lactose being most beneficial, both in terms of general nutritional consequences as well as in providing a boost to vital calcium absorption, covaried with animal husbandry practices. It was the existence of dairying practices, a product of culture, along with other factors like the relative paucity of sunlight levels in northern Europe that formed the selection filters that drove the mutated gene to fixation. Here culture has been directly implicated as a causal force in an admittedly small, but nonetheless quite concrete, case of human genetic change.

Another example is infanticide, a culturally driven practice that is present in many societies. Gene-culture co-evolutionary modelling shows the potential effects of sex-biased infanticide on sex ratios in future human populations (Laland et al., 1995). The results are not easy to predict because they depend on whether the society in question is patrilineal, whether it is the mother or father who is the principal proponent of sex-biasing the family, and whether parents do or do not adjust family size following the early death of a child. What the modelling certainly does demonstrate is that the culturally driven practice of sex-biased infanticide can, and will, have significant effects on the structure of human populations.

Many other examples have been put forward, not many of them based on empirical study or mathematical modelling. It is thought that genocide in the distant past may have affected human evolution; that the invention of fire and the cooking of food may have led to increased brain size and yet further increases in intelligence and the capacity for entering into ever-more complex culture; that medical advances have kept certain genes in the gene pool that natural selection would have eliminated; and that the burning of fossil fuels is accelerating climate change with potentially catastrophic effects not only for our species but for millions of others as well. These may at present be speculative arguments, but there is no denying that certain diseases have either been entirely eradicated or can now be effectively treated, or that every jet airliner flying from London to New York deposits half a ton of carbon dioxide into the atmosphere. It is an irony that the most enlightened forms of human culture, science and its application in medicine and engineering, may yet have the most profound and opposite effects on future human evolution.

2.5. The architecture of complexity

More than once in the history of life, evolution has given rise to organisms with traits that have the power to enhance the evolutionary process itself. The evolution of sexual reproduction is one example. Phenotypic plasticity is another. The latter takes three forms. One is developmental plasticity. The second is learning or intelligence by which representations of the world are laid down in central nervous systems which serve to generate adaptive behaviour, of which non-human cultures are one of many different representational forms. The third is human culture, in which imagined worlds are made real by collective agreement (Plotkin, 2002). It is because of this tripartite nature of phenotypic plasticity that culture, built upon evolution, phenotypic plasticity and learning, and able to effect changes in all of these more fundamental levels which track a world in continuous flux, is most aptly described by Simon's phrase "the architecture of complexity" (Simon, 1962). It captures well the problem that is faced by any formal attempt to place culture within a structured causal theory. Culture is complexity writ large. Culture is at once a product of the evolution of specific cognitive and motivational mechanisms; at the same time it constitutes an entity, or more correctly a set of entities, into which every member of a social group must enter in order to share agreed knowledge, values and beliefs, and which thus entered is causal in the psychological development of each encultured child; culture also has the power to change our own and other species, as well as the world in which we all live. Thus it is that culture is a force in our own evolution as well as that of other species. How can this whirl of causal powers be captured within a simplifying explanatory model?

Simon offered at least part of the answer in the form of hierarchies, an architecture of complexity that many others came to adopt (Pattee, 1973; Dawkins, 1976; Arnold and Fristrup, 1982; Gould, 1982) as a way of dealing with the complexity of evolution and its products, when they could agree on virtually nothing else. A hierarchy is "a system that is composed of interrelated subsystems, each of the latter being, in turn, hierarchic in structure until we reach some lowest level of elementary subsystem" (Simon, 1962, p. 468). Whilst a number of different types of hierarchy have been described, all fall into one of two types. There are structural hierarchies characterized by containment, as in Chinese boxes or Russian dolls, in which each level of organization is literally contained in another (organelles, cells, organs, organisms, populations, ecosystems). The other is a control or informational hierarchy (as in human organizations like corporations or armed forces) characterized by absence of physical containment with much greater fluidity of causal interaction between levels, though a frequent assumption is that causal power is generally greater within a level than between levels. Culture is a part of a control hierarchy, the four main levels of which are evolution, ontogeny, learning and culture itself. Each main level may comprise multiple sublevels (Campbell, 1974). It is the fluidity of causal interactions in control hierarchies that accounts for the complexity by which culture is at once a product of all three more fundamental levels in the hierarchy, and yet which in turn exerts causal force upon each of those other levels of learning, development and evolution itself.

One elaboration of this scheme is the assumption that each level operates by the same processes that characterize the fundamental level, that is, the generation of variants, the selection of a small subset of these, and their propagation into the future (Lewontin, 1970; Campbell, 1974; Plotkin, 1994). "Levels do not achieve their independence because some fundamentally new genetic process emerges at their scale. Rather, the same processes of variation and selection operate throughout the hierarchy. But they work differently upon the varying materials (individuals) of ascending levels in a discontinuous hierarchy" (Gould, 1982, p. 104). Within this scheme of universal Darwinism, culture is at once a product of Darwinian evolution, whilst itself constantly changing through those same processes. Evolutionary worlds without end.

A final point should be added to this scheme of complexity. Organisms alter the worlds in which they live. Darwin knew this but did not accord it especial importance. Recently Odling-Smee *et al.* (2003) have instituted a major addition to the modern synthesis which Odling-Smee long referred to as niche construction (see Laland, Chapter 4). Odling-Smee understood that niche construction is an element of the evolutionary process at every level, including that of culture. There is no more explicit instance of niche construction than that at the cultural level, niches that exist within the realm of culture and social reality itself, and which also extend into the physical world as human culture cuts a swathe of effects into our planet.

The power of culture is awesome. It is our universal fate that it touches virtually every aspect of our lives. And it does this because it is written deep into the fabric of our biology.

References

Arnold, A. J. and Fristrup, K. (1982) The theory of evolution by natural selection: a hierarchical expansion. *Paleobiology*, 8: 113–129.

Baron-Cohen, S., Tager-Flusberg, H. and Cohen, D. J. (eds) (2000) *Understanding Other Minds*. Oxford University Press, Oxford.

Bartlett, F. C. (1932) *Remembering*. Cambridge University Press, Cambridge.

Bingenheimer, J. B., Brennan, R. T. and Earls, F. J. (2005) Firearm violence exposure and serious violent behaviour. *Science*, 308: 1323–1326.

Boyd, R. and Richerson, P. (1985) *Culture and the Evolutionary Process*. Chicago University Press, Chicago.

Bratman, M. E. (1992) Shared cooperative activity. *The Philosophical Review*, 101: 327–341.

Campbell, D. (1974) Evolutionary epistemology. In P. A. Schilpp (ed.) *The Philosophy of Karl Popper*, pp. 413–463. Open Court Publishing, La Salle, IL.

Cole, M. (1996) *Cultural Psychology*. Harvard University Press, Cambridge, MA.

Cole, M. (in press) Cultural and cognitive development in phylogenetic, historical and ontogenetic perspective. In W. Damon and D. Kuhn (eds) *Handbook of Child Psychology*, Vol. 2: *Cognition, Perception and Language*, 6th edn. Wiley, New York.

Dawkins, R. (1976) Hierarchical organization: a candidate principle for ethology. In P. P. G. Bateson and R. A. Hinde (eds) *Growing Points in Ethology*, pp. 7–54. Cambridge University Press, Cambridge.

Dennett, D. C. (1995) *Darwin's Dangerous Idea*. Penguin, London.

Donald, M. (1991) *Origins of the Modern Mind*. Harvard University Press, Cambridge, MA.

Durham, W. H. (1991) *Coevolution: Genes, Culture and Human Diversity*. Stanford University Press, Stanford.

Frith, C. and Wolpert, D. (eds) (2004) *The Neuroscience of Social Interaction*. Oxford University Press, Oxford.

Goodenough, W. H. (1957) Cultural anthropology and linguistics. In P. Garvin (ed.) *Report of the 7th Annual Roundtable Meeting on Linguistics and Language Study*, pp. 162–184. Georgetown University Monograph Series on Language and Linguistics, Vol. 9.

Gould, S. J. (1982) The meaning of punctuated equilibrium and its role in validating a hierarchical approach to macroevolution. In R. Milkman (ed.) *Perspectives on Evolution*, pp. 83–104. Sinauer, Sunderland, MA.

Grossman, D. (1995) *On Killing*. Little, Brown, New York.

Keesing, R. M. (1974) Theories of Culture. *Annual Review of Anthropology*, 3: 73–97.

Kroeber, A. L. and Kluckhohn, C. (1952) *Culture: A Critical Review of Concepts and Definitions*. Harvard University Press, Cambridge, MA.

Laland, K. N., Kumm, J. and Feldman, M. W. (1995) Gene-culture co-evolutionary theory: a test case. *Current Anthropology*, 36: 131–158.

Lewontin, R. C. (1970) The units of selection. *The Annual Review of Ecology and Systematics*, 1: 1–18.

Lillard, A. (1998) Ethnopsychologies: cultural variations in theories of mind. *Psycholgical Bulletin*, 123: 3–32.

Lloyd, E. A. (2004) Kanzi, evolution, and language. *Biology and Philosophy*, 19: 577–588.

Marler, P. and Slabberkoorn, H. (2004) *Nature's Music: The Science of Birdsong*. Elsevier, London.

Medin, D. L. and Atran, S. (2004). The native mind: biological categorization and reasoning in development and across cultures. *Psychological Review*, 111: 960–983.

Minsky, M. L. (1975) A framework for representing knowledge. In P. H. Winston (ed.) *The Psychology of Computer Vision*, pp. 211–277. McGraw-Hill, New York.

Odling-Smee, F. J., Laland, K. L. and Feldman, M. W. (2003) *Niche Construction: The Neglected Process in Evolution*. Princeton University Press, Princeton.

Pattee, H. (ed.) (1973) *Hierarchy Theory: The Challenge of Complex Systems*. Braziller, New York.

Pearce, J. M. (1987) *An Introduction to Animal Cognition*. Erlbaum, London.

Pinker, S. (1997) *How the Mind Works*. Norton, London.

Plotkin, H. (1994) *The Nature of Knowledge*. Allen Lane, London.

Plotkin, H. (2002) *The Imagined World Made Real*. Allen Lane, London.

Rendell, L. and Whitehead, H. (2001) Culture in whales and dolphins. *The Behavioural and Brain Sciences*, 24: 309–382.

Rummelhart, D. E. and Norman, D. A. (1985) Representation of knowledge. In A. M. Aitkinhead and J. M. Slack (eds) *Issues in Cognitive Modelling*, pp. 15–62. Erlbaum, Hove.

Schank, R. C. and Abelson, R. (1977) *Scripts, Plans, Goals and Understanding*. Erlbaum, Hillsdale, NJ.

Searle, J. (1995) *The Construction of Social Reality*. Allen Lane, London.

Simon, H. A. (1962) The architecture of complexity. *Proceedings of the American Philosophical Society*, 106: 467–482.

Siok, W. T., Perfetti, C. A., Jin, Z. and Tan, L. H. (2004) Biological abnormality of impaired reading is constrained by culture. *Nature*, 431: 71–76.

Sperber, D. (2000) An objection to the memetic approach to culture. In R. Aunger (ed.) *Darwinizing Culture*, pp. 163–173. Oxford University Press, Oxford.

Szathmary, E. and Maynard Smith, J. (1995) The major evolutionary transitions. *Nature*, 374: 227–232.

Tomasello, M. (1999) *The Cultural Origins of Human Cognition*. Harvard University Press, Cambridge, MA.

Tomasello, M. and Call, J. (1997) *Primate Cognition*. Oxford University Press, Oxford.

Tuomela, R. and Miller, K. (1988) We-intentions. *Philosophical Studies*, 53: 367–389.

van Shaik, C. P., Ancrenaz, M., Borgen, G., Galdikas, B., Knott, C. D., Singleton, I., Suzuki, A., Utami, S. S. and Merrill, M. (2003) Orangutan cultures and the evolution of material culture. *Science*, 299: 102–105.

Whiten, A., Goodall, J., McGrew, W. C., Nishida, T., Reynolds, V., Sugiwama, Y., Tutin, C. E. G., Wrangham, R. W. and Boesch, C. (1999) Cultures in chimpanzees. *Nature*, 399: 682–685.

CHAPTER 3

Evolution and psychology in philosophical perspective

Matteo Mameli

3.1. Introduction

Humans are evolved organisms. This means that human minds have an evolutionary origin and that human psychological traits are, in one way or another, the product of evolution. This chapter explores the implications of this deceptively simple fact for the science of psychology. The question we need to address is whether and how knowing that human minds have an evolutionary origin can help us understand the way modern human minds work. The true implications of the evolutionary origins of human minds are not always easy to unravel. Some mistakes can be avoided by steering away from simplistic views of evolution and development, and of the way they interact. Developmental plasticity, environmental change, niche construction and cultural transmission have all played an important role in human evolution. Understanding such factors is thereby crucial for an accurate evolutionary account of human psychological traits.

3.2. The old orthodoxy

According to one view of the relation between human evolution and human minds, the evolu-

tionary process has resulted only in a restricted set of basic innate mental abilities. This basic set comprises sensory skills and a small number of general-purpose rules for learning and reasoning, such as habituation, operant and classical conditioning, imitation, and the basic principles of logic and probabilistic reasoning. All other human psychological traits result from the application of these basic general-purpose rules to the deliverances of the senses. That is, all other human psychological traits are the product of learning and reasoning. On this view, evolved psychological components place only the broadest constraints on what a human mind can become through psychological development. As a consequence, evolutionary thinking is not useful in psychological theorizing. Human psychological traits can only be explained by studying the learning and reasoning processes that generate them. Given that the basic innate components involved in such processes have already been identified, evolutionary studies are not needed. This view was the official orthodoxy in psychology, anthropology, the social sciences and the humanities for much of the twentieth century.

People who hold this view usually also think that culture is very important. They believe that much of human psychological development is determined by the cultural context. Humans absorb the surrounding culture and learn to behave in ways that are similar to those of people in their community. This process of absorption is made possible by the basic biologically evolved machinery but, because of its general-purpose nature, such machinery does not pose any restrictions on cultural absorption, except perhaps for very general restrictions on the quantity of cultural information that humans can absorb and on the rate at which they can absorb it.

Even though there are some disciplines or subdisciplines where the old orthodoxy is still popular, this view has now been abandoned by many researchers in the cognitive and social sciences, and for good reasons. Many ethnographic studies suggest that, despite being large, cultural variation is not as unconstrained as many twentieth-century researchers claimed it to be. At a deep level of analysis, there seem to be many cross-cultural constants. Moreover, a variety of empirical and theoretical considerations (including computer simulations and mathematical models) indicate that the mental architecture posited by the old orthodoxy is unable to explain the acquisition of many standard psychological competences, such as the ability to speak and understand a language, the ability to ascribe mental states to other humans, or the ability to learn a new skill by observing a conspecific. One of the most influential thinkers in this area is Noam Chomsky, who strongly criticized the behaviourist theories of the old orthodoxy according to which language acquisition can be explained by appealing solely to general-purpose learning (Chomsky, 1959, 1987).

3.3. **Chomsky**

Chomsky revolutionized the study of language acquisition by drawing attention to two factors: (1) the speed, ease, and reliability with which most human children in all cultures acquire the ability to understand and speak the language of their community, and (2) the relative paucity of linguistic stimuli that children receive. He argued that the input of the acquisition process is too impoverished for it to be possible that children learn to speak and understand a language as quickly and reliably as they do by means solely of classical and operant conditioning or through unconstrained processes of hypothesis formation and testing (where the hypotheses in question are about the rules that govern the language spoken in the community). This is the famous 'poverty of the stimulus' argument. Chomsky concluded that (1) and (2) can only be explained by assuming that the acquisition process is biased, constrained, and directed by innate knowledge of what syntactic structures can and cannot occur in human languages (Chomsky, 1987). As he famously put it, children have innate knowledge of a universal grammar (UG). The languages with syntactic structures compatible with the rules of UG are only a proper subset of all the logically possible languages. While superficially human languages seem to be radically different from each other, at the level of fundamental rules of syntax there is, according to Chomsky, no variation at all: all human languages are versions of UG because implicit knowledge of UG governs the acquisition of language in every (normal) human child.

Chomsky's view of language has been incredibly influential. But his theory is not uncontroversial. It is certainly true that (1) and (2) indicate the existence of important and universal constraints on language acquisition. But important disagreements exist about whether such constraints are generated by innate knowledge of a UG or by something else (Elman *et al.*, 1996; Tomasello, 2003) and about what such innate knowledge might consist in (Pinker, 1994; Cowie, 1999; Fodor, 2000). One point can be made without going into these controversies. If the process responsible for the acquisition of specific psychological traits is constrained in ways that are not predicted by the general-purpose architecture of the old orthodoxy, then evolutionary theory can in principle help us understand how human minds work by helping us understand these constraints. In recent decades, an increasing number of psychological studies have uncovered evidence for the existence of such constraints on the acquisition of many important human psychological traits. Again, disagreements exist about how such constraints should be conceived of, about how they develop and operate, and about how evolutionary theory can help us understand them (Sperber, 1996; Pinker, 1997;

Bateson and Martin, 1999; Heyes, 2003; Lickliter and Honeycutt, 2003; Sterelny, 2003). But most of the researchers aware of the evidence for the existence of such constraints tend to agree on the usefulness of (some kind of) evolutionary thinking in psychological theorizing.

Curiously, Chomsky is one of those who disagrees (see quotes in Pinker and Bloom, 1990). According to him, innate knowledge of UG is likely to be the byproduct of a single genetic mutation that affected some profound structural features of the human brain and has been inherited by all (normal) modern humans (Chomsky, 1982). Innate knowledge of UG is not the result of a cumulative process of selection driven by long-standing features of the human evolutionary environment and, therefore, studying human evolution will not tell us much about language acquisition, except for the fact that, at some point in time, a lucky macro-mutation occurred.

Chomsky's ideas about the evolution of language are almost certainly incorrect. The chances that something as complex and functionally organized as the human linguistic competence could result from a single lucky macro-mutation (or even a small set of lucky macro-mutations) are "vanishingly small" (Pinker and Bloom, 1990; Pinker, 1994; Dennett, 1995). Many different genes and non-genetic developmental factors are involved in the reliable development of human linguistic abilities. That these factors almost universally combine in members of the human species to reliably give rise to complex developmental patterns can only have resulted from processes of cumulative selection. Attempts to understand the evolutionary and selectional history of language acquisition can, at least in principle, help us understand how the various components of the linguistic competence operate. These attempts may often present epistemic difficulties, which means that we should be careful when using evolutionary thinking in psychological theorizing; but this does not mean that evolutionary thinking in this area is useless.

3.4. Wilson's sociobiology

Genetic selection occurs when:

- a phenotypic variant increases in frequency (in a given population) relative to other variants (also present in the population);

- This increase in frequency is due to the variant conferring higher (inclusive) fitness to the organisms that have it (relative to the fitness of the organisms that have other variants);

- The differences between the competing variants are due (at least in part) to transmissible genetic elements, so that when the genetic differences are transmitted to the following generations, the phenotypic differences caused by these genetic differences are also likely to be transmitted.

As long as these conditions are satisfied, the phenotypic variants in question can be of any kind. They can be, for example, behavioural variants. Behavioural differences, like all other kinds of phenotypic differences, can be the target of genetic selection. In contemporary evolutionary biology, a *genetic adaptation* is any trait for which there has been genetic selection. Behavioural traits, like all other kinds of phenotypic traits, can be genetic adaptations (Futuyma, 1998).

In *Sociobiology*, E. O. Wilson argued that many human behaviours actually are genetic adaptations. For example, he argued that behavioural traits such as incest avoidance, male promiscuity, female coyness, rape, and hostility to strangers are genetic adaptations (Wilson, 1975, 1978). Wilson was accused of being a genetic determinist (Allen *et al.*, 1975). Were the accusers right?

The claim that a phenotypic trait P is a genetic adaptation does not entail that P is genetically determined. That is, it does not entail that there are certain genes such that if an organism has them then the organism necessarily develops P, independently of the environmental circumstances in which the organism finds itself. Nothing in the definition of genetic selection requires this to be the case. The genetic selection of a trait is entirely compatible with the trait being affected by environmental variation. Indeed, this is typically what happens (Dawkins, 1982). Moreover, the definition of genetic selection is entirely compatible with a genetic adaptation being the developmental outcome of complex interactions between genes and environmental factors, independently of whether such factors are also responsible for phenotypic variation or not. Also, one should notice that some genetic adaptations are facultative adaptations. These are adaptations produced by selection favouring variants that are sensitive to differences in environment and use such sensitivity to generate different outcomes in different situations. So, there can be selection for a variant that results in outcome P^1 when in situation S^1, in outcome P^2 when in situation S^2, in P^3 when in S^3, etc. For example, some insects develop different shapes or pigmentation according to the season in which they are born. This is due to selection for developing a given phenotype in spring, a different phenotype in summer, etc. All such phenotypes are genetic adaptations, but their development is environmentally induced.

Wilson knew all these things and so his opponents were wrong in accusing him of genetic determinism. It is true though that some sections of Wilson's writings present the view that the psychological dispositions responsible for behavioural genetic adaptations are not developmentally malleable and that, as a consequence, the behaviours in question may be very difficult to eradicate. Wilson's claims on what he called *biological refractoriness* were based mainly on the assumption that genetic adaptations are always developmentally robust. As we will see below, such an assumption is wrong. Ironically, some of those who accused Wilson of being a genetic determinist were probably making the same mistake. Their opposition to evolutionary explanations of human behaviour was often the result of a combination of two things: (i) a desire to promote political action aimed at changing what they saw as unjust social arrangements, and (ii) a belief that, given that genetic adaptations are hard to modify, such political action is incompatible with the view that human behaviours are genetic adaptations.

However, not all criticisms to Wilson had to do with genetic determinism. Some evolutionary biologists were unhappy with Wilson's evolutionary theories of human behaviour because they saw such theories as speculations with little evidence to support them. For example, Wilson claimed that certain forms of aggressive behaviour are widespread because of their positive contribution to genetic fitness. But he had not conducted any proper analysis of the fitness costs and benefits of the behaviours in question. In the years immediately following the publication of *Sociobiology*, some researchers started doing what Wilson had not done. They developed optimality models of human behaviour and looked for ethnographic data that could provide evidence about whether human behaviour in various societies matches the predictions of the models or not. This was the birth of what is now called *human behavioural ecology*.

Even if Wilson had had good evidence about the positive contribution to fitness of the behaviours he was interested in, many of his claims about such behaviours being genetic adaptations would have been unsupported. In the case of extant humans, even when it is possible to determine the fitness consequences of a given behaviour, it is not easy to use this information to ascertain whether the behaviour is a genetic adaptation. The reason for this is that current human environments differ in many important respects from the environments in which our ancestors evolved. For example, there have been very significant changes in:

- the amounts and compositions of foods eaten by humans (thanks to changes in subsistence practices and in technology);
- the sizes and structures of human social groups;
- the amounts and means of social exchange and mobility;
- the structures of the places where members of our lineage live;
- the daily and yearly rhythms of the lives of members of our lineage (as a result, for example, of artificial lighting).

Many of these changes are the product of human activities. This process is called *niche construction* (Odling-Smee *et al.*, 2003; Laland, Chapter 4). All living organisms are (in one way or another) niche constructors, but human niche construction is particularly powerful. A form of niche construction that is extremely important in humans is *cultural transmission*. Cultural transmission produces environmental changes by generating technological and behavioural evolution. Moreover, cultural transmission and technological innovations such as books and mass media (which are themselves the products of cultural evolution) are responsible for constant changes in the human *cognitive niche*, that is, in the kinds and quantities of salient stimuli that our minds have to deal with.

In this context, environmental change matters in at least two ways. The first has to do with the difference between being adaptive and being an adaptation. A trait is adaptive or maladaptive in a given environment according to whether, respectively, it increases or decreases fitness (on average) in that environment. The fact that a trait is adaptive (or maladaptive) in the current environment does not mean that the trait was adaptive (or maladaptive) in ancestral environments. Traits that are adaptive in the current environment may not be traits that were adaptive in ancestral environments and increased in frequency for that reason. Conversely, traits that are maladaptive in the current environment may be adaptations that have lost their positive contribution to fitness because of environmental change. Thus, even if we can establish that, say, certain kinds of aggressive behaviours are adaptive in current human environments, this fact by itself does not tell us much about whether there was selection for those behaviours in past environments.

The second way in which environmental change matters in relation to the kinds of evolutionary hypotheses put forward by Wilson has to do with the fact that the same psychological mechanism can generate different behaviours in different environments. A behaviour can be highly adaptive in the current environment while at the same time being an evolutionary novelty. It can be the product of evolved psychological mechanisms operating in a novel environment. Evolutionary novelties are traits that never occurred in the past. This means that they were never selected and thereby they cannot possibly be genetic adaptations. A certain form of aggressive behaviour may, for example, be an evolutionary novelty induced by novel social arrangements. Even if adaptive, such behaviour would not be a genetic adaptation.

The fact that a behaviour confers higher fitness in current environments does not guarantee that the behaviour was adaptive in ancestral environments and it does not even guarantee that it occurred in ancestral environments. All this does not mean that measuring the fitness consequences of behaviours—or, more generally, the way specific behaviours contribute to the maximization of some variable usually correlated with fitness—and seeing whether such measurements are consistent with particular optimality models or particular evolutionary hypotheses is not an important tool. Many interesting findings

have been generated through these methods by human behavioural ecologists (Hrdy, 1999; Smith *et al.*, 2001; Shennan, 2002). Yet consistency between observed human behaviour and optimality models only provides limited information about whether the positive contribution to fitness of a given behaviour is due to genetic selection specifically for that behaviour, to learning, or to some other process.

3.5. Cosmides and Tooby's evolutionary psychology

In a series of articles written in the 1980s and the early 1990s, Leda Cosmides and John Tooby elaborated a theory of the relation between human evolution and human minds that aimed at combining evolutionary theory and cognitive psychology. They called it *evolutionary psychology* (Tooby and Cosmides 1990a, 1990b, 1992). Some authors have objected to the use of this label, pointing out that Cosmides and Tooby's views constitute only one possible way of using evolutionary thinking in psychological theorising (e.g. Heyes, 2003). For this reason, it has now become customary to distinguish between *narrow-sense evolutionary psychologists* (i.e. Cosmides and Tooby and those who agree with their specific theoretical commitments) and *broad-sense evolutionary psychologists* (i.e. all those who think that evolutionary thinking can be fruitfully used, but not necessarily in the way suggested by Cosmides and Tooby, in psychological theorizing).

According to Cosmides and Tooby, the problems faced by Wilson's theory can be avoided by concentrating on psychological mechanisms (rather than behaviours) and on ancestral fitness consequences (rather than current adaptiveness). A behaviour can be selected only if there is selection for psychological mechanisms that generate it. Psychological mechanisms produce different behavioural outputs in response to different inputs from experience. A psychological mechanism that has been selected to produce a range of behaviours in a given range of situations may, when confronted with a situation that did not occur in the selective environment, produce an evolutionarily novel output: it can produce a behaviour that was not among those the mechanism produced while it was being selected. According to Cosmides and Tooby, this fact has important implications for the evolutionary study of the human mind.

In order to understand how human minds work, one needs to identify, describe, and explain the psychological mechanisms that compose them. Cosmides and Tooby believe that psychological mechanisms can be studied in the same way that one studies artefacts. A good way to understand how an artefact works is to obtain information about its intended function, the purpose for which it was designed. Similarly, a good way to understand how a psychological mechanism works is to study its evolutionary function, the 'purpose' for which it was selected, the properties and effects that caused the mechanism to increase in frequency in past environments. The way humans behave in the current environment cannot tell us much about what human psychological mechanisms were selected for. The reason for this is that many of these behaviours are likely to be evolutionary novelties, generated by the interaction between evolved mechanisms and new situations. Instead, on this view, the right way to uncover the 'design' of psychological mechanisms is to determine what selection pressures caused their evolution. Current fitness may not be useful in this context. It is *past* fitness that matters. We need to identify the ancestral adaptive problems that human psychological mechanisms evolved to solve. In order to do this, we need to understand what, following John Bowlby, Cosmides and Tooby call the *environment of evolutionary adaptedness* (EEA), the ancestral environment to which the human mind is adapted. According to them:

- the EEA of human-specific psychological adaptations is the Pleistocene (1.8 million to 10 000 years ago);
- selection pressures in the Pleistocene caused the evolution of many different functionally independent psychological mechanisms, or *modules*;
- each module evolved to solve a different recurrent adaptive problem faced by our Pleistocene ancestors;
- many of these modules reached fixation and are now universal in the human species.

On this view, human minds contain many innate universal modules each of which is a genetic adaptation evolved during the Pleistocene to solve a Pleistocene-specific adaptive problem. This account has been endorsed and elaborated by Steven Pinker (1994, 1997, 2002) and others (e.g. Barkow *et al.*, 1992; Daly and Wilson, 1999; Atran, 2002; Buss, 2003, 2005).

The claims made by narrow-sense evolutionary psychologists on modularity and universality are highly controversial (Wilson, 1994; Sterelny and Griffiths, 1999; Fodor, 2000; Barrett *et al.*, 2002; Sterelny, 2003; Buller, 2005), but there is no room to discuss these controversies here. Another debate concerns the way narrow-sense evolutionary psychologists conceive of the environment of evolutionary adaptedness. Arguably, narrow-sense evolutionary psychologists often tend to underestimate the variability of hominin Pleistocene environments and this leads them to simplistic views about the selection pressures that were operating on our ancestors at the time. Moreover, focusing only on Pleistocene selection pressures may not be sufficient, and selection pressures that affected the mental evolution of our lineage both before and after the Pleistocene should also be taken into account (Smith *et al.*, 2001; Laland and Brown, 2002; Laland, Chapter 4).

Independently of whether narrow-sense evolutionary psychologists are right in thinking that the Pleistocene played a prominent role in the evolution of human-specific psychological adaptations, important issues remain concerning how to use hypotheses about Pleistocene selection pressures in psychological theorizing. Cosmides and Tooby claim that such hypotheses should be used according to what they call *adaptive thinking*. This inferential method begins with a reflection on the Pleistocene, whose purpose is to determine the recurrent adaptive problems faced by our Pleistocene ancestors. Once an adaptive problem has been identified, a psychological mechanism that provides an optimal solution to that adaptive problem is sought. This mechanism must be one that in the Pleistocene would have produced adaptive behaviour and that, as a consequence, would have been selected. When such a mechanism has been described in some detail, its existence in the minds of extant humans is posited. The final step is to look for evidence that confirms the existence of the posited mechanism by observing the way modern humans behave both in normal life and in laboratory situations. Cosmides and Tooby claim that adaptive thinking is a reliable method to identify and explain the functional components of extant human minds. In fact, they sometimes suggest that it is the *only* reliable way to do this (Tooby and Cosmides 1992).

The reliability of an inferential method such as adaptive thinking can be studied empirically, since it can be measured in terms of the percentage of cases in which the use of the method leads to true hypotheses. But while Comsides, Tooby and their followers claim to have discovered a good number of previously unknown psychological mechanisms through adaptive thinking, the evidence for the existence of these mechanisms is often ambiguous (Gray *et al.*, 2003; Buller, 2005). Given this, we can ask whether there are any good theoretical reasons for supposing that adaptive thinking is reliable and, more importantly, whether there are ways to increase its chances of being reliable.

3.6. **Developmental environments**

It is undoubtedly true that many human genes were selected because they were more likely than other available genes to result in the development of mechanisms capable of producing adaptive behaviours in ancestral environments. But there is no a priori reason to think that, in the current environment, those selected genes result in the development of the very same psychological mechanisms that they produced in ancestral environments. Psychological mechanisms, like all other traits, are the product of developmental interactions between genes and environments. A gene that was selected because in a given developmental environment it resulted in a given psychological mechanism may, when it operates in a different developmental environment, result in a different psychological mechanism. As mentioned above, the human environment has changed in many important respects. Many of the changed factors probably have a very significant impact on psychological development. Thus, it is not just the human *selective* environment that has changed. The *developmental* environment has changed too.

Even if we still know relatively little about psychological development, we have good reasons—both of an empirical and of a theoretical nature—to believe that these changes in developmental environment may be responsible for important modifications in psychological mechanisms. Some of these reasons have to do with what we know about the human brain, which appears to be very plastic, even though not in an unconstrained way. The plasticity seems to be particularly significant at those levels of organization (medium-levels and micro-levels) at which specific psychological mechanisms are likely to be implemented (Elman *et al.*, 1996; Quartz and Sejnowski, 1997). If many of the psychological mechanisms of extant humans are evolutionary novelties resulting from the developmental interaction between genes selected in ancestral environments and novel niches, then many of these mechanisms are not adaptations and cannot be reliably identified by adaptive thinking *à la* Cosmides and Tooby.

One possible reply is that genetic adaptations are developmentally robust. Thus, changes in the environment are unlikely to have an impact on their development. Consider those human genes that were selected because they resulted in the development of psychological mechanisms adapted to the Pleistocene. On this view, because of the developmental robustness of adaptations, in the current environment these genes usually result in the development of the very same psychological mechanisms they produced in their EEA. Unfortunately, this argument is wrong. Not all genetic adaptations are developmentally robust.

Developmental robustness often confers fitness advantages, but it is also costly. Important developmental resources are needed to buffer the development of a phenotypic trait. There can be selection *for* or *against* the developmental robustness of a trait, depending on the balance of fitness costs and benefits. The fact that there has been selection for a psychological mechanism does not mean that there has also been selection for the developmental robustness of that mechanism. Moreover, when selection for the developmental robustness of a trait occurs, such selection can only be selection for buffering the trait against environmental perturbations that actually occur in the range of environments where the trait is evolving. Natural selection has no foresight, so it cannot select for buffers that protect the development of a trait against future kinds of perturbations. Even if we suppose that there was selection in the Pleistocene for adaptive psychological mechanisms buffered against perturbations that were common in the Pleistocene, we cannot from this infer that such psychological mechanisms are also developmentally buffered against all the profound ways in which the human environment has changed.

If Wilson was wrong in assuming that *in general* behaviours selected in ancestral environments must occur in extant human populations, evolutionary psychologists are wrong in assuming that *in general* psychological mechanisms selected in the Pleistocene must develop in current humans. This does not necessarily mean that adaptive thinking *never* works. It only means that, in order to properly use adaptive thinking for the purpose of identifying structures in the minds of extant humans, we need to know more about how brain development results in psychological mechanisms and about the kinds of developmental buffers which are likely to be involved in such processes.

3.7. The problem of the problem and the problem of the solution

Adaptive thinking *à la* Cosmides and Tooby cannot (at least not by itself) help us identify evolutionarily novel psychological mechanisms. At the moment we do not know how many such mechanisms there are, and whether they are the majority. But can adaptive thinking at least help us identify those psychological mechanisms that are *not* evolutionary novelties?

Let us focus on the first step of adaptive thinking, the one requiring that we ascertain the adaptive problems faced by our Pleistocene ancestors. One thing to notice is that the adaptive problems faced by an organism are in part determined by the phenotypic features of the organism (Lewontin, 1983). There is a sense in which all organisms face the same adaptive problem: to have more descendants than their conspecifics. But this does not tell us anything about what specific features are going to evolve in specific lineages. The evolution of specific features is the product of specific adaptive problems,

and specific adaptive problems are partly determined by existing capacities. For example, fast-running predators are selectively relevant to gazelles, which can run away and (if they are fast enough) out-compete slower conspecifics, but they are not selectively relevant to plants, since plants cannot move. Thus, in order to identify the specific adaptive problems faced by our Pleistocene ancestors, we need information about their physical and psychological traits. The more specific is such information, the more specific our hypotheses about Pleistocene selection pressures can be. At the moment, the information in our possession is not very detailed.

Obviously, the selection pressures acting on an organism are determined not only by the organism's phenotypic traits but also by the organism's environment. Thus, even if we know relatively little about the traits (especially the psychological traits) of our Pleistocene ancestors, do we at least know enough about Pleistocene environments? The answer is that often we do not. One reason for this has to do, once again, with environmental change. Humans have greatly modified their physical and cognitive niche through niche construction and cultural transmission processes. But such profound changes are not just the product of recent historical events. Niche construction and cultural transmission changed the human selective environment throughout the Pleistocene. During the Pleistocene, many important aspects of the human selective environment were *constantly* changing, and each change undoubtedly selected for psychological traits that would then generate further environmental changes.

Our current ignorance of Pleistocene phenotypes and of how exactly the hominin physical and cognitive niche changed during those 1.8 million years makes it difficult for us to identify with enough detail the specific adaptive problems faced by our Pleistocene ancestors. We can call this *the problem of (identifying the adaptive) problem*.

Let us now focus on the second step of adaptive thinking, the one requiring that we give detailed descriptions of the psychological mechanisms that evolved to solve Pleistocene adaptive problems. Suppose that, at least in some circumstances, we are able to determine some important and relatively specific adaptive problems faced by our Pleistocene ancestors. Is this sufficient to allow us to *easily* determine which psychological mechanisms were selected for in response to such adaptive problems? It is not. One reason for this is that genetic selection is a *tinkering process* (Jacob, 1977). Selection can only drive up the frequency of the fittest variants present in a population. Which solution to a given adaptive problem can evolve in a given lineage is constrained by the kinds and number of heritable variants present in that lineage. New variants are always modifications of pre-existing traits. Thus, the kinds and number of variants available in a lineage are a function of the history of the lineage. Moreover, genetic mutations produce new phenotypic variants by producing changes in the organism's developmental system. Thus, the kinds and number of variants available in a lineage are also a function of the developmental and structural constraints that operate on the phenotypic traits present in the lineage, constraints which may themselves be the product of previous runs of selection. This means that, even in those cases in which we are able to identify a specific adaptive problem faced by our ancestors, we can make reliable inferences about what adaptive solution evolved in response to that problem only if we know enough about the previous history of the lineage and the structural and developmental constraints that operated on the generation of new variants. The more we know about these things, the more specific and reliable can our hypothesis be. But, in general, we know little about what variants in psychological mechanisms were available in Pleistocene populations. This makes it difficult for us to infer what psychological mechanisms had the opportunity of being selected. We can call this *the problem of (identifying the adaptive) solution*.

The problem of the problem and the problem of the solution are difficult but not intractable problems. Their existence means that adaptive thinking is often not a very reliable inferential method and that its reliability can be improved substantially by gaining a better understanding of ancestral developmental processes, ancestral phenotypes, and ancestral environments.

3.8. Evolution and culture

From a comparative perspective, one peculiar feature of the human species is the incredible amount of behavioural variation present in the species. The way such variation is distributed is also peculiar. There are large behavioural differences between populations and, in comparison, small behavioural differences within populations. One common explanation of this phenomenon is cultural transmission. Beliefs, values, norms, mental recipes for doing or saying things are intensely transmitted within communities and only relatively rarely transmitted between communities. This generates behavioural homogeneity within communities and behavioural differences between communities. Narrow-sense evolutionary psychologists have challenged this explanation. They distinguish between *evoked* and *transmitted* culture. Transmitted culture is the transfer of beliefs, values, norms, etc., which occurs through social learning. Evoked culture refers instead to behavioural variants generated not by the interpersonal transmission of cultural information but exclusively by the context-dependent action of evolved psychological mechanisms. On this view, many of the observed population-level differences in behaviour are produced by evoked rather than transmitted culture. People all over the world share the same evolved psychological mechanisms and many population-level behavioural differences are due to the fact that many such mechanisms are facultative genetic adaptations. People living in the same community often behave in the same way not because of cultural transmission within populations but because they live in the same environment and their evolved psychological mechanisms react similarly to this common environment. People living in different communities often behave differently not because of lack of cultural transmission between communities but because they inhabit different environments (Tooby and Cosmides, 1992).

Arguably, narrow-sense evolutionary psychologists underestimate the role of transmitted culture. Even though some population-level differences may be environmentally triggered without the mediation of cultural transmission, most of the traits that vary across populations—such as subsistence practices, religious rituals, knowledge about local plants and animals, etc.—cannot simply be evoked by interacting with the environment in a socially unmediated way. Even though in part they depend on the local environment, these traits can only be acquired through intense enculturation.

The importance of cultural transmission in explaining human behaviour is one of the central tenets of the old orthodoxy. But the claim that cultural transmission is important is perfectly compatible with the claim that there are evolved biases and constraints operating on the way cultural information is passed from individual to individual. If such biases and constraints exist—and the evidence suggests that they do—then evolutionary theory can become an important tool for studying how culture affects the development of human minds. Moreover, evolutionary theory can help us understand what are the cognitive mechanisms that allow for cultural transmission and why our species relies so much on culture.

There is also another sense in which an evolutionary approach might help us understand culture. Given that cultural transmission, like genetic transmission, is responsible for the recurrence of phenotypic variants across time and organisms, cultural change can be conceived of as an evolutionary process. One possible way to conceive of culture as an evolutionary process is *memetics* (Dawkins, 1976, 1982; Dennett, 1991, 1995; Blackmore, 1999; Aunger, 2002, and Chapter 41; Distin, 2005). Memes are thought to be mental states embodying discrete chunks of socially transmissible information. Memes are discrete in the sense that when a meme is socially transmitted the information it carries does not usually blend with the information carried by other memes. Genetic transmission and memetic transmission are thought to be very similar processes. Genetic transmission is a copying process in which, in general, genes produce identical genes; the only exception to this is when a genetic mutation occurs. In the same way, memetic transmission is a copying process in which, in general, memes produce identical memes, the exceptions being cases of memetic mutation. According to memeticists, just like genetic evolution can be conceived of in terms of changes in gene frequencies, cultural change can be conceived of in terms of changes in meme frequencies. Moreover, on this view, significant changes in meme frequencies are almost always due to differences in *meme fitness*. Some memes have features that make them more likely—in a given social, biological, and physical environment—to be passed on. Such memes have

higher cultural fitness and, as a consequence, they can increase in frequency. Memes have higher fitness when they are easier to transmit, when they are good at motivating people to pass them on, when they are more likely to be present in influential individuals, when they are particularly memorable or cognitively salient, etc.

Arguably, memetics—at least as conceived by some of its advocates—gives an unsatisfactory account of cultural change. There are empirical studies and mathematical models showing that cultural transmission is not in many ways gene-like. For example, cultural transmission is in general (even though not always) much more noisy and much less reliable than genetic transmission and, at least in some areas of culture, substantial blending occurs. Does this mean that culture is not an evolutionary system? It does not. It just means that the correct way to characterize the similarities between cultural change and biological change is different from what usually suggested by memeticists.

Biological evolution consists in changes in the statistical distributions of phenotypic and genetic traits. Whether and how these statistical distributions change can often be explained in terms of three kinds of factors: *transmission factors*, *selection factors* and *mutation factors*. Let us consider each in turn. Organisms are causally connected to their descendants by means of *inheritance channels*. These channels constitute transmission factors. Genetic transmission is the most important of these channels, but it is not the only one, and it is not even the only one to have evolutionary significance (Mameli, 2004; Mameli, 2005; Jablonka and Lamb, 2005). These causal connections between the generations affect the extent to which and the ways in which organisms resemble their offspring. Thereby, such causal connections can help explain the extent to which and the ways in which the statistical distribution of a trait in a generation depends on the statistical distribution of that trait (or of some related traits) in previous generations. In contrast, explanations of changes in the distribution of traits in terms of selection factors appeal to the way traits affect organisms' chances of survival and reproduction. Selection occurs when a trait increases in frequency because it makes the organisms that have it more likely to do things which result (through reproduction) in the existence of other organisms (biological descendants) with the same (or a similar) trait. Finally, there are cases in which the statistical distribution of traits is affected by factors that generate new phenotypic or genetic variants. These are mutation factors. The agents responsible for genetic mutation are one kind of mutation factor, but they are not the only kind, and they are also not the only kind of mutation factor to have evolutionary significance (West-Eberhard, 2003).

Let us now see what the similarities with culture are. Cultural evolution consists in changes in the statistical distributions of culturally transmissible traits. Similarly to what happens in the general biological case, whether and how these statistical distributions change can often be explained in terms of transmission, selection, and mutation factors. Humans have cognitive mechanisms that allow them to learn from their conspecifics, and they have cognitive mechanisms that allow them to transmit what they have learned. Such cognitive mechanisms constitute *cultural inheritance channels*. These channels affect the extent to which and the ways in which the mental states and behaviours of an individual resemble the mental states and behaviours of some other humans, those with whom the individual has had some cognitive contact. As a consequence, cultural inheritance channels can help explain the extent to which and the ways in which the statistical distribution of a cultural trait at a given time depends on the statistical distribution of that trait (or of some related cultural traits) at an earlier time. Explanations of changes in the distribution of cultural traits that appeal to selection factors, in contrast, refer not to the features of cultural transmission channels but to the ways cultural traits affect the chances that individuals have of being chosen as sources of cultural information by other individuals. Cultural selection occurs when a cultural trait increases in frequency because it makes the individuals who have it more likely to become cultural models and targets of imitation. Finally, there are circumstances in which the statistical distribution of culturally transmissible traits is affected by factors that cause new culturally transmissible variants to appear in the population (through, for example, individual learning). Such factors are mutation factors and they also help explain changes in the distribution of cultural traits.

Cultural change, just like biological change, is an evolutionary process because it can be best understood in terms of the operation of transmission, selection, and mutation factors. The divide between these three kinds of factors is not always a sharp one. This is true both in the biological case and in the cultural case, even though it is perhaps more so in the cultural case. The existence of gene-like particles is an important feature of biological transmission processes, but such particles are not an essential feature of an evolutionary system. This is the reason why culture can be conceived of as an evolutionary process even when discrete memes, strictly speaking, do not exist. When they insist on gene-like cultural particles, memeticists provide the wrong general framework for an evolutionary analysis of cultural processes.

The fact that both cultural change and genetic change are evolutionary processes means that the evolutionary origins of human minds are both genetic and cultural (Tomasello, 1999; Dennett, 2003). Moreover, these two evolutionary processes interact. Changes in the distribution of cultural variants modify the selective and developmental environments of genes; and changes in the distribution of genetic variants modify the selective and developmental environments of cultural variants. Thus, in order to understand the evolutionary history of human minds and to properly use such understanding to explain the workings of extant human minds, we need to study the interactions between cultural and genetic evolution. Many interesting ideas about how to provide a theoretically and predictively useful account of gene–culture coevolution have already been developed (Cavalli Sforza and Feldman, 1981; Boyd and Richerson, 1985, 2005; Durham, 1991; Deacon, 1997; Richerson and Boyd, 2005; Laland *et al.*, 2001; Shennan, 2002; Henrich and McElreath, 2003; Sterelny, 2003, and in press; Odling-Smee *et al.*, 2003; Sperber and Hirschfeld, 2004; McElreath and Henrich, Chapter 38; Mameli, forthcoming). But much remains to be done. Progress in this area will be crucial for making evolutionary theory more useful in psychological theorizing.

Some of the first mathematical models of gene–culture coevolution were developed by

Wilson (Lumsden and Wilson, 1981). Wilson believed that genetic evolution constrains cultural evolution more than the other way around. This led him to make the oft-quoted claim that "genes hold culture on a leash" (Wilson, 1978). Was he right or wrong? Some cultural variants enhance genetic fitness and others do not. Genes that make people more likely to acquire fitness-decreasing cultural variants are selected against. This fact might help explain why certain fitness-decreasing cultural variants are less likely to be transmitted. But the spread of cultural variants is often so fast as to be virtually unaffected—at least in the short and medium term—by genetic fitness. One obvious example is the spread of maladaptive behaviours such as smoking tobacco. This suggests that culture might be on the driver's seat of the coevolutionary process. Moreover, there are many features of human psychology indicating that culture has selected for an increased ability—an increased genetic predisposition, in Wilson's terms—to acquire and transmit cultural variants. There has been culturally generated genetic selection for (more and more) culture. As Richerson and Boyd (2001) put it: "Culture is on a leash all right, but the dog on the end is big, smart, and independent, not a well-trained toy poodle. On any given walk, who is leading whom is not a question with a simple answer."

Many of the existing investigations in gene–culture coevolution are an attempt to use population genetics ideas to model cultural processes and the interaction between cultural processes and genetic processes. This approach has proved fruitful, but other strategies need to be pursued too (e.g. Mesoudi *et al.* 2006). One important and little-studied topic is the way that genes and culture interact developmentally and the transgenerational impact of such developmental interactions. By interacting with their children in specific ways—ways which are heavily influenced by social learning—human parents shape the developmental environment of their offspring. This often causes the children to acquire the same cognitive traits and emotional dispositions as the parents. Similarly, human communities shape the developmental environment of their youngsters in a way that usually results in the youngsters acquiring beliefs, norms and skills that are common in their community. These processes constitute a form of *downstream*

developmental niche construction by means of which human generations (at the individual level, or at the family level, or at the group level) partly construct the developmental niche of the subsequent generations. A proper account of this form of niche construction is extremely important for understanding human psychological development and the way it has changed over time (Griffiths and Gray, 1994; Sterelny, 2003).

3.9. **Innateness**

Many authors interested in the development and evolution of human cognition seem to find utility in the notion of innateness and some have tried to explain and vindicate this notion (Ariew, 1999; Samuels, 2002). Arguably, though, the innate/non-innate distinction hinders a proper understanding of human psychological traits, of how they develop and of how they evolved. The reason for this is that the various properties that are usually taken to be constitutive or strongly indicative of innateness are not equivalent to each other, and the evidential and empirical relations between them seem to be, at least in some important contexts, relatively weak (Griffiths, 2002; Mameli and Bateson, 2006).

Among the properties that biologists and psychologists take to be constitutive or strongly indicative of innateness are things such as: developmental robustness, reduced malleability in post-developmental phase, lack of learning during development, species-typicality, and being a genetic adaptation. We can call them the *i-properties*. The notion of innateness (or at least the way it is usually employed) presupposes that the i-properties form a coherent cluster. That is, it presupposes that the following is true: if a phenotypic trait has one i-property then the trait is also likely to have many other i-properties. But at the moment we do not know whether the i-properties really form a coherent cluster, that is, whether they are strongly correlated with each other or not. The existence of this cluster is an open empirical question, and a difficult one. It is an empirical question that has not been thoroughly investigated. This is partly due to the fact that the widespread use of the innate/non-innate distinction has generated in researchers the illusion that the question has already been answered, while in fact it has not. Here is a list of some of the possible dissociations between i-properties and of the many things we still do not know about how such properties are related:

◆ Not all genetic adaptations are developmentally robust and not all developmentally robust traits are genetic adaptations. At the moment, we do not have a good understanding of how often and to what extent genetic adaptations in psychological traits are developmentally robust.

◆ Not all genetic adaptations are species-typical, or present in all normal members of a species. Currently, we do not have a good understanding of how often and to what extent genetic adaptations in psychological traits are species-typical.

◆ It is often thought that genetic adaptations are necessarily traits whose development does not involve learning. This is wrong. Genetic selection can act on differences in learned traits in the same way that it acts on other phenotypic differences, as long as the differences in question are genetic in origin. At the moment, we do not have a good understanding of how genetic selection affects the evolution of learned traits and of how learning affects genetic evolution.

◆ Learned traits may or may not be developmentally robust, depending on how reliable and buffered the learning process is. We still do not have a good account of how often and in what circumstances learning is developmentally robust. Moreover, we do not have a good account of the kinds of developmental processes that may be responsible for such robustness.

◆ Traits whose development does not involve learning may or may not be developmentally robust. Moreover, such traits may or may not be the product of developmental mechanisms for adaptive plasticity. For many psychological and neural traits, we still do not know whether their development is best described in terms of learning, in terms of other forms of adaptive plasticity, or in other terms. In addition, we do not have a good understanding of the circumstances in which natural selection favours one kind of developmental process over another.

◆ Some psychological traits are malleable during early phases of their development, but become difficult to modify once the process of development reaches a certain stage. Other traits are robust in early stages and become malleable later on. We do not yet have a good

understanding of when and why these phenomena occur.

The use of the innate/non-innate distinction has often led researchers to make unsupported inferences, such as the inference from "it is a genetic adaptation" to "it is developmentally robust", or from "it is developmentally robust" to "it is unlearned", or from "it is learned" to "it is not a genetic adaptation", etc. In order to avoid unreliable inferences and to focus on the important empirical issues, it might be useful to avoid any appeal to the innate/non-innate distinction in scientific contexts, at least until more evidence is gathered about the way the i-properties are related. In the absence of good evidence of strong correlations between i-properties, the various debates that have been framed in terms of innateness are better dealt with by referring to each of the i-properties individually. This would certainly pave the way to a better evolutionary and developmental understanding of psychological traits.

References

Allen *et al.* (1975) Against "Sociobiology". *New York Times Review of Books* 22(18): November 13.

Ariew, A. (1999) Innateness is canalization: a defense of a developmental account of innateness. In V. Hardcastle (ed.) *Where Biology Meets Psychology*, pp. 117–138. MIT Press.

Atran, S. (2002) *In Gods We Trust*. Oxford University Press, Oxford.

Aunger, R. (2002) *The Electric Meme*. Oxford University Press, Oxford.

Barkow, J., Cosmides, L. and Tooby, J. (1992) *The Adapted Mind*. Oxford University Press, Oxford.

Barrett, L., Dunbar, R. and Lycett, J. (2002) *Human Evolutionary Psychology*. Palgrave.

Bateson, P. and Martin, P. (1999) *Design for a Life*. Cape.

Blackmore, S. (1999) *The Meme Machine*. Oxford University Press, Oxford.

Boyd, R. and Richerson, P. (1985) *Culture and the Evolutionary Process*. University of Chicago Press, Chicago.

Boyd, R. and Richerson, P. (2005) *The Origin and Evolution of Cultures*. Oxford University Press.

Buss, D. M. (2003) *Evolutionary Psychology*, 2nd edn. Allyn & Bacon.

Buss, D. M. (ed.) (2005) *Handbook of Evolutionary Psychology*. Wiley.

Buller, D. (2005) *Adapting Minds*. MIT Press.

Cavalli-Sforza, L. L. and Feldman, M. W. (1981) *Cultural Transmission and Evolution*. Princeton University Press.

Chomsky, N. (1959) A review of B. F. Skinner's *Verbal Behaviour*. *Language* 35: 26–58.

Chomsky, N. (1982) *Noam Chomsky on the Generative Enterprise: A Discussion with Riny Hyybregts and Henk van Riemsdijk*. Foris.

Chomsky, N. (1987) *Language and Problems of Knowledge*. MIT Press.

Cowie, F. (1999) *What's Within*. Oxford University Press, Oxford.

Daly, M. and Wilson, M. (1999) Human evolutionary psychology and animal behaviour. *Animal Behaviour* 57: 509–519.

Dawkins, R. (1976) *The Selfish Meme*. Oxford University Press, Oxford.

Dawkins, R. (1982) *The Extended Phenotype*. Oxford University Press, Oxford.

Deacon, T. (1997) *The Symbolic Species*. Norton.

Dennett, D. C. (1991) *Consciousness Explained*. Little, Brown & Co.

Dennett, D. C. (1995) *Darwin's Dangerous Idea*. Simon & Schuster.

Dennett, D. C. (2003) *Freedom Evolves*. Allen Lane.

Distin, K. (2005) *The Selfish Meme*. Cambridge University Press, Cambridge.

Durham, W. H. (1991) *Coevolution*. Stanford University Press.

Elman, J. L., Bates, E. A., Johnson, M. H., Karmiloff-Smith, A., Parisi, D. and Plunkett, K. (1996) *Rethinking Innateness*. MIT Press.

Fodor, J. (2000) *The Mind Doesn't Work That Way*. MIT Press.

Futuyma, D. J. (1998) *Evolutionary Biology*, 3rd edn. Sinauer.

Gray, R., Heaney, M. and Fairhall, S. (2003) Evolutionary Psychology and the challenge of adaptive explanation. In K. Sterelny and J. Fitness (eds) *Front Mating to Mentality*, pp. 247–268. Psychology Press.

Griffiths, P. E. (2002) What is Innateness? *The Monist* 85: 70–85.

Griffiths, P. E. and Gray, R. G. (1994) Developmental systems and evolutionary explanation. *Journal of Philosophy* 91: 277–304.

Henrich, J. and McElreath, R. (2003) The evolution of cultural evolution. *Evolutionary Anthropology* 12: 123–135.

Heyes, C. (2003) Four routes of cognitive evolution. *Psychological Review* 110: 713–727.

Hrdy, S. (1999) *Mother Nature*. Pantheon.

Jablonka, E. and Lamb, M. (2005) *Evolution in Four Dimensions*. MIT.

Jacob, F. (1977) Evolution as tinkering. *Science* 1977: 1161–1166.

Laland, K. N. and Brown, G. R. (2002) *Sense and Nonsense*. Oxford University Press, Oxford.

Lewontin, R. (1983) Genes, organism and environment. In D. S. Bendall (ed.) *From Molecules to Men*. Cambridge University Press, Cambridge.

Lickliter, R. and Honeycutt, H. (2003) Developmental dynamics: toward a biologically plausible evolutionary psychology. *Psychological Bulletin* 129(6): 819–835.

Lumsden, C. J. and Wilson, E. O. (1981) *Genes, Mind, and Culture*. Harvard University Press.

Mameli, M. (2004) Nongenetic selection and nongenetic inheritance. *British Journal for the Philosophy of Science* 55: 37–71.

Mameli, M. (2005) The inheritance of features. *Biology and Philosophy* 20(2–3): 365–399.

Mameli, M. (forthcoming) Understanding culture: a commentary on Richerson and Boyd's *Not By Genes Alone*. *Biology and Philosophy*.

Mameli, M. and Bateson, P. (2006) Innateness and the sciences. *Biology and Philosophy*. 21: 155–188

Mesoudi, A. Whiter, A. and Laland, K. (2006) Towards a unified science of cultural evolution. *Behavioral and Brain Sciences* 29: 329–383.

Odling-Smee, J. F., Laland, K. N. and Feldman, M. W. (2003) *Niche Construction*. Princeton University Press.

Pinker, S. (1994) *The Language Instinct*. Harper.

Pinker, S. (1997) *How the Mind Works*. Norton.

Pinker, S. (2002) *The Blank Slate*. Viking Penguin.

Pinker, S. and Bloom, P. (1990) Natural language and natural selection. *Behavioural and Brain Science* 13: 707–784.

Quartz, S. R. and Sejnowski, T. J. (1997) The neural basis of cognitive development: A constructivist manifesto. *Behavioural and Brain Sciences* 20: 537–596.

Richerson, P. and Boyd, R. (2001) Culture is part of human biology. In S. Maasen and M. Winterhager (eds) *Science Studies: Probing the Dynamics of Scientific Knowledge*. Verlag.

Richerson, P. and Boyd, R. (2005) *Not By Genes Alone*. University of Chicago Press.

Samuels, R. (2002) Nativism in cognitive science. Mind and Language 17: 233–265.

Shennan, S. (2002) *Genes, Memes and Human History*. Thames & Hudson.

Smith, E. A., Borgerhoff-Mulder, M. and Hill, K. (2001) Controversies in the evolutionary social sciences: a guide to the perplexed. *Trends in Ecology and Evolution* 16(3): 128–135.

Sperber, D. (1996) *Explaining Culture*. Blackwell.

Sperber, D. and Hirshfield, L. A. (2004) The cognitive foundations of cultural stability and diversity. *Trends in Cognitive Science* 8: 40–46.

Sterelny, K. (2003) *Thought in a Hostile World*. Blackwell.

Sterelny, K. (in press) The evolution and evolvability of culture. In D. Walsh (ed.) *Twenty-Five Years of Spandrels*. Oxford University Press, Oxford.

Sterelny, K. and Griffiths, P. E. (1999) *Sex and Death*. University of Chicago Press, Chicago.

Tomasello, M. (1999) *The Cultural Origins of Human Cognition*. Harvard University Press.

Tooby J. and Cosmides L. (1990a) The past explains the present: emotional adaptations and the structure of ancestral environments. *Ethology and Sociobiology* 11: 375–424.

Tooby, J. and Cosmides, L. (1990b) On the universality of human nature and the uniqueness of the individual: the role of genetics and adaptation. *Journal of Personality* 58: 17–67.

Tooby, J. and Cosmides, L. (1992) The psychological foundations of culture. In Barkow, J.H., Cosmides, L. and Tooby, J. (eds) *The Adapted Mind*, pp. 19–136. Oxford University Press, Oxford.

West-Eberhard, M. J. (2003) *Developmental Plasticity and Evolution*. Oxford University Press, Oxford.

Wilson, D. S. (1994) Adaptive genetic variation and human evolutionary psychology. *Ethology and Sociobiology* 15: 219–235.

Wilson, E. O. (1975) *Sociobiology*. Belknap Press.

Wilson, E. O. (1978) *Human Nature*. Harvard University Press.

CHAPTER 4

Niche construction, human behavioural ecology and evolutionary psychology

Kevin N. Laland

4.1. Introduction

The niche-construction perspective within evolutionary biology stresses the changes that organisms bring about in their selective environments. Advocates of this viewpoint argue that there is both accuracy and utility in treating niche construction as an evolutionary process in its own right, rather than as merely a product of evolution. Niche construction may be influenced by genetic, ontogenetic and cultural information and feeds back to influence selective processes at each of these levels. In this article I argue that the niche-construction approach is particularly germane to students of human evolution and to researchers using evolutionary methods to interpret human behaviour and society. Reasoning on the basis of niche-construction theory repudiates the suggestion, voiced by some leading evolutionary psychologists, that humans experience an atypically large 'adaptive lag', the idea that modern humans experience a gross discordance in their selective environments compared to those to which they are adapted. The niche-construction perspective is consistent with the philosophy and

methods of human behavioural ecology, and confirms the potential applicability of behavioural ecological methods to all human societies. I will end by sketching how the niche-construction perspective brings with it a suite of novel hypotheses and methods of utility to human scientists.

4.2. Niche construction

Niche construction is one of the most self-apparent features on the natural world. Countless animals manufacture nests, burrows, holes, webs and pupal cases; plants change levels of soil chemicals and modify nutrient cycles; fungi decompose organic matter; bacteria engage in decomposition and nutrient fixation. All of this, and more, is niche construction, the process whereby organisms, through their metabolism, their activities, and their choices, modify niches (Odling-Smee et al., 2003). Organisms also deplete and destroy important components of their world, and the term 'niche construction' incorporates both the positive and negative fitness ramifications of organisms' activities. Furthermore, organisms do not just build environmental components but regulate them to damp out variability in environmental conditions. Beavers, earthworms, ants and countless other animals build complex artefacts, manage temperatures and humidities inside them, control nutrient cycling and stoichiometric ratios around them, and construct and defend suitable nursery environments for their offspring.

The niche-construction perspective was introduced to evolutionary biology in the 1980s through a series of essays by Richard Lewontin (1982, 1983), and has been subject to considerable recent interest (Odling-Smee, 1988; Brandon and Antonovics, 1996; Odling-Smee et al., 1996, 2003; Laland et al., 1996, 1999, 2001; Oyama et al., 2001; Lewens, 2003; Sterelny, 2003; Boni and Feldman, 2005; Donohue, 2005). Advocates of the niche-construction standpoint seek to explain the organism–environment match as a reciprocal interaction between natural selection and niche construction. Niche construction is viewed not just an end product of evolution, but an evolutionary process in its own right. For instance, it is nest building that generates selection for nest elaboration, defence and regulation, and therefore causes such evolutionary episodes (Odling-Smee et al., 2003).

Conversely, the conventional evolutionary perspective explains organism–environment complementarity solely in terms of natural selection. With many complications and caveats, such as frequency dependence and habitat selection (discussed by Odling-Smee et al., 2003), adaptation is usually treated as a process by which selection shapes organisms to be fitted to pre-existing environments. The causal arrow points in one direction only: environments, as the source of selection, determine the features of living creatures. For instance, according to George Williams (1992): "Adaptation is always asymmetrical; organisms adapt to their environment, never *vice versa*". Standard evolutionary theory does not deny niche construction, but interprets it as solely a product of evolution, rather than as a part cause.

The conventional evolutionary approach models the evolutionary consequences of niche construction solely in terms of fitness payoffs to the genes expressed in construction. For instance, the only widely considered feedback from a beaver's dam that is evolutionarily significant is that which affects the fitness of genes that are expressed in building this 'extended phenotype'

(Dawkins, 1982). Niche-construction advocates regard this position as unsatisfactory, since it fails to recognize organisms' activities as a *cause* of evolutionary change. When a beaver builds a dam, creating a lake and influencing river flow, this behaviour not only affects the propagation of dam-building genes but results in major changes in the local environment, affecting nutrient cycling, decomposition dynamics, the structure of the riparian zone, and plant and community composition and diversity (Naiman et al., 1988). It follows that beaver dam building must alter the selection of other beaver traits, co-directing beaver evolution. The active agency of organisms in modifying selection on themselves and other species currently goes unrecognized.

In recent years this feedback from organisms' activities has been subject to intense investigation through mathematical population-genetic analyses (Laland et al., 1996, 1999; Odling-Smee et al., 2003). It is now well established that selection modified by niche construction can be evolutionarily important, and can generate rich micro-evolutionary dynamics. By modifying selection, niche construction can create new evolutionary equilibria, affect the stability of other equilibria, generate momentum effects (populations continue to evolve after selection has stopped), inertia effects (a delayed evolutionary response to selection), as well as opposite and catastrophic responses to selection (Laland et al., 1996, 1999; Odling-Smee et al., 2003). In other words, the feedback that niche construction generates in evolution makes a difference to how organisms evolve. The debate over niche construction now revolves around the expediency of treating niche construction as an evolutionary process, and the practical advantages or disadvantages of this stance (see, for instance, articles in the special edition of *Biology and Philosophy*, volume 20, dedicated to this topic).

4.3. The causes of niche construction

The Galapagos woodpecker finch creates a woodpecker-like niche by learning to use a cactus spine or similar implement to peck for insects under bark (Tebbich et al., 2001). While true woodpeckers' (Picidae) bills are adaptive traits fashioned by natural selection for grubbing, the finch's capacity to use spines to grub for insects is not an adaptation. Rather, the finch, like countless other species, exploits a more general and flexible adaptation, namely the capacity to learn, to develop the skills necessary to grub in environments reliably containing cactus spines and similar implements. The finch's use of spines develops reliably as a consequence of its ability to interact with the environment in a manner that allows it to benefit from its own experience, but is not guaranteed by the presence of naturally selected genes, nor dependent on social learning (Tebbich *et al.*, 2001). The finch's learning opens up resources in the bird's environment that would be unavailable otherwise, and its behaviour probably created a stable selection pressure favouring a bill able to manipulate tools rather than the sharp, pointed bill and long tongue characteristic of woodpeckers.

From the conventional evolutionary perspective, it is of little (evolutionary) consequence if finches improve their foraging through learning. All that counts is the phenotypic effects of the genes that the birds carry, because the only role that phenotypes play in evolution is to survive and reproduce and thereby influence the propagation of the genes they carry. As a result, the only characters that are deemed evolutionarily consequential are adaptations (Dawkins, 1976).

However, all of this changes when niche construction is regarded as an evolutionary process. Now phenotypes play two roles in evolution, they survive and reproduce but they also construct and modify environments, modifying selection pressures. Acquired characters may not directly influence which genes are inherited, but they can nonetheless still play an evolutionary role through modifying selection pressures. In the case of the finches, learned tool use has probably generated selection favouring a manipulative beak, and has seemingly dampened selection for the long pointed bill characteristic of true woodpeckers. The role of acquired characters becomes of particular significance for vertebrate evolution, as a result of their flexible, brain-based learning. There is already considerable interest among evolutionary biologists in the role that imprinting, song learning, social learning, habitat imprinting and various other forms of learning play in evolution, and this interest will surely increase with greater

recognition of the role that learning plays through guiding niche construction.

Organisms gain information that guides their niche construction through processes operating at least three different levels, including population genetic, ontogenetic and cultural. Niche construction is influenced by all such information stores—not just genes—and all feed back to influence selection. The niche construction of every species is informed by naturally selected genes; for many species it is also informed by complex, information-acquiring ontogenetic processes such as learning or the immune system, whereas human niche construction, and perhaps that of a few other species, is also informed by cultural processes. Genetic processes, ontogenetic processes and cultural processes operate at distinct but interconnected levels (Odling-Smee *et al.*, 2003). Each level interacts with, but is not completely determined by, the others: that is, learning is informed, but only loosely, by genetic information, and cultural transmission may be informed, but not completely specified, by both genetic and developmental processes. Genes may affect information gain at the ontogenetic level, which in turn influences information acquisition at the cultural level. In addition, ontogenetic processes, particularly learning, may be affected by cultural processes, while population genetic processes may be affected by both ontogenetic processes and cultural processes when humans modify their selection pressures. These interactions are spelt out in more detail below.

Genetic information is the most fundamental source of information that underpins niche construction. Darwinian evolution comprises a natural algorithm for acquisition of semantic information by organisms. A direct consequence of the differential survival and reproduction of individuals with distinct genotypes is the acquisition and inheritance of genetically encoded information by individuals in populations, expressed in all aspects of the phenotype, including niche construction. Genes comprise a store of information specifying adaptations that were effective in ancestral environments, including niche-constructing adaptations.

Many animal species have also evolved complicated developmental processes that allow individuals to acquire other kinds of information.

These are products of genetic evolution, but they are unusual adaptations because they function to accumulate further relevant information in the current environment. Specialized information-acquiring sub-systems, such as the immune system in vertebrates, or brain-based learning in animals, allow individual organisms to fine tune their defences or behaviour to the idiosyncracies of their local circumstances in a manner that would have been impossible on the basis of inherited genetic knowledge alone.

This is important because some factors in the environment change many times within the lifespan of the animal. Natural selection of genetic variation cannot furnish individuals with specific adaptations for each of these contingencies. What it can do, however, is to furnish them with 'onboard guidance systems' that allow them to learn about their environment and, within some constraints, to adjust their behaviour accordingly during their lives. These systems work through built-in processes such as the 'law of effect' that guides learning in animals. This law states that actions that are followed by a positive outcome are likely to be repeated, while those followed by a negative outcome will be eliminated. Thus, natural selection is more likely to confer on animals a feel-good sensation when they act in a manner that enhances survival and reproduction, and a feel-bad sensation when they act in a way that is detrimental to survival and reproduction. As a consequence individual animals can fine tune their behaviour by learning in a broadly adaptive manner, as they do things that elicit pleasure, and avoid actions that elicit pain.

Ontogenetic processes such as learning and the immune response can also be regarded as operating in a manner loosely analogous to the Darwinian algorithm. In each case, variants (behaviour patterns or antibodies) are produced, their utility is evaluated (e.g. their performance at generating pleasure or avoiding pain, or binding to antigens, is assessed by some kind of system that natural selection has previously selected), and those variants that are most effective are retained while the others are selected out. As a result, these processes acquire and store information about the behaviour patterns or antibodies most effective in dealing with the pathogens in the local environment, and through a process frequently described as 'trial-and-error'

learning, individuals repeatedly generate behavioural variants, test them, eliminate the behavioural errors that produce pain or no positive feelings, and regenerate the successes that elicited more positive sensations. As a result of this process, relevant information pertaining to survival and reproduction is acquired and stored, while the behaviour of individual animals is shaped to be functional and adaptive. For instance, rats given radiation poisoning after eating readily learn that food with that taste leads to illness, but are slow to learn that a buzzer sound or light predicts illness (Garcia and Koelling, 1966). From an evolutionary perspective, this makes a lot of sense, as sickness generally results from eating rather than from sounds or visual cues. In this manner, general learning processes are tailored to the important components of each species' niche. These ontogenetic information-gaining processes are not strictly Darwinian, since the generated variants are guided by evolved aptitudes, biases and constraints. However, the regulation of animal learning by genes is only partial, and genes do not fully determine what is learned.

A few species, including some vertebrates, have evolved a capacity to learn from other individuals. This social learning also has both general and species-specific properties. For example, rhesus macaques acquire a fear of snakes from conspecifics when they see other monkeys behaving fearfully in the presence of a snake, but cannot be conditioned to fear a flower or other arbitrary objects in this manner (Mineka and Cook, 1988). Similarly, when exposed to songs of multiple species, juveniles of a number of bird species preferentially learn conspecific song (Marler and Tamura, 1964; Immelmann, 1969). In humans the ability to learn from others is facilitated by further capabilities (e.g. language) that collectively underlie cultural processes, through which socially learned information is accrued, stored, and transmitted between individuals, both within and between generations. The significance of acquired characters to evolutionary processes becomes further amplified with this stable transgenerational culture, and it is now widely believed that such characters were probably extremely important to hominid evolution (Richerson and Boyd, 2005). Although all cultural knowledge is traceable to innovation and learning by particular individuals, major cultural changes may also occur through learning from neighbouring groups or immigrants, and may be associated with ideological or organizational requirements.

Cultural change can also be regarded as loosely Darwinian in character, in the sense that cultural variants are generated by individuals, and as a result of social learning are culturally 'selected' through their differential adoption. The parallels between genetic and cultural evolution are more impressive than generally appreciated, although they also differ in important respects (Mesoudi *et al.*, 2004). Cultural processes are frequently a short cut to acquiring adaptive information, as individuals rapidly learn, or are shown, what to eat, where to live, or how to avoid danger by doing what other more knowledgeable individuals do. Experienced others such as parents are a reservoir of 'smart variants', allowing naïve individuals to short-cut the many iterations of ontogenetic selection necessary to learn for themselves behaviour patterns appropriate to their environment, and leapfrog to the functional and already-tested solutions established by others. The adoption of cultural variants is also affected by collective experience and social history, including rules of thumb, proverbs, conventions, moral or ethical principles, and other information accrued through prior social learning.

Much of human niche construction is guided by socially learned knowledge and cultural inheritance, but the transmission and acquisition of this knowledge is itself dependent on pre-existing information acquired through genetic evolution, complex ontogenetic processes, or prior social learning. As a result, niche construction that is based on either learned or culturally transmitted information may be expressed 'intentionally' relative to a specific goal. Some aspects of human cultural processes, for instance, science and technology, clearly reflect this goal-directed, intentional quality, while animal protocultures typically lack it. Other components of cultural processes, such as fads and fashions, are less clearly directed, and may be subject to so many complex and frequency-dependent selective processes that their evolution is unpredictable and more difficult to describe quantitatively. Cultural niche construction also creates artefacts and other ecologically inherited resources that not only act as sources of biological selection, but also facilitate learning and perhaps mediate cultural traditions (Aunger, 2000, 2002).

The potency of human niche construction is immediately apparent. Our activities allow us to exist in a fantastically broad range of habitats, and our technology has transformed the planet. To a large extent it is our capacities for culture and technology that make us such effective niche constructors (Boyd and Richerson, 1985; Richerson and Boyd, 2005). Other animals possess traditions for feeding on particular foods or singing songs, for instance, chimpanzee tool use or chaffinch song dialects. Yet human cultural processes are exceptionally potent compared to those in other animals, probably because they possess a cumulative property (Boyd and Richerson, 1985).

Recent mathematical population genetics theory demonstrates that niche construction does not have to be based on genes in order to affect the evolutionary process. Cultural niche construction, in which learned and socially transmitted behaviour modifies environments, can also have major biological evolutionary consequences (Laland *et al.*, 2001; Ihara and Feldman, 2004; Boni and Feldman, 2005). Indeed, mathematical theory suggests that culture amplifies the evolutionary feedback loop generated by niche construction (Laland *et al.*, 2001; Odling-Smee *et al.*, 2003). Human evolution may be unique in that our culture and niche construction have become self-reinforcing, with transgenerational culture modifying the environment in a manner that favours ever-more culture, and niche construction informed by cultural knowledge becoming ever-more powerful (Laland *et al.*, 2000; Odling-Smee *et al.*, 2003).

4.4. The adaptiveness of human behaviour

The niche-construction perspective has evoked both positive and negative responses, and considerable debate, among biologists, and it remains to be seen whether it will become an established feature of evolutionary theory [for a discussion of the issues at the heart of the controversy, see Laland and Sterelny (2006)]. However, irrespective of how this debate pans out, there are compelling reasons why the niche-construction perspective should be more overtly acceptable, less contentious and of immediate utility to researchers studying human behaviour. That is because the clear potency of human niche construction, where there can be no doubt that human technology has massively changed our environments, combined with the comparatively diffuse influence of genes on human behaviour, which means that human niche construction cannot be reduced to prior natural selection, renders the niche-construction perspective of particular significance to human evolution. It also greatly affects the standing of the research philosophies of two contemporary evolutionary approaches to the study of human behaviour and society, namely human behavioural ecology and evolutionary psychology (see Laland and Brown, 2006, for an extended account of this argument).

Human behavioural ecology has been subject to criticism from the dominant modular, adaptationist branch of evolutionary psychologists (e.g. Symons, 1987; Tooby and Cosmides, 1990), leading to a vigorous debate (Smith *et al.*, 2001). One alleged weakness of human behavioural ecology, stressed by these evolutionary psychologists, is that human behaviour will not necessarily be adaptive in industrialized societies. The argument is that modern environments, with their houses, cars, shops, and hospitals, are extremely different from the environments in which the genus *Homo* evolved. Leading evolutionary psychologists from this school argue that, over the last two million years, our ancestors have spent most of their existence hunting and gathering in small groups in Africa and that selection will have fashioned human minds to be adapted to the ancestral world of the Pleistocene, the 'environment of evolutionary adaptedness', rather than its modern counterpart. While all organisms experience a mismatch between current selection pressures and behaviour, evolutionary psychologists apparently believe that the adaptive lag for humans is atypically large, because human technology and innovation have changed human environments so extensively and so quickly.

Human behavioural ecologists typically respond to the putative problem of adaptive lag by stressing the flexibility of human behaviour, which, they claim, allows humans to accommodate themselves to a wide range of circumstances (Smith *et al.*, 2001). Yet even the most adaptable

of creatures will experience limits to its tolerance space, outside of which it is unable to behave adaptively. Do humans behave adaptively in modern industrialized worlds? The fact that human behavioural ecologists primarily study people living in pre-industrial societies only reinforces the view that the adaptive lag hypothesis may be correct, and that modern post-industrial societies may be too different from ancestral selective environments for humans to behave adaptively.

From the niche-construction perspective, the adaptive lag hypothesis is misguided (Laland and Brown, 2006). To the contrary, niche-constructing activity generally increases the match between an animal's behaviour and its environment, and since humans are niche constructors *par excellence*, human behaviour should typically be adaptive. There are three strands to this argument:

First, *humans typically construct their world to suit themselves.* Animals do not perturb their environment at random, but build structures that are extended phenotypes, adaptations that enhance fitness (Dawkins, 1982). Even when they deplete resources and pollute environments this typically increases fitness in the short term, and is often tied to life-history strategies that take account of this activity (Odling-Smee *et al.*, 2003). Animals also regulate structures to damp out variability in environmental conditions, with the result that niche construction can maintain selection pressures and preserve the adaptiveness of behaviour (Odling-Smee *et al.*, 2003). 'Counteractive niche construction' occurs when organisms act to neutralize some prior change in selection pressures. Like the acorn-storing squirrel, or the wasp that cools her nest with water, our ancestors ensured the availability of food by tracking game and storing food, and controlled temperature by building fires and shelters. In principle, modern fridge-freezers and air-conditioning are no different. Such niche construction may change environments, but it actually functions to negate a modified or fluctuating selection pressure, thereby reducing selection (Odling-Smee *et al.*, 2003).

Human-built environments might be different from African savanna, but many selection pressures acting on us could be broadly similar, since our constructions were built to be suited to our bodies and their needs. A cup is a useful drinking utensil for a human, but of little utility to most other organisms, lacking, as they do, the manipulative dexterity of a limb with fine motor control within easy reach of a mouth. That is not because cup manufacturers are constrained by genes to design drinking implements with pre-specified characteristics; it is because other designs have proved less useful. Countless other everyday tools, implements and artefacts are obviously specifically designed with human bodies in mind.

Second, *humans frequently buffer adaptive lag through cultural niche construction*. There is extensive evidence of anatomical and behavioural traits that are probably evolutionary responses to ancestral niche construction, including elaborations of niche-constructed artefacts, and physical or behavioural responses for regulating niche-constructed resources (Odling-Smee *et al.*, 2003). Unlike most other species, humans can respond not only to ancestral niche construction through genetic evolution but also through further (usually cultural) niche construction.

This is illustrated in Figure 4.1(a) (taken from Odling-Smee *et al.*, 2003). Route 1 comprises an adaptive cultural response to a change in the

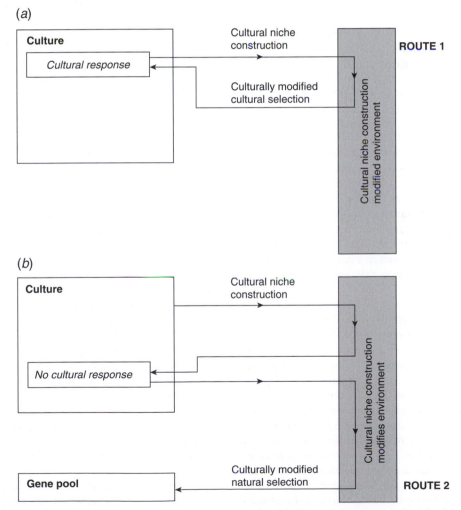

Fig. 4.1 Two routes by which humans can respond to ancestral niche construction (see text for details)

environment that was brought about by earlier cultural niche construction. For example, suppose humans change their environment in a detrimental manner, and this modified environment stimulates the invention and spread of a new technology to cope with the change, alleviating the problem. Provided the response is sufficiently effective to counteract the change in the environment, it should have no effect on human genetics, and there will be no adaptive lag.

Consider the example of human aggregation into large sedentary communities, with the construction of towns and cities, which created, along with countless other challenges, the problem of what to do with human domestic and industrial waste products (Diamond, 1997). At this time, human populations did temporarily experience selection pressures different from those of their African ancestors: for instance, exposure to a host of diseases, including measles, smallpox and typhoid, that thrive in dense populations with poor sanitation (Diamond, 1997). At this juncture there was an adaptive lag, and had the populations lacked the technology to respond, either the adaptive lag would have been maintained, the population would have crashed or genetic evolution would have ensued. However, many human populations did devise solutions, from sewerage plants, to drains, to water purification treatments. Examples of this buffering of adaptive lag through cultural niche construction are commonplace: food shortages alleviated by new agricultural practices, water shortages by irrigation, pipelines and reservoirs, extremes of climate by clothing, fires, and air-conditioning, and so forth.

While there is nothing inevitable about the capacity of humans to construct solutions to self-imposed problems, their capacity for culture and technology renders human niche construction uniquely potent and fast-acting. Theoretical analyses suggest that cultural responses to modified selection pressures will typically occur more rapidly than genetic responses, and will often render genetic responses unnecessary (Laland *et al.*, 2001). By rapidly responding to self-imposed problems through cultural niche construction, humans maintain their adaptiveness.

Third, *where humans are unable completely to buffer adaptive lag through further cultural niche construction, natural selection on genes ensues.*

In recent years, evolutionary biologists have measured rates of response to selection in animals and plants, and the results suggest that selection may often operate faster than hitherto conceived. Indeed, selection experiments and observations of natural selection in the wild have led to the conclusion that biological evolution can be extremely fast, with significant genetic and phenotypic change sometimes observed in a handful of generations (Dwyer *et al.*, 1990; Grant and Grant, 1995; Reznick *et al.*, 1997; Kingsolver *et al.*, 2001). Kingsolver *et al.* reviewed 63 studies that measured the strength of natural selection in 62 species including many vertebrates, reporting that the median selection gradient was 0.16, which would cause a quantitative trait to change by one standard deviation in just 25 generations (approximately 500 years for humans). This suggests that significant human evolution could be measured in thousands of years or less, and opens up the possibility that humans could realistically have evolved solutions to problems self-imposed over the last few millenia. This is illustrated by Route 2 in Figure 4.1(b), where culturally modified environments give rise to modified selection pressures and changes in gene frequencies. Were there no technology available to counter a new problem created by cultural niche construction, then genotypes that were better suited to the modified environment would increase in frequency, leading to evolutionary change.

For instance, there are several examples of culturally induced genetic responses to human agriculture (Odling-Smee *et al.*, 2003). One is provided by a population of yam cultivators in West Africa, who cut clearings in forests to grow crops, with a cascade of consequences (Durham, 1991). The clearings increased the amount of standing water, which provided better breeding grounds for mosquitoes and increased the prevalence of malaria. This in turn modified natural selection pressures in favour of an increase in the frequency of the Sickle-cell *S* allele because, in the heterozygous condition, the *S* allele confers protection against malaria. Here culture has not damped out natural selection but rather induced it.

Once again, this evolutionary change acts to restore adaptiveness. Among malaria-rife regions, being heterozygote for the Sickle-cell *S* allele is adaptive. Similarly, there is now good evidence that dairy farming has created the selection pressures that favoured genes for adult lactose absorption (Feldman and Cavalli-Sforza, 1989; Holden and Mace, 1997). In a dairying society, genes expressed in high lactase activity pay fitness dividends. There are many other examples. Malaria only became a major health problem after the invention of farming, a human cultural niche-constructing practice, yet there are several candidate genes (in addition to sickle-cell) that appear to have been favoured by selection because they provide resistance to malaria, including G6PD, TNFSF5, and alleles coding for haemoglobin C and Duffy blood groups (Balter, 2005). There is also evidence that genes have been selected because they confer resistance to other modern diseases, including AIDS and smallpox (CCR5), and hypertension (AGT, CYP3A) (Balter, 2005). In these cases, human modification of the environment has only temporarily induced adaptive lag, this time alleviated through evolutionary change.

Molecular genetic analyses reveal that small changes in genes, or in their promoters and enhancers, can bring about major changes in the functionality of complex characters (Gilbert, 2003), while among the traits shown to respond quickly to selection are some elaborate, multi-loci characters (Endler, 1986; Kingsolver et al., 2001). Thus, there is little biological support for the argument, put forward by evolutionary psychologists, that human cognitive architecture is too complex to evolve quickly (Tooby and Cosmides, 1990). The data are equally incompatible with the position of anti-evolutionary social scientists, who state that biological evolution is too slow to be relevant to understanding human behaviour and cognition and that these can be explained solely by cultural processes.

4.5. **Implications for the study of human behaviour**

If human traits are largely adaptive, that will be manifest in high absolute fitness, as exemplified by substantive intrinsic growth rates in human populations, while if contemporary human behaviour is largely maladaptive human numbers should decrease. Thus human global population growth (Smil, 1993) provides compelling support for the above argument. Herein lies a problem for advocates of the adaptive lag hypothesis. Why should our ancestors have thrived as soon as they left their environment of evolutionary adaptedness? It is in the Holocene, the period since the Pleistocene, that we see the explosion in human numbers and human colonization of the globe. Neither is this explosion attributable to expansion of hunter-gatherer societies: on the contrary, population growth appears to be linked to agricultural practices, technological advancement, medicine, and so forth—the phenomena that are most strikingly different from the Pleistocene environments of our ancestors. Growth in human populations provides the clearest indication that a major proportion of human characteristics remains adaptive even in modern constructed environments. Even post-demographic transition societies exhibit relatively stable population sizes, or marginal growth or decline, indicative of largely adaptive behaviour. There are theoretical articles proposing niche-construction hypotheses to explain this demographic transition (Ihara and Feldman, 2004; Kendal et al., 2005).

That is not to suggest that human behaviour will always be adaptive. Theoretical analyses reveal that maladaptive cultural traits can spread under a variety of circumstances (Boyd and Richerson, 1985; Feldman and Laland, 1996; Richerson and Boyd, 2005), although adaptive human behaviour will probably be the norm and maladaptation the exception. However, there is no reason to expect greater levels of adaptive behaviour in pre-industrial, small-scale or hunter-gatherer societies than in the fully industrialized urban metropolis. In spite of the massive changes humans have brought about in their worlds, human niche construction maintains a largely adaptive match between human features and the factors in their environment.

If correct, the niche-construction perspective provides evolutionary support for the widespread and general application of behavioural ecology methods to all human societies, including the most modern post-industrial societies (Laland and Brown, 2006). While there may well be circumstances in which these methods are not effective, there is no satisfactory evolutionary basis to the belief that the tools of behavioural ecology will not be successful in modern societies, and no *evolutionary* reason to expect the methods to be less successful in post-industrial than pre-industrial societies. It might be argued that the use of behavioural ecological methods in modern societies is impractical given the widespread use of contraception, and the resulting 'disconnect' between adaptive behaviour and reproductive success. However, reproductive success is itself only a convenient proxy measure for fitness; any such disconnect is largely an unproven assumption, not an established fact (conceivably using contraception may be an adaptive strategy in restricted circumstances), and even if reproductive success were to prove an ineffective currency, behavioural ecologists regularly exploit a range of different currencies, such as foraging success, growth rates, and material wealth, which could still be employed.

In summary, on evolutionary grounds I argue against the hypothesis that modern humans experience an atypically large adaptive lag (Laland and Brown, 2006), a hypothesis that remains widely held within the dominant school of evolutionary psychology, largely because it is regarded as supported by evolutionary theory. The alternative evolutionary theoretical framework provided by niche construction supports the counter-position and hopefully lends it authority. Other evolutionary approaches to psychological phenomena, which place lesser emphasis on human adaptive lag, are entirely compatible with a niche-construction perspective (Boyd and Richerson, 1985; Plotkin, 1997; Barrett *et al.*, 2001; Dunbar and Barrett, Chapter 1). The argument that modern human minds and behaviour are predominantly suited to an ancestral habitat fails to recognize that humans are active constructors of niches, and exceptionally potent constructors too, rather than passive products of selection.

However, if the niche-construction perspective is to prove more than a philosophical position, of minimal biological relevance to the everyday behavioural ecologist or evolutionary psychologist, it must do more than simply provide another way of describing the world. Cultural evolutionary perspectives (e.g. Cavalli-Sforza and Feldman, 1981; Boyd and Richerson, 1985) have already provided us with a reasonable explanation for many of the phenomena described above, so what does niche construction have to offer in addition?

There are three principle benefits of adopting the niche-construction perspective. The first is that, by providing a more accurate description of evolutionary events, and the interplay of behavioural and developmental processes over ecological and evolutionary timescales, the niche-construction perspective contributes to a deeper understanding of evolutionary phenomena. As such, the perspective is not only consistent with modern evolutionary biology, but also with advances in developmental and behavioural biology and ecology. While I am a great admirer and advocate of cultural evolutionary approaches, those analyses that are embedded in a conventional evolutionary perspective are, in my view, retrograde with respect to the treating of humans as a special case. Many cultural evolutionary models fail to recognize that human niche construction is merely one species-specific manifestation of an extremely general process. One ramification of this blinkering is that cultural evolutionary analyses sometimes fail to consider alternative hypotheses and methods that might have some utility (see below). A second ramification is that many human scientists that might otherwise find an evolutionary framework attractive are currently alienated by what they perceive to be an overly gene-centred, overly adaptationist conception of evolution, a conception that fails explicitly to recognize that humans actively construct their material and social worlds. A third ramification is that archaeologists, anthropologists, and psychologists, amongst others, are not themselves contributing to an understanding of human evolution in the manner that they might.

A second major advantage to adopting the niche-construction perspective is that it is a fertile way of thinking about problems, and of generating novel hypotheses. In the same way that the gene's-eye view led to insights by providing researchers with a novel means of thinking about problems within biology, so the niche-construction perspective can be of value by encouraging new avenues of research. This is illustrated by the multitude of human scientists that are rushing to apply niche-construction thinking to their own research, on topics ranging from primate social behaviour (Fragaszy and Perry, 2003; Flack *et al.*, 2006), antibiotic treatment and bacterial evolution (Boni and Feldman, 2005), the demographic transition (Ihara and Feldman 2004; Kendal *et al.*, in press), cognitive evolution (Mameli 2001; Sterelny, 2003) and extra-genetic inheritance (Jablonka and Lamb, 2005), and many others. This work lends credence to the view that the niche-construction perspective is starting to engender a progressive research programme. While it is perfectly possible to account for this work, and to conceive of many of these hypotheses, from a conventional perspective, the niche-construction perspective is advantaged by explicitly bringing the mind- and body-shaping constructive activities of human beings into the foreground. For instance, one important weakness in an otherwise admirable cultural evolutionary treatise is the emphasis of Richerson and Boyd (2005) on independent (e.g. climatic) sources of environmental variation as the primary selection pressure favouring the extensive human capacity for cultural transmission, which operate on entirely the wrong scale, and the failure to consider the alternative hypothesis, in my view far more compelling, that human ancestors constructed the environmental conditions that favoured human reliance on culture (Odling-Smee *et al.*, 2003). There are now many examples of how a niche-construction perspective has broadened the suite of hypotheses available to evolutionary-minded researchers. For instance, the patterns of response in organisms to natural selection can be changed by counteractive niche construction, with more sophisticated niche constructors expected to exhibit weaker structural responses to independent changes in their environments than less-able niche constructors. If we assume that hominid cultural niche construction is more potent than the niche-constructing activities of other mammals, and that more technically advanced hominids enjoy a greater capacity for counteractive niche construction than less technically advanced ones, then a number of hypotheses suggest themselves (see Odling-Smee *et al.*, 2003, for these and other hypotheses).

Third, and most importantly, the niche-construction perspective brings with it new empirical methods. Odling-Smee *et al.* (2003) describe how hypotheses concerning the evolutionary role of niche construction might be tested through laboratory and field experiments, and theoretical studies. These methods include experiments that investigate the consequences of cancelling or enhancing a population's capacity for niche construction, ways to detect the evolutionary consequences of niche construction in natural environments, and direct tests of the predictions of theoretical models. For instance, Odling-Smee *et al.* (2003) describe how, for any clade of organisms, it is possible to differentiate phenotypic traits (or recipient characters) that may have been rendered adaptive in environments that had been subject to niche construction, and how to use comparative methods to test these hypotheses (e.g. Harvey and Pagel, 1991). They also provide examples of genetic and cultural signatures of past inceptive cultural niche construction, which represent the kind of phenomena that might be studied in future. There are rich possibilities for testing the evolutionary credentials of niche construction and these are likely to expose new lines of empirical research in evolutionary biology.

Acknowledgments

I am grateful to Louise Barrett, Gillian Brown and Robin Dunbar for helpful comments on an earlier draft of this article.

References

Aunger, R. (2000) Conclusion. In R. Aunger (ed.) *Darwinizing Culture. The Status of Memetics as a Science*, pp. 205–232. Oxford University Press, Oxford.

Aunger, R. (2002) *The Electric Meme: a New Theory of How We Think and Communicate*. The Free Press, New York.

Balter, M. (2005) Are humans still evolving? *Science*, 309: 234–237.

Barrett, L., Dunbar, R. and Lycett, J. (2001) *Human Evolutionary Psychology*. Macmillan, London.

Boni, M. F. and Feldman, M. W. (2005) Evolution of antibiotic resistance by human and bacterial niche construction. *Evolution* 59(3): 477–491.

Boyd, R. and Richerson, P. J. (1985) *Culture and the Evolutionary Process*. University of Chicago Press, Chicago.

Brandon, R. & Antonovics, J. (1996) The Coevolution of organism and environment. In: R. Brandon (ed) *Concepts and Methods in Evolutionary Biology* pp. 161–178. Cambridge University Press. Cambridge.

Cavalli-Sforza, L. L. and Feldman, M. W. (1981) *Cultural Transmission and Evolution*. Princeton University Press, Cambridge, MA.

Dawkins, R. (1976) *The Selfish Gene*. Oxford University Press, Oxford.

Dawkins, R. (1982) *The Extended Phenotype*. Oxford University Press, Oxford.

Diamond, J. M. (1997) *Guns, Germs and Steel: The Fates of Human Societies*. Norton, New York.

Donohue, K. (2005) Niche construction through phonological plasticity: life history dynamics and ecological consequences. *New Phytologist* 166: 83–92.

Durham, W. H. (1991) *Coevolution: Genes, Culture and Human Diversity*. Stanford University Press.

Dwyer, G., Levin, S. A. and Buttel, L. (1990) A simulation of the population dynamics and evolution of myxomatosis. *Ecological Monographs* 60: 423–447.

Endler, J. A. (1986) *Natural Selection in the Wild*. Princeton University Press, Princeton.

Feldman MW and Cavalli-Sforza LL (1989) On the theory of evolution under genetic and cultural transmission with application to the lactose absorption problem. In M. W. Feldman (ed.) *Mathematical Evolutionary Theory*. Princeton University Press, Princeton.

Feldman, M. W. and Laland, K. N. (1996) Gene–culture coevolutionary theory. *Trends in Ecology and Evolution* 11: 453–457.

Flack, J. C., Girvan, M., de Waal, F. B. M. and Krakauer, D. C. (2006) Policing stabilizes construction of social niches in primates. *Nature* 439: 426–429.

Fragaszy, D. and Perry, S. (eds) (2003) *The Biology of Traditions: Models and Evidence*. Chicago University Press, Chicago.

Garcia, J. and Koelling, R. A. (1966) *Psychon. Sci.*, 4: 123– 124

Gilbert, S. F. (2003) *Developmental Biology*, 7th edn. Sinauer, Sunderland, MA.

Grant, P. R. and Grant, B. R. (1995) Predicting microevolutionary responses to directional selection on heritable variation. *Evolution* 49: 241–251.

Harvey, P. H. and Pagel, M. (1991) *The Comparative Method in Evolutionary Biology*. Oxford University Press, Oxford.

Holden, C. and Mace, R. (1997) Phylogenetic analysis of the evolution of lactose digestion in adults. *Human Biology* 69: 605–628.

Ihara, Y. and Feldman M. W. (2004) Cultural niche construction and the evolution of small family size. *Theoretical Population Biology* 65: 105–111.

Immelmann, K. (1969) In R. A. Hinde (ed.) *Bird Vocalisations*, pp. 61–74. Cambridge University Press, Cambridge.

Jablonka, E. and Lamb M. J. (2005) *Evolution in Four Dimensions*. MIT Press. Cambridge, MA.

Kendal, J. R., Ihara, Y. and Feldman, M. W. (2005) Cultural niche construction with application to fertility control: a model for education and social transmission of contraceptive use. *Morrison Institute Working Papers Series,* Number 102, Stanford University.

Kingsolver, J. G., Hoekstra, H. E., Hoekstra, J. M., Berrigan, D., Vignieri, S. N., Hill, C. E., Hoang, A., Gilbert, P. and Beerli, P. (2001) The strength of phenotypic selection in natural populations. *American Naturalist* 157: 245–261.

Laland, K. N. and Brown, G. R. (2002) *Sense and Nonsense: Evolutionary Perspectives on Human Behaviour*. Oxford University Press, Oxford.

Laland, K. N. and Brown, G. R. (2006) Niche construction, human behaviour and the adaptive-lag hypothesis. *Evolutionary Anthropology* 15: 95–104.

Laland, K. N. and Sterelny, K. (in press) Seven reasons (not) to neglect niche construction. *Evolution*. 60: 1751–1762.

Laland, K. N., Odling-Smee, F. J. and Feldman, M. W. (1996) On the evolutionary consequences of niche construction. *Journal of Evolutionary Biology* 9: 293–316.

Laland, K. N., Odling-Smee, F. J. and Feldman, M. W. (1999) Evolutionary consequences of niche construction and their implications for ecology. *Proceedings of the National Academy of Sciences USA* 96: 10242–10247.

Laland, K. N., Odling-Smee, F. J. and Feldman, M. W. (2000) Niche construction, biological evolution, and cultural change. *Behavioral and Brain Sciences* 23: 131–175.

Lewens, T. (2003) Prospects for evolutionary Policy. *Philosophy* 78: 495–514.

Lewontin, R. C. (1982) Organism and environment. In H. C. Plotkin (ed.) *Learning, Development and Culture*. New York, Wiley.

Lewontin, R. C. (1983) Gene, organism, and environment. In D. S. Bendall (ed.) *Evolution from Molecules to Men*. Cambridge University Press, Cambridge.

Mameli, M. (2001) Mindreading, mindshaping and evolution. *Biology and Philosophy*, 16: 597–628.

Marler, P. and Tamura, M. (1964) *Science*, 146, 1483–1486.

Mesoudi, A., Whiter, A. & Laland, R. N. (2004) Is human cultural evolution Darwinian? Evidence reviewed from the perspective of The Origin of Species. *Evolution* 58: 1–11.

Mineka, S. and Cook, M. (1988) Social learning and the acquisition of snake fear in monkeys. In T. R. Zentall and B. G. Galef, Jr (eds) *Social Learning. Psychological and Biological Perspectives*, pp. 51–74. Earlbaum, Hillsdale, NJ.

Naiman, R. J., Johnston, C. A. and Kelley, J. C. (1988) Alterations of North American streams by beaver. *BioScience* 38: 753–762.

Odling-Smee, F. J. (1988) Niche constructing phenotypes. In H. C. Plotkin (ed.) *The Role of Behavior in Evolution*, pp. 73–132. MIT Press, Cambridge, MA.

Odling-Smee, F. J., Laland, K. N. and Feldman, M. W. (1996) Niche construction. *American Naturalist* 147: 641–648.

Odling-Smee, F.J., Laland, K. N. and Feldman, M. W. (2003) *Niche Construction: the Neglected Process in Evolution*. Monographs in Population Biology 37. Princeton University Press.

Oyama, S., Griffiths, P. E. and Gray, R. D. (2001) *Cycles of Contingency: Developmental Systems and Evolution*. MIT Press, Cambridge, MA.

Plotkin, H. (1997) *Evolution in Mind: An Introduction to Evolutionary Psychology*. Penguin Books, London.

Reznick, D. N., Shaw, F. H., Rodd, H. and Shaw, R. G. (1997) Evaluation of the rate of evolution in natural populations of guppies (*Poecilia reticulata*). *Science* 275: 1934–1936.

Richerson, P. J. and Boyd, R. (2005) *Not by Genes Alone*. University of Chicago Press, Chicago.

Smil, V. (1993) *Global Ecology: Environmental Change and Social Flexibility*. Routledge, New York.

Smith, E. A., Borgerhoff Mulder M. and Hill, K. (2001) Controversies in the evolutionary social sciences: a guide for the perplexed. *Trends in Ecology and Evolution*, 16: 128–135.

Sterelny, K. (2003) Thought in a hostile world: the evolution of human cognition. Blackwell.

Symons, D. (1987) If we're all Darwinians, what's the fuss about? In C. Crawford, M. Smith and D. Krebs (eds) *Sociobiology and Psychology: Ideas, Issues and Applications*. Erlbaum, Hillsdale, NJ.

Tebbich, S., Taborsky, M., Febl, B. and Blomqvist, D. (2001) Do woodpecker finches acquire tool-use by social learning? *Proceedings of the Royal Society of London B* 268: 2189–2193.

Tooby, J. and Cosmides, L. (1990) The past explains the present: emotional adaptations and the structure of ancestral environments. *Ethology and Sociobiology* 11: 375–424.

Williams, G. C. (1992) Gaia, nature worship, and biocentric fallacies. *Quarterly Review of Biology*, 67: 479–486 (p. 484).

CHAPTER 5

Group-level evolutionary processes

David Sloan Wilson

5.1. Introduction

Anyone who studies human evolution, or indeed humans from any perspective, must acknowledge our groupish nature. Our environment has always been largely our *social* environment. Moreover, fitness has always been influenced by interactions among groups in addition to interactions among individuals within groups. Everyone must acknowledge these elementary facts, providing a common foundation for the study of human psychology and behaviour. Unfortunately, efforts to build upon the foundation have resulted in numerous theoretical perspectives that are poorly related to each other. Our students learn about kin selection, reciprocal altruism, game theory, group selection, multi-level selection, selfish genes, by-product mutualisms, and costly signalling as if they are separate concepts. The widespread rejection of group selection in the 1960s still casts a shadow over the entire subject. According to this consensus, groups should almost never be regarded as important units of selection. How can this belief be reconciled with the fact that groups are manifestly important in human evolution?

In short, the current literature is like the Tower of Babel, which cannot be built because so many different theoretical languages are being spoken. There is a common language that integrates all of the concepts listed above, but it requires acknowledging the importance of higher-level selection, especially in the case of human evolution. In this essay I will briefly summarize the common language of multi-level selection theory, providing references to more extensive treatments along the way.

5.2. Natural selection is based on relative fitness

Every student of evolution learns that natural selection is based on relative fitness. It doesn't matter how well a trait enhances survival and reproduction, as long as it does so better than alternative traits. Traits that decrease absolute fitness can evolve if they decrease the fitness of everyone else even more. Traits that increase absolute fitness can fail to evolve if they increase the fitness of everyone else even more. One reason that *Adaptation and Natural Selection* (Williams, 1966) became a classic book is because it emphasized the importance of relative fitness and the irrelevance of absolute fitness in evolutionary thinking.

Whenever a large population is subdivided into groups, relative fitness in the total population can be divided into two components: (1) relative fitness among individuals within single groups; and (2) relative fitness among groups within the larger population (Sober and Wilson, 1998). These are like vectors that can be calculated separately and then combined to yield the net direction of evolutionary change in the total population. As a classic example, consider a single group of birds that includes two types of foragers in equal proportions. Prudent foragers restrain their feeding to manage their resources over the long term. Imprudent foragers eat and reproduce as much as possible over the short term. Imprudent foragers have the highest relative fitness and will increase in frequency within the group. The fact that the group as a whole suffers from resource overexploitation is irrelevant because natural selection is based only on relative fitness.

Now suppose that there are many groups of foragers instead of just one. If the groups vary in their initial composition, then those with the most prudent foragers will persist longer and produce more dispersers, compared to groups with the most imprudent foragers. Relative fitness among groups in the total population favours the prudent foraging trait, in contrast to relative fitness among individuals within each group. Natural selection in the total population is based on the net effect of these two opposing evolutionary forces, which must be added like component vectors to produce a single final vector.

5.3. Naïve group selection and its rejection in the 1960s

Darwin thought clearly about levels of selection, especially with respect to human evolution, as indicated by numerous passages from the *Descent of Man* and elsewhere (Richards, 1987; Borrello, 2005). Ronald Fisher, Sewall Wright and J. B. S. Haldane also thought clearly about multi-level selection, although it was not the most important thing on their minds, compared to even more foundational issues such as the consequences of Mendelian inheritance (see Sober and Wilson, 1988 for more detailed discussion). Most other biologists did not share their clarity and tended to assume that adaptations evolve at all levels of the biological hierarchy, from individuals to ecosystems. This position, which is called 'naïve group selection', is illustrated by the final paragraph of the textbook *Principles of Animal Ecology* (Allee *et al.*, 1949): "The probability of survival of individual living things, or of populations, increases with the degree to which they

harmoniously adjust themselves to each other and their environment. This principle is basic to the concept of the balance of nature, orders the subject matter of ecology and evolution, underlies organismic and developmental biology, and is the foundation for all sociology."

George C. Williams wrote *Adaptation and Natural Selection* to criticize this form of naïve group selection, which he encountered as a postdoctoral associate at the University of Chicago in the late 1950s (G. C. Williams, personal communication). His writing was in progress when V. C. Wynne-Edward's book *Animal Dispersion in Relation to Social Behaviour* was published in 1962. Wynne-Edwards interpreted myriad social behaviours as adaptations to avoid the overexploitation of resources, similar to my example outlined above. He was aware of multi-level selection but assumed that between-group selection was sufficiently strong to oppose within-group selection, citing the work of Sewall Wright for support.

Wynne-Edwards was wrong about the degree of support provided by Sewall Wright. Moreover, the issues surrounding multi-level selection only partially overlap with Wright's better-known shifting balance theory. Williams was by no means the only person to criticize Wynne-Edwards and the broader tradition of naïve group selection, but his book became the most widely read analysis and the basis for a new consensus. *Adaptation and Natural Selection* is largely a tutorial on basic population genetics theory, written in non-mathematical terms for a broad biological audience (G. C. Williams, personal communication). It begins by *affirming* the importance of multi-level selection theory. Natural selection is based on relative fitness. Natural selection within groups is insensitive to the overall fitness of the group. Traits that are 'for the good of the group' are usually selectively disadvantageous within groups and require a process of group-level selection to evolve. The same goes for traits that are 'for the good of the species' and 'for the good of the ecosystem'. The general rule to keep in mind is: *adaptation at level X requires a corresponding process of natural selection at level X and tends to be undermined by selection at lower levels.*

In addition to clarifying multi-level selection theory for a broad audience, Williams also made an empirical claim that *higher-level selection is almost invariably weak compared to lower-level selection.* It is this empirical claim that turned multi-level selection into what became known as the 'the theory of individual selection'. Ever since, students of evolution have been taught that group selection is possible *in principle*; it just happens that it can be ignored *in practice*. Generations of students have learned about group selection with the help of a Gary Larson 'Far Side' cartoon showing a group of lemmings running into the sea, supposedly to regulate their population size, except for one lemming wearing a sly smile and an inner tube (e.g. Alcock, 1989). The caption in one textbook states "Gary Larson's cartoon captures the essential defect of group selection, namely, the selective advantage self-serving 'mutants' would have over self-sacrificing members of their species." Strictly speaking, this is inaccurate. It is not a *defect* that the cartoon illustrates, but rather *one vector* of multi-level selection (within-group selection) that needs to be combined with another vector (between-group selection) to see what evolves in the total population. The interpretation of the cartoon echoes G. C. Williams' conclusion that between-group selection is invariably weak compared to within-group selection. It doesn't matter that the total population includes many groups of lemmings that vary in their genetic and phenotypic composition. Everything we need to know about evolution can be determined on the strength of fitness differences within single groups.

Williams and other critics were so successful that group selection became a taboo subject in evolutionary biology, as anyone who lived through the period can attest. Every subsequent theoretical perspective, including kin selection, reciprocal altruism, game theory, and selfish-gene theory, was explicitly developed as an alternative to group selection. As Richard Dawkins described his motive for writing *The Selfish Gene*, "I would write a book extolling the gene's eye view of evolution. It should concentrate its examples on social behaviour to help correct the unconscious group-selectionism that then pervaded popular Darwinism."

5.4. How the consensus collapsed

The 1960s consensus rested upon three arguments, like the legs of a stool. The first argument was that group selection is theoretically implausible. The second argument was that no convincing empirical examples of group selection had been established. The third argument was that alternative theories (such as kin selection) do not invoke group selection in their own right. One by one, each of these arguments began to collapse, even by the early 1970s.

With respect to theoretical plausibility, I often encounter the sceptical view that theory counts for very little in the absence of good hard evidence. However, a careful examination of the 1960s consensus reveals that it was based almost entirely on theoretical plausibility arguments, such as Maynard Smith's (1964) haystack model and other models reviewed in Chapter 5 of E. O. Wilson's (1975) *Sociobiology*, which made it appear that within-group selection is invariably stronger than between-group selection. We also need to remember that the desktop computing revolution, complexity theory, and appreciation of such things as social control and cultural transmission were barely on the horizon in the 1960s. It therefore means something when more recent theoretical models of higher-level selection have become more plausible.

With respect to empirical examples, Williams used the principle of parsimony to create a dominance hierarchy in which any argument framed in terms of individual selection, no matter how speculative, trumped any argument framed in terms of group selection. The only empirical example in *Adaptation and Natural Selection* that came close to a rigorous test involved sex ratio and led to the prediction that female-biased sex ratios would provide evidence for group selection. The subsequent discovery of many examples of female-biased sex ratio led Williams to change his mind about group selection, at least for this particular trait: "I think it is desirable … to realize that selection in female-biased Mendelian populations favours males, and that it is only the selection among such groups that can favour the female bias." (Williams, 1992, p. 49.) Williams also acknowledged an important role for group selection in disease evolution, as part of his more general interest in Darwinian medicine. The following passage from Williams and Nesse (1991, p. 8) shows how easily Williams reverted from individual selection back to multi-level selection, once he decided that between-group selection might be important after all: "The evolutionary outcome will depend on relative strengths of within-host and between-host competition in pathogen evolution." Dozens of other empirical examples have emerged from field and laboratory studies, (e.g. Goodnight and Stevens, 1997; Velicer, 2003) making it simply false to claim categorically that group selection can be ignored as an important evolutionary force.

With respect to alternative theories, the following statements are true for virtually all models of social behaviour, regardless of what they are called.

(1) *Virtually all models are multi-group models.* Why? Because social interactions almost invariably take place among sets of individuals that are small compared to the total population. No model can ignore this biological reality. In *N*-person game theory, *N* refers to the size of the group within which social interactions occur. In kin selection theory, *r* specifies that individuals are interacting with a subset of the population with whom they share a certain degree of genealogical relatedness, and so on. The groups need not have discrete boundaries; the important feature is that social interactions are *local*, compared to the size of the total population.

(2) *All models must converge on the same definition of groups for any particular trait.* Why? Because all models must calculate the fitness of individuals. With social behaviours, the fitness of an individual depends upon its own phenotype and phenotypes of the others with whom it interacts. These others must be appropriately specified or else the model will simply arrive at the wrong answer. If individuals are interacting in groups of $N = 5$, two-person game theory won't do. Evolutionary models of social behaviour consider many kinds of groups, but that is only because they consider many kinds of traits. For any particular trait, such as sentinel behaviour, resource management, or food sharing, there is an appropriate population structure that must conform to the biology of the situation, regardless of what the model is called. That is the meaning of the term 'trait-group' that I coined in 1975.

(3) *In virtually all cases, traits labelled cooperative and altruistic are selectively disadvantageous within groups and require between-group selection to evolve, once the groups are appropriately identified.* W. D. Hamilton made this discovery for inclusive fitness theory when he encountered the work of

George Price in the early 1970s. Price had derived an equation that partitioned total gene frequency change into within- and between-group components. When Hamilton reformulated his theory in terms of the Price equation, he saw that altruistic traits are selectively disadvantageous within kin groups and evolve only because kin groups with more altruists differentially contribute to the total gene pool. Hamilton's key insight about the importance of genetic relatedness remained intact, but his previous interpretation of inclusive fitness theory as an alternative to group selection was wrong, as he clearly acknowledged in 1975 and in his autobiographical recollection (Hamilton, 1996; see also Schwartz, 2000). For two-person game theory, the cooperative Tit-for-Tat strategy never beats its social partner; it only loses or draws. The only reason that Tit-for-Tat or any other cooperative strategy evolves in a game theory model is because groups of cooperators contribute more to the total gene pool than groups of non-cooperators, as Anatol Rapoport, the political scientist who submitted the Tit-for-Tat strategy to Robert Axelrod's famous computer simulation tournament, clearly recognized (Rapoport, 1991; discussed in Sober and Wilson 1998, pp. 85–86). All of these models obey the following simple rule: 'Selfishness beats altruism within single groups; altruistic groups beat selfish groups'. The main exception to this rule involves models that result in multiple local equilibria, which are internally stable by definition. In this case, group selection can favour the local equilibria that function best at the group level, which is sometimes called 'equilibrium selection' (e.g. Samuelson, 1997).

5.5. The replicator concept is irrelevant to the issues associated with multi-level selection

As part of his effort to interpret basic population genetics theory for a broad audience, Williams (1966) discussed the concept of average effects, which is the fitness of alternative genes at a given locus, averaged across all genotypic, environmental and social contexts. The average effect gives the bottom line of what evolves in the total population, the final vector that reflects the summation of all the component vectors. It became 'the gene's eye view', 'the replicator concept', and 'the gene as the fundamental unit of selection' in Richard Dawkins' 'selfish-gene theory'. These concepts were widely interpreted as arguments against group selection, but they are nothing of the sort. The whole point of multi-level selection theory is to examine the *component vectors* of evolutionary change, and in particular to ask whether genes can evolve on the strength of between-group selection, despite a selective disadvantage within groups. Multi-level selection models calculate the average effects of genes, just like any other population genetics model, but the final vector includes both levels of selection and by itself cannot possibly be used as an argument against group selection. Both Williams and Dawkins eventually acknowledged their error but it is still common to read in articles and textbooks that group selection is wrong because 'the gene is the fundamental unit of selection'.

A similar problem exists with evolutionary models that are not explicitly genetic, such as game theory models, which assume that the various individual strategies 'breed true' in some general sense (Grafen, 1984). The procedure in this case is to average the fitness of the individual strategies across all of the social groupings, yielding an average fitness that is equivalent to the average effect of genes in a population genetics model. Once again, it is the final vector that is interpreted as 'individual fitness' and regarded as an argument against group selection, even though the groups are clearly defined and the component vectors are there for anyone to see, once they know what to look for.

5.6. A single theoretical framework for studying the evolution of social behaviour

The collapse of all three arguments supporting the 1960s consensus requires a re-evaluation that the field as a whole has been reluctant to undertake, in part because the group selection controversy has been taught to generations of students in black-and-white terms. Once we adopt a more nuanced and historically accurate perspective, a simple solution immediately appears. Recall that

Williams made two claims in *Adaptation and Natural Selection*: he *affirmed* the importance of multi-level selection as a theoretical framework and then *denied* the importance of group selection as an empirical claim. If his first claim is correct and his second claim is incorrect, then we can fix the problem by reverting back to multi-level selection theory, just as Williams did for sex ratio and disease virulence. All of the insights that we attribute to inclusive fitness theory, game theory, and other theoretical frameworks remain important, but their significance can be understood in terms of the parameters of multi-level selection theory (such as the balance between levels of selection), without requiring additional parameters. In all cases, we need to identify the appropriate groups and other aspects of population structure, examine selection differentials within groups, and then examine selection differentials among groups in the total population to determine the final vector of evolutionary change. Many evolutionists have already adopted this perspective. For them, evaluating the relative importance of within- versus between-group selection has become as routine as an ecologist who evaluates the relative importance of competition versus predation. Unfortunately, articles and books written from this matter-of-fact multi-level perspective appear alongside other articles and books that are written as if nothing has changed since the 1960s, resulting in the 'Tower of Babel' problem that I discussed at the beginning of this essay. A new consensus needs to be reached, or else the cynical aphorism 'science progresses, funeral by funeral' will become a reality for this important subject.

5.7. Major transitions in evolution

A major event in evolutionary theory occurred with the discovery that individual organisms are the social groups of past ages. Evolution proceeds not only by small mutational change, but also by groups and symbiotic communities becoming so integrated that they become higher-level organisms in their own right. Despite multi-level selection theory's turbulent history, which continues for the traditional study of social behaviour, it is the accepted theoretical framework for studying major transitions. There is universal agreement that selection occurs within and among groups, that the balance between levels of selection can itself evolve, and that a major transition occurs when selection within groups is suppressed, enabling selection among groups to dominate the final vector of evolutionary change. Genetic and developmental phenomena such as chromosomes, the rules of meiosis, a single-cell stage of the life cycle, the early sequestration of the germ line, and programmed death of cell lineages are interpreted as mechanisms for stabilizing the organism and preventing it from becoming a mere group of evolving elements.

Social insect colonies fall easily within the new paradigm of major transitions. Historically, social insect colonies were widely interpreted as 'superorganisms' during the first half of the twentieth century, only to be re-interpreted in terms of inclusive fitness theory in the 1960s. According to Hamilton (1964), the key fact about eusocial insects was the extra-high genetic relatedness among sisters in haplo-diploid species, at least if the queen has mated with only a single male. In retrospect, not only is this one factor neither necessary nor sufficient to explain the evolution of eusociality, but its limited significance can be understood in terms of the parameters of multi-level selection theory, just like all aspects of inclusive fitness theory. Genetic relatedness can even become a disruptive factor in colonies that consist of multiple matrilines and patrilines, requiring mechanisms that prevent nepotism along with individual selfishness, so that the colony as a whole can function as an adaptive unit. As Wilson and Holldobler (2005) conclude in a recent article: "Group selection is the strong binding force in eusocial evolution."

The paradigm of major transitions did not emerge until the 1970's, with Lynn Margulis's (1970) symbiotic theory of the eukaryotic cell. It did not become generalized until the 1990s, with books such as *The Major Transitions of Evolution* (Maynard Smith and Szathmary, 1995). Even though these developments are very recent, it is becoming clear that human evolution falls within the paradigm. Human moral systems can be regarded as mechanisms that suppress selection within groups, enabling between-group selection to become the primary evolutionary

force, just like chromosomes and the rules of meiosis (Boehm, 1999). Our capacities for social transmission, language, and other forms of symbolic thought are fundamentally communal activities that required a shift in the balance between levels of selection before they could evolve. The human major transition was a rare event, but once established it enabled our species to achieve worldwide ecological dominance. Wilson and Holldobler (2005) stress the parallels with social insect evolution as follows: "Rarity of occurrence and unusual pre-adaptations characterized the early species of *Homo* and were followed in a similar manner during the advancements of the ants and termites by the spectacular ecological success and preemptive exclusion of competing forms by *Homo sapiens*."

One reason that group selection is an important force in human evolution is because cultural processes have a way of increasing phenotypic variation among groups and decreasing it within groups. If a new behaviour arises by a genetic mutation, it remains at a low frequency within its group in the absence of clustering mechanisms such as associations among kin. If a new behaviour arises by a cultural mutation, it can quickly becoming the most common behaviour within the group. Evolutionary biologists who study cultural evolution are largely in agreement about the importance of cultural group selection in human evolution (e.g. Henrich, 2003; Richerson and Boyd, 2004; Gintis *et al.*, 2005; see also Henrich and McElreath, Chapter 38 and McElreath & Henrich Chapter 39 of this volume). A recent edited volume titled *Genetic and Cultural Evolution of Cooperation* (Hammerstein, 2003) shows how human cultural evolution is being studied in exactly the same way as other major evolutionary transitions.

5.8. **The future study of group-level evolutionary processes**

I began this essay by saying that anyone who studies humans must acknowledge the importance of group-level evolutionary processes. Yet, a consensus formed in the 1960s that groups are not important units of selection. Evolutionists have been struggling with this massive contradiction ever since. Some progress has been made, but much more can be made in the future by revisiting the past and forming a new consensus about the importance of higher-level selection, especially in the case of human evolution.

References

Alcock, J. (1989) *Animal Behaviour*. Sinauer, Sunderland, MA.

Allee, W. C., Emerson, A. E., Park, O., Park T. and Schmidt K. P. (1949) *Principles of Animal Ecology*. Saunders, Philadelphia.

Boehm, C. (1999) *Hierarchy in the Forest: Egalitarianism and the Evolution of Human Altruism*. Harvard University Press, Cambridge, MA.

Borrello, M. E. (2005) The rise, fall and resurrection of group selection. *Endeavor*, 29: 43–47.

Dawkins, R. (1976) *The Selfish Gene*. Oxford, Oxford University Press.

Gintis, H., S. Bowles, R. T. Boyd and E. Fehr (eds) (2005) Moral sentiments and material interests: the foundations of cooperation in economic life. MIT Press, Cambridge, MA.

Goodnight, C. J. and Stevens, L. (1997) Experimental studies of group selection: What do they tell us about group selection in nature? *American Naturalist*, 150: S59–S79.

Grafen, A. (1984) Natural selection, kin selection and group selection. In J. Krebs and N. Davies (eds) *Behavioural Ecology: An Evolutionary Approach*, pp. 62–84. Blackwell, Oxford.

Hamilton, W. D. (1964) The genetical evolution of social behaviour: I and II. *Journal of Theoretical Biology*, 7: 1–52.

Hamilton, W. D. (1975) Innate social aptitudes in man, an approach from evolutionary genetics. In: R. Fox (ed) *Biosocial Anthropology*. John Wiley, New York.

Hamilton, W. D. (1996) *The Narrow Roads of Gene Land*. W. H. Freeman/Spektrum, Oxford.

Hammerstein, P. (ed.) (2003) *Genetic and Cultural Evolution of Cooperation*. MIT Press, Cambridge, MA.

Henrich, J. (2003) Cultural group selection, coevolutionary processes and large-scale cooperation. *Journal of Economic Behaviour and Organization*, 53: 3–35.

Margulis, L. (1970) *Origin of Eukaryotic Cells*. Yale University Press, New Haven.

Maynard Smith, J. (1964) Group selection and kin selection. *Nature*, 201: 1145–1146.

Maynard Smith, J. and Szathmary, E. (1995) *The Major Transitions of Life*. W. H. Freeman, New York.

Price, G. R. (1970) Selection and covariance. *Nature*, 277: 520–521.

Price, G. R. (1972) Extension of covariance selection mathematics. *Annals of Human Genetics*, 35: 485–490.

Rapoport, A. (1991) Ideological commitments and evolutionary theory. *Journal of Social Issues*, 47: 83–100.

Richards, R. J. (1987) Darwin and the emergence of evolutionary theories of mind and behaviour. Chicago, University of Chicago.

Richerson, P. J. and Boyd, R. (2004) *Not by Genes Alone: How Culture Transformed Human Evolution*. University of Chicago Press, Chicago.

Samuelson, L. (1997) *Evolutionary Games and Equilibrium Selection*. MIT Press, Cambridge, MA.

Sober, E. and Wilson, D. S. (1998) *Unto Others: The Evolution and Psychology of Unselfish Behaviour*. Harvard University Press, Cambridge, MA.

Schwartz, J. (2000) Death of an altruist. *Lingua franca*, 10: 51–61.

Velicer, G. J. (2003) Social strife in the microbial world. *Trends in Microbiology*, 11: 330–337.

Williams, G. C. (1966) *Adaptation and Natural Selection: A Critique of Some Current Evolutionary Thought*. Princeton University Press, Princeton.

Williams, G. C. (1992) *Natural Selection: Domains, Levels and Challenges*. Oxford University Press, Oxford.

Williams, G. C. and Nesse R. M. (1991) The dawn of Darwinian medicine. 66: 1–22.

Wilson, D. S. (1975) A theory of group selection. *Proceedings of the National Academy of Sciences of the USA*, 72: 143–146.

Wilson, E. O. (1975) *Sociobiology: The New Synthesis*. Harvard University Press, Cambridge, MA.

Wilson, E. O. and B. Holldobler (2005) Eusociality: origin and consequences. *Proceedings of the National Academy of Sciences of the USA* 102: 13367–13371.

Wynne-Edwards, V. C. (1962) *Animal Disperson in Relation to Social Behaviour*. Oliver & Boyd, Edinburgh.

SECTION II
The comparative approach

We have already emphasized the way in which evolutionary theory provides us with a broad framework in which to situate questions of psychological interest. Given evolutionary continuity across species, it is obvious that these questions can and should be extended to other species besides ourselves; after all, humans did not drop into the Pleistocene fully formed, and our cognitive mechanisms and the behaviours they produce have a much longer evolutionary history than the last 10 000 years.

As an anthropocentric endeavour designed to shed light on how we came to be, studies of non-human primates have tended to take centre-stage in comparative studies of cognition, as befits their close evolutionary relationship to us. However, as Rendall *et al.* remind us, our anthropocentric assumptions may often be misplaced when we try to 'homologize the mind' in this way, at least partly because we fail to recognise the 'bushiness' of the evolutionary family tree, and the varying evolutionary paths that different species have taken. Assuming that other primate species will possess the precursors of human behaviour and cognition reflects an (often unrecognized) assumption that other species' abilities must be the evolutionary stepping stones by which our own cognitive abilities were gradually built up, as well as assuming that our selective environments have been fundamentally the same. Rendall *et al.* thus draw on some of the themes raised by Mameli and Laland in the previous section in order to place our views of ourselves, and other primate species, under close scrutiny.

These arguments obviously extend beyond the primates, and also raise the issue of whether, given our massively enlarged brains, primates, including humans, are as cognitively 'special' as we so often assume. The answer to this question obviously requires that we investigate the abilities of other, non-primate, species, and focus on identifying the kinds of evolutionary pressures that are associated with particular cognitive abilities. As Bshary *et al.* argue, this 'ecological approach' moves us beyond our rather narrow anthropocentric concerns, as well as enabling more controlled and detailed investigations of the links between behaviour and cognition through the use of 'model' species more amenable to study than ourselves. At the same time, we shouldn't lose sight of the real animal, acting in its natural environment, for without such data we would have little idea of what experiments to perform. Behavioural, ecological and evolutionary studies of animal behaviour can inform the field of comparative cognition in crucially important ways: we should not forget the intellectual sterility of radical behaviourism, and the importance of thinking outside of the (Skinner) box.

In some instances, an ecological approach may include anthropocentrically relevant elements, especially among highly social species where getting along with one's fellows is likely to have exerted a very strong selection pressure. The degree to which such social manoeuvring can be explained by 'knowledge-based' as opposed to 'cue-based' (i.e. associative) mechanisms is one of the key issues at stake in this respect, and Call argues that the weight of evidence lies with the former rather than the latter, at least among the Great Apes. Van Schaik adds weight to this conclusion in his discussion of the evolutionary relevance of ontogeny among these long-lived species, arguing that the 'scaffolding' of learning by other, more experienced, individuals over long periods of development may be the key to explaining the greater cultural capacities of the apes compared to other species. The social support of learning is, however, likely to differ from that shown by human mothers to their offspring in important respects: a lack of 'other-regarding' preferences among the Great Apes, as discussed by Silk, would seem to suggest that, whatever mechanisms underlie these social learning processes, an empathic concern for others is unlikely to be among them.

CHAPTER 6

Homologizing the mind

Drew Rendall, Hugh Notman and John R. Vokey

6.1. Evolution and adaptation: descent with modification

Theodosius Dobzhansky famously said, "Nothing in biology makes sense except in the light of evolution." (Dobzhansky 1973, p. 125). Sometime later a colleague cleverly quipped, "Nothing in evolution makes sense except in the light of constraint." Just so. Evolutionary processes play a central role in the design of all living things, producing a diversity of extraordinary adaptations "which justly excites our admiration" (Darwin, 1859: Introduction, p. 2). Equally true, but more often neglected, such adaptations seldom arise *de novo*. The details of evolutionary design can only be fully understood in historical context, with the broader perspective it offers on how design solutions to recent specific environmental pressures are critically shaped (either facilitated or constrained) by species' history—that is, by the requirement that they be integrated with the myriad pre-existing physical, physiological, and behavioural solutions to other adaptive challenges that species' history entails. In short, organisms are a blend of adaptive potential and historical inertia; the degrees of freedom are not infinite and so what is evolutionarily possible over most timeframes depends critically on the starting conditions.

These points are not controversial, either in principle or in the abstract. However, in practice, and with respect to specific trait systems, they are frequently debated, and attention to the inevitable mix often takes a back seat to emphasizing one dimension over the other, as evidenced in the often polarized perspectives that pervade biology: ecology versus phylogeny, adaptation versus constraint, optimizing versus satisficing. A similar tension pervades comparative psychology which seeks to homologize the mind by providing a comprehensive evolutionary account of continuity and diversification in psychological structure and function across species. Most current efforts to homologize the mind can be seen to be guided by one of two general frameworks that loosely track this same push-and-pull between history/continuity and adaptation/diversification.

In what follows, we outline briefly these frameworks and highlight broad conceptual weaknesses in them. But before we do, we need to attach a few important qualifiers. First, few of the concerns we raise are novel but rather have been anticipated, in some fashion and to at least some degree, by many others. In acknowledging a significant precedent for some of our concerns, we do not mean to imply that the concerns are thus widely appreciated or endorsed by most practitioners. Indeed, we raise these concerns again precisely because they seem not to be widely or fully appreciated—but should be. Second, our sketches of the two general frameworks guiding comparative psychological research are necessarily somewhat simplified. We simply cannot elaborate more subtle or nuanced positions in the space we have here.

This point affords no comfort, however, in the obvious objection that our brief characterizations of the frameworks are somehow at best caricatures that fail to capture what practitioners of comparative psychology are really doing and that, as a result, our concerns are misplaced. Quite the opposite. Our concerns are quite broad and independent of the finer conceptual points of either framework; they apply to the broad sweep of research conducted under both. Third, both frameworks assume a priori that important elements of mind structure and function evolve and so can be meaningfully homologized. But this basic assumption is not above questioning. Indeed other contributors to this volume provide compelling reasons not to accept it too uncritically. Mindful of these concerns, we will nevertheless accept the assumption that minds evolve for the sake of elucidating additional concerns about the frameworks that are commonly used to explain how such mind evolution is likely to have occurred and what its products are likely to be.

6.2. **Frameworks for understanding the evolution of mind design**

The first framework commonly used to model psychological evolution is not recognized by any formal name and indeed may not be recognized explicitly by most of its practitioners. We introduce the approach by way of example and, for reasons that will become immediately clear, give it the label 'Frodoian Psychology'.

6.2.1. **'Frodoian Psychology'**

Early in this new millennium, Hollywood breathed life into J. R. Tolkien's legendary Frodo Baggins and the many other dwarfed and furry-footed, hobbit denizens of middle-earth using the suitably other-worldly mountains and fiordes of southern New Zealand as the backdrop. At about the same time, and not far away, paleontologists actually discovered fossils representing a dwarfed hominin that might have lived as recently as 12 000 years ago in southeast Asia (Brown *et al.*, 2004; Morwood *et al.*, 2004). This species was not only entirely new to science, it

was also remarkable in several important respects, not least in being dwarfed (only 1 m tall) and having an extremely small brain for a temporally modern hominin (380 cc) that was more in line with the size of a chimpanzee's brain. Nevertheless, it showed evidence of complex, human-like behaviours, including the manufacture and use of tools, the use of fire, and possibly also the ability to construct crude watercraft. The species was named *Homo floresiensis* after the Indonesian island of Flores on which its remains were found, but the fossils were quickly nicknamed the *hobbit*.

Some of this is coincidence, some of it is not. What is not coincidence is that the behaviour of the new species was rather speculatively elaborated by investigators to include complex cognitive abilities, cooperative hunting, and communicating with language (Morewood *et al.*, 2004). For example, in one media interview following publication of the fossil find, study co-author Richard Roberts reiterated the suspected intelligence of *H. floresiensis*, "as they were manufacturing sophisticated stone tools, hunting pygmy elephants and crossing at least two water barriers to reach Flores ... The latter two activities must surely have been group activities, which implies communicative skills and use of language ... all with a brain the size of a grapefruit." (Vergano, 2004).

Future discoveries might ultimately confirm (or contradict) many of these attributions, or indeed any of the original findings. Perhaps *H. floresiensis*, as a distinct species, will not even survive the test of time. But none of that actually matters. The point of the example is simply to highlight the evolutionary psychological framework that is being invoked, at least implicitly. In attributing language, hunting, and complex societies to the hobbits, we are clearly taking the evidence of certain human-like traits (e.g. stone tools) and projecting several others. In doing so, we are being anthropomorphic, possibly a very long-standing mode of human reasoning (see below), but also a specific manifestation of a broader evolutionary psychological framework (loosely grounded in the formerly popular, but now largely discredited, *Scala Naturae*) that espouses gradistic notions of linear psychological continuity according to which ancestors are viewed as scaled-down versions of their descendants, possessing the same basic abilities, although perhaps in somewhat simpler form (c.f. Hodos and Campbell, 1990). The anthropomorphic variant of psychological gradism involves the additional element of projecting specifically human traits backwards onto ancestral taxa, or extant taxa that are taken to approximate them.

Space limits prohibit rehearsing the many acknowledged powers and pitfalls of the gradistic (or anthropomorphic) approach. Suffice it to say that:

1. It is entirely natural, perhaps inevitable. We are, after all, human, and only human: we experience the world around us from this particular, anthropocentric, perspective, and we can by definition then investigate worldly phenomena only from this same anthropocentric perspective.

2. It may even be adaptive, at least as applied to our human companions, in as much as conspecific humans have been an important part of our selective history, and understanding them, so as to interact profitably with them, has very probably been aided by thinking about them anthropomorphically (a practice sometimes also labelled 'folk psychology').

3. It is, to some degree, theoretically sensible in emphasizing the continuity dimension inherent in evolutionary descent. All else being equal, a recent, even hobbit-like, species of human should be a lot like us.

4. However, this approach is also fatally teleological and therefore increasingly dangerous as the ancestral distance from us increases. The diversity of known taxa are simply not waypoints on the journey to person-hood, perhaps not even taxa closely related to us. The evolutionary process is by now famously understood to be more like a bush than it is like a ladder. And so, and perhaps obviously, anthropomorphism as folk psychological strategy for *understanding* others must be distinguished from anthropomorphism as scientific *explanation* of others.

This is all familiar ground, and, as a result, the notion of anthropomorphism—and gradistic psychological evolution more generally—is deemed naively simplistic. Or at least it is among scientists who seek an objective explanation of other minds which they realize might not bear much relation to our own minds, much less to how we ourselves understand our own minds. We acknowledge that this contemporary scientific proscription on anthropomorphism might not generalize fully. For example, it might not hold among many lay people. Indeed, the general public might well prefer an anthropomorphic to an objective scientific account of the minds of other species because they might not be particularly invested in what other species are *truly* like (inherent barriers to the latter notwithstanding; Nagel, 1974, but see also Akins, 1993), only whether, and in what degree, they are human-like; any discrepancies between these two 'realities' quite understandably being of little practical day-to-day significance to them.

However, although such a preference for deliberately anthropomorphic accounts of other species might characterize a substantial section of the general public, we doubt that it accounts for anthropomorphism among scientists. Rather, we guess that anthropomorphism among scientists, when it occurs, is unintentional: it reflects either the inherent anthropomorphic bias that we humans naturally bring to any endeavour, or an additional but unwitting seepage into formal research programmes of an element of the anthropomorphism deliberately indulged in to popularize science for the general public. We suggest that any scientific anthropomorphism that occurs must thus be unintentional because a deliberate anthropomorphic account of another species must be without any meaningful scientific justification. If (i) we acknowledge that our anthropocentric, or folk psychological, accounts of our own mental life probably seriously distort the objective reality of our own minds; and (ii) we further acknowledge that our anthropocentric understanding of the minds of other species very likely seriously distorts the objective reality of those minds; then, what scientific justification could there possibly be for knowingly seeking a distorted anthropomorphic account of the human-like nature of another species based on a folk psychological model of human nature that seriously distorts that nature to begin with?

As we said, no researcher today subscribes to this brand of homologizing, or at least not explicitly. Of course, if this were really true, then no researcher would be tempted to assume that a newly discovered species of tool-using hominin must, like us, also have lived in complex societies and communicated with language. No researcher would seek to test whether monkeys, apes and elephants can, like people, recognize themselves in a mirror. No researcher would seek evidence of a sense of justice, fairness, or morality in animals. No researcher would go to the trouble of designing artificial languages to test chimpanzees', dolphins' or parrots' understanding of language-like symbolism and syntax, etc. ... But they do. We all do. (For additional topical examples, see Silk, this volume, Chapter 10.)

6.2.2. 'Fodorian Psychology'

A second, and currently central, evolutionary psychological framework is based on the early mind design insights of philosopher, Jerry Fodor. His profoundly influential book, *Modularity of Mind*, proposed a broad outline of mind architecture that involved multiple peripheral mental modules operating largely independently of one another and in functionally specialized ways on worldly input. These modules then forward their processed content to a more general, centralized executive processing system (Fodor, 1983). One kernel of Fodor's framework—functionally specialized, informationally encapsulated mental modules—resonated particularly strongly with evolutionary psychologists (Tooby and Cosmides, 1992). For evolutionary psychologists (in the narrow-sense; see Mameli, this volume, Chapter 10), the idea of modules brilliantly captured both the natural level at which mental processes must be organized in the brain and specifically also the adaptive and diversifying element of the evolutionary process that must have shaped them. Via such modularity, the evolved architecture of the mind—the natural joints at which the mind is carved—could be revealed by identifying its constituent, functionally distinct mental modules that would have arisen as psychological adaptations tailored to the processing demands of the many specific problems posed by the environments in which the species evolved (Pinker, 1997). For humans, the critical environment that shaped our minds is proposed to have been the Pleistocene period (1.8 million years ago to 10 000 years ago) during which were crystallized adaptive modules related to hunting,

foraging, navigating space, choosing mates, detecting signs of health and symmetry, developing social alliances, detecting cheaters, and many other social, ecological, and technological challenges (reviewed in Barkow *et al.*, 1992). These various adaptive modules are deployed by contemporary humans, to greater or lesser effect, depending on how faithfully modern environments and the challenges they pose replicate the environments and challenges of the Pleistocene.

This more modern evolutionary psychological framework, based on extensive elaboration of Fodor's idea of modules[1], is intuitively appealing and has been extremely productive. It is not without problems, however. Consider the hobbit example again, portrayed in the simplified cladogram in Figure 6.1. If the B of *H. floresiensis* is the same as the B of modern *H. sapiens* (as some speculations about the hobbits' use of tools, language, and cooperative hunting have suggested), then there is a serious hole in our theories of mind/brain function. That is, the same behaviour (B) is being generated from very different brains (and perhaps minds; see next Section 6.3), while different behaviours, specifically the b of chimpanzees (who lack language, sophisticated tools, and cooperative hunting) versus the B of *H. floresiensis* (who apparently possess these traits), are being generated from similar brains (at least in size). Of course, the B of *H. floresiensis* may not be the same as the B of *H. sapiens* (as seems plausible); in which case, recent speculations about the human-like behaviour of the hobbit are misguided, as per the previous section. However, if this is true, then why do we attach such importance to Pleistocene conditions *per se* in having forged the modern human mind? If an offshoot hominin can completely remodel itself—body and brain—in such short order, then could not the same be true of *H. sapiens* over a similar time period? (For evidence consistent with this possibility, suggesting recent and extensive changes in the human genome, see Voight *et al.*, 2006.) And if this is possible,

---

[1] We think Jerry Fodor might not endorse this elaborated version of modularity (i.e. Massive Modularity, MM; Fodor, 2000) and so would not actually consider himself a Fodorian psychologist in the sense described. And that's the point. If Fodor would not march with the Fodorians, should we?

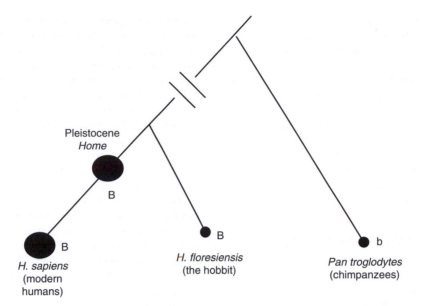

Fig. 6.1 Schematic cladogram illustrating the branching relationships between chimpanzees, modern humans, and the recently discovered hobbit. The putative Pleistocene ancestor to modern humans is also shown. Upper- and lower-case B letters refer to the behaviour of the different species, while the size of the circle represents their relative brain size.

why do we assume that *H. sapiens* minds were forged and then frozen in the Pleistocene?

No doubt there are ways out of this dilemma, but the example serves simply to point up potential chinks in the elaborated Fodorian framework as well, in the form of troubling disconnects between brains, minds and behaviour. Incidentally, it is of no help in the above example to object that, in fact, chimpanzees do, by some definition, have language and sophisticated tools, and hunt cooperatively. By such objection, all species illustrated in Figure 6.1 would then have the same behaviour, B, yet very different brains—at least in size—which would then make even more mysterious how minds, brains, and behaviours evolve.

Consider another, more concrete, example. One major focus in current evolutionary psychological research, particularly that focused on human and non-human primates, concerns a proposed social-cognitive module labelled 'theory of mind' (ToM; Premack and Woodruff, 1978; see Call, this volume, Chapter 7). ToM is characterized by an ability to treat other individuals as mental agents—to impute to them specific types of mental state (e.g. motives, beliefs, wants, desires, states of knowledge) and to assume that these play a causal role in determining their behaviour. ToM abilities are held to be foundational to a whole spectrum of complex social behaviours (e.g. cooperation, deception, pedagogy, even language in humans) that hinge on accurately modelling the intentions and motivations of others, as well as what they might or might not know or believe about some state of affairs, so as to better predict and manage what they are likely to do. ToM is proposed to have arisen as an adaptive response to the problems posed by living in large social groups, namely the need to negotiate successfully a complex web of social network opportunities and challenges (Jolly, 1966; Humphrey, 1976; Byrne and Whiten, 1988). There is arguably no other potential mind adaptation that is currently attributed such significance in the evolution of primate sociality.

Nevertheless, if this is so, we are now faced with two problems, one of them empirical and the other theoretical. The empirical problem involves an apparent disconnect between complex social living and ToM abilities among primates. For example, among non-human primates, the cercopithecine monkeys of the Old World (e.g. macaques and baboons) live in large, cohesive groups and have long distinguished themselves from other primate taxa for being exceptionally sociable and deft in their management of tangled webs of overlapping short- and long-term friendships, alliances and coalitions (Cheney *et al.*, 1986). The complex social dynamics of these monkeys were the original inspiration for the popular Social Intelligence (or Machiavellian Intelligence) hypothesis that currently dominates theorizing on the evolution of primate sociality and cognition, and that has culminated in the proposal of a ToM module to allow effective management of such complex social relationships (Humphrey, 1976; Byrne and Whiten, 1988; Dunbar, 1998). Surprisingly, then, these same monkeys routinely fare poorly in many of the social-cognitive tests that are believed to comprise the functional capacities of the proposed ToM module.

For example, one experimental design has involved testing whether or not animals can recognize themselves in a mirror, the assumption being that this task might reveal some sense of self-awareness that would be foundational to a mentalistic understanding of others (Gallup, 1970, 1977; Povinelli *et al.*, 1993). Another has involved testing how well these same animals can coordinate their behaviour with a partner in a cooperative foraging task, where success hinges on understanding both your own role in the task and also your partner's role (Mason and Hollis, 1962; Povinelli *et al.*, 1992a,b). Still others have involved testing whether study animals can predict what a partner knows about the location of food, for example, based on what that partner has or has not seen; or whether they can adjust their own foraging behaviour based on what partners do or do not know about where food is located (Povinelli and Eddy, 1996; Hare *et al.*, 2000, 2001). In most of these tests, the highly social primates, such as Old World macaques, fare relatively poorly. In contrast, the great apes, particularly chimpanzees and orangutans, have fared much better on the same tests despite being far less intensely social under natural conditions in the wild.

Some creative ideas have been offered to reconcile the discordance between social living and social cognitive abilities in monkeys versus apes, for example, that the spatially dispersed and fluid communities of chimpanzees and orangutans actually represent a more complicated social problem than the permanent and cohesive groups of monkeys (e.g. Galdikas and Vasey, 1992). Another possibility is that the ToM module is not actually a single module but a constellation of component sub-modules (e.g. Baron-Cohen, 1995) that may be realized in varying degrees and combinations of the relevant skills (e.g. sensitivity to eyes, gaze following, want-belief attribution, knowledge attribution). But, of course, these kinds of arguments, however plausible, just confirm how poorly we understand what the key dimensions of social-life challenges are that drive social-cognitive adaptations and at what processing level they contact the cognitive machinery. As a result, the connection between *functional adaptive problems* (e.g. social complexity) and *specialized cognitive modules* (e.g. ToM) that represents the very core of Fodorian evolutionary psychology remains tenous. Not only do we not know exactly where the mind's natural joints are, but we do not have any very clear sense of how to find them.

We may, of course, be mischaracterizing social complexity in these different species, or we may be mischaracterizing their different social cognitive abilities, or both. Or, it may be that what matters more is the sort of organism you are and the sort of cognitive tools you have to begin with (i.e. history matters; e.g. Barrett *et al.*, submitted). Perhaps ToM abilities will prove to be epiphenomenal of other (more generalized) abstract reasoning abilities that come with some threshold expansion of the brain, or more particularly the frontal cortex, that occurs other reasons entirely including some form of allometric scaling that cannot be linked very directly with any specific adaptive challenges (Finlay *et al.*, 2001). In which case, chimpanzees and organutans might be better than monkeys on ToM tasks simply because each of the former has a more elaborated frontal cortex than any of the latter.

Notwithstanding these considerable empirical ambiguities in the manifestation and evolution of ToM, there seems to be an a priori theoretical problem in our investigation of it among primates *vis-à-vis* the Fodorian, adaptive modularity framework. According to the logic of Fodorian evolutionary psychology, the ToM module represents a social-cognitive adaptation to living in large social groups and managing the competing social pressures of cooperation and competition that life in such groups entails. These challenges are proposed to have represented an especially important selective pressure in human evolution as inter-group warfare selected for social groups of increasing size throughout the Pleistocene, yielding groups that were routinely much larger than those of ancestral hominins or non-human primates (Aiello and Dunbar, 1993; Dunbar, 1993). In such groups, the intensity and complexity of social problems was greatly magnified because the number of individuals and social relationships that had to be managed increased exponentially with increasing group size. Effective social functioning in such large groups hinged on an ability to efficiently predict what other individuals knew or believed so as to anticipate how they were likely to behave based on their knowledge or beliefs. It is proposed to have been particularly important to be able to detect and avoid potential cheaters—individuals who were likely to defect on social obligations or contracts, thereby negating the benefits of cooperation (Cosmides and Tooby, 1992)—and ultimately to share this and other relevant social information with other group members, perhaps culminating in the evolution of language for the efficient exchange of social information (Dunbar, 1998).

This comprehensive evolutionary account of human social cognition now holds a central place in human cognitive psychology where a great deal of research is focused on documenting various ToM abilities and describing the timecourse of their development in young children (see, for example, essays in Carruthers and Smith, 1996). Although the details of many of the abilities, and even the broader theory to account for them, are subject to debate, what is more problematic for present purposes is that the general research programme has been extended directly to non-human primates.

The theoretical problem here is obvious. If social groups of increasing size were a critical part of the hominin adaptive landscape that selected for specialized, modular social-cognitive adaptations (e.g. knowledge attribution and 'cheater-detection'), then why would we subsequently test extant non-human primates—which have had a very different selective history—for the same social-cognitive adaptations? The answer must be that we want to test whether non-human primates show evidence of the same abilities to see whether and to what extent these abilities might have evolved incrementally from more distant, non-human primate ancestors (that extant non-human primate taxa are accepted as models of). But here we are now applying a gradistic approach, and an explicitly anthropomorphic variant of it, by backward-modelling human ToM abilities in non-human primates. Having derived an evolutionarily intuitive account for the emergence of specialized social-cognitive adaptations subserving major dimensions of contemporary human behaviour (pedagogy, deception, cheater detection, language) that appeared to distinguish human from non-human primates and thus to require special explanation, we now invert the logic, and the evolutionary process, by testing for the same social cognitive abilities in non-human primates, many of which did not evidence patterns of social behaviour that would require such mechanisms to begin with. In the process, we both mangle the logic of Fodorian evolutionary psychology that inspired the proposal of specialized social-cognitive modules in response to specific social pressures to begin with, and blend it with the logic of the gradistic, Frodoian framework which models ancestors as scaled-down versions of their descendants, thereby thoroughly conflating processes of continuity and processes of diversification.

6.3. Homologizing the mind

How do minds evolve exactly, if they evolve at all? We do not know. We do not entirely understand how brains evolve, which would be a good start (see Panksepp, this volume, Chapter 12). But even if we knew that, we might not be much better off because we do not know much about how minds map onto brains, or even how complex behaviours—which is generally all that we have to go on—map onto minds.

We do know that some aspects of central nervous system layout and design are common to most organisms, from fruit flies to humans (Reichert and Simeone, 1999), implying that some dimensions of brain evolution are remarkably conservative. There is some evidence that certain neural circuits can be similarly conservative (Kavanau, 1990). Furthermore, the broadly networked nature of neural functioning itself seems to point to a degree of structural and functional brain integration that might be inherently resistant to any ripple effect that would be entailed by wholesale design modifications required to support novel, narrowly tuned adaptive processing routines.

However, at the same time, there is some reason to think that the same neural circuits, under different states of activation, can support widely different functions (Lauder, 1980; Kavanau, 1990; Katz and Harris-Warrick, 1999), implying that functional mental flexibility can coexist with structural conservativism. We also know that, in response to developmental disturbance or acute injury, some high-level behavioural functions (e.g. language) can shift to, or be appropriated by, disparate brain regions, at least within species. Unfortunately, the significance of this plasticity vis-à-vis mind/brain evolution is unclear. On the one hand, such plasticity might point to a capacity for rapid evolutionary specialization of mind/brain in response to new processing demands. On the other hand, it could confirm just the opposite, namely that brain tissue manifests significant neuro-functional pluripotence: it could be a highly conserved mechanism that provides for processing flexibility but specifically without structural or operational specialization for, or dedication to, any particular processing demand.

Ultimately, then, we cannot be entirely certain whether brain design is inherently evolutionarily conservative or evolutionarily plastic. More problematic, though, we cannot be entirely certain whether the result here would necessarily have any clear implications for the evolution of mind. That it would, implies that mind change reflects brain change and vice versa. But this need not be true (recall the hobbit example), if, as seems plausible, mental routines enjoy a degree of emancipation from the neural architecture supporting them—just as computer software is partially emancipated from the details of the structural platforms on which it can be implemented.

Exactly the same kind of structural emancipation characterizes many forms of behaviour which are not easily traced to tangible structural substrates. For example, many behaviours related to courtship and mating, to parenting, to territoriality, to spatial navigation, or to temperament and demeanor have no direct morphological underpinnings. In other cases, there may be structural links to behaviour but the links are different in different species even though the behaviour itself is similarly motivated and serves a similar function in all of them. For example, among primates, some species mark or advertise their territories using deposits of urine, faeces or the product of some specific scent gland, while others do so using loud, conspicuous vocalizations. Hence, the territory advertisement behaviour serves the same function in the different species although it is supported by different anatomical systems. Critics have argued that behaviours like these that either have only loose or ephemeral connections to structural substrates, or that are supported by different structures in different species, cannot be meaningfully homologized at all, no matter what functional commonality they might share (Atz, 1970; Hodos, 1976). They argue that what evolves, and so what can be homologized, is structure, not the behaviour it supports nor its behavioural functions, which could arise through epigenetic processes.

The latter conclusions seem too bleak because they are tantamount to saying that behaviour does not evolve. Perhaps this is true for many behaviours, including some that we naïvely model the evolution of, and so we should be mindful of the cautionary prescriptions. However, as a blanket prescription for behaviour, it is pretty unsatisfying. Despite sometimes being structurally enigmatic, there is ample evidence that some behaviours evolve and so they can, at least in principle, be meaningfully homologized (reviewed in Rendall and Di Fiore, 2007). Of course, behavioural evolution, like the evolution of other trait systems (e.g. morphology, genes), can be in either a conservative or a diversifying way and quite independent of structure (Brooks and McLennan, 1991; Streidter and Northcutt, 1991): in some cases behaviour is extremely conserved, even in the face of substantial environmental change that can be remodelling the organism in other ways (Brooks and McLennan, 1991; Di Fiore and Rendall, 1994); in other cases, behavioural modification can be rapid and precede, and perhaps even drive, structural change (Mayr, 1958; West-Eberhard, 1989).

There are obviously instructive parallels here for the evolution of minds. Many of the same problems that characterize attempts to homologize structurally enigmatic behaviours apply to structurally enigmatic minds as well and so many of the same cautions and criticisms could be levelled. But the example of behaviour here represents more than just an analogy for minds both because minds and the behaviours they produce are causally connected and because our inferences of mind design are generally based only on interpretations of the behaviour patterns that we can observe. And, as others have compellingly argued (e.g. Povinelli *et al.*, 2000), evidence for behavioural similarity among organisms does not necessarily constitute evidence for mind similarity among them. Just as functionally similar territorial advertisement in different primate taxa can be supported by different anatomical structures, so too could similarly complex social behaviours in various species be supported by different mental processes. The converse may also be true, namely that behavioural differences do not necessarily reflect mind differences. This may be because much of the behavioural variation we observe is actually epigenetic in origin and reflects developmental, rather than evolutionary, plasticity and such behavioural plasticity effectively buffers other trait systems, including the mind, from environmental exigencies that might otherwise drive evolutionary changes (Rendall and Di Fiore 2007; see also Laland, this volume, Chapter 4).

So, ultimately, how do we use the evidence from structurally enigmatic behaviours to homologize structurally enigmatic minds? The answer must be with caution, obviously, because we lack any well worked-out theory of brain–mind–behaviour evolution. The two general frameworks of mind evolution considered above each have merit, but neither is entirely satisfying. The practice of using human behaviours or human mental abilities (even where known) to model those of other species may be irresistably seductive, but it is potentially deeply

misleading. At best, it prematurely narrows the options we entertain in our attempts to understand other species and their minds. Despite our folk psychological reflexes, and popular literary representations (Tolkien, 1937), most other species simply are not smaller, hairier versions of us. The alternative, adaptive modularity, approach is intuitively appealing, but it is plagued by conceptual ambiguities: as applied to humans, the historical precedence of the Pleistocene, or any other epoch, in forging mind adaptations is not entirely substantiated; the characteristics of the proposed environment(s) of evolutionary adaptedness remain unspecified then; and the specific adaptive problems those environments represented, for which specialized cognitive routines are proposed to have evolved, are therefore unclear. (The ambiguities are at least as great for other species, particularly when modules relevant to humans are then applied to non-humans.) Furthermore, the paradigms' fundamental theoretical pillar—that cognition is structuro-functionally compartmentalized according to tightly circumscribed behavioural problems (e.g. detecting cheaters)—does not yet enjoy overwhelming empirical support.

Ultimately, we crave some alternative that is faithful both to the continuity inherent in descent and to the diversification inherent in adaptation, but that is also better informed by the reality of how mental processing routines are actually realized in the physics of particular brains. We are impotent to suggest exactly what this kind of framework should look like. However, given the substantial concerns outlined above, one sensible strategy might be to adopt a conservative approach that explicitly embraces well-established processes of perception and learning and that subsequently builds on and elaborates these only as the evidence clearly requires it (e.g. Pearce and Boutin, 2001). This strategy need not entail a wholesale return to behaviourist psychology and its ecological sterility which was, after all, anathema to a proper evolutionary framework. But nor would it involve ignoring or bypassing the powerful and taxonomically widespread learning mechanisms that behaviourists and their successors elucidated in favour of loosely defined, high-level cognitive processing routines whose reality remains largely hypothetical. Instead, this alternative approach would be grounded in the closest thing we have to psychological first principles, which it would then explore and elaborate in ecologically informed ways.

Garcia and Koelling's (1966) landmark work on conditioned taste aversions famously illustrates the fruits of exactly this approach, demonstrating how general learning mechanisms and the environmental dimensions to which they are responsive can be subtly but adaptively modified to reflect the sometimes peculiar task demands of species-specific foraging problems. Subsequent research on the neuro-cognitive processes subserving the elaborated memory demands faced by food-storing birds (e.g. Clayton and Dickinson, 1998; reviewed in Sherry, 2006) represents a natural and productive extension of the same approach.

It is not clear just how far this sort of conservative, bottom-up approach, grounded in general mechanisms of learning and perception, could be pushed. Studies of language learnability in human children, as well as in artificial neural networks, certainly suggest that these mechanisms could yet prove extremely powerful and at least partially responsible for what have long been considered some of our own most complicated psychological and behavioural abilities (e.g. Rumelhart and McLelland, 1986; Elman, 1991; Kuhl, 2000; Landauer, 2002; Saffran, 2003). Still, in the end, they might often yield to qualitatively specialized processing routines. But whenever and wherever they yield, it seems likely that the details of their yielding, when revealed from a grounded bottom-up perspective rather than from an unbounded top-down perspective, will make much clearer exactly how they have been specialized.

Acknowledgments

Two of us are not actually psychologists and most certainly know nothing about how minds work, while the third is a psychologist, but has no clearer idea. We are therefore all the more grateful that the Natural Sciences and Engineering Research Council (NSERC) of Canada has nevertheless generously supported our work.

References

Aiello, L.C. and Dunbar, R.I.M. (1993) Neocortex size, group size, and the evolution of language. *Current Anthropology*, 34: 184–193.

Akins, K. (1993) What is it like to be boring and myopic? In B. Dahlbom, *Dennett and His Critics*, pp. 124–160. Blackwell/Oxford University Press, Oxford.

Atz, J.W. (1970) The application of the idea of homology to behavior. In L. R. Aronson, E. Tobach, D. S. Lehrman and J. S. Rosenblatt (eds) *Development and Evolution of Behavior: Essays in memory of T. C. Schnierla*, pp. 53–74. W. H. Freeman, San Francisco.

Barkow, J. H., Cosmides, L. and Tooby, J. (eds) (1992) *The Adapted Mind: Evolutionary Psychology and the Generation of Culture*. Oxford University Press, New York, NY.

Baron-Cohen, S. (1995) *Mind-Blindness*. MIT Press, Cambridge, MA.

Barrett, L., Aureli, F., Call, J., Connor, R. and Holekamp, K. (submitted) Cognitive demands of fission–fusion dynamics. *Current Anthropology*.

Brooks, D. R. and McLennan, D. A. (1991) *Phylogeny, Ecology, and Behavior*. University of Chicago Press, Chicago.

Brown, P., Sutikna, T., Morwood, M. J., Soejono, R. P., Jatmiko, Wayhu Saptomo, E. and Due, R. A. (2004) A new small-bodied hominin from the Late Pleistocene of Flores, Indonesia. *Nature* 431: 1055–1061.

Byrne, R. W. and Whiten, A. (eds) (1988) *Machiavellian Intelligence. Social Expertise and the Evolution of Intellect in Monkeys, Apes, and Humans*. Oxford University Press, Oxford.

Carruthers, P. and Smith, P. K. (eds) (1996) *Theories of Theories of Mind*. Cambridge University Press, Cambridge.

Cheney, D. L., Seyfarth, R. M. and Smuts, B. B. (1986) Social relationships and social cognition in non-human primates. *Science* 234: 1361–1366.

Clayton, N. S. and Dickinson, A. (1998) Episodic-like memory during cache recovery by scrub jays. *Nature* 395: 272–278.

Cosmides, L. and Tooby, J. (1992) Cognitive adaptations for social exchange. In J. Barkow, L. Cosmides and J. Tooby (eds). *The Adapted Mind*, pp. 163–228. Oxford University Press, New York.

Darwin, C. 1859. *On the Origin of Species*. The Modern Library, New York.

Di Fiore, A. F. and Rendall, D. (1994) Evolution of social organization: A reappraisal for primates by using phylogenetic methods. *Proceedings of the National Academy of Sciences of the USA* 91: 9941–9945.

Dobzhansky, T. (1973) Nothing in biology makes sense except in the light of evolution. *The Biology Teacher* 35: 125–129.

Dunbar, R. I. M. (1993) Coevolution of neocortex size, group size and language in humans. *Behavioral and Brain Sciences* 16: 681–735.

Dunbar, R. I. M. (1998) The social brain hypothesis. *Evolutionary Anthropology* 6: 178–190.

Elman, J. L. (1991) Distributed representations, simple recurrent networks, and grammatical structure. In D. Touretzky (ed.) *Connectionist Approaches to Language Learning*, pp. 91–122. Kluwer, Dordrecht.

Finlay, B. L., Darlington, R. B. and Nicastro, N. (2001) Developmental structure in brain evolution. *Behavioral and Brain Sciences* 24: 263–308.

Fodor, J. (1983) *The Modularity of Mind: An Essay on Faculty Psychology*. MIT Press, Cambridge, MA.

Fodor, J. (2000) *The Mind Doesn't Work that Way*. MIT Press, Cambridge, MA.

Galdikas, B. F. M. and Vasey, P. (1992) Why are orangutans so smart? Ecological and social hypothesis. In F. D. Burton (ed.) *Social Processes and Mental Abilities in Nonhuman Primates*, pp. 183–224. Edwin Mellen Press, Lewiston, New York.

Gallup, G. Jr. (1970) Chimpanzees: self-recognition. *Science* 167: 86–87.

Gallup, G. Jr (1977) Absence of self-recognition in a monkey (Macaca fascicularis) following prolonged exposure to a mirror. *Developmental Psychobiology* 10: 281–284.

Garcia, J. and Koelling, R. A. (1966) Relation of cue to consequence in avoidance learning. *Psychonomic Science* 4: 123–124.

Hall, B. K. (ed.) (1994) *Homology: The Hierarchical Basis of Comparative Biology*. Academic Press, New York.

Hare, B., Call, J., Agnetta, B. and Tomasello, M. (2000) Chimpanzees know what conspecifics do and do not see. *Animal Behaviour* 59: 771–786.

Hare, B., Call, J. and Tomasello, M. (2001) Do chimpanzees know what conspecifics know? *Animal Behaviour* 61, 139–151.

Hodos, W. (1976) The concept of homology and the evolution of behavior. In R. B. Masterton, W. Hodos and H. Jerison (eds) *Evolution, Brain, and Behavior: Persistent Problems*. Hillsdale, NJ: John Wiley and Sons. Pp. 153–167.

Hodos, W. and Campbell, C. B. G. (1990) Evolutionary scales and comparative studies of animal cognition. In R. P. Kesner and D. S. Olton (eds), *Neurobiology of Comparative Cognition*, pp. 1–20. Lawrence Erlbaum Associates, Hillsdale, NJ.

Humphrey, N. K. (1976) The social function of intellect. In P. P. G. Bateson and R. A. Hinde (eds) *Growing Points in Ethology*, pp. 303–317. Cambridge University Press. Cambridge.

Jolly, A. (1966) Lemur social behavior and primate intelligence. *Science* 153: 501–506.

Kavanau, J. L. (1990. Conservative behavioral evolution, the neural substrate. *Animal Behaviour* 39: 758–767.

Katz, P. S. and Harris-Warrick, R. M. (1999) The evolution of neuronal circuits underlying species-specific behavior. *Current Opinion in Neurobiology* 9: 628–633.

Kuhl, P. (2000) A new view of language acquisition. *Proceedings of the National Academy of Sciences of the USA* 97: 11850–11857.

Landauer, T.K. (2002) On the computational basis of learning and cognition: arguments from LSA. In N. Ross (ed.), *The Psychology of Learning and Motivation* 41: 43–84.

Lauder, G. V. (1986) Homology, analogy, and the evolution of behavior. In M. H. Nitecki and J. A. Kitchell (eds) *Evolution of Animal Behavior: Paleontological and Field Approaches*, pp. 9–40. Oxford University Press, Oxford.

Mason, W. A. and Hollis, J. H. (1962) Communication between young rhesus monkeys. *Animal Behavior* 10: 211–221.

Mayr, E. (1958) Behavior and systematics. In A. Roe and G. G. Simpson (eds) Behavior and Evolution. Yale University Press, New Haven, CT.

Morwood, M. J., Soejono, R. P., Roberts, R. G. *et al.* (2004) Archaeology and age of a new hominin from Flores in eastern Indonesia. *Nature* 431: 1087–1091.

Nagel, T. (1974) What is it like to be a bat? *The Philosophical Review* 83(4): 435–450.

Pearce, J. M. and Bouton, M. E. (2001) Theories of associative learning in animals. *Annual Review of Psychology* 52: 111–139.

Pinker, S. (1997) *How the Mind Works*. W. W. Norton & Co., New York.

Povinelli, D. J. and Eddy, T. J. (1996) What young chimpanzees know about seeing. *Monographs of the Society for Research in Child Development* 62: 3.

Povinelli, D. J., Nelson, K. E. and Boysen, S. T. (1992a) Comprehension of role reversal in chimpanzees: evidence of empathy? *Animal Behaviour* 43: 633–640.

Povinelli, D. J., Parks, K. A. and Novak, M.A. (1992b) Role reversal by rhesus monkeys, but no evidence of empathy. *Animal Behaviour* 44: 269–281.

Povinelli, D. J., Rulf, A. B., Landau, K. R. and Bierschwale, D. T. (1993) Self-recognition in chimpanzees (*Pan troglodytes*): distribution, ontogeny, and patterns of emergence. *Journal of Comparative Psychology* 107: 347–372.

Povinelli, D. J., Bering, J. and Giambrone, S. (2000) Toward a science of other minds: escaping the argument by analogy. *Cognitive Science* 24: 509–541.

Premack, D. and Woodruff, G. (1978) Does the chimpanzee have a Theory of Mind? *Behavioral and Brain Sciences* 1: 515–526.

Reichert, H. and Simeone, A. (1999) Conserved usage of gap and homeotic genes in patterning the CNS. *Current Opinion in Neurobiology* 9: 589–595.

Rendall, D. and Di Fiore, A. (2007) Homoplasy, homology and the perceived special status of behavior in evolution. *Journal of Human Evolution*.

Rumelhart, D. and McClelland, J. (1986) On learning the past tenses of english verbs. In J. McClelland, D. Rumelhart *et al.* (eds) *Parallel Distributed Processing*, vol. II, pp. 216–271. MIT Press, Cambridge, MA.

Saffran, J. R. (2003) Statistical language learning: mechanisms and constraints. *Current Directions in Psychological Science* 12: 110–114.

Sherry, D. F. (2006) Neuroecology. In Fiske, S. T., Schacter, D. L. and Zahn-Waxler C. (eds) *Annual Review of Psychology* 57: 167–197.

Streidter, G. F. and Northcutt, R. G. (1991) Biological hierarchies and the concept of homology. *Brain, Behavior and Evolution* 38: 177–189.

Tolkien, J. R. (1937) *The Hobbit: or There and Back Again*. George Allen & Unwin, London.

Tooby, J. and Cosmides, L. (1992) The psychological foundations of culture. In J. Barkow, L. Cosmides and J. Tooby (eds), *The Adapted Mind: Evolutionary Psychology and the Generation of Culture*, pp. 19–136. Oxford University Press, New York.

Vergano, D. (2004) *USA Today*, October 27. Available at: http://www.usatoday.com/news/science/2004–10–27-hobbitts_x.htm

Voight, B. F., Kudaravalli, S., Wen, X. and Pritchard, J. K. (2006) A map of recent positive selection in the human genome. *PLoS Biology* 4(3), e72: 446–458.

West-Eberhard, M. J. (1989) Phenotypic plasticity and the origins of diversity. *Annual Review of Ecology and Systematics* 20: 249–278.

CHAPTER 7

Social knowledge in primates

Josep Call

7.1. Introduction

The last two decades has seen an unprecedented growth in some areas of social cognition and knowledge in primates and other animals. Historically, social knowledge has been used with two different meanings. One meaning is knowledge about the individual's group, an orientation that emanates from an ethological tradition (e.g. Kummer, 1982; Cheney and Seyfarth, 1990) The individual's knowledge about group membership, dominance, affiliation, or kinship relations between group members, the formation of coalitions and alliances including the motives for those interactions are some of the questions that this orientation has addressed.

Another meaning of social knowledge emanates from the psychological tradition and it has focused its attention on the individual as a unit of analysis rather than the group (e.g. Menzel, 1974; Premack and Woodruff, 1978) Thus, the focus here is on the individual's knowledge about the psychological states of other individuals that govern their behaviour. Premack and Woodruff's (1978) seminal paper on whether the chimpanzee has a theory of mind set the stage for this line of research by asking the question of whether chimpanzees attribute intentions to others in problem-solving situations. Since then this orientation has extended its scope and included other psychological states such as perceptions, desires, knowledge, or beliefs. Note that to function properly in the

social world, both types of social knowledge are important. For instance, when an individual is competing for food, she needs to know not only who outranks her, but also whether those animals can or cannot see the contested food. However, the focus of this chapter will be on the latter sense of social knowledge, what is usually referred to as theory-of-mind research or mind-reading, or mental state attribution.

Before reviewing the evidence available, there are two points that need to be emphasized from the outset. First, 'theory of mind' is a multifaceted concept that includes attributing perception, attention, desires, goals, intentions, knowledge, and beliefs. Whereas the comparative study of some areas, such as perception and attention, have developed tremendously in recent years, other areas such as desires or beliefs remain largely unexplored. Partly, this may be explained by the difficulty of posing questions that can effectively distinguish between attribution of perceptual and epistemic states without using verbal responses. In this chapter, I will focus on the areas of attribution of attention and goals to others, which are the ones that have changed the most in recent years. For other areas within theory-of-mind research, the reader is directed to texts that have already covered those areas (e.g. Tomasello and Call, 1997; Suddendorf and Whiten, 2001; Call and Tomasello, 2003)

Second, when one investigates the cognitive processes underlying behaviour, no single experiment in isolation can be taken as the definitive support for a given hypothesis. Although this is obviously true for other subjects of study, it is particularly important in comparative cognition. Instead a conglomerate of experiments and observations, ideally encompassing multiple paradigms, is required. Similarly, experiments within a given paradigm often require multiple control conditions to rule out alternative explanations. For this reason, the strongest support comes from a combination of multiple conditions within a given paradigm, and from the combination of different paradigms including experimental and observational data. It is in this spirit that the evidence presented in this chapter will include multiple paradigms aiming at the same question: what do individuals know about the psychological states of attention and intention in others?

7.2. Perception and attention

Gaze following, gestural communication, and food competition are the three main areas that have witnessed the most notable advances in attributing perception and attention to others. Below I review each of them in turn.

7.2.1. Gaze following

Field workers have known for a long time that individuals react to the sight of others looking in the distance by looking in the same direction. However, experimental support for these observations, *let alone* the cognitive processes underlying this behaviour, has only recently become available for a number of species. Leaving aside the pioneering work of Menzel (1974) in which he described chimpanzees using the body orientation, gaze direction, and travel direction of others to locate food in their outdoor enclosure, Itakura (1996) and Povinelli and Eddy (1996a) reported that several species of monkeys and apes and chimpanzees, respectively, followed the gaze of a human experimenter to locations above and behind themselves under controlled conditions. Call *et al.* (1998) replicated this result with chimpanzees and Anderson and Mitchell (1999) reported similar results for macaques, but not for lemurs. Other species such as dogs, dolphins, fur seals, and ravens can also follow gaze of humans to various locations

(Hare *et al.*, 1998; Miklósi *et al.*, 1998; Tschudin *et al.*, 2001; Bugnyar *et al.*, 2004; Scheumann and Call, 2004)

Emery *et al.* (1997) described rhesus macaques following the gaze of conspecifics to locations situated in front and to the side of the subject whereas Tomasello *et al.* (1998) extended this result to conspecifics in several primate species including chimpanzees, mangabeys and three macaque species to locations above and behind subjects. Goats also follow the gaze of conspecifics to locations above and behind themselves (Kaminski *et al.*, 2005)

Thus, a variety of species follow the gaze of humans or conspecifics to locations that are out of sight. There has also been some progress on the mechanisms governing this behaviour. One possibility is that gaze following only reflects an orientation response, be it hardwired or learned, but in both cases subjects may turn in a certain direction depending on the orientation of their partners. Another alternative, which builds on this orientation response, and goes beyond it, is that subjects also expect to detect something that they cannot see from their current location; a richer psychological interpretation than the mere orientation response. Tomasello *et al.* (1999) found that chimpanzees followed the gaze of a human geometrically as they bypassed a distracter object on their way to the location where the human was looking. If subjects had operated on the basis of an orientation model of the kind 'search until you find something novel', they should have stopped searching upon detection of any novel object. Instead, they continued to turn in the direction that the informant was looking, suggesting that they followed gaze geometrically (Butterworth and Jarred, 1991) Povinelli and Eddy (1996a) reported that when a human looked to a location situated behind an opaque barrier, chimpanzees moved around the barrier and looked at the same spot where the human was focusing her attention. Tomasello *et al.* (1999) confirmed this finding with chimpanzees, while Bräuer *et al.* (2005) and Bugnyar *et al.* (2004) extended it to other great apes and ravens, respectively.

Call *et al.* (1998) reported another interesting finding, this time in the absence of barriers. They observed that upon following the gaze of a human experimenter to the ceiling and finding nothing, chimpanzees checked back to the face of the experimenter and looked back up again. Bräuer *et al.* (2005) confirmed the existence of such double looks in chimpanzees and extended this finding to other apes. However, only juveniles and adults displayed double looks. Double looks were virtually absent in individuals younger than 6 years of age, even though they followed gaze perfectly well. Scerif *et al.* (2004) have also reported double looks in Diana monkeys when the informant was not looking at the location where a target object was located. This effect, however, was only found in adult animals. Other data available also fit with the developmental pattern reported above: when exposed to a human looking repeatedly to a location above the subjects in which nothing could be detected, adult rhesus and adult chimpanzees decreased their responses, whereas infants of both species continued to look (Tomasello *et al.*, 2001; see also Okamoto *et al.*, 2004) One possibility is that infants follow gaze as an orientation response, whereas adults have another regulatory process on top of this orienting response.

In sum, these findings suggest that the orientation model is insufficient to account for the gaze-following results of adult monkeys and apes. Looking around barriers (and past distracters) suggests that individuals expect to see some target. When the potential target is occluded by a barrier, they change their location to see the target. When there is no occlusion but they cannot find the target, they check back to the informant and then look again. Similarly, when the orientation of the informant is inconsistent with the location of the target, individuals check back to the informant, and after looking up repeatedly and seeing nothing, they decrease their responses. If gaze following is solely governed by an automatic orientation response, subjects should stop after the first look or continue responding after observing an informant repeatedly. Instead, these data suggest that, after following the gaze of an informant, individuals are expecting to see something.

7.2.2. Gestural communication

Initial observations suggested that chimpanzees are sensitive to what others can see regarding their communicative signals. For instance, de Waal (1982) observed a chimpanzee covering his fear-grinning facial expression from opponents during agonistic interactions. Although such observations possess great heuristic value they do not constitute systematic observations. Tomasello *et al.* (1994) found that chimpanzees systematically used visual gestures when others were oriented towards them (so that they could see them) In contrast, chimpanzees did not take into account body orientation when they used tactile gestures. Since then, these results have been replicated in a different group of chimpanzees (Tomasello *et al.*, 1997; Liebal *et al.*, 2004) and extended to other ape species (Pika, in press a, b; Liebal, in press a, b)

Furthermore, several experimental studies have confirmed these findings. Call and Tomasello (1994) showed that orangutans gestured less frequently to someone who had his back turned to them compared to someone facing them. Povinelli and Eddy (1996b) also found that chimpanzees spontaneously begged food from a human that was facing them significantly more often than from a human with the back turned. Kaminski *et al.* (2005) replicated this result with orangutans, chimpanzees, and bonobos. In contrast, Povinelli and Eddy (1996b) found that chimpanzees failed to spontaneously discriminate between (1) a human with her face visible and one with a bucket over her head, (2) a human with her eyes visible (and a blindfold over her mouth) and a human with her eyes covered by the blindfold, or (3) with her back turned but looking over her shoulder.

Some of these results, however, have been recently challenged using other paradigms. Kaminski *et al.* (2005) found that apes begging from a human were sensitive to her face orientation but only when the human's body was oriented toward them, but not when the body was oriented away. In other words, confronted with two situations in which the human's body was facing forward, they responded more when the human's face was also facing forward compared to facing away. In contrast, they made no distinction between the orientation of the face when the human's body was facing away. Kaminski *et al.* (2005) hypothesized that individuals focused both on face and body orientation and extracted different information from each stimulus. Whereas face orientation informed them about whether someone was able to see them, body orientation informed them about their disposition to give them food—someone with the back turned away was not going to transfer food unless she first turned around, and therefore begging was unlikely to be effective. Povinelli *et al.* (2003) also found that chimpanzees directed their begging gestures toward the location that a human experimenter's face was oriented and Gómez (1996) reported that chimpanzees raised by humans were sensitive to the face (and the eyes)

Although previous studies have indicated that apes are sensitive to the attentional state of others, it is unclear whether individuals can also manipulate the attention of others when they want to communicate with them. Liebal *et al.* (2004a) reported that chimpanzees did not use auditory gestures such as slapping the ground or vocalizations to call others' attention before using purely visual gestures. Instead, they used tactile gestures to convey their message or walked around an inattentive recipient to face her and then use a visual gesture. Liebal *et al.* (2004b) tested these observations experimentally by confronting apes with a human with food but with the experimenter's back turned to them. The question was whether apes would use a gesture to call the human's attention or walk around to face her before they begged for food. Results showed that apes did not use auditory gestures to call the attention of the experimenter when she had her back turned. Instead, all species moved around to face the experimenter, thus corroborating the observational findings.

This does not mean that apes are unable to use auditory gestures or vocalizations to call the attention of others when their preferred options are unavailable. Hostetter *et al.* (2001) found that chimpanzees uttered vocalizations faster and were more likely to produce vocalizations as their first communicative behaviour when a human holding food was oriented away from them. In contrast, chimpanzees used manual gestures more frequently and faster when the human holding the food was facing the chimpanzee.

In sum, chimpanzees and other apes use visual gestures preferentially when others are oriented to them. They are particularly sensitive to the orientation of the face, and some studies suggest that they also pay special attention to the

eyes, although the results here are mixed. Confronted with inattentive recipients, apes seem to prefer to use non-visual gestures or change their position so that potential recipients can see them. It is much less common for them to use auditory signals to call the attention of non-attentive recipients, although they can do this when other options are not available.

7.2.3. Food competition

There are numerous observations to suggest that food competition is a third area in which several species have shown their perspective taking skills (e.g. Whiten and Byrne, 1988) Although experimental studies have confirmed these observations, and have even documented the development of certain types of tactical deception, the cognitive processes underlying these observations remain unclear. For instance, it has been shown that subordinate chimpanzees or mangabeys refrain from taking hidden food in the presence of dominant animals (e.g. Menzel, 1974; Coussi-Korbel, 1994) However, it is unclear whether subordinate animals react to the presence of the dominant animal, the dominant's current behaviour, or the dominant's visual access to the food.

Recently, this question has received close attention. Hare *et al.* (2000) placed a subordinate and a dominant chimpanzee into rooms on opposite sides of a third room in which there were two pieces of food. The subordinate could see a piece of food that the dominant could not see—because it was on her side of a small barrier. Subordinate chimpanzees preferred to approach a piece of food that only they could see much more often than the food that both they and the dominant could see. Several control conditions ruled out the possibility that subordinate chimpanzees were reacting to the behaviour of the dominant animal before deciding which piece to approach—a strategy that can explain the results obtained with capuchin monkeys (Hare *et al.*, 2002) Karin-D'Arcy and Povinelli (2002), however, failed to replicate these results with another group of chimpanzees. In contrast, Bräuer *et al.* (in press) replicated Hare *et al.*'s (2000) original results and suggested that Karin-D'Arcy and Povinelli (2002) had been unsuccessful because the arena where the competition took place, as well as the distances between the food pieces, were too small compared to the ones originally used by Hare *et al.* (2000). Indeed, Bräuer *et al.* (in press) showed that manipulating the distances affected the likelihood of obtaining positive results.

In a follow-up study, Hare *et al.* (2001) investigated whether chimpanzees were also able to take into account past information such as whether the dominant had seen the baiting. In this case, the set-up consisted of two barriers and one piece of food. In experimental trials dominants had not seen the food hidden, or food they had seen hidden was moved to a different location when they were not watching (whereas in control trials they saw the food being hidden or moved). Subordinates always saw the entire baiting procedure and whether the dominant had visual access to the baiting. Subordinates preferentially retrieved and approached the food that dominants had not seen hidden or moved, which suggests that subordinates were sensitive to what dominants had or had not see during baiting a few moments before. This study also ruled out the so-called peripheral feeding hypothesis (Karin-D'Arcy and Povinelli, 2002) according to which chimpanzees solved the Hare *et al.* (2000) tasks because they preferred to feed close to barriers, independently of whether others had any visual access to the food. Hare *et al.* (2001) always used two barriers which makes the peripheral hypothesis moot because, unlike the set-up in Hare *et al.* (2000) where there was one piece of food behind the barrier and the other in the open, here the food was always behind a barrier and chimpanzees had to decide whether to take it or not. In a final experiment, we allowed a dominant A to witness the baiting procedure and then exchanged her with dominant B, who had not seen the baiting. We then released B and allowed her to compete with the subordinate animal. We compared this condition with one in which the dominant who had seen the baiting was the same individual that competed with the subordinate. Subordinate chimpanzees were more likely to take food from ignorant dominants compared to knowledgeable dominants, suggesting that chimpanzees attribute information to particular individuals who have had visual access to certain events.

These studies are silent regarding the particular stimuli that control the behaviour of individuals. For instance, it is unclear whether the face or the eyes play a privileged role regulating these interactions. Recently, several studies have addressed this issue. Chimpanzees and rhesus macaques preferentially steal food from a human competitor whose face is not directed towards them (Flombaum and Santos, 2005; Hare *et al.*, in press) One interesting outcome of these studies is that, when combined with those on food begging reviewed earlier, individuals either seek or avoid their partner's face depending on whether their goal is to communicate or outwit them, respectively. Flombaum and Santos (2005) have even shown that rhesus macaques are sensitive to the state of the eyes (open, closed or averted) when trying to outwit humans. Call *et al.* (2003) found that domestic dogs also take into account the state of the eyes when trying to take forbidden food. Dogs were less likely to take forbidden food in front of a human who had her eyes open and directed to them than from someone who had her eyes open but directed down to her lap, or who had her eyes closed, or her back turned.

However, seeing the face or the eyes is not critical to solving these kinds of problems. Some species can make inferences about what others can see, even without having direct access to the face or eyes of others. For instance, Melis *et al.* (2006) found that chimpanzees preferentially reached through an opaque tunnel (as opposed to a transparent one) that blocked a human's visual access to the chimpanzee's hand when trying to steal food. Similarly, chimpanzees will open a silent trap door (as opposed to a noisy one) to get access and steal a piece of food without alerting a distracted human (Melis *et al.*, 2006) This means that chimpanzees are sensitive not only what others can or cannot see, but also what others may hear—a finding that had been suggested by some observational studies (e.g. Hauser, 1990; Boesch and Boesch-Achermann, 2000) Dogs can also make inferences about what others can see from their perspective. Bräuer *et al.* (2004) found that dogs were more likely to take forbidden food from behind a large barrier than from a barrier with a window in front of the food, which enabled a human experimenter to see them take the food.

Critically, dogs were not able to see the human when they made the decision to take the food in either condition, and once they had decided to take the food they did not stop even after they saw the human in the window condition. This means that taking more food in the opaque condition cannot be a result of aborting the food grabbing at the last minute when the human comes into sight through the window.

In sum, the findings of these studies suggest that chimpanzees know what conspecifics can and cannot see, even what they have or have not seen in the immediate past, and that this knowledge is attached to particular individuals. Moreover, individuals are sensitive to certain stimuli like the face or the eyes, but the sight of these is not strictly necessary to solve perspective-taking problems. There is also some evidence that other species such as rhesus macaques and dogs may possess comparable abilities to those shown in chimpanzees.

7.3. **Goals and intentions**

Compared to the notable changes that the comparative study of perspective-taking has experienced in recent years, there has been little progress in the area of goal and intention attribution, even though Premack and Woodruff's (1978) study on intention attribution in the chimpanzee signalled the starting point to the now vast literature on theory of mind. In their seminal study, Premack and Woodruff (1978) found that the laboratory-trained, language-trained chimpanzee Sarah was capable of completing video sequences in which a human was shown trying to solve a problem. For instance, Sarah saw a human looking up to an out-of-reach banana hanging from the ceiling, and she had to choose the photograph in which the human completed the goal of gaining access to the banana (i.e. climbed on a box) Premack and Woodruff argued that Sarah "recognized the videotape as representing a problem, understood the actor's purpose, and chose alternatives compatible with that purpose." However, Savage-Rumbaugh et al. (1978) argued that she may have chosen based on associating commonplace situations with certain objects. In fact, Sarah performed better in those situations for which associative procedures were most

straightforward (e.g. key with lock) compared to those that were less straightforward. Moreover, Savage-Rumbaugh et al. reported that two language-trained chimpanzees were capable of solving the problems presented to Sarah using a matching-to-sample paradigm without training.

Subsequent research on chimpanzees' understanding of intentions produced mixed results. Thus, Premack (1988) reported an attempt to train Sarah to discriminate between videotaped sequences that depicted intentional actions versus those that depicted non-intentional actions. Sarah never learned the discrimination. Similarly, Povinelli et al. (1998) presented six juvenile chimpanzees with one experimenter who accidentally spilled the juice that she was about to deliver to the chimpanzee, whereas the other experimenter intentionally poured the juice on the floor. When chimpanzees were later asked to choose between experimenters from whom they would receive juice, none of the six chimpanzees showed a preference for the 'clumsy' over the 'mean' human experimenter. If chimpanzees understood the intentions of the two actors, they should have chosen to receive the juice from the well-intentioned one. However, since they received no juice from any experimenter, it is unclear whether there was any motivation to choose between any of them.

Call and Tomasello (1998) trained chimpanzees and orangutans to use a landmark placed on top of one of three opaque containers as an indicator for the location of hidden food. During training, the apes never saw the human actually place the marker on the container: the marker was already on top of one of the containers when they were presented to the ape. On test trials, a human experimenter then placed the marker on one of the containers intentionally, but either before or after this, he let the marker fall accidentally onto one of the other containers. The marker was removed at the point where the ape had to make his choice, so for test trials the ape was faced with a choice in which one bucket had been marked intentionally and the other accidentally. Apes as a group chose the container that was marked intentionally, although no individual was above chance on his own (except for one language-trained orangutan) The apes' performance was comparable to that of 2.5-year-old children presented with the same task and worse than that of 3-year-old children. In contrast, we found no evidence that dogs tested with the same paradigm distinguished between intentional and accidental actions (Riedel *et al.*, 2006). Jellema *et al.* (2000) found some neurophysiological data supporting the idea that primates do indeed perceive the distinction between intentional and accidental actions. These authors described a population of cells in the superior temporal sulcus (STS) of the macaque that respond to the orientation of the face in combination with an action, but that do not activate if those same actions are performed while the subject's attention is focused elsewhere. Recall that in the previous experiment, the focus of attention was one of the main indicators of intention. Intentional actions were those that were attended to, whereas accidental actions invariably occurred when attention was averted from the action.

Call *et al.* (2004) tested whether chimpanzees in a food-sharing situation can distinguish between a human who is unwilling to give them food from one that is unable to do so. After the experimenter had passed a few grapes to the subject, he took another grape but did not pass it to the subject, and the reason for stopping the transfer was then manipulated. In some cases, he was unable because the grape kept falling off his hand, he was occupied with other tasks, or did not see the food. In other cases, he was unwilling to give the food, for instance, he would put the food close to the ape but then pull it back, or would leave the food on the platform and stare at the ape for no apparent reason, or he just ate the food himself. The presentation of multiple conditions minimized the possibility that subjects may have reacted to certain superficial features of the experimenter's behaviour and also allowed us to control certain types of information such as the movement of the reward or the experimenter's gazing patterns. Chimpanzees spontaneously (without training and without differential reinforcement) behaved differently depending on whether a human was unwilling or unable to give them food. Chimpanzees produced more behaviours and left the testing station earlier with an unwilling compared with an unable (but willing) experimenter. Behne *et al.* (2005) found comparable results with 9–18-month-old human infants, but not with 6-month-olds.

In sum, Sarah, the language-trained chimpanzee, was able to complete sequences of actors solving problems, although other interpretations for these findings are possible. Chimpanzees and orangutans were able to disregard certain actions when they have been performed accidentally—a finding that has also received some neurophysiological support in monkeys. Chimpanzees were able to distinguish between an experimenter who was unwilling from one who was unable to give them food. Thus, it appears that primates—or at least chimpanzees and other apes—are sensitive to the goals of others.

7.4. Conclusions and future directions

Recent developments in the field of comparative cognition support some earlier proposals regarding the mental attribution skills of the great apes (e.g. Premack and Woodruff, 1978; Whiten and Byrne, 1988) Chimpanzees (and other apes) can follow the gaze of others around barriers, past distractors, check back when they do not detect anything remarkable, and stop looking if they find nothing on repeated occasions. Chimpanzees and other apes use visual gestures preferentially when others are oriented to them. They are particularly sensitive to the orientation of the face, and some studies suggest that they also pay special attention to the eyes. Confronted with inattentive recipients, and when other options are unavailable, they can use auditory signals to call the attention to themselves. Chimpanzees know what conspecifics can and cannot see in competitive situations, even what they have or have not seen in the immediate past, and they attach privileged visual access to particular individuals. Moreover, individuals are sensitive to certain stimuli like the face or the eyes, but the sight of those is not strictly necessary to solve perspective-taking problems. In regard to actions, chimpanzees and orangutans distinguish intentional from accidental actions and they can gauge the motives of a human passing them food.

Certainly, some of these data could be explained as responding to key stimuli without having to postulate any sensitivity to the psychological states of others. For instance, individuals distinguish between someone facing them versus someone facing away. However, some other data cannot be explained in the same way because those stimuli (e.g. face orientation) are not present. Obviously, one can postulate another set of perceivable stimuli and learned associations that could explain those data as well, and one can use this logic *ad infinitum*. Unfortunately, the veracity of those postulated mechanisms is rarely verified. More importantly, in many cases they may represent quite remote possibilities considering what we know about the learning capabilities of non-human primates. One has to explain why those sets of learned associations often transfer to novel situations, or why some of those stimuli are positive in some contexts and negative in others (e.g. subjects seek or avoid the face of the experimenter when begging or trying to steal the food from her, respectively). Although processes of generalization and conditional discrimination are often invoked to explain those findings, the truth is that numerous studies have shown that mastering conditional discrimination is not so easy, particularly when the cues to be associated are displaced in space and time, as many of the current findings would require.

Therefore, we face a dilemma. One can postulate multiple sets of learned contingencies in specific situations or one can postulate a more general knowledge about some psychological states in others (Tomasello and Call, 2006; Whiten, 1994) It is hard to decide between these two alternatives. Explanations based on learned associations are often preferred over their 'mindreading' counterpart because they are said to be more parsimonious—they make fewer assumptions. Leaving aside the issue of whether individuals are indeed capable of solving such problems by association, can parsimony still be invoked when one has to use no less than a dozen different learned associations to explain the data available as an alternative to a single mechanism that can explain most (if not all) of the data (see Tomasello and Call, 2006, for a detailed analysis)? To be clear, it is still possible that the various specific learned associations are correct and the single general explanation is not. However, parsimony does not seem a plausible argument to invoke to distinguish between

those two alternatives. At this point, we and others (e.g. Suddendorf and Whiten, 2001; Tomasello *et al.*, 2003, but see Povinelli and Vonk, 2003) see the current results as evidence that apes have some understanding of attention and intention.

Future research should advance in at least four directions. First, it is necessary to investigate the distribution of attributional skills among species to be able to make inferences about the evolution of such skills. Currently, there is some evidence that various species including ravens, some species of monkeys, and dogs may possess quite sophisticated perspective-taking abilities, but the picture is still too fragmentary to derive solid conclusions on how these skills may have evolved. Second, more research attention should be devoted to the various processes that fall under the umbrella of theory of mind. Although we have learned quite a lot about attention and perspective taking (and some things about intentions) in the last few years, we still know virtually nothing about other psychological constructs such as desires, knowledge, or beliefs. Such a piecemeal approach reflects the need to treat the different psychological states separately because each informs us about different components of a social cognitive suite (Whiten, 1994; Tomasello *et al.*, 2003)

Third, there is a need to investigate in greater depth those psychological states for which there is some evidence available such as attention and perspective taking. Currently, the evidence on attributing attention to others can be explained as an appreciation of what others can or cannot see (so-called level I perspective taking, Flavell, 1992) It is unclear whether individuals also display level II perspective taking, that is, they appreciate how others will see certain events. This would involve imagining how a given object would look from a different angle, not just whether it would be visible or not. Finally, it would be desirable to shift some research attention from attribution to others to self-attribution skills. Most of the research has been devoted to the psychological states of other individuals and little effort have been devoted to investigate whether individuals have access to their own psychological states (but see Call and Carpenter, 2001; Hampton, 2001;

Smith *et al.*, 2003; Call, 2005) Since many theories have postulated some relation between self- and other-attribution, it is important to see how self-attribution skills are distributed in nonhuman animals and how relate to skills of other-attribution.

References

Anderson, J. R. and Mitchell, R. W. (1999) Macaques but not lemurs co-orient visually with humans. *Folia Primatologica*, 70: 17–22.

Behne, T. Carpenter, M., Call, J. and Tomasello, M. (2005) Unwilling or unable? Infants' understanding of others' intentions. *Developmental Psychology*. 41: 328–337

Boesch, C. and Boesch-Achermann, H. (2000) *The Chimpanzees of the Tai Forest*. Oxford University Press, New York.

Bräuer, J., Call, J. and Tomasello, M. (2004) Visual perspective taking in dogs (*Canis familiaris*) in the presence of barriers. *Applied Animal Behaviour Science*, 88: 299–317.

Bräuer, J., Call, J. and Tomasello, M. (2005) All great ape species follow gaze to distant locations and around barriers. *Journal of Comparative Psychology*, 119: 145–154.

Bräuer, J., Call, J. and Tomasello, M. (submitted) Chimpanzees really know what others can see in a competitive situation. *Animal Cognition*.

Bugnyar, T., Stowe, M. and Heinrich, B. (2004) Ravens, *Corvus corax*, follow gaze direction of humans around obstacles. *Proceedings of the Royal Society of London Series B: Biological Sciences*, 271: 1331–1336.

Butterworth, G. and Jarred, N. (1991) What minds have in common is space: spatial mechanisms serving joint visual attention in infancy. *British Journal of Developmental Psychology*, 9: 55–72.

Call, J. (2005) The self and the other: a missing link in comparative social cognition. In H. Terrace and J. Metcalfe (eds) *The Evolution of Consciousness in Animals and Humans*, pp. 321–341. Oxford University Press, New York.

Call, J. and Carpenter, M. (2001) Do chimpanzees and children know what they have seen? *Animal Cognition*, 4: 207–220.

Call, J. and Tomasello, M. (1994) Production and comprehension of referential pointing by orangutans (*Pongo pygmaeus*). *Journal of Comparative Psychology*, 108: 307–317.

Call, J. and Tomasello, M. (1998) Distinguishing intentional from accidental actions in orangutans (*Pongo pygmaeus*), chimpanzees (*Pan troglodytes*) and human children (*Homo sapiens*). *Journal of Comparative Psychology*, 112: 192–206.

Call, J. and Tomasello, M. (2003) Social cognition. In D. Maestripieri (ed.) *Primate Psychology*, pp. 234–253. Harvard University Press, Cambridge, MA.

Call, J., Hare, B. H. and Tomasello, M. (1998) Chimpanzee gaze following in an object-choice task. *Animal Cognition*, 1: 89–99.

Call, J., Bräuer, J., Kaminski, J. and Tomasello, M. (2003) Domestic dogs are sensitive to the attentional state of humans. *Journal of Comparative Psychology*, 117: 257–263.

Call, J., Hare, B. H., Carpenter, M. and Tomasello, M. (2004) Unwilling or unable: chimpanzees' understanding of human intentional action. *Developmental Science*, 7: 488–498.

Cheney, D. L. and Seyfarth, R. M. (1990) *How Monkeys See the World*. University of Chicago Press, Chicago.

Coussi-Korbel, S (1994) Learning to outwit a competitor in mangabeys (*Cercocebus torquatus torquatus*) *Journal of Comparative Psychology* 108: 164–171.

de Waal, F. B. M. (1982) *Chimpanzee Politics*. Jonathan Cape, London.

Emery, N. J., Lorincz, E. N., Perrett, D. I. and Oram, M. W. (1997) Gaze following and joint attention in rhesus monkeys (*Macaca mulatta*). *Journal of Comparative Psychology*, 111: 286–293.

Flavell, J. H. (1992) Perspectives on perspective taking. In H. Beilin and P. B. Pufall (eds) *Piaget's Theory: Prospects and Possibilities*, pp. 107–39. Lawrence Erlbaum, Hillsdale, NJ.

Flombaum, J. I. and Santos, L. (2005) Rhesus monkeys attribute perceptions to others. *Current Biology*, 15: 447–452.

Gómez, J. C. (1996) Non-human primate theories of (non-human primate) minds: some issues concerning the origins of mind-reading. In P. Carruthers and P. K. Smith (eds) *Theories of Theories of Mind*, pp. 330–343. Cambridge University Press, Cambridge.

Hampton, R. R. (2001) Rhesus monkeys know when they remember. *Proceedings of the National Academy of Sciences of the USA*, 98: 5359–5362.

Hare, B. H., Call, J. and Tomasello, M. (1998) Communication of food location between human and dog (*Canis familiaris*). *Evolution of Communication*, 2: 137–159.

Hare, B., Call, J., Agnetta, B. and Tomasello, M. (2000) Chimpanzees know what conspecifics do and do not see. *Animal Behaviour*, 59: 771–785.

Hare, B., Call, J. and Tomasello, M. (2001) Do chimpanzees know what conspecifics know and do not know? *Animal Behaviour*, 61: 139–151.

Hare, B., Adessi, E., Call, J., Tomasello, M. and Visalberghi, E. (2002) Do capuchin monkeys, *Cebus apella*, know what conspecifics do and do not see? *Animal Behaviour*, 63: 131–142.

Hare, B., Call, J. and Tomasello, M. (in press) Chimpanzees deceive a human competitor by hiding. *Cognition*.

Hauser, M. D. (1990) Do chimpanzee copulatory calls incite male-male competition? *Animal Behaviour*, 39: 596–597.

Hostetter, A. B., Cantero, M. and Hopkins, W. D. (2001) Differential use of vocal and gestural communication by chimpanzees (*Pan troglodytes*) in response to the attentional status of a human (*Homo sapiens*). *Journal of Comparative Psychology*, 115: 337–343.

Itakura, S. (1996) An exploratory study of gaze-monitoring in nonhuman primates. *Japanese Psychological Research*, 38: 174–180.

Jellema, T., Baker, C. I., Wicker, B. and Perrett, D. I. (2000) Neural representation for the perception of the intentionality of actions. *Brain and Cognition*, 44: 280–302.

Kaminski, J., Riedel, J., Call, J. and Tomasello, M. (2005) Domestic goats (*Capra hircus*) follow gaze direction and use social cues in an object choice task. *Animal Behaviour*, 69: 11–18.

Karin-D'Arcy, M. R. and Povinelli, D. J. (2002) Do chimpanzees know what each other see? A closer look. *International Journal of Comparative Psychology*, 15: 21–54.

Kummer, H. (1982) Social knowledge in free-ranging primates. In D. R. Griffin (ed.) *Animal Mind – Human Mind*, pp. 113–130.

Liebal, K. (in press a) The gestural communication of siamangs. In J. Call and M. Tomasello (eds) *The Gestural Communication of Apes and Monkeys*. Lawrence Earlbaum, Hillsdale, NJ.

Liebal, K. (in press b) The gestural communication of orangutans. In J. Call and M. Tomasello (eds) *The Gestural Communication of Apes and Monkeys*. Lawrence Earlbaum, Hillsdale, NJ.

Liebal, K., Call, J. and Tomasello, M. (2004a) The use of gesture sequences in chimpanzees. *American Journal of Primatology*, 64: 377–396.

Liebal, K., Pika, S., Call, J. and Tomasello, M. (2004b) To move or not to move: how apes alter the attentional states of humans when begging for food. *Interaction Studies*, 5: 199–219.

Melis, A. P., Call, J. and Tomasello, M. (2006) Chimpanzees conceal visual and auditory information from others. *Journal of Comparative Psychology*, 120: 154–162.

Menzel, E. W. (1974) A group of young chimpanzees in a one-acre field: leadership and communication. In A. M. Schrier and F. Stollnitz (eds) *Behavior of Nonhuman Primates*, pp. 83–153. Academic Press, New York.

Miklósi, A., Polgárdi, R., Topál, J. and Csányi, V. (1998) Use of experimenter-given cues in dogs. *Animal Cognition*, 1: 113–121.

Okamoto, S., Tanaka, M. and Tomonaga, M. (2004) Looking back: The "representational mechanism" of joint attention in an infant chimpanzee (*Pan troglodytes*). *Japanese Psychological Research*, 46: 236–245.

Pika, S. (in press a) The gestural communication of gorillas. In J. Call and M. Tomasello (eds) *The Gestural Communication of Apes and Monkeys*. Lawrence Earlbaum, Hillsdale, NJ.

Pika, S. (in press b) The gestural communication of bonobos. In J. Call and M. Tomasello (eds) *The Gestural Communication of Apes and Monkeys*. Lawrence Earlbaum Associates, Hillsdale, NJ.

Povinelli, D. J. and Eddy, T. J. (1996a) Chimpanzees: joint visual attention. *Psychological Science*, 7: 129–135.

Povinelli, D. J. and Eddy, T. J. (1996b) What young chimpanzees know about seeing. *Monographs of the Society for Research in Child Development*, 61: 1–152.

Povinelli, D. J., Perilloux, H., Reaux, J. and Bierschwale, D. (1998) Young chimpanzees' reactions to intentional versus accidental and inadvertent actions. *Behavioural Processes*, 42: 205–218.

Povinelli, D. J., Theall, L. A., Reaux, J. E. & Dunphy-Lelii, S. (2003) Chimpanzees spontaneously alter the location of their gestures to match the attentional orientation of others. *Animal Behaviour*, 66: 71–79.

Povinelli, D. J. and Vonk, J. (2003) Chimpanzee minds: Suspiciously human? *Trends in Cognitive Sciences*, 7: 157–160.

Premack, D. (1988) 'Does the chimpanzee have a theory of mind?' Revisited in R. W. Byrne and A. Whiten (eds) *Machiavellian Intelligence. Social Expertise and the Evolution of Intellect in Monkeys, Apes, and Humans*, pp. 160–179. Oxford University Press, New York.

Premack, D. and Woodruff, G. (1978) Does the chimpanzee have a theory of mind? *Behavioral and Brain Sciences*, 4: 515–526.

Riedel, J., Buttlemann, D., Call, J. and Tomasello, M. (2006) Domestic dogs (*Canis familiaris*) use a physical marker to locate hidden food. *Animal Cognition*, 9: 27–35.

Savage-Rumbaugh, E. S., Rumbaugh, D. and Boysen, S. T. (1978) Sarah's problems in comprehension. *Behavioral and Brain Sciences*, 1: 555–557.

Scerif, G., Gómez, J. C. and Byrne, R. W. (2004) What do Diana monkeys know about the focus of attention of a conspecific? *Animal Behaviour*, 68: 1239–1247.

Scheumann, M. and Call, J. (2004) The use of experimenter-given cues by South African fur seals (*Arctocephalus pusillus*). *Animal Cognition*, 7: 224–230.

Smith, J. D., Shields, W. E. and Washburn, D. A. (2003) The comparative psychology of uncertainty monitoring and metacognition. *Behavioral and Brain Sciences*, 26: 317–373.

Suddendorf, T. and Whiten, A. (2001) Mental evolution and development: evidence for secondary representation in children, great apes, and other animals. *Psychological Bulletin*, 127: 629–650.

Tomasello, M. and Call, J. (1997) *Primate Cognition*. Oxford University Press, New York.

Tomasello, M. and Call, J. (2006) Do chimpanzees know what others see—or only what they are looking at? In S. Hurley and M. Nudds (eds) *Rational Animals*. Oxford University Press, Oxford.

Tomasello, M., Call, J. and Hare, B. (1998) Five primate species follow the visual gaze of conspecifics. *Animal Behaviour*, 55: 1063–1069.

Tomasello, M., Call, J., Nagell, K., Olguin, R. and Carpenter, M. (1994) The learning and use of gestural signals by young chimpanzees: a trans-generational study. *Primates*, 35: 137–154.

Tomasello, M., Call, J., Warren, J., Frost, G.T., Carpenter, M. and Nagell, K. (1997) The ontogeny of chimpanzee gestural signals: a comparison across groups and generations. *Evolution of Communication*, 1: 223–259.

Tomasello, M., Hare, B. and Agnetta, B. (1999) Chimpanzees, *Pan troglodytes*, follow gaze direction geometrically. *Animal Behaviour*, 58: 769–777.

Tomasello, M., Hare, B. and Fogleman, T. (2001) The ontogeny of gaze following in chimpanzees and rhesus macaques. *Animal Behaviour*, 61: 335–343.

Tomasello, M., Call, J. and Hare, B. (2003) Chimpanzees understand psychological states—the question is which ones and to what extent. *Trends in Cognitive Sciences*, 7: 153–156.

Tschudin, A., Call, J., Dunbar, R. I. M., Harris, G. and van der Elst, C. (2001) Comprehension of signs by dolphins (*Tursiops truncatus*). *Journal of Comparative Psychology*, 115: 100–105.

Whiten, A. (1994) Grades of mindreading. In C. Lewis and P. Mitchell (eds) *Children's Early Understanding of Mind*, pp. 47–70. Lawrence Erlbaum, Hillsdale, New Jersey.

Whiten, A. and Byrne, R.W. (1988) The manipulation of attention in primate tactical deception. In R.W. Byrne and A. Whiten (eds) *Machiavellian Intelligence. Social Expertise and the Evolution of Intellect in Monkeys, Apes, and Humans*, pp. 211–223. Oxford University Press, New York.

CHAPTER 8

Social cognition in non-primates

Redouan Bshary, Lucie H. Salwiczek and
Wolfgang Wickler

8.1. Introduction

The ultimate goal of evolutionary psychology is to understand the human mind/brain mechanisms in evolutionary perspective (Buss, 1999; Workman and Reader, 2004) focusing on key questions like: "*how* is the human mind designed" (what are its mechanisms or component parts, and how are they organized); "*what* is the mind designed to do" (what are the functions of the component parts and their organized structure) and "*how* does input from the current environment interact with the design of the human mind to produce an observable behaviour" (Buss, 1999). To not just describe, but also understand how the human mind is structured and why it is structured that way, an evolutionary view is necessary (Salwiczek and Wickler 2004, 2005). Consequently evolutionary psychology is a synthesis of modern psychology and evolutionary biology, and, as a synthesis, has always benefited from new developments in biology.

Konrad Lorenz emphasized in 1941 that "our cognitive and perceptual categories, given to us prior to individual experience, are adapted to the environment for the same reasons that the horse's hoof is suited to the plains before the horse is born, and the fin of a fish is adapted for the water before the fish hatches from the egg" (translation by Eibl-Eibesfeldt, 1989, p. 8).

Consistent with the ethological view, Tooby and Cosmides, drawing on the differences between "genotype and phenotype", proposed an analogous distinction between 'an individual's innate psychology and an individual's manifest psychology and behaviour' (quoted from Plotkin, 1997). Equally influential on evolutionary psychology had been inclusive fitness theory (Hamilton, 1964), which marshalled a new era that might be described in terms of "thinking about selection from the perspective of the genes" (Buss, 1999, p. 14). As a result, analyses always focus on the pay-offs at an individual level, even under conditions where strong inter-group competition favours the evolution of within-group altruism (Wilson, 1980; Gintis *et al.*, 2003).

With the downfall of behaviourism, explaining human and non-human animals' behaviour only in terms of environmental contingencies of reinforcement, and the rise of the cognitive revolution, psychology returned to looking inside the head and is now more or less equated with information processing (Pearce, 1997; Buss, 1999). If the current edited volume represents a fair reflection of evolutionary psychology, then the research focus will clearly be on humans, and to a lesser extent on the comparison between humans and primates. We argue, however, that the research focus should become much broader in the future because we think that broad species comparisons including non-primate species provide the (only) key to several important issues for psychologists taking an evolutionary view/approach.

Reviewing the entire literature on cognition in non-primates is an impossible task for a book chapter. For readers who are interested in more detailed information on cognitive abilities in non-primates we refer to the following textbooks: Mackintosh (1994), Balda *et al.* (1998), Shettleworth (1998), Heyes and Huber (2000), Mann *et al.* (2000), Roth and Wullimann (2001), Bekoff *et al.* (2002), Reader and Laland (2003), Rogers and Kaplan (2004) and Brown *et al.* (in press), and very general reviews on birds (Emery, 2006) and fish (Bshary *et al.*, 2002).

8.2. Why an evolutionary approach to human cognition should entail a comparison with other animals

Many interesting theories in evolutionary psychology, like the social brain hypothesis (Dunbar, 1993) or the modular mind hypothesis (Fodor, 1983; Barkow *et al.*, 1992) can only be tested with a comparative approach because working on humans alone means that sample size is 1 with respect to the evolutionary experiment that we are investigating. In other words, we can apply evolutionary logic to better understand human cognition, but we cannot verify the logic and test whether we are dealing with general evolutionary principles. The social brain hypothesis has been widely accepted because several broad comparisons in vertebrate taxa have found a positive association between group size and relative forebrain size (Barton and Dunbar, 1997; Emery and Clayton, 2004).

Evolutionary theory provides two alternative concepts that generate different predictions for the cognitive abilities of animals. First, studying the cognitive capacities of closely related species may allow us to trace the evolutionary roots of these abilities due to shared ancestry (homologous traits). This approach emphasizes phylogenetic constraints/inertia, in particular with respect to brain structure as the anatomical

basis for cognitive abilities. This approach is currently predominant in evolutionary psychology; hence the research focus is on apes and monkeys. We will focus on the second concept, which deals with the comparison of distantly related species that live in similar environments. Any similarities in their cognitive abilities would thus reveal independently evolved (analogous) traits. Both concepts are unified in the 'ethological approach', which has been developed largely in the 1980s (Kamil, 1998; Shettleworth, 1994). Applied to animal cognition, the logic of evolutionary theory can be used as follows.

1. All individuals of any species are adapted to their specific ecological niche, due to selection of their ancestors.

2. Therefore, if the environment poses challenges that can only be solved with learning (cognitive?) processes rather than with fixed genetic strategies, individuals will be able to solve these problems with learning and memory.

3. Individuals belonging to species of different taxa but who share similar cognitive challenges in their environment will be similar in their ability to solve these challenges.

4. Closely related species with different cognitive challenges in their environment will be different in their cognitive abilities.

In conclusion, this 'ecological approach' predicts analogous capacities in distantly related species due to common ecology, rather than homologous capacities in closely related species due to common ancestry. Note that according to this view, evolution selects only for outcomes, not for mechanisms, thus analogous similarity may be achieved with different mechanisms that thereby reveal their functional relevance for the property in question (Salwiczek and Wickler, 2004). This is in contrast to the view promoted by Cosmides and Tooby (1987) who propose that selection works directly on existing mechanisms.

The great heuristic value of a "purist adaptationist" approach is that it helps to generate very precise predictions based on the ecology of a species. Its predictions will therefore often contrast with an approach that predicts similar abilities in closely related species due to common ancestry. For example, the adaptationist approach would predict that highly social carnivores like hyenas (East and Hofer, 2002) or highly social cetaceans like bottlenose dolphins (Herman, 2002) have more elaborate social cognitive skills than the mostly solitary orang-utans. In particular, in the field of cognition, the relative importance of adaptation to the environment versus phylogenetic constraints remains one of the most important issues to solve. Currently, we do not know enough to give a good answer to this question. A possible result, after more research (but purely speculative at this stage), might be that an animal's ability to solve a specific problem (quantitative aspects like the amount of information processed, speed of learning, accuracy of behaviour) might be closely linked to its ecology (convergent evolution), while the specific mechanisms used to solve such problems may be more similar in closely related species (through common ancestry).

Given the above, we conclude that a 'proper' evolutionary approach to cognition should encompass all animals for three reasons. First, only a broad comparison between species may allow us to identify selective forces on cognitive abilities that might be unique to humans (and hence may explain qualitative or quantitative differences between humans and other animals). Second, only a broad comparison allows us to distinguish between the two evolutionary hypotheses that put emphasis either on homology due to common ancestry or on analogy due to similarities in ecology. Third, a broad comparison helps us to situate humans within the animal kingdom. After all, we are not superior to other animals with respect to all cognitive problems, and our shortcomings and the amazing abilities of some animals are closely linked to the selective forces in the environment.

8.3. An important precondition for a fruitful broad comparison between species

Traditionally, the field of cognition has been dominated by studies on humans. This is not only due to a research focus on our own species, but also because philosophers, theologians, lawyers and social scientists have been interested in questions regarding human nature. As a consequence, cognition is full of definitions which, unfortunately, do not distinguish between two aspects that should be kept separate, namely the phenomenon itself and the underlying cognitive mechanism. For example, tactical deception can be described purely at a functional level, as a signal that is produced out of context, which produces context-specific responses by the signal recipient to its own disadvantage, but to the advantage of the signaller (Hauser, 1997). On this level, we can compare the phenomenon between many different species. However, the definition of tactical deception is usually linked to the underlying cognitive mechanism, which requires that an individual is conscious of its actions, understands why the signal works and knows that it will inflict costs on the signal recipient. However, no such mechanism has been shown for any species that is known to produce signals out of context, but, on the other hand, neither can we conclusively state that tactical deception is solely due to non-mentalistic associative learning processes. Similarly, the terminology used for social interactions (using our everyday language) implicitly assumes the operation of cognitive processes that preclude broad species comparisons. Phenomena like punishment, reconciliation, cheating and social support are all linked to theory of mind and empathy, while definitions for traditions are often coupled with imitation learning (McFarland, 1993). We would prefer definitions where any form of social learning is enough (Galef, 1988). Evidence for social learning can be collected in the field, but the distinction between imitation learning and the supposedly simpler mechanism of 'stimulus enhancement' is virtually impossible to make according to proper scientific standards.

Elucidating the precise cognitive mechanisms that underlie a specific behaviour is the ultimate goal of animal cognition. But this goal is still far away. In the absence of conclusive evidence for underlying mechanisms, the creation of new labels ('pseudo-tactical deception' or 'tactical deception-like') does not help. A possible addition could be 'functional' but this means only that the mechanism is not known. Instead, we propose that whenever possible, definitions should be kept purely descriptive, and the mechanism added separately if known. That is, we promote an approach where phenomena and underlying mechanisms are treated separately.

Focusing on the phenomena first allows us to draw from the wealth of knowledge on animal behaviour. Once we have identified similar phenomena in various species or even taxa, we can go on and ask how the different species produce the phenomenon in question. In Section 8.4, we provide evidence that very interesting behavioural phenomena exist in a large variety of non-primate species. Evidence for the existence of selected cognitive mechanisms in non-primate animals is given in Section 8.5.

8.4. **Interesting phenomena that can be found in a broad range of taxa**

8.4.1. **Phenomena linked to social complexity**

Currently, the most widely accepted theory for why primates (including humans) evolved a large brain (and specifically a large neocortex) is the so-called Machiavellian intelligence hypothesis (Byrne and Whiten, 1988: based on Jolly, 1966 and Humphrey, 1976). The hypothesis states that ability to cope with its social environment is the main challenge that a primate must overcome in order to reproduce. In an interspecific comparison, group size (as an index of a largely unspecified social complexity) correlates strongly with neocortex ratio (the size of the neocortex relative to the rest of the brain) (Dunbar, 1993).

While primates are highly social as a taxon, there are many other species that also live in large, stable and structured groups. Most prominent examples are social carnivores, elephants and cetaceans. Among birds, corvids are well known for their social skills (Emery and Clayton, 2004), while parrots have long been suspected to possess similar skills (Pepperberg, 1998; Emery, 2006), although more field studies are needed. Unfortunately, reptiles and amphibians are little studied, and we do not know of any species living in large stable groups. Sociality is also rare in fish but there are few exceptions, e.g. some cichlids (Taborsky, 1984; Kohler, 1997). A special case of social complexity can be found in some 'cleaner'-fish species that remove ectoparasites, mucus and scales

from so-called 'client' fish (Côté, 2000). The best-studied species, *Labroides dimidiatus*, has about 2000 interactions per day with about 100–500 individual clients belonging to about 30–50 different species (review by Bshary and Noë, 2003). Below, we give evidence that in these various social non-primate species, all the aspects of social complexity that interest primatologists exist: nepotism, social prestige, reciprocity, alliance formation, tactical deception, punishment and reconciliation (all terms operationally defined without underlying cognitive mechanism), as well as individual recognition and knowledge about the relationships between other individuals, which is a necessary precondition to successfully manage social complexity (Cheney and Seyfarth, 1990).

Individual recognition has been shown to exist in a wide variety of vertebrate species. The most detailed study was conducted on sheep. Kendrick *et al.* (2001) showed that individuals can recognize up to 50 group members from photos and remember them over a period of 2 years. In elephants, the fourth commandment ('honour the elders') was shown to have a strong biological basis: groups with an old cow had higher reproductive output than groups that lacked old individuals (McComb *et al.*, 2001). Apparently, the entire group benefits from the knowledge of other groups that old cows possess, as tension is reduced during encounters if old cows are present. Several studies have found positive evidence for individual recognition in fishes, including inter-specific individual recognition in a cleaner fish mutualism (reviewed by Bshary *et al.*, 2002). Studies on invertebrates are clearly needed, but there is one example for individual recognition among painted shrimps (Seibt and Wickler, 1972).

The question of how much individuals know about the *relationships between other group members* has hardly been touched among non-primate animals that live in stable social groups. Clearly, being able to incorporate information about the relationships between group members in one's own decision-making adds a significant level of complexity to the decision-making process compared with only using information from direct interactions with each group member. For example, in nepotistic societies, where rank order is not based on individual strength but on the ranks of individuals belonging to the same matriline, the manner in which animals group can be taken as evidence that individuals at least know the matriline to which each group member belongs. There are some further observational indications that hyenas know the relationships between unrelated group members (Engh et al., 2005) but this has to be confirmed experimentally. While systematic studies on the issue are lacking, there is ample evidence that non-primate animals pay attention to interactions between third parties. Such eavesdropping has been found in species as diverse as dolphins, elephants, black tits, choruses of anurans, Siamese fighting fish, guppies and fiddler crabs, as summarized in a recent edited volume (McGregor, 2005). Eavesdropping may cause adjustment in the behaviour of observed animals (so-called audience effects: summary by Matos and Schlupp, 2005). For example, there is experimental evidence that cleaner fish behave more cooperatively towards a current client in the presence of bystanders as that increases the probability of getting access to these bystanders (Bshary and Grutter, 2006). Basic knowledge for complex social decisions thus exists in a large variety of species. The equivalent of a baboon, simultaneously presenting to a male while threatening a harassing animal (protected threat; Kummer, 1957), has been repeatedly observed in cleaner fish. On five occasions in 96 h of observation, individuals that were being chased by a non-predatory client approached a passing predatory client and started an interaction, which terminated the chase by the non-predatory client. During the same observations, cleaners approached a non-predatory client when chased only once (Bshary et al., 2002). Cleaners thus use predators as a social tool in a conflict with a client. Experiments are still needed, however, to clarify how cleaners acquire this behaviour and how much they know about the relationship between predators and prey species.

Alliances in non-primate animals (as well as in primates) are usually formed between related individuals (Franck et al., 1995). Societies where nepotism is based on kin selection do not seem to be of great interest to us because the decision rule "help relatives against non-relatives in a conflict" seems to be very simple (but see Byrne

and Whiten, 1997 for their view on that issue). In contrast, alliances between unrelated individuals in varying combinations seem to be cognitively demanding because partners are exchangeable and the stability of partnerships is not guaranteed by relatedness. Such alliances are rare both in primates and in non-primates. One example is the bottlenose dolphin where males form meta-alliances of up to 20 individuals in order to monopolize females (Connor et al., 1998).

Reconciliation between partners after a conflict has received little attention outside primatology but it has been observed in various mammals, such as dolphins, hyenas, goats and sheep (references in Aureli and de Waal, 2000) and in the cleaner fish *Labroides dimidiatus* (Bshary and Würth, 2001).

Evidence for the production of a signal out of context to the signaller's advantage and at the receiver's expense has been found in a variety of taxa. False alarm calls have been described in birds (Munn, 1986; Moeller, 1988) and snow foxes, *Alopex lagopus* (Rüppell, 1969). Domestic cocks have a food call, which is usually given when they find food. The call attracts hens to the food source. However, the cocks sometimes produce the call in the absence of food and copulate with an approaching hen (Hauser, 1997). Very intriguing cases of deception and counter-deception have been described in food-caching birds, like scrub jays (Emery, 2006) and ravens (Bugnyar and Heinrich, 2005). Caching individuals must avoid being observed during this process in order to avoid raids by observer birds. This conflict leads to fake caching, re-caching and hiding by observers as well as observers apparently attributing knowledge to other observers (Bugnyar and Heinrich, 2005; Emery, 2006). In the cleaner fish *L. dimidiatus*, individuals that bite their clients rather than removing ectoparasites actively seek small clients and provide them with a 'massage' (applied to the clients' body with the pelvic and pectoral fins). While massages are normally used to manipulate the decisions of the recipient, the function of the biting cleaners' massages is to attract larger clients that can then be exploited (Bshary and D'Souza, 2005). This is possible because passing clients attribute an image score to a cleaner fish depending on how the cleaner treats its current client and invite inspection mainly if they witness a cooperative interaction. In return, cleaners are generally more cooperative to a current client if other potential clients are present (Bshary and D'Souza, 2005). This is the first observational evidence for the existence of a simple form of indirect reciprocity based on image scoring (Alexander, 1987) outside humans. The cleaner-client system has also yielded the first experimental evidence for *punishment* in non-human animals (Bshary and Grutter, 2005). While punishment is suspected to occur across a broad variety of species (Clutton-Brock and Parker, 1995), the main challenge to prove its existence is methodological, as one has to exclude immediate benefits of the action, show delayed benefits, and show immediate costs of the action.

A relatively independent sub-field of cooperation is the occurrence of *cooperative hunting*. Cooperative hunting in chimpanzees has received a lot of attention (Boesch and Boesch, 1989; Stanford *et al.*, 1994; Mitani and Watts, 2001), at least partly because one hypothesis for human cognitive evolution proposes that complex cooperative hunting was a key selective force (though evidence is scarce: see Dunbar, 1993). Key components of hunting complexity proposed by Boesch and Boesch (1989) are the coordination between individuals that play different roles, the persistence of role division across various hunts, the decision to hunt before a potential prey has been encountered (termed 'intentional hunting'), and the sharing of meat after a successful hunt. *Coordinated cooperative hunting* where individuals adopt different roles has been described for a variety of mammals, including lions, dolphins, and whales and harrier hawks (reviewed by Gazda *et al.*, 2005). *Role specialization* (individual consistency) has been observed in dolphins (Gazda *et al.*, 2005). In fish, group hunting with coordinated actions has been observed in several species, and recently the first evidence for stable hunting parties has been found in *Mormyrops anguilloides*, a mormyrid species in Lake Malawi (Arnegard and Carlson, 2005). However, role division has not been described in any of these species. Unpublished observations (Laure Bize and Redouan Bshary) suggest role division in yellow saddle goatfish, *Parupeneus cyclostoma*. One individual accelerates to catch a prey, but its

partner(s) often does not follow directly but instead deviates and hence blocks a possible escape route of the prey. In fish, inter-specific cooperative hunting with evolved complementary roles seems to be quite common. For example, groupers hunt with moray eels (Bshary *et al.*, 2002) and Napoleon wrasses with trevallies (Elodie Peingeon and Redouan Bshary, unpublished data). Groupers and trevallies hunt with speed while moray eels and Napoleon wrasses may catch prey hiding in crevices. One aspect about the grouper–moray system is particularly interesting: the groupers visit the morays that are normally resting during daytime and signal with a quick shaking of their heads (Bshary *et al.*, 2002). Thus, the decision to hunt jointly is taken before a prey has been singled out. As such 'intentional' hunting has been described for chimpanzees at Taï National Park but not for other populations, Boesch (1994) proposed that the phenomenon may be linked to cognition and human evolution, but the moray example would suggest otherwise. *Food sharing* has never been described in fish, where prey is small enough to be swallowed immediately and whole. The phenomenon is more common among the social carnivores, in particular between female lions where ownership is also respected (Packer and Pusey, 1985). In other carnivores, food sharing often interacts with rank hierarchies and priority of access (Franck *et al.*, 1995).

The social brain hypothesis has been evaluated in carnivores and bats (Barton and Dunbar, 1997). In both cases, group size correlated positively with neocortex ratio. In birds, the neopallium seems to be larger in the relatively social corvids than in other taxa (Emery and Clayton, 2004). Thus, it seems at the moment that the link between social complexity and an increased forebrain size is a general phenomenon. However, there is evidence for correlations between increased brain areas and ecological correlates or skills as well. Feeding innovation frequency is positively correlated with forebrain size in birds (Lefebvre *et al.*, 1998) and enhanced performance in spatial tasks is positively correlated with hippocampus volume or size in mammals and birds [e.g. Krebs *et al.*, 1996, Pravosudov and de Kort (2006)]. Roth *et al.* (2006) demonstrate volumetric sex differences in snakes' putative homologue to the avian/mammalian hippocampus, the medial cortex, which is positively correlated with spatial ecology. They found that males, which occupy larger home ranges than females, also had significantly larger medial cortices relative to telencephalon volume than females, while there were no differences in the other analysed cortex structures. Comparisons between the mushroom bodies of annelids/arthropods and the vertebrate hippocampus have also been proposed (Mizunami *et al.*, 1993), because both play roles in similar types of learning and memory, such as place memory in mammals (for review, see Muller, 1996). Most intriguingly, mushroom bodies positively correlate in size with foraging ranges and behavior in butterflies (Sivinski, 1989) and wood ants (Bernstein and Bernstein, 1969).

Recently, Macphail and Bolhuis (2001) have argued that this kind of approach where some features or skills of an animal are correlated with certain brain areas is too simplistic, because each area may serve several functions in different situations. While the debate is ongoing and more data are needed, we think that the general logic still holds as long as we look for general principles, rather than trying to understand any given species' exact value relative to the others. Again, large sample sizes of species are needed, in this case to allow for variance that is currently unexplained. The unexplained variance could be due to a brain structure being responsible not only for the performance of the behavioural/cognitive correlate being investigated but for other tasks as well, or it could even be currently misidentified in its function (Macphail and Bolhuis, 2001). Further studies on brain anatomy, physiology and function are clearly necessary.

8.4.2. Traditions in non-primate animals

Two entire textbooks deal with the long list of traditions (defined as "distinctive behaviour patterns shared by two or more individuals, which persist over time acquired in part by social learning") and culture in animals (Avital and Jablonka, 2000; Fragaszy and Perry, 2003). Three classic examples are the cultural transmission of enemy recognition in birds, the repeated migrations of reef fishes and the dialects in songbirds. Curio *et al.* (1978) in a famous experiment proved that adult birds' mobbing towards a predator serves to transmit predator recognition to inexperienced young. Later, those young that, by a trick in the experimental design, had learned to identify a plastic bottle as predator were shown to pass this mistaken information on to their own offspring. Helfman and Schultz (1984) provided experimental evidence in the field that the repeated use of specific daytime schooling sites and twilight migration routes in French grunts, *Haemulon flavolineatum*, was due to social learning. Translocated individual grunts adopted the behaviour of resident grunts and later performed this behaviour after the removal of the residents as well. If grunts were translocated into an area where residents had been removed they could not find the migration routes by themselves. Warner (1988, 1990) studied traditions in mating site preferences in the blueheaded wrasse, *Thalassoma bifasciatum*. He removed entire populations and replaced them with new individuals. He observed the establishment and long-term maintenance of new mating sites. Not once in a 12-year study on 22 patches of reef was a new mating site established except for the initial experimental manipulation. This provides compelling evidence that mating sites are maintained by social learning rather than through aggregation at sites particularly suited for mating.

In songbirds, it has been shown that local dialects reduce gene flow in populations due to female mate choice. The reason is that females are imprinted on the song of their fathers or neighbouring males (Nicolai, 1964; Payne, 1973). Studies that tried to link local differences in song to differences in habitat structure failed to produce positive results (discussed in Wickler, 1988; Seibt *et al.*, 2002). Thus, differences between dialects are not functional and are maintained through social learning.

In the context of culture and traditions, one can also ask whether animals teach each other, i.e. an individual (instructor) changes its behaviour in the presence of a naïve individual (pupil), facilitating the pupil's learning as a direct consequence of the teacher's act. Teaching incurs some immediate costs for the instructor, but benefits in the long term (Shettleworth, 1998). Caro and Hauser (1992) distinguish between two cases of teaching: 'opportunity teaching', where an instructor creates a situation that allows others to learn by themselves through trial and error, and 'coaching' (or true teaching), where the behaviour of the pupil is either encouraged or punished by the instructor. Opportunity teaching exists in cheetahs, for example. Mothers bring live prey to offspring and let them try to hunt the prey, only stopping the prey from a complete escape (Ewer, 1969). The best evidence for true teaching has been provided by a study on white-tailed ptarmigan, *Lagopus leucurus* (Allen and Clarke, 2005). In this species, mothers teach their offspring what plants to eat by actively calling them to an edible food item and then pecking on the item for proper illustration. The first example of teaching in a non-human animal that involves bidirectional feedback between teacher and pupil comes from the ant-species *Temnothorax albipennis* (Franks and Richardson, 2006). Members, knowing the location of food, use 'tandem running' to lead a naive ant (pupil) from the nest to the food location.

8.4.3. Complex communication

Language is supposedly one of the key differences between humans and other animals. This may be partly due to the apparent lack of complex communication in other primates (but see Zuberbühler 2003 for recent developments in primatology). The well-established symbolic language in honeybees (von Frisch, 1965) is seen as an idiosyncrasy and as something very simplistic compared to human language. Beyond mammals, songbirds seem to have the most elaborate vocal communication system. It has been argued that the development of speech in human infants largely parallels that of song in young songbirds (Marler, 1970, 1973; Marler and Peters, 1981). Indeed the learning of language structure, that is, the grammar and syntax that characterize every language, occurs without the child having any idea of exactly what it learns. As Plotkin (1997) puts it: "I do not know that I know how to use the conditional subjunc-

tive because I do not know what conditional subjunctive is, yet linguists tell me that I must know it, because I use it correctly". The demonstration of imprinting learning and the detailed studies of song learning in birds give us a broader view on the phenomenon as well on possible mechanisms of learning the rules of a complex—vocal—communication system without 'conscious' guidance and instructions (Salwiczek and Wickler, 2004). It is also a songbird family that offers the best example in the non-human animal kingdom where memes keep genes on a leash (for a detailed discussion see Salwiczek, 2001).

Cetaceans are another taxon where communication appears to be much more complex than in non-human primates (see contributions in Mann *et al.*, 2000). For several whale species, there is evidence for local (group) dialects (Baird, 2000; Rendell and Whitehead, 2001; Whitehead, 2003). Bottlenose dolphins develop their individualised signature whistle and copy the whistle of close associates (Tyack, 1997). Laboratory experiments have revealed that bottlenose dolphins can learn to follow instructions given by humans using a gestural language with a grammar (Herman *et al.*, 1984). A female dolphin first learned some 50 signs, which were then used to test the dolphin's ability to solve displaced reference and syntax tasks. In both tasks, each situation was novel and presented only once. She performed significantly above chance in both tasks.

8.4.4. Tool use

We only discuss tool use according to the strict definition given that an animal has to handle a neutral object to manipulate the object it is interested in (Beck, 1980). Such behaviour has been observed in a large variety of species (Pierce, 1986; Lefebvre *et al.*, 2002). While tool use raises important questions regarding the environmental intelligence of animals, the question of whether tool use is acquired socially has also been a research focus. Examples among mammals include elephants that use a variety of objects to scratch the body or throw them at other animals (Chevalier-Skolnikoff and Liska, 1993) and dolphins using baits and sponges for hunting (Kuttin and Goldblatt, 1992; Smolker et al., 1997). In birds, herons may bait fish by throwing floating objects into the water (Higuchi, 1986, 1988), vultures throw stones on ostrich eggs (Thouless et al., 1989), and both New Caledonian crows and woodpecker finches use spines and twigs to pry invertebrates out from underneath bark (Hunt, 1996; Tebbich et al., 2001). Schultz (1982) described how pavement ants, *Tetranorium caespitum*, respond to a bee guarding the entrance to their nest, by searching for pieces of soil and dropping them onto the bee's head. In what can be seen as the equivalent of chimpanzees using leaf sponges to collect water from tree holes, individuals of the ant species *Aphaenogaster rudis* use leaves to soak liquid food and then carry the food with the leaves back to the colony (Fellers and Fellers, 1976).

These field observations have inspired laboratory experiments similar to primate studies to investigate how far animals understand the physics of tool use (Visalberghi, 1995; Chappell and Kacelnik, 2002; Tebbich and Bshary, 2004). All in all, the abilities and shortcomings of primates and bird species are quite similar, though one crow became famous for its spontaneous construction of a hook to retrieve food (Weir et al., 2002). An intriguing analogue to the famous termite fishing of chimpanzees (using twigs) is the termite-fishing assassin bug *Salyavata variegata* of Costa Rica (McMahan, 1982, 1983a,b). The bug first catches a worker termite (which is six times smaller), injects paralytic toxin and consumes the inner part but hollows the carcass. The bug then holds the carcass in front of its head with its forelegs and moves back to the termite mound. It slowly pushes the carcass into the opening, jiggling it slightly in a movement that might described as 'tantalizing'. Since termites consume their own dead and dying nest mates, usually one or more termites will try to pull the dangling carcass into the hole using their mandibles. The bug then pulls the grasping worker steadily backwards, and draws it slowly from the nest. When the worker's head is in an accessible position, the bug grasps it quickly with its forelegs and kills the termite. The new carcass is used for the next termite baiting. In one episode, one bug successfully baited and captured 31 termites within three hours. Nobody has looked for individual variation in this behaviour or its basis (learned or genetic).

8.4.5. Solving a problem 'backwards'

Solving a problem backwards means that the correct sequence of steps has to be deduced from the final step, working backwards over the intermediate steps. Evidence—parallel to that from a chimpanzee that had to open as many as 14 boxes in the right sequence to obtain food (Döhl, 1968)—has been collected in jumping spiders (Hill, 1979; Tarsitano and Andrew, 1999; Harland and Jackson, 2004). Jumping spiders often have to perform detours to catch prey after they spot it. During the detour, the prey is out of sight. Therefore, the spiders have to choose the appropriate path to the prey and remember the right path (that may repeatedly lead away from the prey's location) that leads to the prey. In experiments on *Phidippus pulcherrimus* (Hill, 1979) the prey (a dead fly cemented to the end of a long, thin strand of hair) was removed immediately after the spider's initial orientation to the prey, but the spiders nevertheless selected an appropriate three-dimensional detour with respect to the position of the prey. They apparently kept a memory of that position in space (Hill, 1979), as shown by intermediate reorientation to the expected prey position. Secondary objectives (e.g. a sighted plant configuration) can also replace the primary objective (prey position) as a determinant of immediate behaviour. This seems to be because jumping spiders often cannot approach their prey directly but have to climb a structure above the prey so that they can drop from above.

In experiments conducted by Tarsitano and Andrew (1999), *Portia labiata*, another jumping spider, was shown to discriminate between detour routes that did and did not lead to prey. Individuals first 'scanned' the available rampways by standing more or less in one place while pivoting about and repeatedly fixating its principal eyes on objects in its environment.

After the spiders had scanned the complete route, they overwhelmingly chose to head towards the route leading to the lure. Selecting a route ahead of time—planning ahead—is called a putative cognitive ability when manifested by vertebrates. As with many previous phenomena, the spider example should caution us against assuming high-level cognitive abilities on the basis of behavioural phenomena alone, rather than a detailed study of underlying mechanisms.

8.4.6. Alex the parrot

Alex, an African grey parrot, *Psittacus erithacus*, is the most famous example of a non-primate animal whose cognitive abilities have been amplified through constant interactions with a human scientist (Pepperberg, 1999). Hand-raised by Irene Pepperberg, he has been trained to understand and produce human words and use them in a 'naming' game, associating a word with a specific object or category. He can label many objects and categorize them according to shape, material or colour, using human words as labels. Parrots and some other social birds normally mimic vocalizations within their group (Nottebohm, 1970; Price, 1998). This suggests that the original advantage of vocal copying was to address individually known conspecifics and to name them, rather than objects.

When confronted with collections of unique combinations of items that differ in colour and shape, and asked "What colour?" or "What shape?", Alex has been shown to categorize the same item with respect to colour on one trial and shape on another. Furthermore, the bird proved able to answer correctly when queried "What colour is object X?", "What shape is object Y?", "What object is colour A?", "What object is shape B?" and even "What object is colour A and shape C?". Thus, the bird understands all elements in the query and categorizes conjunctively. There are many more fascinating details (Pepperberg, 1999). Drawing a comparative conclusion, Pepperberg (2001, p. 59) provocatively states "that a non-human, non-primate, non-mammal has a level of competence that, in an ape, would be taken to indicate that equal to a human".

8.5. Complex cognitive mechanisms found in non-primate animals

8.5.1. Episodic-like memory

Current theories of human episodic memory refer to the conscious experience of self that accompanies episodic recall. As this state has no obvious manifestation in non-linguistic behaviour (Tulving, 1983; Tulving and Markowitsch, 1998), it is currently (forever?) undetectable in non-human species. In terms of criteria that can be deduced from behaviour alone, Clayton and Dickinson (1998) suggest that episodic recall should comprise evidence that an animal remembers the 'what', 'where' and 'when' of an episode. Clayton and Dickinson (1998) took advantage of the fact that scrub jays hide both perishable and non-perishable food for later recovery under both natural and laboratory conditions. They demonstrated in subsequent experiments that scrub jays possess an episodic-like memory (Clayton and Dickinson, 1998, 1999a; Clayton *et al.*, 2001a), that individuals differentiate between memories of caching and recovery events (Clayton and Dickinson, 1999b), and update information about the current status of their caches. Furthermore, scrub jays can remember information about the social context of the caching event based on whether they have a personal experience of food caching or have observed another bird doing so (Clayton *et al.*, 2001b).

Brood care in parasitoid wasps provides another interesting system in which to look for the basis of episodic-like memory in an invertebrate. The following observations were made by Baerends (1941) on *Ammophila campestris*. The wasp builds many locally distributed burrows, each for one larva, with caterpillars as food. A female closes a newly prepared ('virgin') burrow to hunt for the first caterpillar and lays an egg on it. If successful, she will leave this burrow unvisited for two days. In the meantime she visits other, older nests (up to six) each in a different stage requiring age-specific activities, e.g. one burrow only requires inspection while others need to be filled with several caterpillars before definite closing. This variability in brood care makes timing via 'trapline nest visiting' impossible. Baerends showed that the wasp has an expectation about what to find in a virgin nest; if the experimenter placed a caterpillar with an egg in a virgin nest before the wasp's first return, she would remove both and replace them with her own ones, even though later on she does not differentiate between own and foreign larvae. Clearly, this system deserves further experimental study.

8.5.2. Theory of mind

Theory of mind describes the ability to attribute mental states to other individuals (Premack and Woodruff, 1978). Clearly, such a mechanism would enhance the ability to predict the behaviour of others in new situations and thus enhance the social competence of an individual. Unfortunately, proving its existence in non-human animals has turned out to be virtually impossible, due to methodological constraints. There is as yet no agreement regarding the kind of experiment that could decisively prove or disprove the existence of theory of mind in animals (Heyes, 1998). It is possible that the food-caching behaviour of birds provides a framework for the study of theory of mind. Emery and Clayton (2001) observed that jays who had previously been allowed to raid caches of other jays "disliked" being observed while caching and re-cached food significantly more often afterwards than individuals who had never raided food from others. Other results suggest that scrub-jays use flexible, cognitive caching and recovery strategies to aid in reducing potential future pilfering of caches by conspecifics (Emery et al., 2004). In conclusion, jays might learn that the world is evil (others might raid their caches) because they are evil themselves (they raid the caches of others).

8.5.3. Imitation and emulation

Imitation refers to the reproduction of the behaviour of a demonstrator, while emulation refers to the observer trying to reproduce the goal of the model's action, and the combination of both has been termed true imitation (Wynne, 2001). Since Heyes (1993) pointed out that imitation can only be shown convincingly under very strict experimental conditions, a few examples have emerged in non-primate animals.

A brilliant example is a study on Japanese quails (Akins et al., 1996; Zentall, 1996). Observers were placed in four different situations with demonstrators that either pecked a treadle or stepped onto it, and were either observed feeding or not. The observers imitated the models' action and were more likely to do so if they saw the demonstrator being rewarded. Thus, both the behaviour and the goal seem to have influenced the behaviour of observers. This is a wonderful example for true imitation. Some authors, however, suggest that for true imitation, observers have to understand the motivation of another animal and hence have a theory of mind (Wynne, 2001).

8.5.4. Transitive inference

Transitive inference means that an animal understands the logic of "if A > B and B > C, then A > C" (= C < A). Bond et al. (2003) proposed that such ability should be particularly important for animals living in large stable groups in order to be able to monitor the (rank) relationships between other group members. They found experimental evidence that highly social pinyon jays use transitive inference with high efficiency in a task where a rank order was attributed to different symbols.

8.6. Discussion

8.6.1. The link between ecology and an animal's cognitive abilities

We have shown that there exist many phenomena, previously considered to be unique to primates, and requiring their advanced cognitive abilities, that are in fact widespread among non-primate species. Currently, the ecological approach is most successful in allowing scientists to choose model systems to investigate specific questions, as will be discussed in Section 8.6.2. Conclusive evidence for the purist adaptationist approach that links specific abilities to specific ecological problems is still very rare, however. To prove that the adaptationist approach is valid means that we not only have to find evidence that, for example, animals that live in complex social environments (dolphins, elephants, social carnivores, parrots, corvids and cleaner fish) have important social skills and are similar in their abilities to solve social tasks (still ignoring potential mechanisms). We also have to show that animals that have a more solitary lifestyle lack such social skills.

Only a very few studies have used a comparative approach to investigate the same skill in several species that differ with respect to the ecological relevance of the skill in question. Balda and Kamil (1989), for example, compared the memory capacities of three species of corvids that differ with respect to their dependence on retrieval of food caches for survival under natural conditions. The most specialized species, Clark's nutcracker, performed best in spatial memory tasks, as predicted by an adaptationist approach. In addition, the nutcrackers were outstanding only in the spatial memory task but average in a colour memory task, indicating that memory abilities are specific rather than general in these birds. Bond et al. (2003) explicitly tested two closely related jay species that differed with respect to the complexity of social life, to investigate whether these differences have selected for different mechanisms to track social relationships between third parties. The highly social pinyon jays (*Gymnorhinus cyanocephalus*) solved the tasks more rapidly, due to the use of relational learning, while western scrub jays (*Aphelocoma californica*) learned tasks more slowly using associative learning. However, as birds were captured as adults, one cannot distinguish between an evolutionary explanation and ontogenetic differences that may explain these findings.

The corvid studies cited above show the path for future studies. An important further step is to increase the sample size for the number of species tested, either through collaboration between research groups or through an augmentation of species studied within a laboratory. Eventually, as studies on specific questions accumulate, meta-analysis techniques can be used to test whether or not the results are consistent with the adaptationist approach across studies.

For the use of meta-analyses, researchers need to see the importance of conducting studies on species that are predicted to fail at solving tasks and present a lack of evidence for a certain cognitive mechanism. Negative results should be published/publishable and regarded as important contributions to our general understanding. We are aware that 'proving failure' is like trying to prove the null-hypothesis. However, as long as researchers try to adjust each experiment as much as possible to the ecology and sensory systems of the species tested, we see no obvious reason why the results should be biased in favour of certain species or taxons. In any case, basing general concepts in part on negative evidence is clearly better than an approach that assumes that the absence of positive evidence for certain abilities or mechanisms in a taxon (or all non-human animals) can be taken as evidence for the non-existence of those abilities or mechanisms in that taxon. Such a conclusion is clearly immature in the absence of negative evidence.

Broad comparisons between species with respect to their cognitive abilities should be conducted both on a quantitative level and on the mechanistic (qualitiative) level. Quantitative studies address questions like 'how much can be learned', 'how fast is a solution learned', and 'with what accuracy is a problem solved'. Mechanistic questions focus on how a problem is solved. While the extreme position that there are no cognitive differences between non-human animals (Macphail, 1982) is not supported by current evidence, we know little about whether observed differences are more of a quantitative or qualitative nature. In particular the various examples of invertebrates showing tool use, 'detour planning', and possibly episodic-like memory, warrant detailed studies on the underlying mechanisms. Perhaps such studies can reveal the most basic processes necessary to produce such interesting behaviour.

What is clear from current evidence is that even if the adaptationist approach can explain general principles, it often fails to predict the presence or absence of specific abilities in any species. Why do we find termite fishing in one predatory bug species but not in other invertebrate termite predators? Why do we know of only a few species of heron throwing bait into the water to attract fish, while other species benefit from the very same trick that could do not use it? Nature seems to be quite full of idiosyncratic examples of cognitive phenomena. On the other hand, recent evidence from field studies sometimes backs up the link between ecology and cognition in species where old laboratory studies have provided amazing cognitive skills in the apparent absence of an ecological background. For example, it has been observed only quite recently that both orang-utans and gorillas use tools under natural conditions (van Schaik *et al.*, 2003; Breuer *et al.*, 2005).

8.6.2. The ecological approach and choosing the right study species

To date, knowledge about the ecology of a species has been most helpful in identifying model systems to address specific cognitive questions. The main challenge for cognitive scientists working on animals is often to find the adequate experimental paradigm that can provide conclusive evidence when it is not possible literally to ask the subject how it solved a given problem. The great success of Pepperberg's work is certainly due in part to the fact that she was able to teach Alex the use of human language. Clayton and colleagues (Clayton and Dickinson, 1998; Emery and Clayton, 2001) have used the food-caching behaviour of jays to develop experimental set-ups that can be used not only for studies on mental 'time travel' but also for studies that investigate the mechanisms underlying apparently complex social behaviour. Also the spontaneous construction of a tool to solve an otherwise impossible task has been observed in a bird species that was known to use and to modify a variety of tools under natural conditions (Hunt, 1996). More generally, if one wants to investigate an animal's ability to understand aspects of 'folk physics', the easiest way to set up experiments is to choose species that use tools under natural conditions and explore the cognitive aspects of tool use (Weir *et al.*, 2002; Tebbich and Bshary, 2004).

At the phenomenal level, it is obvious that interesting social behaviours like alliance formation, tactical deception, etc., have a higher probability of being observed in highly social species than in less social species. In the case of animal traditions, the migrations of some coral reef fish species have provided an ideal set-up for experimental manipulation in the field (Helfman and Schulz, 1984; Warner, 1988, 1990). Imagine a similar experiment on chimpanzees, where a

group from Gombe, Tanzania, is exchanged with a group from Taï, Ivory Coast. On the one hand, it is clear that such experiments should be conducted in order to gain conclusive evidence that knowledge is transferred socially from one generation to the next. On the other hand, it is clear that such experiments cannot be conducted on apes for ethical reasons, as well as logistic ones. What these kinds of thought experiment make clear is that if we want to know more about our closest relatives, we also have to accept correlative evidence. Applied to the many potential examples for chimpanzee culture (Whiten *et al.*, 1999), the logic of the argument can be developed as follows: (a) studies on fish migrations and on bird song have already shown that culture is not unique to humans. (b) Thus, if we observe differences in the behaviour of animals between populations and do not find functional explanations for these differences, cultural differences become a (or the most) likely explanation. (c) Most of the examples for chimpanzee culture fulfil these requirements. Nevertheless, each single potential example has to be treated with caution. For example, Tebbich *et al.* (2001) have shown that woodpecker finches learn their elaborate usage of tools through individual learning during a sensitive phase of development, rather than socially. Thus, the observation that all individuals in a population use tools is not necessarily evidence for a social learning mechanism.

In conclusion, whenever we ask whether a certain characteristic of humans also exists in animals, the most promising approach may not be to start on our closest relatives but to use our knowledge of animal behaviour and ecology to choose a species that offers the possibility for a suitable experimental approach. Perhaps the most recent example is a study on the evolution of learning abilities in *Drosophila* (Mery and Kawecki, 2002, 2005). Due to the short generation times, it is relatively easy to conduct selection experiments. The experiments showed that one can select for discriminatory abilities and long-term memory (Mery and Kawecki, 2002). However, using long-term memory turned out to be quite costly to the flies as it reduced life expectancy significantly (Mery and Kawecki, 2005). We sincerely hope that future studies will explain why this result is *not* applicable to humans.

8.6.3. **Our place in nature**

While there seem to be good reasons to claim highly evolved cognitive skills for humans, the evolutionary approach helps to embed us in the animal world of which we are (and always have been) a part. Humans are social, omnivorous, diurnal and terrestrial, and these features are certainly reflected in our cognitive abilities, as well highlighting the abilities we lack. Most basically, our sensory system is adapted to a terrestrial and diurnal life. As a consequence, many animal species can solve cognitive tasks that we cannot because they have sensory systems with a higher resolution than ours (a dog's smelling abilities) or because they have sensory systems that we lack entirely (see Wynne, 2001 for a useful summary). Rather than playing down the importance of sensory systems and the associated lack of certain cognitive abilities, we should appreciate the link between these variables and the ecology of a species.

However, it is not just that animals have superior or different senses to humans: animals may excel also in tasks where we like to think that we excel. For example, humans have well-developed spatial memory skills and often use a cognitive map for orientation. Nevertheless, the abilities of food-caching birds to retrieve hidden food items after month, often in seemingly unstructured areas (meadow), clearly surpass human abilities. Clark's nutcrackers store about 30 000 food items in 6000–8000 caches. They rely on their caches between 80–100% during winter and spring (up to 6–7 months), when they already raise their first brood (Van der Wall and Balda, 1977; Tomback, 1982). Tomback (1980) suggests that nutcrackers find most of their caches by means of memory.

The most intriguing example for animal superiority in a human domain is provided by Vickrey and Neuringer (2000), who found that pigeons beat humans in the Hick's test, a choice task in which a subject's performance correlates very well with the subject's performance in IQ tests. Following the 'different intelligences' hypothesis (Carlson and Widaman, 1987; Gardner, 1983; Sternberg, 1985), the authors propose that pigeons perform better than humans because "To survive, pigeons forage, often in flocks, for small pieces of grain, as well as for insects that move and fly. Such foraging requires rapid choices to be made from simultaneously available objects. Thus, the pigeon might, in fact, be capable of more rapid choices among potential food items than are people." (Vickrey and Neuringer, 2000, p. 291.) The experiment should be extended to other species to test this proposed link between ecology and performance in the test.

8.7. **Conclusions**

There are plenty of indications for a strong link between the ecology of a species and its cognitive abilities. However, we are still very far from being able to understand how specific cognitive abilities correspond to ecology, and whether the underlying cognitive mechanisms are also linked to ecology or to phylogenetic relatedness. To answer these questions, we need broad comparisons between species that address the following issues:

1. The link between a phenomenon and its underlying mechanism.

2. Quantitative comparison between species with respect to each ability.

3. Experiments on closely related species with a different ecology.

4. The specificity of abilities.

5. The link between cognitive abilities and the structure and size of corresponding brain areas.

For the success of this approach, we need increased awareness that negative results are as important as positive results. Only broad comparisons will reveal where humans fit general rules and where they are exceptions to general rules.

Acknowledgments

We thank Ralph Bergmüller and Nick Mackintosh for discussions. L.S. is financed with a postdoctorate grant by the Max Planck Society. R. B. is financed by the Swiss Science Foundation, grant 3100A0–108019.

References

Akins, C. K, Zentall, T. R. and Thomas, R. (1996) Imitative learning in male Japanese quail (*Coturnix japonica*) using the two-action method. *Journal of Comparative Psychology*, 110: 316–320.

Alexander, R. D. (1987) *The Biology of Moral Systems.* Aldine de Gruyter, New York.

Allen, T. and Clarke, J. A. (2005) Social learning of food preferences by white-tailed ptarmigan chicks. *Animal Behaviour*, 70: 305–310.

Arnegard, M. E. and Carlson, B. A. (2005) Electric organ discharge patterns during group hunting by a mormyrid fish. *Proceedings of the Royal Society of London B*, 272: 1305–1314.

Aureli, F. and de Waal, F. B. M. (eds) (2000) *Natural Conflict Resolution.* University of California Press. Berkeley.

Avital, E. and Jablonka, E. (2000) *Animal Traditions. Behavioural Inheritance in Evolution.* Cambridge University Press, Cambridge.

Baerends, G. P. (1941) Fortpflanzungsverhalten und Orientierung der Grabwespe *Ammophila campestris* Jur. *Tijdschrift voor Entomologie*, 84: 68–275.

Baird, R. W. (2000) The killer whale: foraging specializations and group hunting. In J. Mann, R. C. Connor, P. L. Tyack and H. Whitehead (eds) *Cetacean Societies*, pp. 127–153. University of Chicago Press, Chicago.

Balda, R. P. and Kamil, A. C. (1989) A comparative study on cache recovery by three corvid species. *Animal Behaviour*, 38: 486–495.

Balda, R. P., Pepperberg, I. M. and Kamil, A. C. (eds) (1998) *Animal Cognition in Nature.* Academic Press, San Diego.

Barkow, J. H., Cosmides, L. and Tooby, J. (1992) *The Adapted Mind.* Oxford University Press, Oxford.

Barton, R. A. and Dunbar, R. (1997) Evolution of the social brain. In A. Whiten and R. W. Byrne, (eds) *Machiavellian Intelligence II*, pp. 240–263. Cambridge University Press, Cambridge.

Beck, B. B. (1980) *Animal Tool Behavior: The Use and Manufacture of Tools by Animals.* Garland, London.

Bekoff, M., Allen, C. and Burghardt, G. M. (eds) (2002) *The Cognitive Animal.* Bradford, Cambridge, MA.

Bernstein, S. and Bernstein, R. A. (1969) Relationships between foraging efficiency and the size of the head and component brain and sensory structures in the red wood ant. *Brain Research*, 16: 85–104.

Boesch, C. (1994) Cooperative hunting in wild chimpanzees. *Animal Behaviour*, 48: 653–667.

Boesch, C. and Boesch, H. (1989) Hunting behavior of wild chimpanzees in the Taï National Park. *American Journal of Physical Anthropology*, 78: 547–573.

Bond, A. B., Kamil, A. C. and Balda, R. P. (2003) Social complexity and transitive inference in corvids. *Animal Behaviour*, 65: 479–487.

Breuer, T., Ndoundou-Hockemba, M. and Fishlock, V. (2005) First observation of tool use in wild gorillas. *PLoS* 3(11): 2041–2043.

Brown, C., Laland, K. and Krause, J. (eds) (in press) *Fish Cognition and Behaviour.* Blackwell, Oxford.

Bshary, R. and D'Souza, A. (2005) Cooperation in communication networks: indirect reciprocity in interactions between cleaner fish and client reef fish. In P. McGregor (ed.) *Communication Networks*, pp. 521–539. Cambridge University Press, Cambridge.

Bshary, R. and Grutter, A. S. (2005) Punishment and partner switching cause cooperative behaviour in a cleaning mutualism. *Biology Letters*, 1: 396–399.

Bshary, R. and Grutter, A. S. (2006) Image scoring and cooperation in a cleaner fish mutualism. *Nature* 441: 975–978.

Bshary, R. and Noë, R. (2003) Biological markets: the ubiquitous influence of partner choice on cooperation and mutualism. In P. Hammerstein (ed.) *Genetic and Cultural Evolution of Cooperation*, pp. 167–184. MIT Press, Cambridge.

Bshary, R. and Würth, M. (2001) Cleaner fish *Labroides dimidiatus* manipulate client reef fish by providing tactile stimulation. *Proceedings of the Royal Society of London B*, 268: 1495–1501.

Bshary, R., Wickler, W. and Fricke, H. (2002) Fish cognition: a primate's eye view. *Animal Cognition* 5: 1–13.

Bugnyar, T. and Heinrich, B. (2005) Ravens, *Corvus corax*, differentiate between knowledgeable and ignorant competitors. *Proceedings of the Royal Society of London B* online, doi: 10.1098/rspb.2005.3144.

Buss, D. M. (1999) *Evolutionary Psychology. The New Science of the Mind.* Allyn & Bacon, Boston.

Byrne, R. W. and Whiten, A. (1988) *Machiavellian Intelligence.* Clarendon Press, Oxford.

Byrne, R. W. and Whiten, A. (1997) Machiavellian intelligence. In A. Whiten and R. W. Byrne (eds) *Machiavellian Intelligence II*, pp. 1–23. Cambridge University Press, Cambridge.

Carlson, J. S. and Widaman, K. F. (1987) Elementary cognitive correlates of *G*: progress and prospects. In P. A. Vernon (ed.) *Speed of Information-processing and Intelligence*, pp. 69–99. Ablex, Norwood, NJ.

Caro, T. M. and Hauser, M. D. (1992) Is there teaching in nonhuman animals? *Quarterly Review of Biology*, 67: 151–174.

Chappell, J. and Kacelnik, A. (2002) Tool selectivity in a non-primate, the New Caledonian crow (*Corvus moneduloides*). *Animal Cognition*, 5: 71–78.

Chevalier-Skolnikoff, S. and Liska, J. (1993) Tool use by wild and captive elephants. *Animal Behaviour*, 46: 209–219.

Cheney, D. L. and Seyfarth, R. M. (1990) *How Monkeys see the World.* University of Chicago Press, Chicago.

Clayton, N. S. and Dickinson, A. (1998) Episodic-like memory during cache recovery by scrub jays. *Nature*, 395: 272–274.

Clayton, N. S. and Dickinson, A. (1999a) Scrub jays (*Aphelocoma coerulescens*) remember when as well as where and what food items they cached. *Journal of Comparative Psychology*, 113: 403–416.

Clayton, N. S. and Dickinson, A. (1999b) Motivational control of food storing in the scrub jay (*Aphelocoma coerulescens*). *Animal Behaviour*, 57: 435–444.

Clayton, N. S., Emery, N. J. and Dickinson, A. (2001a) Elements of episodic-like memory in animals. In A. Baddeley, M. Conway and J. Aggleton (eds) *Episodic Memory. New Direction in Research*, pp. 232–248. Oxford University Press, Oxford.

Clayton, N. S., Yu, K. and Dickinson, A. (2001b) Scrub jays (*Aphelocoma coerulescens*) can form integrated memory for multiple features of caching episodes. *Journal of Experimental Psychology: Animal Behaviour Processes*, 27: 17–29.

Clutton-Brock, T. H. and Parker, G. A. (1995) Punishment in animal societies. *Nature*, 373: 209–216.

Connor, R. C., Mann, J., Tyack, P. L. and Whitehead, H. (1998) Social evolution in toothed whales. *Trends in Ecology and Evolution*, 13: 228–232.

Cosmides, L. and Tooby, J. (1987) From evolution to behaviour: evolutionary psychology as the missing link. In J. Dupré (ed.) *The Latest on the Best: Essays on Evolution and Optimality*, pp. 277–306. MIT Press, Cambridge.

Cosmides, L. and Tooby, J. (1987) From evolution to behaviour: evolutionary psychology as the missing link. In: Dupré, J. (ed) *The latest on the best: essays on evolution and optimality*. Cambridge, MA. MIT Press. pp. 277–306.

Côté, I. M. (2000) Evolution and ecology of cleaning symbioses in the sea. *Oceanography and Marine Biology*, 38: 311–355.

Curio, E., Ernst, U. and Vieth, W. (1978) Cultural transmission of enemy recognition: one function of mobbing. *Science*, 202: 899–901.

Döhl, J. (1968) Über die Fähigkeit einer Schimpansin, Umwege mit selbständigen Zwischenzielen zu überblicken. *Zeitschrift für Tierpsychologie*, 25: 89–103.

Dunbar, R. I. M. (1993) Coevolution of neocortical size, group size and language in humans. *Behaviour and Brain Science*, 16: 681–735.

East, M. L. and Hofer, H. (2002) Conflict and cooperation in a female-dominated society: a reassessment of the "hyperaggressive" image of spotted hyenas. *Advances in the Study of Behavior*, 31: 1–30.

Eibl-Eibesfeldt, I. (1989) *Human Ethology*. Aldine de Gruyter, New York.

Emery, N. J. (2006) Cognitive ornithology: the evolution of avian intelligence. *Philosophical Transactions of the Royal Society of London B*, 361: 23–43.

Emery, N. J. and Clayton, N. S. (2001) Effects of experience and social context on prospective caching strategies in scrub jays. *Nature*, 414: 443–446.

Emery, N. J. and Clayton, N. S. (2004) The mentality of crows. Convergent evolution of intelligence in corvids and apes. *Science*, 306: 1903–1907.

Emery N. J., Dally J. M. and Clayton N. S. (2004) Western scrub jays (*Aphelocoma californica*) use cognitive strategies to protect their caches from thieving conspecifics. *Animal Cognition*, 7: 37–43.

Engh, A. L., Siebert, E. R., Greenberg, D. A. and Holekamp, K. E. (2005) Patterns of alliance formation and post-conflict aggression indicate spotted hyaenas recognize third-party relationships. *Animal Behaviour*, 69: 209–217.

Ewer, R. F. (1969) The "instinct to teach". *Nature*, 223: 698.

Fellers, J.-H. and Fellers, G.-M. (1976) Tool use in a social insect and its implications for competitive interactions. *Science*, 192: 70–72.

Fodor, F. J. (1983) *The Modularity of Mind*. MIT Press, Cambridge, MA.

Fragaszy, D. M. and Perry, S. (eds) (2003) *The Biology of Traditions. Models and Evidence*. Cambridge University Press, Cambridge.

Franck, L. G., Holekamp, K. E. and Smale, L. (1995) Dominance, demography, and reproductive success of spotted hyenas. In A. R. E. Sinclair and P. Arcsese (eds) *Serengeti II: Dynamics, Management, and Conservation of an Ecosystem*, pp. 364–384. University of Chicago Press, Chicago.

Franks, N. R. and Richardson, T. (2006) Teaching in tandem-running ants. *Nature* 439: 153.

Galef, B. G. (1988) Imitation in animals: history, definition and interpretation of data from physiological laboratory. In T. R. Zentall and B. G. Galef (eds) *Social Learning. Psychological and Biological Perspectives*, pp. 3–28. Lawrence Erlbaum, Hillsdale, NJ.

Gardner, H. (1983) *Frames of Mind: The Theory of Multiple Intelligences*. Basic Books, New York.

Gazda, S. K., Connor, R. C., Edgar, R. K. and Cox, F. (2005) A division of labour with role specialization in group-hunting bottlenose dolphins (*Tursiops truncatus*) off Cedar Key, Florida. *Proceedings of the Royal Society of London B*, 272: 135–140.

Gintis, H., Bowles, S., Boyd, R. & Tehr, E. (2003) Explaining altruistic behaviour in humans. *Evolution and Human Behaviour* 24: 153–172.

Hamilton, W. D. (1964) The genetical evolution of social behaviour. I. and II. *Journal of Theoretical Biology*, 7: 1–52.

Harland, D. P. and Jackson, R. R. (2004) *Portia* perceptions: the *Umwelt* of an araneophagic jumping spider. In F. R. Prete (ed.) *Complex Worlds from Simpler Nervous Systems*, pp. 5–40. MIT Press, Cambridge, MA.

Hauser, M. D. (1997) Minding the behaviour of deception. In A. Whiten and R. W. Byrne (eds) *Machiavellian Intelligence II*, pp. 112–143. Cambridge University Press, Cambridge.

Helfman, G. S. and Schultz, E. T. (1984) Social transmission of behavioural traditions in a coral reef fish. *Animal Behaviour*, 32: 379–84.

Herman, L. M. (2002) Exploring the cognitive world of the bottlenosed dolphin. In M. Bekoff, C. Allen and G. M. Burghardt (eds) *The Cognitive Animal*, pp. 275–283. MIT Press, Cambridge, MA.

Herman, L. M., Richards, D. G. and Wolz, J. P. (1984) Comprehension of sentences by bottlenosed dolphins. *Cognition*, 16: 129–219.

Heyes, C. M. (1993) Imitation, culture and tradition. *Animal Behaviour*, 46: 999–1010.

Heyes, C. M. (1998) Theory of mind in nonhuman primates. *Behavioral and Brain Sciences*, 21: 101–148.

Heyes, C. M. and Huber, L. (eds) (2000) *The Evolution of Cognition*. Bradford, Cambridge MA.

Higuchi, H. (1986) Bait-fishing by the green-backed heron *Ardeola striata* in Japan. *Ibis*, 128: 285–290.

Higuchi, H. (1988) Individual differences in bait-fishing by the Green-backed Heron *Ardeola striata* associated with territory quality. *Ibis*, 130: 39–44.

Hill, D. E. (1979) Orientation by jumping spiders of the genus *Phidippus* (Araneae: Salticidae) during the pursuit of prey. *Behavioral Ecology and Sociobiology*, 5: 301–322.

Humphrey, N. K. (1976) The social function of intellect. In P. P. Bateson and R. A. Hinde (eds) *Growing Points in Ethology*, pp. 303–317. Cambridge University Press, Cambridge.

Hunt, G. R. (1996) Manufacture and use of hook-tools by New Caledonian crows. *Nature*, 379: 249–251.

Jolly, A. (1966) Lemur social behavior and primate intelligence. *Science*, 153: 501–506.

Kamil, A. C. (1998) On the proper definition of cognitive ethology. In R. P. Balda, I. M. Pepperberg and A. C. Kamil (eds) *Animal Cognition in Nature*, pp. 1–28. Academic Press, San Diego.

Kendrick, K. M., da Costa, A. P., Leigh, A. E., Hinton, M. R. and Peirce, J. W. (2001) Sheep don't forget a face. *Nature*, 414: 165–166.

Kohler, U. (1997) Zur Struktur und Evolution des Sozialsystems von *Neolamprologus multifasciatus* (Cichlidae, Pisces), dem kleinsten Schneckenbuntbarsch des Tanganjikasees. PhD thesis, Ludwig-Maximilian-Universität, Munich.

Krebs, J. R., Clayton, N. S., Healy, S. D., Cristol, D. A., Patel, S. N. and Jolliffe, A. R. (1996) The ecology of the avian brain: food-storing memory and the hippocampus. *Ibis*, 138: 34–46.

Kummer, H. (1957) Soziales Verhalten einer Mantelpavian-Gruppe. *Schweizerische Zeitschrift für Psychologie und ihre Anwendungen*. 33: 1–91.

Kuttin, E. S. and Goldblatt, A. (1992) Bait-fishing by dolphins: a documented anecdote. *Aquatic Mammals*, 18: 89–90.

Lefebvre, L., Gaxiola, A., Dawson, S., Timmermans, S., Rosza, L. and Kabai, P. (1998) Feeding innovations and forebrain size in Australasian birds. *Behaviour*, 135: 1077–1097.

Lefebvre, L., Nicolakakis, N. and Boire, D. (2002) Tools and brains in birds. *Behaviour*, 139: 939–973.

Lorenz, K. (1941) Vergleichende Bewegungsstudien an Anatinen. *Journal für Ornithologie*, 89: 194–294.

Mackintosh, N. J. (ed.) (1994) *Animal Learning and Cognition*. Academic Press, San Diego.

Macphail, E. M. (1982) *Brain and Intelligence in Vertebrates*. Clarendon Press, Oxford.

Macphail, E. M. and Bolhuis, J. J. (2001) The evolution of intelligence: adaptive specializations versus general process. *Biological Reviews*, 76: 341–364.

Mann, J., Connor, R. C., Tyack, P. I. and Whitehead, H. (eds) (2000) *Cetacean Societies*. University of Chicago Press, Chicago.

Marler, P. (1970) Bird song and speech development: could there be parallels? *American Scientist*, 58: 669–673.

Marler, P. (1973) Speech development and bird song: are there any parallels? In G. A. Miller (ed.) *Communication, Language, and Meaning*, pp. 73–83. Basic Books, New York.

Marler, P. and Peters, S. (1981) Birdsong and speech: evidence for special processing. In P. Eimas and J. Miller (eds) *Perspectives on the Study of Speech*, pp. 75–112. Lawrence Erlbaum, Hillsdale.

Matos, R. J. and Schlupp, I. (2005) Performing in front of an audience. In P. K. McGregor (ed.) *Animal Communication Networks*, pp. 63–83. Cambridge University Press, Cambridge.

McComb, K., Moss, C. J., Durant, S. M., Baker, L. and Sayialel, S. (2001) Matriarchs as repositories of social knowledge in African elephants. *Science*, 292: 491–494.

McFarland, D. (1993) *Animal Behaviour*. Wiley, New York.

McGregor, P. K. (ed.) (2005) *Animal Communication Networks*. Cambridge University Press, Cambridge.

McMahan, E. A. (1982) Bait-and-capture strategy of a termite-eating assassin bug. *Insectes sociaux*, 29: 346–351.

McMahan, E. A. (1983a) Bugs angle for termites. *Natural History (NY)*, 92: 40–46.

McMahan, E. A. (1983b) Adaptations, feeding preferences, and biometrics of a termite-baiting assassin bug (Hymenoptera: Reduviidae). *Annals of the Entomological Society of America*, 76: 483–486.

Mery, F. and Kawecki, T. J. (2002) Experimental evolution of learning ability in fruit flies. *Proceedings of the National Academy of Sciences of the United States of America*, 99: 14274–14279.

Mery, F. and Kawecki, T. J. (2005) A cost of long-term memory in Drosophila. *Science*, 308: 1148.

Mitani, J. C. and Watts, D. P. (2001) Why do chimpanzees hunt and share meat? *Animal Behaviour*, 61: 915–924.

Mizunami, M., Weibrecht, J. M. and Strausfeld, N. J. (1993) A new role for the insect mushroom bodies: Place memory and motor control. In R. D. Beer, R. Ritzmann and T. McKenna (eds) *Biological Neural Networks in Invertebrate Neuroethology and Robotics*, pp. 199–225. Academic Press, Cambridge, MA.

Moeller, A. P. (1988) False alarm calls as a means of resource usurpation in the great tit *Parus major*. *Ethology*, 79: 25–30.

Moore, B. R. (1992) Avian movement imitation and a new form of mimicry: tracing the evolution of a complex form of learning. *Behaviour*, 122: 231–263.

Muller, R. (1996) A quarter of a century of place cells. *Neuron*, 17: 813–822.

Munn, C. A. (1986) Birds that "cry wolf". *Nature*, 319: 143–145.

Nicolai, J. (1964) Der Brutparasitismus der Viduinae als ethologisches Problem. Prägungsphänomene als Faktoren der Rassen und Artbildung. *Zeitschrift für Tierpsychologie*, 21: 129–204.

Nottebohm, F. (1970) Ontogeny of bird song. *Science*, 167: 948–956.

Packer, C. and Pusey, A. E. (1985) Asymmetric contests in social mammals: respect, manipulation and age-specific aspects. In P. J. Greenwood and M. Slatkin (eds) *Evolution, Essays in Honour of John Maynard Smith*, pp. 173–186. Cambridge University Press, Cambridge.

Payne, R. B. (1973) Behavior, mimetic songs and song dialects, and relationships of the parasitic indigobirds (*Vidua*) of Africa. *Ornithological Monographs*, 11: 1–333.

Pearce, J. M. (1997) *Animal Learning and Cognition*. East Sussex, Psychology Press.

Pepperberg, I. M. (1998) The African grey parrot: how cognitive processing might affect allospecific vocal learning. In R. P. Balda, I. M. Pepperberg and A. C. Kamil (eds) *Animal Cognition in Nature*, pp. 381–410. Academic Press, San Diego.

Pepperberg, I. M. (1999) *The Alex Studies.* Harvard University Press, Cambridge, MA.

Pepperberg, I. M. (2001) Millennium review—avian cognitive abilities. *Bird Behavior,* 14: 51–70.

Pierce, J. D. (1986) A review of tool use in insects. *Florida Entomologist,* 69: 95–104.

Plotkin, H. (1997) *Evolution in Mind. An Introduction to Evolutionary Psychology.* Penguin, London.

Pravosudov, V. V. and de Kort, S. R. (2006) Is the Western scrub-jay (*Aphelocoma california*) really an underdog among food-caching corvids when it comes to hippocampal volume and food caching propensity? *Brain, Behavior and Evolution,* 513, online.

Premack, D. and Woodruff, G. (1978) Does the chimpanzee have a theory of mind? *Behavioural and Brain Sciences,* 1: 515–26.

Price, J. J. (1998) Family- and sex-specific vocal traditions in a cooperatively breeding songbird. *Proceedings of the Royal Society of London B,* 265: 497–502.

Reader, S. M. and Laland, K. N. (eds) (2003) *Animal Innovation.* Oxford University Press, Oxford.

Rendell, L. and Whitehead, H. (2001) Culture in whales and dolphins. *Behavioral and Brain Sciences,* 24: 308–382.

Rogers, L. J. and Kaplan, G. (eds) (2004) *Comparative Vertebrate Cognition.* Kluwer Academic/Plenum Publishers, New York.

Roth, G. and Wullimann, M. F. (eds) (2001) *Brain Evolution and Cognition.* Wiley, New York.

Roth, E. D., Lutterschmidt, W. I. and Wilson, D. A. (2006) Relative medial and dorsal cortex volume in relation to sex differences in spatial ecology of a snake population. *Brain, Behavior and Evolution,* 67: 103–110.

Rüppell, G. (1969) Eine "Lüge" als gerichtete Mitteilung beim Eisfuchs (*Alopex lagopus* L.). *Zeitschrift für Tierpsychologie,* 26: 371–374.

Salwiczek, L. (2001) Grundzüge der Memtheorie. In W. Wickler and L. Salwiczek (eds) *Wie wir die Welt erkennen,* pp. 119–201. Verlag Karl Alber, Freiburg.

Salwiczek, L. H. and Wickler, W. (2004) Birdsong: an evolutionary parallel to human language. *Semiotica,* 151: 163–182.

Salwiczek, L. H. and Wickler, W. (2005) The shaping of animals' minds. *Interaction Studies,* 6: 393–411.

Schultz, G. W. (1982) Soil dropping behavior of the pavement ant *Tetranorium-caespitum* (Hymenoptera: Formicidae) against the alkali bee *Nomia melanderi* (Hymenoptera: Halictidae). *Journal of the Kansas Entomological Society,* 55: 277–282.

Seibt, U. and Wickler, W. (1972) Individuen-Erkennen und Partnerbevorzugung bei der Garnele *Hymenocera picta* Dana. *Naturwissenschaften,* 59: 40–41.

Seibt, U., Wickler, W., Kleindienst, H.-U. and Sonnenschein, E. (2002) Structure, geography and origin of dialects in the traditive song of the forest weaver *Ploceus bicolor sclateri* in Natal, S.Africa. *Behaviour,* 139: 1237–1265.

Shettleworth, S. J. (1994) Biological approaches to the study of learning. In N. J. Mackintosh (ed.) *Animal Learning and Cognition,* pp. 185–219. Academic Press, San Diego.

Shettleworth, S. J. (1998) *Cognition, Evolution, and Behavior.* Oxford University Press, New York.

Sivinski, J. (1989) Mushroom body development in nymphalid butterflies: a correlate to learning? *Journal of Insect Behaviour,* 2: 277–283.

Smolker, R., Richards, A., Connor, R., Mann, J. and Berggren, P. (1997) Sponge-carrying by Indian Ocean bottlenose dolphins: possible tool-use by a delphinid. *Ethology,* 103: 454–465.

Stanford, C. B., Wallis, J., Mpongo, E. and Goodall, J. (1994) Hunting decisions in wild chimpanzees. *Behaviour,* 131: 1–18.

Sternberg, R. J. (1985) *Beyond IQ.* Cambridge University Press, Cambridge.

Taborsky, M. (1984) Broodcare helpers in the cichlid fish *Lamprologus brichardi*: their costs and benefits. *Animal Behaviour,* 32: 1236–1252.

Tarsitano, M. S. and Andrew, R. (1999) Scanning and route selection in the jumping spider *Portia labiata. Animal Behaviour,* 58: 255–265.

Tebbich, S., Taborsky, M., Fessl, B. and Blomqvist, D. (2001) Do woodpecker finches acquire tool-use by social learning? *Proceedings of the Royal Society of London B,* 268: 2189–2193.

Tebbich, S. and Bshary, R. (2004) Cognitive abilities related to tool use in the woodpecker finch, *Cactospiza pallida. Animal Behaviour,* 67: 689–697.

Thouless, C. R., Fanshawe, J. H. and Bertram, B. C. R. (1989) Egyptian vultures *Neophron percnopterus* and ostrich *Struthio camelus* eggs: the origin of stone-throwing behaviour. *Ibis,* 131: 9–15.

Tomback, D. F. (1980) How nutcrackers find their seed stores. *Condor,* 82: 10–19.

Tomback, D. F. (1982) Dispersal of whitebark pine seeds by Clark's nutcracker: a mutualism hypothesis. *Journal of Animal Ecology,* 51: 451–467.

Tulving, E. (1983) *Elements of Episodic Memory.* Oxford University Press, New York.

Tulving, E. and Markowitsch, H. J. (1998) Episodic and declarative memory: role of the hippocampus. *Hippocampus,* 8: 198–204.

Tyack, P. L. (1997) Development and social functions of signature whistles in bottlenose dolphins *Tursiops truncatus. Bioacoustics,* 8: 21–46.

Van der Wall, S. B. and Balda, R. P. (1977) Coadaptations of the Clark's nutcracker and the pinon pine for efficient seed harvest and dispersal. *Ecological Monographs,* 47: 89–111.

van Schaik, C. P., Ancrenaz, M., Borgen, G. *et al.* (2003) Orangutan cultures and the evolution of material culture. *Science,* 299: 102–105.

Vickrey, C. and Neuringer, A. (2000) Pigeon reaction time, Hick's law, and intelligence. *Psychonomic Bulletin and Review,* 7: 284–291.

Visalberghi, E., Fragaszy, D. M. and Savage-Rumbaugh, E. S. (1995) Performance in a tool-using task by common chimpanzees (*Pan troglodytes*), bonobos (*Pan paniscus*), an orangutan (*Pongo pygmaeus*), and capuchin monkeys (*Cebus apella*). *Journal of Comparative Psychology,* 109: 52–60.

von Frisch, K. (1965) *Tanzsprache und Orientierung der Bienen*. Springer-Verlag, Berlin.

Warner, R. R. (1988) Traditionality of mating site preferences in a coral reef fish. *Nature*, 335: 719–721.

Warner, R. R. (1990) Resource assessment versus traditionality in mating site determination. *American Naturalist*, 135: 205–217.

Weir, A. A.S., Chappell, J. and Kacelnik, A. (2002) Shaping of hooks in New Caledonian crows. *Science*, 297: 981.

Whitehead, H. (2003) *Sperm Whales. Social Evolution in the Ocean*. The University of Chicago Press, Chicago.

Whiten, A., Goodall, J., McGrew, W. C. *et al.* (1999) Cultures in chimpanzees. *Nature*, 399: 682–685.

Wickler, W. (1988) *I dialetti degli animali*. Bollati Boringhieri, Turin.

Wilson, D. S. (1980) *The Natural Selection of Populations and Communities*. Benjamin Cunnings, Mello Park.

Workman, L. and Reader, W. (2004) *Evolutionary Psychology. An Introduction*. Cambridge University Press, Cambridge.

Wynne, C. D. L. (2001) *Animal Cognition*. Palgrave, New York

Zentall, T. R., Sutton, J. E. and Sherburne, L. M. (1996) True imitative learning in pigeons. *Psychological Science*, 7: 343–346.

Zuberbühler, K. (2003) Referential signalling in non-human primates: cognitive precursors and limitations for the evolution of language. *Advances in the Study of Behaviour*, 33: 265–307.

CHAPTER 9

Culture in primates and other animals

Carel P. van Schaik

9.1. Defining culture

Mention the word 'culture' and the image conjured up in most people's minds is one of an elegantly dressed elite enjoying classical music or visiting the art museum. But culture is much more than art, music and cherished traditions—it also encompasses basic subsistence techniques, technology and of course language. Indeed, culture affects how we do things, and perhaps even how we think. For many people, culture also has a normative component, prescribing the acceptable and desired behaviours of a member of a given society. Culture, then, is almost synonymous with being human, and may be our most successful adaptation. Little wonder that most definitions in cultural anthropology, the discipline that invented the concept of culture, implicitly or explicitly consider it a phenomenon uniquely human (McGrew, 1998).

In its present form, culture is indeed unique to our own species. No other species produces artefacts anywhere near as complex as we do, or manipulates symbols that convey arbitrary, but very deeply held, meanings, or developed rituals and institutions based on these symbols that provide moral prescriptions for the behaviour of the members of a given society. Yet, ever since Darwin (1871), evolutionary biologists insist that every unique feature in any species has its antecedents, a foundation upon which it is built. Where is this foundation for human culture to be found?

A broader, biological definition of culture would argue that it contains socially transmitted innovations (Imanishi, 1952, cited in de Waal, 2001; Kummer, 1971). Social transmission is critical for any definition, because it creates heritability, the passing on of traits to the next generation, in a fundamentally new way: through behavioural induction rather than genetic prescription. Many definitions of culture are silent on exactly what is being transmitted socially. Socially transmitted information about the environment, such as the location of food ('public information'), is probably the simplest form, but the potential for culture is greatest when the social transmission concerns innovations, because it may produce both geographic variation and cumulative cultural change, where innovations gradually increase in complexity.

This definition is broad enough to encompass both animal and human culture, without of course denying the abyss that separates human culture from that of animals. Here, I will first examine the mechanism of social transmission, social learning, then examine the source of culture, innovation, and finally discuss evolutionary aspects.

9.2. Social learning

Social learning, or socially mediated learning, is learning under the influence of conspecifics (Fragaszy and Perry, 2003). The nature of this influence can vary widely, from the traces or smells left behind by the activities of con-specifics, to attraction to the spots visited, or stimuli attended to by others, to copying of novel actions of experts that are carefully observed.

The key advance due to social learning is that the naïve individual is made aware of some pos-sibility by the presence of a conspecific, i.e. its attention is selectively drawn to some object, location or stimulus, allowing it to learn about a situation or the affordances of an object that it might otherwise have ignored altogether (local or stimulus enhancement). Social learning therefore does not need to involve copying of behaviour patterns, because the naïve animal often invents the same new behavioural skills independently. Some forms, however, do involve direct observation: copying of goals or outcomes, often referred to as emulation, or of the actual actions, usually called imitation, or some mix. These observational forms of social learning are more likely to be linked to innova-tions rather than mere information, but one must be careful to infer their presence. For instance, the famous opening of milk-bottle tops by blue tits can be induced in naïve birds by the mere presence of opened bottles (Sherry and Galef, 1984).

Some have argued that there are no special mechanisms involved in social learning, and that it is just selective attention (Fragaszy and Perry, 2003). That may be true for most, but almost certainly not all, mechanisms, and it is generally assumed that those forms that involve observations of behaviour patterns or outcomes rely on specialized cell types. Thus, mirror neu-rons in the pre-motor cortex of macaques fire not only when a particular act is performed, but also when the individual sees another engage in the same act; interestingly, if an object is moved by an actor, the neurons fire too, but when the object moves in exactly the same way, but with-out the involvement of an actor, they do not (Gallese *et al.*, 1996).

Vocal learning is a special class of social learn-ing; it is widespread in birds and a few mammals (e.g. cetaceans, humans), but its ability does not show any clear correlation with that of social learning of actions, perhaps because it depends on special modules in the brain. We will concen-trate here on non-vocal social learning.

Simple kinds of social learning are presumably quite common. Most evidence for social learning in nature can be explained by these non-obser-vational kinds of social learning: what the naïve animal learns it could have learned on its own, but it would have taken longer. However, for other kinds some observation is needed. Alarm calls tend to be functionally referential, in that different call types refer to different classes of predators to whom differential responses are adaptive. The ability to produce each of these alarm calls is innate, but the nature of the elicit-ing stimuli is socially learned through observa-tional conditioning, often with a high degree of preparedness, as shown by elegant experiments (see examples in Galef and Laland, 2005), and by natural experiments (e.g. Fichtel and van Schaik, 2006). The mate-copying behaviour that may be common in numerous species (Danchin *et al.*, 2004) is another common context for observa-tional conditioning.

Opinions about the presence of observational forms of social learning have swung wildly. Until the 1980s, it was generally agreed that many animals were capable of the most complex form of observational learning (imitation), encapsulated in the adage 'monkey see, monkey do.' However, scepticism spread when rigorous studies failed to find evidence for imitation even in apes and after it was noted that some of the classic examples in monkeys and birds had sim-pler explanations. The most recent wave of stud-ies over the past 10 years, however, has reinstated apes as imitators, along with several other taxa from monkeys and ravens to dolphins and even cephalopods (Whiten *et al.*, 2004). Over the last few years, most observers have come to agree that animals that learn by obser-vation use a whole array of social learning tech-niques, as well as individual practice of parts that are by necessity unobservable. Thus, active inference of functions plays a major role, even if animals 'just' imitate.

9.3. **The acquisition of culture**

While there has been much work on revealing the mechanisms of social learning, much less is known about the contexts in which it is deployed and why it is done at all (Laland, 2004). Most cul-tural variants are learned by young animals rather than by adults. In many species, young behave as if they were apprentices: following their mother or other caretakers around with intense curiosity, and paying special attention when difficult skills are being demonstrated. Foraging skills are often learned because the infant scrounges partly processed foods from the mother (e.g. in rats: Terkel, 1996). Thus, most skill transfer is from parents (vertical transmission) or helpers (oblique transmission) to young, with no examples of active transfer among peers (horizontal transmission). Perhaps the most striking feature of species with extensive cultural repertoires, such as great apes, is that adults continue to be interested in, and capable of, social learning (e.g. Whiten *et al.*, 2004).

If there is a clear asymmetry in skill or knowledge, as between adult (parent or helper) and immature, it is obvious why social learning happens: the expert knows something the youngster does not. In chimpanzees, immatures selectively attend to the behaviour of older experts and ignore the behaviour of peers or younger infants (Matsuzawa *et al.*, 2001). Psychologically, this means that the naïve individual looks at the expert as a role model, applying a so-called model-based bias (Henrich and McElreath, 2003). Where adults continue to learn socially, this bias may also extend toward successful or prestigious group members. An alternative transmission rule is that an animal simply adopts whatever behaviour is demonstrated most commonly, or is demonstrated by the largest number of individuals. At this stage, there is no evidence for animals that such conformity is more than just a passive byproduct of the tendency to adopt the most commonly demonstrated form, rather than a socially imposed norm (as in humans). Finally, it is possible that the naïve animal simply decides whether or not to adopt some novel variant simply on the basis of how well it likes it (content bias). This is evident for the simplest variants, involving food choice or predator recognition, but may also be relevant where learners carefully evaluate a new feeding skill.

There is generally no need for active teaching (Caro and Hauser, 1992) on the part of the adults. At best, the mother modifies the situation in such a way that the learning of the offspring is facilitated (opportunity teaching or scaffolding). However, although some have suggested that active teaching is limited to humans, there are some indications for it, from chimpanzees to ants (Boesch, 1991; Franks and Richardson, 2006), suggesting that parents or caretakers adjust their behaviour to the needs of their charges. Moreover, experiments in multiple species have suggested that adults chase immatures away from food or sites that have become dangerous, even in species with very limited evidence for social learning (but see Galef *et al.*, 2005). The irony is that teaching may also have been overestimated in humans. The ethnological literature on hunter-gatherers is remarkably silent on the teaching of skills; most skill transfer is in the form of apprenticeships. Where teaching does seem to be important, and where language plays an essential role, is in the transmission of the tribe's norms and myths.

9.4. Culture in nature

The mechanistic aspects of social learning have predominantly been studied in laboratory conditions, which allow control over exposure history and conditions. However, no matter how ingenious the laboratory studies, they cannot tell us what is happening in the wild. The abilities may be a byproduct of other processes, or may be an essential component of the animals' lives. We must turn to the wild to answer these basic questions. Yet, although the Japanese zoologist Kinji Imanishi (1952, cited in de Waal, 2001) drew attention to the possibility that animals have the basics of culture over half a century ago, field studies remained remarkably rare for several decades. The reason is that studying culture in nature faces major obstacles (Galef, 1992). Only rarely can we demonstrate convincingly that an animal we observe is inventing some new trick rather than simply using a well-remembered but rarely practised habit. Neither can we ever prove to everyone's satisfaction that she learned a new skill from another group member who already had it rather than figured it out all by herself. On the other hand, while we can show that animals in the laboratory are capable of observational forms of social learning, such studies tell us nothing about culture in nature: neither what it is generally about nor how much of it is there. Thus, studies in the laboratory and in nature are complementary and thus both necessary.

The usual trigger for considering culture in an animal species is the documentation of geographical variation in behaviour, in cases where local adaptation through natural selection of mutant genotypes is less plausible. Ideally, one then takes the animals into the laboratory and studies the social transmission of innovations experimentally to control for ecological and genetic factors, as done so elegantly for black rats feeding on pine cones (Terkel, 1996). Alternatively, one exchanges animals or entire populations between sites (Laland and Hoppitt, 2003). However, we should not count on many of these experiments being performed in the near future. For many species, such experiments would not only be illegal, they would also introduce massive confounding effects among animals that live in stable societies with individualized relationships. On the other hand, more systematic use can be made of the inadvertent experiments created by reintroduction programmes.

Where field studies must remain descriptive, they need a heuristic to demonstrate that a behavioural variant has a cultural basis. Most commonly used is the geographic method, also called the method of elimination (Boesch, 1996; Whiten et al., 1999; van Schaik, 2003), which consists of various steps. First, the geographic variation must be of the all-or-nothing variety, with the variant being common wherever it occurs, consistent with its spread and maintenance by social learning. It also helps if the variant is adopted by maturing individuals wherever it is found, indicating intergenerational transfer. The second step is to eliminate alternative explanations that produce the same spatial pattern but do not involve social learning. An ecological explanation would claim that all individuals exposed to a particular set of habitat features independently converge on the same skill. A genetic explanation would argue that all individuals in a particular region have a strong genetic predisposition to develop the behaviour, implying that the behaviour is not a clear innovation that must be socially learned. This would generally lead to clear-cut geographic clusters, whose boundaries coincide with subspecies boundaries or long-term dispersal barriers.

Although the geographic method has been criticized (e.g. Galef, 2003; Laland and Hoppitt, 2003; Fragaszy and Perry, 2003), it does generally serve to demonstrate the existence of culture, at least in the great apes that have been studied most extensively. It relies on identifying patterns produced by cultural processes. Its validity can therefore be evaluated by additional, more stringent tests. The patterns in the geographically variable behavioural variants should be consistent with a cultural explanation. If they always are, the likelihood that they are instead caused by convergent development of many individuals, without any social inputs, due to ecological conditions or genetic predisposition, becomes increasingly remote. Several such tests have been done. First, the variants that are most likely to be observed by others should be most likely to reach cultural status. This was indeed found for orangutans (van Schaik et al., 2006). Second, the presence of different variants on either side of a dispersal barrier in orang-utans (van Schaik 2004) is consistent with a cultural interpretation, although obviously a genetic explanation cannot be excluded. However, if the behaviour at issue is some tool use, the genetic explanation is less plausible, since in captivity all orangutans readily learn to use and make tools. Third, if culture is indeed responsible for the geographically patchy behavioural variants, then the number of local cultural variants should somehow be linked to the wealth of opportunities for social learning—how often or how well animals can observe others—and hence to measures of association and social tolerance. Sites in which individuals spend more time in association with others have greater cultural repertoires in both orangutans and chimpanzees (van Schaik et al., 2003). As expected, this effect was strongest for food-related variants, because acquiring feeding skills from somebody else must require more close-range observation than picking up some conspicuous communication signal. These tests underscore the validity of the geographic method to identify culture in nature.

Other non-experimental methods also exist. First, where multiple variants coexist within a population, one can show the operation of cultural transmission if one finds a strong correlation between a maturing individual's exposure to a variant and its subsequent adoption (cf. Perry et al., 2003). This correlation is most convincing if the exposure is to individuals who are not close kin. Second, documentation of the spread of newly minted innovations would seem to be an obvious and convincing approach to demonstrating the presence of social transmission in a particular population. Although this has been done in the past, various processes, including repeated independent innovations by individuals, produce very similar patterns of spread (Reader, 2004), thus making this method ineffective without additional information.

Use of the geographic method has suggested the widespread presence of cultural variation in chimpanzees (Whiten *et al.*, 1999), cetaceans (Rendell and Whitehead, 2001), orang-utans (van Schaik *et al.*, 2003), and capuchin monkeys (Perry *et al.*, 2003). However, the geographic method is conservative, in that it misses most behaviours that show a perfect correlation with ecological variables or genetic discontinuities, e.g. inclusion in the diet of a particular food item, even if they are dependent on social learning for their maintenance (cf. Humle and Matsuzawa, 2002). The emphasis on the absence of ecological or genetic influences is an attempt to attain the methodological cleanliness of a rigorous experiment in a situation where one cannot do a real experiment rather than a reflection of the real world. But, of course, this does not mean that genetics and ecology are irrelevant to culture. We must therefore expect to find that more geographic variation in behaviour is cultural than we know at present. Despite the recent surge of studies, however, it is perhaps more remarkable how little evidence we have for culture in nature. Why are there no examples from such well-studied animals as baboons, horses and great tits? Time will tell whether the current evidence for culture in animals is the tip of a giant iceberg, or whether animal culture is a mere molehill.

To turn to what we know about the content of animal culture in the wild, most cultural variants are simple because the innovations upon which they are based are simple, e.g. the recognition of a new food or a new predator, and hence the social-learning techniques needed to adopt them from others are simple too. Other variants represent more complex innovations, and thus generally require observational learning to be spread and maintained. Examples include skills related to subsistence, comfort, or social behaviour (e.g. extractive tool use or building roofs on a night nest, or coercing an unwilling female using a club, in great apes). Signal variants, to spread, definitely require observational or vocal learning, such as the various forms of kiss-squeaks found in orang-utans. Some signal variants show geographically varying meaning, and are thus symbolic. To date, there are only some tentative examples of those in chimpanzees (e.g. leaf clipping, described by Boesch, 1996).

In the end, cognitive abilities limit the complexity of both innovation and social learning, and thus the content and extent of cultural repertoires. The variants that are easily innovated and transmitted through simple mechanisms such as social facilitation or stimulus or local enhancement may be most widespread, although where innovations arise so easily we may not observe any geographic variation. As the cognitive complexity of the innovation increases, more dedicated mechanisms of social learning are required for social transmission. These make the most interesting cultural variants, because social transmission is likely to be essential for their spread and maintenance, and geographic variation almost inevitably arises.

Transmission pathways and dispersal together should determine the spatial patterning of culture (Whitehead *et al.*, 2002). If transmission is exclusively vertical, from mother to offspring, patchy geographic distribution is unlikely, because multiple cultural variants may coexist in the same region. At the other extreme, purely horizontal transmission should lead to large geographic homogeneity. Likewise, if animals are nomadic, no geographic clustering of variants is expected, whereas strong philopatric tendencies are more likely to produce such clusters. Where most transmission is vertical and mothers only care for offspring, strict female philopatry will tend to produce stronger geographic clustering. In general, birds may show greater spatial homogeneity if biparental care allows transmission by both parents. At present, however, these patterns are predicted rather than observed.

9.5. Innovation

Innovation is the ultimate source of all cultural change and of all geographic variation in behaviour that is maintained by social transmission.

The study of cultural systems must therefore include the study of innovation, although its systematic study is only just beginning.

An innovation is a solution to a novel problem or a novel solution to an old one (Kummer and Goodall, 1985; see also Reader and Laland, 2003). A 'solution to a novel problem' is often the result of some major environmental change, which nowadays is often human-induced. Such innovations may be based on innate predispositions in the response to external stimuli and may therefore arise in many individuals. As a result, they need not have cultural consequences. However, some of these solutions to novel problems may be rare. Thus, only 3% of wild rats tested by Terkel (1996) spontaneously adopted pinecone stripping, a skill that was customary in a particular local population. Likewise, the sweet potato washing and wheat sluicing induced in Japanese macaques in the 1950s by provisioning on the beach of their forest island (Kawai, 1965) were both invented by one and the same individual. The second class of innovations (novel solution to old problem) is bound to be rare, because there are no obvious new stimuli or new affordances that predictably elicit the novel behaviour. Thus, on average, they may also have a richer cognitive component, and are likely to spread through social transmission rather than parallel innovation.

Because spontaneous innovation under changing conditions is rare, we know most about innovations in response to novel conditions. Individuals and species vary in their tendency to innovate. Within species, individual attributes, ecological conditions and the social structure are thought to play a role. Individual variation in temperament, summarized in contrasts such as bold-shy or reactive-proactive, does affect responses to novel objects (e.g. Marchetti and Drent, 2000) and may therefore also affect innovation. Social position may also be relevant (Reader and Laland, 2001): low-ranking or peripheralized members of society may have the greatest incentive to innovate because they are excluded from limiting resources. The influence of ecological conditions parallels this effect of social position. The most plausible and best-supported idea is that exploration and thus innovation is favoured when the regular behavioural routines no longer yield their expected benefits. There is less evidence for the alternative that well-fed animals with much spare time are more innovative. Finally, the effect of social structure on innovation has not been studied, but the finding that object exploration is more common in species with tolerant social structures (Thierry, 1994) suggests such an influence.

Different species also vary considerably in the tendency to explore novel objects (Glickman and Sroges, 1966). By and large, this tendency also covaries with the tendency to innovate, as estimated from reports in the literature on novel solutions (mostly innovations of the first kind: e.g. Lefebvre *et al.*, 1997). Moreover, this tendency is correlated with relative brain size and how well animals solve problems that are formulated in such a way that differences in perception, motor abilities and motivation are controlled for: innovative species tend to be intelligent species (Lefebvre *et al.*, 1997; Reader and Laland, 2002). These same species are also more likely to be successful colonizers (Sol *et al.*, 2005), and to show social learning (Reader and Laland, 2002), and thus to be cultural.

This work, however, is plagued by the same problem as that on social learning. We can study innovation in the laboratory by eliciting it in novel situations, but systematic observational study of the innovation process in the field will remain difficult, and thus our insight into the individual characteristics that facilitate innovation, such as dominance rank, age, sex, and personality, will in the end stem mainly from experiments.

The content of innovation is not open-ended. Every species can be thought of as having an innovation space that contains all potential innovations. Given the species-specific predispositions, some innovations are much more likely than others, and species show predictable differences in their innovation repertoires. Take one of the most bizarre behaviours to reach cultural status in chimpanzees, medicinal plant use. Among the best-studied forms is whole-leaf swallowing, in which a leaf of a plant species with very rough leaves is carefully brought into the mouth, and then swallowed whole, without any chewing, although it may have been folded. Leaf swallowing is occasionally seen in all African great apes, but the plant species used for it may vary from site to site (Huffman and Hirata, 2004). In each of the three captive groups of chimpanzees tested, at least one individual accepted the sandpapery leaf and swallowed it, although none of the animals was likely to be familiar with it. This ready acceptance strongly suggests a genetic predisposition for this behaviour. Others subsequently learned it from the leaf-swallowers, with the pattern of spread reflecting the social network. This kind of innovation—swallowing rough leaves without chewing—may therefore arise rather easily, and therefore rather frequently, in natural populations. Copying behaviour then may serve to reinforce and maintain the choice of species selected more or less accidentally by the first animal to try. The familiarity with particular actions or the properties of objects may then facilitate new innovations that build on these. Tool use, for instance, tends to come in clusters, at least in great apes.

9.6. The evolutionary origins of animal culture

How did the cultural capacity arise? The intuitively obvious answer is that it saves the naïve animal the trouble of time-consuming and risky individual learning, suggesting it is a straightforward correlate of gregariousness. However, Rogers (1988; see also Boyd and Richerson, 1985; Laland, 2004) suggested this need not be so. Social learning is most beneficial when it is rare: when all rely on taking information from others, the quality of this information will inevitably deteriorate to the point of becoming useless. However, this conclusion applies to (perishable) information rather than (permanent) skills that are subject to individual evaluation by new adopters (Galef, 1995), and to horizontal transmission among adult individuals, rather than vertical transmission. Thus, the social learning ability most relevant to culture (acquiring innovations, as opposed to obtaining public information through 'eavesdropping') may have evolved for a very mundane purpose: skill learning by immatures. In such a context, social learning is inevitably more efficient than individual learning and nearly cost-free in that one is unlikely to learn worthless features from one's parent.

Most cases of social transmission in nature may concern the acquisition during development of species-wide foraging patterns or predator recognition (cf. Galef and Giraldeau, 2001), with its main effect one of speeding up their acquisition. In most species, the learning processes involved need not be any different from the ones an animal would use when alone (witness the pinecone-stripping rats), but such social learning may be extremely common in nature. We only tend to regard social learning as special because we are so used to cognitive tests in laboratories, where animals (often adults) are presented with puzzles they must solve on their own. In nature, however, much of the exploration and learning by immatures is socially guided: infants of the slower-developing taxa, such as primates, are intensely curious about everything the mother does, particularly with regard to feeding. The importance of such apprenticeships (Matsuzawa et al., 2001) is beautifully illustrated by the sex difference in acquisition rate of termite fishing in Gombe chimpanzees, where the highly attentive female infants use techniques more similar to the ones demonstrated to them and reach adult-level proficiency years ahead of the sons, whose attention tends to be directed elsewhere (Lonsdorf et al., 2004).

At least in mammals, slow developers also grow much of their brain after birth, and their brains tend to be large, relative to others with faster development (Ross and Jones, 1999). Brain development involves practice, exploration and play, with both objects and social partners. Skills in large-brained animals require practice to be fully expressed—as shown by the deprivation experiments of the mid-twentieth century, there are few instinctive behaviours that simply mature and emerge perfectly formed. On the other hand, some rapidly developing species may require little social input to acquire adult-level skills. This contrast can be illustrated by developmental differences between aye-ayes (*Daubentonia madagascariensis*) and ruffed lemurs (*Varecia variegata*), both similar-sized lemurs that leave their young in a nest (Krakauer, 2005). Aye-ayes show species-specific but complex extractive foraging technique, which involves a sequence of tapping and listening, gnawing a narrow hole upon acoustic location of wood-boring prey, and finally extracting the larva using their elongated third digit. Immatures develop very slowly. They build up this skill by deploying a mix of individual practice and attention to their mother's foraging, expressed in selective curiosity toward tap foraging and examination of adult feeding traces. They avoid novel foods unless eaten first by their mother. Parents become increasingly tolerant of food-motivated offspring, allowing them to scrounge food as they acquire their foraging skills. Ruffed lemur infants, in contrast, develop rapidly, show no special interest in foraging adults, and individually explore novel foods without much hesitation.

Slow growth and development, and hence years of close association with the mother, as seen in great apes, cetaceans or elephants, form the perfect setting for developing immatures to learn not only the regular, species-wide skills but also the locally cultural innovations (i.e. culture). Under these conditions, it is also possible for selection to have favoured the evolution of special social-learning skills that involve direct observation, such as imitation, that enable the young to learn these more complex skills, suggesting that the more advanced forms of social learning evolved in this context. Routine deployment of observational social learning may produce a watershed in cultural evolution, because cognitively complex innovations that involve fundamentally novel actions can now be acquired by alert youngsters.

How can this vertical transmission system evolve into full-blown culture? Evolution can have proceeded in two steps. First, if the novel skills learned in this way have a strong enough positive impact on fitness, some form of buffering can easily evolve. Kin selection is expected to favour social tolerance by relatives, be they older siblings or relatives of the mother, whenever the costs of having a distracting poky infant around while feeding are unlikely to outweigh the benefits to their kin (the curious immatures soon learn not to steal food from individuals other than their mother). Second, if innovations arise commonly and adults roam widely or the environment is very heterogeneous in space and time, we expect selection to favour the continuation of such tolerance during adulthood and towards non-relative friends through mutualistic benefits. A tolerant social structure is more

amenable to social learning (Coussi-Korbel and Fragaszy, 1995; van Schaik, 2003), and can be seen as both evolutionary cause and consequence of culture. The origin of extensive culture, then, requires that innovations improve fitness, are frequent, and can be learned socially. All of these conditions are more likely to be met where animals are intelligent, i.e. innovate frequently, and use observational learning.

9.7. The impact of culture on intelligence

Innovation is the source of all culture, so there must be some connection between innovative abilities (and thus exploratory tendencies and intelligence) and social learning abilities. Indeed, the species for which we have evidence for culture are obviously among the more intelligent species in nature (Reader and Laland, 2002). But is this connection a coincidence, or is it the result of a predictable evolutionary process?

Developmentally, there is a connection between rich environmental inputs and cognitive performance once adult, as suggested by numerous deprivation experiments. Environmental inputs that are social in nature are much more effective in leading to learning, and one would therefore predict that animals growing up in populations with richer opportunities for social learning become more intelligent adults. As predicted, we see a positive correlation between the complexity of innovations in a population and the degree of tolerant proximity in orang-utans and chimpanzees (van Schaik 2006), both species in which mothers have a variable tendency toward solitary foraging.

The same connection between culture and intelligence may also arise during evolution. It is not easy for natural selection to directly favour improvements in innovativeness, i.e. intelligence. Imagine the extreme case of no contact between generations. An individual that made a major, fitness-enhancing innovation is likely to leave more offspring than one that did not, but because only the capacity is inherited and not the actual invention, chances are that the offspring will never acquire the special skill. As soon as there is contact between generations (vertical transmission), the special skill will not disappear, if the social learning is such that offspring are likely to acquire it. Without social learning, then, rarely invented fitness-enhancing skills will not remain in a lineage, but social learning makes it possible for innovativeness to bring lasting fitness benefits. More buffering is provided if, in addition to one parent, other knowledgeable, and thus usually older, individuals act as models to naïve youngsters. Thus, selection on innovative abilities is only expected when social learning is common. Indeed, selection on social-learning abilities will usually be more efficient than selection on innovative abilities (van Schaik and Pradhan, 2003), but because of the cognitive overlap between the cognitively rich forms of innovation and social learning, selection on social learning automatically also enhances innovative abilities. This argument suggests that the taxonomic correlation between intelligence and culture has arisen because culture based on socially transmitted skills favours selection on cognitive abilities, which improve both the innovation and the acquisition through social learning of valuable skills.

9.8. The origins of human culture

The argument from evolutionary continuity suggests that human cultures are in some way connected to those found among great apes. Now that great-ape cultures have been documented in some detail, we see two main differences. The first is that human skills and the artefacts they produce show strong evidence of cumulative cultural evolution, in that many of the skills or artefacts routinely acquired during development by humans are far beyond the cognitive range of normal individual development, i.e. individual humans in most societies would be very unlikely to invent many of the skills or artefacts they use routinely on a daily basis. The presence of such skills is referred to as the ratchet effect (Tomasello, 1999). In contrast, the skills of wild great apes tend to be within the cognitive reach of individuals, i.e. the skills are not more complex than a reasonably intelligent individual great ape could be expected to invent in its own lifetime, with the possible exception of nut cracking using stone tools in chimpanzees. Thus, even the technologically simplest human foragers have

many more and vastly more complex skills, as expressed in artefacts well beyond the range produced by any great ape. For instance, the most complex great-ape tools, the hammer-and-anvil, with the anvil supported by a prop, is still far removed from even fairly early hominin tools such as Oldowan flakes in terms of the number of steps involved in production or the cognitive complexity as estimated by the degree of embedding in an organizational hierarchy. Moreover, there are very few examples of 'tool sets', i.e. use of more tools in integrated sequence in a single task (but see Sanz et al., 2004).

The second major difference is that human culture is characterized by extensive use of symbols (Kuper, 1994; Tuttle, 2001) that have a moral connotation and often serve as ethnic markers. Use of symbols among humans is incomparably richer than among great apes, where it is perhaps present in some very basic form in the odd cultural variant (e.g. leaf clipping in chimpanzees: Boesch, 1996). This second difference focuses on social organization, institutions and social norms.

Given the ubiquity of culture in great apes, it seems fair to assume that the first hominins started out with the general great ape form of culture (van Schaik, 2004). Hence, the major differences must have arisen during hominin evolution, most likely after the origin of the genus *Homo*, which coincides with occupation of the open savanna habitat, anatomical and physiological specialization on exclusive bipedality and long-distance walking and running, as well as far stronger reliance on meat and underground tubers (Klein, 2000). This lineage gave rise to us, so different from the rest of the great ape clade that we had to wait for modern molecular biology and a slew of recent fossil discoveries to convince scholars and lay people alike that we were indeed members of the same clade. What spawned the cultural spiral may well have been the reliance on tolerance-enhancing cooperation to procure and defend food that could be shared, relying on cunning and technology in this new niche rather than on size, speed or strength. Culture, therefore, may well have been the essential ingredient that set us on the way toward humanity.

The unusual status of humans among our fellow great apes indicates that cultural evolution has become a second major force in evolution. It is much faster, albeit less reliable, because the equivalent of mutation, the innovation, is often directed rather than random, and usually beneficial rather than usually deleterious, and because transmission can be immediate rather than through differential reproduction. Cultural evolution therefore can take a population to local adaptation much faster and even in the face of migration that would normally swamp any local adaptations. On the other hand, culture is not necessarily stable. Breakdown of social organization means interruption of transmission, even if only for a single generation, and thus utter loss of any and all cultural achievements. It can also misfire spectacularly, as is perhaps evident in the demographic transition or ballooning membership of suicide sects, suicide bombing, or celibacy, where influential role models spread maladaptive habits.

References

Boesch, C. (1991) Teaching among wild chimpanzees. *Animal Behaviour*, 41: 530–532.

Boesch, C. (1996) Three approaches for assessing chimpanzee culture. In A. E. Russon, K. A. Bard and S. T. Parker (eds) *Reaching into Thought: The Minds of the Great Apes*, pp. 404–429. Cambridge University Press, Cambridge.

Boyd, R. and Richerson, P. J. (1985) *Culture and the Evolutionary Process*. University of Chicago Press, Chicago.

Caro, T. M. and Hauser, M. D. (1992) Is there teaching in nonhuman animals? *Quarterly Review of Biology*, 67: 151–174.

Coussi-Korbel, S. and Fragaszy, D. M. (1995) On the relation between social dynamics and social learning. *Animal Behaviour*, 50: 1441–1453.

Danchin, E., Giraldeau, L.-A., Vallone, T. J. and Wagner, R. H. (2004) Public information: from nosy neighbors to cultural evolution. *Science*, 305: 487–491.

Darwin, C. (1871) *The Descent of Man and Selection in Relation to Sex*. Murray, London.

de Waal, F. B. M. (2001) *The Ape and the Sushi Master: Cultural Reflections by a Primatologist*. Basic Books, New York.

Fichtel, C. and van Schaik, C. P. (2006) Semantic differences in sifaka (Propithecus verreauxi) alarm calls: a reflection of genetic or cultural variants? *Ethology*, 112: 839–849.

Fragaszy, D. M. and Perry, S. (2003) Towards a biology of traditions. In D. M. Fragaszy and S. Perry (eds) *The Biology of Traditions: Models and Evidence*, pp. 1–32. Cambridge University Press, Cambridge.

Franks, N. R. and Richardson, T. (2006) Teaching in tandem-running ants: tapping into the dialogue between leader and follower reveals an unexpected social skill. *Nature*, 439: 153.

Galef, B. G., Jr (1992) The question of animal culture. *Human Nature*, 3: 157–178.

Galef, B. G., Jr (1995) Why behaviour patterns that animals learn socially are locally adaptive. *Animal Behaviour*, 49: 1325–1334.

Galef, B. G., Jr (2003) "Traditional" foraging behaviors of brown and black rats (*Rattus norvegicus* and *Rattus rattus*). In Fragaszy, D. M. and Perry, S. (eds) *The Biology of Traditions: Models and Evidence*, pp. 159–186. Cambridge University Press, Cambridge.

Galef, B. G., Jr and Giraldeau, L.-A. (2001) Social influences on foraging in vertebrates: causal mechanisms and adaptive functions. *Animal Behaviour*, 61: 3–15.

Galef, B. G. J. and Laland, K. N. (2005) Social learning in animals: empirical studies and theoretical models. *Bioscience*, 55: 489–499.

Galef, B. G. J., Whiskin, E. E. and Dewar, G. (2005) A new way to study teaching in animals: despite demonstrable benefits, rat dams do not teach their young what to eat. *Animal Behaviour*, 70: 91–96.

Gallese, V., Fadiga, L., Fogassi, L. and Rizzolatti, G. (1996) Action recognition in the premotor cortex. *Brain*, 119: 593–609.

Glickman, S. E. and Sroges, R. W. (1966) Curiosity in zoo animals. *Behaviour*, 26: 151–188.

Henrich, J. and McElreath, R. (2003) The evolution of cultural evolution. Evolutionary Anthropology [CHECK], 12: 123–135.

Huffman, M. A. and Hirata, S. (2004) An experimental study of leaf swallowing in captive chimpanzees: insights into the origin of a self-medicative behavior and the role of social learning. *Primates*, 45: 113–118.

Humle, T. and Matsuzawa, T. (2002) Ant-dipping among chimpanzees of Bossou, Guinea, and some comparisons with other sites. *American Journal of Primatology*, 58: 133–148.

Kawai, M. (1965) Newly-acquired pre-cultural behavior of the natural troop of Japanese monkeys on Koshima Islet. *Primates*, 6: 1–30.

Klein, R. G. (2000) Archeology and the evolution of human behavior. *Evolutionary Anthropology* [CHECK], 9: 17–36.

Krakauer, E. (2005) Development of Aye-aye (*Daubentonia madagascariensis*) foraging skills: independent exploration and social learning. PhD dissertation, Duke University, Durham, NC.

Kummer, H. (1971) *Primate Societies: Group Techniques of Ecological Adaptation*. AHM, Arlington Heights, IL.

Kummer, H. and Goodall, J. (1985) Conditions of innovative behaviour in primates. *Philosophical Transactions of the Royal Society of London*, B, 308: 203–214.

Kuper, A. (1994) *The Chosen Primate: Human Nature and Cultural Diversity*. Harvard University Press, Cambridge, MA.

Laland, K. N. (2004) Social learning strategies. *Learning & Behavior*, 32: 4–14.

Laland, K. N. and Hoppitt, W. (2003) Do animals have culture? *Evolutionary Anthropology*, 12: 150–159.

Lefebvre, L., Whittle, P., Lascaris, E. and Finkelstein, A. (1997) Feeding innovations and forebrain size in birds. *Animal Behaviour*, 53: 549–560.

Lonsdorf, E. V., Eberly, L. E. and Pusey, A. E. (2004) Sex differences in learning in chimpanzees. *Nature*, 428: 715–716.

Marchetti, C. and Drent, P. J. (2000) Individual differences in the use of social information in foraging by captive great tits. *Animal Behaviour*, 60: 131–140.

Matsuzawa, T., Biro, D., Humle, T., Inoue-Nakamura, N., Tonooka, R. and Yamakoshi, G. (2001) Emergence of culture in wild chimpanzees: education by master-apprenticeship. In T. Matsuzawa (ed.) *Primate Origins of Human Cognition and Behavior*, pp. 557–574. Springer, Tokyo.

McGrew, W. C. (1998) Culture in nonhuman primates? *Annual Review of Anthropology*, 27: 310–328.

Perry, S., Panger, M., Rose, L. M. *et al.* (2003) Traditions in wild white-faced capuchin monkeys. In D. M. Fragaszy and S. Perry (eds) *The Biology of Traditions: Models and Evidence*. Cambridge University Press, Cambridge, pp. 391–425.

Reader, S. M. (2004) Distinguishing social and asocial learning using diffusion dynamics. *Learning & Behavior*, 32: 90–104.

Reader, S. M. and Laland, K. N. (2001) Primate innovation: sex, age and social rank differences. *International Journal of Primatology*, 22: 787–805.

Reader, S. M. and Laland, K. N. (2002) Social intelligence, innovation, and enhanced brain size in primates. *Proceedings of the National Academy of Sciences of the USA*, 99: 4436–4441.

Reader, S. M. and Laland, K. N. (eds) (2003) Animal Innovation. Oxford University Press, Oxford.

Rendell, L. and Whitehead, H. (2001) Culture in whales and dolphins. *Behaviour Brain Science*, 24: 309–382.

Rogers, A. R. (1988) Does biology constrain culture? American Anthropologist, 90: 819–831.

Ross, C. and Jones, K. E. (1999) Socioecology and the evolution of primate reproductive rates. In P. C. Lee (ed.) *Comparative Primate Socioecology*, pp. 73–110. Cambridge University Press, Cambridge.

Sanz, C., Morgan, D. and Gulick, S. (2004) New insights into chimpanzees, tools, and termites from the Congo Basin. *American Naturalist*, 164: 567–581.

Sherry, D. F. and Galef, B. G., Jr (1984) Cultural transmission without imitation: milk bottle opening by birds. *Animal Behaviour*, 32: 937.

Sol, D., Duncan, R. P., Blackburn, T. M., Cassey, P. and Lefebvre, L. (2005) Big brains, enhanced cognition, and response of birds to novel environments. *Proceedings of the National Academy of Sciences of the USA*, 102: 5460–5465.

Terkel, J. (1996) Cultural transmission of feeding behavior in the black rat (Rattus rattus). In *Social Learning in Animals: The Roots of Culture*. Academic Press, San Diego, pp. 17–47. [EDS?]

Thierry, B. (1994) Social transmission, tradition and culture in primates: from the epiphenomenon to the phenomenon. *Techniques & Culture*, 23–24: 91–119.

Tomasello, M. (1999) *The Cultural Origins of Human Cognition*. Harvard University Press, Cambridge, MA.

Tuttle, R. (2001) Culture and traditional chimpanzees. *Current Anthropology*, [CHECK] 42:407–409.

van Schaik, C. P. (2003) Local traditions in orangutans and chimpanzees: social learning and social tolerance. In D. M. Fragaszy and S. Perry (eds) *The Biology of Traditions: Models and Evidence*, pp. 297–328. Cambridge University Press, Cambridge.

van Schaik, C. P. (2004) *Among Orangutans: Red Apes and the Rise of Human Culture*. Harvard University Press (Belknap), Cambridge, MA.

van Schaik, C. P. (2006) Why are some animals so smart? *Scientific American*, 294(4): 64–71.

van Schaik, C. P. and Pradhan, G. R. (2003) A model for tool-use traditions in primates: implications for the evolution of culture and cognition. *Journal of Human Evolution*, 44: 645–664.

van Schaik, C. P., Ancrenaz, M., Borgen, G. *et al.* (2003) Orangutan cultures and the evolution of material culture. *Science*, 299: 102–105.

van Schaik, C. P., van Noordwijk, M. A. and Wich, S. (2006) Innovation in wild Bornean orangutans (*Pongo pygmaeus wurmbii*). *Behaviour*, 7: 839–876.

Whitehead, H., Richerson, P. J. and Boyd, R. (2002) Cultural selection and genetic diversity in humans. *Selection*, 3: 115–125.

Whiten, A., Goodall, J., McGrew, W. C. *et al.* (1999) Cultures in chimpanzees. *Nature*, 399: 682–685.

Whiten, A., Horner, V., Litchfield, C. A. and Marshall-Pescini, S. (2004) How do apes ape? *Learning & Behavior*, 32: 36–52.

CHAPTER 10

Empathy, sympathy, and prosocial preferences in primates

Joan B. Silk

10.1. Introduction

Humans differ from most other animals, and from virtually all other primates, in the extent of our dependence on cooperation. In foraging societies, parents typically provide food for their offspring until they reach adulthood; men and women perform different tasks and share the proceeds of their labour; and food is exchanged among families within communities (Kaplan and Gurven, 2005). Humans are able to solve public goods problems, punish transgressors of social rules and moral norms, and create institutions that protect the welfare of the poor, the sick, and the aged (Richerson and Boyd, 2004). Humans do not limit altruism to family and close acquaintances. We donate to charity, give blood, vote, avoid littering, join political demonstrations, and participate in conservation initiatives. In a series of experiments devised by behavioural economists that have been performed in both developed and subsistence level societies around the world, people willingly sacrifice substantial monetary rewards in order to provide benefits to other individuals in strictly anonymous interactions (Fehr and Fischbacher, 2003, 2005; Henrich *et al.*, 2004). In humans, altruism seems to be at least partly based on empathy and genuine concern for the welfare of

others (Batson and Powell, 1998; Fehr and Fischbacher, 2003). Empathy and other-regarding sentiments are part of a system of moral emotions that guide our preferences and behavioural responses. We may also be motivated by a concern for reputation (Haley and Fessler, 2005), that makes us want others to think that we are generous, fair, or charitable.

Non-human primates also act altruistically, but the extent and deployment of altruism in primate groups is much more limited than it is in human societies. Within the primate order, a relatively small number of altruistic interactions has been described. The list includes grooming, food sharing, allo-maternal care, territorial defence, predator defence and deterrence, joint mate guarding, and coalitionary aggression. In most species, only a subset of these forms of altruism occurs. Moreover, altruistic interactions usually involve very small numbers of individuals (usually dyads) and are strongly biased by kinship (Chapais, 1992, 2001; Kapsalis, 2004; Silk, 2002, 2005a,b; Strier, 2004). There is some evidence for reciprocity among unrelated individuals, but these exchanges are generally restricted to short-term exchanges of low-cost commodities (T. H. Clutton-Brock, personal communication). The dynamics of cooperation in non-human primates may be driven by the benefits that individuals receive themselves, via inclusive fitness or reciprocity, not the benefits that they provide to others.

Differences in the deployment of altruism in human and non-human primate groups raise two different questions. We might ask: why are humans so altruistic? But given the obvious advantages humans gain by cooperating, we might also ask: why do other primates cooperate so little? Here, I consider some of the factors that may limit the extent of cooperation in non-human primate groups. In particular, I will focus on the evidence for the features that are associated with altruistic behaviour in humans: the capacity for empathy, the existence of moral sentiments, and the concern for the welfare of others.

Before we begin, it is important to clarify some terminological issues. Here, I define cooperation as "costly behavior performed by one individual that increases the payoff of others" (Boyd and Richerson, 2006). Cooperation is thus equivalent to the biological definition of altruism, and I use these terms interchangeably. I use the term 'prosocial' to refer to behaviour that increases the welfare of the recipient, regardless of the cost to the actor (Eisenberg and Mussen, 1995). I will distinguish between empathy (the ability to understand the feelings, motives, and thoughts of others and to appreciate the distinction between self and others) and sympathy (feelings of concern about the welfare of others). This definition of empathy corresponds to Preston and de Waal's (2002) concept of 'cognitive empathy'. While we often conflate empathy and sympathy, the two can be uncoupled (i.e. both teasing and torture involve empathy, but not sympathy). Thus, empathy is a necessary, but not sufficient, condition for sympathy.

10.2. **Evidence for empathy and sympathy**

The literature on empathy and sympathy consists of a number of anecdotes, descriptions of several types of common behaviours, and a very small number of systematic analyses and experiments. I describe these data in some detail below because I think it is important to evaluate the quality of the data that are available.

10.2.1. **Singular events**

Many of the anecdotes about empathy have been compiled and described elsewhere (O'Connell, 1995; de Waal, 1996; Preston and de Waal, 2002). O'Connell's sample was based on surveys completed by 16 scientists, 18 papers, and six books. From these sources, O'Connell (1995) extracted 171 "case studies" and 2252 instances of empathy or sympathy (she does not clearly distinguish between the two). The latter is the number that is often cited (e.g. Preston and de Waal, 2002). However, the sample size is inflated by repeated instances of the same type of behaviour and includes some types of behaviours that most other observers do not treat as evidence for empathy or sympathy. For example, O'Connell notes that her sample "contains 93 instances of reconciliation behaviour". Because O'Connell has not published a full description of her data set or the operational definitions that she used to assess the data that she compiled, it is difficult to evaluate the merits of her analysis.

One problem with all of these anecdotes is that they require interpretation and that interpretation is necessarily subjective. For example, consider the case of Binti Jua, the gorilla at the Brookfield Zoo who picked up and held a 3-year-old child that tumbled into her enclosure. How can we tell why the gorilla picked up the child that fell into her enclosure? She might have realized that the child was injured or in danger, and acted to protect it. This is certainly possible, and if this is the case then we might agree with Preston and de Waal's (2002) conclusion that her behaviour was motivated by empathy and sympathy. But suppose this gorilla had been coached to care for infants using a doll, something that is sometimes done when apes don't display appropriate maternal responses? If so, the gorilla might have been responding to the child as she had been trained to respond to the doll. Then, we would not conclude that the gorilla's response was based on understanding of the child's predicament or concern for its welfare. Furthermore, what if this gorilla's response was atypical, and was not observed in similar situations in other gorilla groups or by other individuals in the same group? To find this out, we would have to drop 100 children into gorilla enclosures.

For obvious reasons, this experiment will not be done, leaving us to speculate about why the gorilla picked up the child.

Another problem with these anecdotes is that they conflate empathy with sympathy. It is possible that the differences between the behaviour of monkeys and apes when a group member is injured are due to differences in concern for the welfare of others, not differences in their capacity for empathy. While there is good reason to suspect that the differences between monkeys and apes may reflect real differences in their cognitive abilities and the quality of their theories of mind (Hare *et al.*, 2000, 2001; Povinelli, 1992a,b; Tomasello and Call, 1997; Tomasello *et al.*, 2003), the anecdotes themselves do not help us to distinguish between these two possibilities.

Finally, the anecdotes suffer from the same problem that plagues all *ad libitum* data collection schemes—they are subject to various sorts of bias (Altmann, 1974). In this case, it seems plausible that observers may be more likely to notice and remember incidents that seem to indicate that monkeys or apes are empathetic or sympathetic about the welfare of others than they are to take note when they seem oblivious and indifferent. Further, it is possible that we are more likely to offer 'cognitively generous' interpretations of the behaviour of apes (or dogs) than monkeys or prosimians.

10.2.2. Common events

Some forms of common behaviours have been interpreted as evidence of empathy and sympathy. These include wound cleaning (Boesch, 1992), reconciliation (O'Connell, 1995), and consolation (O'Connell, 1995; de Waal, 1996). Non-human primates often lick and groom others' wounds, and this may play a role in keeping the wounds clean and preventing infection. But Boesch (1992, cited in de Waal, 1996) goes further. He argues that in chimpanzees this behaviour implies that they "are aware of the needs of the wounded" and have "empathy for the pain resulting from such wounds". De Waal (1996, p. 58) acknowledges the difficulty of interpreting wound-cleaning behaviour, but concludes that Boesch's interpretation is correct:

> Unfortunately, the tending of wounds *per se* tells us nothing about the underlying mental processes.

A skeptic could argue that it only proves that blood tastes good; indeed, it is not unusual for primates to lick blood off plants or branches spattered during a fight or birth. I believe there is more to the cleaning of wounds; many hard-to-convey details in the behaviour of chimpanzees (the way they approach an injured individual; the concerned look in their eyes; the care they take not to hurt) make me intuitively agree with the views of … Boesch. That such details are less obvious in monkeys does not necessarily mean that they perform the same actions devoid of feelings, or any understanding of what happened to the victim; monkeys are harder to read because of their greater evolutionary distance from us.

O'Connell's (1995) compendium includes a number of instances of reconciliation. This classification of reconciliation is idiosyncratic, but it is likely derived from the idea that reconciliation repairs valued relationships that have been damaged by conflict (reviewed in Aureli and de Waal, 2000). The ability to appreciate the impact of aggression on the quality of social bonds might require some knowledge of others' thoughts and feelings, and this might in turn be based on empathy. However, to my knowledge no one else has endorsed this interpretation and invoked reconciliation as direct evidence for empathy or sympathy.

Consolation behaviour occurs when bystanders approach, embrace, touch, and groom the victims of aggression, particularly after episodes that include aggressive vocalizations or physical contact (de Waal and Aureli, 1996). Preston and de Waal (2002) note that bystanders do not show evidence of distress themselves, although this has not been systematically investigated. Chimpanzees may console victims of aggression because they empathize with their pain or distress and want to make them feel better. Consolation behaviour has now been described in several groups of chimpanzees and bonobos (Arnold and Whiten, 2001; Palagi *et al.*, 2004; Wittig and Boesch, 2003), but there is very limited evidence for similar types of behaviour in monkeys (but see Call *et al.*, 2002).

Surprisingly, one common type of interaction is absent from the list of behaviours that provide evidence of empathy and sympathy. Other primates sometimes intervene on behalf of other group members who are involved in ongoing conflicts. In some cases, the victims of aggression advertise their plight by screaming loudly, and they sometimes solicit support from particular group members (Perry *et al.*, 2004; Silk, 1999). We know that intervention is strongly biased by kinship (Buchan *et al.*, 2003; Kapsalis, 2004; Silk, 2001, 2005a,b). However, to my knowledge no one has suggested that monkeys are motivated by empathy or sympathy when they intervene on behalf of the victims of aggression. Why not?

The problem is not that these interpretations are wrong. The problem is, how would we know if they were right? Even though we can readily identify with the feelings of chimpanzees who see other chimpanzees being attacked or chimpanzees that painstakingly groom others' wounds, how do we know that the chimpanzees feel the same things that we do? De Waal (1996) argues that it is parsimonious to assume that "if closely related species act the same the underlying process is probably the same too". But natural selection can produce rapid change and closely related species can differ in important ways. This means that we need to entertain the possibility that anthropomorphic projections might be misplaced. Perhaps consolation occurs in chimpanzees because conflict evokes feelings of distress in bystanders, who then act to reduce stimuli that cause distress to themselves. Call *et al.* (2002) speculated that in stumptailed macaques bystanders may initiate contact with aggressors to signal solidarity and may initiate contact with victims to forestall redirected aggression. These kinds of explanations might apply to chimpanzees as well.

Despite my concerns, I think that it is a mistake to dismiss these kinds of data simply because they are based on singular observations or subjective interpretations of behaviour. Although as Bernstein sternly warned, "the plural of anecdote is not data", a datum *is* a single observation. Anecdotal observations can provide a useful starting point for more systematic analyses.

An excellent example of the successful application of this kind of approach is provided by a recent study of macaque females' responses when their infants are harassed (Schino *et al.*, 2004). Primate females emphasize quality over quantity in offspring, and each offspring represents a

major proportion of a female's lifetime fitness. Thus, mothers have every reason to be concerned when their infants are threatened, chased, or attacked by other group members. Schino and his colleagues speculated that if mothers appreciate their infants' plight, then they will display concern when their infants receive aggression and make efforts to comfort them. They tested these predictions in a large group of Japanese macaques housed at the Rome Zoo. Although macaques and baboons typically display elevated rates of self-directed behaviours, such as scratching, after they receive aggression (Aureli and van Schaik, 1991; Castles and Whiten, 1998), mothers showed no changes in the rate of self-directed behaviours after their infants were involved in aggressive conflicts. Mothers were no more likely to approach their infants in the minutes that followed conflicts than they were at other times. Moreover, mothers' responses to their infants were not influenced by the risks their infants faced or the severity of the aggression that they received. The absence of empathy and sympathetic responses in a situation in which they would seem most likely to be manifest provides strong evidence that macaques may not have the capacity for empathy.

The results that Schino *et al.* (2004) obtained are consistent with the results from a study of mothers' reactions when their infants were exposed to danger (Cheney and Seyfarth, 1990). In these experiments, mothers knew that a dangerous or frightening object, such as a model of a snake, was concealed in a box in their enclosure. When their infants—who had not seen the contents of the box—approached, mothers made no effort to stop their infants or to warn them of the danger. Apparently, these mothers did not appreciate the difference between their own knowledge and the knowledge of their infants.

10.2.3. Experimental data

Two sets of experiments, conducted long before institutional review boards were mandatory parts of the research process, were designed to assess monkeys' responses to the sight of conspecifics' distress. In one experiment, monkeys were trained to associate the presence of another monkey in an adjoining cage with a painful shock to themselves. They could terminate the shock by pressing a lever. Later, the same monkeys were exposed to the sight (or photographic image) of another monkey being shocked. The monkeys responded to the sight of others' being shocked in the same way that they responded when they received shocks themselves (Mirsky et al., 1958; Miller et al., 1959a,b).

In another set of experiments, macaques were trained to pull one chain in response to a blue light and another chain in response to a red light (Masserman et al., 1964; Wechkin et al., 1964). When the monkeys pulled the right chains in response to the appropriate cues, they were rewarded with food. During these training sessions, another monkey was housed in an adjacent cage. After the monkeys mastered the task, the experimenters rigged the experimental apparatus so that the monkey in the adjacent cage received a shock each time one of the two chains was pulled. The majority of monkeys that Masserman and his colleagues tested avoided the response that delivered a shock, thereby depriving themselves of the food rewards they would have obtained by pulling the chain. They were especially likely to show this response if they had received shocks themselves in the past.

Preston and de Waal (2002) interpret the results of these two sets of experiments as examples of instances of emotional contagion in which the "perception of a behavior in another automatically activates one's own representations for the behaviour, and output from this shared representation automatically proceeds to motor areas of the brain where responses are prepared and executed." In this instance, monkeys who had been shocked in the past became distressed when they saw another monkey being shocked, and acted to eliminate the stressful stimulus. If this is an accurate representation of events, then the monkeys did not feel empathy or sympathy. That is, they did not appreciate the feelings of the other individual in a way that was independent of their own feelings, and acted out of concern for themselves rather than concern for the monkey who was being shocked.

Further evidence for emotional contagion comes from experimental studies of chimpanzees. Parr (2001) measured the physiological responses of three adult chimpanzees who were shown four different types of images: (1) hypodermic needles and dart guns, (2) a chimpanzee being darted or injected with a needle, (3) a veterinarian pursuing a chimpanzee with a dart gun, and (4) scenes from the home environment (including activity by caretakers, unfamiliar chimpanzees in neutral activities, cage mesh and transport boxes). The scenes from the home environment were meant to serve as a set of control images. The three subjects had all been treated by veterinarians and had experience with dart guns and needles. Using skin conductance to measure arousal, Parr found that the chimpanzees responded most strongly to the images of the chimp being injected or darted and to the images of the dartgun and needles alone. However, they did not differentiate between these two sets of images. The needles and dartguns created as strong a response as the images of chimpanzees being injected or darted. The chimpanzees showed a considerably weaker response to the image of the chimpanzee being pursued by the veterinarian. Oddly, the chimpanzees responded as strongly to the control images as they did to the other images with which they were paired. Parr suggests that this may be a methodological artefact of the experimental design. It is possible that the chimpanzees' physiological responses changed too slowly to discriminate accurately between the experimental and control conditions.

The fact that these three chimpanzees were as disturbed by the images of needles and dart-guns as they were by images of other chimpanzees being injected or darted suggests that the chimpanzees' responses represent an example of emotional contagion, rather than empathy or sympathy. If the chimpanzees' responses were influenced by an understanding of other individuals' feelings or desires, and if they were concerned about the welfare of others, they should have been more strongly affected by the images of other chimpanzees being injected or darted than by the needles or dart-guns alone.

In another series of experiments, which were designed to test other primates' capacity for perspective taking and empathy, individuals must exchange information to obtain rewards (Povinelli, 1992a,b). One individual (the informant) knows where food is located, but cannot obtain access to the food itself. The other individual (the operator) does not know where the food is located, but can gain access to the food if it knows where it is located. In order to obtain food, the informant must provide some kind of information to the operator about which of several identical devices is baited. Both chimpanzees (Povinelli *et al.*, 1992a) and rhesus macaques (Povinelli *et al.*, 1992b) succeeded at this task when paired with human partners. In a very similar experiment conducted by Mason and Hollis (1962), who originally designed the apparatus that Povinelli and his colleagues adapted for their own experiments, young rhesus monkeys also succeeded in the task when they were paired with other monkeys.

Although both monkeys and chimpanzees succeeded in obtaining rewards, there seems to have been a difference in their understanding of the task. Thus, three of the four chimpanzees that Povinelli and his colleagues tested succeeded immediately when they switched roles (Povinelli 1992a), but monkeys do not seem to be able to do this as readily (Hattori *et al.*, 2005; Hess *et al.*, 1993; Mason and Hollis, 1962; Povinelli *et al.*, 1992b). For chimpanzees, the data are consistent with the hypothesis that "during the role training phases, the subjects learned the requirements of both roles through social attribution, thus enabling them to immediately perform their new role." (Povinelli *et al.*, 1992a; but see Heyes, 1993 for a more sceptical interpretation.)

If chimpanzees can master perspective-taking tasks, then they may be capable of empathy. Their responses in this experiment, however, do not provide any evidence for sympathy. In order to obtain food for itself, the informant must provide information to the operator. And when the operator responds, it automatically provides food to both itself and the informant. The behaviour of both individuals may be entirely self-interested.

10.3. **Moral emotions in other primates**

Flack and de Waal (2000) argue that there are important parallels between human moral conduct and social behaviours that are commonly seen in other primates. They argue that critical components of human morality can be detected in other animals, and that these components include conflict resolution, reciprocity, empathy, sympathy, community concern, a sense of justice, and perhaps the internalization of social norms. This claim suffers from some of the same problems that we encounter when we evaluate the data on empathy and sympathy. Much of the evidence is anecdotal, and the assessment of moral content rests on subjective interpretations about the motives underlying behaviour.

In human societies, transgressions of social norms are often punished. Punishment is meted out by uninvolved bystanders or group members that suffered no immediate harm. Animals often use aggression or other forms of costly sanctions to shape the behaviour of group members (Clutton-Brock and Parker, 1995a,b) or to exact revenge on rivals (de Waal and Luttrell, 1988; Silk, 1992). But primates rarely use aggression or negative sanctions to shape the behaviour of third parties. In one case, a young adult male chimpanzee in the Mahale Mountains of Tanzania was attacked by eight members of his own group (Nishida *et al.*, 1995). The authors speculated that he may have been attacked because he violated social norms by not deferring to dominant males and launching unprovoked attacks on females.

More systematic evidence of third party punishment comes from an experimental study on rhesus macaques conducted by Hauser and Marler (1993a,b; Hauser, 1997). Rhesus macaques give characteristic calls when they discover novel food items (Hauser and Marler, 1993a). Taking advantage of this situation, Hauser and Marler conducted an experiment in which observers surreptitiously dropped handfuls of coconut or monkey chow and waited for monkeys to find it (Hauser and Marler, 1993b). Finders sometimes called, but sometimes remained silent. Calling significantly reduced the likelihood of being harassed after discovery by other group members. Monkeys who discovered food and subsequently called were less likely to be harassed by higher-ranking monkeys than monkeys who remained silent after they found food (M. D. Hauser, personal communication). Sanctions are only directed at females. Males virtually never call when they find food, and are not punished (Hauser and Marler, 1993b; Hauser, 1997).

In a more recent attempt to systematically study the existence of moral emotions, Brosnan and de Waal (2003) evaluated capuchins' responses to inequity. They trained capuchins to exchange tokens for food rewards. Capuchins readily handed pebbles to human experimenters who offered them cucumbers, apples, and grapes in return. However, they refused to accept cucumbers in exchange for tokens, if they saw other group members obtain grapes for cucumbers, or if other group members received grapes without providing a token at all. (Capuchins generally prefer grapes over apples and apples over cucumbers.) Brosnan and de Waal (2003) concluded that "tolerant species with well-developed food sharing and cooperation, such as capuchins, may hold emotionally charged expectations about reward distribution and social exchange that lead them to dislike inequity."

These results have been widely cited as evidence for a 'sense of fairness' in other primates (e.g. Rapaport and Bearden, 2005; Vogel, 2004). Fairness is a prosocial value, and evidence that monkeys have a sense of fairness would provide strong evidence of concern for the welfare of others. However, Henrich (2004) pointed out that if monkeys were truly averse to inequity, they would have refused to accept rewards that were better than the rewards their partners received. The monkeys never did this; they only rejected exchanges in which they were disadvantaged themselves. Moreover, the monkeys' reaction to being shortchanged exaggerated the inequity, it did not diminish it. By flinging the cucumber back at the experimenter rather than eating it, the capuchins increased the magnitude of the gap between their own rewards and the rewards of others.

Brosnan et al. (2005) also conducted very similar experiments among chimpanzees. Members of one group that had lived together for 30 years exchanged tokens for food, and were unaffected by the nature of rewards that others received. Members of another group, which had lived together for only 8 years and had less stable social relationships, behaved more like the capuchins. They refused to participate in exchanges in which they received rewards of lower value than other group members received. Like the capuchins, none of the chimpanzees showed any reluctance to reject rewards that were of higher value than other group members received, and the chimpanzees that rejected exchanges actually increased the extent of inequity between themselves and others.

Although these data may fall short of demonstrating that capuchins or chimpanzees demonstrate a sense of fairness, the tendency to reject disadvantageous exchanges may represent one of many stages in the evolution of inequity aversion in humans (Brosnan et al., 2005). In order to react to inequity, animals must first be able to assess the value of what they are offered and the value of what is offered to others. Experimental studies of a number of primates suggests that they can assess the value of commodities, and adjust their expectations about value based on local conditions (Hyatt and Hopkins, 1998; Sousa and Matsuzawa, 2001; Brosnan and De Waal, 2003, 2005; Brosnan et al., 2005; Drapier et al., 2005; Ramseyer et al., 2005). This capacity is a necessary condition for evaluating equity. It is also a necessary condition for reciprocal exchanges, particularly the kinds of subtle negotiations that market models rely on (Noë, 2005). These models rely on the assumption that other animals adjust their expectations as the supply and demand of resources shifts, and these data suggest that other primates can and do make such calculations. This protocol represents an important methodological innovation because it allows researchers to systematically examine preferences for a range of economic outcomes.

10.4. Other-regarding preferences in non-human primates

In humans, altruism seems to be motivated at least in part by genuine concern for the welfare of others, or other-regarding preferences. If chimpanzees can "comprehend the emotions, attitude, and situation of another" (Preston and de Waal, 2002), and if chimpanzees are motivated by moral sentiments that are homologous to our own (Flack and de Waal, 2000), then we might expect chimpanzees to display other-regarding preferences. We might even expect chimpanzees to display empathic and sympathetic responses to unfamiliar individuals. De Waal (1996, p. 233) cited a male chimpanzee's response to the sight of technicians trying to capture a rhesus macaque that had escaped from its enclosure at the Yerkes field station, and suggested that "he appeared to empathize with the monkey". If de Waal's intuition is correct, then we would expect chimpanzees to display concern for the welfare of others, particularly familiar group members.

To test this notion, my colleagues and I have conducted a series of experiments on chimpanzees (Silk *et al.*, 2005). Our experiments were designed to determine whether chimpanzees would take advantage of opportunities to provide benefits to others at no cost to themselves. In our experiments, actors were faced with a choice between two options: Option 1 provided a reward only to the actor, and Option 2 delivered a reward to the actor and simultaneously delivered an identical reward to another member of the subject's group. Of course, actors might prefer Option 2 simply because they preferred two rewards over one reward (regardless of the distribution), so we included a control condition in which no potential recipients were present. If individuals are concerned about the welfare of others, they are expected to prefer Option 2 over Option 1 and this preference is expected to be stronger when another individual is present than when the actor is alone. If individuals are indifferent about the welfare of others, they are expected to choose Option 1 and Option 2 with equal frequencies in both conditions. Finally, if individuals are motivated to reduce welfare of others, they will choose Option 1 less often than Option 2, and this preference will be more pronounced when another individual is present than when they are alone.

In this experiment, the bar for prosocial responses was deliberately set very low. Actors incur no cost when they behave prosocially. They obtain the same reward no matter which option they choose. This means that other-regarding sentiments do not conflict with selfish motives to obtain rewards because actors' choices do not affect their own payoffs. In addition, the experiments involve animals who have long-term social bonds. Actors might behave generously toward group members with whom they cooperate outside the experiment, even if they lack genuine concern for the welfare of their partners. By the same token, the absence of prosocial behaviour would provide compelling evidence that actors do not possess prosocial preferences.

We conducted work on chimpanzees at two different sites using two different apparatuses. In Louisiana, we worked with seven adults (six females, one male). These chimpanzees have lived together as a group since they were juveniles, and have considerable experience with cognitive and behavioural testing. In Louisiana, the chimpanzees used an expanding device attached to two trays. When the handle was pulled, one tray moved toward the actor and the other tray moved toward the opposite enclosure. In Texas, we worked with 11 same-sexed pairs of adults. These animals were all reared by their own mothers and live in stable social groups, but had very little experience with behavioural or cognitive testing before our experiments began. In this set of experiments, the animals were ushered into adjacent enclosures, and one individual manipulated a two-tiered bar-pull device. When a handle attached to one tray was pulled, food rewards were moved to within reach of the chimpanzees. (For additional details about these experiments, see Silk *et al.*, 2005 and associated online materials).

All of the animals were strongly motivated to obtain rewards for themselves. When the chimpanzees were paired with a potential recipient, they chose the option that delivered rewards to the other chimpanzee about half the time. But *none* of the 18 chimpanzees that we tested chose the prosocial option significantly more often when another chimpanzee was present than when they were alone.

We have also conducted a second set of experiments on the same sets of chimpanzees using a different protocol and a different apparatus (J. Vonk *et al.*, unpublished). In this case, the chimpanzees were able to choose one option that provided a reward for themselves *and* a second option that provided a reward to the chimpanzee sitting beside them or opposite them. In these experiments, the actor needs to make a separate response to provide rewards for its partner and itself, so there is a small cost associated with providing rewards to others.

Again, we found that the presence of a potential recipient had no effect on the chimpanzees' behaviour.

These results have been replicated in a series of strikingly similar experiments conducted by Jensen *et al.* (2006) in Leipzig. Again, the chimpanzees could choose between two options. One option provided rewards only to the actor, and the other option provided rewards to the actor and to another group member. The chimpanzees were strongly motivated to obtain rewards for themselves, but unaffected by the presence or absence of other group members. Thus, the chimpanzees in Leipzig were also indifferent to the welfare of other group members in a very similar experimental setting.

Monkeys seem to behave in similar ways in similar situations. Mason and Hollis (1962), who originally designed the prototype of the apparatus that we used in our experiments in Louisiana, conducted an experiment that was quite similar to our experiments. They divided the enclosure that housed the Informant into two halves. When the actor pulled the handle on one side, the opposing tray was moved to within reach of the other monkeys, but when the actor pulled the handle on the other side, the opposing tray was delivered to the empty half of the enclosure. Mason and Hollis baited all four trays with identical rewards and allowed the actor to choose between the two handles. The monkeys did not differentiate between the two options; they were equally likely to deliver rewards to their partners and to an empty cage.

In another early experiment that was also very like the experiments that my colleagues and I conducted on chimpanzees, four pairs of macaques were trained to press a pair of levers to obtain food (Colman *et al.*, 1969). One lever delivered food to the monkey pressing the lever, the other lever delivered food to the monkey pressing the lever and to another monkey in an adjacent cage. One of the macaques typically fed himself and the other monkey, one monkey systematically fed only himself, and two monkeys pressed both levers with equal frequency.

Young children seem to behave very differently in similar situations. Children 3–5 years old were asked whether they would prefer one sticker for themselves or one sticker for themselves and one sticker for a 16-year-old female research assistant that they had not met before (Thompson *et al.*, 1997). Nearly all of the children chose the prosocial option. A smaller majority of children also preferred one sticker for themselves and one sticker for the research assistant over two stickers for themselves. Children's generosity may well be the product of socialization which emphasizes the value of sharing and generosity. It might also reflect children's desire to please or ingratiate themselves with adults. Thus, we are now replicating our experiments with preschool-aged children, giving them the chance to provide food rewards to other children.

10.5. Conclusions

Current claims for the existence of empathy, sympathy, moral sentiments, and other-regarding preferences in other primates rest on an insecure empirical foundation. The anecdotal accounts and *post hoc* interpretations of behaviour have limited probative value because they rely on subjective interpretations of animals' intentions and motivations and they are not systematically collected or analysed. This means that we cannot be certain whether any given interpretation is right or wrong, and we have no means of discriminating between competing claims.

To transform singular observations and subjective interpretations of behaviour into more robust findings, we need to develop theoretically grounded hypotheses that we can subject to empirical testing. As de Waal (1996, pp. 46–47) has noted, "Although it is hard to know the intentions of animals, we can speculate about them and may one day reach the point of testing one interpretation against another. For a research program into animal empathy, it is not enough to review the highlights of succorant behaviour, it is equally important to consider the absence of such behaviour when it might have been expected."

The kind of well-designed experiments and carefully constructed analyses of naturally occurring behaviour that I have described here do allow us to test competing interpretations of behaviour. If the interpretations of consolation behaviour in chimpanzees are correct, then we would expect female chimpanzees to become agitated when their infants are harassed and to make efforts to comfort them. The protocol that Schino and his colleagues develops provides an elegant way to test this prediction. Call *et al.*'s (2002) careful dissection of the kinds of behaviours that are performed by bystanders could be extended to other species in which consolation behaviour has not been detected. Our study of other-regarding preferences ought to be extended to other species, particularly ones in which cooperation plays an important role.

These data will make an important contribution to ongoing efforts to understand the origins of prosocial preferences and moral sentiments in our own species. Evidence of empathy, sympathy, moral sentiments, and prosocial preferences in chimpanzees or other primates would demonstrate that these traits have deep roots within the primate order. At the same time, the absence of these traits would indicate that the moral emotions and other-regarding sentiments that underlie prosocial behaviour may be an emergent property of human societies, linked to the capacity for culture, language, and a well-developed theory of mind.

Acknowledgments

I thank Sarah Brosnan for sharing the Colman *et al.* experiment with me. The experimental work which stimulated my thinking on this topic was supported by a grant from the MacArthur Foundation Preferences Network. I thank Rob Boyd, Ernst Fehr, Dan Fessler, Josep Call, Joe Henrich, Sarah Brosnan, Daniel Povinelli, and Jennifer Vonk for stimulating conversations about many of the ideas explored in this paper. This paper was written while I was a Visiting Professor in the Department of Zoology and a Visiting Professorial Fellow of Madgalene College, Cambridge University. I thank my hosts for their hospitality and fellowship.

References

Altmann, J. (1974) Observational study of behavior: sampling methods. *Behaviour*, 49: 227–267.

Arnold, K. and Whiten, A. (2001) Post-conflict behaviour of wild chimpanzees (*Pan troglodytes schweinfurthii*) in the Budongo forest, Uganda. *Behaviour*, 138: 649–690.

Aureli, F. and De Waal, F. B. M. (eds) (2000) *Natural Conflict Resolution*. University of California Press, Berkeley.

Aureli, F. and van Schaik, C. P. (1991) Post conflict behaviour in long-tailed macaques (*Macaca fasicularis*). II. Coping with the uncertainty. *Ethology*, 89: 101–114.

Batson, C. D. and Powell, A. A. (1998) Altruism and prosocial behavior. In T. Millon and M. J. Lerner (eds) *Handbook of Psychology: Personality and Social Psychology*, vol. 5, pp. 463–484. Wiley, Hoboken.

Boesch, C. (1992) New elements of a theory of mind in wild chimpanzees. *Behavioral and Brain Sciences*, 15: 149–150.

Boyd, R. and Richerson, P. J. (in press) Culture and the Evolution of the Human Social Instincts. In: Levinson, S. and Enfield, N. (eds) *Roots of Human Sociality*. pp. 453–477 Berg, Oxford.

Brosnan, S. F. and de Waal, F. B. M. (2003) Monkeys reject unequal pay. *Nature*, 425: 297–299.

Brosnan, S. F. and de Waal, F. B. M. (2005) Responses to a simple barter task in chimpanzees, *Pan troglodytes*. *Primates*, 46: 173–182.

Brosnan, S. F., Schiff, H. C. and de Waal, F. B. M. (2005) Tolerance for inequity may increase with social closeness in chimpanzees. *Proceedings of the Royal Society of London, B*, 272: 253–258.

Buchan, J. C., Alberts, S. C., Silk, J. B. and Altmann, J. (2003) True paternal care in a multi-male primate society. *Nature* 425: 179–181.

Call, J., Aureli, F. and de Waal, F. B. M. (2002) Postconflict third-party affiliation in stumptailed macaques. *Animal Behaviour*, 63: 209–216.

Castles, D. L. and Whiten, A. (1998) Post-conflict behaviour of wild olive baboons. II. Stress and self-directed behaviour. *Ethology*, 104: 148–160.

Chapais, B. (1992) The role of alliances in social inheritance of rank among female primates. In A. H. Harcourt and F. B. M. de Waal (eds) *Coalitions and Alliances in Humans and Other Animals*, pp. 29–59. Oxford Science Publications, Oxford.

Chapais, B. (2001) Primate nepotism: what is the explanatory value of kin selection? *International Journal of Primatology*, 22: 203–229.

Cheney, D. and Seyfarth, R. (1990) Attending to behaviour versus attending to knowledge: examining monkeys' attribution of mental states. *Animal Behaviour*, 40: 742–753.

Clutton-Brock, T. H. and Parker, G. A. (1995a) Punishment in animal societies. *Nature* 373: 209–216.

Clutton-Brock, T. H. and Parker, G. A. (1995b) Sexual coercion in animal societies. *Animal Behaviour*, 49: 1345–1365.

Colman, A. D., Liebold, K. E. and Boren, J. J. (1969) A method for studying altruism in monkeys. *The Psychological Record*, 19: 401–405.

De Waal, F. B. M. (1996) *Good Natured*. Harvard University Press, Cambridge, MA.

De Waal, F. B. M. and Aureli, F. (1996) Consolation, reconciliation, and a possible cognitive difference between macaques and chimpanzees. In A. E. Russon, K. A. Bard and S. T. Parker (eds) *Reaching into Thought*, pp. 80–110. Cambridge University Press, Cambridge.

De Waal, F. B. M. and Luttrell, L. M. (1988) Mechanisms of social reciprocity in three primate species: symmetrical relationship characteristics or cognition? *Ethology and Sociobiology*, 9: 101–118.

Drapier, M., Chauvin, C., Dufour, V., Uhlrich, P. and Thierry, B. (2005) Food-exchange with humans in brown capuchin monkeys. *Primates*, 46: 241–248.

Eisenberg, N. and Mussen, P. H. (1995) *The Roots of Prosocial Behavior in Children*. Cambridge University Press, Cambridge.

Fehr, E. and Fischbacher, U. (2003) The nature of human altruism. *Nature*, 425: 785–791.

Fehr, E. and Fischbacher, U. (2005) The economics of strong reciprocity. In H. Gintis, S. Bowles, R. Boyd and E. Fehr (eds) *Moral Sentiments and Material Interests: On the Foundations of Cooperation in Economic Life*, pp. 151–191. MIT Press, Cambridge, MA.

Flack, J. C. and de Waal, F. B. M. (2000) 'Any animal whatever'. Darwinian building blocks of morality in monkeys and apes. *J. Consciousness Studies*, 7: 1–29.

Haley, K. J. and Fessler, D. M. T. (2005) Nobody's watching? Subtle cues affect generosity in an anonymous economic game. *Evolution and Human Behavior*, 26: 245–256.

Hare, B., Call, J., Agnetta, B. and Tomasello, M. (2000) Chimpanzees know what conspecifics do and do not see. *Animal Behaviour*, 59: 771–785.

Hare, B., Call, J. and Tomasello, M. (2001) Do chimpanzees know what conspecifics know? *Anim. Behav.*, 61: 139–151.

Hauser, M. D. (1997) Minding the behaviour of deception. In A. Whiten and R. W. Byrne (eds) *Machiavellian Intelligence II*, pp. 112–143. Cambridge University Press, Cambridge.

Hauser, M. D. and Marler, P. (1993a) Food-associated calls in rhesus macaques (*Macaca mulatta*): I. Socioecological factors. *Behavioral Ecology*, 4: 194–205.

Hauser, M. D. and Marler, P. (1993b) Food-associated calls in rhesus macaques (*Macaca mulatta*): II. Costs and benefits of call production and suppression. *Behavioral Ecology*, 4: 206–212.

Hattori, Y., Kuroshima, H. and Fujito, K. (2005) Cooperative problem solving by tufted capuchin monkeys (*Cebus apella*): spontaneous division of labor, communication, and reciprocal altruism. *Journal of Comparative Psychology*, 119: 335–342.

Henrich, J., (2004) Inequity aversion in capuchins? *Nature* 428: 139.

Henrich, J. , Boyd, R., Bowles, S., Camerer, C., Fehr, E. and Gintis, H. (eds) (2004) *Foundations of Human Sociality*. Oxford University Press, Oxford.

Hess, J., Novak, M. A. and Povinelli, D. P. (1993) 'Natural pointing' in a rhesus monkeys, but not evidence of empathy. *Animal Behaviour*, 46: 1023–1025.

Heyes, C. M. (1993) Anecdotes, training, trapping and triangulating: do animals attribute mental states? *Animal Behaviour*, 46: 177–188.

Hyatt, C. W. and Hopkins, W. D. (1998) Interspecies object exchange: bartering in apes? *Behaviorial Processes*, 42: 177–187.

Jensen, K., Hare, B., Call, J. and Tomasello, M. (2006) What's in it for me? Self-regard precludes altruism and spite in chimpanzees. *Proceedings of the Royal Society, London, Series B*. 273: 1013–1021.

Kaplan, H. and Gurven, M. (2005) The natural history of human food sharing and cooperation: a review and new multi-individual approach to the negotiation of norms.

In H. Gintis, S. Bowles, R. Boyd and E. Fehr (eds) *Moral Sentiments and Material Interests: On the Foundations of Cooperation in Economic Life*, pp. 75–113. MIT Press, Cambridge.

Kapsalis, E. (2004) Matrilineal kinship and primate behavior. In B. Chapais and C. M. Berman (eds) *Kinship and Behavior in Primates*, pp. 153–176. Oxford University Press, Oxford.

Mason, W. A. and Hollis, J. H. (1962) Communication between young rhesus macaques. *Animal Behaviour*, 10: 211–221.

Masserman, J. H., Wechkin, S. and Terris, W. (1964) "Altruistic" behavior in rhesus monkeys. *American Journal of Psychiatry*, 121: 584–585.

Miller, R. E., Murphy, J. V. and Mirsky, I. A. (1959a) Nonverbal communication of affect. *Journal of Clinical Psychology*, 15: 155–158.

Miller, R. E., Murphy, J. V. and Mirsky, I. A. (1959b) Relevance of facial expressions and posture as cues in communication of affect between monkeys. *Archives of General Psychiatry*, 1: 480–488.

Mirsky, I. A., Miller, R. E. and Murphy, J. V. (1958) The communication of affect in rhesus monkeys. *Journal of the American Psychoanalytic Association*, 6: 433–441.

Nishida, T., Hosaka, K., Nakamura, M. and Hamai, M. (1995) A within-group gang attack on a young adult male chimpanzee: ostracism of an ill-mannered member? *Primates*, 36: 207–211.

Noë, R. (2005) Digging for the roots of trading. In P. M. Kappeler and C. P. van Schaik (eds) *Cooperation in Primates and Humans: Mechanisms and Evolution*, pp. 223–251. Springer, Berlin.

O'Connell, S. (1995) Empathy in chimpanzees: evidence for theory of mind. *Primates*, 36: 397–410.

Palagi, E., Paoli, T. and Borgognini Tarli, S. (2004) Reconciliation and consolation in captive bonobos (*Pan paniscus*). *American Journal of Primatology*, 62: 15–30.

Parr, L. (2001) Cognitive and physiological markers of emotional awareness in chimpanzees (*Pan trogloydytes*). *Animal Cognition*, 4: 223–229.

Perry, S., Barrett, H. C. and Manson, J. H. (2004) White-faced capuchin monkeys show triadic awareness in their choice of allies. *Animal Behaviour*, 67: 165–170.

Povinelli, D. J., Nelson, K. E. and Boysen, S. T. (1992a) Comprehension of role reversal in chimpanzees: evidence of empathy? *Animal Behaviour*, 43: 633–640.

Povinelli, D. J., Parks, K. A., Novak, M. A. (1992b) Role reversal by rhesus monkeys, but no evidence of empathy. *Animal Behaviour*, 44: 269–281.

Preston, S. D. and de Waal, F. B.M. (2002) Empathy: its ultimate and proximate bases. *Brain and Behavioral Sciences*, 25: 1–72.

Ramseyer, A., Pelé, M., Dufour, V., Chauvin, C. and Thierry, B. (2005) Accepting loss: the temporal limits of reciprocity in brown capuchin monkeys. *Proceedings of the Royal Society of London, B.*, published online (doi:10.1098/rspb.2005.3300).

Rapaport, A. and Bearden, J. N. (2005) Strategic behavior in monkeys. *Trends in Cognitive Sciences*, 9: 213–215.

Richerson, P. J. and Boyd, R. (2004) *Not by Genes Alone: How Culture Transformed Human Evolution*. University of Chicago Press, Chicago.

Schino, G., Gemiani, S., Rosati, L. and Aureli, F. (2004) Behavioral and emotional response of Japanese macaque (*Macaca fuscata*) mothers after their offspring receive aggression. *Journal of Comparative Psychology*, 118: 340–346.

Silk, J. B. (1992) The patterning of intervention among male bonnet macaque: reciprocity, revenge, and loyalty. *Current Anthropology*, 33: 318–325.

Silk, J. B. (1999) Male bonnet macaques use information about third party rank relationships to recruit allies. *Animal Behaviour*, 58: 45–51.

Silk, J. B. (2002) Kin selection in primate groups. *International Journal of Primatology*, 23: 849–875.

Silk, J. B. (2005a) The evolution of cooperation in primate groups. In H. Gintis, S. Bowles, R. Boyd and E. Fehr (eds) *Moral Sentiments and Material Interests: On the Foundations of Cooperation in Economic Life*, pp. 43–73. MIT Press, Cambridge, MA.

Silk, J. B. (2005b) Practicing Hamilton's rule: kin selection in primate groups. In P. M. Kappeler and C. P. van Schaik (eds) *Cooperation in Primates and Humans: Mechanisms and Evolution*, pp. 21–42. Springer, Berlin.

Silk, J. B., Brosnan, S. F., Vonk, J., Henrich, J., Povinelli, D. J., Richardson, A. F., Lambeth, S. P., Mascaro, J. and

Schapiro, S. J. (2005) Chimpanzees are indifferent to the welfare of other group members. *Nature*, 435: 1357–1359.

Sousa, C. and Matsuzawa, T. (2001) The use of tokens as rewards and tools by chimpanzees (*Pan troglodytes*). *Animal Cognition*, 4: 213–221.

Strier, K. B. (2004) Patrilineal kinship and primate behavior. In B. Chapais and C. M. Berman (eds) *Kinship and Behavior in Primates*, pp. 177–199. Oxford University Press, Oxford.

Thompson, C., Barresi, J. and Moore, C. (1997) The development of future-oriented prudence and altruism in preschoolers. *Cognitive Development*, 12: 199–212.

Tomasello, M. and Call, J. (1997) *Primate Cognition*. Oxford University Press, Oxford.

Tomasello, M., Call, J. and Hare, B. (2003) Chimpanzees understand psychological states-the question is which ones and to what extent. *Trends in Cognitive Sciences*, 7: 153–156.

Vogel, E. (2004) Evolution of the golden rule. *Science*, 303: 1128–1130.

Wechkin, S., Massserman, J. H. and Terris, W. Jr (1964) Shock to a conspecific as an aversive stimulus. *Psychonomic Science*, 1: 47–48.

Wittig, R. and Boesch, C. (2003) The choice of post-conflict interactions in wild chimpanzees (*Pan troglodytes*). *Behaviour*, 140: 1527–1559.

SECTION III

Evolutionary neurobiology and cognition

Understanding brain evolution has obvious implications for psychology and cognition. One of the most important is that it reminds us not to expect perfection in our evolved cognitive architecture. Evolutionary design is never perfect because nothing is ever designed from scratch: evolution tinkers with what is already present. In this sense, evolutionary processes are constrained. At the same time, they are also liberated by the vast periods of time over which they operate. Cost-effective, but non-obvious, often somewhat messy, solutions, are the result. This is as true of the brain as it is for any other organ or anatomical structure, which means that understanding the evolved architecture and function of the brain is essential if we are to frame our theories of cognitive evolution appropriately.

For example, most of evolutionary history has been spent perfecting the perceptual and action-based mechanisms that allow an animal to deal effectively with its environment (Brooks, 1999)—as Barton points out, the fundamental behavioural function of the brain is to move bodies around the world in an adaptive manner, rather than act as a "disembodied, logical reasoning device" (Clark, 1997). Given this, it should be apparent that, over evolutionary time, the perception–action mechanisms that are in place will inevitably constrain the manner in which higher-level cognitive processes evolve and help to explain why cognition is structured in a particular way. The recent discovery of mirror neurons in the motor system of primates, and the implications they hold for the evolution of more sophisticated forms of social cognition, are a case in point, as discussed by Rizzolatti and Fogassi. Jellema and Perrett put forward a similar argument with respect to aspects of the visual sensory system. It is clear that paying attention to the evolution and function of perceptual and motor processes will shed light on how and why we think in the ways that we do.

Moreover, it is evident that an understanding of brain evolution helps to refocus our attention on the selection of particular networks and systems within the brain. The influential 'social brain' hypothesis (Dunbar, 1998) has, to date, focused attention on the neocortex due to its evolutionary expansion within the primate order. Both Barton and Panksepp, however, emphasise the importance of moving away from a focus on one particular brain area to one where the "social brain" is seen as a distributed neural (and neurochemical) system, in which several of the pathways involved can be traced back to our more distant mammalian ancestors, and are thus very ancient systems indeed.

Finally, it is also clear that, as well as being constrained by brain architecture and perceptuo-motor systems, cognitive structures will themselves be constrained by evolutionary processes. As Todd and Gigerenzer argue, we should expect humans and other animals to show 'ecological rationality', rather than the economists' perfect rationality. Solutions which, in the confines of certain laboratory set-ups, appear clunky or prone to mistakes may still be good enough to produce adaptive solutions under more evolutionarily relevant conditions. Expecting highly tuned perfection in either brain processes or cognitive processes, and theorizing on that basis, is simply not an evolutionarily sound position to take. Instead, we need to roll up our sleeves and get into the messy stuff of real life.

References

Brooks, R. A. (1999) *Cambrian Intelligence: The Early History of the New AI.* MIT Press, Cambridge, MA.

Clark, A. (1997) *Being There: Putting Brain, Body, and World Together Again.* MIT Press, Cambridge, MA.

Dunbar, R. I. M. (1998) The Social Brain Hypothesis. *Evolutionary.Anthropology 6:* 178–190.

CHAPTER 11

Evolution of the social brain as a distributed neural system

Robert A. Barton

11.1. Introduction

Amid the excitement of technological developments in molecular neurobiology and brain imaging, it is easy to lose sight of the broader issues within which these developments must be placed. Ultimately, the diverse methods and models of neuroscience are aimed at answering basic questions such as: what are brains for, how are they organized, and how does this organization support adaptive behaviour? A key biological fact to bear in mind in constructing answers to those questions is that brains evolved. Brains are quintessential Darwinian "organs of extreme complication and perfection" (Darwin, 1859), suggesting that their structure and mechanisms are adaptations that fit the animal's behaviour and cognitive capacities to its ecological niche. In some sense the animal's behaviour may also construct its niche (see Laland, this volume, Chapter 4), creating a dynamic interaction between behaviour and evolution. The key point that will be emphasized here, however, is that understanding species differences in cognitive mechanisms requires a close relationship between evolutionary biology and cognitive neuroscience.

11.2. Comparative cognition and brain evolution

The distinctive cognitive attributes of primates, including humans, are widely assumed to relate in some way to their large brains. But what exactly are these distinctive cognitive attributes, and what are the functional properties of large brains that support them? Despite decades of experimental comparative psychology, there appears to be little consensus on how cognitive capacities differ between species. This lack of consensus is exemplified by studies of primates. Macphail (1982), Heyes (1998), Tomasello and Call (1997) and Povinelli and Vonk (2003) all question the evidence for cognitive differences between non-human primate species, emphasizing that only humans are clearly different. Tomasello and Call (1997), however, differ from some other authors in arguing that there is sufficient evidence to conclude that primates have cognitive skills lacking in other mammals. More recently, Tomasello *et al.* (2005), revising the opinion in Tomasello and Call (1997), argue that new data suggest that great apes differ from other non-human primates in being able to understand others' perceptions and goals, whereas Povinelli and co-workers (Povinelli and Vonk, 2003, 2004; Povinelli and Barth, 2005) continue to dispute this, arguing that apes have a more concrete understanding of both the world and other individuals, and can reason only about observable properties of events and interactions.

One of the main difficulties is that researchers have failed to agree on what constitutes valid evidence for cognitive differences. Macphail (1982) takes an extreme position, arguing that we cannot reject the null hypothesis (that there are no species differences in intelligence amongst *any* non-human species) until the effects of 'contextual variables' on task performance have been ruled out. Contextual variables are motivational, sensory and motor differences that confound attempts to create a level playing field in assessing differences in intelligence. Since any task must in some way depend on motivating the animal and engaging its sensory and motor capacities, and since the effects of these are unquantifiable, it may be impossible to fully and unambiguously satisfy Macphail's criterion. The key point is this: the intellect of an animal cannot be entirely isolated from the rest of its biology. Yet, to some extent, all experiments carried out in the laboratory are attempts to do precisely that, in that the point of experiments *is* to isolate a phenomenon of interest by controlling confounding variables. Hence, the implicit (or explicit) assumption that it is necessary to separate out the effects of cognitive, perceptual and motivational factors underlies virtually all comparative psychology.

The failure to unambiguously demonstrate cognitive differences between species is at odds with clear differences in brain size and behaviour in the wild. Relative to body size, there are statistically significant differences in brain size among mammalian orders and sub-orders (Jerison, 1973; Martin, 1990). Primates, for example, are significantly larger-brained than many other mammals and, within the primates, monkeys and apes are larger-brained than lemurs and lorises (Jerison, 1973; Barton, 1999). The suggestion that these differences may be due to natural selection on body size rather than on brain size (Gould, 1975; Riska and Atchley, 1975; Deacon, 1997) does not appear to be true (Deaner and Nunn, 1999; Barton, in press).

Theoretically, it seems likely that the differences between species in their behavioural patterns in the wild, whether, for example, they are nocturnal and solitary or diurnal and gregarious, is in some way manifested in differences in their brains. Indeed, brain size evolution correlates with ecology and behavioural specializations in ways likely to reflect selection on cognitive capacities (Harvey and Krebs, 1990; Barton, 1999).

11.3. Correlations between brain size and behavioural ecology

Early studies of brain size found correlations with diet and foraging behaviour: in both primates and bats, fruit-eating species are larger-brained than species with other types of diets, such as leaf-eaters (Eisenberg and Wilson, 1978; Clutton-Brock and Harvey, 1980), leading to the suggestion that large brains reflect selection on the cognitive abilities underpinning exploitation of the environment. Fruit is generally more patchily and less predictably distributed in the environment than are leaves or insects, perhaps requiring a better spatial memory in frugivores (Milton, 1988). This conclusion is bolstered by the fact that frugivores have relatively large home ranges (Nunn and Barton, 2000), and the fact that brain size also correlates positively with home range size (Clutton-Brock and Harvey, 1980; Deaner *et al.*, 2000).

Subsequent studies on primates have not, however, provided unequivocal support for the foraging hypothesis. Notably, Dunbar (1998) found that social group size was the best predictor of neocortex size, and argued that sociality was the main selection pressure on primate brain size and intelligence. A difficulty in distinguishing between the rival hypotheses is that lifestyle variables, such as social group size and diet, are often correlated with each other and are measured with considerable error. More confidence can be placed in a particular lifestyle correlate if it is possible, as has been the case with sociality, to find convergent evidence from different data sets (Aiello and Dunbar, 1993), different types of analysis (Barton, 1996; Lindenfors, 2005), and different taxonomic groups (Dunbar and Bever, 1998; Perez-Barberia and Gordon, 2005; Shultz and Dunbar, 2005).

On the other hand, it is perfectly reasonable to suppose that there may have been multiple influences on brain size evolution, given that a variety of neural systems are potentially involved. Correlates of brain and neocortex size therefore need to be interpreted in the light of underlying variation in specific neurocognitive systems.

The problem, then, is that brain size and natural behaviour vary substantially, but it is unclear what the cognitive implications of such variation are. Experimental evidence for cognitive differences between species is disputed, and variation in brain size, although suggestive, is open to a variety of possible interpretations. Progress in resolving this problem will depend on a deeper understanding of brain evolution than can be achieved through study of brain size alone. Does large brain size reflect the selective expansion of specific neural systems (mosaic brain evolution) or merely the global enlargement of all systems? If the former, then identifying which specific neural systems are associated with brain size evolution is clearly critical for understanding the correlations between brain size and lifestyle.

11.4. How did brains evolve?

Organisms tend to evolve in a coordinated fashion. Hence, as overall size increases, so does the size of limbs, muscles, tendons and internal organs: this is necessary for the organism to function efficiently. A large proportion of the variance in the size of individual body parts is therefore in some sense explained by overall size. On the other hand, parts also vary independently of overall size:

"The concept of mosaic evolution dictates that organs will evolve in different ways to meet varying selective pressures" (Gould, 1978, p. 66).

For example, whilst the size of the testes correlates closely with the size of other organs and overall body size, testes of promiscuously mating species are large relative to body size as an adaptation for sperm competition (Harcourt et al., 1996). As with the organs of the body, individual brain components may vary in adaptively specialized ways, independently of variation in whole brain size. Unlike bodily organs, however, brain components have extensive

neural interconnections to support the integrated processing of information, potentially limiting the importance of mosaic evolution. Nevertheless, individual components are grouped within structurally and functionally differentiated neural systems specialized for handling particular cognitive operations, upon which natural selection might act at least partly independently of evolutionary change in other systems:

> ... a relatively large brain may result from differential increase in the size of [specific components] ... those areas of the brain that do increase in size are often related to specializations in certain sense organs, and correlate with the collection, storage and retrieval of specific kinds of data relevant to the niches the animals exploit. (Eisenberg, 1981) p.276

There is evidence for this hypothesis, even at the level of the gross anatomical subdivisions of the brain (Barton, in press). Some components (e.g. the neocortex and cerebellum) show clear 'grade' differences between taxonomic groups, whereas others (e.g. the medulla) do not. Furthermore, there are different grade effects for different structures: both the neocortex and cerebellum are larger in primates than in insectivores, but only neocortex size also differentiates between strepsirhines (lemurs and lorises) and anthropoids (monkeys and apes). Within anthropoids, however, the cerebellum is relatively enlarged in apes compared with monkeys (Rilling and Insel, 1998; Rilling, 2006). The main olfactory bulbs are larger in strepsirhine primates and insectivores than in haplorhine primates, a difference that is at least partly associated with adaptive radiation into nocturnal and diurnal niches (Barton et al., 1995; Barton, 2006). During primate evolution, therefore, different brain components have changed in size to different extents, at different times and in different directions.

Although these differences among major anatomical regions of the brain support the general proposition that brains evolved in a mosaic fashion, they reveal comparatively little about natural selection on specific neurocognitive systems. First, major subdivisions of the brain, such as the neocortex and cerebellum, are highly heterogeneous structures containing pharmacologically and anatomically distinct areas with different connections and diverse functions. Second, the components of functionally integrated neurocognitive systems are distributed across major subdivisions of the brain, potentially limiting the extent to which these subdivisions vary independently of one another. The visuo-motor system, for example, involves connected nuclei in many brain areas. Hence, selection on the visuo-motor system would be expected to cause correlated size change in sub-cortical visual pathways, in cortical visual and motor areas, in cerebellum, in relays between cortex and cerebellum located in the thalamus and pons, and possibly also in vestibular nuclei in the medulla.

Testing whether brain evolution involves size change in specific neurocognitive systems therefore requires more fine-grained comparative analysis. The hypothesis predicts that the components of such systems exhibit correlated evolution: they should have changed in size together, but independently of change in other systems. This prediction has been borne out by several comparative studies using phylogenetic methods for detecting correlated evolution. For example, separate components of the visual system have evolved together independently of size change in other brain structures (Barton *et al.*, 1995). In general, positive correlations between structures within neural systems are ubiquitous: among a range of brain systems and within separate taxonomic groups, anatomical and functional connections closely predicted significant positive correlations between pairs of structures (Barton and Harvey, 2000).

In some cases it has been possible to test the prediction of correlated evolution at the level of individual nuclei. As suggested above, connected nuclei in the hind-, mid- and fore-brain of the cortico-cerebellar system evolved together independently of variation in other systems (Whiting and Barton, 2003). Within this system, the four vestibular and three cerebellar nuclei have one direct connection (between the lateral vestibular and middle cerebellar nuclei), and it is these that show correlated evolution after controlling for the size of other structures (Whiting and Barton, 2003). Hence, functional and anatomical connections in the brain closely predict fine-grained patterns of correlated evolution.

11.5. From evolutionary biology to neuroscience …

It should, in principle, be possible to turn the process of predicting correlated evolution from neuroscientific data on its head. The fact that brain nuclei evolve together according to their functional connections could be used to help resolve uncertainty about aspects of brain organization. An example concerns debate about the structural and functional integrity of the amygdala. The amygdala is a small temporal lobe structure with extensive connections to neocortical areas, including those involved in processing social information. In primates more than in other species, the amygdala 'sprays' connections to many neocortical areas (Young *et al.*, 1994). Electrophysiological, clinical and functional imaging studies have implicated the amygdala in responses to emotional stimuli, particularly fear and anger (Brothers, 1990; Adolphs, 2001). Despite great interest in the role of the amygdala in animal and human behaviour and its potential role in 'the social brain' (Brothers, 1990; Adolphs, 2001), its very existence as a structurally and functionally unified brain component has been questioned, because different regions within it have divergent pharmacological and connectional characteristics. Swanson and Petrovich (1998) argued that the term 'amygdala' refers to a collection of disparate nuclei that are really parts of quite separate neural systems. On the other hand, some researchers consider that dense connections between nuclei within the amygdala indicate a coordination of neural activity consonant with its being part of an integrated system (see Aggleton and Saunders, 2000).

It would be easy to envisage a perpetual cycle of claim and counter-claim about the neurobiological validity of the amygdala, based on affinities among nuclei and differences between them, respectively. The problem lies in deciding what constitutes sufficient evidence to conclude that the amygdala either does, or does not, exist as a structurally and functionally integrated entity. Whether or not the amygdala is deemed to exist is not, however, simply a matter of taste, but lies at the heart of the systems neuroscience project: what is the organization of the brain? I argue that this question is inherently an evolutionary one (Barton *et al.*, 2003). Like all complex biological traits that function conspicuously well, neural systems exist because they evolved by the process of natural selection (Young *et al.*, 2000). The question of whether particular components constitute parts of a unified neural system or structure therefore amounts to a question about how they evolved. If two or more brain structures evolved together in a closely coordinated fashion, in a way that cannot be attributed merely to their integration within a larger, more global system (such as the limbic system or even the brain as a whole), it is difficult to escape the conclusion that they are components of a structurally and functionally unified system.

Phylogenetic analysis of comparative data on brain structure volumes in primates and insectivores clearly shows that the amygdala coheres as an evolutionary unit: after controlling for variation in a range of other brain structures, including other limbic structures, separate groups of nuclei in the amygdala show significantly correlated volumetric evolution (Barton *et al.*, 2003). Amygdala nuclei also correlate with other structures outside the amygdala, and these correlations differ slightly in different taxonomic groups (Barton *et al.*, 2003), reflecting taxonomic differences in the extrinsic connectivity of the amygdala (Young *et al.*, 1994). The strongest and most consistent correlations, however, are between components of the amygdala, hence refuting the claim that they are parts of entirely different neural systems.

Evolutionary analysis, whether based on volumetric data, neuron numbers, connectivity, gene expression or other data, therefore has considerable potential to shed light on the architecture of the brain. Extending his analysis of the amygdala to the broader question of the overall organization of the vertebrate brain, Swanson (2000) notes that the basic parts have been grouped in several different ways corresponding to different theories of brain architecture, and that, even today, there is no undisputed model of the fundamental relationships between brain structures. Swanson suggests that molecular techniques have the potential to unlock the secrets of brain organization. Whilst surely important, such an approach must be placed in phylogenetic context in order to understand how the relevant genes evolved and gave rise over time to distinctively different patterns of brain organization in different species. Meanwhile, analysis of volumetric data reveals some fundamental similarities, as well as some differences, in the evolutionary relationships among basic brain structures. Analysis of bivariate relationships suggests that all major structures evolve in a quite strongly coordinated fashion, suggesting that brain size may capture much of the variability in specific systems (Finlay and Darlington, 1995). Teasing apart these relationships further, however, using phylogenetic methods (Harvey and Pagel, 1991) and multivariate analyses reveals more fine-grained patterns (Figure 11.1). The chain of structures along the main axis in the diagrams (medulla–mesencephalon–diencephalon–neocortex) corresponds to a basic anatomical sequence from posterior (medulla) to anterior (neocortex) parts of the brain, and major projections are found between each of the links in this chain. For example, the main part of the diencephalon, the thalamus, is the site of many major relays to and from the neocortex. The triangular relationship between diencephalon, neocortex and cerebellum reflects the presence of major thalamo-cortico-cerebellar circuits. Hence, the evolutionary patterns are consistent with anatomical data at the level of basic brain subdivisions. On the other hand, the taxonomic differences in the patterns observed suggest that the constraints on how brains evolve are not rigid, and, as with the differing correlations for extrinsic connections of the amygdala, imply hypotheses about taxonomic differences in brain architecture. It is important to emphasize that these patterns are empirically derived. Although the choice of structures to include and how they are demarcated will inevitably influence the statistical outcomes, the similarities among different mammalian orders are striking and imply some fundamental underlying rules of mammalian brain organization.

Phylogenetic comparative analysis therefore reveals how brain structures evolved in relation to one another within taxonomic groups, and thereby provides evolutionary models of brain organization meriting further investigation. Such models may be framed at the level of fundamental relationships among major brain components or at the level of more fine-grained relationships among specific nuclei. In terms of understanding how natural selection modified brains, the existence of neural systems distributed across different brain regions, and the patterns of coordinated evolution among components that

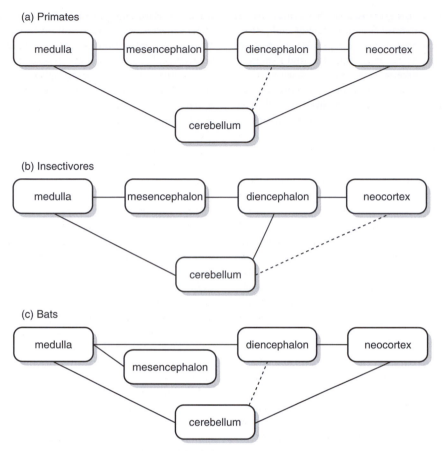

Fig. 11.1 Empirical patterns of correlated evolution among major brain structures in three mammalian orders. Phylogenetically independent contrasts were calculated from the volumetric data of Stephan *et al.* (1981). Partial correlations were then calculated between pairs of structures, controlling for variation in the other structures (see Barton and Harvey, 2000). Solid lines signify significant positive correlations ($P < 0.05$). Dotted lines between cerebellum and either neocortex or diencephalon represent correlations that were significant only when the third structure in this triangular relationship was removed. Hence, there is a tight, three-way evolutionary relationship among these structures. See Barton and Harvey (2000) for further details of methods.

these distributed systems reflect, demand that variation in the size of any particular component be interpreted at least partly in the context of variation in other components.

11.6. ... and back again: primate brain evolution and the neocortex

Variation in neocortex size is a prominent feature of brain structure variation in mammals (Kaas, 1995; Allman, 1999; Barton in press). In humans, the neocortex comprises about 75% of total brain volume, whereas in some shrews the equivalent figure is under 10% (Frahm *et al.*, 1982), These percentage differences are, to some extent, simply a reflection of the general tendency for the neocortex to increase relatively quickly with increases in overall brain size (Finlay and Darlington, 1995; Barton and Harvey, 2000). After controlling for the size of other brain structures, the neocortex is, on average, approximately five times larger in primates than in insectivores, with some comparisons of individual species yielding 10-fold differences (Barton and Harvey, 2000). Further variation is evident within the primate order: monkeys and apes have a significantly larger neocortex, relative to the size of the rest of the brain, than do lemurs and lorises (Barton, 1996), and overall brain size correlates positively with the extent of neocortical expansion relative to the rest of the brain (Barton, 2000, p. 225). Hence, large-brained primates tend to have a disproportionately enlarged neocortex. As the neocortex is often associated with 'higher cognition', these patterns are often taken as an indication that primates in general, and anthropoid primates in particular, are smart. The fact that relative neocortex size correlates with indices of social complexity such as group size in primates and in some other taxonomic groups has been taken to indicate that it is social smartness in particular that underlies large neocortex size in primates (Dunbar, 1998).

As we have seen, however, variation in neocortex size alone is unlikely to be the whole story, because of the correlated variation in other structures. This correlated variation accords with the way that the functional systems of the brain cut across the major subdivisions (Arbib et al., 1998; Ramnani, 2006), and with the fact that there is no known cognitive process mediated exclusively by the neocortex. Complex cognitive processes are mediated by networks that link the neocortex with many other structures. Furthermore, the neocortex is a highly heterogeneous organ, processing information from all the senses and being involved in many different aspects of sensory, motor and cognitive processing (Allman, 1999; Bond, 2004). Understanding the functional significance of neocortex size therefore requires that we narrow the field of candidate neural systems implicated by considering which other structures show correlated variation. In addition, we must consider the possibility that selection has acted on different neural systems in different lineages, such that no single cognitive or behavioural trait explains all of the observed variation in brain and neocortex size.

The general patterns of correlated variation between neocortex and other brain structures, derived from several comparative studies,

are summarized in Figure 11.2. One clear finding of these studies has been the relationship between neocortical evolution and visual specialization. Features of primate visual specialization include the following: relatively large, frontally directed eyes with a high degree of binocular overlap, facilitating stereopsis; high visual acuity—particularly in diurnal anthropoids—associated with a well-developed retinal fovea containing a high density of photoreceptors; and a lateral geniculate nucleus (LGN) with up to six distinct layers, including both the two magnocellular layers common to all mammals and two to four parvocellular layers not found in other mammals (Allman, 1987; Allmann and McGuinness, 1988). These visual specializations are associated with a complex arrangement of highly interconnected and numerous cortical visual areas. In macaques, visual areas make up about half of the neocortex (van Essen et al., 1992), and also have extensive inputs into 'non-visual' areas, such as those in frontal cortical regions.

Comparative analysis shows that these elaborations of the visual system in primates contributed substantially to variation in neocortex and brain size. Among mammalian species, Striedter (2005, p. 211) notes a correlation between the number of visual areas and total neocortex size in mammals, whilst Kirk (2006) demonstrates correlated evolution between brain size and the size of the optic foramen (which is closely related to optic nerve size) in carnivores and primates. Within primates, neocortical expansion correlates with the relative size of the LGN, and neocortex and LGN size correlate with the same behavioural traits (Barton, 1998). Several characteristics of the eyes correlate with neocortex and brain size: binocularity (the degree of convergence of the orbits, which determines the area of overlap of the visual fields of each eye); density of retinal ganglion cells; eye size (which partly determines acuity); and relative size of the optic nerve (Barton, 2004; Barton, unpublished). Within the LGN, the functional dissociation between parvocellular layers (which project to ventral cortical areas involved in high-acuity colour vision and fine-grained stereopsis), and magnocellular layers (which project primarily to dorsal areas involved in movement detection and the analysis of dynamic form) is reflected in

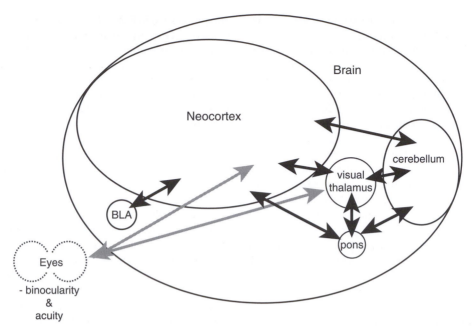

Fig. 11.2 Empirical patterns of correlated volumetric evolution among components of the cortico-cerebellar network, basolateral amygdala (BLA) and visual system. Arrows represent significant positive partial correlations between the structures after controlling for variation in other structures. Black arrows: correlations among brain structures. Grey arrow: correlation between peripheral visual traits and neocortex. See Figure 11.1 for methods.

an evolutionary dissociation: the volume and neuron number of parvocellular layers, and not magnocellular layers, correlate with binocularity, with neocortex and overall brain size, and with ecological factors (Barton, 1998, 1999, 2004).

Because no apes (including humans) were included in the comparative studies of the lateral geniculate nucleus layers, it is not known whether the relationship between parvocellular expansion and brain size generalizes to that group. In fact, there is some evidence for a relative reduction in lateral geniculate nucleus and primary visual cortex in apes (Dunbar, 2003), that is particularly marked in humans (Striedter, 2005). However, a relative reduction of these specific visual areas does not necessarily preclude the possibility of visual specialization, because there are other visual pathways. Intriguingly, there is evidence for elaboration of the dorsal rather than ventral visual stream. Humans, compared with macaques, show a marked expansion of parietal visual areas in the dorsal stream (van Essen *et al.*, 2001).

The expansion of these parietal visual areas, which receive only magnocellular projections from the LGN, fits nicely with the discovery that, in humans, area V1 has a distinctive organization, involving enhancement of the magnocellular rather than parvocellular inputs (Preuss and Coleman, 2002).

Also represented in Figure 11.2 are correlations among components of the cortico-cerebellar circuits via pons and thalamus, based on the comparative study of Whiting and Barton (2003). These correlations reflect the existence in primates of extensive cortico-ponto-cerebellar projections originating throughout the neocortex (Allen *et al.*, 2005; Ramnani *et al.*, 2005; Ramnani, 2006). In a nice parallel to these evolutionary correlations, a recent functional imaging study shows correlated spontaneous activation of the cerebellum, neocortex, thalamus, and some other subcortical regions (Allen *et al.*, 2005). The evolution of this system is likely to be related to the kinds of visual specializations discussed above. Cortico-cerebellar functions include visually guided reaching and manipulation, and programming of complex motor skills (Glickstein, 1998). Thier and Ilg (2005) note that smooth-pursuit eye-movements in primates are based on a unique cortico-ponto-cerebellar pathway that evolved in parallel with foveal vision, whilst Preuss (1993) notes that a substantial proportion of frontal and parietal cortex in macaques is involved in the organization of visually guided reaching and grasping, and that another cortical area involved in this task, the ventral premotor area, may be unique to primates. Taken together, therefore, the comparative and experimental data suggest that one of the factors underlying neocortical and cerebellar enlargement in primates was specialization for visually guided bodily control, especially of hand movements, and this is consistent with evolutionary models of the origins of primate adaptations that emphasize visually-guided grasping and manipulation (Cartmill, 1974; Sussman, 1991). Significant cerebellar enlargement in great apes (Rilling, 2006) fits with Byrne's (1995) argument that cognitive specialization in great apes is associated with the learning and execution of complex, planned, visually guided food-processing tasks (including tool use). However, emerging evidence for the role of the cerebellum in a wide range of functions, including sensory discrimination, working memory, imitation, language and emotion (e.g. Mulle et al., 1998; Chaminade et al., 2002; Allen et al., 2005; Schutter and von Honk, 2005; Ramnani, 2006) suggests that the cognitive significance of cerebellar evolution may be much broader than visuo-motor control and programming.

Two general implications of Figure 11.2 are important. First, the evolution of central and peripheral neural mechanisms were intimately related: in primates, the evolution of sophisticated visual mechanisms based on fine-grained stereoscopic vision required both specialized eyes and specialized brains. The association between neocortex size and peripheral sensory specializations supporting stereopsis and acuity, calls into question the assumption that anthropoid cognitive adaptations and neocortical evolution are based primarily on frontal brain regions (Falk, 1992; Dunbar, 1998). Frontal regions do have important visual and cerebellar

connections (e.g. Ramnani et al., 2005; Ramnani, 2006) and so are likely to be involved in the networks represented in Figure 11.2, but together with connected areas in temporal, occipital and parietal cortex, and in cerebellum, not in isolation (see also Striedter, 2005). Even in humans, it has proved difficult to show that it is frontal regions of the neocortex that are particularly expanded (Semendeferi et al., 1997, 2001, 2002; Rilling and Seligman, 2002; Schenker et al., 2005; Schoenemann et al., 2005; Striedter, 2005). Whilst Semendeferi et al. (2001) claimed that Area 10 of prefrontal cortex is relatively enlarged in humans compared with great apes, this was directly contradicted by their own data: on a log–log plot of Area 10 size compared to the rest of the brain, humans fell exactly on the line of best fit. One study even found that anthropoids have smaller frontal cortices relative to the rest of the cortex than do lemurs and lorises (Bush and Allman, 2004), probably reflecting the relative expansion in anthropoids of occipital and temporal visual cortices.

The second general implication is that the evolution of the neocortex (or of any brain component) cannot be adequately understood in isolation from those other components with which it shares the neural pathways upon which selection acted. This does not mean that all structures with direct connections to the neocortex contribute to primate cognitive specialization. Interestingly, the size of the hippocampal complex, which is important in learning and memory and which has major connections with the neocortex, does not differ significantly in size between primate sub-orders, nor between primates and insectivores (Barton, 2000), and does not correlate with neocortex size independently of variation in other structures (Barton and Harvey, 2000). And even those structures that have tended to evolve closely together, such as the neocortex and cerebellum, need not have done so in a rigidly constrained way. The extent of correlated evolution will depend on which specific sub-systems within these structures, with what connections to other structures, selection acted on. It is not therefore anomalous that the neocortex and cerebellum show both correlated evolution and a degree of evolutionary dissociation: both are enlarged in primates compared with insectivores, but neocortex size differs more, and only neocortex size distinguishes anthropoids from lemurs and lorises (Barton, in press), whereas only cerebellum size distinguishes apes from other anthropoid primates (Rilling, 2006). There may also be differences between phylogenetic lineages in which specific cortical and cerebellar regions evolved together: Ramnani *et al.* (2005) found that humans have a larger prefrontal cortical input to the cerebellum compared with macaques. Observed patterns of correlated evolution among major brain components do not therefore reflect obligate neurobiological constraints, but are simply indicative of functional connections and the distributed nature of the neural systems on which selection acted.

In summary, the patterns of primate brain evolution are complex but intelligible. Relative change in neocortex size was a major feature, but did not occur in isolation. The variability in which structures changed across different evolutionary radiations presumably reflects differences in the selection pressures associated with these radiations, a supposition consistent with the fact that overall brain and neocortex size correlate with multiple ecological factors (Barton, 1999; Deaner *et al.*, 2000; Shultz and Dunbar, 2005).

11.7. Cognitive implications

The comparative studies summarized above make clear that the neural systems implicated in primate brain evolution are not exclusively neocortical, but are distributed across multiple brain regions. They involve networks that integrate sensory (e.g. social) information, motor control and emotional significance. The question may then be raised in some people's minds: this is all very well in terms of the basic sensory–motor and emotional responses, but what about *cognition*? Isn't the really interesting stuff that primates do, like reasoning, deception and theory of mind, located in 'higher' cortical regions? I suggest, however, that this way of framing the question, in terms of cognition as distinct from 'basic' sensory–motor control, is fundamentally misconceived.

The distinction between cognition as a process of interpreting and integrating information about the outside world on one hand, and the

information that this process is about on the other, is ubiquitous. Classically in the cognitive sciences, distinctions are made between 'peripheral' and 'central' neural processes, between sensory inputs, cognition and behavioural outputs. Hence, cognitive ('thinking') processes tend to be treated as something distinct from both sensory–motor control and emotion. These distinctions are common, probably because it subjectively seems that this is how our own mental processes work: 'we' (our conscious, cognitive selves) interpret and act upon information received from the environment (Crick, 1990). Fodor's (1983) influential treatment, for example, distinguishes between modular input systems and a general-purpose 'higher' cognitive system that can make inferences about information received from the input systems. Similarly, comparative psychologists have sought to test for species differences in intelligence and reasoning abilities as abstractions from their context within the natural sensory–motor capacities and emotional predispositions of each species.

The social intelligence industry has also absorbed this way of constructing the problem: social cognition is construed in terms of cognitive mechanisms that analyse environmental information (what is happening in your social group) and compute abstract conceptual representations and relationships (e.g. Premack and Woodruffe, 1978; Dasser, 1988; Cosmides, 1989) which then inform the animal's decisions about how to act. Nevertheless, a growing body of opinion suggests that the view of cognition as distinct from perception, action and emotion has no theoretical or empirical foundation, and actually hinders advances in understanding brain-behaviour relationships and the nature of cognitive processes (Damasio, 1994; Clark, 1997; Chiel and Beer, 1997; Gigerenzer, 1997; Brooks, 1999; Barrett and Henzi, 2005; Barrett *et al.*, in press; Gallese, in press, a,b).

As Clark (1997) makes clear in his elegant treatment of the problem, at the root of these distinctions is a fundamentally disembodied and dualist view of the mind. The notion of a central executor, an intelligent being, a 'we' that is distinct from the information acquired from the environment, is a version of the Cartesian 'ghost in the machine', the homunculus that sits within us peering out at the world and pulling the strings to make our bodies move. As remarked above, this dualism is probably an inference from introspection: it does subjectively feel as though we have minds that exist independently of the information they receive and the actions they generate. But one of the lessons of cognitive neuroscience is that introspection is a poor guide to how minds actually work. For example, introspection would not have predicted the surprising dissociations between functions such as the ability to recognize a familiar person's physical features and the feeling that those features do indeed belong to that same person rather than to a physically identical imposter (Ellis and Lewis, 2001), nor the finding that the visual properties of a stimulus, such as its movements and its shape, are processed in separate parts of the brain (e.g. Livingstone and Hubel, 1988; Milner and Goodale, 1995). Furthermore, the distinctions do not correspond to the structure of the nervous system or to how its functions are physiologically implemented. One only has to ask where in the nervous system the transition between perception and cognition is supposed to occur to realize that the distinction is of no help in understanding the functional organization of the brain or the nature of real-world biological cognition (Clark, 1997).

An alternative approach starts from the proposition that, fundamentally, the behavioural function of the brain is to perform adaptive sensory–motor transformations (Chiel and Beer, 1997; Clark, 1997; Barton and Dunbar, 1997). As Clark (1997, p. 1) says "... the biological mind is, first and foremost, an organ for controlling the biological body. Minds make motions, and they must make them fast—before the predator catches you, or before your prey gets away from you. Minds are *not* disembodied logical reasoning devices." The lack of a need to postulate separate 'cognitive' and 'sensory–motor' processes is supported by research in robotics: when animate robots have been designed that can successfully carry out simple behavioural tasks, they do so not through a system of internal representations and central control, but using a number of interacting sensory–motor systems without any explicit symbolic encoding

or recoding of inputs (Brooks, 1999). In the real world inhabited by organic organisms, making the right (i.e. adaptive) sensory–motor transformation is of course inextricably linked to the animal's emotional response to it, and to the possible alternative courses of action. Damasio (1994) therefore argues convincingly that emotional processes are an intrinsic part of cognition, not supplementary to it: contrary to *Star Trek*'s Mr Spock, one cannot act rationally in the absence of an emotional valence to the alternative courses of action. Cognition can therefore be thought of as an array of embodied, emotionally valent and interacting sensory–motor processes.

The tendency to view sensory–motor control as non-cognitive may be linked to the assumption that it is computationally and neurobiologically trivial. And yet the lesson of artificial intelligence and robotics is the reverse. Whilst programmes designed to calculate chess moves are capable of beating grand masters, when it comes to picking up, manipulating and accurately moving the pieces, the current state of the art cannot match the dexterity of a small child (Wolpert *et al.*, 2003). Similarly, although we may tend to think of vision and visuo-motor control as something rather prosaic and straightforward, neuroscientists' attempts to unravel the visual system of primates have revealed startling complexity, with correspondingly extensive neural tissue devoted to it (Crick, 1990; van Essen *et al.*, 1992; Young, 1992). A key design feature is the presence of two distinct cortical processing streams, one projecting across the dorsal neocortex and the other across ventral areas (Allman and McGuinness, 1988; Livingstone and Hubel, 1988; Young *et al.*, 1994). Whilst the exact organization and functional division of labour between these two streams is still under review (e.g. Milner and Goodale, 1995; Gallese, in press a), it is clear that the ventral stream includes temporal lobe areas that are crucially important in social interaction. Neurons in infero-temporal cortex respond selectively to faces, and major connections have been discovered between this cortical region and the amygdala (Brothers, 1990). The amygdala also contains cells that respond selectively to faces and is involved in recognizing and responding to emotional signals such as fear and anger in both facial expressions (Brothers, 1990; Adolphs, 2001) and bodily movements (de Gelder, 2006). Temporal lobe damage causes a variety of deficits in social interaction, such as inability to recognize familiar faces, inability to distinguish different types of emotional expressions, and inappropriate responses to social signals (Adolphs, 2001). Temporal cortex also projects to prefrontal cortex, where social information can be processed whilst held in working memory (Goldman-Rakic, 1994). This ventral stream–prefrontal network may therefore be best characterized as a system for processing complex social signals in an emotional context. The signals need not be exclusively visual, and recent evidence shows that parallel auditory pathways exist with a division of labour similar to that of the visual pathways (Kraus, 2005), and that amygdala damage leads to auditory as well as visual deficits in recognizing emotions (Scott et al., 1997). Nevertheless, visual inputs are clearly a major part of the temporal–prefrontal network in primates and probably explain the temporal lobe expansion observed in fossil endocasts of early primate crania (Jerison, 1973; Preuss, 1993).

These supposedly 'low-level' sensory–cognitive processes have been largely ignored in discussions of primate social cognition, although they were explicit in Leslie Brothers' original formulation of the social brain hypothesis (Brothers, 1990). This neglect is perhaps surprising given that field primatologists are so familiar with the richness and complexity of the constant stream of visual signals that a successful group member must be able to process and respond to appropriately, including facial and postural stimuli, subtle gradations of emotions such as fear and anger, temporally sequenced events, and polyadic contexts such as coalition formation.

What is the neural basis of the individual's understanding of this stream of social information? Recent studies strongly suggest that social understanding is based on linkages between the neural systems for perceiving the behaviour of others and the systems for producing the same behaviour. The best known manifestation of these linkages is in the 'mirror neuron' system, in which the same regions in parietal cortex are activated when an individual observes another

making a specific action and when the individual performs the action itself (Gallese, in press a; Rizollati and Fogassi, this volume, Chapter 14). There is also linkage between the control of actions and the prediction of the actions of others, both being associated with activation of the motor system (Ramnani and Miall, 2004). Oztop et al. (2005) have developed a computational model showing that control mechanisms for manual manipulation are 'pre-adapted' for visual and predictive processing capabilities, and thus provide a basis for the understanding of movements by others through mental simulation. They conclude that "computational elements developed for sensorimotor control are effective in inferring the mental states of others" (p. 129). Hence, these studies of the linkages between motor control, action perception and action prediction are beginning to provide a concrete, computationally explicit and neurobiologically realistic basis for social understanding. They point to 'embodied simulation' as a key mechanism in primate social cognition, imitation and possibly even human language (Gallese, in press a,b).

Mirror neuron research has concentrated on goal-directed movements, particularly of the hands. Emotional expressions and body language are also subject to mirroring, however (Gallese et al., 2004). Regions within the amygdala and associated cortical regions, for example, are activated both when the individual experiences an emotion such as fear, and when perceiving the fearful reactions of others. This emotional mirror system may well be the basis for the contagiousness of emotional behaviour (de Gelder, 2006). It may also be a key component of imitation. Williams et al. (2006) found that, in autistic spectrum disorder (ASD), deficits in imitation were associated with both decreased activity in classic mirror neuron cortical areas and lack of modulation of neural activity in the amygdala. The amygdala appears to have a central role in autistic syndrome (Baron-Cohen et al., 2000), and Williams et al. (2006) relate the observed neural correlates of imitation deficits to a failure to engage emotionally with the actions or goal of the model. In line with the arguments developed here, they suggest that ASD involves "abnormal patterns of integration ... between areas involved in visual analysis, motor action, proprioception and emotional processing" (p. 620).

The physiological and neuroimaging data indicating an intimate relationship between action production, action perception, action understanding and mental state attribution in primates converge neatly on the comparative neuroanatomical evidence for correlated evolution of visual systems, neocortex and cerebellum. Recent functional imaging studies, for example, show that the cortico-cerebellar system is involved in the capacity to model both the motor action patterns of others (Chaminade et al., 2002; Muhlau et al., 2005) and also their mental states (Jackson et al., 2005; Shamay-Tsoory et al., 2005). The cognitive implications of visuo-motor specialization based on cortico-cerebellar circuits are thus likely to extend to social learning and cultural transmission. These require the capacity for shared visual attention, monitoring of gaze direction (Baron-Cohen, 1994), and for mapping the visual model onto a corresponding motor action pattern (Wolpert et al., 2003), which are all capacities associated with cortico-cerebellar circuits. Mirror neurons have so far been found in cortical motor regions such as ventral premotor cortex (Rizollati and Fogassi, this volume, Chapter 14). Given, however, the connectivity and coevolution of these cortical regions with the cerebellum, and the involvement of the cerebellum in sensorily guided movement, it seems reasonable to predict that mirror neurons will eventually be found in the cerebellum. The emerging role of the cerebellum in emotion (Schutter and van Honk, 2005), including the simulation and attribution of emotional states in others (Shamay-Tsoory et al., 2005) is intriguing, and further supports the idea that the social brain comprises a highly distributed neural system with the capacity to perceive, model, empathize with and predict the behaviour of others.

11.8. Conclusion

Patterns of neural system evolution, neuroanatomical connectivity and functional brain activation all indicate that the social brain is not, as sometimes implied, localized in a homunculus-like way in 'higher' cortical areas. Instead it consists of a network of components distributed among a variety of cortical and non-cortical structures, forming the neural basis of sensory–emotional–motor systems for decoding and responding to social situations. Although the evolution of these systems had a marked impact on the size of the neocortex as a whole, cortical connections from neocortex to cerebellum, and to sub-cortical temporal lobe structures such as the amygdala, have also played an important role in the evolutionary diversification of the primate brain. This 'distributed' view of the neural basis of primate cognition, together with the emerging evidence for the continuity between sensory–motor, emotional and cognitive processes, implies that we should cease to think of the neocortex as the 'intelligent' bit of the brain, and cease to study cognitive evolution in terms of abstract conceptual and representational abilities divorced from the natural behavioural contexts in which information processing specializations evolved.

References

Adolphs, R. (2001) The neurobiology of social cognition. *Current Opinion in Neurobiology*, 11: 231–239.

Aggleton, J. P. and Saunders, R. C. (2000) The amygdala: what's happened in the last decade? In J. P. Aggleton (ed.) *The Amygdala: A Functional Approach*. Oxford University Press.

Aiello, L. C. and Dunbar, R. I. M. (1993) Neocortex size, group-size, and the evolution of language. *Current Anthropology*, 34: 184–193.

Allen, G., McColl, R., Barnard, H., Ringe, W. K., Fleckenstein, J. and Cullum, C. M. (2005) Magnetic resonance imaging of cerebellar–prefrontal and cerebellar–parietal functional connectivity. *Neuroimage*, 28: 39–48.

Allman, J. and McGuinness, E. (1988) Visual cortex in primates. In H. Steklis (ed.) *Comparative Primate Biology*, vol. 4, pp. 279–326. Alan R. Liss, New York.

Allman, J. M. (1999) *Evolving Brains*. Scientific American Publications, New York.

Arbib, M. A., Erdi, P. and Szentagothai, J. (1998) *Neural Organization*. MIT Press, Cambridge, MA.

Baron-Cohen, S. (1994) A model of the mindreading system: neuropsychological and neurobiological perspectives. In P. Mitchell and C. Lewis (eds) *Origins of An Understanding of Mind*. Lawrence Erlbaum, New York.

Baron-Cohen, S., Ring, H. A., Bullmore, E. T., Wheelwright, S., Ashwin, C. and Williams, S. C. (2000) The amygdala theory of autism. *Neuroscience and Biobehavioral Reviews* 24: 355–364.

Barrett, L. and Henzi, P. (2005) The social nature of primate cognition. *Proceedings of the Royal Society* B, 272: 1865–1875.

Barrett, L., Henzi, P. and Rendall, D. (in press) Social cognition and the sources of complexity. *Philosophical Transactions of the Royal Society B*.

Barton, R. A. (1996) Neocortex size and behavioural ecology in primates. *Proceedings of the Royal Society B*, 263: 173–177.

Barton, R. A. (1998) Visual specialization and brain evolution in primates. *Proceedings of the Royal Society B*, 265: 1933–1937.

Barton, R. A. (1999) The evolutionary ecology of the primate brain. In P. C. Lee (ed.) *Comparative Primate Socioecology*, pp. 167–203. Cambridge University Press, Cambridge.

Barton, R. A. (2004) Binocularity and brain evolution in primates *Proceedings of the National Academy of Sciences*, 101: 10113–10115.

Barton, R. A. (2006) Olfactory evolution and behavioural ecology in primates. *American Journal of Primatology*, 68: 545–558.

Barton, R. A. (in press) Primate brain evolution: integrating comparative, neurophysiological and ethological data. *Evolutionary Anthropology*.

Barton, R. A. and Aggleton, J. (2000) Primate evolution and the amygdala. In J. P. Aggleton (ed.) *The Amygdala: A Functional Analysis*, pp. 480–508. Oxford University Press, Oxford.

Barton, R. A. and Harvey, P. H. (2000) Mosaic evolution of brain structure in mammals. *Nature*, 405: 1055–1058.

Barton, R. A., Purvis, A. and Harvey, P. H. (1995) Evolutionary radiation of visual and olfactory brain systems in primates, bats and insectivores. *Philosophical Transactions of the Royal Society, B*, 348: 381–392.

Barton, R. A., Aggleton, J. and Grenyer, R. (2003) Evolutionary coherence of the mammalian amygdala. *Proceedings of the Royal Society of London, B* 270: 539–544.

Bond, A. H. (2004) An information-processing analysis of the functional architecture of the primate neocortex. *Journal of Theoretical Biology*, 227: 51–79.

Brooks, R. A. (1999) *Cambrian Intelligence: The Early History of the New AI*. MIT Press, Cambridge, MA.

Brothers, L. (1990) The social brain: a project for integrating primate behavior and neurophysiology in a new domain. *Concepts in Neuroscience*, 1: 27–51.

Bush, E. C. and Allman, J. M. (2004) The scaling of frontal cortex in primates and carnivores. *Proceedings of the National Academy of Sciences*, 101: 3962–3966.

Byrne, R. W. (1995) *The Thinking Ape: Evolutionary Origins of Intelligence*. Oxford University Press, Oxford.

Cartmill, M. (1974) Rethinking primate origins. *Science*, 184: 436–443.

Chaminade, T., Meltzoff, A. N. and Decety, J. (2002) Does the end justify the means? A PET exploration of the mechanisms involved in human imitation. *Neuroimage* 15: 318–328.

Chiel, H. J. and Beer, R. D. (1997) The brain has a body: adaptive behavior emerges from interactions of nervous system, body and environment. *Trends in Neurosciences*, 20: 553–557.

Clark, A. (1997) *Being there: Putting Brain, Body, and World Together Again*. MIT Press, Cambridge, MA.

Clutton-Brock, T. H. and Harvey, P. H. (1980) Primates, brains and ecology. *Journal of Zoology*, 207: 151–169.

Cosmides, L. (1989) The logic of social exchange: has natural selection shaped how humans reason? *Cognition* 31: 187–276.

Crick, F. (1990) *The Astonishing Hypothesis: The Scientific Search for the Soul*. Simon and Schuster, New York.

Damasio, A. (1994) *Descartes' Error: Emotion, Reason and the Human Brain*. Putnam, New York.

Dasser, V. (1988) A social concept in Java monkeys. *Animal Behaviour*, 36: 225–230.

Darwin, C. (1859) *On the Origin of Species*. John Murray, London.

Deacon, T. (1997) *The Symbolic Species*. Penguin, London.

Deaner, R. O. and Nunn, C. L. (1999) How quickly do brains catch up with bodies? A comparative method for detecting evolutionary lag. *Proceedings of the Royal Society of London, B*, 266: 687–694.

Deaner, R. O., Nunn, C. L. and van Schaik, C. P. (2000) Comparative tests of primate cognition: different scaling methods produce different results. *Brain Behavior and Evolution*, 55: 44–52.

de Gelder, B. (2006) Towards the neurobiology of emotional body language. *Nature Review of Neuroscience*, 7: 242–249.

Dunbar, R. I. M. (1998) The social brain hypothesis. *Evolutionary Anthropology* 6: 178–190.

Dunbar, R. I. M. (2003) Why are apes so smart? In P. M. Kappeler and M. E. Perreira (eds) *Primate Life Histories and Socioecology*, pp. 285–298. Chicago University Press, Chicago.

Dunbar, R. I. M. and Bever, J. (1998) Neocortex size predicts group size in carnivores and some insectivores. *Ethology*, 104: 695–708.

Eisenberg, J. F. and Wilson, D. E. (1978) Relative brain size and feeding strategies in the chiroptera. *American Naturalist*, 32: 740–751.

Ellis, H. D. and Lewis, M. B. (2001) Capgras delusion: a window on face recognition. *Trends in Cognitive Sciences* 5: 149–156.

Falk, D. (1992) *Braindance: New Discoveries about Human Origins and Brain Evolution*. Henry Holt, New York.

Finlay, B. L. and Darlington, R. B. (1995) Linked regularities in the development and evolution of mammalian brains. *Science*, 268: 1578–1584.

Fodor, J. A. (1983) *The Modularity of Mind*. MIT Press, Cambridge, MA.

Frahm, H. D., Stephan, H. and Stephan, M. (1982) Comparison of brain structure volumes in Insectivora and Primates. I. Neocortex. *Journal fur Hirnforschung*, 23: 375–389.

Gallese, V. (in press a) The "conscious" dorsal stream: Embodied simulation and its role in space and action conscious awareness. *Psyche*.

Gallese, V. (in press b) Before and below Theory of Mind: embodied simulation and the neural correlates of social cognition. *Philosophical Transactions of the Royal Society, B*.

Gallese, V., Keysers, C. and Rizzolatti, G. (2004) A unifying view of the basis of social cognition. *Trends in Cognitive Sciences* 8: 396–403.

Gigerenzer, G. (1997) The modularity of social intelligence. In A. Whiten and R. W. Byrne (eds) *Machiavellian Intelligence II: Extensions and Evaluations*. Cambridge University Press, Cambridge.

Glickstein, M. (1998) Cerebellum and the sensory guidance of movement. *Novartis Foundation Symposium*, 218: 252–271.

Goldman-Rakic, P. S. (1996) The prefrontal landscape: implications of functional architecture for understanding human mentation and the central executive. *Philosophical Transactions of the Royal Society of London, B*, 351: 1445–1453.

Gould, S. J. (1975) Allometry in primates with emphasis on scaling and the evolution of the brain. *Contributions to Primatology*, 5: 244–292.

Gould, S. J. (1978) *Ever Since Darwin*. Pelican, London.

Harcourt, A. H., Purvis, A. and Liles, L. (1996) Sperm competition: mating systems, not breeding season, affects testes size of primates. *Functional Ecology*, 10: 306–306.

Harvey, P. H. and Krebs, J. R. (1990) Comparing brains. *Science*, 249: 140–146.

Harvey, P. H. and Pagel, M. D. (1991) *The Comparative Method in Evolutionary Biology*. Oxford University Press, Oxford.

Heyes, C. M. (1998) Theory of mind in nonhuman primates. *Behavioral and Brain Sciences*, 21: 101–.

Jackson, P. L., Meltzoff, A. N. and Decety, J. (2005) How do we perceive the pain of others? A window into the neural processes involved in empathy. *Neuroimage* 24: 771–779.

Jerison, H. J. (1973) *Evolution of the Brain and Intelligence*. Academic Press, New York.

Kaas, J. H. (1995) The evolution of isocortex. *Brain Behavior and Evolution*, 46: 187–196.

Kirk, E. C. (2006) Visual influences on primate encephalization. *Journal of Human Evolution* 51: 76–90.

Kraus, N. F. (2005) Brainstem origins for cortical 'what' and 'where' pathways in the auditory system. *Trends in Neuroscience*, 28: 176–181.

Lindenfors, P. (2005) Neocortex evolution in primates: the 'social brain' is for females. *Biology letters*, 1: 407–410.

Livingstone, M. S. and Hubel, D. H. (1988) Segregation of form, color, movement and depth: anatomy, physiology and perception. *Science*, 240: 740–749.

Macphail, E. M. (1982) *Brain and Intelligence in Vertebrates*. Clarendon Press, Oxford.

Martin, R. D. (1990) *Primate Origins and Evolution: A Phylogenetic Reconstruction*. Princeton University Press.

Milner, A. D. and Goodale, M. A. (1995) *The Visual Brain in Action*. Oxford University Press, Oxford.

Milton, K. (1988) Foraging behaviour and the evolution of primate intelligence. In R. W. Byrne and A. Whiten (eds) *Machiavellian Intelligence*, pp. 285–306. Clarendon Press, Oxford.

Muhlau, M., Hermsdorfer, J., Goldenberg, G. *et al.* (2005) Left inferior parietal dominance in gesture imitation: an fMRI study. *Neuropsychologia*, 43: 1086–1098.

Nunn, C. L. & Barton, R. A. (2000) Allometric slopes and independent contrasts: a comparative test of Kleiber's law in primates. *American Naturalist*, 156: 519–533.

Oztop, E., Wolpert, D., Kawato, M. (2005) Mental State inference using visual control parameters. *Cognitive Brain Research*, 22: 129–151.

Perez-Barberia, F. J. and Gordon, I. J. (2005) Gregariousness increases brain size in ungulates. *Oecologia*, 145: 41–52.

Povinelli, D. J. and Barth (2005) Reinterpreting behavior: a human specialization? *Behavioral and Brain Sciences*, 28: 712.

Povinelli, D. J. and Vonk, J. (2003) Chimpanzee minds: suspiciously human? *Trends in Cognitive Sciences*, 7: 157–160.

Premack, D. and Woodruffe, G. (1978) Does the chimpanzee have a theory of mind? *Behavioral and Brain Sciences* 1: 515–526.

Preuss, T. M. (1993) The role of the neurosciences in primate evolutionary biology. In R. S. D. E. Macphee (ed.) *Primates and Their Relatives in Phylogenetic Perspective*, pp. 333–362. Plenum Press, New York.

Preuss, T. M. and Coleman, G. Q. (2002) Human-specific organization of primary visual cortex: Alternating compartments of dense Cat-301 and calbindin immunoreactivity in layer 4A. *Cerebral Cortex* 12: 671–691.

Ramnani, N. (2006) The primate cortico-cerebellar system: anatomy and function. *Nature reviews in Neuroscience* 7: 511–522.

Ramnani, N. and Miall, C. (2004) A system in the human brain for predicting the actions of others. *Nature Neuroscience* 7: 85–89.

Ramnani, N., Behrens, T. E. J., Johansen-Berg, H. *et al.* (2005) The Cortico-pontine System: Diffusion Imaging Evidence from Macaque monkeys and humans. *Cerebral Cortex*, 16: 811–818.

Rilling, J. K. (2006) human and non-human primate brains: are they allometrically scaled versions of the same design? *Evolutionary Anthropology*, 15: 65–77.

Rilling, J. K. and Insel, T. R. (1998) Evolution of the cerebellum in primates: differences in relative volume among monkeys, apes and humans. *Brain Behavior and Evolution*, 52: 308–314.

Rilling, J. K. and Seligman, R. A. (2002) *Journal of Human Evolution*, 42: 505–533

Riska, B. and Atchley, W. R. (1985) Genetics of growth predicts patterns of brain size evolution. *Science*, 229: 1302–1304.

Schenker, N. M., Desgouttes, A. M. and Semendeferi, K. (2005) Neural connectivity and cortical substrates of cognition in hominoids. *Journal of Human Evolution*, 49: 547–569.

Schoenemann, P. T., Sheehan, M. J. and Glotzer, L. D. (2005) Prefrontal white matter volume is disproportionately larger in humans than in other primates. *Nature Neuroscience*, 8: 242–252.

Schutter, D. J. L. G., Van Honk, J. (2005) The cerebellum on the rise in human emotion. *Cerebellum*, 4: 290–294.

Scott, S., Young, A. W., Calder, A. J., Hellawell, D. J., Aggleton, J. P. and Johnson, M. (1997) Auditory recognition of emotion after amygdalotomy: impairment of fear and anger. *Nature*, 385, 254–257.

Semendeferi, K., Damasio, H. and Frank, R. (1997) The evolution of the frontal lobes: A volumetric analysis based on three-dimensional reconstructions of magnetic resonance scans of human and ape brains. *Journal of Human Evolution*, 32: 375–388.

Semendeferi, K. Armstrong, E., Schleicher, A., Zilles, K. and Van Hoesen, G. W. (2001) Prefrontal Cortex in humans and apes: a comparative study of Area 10. *American Journal of Physical Anthropology*, 114: 224–241.

Semendeferi, K., Lu, A., Schenker, N. *et al.* (2002) Humans and great apes share a large frontal cortex. *Nature Neuroscience*, 5: 272–276.

Shamay-Tsoory, S. G., Lester, H., Chisin, R. *et al.* (2005) The neural correlates of understanding the other's distress: a positron emission tomography investigation of accurate empathy. *Neuroimage*, 27, 468–472.

Shultz, S. and Dunbar, R. I. M. (2005) Both social and ecological factors predict ungulate brain size. *Proceedings of the Royal Society of London, B*, 273: 207–215.

Stephan, H., Frahm, H. D. and Baron, G. (1981) New and revised data on volumes of brain structures in Insectivores and Primates. *Folia Primatologica*, 35: 1–29.

Striedter, G. F. (2005) *Principles of Brain Evolution*. Sinauer, Sunderland, MA.

Sussman, R. W. (1991) Primate Origins and the evolution of angiosperms. *American Journal of Primatology*, 23: 209–223.

Swanson, L. W. (2000) What is the brain? *Trends in Neurosciences*, 23: 519–527.

Swanson, L. W. and Petrovich, G. D. (1998) What is the amygdala? *Trends in Neurosciences*, 21: 323–331.

Thier and Ilg (2005) The neural basis of smooth-pursuit eye movements. *Current Opinion in Neurobiology*, 15: 645–652.

Tomasello, M. and Call, J. (1997) *Primate Cognition*. Oxford University Press, Oxford.

Tomasello, M., Carpenter, M., Call, J., Behne, T. and Moll, H. (2005) Understanding and sharing intentions: the origins of cultural cognition. *Behavioral and Brain Sciences*, 28: 675–735.

van Essen, D. C., Anderson, C. H. and Felleman, D. J. (1992) Information processing in the primate visual system: an integrated systems perspective. *Science*, 255: 419–423.

Van Essen, D. C., Lewis, J. W., Drury, H. A., Hadjikhani, N., Tootell, R. B.H., Bakircioglu, M. and Miller, M. I. (2001) Mapping visual cortex in monkeys and humans using surface-based atlases. *Vision Research* 41: 1359–1378.

Whiting, B. and Barton, R. A. (2003) Evolution of the cortico-cerebellar system in primates: anatomical projections predict patterns of correlated evolution. *Journal of Human Evolution*, 44: 3–10.

Williams, J. H.G., Waiter, G. D., Gilchrist, A., Perrett, D. I., Murray, A. D. and Whiten, A. (2006) Neural mechanisms of imitation and 'mirror neuron' functioning in autistic spectrum disorder. *Neuropsychologia* 44: 610–621.

Wolpert, D. M., Doya, K. and Kawato (2003) A unifying computational framework for motor control and social interaction. *Proceedings of the Royal Society of London, B*, 593–602.

Young, M. P. (1992) Objective analysis of the topological organization of the primate cortical visual-system. *Nature*, 358: 152–155.

Young, M. P., Scannell, J. W., Burns, G. A. P. C. and Blakemore, C. (1994) *Reviews in Neuroscience*, 5: 227–249.

Young, M. P., Hilgetag, C. and Scannell, J. W. (2000) On imputing function to structure from the behavioural effects of brain lesions. *Philosophical Transactions of the Royal Society, B*, 355: 147–161.

CHAPTER 12

The neuroevolutionary and neuroaffective psychobiology of the prosocial brain

Jaak Panksepp

12.1. Introduction

The human social brain arises from a set of innate emotional tendencies, including separation distress, playfulness, sexual and maternal urges. These ancient tools for living, shared homologously by all mammals, are found in the deep sub-neocortical midline recesses of the brain reaching upward to limbic cortices. These foundational social processes guide key aspects of attention, emotion and motivation, permitting the gradual epigenetic development of the fully social brain. One can observe behavioural manifestations of these brain processes more clearly in our mammalian cousins than in our fellow humans; other animals do not posses the neocortical capacity to inhibit and alter emotional expression to the degree that is common in human adults. To the best of our knowledge, all mammalian brains can elaborate a host of affective processes from anger to sexual urges. Thus, paradoxically, we can learn most about the core neurobiology of human emotions from the study of brain–behaviour relations in lower mammals.

These foundational urges interact with a variety of associative and higher cognitive processes that help mould acquired behaviour patterns that vary more considerably across species than the instinctual substrates. As neocortical endowments increase, with probably few major genetic changes aside from those dictating cortical columnar proliferation, the environmentally and culturally channelled developmental landscapes become vastly more complex. Most of these cognitive complexities are probably not controlled by detailed genetic rules, but by the capacity of different species to see the world differently depending upon their perceptual strengths and learning abilities intermixing with the ancient genetic–instinctual tools for living. These cognition–emotion interactions notwithstanding, at their most basic level, core emotions are so ancient that it is scientifically wise to conceptualize them independently of cognition. In their raw form, they are innate tools for living. Here I will be concerned mainly with those core emotions that are the genetic endowments of the mammalian brain, homologous albeit not identical, in all mammalian species.

Evolutionary psychology (EP) must recognize the ancient sub-neocortical emotional *forces* of the animal mind in order to provide coherent guidance for conceptualizing the additional neuroevolutionary developments that promoted what seems to be unique about the emergence of human mentality. The central question for all behavioural choices, of humans and other animals, is the nature of the genetically provided value system that index major survival concerns. Our capacity for complex cognitive evaluation of our behavioural choices and our place in the world is dependent on a host of pre-humanoid affective feelings that sink deeply into the ancient history of vertebrate brain evolution.

12.2. **Toward a neuroevolutionary affective neuroscience**

An evolutionary view of human social urges requires adequate conceptualization of the universal cross-mammalian brain–mind processes, including traditional behaviouristic concepts such as rewards, punishments and reinforcements, recast in the concepts of real brain systems. We must also envision how basic affective feelings emerge from brain and body physiologies, but most especially the instinctual underpinnings of mind (Panksepp, 2005a,b). Experiential consciousness seems to be an intrinsic capacity of mammalian brains. Here I will focus on the core prosocial emotional systems of mammalian brains, at the expense of the higher cognitive functions with which they interact. For instance, while developmental emergence of theory-of-mind capacities in human children is facilitated by maternal emotional sensitivities (Meins *et al.*, 2002), we have no good data that our capacity to think about other minds emerges from evolutionarily preordained modules. Perceptual mirror neuron systems along with the capacity for emotional resonances, probably existing in all mammals, may suffice (Rizzolatti and Craigero, 2004). Since we should remain suspicious of premature conclusions about what did or did not evolve in the higher reaches of the brain, I will not dwell

on such higher social brain functions here. I will also ignore certain lower ones, such aggressive-dominance and social-disgust tendencies, which may derive their coherence developmentally from a variety of more primitive emotional urges.

First and foremost, a scientific understanding of the social brain requires a clear vision of what is fundamental and genetically preordained, and what may be derivative and epigenetically emergent. It is becoming increasingly evident that basic prosocial feelings arise from the dynamics of a limited number of genetically provided 'instinctual' brain systems. A central tenet of the affective neuroscience strategy is that we can scientifically decipher the basic nature of core social feelings as well as the various non-social affects by cross-species triangulation among three critical lines of evidence: behavioural, psychological and neuroscientific (Panksepp, 1998a). My overall position is that affective consciousness, the non-reflective subjective experience of being a living creature in the world, is much older in brain evolution than cognitive forms of consciousness that allow us to think about the world (Panksepp, 2005a,b). Indeed, it is possible that cognitive consciousness is heavily dependent on, perhaps even partly an outgrowth of, the more primal capacity to experience living affectively.

Seven core emotional systems have been provisionally identified through empirically robust affective neuroscience strategies, such as evocation of coherent emotional responses by localized electrical stimulation of the brain. Four are substantially pre-mammalian, since they are evident in all vertebrates: FEAR, RAGE, SEEKING and LUST which are essential ingredients for feelings of anxiety, anger, desire and eroticism in mammals. With the expansion of mammalian limbic circuits (Heimer, 2003; MacLean, 1990), there emerged robust CARE, PANIC and PLAY systems, which are fundamental brain substrates for the affective feelings of nurturance, separation distress/sadness, and social joy, respectively. These *social* systems have deep ancestral roots in other fundamental brain processes: based on shared opioid, oxytocinergic/vasotocinergic and prolactinergic neurochemical controls, it seems likely that the nurturant dynamics of the CARE system evolved from the pre-existing substrates of sexual LUST systems. The sting of social separation distress (PANIC), which is the antecedent to loneliness, sadness and grief (emotional terrain that is prepared by, but perhaps distinguishable from, separation distress), emerged partly from pre-existing systems that controlled physical pain, and opiates, oxytocin and prolactin are very effective in reducing separation distress (Panksepp, 1998a). In addition there is a variety of arousal-regulating systems—norepinephrine, epinephrine, dopamine, histamine, acetylcholine—in the brain that modulate all of the more specific emotional processes.

The 'big seven' may not be a comprehensive list, but each can be defended with solid *affective neuroscientific* evidence (Panksepp, 1998a). Additions should be based on solid neurobehavioural evidence rather than conceptual arguments. 'Dominance' should not yet be considered a primary emotional system, as advocated by Ellis and Toronchuk (2005), because it could easily emerge from the interactions of several others, especially PLAY, SEEKING, RAGE, and FEAR. 'Disgust' is not a basic emotion because it is a fundamental *sensory* rather than *emotional* affect. This is not to say that the feeling of sensory disgust is not basic. But just like feelings of tiredness, sweetness, etc., they simply are not *emotional* affects, namely ones that require a flexibly complex instinctual action apparatus (one that is dynamically responsive to relevant sensory events). However, through social learning, the feeling of revulsion can be re-symbolized into the emotional domain, as social disgust/distain/scorn, but there is no clear data that brain evolution engendered that re-symbolization. Human imagination and social learning may have sufficed. Similar arguments could be made for emotions such as jealousy, shame and many others.

Why capitalize the labels for emotional primes? I adopted this convention to provide a convenient vernacular heuristic for the pre-propositional systems we need to understand if we are ever going to really explain emotions. Also, the evidence indicates that such brain systems generate core affective states that are essential evolutionary solutions for guiding anticipatory behaviours. Unlike cognitions, affects do not lend themselves easily to further linguistic analysis. Probably affects could best be described in artistic terms. One could imagine that tender music might best represent the CARE system. A dramatic sculpture might best capture PANIC, while joyous dance like an Irish jig may depict PLAY. However, in mind science we are confined to verbal symbols, so I have chosen capitalized descriptors to indicate that each symbolizes an emotional system. This convention also aims to minimize mereological fallacies (part-whole confusions), so prevalent in cognitive neuroscience (Bennett and Hacker, 2003). We do not know how far emotional systems extend in the brain. We know that they interpenetrate into many cognitive domains, to the extent that many would like to see emotions and cognitions as different sides of the same neural domain (Lane and Garfield, 2005). This phenomenological 'insight' that focuses more on emotional *awareness* rather than raw emotional *experience,* is not very useful for elucidating the ancient, neuroevolutionary substrates of raw emotionality. For instance, the many cognitive changes that accompany pain do not tell us much about the nature of pain, which has deep and diverse genetic controls (Mogi, 2004).

In human experience, cognition and emotion are invariably intertwined. For this reason, we tend to think that they are a single psychic entity. In part, my use of capitalized labels is aimed at alerting us to the fact that these emotional brain-operating systems are fundamentally distinct from higher cognitive processes. Robust evidence supports this hypothesis: as summarized elsewhere (Panksepp, 1998a,b 2005a), we can evoke these distinct emotional behaviour patterns (e.g. fear, rage, seeking, sexuality, maternal behaviours and separation distress calls) from all mammals by electrically and chemically stimulating essentially identical brain circuits concentrated in sub-neocortical areas of the brain. These energetic states of the brain, in their most intense forms, are well represented in various instinctual behaviours, and there is much to commend the view that these global brain–body states are the primal sources of raw emotional feelings, brain processes that were hard for behavioural scientists to accept during the twentieth century to the detriment of a full understanding of what brain tissues actually do. They create raw feelings that are critically linked with instinctual emotional action urges.

In any event, animals are not psychologically neutral about such evoked brain changes. Their feelings can be evaluated by the emotional sounds and behavioural choices they make. When allowed to sustain or terminate such emotional states, all animals tested give clear answers. They will readily either turn them on or off. Apparently they either like or dislike such states, even though a great deal more work needs to be done to determine the extent to which animals can cognitively discriminate among them. Although such brain stimulation data are decidedly more limited for our species, humans do consistently report the sudden arousal of the appropriate emotional feelings when homologous brain areas are artificially aroused with localized brain stimulation. In other words, the brain regions that can trigger dramatic emotional outbursts in other animals do generate the corresponding affective feelings in humans. Also, the varieties of affect-congruent cognitive changes that ensue highlight how human thoughts can be driven by sub-neocortical large-scale *energetic* states (Heath, 1996; Panksepp, 1985).

Sadly, energy metaphors of mind were discarded a long time ago, to the great detriment of understanding what emotions really are (Ciompi and Panksepp, 2004). However, information-processing metaphors fail miserably when we seek to envision the actions of such visceral–emotional brain systems. Energetic dynamics are clearly reflected in emotional actions of both brain and body, as large ensembles of neurons are brought into distinct but coherent action modes by executive neuropeptides (Panksepp, 1993; Panksepp and Harro, 2004). To understand such global functions of the brain, we need functional 'network doctrines' as much as we need a 'neuron doctrine'. The failure to recognize the foundational importance of such energetic *state* processes of the brain reflects the long-standing failure of the computational revolution, as well as certain EP spin-offs, to come to terms with ancestral sources of mind. As every milk-maid knows, you will not get milk from the udder with mere mechanical yanking of the teats; one must firmly caress them with a suckling dynamic that

coaxes the oxytocinergic reflexes of the paraventricular hypothalamus to release the milk. The fact that mechanical milking machines have been created to simulate the energetic dynamic of a suckling animal only indicates that the dynamics of such mechanisms are not infinitely complex but do have objective control parameters, which are often evident in whole body emotional dynamics. Such large-scale network functions have been woefully neglected in modern cognitive-sciences, to the detriment of both neuroscience and EP.

If we recognize that the basic emotional systems of the brain are built around neuropeptide systems that are enriched in the visceral organs of the body, we can envision that the evolutionary roots of many emotional feelings go back to the large-scale dynamic visceral changes that characterize emotional states. Just consider the propulsion of food through the gastrointestinal system or the oxytocin-mediated 'caressive' squeezing of milk from the mammary glands, and many others, all controlled by various neuropeptides of the visceral enteric nervous systems (Panksepp, 1993; Panksepp and Harro, 2004). Consider that about 95% of bodily serotonin is contained in the gastrointestinal system, and only 5% of this mood-regulating molecule is contained within the brain. Clearly, the energetic regulators of visceral organ activities are still represented in the emotional circuits of the brain, helping to explain why all basic emotions have such a visceral feel to them and why psychosomatic disorders can lead to imbalances in our vital organs. William James was correct that our emotions are linked to our visceral arousals, but he had no way of knowing that a host of chemical systems was robustly represented within visceral regions of the brain, leading to a century of mistaken belief that feelings were simply the sensory readouts of peripheral states of the body. In fact, they are created by brain circuits that sustain a rich interchange with the visceral changes within the body.

The evidence strongly suggests that core emotional affects are created by large-scale brain neurodynamics that mould whole-body energetic expressiveness. To understand the neurology of the affective mind, it may be essential to distinguish these energetic *state* functions from informational *channel* functions of the brain (Mesulam, 2000). Global emotional *states* are created by a variety of neurochemistries, from biogenic amine arousal networks to more functionally precise peptidergic controls, that control vast regions of the brain simultaneously. These global psychobehavioural states are not 'meaningfully' computable digitally. It seems that such non-linear, large-scale analogue neurodynamics are the bedrock of emotional experiences, and perhaps of consciousness itself.

Channel functions, on the other hand, refer to more discrete, cognitive processing of extero-ceptive information, where fast and precise glutamatergic transmission of information may allow classical computational metaphors to be realistic guides to modelling how much of think-ing occurs. In other words, there are important psychobiological differences in the way cogni-tions and emotions are instantiated in brain mechanisms (Panksepp, 2003a). Thus, we should not conflate cognitive and affective processes in our desire to understand mind. Their intimate interactions and interpenetrations do not mean they are one and the same thing, as many cogni-tive neuroscientists are prone to claim (Lane and Garfield, 2005; for critique see Panksepp, 2005d). The kidney and liver are also meaningfully differ-ent organic entities even though they could not survive without each other.

The study of the distinct *state* and *channel* functions of the mind may require rather differ-ent empirical strategies for adequate illumina-tion of the underlying neurobiology of mind. It is comparatively easy to envision how evolutionarily specific emotional values were generated within the state functions of the brain (genes can code for network dynamics con-trolled by command chemistries). Likewise, one can also envision how sensory values obtain their affective impact. It is much harder to imag-ine how evolution could have constructed *specific* cognitive strategies into brain circuits. It is possible that cognitive resolution is achieved epigenetically by the interplay of mas-sive exteroceptive sensory fields interacting with the various affective value states of the brain. The way in which affective values guide learning may require more complex and dynamic visions of brain activity than could ever be generated by the behaviouristic concepts of reinforcement and punishment (Panksepp, 2005a).

12.3. The neuroevolutionary psychobiology of lower and higher social brains

The cognitive accompaniments of emotional arousal will continue to be best studied through human first person self-reports, but for the foreseeable future, emotional vocal signals, bod-ily expressions of emotions and the behavioural choices exhibited by other animals will remain essential for identifying the material substrates from which affective states first arose in brain evolution. Human research has no ready access to the relevant brain systems. Even modern brain imaging can only envision the tips of the icebergs (perhaps a better metaphor being 'eyes of the hurricane') of the underlying brain com-plexities, pointing only to areas where more precise neuroscience tools need to be applied. For instance, we do not even know whether most modern brain imaging 'hotspots' largely reflect excitatory or inhibitory foci of the large networks which actually generate mentality. At present, the underlying neural principles that generate raw affective experiences are best deciphered through the study of animal models.

The knowledge derived from the animal work can guide insightful causal analysis of human affective changes, especially coupled to neuro-chemical manipulations (Panksepp, 1999; Panksepp and Harro 2004). For instance, abun-dant work with animals has revealed that the neuropeptide, oxytocin, reduces separation dis-tress and facilitates social bonding and nurtu-rance (Nelson and Panksepp, 1998; Panksepp, 1998a; Insel and Young, 2001; Young and Wang, 2004). It has recently been demonstrated that intranasally applied oxytocin can increase feel-ings of trust in humans (Kosfeld *et al.*, 2005), which may be a variant of social confidence. Perhaps 'trust' as well as 'confidence' are concep-tual parsings of the more basic social–affective changes already observed in animals, namely the reduced ability to feel the distressing sting of social isolation.

A solid EP of the social brain must be based on a blend of animal and human research, led by an understanding of the evolved adaptations humans still share with other animals, and fol-lowed by an analysis of human cognitive changes, perhaps promoted by some yet unfathomed neuroevolutionary epistemology, but most certainly solidified by social learning. Our earlier critiques of EP asserted that if we do not pay sufficient attention to the foundational issues, such as the sub-neocortical socio-emotional circuits shared by all mammals, then we may easily mistake the diverse epigenetic emergents of human cognitive abilities for basic evolutionary adaptations (Panksepp and Panksepp, 2000; Panksepp et al., 2002).

The classic EP findings have been harvested from adults using pencil-and-paper tests, methods that cannot discriminate learned stuff from evolutionarily inherent stuff. There is very little 'classic' EP work that pursues investigations in young children, the only members of our species from whom one might obtain optimal estimates of ancestral solutions. Most of the major findings of EP, from gender-specific jealousies to cheater detection modules and heightened aggression among non-kin, are not surprising to any intelligent observer of human behaviour, but they could easily emerge through the core affective landscapes that interpenetrate with developmental–associative–cognitive–cultural learning. If there exist additional genetic channellings of higher affective–cognitive processes in humans—an evolutionary epistemology built into brain circuits—they must be demonstrated with empirical strategies other than mere statistical trends in how groups of people behave. The power of epigenetic processes and brain/mind plasticity should not be minimized in EP. The power of animal brain research to clarify evolutionary foundations of human nature should no longer be ignored.

Why has such an alternative vision been so slow to emerge in EP? Partly it is surely because those working on animal models are rarely willing to discuss the nature of emotional feelings. Many remain afraid of being accused of anthropomorphism; others cannot conceptualize how mental change (which was once falsely believed to be immaterial) can emerge from mere neural activities. This, of course, should no longer be problematic. Surely the biological complexity of mammalian brain dynamics has the right stuff to formulate mentality from its ability to represent the body and its place in world affairs. However, many behavioural neuroscientists continue to assert that psychology has no role in brain functions. The fear of subjectivity is pervasive (Wallace, 2000). Many remain convinced that *eliminative neural materialism* is the only cogent ontological view, and if so, a discussion of psychological processes cannot be deemed to be part of any scientifically coherent explanatory framework for how the brain works. A study of neuronal processes will suffice. This view is deeply flawed, for is overlooks a critical issue—one product of complex neuronal processes is the generation of adaptive psychological states.

The capacity to experience oneself in the world (primary-process mentality) is a remarkably useful survival device. I suspect that a non-feeling bio-robot would run into competitive brick walls pretty rapidly in the struggle for survival against organisms that have subjective experiences. Affects are part of primary-process consciousness, which may have been the precondition for the eventual emergence of thoughts and a self-reflective, self-awareness (secondary and tertiary forms of consciousness) that can only be well studied in humans. However, before we ever understand the latter functions neuroscientifically, we may have to understand primary process forms of consciousness, such as raw emotional feelings Panksepp (1998b).

I side with the view that emotional brain functions need to be viewed from two complementary perspectives—the neurodynamic and the psychodynamic—using a *dual-aspect monism* strategy (Panksepp, 1998a,b 2005b). In the present context, that means raw affective feelings are an intrinsic part of the complex neurodynamics that generate instinctual action tendencies. A striking recent example of this from modern human brain imaging is evident in the neural changes that accompany human orgasm, which appears to arise from brain regions that are known to control instinctual sexual behaviours in animals (Holstege et al., 2003), a pattern that is emulated for all major basic emotional systems (Damasio et al., 2000). Organisms that can encode key survival issues in raw affective feelings possess incredibly effective intrinsic tools to compete effectively against organisms that have no intrinsic capacity to sustain critical survival issues in mind, as evolutionarily symbolized by raw affective feelings. To have affective feelings, animals need not be cognitively *aware* of the adaptive goals of their behaviours. Various feelings of goodness and badness may act as a short-hand for making critically important life choices.

To cogently argue that basic social–affective processes exist in other animals, one must address what adaptive functions such evolved processes served in enhancing survival. A straightforward answer is that affects are *evolutionary memories* (i.e. core affective feelings are not learned). They are aspects of the instinctual emotional action systems that intrinsically allow organisms to anticipate and effectively deal with various life-detracting and life-supporting circumstances. In other words, core affective feelings are not created during the lifespans of individual members of species. They were 'learned' through past genetic capacities to build certain kinds of brains, linked to certain kinds of bodies, subsisting in certain kinds of environments. These raw affects are further parsed through social learning, leading to emotional complexities in humans that we cannot study credibly in animals.

The primary affective brain systems facilitate survival unconditionally, by *anticipating* major survival issues. For instance, congenital pain insensitivity reduces ones lifespan (Brand and Yancey, 1997). The experience of pain is an evolutionary heuristic that allows the body to instinctually avoid further harm. Without pain, all organisms would die prematurely. Similarly, fluctuating affects may reside at the core of *reinforcement processes* that fine-tune behaviours through individual learning. In other words, value codes within the brain need to be felt if they are going to be optimal heuristics for learning. Very simple learning may be mindless (i.e. even some plants exhibit classical conditioning), but sophisticated behavioural choices are only efficiently moulded by the ability of animals to experience comfort and satisfaction when world events support survival, and to experience discomfort and distress when the probability of survival diminishes.

In the rest of this essay I will first discuss the neural nature of raw affects and focus on two core, prosocial adaptations of the youthful social brain–separation distress (PANIC) and PLAYfulness. Then, more briefly, I will focus on two adult emotional adaptations—the basic brain systems that mediate adult sexual (LUST) and maternal–nurturant (CARE) urges.

These interdigitating social circuits, which can be deemed to be emotional endophenotypes of prosocial brains (Panksepp, 2006), contribute to the emergence of social bonds and friendships. It is easy to envision how various higher prosocial functions, so evident in humans, emerge developmentally, ranging from mundane issues such as jealousy and shame, to the more subtle issues such as sympathetic fellow-feelings of empathy to the social bonding symbolically encapsulated in certain religious traditions (Ostow, 2006; Watt, 2005).

The few that accept the affective foundations of mentality are often tempted to conclude that only two primal forms of feeling, negative and positive affect, suffice to jump-start the whole complexity of affective life (e.g. Russell, 2003). The argument that all emotional complexities arise simply from a primordial bivalent affective and arousal brain functions, present at birth, is currently without neurobiological substance. Existing evidence suggests that many affective states are gifts of nature, even though some, such as fully nurturant (CARE) and sexual (LUST) feelings, emerge developmentally more slowly than others, such as separation distress (PANIC) and interactive juvenile joy (PLAY). The focus here will be on such basic prosocial emotional affects, without considering fear and anger, hunger and thirst, and the various sensory delights and disgusts.

12.4. The socio-affective mammalian brain

The past three decades of affective neuroscience research have clarified basic brain processes that make mammals the highly social creatures that they are. The conceptual and behavioural understanding of social bonds advanced in the 1960s–1970s by pioneers such as Bowlby (1960; also see Holms, 1993), Harlow (1958) and Scott and Fuller (1965) has now been enriched by a depth of neuroscientific understanding unimaginable in previous eras.

The transition to a substantive affective and social neuroscience was initiated by the definitive identification of the first neurotransmitter receptor, the *mu* opioid receptor, which mediates narcotic addiction, in the early 1970s.

These seminal findings provided the first neuro-chemical substrata for prosocial feelings (Herman and Panksepp, 1978; Panksepp *et al.*, 1978a,b). Brain opioid regulation of social affect has now been supplemented by the discovery of several additional 'social neuropeptides'—including oxytocin, vasopressin, prolactin, and several others, which have enriched our under-standing of the evolutionary substrates of socio-emotional processes (Carter, 1998; Insel, 1997; Weller and Feldman, 2003). Our initial work was guided by the idea that there are deep simi-larities between narcotic dependencies and addictive social attachments (Panksepp, 1981; Panksepp *et al.*, 1980). This concept remains a robust bridge to important human psycholog-ical and cultural issues. This relationship helps to explain the evolutionary allure of narcotics—a great deal of addiction may be self-medication to sustain affective homeostasis. However, opioids are only one of many sub-neocortical neuropeptide systems that regulate feelings, but one that can currently be effectively manipulated in humans.

This research suggests that the earliest social–emotional capacities are (i) the ability to experience distress when loss of social support is detected, and to vocally communicate such states so that the probability of reunion is increased, and (ii) the proclivity to feel comfort in the presence of social support, which is behaviourally reflected in elevated levels of smiling and laughing. At juvenile ages, organ-isms also develop dynamic urges for positive social engagements that are most evident in rough-and-tumble play activities. These core emotions of youth—separation distress and playfulness—are critical for the epigenetic emergence of the quality of social bonds to care-takers and, at later stages of development, friendships with others, thereby setting the stage for competent socio-sexual abilities. Conversely, sexuality may also have served as the evolution-ary precondition from which maternal urges eventually emerged. As already noted, the brain substrates of sexuality may be the primordial neural matrix from which many other prosocial processes emerged in brain evolution. Similarly, ancient mechanisms of pain may have been the source of separation distress (Panksepp, 2005b). Evolution uses old parts to create new solutions, and every core emotional system surely has his-torical antecedents in more simple-minded solutions.

This complex genetically dictated matrix of basic social processes, shared by all mammals, may be the fundamental substrate from which much of the rest of the social brain emerges through epigenetic learning processes. For EP, the lesson may be that a great deal of psycholog-ical complexity can emerge from a few primor-dial neuropsychological tools, such as the core affects, interacting with learning and related cognitive processes. If we accept such an epige-netic view, we need to question some of the central tenets of EP, such as a host of genetically specified universal *modules*, elaborating com-plex cognitive abilities that appear in all of us in similar ways, residing in higher regions of the brain.

If this is true, then the EP project needs to envision the ancestral forces underlying human nature that are rather more ancient than Pleistocene neocortical expansions, whose repetitive columnar structures resemble prolif-erative random access memory, rather than functionally specialized modules. Structurally, the neocortical *columns* are highly similar, and even though their interconnections mediate enormous networks of associations, there appear to be few specializations in these systems until they are moulded by sensory experiences. Such cognitive/perceptual capacities ultimately permitted human culture and the full flowering of the human mind, but those functions would collapse without the sub-neocortical affective substrates.

However, the lower brain can sustain organis-mic coherence on their own, in humans (Shewmon *et al.*, 1999) and other animals (Kolb and Tees, 1990; Panksepp *et al.*, 1994b). The social brain appears to start life with a rather limited set of genetically provided sub-neocortical social–emotional tools, and the fully social adult brain surely emerges largely through develop-mental and cultural learning processes, as most of psychology has long accepted. Why this realis-tic possibility has been neglected in standard EP is puzzling and may be partly due to its exces-sively anthropocentric attitude, and its failure to confront the challenges that existing genetic and neuroscientific perspectives entail.

There is little evidence that genetically provided social–emotional tools exist in humans above and beyond those provided by systems we share with the other mammals. There are undoubtedly refinements in sensory–perceptual processing of emotions, as might be achieved with mirror-neuron systems (see Rizzolatti and Fogassi, this volume, Chapter 14, for a review), and the resulting sophisticated theory of mind capacities, but there is presently no evidence that human genes generate totally new types of emotional feelings. As long as there is no such evidence, our understanding of the basic tools for the emergence of social bonds and more complex social relations and cognitions (i.e. the construction of social brains) may be largely based on our understanding of separation distress and playfulness of the young on one hand, and sexual and maternal urges of adults on the other.

12.5. **The emergence of a social–affective neuroscience**

The first major, research-promoting theoretical idea that emerged at the outset of the affective/social neuroscience revolution was the possibility that social attachments had fundamental brain relations to opiate addiction. Opiates were uniquely efficacious in quelling separation distress across a variety of species (Herman and Panksepp, 1978; Panksepp et al., 1978a,b), which was matched, after the study of scores of other neurochemical agents, with intracerebral administration of oxytocin (Panksepp et al., 1988). The idea that early social attachments may be a drug-'dependence' type of phenomenon arose from the recognition that both social attachments and narcotic dependence were characterized by an initial affectively intense and emotionally positive attraction phase, followed by tolerance phase, during which the intensity of affect diminished, so that positive affective arousal could only by sustained by higher and higher doses of drugs or an increasing variety of socio-sexual engagements. However, when opiate or social dependence had been solidified, and even as the positive affective experience from the attachments had diminished (i.e. tolerance had occurred), a dramatic

emotional response emerged when individuals were separated from those to whom they are attached. Likewise, when narcotics were no longer available, there was a powerful withdrawal response which symptomatically resembled the distress arising from the loss of a loved one: irritability, insomnia, loss of appetite, crying and feelings of isolation and loneliness, namely depressive responses accompanied by a profound psychic pain (Panksepp, 1981).

These similarities led naturally to the idea that the pain of social loss was evolutionarily related to more ancient physical pain mechanisms of the brain, and that both were opioid-regulated. This has been repeatedly affirmed in various species (for summary, see Panksepp, 2003b, 2005,a,b,c). This theoretical perspective also envisioned social attachments to be linked to ancient thermoregulatory rewards (feelings of coldness when socially alone) and to place attachment mechanisms, both of which are partly opioid-mediated (Panksepp, 1981, 1998a). Additional evidence emerged that infant social attachments had both endogenous opioid and oxytocinergic components (Nelson and Panksepp, 1998).

Of course, young animals, as well as their mothers, should not become 'tolerant' (i.e. insensitive) to social rewards, as rapidly as adults do to narcotic drugs. When it was discovered that opioid sensitivity in the brain could be sustained by nurturance-promoting brain chemicals such as oxytocin (Kovacs et al., 1998), a potential mechanism was revealed by which opioid reward, and hence social bonds, could be sustained for extended periods on both sides of the mother–infant bond. Attachment was sustained by the undiminished neurochemical pleasures of friendly and supportive social contacts, as well as the distress-alleviating effects of such bonding chemistries. It was demonstrated that opioids were released during prosocial activities such as play (Panksepp and Bishop, 1981), being held (Panksepp et al., 1980a,b), and grooming (Keverne et al., 1989). Thereby, social attachments were solidified partly through the neurochemistries that alleviate separation distress.

The separation distress mechanisms, probably evolutionarily derived from more ancient pain systems of the brain, were mapped with localized electrical brain stimulation in several species, including monkeys, guinea pigs, and domestic chicks (Herman and Panksepp, 1981; Jürgens, 1994, 1998; Panksepp *et al.*, 1988), and the sub-cortical anatomies were remarkably similar, including prominently the periaqueductal gray, dorsomedial thalamus, preoptic–septal regions and the bed nucleus of the stria terminalis. The general anatomical trajectories correspond well to those that were eventually revealed with positron emission tomography (PET) brain-imaging of human sadness (Damasio *et al.*, 2000; Panksepp, 2003c). Recently, PET studies verified that human sadness, just like animal separation distress, is associated with low brain opioid activity (Zubieta *et al.*, 2003). This also fits well with the long established fact that opiate receptor stimulants are excellent antidepressants (Bodkin *et al.*, 1995). Indeed, brain tissues from suicides strongly suggest deficiencies in pleasure-facilitating endogenous opioids (Gross-Isseroff *et al.*, 1990). It is reasonable that a deficit in chemistries that promote positive social feelings would be experienced as painful and hence a major source of depression and suicidal mentation. It is likely that the neuronal circuitries of separation distress arose evolutionarily from pre-existing physical pain systems. This allows clinicians to understand why social loss is experienced as painful, and why individuals with congenital pain insensitivity might begin to experience pain when grieving (Danziger and Willer, 2005).

The association of social processes with brain opioid activity provides a conceptual structure for understanding placebo effects, now well demonstrated to rely on the release of endogenous opioids (Petrovic *et al.*, 2002). From a brain socio-emotional circuit perspective, placebo effects may reflect the kinds of positive social feelings that underlie the traditional 'best-tool' available to all sensitive physicians—the 'healing touch'. In animals, social touch does release brain opioids (Keverne *et al.*, 1989; Panksepp and Bishop, 1981). It is possible that placebo effects simply would not exist without the prosocial circuits of the brain.

In sum, an overarching idea for all of these findings is that the primal sources of affective experience arise from the dynamics of the instinctual emotional operating systems that are a birthright of all mammals (Panksepp, 2005a,b). Thereby, the dual-aspect monism strategy provides a credible epistemology for decoding the nature of core affects through the diligent use of appropriate animals models, which can yield a host of novel psychological predictions that could bridge the remarkable findings of behavioural neuroscience and psychobiological studies of the human brain–mind (Panksepp, 1999, 2004; Panksepp and Harro, 2004).

12.6. **More recent neurochemical advances in social–affective neuroscience**

With the solid start afforded by the opioid model of social affects, our understanding of the basic neurobiology of social processes expanded with the clarification of additional prosocial neurochemical systems: (i) the discovery that brain oxytocin networks, enriched in the female brain, were influential in maternal urges and both adult and infant social bonds (Carter, 1998; Insel, 1997; Insel and Young, 2001), (ii) the recognition that related neuropeptides, such as vasopressin, enriched in male brains, helped foster male sexual urgency and dominance (Winslow *et al.*, 1993), and (iii) the role of many other general-purpose neurochemicals such as dopamine, norepinephrine and serotonin in the regulation of all appetitive behaviour, including social ones (Nelson and Panksepp, 1998). There are yet other social neurochemistries on the horizon that will eventually help round off our understanding of the lower social brain (Weller and Feldman, 2003). After a century of neglect, social neuroscience is finally on the intellectual map of brain researchers, and should increasingly coax evolutionary psychologists to try their hand at neuroscientific analysis.

Briefly, the major advances of the last few years have been in the analysis of adult social bonds, with demonstrations that partner preferences are mediated by both oxytocin and vasopressin systems (Cho *et al.*, 1999; Lim *et al.*, 2004a), and that the variability of social behaviour in different species and sub-species is substantially due to differential brain distributions of these receptors (Young and Wang, 2004). The ability to genetically transfect vasopressin promoter regions from the highly social prairie vole to the more solitary montane vole (Lim *et al.*, 2004b) became the first successful genetic engineering of social dispositions, even though it has long been known that social tendencies have strong genetic underpinnings (Scott and Fuller, 1965). The possibility that imbalance of oxytocin systems also contributes to symptoms of autism has been raised and partially supported (Panksepp, 1992; Bouvard *et al.*, 1995; Hollander *et al.*, 2003; Kim *et al.*, 2005).

The idea that adult pair-bonds are an addictive phenomenon based on addictive dopamine dynamics is taking hold (Wang *et al.*, 1999; Insel, 2003), even though we must reserve opinion on whether the data used to support such ideas translates well into long-term social partnerships that are evident in nature. It is possible that so far the data only reflect the well-demonstrated phenomenon of conditioned place preferences, using social choice, as opposed to environmental choice, as the behavioural endpoint. A critical question is whether dopamine 'reward' operates more acutely in social situations than in non-social ones, and there is no answer to this yet. There are yet other social neurochemistries on the horizon that will complement our understanding of the lower social brain (Weller and Feldman, 2003). It is quite remarkable that 'love' is no longer ignored in neuroscience, and there is evidence that endogenous opioids do facilitate social bonds in several species (Panksepp *et al.*, 1982, 1994a; Shayit *et al.*, 2003; Moles *et al.*, 2004). I personally suspect that these will eventually be found to be deeper, long-term, nurturant bonds than those facilitated by dopamine, which may be shorter-term sexual bonds.

As mentioned above, the study of oxytocin dynamics in humans has now yielded evidence that intranasal oxytocin can facilitate feelings of trust (Kosfeld *et al.*, 2005). Many have confidence that this neuropeptide contributes to feelings of love (Carter, 1998; Panksepp, 1998), and human brain imaging of such processes is flourishing (e.g. Fisher *et al.*, 2002; Lorberbaum *et al.*, 2002; Bartels and Zeki, 2004). Indeed, similar brain regions are activated by emotionally moving music that evokes chills (Panksepp and Bernatzky, 2002), which is often ideally suited to arouse social–affective feelings (Blood and Zatorre, 2001). However, human brain imaging only yields correlates of affective states—often just the cognitive tips of affective 'icebergs' that

cannot be imaged because those slowly shifting global brain states are often subtracted out of the brain imaging equations. Such measures also often miss ancient brain areas with low metabolic activity where the power of molecules is more important than the frequency of action potentials, yielding many false negatives. Indeed, the modern image of the 'computational brain' in EP, where it is assumed that one needs to simply envision the flow of information within circuits, without taking full account of brain 'states' generated by chemical communication/ neuromodulation channels, is giving us a faulty image of the human mind.

In a sense, the empirical resolution of modern brain-imaging techniques is more comparable to the telescopes that Galileo constructed than to the Hubble telescope of the current era, which is why psychological functions seem to be localized to discrete brain areas with such precision – because the machines are so crude, and have such low resolution, only large differences in activation are significant using the subtraction methods (Toga and Mazziotta, 2000), even though some intriguing patterns are emerging in emotion research (Phan *et al.*, 2002; Murphy *et al.*, 2003). With better machines, we will no doubt find more and more areas of the brain being involved in various psychological processes, making it harder to argue for discrete neuroanatomical modules, as opposed to highly overlapping and interactive networks (see also Barton, this volume, Chapter 11).

Although there is not sufficient space to highlight advances in our understanding of sexual and maternal systems of the mammalian brain, both have recently been intensively studied and well summarized (Pfaff, 1999; Numan and Insel, 2003). Brain opioids and oxytocin also figure heavily in erotic and nurturant social gratifications, but those passions seem to be concentrated in brain regions different from those that regulate separation distress and play. It is especially noteworthy how plastic some of these systems are. Lifelong changes in emotionality emerge in young animals raised with consistent tender loving care (Suomi, 1997; Suomi and Levine, 1998). Some of the most dramatic effects have been obtained in the analysis of ano-genetical grooming/affection that good rat mothers lavish on their offspring. Such care behaviours permanently modify the emotional personalities (psycho-phenotypes) of rats throughout the lifespan (Meaney, 2001; Champagne *et al.*, 2003). These effects are due to modified methylation of genes that are important in regulating brain stress responsivity (Weaver *et al.*, 2004).

Also, the idea that social bonds may partly reflect addictive processes of the brain has gar-nered further support by the finding that brain dopamine systems, which are important in all kinds of reward-seeking urges, can promote social preferences (Insel, 2003). Brain dopamine deficiencies promote attraction to psychostimu-lants such as cocaine (Morgan *et al.*, 2002). Indeed, attractions of cocaine vary as function of social status. Submissive animals find cocaine more desirable than dominant animals (Heyne and Wolffgramm, 1998; Morgan *et al.*, 2002). And the satisfactions of maternal behaviour seem to outweigh cocaine reward in similar regions of the brain (Febo *et al.*, 2005). In this context, it is worth noting that juvenile social dominance can be regulated by opioids. Opioid receptor blockade promotes submissiveness in play encounters, perhaps by reducing social dominance, while low doses of morphine facili-tate dominance, perhaps by increasing social confidence (Panksepp *et al.*, 1985).

Finally, the existence of a laughter-type 50 kHz vocalization in rats (Panksepp and Burgdorf, 1999, 2003), first discovered by listen-ing in to rats playing, offers a vocal measure of positive social affect in the same way that sepa-ration-distress calls reflect negative social affect (Knutson *et al.*, 2002). This response is strongly modulated by brain dopamine activity, and the 50 kHz vocal response is facilitated by dopamine energized reward-seeking circuitry (Burgdorf and Panksepp, 2006). One prediction from an inclusive-fitness perspective is that these 'happy' vocalizations may facilitate social attractiveness and hence reproductive success. This could be achieved by directly enticing the opposite sex, or perhaps just from gaining the benefits of being socially attractive by exhibiting a willingness to participate in positive social interchange. Indeed, this measure could potentially be used as a gen-eral measure of social desire, and we would note that the SEEKING system that is so intimately linked to 'happy/eager' 50 kHz vocalizations is probably a generalized emotional system that is

foundational for all motivational and emotional processes (Burgdorf and Panksepp, 2006). Arousal of this system can promote the seeking of all kinds of rewards, both social and non-social (Panksepp, 1981, 1986), as well as the seeking of safety in dangerous situations (Ikemoto and Panksepp, 1999).

In sum, we now have a solid understanding of the nature of the *lower social brain* and this kind of knowledge needs to integrated with our understanding of the *higher social brain* (e.g. Dunbar, 1993; Preston and de Waal, 2002). With the emergence of sophisticated ways to image the cognitive functions of higher brain regions in humans within the past dozen years, an under-standing of the neurogeographies of some human *social* processes—for instance, the sources of empathy, love, jealousy and shame—is accumulating. There is insufficient space here to try to weave these threads into a coherent story, but a recent synthesis is available (Watt, 2005).

In closing, I would simply re-emphasize that the four basic mammalian social–emotional systems (separation distress/PANIC, the basic social engagement PLAY system, the male and female LUST systems, and nurturant CARE sys-tem (Panksepp, 1998a, 2005a), provide enough social–affective complexity at the intrinsic, geneti-cally provided motivational level to serve as a solid foundation for the emergence of many subtle human social processes. We can be confident that the above systems have strong genetic constraints since, to the best of our knowledge, they are situ-ated in the same regions of all mammalian brains and contain the same neurochemical messengers and regulators (with, of course, abundant cross-species variability in fine details, including the precise nature of each emotional response, which cannot monitored in fine detail any more than the weather patterns that sweep across the landscape).

How might the basic emotional 'energies' play out in the higher, more cognitive, regions of the brain? If we imagine the force of the ancient separation distress/PANIC system in the genera-tion of human grief, loneliness and heartache, we can imagine how this could be a force for art, music, literature and our obsessive desire to be part of a larger supportive whole, such as insti-tutionalized religions (Ostow, 2006). Indeed, it might be worth considering that the two basic religious postures, namely the hunched supplication of prayer, and the feelings of reverent awe expressed in the outreached arms of religious exaltation, have basic similarities to two fundamental social postures—the ancient hunched postures following prolonged separation distress (so evident in Harlow's motherless young monkeys) and infants reaching eagerly upward to be picked up by caretakers. Likewise, if we consider the power of play in helping to construct social brains by allowing organisms to explore the boundaries of their social knowledge, we can envision how the prosocial brain is constructed from the genetic birthrights of a few basic social–affective tendencies and our massive capacity for associative learning.

12.7. From social emotions to social cognitions: the 'objectless' genetics of socio-affective processes

In sum, what has evolution provided as genetic birthrights to social brains? The molecules of inheritance *only* contain codes for manufacturing hordes of proteins which, through environmentally channelled developmental pathways, lead to the construction of complex brains that do have certain intrinsic skills (types of sensory, behavioural and affective urges), all of which become effective psychobehavioural skills when refined by experience. Brains do not contain intrinsic cognitions/thoughts, only dispositions to behave, feel, and, with a sufficiently complex cognitive apparatus, perhaps to think in certain ways. Emotional feelings are attached to most objects and events via learning (LeDoux, 1996).

Thus, most of the genetically provided affects are initially largely 'objectless'. The brain can contain the potentials for certain types of emotional, homeostatic and sensory affects, without having any clear-headed idea what those affects are all about. There are, of course, some pre-ordained exteroceptive and interoceptive sensory pathways into these affective–instinctual psychobehavioural systems, especially the sensory and homeostatic affects (e.g. the delight of sugar and the pain of hunger). However, few of the neurodynamics that become resolved into emotional feelings have any robust and complex

perceptual inputs with which they are genetically linked. For instance, primates do not intrinsically fear snakes and spiders, even though such fears are rapidly learned through social observations (Mineka and Cook, 1988). At best, there are linkages, such as the capacity of the smell of a cat and pain to evoke a fearful neurodynamic in rats. However, the negative affect of fearfulness can be rapidly connected to most world events by learning. Perhaps the most likely systems to have intrinsic sensory inputs are those of LUST, mediating reproductive urges. There is much evidence for sensory driving of sexual arousal, from various pheromones in many species to visual attractions in primates, but we should be hesitant to assume that erotic feelings that can so easily be aroused in adult human males by female body parts are intrinsically built into the visual apparatus. They may developmentally reflect conditioned associations to relatively objectless erotic feelings.

According to the present view, the core emotional affects are the 'ancestral voices of the genes' reflecting brain potentials that are built into the instinctual emotional action apparatus. These operating systems interface powerfully with higher cognitive systems, which allow the inherited psychobehavioural tools of the brain to be linked up with the propositional events of the world and the cultural evolution that characterizes the human species. It is probably a mistake to assume that evolution has provided the core emotional systems of organisms with any intrinsic propositional knowledge of the world. Since organisms are never, at any point, separated from the world, it may have been pointless to build in knowledge that can easily be harvested through affective associations. Such views are increasingly being accepted by many scholars who are pursuing the agenda of embodiment and embeddedness in the study of mind (see Colombetti and Thompson, 2005). However, as we discard false separations between organisms and their environments, there is still abundant room for conceptualizing the tools that genetic inheritance provides each species to facilitate survival. There is much evidence to suggest that, for all mammals, many of the essential tools for living and learning are deeply affective, and do not differ so substantially across different organisms that useful cross-species inferences cannot be derived, despite their distinct sensory and motor abilities, adapted for different ecological niches.

While most core emotional systems may initially be without objects, they rapidly become linked to the world through individual and cultural learning. This learning transpires via the systematic application of rewards and punishments (i.e. through the use of traditional, behaviouristic reinforcement procedures), but I would suggest that that learning would not proceed very rapidly if there were no accompanying affective changes. As already noted, how the *process* of reinforcement is elaborated within the brain remains largely a mystery, but it is noteworthy that the most effective reinforcers are always accompanied by affective experiences in humans. This mystery spawns a chicken-and-egg type of dilemma. Are emotional feelings created by reinforcement principles? Or is 'reinforcement' simply a short-hand term for describing how core affective systems regulate learning? I would suggest that it is the latter—that the epigenetic 'grooves' and channellings provided by ancient core affective processes are perhaps the main way that the social brain is constructed during child development. For instance, the joyous urge to play, often resulting in affectively negative consequences, allows young organisms to learn a great deal about the behavioural tendencies and expectations of others of their kind. It is increasingly clear that, in addition to genetically provided sensory–perceptual processes, much of human cognitive activity relies on a general purpose neocortex, which provides the essential substrate, a vast neuronal associative 'playground' for the generation of most cognitive activities.

Consider the basic power of love. An increasing number of investigators accepts that we might be able to make progress on this slippery topic if we pay attention to the prosocial chemistries we share with the other animals. At present one can do this this by: (i) looking at the neurochemical systems underlying prosocial emotions: oxytocin linked with nurturance, vasopressin with protectiveness, gonadotropin-releasing hormone with erotic feelings, the endorphins with play and bonding, corticotropin-releasing factor with separation anxiety, etc.; and (ii) looking at the developmental unfolding of these feelings from infancy, and how these feelings relate critically to communicative interchanges with others. In other words, all mammals have nurturant-bonding chemistries in their brain, and love, as we humans understand it, may be created in higher cognitive brain regions by lower affective functions of the ancestral neuro-mental apparatus. The same goes for many higher socially constructed emotions (Manstead *et al.*, 2004).

To try to put more into those higher brain systems than is supported by solid neurobio-behavioural evidence is premature, and may be woefully incorrect. Whether those aspects of the higher social–emotional brain, such as orbitofrontal cortex and anterior cingulate, can generate affective experience on their own is simply unknown. It is possible, however, that higher brain evolution only provided the capacity for sensory–perceptual parsing of incoming cognitive information into the old affective strata of the brain. At the very least, I would suggest that we resist belief statements on how affective experience may be a higher brain function that is unique to humans (e.g. Lane and Garfield, 2005; Rolls, 2005). There was much more to affective brain circuit evolution than the reflective capacities of neocortical computations.

There need to be vigorous discussions within EP with respect to how affect is constructed within brain. We must consider how the various possibilities can be *empirically* resolved. To merely accept *conceptual* points of view in this area, just because they seem so compelling from cross-cultural analyses of adult psychological tendencies, can transform guesswork into apparent knowledge. The statistical, cross-cultural, psychological trends on which classic EP is based should be reconsidered with respect to all the other reasonable developmental trajectories that might lead to the kinds of end results that evolutionary psychologists have documented. The plasticities of epigenetic landscapes are likely to explain more of those exciting findings than mere genetic determinism (Buller, 2004). However, there are at least seven genetically provided emotional processes (whose massive intrinsic complexities become epigenetically refined) that are critically important in constructing social brain. So far, a balanced analysis of *all* the available evidence suggests that the most important evolutionary tools we have for survival are the ones we share with the other mammals. An increasing respect for the basic psychological processes of other animals may help us untangle the "world-knot" (Griffin, 1998) that we have created for ourselves through the deceptive magic of words that arise from our uniquely expansive neocortex working in long-standing historical circumstances, constrained by cultural landscapes that our ancestors constructed.

References

Bartels, A. and Zeki, S. (2004) The neural correlates of maternal and romantic love. *Neurimage*, 21: 1155–1166.

Bennett, M. R. and Hacker, P. M.S. (2003) *Philosophical Foundations of Neuroscience*. Blackwell, Malden, MA.

Blood, A. J. and Zatorre, R. J. (2001) Intensely pleasurable responses to music correlate with activity in brain regions implicated in reward and emotion. *Proceedings of the National Academy of Sciences*, 98: 11818–11823.

Bodkin, J. L., Zornberg, G. L., Lucas, S. E. and Cole, J. O. (1995) Buprenorphine treatment of refractory depression. *Journal of Clinical Psychopharmacology*, 16: 49–57.

Bouvard, M. P., Leboyer, M., Launay, J.-M. *et al.* (1995) Low-dose naltrexone effects on plasma chemistries and clinical symptoms in autism: a double-blind, placebo-controlled study. *Psychiatry Research*, 58: 191–201.

Bowlby, J. (1960) Separation anxiety. *International Journal of Psychoanalysis*, 41: 89–113.

Brand, P. and Yancey, P. (1997) *The Gift of Pain*. Zondervan Publishing House, Grand Rapids, MI.

Buller, D. J. (2004) *Adapting Minds, Evolutionary Psychology and the Persistent Quest for Human Nature*. MIT Press, Cambridge, MA.

Burgdorf, J. and Panksepp, J. (2006) The neurobiology of positive emotions. *Neuroscience and Biobehavioral Reviews*, 30: 173–187.

Carter, C. S. (1998) Neuroendocrine perspectives on social attachment and love. *Psychoneuroendocrinology*, 23: 779–818.

Champagne, F. A., Francis, D. D., Mar, A. and Meaney, M. J. (2003) Variations in maternal care in the rat as a mediating influence for the effects of environment on development. *Physiology and Behavior*, 79: 359–371.

Cho, M. M., DeVries, A. C., Williams, J. R. and Carter, C. S. (1999) The effects of oxytocin and vasopressin on partner preferences in male and female prairie voles (*Microtus ochrogaster*) *Behavioral Neuroscience*, 113: 1071–1079.

Ciompi, L. and Panksepp, J. (2004) Energetic effects of emotions on cognitions— complementary psychobiological and psychosocial finding. In R. Ellis and N. Newton (eds) *Consciousness & Emotions*, vol. 1, pp. 23–55. John Benjamins, Amsterdam.

Colombetti, G. and Thompson, E. (eds) (2005) Emotion experience. *Journal of Consciousness Studies*, 12: 1–250.

Damasio, A. R., Grabowski, T. J., Bechara, A. *et al.* (2000) Subcortical and cortical brain activity during the feeling of self-generated emotions. *Nature Neuroscience*, 3: 1049–1056.

Danziger, N. and Willer, J.-C. (2005) Tension-type headache as the unique pain experience of a patient with congenital insensitivity to pain. *Pain*, 117: 478–483.

Dunbar, R. I. M. (1993) Coevolution of neocortical size, group size and language in humans. *Behavioral and Brain Sciences*, 16: 681–735.

Ellis, G. F. R. and Toronchuk, J. (2005) Neural development: Affective and immune system influences. In N. Newton and R. Ellis (eds) *Consciousness and Emotion: Agency, Conscious Choice and Selective Perception*, pp. 81–119. John Benjamins, Philadelphia, PA.

Febo, M., Numan, M. and Ferris, C. F. (2005) Functional magnetic resonance imaging shows oxytocin activates brain regions associated with mother-pup bonding during suckling. *Journal of Neuroscience*, 25: 11637–11644.

Fisher, H. E., Aron, A., Mashek, D., Li, H. and Brown, L. L. (2002) Defining the brain systems of lust, romantic attraction, and attachment. *Archives of Sexual Behavior*, 3: 413–419.

Griffin, D. R. (1998) *Unsnarling the World-Knot*. University of California Press, Berkeley.

Gross-Isseroff, R., Dillon, K. A., Israli, M. and Biegon, A. (1990) Regionally selective increases in opioid receptor density in the brains of victims. *Brain Research*, 530: 312–316.

Harlow, H. F. (1958) The nature of love. *American Psychologist*, 13: 673–685.

Heath, R. G. (1996) *Exploring the Mind–Body Relationship*. Moran Printing, Baton Rouge, LA.

Heimer, L. (2003) A new anatomical framework for neuropsychiatric disorders and drug abuse. *American Journal of Psychiatry*, 160: 1726–1739.

Herman, B. H. and Panksepp, J. (1978) Effects of morphine and naloxone on separation distress and approach attachment: evidence for opiate mediation of social affect. *Pharmacology, Biochemistry & Behavior*, 9: 213–220.

Herman, B. H. and Panksepp, J. (1981) Ascending endorphinergic inhibition of distress vocalization. *Science*, 211: 1060–1062.

Heyne, A. and Wolffgramm, J. (1998) The development of addiction to d-amphetamine in an animal model: same principles as for alcohol and opiate. *Psychopharmacology*, 140: 510–518.

Hollander, E., Novotny, S., Hanratty, M. *et al.* (2003) Oxytocin infusion reduces repetitive behaviors in adults with autistic and Asperger's disorders. *Neuropsychopharmacology*, 28: 193–198.

Holms, J. (1993) *John Bowlby and Attachment Theory*. Routledge, London.

Holstege, G., Georgiadis, J. R., Paans, A. M., Meiners, L. C., van der Graaf, F. H. and Reinders, A. A. (2003) Brain activation during human male ejaculation. *Journal of Neuroscience*, 23: 9185–9193.

Ikemoto, S. and Panksepp, J. (1999) The role of nucleus accumbens DA in motivated behavior: a unifying interpretation with special reference to reward-seeking. *Brain Research Reviews*, 31: 6–41.

Insel, T. R. (1997) The neurobiology of social attachment. *American Journal of Psychiatry*, 154: 726–735.

Insel, T. R. (2003) Is social attachment an addictive disorder? *Physiology & Behavior*, 79: 351–357.

Insel, T. R. and Young, L. J. (2001) The neurobiology of attachment. *Nature Reviews Neuroscience*, 2: 129–136.

Jürgens, U. (1994) The role of the periaqueductal grey in vocal behaviour. *Behavioral Brain Research*, 62: 107–117.

Jürgens, U. (1998) Neuronal control of mammalian vocalization, with special reference to the squirrel monkey. *Naturwissenschaften*, 85: 376–388.

Keverne, E. B., Martensz, N. and Tuite, B. (1989) β-Endorphin concentrations in CSF of monkeys are influenced by grooming relationships. *Psychoneuroendocrinology*, 14: 155–161.

Kim, S. J., Young, L. J., Gonen, D. *et al.* (2005) Transmission disequilibrium testing of arginine vasopressin receptor 1A (AVPR1A) polymorphisms in autism. *Molecular Psychiatry*, 7: 503–507.

Knutson, B., Burgdorf, J. and Panksepp, J. (2002) Ultrasonic vocalizations as indices of affective states in rats. *Psychological Bulletin*, 128: 961–977.

Kolb, B. and Tees, C. (eds) (1990) *The cerebral cortex of the rat.* Cambridge, MA: MIT Press.

Kosfeld, M., Heirichs, M., Zak, P. J. and Fehr, E. (2005) Oxytocin increases trust in humans. Nature, 435: 673–676.

Kovacs, G. L., Sarnyai, Z. and Szabo, G. (1998) Oxytocin and addiction: a review. *Psychoneuroendocrinology*, 23: 945–962.

Lane, R. D. and Garfield, D. A. S. (2005) Becoming aware of feelings: integration of cognitive–developmental, neuroscientific and psychoanalytic perspectives, *Neuro-Psychoanalysis*, 7: 5–30.

LeDoux, J. E. (1996) *The Emotional Brain* Simon & Schuster, New York.

Lim, M. M., Wang, Z., Olazabal, D. E., Ren, X., Terwilliger, E. F. and Young. L. J. (2004a) Enhanced partner preference in a promiscuous species by manipulating the expression of a single gene. *Nature*, 429: 754–757.

Lim, M. M., Murphy, A. Z. and Young, L. J. (2004b) Ventral striatopallidal oxytocin and vasopressin V1a receptors in the monogamous prairie vole (*Microtus ochrogaster*). *Journal of Comparative Neurology*, 468: 555–570.

Lorberbaum, J. P., Newman, J. D., Horwitz, A. R. *et al.* (2002) A potential role for thalamocingulate circuitry in human maternal behavior. *Biological Psychiatry*, 51: 431–445.

MacLean, P. D. (1990) *The Triune Brain in Evolution.* Plenum, New York.

Manstead, A. S. R., Frijda, N. and Fischer, A. (2004) *Feelings and Emotions: The Amsterdam Symposium.* Cambridge University Press, Cambridge, UK.

Meaney, M. J. (2001) Maternal care, gene expression, and the transmission of individual differences in stress reactivity across generations. *Annual Review of Neuroscience*, 24: 1161–1192.

Meins, E., Fernyhough, C. M., Wainwrith, R., Gupta, M. D., Fradley, E. and Tuckey, M. (2002) Maternal mind-mindedness and attachment security as predictors of theory of mind understanding. *Child Development*, 73: 1715–1726.

Mesulam, M. (ed.) (2000) *Principles of Behavior and Cognitive Neurology*, 2nd edn. Oxford University Press, New York.

Mineka, S. and Cook, M. (1988) Social learning and the acquisition of snake fear in monkeys. In T. R. Zentall and B. G. Galef (eds) *Social Learning*, pp. 51–73. Lawrence Erlbaum, Hillsdale, NJ.

Mogil, J. S. (ed.) (2004) *The Genetics of Pain.* IASP Press. Seattle, WA.

Moles, A., Kieffer, B. L. and D'Amato, F. R. (2004) Deficit in attachment behavior in mice lacking the mu-opioid receptor gene. *Science*, 304: 1983–1986.

Morgan, D., Grant, K. A., Gage, H. D. *et al.* (2002) Social dominance in monkeys: dopamine D2 receptors and cocaine self-administration. *Nature Neuroscience*, 5: 169–174.

Murphy, F. C., Nimmo-Smith, I. and Lawrence, D. (2003) Functional neuroanatomy of emotions: a meta-analysis. *Cognitive, Affective, & Behavioral Neuroscience*, 3: 207–233.

Nelson, E. E. and Panksepp, J. (1998) Brain substrates of infant–mother attachment: contributions of opioids, oxytocin, and norepinephrine. *Neuroscience & Biobehavioral Reviews*, 22: 437–452.

Numan, M. and Insel, T. R. (2003) *The Neurobiology of Parental Behavior.* Springer, New York.

Ostow, M. (2006) *Spirit, Mind and Brain.* Columbia University Press, New York.

Panksepp, J. (1981) Brain opioids: a neurochemical substrate for narcotic and social dependence. In S. Cooper (ed.) *Progress in Theory in Psychopharmacology.* Academic Press, London, pp. 149–175.

Panksepp, J. (1985) Mood changes. In *Handbook of Clinical Neurology*, vol. 1(45), *Clinical Neuropsychology*, pp. 271–285. Elsevier, Amsterdam.

Panksepp, J. (1992) Oxytocin effects on emotional processes: separation distress, social bonding, and relationships to psychiatric disorders. *Annals of the New York Academy of Sciences*, 652: 243–252.

Panksepp, J. (1993) Neurochemical control of moods and emotions: Amino acids to neuropeptides. In M. Lewis and J. Haviland (eds) *Handbook of Emotions*, pp. 87–107. Guilford Press, New York.

Panksepp, J. (1998a) *Affective Neuroscience. The Foundation of Human and Animal Emotions.* Oxford University Press, New York.

Panksepp, J. (1998b) The periconscious substrates of consciousness: affective states and the evolutionary origins of the SELF. *Journal of Consciousness Studies*, 5: 566–582.

Panksepp, J. (1999) Emotions as viewed by psychoanalysis and neuroscience: an exercise in consilience, and accompanying commentaries. *NeuroPsychoanalysis*, 1: 15–89.

Panksepp, J. (2003a) At the interface of affective, behavioral and cognitive neurosciences. Decoding the emotional feelings of the brain. *Brain and Cognition*, 52: 4–14.

Panksepp, J. (2003b) Can anthropomorphic analyses of "separation cries" in other animals inform us about the emotional nature of social loss in humans? *Psychological Review*, 110: 376–388.

Panksepp, J. (2003c) Feeling the pain of social loss. *Science*, 302: 237–239.

Panksepp, J. (ed.) (2004) *Textbook of Biological Psychiatry*. Wiley, Hoboken, NJ.

Panksepp, J. (2005a) Affective consciousness: core emotional feelings in animals and humans. *Consciousness and Cognition*, 14: 19–69.

Panksepp, J. (2005b) Feelings of social loss: the evolution of pain and the ache of a broken heart. In R. Ellis and N. Newton (eds) *Consciousness & Emotions*, vol. 1, pp. 23–55. John Benjamins, Amsterdam.

Panksepp, J. (2005c) On the neuro-evolutionary nature of social pain, support, and empathy. In M. Aydede (ed.) *Pain: New Essays on Its Nature & the Methodology of Its Study*, pp. 367–387. MIT Press, Cambridge, MA.

Panksepp, J. (2005d) On the primal nature of affective consciousness: what are the relations between emotional awareness and affective experience? *Neuro-Psychoanalysis*, 7: 40–55.

Panksepp, J. (2006) Emotional endophenotypes in evolutionary psychiatry. *Progress in Neuro-Psychopharmacology & Biological Psychiatry*.

Panksepp, J. and Bernatzky, G. (2002) Emotional sounds and the brain: the neuro-affective foundations of musical appreciation. *Behavioural Processes*, 60: 133–155.

Panksepp, J. and Bishop, P. (1981) An autoradiographic map of (3H)diprenorphine binding in rat brain: effects of social interaction. *Brain Research Bulletin*, 7: 405–410.

Panksepp, J. and Burgdorf, J. (1999) Laughing rats? Playful tickling arouses high frequency ultrasonic chirping in young rodents. In S. Hameroff, D. Chalmers and A. Kazniak, *Toward a Science of Consciousness III*, pp. 231–244. MIT Press, Cambridge, MA.

Panksepp, J. and Burgdorf, J. (2003) "Laughing" rats and the evolutionary antecedents of human joy? *Physiology & Behavior*, 79: 533–547.

Panksepp, J. and Harro, J. (2004) Future prospects in psychopharmacology. In J. Panksepp (ed.) *Textbook of Biological Psychiatry*, pp. 627–660. Wiley, Hoboken, NJ.

Panksepp, J. and Panksepp, J. B. (2000) The seven sins of evolutionary psychology. *Evolution and Cognition*, 6: 108–131.

Panksepp, J., Herman, B., Conner, R., Bishop, P. and Scott, J. P. (1978a) The biology of social attachments: Opiates alleviate separation distress. *Biological Psychiatry*, 9: 213–220.

Panksepp, J., Vilberg, T., Bean, N. J., Coy, D. H. and Kastin, A. J. (1978b) Reduction of distress vocalization in chicks by opiate-like peptides. *Brain Research Bulletin*, 3: 663–667.

Panksepp, J., Bean, N. J., Bishop, P., Vilberg, T. and Sahley, T. L. (1980a) Opioid blockade and social comfort in chicks. *Pharmacology Biochemistry & Behavior*, 13: 673–683.

Panksepp, J., Herman, B. H., Villberg, T., Bishop, P. and DeEskinazi, F. G. (1980b) Endogenous opioids and social behavior. *Neuroscience and Biobehavioral Reviews*, 4: 473–487.

Panksepp, J., Siviy, S., Normansell, L. A., White, K. and Bishop, P. (1982) Effects of B-chlornaltexamine on separation distress in chicks. *Life Sciences*, 31: 2387–2390.

Panksepp, J., Jalowiec, J., DeEskinazi, F. G. and Bishop, P. (1985) Opiates and play dominance in juvenile rats. *Behavioral Neuroscience*, 99: 441–453.

Panksepp, J., Normansell, L. A., Herman, B., Bishop, P. and Crepeau, L. (1988) Neural and neurochemical control of the separation distress call. In J. D. Newman (ed.) *The Physiological Control of Mammalian Vocalizations*, pp. 263–299. Plenum Press, New York.

Panksepp, J., Nelson, E. and Siviy, S. (1994a) Brain opioids and mother–infant social motivation. *Acta Paediatrica*, 397: 40–46.

Panksepp, J., Normansell, L. A., Cox, J. F. and Siviy, S. (1994b) Effects of neonatal decortication on the social play of juvenile rats. *Physiology & Behavior*, 56: 429–443.

Panksepp, J., Moskal, J., Panksepp, J. B. and Kroes, R. (2002) Comparative approaches in evolutionary psychology: Molecular neuroscience meets the mind. *Neuroendocrinology Letters*, 23: 105–115.

Petrovic, P., Kalso, E., Petersson, K. M. and Ingvar, M. (2002) Placebo and opioid analgesia: imaging a shared neuronal network. *Science*, 295: 1737–1740.

Pfaff, D. W. (1999) *Drive: Neurobiological and Molecular Mechanisms of Sexual Behavior*. MIT Press, Cambridge, MA.

Phan, K. L., Wager, T., Taylor, S. F. and Liberzon, I. (2002) Functional neuroanatomy of emotion, A meta-analysis of emotion activation studies in PET and fMRI. *Neuroimage*, 16: 331–348.

Preston, S. D. and de Waal, B. M. (2002) Empathy: Its ultimate and proximate bases. *Behavioral and Brain Sciences*, 25: 1–72.

Rizzolatti, G. and Craigero, L. (2004) The mirror-neuron system. *Annual Review of Neuroscience*, 27: 169–192.

Rolls, E. (2005) *Emotions Explained*. Oxford University Press, New York.

Russell, J. A. (2003) Core affect and the psychological construction of emotion. *Psychological Review*, 110: 145–172.

Scott, J. P. and Fuller, J. L. (1965) *Genetics and the Social Behavior of the Dog*. University of Chicago Press, Chicago, IL.

Shayit, M., Nowak, R., Keller, M. and Weller, A. (2003) Establishment of a preference by the newborn lamb for its mother: the role of opioids. *Behavioral Neuroscience*, 117: 446–454.

Shewmon, D. A., Holmes, D. A. and Byrne, P. A. (1999) Consciousness in congenitally decorticate children: developmental vegetative state as self-fulfilling prophecy. *Developmental Medicine and Child Neurology*, 41: 364–374.

Suomi, S. J. (1997) Early determinants of behaviour: evidence from primate studies. *British Medical Bulletin*, 53: 170–184.

Suomi, S. J. and Levine, S. (1998) Psychobiology of intergenerational effects of trauma: evidence from animal studies. In Y. Danieli (ed.), *Intergenerational Handbook of Multigenerational Legacies*, pp. 623–637. Plenum Press, New York.

Toga, A. W. and Mazziotta, J. C. (eds) (2000) *Brain Mapping: The Systems*. Academic Press, San Diego.

Wallace, B. A. (2000) *The Taboo of Subjectivity*. Oxford University Press, New York.

Wang, Z., Yu, G.-Z, Cascio, C., Liu, Y., Gingrich, B. and Insel, T. R. (1999) D2 receptor-mediated regulation of partner preferences in female prairie voles: a mechanism for pair bonding. *Behavioral Neuroscience*, 113: 602–611.

Watt, D. F. (2005) Social bonds and the nature of empathy. *Journal of Consciousness Studies*, 12: 188–212.

Weaver, I. C.G., Cervoni, N., Champagne, F. A. *et al*. (2004) Epigenetic programming by maternal behavior. *Nature Neuroscience*. 7: 847–854.

Weller, A. and Feldman, R. (2003) Emotion regulation and touch in infants: the role of cholecystokinin and opioids. *Peptides*, 24: 779–788.

Winslow, J. T., Hastings, N., Carter, C. S., Harbaugh, C. R. and Insel, T. R. (1993) A role for central vasopressin in pair bonding in monogamous prairie voles. *Nature*, 365: 544–548.

Young, L. J. and Wang, Z. (2004) The neurobiology of pair bonding. *Nature Neuroscience*, 7: 1048–54.

Zubieta, J. K., Ketter, T. A., Bueller, J. A. *et al*. (2003) Regulation of human affective responses by anterior cingulate and limbic mu-opioid neurotransmission. *Archives of General Psychiatry*, 60: 1145–1153.

CHAPTER 13

Neural pathways of social cognition

Tjeerd Jellema and David I. Perrett

13.1. A visual analysis of social behaviour without telepathy

This chapter reviews recent ideas about visual processing pathways and mechanisms in the brains of human and non-human primates that support social cognition. We will attempt to show how detection of visual cues provides a basis for guiding the observer's behaviour in ways that are based on the current and likely future behaviour of others. These visual mechanisms underpin social cognition, but do not rely on understanding others' minds. They provide what one could call a 'mechanistic' description of others' behaviour and of social events in terms of constituent components of actions, their causes and consequences, and expected future occurrence.

There are at least two features crucial for enabling such visual processing to produce descriptions of the 'mechanics' of social events.

1. It should be able to combine the description of an action with the description of contextual cues that relate to the action, because only then can the action be put in a causal setting. These contextual cues can be derived either from the agent that performed the action (such as the agent's direction of attention), or from the immediate environment

where the action took place. Examples of the latter include objects the action is directed at, or the relative spatial locations occupied by the agents and observer involved.

2. Processing should be sensitive to immediate perceptual history, because this can form the basis from which likely events or outcomes can be predicted. After all, actions within a social context evolve over time; witnessing actions and their consequences typically spans several seconds.

We will argue that the superior temporal sulcus (STS) forms the prime neural substrate for forming descriptions of the 'mechanics' of social events. This deviates from the usual view on the role of the STS, which centres on the forming of pictorial descriptions of someone's actions without any account of the physical causes. A role of the STS in forming the higher-order visual descriptions of observed actions is well documented and not disputed (cf. Allison *et al.*, 2000; Karnath, 2001). In this chapter we will qualify the nature of the higher-order descriptions by highlighting findings from single-cell recordings in the macaque monkey. These findings suggest that cell populations in the banks of the STS incorporate both features mentioned above, i.e. sensitivity to both actions and contextual cues (Jellema and Perrett, 2002, 2005, Jellema *et al.*, 2002) and sensitivity to the perceptual history

(Zacks *et al.*, 2001; Jellema and Perrett, 2003a), which might enable the prediction of future actions. We also note the interplay between the STS and mirror neurons in the parietal lobe, which have also been reported to code for the most likely future actions of others on the basis of the current visual input, both in macaques (Fogassi *et al.*, 2005) and humans (Iacoboni *et al.*, 2005).

A more sophisticated understanding of actions of conspecifics, and of social events in general, involves the attribution of mental states to the agents involved. A purely literal description of others' actions and social events will not allow the observer to understand the behaviour of others when their goals are complex and do not bear a one-to-one relationship with the directly visible events. An example is deceit, when an agent desires object A, but deliberately pays attention to object B so as to draw the attention of a rival agent away from object A. Attribution of mental states such as intentions, beliefs, and feelings towards others, in order to explain their behaviour beyond mere physical causal relationships, is an important capacity provided potentially by phylogenetic and/or ontogenetic development (Tooby and Cosmides, 1990; Baron-Cohen, 1995, and this volume, Chapter 16; Wyman and Tomasello, this volume, Chapter 17). In essence, 'mentalistic' descriptions (intentions, beliefs etc.) are often referred to as theory-of-mind (ToM) capacities. They resemble mechanistic descriptions, except that the physical causes have been replaced by abstract 'mental' causes. Mentalistic descriptions of others' behaviour may well be built on top of mechanistic descriptions by linking the STS with descriptions of the mental states of others. The STS may allow prediction of behaviour, whereas systems built on top of it (ToM) may allow *explanation* of behaviour.

The idea of the STS as part of a core system, which communicates with an extended system in order to accomplish the more sophisticated aspects of social cognition, such as social learning, imitation, empathy and theory of mind, is incorporated in several neural models (Adolphs, 1999; Haxby *et al.*, 2000, 2002; Gallese *et al.*, 2004; Iacoboni, 2005). The extended system typically includes structures such as the amygdala, insula, orbitofrontal, cingulate and parietal cortices.

We will discuss relationships of the STS to this system and the merits of the models.

Thus, a basic principle according to which the visual system may operate to support social cognition is that it is tuned to detect contingencies between causes (be they physical or mental) and outcomes of others' behaviour, so as to allow the prediction of their most likely future behaviour. These predictions are in turn used to guide the observer's behaviour towards others. We speculate that in neurodevelopmental disorders such as autism, malfunctioning of the extended system compromises the formation of mentalistic descriptions, while the mechanistic ones are still intact. As a result, the autistic mind tries to explain the world—including others' behaviour—in terms of physical, literal contingencies, and guides behaviour accordingly.

13.2. **Breaking down bodies and reassembling them**

Current ideas about where in the brain the different features of moving complex visual stimuli, such as the self-propelled actions of animate objects, are processed still rely heavily on the Ungerleider and Mishkin model (1982). This model envisaged a separation of visual processing into two distinct cortical streams: a dorsal 'where' stream, extending from V1 into the inferior parietal cortex, primarily dealing with the spatial relationships of objects; and a ventral 'what' stream, extending from V1 into the inferior temporal cortex (IT), dealing with the shape and identity of objects (Desimone and Ungerleider, 1989). A subsequent adaptation by Milner and Goodale (1995) questioned the strict 'what–where' dichotomy, and suggested that space and form are processed in both parietal and temporal areas but for different purposes (Goodale *et al.*, 1991). In their view, the ventral stream subserves visual 'perception', i.e. object and scene recognition, requiring allocentric spatial coding to represent the enduring characteristics of objects, while the dorsal stream subserves the visual control of 'action', requiring egocentric spatial coding for short-lived representations (vision for perception versus vision for action). The role of the ventral stream in the recognition of complex objects is supported by findings showing a gradual increase in the complexity of stimuli analysed by cells from primary visual cortex to temporal cortex (Perrett and Oram, 1993). Across primate species, the size of ventral pathway is related to social group size (Barton, this volume, Chapter 11), perhaps because, as group size increases, so does the necessity to recognize more social signals and behaviour.

Understanding the motion of animate objects is less straightforward than that of non-animate objects, whose motion can be explained by physical causality. If the animated objects are primates, they may well have a mental life, with the accompanying beliefs (both true and false), desires and fears, all of which make understanding the goals of actions uncertain. We will describe ideas about how the visual system has 'solved' this problem.

An initial step in understanding others from sight comes from a fractionation of the body into key parts such as the eye, mouth, head, finger, hand and arm. These are represented in specific regions of the visual association cortex within the ventral stream, in a constellation of areas often referred to as the 'core system'. They include in humans the fusiform face area (FFA; Kanwisher et al., 1997) and extrastriate body area (Downing et al., 2001), and in monkeys the inferotemporal cortex and cortex surrounding the STS. The motion of body parts is analysed separately in the dorsal stream. In humans and monkeys, processing in the posterior STS sees a confluence of the two streams of information, and the behaviour of others is specified in terms of key postures and animations.

In most neural models of social cognition, the STS features at the top of the hierarchy within a core system. The core system is not itself concerned with social meaning, but communicates with an extended system, which serves to extract social meaning from the core system output in order to accomplish the more sophisticated aspects of social cognition such as social learning, imitation, action and emotion understanding, empathy, intentionality and theory of mind.

A wealth of information about the visual analysis performed in the core system, and in the STS in particular, has come from single-cell studies in the macaque monkey. Gross et al. (1972) made the first startling finding of temporal cortex cells that responded selectively to the sight of one specific body part, a hand. Subsequent work, much of which was done in the anterior part of the STS (STSa, corresponding to area STPa; Bruce et al., 1981), revealed populations of cells selectively responsive to specific parts of the body, such as a head, hand, eye, leg or arm and often required that part to make a specific action (e.g. Bruce et al., 1981; Perrett et al., 1982; Hasselmo et al., 1989a; Oram and Perrett, 1996). Other populations of cells within the STSa respond selectively to particular whole-body actions, such as walking, crouching or jumping and not to movements of isolated body parts (Perrett et al., 1989; Oram and Perrett, 1996; Jellema and Perrett, 2003a, 2005). Single-cell coding for whole-body actions presumably results from a complex pooling of the outputs of the cells coding for individual body parts and their movement (Perrett et al., 1989). Thus, apparently, after the initial breakdown of bodies, the parts are reassembled in the STS.

Other STSa cells are tuned to multiple views of the same animate object (Perrett et al., 1985, 1987; Logothetis et al., 1995) or of the same action (Jellema and Perrett, 2002a), or are tuned to conceptually related visual stimuli, such as multiple body signals of attention directed to one point (Perrett et al., 1985, 1992). Such response selectivity is most likely obtained through pooling of the outputs of cells coding for separate views of distinct stimuli. Characteristic of many STSa cells is that they integrate information about form and motion of animate objects (Oram and Perrett, 1996; Tanaka et al., 1999).

13.3. The face: a special case

The neural representation of the face has received a disproportionately large amount of scientific investigation because faces convey a wide variety of social information, most of it via dynamic changes in parts of the face, such as lip shape and gaze direction. These changeable or variant facial aspects are not confined to a particular individual. By contrast, the invariant facial aspects remain constant across facial movements, and carry information about identity, sex and age. In the model put forward by

Haxby and colleagues (Haxby *et al.*, 2000, 2002; Hoffman and Haxby, 2000), the invariant face aspects are analysed in the fusiform gyrus, the variable face aspects in the STS, while the lateral inferior occipital gyri provide input to both fusiform and STS.

It makes sense that the representations of identity and of the changeable aspects of a face are relatively independent, because a change in expression should not be misinterpreted as a change in identity (Bruce and Young, 1986). Indeed, the two types of information processing can be experimentally disentangled, e.g. repetition-priming paradigms, which enhance face processing when identity is involved but not when expression is involved (Ellis *et al.*, 1990). The separation of expression and identity processing is, however, controversial (Calder and Young, 2005). Long before the introduction of brain-imaging techniques, two types of research had already produced indications that specialized module(s) for face processing existed: (i) neuropsychological studies of people with prosopagnosia (Bodamer, 1947; Hecaen and Angelergues, 1962), who do not recognize familiar faces, but have no clear problem recognizing other categories of object, and (ii) single-unit studies in monkey temporal cortex, which revealed the existence of neurons specifically sensitive to faces (Desimone, 1991; Perrett *et al.*, 1982, 1984, 1985). Single-unit studies also provided clues as to the different aspects of the face that different brain regions were tuned to: expressions and other changeable aspects of the face (e.g. gaze direction) seemed to be analysed in the STS, while the non-changeable aspects such as identity are analysed to a greater extent in the inferior temporal cortex (Perrett *et al.*, 1984; Hasselmo *et al.*, 1989a; Young and Yamane, 1992). Single-cell studies indicate that identity coding proceeds in a similar fashion in humans, with semantic integration of names and familiar faces occurring within the medial temporal lobe limbic structures (Quiroga *et al.*, 2005).

Recent imaging studies of the human brain have shown activation of three areas in response to the viewing of faces: the lateral fusiform gyrus, which has also been dubbed the fusiform face area (FFA; Kanwisher *et al.*, 1997), the posterior STS, and the lateral inferior occipital gyri

(e.g. Hoffman and Haxby, 2000). Although the FFA consistently shows greater activation to faces than to any other object category, it has been asserted that the FFA is engaged in the discrimination between individual objects belonging to the same category (be it faces, birds, cars or any other category of object; Gauthier *et al.*, 1999). Recent evidence shows that this assertion is wrong. Increased depth of processing (subtle discrimination of object identity rather than general recognition of object class) does enhance FFA processing, but enhancement only occurs for faces and birds (which have faces). Enhancement does not occur for flowers, cars or guitars (Grill-Spector *et al.*, 2004; see also Xu *et al.*, 2005).

In humans, the posterior STS is activated by movements of face parts, such as mouth and eyes (e.g. Decety and Grezes, 1999; Puce *et al.*, 1998; Puce and Perrett; 2003). These findings suggest that the face-processing areas identified in the monkey STS and inferior temporal (IT) cortex most likely correspond to the human posterior STS and FFA, respectively. The Hoffman and Haxby (2000) scheme of the STS processing variable face aspects and the FFA processing invariant face aspects is likely to be a simplification because single-cell, anatomical and functional imaging all suggest an organization with several patches of cortex processing faces within the STS and IT of the monkey (Harries and Perrett, 1991; Tsao *et al.*, 2006).

13.4. **Actions as they pertain to the observer**

Perhaps it is most important to comprehend how the actions of others impinge on ourselves. Prior experience coupled with an egocentric visual analysis can suffice for a limited social competence. Fortunately, most visual analyses begin with an egocentric frame of reference; such viewer-referenced coding is a defining feature of the way faces, body postures and bodily actions are coded for in the STS.

Perceived bodily actions can, in principle, be described within two different coordinate systems: a viewer- or an object-centred system (e.g. Perrett *et al.*, 1989, 1991; Hasselmo *et al.*, 1989b; Jellema and Perrett, 2006). For a viewer-centred system, the view and direction of motion or articulation of the object are defined relative to the observer. For an object-centred description, the principal axis of the object, or another part of the object, is taken as a reference point to define the action. Object-centred descriptions therefore remain constant across different vantage points of the observer.

The neural implementation of these coordinate systems has been the subject of intense research. Coding in STS is typically viewer-centred. For example, an STS cell may respond to an agent advancing (i.e. following its nose) to the right of the observer (from the observer's perspective the right profile is visible and motion is to the right), but not to the agent retreating to the right (left profile view and motion to the right), nor to the agent retreating to the left (right profile view and motion to the left). Such cells require a specific combination of body view and motion direction, defined from the observer's perspective. Although these cells do not generalize across changes in perspective view, they usually generalize very well across changes in illumination and size.

In contrast, object-centred cells have received relatively little study, probably because they are rare: only about 5% of STS cells that respond to an action or static posture do so in an object-centred manner, the other 95% use a viewer-centred frame (e.g. Oram and Perrett, 1996). An example of object-centred coding would be selectivity for all examples of walking forward (i.e. when the body moves in the same direction as the nose), but lack of response to all backward walking. In the macaque, object-centred cells are perhaps more prevalent towards the pole of the temporal lobe, whereas viewer-centred cells may be more equally distributed along the STS (Jellema and Perrett, 2006).

Theories of ventral stream function, as well as psychological and computational models of object recognition, postulated object-centred (viewpoint-independent) coding of objects as the most efficient way of storing object information (Marr and Nishihara, 1978). Such coding would enable the neural system to achieve object constancy, which facilitates object recognition. In this light, it has been somewhat puzzling as to why most electrophysiological studies in the temporal cortex report viewpoint-dependent coding (e.g. Perrett et al., 1985, 1991; Wachsmuth et al., 1994; Logothetis et al., 1995).

There are at least two functions for viewer-centred representations which may account for their prevalence: (i) understanding an action sequence from momentary postures that constitute key components of that action (e.g. how to put on a lifejacket can be understood from poses depicted on safety instructions) (Byrne, 1995; Perrett, 1999) and (ii) inferring the direction of attention of others (are their actions directed at me or at someone or something else?) (Perrett et al., 1992). A cell responding to the left profile, but not to the right, may code for the abstract notion of 'attention directed to the observer's left', instead of the geometric characteristics of the left side of the face. The visual information arising from gaze and body cues appears to contribute to cell sensitivity in a way that is consistent with the cells' role in analysing the direction of attention. For example, cells tuned to the left profile view of the head are often additionally tuned to left eye gaze and the left profile view of the body (Wachsmuth et al., 1994). Despite the findings of cellular sensitivity to attention direction in macaques, the extent to which Old World monkeys are able to use information about the gaze direction of others is still a matter of some debate (e.g. Anderson et al., 1996; Emery et al., 1997; Lorincz et al., 1999). None the less monkeys are acutely sensitive to eye contact, particularly from dominant individuals in close proximity (Perrett and Mistlin, 1990).

13.5. Actions as they pertain to others

Actions are more than simple movements—they typically involve goal direction. This means that an action is functionally related to aspects of the environment, to its cause and/or consequence. Hence, a more abstract representation of actions can be gleaned by relating actions to environmental cues such as position (defined with respect to landmarks), goal objects, and other individuals. Such analysis appears to be conducted in sub-regions of the temporal cortex (Perrett et al., 1989, 1990).

Recent findings have made it increasingly clear that the sensitivity of cell populations in STSa exceeds that which would be required to form merely a 'pictorial' description of complex actions. STS cells respond, in intricate ways, to the sight of actions in conjunction with other visual cues. The response characteristics suggest that the cells are involved in computing (or predicting) the most likely next action or event. The cues used can be derived from the agent performing the action, or from the environment where the action took place. As such, these cells show sensitivity to the context in which the action was performed. Examples detailed below include STS cells that combine sensitivity for actions with sensitivity for the gaze direction of the performing agent (Section 13.5.1), the object the action was directed at (Section 13.5.2), or the spatial location where the action took place (Section 13.5.3). Such joint coding for actions and related contextual cues can be informative about the goals of the agent's actions.

13.5.1. Sensitivity to actions and gaze direction

A subset of STSa cells responds only to the sight of an actor performing a reaching action on the condition that the direction of head and eye gaze of the actor matched the direction of reaching (Jellema *et al.*, 2000). In other words, the agent performing the action needed to attend to the target position of his/her action in order to excite the cells. Such a combined analysis of action and gaze may well support the detection of intentional or purposive actions. That is, when an agent reaches out and knocks over an object while looking at the object, then a good guess is that it was this agent's intention to knock the object over, whereas if the agent's attention is directed elsewhere during the same reaching action then it is more likely that knocking the object over was unintentional and accidental.

13.5.2. Sensitivity to actions and their goals

Sensitivity to action goals is most clear for cells sensitive to hand–object interactions, such as reaching for, picking, tearing and manipulating objects (Perrett *et al.*, 1989, 1990; Jellema *et al.*, 2000). These cells are sensitive to the form of the

hand performing the action, and are unresponsive to the sight of tools manipulating objects in the same manner as hands. Furthermore, the cells code the spatio-temporal interaction between the agent performing the action and the object of the action. For example, cells tuned to hands manipulating an object cease to respond if: (i) the object is removed, (ii) the hand action is made in a direction away from the object, or (iii) the hands and object move appropriately but remain spatially separated (Perrett *et al.*, 1989). This selectivity ensures that the cells are more responsive in situations where the agent's motion is causally related to the object's motion.

Cells with strikingly similar sensitivity to the sight of goal-directed hand actions are found in the premotor and parietal cortex (F5, see Keysers and Perrett, 2004 for comparison). Cells in these latter areas are known as 'mirror neurons' because they respond when the monkey prepares to and executes the same hand action (i.e. the cells may respond during grasping and to the sight of grasping; see Rizzolatti and Fogassi, this volume, Chapter 14).

13.5.3. Sensitivity to actions and location

Milner and Goodale suggested that spatial position might be processed in both dorsal (parietal) and ventral (temporal) streams but for different purposes (e.g. Goodale *et al.*, 1991; Milner and Goodale, 1995). Consistent with ventral coding of position, cell populations in STSa are sensitive to the spatial location of animate objects after they move out of sight behind a screen (Baker *et al.*, 2001). Additionally the activity of cell populations sensitive to the action of walking is strongly modulated by the position of walking with respect to the observer: some cells respond only to walking at locations near to the subject, others only to walking at far-away locations (Jellema *et al.*, 2004).

Marr and Nishihara (1978) noted that to recognize an object one needs to generalize across viewing conditions (ignoring whether the object is far, near, seen from the front or side). Under this scheme it is surprising that the STS cells care so much about view and distance to objects and agents. We argue that recognizing the nature and purpose of actions requires specification of how those actions are related to objects and the observer. For this coding of the location and orientation of actions within the environment is crucial.

The combined sensitivity for actions and spatial location could enable the STS cell populations to represent meaningful aspects of social actions and interactions. The spatial positions people occupy with respect to each other and to objects often provide important clues to the meaning of the social event and to the goals or intentions of the people involved. Imaging studies in humans support the suggested role of the STS in using environmental cues to represent the goal-directedness and other contingencies related to biological actions (Castelli *et al.*, 2000; Zacks *et al.*, 2001). Saxe *et al.* (2004) showed that the right posterior STS is especially involved when the relationship of the action with the environment is manipulated to implicate different intentions of the agent.

An obvious question is, of course, whether there is any behavioural evidence that non-human primates can discriminate between intentional and non-intentional actions. A study by Call and Tomasello (1998) showed that great apes preferentially follow intentional actions performed by the experimenter, rather than non-intentional actions. In reviewing behavioural evidence, Barrett and Henzi (2005) conclude that monkeys have a limited understanding of others' minds; monkeys do not behave in a Machiavellian manner using a theory of others' minds. None the less, the actions that monkeys do perform that are designed to promote short-term selfish goals (which can result paradoxically in cooperation) still need a sophisticated analysis of the behaviour of others and its context, one that we argue could be supplied by the representations of the type we are describing.

13.6. Systems for predicting behaviour

Recent discoveries in temporal and parietal cortex show that the context of recently witnessed behaviour can have a profound effect on the visual analysis of currently seen behaviour. In effect, these brain systems allow prior behaviour to be taken into account to predict future actions of others. Such contextual analysis means that the understanding of others moves to a new level of sophistication (see also Rizzolatti and Fogassi, this volume, Chapter 14).

13.6.1. Predicting actions from static body postures

Articulation seen in point light or biological motion displays seems to be preferentially processed in human and monkey STS (Beauchamp *et al.*, 2003; Puce and Perrett, 2003). To understand an articulated action performed by another individual, however, does not require that we witness the entire action sequence. A single momentary view is often enough to identify the action and its goal. This capacity allows us to understand another's actions in a situation where the other is intermittently occluded from view. In instruction manuals, for example, the performance of dexterous manual tasks is often specified as a series of static pictures, each demonstrating particular sub-goals or stages in the action sequence. The momentary postures allow us to infer the dynamics of the whole action.

The formation of associations between an action and its end-posture might well underlie the ability of the brain to infer impending or prior action from static 'snapshots' of the body. We have found that populations of STSa cells responsive to the sight of specific articulated body actions also code for the consequent articulated static body postures when presented in isolation (Jellema and Perrett, 2003b). Such actions occur when one body part (e.g. a limb or head) moves with respect to the remainder of the body; conversely, non-articulated actions occur when equivalent body parts move as one. Articulated postures contain a torsion or rotation between parts, while non-articulated postures do not.

For the population of cells described it was notable that similar postures, which did not form the logical end-point of the effective articulated action, did not evoke responses. Starting postures, even of the effective articulated actions, also failed to evoke a response. Moreover, the cells also did not respond to unusual body actions that culminated in the effective end-posture. Together the data suggest that the cells' responses were related to the implied prior action, rather than the static posture alone. It seems that the neural representations in STSa for *actual* biological motion may extend to biological motion *implied* from static postures.

These implied motion representations could play a role in producing the activity in the medial temporal/medial superior temporal [V5(MT)/MST] areas reported in functional magnetic resonance imaging (fMRI) studies when subjects viewed still photographs of people in action (e.g. a snapshot of a running athlete; Kourtzi and Kanwisher, 2000; Senior et al., 2000). It is well established that the V5(MT)/ MST complex plays a primary role in the analysis of the direction and speed of moving objects (Maunsell and Van Essen, 1983). Its activation in response to implied motion suggests that it receives a top-down influence, since the object and context first need to be identified before the associated movement can be identified. The cell populations in STS sensitive to the articulated postures and associated preceding actions could well provide this top-down input (Barraclough et al., 2006; cf. Lorteije et al., 2006). Thus, the visual processing of static form may contribute to the comprehension of dynamic actions: sensitivity to associations between image form and motion could form the basis of the ability of the nervous system to retrieve likely motion given entirely static images.

13.6.2. **Prediction based on perceptual history**

Some STS cell populations seem to be tuned to impending behaviours of others, based on their immediate perceptual history (Jellema and Perrett, 2003a). Seeing events prior to a body assuming a static posture can allow one to predict the likelihood and nature of the body's next movement.

Under natural viewing conditions the responses of some STSa cells to the sight of static body postures is controlled by the actions performed by that body (agent) in the one or two seconds directly preceding the onset of the static posture. In other words, the perceptual history can enable or prevent a cell's response to the current retinal input (Jellema and Perrett, 2003a).

One example is that of cells responding to the front view of a static body when preceded by walking towards the observer. Other actions such as walking backward and stopping or body rotation that culminate in the same static body view at the same location in the testing room failed to result in a response. Although the type of preceding motion was crucial for evoking a response during the static phase, the cells did not respond during this prior movement.

These neural representations for sequences of events may play a role in predicting or anticipating the next move or posture. For example, the sight of a body that has just stopped walking forward may invoke an expectation that, should walking commence again, it is likely to resume a forward direction. The same view of a static body that has just stopped walking backward, by contrast, may be expected to move in a backward direction should walking resume.

13.6.2.1. Prediction during unseen actions

The actions of others are not always fully visible; for example, someone may become hidden from our sight as they move behind a tree, or their hands may not remain fully in view as they reach to retrieve an object. Within STS it is now apparent that specific cell populations are activated when the presence of a hidden agent can be inferred from the preceding visual events (i.e. the agent was witnessed passing out of sight behind a screen and has not yet been witnessed re-emerging into sight, therefore the agent is likely to remain behind the screen; see Baker et al., 2001). These STSa cells respond maximally to the sight of individuals 'hiding' behind an occluding screen. In the 3s following disappearance from sight behind a screen, the population response is significantly larger than in the prior 3s when the agent was visible and moving towards the screen. The cells responding to occlusion additionally showed spatial sensitivity, discriminating between locations where the agent was hidden (at the left, right or middle of the room; Baker et al., 2001). Cell responses to the experimenter walking in-sight were consistent with the out-of-sight responses. For example, if hiding behind a screen located at the right-hand side of the testing room evoked significantly larger responses than hiding behind a screen at the left-hand side, then walking towards the right-hand screen would also evoke a larger response than walking towards the left-hand screen, with walking in both cases from left to right. These responses are consistent with the idea that the cells coded not only for the presence of the experimenter behind the right-hand screen, but also for the intention/goal of the experimenter to go behind that screen. For this interpretation, we need only assume that walking towards the right screen reflects the intention to move behind that screen. Saxe *et al.* (2004) have argued similarly that a region of posterior STS is activated when human observers interpret events in actions as intentional as opposed to incidental.

Corresponding cell properties are seen in F5 (Umilta *et al.*, 2001). If a monkey sees an object hidden behind a screen, the monkey can 'believe' the object continues to exist. F5 cells responding to the sight of the experimenter reaching and grasping objects in full view will also respond to the sight of the experimenter reaching to grasp an object behind the screen (so long as the monkey has seen the object hidden behind the screen). In this instance the coding of the agent's action and goal includes 'belief' (see Rizzolatti and Fogassi, this volume, Chapter 14).

13.7. **The will and capacity to learn about others**

Humans preferentially look at faces and react to them in the first hours of life (Goren *et al.*, 1975). This capacity appears widespread amongst primates (K. Fujita, personal communication). Faces and facial expressions become (or perhaps are) intrinsically reinforcing for behaviour, encouraging or discouraging the observer to react in stereotyped or subtle ways. Brain systems (including the amygdala, ventral striatum, insular cortex, and orbitofrontal cortex) support: (a) the drawing of attention towards faces, (b) the extraction of meaning from faces, and (c) the reinforcement of social behaviour by face cues. For adults the sight of facial and bodily cues (infantile features, or sexually dimorphic adult features) can provide secondary reinforcement for social behaviour. A full treatment of the brain pathways underlying

social cognition should incorporate details of how such social cues come to activate 'reward systems' in the brain (Kampe *et al.*, 2001; O'Doherty *et al.*, 2003) and hence can guide social interactions.

Most neural models of social cognition see the STS as part of a core system dealing with social perception *per se* (cf Allison *et al.*, 2000), and postulate that connections with the 'extended' system (including insula, orbitofrontal, cingulate, anterior temporal, somatosensory and parietal cortices and the amygdala) serve to extract meaning from social perceptions and control reactions (Haxby *et al.*, 2000).

For example, the ability to follow gaze, and, in cases where the other's attention is directed at a specific object, the ability to share attention with the observed agent, is likely to be underpinned by connections between the STS and the intraparietal sulcus (Harries and Perrett, 1991). The direction, or target, of another's attention is computed by neurons in the STS specifically responsive to eye-gaze direction, head orientation and bodily orientation (Perrett *et al.*, 1985, 1992), while the parietal cortex is involved in (covertly) directing the observer's spatial attention (cf. Corbetta, 1998). It has been shown that the judgment of gaze direction indeed activates both the intraparietal sulcus and the posterior STS (Hoffman and Haxby, 2000).

Another example is the connection between the STS and the superior temporal gyrus (STG). The perception of mouth and lip movements typically activates the STS, whether or not the movements are related to speech (Puce *et al.*, 1998). To extract meaning from the lip movements, connections from the STS with the auditory cortex in the STG are recruited (STG typically responds to heard vocalizations). This was shown in experiments using silent lip-reading tasks, which produced activity in both the STS and STG (Calvert *et al.*, 1997).

The STS is reciprocally connected with the amygdala to support the extraction of meaning from stimuli and to highlight those social stimuli that have an emotional significance for the observer on the basis of past life experiences or genetically determined strategies (Adolphs, 1999; Barton, this volume, Chapter 11). Fearful facial expressions are well known to excite the amygdala (Morris *et al.*, 1996) but amygdala function is also implicated in other emotions and aspects of social cognition. Amygdala activity in response to processing faces is modulated by the gaze direction of these faces (probably computed in the STS), with direct gaze producing larger activation than averted gaze (Kawashima *et al.*, 1999). This modulation could be related to an inherent ambiguity because direct gaze can reflect interest/attraction as well as a threat. Furthermore, it has been suggested that the amygdala is involved when an observer interprets the mental state of an agent on the basis of the eye region (Baron-Cohen *et al.*, 1999), and may, in fact, be vital for developing a theory of mind (Baron-Cohen *et al.*, 2000).

Other parts of the extended system for extracting meaning from faces include the orbitofrontal and somatosensory cortex. The orbitofrontal cortex is known from single-cell studies in the macaque to contain face-responsive neurons (Thorpe *et al.*, 1983) and to evaluate rewards associated with stimuli (Rolls, 1996, 2000). This role, applied to social stimuli such as facial expressions, could guide behaviour in a socially acceptable manner. Dysfunction of this area results in inappropriate responses to social stimuli, presumably because an assessment of the positive/negative social value of social stimuli can no longer be made (Damasio *et al.*, 1994).

Somatosensory cortex also aids interpretation of faces (Adolphs, 1999). To understand emotional expressions of others we may refer to how the expressions would feel on our own faces (a kind of mental rehearsal without outward sign, see below). Through activity in the somatosensory cortex we can perhaps sense the position and stretch in the muscle movements required to produce the expressions. This simulation would tell us how the outward manifestation of an emotion state would feel if it were occurring in ourselves (cf. Wicker *et al.*, 2003).

The FFA, part of the core face-processing system identified by Haxby *et al.* (2000), also connects to an extended system of brain areas in order to extract information related to the identity of the face. This system includes the anterior middle temporal gyrus, which becomes active when the identity or name belonging to familiar faces is determined (e.g. Nakamura *et al.*, 2000; see also Quiroga *et al.*, 2005). This area is not exclusively involved in extracting social knowledge about

people, it is also activated by the perception of, for example, familiar outdoor scenes (Nakamura *et al.*, 2000), suggesting a more general function in representing autobiographical information.

13.8. **The mirror neuron system as a guiding principle**

Gallese *et al.* (2004) suggest that our understanding of others' actions depends on the STS in close association with the mirror neuron system (Di Pellegrino *et al.*, 1992). The human mirror neuron system is comprised of frontal components: the posterior inferior frontal gyrus and the adjacent ventral premotor cortex (area F5), and posterior parietal components in the rostral section of the inferior parietal lobule (area PF; Rizzolatti and Fogassi, this volume, Chapter 14). The posterior STS forms one of the main inputs of this mirror neuron system, through its connections with area PF (Seltzer and Pandya, 1994).

Since the mirror system responds during execution and observation of the same action, this system is thought to underlie imitative behaviour, which is a driving force behind the development of our social cognitive abilities (Hurley and Chater, 2005). Overt imitation may arise through interactions of the core system with the amygdala to enable social mirroring (Meltzoff and Decety, 2003), while imitation as a form of social learning is supported by dorsolateral prefrontal cortex and other motor preparation areas (Iacoboni, 2005).

The mirror neuron mechanisms may allow us to understand the meaning of others' actions by internally simulating these actions, without the need for any conceptual reasoning (see Rizzolatti and Fogassi, this volume, Chapter 14). The internal simulation happens at a sub-threshold level, i.e. not strong enough to actually cause a motor pattern through activation of muscles, but nevertheless strong enough to produce a cortical representation and an intuitive grasp of what the other does.

'Mirroring' may happen not only for actions but also for emotions. fMRI data indicates that the neural substrates for the perception of disgust in others and those for the experience of disgust overlap in the anterior insula (Wicker *et al.*, 2003).

The activity in the insula following the perception of others' disgust is probably mediated by projections arising initially in face-responsive cell populations of the STS (Phillips *et al.*, 1997), while insula activity during the experience of disgust is mediated by connections from olfactory and gustatory centres (Augustine, 1996) combined with information about the interoceptive state of the body (Craig, 2002). This connectivity allows the same insula area to be active when we witness the disgusted facial expression of someone else and when we experience disgust. Similar matching mechanisms for the perception and experience of other emotions probably exist. In this way the mirror mechanism allows us to fuse our third- and first-person experiences of actions or emotions. Thus we can begin to realize the experience of others.

Understanding the minds of others might depend on mirror mechanisms (Gallese and Goldman, 1998; Gallese *et al.*, 2002). It has further been argued that a simulation of another's feelings is necessary to develop the capacity of empathy. This is one of the reasons why a mirror-system deficit features in models of autism (Williams *et al.*, 2001; Dapretto *et al.*, 2006). Lack of empathy is one of the most striking characteristics of the autistic syndrome (Baron-Cohen, 2002, 2005). Empathy has also been described as a social-mirroring process with a sensory–motor basis, supported by the core system (STS plus mirror neuron system) and the limbic system (Carr *et al.*, 2003).

13.9. Taking things literally

According to the 'social brain hypothesis' (Brothers *et al.*, 1990; Dunbar, 1998), the advantage gained by understanding others' behaviour and intentions constituted a major driving force behind the primate brain evolution. We argued that the STS forms the prime neural substrate for descriptions of the 'mechanics' of social events. This description goes beyond pictorial descriptions of others' actions. Instead the STS embodies physical causes and consequences of actions allowing prediction within action sequences. This description provides a basis for guiding the observer's reactions and planning contingencies based on the likely future behaviour of others. A purely mechanistic description

of others' actions and social events will not suffice to understand the reasons agents have for doing what they do; a more sophisticated understanding of others' actions could be based on the attribution of mental states to the agents involved. As noted, the STS communicates with an extended system that in humans may accomplish the more sophisticated mentalistic aspects of social cognition. The two stages of interpretation (mechanistic and mentalistic) are thus anatomically distinct and can therefore be affected differentially.

The study of developmental disorders has proved helpful in dissecting the neural basis of social cognition. Aspects of social cognition can be selectively impaired, while many other cognitive abilities are spared in autistic individuals (Frith, 2001). By the same token, in Williams' Syndrome some aspects of social cognition can be spared (or even enhanced) in the presence of many impaired non-social abilities (Bellugi *et al.*, 2000). These findings support the notion that social and non-social stimuli are represented by distinct neural substrates. The impairment in social cognition encountered in autism becomes most visible in difficulties establishing a theory of mind, i.e. the ability read the behaviour of others (and possibly of oneself) in terms of mental states (such as desires, beliefs and intentions; Frith *et al.*, 1991; Baron-Cohen, 1995) and to empathize with others (Baron-Cohen, 2002, 2005).

Presumably in typical people the processing of social cues is fully automated. One can imagine that, if mentalistic interpretation fails, daily social interactions become extremely puzzling. One idea is that the autistic mind cannot keep up with the pace and complexity of social interactions and resorts to the mode of operation that does work properly: the literal–mechanistic mode.

The basic operations of the STS may be intact in autism. In fact, autistic people may rely too much on the STS for their interpretation of the (social) world, due to failures to recruit the extended systems. This leads to a focusing on the physical attributes of a social stimulus at the expense of social meaning or consequence. One of the characteristic features of the autistic mind is indeed the tendency to take things too literally (Grandin, 1995). One domain where it is particularly evident is language: people often do not speak literally: there may be a discrepancy between what the speaker intends to convey and what his or her words mean in terms of dictionary definitions. The ability to detect such discrepancies and go beyond the literal spoken word is crucial for conducting an intelligible conversation. People with autism, even those who have a good grasp of grammar and ample vocabulary, take words literally. For example, an autistic child may become upset when asked, "give me your hand" (Frith, 1995). Not surprisingly, such misunderstandings are not limited to the language domain. Social cues conveyed by bodily postures and actions can also be misunderstood by taking them literally.

In this review we have focused on the properties of a core system for describing the behaviour of others. We have documented how the system achieves a visual representation of the mechanics of social interaction in terms that go beyond a pictorial description and embody causes and consequences of actions. This system utilizes visual cues in a hierarchical manner to achieve a relatively sophisticated interpretation of the social world. In concert with an extended system it is possible to begin to understand how neural mechanisms provide a basis for social cognition and how system dysfunction might underlie problems in comprehension of the social world.

References

Adolphs, R. (1999) Social cognition and the human brain. *Trends in Cognitive Sciences*, 3: 469–479.

Allison, T., Puce, A. and McCarthy, G. (2000) Social perception from visual cues: role of the STS region. *Trends in Cognitive Sciences*, 4: 267–278.

Anderson, J. R., Montant, M. and Schmitt, D. (1996) Rhesus monkeys fail to use gaze direction as an experimenter-given cue in an object-choice task. *Behavioral Processes*, 37: 47–55.

Augustine, J. R. (1996) Circuitry and functional aspects of the insular lobe in primates including humans. *Brain Research Reviews*, 22: 229–244.

Baker, C. I., Keysers, C., Jellema, T., Wicker, B. and Perrett, D. I. (2001) Neuronal representation of disappearing and hidden objects in temporal cortex of the macaque. *Experimental Brain Research*, 140: 375–381.

Barraclough, N. E., Xiao, D., Oram, M. W. and Perrett, D. I. (2006) The sensitivity of primate STS neurons to walking sequences and to the degree of articulation in static images. *Progress in Brain Research*, 154: 135–148.

Barrett, L. and Henzi, S. P. (2005) The social nature of primate cognition. *Proceedings of the Royal Society of London, B*, 272: 1865–1875.

Baron-Cohen, S. (1995) *Mindblindness: An Essay on Autism and Theory of Mind*. MIT Press, Cambridge, MA.

Baron-Cohen, S. (2002) The extreme male brain theory of autism. *Trends in Cognitive Sciences*, 6: 248–254.

Baron-Cohen, S. (2005) Autism and the origins of social neuroscience. In A. Easton and N. J. Emery (eds) *The Cognitive Neuroscience of Social Behaviour*, pp. 239–255, Studies in Cognition Series. Psychology Press, New York.

Baron-Cohen, S., Ring, H. A., Wheelwright, S. *et al.* (1999) Social intelligence in the normal and autistic brain: an fMRI study. *European Journal of Neuroscience*, 11: 1891–1898.

Baron-Cohen, S., Ring, H. A., Bullmore, E. T., Wheelwright, S., Ashwin, C. and Williams, S. C. R. (2000) The amygdala theory of autism. *Neuroscience and Biobehavioral Reviews*, 24: 355–364.

Beauchamp, M. S., Lee, K. E., Haxby, J. V. and Martin, A. (2003) Parallel visual motion processing streams for manipulable objects and human movements. *Neuron*, 34: 149–159.

Bellugi, U., Lichtenberger, L., Jones, W., Lai, Z. and St George, M. (2000) The neurocognitive profile of Williams Syndrome: a complex pattern of strengths and weaknesses. *Journal of Cognitive Neuroscience*, 12: 7–29.

Bodamer, J. (1947) Die-Prosop-agnosie. *Archiv für Psychiatrie und Nervenkrankheiten*, 179: 6–54. [partial English translation by Ellis HD, and Florence M (1990) *Cognitive Neuropsychology*, 7: 81–105.]

Brothers, L., Ring, B. and Kling, A. (1990) Responses of neurons in the macaque amygdala to complex social stimuli. *Behavioral Brain Research*, 41: 199–213.

Bruce, C., Desimone, R. and Gross, C. G. (1981) Visual properties of neurons in a polysensory area in superior temporal sulcus of the macaque. *Journal of Neurophysiology*, 46: 369–384.

Bruce, V. and Young, A. (1986) Understanding face recognition. *British Journal of Psychology*, 77: 305–327.

Byrne, R. W. (1995) *The Thinking Ape: Evolutionary Origins of Intelligence*. Oxford University Press, New York.

Calder, A. J. and Young, A. W. (2005) Understanding the recognition of facial identity and facial expression. *Nature Reviews Neuroscience*, 6: 641–651.

Call, J. and Tomasello, M. (1998) Distinguishing intentional from accidental actions in orangutans (*Pongo pygmaeus*), chimpanzees (*Pan troglodytes*) and human children (*Homo sapiens*) *Journal of Comparative Psychology*, 112: 192–206.

Calvert, G., Bullmore, E. T., Brammer, M. J., Campbell, R., Williams, S. C. R. and McGuire, P. K. (1997) Activation of auditory cortex during silent lipreading. *Science*, 276: 593–596.

Carr, L., Iacoboni, M., Dubeau, M. C., Mazziotta, J. C. and Lenzi, G. L. (2003) Neural mechanisms of empathy in humans: a relay from neural systems for imitation to limbic areas. *Proceedings of the National Academy of Sciences of the USA*, 100: 5497–5502.

Castelli, F., Happe, F., Frith, U. and Frith, C. (2000) Movement and mind: a functional imaging study of perception and interpretation of complex intentional movement patterns. *Neuroimage*, 12: 314–325.

Corbetta, M. (1998) Frontoparietal cortical networks for directing attention and the eye to visual locations: identical, independent, or overlapping neural systems? *Proceedings of the National Academy of Sciences of the USA*, 95: 831–838.

Craig, A. D. (2002) How do you feel? Interoception: the sense of the physiological condition of the body. *Nature Review Neuroscience*, 3: 655–666.

Dapretto, M., Davies, M. S. and Pfeifer, J. H. *et al.* (2006) Understanding emotions in others: mirror neuron dysfunction in children with autism spectrum disorders. *Nature Neuroscience*, 9: 28–30.

Damasio, H., Grabowski, T., Frank, R., Galaburda, A. M. and Damasio, A. R. (1994) The return of Phineas Gage: clues about the brain from the skull of a famous patient. *Science*, 264: 1102–1104.

Decety, J. and Grezes, J. (1999) Neural mechanisms subserving the perception of human actions. *Trends in Cognitive Sciences*, 3: 172–178.

Desimone, R. (1991) Face-selective neurons in the temporal cortex of monkeys. *Journal of Cognitive Neuroscience*, 3: 1–8.

Desimone, R. and Ungerleider, L. G. (1989) Neural mechanisms of visual processing in monkeys. In F. Boller and J. Grafman (eds) *Handbook of Neuropsychology*, vol. 2, pp. 267–299. Elsevier, Amsterdam.

Di Pellegrino, G., Fadiga, L., Fogassi, V., Gallese, V. and Rizzolatti, G. (1992) Understanding motor events: a neurophysiological study. *Experimental Brain Research*, 91: 176–180.

Downing, P. E., Jiang, Y. H., Shuman, M. and Kanwisher, N. (2001) A cortical area selective for visual processing of the human body. *Science*, 293: 2470–2473.

Dunbar, R. I. M. (1998) The social brain hypothesis. *Evolutionary Anthropology*, 6: 178–190.

Ellis, A. W., Young, A. W. and Flude, B. M. (1990) Repetition priming and face processing: priming occurs within the system that responds to the identity of a face. *Quarterly Journal of Experimental Psychology*, 42: 495–512.

Emery, N. J., Lorincz, E. N., Perrett, D. I., Oram, M. W. and Baker, C. I. (1997) Gaze following and joint attention in rhesus monkeys (*Macaca mulatta*). *Journal of Comparative Psychology*, 111: 286–293.

Frith, U. (1995) *Autism. Explaining the Enigma*. Blackwell, Oxford.

Frith, U. (2001) Mind blindness and the brain in autism. *Neuron*, 32: 969–979.

Frith, U., Morton, J. and Leslie, A. M. (1991) The cognitive basis of a biological disorder—autism. *Trends in Neurosciences*, 14: 433–438.

Fogassi, L., Ferrari, P. F., Gesierich, B., Rozzi, S., Chersi, F. and Rizzolatti, G. (2005) Parietal lobe: from action organization to intention understanding. *Science*, 308: 662–667.

Gallese, V. and Goldman, A. (1998) Mirror neurons and the simulation theory of mind-reading. *Trends in Cognitive Sciences*, 2: 493–501.

Gallese, V., Fadiga, L., Fogassi, L. and Rizzolatti, G. (2002) Action representation and the inferior parietal lobule. *Attention and Performance*, 19: 334–355.

Gallese, V., Keysers, C. and Rizzolatti, G. (2004) A unifying view of the basis of social cognition. *Trends in Cognitive Sciences*, 8: 398–403.

Gauthier, I., Tarr, M. J., Anderson, A. W., Skudlarski, P. and Gore, J. C. (1999) Activation of the middle fusiform "face area" increases with expertise in recognizing novel objects. *Nature Neuroscience*, 2: 568–573.

Goodale, M. A., Milner, A. D., Jakobson, L. S. and Carey, D. P. (1991) A neurological dissociation between perceiving objects and grasping them. *Nature*, 349: 154–156.

Goren, C. C., Sarty, M. and Wu, P. Y. K. (1975) Visual following and pattern discrimination of face like stimuli by newborn infants. *Paediactrics*, 56: 544–549.

Grandin, T. (1995) *Thinking in Pictures and Other Reports from My Life with Autism*. Vintage Books, New York.

Grill-Spector, K., Knouf, N. and Kanwisher, N. (2004) The fusiform face area subserves face perception, not generic within-category identification. *Nature Neuroscience*, 7: 555–562.

Gross, C. G., Rocha-Miranda, C. E. and Bender, D. B. (1972) Visual properties of neurons in inferotemporal cortex of the macaque. *Journal of Neurophysiology*, 35: 96–111.

Harries, M. H. and Perrett, D. I. (1991) Visual processing of faces in temporal cortex: physiological evidence for a modular organization and possible anatomical correlates. *Journal of Cognitive Neuroscience*, 3: 9–24.

Hasselmo, M. E., Rolls, E. T. and Baylis, G. C. (1989a) The role of expression and identity in the face-selective responses of neurons in the temporal visual cortex of the monkey. *Behavioural Brain Research*, 32: 203–218.

Hasselmo, M. E., Rolls, E. T., Baylis, G. C. and Nalwa, V. (1989b) Object-centred encoding by face-selective neurons in the cortex in the superior temporal sulcus of the monkey. *Experimental Brain Research*, 75: 417–429.

Haxby, J. V., Hoffman, E. A. and Gobbini, M. I. (2000) The distributed human neural system for face perception. *Trends in Cognitive Sciences*, 4: 223–233.

Haxby, J. V., Hoffman, E. A. and Gobbini, M. I. (2002) Human neural systems for face recognition and social communication. *Biological Psychiatry*, 51: 59–67.

Hecaen, H. and Angelergues, R. (1962) Agnosia for faces (Prosopagnosia). *Archives of Neurology*, 7: 24–32.

Hoffman, E. A. and Haxby, J. V. (2000) Distinct representations of eye gaze and identity in the distributed human neural system for face perception, *Nature Neuroscience*, 3: 80–84.

Hurley, S. and Chater, N. (2005) *Perspective on Imitation: From Neuroscience to Social Science*, vol. 1. MIT Press, Cambridge, MA.

Iacoboni, M. (2005) Neural mechanisms of imitation. *Current Opinion in Neurobiology*, 15: 632–637.

Iacoboni, M., Molnar-Szakacs, I., Gallese, V., Buccino, G., Mazziotta, J. C. and Rizzolatti, G. (2005) Grasping the attention of others with one's own mirror neuron system. *Public Library of Science Biology*, 3: 529–535.

Jellema, T. and Perrett, D. I. (2002) Coding of visible and hidden objects. *Attention and Performance*, 19: 356–380.

Jellema, T. and Perrett, D. I. (2003a) Perceptual history influences neural responses to face and body postures. *Journal of Cognitive Neuroscience*, 15: 961–971.

Jellema, T. and Perrett, D. I. (2003b) Cells in monkey STS responsive to articulated body motions and consequent static posture: a case of implied motion? *Neuropsychologia*, 41: 1728–1737.

Jellema, T. and Perrett, D. I. (2005) Neural basis for the perception of goal-directed actions. In A. Easton and N. J. Emery (eds) *The Cognitive Neuroscience of Social Behaviour*, pp. 81–112, Studies in Cognition Series. Psychology Press, New York.

Jellema, T. and Perrett, D. I. (2006) Neural representations of perceived bodily actions using a categorical frame of reference. *Neuropsychologia*, 44: 1535–1546.

Jellema, T., Baker, C. I., Wicker, B. and Perrett, D. I. (2000) Neural representation for the perception of the intentionality of actions. *Brain and Cognition*, 44: 280–302.

Jellema, T., Baker, C. I., Oram, M. W. and Perrett, D. I. (2002) Cell populations in the superior temporal sulcus of the macaque and imitation. In A. N. Meltzoff and W. Prinz (eds) *The Imitative Mind: Development, Evolution, and Brain Bases*, pp. 267–290. Cambridge University Press, Cambridge.

Jellema, T., Maassen, G. and Perrett, D. I. (2004) Single cell integration of animate form, motion, and location in the superior temporal sulcus of the macaque monkey. *Cerebral Cortex*, 14: 781–790.

Kampe, K. K., Frith, C. D., Dolan, R. J. and Frith, U. (2001) Reward value of attractiveness and gaze. *Nature* 413: 589.

Kanwisher, N., McDermott, J. and Chun, M. M. (1997) The Fusiform Face Area: a module in human extrastriate cortex specialized for face perception. *Journal of Neuroscience*, 17: 4302–4311.

Karnath, H.-O. (2001) New insights into the functions of the superior temporal cortex. *Nature Reviews Neuroscience*, 2: 568–576.

Kawashima, R., Sigiura, M., Kato, T. et al. (1999) The human amygdala plays an important role in gaze monitoring: a PET study. *Brain*, 122: 779–783.

Keysers, C. and Perrett, D. I. (2004) Demystifying social cognition: a Hebbian perspective, *Trends in Cognitive Science*, 8: 501–507.

Kourtzi, Z. and Kanwisher, N. (2000) Activation in human MT/MST by static images with implied motion. *Journal of Cognitive Neuroscience*, 12: 48–55.

Logothetis, N. K., Pauls, J. and Poggio, T. (1995) Shape representation in the inferior temporal cortex of monkeys, *Current Biology*, 5: 552–563.

Lorincz, E. N., Baker, C. I. and Perrett, D. I. (1999) Visual cues for attention following in rhesus monkeys. *Current Psychology of Cognition*, 18: 973–1001.

Lorteije, J., Kenemans, J. L., Jellema, T., Van der Lubbe, R. H. J., De Heer, F. and Van Wezel, R. J. A. (2006) Delayed response to implied motion in human motion processing areas. *Journal of Cognitive Neuroscience*, 18: 158–168.

Marr, D. and Nishihara, H. K. (1978) Representation and recognition of the spatial organization from single two-dimensional images. *Proceedings of the Royal Society of London, B*, 200: 269–294.

Maunsell, J. H. R. and Van Essen, D. C. (1983) Functional properties of neurons in the middle visual temporal area of the macaque monkey. I. Selectivity for stimulus direction, speed, and orientation. *Journal of Neurophysiology*, 49: 1127–1147.

Meltzoff, A. N. and Decety, J. (2003) What imitation tells us about social cognition: A rapprochement between developmental psychology and cognitive neuroscience. *Philosophical Transactions of the Royal Society of London, B*, 358: 491–500.

Milner, A. D. and Goodale, M. A. (1995) *The Visual Brain in Action*. Oxford University Press, Oxford.

Morris, J. S., Frith, C. D., Perrett, D. I. et al. (1996) A differential neural response in the human amygdala to fearful and happy facial expressions. *Nature*, 383: 812–815.

Nakamura, K., Kawashima, R., Sato, N., Nakamura, A. and Sugiura, M. (2000) Functional delineation of the human occipito-temporal areas related to face and scene processing: a PET study. *Brain*, 123: 1903–1912.

O'Doherty, J., Winston, J., Critchley, H., Perrett, D. I., Burt, D. M. and Dolan, R. J. (2003) Beauty in a smile: the role of medial orbitofrontal cortex in facial attractiveness. *Neuropsychologia*, 41: 147–155.

Oram, M. W. and Perrett, D. I. (1996) Integration of form and motion in the anterior superior temporal polysensory area (STPa) of the macaque monkey. *Journal of Neurophysiology*, 76: 109–129.

Phillips, M. L., Young, A. W., Senior, C. et al. (1997) A specific neural substrate for perceiving facial expressions of disgust. *Nature*, 389: 495–498.

Perrett, D. I. (1999) A cellular basis for reading minds from faces and actions. In M. Hauser and M. Konishi (eds), *Behavioural and Neural Mechanisms of Communication*. MIT Press, Cambridge, MA.

Perrett, D. I. and Mistlin, A. J. (1990) Perception of facial attributes. In W. C. Stebbins and M. A. Berkley (eds) *Comparative Perception*, vol. II, *Complex Signals*, pp. 187–215. John Wiley, New York.

Perrett, D. I. and Oram, M. W. (1993) Neurophysiology of shape processing. *Image and Vision Computing*, 11: 317–333.

Perrett, D. I., Rolls, E. T. and Caan, W. (1982) Visual neurones responsive to faces in the monkey temporal cortex. *Experimental Brain Research*, 47: 329–342.

Perrett, D. I., Smith, P. A. J., Potter, D. D. et al. (1984) Neurones responsive to faces in the temporal cortex: studies of functional organization, sensitivity to identity and relation to perception, *Human Neurobiology*, 3: 197–208.

Perrett, D. I., Smith, P. A. J., Potter, D. D. *et al.* (1985) Visual cells in the temporal cortex sensitive to face view and gaze direction. *Proceedings of the Royal Society of London, B*, 223: 293–317.

Perrett, D. I., Mistlin, A. J. and Chitty, A. J. (1987) Visual cells responsive to faces. *Trends in Neurosciences*, 10: 358–364.

Perrett, D. I., Harries, M. H., Bevan, R. *et al.* (1989) Frameworks of analysis for the neural representation of animate objects and actions. *Journal of Experimental Biology*, 146: 87–113.

Perrett, D. I., Mistlin, A. J., Harries, M. H. and Chitty, A. J. (1990) Understanding the visual appearance and consequences of hand actions. In M. A. Goodale (ed.) *Vision and Action: The Control of Grasping*, pp. 163–180. Ablex Publishing, Norwood, NJ.

Perrett, D. I., Oram, M. W., Harries, M. H. *et al.* (1991) Viewer-centred and object-centred coding of heads in the macaque temporal cortex. *Experimental Brain Research*, 86: 159–173.

Perrett, D. I., Hietanen, J. K., Oram, M. W. and Benson, P. J. (1992) Organization and functions of cells responsive to faces in the temporal cortex. *Philosophical Transactions of the Royal Society of London, B*, 335: 23–30.

Puce, A. and Perrett, D. I. (2003) Electrophysiology and brain imaging of biological motion. *Philosophical Transactions of the Royal Society of London, B*, 358: 435–445.

Puce, A., Allison, T., Bentin, S., Gore, J. C. and McCarthy, G. (1998) Temporal cortex activation in humans viewing eye and mouth movements. *Journal of Neuroscience*, 18: 2188–2199.

Quiroga, R. Q., Reddy, L., Kreiman, G., Koch, C. and Fried, I. (2005) Invariant visual representation by single neurons in the human brain. *Nature*, 435: 1102–1107.

Rolls, E. T. (1996) The orbitofrontal cortex. *Philosophical Transactions of the Royal Society of London, B*, 351: 1433–1444.

Rolls, E. T. (2000) The orbitofrontal cortex and reward. *Cerebral Cortex*, 10: 284–294.

Saxe, R., Xiao, D.-K., Kovacs, G., Perrett, D. I. and Kanwisher, N. (2004) A region of right superior temporal sulcus responds to observed intentional actions. *Neuropsychologia*, 42: 1435–1446.

Seltzer, B. and Pandya, D. N. (1994) Parietal, temporal and occipital projections to cortex of the superior temporal sulcus in the rhesus monkey: a retrograde tracer study. *Journal of Comparative Neurology*, 243: 445–463.

Senior, C., Barnes, J., Giampietro, V. *et al.* (2000) The functional neuroanatomy of implicit-motion perception or 'representational momentum'. *Current Biology*, 10: 16–22.

Tanaka, Y. Z., Koyama, T. and Mikami, A. (1999) Neurons in the temporal cortex changed their preferred direction of motion dependent on shape. *Neuroreport*, 10: 393–397.

Thorpe, S. J., Rolls, E. T. and Maddison, S. (1983) The orbitofrontal cortex: neuronal activity in the behaving monkey. *Experimental Brain Research*, 49: 93–115.

Tooby, J. and Cosmides, L. (1990) The past explains the present—emotional adaptations and the structure of ancestral environments. *Ethology and Sociobiology*, 11: 375–424.

Tsao, D. Y., Freiwald, W. A., Tootell, R. B. H. and Livingstone, M. S. (2006) A cortical region consisting entirely of face selective cells. *Science*, 311: 670–674.

Ungerleider, L. G. and Mishkin, M. (1982) Two cortical visual systems. In D. J. Ingle, M. A. Goodale and R. J. W. Mansfield (eds) *Analysis of Visual Behavior*, pp. 549–586. MIT Press, Cambridge, MA.

Umilta, M. A., Kohler, E., Gallese, V. *et al.* (2001) I know what you are doing: a neurophysiological study. *Neuron*, 31: 155–165.

Wachsmuth, E., Oram, M. W. and Perrett, D. I. (1994) Recognition of objects and their component parts: responses of single units in the temporal cortex of the macaque. *Cerebral Cortex*, 5: 509–522.

Wicker, B., Keysers, C., Plailly, J., Royet, J. P., Gallese, V. and Rizzolatti, G. (2003) Both of us disgusted in my insula: the common neural basis of seeing and feeling disgust. *Neuron*, 40: 655–664.

Williams, J. H. G., Whiten, A., Suddendorf, T. and Perrett, D. I. (2001) Imitation, mirror neurons and autism. *Neuroscience and Behavioural Reviews*, 25: 287–295.

Young, M. P. and Yamane, S. (1992) Sparse population coding of faces in the inferotemporal cortex. *Science* 256: 1327–1331.

Xu, Y. D., Liu, J. and Kanwisher, N. (2005) The M170 is selective for faces, not for expertise. *Neuropsychologia*, 43: 588–597.

Zacks, J. M., Braver, T. S., Sheridan, M. A. *et al.* (2001) Human brain activity time-locked to perceptual event boundaries. *Nature Neuroscience*, 4: 651–655.

CHAPTER 14

Mirror neurons and social cognition

Giacomo Rizzolatti and Leonardo Fogassi

14.1. Introduction

In spite of great progress in neuroscience over the last decade, it would be excessive to claim that neurophysiology can offer a scientific account of social cognition. Yet, there is little doubt that the discovery of mirror neurons represents an important step towards providing a biological substrate for some of the basic phenomena on which social cognition is built. Our aim here is to give a general overview of the properties of mirror neurons, to discuss the basic functional role of the mirror neuron system, and to examine which cognitive functions are built on top of it.

14.2. Mirror neurons

Mirror neurons are a specific set of motor neurons first discovered in area F5 (a part of the ventral premotor cortex) of the macaque monkey (Gallese *et al.*, 1996; Rizzolatti *et al.*, 1996a). F5 neurons discharge in association with active monkey movements. Their main characteristics are that they do not code elementary movements, as for example the neurons of the primary motor cortex do, but discharge in relation to goal-related *motor acts* such as grasping, manipulating, holding, tearing objects. Among these acts, grasping is the most heavily represented (Rizzolatti *et al.*, 1988).

Some F5 neurons are merely motor neurons. Others also respond to visual stimuli (visuo-motor neurons). There are two categories of visuo-motor neurons. One is formed by neurons that respond to the presentation of three-dimensional (3D) objects. These neurons are called *canonical* neurons (see Rizzolatti *et al.*, 2004). The second is constituted by neurons that discharge when a monkey observes another individual (a human being or another monkey) performing a hand action and when it executes the same or a similar action (Gallese *et al.*, 1996; Rizzolatti *et al.*, 1996a). These neurons have been named *mirror* neurons (Figure 14.1).

Unlike canonical neurons, mirror neurons do not discharge to presentation of 3D objects, including food. They also do not discharge, or discharge very poorly, when the monkey observes the experimenter performing the grasping action without any object present (mimed actions). Mirror neurons show a large degree of stimulus generalization, their response being, to a large extent, independent of the distance from the monkey at which the observed action is performed and its location in space. In some neurons, however, response intensity depends on the spatial location of the observed action, or its direction, or the hand used by the observed individual. Depending on the action to which they respond best, mirror neurons have been categorized into grasping, manipulating,

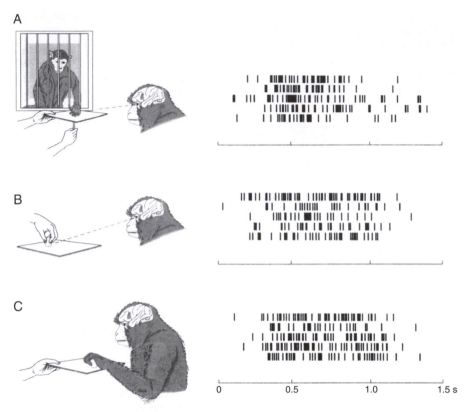

Fig. 14.1 Example of mirror neuron. (**A**) Neuron activation during observation of grasping performed by another monkey or (**B**) by an experimenter in front of the recorded monkey. (**C**) Neuron activation during grasping execution performed by the recorded monkey. Each panel shows the neuron activity recorded in five trials of 1.5 s each. Note that spontaneous activity was virtually absent. Modified from Rizzolatti *et al.* (1996a).

tearing, and holding neurons. More than half of F5 mirror neurons respond to the observation of only one action, while the remaining ones respond to the observation of two or more actions.

Comparison between the effective observed actions and effective executed actions reveals that most mirror neurons show congruence between their visual and motor responses. Two sets of mirror neurons have been distinguished: 'strictly congruent' and 'broadly congruent' neurons. 'Strictly congruent' neurons are those neurons in which the observed and executed actions coincide exactly. They represent about 30% of all F5 mirror neurons. 'Broadly congruent' neurons are those in which the coded observed action and the coded executed

action, although similar, are not identical. For example, a neuron could discharge when the monkey grasps objects using a precision grip, but also respond when the observed individual grasps food using other types of prehensions as well. Broadly congruent neurons represent about 60% of F5 mirror neurons.

In addition to mirror neurons related to hand actions, there are mirror neurons that become active when the monkey observes and executes mouth actions ('mouth mirror neurons', Ferrari *et al.*, 2003a). Most mouth mirror neurons respond to the observation of ingestive actions such as biting, tearing with the teeth, sucking, licking, etc. Their characteristics appear to be identical to that of hand mirror neurons. They do not respond to simple object presentation or to mouth mimed actions and their visual response is often very specific for certain mouth acts. As with hand mirror neurons, mouth mirror neurons also can be subdivided into 'strictly congruent' and 'broadly congruent' neurons. Finally, there is a small, but very interesting, set of mouth mirror neurons that discharges during active ingestive movements, and responds specifically to the observation of mouth communicative actions belonging to the monkey repertoire, such as lips-smacking, lips protrusion or tongue protrusion ('communicative mouth mirror neurons') (Figure 14.2). We will discuss their possible evolutionary importance below.

14.3. **Mirror neuron system of the monkey**

There are other monkey cortical areas, besides F5, that contain mirror neurons. A recent functional magnetic resonance imaging (fMRI) study (Nelissen *et al.*, 2005) showed that the observation of grasping hand actions activates, besides visual areas, the region of the superior temporal sulcus (STS), the rostral part of the inferior parietal lobule (IPL) including the cortex within the intraparietal sulcus, different sectors of area F5, and area 45.

There is no convincing evidence that STS neurons have motor properties. Although they code biological actions, including hand–object interactions, their coding appears to be exclusively visual (Perrett *et al.*, 1989; Jellema *et al.*, 2002; Jellema and Perrett, this volume, Chapter 13). Similarly it is plausible that area 45, giving its granular structure, is not endowed with motor properties, strictly defined. Thus, it is parsimonious, at least at present, not to include these two regions in the *mirror neuron system*, defined as the cortical system where neurons with mirror properties are located. The situation is quite different for the rostral part of IPL.

IPL has been traditionally considered to be an association area. The classic studies of Mountcastle *et al.* (1975) and Hyvärinen (1981) showed, however, that many IPL neurons discharge in association with movements. These findings were recently confirmed and extended by experiments in which IPL neurons were tested during active behaviour of the monkey and in response to sensory stimulation (Ferrari *et al.*, 2003b). These experiments showed that many IPL neurons are active during the execution of specific motor acts. By using the motor responses as a physiological variable, it was found that the convexity of IPL is somatotopically organized with the mouth field located rostrally, followed, in caudal sequence, by the hand, arm and eye fields.

Many IPL motor neurons respond to somatosensory and visual stimuli. Among them there are also neurons with mirror properties very similar to those of F5 mirror neurons. The most effective observed actions are grasping, holding, manipulating and bimanual interactions. Thus, the mirror system of the monkey appears to be formed by two main nodes, one located in F5, the other in the rostral part of IPL.

14.4. **Mirror neuron system in humans**

A large amount of data indicates that, in humans, the observation of actions done by others activates cortical areas that are involved in motor activity. Evidence for this comes from electroencephalographic (EEG) and magnetoencephalographic (MEG) investigations, transcranial magnetic stimulation experiments (TMS), and brain-imaging studies (Fadiga *et al.*, 1995; Rizzolatti *et al.*, 1996b; Grafton *et al.*, 1996; Grèzes *et al.*, 1998, 2003; Hari *et al.*, 1998; Cochin *et al.*, 1999; Iacoboni *et al.*, 1999, 2001; Strafella and Paus, 2000; Nishitani and Hari, 2000, 2002; Buccino *et al.*, 2001; Koski *et al.*, 2002, 2003; Manthey *et al.*, 2003, Johnson-Frey *et al.*, 2003; Gangitano *et al.*, 2004).

Brain-imaging studies have shown that the localization of the mirror neuron system in humans is very similar to that of the monkey. Besides visual areas and the STS region, activations have been found in the inferior parietal lobule and the lower part of the precentral gyrus (ventral premotor cortex), plus the posterior part of the inferior frontal gyrus (IFG). These parietal and frontal regions form the core of the mirror neuron system in humans (see Figure 14.3).

Both the parietal and frontal human mirror neuron regions show somatotopic organization.

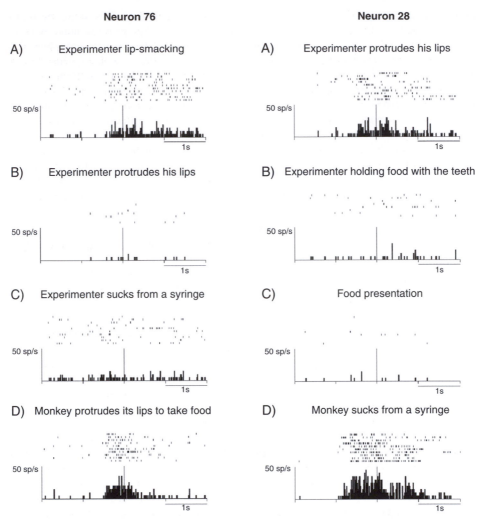

Fig. 14.2 Examples of two 'communicative' mirror neurons. Neuron 76 activates (**A**) when the monkey observes a lip-smacking action made by an experimenter in front of it and (**D**) when the monkey protrudes its lips to take food. Other communicative (**B**) or ingestive (**C**) actions made by the experimenter in front of the recorded monkey are not effective in activating the neuron. Neuron 28 activates (**A**) when the monkey observes a lip-protruded action made by an experimenter in front of it and (**D**) when the monkey sucks juice from a syringe. The neuron does not activate when the monkey observes an experimenter performing an ingestive action (**B**) and when it simply observes an object (food) (**C**). Each panel shows, in the top part, the neuron activity recorded in ten consecutive trials (raster), in the bottom part the averaged activity represented as a histogram. Rasters and histograms are aligned with the moment at which the mouth of the experimenter (observation condition) or of the monkey (execution condition) touched the food or when the food was abruptly presented (presentation condition). During observation of communicative actions the alignment is with the moment at which the action is fully expressed. Abscissa: time; bin width = 20 ms. Ordinate: discharge frequency in spikes/s. Modified from Ferrari *et al.* (2003a).

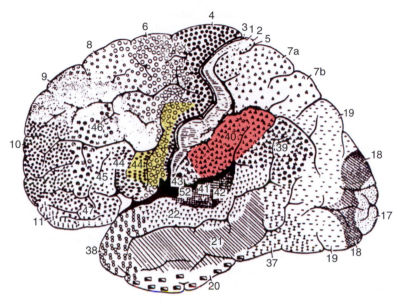

Fig. 14.3 Lateral view of the human cortex showing the frontal and parietal regions constituting the core of the mirror neuron system in humans. The first are indicated in yellow, the second in red. Numbers and symbols indicate the different cytoarchitectonic areas according to the parcellation of Brodmann (1905).

In a recent fMRI study, normal volunteers were presented with video-clips showing actions performed with the mouth, hand/arm, and foot/leg. Action observation was contrasted with the observation of a static face, hand, and foot respectively (Buccino *et al.*, 2001). The results showed that in the frontal lobe, mouth movements were represented laterally in the pars opercularis of IFG, hand/arm movements were represented in the dorsal part of the pars opercularis, partially overlapping with the mouth field, and in the ventral premotor cortex, while the foot movements were also represented in the premotor cortex, but more medially. Each type of observed action determined two activations in the parietal lobe: one located rostrally adjacent to the intraparietal sulcus and extending into it, the other more caudally also close to the intraparietal sulcus. While the latter activation was present with all the types of observed actions, the former showed a clear somatotopy. Mouth actions determined rostral activation, hand/arm actions activated a more caudal region, while foot actions produced a signal increase even more caudally, as well as within

the intraparietal sulcus. Note the similarity between human somatotopy and that found in the monkey using motor-related neuron responses.

14.5. Mirror neurons and action understanding

From the moment they were first discovered, it was suggested that mirror neurons play a fundamental role in action recognition (Gallese *et al.*, 1996; Rizzolatti *et al.*, 1996a, 2001). The proposed mechanism is as follows: each individual has a representation—a 'vocabulary'—of motor acts coded in the parietal and premotor cortices. These acts can be retrieved endogenously when the individual decides to perform an action. In this case the agent knows (predicts) the action outcome. When the same motor representation is activated by observing another individual performing that motor act, the observer knows what the other is doing, because the observed act activates, in its frontal and parietal cortices, the motor representation of that action.

Thus, the action of another individual becomes 'my action'. Its goal is now transparent.

Evidence supporting this notion comes from a recent series of studies in which F5 mirror neurons were tested in experimental conditions in which the monkey could understand the meaning of an occurring action, but had no information or only partial visual information about it. The rationale of these studies was the following. If mirror neurons mediate action understanding, they should become active when the meaning of the observed action is understood, even in the absence of visual information.

The results showed that this was the case. In the first of these studies (Umiltà *et al.*, 2001) neurons were tested in the following two experimental conditions. In one, the monkey could see the whole action directed towards the object ('Full vision' condition), while in the other, the same action was presented, but with its final, critical part (hand–object interaction) hidden behind a screen ('Hidden' condition). There were also two control conditions ('Mimicking in full vision', and 'Hidden mimicking') in which the same action was performed without the object actually present, either in full vision or behind the occluding screen, respectively. The results showed that the majority of tested mirror neurons responded to the observation of hand actions even when the final part of the action, that evoking the response in full vision, was hidden from the monkey's sight. However, when the hidden action was performed with no object present behind the occluding screen, there was no response. Thus, in the Hidden condition the mirror neurons were able to generate a motor representation of an observed action, not only when the monkey saw that action, but also when it 'knew' its outcome without seeing its most crucial part (i.e. hand–object interaction).

In another study, F5 mirror neurons were recorded while the monkey was observing a 'noisy' action (e.g. ripping a piece of paper) and when it was presented with the noise of that action without seeing it. The results showed that a large number of mirror neurons, responsive to the observation of noisy actions, also responded to the presentation of the sound of that action, alone. The responses of these neurons were specific for the type of action seen and heard. For example, they responded to peanut breaking when the action was only observed, only heard or both heard and observed, and did not respond to the vision and sound of another action, or to non-specific sounds. Neurons responding selectively to specific action sounds were named 'audio-visual' mirror neurons (Kohler *et al.*, 2002).

These data indicate that the acoustic input reaching the motor cortex of a listener elicits the action representation present in this cortical region. Furthermore, they indicate that mirror neurons allow the understanding of actions independently of whether these actions are seen, heard or performed. In conclusion, the activity of mirror neurons correlates with action understanding. The visual features of the observed actions are necessary to trigger mirror neurons only insofar as they allow the understanding of the observed actions. If action comprehension is possible on other bases, mirror neurons signal the action, even in the absence of visual stimuli.

14.6. **First person knowledge**

Why do we need a motor activation in order to understand what others are doing? Why is visual activation not sufficient? The traditional view is that actions performed by others are understood in the same way as other visual stimuli. Thus, according to this view, action understanding would be based on the visual analysis of the different elements that form an action. For example, when we observe a boy grasping a ball, the analysed elements would be his hand, the ball and the movement of the hand towards the ball. The association of these elements and inferences about their interaction would enable the observer to understand the witnessed action. The cortical areas specifically involved in the process of action recognition would be some extrastriate visual areas and the region of the STS.

It has been recently argued that the visual information alone does not provide a *full* understanding of the observed action (Rizzolatti *et al.*, 2001; Jeannerod, 2004). The main reason for this is that, in order to fully understand an action performed by another individual, that action must activate its representation in the observer's motor repertoire. Mere visual information, without involvement of the motor system, provides a description of the visible aspects of the movements of the agent, but does not give information critical for understanding what it means to undertake that action, how it relates to other actions, and finally how it can be replicated.

There is clear evidence that the observation of actions belonging to the motor repertoire of the observer produces a stronger activation of the mirror neuron system than actions that are not part of it. Calvo-Merino *et al.* (2005) presented capoeira (a Brazilian fight-dance) dancers, expert classical ballet dancers and non-dancer controls with video sequences showing capoeira and ballet movements. The capoeira dancers showed stronger activation in the premotor and parietal areas (mirror neuron areas) and in the STS region, when observing capoeira movements than when observing classical ballet movements. Conversely, the classical ballet dancers showed a stronger activation of the same areas during the observation of classical ballet movements than during the observation of capoeira movements. Similarly, Haslinger *et al.* (2005) found that during the observation of piano playing there is a stronger activation of the motor system in professional pianists than in musically naïve controls.

Even stronger evidence showing the importance of internal representation of actions to the understanding of actions performed by other individuals is provided by a recent fMRI experiment (Buccino *et al.*, 2004a). Video-clips showing mouth actions performed by a man, a monkey and a dog were presented to normal volunteers. Two types of actions were shown: biting a piece of food and oral, silent, communicative actions (speech reading, lip smacking, barking). Static images of the same actions were presented as a control.

The results showed that actions performed by an individual of another species (e.g. a dog or a monkey) activate the mirror neuron system, when actions are also part of the observer's own motor repertoire (like biting a piece of food). However, when the observed actions were communicative gestures, those performed by a human activated the mirror neuron system, whereas those performed by non-conspecifics (e.g. silent barking, or lip smacking), did not activate it. In these cases, only visual areas showed signal increase.

Taken together, these findings indicate that while all observed actions activate higher-order visual areas, only those actions that the individuals know how to perform enter into their motor network. This additional representation provides the observer with a specific 'first person' motor knowledge, i.e. with the knowledge of what means *to do* the observed action. That is, we know what biting means because this is something that we all do, but we do not know what barking means, although we recognize this action when a dog barks. This neurophysiological distinction is reminiscent of that made by phenomenologists (see Merleau-Ponty, 1962) between personal knowledge and objective knowledge.

14.7. Intention understanding

There is a second reason why activation of the motor network during observation of actions performed by others gives advantages to individuals endowed with this mechanism, and it is related to understanding the intentions of others. In fact, by activating this network it is possible not only to understand the 'what' of the observed action (e.g. an individual is grasping a cup of coffee), but also the 'why' of it (the individual is grasping it for drinking, for moving, or for throwing).

Before discussing the mechanism leading from mirror neurons to intention understanding, we need to first describe the motor organization of the inferior parietal lobule. It has already been mentioned that IPL neurons discharge in association with specific motor acts. Motor acts are defined as movements with a specific, restricted goal. Examples are reaching, grasping, holding, bringing to the mouth etc. The reinforcement of such motor acts consists in their success. Reaching, for example, is reinforced by the sensory information that the hand has reached the object, and so is grasping. Actions result from sequences of motor acts. Their final outcomes provide a *reward* to the acting individuals. Grasping a piece of food, bringing it to the mouth and eating it comprise an action. Getting food is its reward.

The same motor act (for example, grasping) may be part of different actions leading to different final goals. Recent work by Fogassi *et al.* (2005) has addressed the issue of whether the discharge of IPL neurons coding grasping is influenced by the action of which the grasping movement is a part. The recorded neurons were tested in two main conditions. In one, the monkey reached and grasped a piece of food located in front of it and brought it to its mouth. In the other, the monkey reached and grasped an object and placed it into a container. In the first condition, the monkey was rewarded by eating the food. In the second condition, the monkey was rewarded with food given to it by the experimenter after task accomplishment.

The results showed that the majority of IPL grasping neurons discharged with a different intensity depending on the final goal of the action in which grasping was embedded (see Figure 14.4). A series of controls for grasping force, kinematics of reaching movements, and type of stimuli showed that neuron selectivity was not due to these factors. Thus, the differential discharge of these grasping neurons appeared to reflect the intention of the acting agent.

These neural properties suggest that motor actions are coded in IPL in the following way: neurons coding individual motor acts (e.g. grasping), instead of being used in a multiplicity of actions, are part of pre-wired chains, each

coding a specific action. This organization is appropriate for providing fluidity to action execution, because each neuron not only codes a specific motor act, but, being embedded into a specific action, is also linked with neurons coding the next motor acts and possibly facilitates them (see Yokochi *et al.*, 2003).

In the study just discussed, Fogassi *et al.* (2005) tested IPL neurons that discharged during active gasping and were activated by grasping observation (IPL mirror neurons), under the same two conditions used for studying the motor properties of IPL grasping neurons (grasping for eating and grasping for placing). The observed actions were performed by one of the experimenters in front of the monkey. The context (presence or absence of the container) and the repetition of the same action by the experimenter (blocked design) gave clues to the monkey about what action the experimenter was going to perform.

The results showed that the majority of IPL mirror neurons was differentially activated when the observed grasping motor act belonged to different actions (see Figure 14.5). Thus, the visual response of these mirror neurons appears

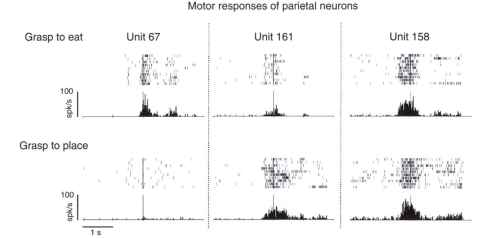

Fig. 14.4 Examples of inferior parietal lobule (IPL) motor neuron activity during motor task performance. Neuron 67 discharges when the monkey grasps for eating, but not when it grasps for placing. Neuron 161 shows the opposite preference. Neuron 158 does not show any differential activation during grasping in both action sequences. Rasters and histograms are synchronized with the moment when the monkey touched the object to be grasped. Conventions as in Figure 14.2. Modified from Fogassi *et al.* (2005).

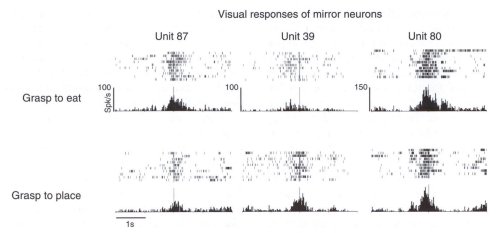

Fig. 14.5 Examples of inferior parietal lobule (IPL) mirror neuron activity during observation of the two actions of the task (grasping for eating and grasping for placing). Neuron 87 activates when the monkey observes the experimenter grasping a piece of food for eating, but not when he grasps it for placing. Neuron 39 shows the opposite preference. Neuron 80 does not show any differential activation during observation of grasping in both action sequences. Rasters and histograms are synchronized with the moment when the experimenter touched the food to be grasped. Conventions as in Figure 14.2. Modified from Fogassi *et al.* (2005).

to predict what will be the next motor act of the experimenter, that is, his intention. Furthermore, by comparing the visual and motor properties of these neurons, it became clear that those neurons that discharged more intensely during grasping for eating compared to grasping for placing, also discharged more intensely during the observation of grasping for the eating. The same congruence was found for neurons specific for grasping to place.

Altogether, these data suggest that the chained organization of IPL neurons, and the capacity also to activate specific chains when observing others' actions, represents a mechanism for understanding the intentions of others. Mirror neurons, therefore, are not only involved in understanding observed motor acts (e.g. the boy is grasping the ball), but also by predicting impending motor acts, or in other words, the agent's intention (e.g. the boy is grasping the ball to throw it).

A recent experiment by Iacoboni *et al.* (2005) indicates that humans also use the mirror neuron system in order to understand the intentions of others. In an fMRI experiment, they presented volunteers with three kinds of stimuli: a hand grasping a cup without a context, context only (scenes containing objects), and a hand grasping a cup in two different contexts. The contexts consisted of two scenes with objects arranged either as just before having tea ('drinking' context) or as just after having tea ('cleaning' context). The results showed that hand actions embedded in contexts, compared with the other two conditions, produced a higher activation of caudal IFG.

In conclusion, both monkey and human data show that the intentions behind the actions of others can be recognized by the motor system using the mirror neuron mechanism. This does not imply, of course, that other more cognitive ways of 'reading minds' do not exist. However, the present data show for the first time a neural mechanism by which an important aspect of mind reading, understanding the intention of others, is achieved.

14.8. Imitation

From the very beginning of the discovery of mirror neurons, it was suggested that these neurons might underlie imitation. In fact, the mirror neuron mechanism can solve one of the most difficult problems related to imitation, the so-called 'translation' problem: information about actions to be imitated is captured by the visual system and coded in visual parameters, yet the observer is able to translate this information immediately into the motor parameters necessary for the execution of the observed action. The fact that the monkey does not imitate or has very little capacity in this regard suggests that imitation is not the primary function of mirror neurons. However, this does not exclude the possibility that mirror neurons may represent the building blocks from which imitation proceeds in humans. Indeed, a series of experiments has shown that this is the case.

In an fMRI experiment, Iacoboni *et al.* (1999) tested volunteers in three experimental conditions. In one, they lifted a finger in response to finger lifting performed by another individual (imitation condition), while in the other two conditions (control conditions) they performed the same movement in response to the presentation of a small cross which could be shown either on the computer screen or on a picture showing a still finger. The main result of the study was a stronger signal increase in the *pars opercularis* of the left inferior frontal gyrus (IFG) during the imitation condition than in the other two conditions. Experiments by Koski *et al.* (2002) confirmed the importance of this region in imitation, in particular when the action to be imitated had a specific goal (i.e. touching a target versus simply moving the finger). Grèzes *et al.* (2003) obtained similar results.

The importance of IFG for imitation has also been shown by Nishitani and Hari (2000) using the event-related neuromagnetic (MEG) technique. Normal volunteers were asked to grasp a manipulandum with their right hand, to observe the same movement performed by an experimenter, or to observe and replicate the observed action. The results showed that during the active grasping condition, there was an early activation in the left posterior IFG with a response peak appearing approximately 250 ms before the touching of the target. This activation was followed within 100–200 ms by activation of the left pre-central motor area. During observation and imitation, the pattern and sequence of frontal activations were similar to those found during execution, but area IFG activation was preceded by an occipital activation due to

visual stimulation present in these two conditions. Activation was stronger during action imitation.

The importance of the *pars opercularis* of IFG in imitation was recently further demonstrated by Heiser *et al.* (2003), using repetitive TMS, a technique that transiently disrupts the functions of the stimulated area. The task used in the study was, essentially, the same as that of the fMRI study by Iacoboni *et al.* (1999). The results showed that, following stimulation of both left and right posterior IFG, there was significant impairment in imitation of finger movements. The effect was absent when finger movements were performed in response to spatial cues.

In the experiments reviewed above, individuals were asked to repeat 'on line' highly practised actions performed by another individual. Buccino *et al.* (2004b) recently investigated which cortical areas become active when individuals are required to learn, on the basis of action observation, a *novel motor pattern*, rather than simply repeating an action already present in their motor repertoire. The basic task was imitation by naïve participants of guitar chords played by an expert guitarist. By using an event-related fMRI paradigm, cortical activations were mapped during the following events: (a) observation of the chords made by the expert player, (b) pause, (c) execution of the observed chords, and (d) rest. In addition to the imitation condition, there were other conditions to control for observation not followed by imitation and for non-imitative motor activity.

The results showed that during observation for imitation there was activation of a cortical network formed by the inferior parietal lobule and the dorsal part of ventral premotor cortex, plus the *pars opercularis* of IFG. This circuit was also active during observation in the control conditions in which participants merely observed the chords, or observed them with the instruction to subsequently perform an action not related to guitar chord execution. During the pause in the imitation condition, activation was found in the same circuit as during observation, but, most interestingly, also in the middle frontal cortex (area 46) and in the anterior mesial cortex (i.e., the cortex buried inside the interhemispheric fissure).

These data show that during new motor pattern formation there is a strong activation of the mirror neuron system. The authors suggested a two-step mechanism for imitation learning. First, the observed actions are decomposed into elementary motor acts that activate, via mirror mechanisms, the corresponding motor representations in the parietal and frontal lobes. Once these motor representations are activated, they are recombined to fit the observed model. For this recombination, a crucial role is played by frontal area 46.

As mentioned above, monkey capacity for learning by imitation is minimal, if any exists at all (see Visalberghi and Fragaszy, 2002). How is it possible to reconcile this finding with the presence in the monkey of a well-developed mirror neuron system? Imitation, strictly defined, is the capacity to reproduce not only the goal of the observed action, but also the means by which the goal is achieved. As described at the beginning of this chapter, monkeys have relatively few mirror neurons describing actions in detail (strictly congruent mirror neurons). The majority actually code the action goal. Furthermore, unlike the monkey mirror neuron system, that of humans also codes meaningless movements (Fadiga *et al.*, 1995; Grèzes *et al.*, 1998), thus suggesting the existence of a mirror system for copying movements independent of the presence of a goal. In addition, as shown by the experiment on guitar chord learning, a crucial role in imitation learning is played by the prefrontal cortex. It is well known that this cortical region has grown tremendously in the evolution of human brain.

These considerations do not explain, however, the great difficulties that monkeys have repeating actions *already* present in their repertoire (Kumashiro *et al.*, 2003). An explanation for this might be found in the mechanisms that control action production in humans and monkeys. There is convincing evidence that the action representations, coded in the parieto-premotor circuits, are under complex excitatory and inhibitory control exerted on them by the mesial motor areas (e.g. pre-SMA) and the prefrontal lobe (Rizzolatti and Luppino, 2001). Action representation becomes overt action only when these areas allow it. All species endowed with a mirror neuron system must have a tonic inhibitory mechanism that prevents the overt occurrence of the observed actions.

This is because, while action representation and therefore action understanding through the mirror system is advantageous for the individual, imitation of the observed actions may be dangerous. It is likely that humans, due to the expansion of the frontal lobe, acquired the capacity to use the frontal lobe control system in a flexible way, allowing the overt action occurrence when the external contingencies are such that imitation is useful for the observing individual, and blocking it when they are not.

14.9. **Language**

Communication may be intentional and non-intentional. The difference is that in the case of intentional communication the sender plays the leading role and imposes the communication on the receiver, while in the case of non-intentional communication, the sender sends a message without having any intention to do so. Of these two types of communication, the non-intentional one is the most basic and primitive. It is evolutionarily necessary because, in social life, individuals have to understand what the others are doing, regardless of whether the acting individuals wish to be understood or not. It is quite plausible to suppose that intentional communication has been an evolutionary elaboration of non-intentional communication.

If this is accepted, the question immediately becomes one of whether there is an association between the mirror neuron system and language. The mirror neuron system, in essence, is a mechanism that creates a direct link between the sender of a message and its receiver. Thanks to this system, actions performed by other individuals become messages that are understood by an observer without any cognitive mediation. On the basis of this fundamental property, Rizzolatti and Arbib (1998) proposed that the mirror mechanism underlies language evolution. Indeed, mirror mechanisms solve two fundamental communication problems: parity and direct comprehension of the action. Parity requires that what counts for the sender of the message also counts for the receiver. Direct comprehension means that there is no need for any negotiation and agreement of terms in order for individuals to understand each other; comprehension is inherent to the neural organization of the individuals concerned. The mirror neuron mechanism appears therefore to be the natural communication system on top of which more sophisticated systems evolved.

A further reason for linking the mirror neuron system to language is the generally accepted homology between the motor areas mediating language in humans and the areas that form the mirror neuron system in monkeys. There is a consensus that area F5 (in particular area F5a, see Nelissen *et al.*, 2005) represents the monkey homologue of posterior sector (area 44) of human Broca's area (Petrides and Pandya, 1997; Rizzolatti and Arbib, 1998; Nelissen *et al.*, 2005). The mirror neuron system parietal node does not correspond, of course, to the auditory centres mediating vocal analysis for communication. The issue at stake here, however, is not how phonology evolved, but how communicative signals link to the origin of language. In this respect, the evidence presented above clearly indicates that the inferior parietal lobule has a similar organization in humans and monkeys and plays a fundamental role in action understanding in both species.

A criticism against the hypothesis that the mirror neuron system forms the basis of language evolution is that, in the monkey, the mirror neuron system consists of neurons coding object-directed actions. Thus, the monkey mirror neuron system forms a closed system, which cannot be involved in intentional communication. But if this is true for the monkey, this is not the case for the mirror neuron system in humans. Evidence from TMS and brain-imaging experiments has shown that, in humans, the activation of the mirror system occurs also when intransitive actions, for example meaningless arm movements (Fadiga *et al.*, 1995; Maeda *et al.*, 2002) or action pantomimes (Buccino *et al.*, 2001, Grèzes *et al.*, 2003), are presented.

The shift from a closed system to an open, intentionally communicative system most likely occurred through a process of ritualization. This suggestion is in line with the proposal of Van Hooff (1967) that many of the most common communicative gestures of monkeys, such as lip smacking or the lips-protruded face, are ritualizations of ingestive actions that have evolved into actions with affiliative purposes. The properties of communicative mouth mirror neurons

responding to the sight of communicative actions and discharging during active ingestive actions appear to give neurophysiological support to this idea (Ferrari *et al.*, 2003a).

In monkeys, dyadic inter-individual communication is mostly based on oro-facial gestures, rather than sounds. Thus, it is in humans, and not in monkeys, that one has to look for the presence of a mirror neuron system activated by sounds. Recent evidence has shown that a motor system that resonates selectively in response to speech sounds ('echo mirror neuron system') indeed exists in humans. Fadiga *et al.* (2002) recorded motor-evoked potentials (MEPs) from the tongue muscles in normal volunteers instructed to listen to acoustically presented verbal and non-verbal stimuli. The stimuli were words, regular pseudo-words, and bitonal sounds. In the middle of words and pseudo-words there was either a double 'f' or a double 'r'. 'F' is a labio-dental fricative consonant that, when pronounced, requires virtually no tongue movements, while 'r' is linguo-palatal fricative consonant that, in contrast, requires a marked tongue muscle involvement to be pronounced. During stimulus presentation, the left motor cortex of the participants was stimulated with single TMS pulses. The results showed that listening to words and pseudo-words containing the double 'r' resulted in a significant increase in the amplitude of MEPs recorded from the tongue muscles, as compared to listening to words and pseudo-words containing the double 'f' and bitonal sounds (see Figure 14.6).

Results congruent with those of Fadiga *et al.* (2002) were obtained by Watkins *et al.* (2003). By using a single pulse TMS technique, they recorded MEPs from a lip (*orbicularis oris*) and a hand muscle (first *interosseus*), respectively, in four conditions: listening to continuous prose, viewing speech-related lip movements, listening to non-verbal sounds, and viewing eye and brow movements. Compared to the viewing eye and brow condition, listening to and viewing speech enhanced the MEP amplitude recorded from the *orbicularis oris* muscle. All these changes were seen only in response to stimulation of the left hemisphere.

Finally, recent brain-imaging experiments show that reading or listening to action words activates premotor areas that are part of the

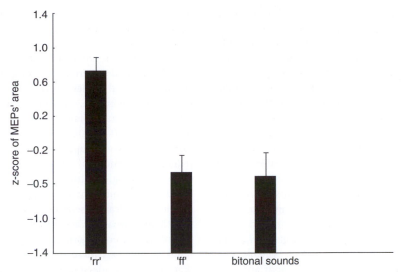

Fig. 14.6 Average value (+ standard error) of normalized motor-evoked potentials' (MEPs') total areas recorded from all volunteers in three different conditions: listening to words and pseudo-words containing a double 'r', to words and pseudo-words containing a double 'f' and to bitonal sounds. Modified from Fadiga *et al.* (2002).

mirror system. Although the activated areas only roughly correspond to those activated during action observation, they appear to suggest a link between mirror neuron system and language understanding (Hauk *et al.*, 2004, Tettamanti *et al.*, 2005).

14.10. **Emotion and mirror system**

Up to now we have discussed neural mechanisms that enable individuals to understand actions devoid of any obvious emotional content. In social life, however, the capacity to understand emotions is equally important. What mechanisms enable us to understand what others feel? Is there a mirror mechanism for emotions similar to that described for action understanding?

As in the case of action understanding, it is likely that emotions are understood in two ways. The first is through a cognitive elaboration of the sensory information captured during the observation of others' emotions, the other is through a direct mapping of this sensory information onto the motor structures that determine

the experience of the observed emotion in the observer. These two ways of recognizing emotions are profoundly different. With the first, the observer understands the emotion expressed by others, but does not feel it. He deduces it. A certain facial or body pattern means fear, another happiness. There is no emotional involvement. With the other mechanism, the recognition occurs because the observed emotion triggers in the observer the same emotional state. It is direct first-person recognition.

In this section, we will examine the neural mechanisms underlying this second type of emotion understanding. For the sake of space, we will review data on one form of emotion only—disgust—for which there is rich empirical evidence. Disgust is a basic emotion whose expression has important survival value for conspecifics (but see Panksepp, this volume, Chapter 12, for a different perspective). In its most basic, primitive form ('core disgust'; Rozin *et al.*, 2000) it indicates that something that the individual tastes or smells is bad and, most likely, dangerous.

Brain-imaging studies have shown that when an individual is exposed to disgusting odours or tastes, there is an intense activation of two structures: the amygdala and the insula (Augustine, 1996; Royet *et al.*, 2001; Small *et al.*, 2003; Zald *et al.*, 1998; Zald and Pardo, 2000). The insula is currently the focus of many studies. Among them, one of particular interest is that by Craig (2002), which demonstrated that the insula is the main cortical target of interoceptive afferents, that is for information coming from the inside of our body. Thus, besides being the primary cortical area for chemical exteroception (e.g. taste and olfaction), the insula is also the cortical region where 'body states' are represented. Furthermore, the insula, in addition to being excited by disgusting stimuli, also becomes active during the observation of disgusted facial expressions (Phillips *et al.*, 1997, 1998; Sprengelmeyer *et al.*, 1998; Schienle *et al.*, 2002; Wicker *et al.*, 2003). It is important, however, to remember that the insula is not exclusively a sensory area. In both monkeys and humans, its electrical stimulation produces body movements, which, unlike those evoked by stimulation of classical motor areas, are typically accompanied by autonomic and visceral responses (Penfield and Faulk, 1955; Showers and Lauer, 1961; Krolak-Salmon *et al.*, 2003).

Particularly interesting for the relation between the mirror system and emotion understanding is the fMRI study by Wicker *et al.* (2003). The study consisted of olfactory and visual runs. In the *olfactory* runs, individuals inhaled disgusting and pleasant odorants. In the *visual* runs, the same participants viewed videoclips of individuals smelling a glass containing disgusting, pleasant and neutral odorants and expressing their emotions. Inhalation of disgusting odorants produced a very strong signal increase in the amygdala, in the anterior part of the insula, bilaterally and in the anterior cingulate. The observation of disgust activated various cortical areas, including the anterior cingulate and the anterior sector of the left insula. The amygdala was not activated.

The most important result of the study was the demonstration that *precisely* the same parts within the anterior insula that were activated by the exposure to disgusting odorants were also activated by the observation of disgust in others. A similar, but smaller overlap, was also observed in the cingulate. These data strongly suggest that there are neural populations, especially in the insula, that become active both when the participants experience disgust and when they see it in others.

The notion that the insula mediates both the recognition and experience of disgust is supported by clinical studies showing that, following lesions of the insula, patients have a severe deficit in understanding disgust expressed by others (Calder *et al.*, 2000; Adolphs *et al.*, 2003). This deficit is accompanied by blunted and reduced sensation of disgust. In addition, electrophysiological studies showed that sites in the anterior insula, whose electrical stimulation produced unpleasant sensations in the patient's mouth and throat, are activated by the observation of faces expressing disgust.

Taken together, these data strongly suggest that humans understand disgust, and most likely other emotions (see Carr *et al.*, 2003, Singer *et al.*, 2004), through a direct mapping mechanism. The observation of emotionally laden actions activates those structures that give a first-person experience of the same actions. By means of this activation a bridge is created between ourselves and others.

The hypothesis that we perceive emotion in others by activating the same emotion in ourselves has been advanced previously by various authors (e.g. Phillips *et al.*, 1997; Adolphs *et al.*, 2003; Damasio, 2003a; Calder *et al.*, 2000; Carr *et al.*, 2003; Goldman and Sripada, 2004; Gallese *et al.*, 2004). The studies of Damasio and his co-workers have been particularly influential (Adolphs *et al.*, 2000; Damasio, 2003a,b). According to them, first-person understanding of emotions depends on the activation of somatosensory cortices and the insula. We fully agree with Damasio on the crucial importance of insula. We are not convinced, however, that the activation of the somatosensory cortices is necessary for first person understanding of emotions. Fundamental for first person understanding of emotion is the activation of a mechanism that generates this emotion in its full-fledged form, including its visceromotor aspects, in the observer. Sensory cortices do not have this ability. The insula has it.

The data we have reviewed offer a basis for explaining some aspects of social behaviour. One should be very cautious, however, before concluding that they also enable one to give the neurophysiological explanation of our capacity to have a conscious empathic feeling (or sympathy) toward others. The first-person comprehension of others' emotions, made possible by mirror neuron mechanisms, undoubtedly represents the necessary prerequisite for establishing empathic relations with others, but it is not sufficient. To share an emotional state with another is not the same as having a sympathetic feeling for that person. For example, if we see a person expressing pain, this does not mean that we are forced to feel compassion, that is, sympathy, for them. This may occur, but the processes of empathy and sympathy are distinct. Sympathy depends on many other factors such as the identity of the other person, our relationship with him and our capacity to understand the reason for his state. If the person in pain is a person who is close to us we will feel both empathy and sympathy for him, while it is much less likely that this will happen if the other person is not known to us or is our enemy.

In conclusion, and in analogy with action understanding, the mirror mechanism for emotion understanding only provides the *basis* of interpersonal relationships on which more complex social behaviors are built. These behaviours require the intervention of other cortical areas and subcortical centres.

Acknowledgments

This work was supported by Italian FIRB n. RBNE018ET9_002, PRIN prot. 2004057380, and prot. 2004053812, and by the European Projects Neurocom, n. 12738. 2005–2008, OMLL n. JA12F05 and n. JA05R03.

References

Adolphs, R., Damasio, H., Tranel, D., Cooper, G. and Damasio, A. R. (2000) A role for somatosensory cortices in the visual recognition of emotion as revealed by three-dimensional lesion mapping. *Journal of Neuroscience*, 20: 2683–2690.

Adolphs, R., Tranel, D. and Damasio, A. R. (2003) Dissociable neural systems for recognizing emotions. *Brain Cognition*, 52: 61–69.

Augustine, J. R. (1996) Circuitry and functional aspects of the insular lobe in primates including humans. *Brain Research Reviews*, 22: 229–244.

Brodmann, K. (1905) Beitrage zur histologischen lokalisation der grosshirnrinde. III. Mitteilung: die rindenfelder der niedere affen. *Journal für Psychologie und Neurologie*, 4: 177–226.

Buccino, G., Binkofski, F., Fink, G. R. *et al.* (2001) Action observation activates premotor and parietal areas in a somatotopic manner: an fMRI study. *European Journal of Neuroscience*, 13: 400–404.

Buccino, G., Lui, F., Canessa, N. *et al.* (2004a) Neural circuits involved in the recognition of actions performed by non-conspecifics: an fMRI study. *Journal of Cognitive Neuroscience*, 16: 114–126.

Buccino, G., Vogt, S., Ritzl, A. *et al.* (2004b) Neural circuits underlying imitation of hand actions: an event related fMRI study. *Neuron*, 42: 323–334.

Calder, A. J., Keane, J., Manes, F., Antoun, N. and Young, A. W. (2000) Impaired recognition and experience of disgust following brain injury. *Nature Neuroscience*, 3: 1077–1088.

Calvo-Merino, B., Glaser, D. E., Grezes, J., Passingham, R. E. and Haggard, P. (2005) Action observation and acquired motor skills: an FMRI study with expert dancers. *Cerebral Cortex*, 15: 1243–1249.

Carr, L., Iacoboni, M., Dubeau, M. C., Mazziotta, J. C. and Lenzi, G. L. (2003) Neural mechanisms of empathy in humans: a relay from neural systems for imitation to limbic areas. *Proceedings of the National Academy of Science USA*, 100: 5497–5502.

Cochin, S., Barthelemy, C., Roux, S. and Martineau, J. (1999) Observation and execution of movement: similarities demonstrated by quantified electroencephalography. *European Journal of Neuroscience*, 11: 1839–1842.

Craig, A. D. (2002) How do you feel? Interoception: the sense of the physiological condition of the body. *Nature Reviews Neuroscience*, 3: 655–666.

Damasio, A. (2003a) *Looking for Spinoza*. Vintage, London.

Damasio, A. (2003b) Feeling of emotion and the self. *Annals of the New York Academy of Sciences*, 1001: 253–261.

Fadiga, L., Fogassi, L., Pavesi, G. and Rizzolatti, G. (1995) Motor facilitation during action observation: A magnetic stimulation study. *Journal of Neurophysiology*, 73: 2608–2611.

Fadiga, L., Craighero, L., Buccino, G. and Rizzolatti, G. (2002) Speech listening specifically modulates the excitability of tongue muscles: a TMS study. *European. Journal of Neuroscience*, 15: 399–402.

Ferrari, P. F., Gallese, V., Rizzolatti, G. and Fogassi, L. (2003a) Mirror neurons responding to the observation of ingestive and communicative mouth actions in the monkey ventral premotor cortex. *European Journal of Neuroscience*, 17: 1703–1714.

Ferrari, P. F., Gregoriou, G., Rozzi, S., Pagliara, S., Rizzolatti, G. and Fogassi, L. (2003b) Functional organization of the inferior parietal lobule of the macaque monkey. *Society for Neuroscience Abstracts*, 919.7.

Fogassi, L., Ferrari, P. F., Gesierich, B., Rozzi, S., Chersi, F. and Rizzolatti, G. (2005) Parietal Lobe: from Action Organization to Intention Understanding. *Science*, 308: 662–667.

Gallese, V., Fadiga, L., Fogassi, L. and Rizzolatti, G. (1996) Action recognition in the premotor cortex. *Brain*, 119: 593–609.

Gallese, V., Keysers, C. and Rizzolatti, G. (2004) A unifying view of the basis of social cognition. *Trends in Cognitive Sciences*, 8: 396–403.

Gangitano, M., Mottaghy, F. M. and Pascual-Leone, A. (2004) Modulation of premotor mirror neuron activity during observation of unpredictable grasping movements. *European Journal of Neuroscience*, 20: 2193–2202.

Goldman, A. I. and Sripada, C. S. (2004) Simulationist models of face-based emotion recognition. *Cognition*, 94: 193–213.

Grafton, S. T., Arbib, M. A., Fadiga, L. and Rizzolatti, G. (1996) Localization of grasp representations in humans by PET: 2. Observation compared with imagination. *Experimental Brain Research*, 112: 103–111.

Grèzes, J., Costes, N. and Decety, J. (1998) Top-down effect of strategy on the perception of human biological motion: a PET investigation. *Cognitive Neuropsychology*, 15: 553–582.

Grèzes, J., Armony, J. L., Rowe, J. and Passingham, R. E. (2003) Activations related to "mirror" and "canonical" neurones in the human brain: an fMRI study. *Neuroimage*, 18: 928–937.

Hari, R., Forss, N., Avikainen, S., Kirveskari, S., Salenius, S. and Rizzolatti, G. (1998) Activation of human primary motor cortex during action observation: a neuromagnetic study. *Proceedings of the National Academy of Sciences USA*, 95: 15061–15065.

Haslinger, B., Erhard, P., Altenmuller, E., Scroeder, U., Boecker, H. and Ceballos-Baumann, A. O. (2005) Transmodal sensorimotor networks during action observation in professional pianists. *Journal of Cognitive Neuroscience*, 17: 282–293.

Hauk, O., Johnsrude, I. and Pulvermuller, F. (2004) Somatotopic representation of action words in human motor and premotor cortex. *Neuron*, 41: 301–307.

Heiser, M., Iacoboni, M., Maeda, F., Marcus, J. and Mazziotta, J. C. (2003) The essential role of Broca's area in imitation. *European Journal of Neuroscience*, 17: 1123–1128.

Hyvärinen, J. (1981) Regional distribution of functions in parietal association area 7 of the monkey. *Brain Research*, 206: 287–303.

Iacoboni, M., Woods, R. P., Brass, M., Bekkering, H., Mazziotta, J. C. and Rizzolatti, G. (1999) Cortical mechanisms of human imitation. *Science*, 286: 2526–2528.

Iacoboni, M., Koski, L. M., Brass, M. *et al.* (2001) Reafferent copies of imitated actions in the right superior temporal cortex. *Proceedings of the National Academy of Sciences of the USA*, 98: 13995–13999.

Iacoboni, M., Molnar-Szakacs, I., Gallese, V., Buccino, G., Mazziotta, J. C. and Rizzolatti, G. (2005) Grasping the intentions of others with one's own mirror neuron system. *PloS Biology*, 3: 529–535.

Jeannerod, M. (2004) Visual and action cues contribute to the self-other distinction. *Nature Neuroscience*, 7: 422–423.

Jellema, T., Baker, C. I., Oram, M. W. and D. I. Perrett (2002) Cell populations in the banks of the superior temporal sulcus of the macaque monkey and imitation. In A. N. Melzoff and W. Prinz (eds) *The Imitative Mind. Development, Evolution and Brain Bases*, pp. 143–162. Cambridge University Press, Cambridge.

Johnson-Frey, S. H., Maloof, F. R., Newman-Norlund, R., Farrer, C., Inati, S. and Grafton, S. T. (2003) Actions or hand-objects interactions? Human inferior frontal cortex and action observation. *Neuron*, 39: 1053–1058.

Kohler, E., Keysers, C., Umiltà, M. A., Fogassi, L., Gallese, V. and Rizzolatti, G. (2002) Hearing sounds, understanding actions: action representation in mirror neurons. *Science*, 297: 846–848.

Koski, L., Wohlschlager, A., Bekkering, H., Woods, R. P. and Dubeau, M. C. (2002) Modulation of motor and premotor activity during imitation of target-directed actions. *Cerebral Cortex*, 12: 847–855.

Koski, L., Iacoboni, M., Dubeau, M. C., Woods, R. P. and Mazziotta, J. C. (2003) Modulation of cortical activity during different imitative behaviors. *Journal of Neurophysiology*, 89: 460–471.

Krolak-Salmon, P., Henaff, M. A., Isnard, J. *et al.* (2003) An attention modulated response to disgust in human ventral anterior insula. *Annals of Neurology*, 53: 446–453.

Kumashiro, M., Ishibashi, H., Uchiyama, Y., Itakura, S., Murata, A. and Iriki, A. (2003) Natural imitation induced by joint attention in japanese monkeys. *International Journal of Psychophysiology*, 50: 81–99.

Maeda, F., Kleiner-Fisman, G. and Pascual-Leone, A. (2002) Motor facilitation while observing hand actions: specificity of the effect and role of observer's orientation. *Journal of Neurophysiology*, 87: 1329–1325.

Manthey, S., Schubotz, R. I. and von Cramon, D. Y. (2003) Premotor cortex in observing erroneous action: an fMRI study. *Brain Research Cognitive Brain Research*, 15: 296–307.

Merleau-Ponty, M. (1962) *Phenomenology of Perception* (translated from the French by C. Smith). Routledge, London.

Mountcastle, V. B., Lynch, J. C. G. A., Sakata, H. and Acuna, C. (1975) Posterior parietal association cortex of the monkey: command functions for operations within extrapersonal space. *Journal of Neurophysiology*, 38: 871–908.

Nelissen, K., Luppino, G., Vanduffel, W., Rizzolatti, G. and Orban, G. (2005) Observing others: multiple action representation in the frontal lobe. *Science*, 310: 332–336.

Nishitani, N. and Hari, R. (2000) Temporal dynamics of cortical representation for action. *Proceedings of the National Academy of Sciences of the USA*, 97: 913–918.

Nishitani, N. and Hari, R. (2002) Viewing lip forms: cortical dynamics. *Neuron*, 36: 1211–1220.

Penfield, W. and Faulk, M. E. (1955) The insula: further observations on its function. *Brain*, 78: 445–470.

Perrett, D. I., Harries, M. H., Bevan, R. *et al.* (1989) Frameworks of analysis for the neural representation of animate objects and actions. *Journal of Experimental Biology*, 146: 87–113.

Petrides, M. and Pandya, D. N. (1997) Comparative architectonic analysis of the human and the macaque frontal cortex. In F. Boller and J. Grafman (eds) *Handbook of Neuropsychology*, vol. IX, pp. 17–58. Elsevier, New York.

Phillips, M. L., Young, A. W., Senior, C. *et al.* (1997) A specific neural substrate for perceiving facial expressions of disgust. *Nature*, 389: 495–498.

Phillips, M. L., Young, A. W., Scott, S. K. *et al.* (1998) Neural responses to facial and vocal expressions of fear and disgust. *Proceedings Biological Sciences of the Royal Society of London*, 265: 1809–1817.

Rizzolatti, G. and Arbib, M. A. (1998) Language within our grasp. *Trends in Neuroscience*, 21: 188–194.

Rizzolatti, G. and Luppino, G. (2001) The cortical motor system. *Neuron*, 31: 889–901.

Rizzolatti, G., Camarda, R., Fogassi, L., Gentilucci, M., Luppino, G. and Matelli, M. (1988) Functional organization of inferior area 6 in the macaque monkey: II. Area F5 and the control of distal movements. *Experimental Brain Research*, 71: 491–507.

Rizzolatti, G., Fadiga, L., Fogassi, L. and Gallese, V. (1996a) Premotor cortex and the recognition of motor actions. *Cognitive Brain Research* 3: 131–141.

Rizzolatti, G., Fadiga, L., Matelli, M. *et al.* (1996b) Localization of grasp representation in humans by PET: 1. Observation versus execution. *Experimental Brain Research*, 111: 246–252.

Rizzolatti, G., Fogassi, L. and Gallese, V. (2001) Neurophysiological mechanisms underlying the understanding and imitation of action. *Nature Reviews Neuroscience*, 2: 661–670.

Rizzolatti, G., Fogassi, L. and Gallese, V. (2002) Motor and cognitive functions of the ventral premotor cortex. *Current Opinion in Neurobiology*, 12: 149–154.

Rizzolatti, G., Fogassi, L. and Gallese, V. (2004) Cortical mechanisms subserving object grasping, action understanding, and imitation. In M. S. Gazzaniga (ed.) *The Cognitive Neurosciences III*, pp. 427–440. MIT Press, Cambridge, MA.

Rozin, R., Haidt, J. and McCauley, C. R. (2000) Disgust. In M. Lewis and J. M. Haviland-Jones (eds) *Handbook of emotion*, 2nd edn, pp. 637–653. Guilford Press, New York.

Royet, J. P., Hudry, J., Zald, D. H. *et al.* (2001) Functional neuroanatomy of different olfactory judgments. *Neuroimage*, 13: 506–519.

Schienle, A., Stark, R., Walter, B. *et al.* (2002) The insula is not specifically involved in disgust processing: an fMRI study. *Neuroreport*, 13: 2023–2026.

Showers, M. J. C. and Lauer, E. W. (1961) Somatovisceral motor patterns in the insula. *Journal of Comparative Neurology*, 117: 107–115.

Singer, T., Seymour, B, O'Doherty, J., Kaube, H., Dolan, R. J. and Frith, C. D. (2004) Empathy for pain involves the affective but not the sensory components of pain. *Science*, 303: 1157–1162.

Small, D. M., Gregory, M. D., Mak, Y. E., Gitelman, D., Mesulam, M. M. and Parrish, T. (2003) Dissociation of neural representation of intensity and affective valuation in human gustation. *Neuron*, 39: 701–711.

Sprengelmeyer, R., Rausch, M., Eysel, U. T. and Przuntek, H. (1998) Neural structures associated with recognition of facial expressions of basic emotions. *Proceedings Biological Sciences of the Royal Society of London*, 265: 1927–1931.

Strafella, A. P. and Paus, T. (2000) Modulation of cortical excitability during action observation: a transcranial magnetic stimulation study. *NeuroReport*, 11: 2289–2292.

Tettamanti, M., Buccino, G., Saccuman, M. C. *et al.* (2005) Listening to action-related sentences activates fronto-parietal motor circuits. *Journal of Cognitive Neuroscience*, 17: 273–281.

Umiltà, M. A., Kohler, E., Gallese, V. *et al.* (2001) "I know what you are doing": a neurophysiological study. *Neuron*, 32: 91–101.

Van Hoof, J. A. R. A. M. (1967) The facial displays of the catarrhine monkeys and apes. In D. Morris (ed.) *Primate Ethology*, pp. 7–68. Weidenfield & Nicolson, London.

Visalberghi, E. and Fragaszy, D. M. (2002) "Do monkeys ape?" Ten years after. In K. Dautenhahn and C. Nehaniv (eds) *Imitation in Animals and Artifacts*. MIT Press, Cambridge, MA.

Watkins, K. E., Strafella, A. P. and Paus, T. (2003) Seeing and hearing speech excites the motor system involved in speech production. *Neuropsychologia*, 41: 989–994.

Wicker, B., Keysers, C., Plailly, J., Royet, J. P., Gallese, V. and Rizzolatti, G. (2003) Both of us disgusted in my insula: the common neural basis of seeing and feeling disgust. *Neuron*, 40: 655–664.

Yokochi, H., Tanaka, M., Kumashiro, M. and Iriki, A. (2003) Inferior parietal somatosensory neurons coding face-hand coordination in Japanese macaques. *Somatosensory Motor Research*, 20: 115–125.

Zald, D. H. and Pardo, J. V. (2000) Functional neuroimaging of the olfactory system in humans. *International Journal of Psychophysiology*, 36: 165–181.

Zald, D. H., Lee, J. T., Fluegel, K. W. and Pardo, J. V. (1998) Aversive gustatory stimulation activates limbic circuits in humans. *Brain* 121: 1143–1154.

CHAPTER 15

Mechanisms of ecological rationality: heuristics and environments that make us smart

Peter M. Todd and Gerd Gigerenzer

15.1. Introduction: making quick decisions well

A high fly ball comes down towards centre field. Wind is blowing, the ball is spinning, and gravity exerts its parabolic pull, but still the fielder smoothly runs to make the catch. A diner confronts two dishes at a new restaurant, ignores the extensive menu descriptions and offer of input from the waiter, and quickly decides to go with the one she recognizes. A doctor just starting a rotation in a different city assesses a man brought to the emergency room, checks two vital signs without consulting the banks of sophisticated test machinery available, and makes a fast assignment of the patient to the operating room, saving a life.

Most of the decisions we make spring relatively effortlessly from our minds. We make snap judgments, jump to conclusions, choose quickly—indeed, if a decision takes more than minimal time and effort, it becomes worthy of comment (and possibly aversive). And yet, our frequent fast decisions end up working out more often than not—the fielder catches the ball, the diner chooses an acceptable meal, the doctor saves her patient. We do not typically need to gather a great amount of information and process it extensively, as traditional maxims of rationality would instruct us to do, before successfully making up our minds. How are we able to make adaptive choices in our more limited fashion?

The answer is that we can often draw on a collection of simple 'fast and frugal' heuristics for inference and choice that enable us to make quick and accurate decisions using little information (making them frugal) and little mental computation (making them fast). These and other mechanisms filling the mind's *adaptive toolbox* (Gigerenzer *et al.*, 1999) can accomplish their trick of good performance without high information and processing demands because of three main features. First, they are built on evolved capacities that synthesize multiple environmental features into single cues for decision making, and simple building blocks that limit how many cues are considered. Second, they exploit the structure of information patterns in the environment to let the world do some of their work, allowing the internal mechanisms to be simpler and quicker. Third, their use of less information enables heuristics to avoid overfitting meaningless noise in the environment and leads to better generalization to new situations.

Thus, the fielder is able to catch balls without stopping to account for wind speed, drag, spin, and the like by using a *gaze heuristic* that capitalizes on our underlying evolved ability to track moving objects and uses the angle of gaze between ball and horizon as the only piece of information to guide where to run (Raab and Gigerenzer, 2005). The diner exploits only her pattern of systematic recognition of some foods and not others to reason with the *recognition heuristic* and conclude that those dishes she recognizes are known to her because they are more often talked about and hence probably tastier (Todd, 2000). And the doctor uses the *'Take The Best' heuristic* or decision tree to check only those cues necessary to make a quick diagnosis, focusing on the most valid pieces of information and ignoring the other possible tests that may not generalize well from her previous experience in another city (Gigerenzer *et al.*, 1999).

In this chapter, we describe some of these simple heuristics that we believe the human mind has evolved to use in particular circumstances, and the pressures on decision making that may have shaped the contents of the mind's adaptive toolbox. We begin by considering the notion of bounded rationality—the assumption that human cognition is constrained by limits of some sort—and just which types of bounds have been most important in cognitive evolution. We then look at the components that our decision mechanisms are built up from and examine how they enable simple and fast choices to be made. Next, we present four main classes of simple heuristics that have been explored in depth: ignorance-based heuristics, one-reason decision mechanisms, elimination strategies, and satisficing search methods. Finally, we consider some of the challenges facing the understanding of simple heuristics and why they can work so well.

15.2. **From bounded rationality to ecological rationality**

Traditional notions of *unbounded rationality* have posited that the appropriate way to make decisions is to gather all of the available information, weight each piece appropriately according to its importance for the current decision, and combine all this weighted information in an optimal fashion to find the option with the greatest utility (Edwards and Fasolo, 2001); furthermore, it is commonly assumed that people behave as if they are maximizing their utility in this way. But to make choices in most common everyday contexts, real decision makers must employ limited search for information and limited processing of what they find, because they have only a finite amount of time, knowledge, attention, or money to spend on a particular decision (Todd, 2001). As such, people are usually acting in accordance with what Herbert Simon called *bounded rationality*—making decisions within the bounds of time, information, and computational ability that the task environment and human cognitive capacities impose on us (Simon, 1990). The notion of unbounded rationality, following the tenets of logic and probability theory, is a convenient fiction for constructing mathematical models of behaviour, but to understand real human behaviour, we must consider the actual bounded psychological processes that guide our decision making.

But what are the most critical bounds on our cognitive mechanisms? The usual assumption is that human cognitive abilities are bounded by the hard mental constraints of our limited memory and information-processing power. However, given sufficient adaptive pressure to succeed in complex tasks, evolution could build complex information-processing structures to handle those tasks. That is, cognitive limitations on memory and processing could be circumvented over the course of evolution, if the benefit outweighs the cost. For instance, our ability to store and retrieve information from memory could be much greater, as the skills of mnemonists attest (Luria, 1968). The amount of information that can be held and processed in working memory can be greatly increased through practice (Ericsson and Kintsch, 1995). And the processing of information itself could be more rapid and sophisticated, as evidenced both by the great processing power that the visual system already possesses, and by the ability of some individuals to solve complex problems rapidly that most of us would find impossible (e.g. chess masters, or horse-race experts—see Ceci and Liker, 1986). Thus, human cognitive boundaries could have been extended, if that had been adaptive for our ancestors. What then *did* lead to our highly constrained decision mechanisms in so many situations?

This typical assumption, that the constraints bounding our rationality are internal ones such as limited memory and computational power, leaves out most of the picture—namely, the external world and the constraints that it imposes on decision makers. There are two particularly important classes of constraints that stem from the nature of the world. First, because the external world is uncertain—we never face exactly the same situation twice—our mental mechanisms must be robust, that is, they must generalize well from old instances to new ones. One of the best ways to be robust is to be simple, for instance, by employing a mechanism containing few parameters. As a consequence, external uncertainty can impose a bound of simplicity on our mental mechanisms.

Second, because the world is competitive and time is short, our decision mechanisms must generally be fast. The more time we spend on a given decision, the less time we have available for other activities, and the less likely we are to outcompete our rivals in the endless arms race of life. Because it takes time to find and assess the informative cues or choice alternatives (external in the world or internal in memory) we need to make a decision; there is pressure to base decisions on fewer cues. And even if the search for more information could be accomplished quickly, it might not do the decision maker much good: cues are often highly intercorrelated (Brunswik, 1943), so that searching for additional cues provides rapidly diminishing returns in terms of useful data. Thus, to be fast, we must minimize the information or alternatives we search for in making our decisions. In other words, the external world also constrains us to be frugal in what we search for.

But the external world does not just impose the bounds of simplicity, speed, and frugality on us—it also provides the means for staying within these bounds. A decision mechanism can stay simple and robust by relying on some of its work being done by the external world—that is, by counting on the presence of certain useful patterns of information in the environment. Some observable cues are useful indicators of particular aspects of the world, such as red colour usually indicating ripe fruit. Our minds are built to exploit such patterns and thereby reduce the need for gathering and processing extra information. As we will show in the following sections, heuristics that use just a little of the patterned information and process it in simple ways can make decisions that are fast, accurate, and adaptive. However, as research in both evolutionary psychology and the heuristics-and-biases programme has demonstrated, the reliance on particular expected information patterns can lead us astray if we are presented with environments that violate our expectations (such as environments where fatty foods are readily obtained, or where the representativeness of the choices we encounter in a laboratory setting are made to violate distributions familiar from daily life). Adaptive behaviour emerges just when the mechanisms of the mind are properly matched to the (information) structures of the environment—producing what we call *ecological rationality*.

The importance of looking at the world to understand the mind has long been appreciated, though not very widely. Charles Darwin held that environmental forces had shaped human behaviour through natural selection, leading to the modern call by evolutionary psychologists to look to our ancestral world for the problems our mind is designed to solve. Egon Brunswik, half a century ago, urged studying the array of noisy cues available in the environment and how the mind adjusts its use of them, like a husband and wife coming to mutual agreement; Roger Shepard spoke of the mind more as a mirror, reflecting long-standing physical aspects of the world such as the 24-hour light–dark cycle (Brunswik, 1943; Shepard, 2001). Herbert Simon (1990) proposed the metaphor of the mind and world fitting together like the blades of a pair of scissors—the two must be well-matched for effective behaviour to be produced. In each case, looking for structure in the world will help us find corresponding structure in the mind, and considering the latter without the former, like a solitary husband or single scissor-blade, can lead to much misapplied effort.

Research on ecological rationality builds on these foundations to create a framework for understanding how patterns of information in the world can be exploited by decision mechanisms in the head to produce adaptive behaviour (Gigerenzer *et al.*, 1999; Todd *et al.*, in press). Rather than studying how the mind may employ or deviate from unbounded logical rationality via domain-general, normatively optimal reasoning systems, bounded ecological rationality explores how the mind uses simple, domain-specific decision heuristics that expect the world to do some of the work in providing useful structure for making choices. The fact that there is structure to be relied on in the world implies that the mind can get away with using less extensive, though more problem-specific, computations, leading to an emphasis on studying simple, psychologically plausible heuristics. In this view, a decision mechanism cannot be deemed good or bad on its own—it is only the match between a mechanism and an environment in which it is employed that can be assessed as yielding good or bad performance. This notion of mind–world match is missing from most logical and mathematical principles of rationality and their corresponding theories of cognition, which posit what is correct behaviour independent of any application domain.

How is ecological rationality possible? That is, how can fast and frugal heuristics work as well as they do and escape the trade-offs between different real-world criteria including speed and accuracy? The main reason for their success is that they make a trade-off on another dimension: that of generality versus specificity. While internal criteria for the coherence of decisions are very general—logical consistency, for instance, can be applied to any domain—the correspondence criteria that measure a heuristic's performance against the real world require much more domain-specific solutions. What works to make quick and accurate inferences in one domain may well not work in another. Thus, different environments can have different specific fast and frugal heuristics that exploit their particular information structure to make adaptive decisions. But specificity can also be a danger: if a different heuristic were required for every slightly different decision-making environment, we would need an unworkable multitude

of heuristics to reason with, and we would not be able to generalize to previously unencountered environments. Fast and frugal heuristics can avoid this trap by their very simplicity, which allows them to be robust in the face of environmental change and enables them to generalize well to new situations.

Robustness goes hand in hand with speed, accuracy, and especially information frugality. Simple heuristics can reduce overfitting (focusing too much on the specific details in a particular data set) by ignoring the noise inherent in many cues and looking instead for the 'swamping forces' reflected in the most important cues. Thus, simply using only one or a few of the most useful cues can automatically yield robustness—more information, like more processing, is not necessarily better (Hertwig and Todd, 2003). Furthermore, important cues are likely to remain important. The informative relationships in the environment are likely to hold true when the environment changes. Because of this pattern, fast and frugal heuristics that pay attention to systematic informative cues while overlooking more variable uninformative cues can ride out environmental change without suffering much decrement in performance.

The study of ecological rationality thus requires analysing the structure of environments, the structure of heuristics, and the match between them. The research programme proposed by Gigerenzer *et al.* (1999) for studying the simple ecologically rational heuristics that humans and animals use involves (i) proposing and specifying computational models of candidate simple heuristics, (ii) analysing the environmental structures in which they perform well, (iii) testing their performance in real-world environments (often via computer simulation), and (iv) determining whether and when people really use these heuristics (both experimentally in the laboratory and empirically in the field). This process is similar to that proposed for studying the Darwinian algorithms of evolutionary psychology (Cosmides and Tooby, 1987). We now turn to the first step in this process, exploring the components that go into a proposed heuristic model, before considering some specific heuristics and the ways they have been tested in the further steps of this research programme.

15.3. Creating simple heuristics from capacities and building blocks

To study particular heuristics in detail, computational models must be developed that specify the precise steps of information gathering and processing that are involved in generating a decision, allowing the heuristic to be instantiated as a computer program. In particular, simple fast and frugal heuristics are made up of building blocks that guide the search for alternatives, information, or both, stop that search, and make a decision. But 'below' these building blocks comes a foundation of evolved capacities that provides many of the cues that the building blocks (and heuristics) process. This evolved foundation distinguishes human and other animal minds from artificial computational models that focus on abstract information-processing abilities.

15.3.1. Evolved capacities

The various simple heuristics that are built up from building blocks and other nested heuristics can all be thought of as making up part of the adaptive toolbox: the collection of specialized cognitive mechanisms that evolution has built into the human mind for specific domains of inference and reasoning (Gigerenzer *et al.*, 1999; see also Cosmides and Tooby, 1992; Payne *et al.*, 1993). The adaptive toolbox contains all manner of psychological (as opposed to morphological or physiological) adaptations. These include so-called 'lower-order' perceptual and memory processes that can be fairly automatic, such as depth perception, auditory scene analysis, and face recognition, as well as 'higher-order' processes that are based on the 'lower' processes and can be at least partly accessible to consciousness. Within the class of higher-order mental processes fall fast and frugal heuristics for decision making, which themselves often call upon lower-order processes of cue perception and memory.

The lower-order processes are typically evolved capacities that operate quickly and effortlessly to distill multiple pieces of information from the environment or from memory into more compact representations, often even single cues, that can be used in further decision making. There are many of these capacities; here we list just a few for illustration, grouping them into rough classes. Among search capacities are exploring (quasi-random search for information), tracking (following a specific moving object), and observing other people (vicarious search). Memory capacities include recognition (noticing that one has seen/heard/smelled an object before), recall (when knowledge beyond mere recognition comes to mind about an encountered object), and forgetting (losing information from memory). Learning capacities cover, among other things, Pavlovian and operant conditioning (e.g. learning to avoid unpleasant stimuli), preparedness (enabling one-trial learning of evolutionarily important stimulus–reaction associations), and imitation (copying the behaviour of others). And basic evolved social capacities, while perhaps not being lower-order in the same sense (and themselves being built on other primitives such as face recognition and memory for features of individuals), may include reciprocal altruism and ability to trust (cooperating with non-related others to achieve a common goal), reputation memory (ability to recall an individual's relative score or rank on a socially important trait), and group identification (aligning one's values and identity to that of a group).

Lower-order perceptual and memory processes such as these are complex and difficult to unravel, in part because they may make use of massively parallel computations. No one has yet managed to build a machine that recognizes faces as well as a 2-year-old child. Now consider a higher-order decision mechanism that makes inferences based on these processes, the recognition heuristic mentioned earlier. This fast and frugal heuristic uses recognition to make rapid inferences about unknown aspects of the world: for instance, food whose taste one recognizes is probably safer than unrecognized food, and a university whose name one has heard of probably provides a more prestigious education than one whose name is unfamiliar. Although the mechanisms of recognition memory may be intricate and complex, the recognition heuristic can be described as an algorithm just a few steps long. We do not need to know precisely how recognition memory works to describe a heuristic that relies on recognition. This example illustrates an apparently paradoxical thesis: higher-order cognitive mechanisms can often be modelled by simpler algorithms than can lower-order mechanisms. This thesis is not new, having been proposed in various forms over the past century (e.g. by proponents of the Würzburg school of psychology in the early 1900s—see Kusch, 1999). But it is central to the discussion of when we should postulate simple versus complex decision mechanisms in the adaptive toolbox.

15.3.2. **Building blocks**

Our evolved capacities provide our decision mechanisms with inputs distilled and compiled from multiple environmental features. The decision mechanisms in the adaptive toolbox, including simple heuristics, process those information inputs through a series of steps that can be characterized in many instances as three types of building blocks: for guiding information search, stopping that search, and making the decision on the basis of the search results.

15.3.2.1. Building blocks for guiding search

Decisions must be made between alternatives, and based on information about those alternatives. In different situations, those alternatives and pieces of information may need to be found through active search. The building blocks for guiding search, whether across alternatives or information, are what give search its direction (if it has one). For instance, search for cues can be simply random, or in the order of some precomputed criterion related to their usefulness, or based on a recollection about which cues worked previously when making the same decision. Search for alternatives can similarly be random or ordered. Fast and frugal search-guiding principles do not use extensive computations or knowledge to figure out where to look next.

15.3.2.2. Building blocks for stopping search

To fit within the temporal limitations of the human mind, search for alternatives or information must be terminated at some point. Moreover, owing to the computational limitations of boundedly rational agents, the method for determining when to stop search should not be overly complicated. For example, one simple stopping rule is to cease searching for information and make a decision as soon as the first cue or reason that favours one alternative is found (as embodied in one-reason decision making, described below). This and other cue-based stopping rules do not need to compute an optimal cost–benefit trade-off for determining when enough information has been found; in fact, they need not compute any costs or benefits at all. For search among alternatives, simple aspiration-level stopping rules can be used (see Section 15.4.4 below on satisficing search).

15.3.2.3. Building blocks for decision making

Once search has been guided to find the appropriate alternatives or information and has then been stopped, a final type of building block can be called upon to make the decision or inference based on the results of the search. These components can also be very simple and computationally bounded. For instance, a decision or inference can be based on only one cue or reason, whatever the total number of cues found during search (as in the ignorance-based and one-reason decision mechanisms). Such single-cue decision making does not need to weight or combine cues, and so no common currency between cues need be determined. Decisions can also be made through a simple elimination process, in which alternatives are thrown out by successive cues until only one final choice remains (see Section 15.4.3 on elimination heuristics).

15.3.3. **Heuristics**

These building blocks can be put together to form a variety of fast and frugal heuristics. Given that the mind is a biological rather than a purely logical entity, formed through a process of successive accrual, borrowing, and refinement of components, it seems reasonable to assume that new heuristics are built from the parts of old ones, rather than from scratch (Pinker, 1998). Following this assumption, two main methods can be used to construct computational models of fast and frugal heuristics: combining building blocks and nesting existing heuristics. Building blocks can be combined in multiple ways, though not arbitrarily: for instance, a fast and frugal heuristic for two-alternative choice that stops information search at the first cue on which the alternatives differ must also use a decision principle based on one-reason decision making. Whole fast and frugal heuristics can themselves be combined by nesting one inside another. As an example, the recognition heuristic can also serve as the first step of one-reason decision heuristics that draw on other capacities beyond recognition, such as recall memory. Recognition memory develops earlier than recall memory both ontogenetically and evolutionarily, and the nesting of heuristics can similarly be seen as analogous to the addition of a new adaptation on top of an existing one.

Heuristics are the most flexible of the contents of the adaptive toolbox. This is because the heuristics, not the evolved capacities or building blocks, act directly on the environment and hence need to be adaptive and adapted. The flexibility of a given heuristic seems to be linked with the way it has entered into the adaptive toolbox. Evolution leads to the most inflexible heuristics, as the unconscious inferences of the gaze heuristic and other perceptual heuristics illustrate. Social and cultural learning leads to more flexible use of heuristics, applying them in different domains according to what others have found to be useful. Finally, individual learning, such as reinforcement learning, seems to lead to the most context-sensitive and rapidly adjusted use of heuristics (Rieskamp and Otto, 2006), which is highly dependent on the specific circumstances of the learned task environment.

15.4. Four families of simple heuristics

The decision-making building blocks just described can be put together to form classes or families of heuristics whose members are related by the particular search, stop, or decision rules they use. In this section we briefly introduce four such families of heuristics (out of many possible) covering decision situations that vary in the amount of information available, the number of options to choose between, and the distribution of options in time or space. These algorithmic models are intended to capture how real minds make decisions under constraints of limited time and knowledge.

15.4.1. Ignorance-based decision mechanisms

One of the simplest forms of decision that can be made is to select one option from two possibilities, according to some criterion on which the two can be compared. What simple cognitive mechanisms can be used to make this type of decision? This will depend on the amount and type of information that is available in the environment. If the only information available is whether or not each possibility has ever been encountered before, then the decision maker can do little better than rely on his or her own partial ignorance, choosing either recognized options or unrecognized ones. For heuristics applicable to such situations, their information-search building block merely specifies that recognition should be assessed for the alternatives being compared; the search-stopping building block limits consideration to this recognition information alone; and the decision building block indicates exactly how recognition information determines the final choice. This 'ignorance-based reasoning' is embodied in the recognition heuristic (Goldstein and Gigerenzer, 1999, 2002), which uses the following decision rule: when choosing between two objects (according to some criterion), if one is recognized and the other is not, then select the former. For instance, Norway rats have evolved to behave according to a rule of this type, preferring to eat things they recognize through past experience with other rats (e.g. items they have smelled on the breath of others) over novel items (Galef, 1987).

Following the recognition heuristic will be ecologically rational—that is, will yield correct responses more often than would random choice—in those decision environments in which exposure to different possibilities is positively correlated with their ranking along the decision criterion being used. Thus, the rats' food preference copying presumably evolved because the things that other rats have eaten (i.e. recognized items) are more often palatable than are random (unrecognized) items sampled from the environment. Such useable correlations are likely to be present for species with social information exchange where important environmental objects are communicated and unimportant ones are ignored, as well as for species in environments where important environmental objects are simply encountered more often or earlier in life.

People have been shown to make decisions in accordance with the recognition heuristic in domains such as choosing the larger of two cities, the deadlier of two diseases, or the more successful of two sports teams (Goldstein and Gigerenzer, 2002), where socially transmitted information is indeed typically about items at one end of the criterion range (large cities or successful teams). Recent research has also shown that people put considerable stock in the value of recognition information for making decisions, even being swayed more in a group decision setting by colleagues who only recognize one available option (and choose that option on the basis of their recognition) than by those who have more information and recognize all available options (Reimer and Katsikopoulos, 2004). Situations in which the recognition heuristic can be applied arise in daily life as well: companies vie for name recognition among consumers in the hope that this will guide their purchase decisions (Borges *et al.*, 1999). In fact, in the modern environment, our recognition memory has become rather easily manipulable by the steady stream of media we are exposed to. Whereas in ancestral environments, we would only recognize people whom we had actually encountered in person, television shows and movies can now trick us into thinking the faces we recognize belong to people we actually know (Kanazawa, 2002). As a consequence, using the recognition heuristic may no longer be ecologically rational in some settings, particularly those where other agents aim to influence what we recognize.

15.4.2. **One-reason decision mechanisms**

Of course, we often have more information than just recognition available for making our decisions. What kinds of fast and frugal heuristics are appropriate in situations like the following? Imagine trying to decide between two restaurants

for taking a guest to dinner. The traditional and normatively prescribed method would be to collect all the information or cues that you know or could find out about each restaurant, such as the average meal cost, distance from home, and amount of garlic in the dishes; then weight each of these cues by its importance for this decision; and finally combine all the weighted values for each alternative to come up with a final total criterion value for each. Whichever restaurant has the higher final criterion value is the one to go to, according to this weighted-additive approach to computing the expected utility of the two choices (Edwards and Fasolo, 2001).

A simpler and faster method is the following. Consider a single cue for the two alternatives, such as meal cost. Does this cue distinguish between the restaurants? If it does, then stop and choose the restaurant pointed to by the cue (e.g. the cheaper one, or the more expensive one, depending on if you want to conserve your resources or impress the guest). If the first cue does not distinguish between the alternatives, then consider a second cue, such as distance. If that cue distinguishes, then stop at this point and go with the indicated choice (e.g. the nearer restaurant). If not, consider a third cue, and so on, stopping this search for cues at the first distinguishing one found and using that cue alone to make the final decision. Mechanisms that operate in this way are called 'one-reason decision heuristics', because their final decision is made on the basis of a single cue or reason alone (Gigerenzer and Goldstein, 1999). A one-reason decision heuristic works as follows.

1. Select a cue dimension using some search building block and look for the corresponding cue values of each option.

2. Compare the two options on their values for that cue dimension.

3. If they differ, then stop (this is the stop-search building block) and choose the option with the cue value indicating a greater value on the choice criterion (the decision building block).

4. If the options do not differ, then return to the beginning of this loop (Step 1) to look for another cue dimension.

Such a heuristic will often have to look up more than one cue before making a decision, but the simple stopping rule (in Step 3) ensures that as few cues as possible will be sought, minimizing the time needed for information search. Furthermore, ultimately only a single cue will be used to determine the choice, minimizing the amount of computation that must be done.

To finish specifying a particular simple heuristic of this type, we must also determine exactly how cue dimensions are 'looked for' in Step 1—that is, we must choose a specific information search building block. For instance, the Take The Best heuristic searches for cues in the order of their validity—that is, their correlation with the decision criterion, while the Minimalist heuristic selects cues in a random order (Gigerenzer and Goldstein, 1996, 1999). Again, both stop their information search as soon as a cue is found that allows a decision to be made between the two options. Particular cue orders will influence just how quickly and how accurately a decision can be made. (The open question of determining which cues and cue order to use will be considered below.)

Despite (or often because of) their simplicity and disregard for most of the available information, these two fast and frugal heuristics can make very accurate choices. A set of 20 environments was collected to test the performance of these heuristics, varying in number of objects and number of available cues, and ranging in content from the German cities data set mentioned earlier to fish fertility to high-school drop-out rates (Czerlinski *et al.*, 1999). The decision accuracies of Take The Best and Minimalist were compared with those of two more traditional decision mechanisms that use all available information and combine it in more or less sophisticated ways: multiple regression, which weights and sums all cues in an optimal linear fashion, and Dawes's Rule, which counts up the positive and negative cues and subtracts the latter from the former. The two fast and frugal heuristics always came close to, and often exceeded, the performance of the traditional algorithms when all were tested on the data they were trained on (data fitting). This surprising performance on the part of Take The Best and Minimalist was achieved even though they only looked through a third of the cues on average (and only decided using one of them), while multiple regression and Dawes's Rule used them all.

The advantages of simplicity grew in the more behaviourally important test of generalization performance, where the decision mechanisms were assessed on a portion of each data set that they had not seen during training; in that case, Take The Best outperformed all three other algorithms by a clear margin. Thus, making good decisions need not rely on the standard rational approach of collecting all available information and combining it according to the relative importance of each cue—simply betting on one good reason, even one selected at random, can provide a competitive level of accuracy in a range of environments. Just what environments allow one-reason decision mechanisms to excel—that is, what conditions lead them to be ecologically rational—is still being explored, but some are known: Take The Best, for instance, seems to do well in environments where cue validities are distributed in a highly skewed fashion, with some cues being much more useful than others (Martignon and Hoffrage, 2002), and where learning samples are small.

Not only are simple one-reason decision mechanisms accurate and robust, they also correspond to how people (and other animals) make decisions in a variety of circumstances. People use these fast and frugal algorithms in environments that have the appropriate structure, even when they must first learn how the environment is structured (Rieskamp and Otto, 2006). Heuristics such as Take The Best are also particularly used where information is costly or time consuming to acquire (Rieskamp and Hoffrage, 1999; Bröder, 2000; Newell and Shanks, 2003), whether the costs come from searching for cues in the environment or from searching in memory (Bröder and Schiffer, 2003).

There is a problem, though, in applying one-reason decision strategies: how can we tell what cues a heuristic should use, and in what order? Take The Best's validity-ordered cue search does considerably better than Minimalist's random search—but how do we come to know a more-or-less validity-ordered set of cues? In evolutionarily important decision contexts like choosing a mate or selecting something to eat, we might have some built-in knowledge of valid cues to use, such as facial symmetry or sweet taste. But we are unlikely to have innately specified cues to use, for instance, in deciding between restaurants. For decisions like this in modern environments, people must learn what cues are most useful or valid. This can be done through individual experience using simple learning rules, for instance, keeping an ordered list of possible cues and moving a cue up in the list every time it leads to a correct decision and down in the list every time it fails (Dieckmann and Todd, 2004). While such learning could happen relatively quickly (i.e. with few learning trials), in some cases people can arrive at a good cue order more quickly by learning it socially from other decision makers, or through culturally transmitted rules.

15.4.3. Heuristics for multiple-option choices

When there are more than two options to choose from, then more than a single binary cue must typically be used to determine a single choice. But here, too, in these situations of multi-attribute decision making it is possible to reach quick decisions using a minimal amount of information, rather than gathering and combining a large number of cues or attributes. A fast and frugal approach to these decision situations is to use the process of elimination, as incorporated by Tversky (1972) in his Elimination By Aspects (or EBA) choice mechanism. For instance, if there are several restaurants to be decided among, first select a cue (or aspect) dimension somehow, and a way of using that cue to discard some of the available options. In the case of EBA, the cues are selected probabilistically, and a threshold is set for determining which options are eliminated from further consideration, such as discarding all restaurants that are more than 10 kilometres away. If there are still multiple options left to be considered, then select another cue and use it to eliminate some more possibilities—such as all restaurants not serving fish tonight. Proceed in this way, using successive cues to whittle down the set of remaining options, until only a single one remains, which is the final choice. Tversky found that this process describes well what people do in these types of preferential choice tasks.

A similar elimination process can be used to categorize objects or stimuli, where the task can

be conceived of as deciding which of several possible categories the object best fits into (Berretty et al., 1999). When information may be difficult to come by, and decisions should be made quickly, a fast and frugal categorization process can be adaptive. Consider the situation of trying to decide about another's intentions as that person approaches. Does this person want to greet me, dance with me, or take my wallet? How can one judge this, especially if the person is a stranger and is not announcing any aims verbally or facially? One way is to come to a quick first guess on the basis of how the person is moving, that is, using motion cues alone and an elimination process to limit the number of cues considered, to make a rapid yet accurate categorization (Blythe et al., 1999; Barrett et al., 2005).

Estimation is another related task that can also be performed accurately with few cues by a simple algorithm that exploits environments with a particular structure. The QuickEst heuristic (Hertwig et al., 1999) is designed to estimate the values of objects along some criterion while using as little information as possible. To estimate the criterion value of a particular object, the heuristic looks through the available cues or features in a criterion-determined order, until it comes to the first one that the object does not possess. At this point, QuickEst stops searching for any further information and produces an estimate based on criterion values associated with the absence of the last cue. QuickEst proves to be fast and frugal, as well as accurate, in environments characterized by a distribution of criterion values in which small values are common and big values are rare (a so-called 'J-shaped' distribution). Such distributions characterize a variety of naturally occurring phenomena including many formed by accretionary growth (e.g. cities, some businesses, etc.).

15.4.4. Satisficing heuristics for sequential choices

The heuristics presented so far assume that all of the possible options to be chosen between are presently available to the decision maker. But a different strategy is called for when alternatives (as opposed to information about the alternatives) take time to find, appearing sequentially over an extended period. This is an important type of decision to study, because sequential search is ubiquitous, occurring whenever resources being sought are distributed in time or space and so cannot be considered (or at least not encountered) simultaneously. Searching for mates or friends, houses or habitats, jobs, parking spaces, shopping bargains, or restaurants to eat at all involve sequential decisions of this sort. The problem is that, whatever option you currently have available—for instance, the restaurant that you are standing in front of—another possibly better option could become available in the future, so how can you decide when to stop searching and stick with the current (or some previous) option?

In this type of choice task, a fast and frugal reasoner need not (only) limit information search, but (also) must have a stopping rule for ending the search for alternatives themselves. Here, Herbert Simon's (1955, 1990) notion of a satisficing heuristic is applicable: an aspiration level is set for the selection criterion being used, and the search for alternatives is stopped as soon as the aspiration is met. Simple mechanisms can be used to set the aspiration level in the first place, such as checking the first few alternatives and taking the best value seen in that set as the level to beat in further search (Todd and Miller, 1999). The trick here is to balance the desire for a short, fast and frugal search on the one hand (achieved by checking as few initial alternatives as possible), against the need for enough information about the potential alternatives to set an appropriate aspiration level on the other hand (achieved by checking as many initial alternatives as possible). People seem relatively adept at striking this kind of balance (Seale and Rapoport, 1997; Dudey and Todd, 2002).

But many sequential choice problems involve an added complication: they are two-sided, which means the searchers are being searched by others at the same time, and choice must therefore be mutual. Job applicants must select their employer and be selected in return; men and women on the marriage market must both decide to take the plunge together. This additional challenge can be solved by the searchers learning their own value or rank position within their pool of fellow searchers and using this self-knowledge to determine how high they should aim their search aspirations (Kalick and Hamilton, 1986), rather than merely setting an aspiration level based on the values of a small sample of available options, as in the one-sided approaches covered above. Todd and Miller (1999) presented a range of simple heuristics that do just this, for instance, heuristics for learning one's mate value through the acceptances and rejections encountered during an adolescent dating period or more generally a phase 1 search period. These heuristics, like the one-sided mechanisms already mentioned, can perform well with little search, quickly learning appropriate aspiration levels based on the searcher's own quality. Evidence for their use can be obtained both via population-level demographic measures (Todd *et al.*, 2005a) and in laboratory experiments of sequential dating.

15.5. The challenge ahead for ecological rationality

Studying ecological rationality as the fit between structures in information-processing mechanisms in the mind and structures in information in the world gives us three things to focus on: the mind (decision heuristics), the world (information patterns), and how they can match. As we have shown in this chapter, the heuristics that have been studied so far cover a wide range of possible types of choice tasks that people face, such as choosing one option from two or more, or finding a good option from a sequence of alternatives. However, another way to think of the organization of the adaptive toolbox is in terms of content domains, such as heuristics for finding food or for choosing mates (Todd, 2000). Some of the same sorts of heuristics (e.g., satisficing mechanisms for sequential search) are, as indicated earlier, likely applied in multiple domains (e.g., in mate search and habitat search), so it will be beneficial to explore the adaptive toolbox from both the decision task and the content domain perspectives, combining cognitive psychology approaches with evolutionary psychology (Todd *et al.*, 2005).

To discover more about the tools in the mind's toolbox, we should also proceed in two additional directions. Delving downward, we need to expand our understanding of the set of building blocks and deeper evolved abilities (e.g., the capacity for recognition or for trust) that can combine to create decision mechanisms. Connecting upward, we must consider how the adaptive toolbox of heuristics for inference and preference ties in with other cognitive, memory, perceptual, and motor systems to produce adaptive behaviour (as has been done in implementing the recognition heuristic within a broader cognitive modelling framework, ACT-R—see Schooler and Hertwig, 2005).

As indicated in earlier examples, researchers have also started to put together a vocabulary for describing environment structures, for instance, in terms of cue validities and distributions of objects. But this effort is still largely incomplete and disconnected. Useful ways to describe psychologically relevant aspects of spatial structure, temporal patterns, and social environments must still be developed, or imported from other disciplines. And the different sources of environment structure—long-term physical and biological aspects of our world, social environments composed of other people, cultural and institutional structures created by others to influence us, and emergent patterns arising from the interactions of populations of individuals each following their own decision heuristics—must all be mapped out and placed in a coherent framework so that their commonalities and differences can be made evident.

The greatest challenge remains in tying the two types of structure, mental and environmental, together. Heuristics often lead to correct answers, but sometimes lead to errors, as emphasized in the heuristics-and-biases research tradition (Kahneman *et al.*, 1982); the work ahead needs to focus on when, where and why they succeed or fail—their ecological rationality. This is only possible if we have precise models of these heuristics, as in terms of the building blocks described earlier. Uncovering the ecological rationality of particular decision mechanisms can be a matter of predicting their performance based on how well their specific building blocks fit to certain information patterns, and then testing them via experimentation, simulation, or mathematical analysis in different environments. However, explaining *why* a heuristic matches some environments and

not others largely remains a conundrum at the centre of ongoing research (Todd *et al.*, in press).

The adaptive processes of evolution, learning, and culture have shaped human minds to be ecologically rational, relying on simple decision heuristics that confer the twin advantages of speed and accuracy in particular environments bearing exploitable patterns of information. Individuals can certainly be led to use heuristics in inappropriate environments and consequently make errors in reasoning, but this serves to show the boundaries of a mechanism's ecological rationality, rather than its irrationality. When mind and world fit together, the evolved capacities, building blocks, and simple heuristics in our adaptive toolbox can guide us to make good choices in a fast and frugal manner.

References

Barrett, H. C., Todd, P. M., Miller, G. F. and Blythe, P. W. (2005) Accurate judgments of intention from motion cues alone: a cross-cultural study. *Evolution and Human Behavior*, 26: 313–331.

Berretty, P. M., Todd, P. M. and Martignon, L. (1999) Categorization by elimination: using few cues to choose. In G. Gigerenzer, P. M. Todd and the ABC Research Group, *Simple Heuristics that Make Us Smart*, pp. 235–254. Oxford University Press, New York.

Blythe, P. W., Todd, P. M. and Miller, G. F. (1999) How motion reveals intention: Categorizing social interactions. In G. Gigerenzer, P. M. Todd and the ABC Research Group, *Simple Heuristics that Make Us Smart*, pp. 257–285. Oxford University Press, New York.

Borges, B., Goldstein, D. G., Ortmann, A. and Gigerenzer, G. (1999) Can ignorance beat the stock market? In G. Gigerenzer, P. M. Todd and the ABC Research Group, *Simple Heuristics that Make Us Smart*, pp. 59–72. Oxford University Press, New York.

Bröder, A. (2000) Assessing the empirical validity of the "Take The Best" heuristic as a model of human probabilistic inference. *Journal of Experimental Psychology: Learning, Memory, and Cognition*, 26: 1332–1346.

Bröder, A. and Schiffer, S. (2003) "Take the best" versus simultaneous feature matching: Probabilistic inferences from memory and effects of representation format. *Journal of Experimental Psychology: General*, 132: 277–293.

Brunswik, E. (1943) Organismic achievement and environmental probability. *Psychological Review*, 50: 255–272.

Ceci, S. J. and Liker, J. K. (1986) A day at the races: a study of IQ, expertise, and cognitive complexity. *Journal of Experimental Psychology: General*, 115: 255–266.

Cosmides, L. and Tooby, J. (1987) From evolution to behavior: evolutionary psychology as the missing link. In J. Dupré (ed.) *The Latest on the Best: Essays on Evolution and Optimization*, pp. 277–306. MIT Press/Bradford Books, Cambridge, MA.

Cosmides, L. and Tooby, J. (1992) Cognitive adaptations for social exchange. In J. Barkow, L. Cosmides and J. Tooby (eds) *The Adapted Mind: Evolutionary Psychology and the Generation of Culture*, pp. 163–228. Oxford University Press, New York.

Czerlinski, J., Gigerenzer, G. and Goldstein, D. G. (1999) How good are simple heuristics? In G. Gigerenzer, P. M. Todd and the ABC Research Group, *Simple Heuristics that Make Us Smart*, pp. 97–118. Oxford University Press, New York.

Dieckmann, A. and Todd, P. M. (2004) Simple ways to construct search orders. In K. Forbus, D. Gentner and T. Regier (eds) *Proceedings of the 26th Annual Conference of the Cognitive Science Society*, pp. 309–314. Lawrence Erlbaum, Mahwah, NJ.

Dudey, T. and Todd, P. M. (2002) Making good decisions with minimal information: simultaneous and sequential choice. *Journal of Bioeconomics*, 3: 195–215.

Edwards, W. and Fasolo, B. (2001) Decision technology. *Annual Review of Psychology*, 52: 581–606.

Ericsson, K. A. and Kintsch, W. (1995) Long-term working memory. *Psychological Review*, 102: 211–245.

Galef, B. G., Jr (1987) Social influences on the identification of toxic foods by Norway rats. *Animal Learning and Behavior*, 18: 199–205.

Gigerenzer, G. and Goldstein, D. G. (1996) Reasoning the fast and frugal way: models of bounded rationality. *Psychological Review*, 103: 650–669.

Gigerenzer, G. and Goldstein, D. G. (1999) Betting on one good reason: the take the best heuristic. In G. Gigerenzer, P. M. Todd and the ABC Research Group, *Simple Heuristics that Make Us Smart*, pp. 75–95. Oxford University Press, New York.

Gigerenzer, G., Todd, P. M. and the ABC Research Group (1999) *Simple Heuristics that Make Us Smart*. Oxford University Press, New York.

Goldstein, D. G. and Gigerenzer, G. (1999) The recognition heuristic: how ignorance makes us smart. In G. Gigerenzer, P. M. Todd and the ABC Research Group, *Simple Heuristics that Make Us Smart*, pp. 37–58. Oxford University Press, New York.

Goldstein, D. G. and Gigerenzer, G. (2002) Models of ecological rationality: the recognition heuristic. *Psychological Review*, 109: 75–90.

Hertwig, R. and Todd, P. M. (2003) More is not always better: the benefits of cognitive limits. In D. Hardman and L. Macchi (eds) *Thinking: Psychological Perspectives on Reasoning, Judgment and Decision Making*, pp. 213–231. Wiley, Chichester, UK.

Hertwig, R., Hoffrage, U. and Martignon, L. (1999) Quick estimation: letting the environment do some of the work. In G. Gigerenzer, P. M. Todd and the ABC Research Group, *Simple Heuristics that Make Us Smart*, pp. 209–234. Oxford University Press, New York.

Kahneman, D., Slovic, P. and Tversky, A. (1982) *Judgment under Uncertainty: Heuristics and Biases*. Cambridge University Press, Cambridge, UK.

Kalick, S. M. and Hamilton, T. E. (1986) The matching hypothesis reexamined. *Journal of Personality and Social Psychology*, 51: 673–682.

Kanazawa, S. (2002) Bowling with our imaginary friends. *Evolution and Human Behavior*, 23: 167–171.

Kusch, M. (1999) Psychological knowledge: a social history and philosophy. Routledge, London.

Luria, A. R. (1968) *The Mind of a Mnemonist*. (translated into English by L. Solotaroff). Basic Books, New York.

Martignon, L. and Hoffrage, U. (2002) Fast, frugal and fit: simple heuristics for paired comparison. *Theory and Decision*, 52: 29–71.

Newell, B. R. and Shanks, D. R. (2003) Take the best or look at the rest? Factors influencing "one-reason" decision-making. *Journal of Experimental Psychology: Learning, Memory, and Cognition*, 29: 53–65.

Payne, J. W., Bettman, J. R. and Johnson, E. J. (1993) *The Adaptive Decision Maker*. Cambridge University Press, New York.

Pinker, S. (1998) *How the Mind Works*. Norton, New York.

Raab, M. and Gigerenzer, G. (2005) Intelligence as smart heuristics. In R. J. Sternberg, J. Davidson and J. Pretz (eds), *Cognition and Intelligence*, pp. 188–207. Cambridge University Press, Cambridge, UK.

Reimer, T. and Katsikopoulos, K. V. (2004) The use of recognition in group decision-making. *Cognitive Science*, 28: 1009–1029.

Rieskamp, J. and Hoffrage, U. (1999) When do people use simple heuristics and how can we tell? In G. Gigerenzer, P. M. Todd and the ABC Research Group, *Simple Heuristics that Make Us Smart*, pp. 141–167. Oxford University Press, New York.

Rieskamp, J. and Otto, P. E. (2006) SSL: a theory of how people learn to select strategies. *Journal of Experimental Psychology: General*, 135: 207–236.

Schooler, L. J. and Hertwig, R. (2005) How forgetting aids heuristic inference. *Psychological Review*, 112: 610–628.

Seale, D. A. and Rapoport, A. (1997) Sequential decision making with relative ranks: an experimental investigation of the 'secretary problem'. *Organizational Behavior and Human Decision Processes*, 69: 221–236.

Shepard, R. N. (2001) Perceptual–cognitive universals as reflections of the world. *Behavioral and Brain Sciences*, 24: 581–601.

Simon, H. A. (1955) A behavioral model of rational choice. *Quarterly Journal of Economics*, 69: 99–118.

Simon, H. A. (1990) Invariants of human behavior. *Annual Review of Psychology*, 41: 1–19.

Todd, P. M. (2000) The ecological rationality of mechanisms evolved to make up minds. *American Behavioral Scientist*, 43: 940–956.

Todd, P. M. (2001) Fast and frugal heuristics for environmentally bounded minds. In G. Gigerenzer and R. Selten (eds), *Bounded Rationality: The Adaptive Toolbox* (Dahlem Workshop Report, pp. 51–70. MIT Press, Cambridge, MA.

Todd, P. M. and Miller, G. F. (1999) From pride and prejudice to persuasion: satisficing in mate search. In G. Gigerenzer, P. M. Todd and the ABC Research Group, *Simple Heuristics that Make Us Smart*, pp. 287–308. Oxford University Press, New York.

Todd, P. M., Billari, F. C. and Simāo, J. (2005a) Aggregate age-at-marriage patterns from individual mate-search heuristics. *Demography*, 42: 559–574.

Todd, P. M., Hertwig, R. and Hoffrage, U. (2005b) The evolutionary psychology of cognition. In D. M. Buss (ed.) *The Handbook of Evolutionary Psychology*, pp. 776–802. Wiley, Hoboken, NJ.

Todd, P. M., Gigerenzer, G. and the ABC Research Group (in press) *Ecological Rationality: Intelligence in the World*. Oxford University Press, New York.

Tversky, A. (1972) Elimination by aspects: a theory of choice. *Psychological Review*, 79: 281–299.

SECTION IV
Development

OVER the preceding sections, a theme has been developing which now comes into sharp focus: namely, that understanding the evolved psychology of ourselves and other animals requires a much better understanding of the process of ontogeny and the selective pressures that have acted on it. Issues of developmental robustness raised by Mameli, ecological inheritance as discussed by Laland, and the notion that the phylogenetic origins of culture are to be found in ontogenetic processes (put forward by van Schaik and Silk) all receive elaboration here, in the context of explaining various aspects of normal human development.

For humans, in particular, an understanding of ontogenetic processes is crucial given the cultural niche we occupy: it means that we live in worlds almost entirely of our own construction, both literally and imaginatively. The means by which children come to appreciate the nature of their world has been canalized over the course of our evolution, enabling them to attend to the social information that is crucial for normal functioning almost from the moment they enter the world, as Baron-Cohen argues, and which can lead to the disabilities of autism when such mechanisms fail.

However, it is also clear that, despite this canalization, evolution has provided us with mechanisms that are highly 'experience-expectant' and require input from the world in order to refine the categories of stimuli to which they respond. Wyman and Tomasello argue that, if these early social mechanisms are in place, in particular the ability to engage in joint attention, the rest then follows in a cascade, as knowledge gained at one stage bootstraps the development of subsequent stages: a combination of classic Piagetian and Vygotskian approaches, but with the added evolutionary suggestion that the ability to enter into cooperative, collaborative interactions from the earliest stages of life is what differentiates us from the other apes.

The peculiar life history of humans (see Section V), and the long developmental periods we experience relative to other species, also provides a rich source of ideas concerning the links between phylogeny and ontogeny. While more research is still needed, it is becoming clear that, as Belsky argues, childhood experiences have a strong influence on the reproductive strategy an individual is likely to adopt as an adult, and that such choices are often highly adaptive in a given environment. Family environments, in particular, seem to play a strong, yet synergistic, role in shaping individual development, as both Sulloway and Bereczkei suggest using various examples to illustrate the 'evocative' nature of development.

The proximate mechanisms that underlie the life trajectories and reproductive strategies followed, and which allow individuals to respond flexibly to prevailing circumstances, often have deep physiological roots, as both Bereczkei and Flinn argue. Flinn, in particular, echoes the arguments put forward by Panksepp (Chapter 12), that hormonal/neurochemical responses are crucial for understanding neurological and psychological development, both evolutionarily and over the course of individual lifespans. Bereczkei also illustrates how sociality and social contact itself are crucial for the development of healthy, normally functioning individuals, while, at the same time, the mechanisms that rely on these social inputs are fairly robust; human children can show remarkable resilience in the face of social and other stressors. This is what we should expect from evolution—mechanisms that are heavily dependent on highly specified inputs would be at a disadvantage in competition with more broadly constrained mechanisms. A loving family seems to be the key to normal human development, but its precise composition, and the manner in which individuals engage with children and other family members, can be much more variable and fluid. Indeed, this variability can be crucial for the acquisition of culturally specific behaviours that allow individuals to become fully functioning, independent members of society.

CHAPTER 16

The evolution of empathizing and systemizing: assortative mating of two strong systemizers and the cause of autism

Simon Baron-Cohen

16.1. Introduction

In this chapter, I discuss two cognitive processes, empathizing and systemizing, in terms of sex differences and the implications of these for evolutionary psychology. I then discuss the theory that assortative mating of two strong systemizers is a cause of autism, a neurodevelopmental condition involving empathy impairment alongside hyper-systemizing.

16.2. What is empathizing?

Empathizing is the drive to identify another person's emotions and thoughts, and to respond to these with an appropriate emotion (Davis, 1994). Empathy is a skill (or a set of skills). As with any other skill, we all vary in it. In the same way that we can think about why someone is talented or average or even disabled in these other areas, so we can think about individual differences in empathy.

16.2.1. The development of empathizing: the 'mindreading system' (1994)

In 1994, I proposed a model to specify the neurocognitive mechanisms that comprise the 'mindreading system' (Baron-Cohen, 1994, 1995). Mindreading is defined as the ability to interpret one's own or another agent's actions as driven by mental states. The model was proposed in order to explain (a) ontogenesis of a theory of mind, and (b) neurocognitive dissociations that are seen in children with or without autism. The model is shown in Figure 16.1 and contains four components: ID, or the Intentionality Detector; EDD, or the Eye Direction Detector; SAM, or the

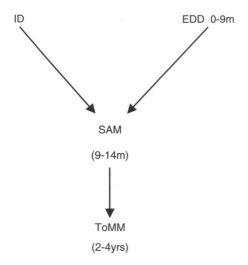

Key: ID = Intentionality Detector
EDD = Eye Direction Detector
SAM = Shared Attention Mechanism
TOMM = Theory of Mind Mechanism

Fig. 16.1 Baron-Cohen's (1994) model of the mindreading system. ID, Intentionality Detector; EDD, Eye Direction Detector; SAM, Shared Attention Mechanism; ToMM, Theory of Mind Mechanism.

Shared Attention Mechanism; and finally ToMM, or the Theory of Mind Mechanism.

ID and EDD build 'dyadic' representations of simple mental states. ID automatically interprets or represents an agent's self-propelled movement as a desire or goal-directed movement, a sign of its agency, or an entity with volition (Premack, 1990). For example, ID interprets an animate-like moving shape as 'it wants x', or 'it has goal y'. EDD automatically interprets or represents eye-like stimuli as 'looking at me' or 'looking at something else'. That is, EDD registers that an entity with eyes can perceive. Both ID and EDD are developmentally prior to the other two mechanisms, and are active early in infancy.

SAM is developmentally more advanced and comes on line at the end of the first year of life. SAM automatically interprets or represents if the self and another agent are (or are not) perceiving the same event. SAM does this by building 'triadic' representations. For example, where ID can build the dyadic representation 'Mother wants the cup' and where EDD can build the dyadic representation 'Mother sees the cup', SAM can build the

triadic representation 'Mother sees that I see the cup'. As is apparent, triadic representations involve embedding or recursion. [A dyadic representation ('I see a cup') is embedded within another dyadic representation ('Mum sees the cup') to produce this triadic representation.] SAM takes its input from ID and EDD, and triadic representations are made out of dyadic representations. SAM typically functions from 9 to 14 months of age, and allows 'joint attention' behaviours such as protodeclarative pointing and gaze monitoring (Scaife and Bruner, 1975).

ToMM allows an epistemic mental state to be represented (e.g. 'Mother thinks this cup contains water' or 'Mother pretends this cup contains water'), and it integrates the full set of mental state concepts (including emotions) into a theory. ToMM develops between 2 and 4 years of age, and allows pretend play (Leslie, 1987), understanding of false belief (Wimmer and Perner, 1983), and understanding of the relationships between mental states (Wellman, 1990). An example of the latter is the seeing-leads-to-knowing principle (Pratt and Bryant, 1990), where the typical 3 year old can infer that if someone has seen an event, then he will know about it.

The model shows the ontogenesis of a theory of mind in the first 4 years of life, and justifies the existence of four components on the basis of developmental competence and neuropsychological dissociation. In terms of developmental competence, joint attention does not appear possible until 9–14 months of age, and joint attention appears to be a necessary but not sufficient condition for understanding epistemic mental states (Baron-Cohen, 1991; Baron-Cohen and Swettenham, 1996). There appears to be a developmental lag between acquiring SAM and ToMM, suggesting that these two mechanisms are dissociable. In terms of neuropsychological dissociation, congenitally blind children can ultimately develop joint (auditory or tactile) attention, using the amodal ID rather than the visual EDD route. Children with autism appear able to represent the dyadic mental states of seeing and wanting, but show delays in shared attention (Baron-Cohen, 1989b) and in understanding false belief (Baron-Cohen et al., 1985; Baron-Cohen, 1989a)—that is, in acquiring SAM and ultimately ToMM. It is this specific developmental delay that suggests that SAM is dissociable from EDD.

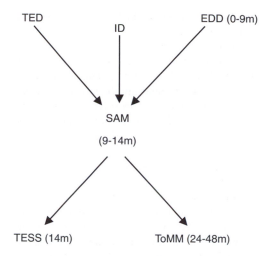

TED

EDD (0-9m)

ID

SAM

(9-14m)

TESS (14m)

ToMM (24-48m)

Key: As in Figure 1, but:
TED = The Emotion Detector; and
TESS = The Empathising SyStem

Fig. 16.2 Baron-Cohen's (2005) model of empathizing. TED, The Emotion Detector; TESS, The Empathizing SyStem. Other abbreviations as in Figure 16.1.

16.2.2. **Short-comings of the 1994 model: the 'empathizing system' (2005)**

The 1994 model of the mindreading system was revised in 2005 because of certain omissions and too narrow a focus. The key omission was that information about affective states, available to the infant perceptual system, had no dedicated neurocognitive mechanism. In Figure 16.2, the revised model (Baron-Cohen, 2005) is shown and now includes a new fifth component: TED, or The Emotion Detector. A particular problem for any account of the distinction between autism and psychopathy is the fact that the concept of mindreading (or theory of mind) makes no reference to the affective state in the observer triggered by recognition of another's mental state. For this reason, the revised model no longer focuses on 'mindreading' but rather focuses on 'empathizing', and also includes a new sixth component, TESS, or The Empathizing SyStem. Where the 1994 mindreading system was a model of a passive observer (all the components had simple decoding functions), the 2005 empathizing system is a model of an observer impelled towards action (because an emotion is triggered

in the observer which typically motivates the observer to respond to the other person).

Like the other infancy perceptual input mechanisms of ID and EDD, the new component of TED can build dyadic representations of a special kind, namely, it can represent affective states. An example would be 'Mother–is unhappy', or even 'Mother–is angry–with me'. Formally, we can describe this as 'agent–affective state–proposition'. We know that infants can represent affective states from as early as 3 months of age (Walker, 1982). As with ID, TED is amodal, in that affective information can be picked up from facial expression, or vocal intonation, 'motherese' being a particularly rich source of the latter (Field, 1979). Another's affective state is presumably also detectable from their touch (e.g. tense, versus relaxed), which implies that congenitally blind infants should find affective information accessible through both auditory and tactile modalities. TED allows the detection of the basic emotions (Ekman and Friesen, 1969). The development of TED is probably aided by simple imitation that is typical of infants (e.g. imitating caregiver's expressions) which in itself would facilitate emotional contagion (Meltzoff and Decety, 2003).

When SAM becomes available, at 9–14 months of age, it can receive inputs from any of the three infancy mechanisms, ID, EDD or TED. Here, we focus on how a dyadic representation of an affective state can be converted into a triadic representation by SAM. An example would be that the dyadic representation 'Mother is unhappy' can be converted into a triadic representation 'I am unhappy that Mother is unhappy', or 'Mother is unhappy that I am unhappy', etc. Again, as with perceptual or volitional states, SAM's triadic representations of affective states have this special embedded, or recursive, property.

ToMM is of major importance in allowing the child to represent the full range of mental states, including epistemic ones (such as false belief), and is important in allowing the child to pull mentalistic knowledge into a useful theory with which to predict behaviour (Baron-Cohen, 1995; Wellman, 1990). But TESS allows more than behavioural explanation and prediction (itself a powerful achievement). TESS allows an empathic reaction to another's emotional state. This is however, not to say that these two modules do not interact. Knowledge of mental states of others made possible by ToMM could certainly influence the way in which an emotion is processed and/or expressed by TESS. TESS also allows for sympathy. It is this element of TESS that gives it the adaptive benefit of ensuring that organisms feel a drive to help each other.

16.2.3. Dissociations between ToMM and TESS from neuropsychiatry

Before leaving this revision of the model, it is worth discussing why the need for this has arisen. First, emotional states are an important class of mental states to detect in others, and yet the earlier model focused only on volitional, perceptual, informational, and epistemic states. Secondly, when it comes to pathology, it would appear that in autism TED may function, although its onset may be delayed (Hobson, 1986; Baron-Cohen et al., 1993, 1997c), at least in terms of detecting basic emotions. Even high-functioning people with autism or Asperger Syndrome have difficulties both in ToMM (when measured with mental-age appropriate tests) (Baron-Cohen et al., 1997a, 2001a; Happe, 1994) and TESS (Attwood, 1997; Baron-Cohen and Wheelwright, 2004; Baron-Cohen et al., 1999a,c, 2003). We discuss autism further later in the chapter. But even at this point, the evidence suggests that TED and TESS may be fractionated.

In contrast, the psychiatric condition of psychopathy may entail an intact TED and ToMM, alongside an impaired TESS. The psychopath (or sociopath) can represent that you are in pain, or that you believe he is the gas-man, thereby gaining access to your house or your credit card. The psychopath can go on to hurt you or cheat you without having the appropriate affective reaction to your affective state. In other words, he or she doesn't care about your affective state (Mealey, 1995; Blair et al., 1997). Lack of guilt or shame or compassion in the presence of another's distress are diagnostic of psychopathy (Cleckley, 1977; Hare et al., 1990). Separating TESS and ToMM thus allows a functional distinction to be drawn between the neurocognitive causes of autism and psychopathy.

16.2.4. Developmental dissociations

Developmentally, one can also distinguish TED from TESS. We know that at 3 months of age, infants can discriminate facial and vocal expressions of emotion (Walker, 1982; Trevarthen, 1989) but that it is not until about 14 months that they can respond with appropriate affect (e.g. a facial expression of concern) to another's apparent pain (Yirmiya et al., 1990) or show 'social referencing'. Clearly, this account is incomplete inasmuch as it does not specify how many emotions TED is capable of recognizing. Our recent survey of emotions identifies 412 discrete emotion concepts that are recognized by the adult English language user (Baron-Cohen et al., submitted). How many of these are recognized in the first year of life is not clear. It is also not clear exactly how empathizing changes during the second year of life. We have assumed that the same mechanism that enables social referencing at 14 months old also allows sympathy and the growth of empathy across development. This is the most parsimonious model, though it may be that future research will justify further mechanisms that affect the development of empathy.

16.3. Sex differences in empathizing—a clue to its evolutionary origins?

Many studies converge on the conclusion that there is a female superiority in empathizing. The evidence includes:

1. *Sharing and turn-taking.* On average, girls show more concern for fairness, whereas boys share less. In one study, boys showed 50 times more competition, whereas girls showed 20 times more turn-taking (Charlesworth and Dzur, 1987).

2. *Rough-and-tumble play* or 'rough housing' (wrestling, mock fighting, etc.). Boys do more of this than girls. Although there's a playful component, it can hurt or be intrusive, so it needs lower empathizing to carry it out (Maccoby, 1999).

3. *Responding empathically to the distress of other people.* Girls from 1 year old show greater concern through more sad looks, sympathetic vocalizations and comforting. More women than men also report frequently sharing the emotional distress of their friends. Women also show more comforting, even of strangers, than men do (Hoffman, 1977).

4. *Using a 'theory of mind'.* By 3 years old, little girls are already ahead of boys in their ability to infer what people might be thinking or intending (Happe, 1995). This sex difference appears in some but not all studies (Charman *et al.*, 2002).

5. *Sensitivity to facial expressions.* Women are better at decoding non-verbal communication, picking up subtle nuances from tone of voice or facial expression, or judging a person's character (Hall, 1978).

6. *Questionnaires measuring empathy.* Many of these find that women score higher than men (Davis, 1994).

7. *Values in relationships.* More women value the development of altruistic, reciprocal relationships, which by definition require empathizing. In contrast, more men value power, politics, and competition (Ahlgren and Johnson, 1979). Girls are more likely to endorse cooperative items on a questionnaire and to rate the establishment of intimacy as more important than the establishment of dominance. Boys are more likely than girls to endorse competitive items and to rate social status as more important than intimacy (Knight *et al.*, 1989).

8. *Disorders of empathy* (such as psychopathic personality disorder, or conduct disorder) are far more common among males (Dodge, 1980; Blair, 1995).

9. *Aggression.* Even in normal quantities, aggression can only occur with reduced empathizing. Here again, there is a clear sex difference. Males tend to show far more 'direct' aggression (pushing, hitting, punching, etc.) whereas females tend to show more 'indirect' (or 'relational', covert) aggression (gossip, exclusion, bitchy remarks, etc.). Direct aggression may require an even lower level of empathy than indirect aggression. Indirect aggression needs better mindreading skills than does direct aggression, because its impact is strategic (Crick and Grotpeter, 1995).

10. *Murder.* This is the ultimate example of a lack of empathy. Daly and Wilson (1988) analysed homicide records dating back over 700 years, from a range of different societies. They found that 'male-on-male' homicide was 30–40 times more frequent than 'female-on-female' homicide.

11. *Establishing a 'dominance hierarchy'.* Males are quicker to establish these. This in part may reflect their lower empathizing skills, because often a hierarchy is established by one person pushing others around, to become the leader (Strayer, 1980).

12. *Language style.* Girls' speech is more co-operative, reciprocal, and collaborative. In concrete terms, this is also reflected in girls being able to keep a conversational exchange with a partner going for longer. When girls disagree, they are more likely to express their different opinion sensitively, in the form of a question, rather than an assertion. Boys' talk is more 'single-voiced discourse' (the speaker presents their own perspective alone). The female speech style is more 'double-voiced discourse' (girls spend more time negotiating with the other person, trying to take the other person's wishes into account) (Smith, 1985).

13. *Talk about emotions.* Women's conversation involves much more talk about feelings, whereas men's conversation with each other tends to be more object- or activity-focused (Tannen, 1991).

14. *Parenting style.* Fathers are less likely than mothers to hold their infant in a face-to-face position. Mothers are more likely to follow through the child's choice of topic in play, whilst fathers are more likely to impose their own topic. And mothers fine-tune their speech more often to match what the child can understand (Power, 1985).

15. *Face preference and eye contact.* From birth, females look longer at faces, and particularly at people's eyes, and males are more likely to look at inanimate objects (Connellan *et al.*, 2001).

16. *Language ability.* Females have also been shown to have better language ability than males. It seems likely that good empathizing would promote language development (Baron-Cohen *et al.*, 1997b) and vice versa, so these may not be independent.

16.4. Natural selection of good empathy among females?

Why might this sex difference in empathy exist? One possibility is that it reflects natural selection of empathy among females during the course of human evolution. If one considers that good empathizing would have led to better care-giving, then since care-giving can be assumed to have been primarily a female activity until very recent history, those mothers who had better empathy would have succeeded better in 'tuning in' to their infant offspring's pre-verbal emotional and physical needs, which may have led to a higher likelihood of the infant surviving to reproductive age. Hence, good empathy in the mother would have promoted her inclusive fitness.

A second explanation is that females with better empathy might have found it easier to socialize—chat, gossip, network—with other females, thereby being more successful in creating social support for themselves whilst engaged in being a care-giver to their infant. Social support from other females is likely also to buffer mothers from the range of life events (illness, poverty, loss, physical attack, etc.) that might otherwise threaten her ability to care for her offspring, and so increase the likelihood of her infant surviving to reproductive age, thereby increasing her inclusive fitness.

From empathizing I want now to turn to systemizing, a very different cognitive process which appears to be stronger in males.

16.5. What is 'systemizing'?

Systemizing is a new concept. By a 'system' I mean something that receives inputs and delivers outputs. To systemize, one uses 'if–then' (correlation) rules. The brain zooms in on a detail or parameter of the system and observes how this varies. That is, it treats a feature of a particular object or event as a variable. Alternately, a person actively, or systematically, manipulates a given variable. One notes the effect(s) of operating on one single input in terms of its effects elsewhere in the system (the output). If I do x, a changes to b. If z occurs, p changes to q. Systemizing therefore requires an exact eye for detail.

Systemizing involves observation of *input–operation–output* relationships, leading to the identification of laws to predict that event x will occur with probability p (Baron-Cohen, 2002). Some systems are 100% lawful (e.g. an electrical light switch, or a mathematical formula). Systems that are 100% lawful have zero variance, or only 1 degree of freedom, and can therefore be predicted (and controlled) 100%. A computer might be an example of a 90% lawful system: the variance is wider or there are more degrees of freedom. The social world may be only 10% lawful. This is why systemizing the social world is of little predictive value.

Systemizing involves five phases:

Phase 1: *Analysis*. Single observations of input and output are recorded in a standardized manner at the lowest level of detail.

Phase 2: *Operation*. An operation is performed on the input and the change to the output is noted.

Phase 3: *Repetition*. The same operation is repeated over and over again to test if the same pattern between input and output is obtained.

Phase 4: *Law derivation*. A law is formulated of the form, 'if X (operation) occurs, A (input) changes to B'.

Phase 5: *Confirmation/disconfirmation*. If the same pattern of input–operation–output holds true for all instances, the law is retained.

If a single instance does not fit the law, Phases 2–5 are repeated leading to modification of the law, or a new law.

Systemizing non-agentive changes is effective because these are *simple* changes: the systems are at least moderately lawful, with narrow variance (or limited degrees of freedom). Agentive change is less suited to systemizing because the changes in the system are *complex* (wide variance, or many degrees of freedom).

There are at least six kinds of systems that the human brain can analyse or construct, as shown in Table 16.1. Systemizing works for phenomena that are ultimately lawful, finite, and deterministic. The explanation is exact, and its truth-value is testable. Systemizing is of almost no use for predicting moment-to-moment changes in a person's behaviour. To predict human behaviour, empathizing is required. Systemizing and empathizing are wholly different kinds of process.

Table 16.1 Main types of analysable systems

Technical systems (e.g. a computer, a musical instrument, a hammer)

Natural systems (e.g. a tide, a weather front, a plant)

Abstract systems (e.g. mathematics, a computer program, syntax)

Social systems (e.g. a political election, a legal system, a business)

Organizable systems (e.g. a taxonomy, a collection, a library)

Motoric systems (e.g. a sports technique, a performance, a musical technique)

16.6. **Sex differences in systemizing**

What is the evidence for a stronger drive to systemize in males?

1. *Toy preferences.* Boys are more interested than girls in toy vehicles, weapons, building blocks, and mechanical toys, all of which are open to being 'systemized' (Jennings, 1977).

2. *Adult occupational choices.* Some occupations are almost entirely male. These include metalworking, weapon making, manufacture of musical instruments, and the construction industries, such as boat building. The focus of these occupations is on creating systems (Geary, 1998).

3. *Mathematics, physics, and engineering.* These disciplines all require high systemizing and are largely male-dominated. The Scholastic Aptitude Math Test (SAT-M) is the mathematics part of the test administered nationally to college applicants in the United States. Males on average score 50 points higher than females on this test (Benbow, 1988). Considering only individuals who score above 700, the sex ratio is 13:1 (men to women) (Geary, 1996).

4. *Constructional abilities.* On average, men score higher than women in an assembly task in which people are asked to put together a 3-dimensional (3D) mechanical apparatus. Boys are also better at constructing block buildings from 2D blueprints. Lego bricks can be combined and recombined into an infinite number of systems. Boys show more interest than girls in playing with Lego. Boys as young as 3 years of age are also faster at copying 3D models of outsized Lego pieces. Older boys, from the age of 9 years, are better than girls at imagining what a 3D object will look like if it is laid out flat. Boys are also better at constructing a 3D structure from just an aerial and frontal view in a picture (Kimura, 1999).

5. *The Water Level Task.* Originally devised by the Swiss child psychologist Jean Piaget, the task involves a bottle that is tipped at an angle. Individuals are asked to predict if the water level will be horizontal or aligned with the angle of the bottle. Women more often draw the water level aligned with the tilt of the bottle and not horizontal, as is correct (Wittig and Allen, 1984).

6. *The Rod and Frame Test.* If people's judgment of vertical is influenced by the tilt of the frame, they are said to be 'field dependent', i.e. their judgment is easily swayed by extraneous input in the surrounding context. If they are not influenced by the tilt of the frame, they are said to be 'field independent'. Most studies indicate that females are more field dependent, i.e. women are relatively more distracted by contextual cues, and they tend not to consider each variable within a system separately. They are more likely than men to state erroneously that a rod is upright if it is aligned with its frame (Witkin *et al.*, 1954).

7. *Good attention to relevant detail.* This is a general feature of systemizing and is clearly a necessary part of it. Attention to relevant detail is superior in males. One measure of this is the Embedded Figures Test. On average, males are quicker and more accurate in locating a target object from a larger, complex pattern (Elliot, 1961). Males, on average, are also better at detecting a particular feature (static or moving) than are women (Voyer *et al.*, 1995).

8. *The Mental Rotation Test.* This test provides another example in which males are quicker and more accurate. It involves systemizing because it is necessary to treat each feature in a display as a variable that can be transformed (e.g. rotated) and then to predict the output, or how it will appear after transformation (Collins and Kimura, 1997).

9. *Reading maps.* This is another everyday test of systemizing, because features from 3D input must be transformed to a 2D representation. In general, boys perform at a higher level than girls in map reading. Men can also learn a route by looking at a map in fewer trials than women, and they are more successful at correctly recalling greater detail about direction and distance. This observation suggests that men treat features in the map as variables that can be transformed into three dimensions. When children are asked to make a map of an area that they have only visited once, boys' maps have a more accurate layout of the features in the environment. More of the girls' maps make serious errors in the location of important landmarks. Boys tend to emphasize routes or roads, whereas girls tend to emphasize specific landmarks (the corner shop, the park, etc). These strategies of using directional cues versus using landmark cues have been widely studied. The directional strategy represents an approach to understanding space as a geometric system. Similarly, the focus on roads or routes is an example of considering space in terms of another system, in this case a transportation system (Galea and Kimura, 1993).

10. *Motoric systems.* When people are asked to throw or catch moving objects (target-directed tasks), such as playing darts or intercepting balls flung from a launcher, males tend to perform better than females. In addition, on average men are more accurate than women in their ability to judge which of two moving objects is travelling faster (Schiff and Oldak, 1990).

11. *Organizable systems.* People in the Aguaruna tribe of northern Peru were asked to classify a hundred or more examples of local specimens into related species. Men's classification systems included more sub-categories (i.e. they introduced greater differentiation) and were more consistent among individuals. Interestingly, the criteria that the Aguaruna men used to decide which animals were more closely related resembled the taxonomic criteria used by Western (mostly male) biologists (Atran, 1994). Classification and organization involves systemizing because categories are predictive. With more fine-grained categories, a system will provide more accurate predictions.

12. *The Systemizing Quotient.* This is a questionnaire that has been tested among adults in the general population. It includes 40 items that ask about a subject's level of interest in a range of different systems that exist in the environment, including technical, abstract, and natural systems. Males score higher than females on this measure (Baron-Cohen *et al.*, 2003).

13. *Mechanics.* The Physical Prediction Questionnaire (PPQ) is based on an established method for selecting applicants to study engineering. The task involves predicting which direction levers will move when an internal mechanism of cog wheels and pulleys is engaged. Men score significantly higher on this test, compared with women (Lawson *et al.*, 2004).

Evolutionary accounts for the male advantage in systemizing include the argument that males were primarily involved in hunting and tracking of prey, and that a male who was a good systemizer would have had greater success in both using and making tools for hunting, or navigating space to explore far afield. Both could have affected a male's reproductive success. Secondly, a good systemizer would have been better placed to acquire wealth or status through being expert in making things, and wealth/status is correlated with reproductive success as a result of sexual selection.

Some might argue that socialization may have caused these sex differences in both empathizing and systemizing. Although evidence exists for differential socialization contributing to sex differences, this is unlikely to be a sufficient explanation. Connellan *et al.* (2001) and colleagues showed that among 1-day-old babies, boys look longer at a mechanical mobile, which is a system with predictable laws of motion, than at a person's face, an object that is almost impossible to systemize. One-day-old girls show the opposite profile. These sex differences are therefore present very early in life.

This raises the possibility that, while culture and socialization may partly determine the development of a male brain with a stronger interest in systems or a female brain with a stronger interest in empathy, biology may also partly determine this. There is ample evidence to support both cultural determinism and biological determinism (Eagley, 1987; Gouchie and Kimura, 1991). For example, the amount of time a 1-year-old child maintains eye contact is inversely related to the prenatal level of testosterone (Lutchmaya *et al.*, 2002). The evidence for the biological basis of sex differences in the mind is reviewed elsewhere (Baron-Cohen, 2003).

We all have both systemizing and empathizing skills. One can envisage five broad types of brain, as Table 16.2 shows. The evidence reviewed here suggests that not all men have the male brain and not all women have the female brain. Expressed differently, some women have the male brain, and some men have the female brain. My claim here is only that *more* males than females have a brain of type S, and *more* females than males have a brain of type E. Data relevant to this claim is summarized elsewhere (Goldenfeld *et al.*, in press).

16.7. **Autism: hyper-systemizing alongside impaired empathizing?**

The autistic spectrum comprises four sub-groups: Asperger Syndrome (AS) (Asperger, 1944; Frith, 1991), and high-, medium- and low-functioning autism (Kanner, 1943). They all share the phenotype of social difficulties and obsessional interests (American Psychological Association, 1994). In AS, the individual has normal or above-average IQ and no language delay. In the three autism sub-groups there is invariably some degree of language delay, and the level of functioning is indexed by overall IQ. These four sub-groups are known as autism spectrum conditions (ASC).

In terms of causes, the consensus is that ASC have a genetic aetiology (Bailey *et al.*, 1995), which leads to altered brain development (Happe *et al.*, 1996; Baron-Cohen *et al.*, 1999b; Frith and Frith, 1999; Courchesne, 2002) affecting social and communication development and leading to the presence of unusual narrow interests and extreme repetitive behaviour (American Psychological Association, 1994). We have already

Table 16.2 The main brain types

Profile	Shorthand equation	Type of brain
Individuals in whom empathizing is more developed than systemizing	E > S	Type E: more common in females
Individuals in whom systemizing is more developed than empathizing	S > E	Type S: more common in males
Individuals in whom systemizing and empathizing are both equally developed	S = E	'Balanced' or Type B
Individuals in whom systemizing is hyper-developed while empathizing is hypo-developed	S >> E	Extreme Type S: the extreme male brain. More common in people with an autism spectrum condition
Individuals who have hyper-developed empathizing skills, while their systemizing is hypo-developed	E >> S	Extreme Type E: the extreme female brain (postulated)

reviewed some evidence for empathy impairments in ASC (but see Baron-Cohen, 1995 for an extensive review). In the next section we review evidence for hyper-systemizing in autism, and in first-degree relatives of people with autism. Such findings are then discussed for their significance for the evolution of systemizing in the general population.

16.7.1. The systemizing mechanism (SM)

The hyper-systemizing theory of ASC posits that all human brains have a systemizing mechanism (SM), and that this is set at different levels in different individuals. In people with ASC, the SM is set too high. The SM is like a volume control. Evidence suggests that within the general population, there are eight degrees of systemizing:

Level 1. Such individuals have little or no drive to systemize, and consequently they can cope with rapid, unlawful change. Their SM is set so low that that they hardly notice if the input is structured or not. Although this would not interfere with their ability to socialize it would lead to a lack of precision over detail when dealing with structured information. We can think of this as *hypo-systemizing.* Such a person would be able to cope with agentive change easily, but may be challenged when dealing with highly lawful non-agentive systems.

Levels 2 and 3. Most people have *some* interest in lawful non-agentive systems, and there are sex differences in this. More females in the general population have the SM set at Level 2, and more males have it set at Level 3 (see the evidence for sex differences reviewed earlier).

Level 4. This corresponds to individuals who systemize at a higher level than average. There is some evidence that above-average systemizers have more autistic traits. Thus, scientists (who by definition have the SM set above average) score higher than non-scientists on the Autism Spectrum Quotient (AQ). Mathematicians score highest of all scientists on the AQ (Baron-Cohen et al., 2001c). Parents of children with ASC also have their SM set higher than average (Baron-Cohen and Hammer, 1997; Happe et al., 2001) and have been described as having the 'broader phenotype' of autism. At Level 4 one would expect a person to be talented at understanding systems with moderate variance or lawfulness.

Level 5. People with AS have their SM set at Level 5: the person can easily systemize lawful systems such as calendars or train timetables (Hermelin, 2002). Experimental evidence for hyper-systemizing in AS includes the following: (i) people with AS score higher than average on the Systemizing Quotient (SQ) (Baron-Cohen et al., 2003); (ii) people with AS perform at a normal or high level on tests of intuitive physics or geometric analysis (Shah and Frith, 1983; Joliffe and Baron-Cohen, 1997; Baron-Cohen et al., 2001b; Lawson et al., 2004); (iii) people with AS can achieve extremely high levels in domains such as mathematics, physics, or computer science (Baron-Cohen et al., 1999c); (iv) people with AS have an 'exact mind' when it comes to art (Myers et al., 2004) and show superior attention to detail (Plaisted et al., 1998; O'Riordan et al., 2001).

Levels 6–8. In people with high-functioning autism (HFA), the SM is set at Level 6, in those with medium-functioning autism (MFA) it is at Level 7, and in low-functioning autism (LFA) it is at the maximum setting (Level 8). Thus, people with HFA try to socialize or empathize by 'hacking' (i.e. systemizing) (Happe, 1994), and on the picture-sequencing task they perform above average on sequences that contain temporal or physical–causal information (Baron-Cohen et al., 1986). People with MFA perform above average on the false photograph task (Leslie and Thaiss, 1992). In LFA, their obsessions cluster in the domain of systems, such as watching electric fans go round (Baron-Cohen and Wheelwright, 1999); and given a set of coloured counters, they show extreme 'pattern imposition' (Frith, 1970).

16.7.2. The assortative mating of two high systemizers

The evidence for systemizing being part of the phenotype for ASC includes the following: fathers and grandfathers of children with ASC are twice as likely to work in the occupation of engineering (a clear example of a systemizing occupation), compared to men in the general population (Baron-Cohen et al., 1997d). The implication is that these fathers and grandfathers have their SM set higher than average (Level 4). Students in the natural sciences (engineering, mathematics, physics) have a higher number of relatives with autism than do students in the humanities (Baron-Cohen *et al.*, 1998). Mathematicians have a higher rate of AS compared to the general population, and so do their siblings (Baron-Cohen *et al.*, in press a).

The evidence that autism could be the genetic result of having *two* high systemizers as parents (assortative mating) includes the following. (a) Both mothers *and* fathers of children with AS have been found to be strong in systemizing on the Embedded Figures Test (Baron-Cohen and Hammer, 1997). (b) Both mothers and fathers of children with autism or AS have elevated rates of systemizing occupations among their fathers (Baron-Cohen *et al.*, 1997d). (c) Both mothers and fathers of children with autism show hyper-masculinized patterns of brain activity during a systemizing task (Baron-Cohen *et al.*, in press b). Whether the current high rates of ASC simply reflect better recognition, growth of services, and widening of diagnostic categories to include AS, or also reflect the increased likelihood of two high systemizers having ASC children, is a question for future research.

16.8. Conclusions

This chapter has reviewed evidence that empathizing and systemizing show strong sex differences, and that these might reflect natural selection operating differently on the two sexes. Also reviewed is the evidence that individuals on the autistic spectrum, which has a genetic basis, have degrees of empathizing difficulties alongside hyper-systemizing. According to the hyper-systemizing theory, autism spectrum conditions (ASC) are the result of a normative systemizing mechanism (SM)—the function of which is to serve as a change-predicting mechanism—being set too high. This theory explains why people with autism prefer either no change, or appear 'change resistant'. It also explains their preference for systems that change in highly lawful or predictable ways (such as mathematics, repetition, objects that spin, routine, music, machines, collections). Finally, it also explains why they become disabled when faced with systems characterized by 'complex' or less lawful change (such as social behaviour, conversation, people's emotions, or fiction), since these cannot be easily systemized.

Whilst ASCs are disabling in the social world, hyper-systemizing can lead to talent in areas that are systemizable. For many people with ASC, their hyper-systemizing never moves beyond Phase 1: massive collection of facts and observations (lists of trains and their departure times, watching the spin-cycle of a washing machine), or Phases 2 and 3: massive repetition of behaviour (spinning a plate or the wheels of a toy car). But for those who go beyond Phase 3 to identify a law or a pattern in the data (Phases 4 and 5), this can constitute original insight. In this sense, it is likely that the genes for increased systemizing have made remarkable contributions to human history (Fitzgerald, 2000, 2002; James, 2003). Finally, the assortative mating theory proposes that the cause of ASC is the genetic combination of having two strong systemizers as parents. This theory remains to be fully tested, but if confirmed, may help to explain why the genes that can cause social disability have also been maintained in the gene pool, as they confer all the fitness advantages that strong systemizing can bring on the first-degree relatives of people with such conditions.

Acknowledgments

I am grateful for the support of the MRC and the Nancy Lurie-Marks Family Foundation during this work. Portions of this paper are taken from elsewhere (Baron-Cohen, 2005, and in press).

References

American Psychological Association (1994) *DSM-IV Diagnostic and Statistical Manual of Mental Disorders*, 4th edn. American Psychiatric Association, Washington, DC.

Ahlgren, A. and Johnson, D. W. (1979) Sex differences in cooperative and competitive attitudes from the 2nd to the 12th grades. *Developmental Psychology*, 15: 45–49.

Asperger, H. (1944) Die "Autistischen Psychopathen" im Kindesalter. *Archiv für Psychiatrie und Nervenkrankheiten*, 117: 76–136.

Atran, S. (1994) Core domains versus scientific theories: evidence from systematics and Itza–Maya folkbiology. In L. A. Hirschfeld and S. A. Gelman (eds) *Mapping the Mind: Domain Specificity in Cognition and Culture*. Cambridge University Press, New York.

Attwood, T. (1997) *Asperger's Syndrome*. Jessica Kingsley, London.

Bailey, A., Le Couteur, A., Gottesman, I. *et al.* (1995) Autism as a strongly genetic disorder: evidence from a British twin study. *Psychological Medicine*, 25: 63–77.

Baron-Cohen, S. (1989a) The autistic child's theory of mind: a case of specific developmental delay. *Journal of Child Psychology and Psychiatry*, 30: 285–298.

Baron-Cohen, S. (1989b) Perceptual role taking and protodeclarative pointing in autism. *British Journal of Developmental Psychology*, 7: 113–127.

Baron-Cohen, S. (1991) Precursors to a theory of mind: understanding attention in others. In A. Whiten (ed.) *Natural Theories of Mind*. Blackwell, Oxford.

Baron-Cohen, S. (1994) The Mindreading System: new directions for research. *Current Psychology of Cognition*, 13: 724–750.

Baron-Cohen, S. (1995) *Mindblindness: An Essay on Autism and Theory of Mind*. MIT Press/Bradford Books, Boston.

Baron-Cohen, S. (2002) The extreme male brain theory of autism. *Trends in Cognitive Science*, 6: 248–254.

Baron-Cohen, S. (2003) *The Essential Difference: Men, Women and the Extreme Male Brain*. Penguin, London.

Baron-Cohen, S. (2005) The Empathizing System: a revision of the 1994 model of the Mindreading System. In Ellis, B. and Bjorklund, D. (eds) *Origins of the Social Mind*. Guilford Press, New York.

Baron-Cohen, S. (in press) The hyper-systemizing, assortative mating theory of autism. *Neuropsychopharmacology and Biological Psychiatry*.

Baron-Cohen, S. and Hammer, J. (1997) Parents of children with Asperger Syndrome: what is the cognitive phenotype? *Journal of Cognitive Neuroscience*, 9: 548–554.

Baron-Cohen, S. and Swettenham, J. (1996) The relationship between SAM and ToMM: the lock and key hypothesis. In Carruthers, P. and Smith, P. (eds) *Theories of Theories of Mind*. Cambridge University Press, Cambridge.

Baron-Cohen, S. and Wheelwright, S. (1999) Obsessions in children with autism or Asperger Syndrome: a content analysis in terms of core domains of cognition. *British Journal of Psychiatry*, 175: 484–490.

Baron-Cohen, S. and Wheelwright, S. (2004) The Empathy Quotient (EQ). An investigation of adults with Asperger Syndrome or High Functioning Autism, and normal sex differences. *Journal of Autism and Developmental Disorders*, 34: 163–175.

Baron-Cohen, S., Leslie, A. M. and Frith, U. (1985) Does the autistic child have a 'theory of mind'? *Cognition*, 21: 37–46.

Baron-Cohen, S., Leslie, A. M. and Frith, U. (1986) Mechanical, behavioural and Intentional understanding of picture stories in autistic children. *British Journal of Developmental Psychology*, 4: 113–125.

Baron-Cohen, S., Spitz A. and Cross P. (1993) Can children with autism recognize surprise? *Cognition and Emotion*, 7: 507–516.

Baron-Cohen, S., Jolliffe, T., Mortimore, C. and Robertson, M. (1997a) Another advanced test of theory of mind: evidence from very high functioning adults with autism or Asperger Syndrome. *Journal of Child Psychology and Psychiatry*, 38: 813–822.

Baron-Cohen, S., Baldwin, D. and Crowson, M. (1997b) Do children with autism use the Speaker's Direction of Gaze (SDG) strategy to crack the code of language? *Child Development*, 68: 48–57.

Baron-Cohen, S., Wheelwright, S. and Joliffe, T. (1997c) Is there a "language of the eyes"? Evidence from normal adults and adults with autism or Asperger syndrome. *Visual Cognition*, 4: 311–331.

Baron-Cohen, S., Wheelwright, S., Stott, C., Bolton, P. and Goodyer, I. (1997d) Is there a link between engineering and autism? *Autism: An International Journal of Research and Practice*, 1: 153–163.

Baron-Cohen, S., Bolton, P., Wheelwright, S. *et al.* (1998) Does autism occurs more often in families of physicists, engineers, and mathematicians? *Autism*, 2: 296–301.

Baron-Cohen, S., O'Riordan, M., Jones, R., Stone, V. and Plaisted, K. (1999a) A new test of social sensitivity: detection of faux pas in normal children and children with Asperger syndrome. *Journal of Autism and Developmental Disorders*, 29: 407–418.

Baron-Cohen, S., Ring, H., Wheelwright *et al.* (1999b) Social intelligence in the normal and autistic brain: an fMRI study. *European Journal of Neuroscience*, 11: 1891–1898.

Baron-Cohen, S., Wheelwright, S., Stone, V. and Rutherford, M. (1999c) A mathematician, a physicist, and a computer scientist with Asperger Syndrome: performance on folk psychology and folk physics test. *Neurocase*, 5: 475–483.

Baron-Cohen, S., Wheelwright, S., Hill, J., Raste, Y. and Plumb, I. (2001a) The 'Reading the Mind in the eyes' test revised version: A study with normal adults, and adults with Asperger Syndrome or High-Functioning autism. *Journal of Child Psychology and Psychiatry*, 42: 241–252.

Baron-Cohen, S., Wheelwright, S., Scahill, V., Lawson, J. and Spong, A. (2001b) Are intuitive physics and intuitive psychology independent? *Journal of Developmental and Learning Disorders*, 5: 47–78.

Baron-Cohen, S., Wheelwright, S., Skinner, R., Martin, J. and Clubley, E. (2001c) The Autism Spectrum Quotient (AQ): evidence from Asperger Syndrome/High Functioning Autism, males and females, scientists and mathematicians. *Journal of Autism and Developmental Disorders*, 31: 5–17.

Baron-Cohen, S., Richler, J., Bisarya, D., Gunathan, N. and Wheelwright, S. (2003) The Systemising Quotient (SQ): an investigation of adults with Asperger Syndrome or High Functioning Autism and normal sex differences. *Philosophical Transactions of the Royal Society of London*, 358: 361–374.

Baron-Cohen, S., Wheelwright, S., Burtenshaw, A. and Hobson, E. (in press a) Mathematical talent is genetically linked to autism. *Human Nature*.

Baron-Cohen, S., Wheelwright, S., Williams, H.R., Bullmore, E. T., Gregory and Chitinis X. (in press b) Parents of children with autism: an fMRI study. *Brain and Cognition*.

Baron-Cohen, S., Wheelwright, S., Hill, J. and Golan, O. (submitted) A New Taxonomy of Human Emotions. *Israeli Journal of Psychiatry*.

Benbow, C. P. (1988) Sex differences in mathematical reasoning ability in intellectually talented preadolescents: their nature, effects and possible causes. *Behavioural and Brain Sciences*, 11: 169–232.

Blair, R. J. (1995) A cognitive developmental approach to morality: investigating the psychopath. *Cognition*, 57: 1–29.

Blair, R. J., Jones, L., Clark, F. and Smith, M. (1997) The psychopathic individual: a lack of responsiveness to distress cues? *Psychophysiology*, 34: 192–198.

Charlesworth, W. R. and Dzur, C. (1987) Gender comparisons of preschoolers' behavior and resource utilization in group problem-solving. *Child Development*, 58: 191–200.

Charman, T., Ruffman, T. and Clements, W. (2002) Is there a gender difference in false belief development. *Social Development*, 11: 1–10.

Cleckley, H. M. (1977) *The Mask of Sanity: An Attempt to Clarify Some Issues about the So-called Psychopathic Personality*. Mosby, St Louis.

Collins, D. W. and Kimura, D. (1997) A large sex difference on a two-dimensional mental rotation task. *Behavioral Neuroscience*, 111: 845–849.

Connellan, J., Baron-Cohen, S., Wheelwright, S., Ba'tki, A. and Ahluwalia, J. (2001) Sex differences in human neonatal social perception. *Infant Behavior and Development*, 23: 113–118.

Courchesne, E. (2002) Abnormal early brain development in autism. *Molecular Psychiatry*, 7: 21–23.

Crick, N. R. and Grotpeter, J. K. (1995) Relational aggression, gender, and social–psychological adjustment. *Child Development*, 66: 710–722.

Daly, M. and Wilson, M. (1988) *Homicide*. Aldine de Gruyter, New York.

Davis, M. H. (1994) *Empathy: A Social Psychological Approach*. Westview Press, Colorado.

Dodge, K. (1980) Social cognition and children's aggressive behaviour. *Child Development*, 51: 162–170.

Eagley, H. (1987) *Sex Differences in Social Behavior: A Social-role Interpretation*. Lawrence Erlbaum, Hillsdale, NJ.

Ekman, P. and Friesen, W. (1969) The repertoire of non-verbal behavior: categories, origins, usage, and coding. *Semiotica*, 1: 49–98.

Elliot, R. (1961) Interrelationship among measures of field dependence, ability, and personality traits. *Journal of Abnormal and Social Psychology*, 63: 27–36.

Field, T. (1979) Visual and cardiac responses to animate and inanimate faces by term and preterm infants. *Child Development*, 50: 188–194.

Fitzgerald, M. (2000) Did Ludwig Wittgenstein have Asperger's Syndrome? *European Child and Adolescent Psychiatry*, 9: 61–65.

Fitzgerald, M. (2002) Did Ramanujan have Asperger's disorder or Asperger's syndrome? *Journal of Medical Biography*, 10: 167–9.

Frith, U. (1970) Studies in pattern detection in normal and autistic children. II. Reproduction and production of color sequences. *Journal of Experimental Child Psychology*, 10: 120–135.

Frith, U. (1991) *Autism and Asperger's Syndrome*. Cambridge University Press, Cambridge.

Frith, C. and Frith, U. (1999) Interacting minds—a biological basis. *Science*, 286: 1692–1695.

Galea, L. A. M. and Kimura, D. (1993) Sex differences in route learning. *Personality and Individual Differences*, 14: 53–65.

Geary, D. (1996) Sexual selection and sex differences in mathematical abilities. *Behavioural and Brain Sciences*, 19: 229–284.

Geary, D. C. (1998) *Male, Female: The Evolution of Human Sex Differences*. American Psychological Association, Washington DC.

Goldenfeld, N., Baron-Cohen, S. and Wheelwright, S. (in press) Empathizing and systemizing in males, females and autism. *Int. J. Clin. Neuropysch.*

Gouchie, C. and Kimura, D. (1991) The relationship between testosterone levels and cognitive ability patterns. *Psychoneuroendocrinology*, 16: 323–334.

Hall, J. A. (1978) Gender effects in decoding nonverbal cues. *Psychological Bulletin*, 85: 845–857.

Happe, F. (1994) An advanced test of theory of mind: understanding of story characters' thoughts and feelings by able autistic, mentally handicapped, and normal children and adults. *Journal of Autism and Development Disorders*, 24: 129–154.

Happe, F. (1995) The role of age and verbal ability in the theory of mind task performance of subjects with autism. *Child Development*, 66: 843–855.

Happe, F. (1994) *Autism an introduction to psychological theory*. UCL Press, Psychology Press, London.

Happe, F., Ehlers, S., Fletcher, P. *et al.* (1996) Theory of mind in the brain. Evidence from a PET scan study of Asperger Syndrome. *NeuroReport*, 8: 197–201.

Happe, F., Briskman, J. and Frith, U. (2001) Exploring the cognitive phenotype of autism: weak "central coherence" in parents and siblings of children with autism: I. Experimental tests. *Journal of Child Psychology and Psychiatry*, 42: 299–308.

Hare, R. D., Hakstian, T. J., Ralph, A., Forth-Adelle, E. and Al, E. (1990) The Revised Psychopathy Checklist: reliability and factor structure. Psychological Assessment, 2: 338–341.

Hermelin, B. (2002) *Bright Splinters of the Mind: A Personal Story of Research with Autistic Savants*. Jessica Kingsley, London.

Hobson, R. P. (1986) The autistic child's appraisal of expressions of emotion. *Journal of Child Psychology and Psychiatry*, 27: 321–342.

Hoffman, M. L. (1977) Sex differences in empathy and related behaviors. *Psychological Bulletin*, 84: 712–722.

James, I. (2003) Singular scientists. *Journal of the Royal Society of Medicine*, 96: 36–39.

Jennings, K. D. (1977) People versus object orientation in preschool children: do sex differences really occur? *Journal of Genetic Psychology*, 131: 65–73.

Joliffe, T. and Baron-Cohen, S. (1997) Are people with autism or Asperger's Syndrome faster than normal on the Embedded Figures Task? *Journal of Child Psychology and Psychiatry*, 38: 527–534.

Kanner, L. (1943) Autistic disturbance of affective contact. *Nervous Child*, 2: 217–250.

Kimura, D. (1999) *Sex and Cognition*. MIT Press, Cambridge, MA.

Knight, G. P., Fabes, R. A. and Higgins, D. A. (1989) Gender differences in the cooperative, competitive, and individualistic social values of children. *Motivation and Emotion*, 13: 125–141.

Lawson, J., Baron-Cohen, S. and Wheelwright, S. (2004) Empathising and systemising in adults with and without Asperger Syndrome. *Journal of Autism and Developmental Disorders*, 34: 301–310.

Leslie, A. M. (1987) Pretence and representation: the origins of "theory of mind". *Psychological Review*, 94: 412–426.

Leslie, A. M. and Thaiss, L. (1992) Domain specificity in conceptual development: evidence from autism. *Cognition*, 43: 225–251.

Lutchmaya, S., Baron-Cohen, S. and Raggatt, P. (2002) Foetal testosterone and eye contact in 12 month old infants. *Infant Behaviour and Development*, 25: 327–335.

Maccoby, E. (1999) *The Two Sexes: Growing Up Apart, Coming Together*. Harvard University Press, Cambridge, MA.

Mealey, L. (1995) The sociobiology of sociopathy: an integrated evolutionary model. *Behavioral and Brain Sciences*, 18: 523–599.

Meltzoff, A. N. and Decety, J. (2003) What imitation tells us about social cognition: a rapprochement between developmental psychology and cognitive neuroscience. *Philosophical Transactions of the Royal Society*, 358: 491–500.

Myers, P., Baron-Cohen, S. and Wheelwright, S. (2004) *An Exact Mind*. Jessica Kingsley, London.

O'Riordan, M., Plaisted, K., Driver, J. and Baron-Cohen, S. (2001) Superior visual search in autism. *Journal of Experimental Psychology: Human Perception and Performance*, 27: 719–730.

Plaisted, K., O'Riordan, M. and Baron-Cohen, S. (1998) Enhanced visual search for a conjunctive target in autism: a research note. *Journal of Child Psychology and Psychiatry*, 39.

Power, T. G. (1985) Mother- and father-infant play: a developmental analysis. *Child Development*, 56: 1514–1524.

Pratt, C. and Bryant, P. (1990) Young children understand that looking leads to knowing (so long as they are looking into a single barrel). *Child Development*, 61: 973–983.

Premack, D. (1990) The infant's theory of self-propelled objects. *Cognition*, 36: 1–16.

Scaife, M. and Bruner, J. (1975) The capacity for joint visual attention in the infant. *Nature*, 253: 265–266.

Schiff, W. and Oldak, R. (1990) Accuracy of judging time to arrival: effects of modality, trajectory and gender. *Journal of Experimental Psychology, Human Perception and Performance*, 16: 303–316.

Shah, A. and Frith, U. (1983) An islet of ability in autism: a research note. *Journal of Child Psychology and Psychiatry*, 24: 613–620.

Smith, P. M. (1985) *Language, the Sexes and Society*. Blackwell, Oxford.

Strayer, F. F. (1980) Child ethology and the study of preschool social relations. IN Foot, H. C., Chapman, A. J. and Smith, J. R. (eds) *Friendship and Social Relations in Children*. New York, John Wiley.

Tannen, D. (1991) *You Just Don't Understand: Women and Men in Conversation*. Virago, London.

Trevarthen, C. (1989) The relation of autism to normal socio-cultural development: the case for a primary disorder in regulation of cognitive growth by emotions. In G. Lelord, J. Muk and M. Petit (eds) *Autisme de troubles du development global de l'enfant*. Expansion Scientifique Francaise, Paris.

Voyer, D., Voyer, S. and Bryden, M. (1995) Magnitude of sex differences in spatial abilities: a meta-analysis and consideration of critical variables. *Psychological Bulletin*, 117: 250–270.

Walker, A. S. (1982) Intermodal perception of expressive behaviours by human infants. *Journal of Experimental Child Psychology*, 33: 514–535.

Wellman, H. (1990) *Children's Theories of Mind*. Bradford/MIT Press Cambridge, USA.

Wimmer, H. and Perner, J. (1983) Beliefs about beliefs: representation and constraining function of wrong beliefs in young children's understanding of deception. *Cognition*, 13: 103–128.

Witkin, H. A., Lewis, H. B., Hertzman, M. *et al.* (1954) *Personality Through Perception*. Harper & Brothers, New York.

Wittig, M. A. and Allen, M. J. (1984) Measurement of adult performance on Piaget's water horizontality task. *Intelligence*, 8: 305–313.

Yirmiya, N., Kasari, C., Sigman, M. and Mundy, P. (1990) Facial expressions of affect in autistic, mentally retarded, and normal children. *Journal of Child Psychology and Psychiatry*, 30: 725–735.

CHAPTER 17

The ontogenetic origins of human cooperation

Emily Wyman and Michael Tomasello

17.1. Introduction

Human beings are inordinately co-operative. While non-human primates regularly engage in collaborative pursuits, humans cooperate with other individuals, including non-kin and even anonymous partners on an astonishingly large scale. In addition, while other primates recognize the social group to which they belong, humans publicly designate different kinds of cooperative group membership with the use of citizenship, uniforms, body markings, and wedding rings, and this occurs before any cooperative activity has even begun. While chimpanzees cooperatively patrol their home ranges, humans collectively agree both on territorial boundaries and on rules for entry into these, using everything from village walls to immigration laws. And while non-human primates have some understanding of familial relatedness, it is only humans that assign social roles such as 'mother' and 'father' that come with social and legal obligations to cooperate in specified ways. In general, humans do not just engage in cooperative activities, they symbolically mark cooperative relations and boundaries and actively prescribe different forms of collaboration based on this.

It is highly unlikely that human beings are biologically adapted specifically for large-scale, anonymous collaboration, which is much too new in evolutionary terms—emerging probably within the last 10 000 years—and much too variable across cultures in its specifics. Much more likely is that humans are biologically adapted for certain kinds of small-scale cooperation, and that as human groups grew, these small-scale cooperative skills and motivations were co-opted by some groups for novel uses. Some scientists attempt to investigate the manifestations of these small-scale cooperative abilities by looking at modern-day hunter-gatherer societies. We believe that another productive way to examine fundamental human skills and tendencies for cooperation is through the observation of very young children as they learn to participate in various kinds of cooperative cultural activities. Our proposal here is that human beings—including young children in their second year of life—cooperate in unique ways because they are able to engage in a unique form of social engagement that is based on 'shared intentionality'.

Shared intentionality, sometimes called 'we' intentionality, refers to collaborative interactions in which participants have (1) a shared goal and (2) coordinated action roles for pursuing that goal (Searle, 1995; Tuomela, 1995). The collaborative activity itself may be complex, for instance, building a skyscraper or playing a symphony.

However, it may also be simple, as in the case of taking a walk together or engaging in a conversation. Commitment to a shared goal in these types of interaction means that each individual's intention 'I intend to X' is secondary to, and derives from, their joint intention 'We intend to X' (Searle, 1995, 2005). In practical terms, this means 'it is because we intend to do this together that I intend to do it at all'. To illustrate, consider the example of two strangers who meet in a park, become friends, and decide to take a walk together (Gilbert, 1989). An alternative to this simple scenario is that the two individuals never actually meet but incidentally happen to walk the same path, side-by-side, at the same time. From an external perspective the two tandem walks look identical but in one case their action is based on a shared goal to walk together and in the other it is based upon unrelated individual goals. Telling them apart is easy, in principle, given the right perturbation: If we have a shared goal to take a walk together, neither of us can simply change our mind and walk in the other direction without some kind of explanation or excuse to the partner. We are committed. The existence of a shared goal in a cooperative activity enables the participants to formulate differentiated action plans or complementary 'roles' towards its achievement (Bratman, 1992). Thus, if we decide to build a block tower together, you may steady the base while I place blocks on top. But, because we have a shared goal, we conceive of these roles as interdependent and so we are mutually responsive to one another in that I help you if you encounter problems and you do the same for me.

When social groups are composed of individuals who regularly engage with one another in activities with shared goals and designated roles, they create habitual social and cultural practices. For example, when groups trade goods frequently with one another or when couples cooperate repeatedly with officials in order to accomplish wedding ceremonies, habitual cultural practices associated with exchange and marriage develop. These practices give rise to what Searle (1995) terms social or 'institutional facts' that refer to phenomena such as money and marriage. These may have material manifestations in the form of dollar bills and wedding rings but essentially owe their existence and social influence to the shared beliefs, intentions and practices (see also Plotkin, Chapter 2, this volume) of the group.

In our view, the ontogenetic emergence of shared intentionality depends on the developmentally primitive phenomenon of 'joint attention'. This is the ability of the infant to understand that they and other individuals can *attend to the same object and each other's attention simultaneously* and provides a shared, interpersonal frame in which young infants can share experience with others. In this chapter we compare the skills and motivations involved in shared intentionality between humans and chimpanzees and emphasize a marked difference in their joint attention abilities. We suggest that this may explain various differences in social–cognitive skills between the two species, and propose that the phylogenetic emergence of joint attention may account for the evolution of complex forms of cooperation and uniquely human cultural practices.

17.2. **Cooperation**

Animal species engage in different types of cooperative activity depending on the underlying social–cognitive skills and motivations involved: social insects such as ants and honeybees build nests and gather foodstuffs by coordinating their movements in intricate ways (Dugatkin, 1997), activities that are presumably under fairly tight genetic control. Social mammals such as lionesses are able to coordinate their actions efficiently to collectively hunt other mammals (Packer and Ruttan, 1988), and chimpanzees do the same during their group hunting activities (Boesch and Boesch, 1989). Human cooperative activity lies on this continuum but stands out as unique because it is underpinned by a *cooperative form of intentionality*. This can be seen even in very young toddlers who competently engage in shared intentional interaction, despite being unable to provide for themselves in even the simplest ways.

Infants start to cooperate with peers between 18 and 24 months of age on problem-solving tasks (Brownell and Carriger, 1990) and in social games (Eckerman *et al.*, 1989; Hay, 1979). However, as in the case of a couple taking a walk through the park, it is often unclear as to whether these activities are based on shared or individual goals. It is possible, for instance, that when an infant builds a block tower with a partner, her goal is jointly formed with that person, without whom she would not even attempt the task. But it is equally plausible that she simply wants to build the tower for herself and that the other individual is incidental to her overall plan, appearing as a 'cooperative partner' from an external observer's perspective only. In order to assess how infants themselves conceive of their joint activities with others, Warneken et al. (2006) invented a set of simple games and problem-solving tasks. These were used to elicit cooperation between 18- and 24-month-olds and a human experimenter whose behaviour was systematically manipulated. Predictably, it was found that even the youngest children were able to coordinate their actions competently with the adult. However, interruption periods were introduced in which, for no apparent reason, the experimenter ceased to act, and children's responses to these were highly revealing. Rather than abandon the task or attempt it individually (as might be expected if the children were acting according to individual goals) children waited for the adult to resume. In fact, they often attempted to make eye contact as they waited and, more importantly, all of them made active gestural and vocal attempts to re-engage the adult. This suggests that children at this age not only coordinate their actions with others but actually form shared goals with them. Interestingly, after completing the problem-solving tasks in which the goal was to retrieve a toy, many children replaced the toy in its original location, in an apparent effort to restart the activity. Toddlers thus appear to see cooperative activity as rewarding in itself and not just as a means to an end.

In addition to forming shared goals, other evidence suggests that 18-month-old infants, and even some as young as 12 months, understand collaborative interactions as involving two differentiated roles. Carpenter et al. (2005) developed a number of simple games that were composed of two complementary roles. For instance, in one game an experimenter offered a toy base to the infant who placed a toy tiger on top. After this, the infant was given a chance to play the opposite role, by offering the base back to the experimenter. Carpenter et al. found that

after playing one role, the subjects often switched to the other and so demonstrated a nascent ability to understand and to reverse roles. It thus seems that infants can understand cooperative activity as involving interdependent and interchangeable roles that may be coordinated towards the achievement of a shared goal.

At this point, the question naturally arises as to whether chimpanzees also cooperate with shared intentions by way of shared goals and reversible roles. Crucial observations from the wild confirm that chimpanzees do engage in complex and effective group hunting in their natural habitats (Boesch and Boesch, 1989), and some observers have proposed that chimpanzee hunting is indeed based on skills of shared intentionality (Boesch, 2005). However, the possibility remains that this group hunting behaviour might be motivated by the individual goals of members of the hunting troop. It may be, for example, that during a hunt each individual assesses the state of the chase, moment-by-moment, in pursuit of his own goal and decides the best course of action for himself. In line with this, many observers see chimpanzee hunting as essentially equivalent to the group hunting of other social mammals such as lions and wolves (Cheney and Seyfarth, 1990; Tomasello and Call, 1997) and as involving nothing that would be called shared intentionality in the narrow sense of shared goals and coordinated action plans or roles.

Clearly, only experimental data can begin to tease apart these possibilities, and a direct comparison with the data on children's cooperation suggests that the hunting behaviour of chimpanzees may in reality be driven by the individual motivations of groups members rather than any form of shared goal. On the same problem-solving tasks given to young children, Warneken et al. (2006) found that chimpanzees were reasonably skilful in coordinating their actions with a cooperative human partner. However, during interruption periods, when the experimenter ceased to cooperate, the chimpanzees made no attempts to re-engage their recalcitrant partner and often resorted instead to individual attempts to retrieve the food. Another marked species difference was that, unlike the children, the chimpanzees showed little interest in the shared games, perhaps because they perceived no tangible goal, and did not spontaneously attempt to restart any of the activities. In contrast to children, who appear to take delight in cooperating with a shared goal for its own sake, cooperation in chimpanzees in these situations may be more accurately characterized as the complex coordination of individual objectives and goals.

In another direct interspecies comparison, Tomasello and Carpenter (2005) investigated differences in chimpanzee and human infant role understanding and their capacity for role reversal. Here, human-raised chimpanzees were shown the same game as the children in which one role involved offering a toy base to a partner and the other role involved placing a toy tiger on top. After some encouragement, the chimpanzees did indicate a degree of involvement in the game as, after placing the toy in the correct position, they successfully re-enacted some of the demonstrator's actions (by offering the base out). However, there was no suggestion that these actions were actually conceived of as roles in the sense that they were intended 'for' the partner. In particular, there was a conspicuous absence of any accompanying looks to the partner. This suggest that chimpanzees coordinate their actions with others but may not conceive of the interaction as composed of designated roles that are interdependent or, therefore, reversible.

These studies point towards a qualitative difference between human and chimpanzee cooperation: children are motivated in their cooperative activity to form shared goals and achieve them through the adoption and reversal of designated roles. By contrast, chimpanzee cooperation—while sophisticated in itself—may be better characterized as the coordination of individual goals and their accompanying actions. So, what might account for this difference in cooperative capacities? One experiment aimed at exploring chimpanzee cooperative competence reveals a possible, proximate explanation to this question. Melis *et al.* (2006a) presented pairs of chimpanzees with food laid on a platform that was out of reach. The platform was connected to two ropes and both individuals were required to pull these ropes simultaneously in order to retrieve the food. Each chimpanzee dyad released into the room was, therefore, faced with the option of either pulling together or else receiving nothing at all. Interestingly, two constraints

were identified that critically affected the tendency of chimpanzee dyads to cooperate. The first was how easily the secured food could be shared once it had been retrieved (i.e. how dispersed it was on the platform). The second finding was that the level of tolerance shown by any two chimpanzees in a separate feeding situation accurately predicted each dyad's ability to cooperate in the test situation. This leads Hare and Tomasello (2005) to propose that, unless the conditions are favourable, chimpanzees are unwilling to risk aggression or conflict for potential cooperative gain. Indeed, the discovery that low tolerance levels limit chimpanzee tendencies to cooperate implies that the cooperative activity of chimpanzees generally is more tightly constrained by competitive motivations than are the activities of very young children.

There is, however, an additional and perhaps complementary explanation as to why chimpanzees may not engage in cooperative activity based on shared intentions. Experimental evidence suggests that chimpanzees fail to develop a more primary group of collaborative abilities that emerge in human ontogeny between 9 and 12 months, and that are referred to collectively as 'joint attention'. The emergence of joint attention in human ontogeny is signalled towards the end of infants' first year when they begin to both follow into and also to direct the attention of others. Infants at this age begin to reliably and flexibly look where adults look through their gaze-following behaviours; to engage in extended bouts of interaction with others that are mediated by an external object in 'joint engagement'; to use adults as reference points when they encounter unfamiliar stimuli in the environments during 'social referencing'; and to act on objects in the ways that they observe adults acting on them through imitation. Around this same time they also begin to invite others to tune into their own attention frame by holding objects out for show, thus bringing them into common view. In addition, they begin directing the attention of others through indicative gestures, in particular, by pointing to objects and events in the environment. These skills emerge in quick succession towards the end of the first year (Carpenter *et al.*, 1998) and collectively represent the child's emergent ability to understand that both self and other attend to the same object and can monitor each other's attention to that object simultaneously.

The development of joint attention demonstrates the child's emergent understanding of attention in others. That is, that others not only perceive things in their environment but also intentionally focus on a subset of those things. In addition, their indicating, pointing and showing behaviours evidence an early ability to form and navigate a *shared frame* with others based on mutual attention. These developmental achievements have been termed nothing short of revolutionary in the child's development (Tomasello, 1999) because they enable at least two further ontogenetic advances: firstly, joint attention allows infants to jointly focus on entities or events with others that can, therefore, become the object of a shared goal. For instance, it enables two individuals to intentionally focus on a block tower and one another's relation to the construction. They may then take the interdependent roles of, say, 'stabilizer' and 'builder', facilitating the achievement of a goal that neither would have been able to achieve alone. Second, it provides a shared attentional format in which an infant and her partner can communicate intentionally about aspects of their environment (see Section 17.3). It is also worth noting that there is a sense in which, evolutionarily, joint attention presupposes a level of community cooperation or 'trust'. The signalling of one's attentional focus for the express reason of sharing it implies a level of protection from the competitive exploitation of conspecifics and perhaps even a community-wide predisposition to cooperate. In sum, joint attention represents a common attentional framework that allows human infants and, later, adults to form shared goals, to intentionally communicate with others, and to respond sensitively to one another's actions during a cooperative activity. It may also, theoretically, imply a community-wide level of cooperative motive that enables individuals to advertise their attentional focus without fear of exploitation. It is essentially a shared cooperative frame that provides a foundation for cooperative action.

Against this background, it seems highly significant that chimpanzees do not appear to develop any significant joint attentional skills. Tomasello and Carpenter (2005) directly compared the ontogenetic emergence of social–cognitive skills in three human-raised, infant chimpanzees with that of human infants and found a key difference. Human infants first develop skills of 'joint engagement' in which they check back-and-forth between an object and an adult's face. They then begin to engage in communicative gesturing and attention following behaviours and, lastly, engage in imitative learning. Chimpanzees, by contrast, fail to develop any joint engagement behaviours at all. They first produce some imitative behaviours and their attention following and communicative gesture skills develop afterwards. This difference may account for limits in their propensity to actively establish any joint forms of attention as they subsequently fail to use indicative gestures in order to share attention with other individuals or to show things to others for this purpose. Indeed, chimpanzees, in contrast to children, seem to demonstrate their most sophisticated perception reading skills in contexts, not of sharing or cooperation, but of direct social competition (Hare *et al.*, 2000, 2001).

17.3. Communication

Human toddlers use their communicative skills in a variety of cooperative contexts by employing gestures, vocalizations, and primitive language to coordinate social engagement with others (Ashley and Tomasello, 1996; Eckerman and Didow, 1996; Warnekan *et al.*, in press). However, the actual process of communication in humans is collaborative in a more fundamental way because much of it is founded upon joint attentional abilities. When young infants learn to communicate gesturally, for example, they are essentially learning that other people intend to direct their attention within the joint attentional frame and that they can direct the attention of others in the same way. Similarly, when they begin to acquire language, infants learn that words can be used in place of gestures as attention-directing devices (Tomasello, 1999). In contrast to this, chimpanzee cooperation is marked by a general absence of any intentional communication (Melis *et al.*, 2006a,b; Povinelli and O'Neil, 2000). It is proposed here that what may limit the scope and extent of chimpanzee communicative behaviour is both the absence of any joint attentional framework and the absence of any default cooperative tendency (Silk, this volume, Chapter 10; Jensen *et al.*, 2006) or, conversely, the presence of a more highly competitive one.

Consider, for example, the case of an infant who plays a hiding-and-finding game with an adult. The adult points to one of two containers and looks back and forth from the infant to the container. Infants as early as 14 months are able to attend to the adult's point as a communicative cue, identify the referent and infer the relevance of the gesture to their goal, successfully finding the hidden toy (Behne *et al.*, 2005; see Sperber and Wilson, 1986, on relevance). They understand that the adult's motive is to help them and that she intends for them to attend to something. That is, meaning that they understand 'communicative intentions' (Grice, 1957). Strikingly, this simple task proves difficult for chimpanzees. Despite being able to follow the gaze of another individual in order to find hidden food (Call *et al.*, 1998) they are unable to use intentionally produced communicative cues to do the same (Tomasello *et al.*, 1997).

So why, when highly motivated to find food, are chimpanzees are unable to utilize a cooperative human point in order to locate it? An experiment relevant to this question was conducted by Hare and Tomasello (2004) who directly compared chimpanzees' communicative abilities in cooperative and competitive situations and found a clear asymmetry: an experimenter established either a cooperative relationship with the chimpanzees (showing them various food stashes) or a competitive relationship with them (taking food stashes away and devouring them in the animal's full sight). Subjects then interacted with the experimenter who played the role either of a cooperative partner by pointing to the container hiding food or of a competitive partner by reaching to grab the hidden food for herself. Despite the fact that the surface actions were similar in both cases, chimpanzees were significantly more successful in finding the hidden food in the competitive situation than in the cooperative one. Furthermore, a related study suggests that it was not the experimenter's attempt to communicate *per se* that chimpanzees found difficult to comprehend in the case of pointing, but rather the type of communicative gesture used.

Herrman and Tomasello (in press) also found that chimpanzees were unable to find food to which a cooperative experimenter pointed. However, if the experimenter turned her hand from a point into a stop signal (a gesture these animals are somewhat familiar with) and said 'No!' with prohibitive verbal intonation, the chimpanzees were more than able to infer where the food was and secure it. This implies that chimpanzees, at the very least, comprehend that the human has an intention towards the container and can infer the location of the hidden food from this. It may also signify an understanding that the human intends to affect the chimpanzee's ensuing action prohibitively for some reason, which the chimpanzee infers to be the presence of food. But the fact that chimpanzees cannot use a cooperative point to do the same suggests that they simply do not understand that the point is an attempt to *affect their attention*. Without joint attention, chimpanzees seem unable to utilize ostensively and intentionally signalled information from others who attempt to help them by informatively directing their attention in some way.

This basic social–cognitive difference between chimpanzees and humans gives rise to variation in the frequency and type of communicative gestures produced. Infants point imperatively, in order to get things they want, and informatively, in order to help others by providing information for them (Liskowski *et al.*, 2006). In addition, they engage in 'declarative' pointing in which there is no goal other than the emotional reward of socially sharing interest with another person. For instance, Liskowski *et al.* (2004) found that in certain cases of infant pointing, when the adult looked to the object, expressed excitement or showed no reaction at all, the infants expressed discontent. They were satisfied only when the adult both looked to the referent and expressed positive emotion towards them implying that their goal had been to share attention and interest with the adult and they had been using their pointing gestures as a means to this end.

In light of the multi-functional uses 12-month-old infants make of the pointing gesture, it seems surprising, at first, that apes to do not point in the wild and do not point for conspecifics. This is particularly so since such a device is well within the physical capabilities of chimpanzees and, in fact, apes who have had extensive human contact have been known to point in some experimental situations (Leavens and Hopkins, 1998; Tomasello *et al.*, 1994; Gomez, 2004). However, the purpose of their pointing gestures appears to be confined to an imperative function in which the apes understand how to direct the behaviour of human experimenters in order to secure food. It seems to be the case that no apes point declaratively or informatively, that is, in order to direct attention.

The restriction of apes' pointing behaviour to a limited range of human-controlled and imperative situations highlights a useful distinction between two types of imperative communication, both verbal and gestural: as mentioned, it may be that chimpanzee imperative points are aimed at affecting the actions of other individuals in order to get what they want and, in the case of a human addressee, they expect that individual to help them (which they would presumably never predict with conspecifics in the wild). Similarly, human children may also use imperative gestures in order to achieve some effect in the environment. However, experimental evidence indicates that they may try to do so by informing others of their goals or desires. Imagine, for example, a young child who requests gesturally or verbally that one of two toys be passed to her. An adult misunderstands, picks up the incorrect toy and says "Hmm this one? No, I'll give you this other [correct] toy." She then passes the toy that the child had originally requested. If this child wants simply to produce an effect in the environment by getting her toy, she should at this point be contented, despite the misunderstanding. Schwe and Markman (1997) found, however, that 2-year-old children in just this situation repeat their request and to clarify their communicative attempts, suggesting that, in addition to retrieving the toy, their goal was to successfully inform the adult of their desire. It seems that apes who have experienced extensive human contact learn to produce imperative communicative gestures in order affect the actions of others but that only humans produce informative communicative gestures in which they inform others of their goals and desires and understand when others do the same for them (Tomasello, 2006).

Formally speaking, this means that only infants are able to deal with communicative intentions.

This insight has significant consequences for the development of symbolic functioning in humans and chimpanzees because in order to understand or use a symbol, one must recognize the communicative intention that lies behind it (Tomasello, 1999). This results from the principle that objects in the world do not have intrinsic symbolic value but are invested with this value when used by a person or community in order to *communicate* something (see Rakoczy *et al.*, 2006, for discussion). Thus, an item such as a wedding ring only symbolizes the institution of marriage when we, a symbolic community, invest it with this value. The ring can then be used as a device to signify a couple's intention to communicate their marriage status to the rest of the community who understand this communicative intention and, therefore, recognize them as married. In a similar way, linguistic symbols embody the communicative intentions that a person wishes to express and when children learn to use both language and symbolic artefacts, they are learning the conventional ways in which ancestral populations have found it useful to express those intentions (Tomasello, 1999). Without joint attention, chimpanzees may not grasp the basic structure of communicative intentions and without communicative intentions, chimpanzees do not, as a community, collectively invest objects (including vocal sounds) with symbolic value.

17.4. A phylogenetic hypothesis

The social lives of Old World monkeys and apes involve negotiating a complex and shifting balance between the forces of competition and cooperation. The proposal here is that human beings evolved especially enhanced skills and tendencies for collaborating with one another, relative to other primates. These augmented cooperative capacities have been characterized as the ability to form shared goals and to coordinate roles, and, along with joint attention and intentional communication, may be seen as adaptive specializations. However, rather than emphasize the modularity or domain specificity of each skill (see, for example, (Cosmides and Tooby, 1994; Leslie, 1994; Pinker, 1994, 1997;

Spelke and Newport, 1997; Sperber and Wilson, 2002), we stress the way in which interrelated cognitive aptitudes may have arisen as functional dependants. In fact, the emergence of cooperative action in ontogeny reveals a highly complex interaction between multiple pathways: First, an understanding of perception and intentionality converge during development to enable the child to understand attention in others. Later on, joint forms of attention afford a framework within which the child can begin to form shared goals and coordinate roles, and it is in this context that the child comes to need and develop skills of intentional communication.

The functional interrelation between social cognitive skills in ontogeny may parallel complex relationships that have emerged in human phylogeny. With regard to canine species, for example, Hare and Tomasello (2005) propose that the evolution of social cognitive skills may have occurred secondarily to, and as a result of, selection on emotional systems mediating fear and aggression. They note the unexpected result that domestic dogs are more competent than chimpanzees in locating hidden food via a human's point or gaze direction cue (Hare *et al.*, 1998; Hare and Tomasello, 1999), and look to processes of Fox domestication for an explanation. Belyaev (1979) selectively bred an experimental group of foxes on the basis of whether they approached a human fearlessly and non-aggressively as well as a control group of foxes that was bred randomly. When tested on their ability to find hidden food using a human's point or gaze cue, the experimental group succeeded as competently as domestic dogs and significantly better than the control group (Hare *et al.*, 2005). Therefore, in explaining the notable communicative skills of domestic dogs, Hare and Tomasello (2005) advocate a two-stage sequence in which initial selection for a reduction in 'emotional reactivity' placed the animals in a new 'adaptive space'. This then enabled further selection on more cognitive abilities (inherited from pack life in an ancestral wolf population) as those now able to solve novel social–cognitive problems posed by life alongside humans came to an adaptive advantage.

Applying this two-stage model to humans, they propose that the evolution of a less reactive human temperament may have necessarily preceded the evolution of more complex forms of human social cognition. But what could have led to this reduction in emotional reactivity? It is possible that the intense climatic and environmental variability that has characterized hominin evolution (Potts, 1998) led to equally dramatic cycles in the overall availability and density of resources. A plausible consequence of this would have been sporadically increased population densities, and closer proximity during foraging periods, for example. Against this background of environmental change, the emergence of counter-dominant social strategies and egalitarian social systems (see Boehm 1999; Erdal & Whiter 1994) may have created conditions in which a less reactive temperament might potentially evolve. Most recently, Wrangham (in press) proposes a scenario in which early hominins played a directly instrumental role in selecting for enhanced within-group tolerance. He suggests that a first step in the evolution of modern human societies may have occurred when human groups began to ostracize overly aggressive or despotic members, thus engaging in a type of 'self-domestication process' similar to the artificial domestication that has occurred in canine species.

Our tentative addition to this model is that a reduction in emotional reactivity that facilitated closer proximity to conspecifics without a concomitant increase in stress levels may have created social conditions favouring the emergence of joint attention. In these more spatially intimate contexts, individuals operating on common food supplies may have come incidentally to help one another and a resultant rise in foraging efficiency is predicted to have shaped this type of interaction into an increasingly routine behaviour. Furthermore, because increased tolerance would not have removed the threat of conflict altogether, but rather reduced the likelihood of it, individual dyads engaged in helping behaviour may have begun to monitor their partner's attention to common resources as well as the resource itself in order to avoid potential clashes, exploitation, or theft. Thus novel degrees of inter-individual lenience and some kind of mutual attention frame may have enabled further selection for those individuals jointly attending to objects, forming shared goals and adopting cooperative roles. With the roots of a joint attention system in place and some rudimentary form of cooperation based on shared intentions established, the collaborative stage may then have been set for the development of full-blown shared intentionality involving collective cultural institutions and knowledge structures (Plotkin, this volume, Chapter 2).

The classic problem of how systems of cooperation can stabilize despite the fact that these conditions favour the emergence of 'cheaters' also applies here. Theories relying on some form of kin-selection (Hamilton, 1964), group-level selection (Sober and Wilson, 1998) or cultural group selection (Boyd and Richerson, 2002, 2006) that depend on social norms and cultural conformity may provide part of the story. However, a persuasive model that relies on the more prevailing tradition of investigating selection at the individual level is also useful: Roberts (2005) proposes a variation on Hamilton's kin selection formula to show that when individual fitness is positively related to the benefits of group living, individuals through their interdependence have some 'stake' in the welfare and survival of other group members. The result is that tolerance and active cooperation within a group are not subject to the destabilizing threats of freeriders because tolerance and cooperative efforts equate, secondarily, to individual self-investment. Perhaps a combination of reduced emotional reactivity, increasingly attuned joint attention skills, and the indirect self-investment associated with such 'stakeholder altruism' interacted to support the emergence of shared intentional cooperation in the human lineage.

Finally, the evolution of cooperation based on shared intentionality does not, alone, have the potential to explain the observable differences between human cultures today. While joint attention, shared intentionality, and intentional communication enable all humans to symbolically mediate their cooperative relationships through the use of language and cultural artefacts (Vygotsky, 1978), different cultural groups—from the Hadze to the Aché to the Europeans—have created exceptionally different cultural and institutional structures over historical time. To explain human cognition and social life, one needs both the biology of shared intentionality and the psychology of cultural–historical interaction.

References

Ashley, J. and Tomasello, M. (1996) Cooperative problem-solving and teaching in preschoolers. 1998. *Social Development*, 7: 143–163.

Behne, T., Carpenter, M. and Tomasello, M. (2005) One-year-olds comprehend the communicative intentions behind gestures in a hiding game. *Developmental Science*, 8: 492–499.

Belyaev, D. (1979) Destabilising selection as a factor in domestication. *Journal of Heredity*, 70: 301–308.

Boehm, C. (1999) *Hierarchy in the Forest*. Harvard University Press, Cambridge, MA.

Boesch, C. (2005) Joint cooperative hunting among wild chimpanzees: taking natural observations seriously—comment on 'Understanding and sharing intentions: the origins of cultural cognition' by Tomasello *et al.* (2005) *Behavioral and Brain Sciences*, 28: 692–693.

Boesch, C. and Boesch, H. (1989) Cooperative hunting of wild chimpanzees in the tai national park. *American Journal of Physical Anthropology*, 78: 547–573.

Boyd, R. and Richerson, P. J. (2002) Group beneficial norms can spread rapidly in a structured population. *Journal of Theoretical Biology*, 215: 287–296.

Boyd, R. and Richerson, P. J. (2006) Culture and the evolution of human social instincts. In N. Enfield and S. Levinson (eds). *Roots of human sociality: Culture Cognition and Interaction*. Berg, Oxford.

Bratman, M. E. (1992) Shared cooperative activity. *The Philosophical Review*, 101: 327–341.

Brownell, C. A. and Carriger, M. S. (1990) Changes in cooperation and self-other differentiation during the second year. *Child Development*, 61: 1164–1174.

Call, J., Hare, B. and Tomasello, M. (1998) Chimpanzee gaze in an object-choice task. *Animal Cognition*, 1: 89–99.

Carpenter, M., Nagell, K., Tomasello, M. (1998) Social cognition, joint attention, and communicative competence from 9 to 15 months of age. *Monographs of the Society for Research into Child Development*, 63: 1–143.

Carpenter, M., Tomasello, M. and Striano, T. (2005) Role reversal imitation and language in typically developing infants and children with autism. *Infancy*, 8: 253–278.

Cheney, D. L. and Seyfarth, R. M. (1990) *How Monkeys See the World: Inside the Mind of Another Species*. University of Chicago Press, Chicago.

Cosmides, L. and Tooby, J. (1994) Origins of domain specificity: the evolution of functional organisation. In L. A. Hirschfeld and S. A. Gelman (eds) *Mapping the Mind: Domain Specificty in Cognition and Culture*. Cambridge University Press, New York.

Dugatkin, L. A. (1997) *Cooperation Among Animals: An Evolutionary Perspective*. Oxford University Press, New York.

Eckerman, C. O. and Didow, S. M. (1996) Nonverbal imitation and toddler's mastery of verbal means of achieving coordinated action. *Developmental Psychology*, 32: 141–152.

Eckerman, C. O., Davis, C. and Didow, S. (1989) Toddler's emerging ways to achieve social coordination with a peer. *Child Development*, 60: 440–453.

Erdal, D. and Whiter, A. (1994) On human egalitarianism: an evolutionary product of Machiavellian Status Escalation? *Current Anthropology*, 35: 175–183.

Gilbert, M. (1989) *On Social Facts*. Princeton University Press, Oxford.

Gomez, J. C. (2004) *Apes, Monkeys, Children and the Growth of Mind*. Harvard University Press, Cambridge, MA.

Grice, P. (1957) Meaning. *The Philosophical Review*, 66: 377–388.

Hamilton, W. D. (1964) The genetical evolution of social behaviour I and II. *Journal of Theoretical Biology*, 7: 1–52.

Hare, B. and Tomasello, M. (1999) Domestic dogs (canis familiaris) use human and conspecific social cues to locate hidden food. *Journal of Comparative Psychology*, 113: 173–177.

Hare, B. and Tomasello, M. (2005) Human-like social skills in dogs? *Trends in Cognitive Science*, 9: 439–444.

Hare, B. and Tomasello, M. (2004) Chimpanzees are more skilful in competitive than collaborative tasks. *Animal Behaviour*, 68: 571–581.

Hare, B., Call, J. and Tomasello, M. (1998) Communication of food location between human and dog (*canis familiaris*). *Evolution of Cognition*, 2: 137–159.

Hare, B., Call, J., Agnetta, B. and Tomasello, M. (2000) Chimpanzees know what conspecifics do and do not see. *Animal Behaviour*, 59: 771–785.

Hare, B., Call, J. and Tomasello, M. (2001) Do chimpanzees know what conspecifics know? *Animal Behaviour*, 61: 139–151.

Hare, B., Plyusnina, I., Iganacio, N., Wrangham, R. and Trut, L. (2005) Social cognitive evolution in captive foxes is a correlated by-product of experimental domestication. *Current Biology*, 15: 1–20.

Hay, D. (1979) Cooperative interactions and sharing between very young children and their parents. *Developmental Psychology*, 15: 647–653.

Herrmann, E. and Tomasello, M. (in press) Apes' and children's' understanding of cooperative and competitive motives in a communicative situation.

Jensen, K., Hare, B., Call, J. and Tomasello, M. (2006) What's in it for me? Self regard precludes altruism and spite in chimpanzees. *Proceedings of the Royal Society of London, B*, 273: 1013–1021.

Leavens, D. A. and Hopkins, W. D. (1998) Intentional communication by chimpanzees: a cross-sectional study of the use of referential gestures. *Developmental Psychology*, 34: 813–822.

Leslie, A. M. (1994) ToMM, ToBy, and agency: core architecture and domain specificity. In L. A. Hirschfeld and S. A. Gelman (eds), *Mapping the Mind: Domain Specificty in Cognition and Culture*. Cambridge University Press, New York.

Liszkowski, U., Carpenter, M., Henning, A. Striano, T. and Tomasello, M. (2004) Twelve-month-olds point to share attention and interest. *Developmental Science*, 7: 297–307.

Lizkowski, U., Carpenter, M., Striano, T. and Tomasello, M. (2006) 12- and 18- month olds point to provide information for others. *Journal of Cognition and Development*, 7: 173–187.

Melis, A., Hare, B. and Tomasello, M. (2006a) Chimpanzees recruit the best collaborators. *Science*, 311(5765): 1297–1300.

Melis, A., Hare, B. and Tomasello, M. (2006b) Engineering cooperation: tolerance constraints on cooperation. *Animal Behaviour*, 72: 275–286.

Packer, C. and Ruttan, L. (1988) The evolution of cooperative hunting. *The American Naturalist*, 132: 159–198.

Pinker, S. (1994) *The Language Instinct: How the Mind Creates Language*. William Morrow, New York

Pinker, S. (1997) *How the Mind Works*. Penguin, London.

Potts, R. (1998) Variability selection in hominid evolution. *Evolutionary Anthropology*, 7: 81–96.

Povinelli, D. J. and O'Neil, D. K. (2000) Do chimpanzees use their gestures to instruct each other? In S. Baron-Cohen, H. Tager-Flusberg and D. J. Cohen (eds), *Understanding Other Minds: Perspectives from Developmental Cognitive Neuroscience*, pp. 459–487. Oxford University Press, New York.

Rakoczy, H., Tomasello, M. and Striano, T. (2006) How Children Turn Objects into Symbols: A Cultural Learning Account. In: L. Namy (ed) *Symbol use and representation*. pp. 66–97. Lawrence Erlbaum, New York.

Roberts, G. (2005) Cooperation through interdependence. *Animal Behaviour*, 70: 901–908.

Schwe, H. I. and Markman, E. M. (1997) Young children's appreciation of the mental impact of their communicative signals. *Developmental Psychology*, 33: 630–636.

Searle, J. R. (1995) *The Construction of Social Reality*. Free Press, New York.

Searle, J. R. (2005) What is an institution? *Journal of Institutional Economics*, 1: 1–22.

Sober, E. and Wilson, D. S. (1998) *Unto Others: The Evolution and Psychology of Unselfish Behaviour*. Harvard University Press, Cambridge, MA.

Spelke, E. and Newport, E. (1997) Nativism, empiricism and the development of knowledge. In R. Lerner (ed.), *Handbook of Child Psychology*, vol. 1. Wiley, New York.

Sperber, D. and Wilson, D. (1986) *Relevance: Communication and Cognition*. Harvard University Press, Cambridge, MA.

Sperber, D. and Wilson, D. (2002) Pragmatics, modularity and mindreading. *Mind and Language*, 17: 3–23.

Tomasello, M. (2006) *The Cultural Origins of Human Cognition*. Harvard University Press, Cambridge, MA.

Tomasello, M. (2006) Why don't apes point? In N. Enfield and S. Levinson (eds), *Roots of human sociality: culture, cognition and interaction*, pp. 506–524 Berg, Oxford.

Tomasello, M. and Call, J. (1997) *Primate Cognition*: Oxford University Press. New York.

Tomasello, M. and Carpenter, M. (2005) The emergence of social cognition in three young chimpanzees. *Monographs of the Society for Research into Child Development*, 70: 1–152.

Tomasello, M., Call, J., Nagell, K. and Olguin, R. (1994) The learning and use of gestural signals by young chimpanzees: a trans-generational study. *Primates*, 35: 137–154.

Tomasello, M., Call, J. and Gluckman, A. (1997) Comprehension of novel communicative signs by apes and human children. *Child Development*, 68: 1067–1080.

Tuomela, R. (1995) *The Importance of Us: A Philosophical Study of a Basic Social Notion*. Stanford University Press, Palo Alto, CA.

Vygotsky, L. S. (1978) *Mind in Society: The Development of Higher Psychological Processes*. Harvard University Press, Cambridge, MA.

Warneken, F., Chen, F. and Tomasello, T. (2006) Cooperative activities in young children and chimpanzees. *Child Development*, 77: 640–663.

Wrangham, R. (in press) *The Cooking Ape*.

CHAPTER 18

Childhood experiences and reproductive strategies

Jay Belsky

18.1. Introduction

Students of human development, especially those working from traditional psychological perspectives, generally take for granted the biological structure of the life course. Introductory textbooks in developmental psychology routinely point out that humans are born relatively helpless at birth, have an extended juvenile period before reaching reproductive maturity and, in the case of females, experience a rather long post-reproductive life (i.e. menopause). The fact that the very nature of the human life course is something in need of explanation, at least from an evolutionary–biological perspective, is rarely considered. Indeed, it is taken as a given that our species' lengthy period of juvenile dependency evolved in order to facilitate brain development and learning and thereby afford successful functioning in the highly varied physical environments and social contexts in which our ancestors resided (see Kaplan *et al.*, 2000). Not yet appreciated, however, is the competing claim that an extended childhood was an *inadvertent* consequence of the development of a post-reproductive lifespan which enabled grandmothers to increase their reproductive success by assisting daughters in childrearing, and thus that learning represents a mere

secondary effect of a long juvenile period, itself determined by the long lifespan (Hawkes, 2003; Hawkes *et al.*, 2000).

However one views this contest of ideas, it makes clear that from the standpoint of evolutionary anthropology, the main question about human life history concerns selection pressures which led to the emergence of our species, with the central features of that life history more or less taken for granted. Given the field's focus upon cross-species comparisons (e.g. chimpanzees' faster development and shorter lifespans), it is not surprising that little attention has been paid to *within-species* variation in life history. Until perhaps two decades ago, the same was generally true of mainstream developmental–psychological thinking as well.

Even though a variety of theoretical perspectives (e.g. social learning theory, life-course theory, attachment theory) and a huge research literature address the determinants and sequelae of variation in multiple elements of human life history (e.g. onset of sexual behaviour, parenting, marital/partner relations), evolutionary thinking informs little of this work. Indisputably, it is to a history of rewards and punishments or to the child's psychological attachment to a parent or to the quality of important relationships in the child's life (e.g. parent–child, marital, friendship) that students of human development routinely turn when seeking insight into developmental 'outcomes' that evolutionary thinkers would characterize as features of life history and elements of reproductive strategy (e.g. age of first sex, sexual 'promiscuity', quality of parenting). In many respects this is because students of child development, whether trained in psychological, sociological or cultural–anthropological traditions, have been—and remain—concerned principally with proximate questions of how ('How does development operate?') rather than with ultimate questions of *why* ('Why does development operate the way it seems to?').

An excellent example of such an almost exclusive focus upon proximate rather than ultimate influences on development can be found, ironically, in four decades of research on the infant's attachment to its (principal) caregiver, usually the mother. Even though Bowlby (1969), perhaps the first modern practitioner of evolutionary psychology and the theoretician who coined the now well-worn phrase 'environment of evolutionary adaptation' (EEA), drew heavily upon Darwin's insights when formulating attachment theory, his concern with ultimate causation, while mentioned in passing in textbook discussions of infant–parent attachment, has been more or less abandoned entirely in developmental studies of individual differences in attachment, especially the determinants and consequence of this first relationship (but see Chisholm, 1996; Belsky, 1997, 1999). Although an abundance of evidence supports Bowlby's (1969) thesis that secure attachment lays the foundation for general well-being (Thompson, 1999), as well as Ainsworth's (1973) postulate that sensitive (versus insensitive) mothering fosters secure (versus insecure) attachment (de Wolff and van Ijzendoorn 1997), developmentalists fascinated with the attachment bond virtually never wonder why development operates this way rather than some other. Given the risk in the EEA of mother being physically or emotionally compromised and/or even dying during the infant's first years of life, to say nothing of the inherent unpredictability of the future, would it not have made more sense for nature to design a relationship system that was less—if at all—shaped by the quality of care that mother provided or that

would exert less of a developmental impact on the child than attachment theory presupposes? Clearly, such fundamental theoretical issues pertaining to the developmental legacy of early attachment security or childhood experiences more generally arise only when evolutionary 'why' questions about ultimate causation are posed.

Even though mainstream developmental psychology and human development have not, for the most part, applied an evolutionary perspective when asking and answering questions about how experiences in childhood might shape development later in the life course, it is not the case that no such efforts have been made in that direction. In this chapter, one such programme of theory-building dealing with childhood experience and reproductive strategy, along with some relevant evidence, will be reviewed. Before doing so, however, two foundational topics must be addressed. The first is the proposition that experiences early in life might shape developments later in life. The second is life-history theory, as this serves as the higher-level framework on which the chapter builds (Ketelaar and Ellis, 2000; Ellis, 2004).

18.2. **The legacy of childhood experience**

For most students of child development, it is presumed that experiences in the early years of life influence individual differences in later development. This is not say, however, that there is no debate about the power of earlier experiences to shape later development (e.g. determining versus contributing; contingent versus inevitable), the timing of putatively influential experiences (e.g. first year of life, first 5 years, prepubertal years), the nature of these experiences (e.g. prenatal exposure to alcohol, quality of parenting, sib and/or peer relationships), the means by which any such influence is exerted (e.g. direct versus indirect) or the aspects of development which are affected (e.g. intelligence, antisocial behaviour). Nevertheless, it remains the case that only rarely is the specific question already posed with respect to attachment entertained more generally: 'Why should experiences early in life contribute to and forecast developments later in life?' In fact, in recent social-policy-oriented discussions of early-experience effects on brain development (e.g. Schore, 2001; Shonkoff and Phillips, 2000), virtually no attempt has been made to explain why natural selection would have crafted a developmental system whereby what transpires early in life, well before reproductive maturity, would affect functioning later in the lifespan.

Yet almost three decades ago, Kagan *et al.* (1978) argued that the notion that early experiences affect long-term psychological/behavioural development was more a (Western) cultural myth than biological or psychological reality, a theme taken up by Breur (1997) in challenging claims that human research illuminates early-experience effects on brain development and, thereby, provides a basis of crafting social policies. Relatedly, Lewis (1997) has argued that concurrent experience is of far greater consequence to human functioning than experiences and developments earlier in life. Add to these voices the perhaps commonsense logic that it would make much more sense for nature to shape human development so as to be consistent with Lewis's (1997) thesis emphasizing responsiveness to contemporary environmental input rather than to earlier life experiences and it becomes clear why there are grounds for questioning much of what will be the primary focus of this chapter.

But even when plausible arguments against early-experience effects sound convincing, there remains the matter of evidence. Perhaps most noteworthy is recent research showing that antenatal experiences, especially but not exclusively involving nutrition, affect foetal growth and forecast physical health *across the lifespan*, including risk for developing (a) impaired glucose tolerance and reduced insulin sensitivity (Phillips, 1998), (b) impaired immune function (McDade *et al.*, 2001), (c) coronary heart disease (Robinson and Barker, 2002) and (d) even senescence (Sayer *et al.*, 1998). If the very early environment of the womb and foetal growth systematically affect physical health over the ensuing decades of life—and in a manner likened to a 'weather forecast' signalling the unborn child of a poorly nourished woman that it is about to enter a harsh world (Bateson *et al.*, 2004)—why should postnatal experience operate

any differently on psychological and behavioural phenotypes? After all, it is now well appreciated that brain development, to say nothing of psychological and behavioural development, continues well into adolescence and even beyond (Giedd *et al.*, 1999).

Moreover, it would seem just as commonsensical to assume that rather than leaving human functioning to the whim of contemporary circumstances, nature would have crafted an organism capable of modifying its phenotype in response to early environmental inputs provided those inputs afforded a reasonable degree of prediction—in the EEA—about the future that the developing organism would encounter as it grew and developed. (For detailed consideration of this latter point, see Belsky, 2005a,b; Ellis, 2004.) This argument seems even more plausible the moment the possibility is entertained that developmental constraints imposed on the organism as it matured could restrict its future responsiveness to the environment (Boyce and Ellis, in press). In point of fact, many organisms other than humans are strikingly capable of altering their development in response to their environment, including environments encountered early in development (Kaplan and Lancaster, 2003; West-Eberhard, 2003). In sum, although it should be regarded as an empirical question whether any kind of experience early in life influences some particular aspect of development later in life, there seems to be good theoretical and empirical reason for entertaining the prospect that it could. This, of course, is the working assumption on which this chapter is based.

18.3. Life-history theory

The beginning of this chapter made clear that the biological organization of the human life course is something in need of explanation. Life-history theory (LHT) is the metatheoretical framework within more general evolutionary theory that seeks to account for the timing of reproductive and lifespan developments in terms of evolved strategies for distributing metabolic resources between the competing demands of growth, maintenance and reproduction (McArthur and Wilson, 1967; Wilson, 1975; Charnov, 1993; Stearns, 1992; Ellis, 2004;

Kuzawa, 2005). LHT describes an individual's total bioenergetic and material resources as allocated between somatic effort (i.e. resources devoted to the continued survival) and reproductive effort (i.e. resources devoted to producing–supporting offspring). Reproductive effort can itself be further divided into mating effort (i.e. resources devoted to obtaining–retaining sexual partners) and parental effort (i.e. resources devoted to enhancing offspring survival and quality). Life-history traits are the basic units of analysis in LHT and include, for example, age at weaning, age at sexual maturity, adult body size, time to first reproduction, and litter size.

LHT provides a useful means of organizing life-history traits in a manner that highlights costs, benefits and trade-offs of different patterns of development. Such trade-offs are inevitable because time and energy used for one purpose cannot be available for another. In a determinant-growing species like humans (i.e. cease growing at reproductive maturity), the decision of when to switch from investing energy in growth to investing in reproduction is a classic example of such an adaptive trade-off. So, too, is that between number and fitness of offspring. Even though there are benefits, reproductively speaking, of large adult size, risks are associated nevertheless with delaying maturity in order to grow large; this is because there is always the chance of dying before the reproductive benefits of large size are realized (Williams, 1966). At the age when mortality risk associated with delaying maturity outweighs the reproductive benefits of growing larger, LHT predicts that the organism will cease growth and direct energy otherwise devoted to growth into supporting reproduction. These assumptions about the costs and benefits of delaying maturity have been used to predict the timing of reproductive maturity across species (Charnov, 1993).

Natural selection should favour earlier reproduction, *ceterus paribus*, for several reasons (Ellis, 2004). Because the risk of death always exceeds zero, no matter what the time scale, producing offspring earlier in the lifespan lowers the chance of leaving no descendants. Derivatively, the benefits to fitness of early reproduction should be greater the higher the mortality risk (Chisholm, 1999). In addition, earlier reproduction affords a longer period of reproduction, as

onset and termination of reproduction (e.g. menopause) are unrelated (Borgerhoff Mulder, 1989; Peccei, 2000). Finally, early reproduction increases total lineage reproduction, which of course is important from the standpoint of inclusive fitness, due to abbreviated generation times.

All this is not to say that delayed reproduction is without benefit. In fact, competing selection pressures favour delayed reproduction: slower-developing organisms usually attain larger adult body size which itself is generally related to lower risk of death, greater energy production and stores to channel to reproduction across the lifespan and, perhaps most importantly, increased chances of succeeding in intrasexual competition for mates (Charnov, 1993; Hill and Kaplan, 1999). It should be clear, then, that no one means of organizing life-history traits is likely to maximize inclusive fitness across all species and ecological niches.

18.3.1. Variation in human reproductive strategy

Two general life histories reflecting the co-occurrence of a suite of life-history traits are widely discussed when cross-species variation is the focus of consideration (Pianka, 1970). *K*-selected species are relatively long-lived; spend a considerable portion of that lifespan as juveniles; and tend to bear and rear relatively few young while investing heavily in them (e.g. elephants). In contrast, *r*-selected species generally follow the opposite pattern: short lifespan, brief juvenile period, heightened fecundity, and limited parental investment (e.g. rabbits). Although humans obviously qualify more as a *K*- than an *r*-selected species, *r/K* thinking that originally emerged to characterize and explain cross-species variation in life histories has been applied to within-species variation (Stearns and Koella, 1986), including aboriginal human populations (Hill and Hurtado, 1996; see also Rushton, 1985).

When humans become the focus of concern, terminology often shifts to discussions of reproductive strategy. Thus, some individuals are observed to mature sooner than others, mate earlier than others, establish less-enduring pair bonds than others, bear more offspring than others and invest less intensively in them than others. Rather than speaking in terms of *r/K* life histories (but see Rushton, 1985), such variation is typically discussed in terms of quantity/quality reproductive strategies (Figueredo *et al.*, 2005) or, when applied to men, in terms of cads and dads (Draper and Harpending, 1982).

18.3.1.1. The role of heritability

The reality of variation in human reproductive strategy raises the question of determinants. This will be the principle focus of the remainder of this chapter, with emphasis placed on childhood experience. Because individual differences in virtually every measurable psychological and behavioural trait have been shown to be at least partly heritable (Bouchard, 2004), including core life-history traits like pubertal timing (e.g. Treloar and Martin, 1990; Rowe, 2002), the role of the genotype merits consideration as well. But before a simple genetic explanation of variation in reproductive strategy is embraced, three things must be acknowledged.

First, even though variation in the timing of menarche has been linked to an androgen-receptor gene (Comings *et al.*, 2002), an oestrogen receptor gene (Stavrou *et al.*, 2002) and still other genes (Kadlubar *et al.*, 2003), a first effort to replicate Comings *et al.*'s molecular–genetic results in two epidemiological studies using samples drawn from the general population failed to do so (Jorm *et al.*, 2004). This is not an uncommon result in studies endeavouring to link specific genes to development (Caspi *et al.*, 2002).

Second, when Rowe (2000) specifically sought to disconfirm Belsky *et al.*'s (1991) developmental theory of reproductive strategies discussed below in a behaviour–genetic study, he proved unable to administer a 'knock-out punch', as some evidence of environmental influence emerged (see also Ellis, 2004, p. 922). Moreover, as Belsky *et al.* (1991) speculated, the secular trend in pubertal timing that has reduced the age of reproductive maturation over the past 150 years in the Western world, and which is largely attributed to improvements in nutrition and hygiene, may well have attenuated a great deal of variation which had, in ancestral times and beyond, been more susceptible to environmental influence than may appear to be the case in the modern world today (see also, Ellis 2004, p. 922).

Third, Belsky (2000, 2005a) argued that rather than thinking in terms of genetic *or* environmental effects, it might make the most sense to think in terms of nature *and* nurture in the case of reproductive strategies, because for some individuals such suites of life-history traits may be 'born' (i.e. fixed strategists) whereas for others 'made' (i.e. plastic strategists). Within the context of behaviour–genetic research designs, any such 'differential susceptibility' to developmental experiences would attenuate shared environmental effects, because these require different children in the same family to be affected in exactly the same manner *and* to the very same degree by family experiences. Drawing on evolutionary bet-hedging logic, Belsky (2000, 2005a) further argued that such differential susceptibility would make biological sense—to parents, children and siblings—because efforts by parents to shape their children's development could prove misguided, especially from the standpoint of enhancing reproductive fitness, given the inherent unpredictability of the future. For this reason, it would make evolutionary–biological sense for children to vary in the extent to which parental efforts to guide their development proved successful (see also Boyce and Ellis, in press).

Certainly not inconsistent with the notion of differential susceptibility to rearing influence is the ubiquity of non-shared, as opposed to shared, environmental effects in behaviour–genetic studies of development (Bouchard, 2004; Turkheimer and Waldron, 2000); these are effects indicating that shared family experiences (e.g. divorce) affect different children growing up in the same household differently. Also pointing in the same direction (i.e. toward differential susceptibility) is recent molecular–genetic evidence showing that the anticipated effect of child maltreatment in promoting antisocial behaviour in adulthood varies as a function of an individual's genotype (Caspi *et al.*, 2002).

In sum, although it would be foolish to argue that heritability plays no (or even just a marginal) role in human reproductive strategy, there seem to be no grounds for concluding at the current time that developmental programmes are not at least somewhat malleable with respect to life-history traits, though this may be more true for some individuals than others and less in the present than in the past. Indeed, as Ellis (2004, p. 925) recently observed, any number of scholars have argued that "selection can be expected to favour adaptive developmental plasticity of mechanisms (within genetic capacities and constraints) in response to particular ecological conditions (Belsky *et al.*, 1991; Boyce and Ellis, in press; Chisholm, 1996; Ellison, 2001)." Attention is now turned to theory development and some evidence pertaining to humans on just this score.

18.4. **Childhood experience and reproductive strategy**

In a seminal paper that would eventually stimulate a (somewhat delayed) cascade of theoretical developments and empirical studies over the past decade-and-a-half pertaining not just to variation in human reproductive strategies but, more importantly, to the role of childhood experiences in shaping it, Draper and Harpending ('DH'; 1982) argued that girls growing up in father-present and father-absent homes pursue distinctive reproductive strategies. Whereas father-absent girls develop behaviour profiles consistent with an expectation that paternal investment in childrearing will not be forthcoming and that pair bonds will not be enduring, those from father-present households develop as if anticipating the opposite, deferring sexual activity once they reach biological maturity while seeking to establish and maintain enduring, close, heterosexual relationships. What was unique to the DH argument, especially from the standpoint of traditional theories of child development, was the casting of early-experience influences within the family in evolutionary terms, emphasizing reproductive fitness, parental investment, pair bonds, and reproductive strategy. Gone was any moral approbation about 'problem' behaviour and in its place were the potential reproductive-fitness benefits of varying mating and parenting behaviour (i.e. reproductive strategy) to fit the ecological context.

Two things were lacking in this most provocative and original paper, at least from the perspective of students of child development. First, no developmental process was offered to explain *how* the particular childhood experience

in question (i.e. father absence) would shape later functioning in adolescence and adulthood. And second, although the DH argument cast old data linking father-absence in childhood with sexual, mating and parenting behaviour in adulthood in new theoretical terms, it failed to generate any new predictions. Was it more, then, than just old wine in a new bottle? Why, in fact, embrace evolutionary theorizing about 'reproductive strategy' when a myriad of widely acknowledged theoretical perspectives dating back to Sigmund Freud already offered accounts of why the later-life developments addressed by DH would result from father absence in childhood?

18.4.1. **Belsky *et al.*'s (1991) critical prediction: pubertal timing**

Considered reflection on these limitations led Belsky, Steinberg and Draper ('BSD'; 1991) to advance 'an evolutionary theory of socialization' linking childhood experience, interpersonal orientation and reproductive strategy, building directly on the insights of DH. Central to BSD theory was the thesis that stressful and supportive extrafamilial environments influenced family dynamics, most especially parent–child and marital/pair-bond relations, thereby shaping children's early emotional and behavioural development and, through it, subsequent social development, including sexual/mating behaviour, pair bonding and parenting. Moreover, BSD argued, this complex and environmentally sensitive developmental system evolved as a means of fitting the organism to its environment in the service of promoting reproductive fitness (i.e. not psychological well-being).

Of central importance to the BSD theory was the view that parenting, the parent–child relationship and, in particular, the attachment relationship mediated the influence of stressors and supports external to the parent–child relationship on the child's general trustful–mistrustful outlook on the world and opportunistic versus mutually beneficial orientation toward others, as well as his/her behaviour. But what fundamentally distinguished BSD from all other theories of, or perspectives on, early experience and human development was the explicitly labelled 'uncanny prediction' that these developmental experiences and psychological orientations would influence somatic development by affecting the timing of puberty; and that this cascade of developments shaped, in adolescence and adulthood, sexual behaviour, pair-bond orientation and parenting.

More specifically, while noting that it remained unclear whether environmental processes and the development of reproductive strategies should be conceptualized dimensionally or typologically (i.e. continuous versus discrete phenotypic plasticity), BSD posited two distinctive developmental trajectories for purposes of presentation. A quantity-oriented reproductive strategy was most likely to arise, BSD argued, in the context of a variety of stressors which would undermine parental well-being and family relationships, including general stress, marital discord and/or inadequate financial resources. These forces would, probabilistically, give rise to harsh, rejecting, insensitive and/or inconsistent parenting, which would foster insecure attachment, a mistrustful internal working model and an opportunistic, advantage-taking interpersonal orientation. These developments would stimulate an earlier timing of puberty than otherwise would be the case (i.e. within the organism's range of reaction) and an earlier onset of sexual activity, short-term and unstable pair bonds, and limited parental investment.

The alternative, quality-oriented developmental trajectory was fostered by exposure to a supportive rearing environment, characterized by spousal harmony and adequate financial resources. These ecological foundations would give rise, again probabilistically, to sensitive, supportive, responsive and positively affectionate styles of mothering and fathering and, thereby, secure attachments, a trusting internal working model and a reciprocally rewarding interpersonal orientation. Collectively, these developments would delay pubertal maturation (within the range of reaction) and defer the onset of sexual activity while fostering enduring pair bonds and greater parental investment.

As BSD made clear at the time, a great deal of traditional developmental research provided evidence that stressful rearing milieus, whether conceptualized in demographic terms (e.g. low income, lone parenthood), relationships terms (e.g. harsh/neglecting parenting; marital conflict, divorce) or psychological terms (e.g. depressed

mother, insecure attachment), predict developmental 'outcomes' that are regarded by mainstream child developmentalists—and many others—as 'unfavourable' and certainly not 'optimal'. These included, among other things, precocious and promiscuous sexual behaviour; aggressive/antisocial behaviour, depression, relationship instability and unsupportive, if not harsh, parenting. The opposite tends to be true of rearing environments that are well resourced and emotionally and relationally supportive (e.g. Patterson, 1986; Bradley and Caldwell, 1988; Emery, 1988; Cicchetti and Carlson, 1989; Pettit and Bates, 1989; McLoyd, 1990). In the decade-and-a-half since BSD advanced their theory, the publication of evidence highlighting such environmental effects has continued unabated (e.g. Seccombe, 2000; Amato, 2001; Belsky and Fearon, 2002; Buehler and Gerard, 2002; Parke et al., 2004).

As already noted, what made BSD distinctive—and purposefully so—was the hypothesis that social–developmental experiences within the family would influence the timing of sexual maturation (i.e. puberty). Because this is a core life-history variable and because it is a feature of development that no other theory of, or perspective on, human development suggests would be affected by social–developmental experiences in the family, it highlighted the potential 'added value' of an evolutionary approach to human development. According to classic philosophy of science, not only should a good theory, whether it be evolutionarily oriented or not, be parsimonious, it should also be able to account for facts already known while advancing new hypotheses that lead to new discoveries (Belsky et al., 1991; Ketelaar and Ellis, 2000).

A good deal of evidence has emerged which is at least not inconsistent with BSD's 'uncanny' hypothesis. First, greater parent–child warmth, cohesion and positivity predict later pubertal development—in both prospective longitudinal studies (Steinberg, 1988; Graber et al., 1995; Ellis et al., 1999) and retrospective or concurrent ones (Kim and Smith, 1988a; Kim et al., 1997; Miller and Pasta, 2000; Rowe, 2000; Romans et al., 2003). Second, greater parent–child conflict and coercion predict earlier timing of puberty, again in both prospective longitudinal work (Moffitt et al., 1992) and in research adopting retrospective or concurrent-assessment designs (Jorm et al.,

2004; Kim and Smith 1988a,b; Kim *et al.*, 1997; Mezzich *et al.*, 1997; Wierson *et al.*, 1993). Finally, and with respect to marital/partner relations, the happier and/or less conflicted the relationship between mother and father, the more delayed pubertal maturation—in both prospective-longitudinal studies (Ellis *et al.*, 1999; Ellis and Garber, 2000) and investigations adopting weaker research designs in which predictor and outcome data are gathered at the same time and/or retrospectively (Kim *et al.*, 1997; Kim and Smith, 1998b; Romans *et al.*, 2003).

It is important to note that virtually all the relevant findings come from studies of girls, basically due to measurement difficulties in demarcating pubertal development in boys. Also of importance is that while there is a good deal of data linking quality of parent–child and marital relations with pubertal timing, not all tests derived from BSD theory have supported it. Ellis *et al.* (1999), Miller and Pasta (2000) and Steinberg (1988), for example, found no evidence to support the hypothesized linkage between family conflict and coercion and accelerated pubertal timing. Nevertheless, when considered in their entirety, the results of the work cited above led Ellis (2004, pp. 935–936) to conclude in a recent and comprehensive review of research on the determinants of pubertal timing that "empirical research has provided reasonable, though incomplete" support for BSD theory. That said, it must be acknowledged that with rare exception (e.g. Rowe, 2000), relevant work has not been positioned to discount the possibility that common genes account both for why some families function the way they do and why children in the family mature at the rate they do. In fact, one previously cited molecular–genetic inquiry reported evidence indicating that associations like those under consideration might reflect little more than genetic effects, as an X-linked androgen receptor GGC-repeat polymorphism was associated with parental divorce, father absence *and* earlier age of menarche (Comings *et al.*, 2002). The fact, however, that Jorm *et al.*'s (2004) aforementioned effort to replicate such results did not do so cautions against prematurely embracing the conclusion that genetic effects are masquerading in all-too-much of the cited work as environmental effects of rearing experiences on pubertal timing.

18.4.2. **The distinctive influence of the father**

From an empirical perspective, Bruce Ellis has undertaken the most systematic research endeavouring to test propositions derived from BSD theory, especially those dealing with its theory-defining and distinctive pubertal-timing prediction. Notably, Ellis and associates have tracked girls from early childhood into adolescence in a series of investigations (Ellis *et al.*, 1999; Ellis and Garber, 2000; Ellis *et al.*, 2003). One important result of this work and Ellis's (2004) review of pubertal-timing research has been to highlight the potentially unique influence of the father–child relationship and stepfather presence (Ellis, 2004). Whereas DH exclusively addressed the role of father absence during childhood in shaping reproductive strategy, BSD expanded upon the DH model, arguing that father absence was an indicator of a stressful family environment and that DH's narrow conceptualization of the influential rearing milieu could be expanded to consider a larger set of stressors and supports which contribute to the development of reproductive strategy. Thus, BSD called attention to attachment security/insecurity, parental sensitivity/insensitivity, harsh versus warm parenting and harmonious versus conflicted pair bonds, drawing no particular distinction between contributions of mothers and fathers in shaping offspring reproductive strategy.

Upon repeatedly detecting effects of father presence versus absence and even unique effects of the quality of fathering, father–daughter relationships and the presence of a stepfather on pubertal timing (see below), Ellis *et al.* (1999, 2003; Ellis and Garber, 2000) concluded that fathers may have a special role to play in the development of girls' reproductive strategies, or at least their pubertal development. In fact, rather than being a marker of stress, father absence and stepfather presence operate as a paternal-investment cues indicative of low-quality paternal investment: "girls detect and internally encode information specifically about the quality of paternal investment during approximately the first 5 years of life as a basis of calibrating … the timing of pubertal maturation and certain types of sexual behaviour" (Ellis 2004, p. 938). Such processes should be understood in the broader context of human evolution, argued Ellis (2004); not only are humans the only great ape in which males engage in provisioning or care of offspring, but such paternal investment is highly variable, with the contribution of fathers to the family determined by the trade-off between paternal and mating investment in the service of fitness goals (Geary, in press).

Rather consistently, father absence has been related to accelerated pubertal development in girls, demarcated either in terms of age of menarche or the development of secondary sexual characteristics; and this is so across rather diverse studies, including prospective inquiries following girls from childhood into adolescence (Moffitt *et al.*, 1992; Wierson *et al.*, 1993; Campbell and Udry, 1995; Ellis *et al.*, 1999; Ellis and Garber, 2000; Rowe, 2000; Hetherington and Kelly, 2002) and retrospective studies of adult samples (Jones *et al.*, 1972; Surbey, 1990; Kiernan and Hobcraft, 1997; Doughty and Rodgers, 2000; Hoier, 2003; Quinlan, 2003; Romans *et al.*, 2003; Jorm *et al.*, 2004). Although effects of father absence have emerged in research conducted in a variety of Western countries, it is noteworthy that they have not been detected in African-American samples (Campbell and Udry, 1995; Rowe, 2000); Ellis (2004, p. 940) suggests that this could be the result of the "extraordinary secular trend" in this population.

There is evidence to suggest that both timing of father absence and stepfather presence are important to understanding the effects of an absent father. The earlier in the child's life that father absence occurs, perhaps especially in the first 5 years of life, the more potent an impact it appears to have on female pubertal development (Jones *et al.*, 1972; Ellis, 2004; Ellis and Garber, 2000; Quinlan, 2003; Surbey, 1990). The conditions under which stepfather presence exerts its influence may also be important, perhaps even accounting for effects of father absence (Ellis, 2004). Given what has already been stated about relationship quality more generally and father absence in particular, it should not be surprising that conflicted relations between mother and stepfather and early onset of stepfather presence have been found to be particularly influential in accelerating pubertal development in girls (Ellis and Garber, 2000).

Discussion of father absence and stepfather presence should not distract from the fact that biological fathers seem to matter, too. Consistent with BSD's original emphasis on the quality of parent–child relationships, Ellis *et al.* (1999) found that the more time such men spent taking care of their daughters across the child's first 5 years of life and the more they engaged in positive–affectionate interaction with their daughters at age 5 years, the more delayed was girls' pubertal development when followed up around 12 years of age.

Given all the evidence considered so far regarding relationship influences on (female) pubertal development, the apparently important role which males in the family play in influencing girls' pubertal maturation should not be read to imply that mothers and marriages are unimportant. What the work of Ellis and others clearly indicates, however, is that there are strong empirical and theoretical grounds for not treating mother and father as interchangeable agents of influence when it comes to understanding how childhood experiences may shape reproductive strategy and for paying especial attention to the presence of a biologically unrelated male figure in the home of a prepubescent girl.

18.4.3. Mortality rate, time preference and attachment

Not long after BSD extended DH thinking about the role of developmental experience in shaping human reproductive strategies, Chisholm (1993, 1996, 1999) further developed this line of theorising about the human life course; and he did so in three specific ways, each of which is considered in turn.

18.4.3.1. Local mortality rates

First, whereas BSD highlighted economic and marital resources, or the absence thereof, as forces shaping parenting, attachment and thereby nascent reproductive strategies, Chisholm (1999) called attention, following Stearns (1992), to the importance of local mortality rates. Such information, he argued, afforded organisms unconscious if not conscious insight into the relative risk and uncertainty of the developing child surviving until maturity to bear its own offspring. And, as already noted, initiating reproduction earlier rather than later in life makes especially good biological sense when the risk of dying before reproducing is high or, probably more importantly, perceived to be high.

Several notable findings appear consistent with Chisholm's (1999) theorizing, though the research in question was not carried out in direct response to it. First, Wilson and Daly (1997) found that as life expectancy declined across Chicago neighbourhoods, the probability of a woman reproducing by age 30 increased. Similarly, Johns (2003) found that teen mothers in Gloucestershire expected to die at younger ages than did women who became mothers after their teenage years. Such results not only accord with Geronimus's (1996) qualitative interviews with poor, African-American teen mothers which reveal their awareness of their risks for an early death, but also with her 'weathering hypothesis' suggesting that early birth is a strategic response to the rapid decline in health of these women in their third and fourth decade of life. Finally, extending the line of inquiry to parenting and the child's development, meta-analytic research on attachment shows that when a mother experiences the loss of a loved one through death sometime in her life and this loss remains emotionally 'unresolved', the likelihood of her own offspring developing one type of insecure attachment—disorganized—increases (van Ijzendoorn, 1995). Considered together, these illustrative results highlight the value in considering local mortality rates as an important feature of the broader ecology shaping reproductive strategy.

18.4.3.2. Time preference

Whereas BSD highlighted the role of interpersonal orientation, behavioural development and pubertal timing in mediating the effect of rearing environment, parenting and attachment security on future mating and parenting, a second contribution of Chisholm (1999, p. 135) was to call attention to an additional psychological mediator linking childhood experience and reproductive strategy, time preference: "Time preference is the degree to which people prefer to or believe they will achieve their desires (i.e. benefits or consequences of action) now, more-or-less immediately, or later, at some point in the future." Theoretically, individuals living in highly risky and uncertain environments in which waiting for a reward might prove to be a 'fool's errand'

should opt for immediate pay-offs even when delayed ones would be greater. In such circumstances, they are presumed to be hedging their bets against the risk that they may not be around to collect the larger reward. Here, of course, pay-off and reward refer to the likelihood of reproducing.

According to Chisholm (1999), then, time preference should be regarded as an evolutionarily important psychological construct that is sensitive to rearing experience and influences future reproductive functioning, broadly conceived (i.e. mating, parenting). Evidence that children growing up in more economically, socially and psychologically disadvantaged families have a more difficult time waiting to secure a more attractive reward and are more inclined to settle for a lesser reward sooner (i.e. difficulty delaying gratification) would seem consistent with Chisholm's argument about influences on time preference (e.g. Evans and English, 2002; Lengua, 2002).

18.4.3.3. Attachment styles

A third notable contribution that Chisholm (1996) made to thinking about developmental influences on human reproductive strategies involved his elaboration of the role that BSD attributed to attachment security in entraining the development of the most appropriate alternative reproductive strategies. In addition to reiterating the influential role BSD and attachment theory more generally accord warm–sensitive–responsive parenting in shaping attachment security and, thereby, the child's orientation toward others and relationships, Chisholm (1996) distinguished two different manifestations of insensitive parenting while theorizing that each had distinctive developmental consequences. Insecure-resistant attachment, he speculated, arose in reaction to a parent's *inability* to invest, whereas insecure-avoidant attachment derived from a parent's *unwillingness* to invest. In a not unrelated vein, Belsky (1997, 1999) further refined thinking about the opportunistic–advantage-taking interpersonal orientation central to the BSD typology, suggesting that while it was most likely promoted by insecure-avoidant attachment, insecure-resistance may have evolved to promote helper-at-the-nest type behaviour and thus foster in the child emotional and behavioural dependency on the mother well beyond the infancy years.

To date, a rather large body of evidence highlighting the potential role of attachment security in predicting features of reproductive strategy has emerged, though rarely is it cast in such terms or been stimulated by evolutionary thinking. Two different sets of findings merit consideration, one linking adult attachment with sexual behaviour, mating and pair bonding and the other linking adult attachment with parenting. Before summarizing relevant results of this work, it must be noted that very little of the research actually tracks children prospectively from childhood into adulthood.

With this important caveat in mind, it remains of theoretical significance that self-assessments of attachment security in the context of romantic relationships, presumed to be shaped at least in part by rearing history, systematically relate to a variety of aspects of sexual behaviour, mating and pair bonding in a manner consistent with BSD theorizing. With respect to sexual attitudes and behaviour, individuals self-classified as secure are less likely to endorse promiscuous sexual behaviour (Brennan et al., 1998) or to engage in one-night stands or extra-pair sexual liaisons (Brennan and Shaver, 1995; Hazan et al., 1994, as cited in Kirkpatrick, 1998). One study, in fact, showed that over a hypothetical 30-year period, males and females with secure attachment orientation ideally desired only one romantic partner (Miller and Fishkin, 1997), less than those with insecure orientations. Related work further indicates that in the case of females, attachment security is associated with an older age of first sexual intercourse (Bogaert and Sadava, 2002).

Turning to consideration of pair bonding and relationship processes, one consistent finding pertinent to this analysis of attachment and reproductive strategy is that self-reported relationship satisfaction is greater when individuals describe themselves as secure rather than dismissing (i.e. the adult form of insecure-avoidant) or preoccupied (i.e. the adult from of insecure resistant) (e.g. Davila et al., 1999; Feeney, 2000; Mikulincer et al., 2002). Moreover, higher scores on dismissing-avoidant attachment predict lower levels of marital quality, both reported and observed (Shaver and Mikulincer, 2002).

Observational research also indicates that secure partners manifest less negative affect, less avoidant non-verbal behaviour, and more constructive conversation patterns in response to their partners' distancing behaviour (e.g. Feeney, 1998; Rholes et al., 1998). These findings are consistent with related results showing that attachment security predicts greater communication levels within close relationships in adulthood (Collins and Read, 1990), including greater self-disclosure to the romantic partner and responsivity to the partner's self-disclosure (Collins and Read, 1990; Kobak and Hazan, 1991; Mikulincer and Nachson, 1991). Such findings can be meaningfully interpreted as reflecting the BSD view that security promotes a mutually beneficial interpersonal orientation (as opposed to an opportunistic–advantage-taking one). In light of the findings just summarised and the interpretation offered, it seems almost commonsensical that secure individuals prove less likely to get divorced or separated from their romantic partners (e.g. Hazan and Shaver, 1987; Kirkpatrick and Hazan, 1994); have longer-lasting relationships (Hazan and Shaver, 1987; Kirkpatrick and Davis, 1994; Kirkpatrick and Hazan, 1994); and manifest greater levels of commitment to and trust of their partners, irrespective of whether they are dating (Brennan and Shaver, 1995; Levy and Davis, 1988; Pistole, 1989; Pistole and Clark, 1995; Simpson, 1990) or married (Feeney, 1994; Feeney et al., 1994; Fuller and Fincham, 1995; Kobak and Hazan, 1991). In sum, the data suggest, consistent with evolutionary theorizing (Belsky et al., 1991; Belsky, 1997; Chisholm, 1996, 1999) and attachment theory more generally, that attachment orientation in adulthood is systematically related to sexual behaviour, mating and pair-bonding processes.

What about parental investment? When it comes to linking attachment in adulthood with this aspect of reproductive strategy, investigators stand on somewhat firmer ground, basically because the methodology used for measuring adult attachment in this body of work, the Adult Attachment Interview (George et al., 1985), has been found to capture variation that is itself predicted by attachment measured in the opening years of life in prospective longitudinal research (Hamilton, 2000; Waters et al., 2000). It would be mistaken to conclude, however, that continuity inevitably characterises the developmental process with respect to attachment security, as such continuity has not always been detected (Lewis *et al.*, 2000; Weinfield *et al.*, 2000) or has been found to be contingent on events and experiences transpiring—or not transpiring—after early childhood (Hamilton, 2000; Waters *et al.*, 2000).

With respect to the parental investment component of reproductive strategy, evidence indicates that parents classified as autonomous-secure and thus presumed (but not demonstrated) in the relevant studies to have experienced supportive rearing environments while growing up, parent their offspring in a more supportive, sensitive manner, indicative, it would seem, of higher parental investment than others who manifest insecure internal working models of attachment in adulthood. More specifically, security has been linked to more warmth and appropriate structuring of the child's learning environment for both mothers and fathers (Cohn *et al.*, 1992) and to greater provision by mothers of emotional support in a variety of contexts (Crowell and Feldman, 1988, 1991), less negativity (Slade *et al.*, 1999), along with greater sensitivity to the child's needs and states (Das Eiden *et al.*, 1995). In sum, then, not only is adult attachment security related to mating and pair-bonding processes in social–psychological research, it is also related to presumptive indices of parental investment in developmental research.

Work on the intergenerational transmission of parenting that is not carried out within an attachment tradition is also of relevance to this discussion, as a central idea underpinning BSD thinking is that childhood rearing experiences shape psychological, behavioural and even somatic development, including of course attachment security, eventually affecting parental investment when children become parents themselves. Studies pertaining to the intergenerational transmission of parenting typically focus upon child abuse and neglect by means of retrospective designs or involve prospective follow-ups in young adulthood of teenagers at risk for criminal careers (for reviews, see Belsky and Jaffee, 2006; Serbin and Karp, 2003). Consistent with the results of such research, there is evidence from prospective studies beginning in

childhood that harsh, inconsistent and unsupportive parenting (Caspi and Elder, 1988), as well as sensitive-warm-stimulating parenting (Belsky *et al.*, 2005) is transmitted across generations. Importantly, as in the work on the transmission of child maltreatment across generations, continuity is by no means inevitable, underscoring the important point that developments later in life are a function of both early and subsequent experience. Perhaps as important as that observation is that the intergenerational transmission of harsh parenting seems to be mediated by antisocial and problematic child behaviour which can certainly be conceptualized, in the BSD manner, as a form of opportunistic–advantage-taking (e.g. Capaldi *et al.*, 2003; Conger *et al.*, 2003; Thornberry *et al.*, 2003).

18.5. Conclusion

Even though a great deal of mainstream developmental psychology is devoted to understanding whether and how experiences in childhood shape psychological and behavioural development later in life, little theoretical attention has been paid to why such cross-time influences should characterize human development. This is especially true with respect to the well-studied determinants of mating, pair bonding and parenting. Theoretically, DH, BSD, Ellis and Chisholm have all addressed this lacuna, stimulating research on linkages between childhood experience and reproductive strategy. Concern for experiential effects on pubertal timing distinguishes this line of inquiry from more traditional developmental studies because, as already noted, an evolutionary perspective suggests that experiences in the family might affect somatic development. Fifteen years since BSD advanced their 'uncanny' prediction, it seems clear that pubertal timing, at least in females, is related to select aspects of early family experience.

BSD theorized that this would be the case because pubertal timing more or less mediates linkages between experiences in childhood and reproductive functioning later in development. Ellis (2004, p. 947) recently questioned this proposition, arguing that (a) while family experiences do predict pubertal timing (in girls) and, *independently*, other reproductive-strategy-relevant outcomes, (b) pubertal timing itself does not predict important features of reproductive strategy that BSD stipulates it should. Most critically, he commented, "although earlier timing of puberty clearly predicts earlier onset of major forms of sexual experience and reproduction"– meaning age at first dating, kissing, petting, and engaging in sexual intercourse, as well as increased rates of teenage pregnancy and even first birth in natural fertility populations— "there is currently no empirical basis for the hypothesis that earlier timing of puberty leads to a more unrestricted sociosexual orientation, unstable pairbonds, greater number of sexual partners, or lower parental investment." With only six studies addressing the latter issues, none of which longitudinally follow individuals from childhood, Ellis (2004) appropriately acknowledged that "more research is needed."

But even if one supposed that the data base examining linkages between pubertal timing with relevant downstream developmental outcomes pertaining to reproductive strategy was far greater than it is and was as bereft of evidence consistent with BSD predictions as the six available studies seem to be, would there still be grounds for casting aside BSD thinking in exchange for Ellis's (2004) alternative model of adaptive human development to be described below? Were the research carried out in the same manner as the six studies underpinning Ellis's (2004) conclusion, the answer to this question would have to be 'no'; and this is because neither these studies nor Ellis (2004) takes account of a critically important qualification of BSD's evolutionary theory of socialization.

Even though BSD presented their developmental-trajectories' model of reproductive strategies as linearly sequenced with one event or process (e.g. A: attachment security) contributing to the one immediately subsequent to it (e.g. B: interpersonal orientation) in a simple chain of causation (i.e. A → B → C → D ...), they *explicitly* raised the prospect that an alternative, conditional probability model might more accurately characterize the dynamics of human development under consideration (i.e. A × B → C; B × C → D ...). In other words, instead of any link in the causal chain being solely or even principally a function of the immediately preceding link,

or even an earlier link, each development in the sequence could be a function of the co-occurrence of multiple previous links in the chain. Thus, even though pubertal timing might not, in and of itself, directly predict the mating, pair-bonding and/or parenting outcomes that Ellis (2004) regards as critical for substantiating BSD thinking, it might nevertheless do so *in interaction with* developments prior to puberty (e.g. attachment insecurity, opportunistic interpersonal orientation) or thereafter (e.g. early onset of sexual activity). In fact, the latter and highly likely possibility would be perfectly consistent with Sroufe's (1988) argument that development is a function of both early and more contemporaneous experience. Were it to be the case, then, that pubertal timing influences mating, pair bonding and parenting principally in interaction with other factors and forces, assessments of only direct effects of pubertal timing on these features of reproductive strategy—such as those examined in the six available studies— would simply not be in position to detect its impact on reproductively strategic behaviour.

All this is not to say that Ellis's (2004) alternative model of evolutionarily adaptive developmental pathways does not merit serious consideration. According to his penultimate 'child development' theory of pubertal timing, even though family experiences shape age of menarche and, independently, adult reproductive strategy (e.g. pair bonding, parental investment), pubertal timing does not mediate the linkage between childhood experience and adult reproductive strategy, as postulated by BSD. And this is because, as already noted, pubertal timing does not (so far) predict "qualitative aspects of mating and parenting strategies, *independent* of age at onset of sexual and reproductive events" (Ellis, 2004, p. 48, emphasis added). Although it remains unclear why pubertal timing must operate in such a way (i.e. independent of age of first sex) to be legitimately conceived as part and parcel of the development of reproductive strategy, Ellis (2004) provocatively argues that childhood experiences influence *the duration of childhood*, serving to abbreviate it (via accelerated pubertal timing) when family social resources are limited and to extend it (via delayed maturation) when family resources are relatively abundant. Under the former conditions, he theorizes, nature has designed development to move the child out of the family and into the world of peers when the family's capacity to enhance the child's competitive advantage is limited. In contrast, under higher-resource conditions, an extended childhood serves to increase the time that children can benefit from parental investment. Thus, children "should be selected to capitalize on the benefits of high-quality parental investment, and to reduce the costs of low-quality parental investment, by contingently altering the period of growth and development prior to reproductive maturity" (p. 947). Important to note, in closing, is that irrespective of whether one embraces Ellis's (2004) reconceptualization of BSD's 'uncanny' prediction linking social–developmental experiences in the family to pubertal timing (i.e. as just terminating childhood rather than facilitating mating, pair bonding and parenting), the fact remains that he, just like DH, BSD and Chisholm, regards early experiences in the family as playing an influential role in shaping human reproductive strategy. This remains an all-too-uncommon way of thinking about development within the field of developmental psychology.

References

Ainsworth, M. D. (1973) The development of infant-mother attachment. In B. M. Caldwell and H. N. Ricciuti (eds) *Review of Child Development Research*, vol. 3, pp. 1–94. University of Chicago Press, Chicago.

Amato, P. (2001) Children of divorce in the 1990s. *Journal of Family Psychology*, 15: 355–370.

Bateson, P., Barker, D., Clutton-Brock, T. *et al.* (2004) Developmental plasticity and human health. *Nature*, 430: 419–421.

Belsky, J. (1997) Patterns of attachment mating and parenting: an evolutionary interpretation. *Human Nature*, 8: 361–381.

Belsky, J. (1999) Modern evolutionary theory and patterns of attachment. In J. Cassidy and P. Shaver (eds) *Handbook of Attachment: Theory, Research and Clinical Applications*, pp. 141–161. Wiley, New York.

Belsky, J. (2000) Conditional and alternative reproductive strategies. In J. L. Rodgers, D. C. Rowe and W. B. Miller (eds) *Genetic Influences on Human Fertility and Sexuality: Theoretical and Empirical Contributions from the Biological and Behavioural Sciences*, pp. 127–145. Kluwer Academic, Boston.

Belsky, J. (2005a) Differential susceptibility to rearing influence. In B. J. Ellis and D. F. Bjorklund (eds) *Origins of the Social Mind: Evolutionary Psychology and Child Development*, pp. 139–163. Guilford Press, New York.

Belsky, J. (2005b) The developmental and evolutionary psychology of intergenerational transmission of attachment. In C. S. Carter and L. Ahnert (eds) *Attachment and Bonding: A New Synthesis*, pp. 169–198 MIT Press, Cambridge, MA.

Belsky, J. and Jaffee, S. (2006) The multiple determinants of parenting. In D Cicchetti and D Cohen (eds) *Developmental Psychopathology*, 2nd edn. pp. 38–85 Wiley, New York.

Belsky, J. and Fearon, R. M.P. (2002) Infant–mother attachment security, contextual risk and early development. *Development and Psychopathology*, 14: 293–310.

Belsky, J., Steinberg, L. and Draper, P. (1991) Childhood experience, interpersonal development, and reproductive strategy. *Child Development*, 62: 647–670.

Belsky, J., Jaffee, S., Sligo, J., Woodward, L. and Silva, P. (2005) Intergenerational transmission of warm-sensitive-stimulating parenting. *Child Development*, 76: 384–396.

Bogaert, A. F. and Sadava, S. (2002) Adult attachment and sexual behaviour. *Personal Relationships*, 9: 191–204.

Borgerhoff Mulder, M. (1989) Menarche, menopause and reproduction in the Kipsigis of Kenya. *Journal of Biological Science*, 21: 179–192.

Bouchard, T. (2004) Genetic influence on human psychological traits. *Current Directions in Psychological Science*, 13: 148–151.

Boyce, W. T. and Ellis, B. J. (in press) Biological sensitivity to context. *Development and Psychopathology*.

Bowlby, J. (1969) *Attachment and Loss*, vol. 1, *Attachment*. Basic Books, New York.

Bradley, R. H., Caldwell, B. M. and Rock, S. L. (1998) Home environment and school performance. *Child Development*, 59: 852–867.

Brennan, K. A. and Shaver, P.R. (1995) Dimensions of adult attachment, affect regulation, and romantic relationship functioning. *Personality and Social Psychology Bulletin*, 21: 267–283.

Brennan, K. A., Clark, C. and Shaver, P. R. (1998) Self-report measures of adult attachment In J. Simpson and W. S. Rholes (eds) *Attachment Theory and Close Relationships*, pp. 46–76, Guilford Press, New York.

Breur, J. T. (1997) *The Myth of the First Three Years*. Taylor Francis, New York.

Buehler, C. and Gerard, J. (2002) Marital conflict, ineffective parenting, and children's and adolescents adjustment. *Journal of Marriage and the Family*, 64: 78–92.

Campbell, B. C. and Udry, J. R. (1995) Stress and age at menarche of mothers and daughters. *Journal of Biosocial Science*, 27: 127–134.

Capaldi, D., Pears, K., Patterson, G. and Owen, L. (2003) Continuity of parenting practices across generations in an at-risk sample. *Journal of Abnormal Child Psychology*, 31: 127–142.

Caspi, A. and Elder, G. H. (1988) Emergent family patterns. In R. Hinde and J. Stevenson-Hinde (eds) *Relationships Within Families*, pp. 218–240. Oxford University Press, Oxford.

Caspi, A., McClay, J., Moffitt, T. E. *et al.* (2002) Role of genotype in the cycle of violence in maltreated children. *Science*, 297: 851–854.

Charnov, E. L. (1993) *Life History Invariants*. Oxford University Press, Oxford.

Chisholm, J. S. (1993) Death, hope, and sex. *Current Anthropology*, 34: 1–24.

Chisholm, J. S. (1996) The evolutionary ecology of attachment organization. *Human Nature*, 7: 1–38.

Chisholm, J. S. (1999) *Death, Hope and Sex*. Cambridge University Press, New York.

Cicchetti, D. and Carlson, V. (1989) *Child Maltreatment*. Cambridge, New York.

Cohn, D. A., Cowan, P. A., Cowan, C. P. and Pearson, J. (1992) Mothers' and fathers' working models of childhood attachment relationships, parenting styles, and child behavior. *Development and Psychopathology*, 4: 417–431.

Collins, N. L. and Read, S. J. (1990) Adult attachment, working models, and relationship quality in dating couples. *Journal of Personality and Social Psychology*, 58: 644–663.

Comings, D. E., Muhleman, D., Johnson, J. P. and MacMurray, J. P. (2002) Parent-daughter transmission of the androgen receptor gene as an explanation of the effect of father absence on age of menarche. *Child Development*, 73: 1046–1051.

Conger, R., Nell, T., Kim, K. and Scaramella, L. (2003) Angry and aggressive behaviour across three generations. *Journal of Abnormal Child Psychology*, 31: 143–160.

Crowell, J. A. and Feldman, S. S. (1988) Mothers' internal working models of relationships and children's behavioral and developmental status. *Child Development*, 59: 1273–1285.

Crowell, J. A. and Feldman, S. S. (1991) Mothers' internal working models of attachment relationships and mother and child behavior during separation and reunion. *Developmental Psychology*, 27: 597–605.

Das Eiden, R., Teti, D. M. and Corns, K. M. (1995) Maternal working models of attachment, marital adjustment, and the parent-child relationship. *Child Development*, 66: 1504–1518.

Davila, J., Karney, B. R. and Bradbury, T. N. (1999) Attachment change processes in the early years of marriage. *Journal of Personality and Social Psychology*, 76: 783–802.

de Wolff, M. S. and Van Ijzendoorn, M. H. (1997) Sensitivity and attachment. *Child Development*, 68: 571–591.

Doughty, D. and Rodger, J. L. (2000) Behavior genetic modelling of menarche in US females. In J. L. Rodges, D. C. Rowe and W. B. Miller (eds) *Genetic Influences on Human Fertility and Sexuality*, pp. 169–181. Kluwer Academic, Boston.

Draper, P. and Harpending, H. (1982) Father absence and reproductive strategy. *Journal of Anthropological Research*, 38: 255–272.

Ellis, B. J. (2004) Timing of pubertal maturation in girls. *Psychological Bulletin*, 130: 920–958.

Ellis, B. J. and Bjorklund, D. F. (2005) *The Origins of the Social Mind: Evolutionary Psychology and Child Development*. Guilford Press, London.

Ellis, B. J. and Garber, J. (2000) Psychosocial antecedents of variation in girls' pubertal timing. *Child Development*, 71: 485–501.

Ellis, B. J., McFadyen-Ketchum, S., Dodge, K. A., Pettit, G. S. and Bates, J. E. (1999) Quality of early family relationships and individual differences in the timing of pubertal maturation in girls. *Journal of Personality and Social Psychology*, 77: 387–401.

Ellis, B. J., Bates, J.E, Dodge, K. A. *et al.* (2003) Does father absence place daughters at special risk for early sexual activity and teenage pregnancy? *Child Development*, 74: 801–821.

Ellison, P. T. (2001) *On Fertile Ground: A Natural History of Human Reproduction*. Harvard University Press, Cambridge, MA.

Emery, R. (1988) *Marriage, Divorce and Children's Adjustment*. Sage, Beverly Hills, CA.

Evans, G. and English, K. (2002) The environment of poverty. *Child Development*, 73: 1238–1248.

Feeney, J. A. (1994) Attachment style, communication patterns and satisfaction across the life cycle of marriage. *Personal Relationships*, 1: 333–348.

Feeney, J. A. (1998) Adult attachment and relationship-centered anxiety. In J. A. Simpson and W. S. Rholes (eds) *Attachment Theory and Close Relationships*, pp. 189–218. Guilford Press, New York.

Feeney, J. A. (2000) Implications of attachment style for patterns of health and illness. *Child: Care, Health and Human Development*, 26: 277–288.

Feeney, J. A., Noller, P. and Callan, V. J. (1994) Attachment style, communication and satisfaction in the early years of marriage. In K. Bartholomew and D. Perlman (eds) *Advances in Personal Relationships*, vol. 5. pp. 269–308. Jessica Kingsley, London.

Figueredo, A., Vasquez, G., Brumbach, B., Sefcek, J., Kirsner, B. and Jacobs, W. J. (2005) *The K-factor: Individual Differences in Life History Strategies*. Unpublished manuscript. University of Arizona, Tucson, AZ.

Fuller, T. L. and Fincham, F. D. (1995) Attachment style in married couples: Relation to current marital functioning, stability over time, and method of assessment. *Personal Relationships*, 2: 17–34.

Geary, D. C. (in press) Evolution of paternal investment. In D. M. Buss (eds) *The Evolutionary Psychology Handbook*. Wiley, New York.

George, C., Kaplan, N. and Main, M. (1985) *Adult Attachment Interview*. Unpublished manuscript, University of California, Berkeley.

Geronimus, A. T. (1996) What teen mothers know. *Human Nature*, 7: 323–352.

Giedd, J., Blumenthal, J., Jeffries, N. *et al.* (1999) Brain development during childhood and adolescence. *Nature Neuroscience*, 2: 861–863.

Graber, J. A., Brooks-Gunn, J. and Warren, M. P. (1995) The antecedents of menarcheal age. *Child Development*, 66: 346–359.

Hamilton, C. (2000) Continuity and discontinuity of attachment from infancy through adolescence. *Child Development*, 71: 690–694.

Hawkes, K. (2003) Grandmothers and the evolution of human longevity. *American Journal of Human Biology*, 15: 380–400.

Hawkes, K., O'Connell, J. F., Blurton Jones, N. G., Alvarez, H. and Charnov, E. L. (2000) The grandmother hypothesis and human evolution. In L. Cronk, N. Chagnon and W. Irons (eds) *Adaptation and Human Behavior: An Anthropological Perspective*, pp. 231–252. Aldine de Gruyter, New York.

Hazan, C. and Shaver, P. R. (1987) Romantic love conceptualized as an attachment process. *Journal of Personality and Social Psychology*, 52: 511–524.

Hetherington, E. M. and Kelly, J. (2002) *For Better or for Worse*. Norton, New York.

Hill, K. and Hurtado, A. (1996) *Ache Life History*. Aldine De Gruyter, New York.

Hill, K. and Kaplan, H. (1999) Life history traits in humans. *Annual Review of Anthropology*, 28: 397–430.

Hoier, S. (2003) Father absence and age at menarche. *Human Nature*, 14: 209–233.

Johns, S. E. (2003) Environmental risk and the evolutionary psychology of teenage motherhood. PhD thesis, University of Bristol.

Jones, B., Leeton, J., McLeod, I. and Wood, C. (1972) Factors influencing the age of menarche in a lower socio-economic group in Melbourne. *Medical Journal of Australia*, 2: 533–535.

Jorm, A. F., Christensen, H., Rodgers, B., Jacomb, P. A. and Easteal, S. (2004) Association of adverse childhood experiences, age of menarche and adult reproductive behaviour: does the androgen receptor gene play a role? *American Journal of Medical Genetics Part B: Neuropsychiatric Genetics*, 125: 105–111.

Kadlubar, F. F., Berkowitz, G. S., Delongchamp, R. R. *et al.* (2003) The CYP3A4*1B variant is related to the onset of puberty, a known risk factor for the development of breast cancer. *Cancer Epidemiology Biomarkers and Prevention*, 12: 327–331.

Kagan, J., Kearsley, R. and Zelazo, P. (1978) *Infancy*. Harvard University Press, Cambridge, MA.

Kaplan, H. S. and Lancaster, J. B. (2003) An evolutionary and ecological analysis of human fertility, mating patterns and parental investment. In K. W. Wachter and R. A. Bulatao (eds) *National Research Council (2003) Fertility Behaviour in Biodemographic Perspective*, pp. 170–223. National Academics Press, Washington, DC.

Kaplan, H. S., Lancaster, J. and Hurtado, A. M. (2000) A theory of human life history evolution. *Evolutionary Anthropology*, 9: 156–185.

Ketelaar, T. and Ellis, B. J. (2000) Are evolutionary explanations unfalsifiable? *Psychological Inquiry*, 11: 1–21.

Kiernan, K. E. and Hobcraft, J. (1997) Parental divorce during childhood. *Population Studies*, 51: 41–55.

Kim, K. and Smith, P. K. (1998a) Childhood stress, behavioural symptoms and mother-daughter pubertal development. *Journal of Adolescence*, 21: 231–240.

Kim, K. and Smith, P. K. (1998b) Retrospective survey of parental marital relations and child reproductive development. *International Journal of Behavioral Development*, 22: 729–751.

Kim, K., Smith, P. K. and Palermiti, A. L. (1997) Conflict in childhood and reproductive development. *Evolution and Human Behavior*, 18: 109–142.

Kirkpatrick, L. A. (1998) Evolution, pair-bonding, and reproductive strategies. In J. A. Simpson and W. S. Rholes (eds) *Attachment Theory and Close Relationships*, pp. 353–393. Guilford Press, New York.

Kirkpatrick, L. A. and Davis, K. E. (1994) Attachment style, gender and relationship stability. *Journal of Personality and Social Psychology*, 66: 502–512.

Kirkpatrick, L. A. and Hazan, C. (1994) Attachment styles and close relationships. *Personal Relationships*, 1: 123–142.

Kobak, R. R. and Hazan, C. (1991) Attachment in marriage. *Journal of Personality and Social Psychology*, 60: 861–869.

Kuzawa, C. (2005) Fetal origins of developmental plasticity *American Journal of Human Biology*, 17: 5–21.

Lengua, L. (2002) The contribution of emotionality and self-regulation to the understanding of children's response to multiple risk. *Child Development*, 72: 144–161.

Levy, M. B. and Davis, K. E. (1998) Love styles and attachment styles compared. *Journal of Social and Personal Relationships*, 5: 439–471.

Lewis, M. (1997) *Altering Fate*. Guilford Press, New York.

Lewis, M., Feiring, C. and Rosenthal, S. (2000) Attachment over time. *Child Development*, 71: 707–720.

McArthur, R. H. and Wilson, E. O. (1967) *The Theory of Island Biogeography*. Princeton University Press, Princeton, NJ.

McDade, T. W., Beck, M. A., Kuzawa, C. W. and Adair, L. S. (2001) Prenatal nutrition, postnatal environments, and antibody response to vaccination in adolescence. *American Journal of Clinical Nutrition*, 74: 543–548.

McLoyd, V. C. (1990) The impact of economic hardship on black families and children. *Child Development*, 61: 311–346.

Mezzich, A. C., Tarter, R. E., Giancola, P. R., Lu, S., Kirisci, L. and Parks, S. (1997) Substance use and risky sexual behaviour in female adolescents. *Drug and Alcohol Dependence*, 44: 157–166.

Mikulincer, M. and Nachshon, O. (1991) Attachment styles and patterns of self-disclosure. *Journal of Personality and Social Psychology*, 61: 321–331.

Mikulincer, M., Florian, V., Cowan, P. A. and Cowan, C. P. (2002) Attachment Security in Couple Relationships. *Family Process*, 41: 405–434.

Miller, C. and Fishkin, S. A. (1997) On the dynamics of human bonding and reproductive success. In J. A. Simpson and D. T. Kenrick (eds) *Evolutionary Social Psychology*, pp. 197–235. Lawrence Erlbaum, Hillsdale, NJ.

Miller, W. B. and Pasta, D. J. (2000) Early family environment, reproductive strategy and contraceptive behaviour. In J. L. Rodger, D. C. Rowe and W. B. Miller (eds) *Genetic Influences on Human Fertility and Sexuality*, pp. 183–230, Kluwer Academic, Boston.

Moffitt, T. W., Caspi, A., Belsky, J. and Silva, P. A. (1992) Childhood experience and the onset of menarche. *Child Development*, 63: 47–58.

Parke, R., Coltrane, S., Duffy, S., Buriel, R., Dennis, J., Powers, J., French, S. and Widaman, K. (2004) Economic stress, parenting, and child adjustment in Mexican American and European families. *Child Development*, 75: 1613–1909.

Patterson, G. R. (1986) Performance models for antisocial boys. *American Psychologist*, 41: 432–444.

Peccei, J. S. (2000) Genetic correlation between the ages of menarche and menopause. *Human Nature*, 11: 43–63.

Pettit, G. S. and Bates, J. W. (1989) Family interaction patterns and children's behaviour problems from infancy to four years. *Developmental Psychology*, 25: 413–420.

Phillips, D. I.W. (1998) Birth weight and the future development of diabetes. *Diabetes Care*, 21B, 150–155.

Pianka, E. R. (1970) On r and K selection. *American Naturalist*, 104: 592–597.

Pistole, M. C. (1989) Attachment in adult romantic relationships. *Journal of Social and Personal Relationships*, 6: 505–510.

Pistole, M. C. and Clark, E. M. (1995) Love relationships. *Journal of Mental Health Counselling*, 17: 199–210.

Quinlan, R. J. (2003) Father absence, parental care, and female reproductive development. *Evolution and Human Behavior*, 24: 376–390.

Rholes, W. S., Simpson, J. and Stevens, J. G. (1998) Attachment orientations, social support, and conflict resolution in close relationships. In J. Simpson and W. S. Rholes (eds) *Attachment Theory and Close Relationships*, pp. 166–188, Guilford Press, New York.

Robinson, S. M. and Barker, D. J. (2002) Coronary heart disease. *Proceedings of the Nutrition Society*, 61: 537–542.

Romans, S. E., Martin, M., Gendall, K. and Herbison, G. P. (2003) Age of menarche: the role of some psychosocial factors. *Psychological Medicine*, 33: 933–939.

Rowe, D. C. (2000) Environmental and genetic influences on Pubertal development. In JL Rodgers, D. C. Rowe and W. B. Miller (eds) *Genetic Influences on Human Fertility and Sexuality*, pp. 147–168. Kluwer Academic, Boston.

Rowe, D. C. (2002) On genetic variation in menarche and age at first sexual intercourse. *Evolution and Human Behavior*, 23: 365–372.

Rushton, P. (1985) Differential K theory. *Personality and Individual Differences*, 6: 441–452.

Sayer, A. A., Cooper, C., Evans, J. R., Rauf, A., Wormald, R. P., Osmond, C. and Barker, D. J. (1998) Are rates of ageing determined in utero? *Age and Ageing*, 27: 579–583.

Schore, A. (2001) Effects of a secure attachment relationship on right brain development, affect regulation and infant mental health. *Infant Mental Health Journal*, 22: 7–66.

Seccombe, K. (2000) Families in poverty in the 1990s. *Journal of Marriage and the Family*, 62: 1094–1113.

Serbin, L. and Karp, J. (2003) Intergenerational studies of parenting and the transfer of risk from parent to child. *Current Directions in Psychological Science*, 12: 138–142.

Shaver, P. R. and Mikulincer, M. (2002) Attachment-related psychodynamics. *Attachment and Human Development*, 4: 133–161.

Shonkoff, J. and Phillips, D. (2000) *From Neurons to Neighbourhoods: The Science of Early Child Development.* National Academies Press, Washington, DC.

Simpson, J. A. (1990) Influence of attachment styles on romantic relationships. *Journal of Personality and Social Psychology*, 59: 971–980.

Slade, A., Belsky, J., Aber, J. L. and Phelps, J. L. (1999) Maternal representations of their relationship with their toddlers. *Developmental Psychology*, 35: 611–619.

Sroufe, L. A. (1988) The role of infant-caregiver attachment in development. In J Belsky and T Nezworski (eds) *Clinical Implications of Attachment*, pp. 18–40. Lawrence Erlbaum, Hillsdale, NJ.

Stavrou, I., Zois, C., Ioannidis, J. P. and Tsatsoulis, A. (2002) Association of polymorphisms of the oestrogen receptor alpha gene with the age of menarche. *Human Reproduction*, 17: 1101–1105.

Stearns, S. (1992) *The evolution of life histories.* Oxford University Press, Oxford.

Stearns, S. and Koella, J. C. (1986) The evolution of phenotypic plasticity in life-history traits. *Evolution*, 40: 893–913.

Steinberg, L. (1988) Reciprocal relation between parent-child distance and pubertal maturation. *Developmental Psychology*, 24: 122–128.

Surbey, M. K. (1990) Family composition, stress, and the timing of human menarche. In T. E. Ziegler and F. B. Bercovitch (eds) *Monographs in Primatology*, Vol. 13, *Socioendocrinology of Primate Reproduction*, pp. 11–32. Wiley–Liss, New York.

Thompson, R. (1999) Early attachment and later development. In J. Cassidy and P. R. Shaver (eds) *Handbook of Attachment*, pp. 265–286. Guilford Press, New York.

Thornberry, T., Feeeman-Gallant, A., Lizotte, A., Krohn, M. and Smith, C. (2003) Linked lives. *Journal of Abnormal Child Psychology*, 31: 171–184.

Treloar, S. A. and Martin, N. G. (1990) Age at menarche as a fitness trait. *American Journal of Human Genetics*, 47: 89–107.

Turkheimer, E. and Waldron, M. (2000) Non-shared environment. *Psychological Bulletin*, 126: 78–108.

van Ijzendoorn, M. (1995) Adult attachment representations, parental responsiveness, and infant attachment. *Child Development*, 68: 604–609.

Waters, E., Merrick, S., Treboux, D., Crowell, J. and Albersheim, L. (2000) Attachment security in infancy and early adulthood. *Child Development*, 71: 684–689.

Weinfield, N., Sroufe, L. A. and Egeland, B. (2000) Attachment from infancy to early adulthood in a high-risk sample. *Child Development*, 71: 695–702.

West-Eberhard, M. (2003) *Developmental Plasticity and Evolution.* Oxford University Press, Oxford.

Wierson, M., Long, P. J. and Forehand, R. L. (1993) Toward a new understanding of early menarche. *Adolescence*, 28: 913–924.

Williams, G. C. (1966) *Adaptation and Natural Selection.* Princeton University Press, Princeton, NJ.

Wilson, E. O. (1975) *Sociobiology.* Harvard University, Cambridge, MA.

Wilson, M. and Daly, M. (1997) Life expectancy, economic inequality, homicide and reproductive timing in Chicago neighbourhoods. *British Medical Journal*, 314: 1271–1274.

CHAPTER 19

Parental impacts on development: How proximate factors mediate adaptive plans

Tamas Bereczkei

19.1. Introduction

Individuals' reproductive interests are most directly served by having children who grow up and reproduce. From a Darwinian perspective, evolution has operated to select certain forms of parental care in order to ensure that offspring reach sexual maturity and have the potential to carry on the parents' reproductive lineage. This includes not only the physical means necessary for survival, but also the means by which a child develops competencies in his or her social group (Bjorklund and Yunger, 2000).

The impact of parental care on development is especially large and extended in the case of human beings. One of the most striking differences between humans and the rest of the primates is the extent of delayed maturation. Human development is not only prolonged relative to other primates, but also possesses a stage of the life history, namely adolescence, that is unique to *Homo sapiens*. In contrast to other animals, human brain growth continues until adulthood and neural connections continue to

be created under the influence of experience (Bogin, 1999).

An extended period of youth and an enlarged brain are needed to master the increasing complexity of the social environment. Human children are physically dependent on their parents for a long period of time during which they learn vital social skills and practice adult roles. Parents not only provide offspring with resources, but also have a major impact on their social and cognitive development, which deeply influence offspring attitudes and behavioural styles in adulthood (Bowlby, 1965; Bjorklund and Pellegrini, 2002).

In the light of evolutionary theory, parental impacts, like any other environmental stimuli, are hypothesized to be processed by children's evolved psychological mechanisms. Various behavioural algorithms, decision rules, learning programs and epigenetic rules transform input from the family context into behavioural output that presumably solved adaptive problems in evolutionarily relevant environments (Buss, 1995). This is why evolved physiological and psychological processes, considered as proximate mechanisms, are so crucial in the evolutionary explanations of human behaviour. In the present chapter, an attempt is made to clarify the specific ways in which these mechanisms channel behavioural acts into adaptive decisions. A central task is to gain insights into the details of socialization: how children process the information that comes from their parents and how this shapes adaptive patterns and states during development.

19.2. Early mother–child relationships and long-term developmental effects

Well-known (even notorious) experiments with animals have revealed that an infant's need for contact with a familiar figure, especially the mother, is crucial for normal growth and development (Harlow and Mears, 1979). Studies in the 1970s and later suggested that early physical contact facilitates a powerful emotional attraction of a human mother to her child, and influences the child's later development. Mothers who experienced extensive contact with their children immediately after birth displayed more nursing behaviour several months later (Klaus and Kennel, 1976) specifically, they made visual contact with their 3-month-old children more often, as well as kissing them and suckling them more frequently than those who—according to 'traditional' hospital practices—were allowed to see their babies only 12–18 h after delivery. Even 1 year later, these 'early contact' mothers spoke with greater inflection to their children, using more questions and adjectives than commands. The researchers' interpretation of these patterns was that early contact brings about a harmonious relationship and stimulates growth, and perhaps even mental development. In the light of a classical ethological framework, we would say that infants imprinted on the specific cues associated with their mothers—and mothers also imprinted on their infants—during this early, sensitive period, which then ensured the development of long-lasting bonds between them.

Several authors have concluded from these observations that very early contact has a crucial and irreversible effect on a child's later development. However, it has been found that early contact in the first hours after birth has no measurable effects on the mothers' emotional bonds with their infants a year later. In fact, only one group of mothers benefited from early contact; those who were already at risk of abandoning their babies (Hrdy, 1999). Among these women, readiness to accept their babies increased, with the subsequent advantages of later contact, compared to those who did not develop an early bond. In the case of mothers generally, however, a lack of physical contact with their infants immediately after birth does not influence the subsequent security of mother–infant attachment. This suggests that preprogrammed imprinting mechanisms occurring during short sensitive periods, of the kind peculiar to many species of birds and mammals, cannot be fully extended to humans.

Although efforts to relate directly aspects of very early parenting to developmental outcomes have generally met with limited success, several forms of early attachment have been found to predict children's later development. For instance, specialized vocal stimulation from the parent (so-called infant-directed speech) was found to be correlated with 3–4-month-old infants' growth rate, which is, in turn, likely to be associated with health (Monnot, 1999). Young infants who received insensitive maternal care experienced difficulty in recalling representations of attachment as young adults (Beckwith et al., 1999). Prolonged and total emotional deprivation in the first year may lead to further behavioural difficulties in relationships with adults and peers outside the family; deprived children, aged between 7 and 14 years, show over-friendliness toward strangers and more aggression towards class-mates (Hodges and Tizard, 1989). Furthermore, the effects of early adversity do not manifest themselves uniformly across all domains of behaviour. In a study of Romanian orphans, perceptuo-motor skills were found to be less vulnerable to the effects of early deprivation than cognitive and language development (Rutter et al., 1998).

Other studies have indicated that the consequences of parental practices can only be understood by taking into account children's individuality: both their physical condition and various temperamental traits. There is agreement that the interaction of parental characteristics and child characteristics is likely to provide greater explanatory power than either of these two factors alone (Schaffer, 2000). Therefore, just as the mother's condition and psychological preparedness for childbirth influences her relationship with the newborn and its subsequent development, so the child's health and physical condition, as well as their temperament and responsiveness, have a great impact on early attachment and subsequent developmental patterns. For instance, under the influence of risk factors (poverty, parent's mental illness, divorce), children with an 'easy' temperament (high activity and sociability, low anxiousness) develop greater stress resistance than 'difficult' children, probably because they are able to establish supportive relationships with adults more easily, which is beneficial in an adverse environment (Masten, 1994).

Low birth weight and prematurity may be another factor of the infant's initial character that frequently leads to discriminative parental care, which in turn influences development. Mothers tend to smile at and touch such infants less than healthy ones (Goldberg et al., 1986). This may be a response to the infants' inability to participate in some of the mother–child interactions that normally elicit and facilitate maternal attachment (Daly and Wilson, 1987). Premature infants have been found to contribute to difficulties in arousal regulation by providing less clear and easily interpretable behavioural cues to their parents (Bigsby et al., 1996). They tend to have an aversive cry, show poorer motor coordination, smile less, and exhibit more gaze aversion (Furlow, 1997). The physical condition and health status of the newborn appear to strongly influence the parents' perception of the infant and their decision regarding levels of investment. In a study of seven pairs of twins, the healthy twin was found to receive more positive parental behaviour (holding, soothing, gazing) than the poorly twin (Mann, 1992).

This parental discrimination exacerbates the effects of genetic and physiological impairments, such as neurological abnormalities, on the handicapped infant's physical and cognitive development. Low birth weight and premature infants older than 1 year of age show less exploration,

play, and verbal interaction, have more frequent distress behaviour, and engage in more anxious and resistant attachment patterns compared to normal birth weight children, especially if prematurity is associated with another risk factor, such as illness or economic stress (Wille, 1991). Developmental delays and cognitive disabilities, measured at the age of 6 years, have been related to both biomedical disadvantages, such as intra-uterine growth retardation, and a disruption of bonding processes (Korner et al., 1993; Shenkin et al., 2004).

The evolutionary strategy underlying this pattern of parental care and the development of handicapped children is considered as a trade-off between current and future reproductive interests. Parental psychology is shaped by selection to make adaptive decisions about the timing and amount of investment in offspring (Clutton-Brock, 1991; Surbey, 1998; Bjorklund and Pellegrini, 2002). Mothers can optimize their reproductive output with regard to maternal and child health, as well as to their access to resources for child rearing. The reproductive value of a child, i.e. its own expected fitness, is considered to be the primary factor influencing parental investment. Given that an offspring's poor genotypic and phenotypic quality is unlikely to enhance the parents' reproductive prospects, the rejection or neglect of an unhealthy newborn could be a fitness-enhancing strategy. Indeed, there is a considerable amount of evidence that these children are likely to become victims of abuse and infanticide (Daly and Wilson, 1987, 1988). The optimal strategy for parents that have a high-risk child is to reduce investment in that offspring, while increasing long-term fertility by saving resources for a subsequent child (Burgess and Drais, 1999; Chisholm, 1999). As a result, the retention of resources for future reproduction lowers the reproductive value of the current offspring but increases the parents' subsequent reproductive success.

Low birth weight delivery and prematurity have been found to influence strongly a child's reproductive value (Peacock, 1991; Mann, 1992). In the USA, 73.7% of neonatal deaths among white infants and 83.4% among black infants occurred in babies who either weighed less than 2500 g or were born prior to 37 weeks of gestation (Paneth, 1995). Furthermore, low birth weight infants have three times the risk of developmental handicaps and twice the risk of serious congenital anomalies than normal birth weight infants (Abell, 1992). As low birth delivery and prematurity imposes severe costs on mothers, they are expected to reduce, or even terminate, their investment, and minimize their costs in rearing offspring with relatively low prospect of survival and reproduction (Daly and Wilson, 1998).

One longitudinal study has revealed that mothers of high-risk (premature and low birth weight) infants shortened the duration of breastfeeding and interbirth intervals, compared to those with a healthy infant (Bereczkei et al., 2000; Bereczkei, 2001) (Figure 19.1). As a response to the children's lower survival prospect, they diminished birth spacing, gaining 2–4 years across their reproductive lifespan for having additional children. This study also gives some insight into the adaptive significance of this parental bias, especially in the group of subjects living in the most risky environment (in terms of low resource levels, low income and high social uncertainty). Due to their relatively short interbirth intervals, mothers with one or two low birth weight infants were found to have significantly more children, compared to other women with healthy infants. Thus, the mothers

appear to compensate for handicaps associated with low birth weight and prematurity by having a larger number of closely spaced children following the birth of one or more infants with reduced probability of survival. The shift to giving birth to another child in the future might be a beneficial strategy in an environment where morphological and behavioural cues associated with low birth weight (and the possible related prematurity and retardation) signal a high mortality risk.

However, even if mothers are ready to 'replace' high-risk infants, they do not necessarily take less care of them. On the contrary, they can even intensify parental care towards handicapped children. A number of studies have found that mothers of infants with moderately low birth weight make heightened efforts in their interaction with infants. They paid more attention to them, and showed enhanced maternal warmth, as a compensatory strategy against the infant's passivity (Barratt et al., 1996; Tessier et al., 2003; Tully et al., 2004). In general, severe and easily detectable diseases are likely to shift the mother towards a low-investment pattern, while less obvious and more correctable disabilities may encourage them to continue caring behaviour (Mann, 1992). Intensive care for handicapped children is obviously very costly to the parent, but the returns on their investment may be

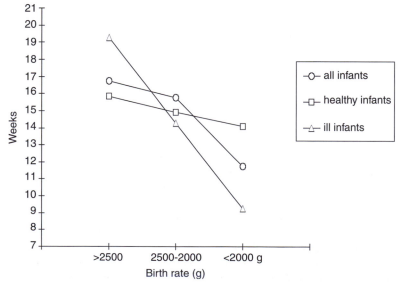

Fig. 19.1 Duration of breastfeeding for high-risk infants in terms of birth weight and health status.

reproductively rewarding in certain cases. Therefore, mothers closely monitor their infant's health status during the early stages of infancy. Low birth weight and premature infants with no signs of severe, discernible deformities may appear 'normal' and healthy, and mothers may not be aware of their handicap. At the same time, because of the infant's unusual responses and unreliable behavioural cues, mothers can feel that something is wrong with the baby. Under such uncertain circumstances, mothers may steadily test the infant's development and continue to provide maternal care, including breast-feeding, up to a point when she can assess accurately the health status of her infant. The point is that mothers monitor infants and make decisions to reduce investment only if these initiatives fail and normal bonding processes cannot be established or restored.

19.3. **Evolutionary and ontogenetic pathways of child social development**

Experiences in the family during childhood have been shown to have an impact on later behavioural styles and attitudes. Children are sensitive to the cues coming from family arrangements and parental behaviour (MacDonald, 1997). Natural selection has favoured learning biases in children for the acquisition of certain forms of social behaviour (Draper and Harpending, 1988). As a result, they have the capacity to adjust life histories in response to environmental conditions, and variations in the life cycle are considered as adaptive answers to different circumstances.

Belsky et al. (1991; see also Belsky, this volume, Chapter 18) argued that the availability of resources, the stability of pair bonds, and the trustworthiness of others during early childhood would affect later mating and parenting effort. Individuals who develop insecure attachment to their parents, experience opportunistic relationships between family members, grow up in a father-absent family, and who face scarce resources and family stress, will shorten the age of biological maturation, accelerate sexual maturation, and tend to engage in short-term pair bonds. Those, on the other hand, who have

more reliable relationships with others and less conflicts in the family will show more stable pair bonds and invest more in child rearing. Indeed, studies have revealed that young children exposed to emotional and financial deprivation and to negative parenting practices show earlier pubertal maturation (e.g. earlier menarche), more non-compliant and 'problem' behaviour, earlier onset of sexual activity, and more frequent marital dissolution than children coming from secure, harmonious, and stable family households (Graber et al., 1995; Bereczkei and Csanaky, 1996, 2001; Belsky, 2004; Ellis, 2004; Bogaert, 2005).

At the beginning of the chapter, I emphasized that an analysis of the proximate mechanisms that mediate evolutionary strategies at the level of manifest behaviour should play a crucial role in evolutionary psychological studies. Several factors have been described that are likely to link family relationships to pubertal development. Cortisol is a key hormone produced in response to physical and psychosocial stressors, and poorer family relations may produce physiological stress responses (Haggerty et al., 1994). A study in a rural village of Dominica indicated complex, sex-specific effects of the family environment on endocrine function. Children living in households with unstable caretaking were more likely to have abnormal cortisol levels. Adult males whose fathers were reportedly absent during their early childhood have higher cortisol levels and lower testosterone levels than father-present males. High levels of family conflicts during childhood were also associated with elevated cortisol levels in adults (Flinn et al., 1996, see also Flinn, Chapter 20, this volume).

The hypothalamic–pituitary–gonadal (HPG) axis is considered as the path linking family stress and pubertal maturation. Persistent activation of the stress response system is associated with immune deficiency, cognitive impairment, inhibited growth, and delayed sexual maturity. Psychosocial stress suppresses activity of HPG, and thereby impairs ovarian functioning in adult women (Marcus et al., 2001). At the same time, stress can stimulate maturation of the HPG axis in prepubertal females. It is possible that there is a curvilinear, U-shaped relation between early exposure to adverse conditions and the development of the stress-reacting system, with higher stress reactivity to both highly stressful and highly protected early social environments (Ellis, 2004).

Several studies have found that single-parent status, especially father absence, is a stronger predictor of daughters' pubertal timing and sexual maturation than conflicts and stress within two-parent families (Ellis et al., 1999). This is because girls may have evolved to show high sensitivity towards the father's role in the family. Over the course of human evolution, the high variability in male reproductive strategies may have afforded important cues to the reproductive opportunities and constraints that young girls were likely to encounter later in life (Ellis et al., 1999). It is unlikely, then, that the same evolved psychological mechanisms have been selected as a response to a father-absent environment and to the physical and psychosocial stressors in a two-parent family. Separate and largely independent paths of the timing of sexual development are involved in these different cases.

One of the causal mechanisms related to the effects of father absence is the daughter's consequent exposure to unrelated adult males. Consistent with this hypothesis, one study found that the length of exposure to stepfathers and mother's boyfriends, rather than years of biological father absence, best accounted for the onset of menarche and other signs of pubertal maturation in girls (Ellis and Graber, 2000). It may be that girls from paternally deprived homes are more likely to become exposed to pheromones of unrelated adult males, which in turn accelerates pubertal development. Research on a variety of mammalian species indicates that exposure to pheromones produced by unfamiliar male conspecifics accelerates female development. Experimental studies have shown that exposure to pheromones produced by men's axillary sweat glands reduced variability in women's ovarian cycles (Cutler et al., 1986). An alternative mechanism may be that increased exposure to biological fathers inhibits sexual maturation. Accordingly, it has been found that higher father–daughter interaction is associated with later pubertal maturation (Ellis et al., 1999). It is highly probable that both mechanisms—inhibition induced by biological father and stimulation caused by stepfathers—play a role in daughters' sexual development. Similarly, the effect of stress and father absence on pubertal

timing—as separate mechanisms—frequently reinforce or counteract each other. A study revealed that girls in families with stepfathers tended to experience early pubertal development only when the relationship between the mother and the stepfather was stressful (Ellis and Graber, 2000).

The above-mentioned hormonal processes (HPG, cortisol, pheromones) are considered as proximate mechanisms by which parental impacts on child development manifest in family environments characterized by stress, insecure attachment, father absence, etc. However, these components of early family environment are also regarded as proximate factors under a slightly different evolutionary explanation, namely that they mediate and express the adaptive problem associated with local mortality rates. In their life-history model, Promislow and Harvey (1990) stated that life-history traits and developmental trajectories vary in accordance with local death rates. If the chances of survival are good, a mother can afford to invest heavily in a limited number of offspring with high competitive ability. If survival is unpredictable or unlikely, a relatively large number of offspring with low levels of parental investment promote the possibility of high fitness in good years but minimize maternal losses in bad years.

Chisholm (1993) argued that children have been selected to be sensitive to environmental cues associated with a high probability of juvenile and adult death. High stress in the family, insensitive and rejecting childrearing practices, insecure attachment and parental feelings of anger, fear, and despair were likely to have been associated with high mortality rates during a major part of human evolution. Facing these cues (or indices) of local mortality, humans have been selected to adopt high-mating-effort reproductive strategies as a form of compensation for increased mortality. Although the relatively low probability of juvenile or adult death is no longer expected to influence the offspring's reproductive value, differential mortality seems to have an impact on developmental trajectories, even in a society following the demographic transition. Humans may be sensitive to the distribution of deaths among relatives and acquaintances, calculate survival probabilities, and make decisions, although not necessarily consciously, on pair-bond and reproductive strategies. On the one hand, sadness and grief represent a kind of psychosocial stress that may lead to the subjective feelings of insecure attachment in adulthood. On the other hand, perceptions of mortality risk, that may signal a shorter expected lifespan, may result in an earlier onset of sexual maturity. Negative correlations were found between early stress and expected lifespan and positive correlations between expected lifespan and age at menarche and first birth (Chisholm *et al.*, 2005)

Among studies that have measured fertility and mortality rates, one found that age of first reproduction, number of children born per woman, mortality risks, and local resource availability were all interrelated in modern-day Chicago (Wilson and Daly, 1997). In neighbourhoods with low resource availability, shorter lifespans were associated with both an earlier age of first reproduction for both men and women and nearly twice as many children born to women, compared with a more favourable neighbourhood. In a more recent Hungarian study, an attempt was made to investigate the possible association between childrearing practices and mortality rates (Bereczkei and Csanaky, 2001). We predicted that differences in family environment would be associated with differential mortality even in an industrialized culture. (Mortality rates were measured as the number of deaths among the subjects' sisters and brothers.)

In accordance with theoretical considerations, higher mortality rates were found for the siblings of 732 Hungarian subjects, close to completed fertility, coming from families with high stress and rejecting, cold parental attitudes when compared with subjects from more favourable family conditions. Parental affection and emotional atmosphere were found to be strongly correlated with adult mortality rates (Figure 19.2). The less parental love the children perceived during childhood, the higher life-long mortality rates they experienced until the age of 45 years. Similarly, high levels of stress during childhood proved to be a strong determinant of the children's low life expectancy. Furthermore, we have found a strong relationship between the subjects' family conditions during childhood and their reproductive output. Mothers from a family environment with a low level of parental affection and a high level of self–parent conflicts started reproduction earlier and gave birth to more live-born infants than those growing up in more favourable households.

These results suggest that children are sensitive to cues in their family environment that are

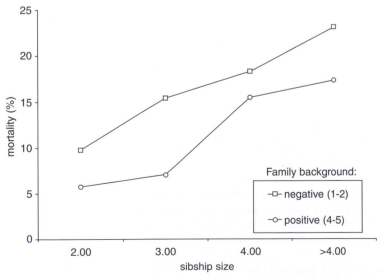

Fig. 19.2 Mortality rates for siblings of subjects aged more than 45 years with a particular birth order.

associated with a high probability of juvenile and adult death. Under the influence of adverse childhood experiences, they are inclined to adopt an opportunistic mating pattern with early maturation and high fertility as a form of compensation for increased mortality. It is remarkable that humans in contemporary societies still seem to follow their reproductive interests, with evolved psychological mechanisms transformed into reproductive output. A possible explanation of the strong correlations between childhood experiences, mortality and fertility patterns is that conditional strategies are involved that enable individuals to follow environmental changes and make reproductively optimal decisions in various environments (Barrett *et al.*, 2002). Both American and Hungarian studies suggest that early and frequent reproduction in certain social contexts might be, at least in part, a facultative response to high mortality rates (Wilson and Daly, 1997; Bereczkei and Csanaky, 2001).

19.4. Sexual imprinting: parental influence on mate choice

Freud (1905) suggested that during the so-called Oedipal phase of development, boys take their mother as their first and primary sexual object, and speculated that, as adults, they look for someone who can represent their mother. Whereas the assumptions on incestuous drives and sexual desires between mothers and infant sons have been falsified by recent theoretical and empirical findings (Daly and Wilson, 1990), the hypothesis that their intimate relationship has a large impact on the child's later sexual development remains plausible. It appears especially true for shaping mate preferences and attitudes.

Imprinting-like mechanisms have been suggested as an explanation for the impact of early experiences on mate criteria in both humans and other animals. Ethologists stated several decades ago that, in addition to fixation on the parents, imprinting also plays a crucial role in shaping sexual behaviour during adulthood (Bateson, 1964; Bolhuis and Horn, 1992; Lorenz, 1965). In the case of sexual imprinting, early exposure to a set of species-specific characteristics is thought

to shape mate preferences that persist until late adulthood. Cross-fostering experiments with various species have revealed that during pair formation adult males tend to prefer sexual partners that are similar to the female that reared them (Immelmann *et al.*, 1991; Oetting *et al.*, 1995; Vos, 1995).

Bateson (1983) argued that sexual imprinting enables individuals to learn the characteristics of their close kin and subsequently to choose mates that appear slightly different, but not too different, from their parents and siblings. This is because both inbreeding and outbreeding have obvious reproductive costs and benefits (Read and Harvey, 1988; Ridley, 1994). On the one hand, inbreeding increases the degree to which parents share genes with offspring, thereby enhancing genetic representation in future generations. It might also prevent genetic complexes co-adapted to the local environment from being disrupted, thereby enhancing reproductive success. On the other hand, an extreme degree of inbreeding can impose serious inbreeding depression effects, and various kinds of outbreeding strategies help to prevent reproductive costs associated with incest. It has been argued that an adaptive compromise (*optimal outbreeding*) has evolved between the opposing selection pressures of inbreeding and outbreeding, with individuals choosing a mate with a moderate degree of similarity (Bateson, 1983). Indeed, experiments have revealed mating preferences for slightly familiar conspecifics in various species (Bateson, 1988; Alcock, 1998).

Several studies have also revealed imprinting-like effects of human parents on children in their later mate choice. People born of mixed ethnicity marriages show a tendency to marry into the ethnic group of the opposite-sex parent more often than into that of the same-sex parent (Jedlicka, 1980). Two studies have shown greater importance of the opposite-sex parent over the same-sex parent in predicting the hair and eye colour of actual partners (Zei *et al.*, 1981; Little *et al.*, 2002). Similarly, women were found to prefer the odours of men with HLA alleles that resembled her father's HLA alleles but not her mother's (Jacob *et al.*, 2002).

Although these studies suggest that imprinting-like mechanisms occur in mate choice, they do not provide evidence of parental impact and developmental processes leading to mating preferences for individuals with similar appearance. A hypothesis was put forward that sexual imprinting during a sensitive period in early childhood is responsible for shaping one's later mate choice criteria through the observed features of the opposite-sex parent (Daly, 1989; Bereczkei et al., 2002). Children are expected to prefer potential mates who are sufficiently similar to the representation of their opposite-sex parent's appearance. During their first 6–8 years of life, children internalize this parent's phenotype as a template for acquiring mates with shared genes. In the process of attachment, young men and women may shape a mental model of their opposite-sex parent's physical appearance and use it in mate choice after reaching adolescence. In the light of this hypothesis, a genetically canalized learning process, rather than direct genetic similarity detection, is responsible for the perceived similarity between spouses.

In a study in which subjects compared more than 300 facial photographs of family members and controls, the subjects correctly matched wives to their mothers-in-law at a significantly higher rate than expected by chance (Bereczkei et al., 2002). Furthermore, using a retrospective attachment test (EMBU), it was found that the more physical and emotional distance from their mothers that sons had experienced during childhood, the less similarity was perceived between their wives and mothers. A regression analysis revealed that men who had been more frequently rejected by their mother during childhood were less likely to choose mates who resembled their mothers in physical appearance. These results suggest that males build up an image of their mother's appearance and search for a partner who fits that perceptual schema.

However, a crucial limitation of these investigations is the difficulty of separating the effects of sexual imprinting from a more direct detection of similarity between mates themselves. It has been suggested that *phenotype matching* could be responsible for controlling mate choice without the help of learning from familiarity or proximity. That is, individuals may be guided to respond to specific phenotypic cues in others and direct altruism selectively towards individuals with shared genes (Dawkins, 1982; Hepper, 1991). Obviously, this can only occur if there is a high correlation between genetic similarity and phenotypic similarity on traits that individuals use to distinguish potential mates. Individuals, equipped with some specific innate algorithm, could then detect some aspect of their own phenotype, match it to new, unfamiliar individuals, and prefer those who possess the same or similar phenotype. Much experimental evidence shows that both lower and higher animals are able to recognize genetic similarity on the basis of shared olfactory and visual cues (Blaustein et al., 1991; Holmes, 1995; Pfennig and Sherman, 1995).

Several authors argue that this mechanism is responsible for homogamy or assortative mating in humans (Rushton, 1989). A number of studies have shown that the majority of mates resemble each other in a high number of traits, such as socioeconomic status, age, intellectual ability, education, personality variables, physical attractiveness, vocational interest and anthropometric measures (Mascie-Taylor, 1988, 1995; Jaffe and Chacon-Puignau, 1995; Bereczkei and Csanaky, 1996; Keller et al., 1996; Bereczkei et al., 1997). However, it is not known what perceptual mechanisms are involved in feature detection associated with phenotype matching, and what part of the similarity detection system is based on innate mechanisms versus associative learning. Several recent studies on the relationship between genetic similarity and mate preferences have yielded controversial results. One has shown that women prefer the odour of men who have significantly more HLA allele matches to her own alleles than to men with the least preferred odour (Jacob et al., 2002). Another study revealed that female students tended to prefer the scent of men who possessed dissimilar HLA genotypes (Wedekind and Furi, 1997; see also Wedekind, this volume, Chapter 22). A very recent study suggested that females find the faces of HLA-heterozygous men more attractive than faces of homozygotes (Roberts et al., 2005), whereas another study detected no such effect (Thornhill et al., 2003).

Despite these controversies, phenotype matching remains plausible as an account of the resemblance between mating partners, and can therefore be considered as a rival explanation of sexual imprinting. This is because similarity between one's spouse and his/her opposite-sex parent may be an artefact, given the 50% overlap between the parents' and offspring's genetic material. Therefore, if homogamy works via phenotype matching, it would be responsible for the similarity between spouse and opposite-sex parent. In this case, our results about resemblances between family members may be due to innate similarity detection between spouses, not sexual imprinting on the mother. In order to disentangle these effects, we conducted another study investigating the mate choices of women from *adoptive* families (Bereczkei *et al.*, 2004). In light of the sexual imprinting hypothesis, early experiences with the opposite-sex parent will have a long-term effect on one's mate choice, whether the child and the caring adult were relatives or not. Women are expected to choose a mate who resembles their father even though he is not a biological relative. Alternatively, if phenotypic matching theory is correct, then women would prefer mates similar to themselves but not to their adoptive father (Bereczkei *et al.*, 2004).

In accordance with the imprinting hypothesis, subjects found a significant resemblance in facial traits between a daughter's husband and her adoptive father, but no resemblance between a daughter's husband and her adoptive mother. This effect

is likely to be modified by the quality of the father–daughter relationship during childhood. Daughters who received more emotional support from their adoptive father were more likely to choose mates similar to their father than those whose father provided a less positive emotional atmosphere (Figure 19.3). These results suggest that individuals acquire mate choice criteria at least partly from the quality of social contact with their opposite-sex parents during childhood, rather than using genetically prescribed mechanisms to detect particular phenotypic cues in unrelated individuals.

However, the operation of phenotype matching in various interpersonal relationships cannot be ruled out. It is highly probable that phenotype matching plays an important role in kin recognition, but that it has less influence on interpersonal relationships beyond the circle of relatives. It may mediate positive affiliation between relatives who share similar detectable facial features or who smell similar. A study found that mothers who had limited contact with their newborns immediately after birth could recognize them by olfactory cues alone (Porter, 1987). (It is worth noting, however, that mothers can also learn the smell of their child during pregnancy, which represents associative

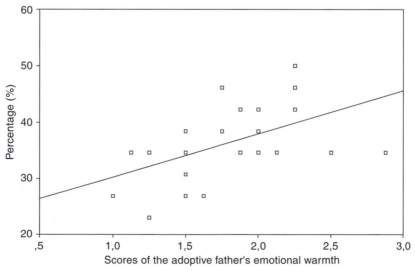

Fig. 19.3 Percentage of husband–wife's adoptive father matching as a function of the father's emotional warmth.

learning, rather than a purely genetic phenotype-matching mechanism.) Adult subjects could also match the odours of mothers with those of their infants, but were unable to match husbands with wives (Porter *et al.*, 1985). Using visual cues, adult subjects could match mothers', fathers', and their newborn infants' facial photographs (Christenfeld and Hill, 1995). In another study, participants were able to identify the odour of most of their first-degree relatives, but mothers could not recognize their stepchildren, nor could children recognize their stepsiblings (Weisfeld *et al.*, 2003).

Recently, DeBruine (2004) and DeBruine *et al.* (2004) argued that humans use facial resemblance as a cue of kinship. She found women's preference for self-resemblance increased during the luteal phases of their cycle, when they were less fertile, and hypothesized that this was a byproduct of a hormonal mechanism for increasing affiliative behaviour towards kin during pregnancy. Furthermore, she revealed that facial self-resemblance increased attractiveness judgments of same-sex faces more than other-sex faces, which may indicate a non-sexual response to family-, kinship- and in-group-related cues. The preference for facial resemblance also appears to influence decisions about social contracts: similarity to the subject's own face raised the incidence of trusting a partner in a two-person sequential trust game (DeBruine, 2002).

In sum, humans may have separate domain-specific mechanisms to deal with social and mating contexts. A preference for self-resemblance seems prevalent in social contexts, and may result from phenotype matching (recognizing certain traits of own phenotype in others). Mate preferences, on the other hand, may lie in mechanisms different from phenotype matching, that is sexual imprinting (exposure to the opposite-sex parent early in life). Alternatively, humans might have been selected for a multiple mechanism that enables individuals to detect similarity in others, and this complex psychological mechanism—that contains both phenotype matching and sexual imprinting—can be used in various contexts of kin recognition and mate choice. Specific conditions, like family circumstances, life-history factors and personality traits can influence the extent to which one matches one's own phenotype to others or uses a template based on experiences with family members.

19.5. Cultural and individual differences of socialization

During socialization parents often teach their children in a way that promotes children's adjustment to the cultural environment. Parents may have evolved psychological mechanisms, expressed as teaching biases, which convey adaptive information to offspring (Barrett *et al.*, 2002). They use socialization techniques and educational rules that increase their children's access to social resources and status. This parental effect, rather than hard-wired, genetically encoded information, would allow the production of diverse cultural variants. A cross-cultural analysis has revealed that boys are taught to be more aggressive, self-reliant and competitive, whereas girls are taught to be more sexually restrained and obedient in cultures where polygamy prevails (Low, 1989). Especially large differences have been found in unstratified highly polygynous societies, where men are expected to compete for resources necessary to have wives, and women are expected to show chastity and obedience as desirable traits for wives who are encouraged to marry up the social scale (hypergyny).

In Hungarian Gypsy villages, daughters are traditionally socialized to help with raising children, and their parents normally expect them to engage in various kinds of duties such as looking after babies, playing with children, cooking for them, etc. (Bereczkei and Dunbar, 2002). In accordance, girls and boys are treated differently; prior to marriage, girls are prepared for maternal roles and provide a valuable service as 'helpers-at-the-nest'. Indeed, studies in rural Gypsy communities have found that (i) first-born girls engage in substantial help in housework related to childcare of their younger siblings; (ii) this assistance both increases the length of the mother's reproductive career and reduces inter-birth intervals for subsequent children; and (iii) Gypsy women with first-born daughters have significantly more children than those who gave birth to sons first (Figure 19.4). These results suggest that a parental bias towards daughters is adaptive in these rural populations

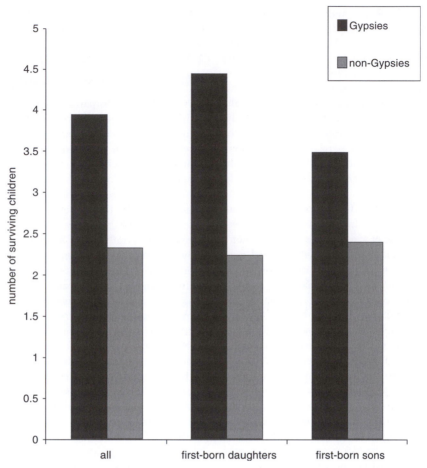

Fig. 19.4 Mean lifetime fertility of Gipsy and non-Gipsy mothers as a function of the sex of their first-born children.

because a first-born daughter reduces the mother's costs of rearing her current infant, thus allowing her to transfer the resulting spare time and energy to producing and raising additional children.

Teaching offspring to behave differently according to their sex is only one kind of differential parental investment. In general, parents apply specific techniques and socialization practices in order to enable their children to adopt the adult roles, values and norms prevalent in a given culture. Ireneus Eibl-Eibesfeldt (1989) found that, in warfaring cultures, such as Eipo, Himba, Yanomami, children are educated early to toughen themselves up by learning to bear

physical pain and to meet aggression with aggression. Children also develop fighting skills in their games in which they frequently imitate the behavioural models displayed by the adults. Adults reinforce certain behaviour through praise and scolding. By contrast, in the more peaceful cultures, as among Bushmen of the Kalahari, parents promote other models for their children. They do not encourage vengeful behaviour, often reprimand the attacker, and comfort the one who was attacked. They rely on appeasement, and rarely use physical force in disciplining their children.

These investigations reveal that in every culture, during socialization, parents provide their children with all the necessary information for them to be able to adapt to the specific social environment. Cross-cultural differences in behaviour patterns are certainly not due to genetic differences, they are rather induced by the diversity of parental rearing strategies. However, within a culture, the diversity of behavioural styles results from socialization processes in which the children's own needs and innate capacities play a more important role. This is important to emphasize, as according to the traditional concept of socialization, developing children are flexible, entirely malleable beings, who—through the impact of their parents—gradually acquire behavioural norms and roles prevailing in the given adult society. While this chain of causation has an undeniable role in children's development, most recent research—evolutionary studies among them—suggest a more complex, multi-causal model. They argue that parents not only shape their offspring's personality, but they also respond to the offsprings' various needs and propensities, and base their decisions concerning their rearing strategies on these endowments (Rowe, 1994; MacDonald, 2005). During this process, individual differences increase in the family.

Lalumière et al. (1996) argue that, in accordance with a Darwinian view, within multi-child families, siblings compete for the same resource: parental investment. They have initial differences due to genetic differences, age, order of birth and their sex. Initial differences on a given characteristic, such as verbal or athletic ability, may give one child an advantage over the other, and the less skilled child may have to display a different or additional type of ability or propensity to receive parental attention and care. Specific sibling characteristics may elicit specific parental reaction that reinforce and extend the original differences. This process places siblings on different developmental trajectories. Socialization processes producing developmental specialization may have been favoured by selection, for two reasons. First, specialization would reduce competition for extrafamilial resources among siblings. Second, specific individual capacities and achievements may make competition with others more efficient in a society that contains a number of niches.

In accordance with this theoretical model, it has been found that siblings grow more dissimilar the more time they spend together, which contradicts most contemporary socialization theories (Bouchard and Loehlin, 2001). Several twin studies have revealed that the length of time twins spend reared in the same family is negatively related to similarity in cognitive abilities and some personality traits, such as extraversion, aggreableness, and openness to experience (Pedersen et al., 1992). Unexpectedly, those twins who had been separated later were more dissimilar than those pairs separated earlier.

This evolutionary explanation closely fits to the recent results of human behavioural genetic studies (Rowe, 1994; Plomin and McClearn, 1997). Theoretically, socialization is not a one-way process in which parents shape children's temperament and personality. Rather, each socialization process involves an interaction between genetically canalized abilities and propensities and environmental effects, such as parental influence, cultural norms, etc. During this process, children play a decisive role in their relationship with their parents and in shaping their own personality characteristics later. One area of the child's activity is the so-called 'evocative' gene–environment correlation that involves an interaction, whereby the innate propensities and temperaments of children influence parental behaviour, which, in turn, affect various aspects of their development. In other words, siblings are treated differently because their genetically influenced patterns elicit or evoke different responses from their parents (Plomin, 1994, see also Sulloway, Chapter 21, this volume). For instance, a highly active child triggers more parental surveillance than an inactive one.

In one study, parent–child dyadic mutuality (cooperation, emotional reciprocity, maternal responsiveness), as an important component of family socialization processes, was measured by both parents and independent observers (Deater-Deckard and O'Connor, 2000). Identical twins were found to be more similar in their relationship with mothers than were fraternal twins, suggesting that child genetic variance was present. Heritability and non-shared environment each accounted for about half of the variance in mother–child dyadic mutuality, whereas the effect of shared environment was negligible.

Furthermore, full siblings (who share 50% of their genes, on average, as do fraternal twins) correlated at the same level as the fraternal twins, whereas adoptive siblings (who are genetically unrelated) were uncorrelated for parent–child mutuality. Since cooperation and emotional reciprocity were rated by parents and observers (not the siblings), the measured similarities and differences between siblings emerge only if parent's ratings are responsive to genetically influenced characteristics of children. This result can be interpreted in the evocative gene–environment correlation by which parents' actual behaviour is affected by genetically influenced characteristics of the children. As a result of this interaction, siblings' developmental paths would diverge and their cognitive and personality traits would be increasingly different.

In general, human behavioural genetics presents a picture of development, learning, and education that is different from the way these processes have been assumed to occur. Most theories of socialization assume that parental effects—and family environment, in general—will mean that children growing up in the same family will be similar to one another. On the contrary, genetic research has shown that environmental influences that affect behavioural development operate to make children in the same family different. There is little evidence that environmental influences shared by siblings, such as global parental style, have a crucial impact on later development. We know this, for example, because genetically unrelated children growing up in the same adoptive family hardly resemble each other for personality, cognitive abilities, and psychopathology in early adulthood (Plomin, 2000). However, this finding does not mean that family environment is unimportant. Rather, it means that environmental influences on development have their effect on an individual level rather than at the family level, and that every moment of human development is the result of an interaction between genetic propensities and environment.

19.6. Conclusions

Parental impacts have a great effect on the child's physical, social, and cognitive development. The main goal of this chapter was to analyse the proximate mechanisms that translate the underlying evolutionary logic into manifest behaviour. An explanation of human behaviour that focuses only on outcome and ultimate gain, and that does not take into account the environmental conditions and the participants' abilities, cannot explain how parents influence their children's development. Thus, the search for psychological mechanisms and their interaction with environmental factors is indispensable to the study of socialization.

References

Abell, T. D. (1992) Low birth weight, intrauterine growth-retarded, and pre-term infants: a research strategy. *Human Nature*, 3: 335–378.

Alcock, J. (1998) *Animal Behaviour. An Evolutionary Approach.* Sinauer, Sunderland, MA.

Barrett, L., Dunbar, R. I. M. and Lycett, J. E. (2002) *Human Evolutionary Psychology.* Palgrave, London.

Barratt, M. S., Roach, M. A. and Leavitt, L. A. (1996) The impact of low-risk prematurity on maternal behaviour and toddler outcomes. *International Journal of Behavioural Development*, 19: 581–602.

Bateson, P. P. G. (1964) An effect of imprinting on the perceptual development of domestic chick. *Nature*, 202: 421–422.

Bateson, P. P.G. (1983) Optimal outbreeding. In P. P. G. Bateson (ed.) *Mate Choice*, pp. 257–277. Cambridge University Press, Cambridge.

Bateson, P. P.G. (1988) Preferences for close relations in Japanese Quail. In H. Quellett (ed.) *Acta XIX. Congressus Internationalis Ornithologici*, vol. 1, pp. 961–972. Ottawa: University of Ottawa Press.

Beckwith, L., Cohen, S. E. and Hamilton, C. E. (1999) Maternal sensitivity during infancy and subsequent life events relate to attachment representation in early childhood. *Developmental Psychology*, 35: 693–700.

Belsky, J. (2004) Differential susceptibility to rearing influence: an evolutionary hypothesis and some evidence. In B. J. Ellis and D. F. Bjorklund (eds) *Origins of the Social Mind: Evolutionary Psychology and Child Development*, pp. 139–163. Guilford Press, New York.

Belsky, J., L. Steinberg and P. Draper (1991) Childhood experience, interpersonal development, and reproductive strategy: An evolutionary theory of socialization. *Child Development*, 62: 647–670.

Bereczkei, T. (2001) Maternal trade-off in treating high-risk children. *Evolution and Human Behaviour*, 22: 197–212.

Bereczkei, T. and A. Csanaky (1996) Evolutionary pathway of child development. Lifestyles of adolescents and adults from father-absent families. *Human Nature*, 7: 268–280.

Bereczkei, T. and Csanaky, A. (2001) Stressful family environment, mortality, and child socialization: life-history strategies among adolescents and adults from unfavourable social circumstances. *International Journal of Behavioural Development*, 25: 501–508.

Bereczkei, T. and R. I. M. Dunbar (2002) Helping-at-the-nest and reproduction in a Hungarian Gypsy population. *Current Anthropology*, 43: 804–809.

Bereczkei, T., Vörös, A., Gál, A. and Bernáth, L. (1997) Resources, attractiveness, family commitment; reproductive decisions in mate choice. *Ethology*, 103: 681–699.

Bereczkei, T., Hofer, A. and Ivan, Z. (2000) Low birth weight, maternal decision on birth spacing, and future reproduction: a cost/benefit analysis. *Human Nature*, 11: 183–205.

Bereczkei, T., Gyuris, P., Koves, P. and Bernath, L. (2002) Homogamy, genetic similarity, and imprinting; parental influence on mate choice preferences. *Personality and Individual Differences*, 33: 677–690.

Bereczkei, T., Gyuris, P. and Weisfeld, G. E. (2004) Sexual imprinting in human mate choice. *Proceedings of the Royal Society of London,* 271: 1129–1134.

Bigsby, R., Coster, W., Lester, B. M. and Peucker, M. R. (1996) Motor behavioural cues of term and preterm infants at 3 months. *Infant Behaviour and Development*, 19: 295–307.

Bjorklund, D. F. and Pellegrini, A. D. (2002) *The Origins of Human Nature: Evolutionary Developmental Psychology*. American Psychological Association, Washington.

Bjorklund, D. F. and Yunger, J. L. (2000) The evolution of parenting and evolutionary approaches to childrearing. In Bornstein, M. (ed.) *Handbook of Parenting*. Lawrence Erlbaum, Mahwah, NJ.

Blaustein, A. R., Bekoff, M., Byers, J. A. and Daniels, T. J. (1991) Kin recognition in vertebrates: what do we really know about adaptive value? *Animal Behaviour*, 41: 1079–1083.

Bolhuis, J. J. and Horn, G. (1992) Generalization of learned preferences in filial imprinting. *Animal Behaviour*, 44: 185–187.

Bogaert, A. F. (2005) Age at puberty and father absence in a national probability sample. *Journal of Adolescence*, 28: 541–546.

Bogin, B. (1999) *Patterns of Human Growth*. Cambridge University Press, Cambridge.

Buss, D. M. (1995) Evolutionary psychology: a new paradigm for psychological science. *Psychological Inquiry*, 6: 1–30.

Bouchard, T. J. and Loehlin, J. C. (2001) Genes, evolution, and personality. *Behaviour Genetics*, 31: 243–273.

Bowlby, J. (1965) *Child Care and the Growth of Love*. Penguin, Harmondsworth.

Burgess, R. L. and Drais, A. A. (1999) Beyond the "Cindarella Effect": life history theory and child maltreatment. *Human Nature*, 10: 373–398.

Chisholm, J. S. (1993) Death, hope and sex: life-history theory and the development of reproductive strategies. *Current Anthropology*, 34: 1–46.

Chisholm, J. S. (1999) Attachment and time preference. Relations between early stress and sexual behaviour in a sample of American University women. *Human Nature*, 10: 51–83.

Christenfeld, N. J. S. and Hill, E. A. (1995) Whose baby are you? *Nature*, 378: 669.

Chisholm, J. S., Quinlivan, J. A., Petersen, R. W. and Coall, D. A. (2005) Early stress predicts age at menarche and first birth, adult attachment, and expected lifespan. *Human Nature*, 16: 233–265.

Clutton-Brock, T. H. (1991) *The Evolution of Parental Care*. Princeton University, Princeton, NJ.

Cutler, W. B., Preti, G., Krieger, A., Huggins, G. R., Garcia, G. R. and Lawley, H. J. (1986) Human axillary secretions influence womenás menstrual cycles: the role of donor extracts from men. *Hormones and Behaviour*, 20: 463–473.

Daly, M. (1989) On distinguishing evolved adaptation from epiphenomena. *Behavioural and Brain Sciences*, 12: 520.

Daly, M. and Wilson, M. (1987) Evolutionary psychology and family violence. In C. Crawford, M. Smith and D. Krebs (eds) *Sociobiology and Psychology: Ideas, Issues, and Applications*, pp. 293–310. Lawrence Erlbaum, Hillsdale, NJ.

Daly, M. and Wilson, M. (1988) *Homicide*. Aldyne de Gruyter, New York.

Daly, M. and Wilson, M. (1998) The evolutionary social psychology of family violence. In Crawford, C. B. and Krebs, D. (eds) *Handbook of Evolutionary Psychology: Ideas, Issues, and Applications*, pp. 431–456. Lawrence Erlbaum, Hillsdale, NJ.

Dawkins, R. (1982) *The Extended Phenotype*. Oxford University Press, Oxford.

Deater-Deckard, K. and O'Connor, T. G. (2000) Parent–child mutuallity in early childhood: two behavioural genetic studies. *Developmental Psychology*, 36: 561–570.

DeBruine, L. M. (2002) Facial resemblance enhances trust. *Proceedings of Royal Society of London,* 269: 1307–1312.

DeBruine, L. M. (2004) Facial resemblance increases the attractiveness of the same-sex faces more than other-sex faces. *Proceedings of Royal Society of London,* 271: 2085–2090.

DeBruine, L. M., Jones, B. C. and Perrett, D. I. (2004) Women's attractiveness judgments of self-resembling faces change across the menstrual cycle. *Hormones and Behaviour*, 47: 379–383.

Draper, P. and H. Harpending (1982) Father absence and reproductive strategy: an evolutionary perspective. *Journal of Anthropological Research*, 38: 255–273.

Eibl-Eibesfeldt, I. (1989) *Human Ethology*. Aldine de Gruyter, New York.

Ellis, B. J. (2004) Timing of pubertal maturation in girls: an integrated life history approach. *Psychological Bulletin*, 130: 920–958.

Ellis, B. J. and Garber, J. (2000) Psychological antecedents of variation in girls' pubertal timing: maternal depression, stepfather presence, and marital and family stress. *Child Development*, 71: 485–501.

Ellis, B. J., McFadyen-Ketchum, S, Dodge, K. A., Pettit, G. S. and Bates, J. E. (1999) Quality of early family relationships and individual differences in the timing of pubertal maturation in girls: a longitudinal test of an evolutionary model. *Journal of Personality and Social Psychology*, 77: 387–401.

Flinn, M. V., Quinlan, R. J., Decker, S. A., Turner, M. T. and England, B. G. (1996) Male–female differences in effects of parental absence on glucocorticoid stress response. *Human Nature*, 7: 125–162.

Freud, S. (1905) Three essays on the theory of sexuality. In J. Strachey, A. Freud, A. Strachery and A. Tyson (eds) *The Complete Psychological Works of Sigmund Freud*, vol. 13, pp. 1–161. Hoghart Press and Institute of Psychoanalysis, London.

Furlow, F. B. (1997) Human neonatal cry quality as an honest signal of fitness. *Evolution and Human Behaviour*, 18: 175–193.

Hodges, J. and Tizard, B. (1989) Social and family relationships of ex-institutional adolescents. *Journal of Child Psychology and Psychiatry*, 30: 77–98.

Goldberg, S., Perrotta, M., Minde, K. and Corter, C. (1986) Maternal behaviour and attachment in low birth weight twins and singletons. *Child Development*, 57: 34–46.

Graber, J. A., Brooks-Gunn, J. and Warren, M. P. (1995) The antecedents of menarcheal age: heredity, family environment, and stressful life events. *Child Development*, 66: 346–359.

Haggerty, R. J., Sherrod, L. R., Garmezy, N. and Rutter, M. (eds) (1994) *Stress, Risk, and Resilience in Children and Adolescents*. Cambridge University Press, Cambridge.

Harlow, H. F. and Mears, C. (1979) *The Human Model: Primate Perspectives*. Wiley, New York.

Hepper, P. G. (ed.) (1991) *Kin Recognition*. Cambridge University Press, Cambridge.

Holmes, W. G. (1995) The ontogeny of littermate preferences in juvenile golden-mantled ground squirrels: effects of rearing and relatedness. *Animal Behaviour*, 50: 309–322.

Hrdy, S. B. (1999) *Mother Nature: A History of Mothers, Infants, and Natural Selection*. Pantheon Books, New York.

Immelmann, K., Pröve, R., Lassek, R. and Bischof, H. (1991) Influence of adult courtship experience on the development of sexual preferences in zebra finch males. *Animal Behaviour*, 42: 83–89.

Jacob, S., McClintock, M. K., Zelano, B. and Ober, C. (2002) Paternally inherited HLA alleles are associated with women's choice of male odor. *Nature Genetics*, 30: 175–179.

Jaffe, K. and Chacon-Puignau, G. (1995) Assortative mating: sex differences in mate selection for married and unmarried couples. *Human Biology*, 67: 11–120.

Jedlicka, D. (1980) A test of the psychoanalytic theory of mate selection. *Journal of Social Psychology*, 112: 295–299.

Keller, M. C., Thiessen, D. and Young, R. K. (1996) Mate assortment in dating and married couples. *Personality and Individual Differences*, 21: 217–221.

Klaus, M. and Kennell, J. (1976) Parent-to-infant attachment. In Hull, D. (ed.) *Recent Adavances in Pediatrics*, pp. 129–152. Churchill Livingstone, Edinburgh.

Korner, A., Stevenson, D., Kraemer, H., Spiker, D., Scott, D., Constantinou, J. and Dimiceli, S. (1993) *Journal of Developmental and Behavioural Pediatrics*, 14: 106–111.

Lalumière, M. L., Quinsey, V. L. and Craig, W. M. (1996) Why children from the same family are so different from one another. *Human Nature*, 7: 281–290.

Little, A. C., Penton-Voak, I. S., Burt, D. M. and Perrett, D. I. (2002) Investigating an imprinting-like phenomenon in humans. Partners and opposite-sex parents have similar hair and eye colour. *Evolution and Human Behaviour*, 24: 43–51.

Lorenz, K. (1965) *Evolution and Modification of Behaviour*. University of Chicago Press, Chicago.

Low, B. S. (1989) Cross-cultural patterns in the training of children: an evolutionary perspective. *Journal of Comparative Psychology*, 103: 311–319.

MacDonald, K. (1997) Life history theory and human reproductive behaviour. *Human Nature*, 8: 327–359.

MacDonald, K. (2005) Personality, evolution, development. In R. L. Burgess and K. MacDonald (eds) *Evolutionary Perspectives on Human Development*, pp. 207–242. Sage, London.

Mann, J. (1992) Nurturance or negligence: maternal psychology and behavioural preference among preterm twins. In J. H. Barkow, L. Cosmides and J. Tooby (eds) *The Adapted Mind. Evolutionary Psychology and the Generation of Culture*, pp. 367–390. Oxford University Press, Oxford.

Marcus, M. D., Loucks, T. L. and Berga, S. L. (2001) Psychological correlates of functional hypothalamic amenorrhea. *Fertility and Sterility*, 76: 310–316.

Mascie-Taylor, C. G. N. (1988) Assortative mating for psychomatric characters. In C. G. Mascie-Taylor and A. J. Boyce (eds) *Human Mating Patterns*, pp. 61–82. Cambridge University Press, Cambridge.

Mascie-Taylor, C. G. N. (1995) Human assortative mating: evidence and genetic implications. In Boyce, A. J. and Reynolds, V. (eds) *Human Populations. Diversity and Adaptations*, pp. 86–105. Oxford University Press, Oxford.

Masten, A. S. (1994) Resilience in individual development: successful adaptation despite risk and adversity. In M. C. Wang and E. W. Gordon (eds) *Educational Resilience in Inner-city America*. Lawrence Erlbaum, Hillsdale, NJ.

Monnot, M. (1999) The adaptive function of infant-directed speech. *Human Nature*, 10: 415–443.

Oetting, S., Pröve, E. and Bischof, H. (1995) Sexual imprinting as two-stage process: mechanisms of information storage and stabilization. *Animal Behaviour*, 50: 393–403.

Paneth, N. (1995) The problem of low birth weight. *The Future of Children*, 5: 1–12.

Peacock, N. (1991) An evolutionary perspective of the patterning of maternal investment in pregnancy. *Human Nature*, 2: 351–385.

Pedersen, N. L., McClearn, G. E., Plomin, R. and Nesselroade, J. R. (1992) Effects of early rearing environment on twin similarity in the last half of the life span. *British Journal of the Developmental Psychology*, 10: 255–267.

Pfennig, D. W. and Sherman, P. W. (1995) Kin recognition. *Scientific American*, 272: 68–73.

Plomin, R. (1994) *Genetic and Experience. The Interplay between Nature and Nurture*. Sage, London.

Plomin, R. (2000) Behavioural genetics in the 21st century. *International Journal of Behavioural Development*, 24: 30–34.

Plomin, R. and McClearn, G. E. (eds) (1997) *Nature, Nurture, and Psychology*. American Psychological Association, Washington, DC.

Porter, R. H. (1987) Kin recognition: functions and mediating mechanisms. In C. H. Crawford, M. Smith and D. Krebs (eds) *Sociobiology and Psychology:*

Ideas, Issues, and Applications, pp. 175–204. Lawrence Erlbaum, London.

Porter, R. H., Cernoch, J. M. and Balogh, R. D. (1985) Odor signatures and kin recognition. *Physiological Behaviour*, 34: 445–448.

Promislow, D. and Harvey P. (1990) Living fast and dying young: a comparative analysis of life-history variation among mammals. *Journal of Zoological Society of London*, 220: 417–437.

Read, A. F. and Harvey, P. H. (1988) Genetic relatedness and the evolution of animal mating patterns. In Mascie-Taylor, C. G. and Boyce, A. J. (eds) *Human Mating Patterns*, pp. 115–131. Cambridge, Cambridge University Press.

Ridley, M. (1994) *Evolution*. Blackwell, Oxford.

Roberts, S. C., Little, A. C., Gosling, L. M., Perrett, D. I., Cartes, V., Jones, B. C., Perton-Voak, I. & Petrie, M. (2005) MHC-heterozygosity and human facial attractiveness. *Evolution and Human Behaviour*, 26: 213–226.

Rowe, D. C. (1994) *The Limits of Family Influence. Genes, Experience, and Behaviour*. Guilford Press, New York.

Rushton, J. P. (1989) Genetic similarity, mate choice, and group selection. *Behavioural and Brain Sciences*, 12: 503–518.

Rutter, M. and the English and Romanian Adoptees Study Team (1998) Developmental catch-up and deficit following adoption after several global early deprivation. *Journal of Child Psychology and Psychiatry*, 39: 465–476.

Schaffer, H. R. (2000) The early experience assumption: past, present, and future. *International Journal of Behavioural Development*, 24: 5–14.

Shenkin, S. D., Starr, J. M. and Deary, I. J. (2004) Birth weight and cognitive ability in childhood: a systematic review. *Psychological Bulletin*, 130: 989–1013.

Surbey, M. K. (1998) Developmental psychology and modern Darwinism. In C. B. Crawford and D. Krebs (eds), *Handbook of Evolutionary Psychology: Ideas, Issues, and Applications*, pp. 369–404. Lawrence Erlbaum, Hillsdale, NJ.

Tessier, R., Cristo, M. B., Velez, S., Giron, M., Nadeau, L., Calume, F., Ruiz-Paláez, J. and Charpak, N. (2003) Kangaroo mother care: a method for protecting high-risk and premature infants against developmental delay. *Infant Behaviour and Development*, 26: 384–397.

Thornhill, R., Gangestad, S. W., Miller, Scheyd, G., McCollough, J. K. and Franklin, M. (2003) Major histocompatibility complex genes, symmetry, and body scent attractiveness in men and women. *Behavioural Ecology*, 14: 668–678.

Tully, L. A., Arseneault, L., Caspi, A., Moffitt, T. E. and Morgan, J. (2004) Does maternal warmth moderate the effect of birth weight on twins' attention-deficit/hyperactivity disorder (ADHD) symptoms and low IQ? *Journal of Consulting and Clinical Psychology*, 72: 218–216.

Vos, D. R. (1995) The role of sexual imprinting for sex recognition in zebra finches: a difference between males and females. *Animal Behaviour*, 50: 645–653.

Wedekind, C. and Furi, S. (1997) Body odour preferences in men and women: do they aim for specific MHC combinations for simply heterozygosity? *Proceedings of Royal Society*, 264: 1471–1479.

Weisfeld, G. E., Czilli, T., Phillips, K. A., Gall, J. A. and Lichtman, C. M. (2003) Possible olfaction-based mechanisms in human kin recognition and inbreeding avoidance. *Journal of Experimental Child Psychology*, 85: 279–295.

Wille, D. E. (1991) Relation of preterm birth with quality of infant-mother attachment at one year. *Infant Behaviour and Development*, 14: 227–240.

Wilson, M. and Daly, M. (1997) Life expectancy, economic inequality, homicide, and reproductive timing in Chicago neighbourhoods. *British Medical Journal*, 314: 1271–1274.

Zei, G., Astofli, P. and Jayakar, S. D. (1981) Correlation between father's age and husband's age: a case of imprinting? *Journal of Biosocial Science*, 13: 409–418.

CHAPTER 20

Evolution of stress response to social threat

Mark V. Flinn

20.1. Introduction

Humans are extraordinarily social creatures. Perhaps as a consequence, our neuroendocrine stress systems are highly sensitive to social challenges. Levels of the glucocorticoid stress hormone cortisol increase acutely in response to events such as public speaking (Kirschbaum and Hellhammer, 1994), school exams (Lindahl *et al.*, 2005), domino matches (Wagner *et al.*, 2002), and a wide variety of other social–cognitive demands (Dickerson and Kemeny, 2004). Elevation of stress hormones can have short- and long-term health costs (McEwen, 1998; Sapolsky, 2005; Ader, 2006), presenting an evolutionary paradox.

We do not have good explanations for why natural selection favoured links between the neuropsychological mechanisms involved with assessment of the social environment and the neuroendocrine mechanisms that regulate stress hormones such as cortisol and norepinephrine. Furthermore, we do not understand why these links are modifiable during ontogeny, such that early experiences may permanently alter neuroendocrine response to social threats (Francis *et al.*, 2002; Mirescu *et al.*, 2004; Weaver *et al.*, 2004; Bartolomucci *et al.*, 2005; Buwalda *et al.*, 2005; Maestripieri *et al.*, 2005).

I approach this paradox of stress response to social threat from the integrative evolutionary paradigm of Nobel laureate Niko Tinbergen (1963), who emphasized the importance of linking proximate physiological explanations with ontogeny, phylogeny, and adaptive function. Here I first briefly review the idea that humans evolved large brains and an extended childhood as adaptations that enable the development of social skills for coping with an increasingly complex and dynamic social and cultural environment. I then explore relations between physiological stress response and the ontogeny of social competencies. Two complementary theoretical models of hormonal stress response are considered: (a) maladaptation to the novelty of chronic stress in social environments (McEwen, 1995; Sapolsky, 2005), and (b) adaptive neural reorganization (Huether, 1998; Meaney, 2001; Kaiser and Sachser, 2005; Rodriguez Manzanares *et al.*, 2005; Ademec *et al.*, 2005; Flinn, 2006a). These two perspectives are interwoven in an evolutionary developmental analysis, complicated by the pleiotropic nature of the key stress hormone, cortisol. Hypotheses are evaluated with a review of an 18-year study of child stress in a rural community on the island of Dominica. The longitudinal depth, large sample size (30 122 salivary cortisol measures from 282 children and their care-givers), and naturalistic paradigm provide a unique research design for investigating relations between social environment and stress response.

My limited objective here is to provide a plausible model and some new pieces for the puzzle linking stress response to the neural plasticity that enables adaptation to the dynamic human social environment. Resolution of this paradox may have significant consequences for public health because it could provide new insights into associations among stress response, social disparities, and psychopathologies such as autism, and perinatal programming.

20.2. **Hormonal stress response to social events**

Danny was roaming the Fond Vert area of the village with two of his closest friends on a rainy Saturday morning. They had eaten their fill of mangoes, after pelting a heavily laden tree with stones for nearly an hour, taking turns testing their skill at knocking down breakfast. Now Danny was up the cashew tree in Mr Pascal's yard, tossing the yellow and red fruits to the smaller children below who had gathered to benefit from this kindness. Suddenly the sharp voice of his stepfather rang out from the nearby footpath. The bird-like chatter and laughter of the children immediately stopped. Danny's hand froze mid-way to its next prize, and his head turned to face the direction of the yell with a mixed expression of surprise and fright. Ordered down from the tree, Danny headed quickly home, head bowed in apparent numb submission (vignette from M.V.F.'s field notes, July 14, 1994). Danny's salivary cortisol level rose from 2.2 to 3.8 µg/dl in little more than an hour. That afternoon, his secretory immunoglobulin-A levels dropped from 5.70 to 3.83 mg/dl. Three days later he had common cold symptoms: runny nose, headache, and fever. His two companions resumed their morning play, exhibiting a normal circadian decline in cortisol, and remained healthy over the next 2 weeks (Figure 20.1).

This anecdotal case example contributes to a common pattern. Children in this rural Dominican community are more than twice as likely to become ill during the week following a stressful event than children who have not recently experienced any significant stressors (Flinn and England, 2003). Humans respond to challenges in their social environments by elevating cortisol levels (Dickerson *et al.*, 2004), often with negative consequences for their health (Mason *et al.*, 1979; Maier *et al.*, 1994;

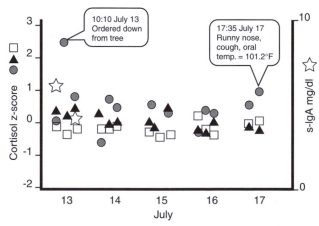

Fig. 20.1 Morning, mid-morning and afternoon cortisol levels of 'Danny' (filled circles) and his two friends (filled triangles; open squares) during summer 1994. Danny's cortisol levels were elevated and his s-IgA levels (open stars) diminished after being reprimanded by his stepfather on the morning of July 13. Danny exhibits symptoms of an upper respiratory infection with slight fever on the afternoon of July 20. Figure adapted from Flinn and England (1997).

Cohen *et al.*, 2003; Marmot, 2004). Morbidity and mortality rates for children in orphanages and hospitals in early 20th century America, lacking the evolutionarily normal intimacy and social contact of the family, were appalling (e.g. Chapin, 1922, p. 214). It is not lack of food or hygienic care, nor just the occurrence of traumatic events, that affect child health, but the lack of social support, including parental warmth and other factors that influence emotional states (Belsky, 1997; Davidson *et al.*, 2001; Field *et al.*, 2003). Why should this be so? Why do social interactions, and a child's perceptions of them, affect stress physiology and morbidity? And, more generally, why is the social environment of such paramount importance in a child's world? From the Tinbergen perspective, these 'why?' questions ultimately involve understanding the evolutionary design of the ontogeny of the mind and brain of the human child (e.g. Frith and Frith, 1999, 2001; Bjorklund and Bering, 2003).

In Danny's village, located on the east coast of the island of Dominica where I have lived and studied part-time over the past 18 years, most of a child's mental efforts seem focused on negotiating social relationships with parents, siblings, grandparents, cousins and other kin, friends, teachers, bus drivers, neighbours, shop owners, and so forth. Foraging for mangos and guavas, hunting birds, or even fishing in the sea from rock cliffs, are relatively simple cognitive enterprises, complicated by conflicts with property owners, and decisions about which companions to garner and share calories with. The mind of the child seems more concerned with solving social puzzles than with utilitarian concerns of collecting food. Other populations may have more difficult subsistence practices that require more extensive learning (e.g. Bock, 2005), but the social chess game none the less appears ubiquitous and cognitively demanding for children in all cultures (Blurton-Jones and Marlowe, 2002; Hewlett and Lamb, 2002, 2005), as it likely was during human evolutionary history (Bowlby, 1969, 1973; Hinde, 1974; Alexander, 1979).

In the following two sections, I review current theories of human life history and the family. I suggest that conspecific social competition was the primary selective pressure shaping the uniquely human combination of physically altricial but mentally and linguistically precocial infancy, extended childhood, and extended adolescence, enabled by extensive bi-parental and kin care. I then turn to the role that the links between psychosocial stimuli and physiological stress response may play in guiding both the acute and long-term neurological plasticity necessary for adapting to the dynamic aspects of human sociality.

20.3. Evolution of the social child

"Most of us see a picture of innocence and helplessness: a clean slate. But, in fact, what we see in the crib is the greatest mind that has ever existed, the most powerful learning machine in the universe." (Gopnik *et al.*, 1999, p. 1.)

The human child is a most extraordinary organism, possessed of 'the greatest mind' and yet 'innocent and helpless'—in effect, a larva equipped with an enormous brain. Even relative to other primates the human infant is unusually altricial, and highly dependent upon parents and other relatives for protection, transport, resources (e.g. food), and information (Lamb *et al.*, 2002). The human child has evolved to rely upon extensive investment over a long period of time, often involving multiple care providers in embedded kin networks (Belsky, 2005; Flinn and Leone, 2006a; Irons, 1983; Lamb, 2005; Lancaster, 1989; Quinlan and Flinn, 2005). Humans stand out as "the species that takes care of children" (Konner, 1991, p. 427).

The selective pressures responsible for this unique suite of life-history characteristics appear central to understanding human evolution (Alexander, 1987, 2005; Hill and Hurtado, 1996a,b; Kaplan *et al.*, 2000; Low, 2001; Bjorklund and Pellegrini, 2002; Flinn and Ward, 2005; Geary, 2005). The delay of reproduction until almost 20 years of age, much longer than that of our hominoid relatives, the chimpanzees and gorillas, involves prolonged exposure to extrinsic causes of mortality and longer generation intervals. What advantages of an extended childhood could have outweighed the heavy costs of reduced fecundity and late reproduction (Williams, 1966; Stearns, 1992) for our hominin ancestors?

The physical growth of the child, although unusual in its temporal pattern (Bogin, 1999; Leigh, 2001), does not appear to involve especially significant challenges. The relatively slow rate of overall body growth during childhood, followed by a rapid growth spurt during puberty, may economize parental resources supporting dependent offspring. A small child requires fewer resources than a large one. Hence delayed physical growth during childhood may have facilitated shortened birth intervals, providing a demographic advantage (Bogin and Marela-Silva, 2003).

Brain growth, however, has a different trend than overall body growth. The baby human has a large brain with high energetic and developmental costs that use more than half (!) of its total metabolism (Holliday, 1986; Armstrong, 1990; Leonard and Robertson, 1994). Although neurogenesis is mostly completed by the third trimester, and synaptogenesis by the third year of life (at a rate of 1.8 million synapses per second!), reproduction is postponed for another 15 years or more. What aspects of the phenotype require so much additional development? And why burden the growing child, and its caregivers, with such a large brain that requires so much energy for so long?

One possibility is that these anomalous patterns of brain and physical growth during human childhood are not adaptations *per se*, but instead are inadvertent outcomes of basic growth processes such as neoteny and heterochrony (Schultz, 1969; Gould, 1977; see also Lovejoy, 1981). Perhaps selection for an extended lifetime or increased body size involved mechanisms that could not adaptively fine-tune life-history stages or growth of different parts of the phenotype. The extended juvenile period, for example, may be interpreted as an incidental outcome of selection for a longer lifespan in general. From this perspective, human childhood and the big brain were viewed in the context of major developmental processes that constrain adaptive solutions.

The recent integration of molecular genetics with evolutionary developmental biology, however, has provided a more nuanced view of the constraints on ontogeny. Detailed knowledge of developmental mechanisms at the genetic and cellular levels (e.g. Kirschner and Gerhart, 2005) has important implications for understanding the evolution of human life histories (Konner, 1991; Finch and Sapolsky, 1999;

Lovejoy *et al.*, 2003). The broad scaling trends among life-history events suggested by Schultz (1969) and Gould (1977), in which all phases of the lifespan remain proportional when lifespan is altered, do not accord with recent comparative analyses that indicate these more specific mechanisms result in diverse and species-specific ontogenies (West-Eberhard, 2003; Leigh, 2004). Human childhood is not likely to be an inadvertent consequence of selection for an extended lifetime or some other life-history constraint (Alexander, 1987). We need a functional evolutionary explanation for this "most powerful learning machine in the universe."

Human childhood has traditionally been viewed as a period of edification: "immatures are enabled to live a protected existence whilst they learn skills necessary for adult life" (Bowlby, 1969, p. 63). The primary question has been: What information is so important and difficult to acquire that many years are needed for its mastery? Most juvenile primates spend considerable effort playing and practising with their physical environment and developing fighting skills (e.g. Symons, 1978; Pellegrini and Archer, 2005). Compared with other primates, our motor skills do not appear especially challenging; a terrestrial environment seems more easily mastered than an arboreal one. Children may need time to acquire knowledge for tool use and complex foraging including hunting (Darwin, 1871; Hill and Kaplan, 1999; see also Byrne, 2002a,b). An extraordinarily long developmental apprenticeship is seen as useful for acquiring learned solutions to ecological problems unique to our niche (Bock, 2005; cf. Blurton Jones and Marlowe, 2002). Investment in 'embodied capital', via an extended childhood, has been suggested to have a fitness pay-off from increased adult foraging ability (Kaplan *et al.*, 2000).

A complementary approach to the problem of the evolution of human childhood involves consideration of the brain as a 'social tool' (Humphrey, 1976, 1983; Byrne and Whiten, 1988; Alexander, 1989; Brothers, 1990; Dunbar, 1998; Bjorklund and Rosenberg, 2005). This hypothesis suggests that many human cognitive and psychological adaptations function primarily to contend with social relationships, with ecological constraints (e.g. hunting or extractive foraging) being a more secondary source of recent evolutionary change. It appears that some human cognitive competencies, such as theory of mind (ToM) and language, are most readily understood in terms of social selection pressures, although cognitive competencies for interacting with the physical (e.g. navigating) and biological world are evident as well (Geary and Huffman, 2002). The primary mental chess game shaping many of the distinctive changes in the neocortex (Allman *et al.*, 2001; Adolphs, 2003) was most likely with other intelligent hominin competitors and cooperators. Human social relationships are complex and variable. Predicting future moves of a social competitor-cooperator, and appropriate countermoves, amplified by networks of multiple relationships, shifting coalitions, and deception, make social success a difficult undertaking (Alexander, 1987, 1990a; Daly and Wilson, 1988a,b; Cummins, 1998; Baumeister, 2005).

Indeed, the potential variety of human social puzzles is apparently infinite; no two social situations are precisely identical, nor are any two individuals ever in exactly the same social environment. Moreover, social relationships can change rapidly, requiring quick modification of strategy. Variability in these dynamics creates conditions that should favour the evolution of brain and cognitive systems above and beyond more traditional modular systems (Fodor, 1983; Tooby and Cosmides, 1995). These systems have been cast in terms of general intelligence, domain-general abilities, fluid-intelligence, and executive functions that are capable of integrating and co-opting information processed by more restricted, domain-specific mechanisms (e.g. Hirschfeld and Gelman, 1994; Adolphs, 2003; Geary, 2005; cf. Quartz and Sejnowski, 1999; La Cerra and Bingham, 2002; Chiappe and MacDonald, 2005) and using mental simulations, or 'scenario-building' (Alexander, 1989) to construct and rehearse potential responses to changing social conditions. These complex cognitive processes would be more capable of contending with, and producing, novelties of cultural change and individual-specific differences (Bjorklund and Rosenberg, 2005; Flinn, 1997, 2006a; MacDonald and Hershberger, 2005; Tomasello, 1999).

Childhood seems to have evolved as a mechanism whereby individuals can develop these necessary social skills (Geary and Bjorklund, 2000; Joffe, 1997). Learning, practice and experience are imperative for social success. The information-processing capacity used in human social competition is considerable, and perhaps significantly greater than that involved with foraging skills (Roth and Dicke, 2005). An extended human childhood may be attributed to the selection for development and necessity of a social brain that requires a lengthy ontogeny to master complex dynamic tasks such as understanding sarcasm (Shamay-Tsoory *et al.*, 2005), moral reasoning (Alexander, 1987; Moll *et al.*, 2005), and cultural novelties (Baumeister, 2005; Flinn, 1997, 2004; Flinn and Alexander, 2006; Flinn and Coe, 2006). The learning environments that facilitate and channel these astonishing aspects of human mental phenotypic plasticity appear to take on a special importance.

20.4. Evolution of the human family as a nest for the child's social development

The human family is extraordinary and unique in many respects (Alexander, 1989, 2005; Flinn *et al.*, 2005b; Geary and Flinn, 2001; Lancaster and Lancaster, 1987). Humans are the only species to live in multi-male groups with complex hierarchical coalitions and extensive paternal care. Humans have concealed ovulation, altricial infants, lengthy child development, female orgasm, and menopause. These traits may be causally linked and provide important clues towards reconstructing the evolution of our (human) unusual life history (Flinn *et al.*, 2005a).

The altricial infant is indicative of a protective environment provided by intense parenting and alloparental care in the context of kin groups (Chisholm, 1999; Flinn and Leone, 2006a,b; Hrdy, 2005). The human baby does not need to be physically precocial. Rather than investing in the development of locomotion, defence, and food acquisition systems that function early in ontogeny, the infant can work instead towards building a more effective adult phenotype. Although humans have a long gestation period like other hominoids, the infant is relatively helpless. The brain continues rapid growth, and the corresponding cognitive competencies largely direct attention toward the social environment. Plastic neural systems adapt to the nuances of the local community (Alexander, 1990b; Bjorklund and Pellegrini, 2002; Bloom, 2000; Fisher, 2005; Geary and Bjorklund, 2000; Geary and Huffman, 2002). In contrast to the slow development of ecological skills of movement, fighting, and foraging, the human infant rapidly acquires skill with the complex communication system of human language (Bloom, 2000; Pinker, 1994; Sakai, 2005). The extraordinary information-transfer abilities enabledby linguistic competency provide a conduit to the knowledge available in other human minds. This emergent capability for intensive and extensive communication potentiates the social dynamics characteristic of human groups (Deacon, 1997a,b; Dunbar, 1997) and provides a new mechanism for social learning and culture. The recursive pattern recognition and abstract symbolic representation central to linguistic competencies enable the open-ended, creative, and flexible information-processing characteristic of humans—especially of children.

An extended childhood appears useful for acquiring the knowledge and practice to hone social skills and to build coalitional relationships necessary for successful negotiation of the increasingly intense social competition of adolescence and adulthood, although ecologically related play and activities (e.g. exploration of the physical environment) occur as well. The unusual scheduling of human reproductive maturity, including an 'adrenarche' and a delay in direct mate competition among males appears to extend the period of practising social roles and extends social ontogeny.

The advantages of intensive parenting, including paternal protection and other care, require a most unusual pattern of mating relationships: moderately exclusive pair bonding in multiple-male groups. No other primate (or mammal) that lives in large, cooperative multiple-reproductive-male groups has extensive male parental care, although some protection by males is evident in baboons (Buchan et al., 2003). The only other primates that have paternal care (e.g. indris, marmosets, tamarins, titi monkeys, night monkeys, and to a lesser extent, gibbons and gorillas—for review see Taub, 1984) do not live in large groups. Competition for females in multiple-male groups usually results in low confidence of paternity (e.g. chimpanzees). Males forming exclusive 'pair bonds' in multiple-male groups would provide cues of non-paternity to other males, and hence place their offspring in great danger of infanticide (Hrdy, 1999). Paternal care is most likely to be favoured by natural selection in conditions where males can identify their offspring with sufficient probability to offset the costs of investment, although reciprocity with mates is also likely to be involved (Smuts, 1985; Smuts and Smuts, 1993). Humans exhibit a unique 'nested family' social structure, involving complex reciprocity among males and females to restrict direct competition for mates among group members. It is difficult to imagine how this system could be maintained in the absence of another unusual human trait: concealed or 'cryptic' ovulation (Alexander and Noonan, 1979). Human groups tend to be male philopatric (males tending to remain in their natal groups), resulting in extensive male kin alliances, useful for competing against other groups of male kin (Chagnon, 1988; LeBlanc, 2003; Wrangham and Peterson, 1996). Females also have complex alliances, but usually are not involved directly in the overt physical aggression characteristic of inter-group relations (Campbell, 2002; Geary and Flinn, 2002). Menopause reduces mortality risks for older women and allows them to concentrate effort on dependent children and other relatives (e.g. grandchildren) with high reproductive value (Williams, 1957; Alexander, 1974; Sherman, 1998; Hawkes, 2003). Parents and other kin may be especially important for the child's mental development of social and cultural maps because they can be relied upon as landmarks who provide relatively honest information. From this perspective, the evolutionary significance of the human family in regard to child development is viewed more as a nest from which social skills may be acquired than just as an economic unit centred on the sexual division of labour. An integration of the attachment paradigm (Bowlby, 1969) with approaches emphasizing relationship networks (e.g. Kerr and Bowen, 1988; Suomi, 2005) would be congruent with this evolutionary logic (Brothers, 2001).

The informational arms race that characterizes human social competition involves substantial novelty (Flinn, 2006b; Flinn and Alexander,

2006) and hence requires unusual phenotypic plasticity. Although knowledge of the basic neuroanatomical structures involved with human social aptitudes has increased considerably (e.g. Allman, 1999; Damasio, 2003; Gallese, 2005; Moll *et al.*, 2005), the mechanisms that guide their ontogeny remain uncertain. Neuroendocrine stress response to stimuli in the social environment may provide important clues.

20.5. **Stress response mechanisms**

Physiological responses to environmental stimuli that are cognitively perceived as 'stressful' are modulated by the limbic system (amygdala and hippocampus) and basal ganglia that interact with the sympathetic and parasympathetic nervous systems and several neuroendocrine axes. Here we are primarily concerned with what has traditionally been termed the limbic hypothalamic–anterior pituitary–adrenal cortex system (HPA). The HPA system affects a wide range of physiological functions in concert with other neuroendocrine mechanisms and involves complex feedback regulation. The HPA system regulates glucocorticoids, primarily cortisol, which is normally released in seven to 15 pulses during a 24 h period (for reviews see: de Kloet *et al.*, 2005; Ellis *et al.*, 2005; Gold and Chrousos, 2002; Gray, 1982; Sapolsky, 1992a,b; Weiner, 1992; McEwen, 1995).

Cortisol is a key hormone produced in response to physical and psychosocial stressors. Cortisol modulates a wide range of somatic functions, including: (a) energy release (e.g. stimulation of hepatic gluconeogenesis in concert with glucagon and inhibition of some effects of insulin), (b) immune activity (e.g. control of inflammatory response and the cytokine cascade, particularly interleukin-2), (c) mental activity (e.g. alertness, memory, and learning), (d) neural modification, (e) growth (e.g. inhibition of growth hormone and somatomedins), and (f) reproductive function (e.g. inhibition of gonadal steroids, including testosterone). These complex multiple effects of cortisol muddle understanding of its adaptive functions. The demands of energy regulation must orchestrate with those of immune function, and so forth.

Cortisol regulation allows the body to respond to changing environmental conditions by preparing for, and recovering from, *specific* short-term demands (Mason, 1971; Munck *et al.*, 1984).

These temporary beneficial effects of glucocorticoid stress response, however, are not without costs. Persistent activation of the HPA system is associated with immune deficiency, cognitive impairment, inhibited growth, delayed sexual maturity, damage to the hippocampus, enhanced sensitivity of amygdala fear circuits, and psychological maladjustment. Stressful life events — such as divorce, death of a family member, change of residence, or loss of a job — are associated with infectious disease and other health problems during adulthood (Maier *et al.*, 1994; Marmot and Wilkinson, 1999; Cohen *et al.*, 2003).

Current psychosocial stress research suggests that cortisol response is stimulated by uncertainty that is perceived as significant and for which behavioural responses will have unknown effects (Dickerson and Kemeny, 2004; Kirschbaum and Hellhammer, 1994). In a child's world, important events are going to happen, the child does not know how to react, but is highly motivated to figure out what should be done. Cortisol release is associated with unpredictable, uncontrollable events that require full alert readiness and mental anticipation. In appropriate circumstances, temporary moderate increases in stress hormones (and associated neurotransmitters such as dopamine) may enhance mental activity for short periods in localized areas and prime memory storage, hence improving cognitive processes for responding to social challenges (Beylin and Shors, 2003; LeDoux, 2000; cf. McEwen and Sapolsky, 1995; McGaugh, 2004). Mental processes unnecessary for appropriate response may be inhibited, perhaps to reduce external and internal 'noise' (Servan-Schreiber *et al.*, 1990; cf. Newcomer *et al.*, 1994; Kirschbaum *et al.*, 1996; Lupien *et al.*, 2005).

Chronically stressed children may develop abnormal cortisol response, possibly via changes in binding globulin levels, and/or reduced affinity or density of glucocorticoid, corticotropin-releasing hormone (CRH), oxytocin and vasopressin receptors in the brain (de Kloet, 1991; Fuchs and Flugge, 1995). Early experience — such as perinatal stimulation of rats (Meaney *et al.*, 1991; Takahashi, 1992;

Weaver *et al.*, 2004), some types of prenatal stress of rhesus macaques (Schneider *et al.*, 1992; Clarke 1993), maternal–infant attachment among humans (Spangler and Grossmann, 1993), and sexual abuse among humans (de Bellis *et al.*, 1994; Heim *et al.*, 2002)—may permanently alter HPA response.

Further complications arise from interaction between HPA stress response and a wide variety of other neuroendocrine and neuroimmune activities, including modulation of catecholamines, melatonin, testosterone, serotonin, β-endorphins, cytokines, and enkephalins (Axelrod and Reisine, 1984; De Kloet, 1991; Miller *et al.*, 2002; Sapolsky, 1990b, 1992b; Saphier *et al.*, 1994). Changes in cortisol for energy allocation and modulation of immune function may be confused with effects of psychosocial stress. Cortisol may be a cofactor priming oxytocin and vasopressin intracerebral binding sites that are associated with familial attachment in mammals (Fleming *et al.*, 2002; Fleming *et al.*, 1997, 1999; Numan and Insel, 2003), and hence may influence distress involving caretaker–child relationships (see also Porges, 1998; Carter, 2003, 2005; Cushing and Kramer, 2005; Wismer Fries *et al.*, 2005). Synergistically, oxytocin has important effects on social cognition and fear (Kirsch *et al.*, 2005). Other components of the HPA axis, such as CRH and melanocyte-stimulating hormone, have additional stress-related effects that are distinct from cortisol. Finally, a variety of hormones and other endogenous chemicals—including 'antiglucocorticoids'—mediate specific actions of cortisol. Concurrent monitoring of all these neuroendocrine activities would provide important information about stress response, but is not possible in a non-clinical setting with current techniques.

Early theoretical models of stress response did not attempt to directly explain the apparent evolutionary paradox of sensitivity to the social environment. For Selye (1976), 'stress' was a general syndrome, and emphasis was placed on understanding the underlying physiological mechanisms. Subsequent analysis of variation in response to different potential 'stressors' suggested that stress theory needed to explain more specific connections (Mason, 1968). Munck *et al.* (1984) proposed that some effects of stress could be incidental consequences of the multiple regulatory

functions of cortisol. Because cortisol modulates (i) immune response, including protection from autoimmune reactions, (ii) mental processes (e.g. energy allocation to the CNS and enhancement of neural circuits vital to flight–fight and some types of memory retention), and (iii) protective responses to damaging effects of catecholamines (sympathetic–adrenal medullary response), immunity could be inadvertently modulated during psychosocial stress. The current picture of HPA stress response is more complex than the Selye model, involving a multitude of interwoven mechanisms and regulatory systems, and a difficult balancing act of trade-offs among competing somatic functions.

Stress response involves an optimal allocation problem (Korte *et al.*, 2005; Sapolsky, 1990a, 1994). Energy resources are diverted to muscular and immediate immune functions and other short-term (stress emergency) functions, at cost to long-term functions of growth, development, and building immunity. Under normal conditions of temporary stress, there would be little effect on health. Indeed, there may be brief enhancement and directed trafficking of immune (Dhabbar and McEwen, 2001) and cognitive function. Persistent stress and associated hyper- or hypo-cortisolaemia, however, is posited to result in pathological immunosuppression, depletion of energy reserves, and damage to or inhibition of neurogenesis in parts of the hippocampus (e.g. Santarelli *et al.*, 2003; Sheline *et al.*, 2003). This perspective highlights the problems with a stress response system that evolved to cope with short-term emergencies. The chronic stress produced by modern human—or other primates with complex relationships—social environments may present novel challenges that the system is not designed to handle, hence potentially resulting in maladaptive pathology (Sapolsky, 1994).

The strict version of the novelty hypothesis, however, is difficult to reconcile with the long evolutionary histories of complex sociality in primates, and especially humans, accompanied by dramatic changes in the brain. Why, given all the extensive modifications of the human brain, would selection not have weeded out this apparent big mistake? Modern human environments have many novelties that elicit stress response, but social challenges in general seem to have a much more ancient evolutionary depth, and, as suggested in previous sections, may be a key selective pressure for the large human brain. One possibility is that the demands of preparing for potential dangers are an unavoidable costly insurance, akin to expensive febrile response to pathogens that are usually benign—the 'smoke-detector' principle (Nesse and Young, 2000). The idea is that although physiological stress response to social challenges is costly, and most often wasteful, it may have helped our ancestors cope with rare and unpredictable serious conflicts often enough to be maintained by selection. The benefit/cost ratio could be improved by fine-tuning stress mechanisms in response to environmental conditions during ontogeny.

A complementary approach to the mismatch hypothesis suggests that neuroendocrine stress response may guide adaptive neural reorganization, such as enhancing predator detection and avoidance mechanisms (Buwalda et al., 2005; Dal Zatto et al., 2003; LeDoux, 2000; Rodriguez Manzanares et al., 2005; Meaney, 2001; Wiedenmayer, 2004). Exposure to cats can have long-term effects on the central amygdala (right side) in mice, resulting in increased fear sensitization (Ademec et al., 2005; see also Knight et al., 2005). The potential evolutionary advantages of this neural phenotypic plasticity are apparent (Rodriguez Manzanares et al., 2005). Prey benefit from adjusting alertness to match the level of risk from predators in their environments. Post-traumatic stress disorder (PTSD) appears analogous to these fear-conditioning models, and involves similar effects of noradrenergic (Pitman et al., 2002) and glucocorticoid systems (Roozendaal et al., 2002) on associative long-term potentiation of the amygdala. Social defeat also affects the amygdala and hippocampus, but in different locations (Koolhaas et al., 1997; Bartolomucci et al., 2005), suggesting that neural remodelling is targeted and domain-specific. Glucocorticoids, perhaps in combination with peptide hormones and catecholamines, appear to facilitate the targeting of domain-specific remodelling and long-term potentiation. The potentiating effects of cortisol on emotional memories and other socially salient information may be of special significance in humans (Fenker et al., 2005; Jackson et al., 2006; Lupien et al., 2005; Pitman, 1989). The neurological effects of stress response may underlie adaptation to both short-term contingencies and guide long-term ontogenetic adjustments of behavioural strategies.

20.5.1. Adaptive phenotypic plasticity in response to social environment

"Environmental stimuli (in children mainly psychosocial challenges and demands) exert profound effects in neuronal activity through repeated or long-lasting changes in the release of transmitters and hormones which contribute, as trophic, organizing signals, to the stabilization [norepinephrine] or destabilization [cortisol] of neuronal networks in the developing brain … destabilization of previously established synaptic connections and neuronal pathways in cortical and limbic structures is a prerequisite for the acquisition of novel patterns of appraisal and coping and for the reorganization of the neuronal connectivity in the developing brain." (Gerald Huether, 1998, p. 297.)

If physiological stress response promotes adaptive modification of neural circuits in the limbic and higher associative centres that function to solve psychosocial problems (Huether et al., 1999), then the paradox of psychosocial stress would be partly resolved. Temporary elevations of cortisol in response to social challenges could have advantageous developmental effects involving synaptogenesis and neural reorganization (Buchanan and Lovallo, 2001; Huether, 1996, 1998) if such changes are useful and necessary for coping with the demands of an unpredictable and dynamic social environment. Elevating stress hormones in response to social challenges makes evolutionary sense if it enhances specific acute mental functions and helps to guide cortical remodelling of 'developmental exuberance' (Innocenti and Price, 2005; Sur and Rubenstein, 2005).

Chronic destabilization of neuronal networks in the hippocampus or cerebral cortex, combined with enhanced fear circuits in the amygdala (e.g. Phan et al., 2006), however, could result in apparently pathological conditions such as PTSD (Yehuda, 2002) and some types of depression (Preussner et al., 2005). Hyporesponsivity may also be problematic. The low cortisol reactivity of autistic children to social challenges may be an impediment to neural reorganization in areas that contribute to the development of social competencies. Even normal (but rather novel) everyday stressors in modern societies, such as social discordance between what we desire and what we have (Dressler, and Bindon, 2000), might generate maladaptive HPA response. Individual differences in perception, emotional control, rumination, reappraisal, self-esteem, and social support networks seem likely cofactors (see also Davis *et al.*, 2001; Ellis *et al.*, 2006).

Testing these ideas about relations between physiological stress response, neural remodeling, and adaptation to the social environment is not a simple or easy task (e.g. Pine *et al.*, 2001). Cortisol can affect cognitive functioning, and cognitive processing can affect cortisol response, all in an ongoing ontogenetic dance. Teasing out the causes and effects in ontogenetic sequence requires sequential data on physiological response profiles, environmental context, and perception. Extensive research on hormonal stress response has been conducted in clinical, experimental, school, and work settings (for reviews see: Weiner, 1992; Stansbury and Gunnar, 1994; Dickerson and Kemeny, 2004). We know relatively little, however, about stress neuroendocrinology among children in normal everyday ('naturalistic') environments, particularly in non-industrial societies (Panter-Brick, 1998). Investigation of childhood stress and its effects on development have been hampered by the lack of non-invasive techniques for measurement of stress hormones. Frequent collection of plasma samples in non-clinical settings is not feasible. The development of saliva immunoassay techniques, however, presents new opportunities for stress research. Saliva is relatively easy to collect and store, especially under adverse field conditions faced by anthropologists and psychologists working in naturalistic research settings (Ellison, 1988). Longitudinal monitoring of a child's daily activities, stress hormones, and psychological conditions provides a powerful research design for investigating naturally occurring stressors. Analysing hormone levels from saliva can be a useful tool for examining the child's imperfect world and its developmental consequences, especially when accompanied by detailed ethnographic, medical, and psychological information. Unfortunately, we do not yet have field techniques for assessment of corresponding ontogenetic changes in the relevant neurological mechanisms.

20.5.2. Ontogeny of stress response to psychosocial stimuli: the Dominica study

"What is missing are long term prospective studies that track the nature and timing of early stress exposure and the linkages to children's later stress exposure, HPA functioning, and behaviors." (Essex *et al.*, 2002, p. 777)

Assessment of relations among psychosocial stressors, hormonal stress response, and health is complex, requiring (a) longitudinal monitoring of social environment, emotional states, hormone levels, immune measures, and health, (b) control of extraneous effects from physical activity, circadian rhythms, and food consumption, (c) knowledge of individual differences in temperament, experience, and perception, and (d) awareness of specific social and cultural contexts. Multi-disciplinary research that integrates human biology, psychology, and ethnography is particularly well suited to these demands. Physiological and medical assessment in concert with ethnography and co-residence with children and their families in anthropological study populations can provide intimate, prospective, longitudinal, naturalistic information that is not feasible to collect in clinical studies. For the past 18 years (1988 to the present) I have conducted such research with the help of many colleagues and students and the extraordinary cooperation of a wonderful study population.

20.5.2.1. The study village

'Bwa Mawego' is a rural community located on the east coast of Dominica. About 500 residents live in 160 structures/households that are loosely clumped into five 'hamlets' or neighbourhoods. The population is of mixed African, Carib and European descent. The community is isolated because it sits at the dead-end of a rough road. Part-time residence is common, with many individuals emigrating for temporary work to other parts of Dominica, other Caribbean islands, the USA, the UK, or Canada. Most residents cultivate bananas and/or bay leaves as cash crops, and plantains, dasheen, and a variety of fruits and vegetables as subsistence crops.

Fish are caught by free-diving with spear-guns and from small boats (hand-built wooden 'canoes' of Carib design) using lines and nets. Land is communally 'owned' by kin groups, but parcelled for long-term individual use.

Most village houses are strung close together along roads and tracks. Older homes are constructed of wooden planks and shingles hewn by hand from local forest trees; concrete block and galvanized roofing are more popular today. Most houses have one or two sleeping rooms, with the kitchen and toilet as outbuildings. Children usually sleep together on foam or rag mats. Wealthier households typically have 'parlours' with sitting furniture. Electricity became available in 1988; during the summer of 1995 about 70% of homes had 'current', 41% had telephones, 11% had refrigerators, and 7% had televisions. Water is obtained from streams, spring catchments, and run-off from roofs; public piped water became available in June 1999, but few households are connected.

The community of Bwa Mawego is appropriate for the study of relations between a child's social environment and physiological stress response for the following reasons: (1) there is substantial variability among individuals in the factors under study (family environments, social challenges, and stress response), (2) the village and housing are relatively open, hence behaviour is easily observable, (3) kin tend to reside locally, (4) the number of economic variables is reduced relative to urban areas, (5) the language and culture are familiar to the investigator, (6) there are useful medical records, and (7) local residents welcome the research and are most helpful.

The study involved 282 children and their caregivers residing in 84 households. This is a nearly complete sample (>98%) of all children living in four of the five village hamlets during the period of fieldwork.

20.5.2.2. Methods and field techniques

Our initial objective, back in 1989, was to assess what each child's general stress level was, as determined by a single measure of the level of cortisol in their saliva. The idea was to see how this hormone was associated with a child's family environment. We assumed, rather naïvely, but in good academic company, that salivary cortisol

levels were a fairly stable 'trait' character. What seemed like an unnecessarily cautious decision at the time to collect and assay additional saliva samples from several of the children resulted in a rather more complex study. We were quite surprised when the results of the additional sample assays indicated that a child's cortisol levels varied substantially from one day to the next. Serendipity provided samples from two siblings in good spirits one day, but sad and upset by a family quarrel the next, in concert with field notes detailing the events. This temporal link between cortisol levels and psychosocial states suggested a dramatic revision of research design. We also were fortunate to have saliva samples from different times of day in this initial collection, and quickly recognized that very precise control of circadian patterns—in particular sleep schedules and wake-up times—was critical to accurate assessment of HPA stress response (Flinn and England, 1992; Flinn and Quinlan, in preparation). More than 30 000 saliva samples later, it seems we have more questions than answers.

In this study, sequential longitudinal monitoring is used to assess physiological stress response to everyday events, including social challenges. Saliva is collected from children by members of the research team at least twice a day, wherever the children happen to be (usually at their household). This direct collection and observation procedure avoids errors that occur with at-home self- or parent-collection and report protocols. The large sample size of cortisol measures for each child (>100 samples for most children) in a variety of naturalistic contexts provides a much more extensive and reliable picture of HPA stress response than small sample designs.

Here I briefly review some of the results from this study that may provide useful insights into the ontogeny of stress response to psychosocial threats.

20.5.2.3. Cortisol response to naturally occurring social threats

Our analyses of naturally occurring stressors in children's lives in Bwa Mawego indicate that social threats are important stressors, with the emphasis upon the family environment as both a primary source and mediator of stressful stimuli (Flinn and England, 1995, 2003; Flinn et al., 1996).

Temporary moderate increases in cortisol are associated with common activities such as eating meals, active play (e.g. cricket), and hard work (e.g. carrying loads of wood to bay oil stills) among healthy children. These moderate stressors—'arousers' might be a more appropriate term—usually have rapid attenuation, with cortisol levels diminished to normal within an hour or two (some stressors have characteristic temporal 'signatures' of cortisol level and duration).

High-stress events (cortisol increases from 100 to 2000%), however, most commonly involved trauma from family conflict or change (Flinn et al., 1996; Flinn and England, 2003). Punishment, quarrelling, and residence change substantially increased cortisol levels, whereas calm, affectionate contact was associated with diminished (−10% to −50%) cortisol levels. Of all cortisol values that were >2 SD above mean levels (i.e. indicative of substantial stress), 19.2% were temporally associated with traumatic family events (residence change of child or parent/caretaker, punishment, 'shame', serious quarrelling,

and/or fighting) within a 24 h period. In addition, 42.1% of traumatic family events were temporally associated with substantially elevated cortisol (i.e. at least one of the saliva samples collected within 24 h was >2 SD above mean levels). Chronic elevations of cortisol levels, as in the example of the Franklin family (Figure 20.2), may also occur, but are more difficult to assess quantitatively.

There was considerable variability among children in cortisol response to family disturbances. Not all individuals had detectable changes in cortisol levels associated with family trauma. Some children had significantly elevated cortisol levels during some episodes of family trauma but not during others. Cortisol response is not a simple or uniform phenomenon. Numerous factors, including preceding events, habituation, specific individual histories, context, and temperament, might affect how children respond to particular situations.

None the less, traumatic family events and social emotions such as guilt and shame (Flinn, in press a;

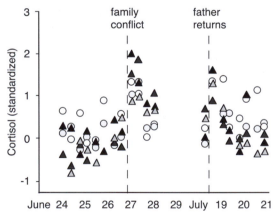

Fig. 20.2 On June 28, 1992, a serious marital conflict erupted in the 'Franklin' household. 'Amanda' was a 34-year-old mother of six children, five of whom (ages 2, 3, 5, 8 and 14 years) were living with her and their father/stepfather, 'Pierre Franklin'. Amanda was angry with Pierre for spending money on rum. Pierre was vexed with Amanda for 'shaming' him in front of his friends. He left the village for several weeks, staying with a relative in town. His three genetic children (ages 2, 3, and 5 years) showed abnormal cortisol levels (in this case, elevated) for a prolonged period following their father's departure. This pattern is typical: children usually became habituated to stressful events, but absence of a parent often resulted in abnormal patterns of elevated and/or subnormal cortisol levels. Following the return of their father, the Franklin children's cortisol levels resumed a more normal profile. Again, this pattern is typical: children living in families with high levels of marital conflict (observed and reported serious quarrelling, fighting, residence absence) were more likely to have abnormal cortisol profiles than children living in more amiable families. Figure redrawn from Flinn and England (1997).

Flinn and Leone, 2006b) were associated with elevated cortisol levels for all ages of children more than any other factor that we examined. These results suggest that family interactions were a critical psychosocial stressor in most children's lives, although the sample collection during periods of relatively intense family interaction (early morning and late afternoon) may have exaggerated this association.

Children residing in households with a stepparent have high cumulative mean cortisol levels relative to their half-siblings in the same household (Flinn, 1999; Flinn and Leone, 2006b). Children in bi-parental households have moderate cortisol levels (Flinn and England, 1995), with a higher proportion of elevations occurring in the context of positive affect situations such as competitive play, physical work, and excitement regarding novel situations.

Although elevated cortisol levels are associated with traumatic events such as family conflict, long-term stress may result in diminished cortisol response. In some cases, chronically stressed children had blunted response to physical activities that normally evoked cortisol elevation. Comparison of cortisol levels during 'non-stressful' periods (no reported or observed crying, punishment, anxiety, residence change, family conflict, or health problem during 24 h period before saliva collection) indicates a striking reduction and, in many cases, reversal of the family environment–stress association (Flinn and England, 2003). Chronically stressed children sometimes had subnormal cortisol levels when they were not in stressful situations. For example, cortisol levels immediately after school (walking home from school) and during non-competitive play were lower among some chronically stressed children (cf. Long et al., 1993). Some chronically stressed children appeared socially 'tough' or withdrawn and exhibited little or no arousal to the novelty of the first few days of the saliva collection procedure. These sub-normal profiles may be similar in some respects to those of individuals with PTSD (e.g. Yehuda et al., 2005).

Although elevated cortisol levels in children are usually associated with negative affect, events that involve excitement and positive affect also stimulate stress response (Flinn, in press, a). For example, cortisol levels on the day before Christmas were >1 SD above normal, with some of the children from two-parent households and those having the most positive expectations exhibiting the highest cortisol (Flinn, in press, b). Cortisol response appears sensitive to social challenges with different affective states. Other studies further suggest that the cognitive effects of cortisol may vary with affective states, such as perceived social support (Ahnert et al., 2004; Quas et al., 2004).

There are some age and sex differences in cortisol profiles, but it is difficult to assess the extent to which this is a consequence of neurological differences (e.g. Butler et al., 2005), physical maturation processes, or the different social environments experienced, for example, during adolescence as compared with early childhood (Flinn et al., 1996; Flinn and Quinlan, in preparation). For instance, young adult women have a higher incidence of depression and associated abnormal cortisol profiles than children or young men in this community.

The emerging picture of HPA stress response in naturalistic context from the Dominica study is one of sensitivity to social threats, consistent with clinical and experimental studies. The results further suggest that family environments are an especially important source and mediator of stressful social challenges for children. In the next section, data on the longitudinal effects of early traumatic experiences are examined to assess the domain-specificity of changes in stress response.

20.5.2.4. Ontogeny: the early trauma causes HPA dysfunction hypothesis

"... the development of individual differences in behavioral and neuroendocrine responses to stress can be influenced by events occurring at multiple stages in development ..." (Francis et al., 2002, p. 7843).

Early experiences can have profound and permanent effects on stress response. Exposure to prenatal maternal stress, or prolonged separation from mother in rodents and non-human primates, can result in life-long changes in HPA stress response (Suomi, 1997; Meaney, 2001; Maccari et al., 2003; cf. Levine, 2005). Research on the developmental pathways has targeted the homeostatic mechanisms of the HPA system, which appear sensitive to exposure to high levels of glucocorticoids during ontogeny. Glucocorticoid receptors (GRs) in the hippocampus that are part of the negative feedback loop regulating release of

CRH and adrenocorticotropic hormone can be damaged by the neurotoxic levels of cortisol associated with traumatic events (Sapolsky, 1991, 2005). Hence early trauma is posited to result in permanent HPA dysregulation and hypercortisolaemia, with consequent deleterious effects on the hippocampus, thymus, and other key neural, metabolic, and immune system components (Mirescu et al., 2004; Zhang et al., 2004). These effects have additional consequences resulting from high density of GRs in the prefrontal cortex in primates (de Kloet et al., 1999; Patel et al., 2000; Sanchez et al., 2000).

Finer-grained analysis of the epigenetic mechanisms involved with maternal effects on glucocorticoid negative feedback on CRH release indicates that DNA methylation affects hippocampal GR exon 1_7 promoter activity (Weaver et al., 2004). The permanence of DNA methylation, set during a sensitive period in the first week after birth, is a mechanism connecting diminished maternal care (licking, grooming, and arched-back nursing in the rat) with long-term elevations of HPA stress response.

The specific mechanisms affecting relations between exposure to trauma early in development and subsequent HPA system function in humans are not as well documented as in animal studies. Nonetheless, a similar causal linkage appears plausible (e.g. Heim et al., 2000;

Essex et al., 2002; O'Conner et al., 2003; Teicher et al., 2003; Lupien et al., 2005).

Children in the Bwa Mawego study who were exposed to the stress of hurricanes and political upheavals during infancy or in utero do not have any apparent differences in cortisol profiles in comparison with children who were not exposed to such stressors. Children exposed to the stress of parental divorce, death, or abuse (hereafter 'early family trauma' or EFT), however, have significantly higher cortisol (Figure 20.3) levels at age 10 years than other children. EFT children also have higher morbidity than no-EFT children (Figure 20.4). Based on analogy with the non-human research discussed previously, two key factors could be involved: (i) diminished hippocampal GR receptor functioning, resulting in less effective negative feedback regulation of cortisol levels; and (ii) enhanced sensitivity to perceived social threats. Children usually elevate cortisol in response to strenuous physical activity, but rapidly return to normal levels. If EFT has affected the negative feedback loop, then recovery to normal cortisol levels would be slower. Resumption of normal cortisol levels after physical stressors, however, is similar regardless of early experience of family trauma (Figure 20.5). Cortisol profiles following social stressors indicate that EFT children sustain elevated cortisol levels longer than non-EFT children (Figure 20.6).

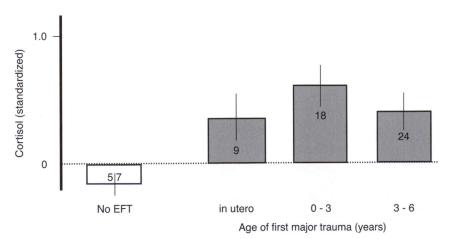

Fig. 20.3 Children exposed to early family trauma *in utero* or postnatally have higher average cortisol levels at age 10 years than children who were not exposed to early family trauma (no EFT). Sample sizes (no. of children) are in bars. Vertical lines represent 95% confidence intervals. Figure adapted from Flinn (2006a).

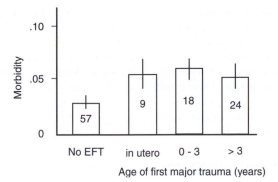

Fig. 20.4 Children exposed to early trauma *in utero* or postnatally have higher average morbidity levels than children who were not exposed to early family trauma (no EFT). Sample sizes (no. of children) are in bars. Vertical lines represent 95% confidence intervals. Figure adapted from Flinn (2006a).

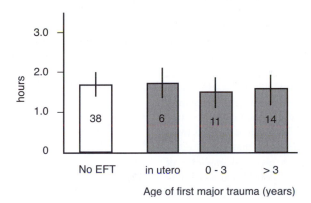

Fig. 20.5 Children exposed to early family trauma (EFT) do not have slower recovery to normal cortisol levels after physical stressors than no-EFT children do. Sample sizes (no. of children) are in bars. Vertical lines represent 95% confidence intervals. Figure adapted from Flinn (2006a).

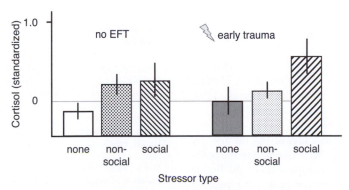

Fig. 20.6 Children exposed to early family trauma (EFT) have higher cortisol levels in response to social stressors, but not non-social stressors, than no-EFT children. Vertical lines represent 95% confidence intervals. Figure adapted from Flinn (2006a).

The enhanced HPA stress response of children in this community who were exposed to EFT appears primarily focused on social challenges, suggesting that the ontogenetic effects of early trauma on stress response may be domain-specific and even context-specific. These results are consistent with studies of the effects of social defeat with non-human models (e.g. Kaiser and Sachser, 2005; Wiedenmayer, 2004).

20.6. **Summary and concluding remarks**

Returning to the paradox of why natural selection favoured sensitivity of stress response to social stimuli in the human child, several points emerge. Childhood is necessary and useful for acquiring the information and practice to build and refine the mental algorithms critical for negotiating the social coalitions that are key to success in our species. Mastering the social environment presents special challenges for the human child (e.g. Lamb, 2005). Social competence is difficult because the target is constantly changing and similarly equipped with theory of mind and other cognitive abilities. Results from the Dominica study indicate that family environment is a primary source and mediator of stressful events in a child's world. The sensitivity of stress physiology to the social environment may facilitate adaptive responses to this most salient and dynamic puzzle.

Coping with social challenges, however, can have significant health consequences, ranging from dysregulation of emotional control and increased risk of psychopathology (Gilbert, 2001; Nesse, 1999) to broader health issues associated with social and economic disparities (Marmot and Wilkinson, 1999). The potential for intergenerational cycles that perpetuate social relationships that affect stress (Belsky, 2005; Belsky *et al.*, 2005; Francis *et al.*, 1999; Maestripieri *et al.*, 2005) and poor health are especially concerning.

We are still far from identifying the specific mechanisms linking stress response to the ontogenetic plasticity of components of the limbic system and prefrontal cortex that are involved with the acquisition of social competencies. An evolutionary developmental perspective can be useful in these efforts to understand this critical aspect of a child's world by integrating knowledge of physiological causes with the logic of adaptive design by natural selection. It reminds us that our biology has been profoundly affected by our evolutionary history as extraordinarily social creatures.

References

Ademec, R. E., Blundell, J. and Burton, P. (2005) Neural circuit changes mediating lasting brain and behavioral response to predator stress. *Neuroscience and Biobehavioral Reviews*, 29: 1225–1241.

Ader, R. (2006) Psychoneuroimmunology. In R. Ader, D. L. Felten and N. Cohen (eds) *Psychoneuroimmunology*, 4th edn, vol. 1. Academic Press, San Diego.

Adolphs, R. (2003) Cognitive neuroscience of human social behavior. *Nature Reviews, Neuroscience*, 4: 165–178.

Ahnert, L., Gunnar, M. R., Lamb, M. E. and Barthel, M. (2004) Transition to child care: Associations with infant-mother attachment, negative emotion, and cortisol elevations. *Child Development*, 75: 639–650.

Alexander, R. D. (1974) The evolution of social behavior. *Annual Review of Ecology and Systematics*, 5: 325–383.

Alexander, R. D. (1979) *Darwinism and Human Affairs.* Seattle: University of Washington Press.

Alexander, R. D. (1987) *The Biology of Moral Systems.* Hawthorne: Aldine de Gruyter.

Alexander, R. D. (1989) Evolution of the human psyche. In P. Mellars and C. Stringer (eds), *The Human Revolution: Behavioural and Biological Perspectives on the Origins of Modern Humans*, pp. 455–513. Princeton University Press, Princeton.

Alexander, R. D. (1990a) Epigenetic rules and Darwinian algorithms: The adaptive study of learning and development. *Ethology and Sociobiology*, 11: 1–63.

Alexander, R. D. (1990b) *How Did Humans Evolve? Reflections on the Uniquely Unique Species.* Museum of Zoology, Special Publication No. 1. University of Michigan, Ann Arbor.

Alexander, R. D. (2005) Evolutionary selection and the nature of humanity. In V. Hosle and Ch. Illies (eds), *Darwinism and Philosophy*, pp. 301–348. University of Notre Dame Press, South Bend, IN.

Alexander, R. D. and Noonan, K. M. (1979) Concealment of ovulation, parental care, and human social evolution. In N. Chagnon and W. Irons (eds) *Evolutionary Biology and Human Social Behavior: An Anthropological Perspective.* Duxbury Press, N. Scituate, MA.

Allman, J. (1999) *Evolving Brains.* Scientific American Library, New York.

Allman, J. M., Hakeem, A., Erwin, J. M., Nimchinsky, E. and Hof, P. (2001) The anterior cingulate cortex: the evolution of an interface between emotion and cognition. *Annals of the New York Academy of Sciences*, 935: 107–117.

Armstrong, E. (1990) Brains, bodies and metabolism. *Brain, Behavior and Evolution*, 36: 166–176.

Axelrod, J. and Reisine, T. D. (1984) Stress hormones: their interaction and regulation. *Science*, 224: 452–459.

Bartolomucci, A., Palanza, P., Sacerdote, P. *et al.* (2005) Social factors and individual vulnerability to chronic stress exposure. *Neuroscience and Biobehavioral Reviews*, 29: 67–81.

Baumeister, R. F. (2005) *The Cultural Animal: Human Nature, Meaning, and Social Life*. Oxford University Press, New York.

Belsky, J. (1997) Attachment, mating, and parenting: an evolutionary interpretation. *Human Nature*, 8: 361–381.

Belsky, J. (2005) The developmental and evolutionary psychology of intergenerational transmission of attachment. In C. S. Carter, L. Ahnert, K. E. Grossmann, S. B. Hrdy, M. E. Lamb, S. W. Porges and N. Sachser (eds) *Attachment and Bonding: A New Synthesis*. Dahlem Workshop Report 92. MIT Press, Cambridge, MA.

Belsky, J., Jaffee, S. R., Sligo, J., Woodward, L. and Silva, P. A. (2005) Intergenerational transmission of warm-sensitive-stimulating parenting: a prospective study of mothers and fathers of 3-year-olds. *Child Development*, 76: 384–96.

Beylin, A. V. and Shors, T. J. (2003) Glucocorticoids are necessary for enhancing the acquisition of associative memories after acute stressful experience. *Hormones and Behavior*, 43: 1124–131.

Bjorklund, D. F. and Bering, J. M. (2003) Big brains, slow development and social complexity: the development and evolutionary origins of social cognition. In M. Brüne, H. Ribbert and W. Schiefenhövel (eds) *The Social Brain: Evolution and Pathology*, pp. 113–151. Wiley, New York.

Bjorklund, D. F. and Pellegrini, A. D. (2002) *The Origins of Human Nature: Evolutionary Developmental Psychology*. American Psychological Association Press, Washington, DC.

Bjorklund, D. F. and Rosenberg, J. S. (2005) The role of developmental plasticity in the evolution of human cognition: evidence from enculturated, juvenile great apes. In B. J. Ellis and D. F. Bjorklund (eds), *Origins of the Social Mind: Evolutionary Psychology and Child Development*, pp. 45–75. Guilford Press, New York.

Bloom, P. (2000) *How Children Learn the Meaning of Words*. MIT Press, Cambridge, MA.

Blurton-Jones, N. G. and Marlowe, F. W. (2002) Selection for delayed maturity: does it take 20 years to learn to hunt and gather? *Human Nature*, 13: 199–238.

Bock, J. A. (2005) Farming, foraging, and children's play in the Okavango Delta, Botswana. In A. D. Pellegrini and P. K. Smith (eds), *The Nature of Play: Great Apes and Humans*, pp. 254–281. Guilford Press, New York.

Bogin, B. (1999) *Patterns of Human Growth*, 2nd edn. Cambridge University Press. Cambridge.

Bogin, B. and Marela-Silva, M. I. V. (2003) Anthropometric variation and health: A biocultural model of human growth. *Journal of Children's Health*, 1: 149–173.

Bowlby, J. (1969) *Attachment*. Basic Books, New York.

Bowlby, J. (1973) *Separation—Anxiety and Anger*. Basic Books, New York.

Brothers, L. (1990) The social brain: a project for integrating primate behavior and neurophysiology in a new domain. *Concepts in Neuroscience* 1: 27–51.

Brothers, L. (2001) *Friday's Footprint: How Society Shapes the Human Mind*. Oxford University Press, Oxford.

Buchan, J. C., Alberts, S. C., Silk, J. B. and Altmann, J. (2003) True paternal care in a multi-male primate society. *Nature*, 425(6954): 179–181.

Buchanan, T. W. and Lovallo, W. R. (2001) Enhanced memory for emotional material following stress-level cortisol treatment in humans. *Psychoneuroendocrinology*, 26: 307–317.

Butler, T., Pan, H., Epstein, J. *et al.* (2005) Fear-related activity in subgenual anterior cingulate differs between men and women. *Neuroreport*, 16: 1233–1236.

Buwalda, B., Kole, M. H. P., Veenema, A. H. *et al.* (2005) Long term effects of social stress on brain and behavior: a focus on hippocampal functioning. *Neuroscience and Biobehavioral Reviews*, 29: 83–97.

Byrne, R. W. (2002a) In J. C. Kaufman (ed.), *The Evolution of Intelligence*, pp. 79–95. Lawrence Erlbaum, Mahwah, NJ.

Byrne, R. W. (2002b) Social and technical forms of primate intelligence. In de Waal, F. B. M. (ed.), *Tree of Origin: What Primate Behavior Can Tell Us About Human Social Evolution*, pp. 145–172. Harvard University Press, Cambridge, MA.

Byrne, R. W. and Whiten, A. (eds) (1988) *Machiavellian Intelligence: Social Expertise and the Evolution of Intellect in Monkeys, Apes, and Humans*. Oxford University Press, Oxford.

Cameron, N. M., Champagne, F. A., Parent, C., Fish, E. W., Ozaki-Kuroda, K. and Meaney, M. J. (2005) The programming of individual differences in defensive responses and reproductive strategies in the rat through variations in maternal care. *Neuroscience and Biobehavioral Reviews*, 29: 843–865.

Campbell, A. (2002) *A Mind of Her Own: The Evolutionary Psychology of Women*. Oxford University Press, London.

Campbell, A. and Muncer, S. (eds) (1998) *The Social Child*. Psychology Press, Hove, East Sussex.

Carter, C. S. (2003) Developmental consequences of oxytocin. *Physiology and Behavior*, 79: 383–397.

Carter, C. S. (2005) The chemistry of child neglect: do oxytocin and vasopressin mediate the effects of early experience? *Proceedings of the National Academy of Sciences of the USA*, 102: 18247–18248.

Chagnon, N. A. (1988) Life histories, blood revenge, and warfare in a tribal population. *Science*, 239: 985–992.

Chapin, H. D. (1922) *Heredity and Child Culture*. E. P. Dutton, New York.

Chiappe, D. and MacDonald, K. (2005) The evolution of domain-general mechanisms in intelligence and learning. *Journal of General Psychology*, 132: 5–40.

Chisholm, J. S. (1999) *Death, Hope and Sex*. Cambridge University Press, Cambridge.

Clarke, A. S. (1993) Social rearing effects on HPA axis activity over early development and in response to stress in rhesus monkeys. *Developmental Psychobiology*, 26: 433–446.

Cohen, S., Doyle, W. J., Turner, R. B., Alper, C. M. and Skoner, D. P. (2003) Emotional style and susceptibility to the common cold. *Psychosomatic Medicine* 65: 652–657.

Cummins D. D. (1998) Social norms and other minds: The evolutionary roots of higher cognition. In D. D. Cummins and C. Allen (eds) *The Evolution of Mind*, pp. 30–50. Oxford University Press, New York, NY.

Cushing, B. F. and Kramer, K. M. (2005) Mechanisms underlying epigenetic effects of early social experience: the role of neuropeptides and steroids. *Neuroscience and Biobehavioral Reviews*, 29: 1089–1105.

Daly, M. and Wilson, M. (1988a) Evolutionary social psychology and family homicide. *Science*, 242: 519–524.

Daly, M. and Wilson, M. (1988b) *Homicide*. Aldine de Gruyter, Hawthorne.

Dal Zatto, S., Marti, O. and Armario, A. (2003) Glucocorticoids are involved in the long-term effects of a single immobilization stress on the hypothalamic–pituitary–adrenal axis. *Psychoneuroendocrinology*, 28: 992–1009.

Damasio, A. (2003) Looking for Spinoza: Joy, Sorrow, and the Feeling Brain. Harcourt, Orlando, FL.

Darwin, C. (1871) *The Descent of Man, and Selection in Relation to Sex*. John Murray, London.

Davidson, R. J., Jackson, D. C. and Kalin, N. H. (2001) Emotion, plasticity, context, and regulation. *Psychological Bulletin*, 126: 890–906.

Davis, E. P., Donzella, B., Krueger, W. K. and Gunnar, M. R. (2001) The start of a new school year: Individual differences in salivary cortisol response in relation to child temperament. *Developmental Psychobiology*, 35: 188–196.

de Bellis, M., Chrousos, G. P., Dorn *et al.* (1994) Hypothalamic–pituitary–adrenal axis dysregulation in sexually abused girls. *Journal of Clinical Endocrinology and Metabolism*, 78: 249–255.

Deacon, T. W. (1997a) What makes the human brain different? *Annual Review of Anthropology* 26: 337–357.

Deacon, T. W. (1997b) *The Symbolic Species: The Co-evolution of Language and the Brain*. Norton, New York.

de Kloet, E. R. (1991) Brain corticosteroid receptor balance and homeostatic control. *Frontiers in Neuroendocrinology*, 12: 95–164.

de Kloet, E. R., Oitzl, M. S. and Joels, M. (1999) Stress and cognition: are corticosteroids good or bad guys? *Trends in Neuroscience*, 22: 422–426.

de Kloet, E. R., Sibug, R. M., Helmerhorst, F. M. and Schmidt, M. (2005) Stress, genes, and the mechanism for programming the brain for later life. *Neuroscience and Biobehavioral Reviews*, 29: 271–281.

Dhabbar, F. S. and McEwen, B. S. (2001) Bidirectional effects of stress and glucocorticoid hormones on immune function: possible explanations for paradoxical observations. In R. Ader, D. L. Felten and N. Cohen (eds) *Psychoneuroendocrinology*, 3rd edn, vol. 1, pp. 301–338. Academic Press, San Diego.

Dickerson, S. S. and Kemeny, M. E. (2004) Acute stressors and cortisol responses: a theoretical integration and synthesis of laboratory research. *Psychological Bulletin*, 130: 355–391.

Dickerson, S. S., Gruenewald, T. L. and Kemeny, M. E. (2004) When the social self is threatened: Shame, physiology, and health. *Journal of Personality*, 72: 1191–1216.

Dressler, W. W. and Bindon, J. R. (2000) The health consequences of cultural dissonance: Cultural dimensions of lifestyle, social support, and arterial blood pressure in an African American community. *American Anthropologist*, 102: 244–260.

Dunbar, R. I. M. (1997) *Gossip, Grooming, and Evolution of Language*. Harvard University Press, Cambridge, MA.

Dunbar, R. I. M. (1998) The social brain hypothesis. *Evolutionary Anthropology*, 6: 178–190.

Duvarci, S., Nader, K. and LeDoux, J. E. (2005) Activation of extracellular signal-regulated kinase- mitogen-activated protein kinase cascade in the amygdala is required for memory reconsolidation of auditory fear conditioning. *European Journal of Neuroscience*, 21: 283–289.

Ellis, B. J. Essex, M. J. and Boyce, W. T. (2005) Biological sensitivity to context: II. Empirical explorations of an evolutionary-developmental theory. *Development and Psychopathology*, 17: 303–328.

Ellis, B. J., Jackson, J. J. and Boyce, W. T. (2006) The stress response systems: universality and adaptive individual differences. *Developmental Review*, 26: 175–212.

Ellison, P. (1988) Human salivary steroids: methodological considerations and applications in physical anthropology. *Yearbook of Physical Anthropology*, 31: 115–142.

Essex, M. J., Klein, M. H., Cho, E. and Kalin N. H. (2002) Maternal stress beginning in infancy may sensitize children to later stress exposure: effects on cortisol and behavior. *Biological Psychiatry*, 52: 776–784.

Fenker, D. T., Schott, B. J., Richardson-Klavehn, A., Heinze, H-J. and Düzel, E. (2005) *European Journal of Neuroscience*, 21: 1–7.

Field, T., Diego, M., Hernandez-Reif, M., Schanberg, S. and Kuhn, C. (2003) Depressed mothers who are "good interaction" partners versus those who are withdrawn or intrusive. *Infant Behavior and Development*, 26: 238–252.

Finch, C. E. and Sapolsky, R. M. (1999) Evolution of Alzheimer's disease the reproductive schedule and apoE isoforms. *Neurobiology of Aging*, 20: 407–428.

Fisher, S. E. (2005) On genes, speech, and language. *New England Journal of Medicine*, 353: 1655–1657.

Fleming, A. S., Steiner, M. and Corter, C. (1997) Cortisol, hedonics, and maternal responsiveness in human mothers. *Hormones and Behavior*, 32: 85–98.

Fleming, A. S., O'Day, D. H. and Kraemer, G. W. (1999) Neurobiology of mother-infant interactions: experience and central nervous system plasticity across development and generations. *Neuroscience and Biobehavioral Reviews*, 23: 673–685.

Fleming, A., Kraemer, G. W., Gonzalez, A., Lovic, V., Rees, S. and Melo, A. (2002) Mothering begets mothering: the transmission of behavior and its neurobiology across generations. *Pharmacology, Biochemistry and Behavior*, 73: 61–75.

Flinn, M. V. (1997) Culture and the evolution of social learning. *Evolution and Human Behavior*, 18: 23–67.

Flinn, M. V. (1999) Family environment, stress, and health during childhood. In: C. Panter-Brick and C. Worthman (eds), *Hormones, Health, and Behavior*, pp. 105–138. Cambridge University Press, Cambridge.

Flinn, M. V. (2004) Culture and developmental plasticity: evolution of the social brain. In R. L. Burgess and K. MacDonald (eds) *Evolutionary Perspectives on Child Development*, pp. 73–98. Sage, Thousand Oaks, CA.

Flinn, M. V. (2006a) Ontogeny and evolution of glucocorticoid stress response in the human child. *Developmental Review*, 17: 138–174.

Flinn, M. V. (in press a) Emotional states and child health. *American Journal of Human Biology*.

Flinn, M. V. (in press b) Cross-cultural universals and variations: the evolutionary paradox of informational novelty. *Psychological Inquiry*, 17: 118–123.

Flinn, M. V. (in press b) 'Twas the day before Christmas, and all through the village children's cortisol levels were high ...' *Family Systems*.

Flinn, M. V. and Alexander, R. D. (2006) Runaway social selection. In S. W. Gangestad and J. A. Simpson (eds), *The Evolution of Mind*, pp. 249–255. Guilford Press, New York.

Flinn, M. V. and Coe, K. (2006) The linked red queens of human cognition, reciprocity, and culture. In S. W. Gangestad and J. A. Simpson (eds), *The Evolution of Mind*, pp. 339–347. Guilford Press, New York.

Flinn, M. V. and England, B. G. (1992) Daily variations in child glucocorticoid stress response. *Proceedings of the International Society of Psychoneuroendocrinology* XXIII: 97.

Flinn, M. V. and England, B. G. (1995) Family environment and childhood stress. *Current Anthropology*, 36: 854–866.

Flinn, M. V. and England, B. G. (1997) Social economics of childhood glucocorticoid stress response and health. *American Journal of Physical Anthropology*, 102: 33–53.

Flinn, M. V. and England, B. G. (2003) Childhood stress: endocrine and immune responses to psychosocial events. In J. M. Wilce (ed.), *Social and Cultural Lives of Immune Systems*, pp. 107–147. Routledge, London.

Flinn, M. V. and Leone, D. V. (2006a) Traumatic early experience and the ontogeny of glucocorticoid stress response in the human child. *Developmental Processes*, 1: 31–68.

Flinn, M. V. and Leone, D. V. (2006b) Alloparental care and the ontogeny of glucocorticoid stress response among stepchildren. In G. Bentley and R. Mace (eds) *Alloparental Care in Diverse Societies*, pp. 212–231. Biosocial Society Series. Berghahn Press, Oxford.

Flinn, M. V. and Ward, C. V. (2005) Evolution of the social child. In B. Ellis and D. Bjorklund (eds) *Origins of the Social Mind: Evolutionary Psychology and Child Development*, pp. 19–44. Guilford Press, London.

Flinn, M. V., Geary, D. C. and Ward, C. V. (2005a) Ecological dominance, social competition, and coalitionary arms races: why humans evolved extraordinary intelligence. *Evolution and Human Behavior*, 26: 10–46.

Flinn, M. V., Ward, C. V. and Noone, R. (2005b) Hormones and the human family. In D. Buss (ed.), *Handbook of Evolutionary Psychology*, pp. 552–580. Wiley, New York.

Flinn, M. V., Turner, M. T., Quinlan, R., Decker, S. D. and England, B. G. (1996) Male-female differences in effects of parental absence on glucocorticoid stress response. *Human Nature*, 7: 125–162.

Fodor, J. A. (1983) *The Modularity of Mind: An Essay on Faculty Psychology*. MIT Press, Cambridge, MA.

Francis, D. D., Diorio, J., Liv, D., and Meaney, M. J. (1999) Nongenomic transmission across generations of maternal behaviour and stress response in the rat. *Science*, 286: 1155–1158.

Francis, D. D., Diorio, J., Plotsky, P. M. and Meaney, M. J. (2002) Environmental enrichment reverses the effects of maternal separation on stress reactivity (2002) *The Journal of Neuroscience*, 22: 7840–7843.

Frith, C. D. and Frith, U. (1999) Interacting minds: a biological basis. *Science*, 286: 1692–1695.

Frith, C. D. and Frith, U. (2001) The biological basis of social interaction. *Current Directions in Psychological Science*, 10: 151–155.

Fuchs, E. and Flugge, G. (1995) Modulation of binding sites for corticotropin-releasing hormone by chronic psychosocial stress. *Psychoneuroendocrinology*, 30: 33–51.

Gallese, V., (2005) Embodied simulation: from neurons to phenomenal experience. *Phenomenology and the Cognitive Sciences*, 4: 23–48.

Geary, D. C. (2005) *The Origin of Mind*. American Psychological Association, Washington, DC.

Geary, D. C. and Bjorklund, D. F. (2000) Evolutionary developmental psychology. *Child Development*, 71: 57–65.

Geary, D. C. and Flinn, M. V. (2001) Evolution of human parental behavior and the human family. *Parenting: Science and Practice*, 1: 5–61.

Geary, D. C. and Flinn, M. V. (2002) Sex differences in behavioral and hormonal response to social threat. *Psychological Review*, 109: 745–750.

Geary, D. C. and Huffman, K. J. (2002) Brain and cognitive evolution: forms of modularity and functions of mind. *Psychological Bulletin*, 128: 667–698.

Gilbert, P. (2001) Evolutionary approaches to psychopathology: the role of natural defences. *Australian and New Zealand Journal of Psychiatry*, 35: 17–27.

Gold, P. W. and Chrousos, G. P. (2002) Organization of the stress system and its dysregulation in melancholic and atypical depression: high vs. low CRH/NE states. *Molecular Psychiatry*, 7: 254–275.

Gopnik, A., Meltzoff, A. N. and Kuhl, P. K. (1999) *The Scientist in the Crib: Minds, Brains, and How Children Learn*. William Morrow, New York.

Gould, S. J. (1977) *Ontogeny and Phylogeny*. Harvard University Press, Cambridge, MA.

Gray, J. A. (1982) *The Neuropsychology of Anxiety: An Enquiry into the Functions of the Septo-hippocampal System*. Oxford University Press, New York.

Hawkes K. (2003) Grandmothers and the evolution of human longevity. *American Journal of Human Biology*, 15: 380–400.

Heim, C., Newport, D. J., Heit, S *et al.* (2000) Pituitary–adrenal and autonomic responses to stress in women after sexual and physical abuse in childhood. *Journal of the American Medical Association*, 284: 592–597.

Hewlett, B. S. and Lamb, M. E. (2002) Integrating evolution, culture and developmental psychology: Explaining caregiver-infant proximity and responsiveness in central

Africa and the USA. In Keller, H., Poortinga, Y. H. and Scholmerich, A. (eds), *Between Culture and Biology: Perspectives on Ontogenetic Development*, pp. 241–269. Cambridge University Press, New York.

Hewlett, B. S. and Lamb, M. E. (2005) (eds) *Hunter-gatherer Childhoods*. Aldine Transaction, New Brunswick, NJ.

Hill, K. and Hurtado, A. M. (1996a) *Ache Life History: The Ecology and Demography of a Foraging People*. Aldine de Gruyter, New York.

Hill, K. and Hurtado, A. M. (1996b) The evolution of premature reproductive senescence and menopause in human females: an evaluation of the grandmother hypothesis. in L. Betzig (ed.) *Human Nature: A Critical Reader*, chapter 15. Oxford University Press, New York.

Hill, K. and Kaplan, H. (1999) Life history traits in humans: theory and empirical studies. *Annual Review of Anthropology*, 28: 397–430.

Hinde, R. A. (1974) *Biological Bases of Human Social Behaviour*. McGraw-Hill, New York.

Hirschfield, C. A. and Gelman, S. A. (1994) *Mapping the mind: domain specificity in cognition and culture*. Cambridge University Press, Cambridge.

Holliday, M. A. (1986) Body composition and energy needs during growth. In F. Falkner and J. M. Tanner (eds), *Human Growth: A Comprehensive Treatise*, 2nd edn, vol. 2, pp. 101–117. Plenum Press, New York.

Hrdy, S. B. (1999) *Mother Nature: A History of Mothers, Infants, and Natural Selection*. Pantheon, New York.

Hrdy, S. B. (2005) Evolutionary context of human development: the cooperative breeding model. In C. S. Carter and L. Ahnert (eds), *Attachment and Bonding: A New Synthesis*. Dahlem Workshop 92. MIT Press, Cambridge, MA.

Huether, G. (1996) The central adaptation syndrome: Psychosocial stress as a trigger for adaptive modifications of brain structure and brain function. *Progress in Neurobiology*, 48: 568–612

Huether, G. (1998) Stress and the adaptive self organization of neuronal connectivity during early childhood. *International Journal of Developmental Neuroscience*, 16: 297–306.

Huether, G., Doering, S., Ruger, U., Ruther, E. and Schussler, G. (1999) The stress-reaction process and the adaptive modification and reorganization of neuronal networks. *Psychiatry Research*, 87: 83–95.

Humphrey, N. K. (1976) The social function of intellect. In P. P. G. Bateson and R. A. Hinde (eds), *Growing Points in Ethology*, pp. 303–317. Cambridge University Press, New York.

Humphrey, N. K. (1983) *Consciousness Regained*. Oxford University Press, Oxford.

Innocenti, G. M. and Price, D. J. (2005) Exuberance in the development of cortical networks. *Nature Reviews Neuroscience*, 6: 955–965.

Irons, W. (1983) Human female reproductive strategies. In S. Wasser and M. Waterhouse (eds), *Social Behavior of Female Vertebrates*, pp. 169–213. Academic Press, New York.

Jackson, E. D., Payne, J. D., Nadel, L. and Jacobs, W. J. (2006) Stress differentially modulates fear conditioning in healthy men and women. *Biological Psychiatry*.

Joffe, T. H. (1997) Social pressures have selected for an extended juvenile period in primates. *Journal of Human Evolution*, 32: 593–605.

Kaiser, S. and Sachser, N. (2005) The effects of prenatal social stress on behaviour: mechanisms and function. *Neuroscience and Biobehavioral Reviews*, 29: 283–294.

Kaplan, H., Hill, K., Lancaster, J. and Hurtado, A. M. (2000) A theory of human life history evolution: diet, intelligence, and longevity. *Evolutionary Anthropology*, 9: 156–185.

Kerr, M. E. and Bowen, M. (1988) *Family Evaluation: An Approach Based on Bowen Theory*. Norton, New York.

Kirsch, P., Esslinger, C., Chen, Q. *et al.* (2005) Oxytocin modulates neural circuitry for social cognition and fear in humans. *Journal of Neuroscience*, 25: 11489–11493.

Kirschbaum, C. and Hellhammer, D. H. (1994) Salivary cortisol in psychneuroendocrine research: recent developments and applications. *Psychoneuroendocrinology*, 19: 313–333.

Kirschbaum, C., Wolf, O. T., May, M. Wippich, W. and Hellhammer, D. H. (1996) Stress- and treatment-induced elevations of cortisol levels associated with impaired declarative memory in healthy adults. *Life Sciences*, 58: 1475–1483.

Kirschner, M. and Gerhart, J. (2005) *The Plausibility of Life: Resolving Darwin's Dilemma*. Yale University Press, New Haven.

Knight, D. C., Nguyen, H. T. and Bandettini, P. A. (2005) The role of the human amygdala in the production of conditioned fear responses. *NeuroImage*, 26: 1193–1200.

Koolhaas, J. M., de Boer, S. F., de Ruiter, A. J. H., Meerlo, P., and Sgoifo, A. (1997) Social stress in rats and mice *Acta Physiologica Scandanavia*, 161: 69–72.

Konner, M. (1991) *Childhood*. Little, Brown, Boston, MA.

Korte, S. M., Koolhaas, J. M., Wingfield, J. C. and McEwen, B. S. (2005) The Darwinian concept of stress: Benefits of allostasis and costs of allostatic load and the trade-offs in health and disease. *Neuroscience and Biobehavioral Reviews*, 29: 3–38.

La Cerra, P. and Bingham, R. (1998) The adaptive nature of the human neurocognitive architecture: an alternative model. *Proceedings of the National Academy of Sciences of the USA*, 95: 11290–11294.

Lamb, M. E. (2005) Attachments, social networks, and developmental contexts. *Human Development*, 48: 108–112.

Lamb, M. E., Bornstein, M. H. and Teti, D. M. (2002) *Development in Infancy*, 4th edn. Lawrence Erlbaum, Mahwah.

Lancaster, J. (1989) Evolutionary and cross cultural perspectives on single parenthood. In: R. W. Bell and N. J. Bell (eds). *Sociobiology and social sciences*. pp. 63–71. Texas Tech University Press. Lubboch USA.

Lancaster, J. and Lancaster, C. S. (1987) The watershed: change in parental-investment and family-formation strategies in the course of human evolution. In J. B. Lancaster, J. Altmann, A. S. Rossi and L. R. Sherrod (eds), *Parenting Across the Lifespan: Biosocial Dimensions*, pp. 187–206. Aldine de Gruyter, New York.

Leblanc, S. A. (2003) *Constant Battles: The Myth of the Peaceful, Noble Savage*. St Martin's Press, New York.

LeDoux, J. E. (2000) Emotion circuits in the brain. *Annual Reviews Neuroscience*, 23: 155–184.

LeDoux, J. E. (2003) The emotional brain, fear, and the amygdala. *Cellular and Molecular Neurobiology*, 23: 727–738.

Leigh, S. R. (2001) The evolution of human growth. *Evolutionary Anthropology* 10: 223–236.

Leigh, S. R. (2004) Brain growth, life history, and cognition in primate and human evolution. *American Journal of Primatology*, 62: 139–64.

Leonard, W. R. and Robertson, M. L. (1994) Evolutionary perspectives on human nutrition: the influence of brain and body size on diet and metabolism. *American Journal of Human Biology*, 4: 77–88.

Levine, S. (2005) Developmental determinants of sensitivity and resistance to stress. *Psychoneuroendocrinology*, 30: 939–946.

Lindahl, M., Theorell, T. and Lindblad, F. (2005) Test performance and self-esteem in relation to experienced stress in Swedish sixth and ninth graders—saliva cortisol levels and psychological reactions to demands. *Acta Paediatrica*, 94: 489–495.

Long, B., Ungpakorn, G. and Harrison, G. A. (1993) Home-school differences in stress hormone levels in a group of Oxford primary school children. *Journal of Biosocial Sciences*, 25: 73–78.

Lovejoy, C. O. (1981) The origin of man. *Science*, 211: 341–350.

Lovejoy, C. O., McCollum, M. A., Reno, P.L and Rosenman, B. A. (2003) Developmental biology and human evolution. *Annual Reviews of Anthropology*, 32: 85–109.

Low, B. S. (2000) *Why Sex Matters*. Princeton University Press, Princeton.

Lupien, S., Fiocco, A., Wan, N., Maheu, F., Lord, C., Schramek and Thahn Tu, M. (2005) Stress hormones and human memory function across the lifespan. *Psychoneuroendocrinology*, 30: 225–242.

MacDonald, K. B. and Hershberger, S. L. (2005) Some theoretical issues in the study of evolution and development. In R. L. Burgess and K. B. MacDonald (eds), *Evolutionary Perspectives on Child Development*, pp. 21–72. Sage, Thousand Oaks, CA.

Maccari, S. Darnaudery M., Morley-Fietcher, S., Zvena, A. R., Cinque, C. and van Reeth, O. (2003) Prenatal stress and long-term consequences: implications of glucocorticoid hormones. *Neuroscience and Biobehavioral Reviews*, 27: 119–227.

Maestripieri, D., Lindell, S. G., Ayala, A., Gold, P. W. and Higley, J. D. (2005) Neurobiological characteristics of rhesus macaque abusive mothers and their relation to social and maternal behavior. *Neuroscience and Biobehavioral Reviews*, 29: 51–57.

Maier, S. F., Watkins, L. R. and Fleshner, M. (1994) Psychoneuroimmunology: the interface between behavior, brain, and immunity. *American Psychologist*, 49: 1004–1017.

Marmot, M. G. (2004) *The Status Syndrome: How Social Standing Affects Our Health and Longevity*. Times Books/Henry Holt, New York.

Marmot, M. and Wilkinson, R. G. (eds) (1999) *Social Determinants of Health*. Oxford University Press, Oxford.

Mason, J. W. (1971) A re-evaluation of the concept of "non-specificity" in stress theory. *Journal of Psychosomatic Research*, 8: 323–334.

Mason, J. W., Buescher, E. L., Belfer, M. L., Artenstein, M. S. and Mougey, E. H. (1979) A prospective study of corticosteroids and catecholamine levels in relation to viral respiratory illness. *Journal of Human Stress* (September, 1979), 18–28.

McEwen, B. S. (1995) Stressful experience, brain, and emotions: developmental, genetic, and hormonal influences. In M. S. Gazzaniga (ed.) *The Cognitive Neurosciences*, pp. 1117–1135. MIT Press, Cambridge, MA.

McEwen, B. S. (1998) Protective and damaging effects of stress mediators. *New England Journal of Medicine*, 338: 171–179.

McEwen, B. S. and Sapolsky, R. (1995) Stress and cognitive function. *Current Opinion in Neurobiology*, 5: 205–216.

McGaugh, J. L. (2004) The amygdala modulates the consolidation of memories of emotionally arousing experiences. *Annual Review of Neuroscience*, 27: 1–28.

Meaney, M. J. (2001) Maternal care, gene expression, and the transmission of individual differences in stress reactivity across generations. *Annual Review of Neuroscience*, 24: 1161–1192.

Meaney, M., Mitchell, J., Aitken, D., Bhat Agar, S., Bodnoff, S., Ivy, L. and Sarriev, A. (1991) The effects of neonatal handling on the development of the adrenocortical response to stress: implications for neuropathology and cognitive deficits later in life. *Psychoneoroendocrinology*, 16: 85–103.

Miller, G. E., Cohen, S. and Ritchey, A. K. (2002) Chronic psychological stress and the regulation of pro-inflammatory cytokines: a glucocorticoid-resistance model. *Health Psychology*, 21: 531–541.

Mirescu, C., Peters, J. D. and Gould, E. (2004) Early life experience alters response of adult neurogenesis to stress. *Nature Neuroscience*, 7: 841–846.

Moll, J., Zahn, R., de Oliveira-Souza, R., Krueger, F. and Grafman, J. (2005) The neural basis of human moral cognition. *Nature Reviews: Neuroscience*, 6: 799–809.

Munck, A., Guyre, P. M. and Holbrook, N. J. (1984) Physiological functions of glucocorticoids in stress and their relation to pharmacological actions. *Endocrine Reviews*, 5: 25–44.

Nesse, R. (1999) Proximate and evolutionary studies of anxiety, stress and depression: synergy at the interface. *Neuroscience and Biobehavioral Reviews*, 23: 895–903.

Nesse, R. M. and Young, E. A. (2000) Evolutionary origins and functions of the stress response. *Encyclopedia of Stress*, vol. 2, pp. 79–84. Academic Press, New York.

Newcomer, J. W., Craft, S., Hershey, T., Askins, K. and Bardgett, M. E. (1994) Glucocorticoid-induced impairment in declarative memory performance in adult humans. *Journal of Neuroscience*, 14: 2047–2053.

Numan, M. and Insel, T. R. (2003) *The Neurobiology of Parental Behavior*. Springer, New York.

O'Conner, T. G., Heron, J., Golding, J., Glover, V. and ALSPAC study team (2003) Maternal antenatal anxiety and behavioral/emotional problems in children: a test of a programming hypothesis. *Journal of Child Psychology and Psychiatry*, 44: 1025–1036.

Panter-Brick, C. (1998) *Biosocial perspectives on children.* Cambridge University Press, New York.

Patel, P. D., Lopez, J. F., Lyons, D. M., Burke, S., Wallace, M. and Shatzberg, A. F. (2000) Glucocorticoid and mineralocorticoid receptor mRNA expression in squirrel monkey brain. *Journal of Psychiatric Research*, 34: 383–392.

Pellegrini, A. D. and Archer, J. (2005) Sex differences in competitive and aggressive behavior: a view from sexual selection theory. In B. Ellis and D. Bjorklund (eds), *Origins of the Social Mind: Evolutionary Psychology and Child Development*, pp. 219–244. Guilford Press, London.

Phan, K. L., Fitzgerald, D. A., Nathan, P. J. and Tancer, M. E. (2006) Association between amygdala hyperactivity to harsh faces and severity of social anxiety in generalized social phobia. *Biological Psychiatry*.

Pine, D. S., Fyer, A., Grun, J., Phelps, E. A., Szeszko, P. R., Koda, V., Li, W., Ardekani, B., Maguire, E. A., Burgess, N. and Bilder, R. M. (2001) Methods for developmental studies of fear conditioning circuitry. *Biological Psychiatry*, 50: 225–228.

Pinker, S. (1994) *The Language Instinct*. New York: William Morrow.

Pitman, R. K. (1989) Post-traumatic stress disorder, hormones, and memory. *Biological Psychiatry*, 26: 221–223.

Pitman, R. K., Sanders, K. M., Zusman, R. M., Healy, A. R., Cheema, F., Lasko, N. B., Cahill, L. and Orr, S. P. (2002) Pilot study of secondary prevention of posttraumatic stress disorder with propranolol. *Biological Psychiatry*, 51: 189–192.

Porges, S. W. (1998) Love: an emergent property of the mammalian autonomic nervous system. *Psychoneuroendocrinology*, 23: 837–861.

Preussner, J. C., Baldwin, M. W., Dedovic, K., Renwick, R., Khalili Mahani, N., Lord, C., Meaney, M. and Lupien, S. (2005) Self-esteem, locus of control, hippocampal volume, and cortisol regulation in young and old adulthood. *NeuroImage*, 28: 815–826.

Quartz, S. and Sejnowski, T. (1999) Constraining constructivism: cortical and sub-cortical constraints on learning in development. *Behavioral and Brain Sciences* 23: 785–792.

Quas, J. A., Bauer, A. and Boyce, W. T. (2004) Physiological reactivity, social support, and memory in early childhood. *Child Development*, 75: 797–814.

Quinlan, R. J. and Flinn, M. V. (2005) Kinship, sex and fitness in a Caribbean community. *Human Nature*, 16: 32–57.

Rodriguez Manzanares, P. A., Isoari, N. A., Carrer, H. F. and Molina, V. A. (2005) Previous stress facilitates fear memory, attenuates GABAergic inhibition, and increases synaptic plasticity in the rat basolateral amygdala. *Journal of Neuroscience*, 25: 8725–8734.

Roozendaal, B. (2002) Stress and memory: opposing effects of glucocorticoids on memory consolidation and memory retrieval. *Learning and Memory*, 78: 578–595.

Roth, G. and Dicke, U. (2005) Evolution of the brain and intelligence. *Trends in Cognitive Sciences*, 9: 250–257.

Rumpel, S., LeDoux, J. E., Zador, A. and Malinow, R. (2005) Postsynaptic receptor trafficking underlying a form of associative learning. *Science*, 308(5718), 83–88.

Sakai, K. L. (2005) Language acquisition and brain development. *Science*, 310: 815–819.

Sanchez, M. M., Young, L. J., Plotsky, P. M. and Insel, T. R. (2000) Distribution of corticosteroid receptors in the hippocampal formation. *Journal of Neuroscience*, 20: 4657–4668.

Santarelli, L., Saxe, M., Gross, C. *et al.* (2003) Requirement of hippocampal neurogenesis for the behavioral effects of antidepressants. *Science*, 301: 805–809.

Saphier, D., Welch, J. E., Farrar, G. E., Ngunen, N. Q., Aguado, F., Thaller, T. R. and Knight, D. S. (1994) Interactions between serotonin, thyrotropin-releasing hormone and substance P in the CNS regulation of adrenocortical secretion. *Psychoneuroendocrinology* 19: 779–797.

Sapolsky, R. M. (1990a) Stress in the wild. *Scientific American* (January 1990), 116–123.

Sapolsky, R. M. (1990b) Adrenocortical function, social rank, and personality among wild baboons. *Biological Psychiatry*, 28: 862–878.

Sapolsky, R. M. (1991) Effects of stress and glucocorticoids on hippocampal neuronal survival. In M. R. Brown, G. F. Koob and C. Rivier (eds), *Stress: Neurobiology and Neuroendocrinology*, pp. 293–322. Dekker, New York.

Sapolsky, R. M. (1992a) Neuroendocrinology of the stress-response. In J. B. Becker, S. M. Breedlove and D. Crews (eds) *Behavioral Endocrinology*, pp. 287–324. MIT Press, Cambridge, MA.

Sapolsky, R. M. (1992b) *Stress, the Aging Brain, and the Mechanisms of Neuron Death*. MIT Press, Cambridge, MA.

Sapolsky, R. M. (1994) *Why Zebras Don't Get Ulcers*. Freeman, New York.

Sapolsky, R. M. (2003) Stress and plasticity in the limbic system. *Neurochemical Research*, 28: 1735–1742.

Sapolsky, R. M. (2005) The influence of social hierarchy on primate health. *Science*, 308(5722): 648–652.

Schneider, M. L., Coe, C. L. and Lubach, G. R. (1992) Endocrine activation mimics the adverse effects of prenatal stress on the neuromotor development of the infant primate. *Developmental psychobiology*, 25: 427–439.

Schultz, A. H. (1969) *The Life of Primates*. Universe Press, New York.

Selye, H. (1976) *The Stress of Life*, revised edn. McGraw-Hill, New York.

Servan-Schreiber, D., Printz, H. and Cohen, S. D. (1990) A network model of catecholamine effects: gain, signal-to-noise ratio, and behavior. *Science*, 249: 892–895.

Shamay-Tsoory, S. G., Tomer, R. and Aharon-Peretz, J. (2005) The neuroanatomical basis of understanding sarcasm and its relationship to social cognition. *Neuropsychology*, 19: 288–300.

Sheline, Y. I., Gado, M. H. and Kraemer, H. C. (2003) Untreated depression and hippocampal volume loss. *American Journal of Psychiatry* 160: 1516–1518.

Sherman, P. W. (1998) The evolution of menopause. *Nature*, 392: 759–760

Smuts, B. (1985) *Sex and Friendship in Baboons*. Aldine de Gruyter, New York.

Smuts, B. B. and Smuts, R. W. (1993) Male aggression and sexual coercion of females in nonhuman primates and other mammals: evidence and theoretical implications. *Advances in the Study of Behavior* 22: 1–63.

Spangler, G. and Grossmann, K. E. (1993) Biobehavioral organization in securely and insecurely attached infants. *Child Development*, 64: 1439–1450.

Stansbury, K. and Gunnar, M. R. (1994) Adrenocortical activity and emotion regulation. *Monographs of the Society for Research in Child Development*, 59: 108–34.

Stearns, S. C. (1992) *The Evolution of Life Histories*. Oxford University Press, Oxford.

Suomi, S. J. (1997) Long-term effects of differential early experiences on social, emotional, and physiological development in nonhuman primates. In M. S. Keshevan and R. M. Murra (eds) *Neurodevelopmental Models of Adult Psychopathology*, pp.104–116. Cambridge University Press, Cambridge.

Suomi, S. J. (2005) Mother–infant attachment, peer relationships, and the development of social networks in rhesus monkeys. *Human Development*, 48: 67–79.

Sur, M. and Rubenstein, J. L. R. (2005) Patterning and plasticity of the cerebral cortex. *Science*, 310: 805–810.

Symons, D. (1978) *Play and Aggression: A Study of Rhesus Monkeys*. Columbia University Press, New York.

Takahashi, L. K. (1992) Prenatal stress and the expression of stress-induced responses throughout the life span. *Clinical Neuropharmacology* 15: 153–154.

Taub, D. (1984) *Primate Paternalism*. Van Nostrand Reinhold, New York

Teicher, M. H., Andersen, S. L., Polcari, Anderson, C. M., Navalta, C. P. and Kim, D. M. (2003) The neurobiological consequences of early stress and childhood maltreatment. *Neuroscience and Biobehavioral Reviews* 27: 33–44.

Tinbergen, N. (1963) On aims and methods of ethology. *Zeitschrift fur Tierpsychologie*, 20: 410–433.

Tomasello, M. (1999) *The Cultural Origins of Human Cognition*. Harvard University Press, Cambridge, MA.

Tooby, J. and Cosmides, L. (1995) Mapping the evolved functional organization of mind and brain. In M. S. Gazzaniga (ed.) *The Cognitive Neurosciences*, pp. 1185–1197. Bradford Books/MIT Press, Cambridge.

Wagner, J. D., Flinn, M. V. and England, B. G. (2002) Hormonal response to competition among male coalitions. *Evolution and Human Behavior*, 23: 437–442.

Weaver, I. C., Cervoni, N., Champagne, F. A., D'Alessio, A. C., Sharma, S., Seckl, J. R., Dymov, S., Szyf, M. and Meaney, M. J. (2004) Epigenetic programming by maternal behavior. *Nature Neuroscience*, 7: 847–854.

Weiner, H. (1992) *Perturbing the Organism*. University of Chicago Press, Chicago.

Wiedenmayer, C. P. (2004) Adaptations or pathologies? Long term changes in brain and behavior after a single exposure to severe threat. *Neuroscience and Biobehavioral Reviews*, 28: 1–12.

Williams, G. C. (1957) Plieotropy, natural selection, and the evolution of senescence. *Evolution*, 11: 398–411.

Williams, G. C. (1996) *Adaptation and natural selection*. Princeton University Press, New Jersey.

Wismer Fries, A. B., Ziegler, T. E., Kurian, J. R., Jacoris, S. and Pollak, S. D. (2005) Early experience in humans is associated with changes in neuropeptides critical for regulating social behavior. *Proceedings of the National Academy of Sciences of the USA*, 102: 17237–17240.

Wrangham, R. W. and Peterson, D. (1996) *Demonic Males*. Houghton Mifflin, New York.

Yehuda, R., Engel, S. M., Brand, S. R., Seckl, J., Marcus, S. M. and Berkowitz, G. S. (2005) Transgenerational effects of posttraumatic stress disorder in babies of mothers exposed to the World Trade Center attacks during pregnancy. *Journal of Clinical Endocrinology and Metabolism*. 90: 4115–4118.

Zhang, T.-Y., Parent, C., Weaver, I. and Meaney, M. J. (2004) Maternal programming of individual differences in defensive responses in the rat. *Annals of the New York Academy of Sciences*, 1032: 85–103.

CHAPTER 21

Birth order and sibling competition

Frank J. Sulloway

21.1. Introduction

Sibling competition is widespread in the natural world, and sometimes ends in siblicide. Order of birth among siblings affects the outcome of such contests, because it is a proxy for disparities in age, size, power, and opportunity. In our own species, birth order combines with the prolonged period of childhood dependence on parents to promote differences in parental investment. In addition, siblings often occupy different niches within the family and employ differing tactics in competition with one another. These disparate experiences influence personality, sentiments about the family, patterns of motivation, and attitudes more generally.

Historically, birth order has long been important in many social customs, including occupational choices, reproductive opportunities, inheritance practices, and royal succession. Birth order has also been implicated in support for, and opposition to, radical social and scientific revolutions. Although the persistence of birth-order effects in adulthood is well established by numerous studies, the extent and magnitude of these effects remains controversial. Compared with their well-documented manifestations within the family, systematic sibling differences are generally less pronounced when expressed in non-family contexts. Moreover, to manifest themselves in extrafamilial contexts, such birth-order effects often require eliciting factors that are linked with familial sentiments or with the familial context in which these behaviours were originally acquired.

21.2. Biological aspects of birth order and sibling competition

On average in sexually reproducing organisms, siblings share half their genes. Hence, with the exception of identical twins, siblings are twice as related to themselves as they are to another sibling. Drawing on this genetic insight, William Hamilton (1964a,b) realized that full siblings ought to compete for scarce resources whenever the benefits of doing so are more than half the costs to another sibling. From this cost/benefit perspective, sibling competition and parent–offspring conflict are opposite sides of the same biological coin. This is because parents are equally related to all of their offspring—present and future—but offspring are twice as related to themselves as they are to siblings or parents. Hence offspring will tend to disagree with parents about the timing of any curtailment of parental investment in themselves in favour of investment in future offspring. Weaning conflicts are a prime example of such dissensions (Trivers, 1974).

Biologists have documented competition between siblings in mammals, birds, amphibians, fish, insects, and even plants (Mock and Parker, 1997; Mock, 2004). Such competitive behaviours are particularly common among seabirds and predatory birds and sometimes lead to siblicide. Among African black eagles (*Aquila verreauxii*) siblicidal competition is 'obligate', occurring in nearly every instance. In this avian species parents are generally not capable, for ecological reasons, of raising more than one chick. The second egg, hatched a few days after the first, serves to ensure that valuable time is not lost in the breeding season should the first chick fail to hatch or die shortly after emerging from the egg. Within a few days, the older of the two black eagle chicks pecks the younger to death. "In all siblicidal species studied to date," note Mock *et al.* (1990), "there is a striking tendency for the victim to be the youngest member of the brood" (p. 445). Parents do not intervene in these lethal contests, as it is not in their biological interests to do so.

Among blue-footed boobies (*Sula nebouxii*), siblicide is 'facultative', meaning that its occurrence depends on ecological factors, which vary from one breeding season to the next. Females of this species lay two or three eggs. Aggressive pecking by an elder chick, directed against a younger, begins when the body weight of the elder chick falls below 80% of normal. In a good year, with plentiful food supplies, blue-footed booby parents can successfully raise two or even three chicks. When food is scarce, siblicide regulates clutch size in a generally adaptive manner (Drummond and García-Chavelas, 1989).

Unlike blue-footed booby parents, parents in some avian species regulate sibling competition in order to produce optimal fledgling numbers. Female canaries (*Serinus canaria*) lay four or five eggs, which hatch on successive days. Relative to older chicks, the younger and smaller ones are at a considerable disadvantage in obtaining food. To equalize competition, canary mothers lace each successive egg with greater amounts of testosterone, which promotes neural growth and makes the younger chicks more pugnacious (Schwabl, 1996; Schwabl *et al.*, 1997). American coots sometimes grab an older offspring by the neck and shake it violently–occasionally even killing it. This seemingly strange behaviour makes it easier for parents to feed younger offspring (Mock, 2004).

Evolution has sometimes given rise to specialized adaptations to help offspring to cope with sibling competition. Piglets are born with eight eye teeth—later shed—which they use in competition for the best maternal teats. Earlier-born piglets fiercely and successfully defend access to the anterior-most teats, which are the richest in milk supply, thereby establishing a dominance hierarchy based on teat order. Owing to differences in nourishment, a piglet born in the second half of the litter is only half as likely as its littermates to survive past the third week (Trivers, 1985). Even plants have sometimes evolved specialized adaptations for sibling competition. The Indian black plum (*Syzygium cuminii*) develops seeds with 25 to 30 ovules, which are botanical siblings. The first ovule to be fertilized secretes a 'death chemical' that prevents the metabolism of sucrose and kills off the other ovules (Krishnamurthy *et al.*, 1997).

21.3. **Social and economic repercussions**

Like many animal species, human offspring are highly dependent on parental investment. As a consequence, sibling strife over parental decisions about how to allocate scarce resources has long been an important consideration in human development. Before 1800, roughly half of all children succumbed to diseases of childhood. Studies have shown that parental discrimination among offspring, by sex and birth order, often affected who lived and who died (Boone, 1986; Voland, 1988, 1990). Having already survived some of the lethal diseases of childhood, elder children were generally better Darwinian bets for passing on their parent's genes to the next generation. In premodern times older offspring generally appear to have been favoured by parents. For example, infanticide is widely practised in traditional societies and is an accepted means of optimally allocating parental investment. No traditional society, however, condones the killing of the elder of two children (Daly and Wilson, 1988).

In a survey of 39 non-Western societies, anthropologists have found that firstborns of both sexes are generally given more elaborate birth ceremonies and privileges than other children. They also usually have authority over their younger siblings. In addition, firstborns–especially males–are generally favoured by inheritance practices and tend, in adulthood, to become the leaders of their family group (Rosenblatt and Skoogberg, 1974). Firstborns are also more likely to be named after a parent, an attribute that is associated with greater parental investment (MacAndrew *et al.*, 2002).

In Western societies, inheritance customs have often reflected discrimination by birth order. Several different systems have commonly been employed, including primogeniture (the policy of leaving all parental assets to the eldest child or eldest son), secundogeniture or (inheritance by the secondborn), and ultimogeniture (inheritance by the youngest child). Local variations in such inheritance strategies are generally understandable in terms of specific geographic and economic circumstances. For example, primogeniture has been common when both land and economic opportunities are limited. Bequeathing all or most of the parental property to the firstborn son avoided the subdivision of family lands and also helped to ensure the survival of the family patronymic (Hrdy and Judge, 1992). Ultimogeniture has usually been practised whenever there are substantial death taxes on property, as inheritance by the youngest child increases the interval between taxations. Equal inheritance is often associated with economic environments in which risk and skill are important factors in success. In Renaissance Venice, for example, economic fortunes were mostly made through speculative trade. Parents wisely gave equal shares to all of their children in the hopes of increasing the chances of having multiple successful offspring, as well as a continuation of the family name (Herlihy, 1977).

21.4. **Why are siblings so different?**

One of the most interesting questions about siblings is why they are so different (Plomin and Daniels, 1987). Although siblings share half their genes and exhibit similarities in personality based on this shared genetic basis, most parents are struck by how different siblings actually are. Research in behavioural genetics has shed extensive light on this topic. Based on studies of twin and non-twin siblings who have either grown up together or been separated at birth, researchers have determined that about 40% of the total variance in personality is genetic, about

35% is attributable to the non-shared environment, and only about 5% is associated with growing up in the same family. (The remaining 20% of the variance in personality is associated with measurement error—see Loehlin, 1992.)

A considerable surprise from these results is that growing up in the same family exerts only a small influence in making siblings more alike. This conclusion has led some commentators to argue that parents have little or no influence on the personalities of their offspring (Harris, 1998; Pinker, 2002). For several reasons, however, this conclusion is overstated. To begin with, these assessments about the importance of the shared environment underestimate its true influence owing to errors of measurement. In addition, even the seemingly modest amount of variance in personality that is currently thought to be explained by the shared environment (5%) represents a more substantial contribution than most people realize. For example, an influence of this magnitude means that a child growing up with relatively extroverted parents is twice as likely as other children to end up in the upper half of the personality distribution for this particular personality attribute (the odds ratio). Couched in these statistical terms, it is difficult to imagine that parents might have any greater influence on the personalities of their offspring than they actually do.

The real surprise from research in behavioural genetics involves the considerable role of the non-shared environment, which exerts roughly seven times as much influence on personality development as does the shared environment. One response to this unexpected finding has been to conclude that personality is mostly shaped by extrafamilial experiences, such as peer group influences (Harris, 1998). Although Harris, following Rowe (1994), has done a considerable service by calling attention to extrafamilial factors in personality formation, her downplaying of parental influences overlooks the fact that the family is not, in its most essential features, a shared environment. In fact, few aspects of family life are truly shared, other than material circumstances such as the number of books contained in the home and the neighbourhood where the home is located. The same shared events, such as a parental divorce, often elicit differing reactions from offspring.

In addition, because children are genetically different, they evoke somewhat different responses from other family members, including parents. More important, siblings notice these differences in behaviour and are sensitive to them (Dunn and Plomin, 1990). Such differing interpersonal interactions between parents and offspring contribute to the family's non-shared environment, not its shared environment. In short, the most important conclusion from research in behavioural genetics is not that parents have little influence on their offspring but rather that the family exerts the bulk of its environmental influence in a very different way than was previously thought.

21.5. Psychological mechanisms

Birth order is one source among many that helps to explain the extensive effects of the non-shared environment. The environmental sources of birth-order differences are best understood as reflecting the operation of several different principles: (1) differences in parental investment (and a cluster of related mechanisms linked with sibling competition); (2) dominance hierarchy effects; (3) niche partitioning within the family; and (4) deidentification, or the tendency for offspring to strive to be different from one another. Each of these four mechanisms leads to somewhat different predictions about the nature of resulting birth-order effects. In addition, (5) birth-order effects may in part reflect stereotypes, which themselves appear to reflect real differences but which are also capable of influencing behaviour independently of reality-based effects (Table 21.1).

21.5.1. Parental investment

Biases in parental investment are expected to foster quadratic or U-shaped trends in birth-order effects, with middleborns being different from other siblings. Such U-shaped distributions are a consequence of what may be termed the 'equity heuristic' and the counterintuitive results that this heuristic produces over time (Hertwig *et al.*, 2002). A variant of resource dilution hypotheses, the equity heuristic refers to the tendency for parents in modern societies

to treat their children in an equitable manner. Because firstborns and lastborns experience a period of exclusive parental investment, when other siblings are not yet born or have grown up and left the home, members of these two sibling positions experience a greater *net* accumulation of parental investment than do middleborns. When a particular parental resource is only important for human development in infancy or early childhood—such as devoting time and financial resources to having offspring vaccinated—the equity heuristic predicts linear rather than U-shaped trends. This is because there is never a period when the youngest child benefits in an exclusive manner from such parental resources, which are no longer developmentally pertinent by the time older siblings have left the home.

In contrast to middleborns, lastborns benefit from another tendency in parental investment. As parents—particularly mothers—reach the end of their reproductive careers, lastborns increasingly represent the last child they will ever have. Under such circumstances, it makes good Darwinian sense to allocate increased parental investment to young and vulnerable offspring that cannot be replaced (Salmon and Daly, 1998; Rohde *et al.*, 2003). Parental favouritism toward lastborns contributes to the U-shaped trends already expected as a consequence of the equity heuristic.

Empirical support for these theoretical perspectives on birth order and parental investment comes from a variety of studies (Hertwig *et al.*, 2002). Lindert (1977) analysed total hours of child care, up to the age of 18 years. In families with more than two children, this investigator found that middleborns were consistently at a disadvantage, receiving about 10% less in cumulative child care relative to firstborns and lastborns. Horton (1988) investigated nutritional status in 1903 Philippine households and found that younger siblings received less total food than older ones, as reflected by their lower height and weight. In addition, several studies have shown that laterborns are less likely to be vaccinated or taken to medical clinics, compared with earlierborn children. One study of 6350 children born in April 1970 in Great Britain found that vaccination rates were 68% for firstborns, 58% for secondborns, 50% for

Table 21.1 A family dynamics model of birth-order differences in human behaviour, health and well-being

Causal mechanisms	Observed birth-order trends
1. Differences in parental investment, which may involve outright discrimination or indirect effects through resource dilution, resulting in unequal *net* investment in offspring owing to the 'equity heuristic'. Historically, such differences in parental investment have often been reinforced by cultural practices such as primogeniture.	Either linear or quadratic (U-shaped) trends, depending on the age at which a parental resource is most important in life. Birth-order differences have been documented for vaccination rates, nutrition, medical care, self-esteem, IQ, and family sentiments (e.g., closeness to parents). See Zajonc and Mullally (1997), Salmon and Daly (1998), Salmon (1999), Hertwig *et al.* (2002)
2. Dominance hierarchy effects.	Linear effects based on sibling differences in age and size, particularly those relating to agreeableness and to some aspects of extraversion, neuroticism, and openness to experience (Sulloway 1996, 2001; Paulhus *et al.*, 1999; Rohde *et al.*, 2003).
3. Niche partitioning within the family system. Niche partitioning reduces competition and sometimes promotes cooperation among siblings.	Predominantly linear trends in attributes related to surrogate parenting, including differences in conscientiousness and in some aspects of extraversion and openness to experience (Sulloway, 1996, 2001).
4. Sibling deidentification.	Pairwise differences, including small zigzag trends, as siblings seek to differentiate themselves from other siblings, especially those who are immediately adjacent in age (Schachter *et al.* 1978; Skinner 1992; Sulloway 1996; Plowman 2005).
5. Birth-order stereotypes.	Stereotypes may create birth-order effects or may reinforce those produced by other mechanisms (Herrera *et al.* 2003).

thirdborns, 39% for fourthborns, and only 34% for fifthborns and higher birth ranks (Lewis and Britton, 1998). Across multiple studies, the odds of being vaccinated decline by 20–30% with each successive child in the family. Not surprisingly, numerous studies have shown that mortality rates in childhood—even in the twentieth century—are typically higher for children of higher birth orders. One study involving 14 192 Swedish children born between 1915 and 1929 found that—compared with firstborns—third- and fourthborns were 2.1 times more likely to die before the age of 10 years (Modin, 2002).

21.5.2. Sibling dominance hierarchies

Siblings reside within a dominance hierarchy based on age, size, and power. In competition, older siblings can physically intimidate younger siblings. Firstborns, in effect, are the 'alpha males' of their sibling group. Differences in linguistics skills also give older siblings an edge in verbal exchanges. Hence firstborns are expected to be dominant over their younger siblings. Some aspects of personality appear to reflect these differences, which present linear trends in traits such as dominance and assertiveness (see Section 21.6).

21.5.3. Niche partitioning

Sibling differences derive in part from niche partitioning within the family, which entails the adoption of diverse roles and domains of expertise. Differences in niche partitioning owe themselves to multiple factors, including genetic disparities between siblings, differences by sex, and differences by birth order. Niche partitioning is a direct consequence of Charles Darwin's (1859) 'principle of divergence'. Specialization within different family niches reduces competition, leads to a division of labour, and also makes it more difficult for parents to make direct comparisons between offspring. This general principle plays a central role in evolutionary biology, where it explains the process of 'adaptive radiation' among evolutionarily successful species such as Darwin's famous Galápagos finches.

Within the family, birth order is relevant to niche partitioning because the age differences between siblings affect the kinds of niches that are usually open to them. Similarly, siblings tend to diverge because they are they use different age-based strategies in dealing with one another. Because niche partitioning is substantially based on differences in age, most birth-order effects deriving from this psychological process are expected to display linear trends. Evidence for such trends is seen in some aspects of personality, such as conscientiousness, extraversion, and openness to experience.

A classic example of niche partitioning involves the consumer advocate and American presidential candidate, Ralph Nader. When Nader was a child, he and his three siblings divided a globe of the world into four sections. Each sibling took one-quarter of the world and thereafter specialized in its languages and history. What the Nader siblings appreciated was that they would all benefit more by cooperatively sharing their diverse domains of world

expertise than by competing to know the most about any single domain (Sulloway, 1996). In general, there is greater pressure on laterborns than on firstborns to diversify their interests and abilities, because firstborns have usually already nailed down the family niche of surrogate parent as well as other parentally valued roles such as being the 'studious' and 'responsible' child.

21.5.4. Deidentification

A fourth class of birth-order effects reflects yet another cause of mutual divergence as sibs seek to differentiate themselves from one another, especially from their immediately adjacent brothers and sisters. This process has been called 'deidentification' (Schachter et al., 1978). The same differentiation process extends to patterns of identification with parents. If one sibling identifies closely with one parent, another sibling will often identify more closely with the other parent (Schachter, 1982). Patterns of deidentification are expected to produce small zigzag trends as adjacent siblings differentiate themselves from one another (Skinner, 1992).

21.5.5. Birth-order stereotypes

There is some evidence that stereotypes about birth order play a role in creating and reinforcing birth-order differences. It should be kept in mind that stereotypes often reflect a perceived reality about the world that is substantially based on valid evidence. Moreover, socially accepted stereotypes, which serve to nurture expectations, exert a considerable influence on human behaviour. Birth-order stereotypes have been shown to exist in a number of different studies (Baskett, 1985; Musun-Miller, 1993; Nyman, 1995; Herrera et al., 2003). These stereotypes about personality and intellectual ability correspond closely with the kinds of birth-order differences that are actually reported in within-family studies. For example, firstborns are widely believed to be more intellectually oriented and conscientious than younger siblings, and to be more likely to attain high occupational status. Considerable evidence supports the higher educational and occupational status of firstborns, as well as the association between these outcomes and the psychological attributes (conscientiousness and intelligence) that are typically assigned to firstborns in studies of birth-order stereotypes (Herrera *et al.*, 2003).

21.6. Human behaviour and personality

More than two thousand publications on the subject of birth order have yielded a sometimes confusing pattern of results, especially about personality. As Ernst and Angst (1983) have rightly pointed out, many of these studies fail to control for differences in family size and social class. Lower-class families are biased for large sibships, so uncontrolled studies showing that laterborns differ from firstborns on some attribute may have detected a spurious cross-correlation rather than a valid birth-order effect.

Even in controlled birth-order studies there is considerable heterogeneity in outcomes. This circumstance has led some commentators, including Ernst and Angst (1983), to dismiss the importance of birth order. The majority of controlled birth-order studies, however, lack sufficient statistical power to demonstrate such effects. When these disparate findings in controlled studies are subject to meta-analysis—a technique for amalgamated findings of a similar nature to gain statistical power—they reveal modest but consistent birth-order differences (Sulloway, 1995, 2002).

Psychologists have usefully classified personality differences under what are known as the 'Big Five' personality dimensions—also sometimes referred to as the 'Five Factor Model' of personality (Costa and McCrae, 1992). These dimensions include Conscientiousness, Agreeableness, Extraversion, Openness to Experience, and Neuroticism. When assessed in terms of the Big Five personality dimensions, research on personality generally reflects the kinds of birth-order trends that are expected based on a family dynamics model.

In within-family studies, firstborns tend to be higher than laterborns in virtually all aspects of Conscientiousness. When siblings rate one another or when parents assess their own offspring—thus controlling for between-family differences—firstborns are described as being more deliberate, organized, dutiful, and self-disciplined than their younger brothers and sisters, and they are also generally considered the 'achiever' of the family (Paulhus *et al.*, 1999;

Plowman, 2005; Sulloway, 1996, 2001). Similarly, firstborns are overrepresented in *Who's Who* and in other standard measures of social and intellectual attainment, including becoming famous writers, world leaders, and winners of prizes for achievement. In addition, firstborns have slightly higher IQs than laterborns. (IQ declines about 1 point with each successive birth rank.) Such differences in intelligence appear to reflect a dilution of intellectual resources: as families increase in size, parents have less time to devote to each child, and children themselves diminish the overall level of the family's intellectual environment (Zajonc, 1976; Zajonc and Mullally, 1997). Some researchers nevertheless maintain that these well-documented effects, which have not been observed in some within-family studies, are artefacts stemming from differences between families (Wichman *et al.*, 2006). In spite of inconsistencies and some unanswered questions, these collective findings appear to reflect the fact that firstborns experience a different family environment than do laterborns. In particular, firstborns often act as surrogate parents toward younger siblings and reap greater parental investment and rewards by occupying this 'responsible' family niche. Owing to their relative immaturity, younger siblings are at a considerable disadvantage in competing for this family role and must generally seek parental favour in other ways—for example, by being affectionate, humorous, or athletic.

Turning to birth-order results for Agreeableness in within-family studies, we find that laterborns tend to score higher than firstborns on most facets of this dimension. Because firstborns are physically bigger and stronger than their siblings, it is easier for them to employ high-powered strategies. By contrast, younger siblings tend to cultivate appeasement strategies and other low-power tactics, including whining and pleading and, when necessary, appealing to parents for protection and assistance.

The unusual status of middleborns, sandwiched between siblings of greater and lesser age and power, appears to lend itself to cooperative and diplomatic skills. Based on within-family assessments, middleborns generally score higher on Agreeableness than do firstborns and lastborns (Sulloway, 2001). Martin Luther King, Jr, the middle of three children, began his career as a champion of non-violent reform by intervening in his younger brother's relentless teasing of their elder sister (Sulloway, 1996).

Traits related to Extraversion exhibit significant heterogeneity by birth order. As expected, firstborns in within-family studies are typically described as being more extraverted in the sense of being assertive and dominant, whereas laterborns are described as being more extraverted in the sense of being fun-loving, affectionate, and excitement seeking. Laterborns also employ humour as a sibling strategy, which exemplifies another facet of Extraversion. One well-designed study of Columbia University students ($N = 1967$) found that laterborns were 1.6 times more likely than firstborns to engage in dangerous sports such as football, rugby, and soccer. These findings appear to reflect laterborn deidentification and divergence from the elder offspring's choice of relatively safe sports such as track, tennis, and swimming (Nisbett, 1968).

Like Extraversion, Openness to Experience exhibits considerable heterogeneity by birth order, especially in within-family studies. Firstborns are more open to experience in the sense of being intelligent and intellectually oriented (reflecting achievement by academic conscientiousness and hence by conformance with the norms of society), whereas laterborns are more open to experience in the sense of being untraditional, unconventional, prone to fantasy, and attracted by novelty. In one study, subjects were asked to list 'the two or three most unconventional or rebellious' aspects about their lives. Laterborns listed more examples than firstborns, and they also listed more behaviours, experiences, and interests that were assessed as being truly unconventional by two independent judges (Sulloway, 2001).

Birth-order differences on the Big Five dimension of Neuroticism are minimal, as expected, because most neurotic traits are not adaptive, and most birth-order differences in personality are expected to reflect a functional—and hence adaptive—role in family dynamics. An exception to this last assertion, however, involves birth-order differences that arise from disparities in parental investment. Biases in parental investment are expected to affect self-confidence. Reduced parental investment, for example, may explain why laterborns—particularly middle

children—display somewhat lower self-esteem than do firstborns (Kidwell, 1982).

In studies of birth order, singletons need to be distinguished from other firstborns. Singletons are a controlled experiment—what it is like to experience childhood without sibling competition or parental discrimination in favour of another sibling. As a result, singletons tend to be intermediate between firstborns and laterborns in many aspects of personality. Owing to greater parental investment than is received by children who have siblings, singletons tend to resemble other firstborns in attributes such as being conscientious and parent-identified, as well as by exhibiting above-average levels of achievement. A portion of these effects can be attributed to small family size rather than to birth order *per se*.

In general, birth-order effects appear to be most pronounced when the age spacing between successive children is 2–4 years, enough to produce inequality in age and size, but not enough to disrupt the competitive dynamics that go on between siblings who are reasonably close in age. Helen Koch's (1955, 1956) pioneering researches on birth order documented the moderating effects of age spacing, as well as sex and sex of sibling. Such moderating effects were generally modest in magnitude and often complex.

In considering birth-order differences in human behaviour, it is important to distinguish between functional and biological birth order. A large age gap between a firstborn and the next younger sibling can effectively transform the younger offspring into a functional firstborn or singleton. Divorce and remarriage, resulting in blended families, can also create disparities between biological and functional birth order. It is functional birth order, not biological birth order, that is important in most aspects of personality development.

Because there are no genes for being a firstborn or a laterborn, most birth-order effects are believed to be environmental in origin. Environmental factors, however, can also be biological, and at least one birth-order effect has been convincingly linked to prenatal biological influences. Among males, the number of older brothers is linearly correlated with a propensity toward homosexual inclinations. These findings, which have been replicated in numerous studies, are consistent with the hypothesis that some mothers develop antibodies to male-specific minor histocompatibility antigens during pregnancy and that these antibodies interfere with the masculinization of subsequent fetuses (Blanchard, 2004).

21.7. **Radical revolutions and world history**

Historically, laterborns have been more likely than firstborns to question the status quo. The Protestant Reformation, for example, was more strongly supported by laterborn rulers and their subjects than by firstborns. Leaders of radical political revolutions, such as Fidel Castro, Georges-Jacques Danton, Vladimir Lenin, Ho Chi Minh and Leon Trotsky, have also tended to be laterborns (Sulloway 1996, 2000). There is some historical evidence that middleborn revolutionaries are less prone to violent tactics than either firstborns or lastborns, which is consistent with within-family assessments of middleborns being higher on Agreeableness. For example, during the French Revolution, which was preferentially supported by laterborns, middleborn deputies to the National Convention were more likely than other deputies to oppose the extreme measures that launched the Reign of Terror (Sulloway, 1996).

Birth order has sometimes been a factor in the instigation and reception of radical scientific innovations. Most radical revolutions in science have been led by laterborns, such as Charles Darwin, who was the fifth of six children. 'Radical revolutions' are defined here as those conceptual transformations that have substantial religious or political implications, that often take many decades to resolve, and that engender extensive public controversy both within and outside of the scientific community. Other radical revolutionaries in science include Copernicus (the youngest of four children), Bacon (the youngest of eight), Descartes (the youngest of three), and Alfred Russel Wallace (the fifth of six). It was Wallace who, in 1858, pushed Darwin into finally publishing the *Origin of Species* after Wallace anticipated the theory of natural selection during a malarial fit in the jungles of faraway Malaysia, where he was collecting natural history specimens. It is noteworthy that laterborn scientists

have not only been more likely than firstborns to support radical conceptual innovations, but they have also been more likely to travel to remote and dangerous parts of the world—as both Darwin and Wallace did.

Although numerous firstborns, including Kepler, Galileo, Newton, Lavoisier, Lyell and Einstein, have led important revolutions in science, the revolutions they have championed have tended to be more technical and less ideologically loaded than those typically championed by laterborns. In addition, compared with first born opponents of scientific revolutions, firstborns who propose or support radical scientific ideas have tended to be young, socially liberal, and to have experienced high levels of conflict with one or both parents—factors that, independently of birth order, are also significant sources of support for radical conceptual innovations (Sulloway 1996, 2001).

In times of 'normal' science, when pushing the dominant paradigm is the usual route to success (Kuhn, 1970), firstborns appear to be favoured over laterborns. Controlled for sibship size, firstborns have won more Nobel Prizes than laterborns (Clark and Rice, 1982). This tendency is more pronounced among laureates in science than it is among those in literature or among winners of the Peace Prize—less structured areas of achievement where laterborns have held their own. Also of interest is the fact that, compared with firstborn scientists, laterborns have tended to have broader interests, as reflected by the number of different fields in which they have achieved distinction (Sulloway, 1996). Darwin, for example, made important contributions to geology, evolutionary biology, botany, ecology, ethology, and psychology.

These birth-order effects in the historical record are confirmed by some contemporary evidence. Salmon and Daly (1998) asked a Canadian sample of middle-aged subjects, "Do you think that you are open to new and radical ideas (such as cold fusion)?" Controlled for age, sex, and sibship size, laterborns were 2.3 times more likely than firstborns to respond in the affirmative to this question ($r = 0.38, N = 100, P < 0.001$). In a series of four within-family studies ($N = 951$), Paulhus *et al.* (1999) found that laterborns were 2.0 times more likely than firstborns to be described as the rebel of the family (see also

Rohde *et al.* 2003, where the corresponding odds ratio was 1.8 to 1). In a real-life study, Zweigenhaft and Von Ammon (2000) found that laterborns were 2.2 times more likely than firstborns to undergo multiple arrests for their involvement in a labour dispute occurring at a Kmart in Greensboro, North Carolina.

In contrast, one well-designed study involving an analysis of social attitudes held by subjects in the General Social Survey showed only three significant birth-order effects out of 33 measures. These three effects were all modest in size and, more notably, were opposite to the predicted direction—laterborns were more patriotic than firstborns and also scored higher on two measures of political tough-mindedness (Freese *et al.*, 1999). In spite of such inconsistent findings about social attitudes, the overall literature on birth order generally supports the existence of modest birth-order differences. In a meta-analysis of 20 relevant studies, including seven studies besides that by Freese *et al.* that have reported non-significant findings, I found a mean-weighted correlation of 0.09 ($n = 11240$) between being laterborn and supporting the radical alternative. Among the eight real-life studies included in this meta-analysis, the effect size was $r = 0.20$ ($n = 1952$). Discrepancies between various study outcomes, including those mentioned here, may reflect the methodological issues discussed below.

21.8. Ongoing methodological considerations

Documentation of significant birth-order effects in human behaviour is most consistent when siblings rate one another, or when parents rate their own offspring (Ernst and Angst, 1983). In such studies, birth order typically accounts for about 1–2% of the variance in predicted scores for specific dimensions of the Five Factor of personality and as much as 4% in predicted scores involving multiple dimensions. Such differences may seem modest or even trivial to some, but 'variance explained' often provides a misleading notion of the real-world consequences of supposedly small effect sizes. For example, a correlation that accounts for just 2% of the variance in some particular attribute is equivalent to a medicine that increases the one's odds of surviving a deadly disease by a factor of 1.6. Most sources of individual differences in personality, including individual genes, explain less than 1% of the variance. It is also important to bear in mind that sex differences, which explain about 2% of the variance in personality traits, are one of the largest known sources of individual differences (Feingold, 1994; Hyde, 2005). Almost no one would argue that sex differences in personality are trivial. In short, in behavioural research, the documentation of any influence on human behaviour that explains just 1% of the variance is a noteworthy result that often has considerable practical importance for people's lives (Rosenthal and Rosnow, 1991).

There are nevertheless reasons for believing that within-family studies of birth order may overestimate effect sizes. In such studies, some of the variance accounted for by birth order may reflect what are known as 'contrast effects'. Such effects denote the tendency for parents and siblings to magnify real differences when making direct comparisons (Saudino, 1997). Another methodological possibility is that within-family evidence on birth order and its relationship to personality may be confusing a difference between personality and family roles. Firstborns may be the most conscientious sibling within the family simply because the task of being a surrogate parent generally falls to them, with all of the customary behavioural expectations that go with this 'responsible' role. What also remains unresolved is whether, independently of personality (or in combination with it), adult firstborns and laterborns retain predilections for adopting certain adult roles, and occupying certain adult family niches, in accordance with role specializations acquired during childhood.

Equally unresolved in birth-order research is the importance of birth-order effects outside the family milieu. Standard personality tests generally indicate little or no birth-order effects when subjects are not comparing themselves with their siblings (Ernst and Angst, 1983; Harris, 1998; Jefferson *et al.*, 1998; Parker, 1998). Such null findings may be contrasted, however, with the documentation of modest but consistent birth-order differences that are found when spouses and room-mates rate themselves, especially in the context of intimate living situations (Sulloway, 2001). In these cases, birth-order effects are about one-third to one-half the magnitude that we typically observe when siblings rate one another. More notably, the birth-order effects found in this class of studies correlate strongly (0.65) with the birth-order effects reported for the same personality attributes in direct sibling comparisons, thereby exhibiting considerable consistency from one behavioural context to another.

21.9. Situation-specific behaviour

Such collective findings suggest that birth-order effects are substantially latent in adult behaviour, expressing themselves only when a specific situation triggers a response based on behavioural repertoires previously learned within the family. As Cervone and Shoda (1999), among others, have shown about personality, much of its expression is subject to context-sensitive effects. This interactionist perspective on behaviour helps to explain some of the otherwise puzzling disparities in the outcomes of birth-order studies. For example, in friendships, dominance is usually not a socially advantageous trait; but, in intimate living situations, differences in dominance are likely to assert themselves in disputes over shared resources. This contextual difference was shown in one study in which subjects were asked to rate themselves and their friends on a measure of dominance (Sulloway, 2001). No birth-order effects were found. Yet when other subjects in the same study rated themselves and either a room-mate or a spouse, firstborns described themselves as more dominant than laterborns.

Unfortunately, only a few birth-order studies have attempted to test this situation-specific behaviour hypothesis. Using an experimental approach, Salmon (1998) played an electronically recorded election campaign speech to 112 college undergraduates. In one version of the speech, the speaker used terms such as 'brothers', 'sisters', and 'brethren' to evoke familial sentiments. In a second version of the speech, references to family terms were electronically replaced with references to 'friends'. As expected based on patterns of cumulative parental investment, firstborns and lastborns preferred the speech with references to

family terms, whereas middleborns preferred the speech containing references to 'friends.' Similarly, in a survey of 236 genealogical researchers in their mid-40s, Salmon and Daly (1998) found that middleborns were significantly underrepresented and were also less likely to nominate their mother as the person to whom they felt closest (for a replication, see Rohde et al., 2003). Such studies show that birth-order effects do manifest themselves outside of the family milieu when the behavioural context provides a link with familial sentiments, motives, or patterns of identification. More studies of this nature are needed to clarify the precise mechanisms, in adulthood, that appear to catalyse the transformation of latent family-based dispositions into manifest behaviour.

The role played by family-related self-conceptions and sentiments in eliciting birth-order effects may explain why evidence from social and scientific controversies is relatively consistent in producing birth-order effects (Sulloway, 1996, 2000, 2001; Numbers, 1998; Salmon and Daly, 1998; Zweigenhaft and Von Ammon, 2000). Many radical social and political revolutions have entailed direct implications for family life. During the Protestant Reformation, Martin Luther called for the abolition of celibacy for nuns and priests, which mainly impacted on laterborns, who were typically shunted into the clergy or the military under the system of primogeniture (Boone, 1986). Leading Protestants also considered primogeniture to be 'un-Christian'. Even in science, radical revolutions often touch on important values and social policies that concern the family. The Copernican and Darwinian revolutions both challenged deeply held religious convictions, which are passed from parents to offspring with a high degree of fidelity (Sulloway et al., 2006). As Darwin himself noted, the Darwinian revolution also gave strong support to equitable parental investment—as opposed to primogeniture—since arbitrary parental favouritism limits the role of competitive superiority in natural selection. To the extent that radical social and scientific revolutions have led to within-family conflicts, or have touched on inequities in parental investment, these sources of controversy are likely to have tapped latent birth-order differences among adults. If this hypothesized mechanism is in fact operative in adult behaviour, then the route by which birth-order effects have expressed themselves in history may depend less exclusively on personality than on a combination of personality differences, familial sentiments, patterns of identification, and consequent differences in motivation, perhaps reinforced by birth-order stereotypes (Plowman, 2005).

One other group of findings is relevant to this discussion about theories and methods in birth-order research. When studies of birth order are collectively examined for the moderating effects of the testing context, several noteworthy trends emerge. First, extrafamilial studies consistently yield smaller and less consistent birth-order effects than do within-family studies. In particular, self-report personality tests conducted without direct sibling comparisons yield the smallest birth-order effects, although these effects are sometimes statistically significant—if not particularly impressive—in samples that are large enough to have adequate statistical power to measure correlations in the range of 0.10 and smaller. Among extrafamilial studies, however, it is notable that experimental designs, which often try to emulate real-life behaviour, exhibit larger and more consistent effect sizes than do self-report personality tests. Finally, studies that involve emotionality and controversy, such as participating in a political protest, also tend to involve larger effect sizes than do studies that use paper-and-pencil methods (Sulloway 2001, 2002). Collectively, these meta-analytic patterns, together with other evidence reviewed here, suggest that birth-order effects—although latent in much of adult behaviour outside the family of origin—are sometimes strongly elicited by situations that involve heightened emotions, controversy, or direct links with familial sentiments. Additional research is needed to answer some of the intriguing questions raised by such methodological trends in birth-order research.

To the extent that the influence of birth order in adult life may turn out to be substantially a matter of person-by-situation interaction effects rather than fixed personality attributes acquired in childhood, then standard psychological tests may often miss these effects. The dilemma facing behavioural scientists is heightened by considerations of statistical power. Given that birth-order effects obtained in within-family assessments typically amount to effect sizes of $r < 0.20$, and given that effects in extrafamilial behaviour are likely to be smaller than these ($r < 0.10$), experimental approaches face the following statistical reality. For an experimenter to be 80% confident of obtaining an expected effect size of $r = 0.10$, the sample size needs to be at least 783 subjects. Expressed another way, experimental designs encompassing only 200 subjects (a reasonably large sample by most experimental standards) risk obtaining a misleading null outcome for such expected effects at least 71% of the time (Cohen, 1988). From a literature exhibiting such a high proportion of null results, most researchers would incorrectly conclude that there was nothing of interest to pursue. Perhaps the use of Internet samples in combination with experimental designs will help to overcome these basic issues of statistical power and thereby shed more light on one of the pressing questions of human psychology, namely, the diverse and so far largely elusive sources of the non-shared environment.

21.10. The overall influence of the family: an evolutionary perspective

One should bear in mind that the influence of birth order is only one component of the overall influence that the family system exerts on children as they are growing up. Although it has become fashionable in the light of recent behavioural genetic studies to minimize the influence that parents and the family have on offspring, researchers are at a considerable disadvantage in assessing all of the varied psychological influences that actually operate within the family. In most behavioural genetic studies, the non-shared environment is not directly measured but is simply what remains statistically unexplained by the effects of genetics and the shared environment (see, however, Reiss et al., 2000). The study of birth order—however modest its effects may seem—provides a useful example of the operation of one systematic within-family dynamic among many. Until behavioural scientists develop new and better methods by which to capture the endless succession of unique and largely non-systematic interactions that characterize the family environment, we can have only a rudimentary idea about how much of the non-shared environment actually resides within the family, as opposed to outside it (Turkheimer and Waldron, 2000; McGuire, 2001; Plomin *et al.*, 2001; Turkheimer, 2004). Based on the amount of time that most family members spend with one another prior to adulthood, the family's total influence—through both shared and non-shared environments—may well amount to 15–20% of the overall variance in personality. An effect of this magnitude would be equivalent to a drug that quadruples one's likelihood of surviving a deadly disease (and hence that quadruples one's likelihood of displaying, or not displaying, a particular personality attribute owing to within-family influences). In the domain of values and social identifications, the influence of the family appears to be even greater (Dunn and Plomin, 1990).

To evolutionary psychologists, as well as to social psychologists, it will come as no surprise that the importance of experiences acquired in early life, and through interactions with other family members, may only be manifested conditionally in interactions occurring later in adulthood—especially with non-family members. Personality substantially reflects adaptation to peer groups, teachers, and other sources of extrafamilial experience. An adaptationist perspective on human behaviour expects just such forms of continuing, context-dependent learning and behaviour. Even blue-footed boobies do not engage in siblicidal aggression unless they are significantly undernourished. Similarly, adult human beings do not generally act towards acquaintances and strangers in the same intimate ways as they do toward siblings and other family members. In adulthood, people appear to carry with them a Darwinian toolkit of learned strategies—some dating from childhood, others acquired subsequently as a result of extrafamilial experiences. We appear to draw as needed on this behavioural toolkit, but only when the tool matches the situation.

Despite many unresolved questions about human development and the role of birth order in this process, one general conclusion has become increasingly certain: the sources of human personality and behaviour, and the story of their expression in the course of development, are much more complex than most of us previously thought. In this revised and multifaceted view of human development there nevertheless appear to be significant and lasting explanatory roles for birth order, sibling competition, and family dynamics more generally.

Acknowledgments

For critical comments on this manuscript I thank Louise Barrett, Ralph Hertwig, Iver Mysterud, Carolyn Phinney, Ian Plowman, Percy Rohde, Catherine Salmon, Eric Turkheimer, and Richard L. Zweigenhaft.

References

Baskett, L. M. (1985) Sibling status: adult expectations. *Developmental Psychology*, 21: 441–445.

Blanchard, R. (2004) Quantitative and theoretical analyses of the relation between older brothers and homosexuality in men. *Journal of Theoretical Biology*, 230: 173–187.

Boone, J. L. (1986) Parental investment and elite family structure in preindustrial states: a case study of late medieval-early modern Portuguese genealogies. *American Anthropologist*, 88: 859–878.

Cervone, D. and Shoda, Y. (1999) *The Coherence of Personality: social–Cognitive Bases of Consistency, Variability, and Organization*. Guilford Press, New York.

Clark, R. D. and Rice, G. A. (1982) Family constellations and eminence: the birth orders of Nobel Prize winners. *The Journal of Psychology*, 110: 281–287.

Cohen, J. (1988) *Statistical Power Analysis for the Behavioral Sciences*, 2nd edn. Lawrence Erlbaum, Hillsdale, NJ.

Costa, P. T., Jr and McCrae, R. R. (1992) *NEO PI-R Professional Manual*. Psychological Assessment Resources, Odessa, Florida.

Daly, M. and Wilson, M. (1988) *Homicide*. Aldine de Gruyter, New York.

Darwin, C. R. (1859) *On the Origin of Species by Means of Natural Selection*. John Murray, London.

Drummond, H. and García-Chavelas, C. (1989) Food shortage influences sibling aggression in the blue-footed booby. *Animal Behavior*, 37: 806–818.

Dunn, J. and Plomin, R. (1990) *Separate Lives: why Siblings Are So Different*. Basic Books, New York.

Ernst, C. and Angst, J. (1983) *Birth Order: its Influence on Personality*. Springer-Verlag, Berlin and New York.

Feingold, A. (1994) Gender differences in personality: a meta-analysis. *Psychological Bulletin*, 116: 429–456.

Freese, J., Powell, B. and Steelman, L. C. (1999) Rebel without a cause or effect: birth order and social attitudes. *American Sociological Review*, 64: 207–231.

Hamilton, W. (1964a) The genetical evolution of social behavior. I. *Journal of Theoretical Biology*, 7: 1–16.

Hamilton, W. (1964b) The genetical evolution of social behavior. II. *Journal of Theoretical Biology*, 7: 17–32.

Harris, J. R. (1998) *The Nurture Assumption: why Children Turn Out the Way They Do*. Free Press, New York.

Herlihy, D. (1977) Family and property in Renaissance Florence. In D. Herlihy and A. L. Udovitch (eds) *The Medieval City*, pp. 3–24. Yale University Press, New Haven.

Herrera, N., Zajonc, R. B., Wieczorkowska, G. and Cichomski, B. (2003) Beliefs about birth rank and their reflections in reality. *Journal of Personality and Social Psychology*, 85: 142–150.

Hertwig, R., Davis, J. and Sulloway, F. J. (2002) Parental investment: how an equity motive can produce inequality. *Psychological Bulletin*, 128: 728–745.

Horton, S. (1988) Birth order and child nutritional status: evidence from the Philippines. *Economic Development and Cultural Change*, 36: 341–354.

Hrdy, S. B. and Judge, D. (1992) Darwin and the puzzle of primogeniture. *Human Nature*, 4: 1–45.

Hyde, J. S. (2005) The gender similarities hypothesis. *American Psychologist*, 60: 581–592.

Jefferson, T., Jr, Herbst, J. H. and McCrae, R. R. (1998) Associations between birth order and personality traits: evidence from self-reports and observer ratings. *Journal of Research on Personality*, 32: 498–508.

Kidwell, J. S. (1982) The neglected birth order: middleborns. *Journal of Marriage and the Family*, 44: 225–235.

Koch, H. (1955) Some personality correlates of sex, sibling position, and sex of sibling among five- and six-year-old children. *Genetic Psychology Monographs*, 52: 3–50.

Koch, H. (1956) Attitudes of young children toward their peers as related to certain characteristics of their siblings. *Psychological Monographs*, 70: 1–41.

Krishnamurthy, K. S., Uma Shaanker, R. and Ganeshaiah, K. N. (1997) Seed abortion in an animal dispersed species, *Syzygium cuminii* (L.) Skeels (Myrtaceae): the chemical basis. *Current Science*, 73: 869–873.

Kuhn, T. (1970) *The Structure of Scientific Revolutions*, 2nd edn. University of Chicago Press, Chicago.

Lewis, S. A. and Britton, J. R. (1998) Measles infection, measles vaccination and the effect of birth order on the aetiology of hay fever. *Clinical and Experimental Allergy*, 28: 1493–1500.

Lindert, P. H. (1977) Sibling position and achievement. *The Journal of Human Resources*, 12: 198–219.

Loehlin, J. C. (1992) *Genes and Environment in Personality Development*. Sage Publications, Newbury Park, CA.

MacAndrew, F. T., King, J. C. and Honoroff, L. R. (2002) A sociobiological analysis of namesaking patterns in 322 American families. *Journal of Applied Social Psychology*, 32: 851–864.

McGuire, S. (2001) Nonshared environment research: what is it and where is it going? *Marriage & Family Review*, 33: 31–56.

Mock, D. W. (2004) *More Than Kin and Less Than Kind: the Evolution of Family Conflict*. Harvard University Press, Cambridge, MA.

Mock, D. W. and Parker, G. A. (1997) *The Evolution of Sibling Rivalry*. Oxford University Press, Oxford and New York.

Mock, D. W., Drummond, H. and Stinson, C. H. (1990) Avian siblicide. *American Scientist*, 78: 438–449.

Modin, B. (2002) Birth order and mortality: a life-long follow-up of 14,200 boys and girls born in early 20th century Sweden. *Social Science & Medicine*, 54: 1051–1064.

Musun-Miller, L. (1993) Sibling status effects: parents' perceptions of their own children. *Journal of Genetic Psychology*, 154: 189–198.

Nisbett, R. E. (1968) Birth order and participation in dangerous sports. *Journal of Personality and Social Psychology*, 8: 351–353.

Numbers, R. L. (1998) *Darwinism Comes to America*, pp. 44–46. Harvard University Press, Cambridge.

Nyman, L. (1995) The identification of birth order personality attributes. *Journal of Psychology*, 129: 51–59.

Parker, W. D. (1998) Birth order effects in the academically talented. *Gifted Child Quarterly*, 42: 29–36.

Paulhus, D. L., Trapnell, P. D. and Chen, D. (1999) Birth order and personality within families. *Psychological Science*, 10: 482–488.

Pinker, S. (2002) *The Blank Slate: the Modern Denial of Human Nature*. Viking, New York.

Plomin, R. and Daniels, D. (1987) Why are children in the same family so different from one another? *Behavioral and Brain Sciences*, 10: 1–60.

Plomin, R., Asbury, K. and Dunn, J. (2001) Why are children in the same family so different? Nonshared environment a decade later. *Canadian Journal of Psychiatry*, 46: 225–233.

Plowman, I. C. (2005) Birth-order, motives, occupational role choice and organizational innovation: an evolutionary perspective. PhD dissertation, University of Queensland.

Reiss, D., Neiderhiser, J., Hetherington, E. M. and Plomin, R. (2000) *The Relationship Code: Deciphering Genetic and Social Patterns in Adolescent Development*. Harvard University Press, Cambridge, MA.

Rohde, P. A., Atzwanger, K., Butovskaya, M., Lampert, A., Mysterud, I., Sanchez-Andres, A. and Sulloway, F. J. (2003) Perceived parental favoritism, closeness to kin, and the rebel of the family: the effects of birth order and sex. *Evolution and Human Behavior*, 24: 261–276.

Rosenblatt, P. C. and Skoogberg, E. L. (1974) Birth order in cross-cultural perspective. *Developmental Psychology*, 10: 48–54.

Rosenthal, R. and Rosnow, R. (1991) *Essentials of Behavioral Research: methods and Data Analysis*. 2nd edn. McGraw-Hill, New York.

Rowe, D. C. (1994) *The limits of family influence: genes, experience, and behavior*. Guilford Press, New York.

Salmon, C. A. (1998) The evocative nature of kin terminology in political rhetoric. *Politics and the Life Sciences*, 17: 51–57.

Salmon, C. A. and Daly, M. (1998) Birth order and familial sentiment: middleborns are different. *Human Behavior and Evolution*, 19: 299–312.

Saudino, K. J. (1997) Moving beyond the heritability question: new directions in behavioral genetic studies of personality. *Current Directions in Psychological Science*, 6: 86–90.

Schachter, F. F. (1982) Sibling deidentification and split-parent identifications: a family tetrad. In M. E. Lamb and B. Sutton-Smith (eds) *Sibling Relationships: Their Nature and Significance Across the Lifespan*, pp. 123–52. Lawrence Erlbaum, Hillsdale, NJ.

Schachter, F. F., Gilutz, G., Shore, E. and Adler, M. (1978) Sibling deidentification judged by mothers: cross-validation and developmental studies. *Child Development*, 49: 543–546.

Schwabl, H. (1996) Environment modifies the testosterone levels of a female bird and its eggs. *Journal of Experimental Zoology*, 276: 157–163.

Schwabl, H., Mock, D. W. and Gieg, J. A. (1997) A hormonal mechanism for parental favouritism. *Nature*, 386: 231.

Skinner, G. W. (1992) Seek a loyal subject in a filial son: family roots of political orientation in Chinese society. In *Family Process and Political Process in Modern Chinese History*, pp. 943–993. Chiang Ching-kuo Foundation for International Scholarly Exchange, Taipei, Republic of China.

Sulloway, F. J. (1995) Birth order and evolutionary psychology: a meta-analytic overview. *Psychological Inquiry*, 6: 75–80.

Sulloway, F. J. (1996) *Born to Rebel: Birth Order, Family Dynamics, and Creative Lives*. Pantheon, New York.

Sulloway, F. J. (2000) *Born to rebel* and its critics. *Politics and the Life Sciences*, 19: 181–202.

Sulloway, F. J. (2001) Birth order, sibling competition, and human behavior. In H. R. Holcomb III (ed.) *Conceptual Challenges in Evolutionary Psychology: Innovative Research Strategies*, pp. 39–83. Kluwer, Dordrecht and Boston.

Sulloway, F. J. (2002) Technical report on a vote-counting meta-analysis of the birth-order literature (1940–1999). Available at: http://www.sulloway.org/metaanalysis.html.

Sulloway, F. J., Starks, P. T.B. and Shermer, M. B. *The Adaptive Significance of Religion: A Mutualistic Relationship Between Memes and Genes*.

Trivers, R. L. (1974) Parent–offspring conflict. *American Zoologist*, 14: 249–264.

Trivers, R. L. (1985) *Social Evolution*. Benjamin/Cummings, Menlo Park, CA.

Turkheimer, E. (2004) Spinach and ice cream: why social science is so difficult. In L. F. DiLalla (ed.) *Behavior Genetics Principles: perspectives in Development, Personality, and Psychopathology*, pp. 161–89. American Psychological Association, Washington, D. C.

Turkheimer, E. and Waldron, M. (2000) Nonshared environment: a theoretical, methodological, and quantitative review. *Psychological Bulletin*, 126: 78–108.

Voland, E. (1988) Differential infant and child mortality in evolutionary perspective: data from the late 17th to 19th century Ostfriesland (Germany). In L. Betzig, M. Borgerhoff Mulder and P. Turke (eds) *Human Reproduction Behaviour: a Darwinian Perspective*, pp. 253–262. Cambridge University Press, Cambridge.

Voland, E. (1990) Differential reproductive success within the Krummhorn population (Germany, 18th and 19th centuries). *Behavioral Ecology and Sociobiology*, 26: 54–72.

Wichman, A. L., Rodgers, J. L. and MacCallum, R. C. (2006) A multilevel approach to the relationship between birth order and intelligence. *Personality and Social Psychology Bulletin*, 32: 117–27.

Zajonc, R. B. (1976) Family configuration and intelligence. *Science*, 192: 227–236.

Zajonc, R. B. and Mullally, P. R. (1997) Birth order: reconciling conflicting effects. *American Psychologist*, 52: 685–699.

Zweigenhaft, R. L. and Von Ammon, J. (2000) Birth order and civil disobedience: a test of Sulloway's "Born to Rebel" hypothesis. *Journal of Social Psychology*, 140: 624–627.

SECTION V
Mating, reproduction and life history

The study of mate preferences and reproductive decision-making are the areas that have, perhaps inevitably, seen the greatest concentration of studies in human evolutionary psychology hitherto. Evolution is all about reproduction, so the means by which individuals select their mates, and the investment decisions they make with respect to offspring, are the obvious evolutionary questions to ask when considering humans in this light.

The first wave of studies in this area established that, like many other animal species, human females' reproductive success rests on access to resources while that of males depends more on access to mates, and that perceptions of attractiveness and mate preferences are consistent with such findings. With time, however, it has become apparent that the picture is much more complex and culturally driven than we suppose. Campbell's consideration of sex differences in aggression is a case in point: sex differences are apparent, but this doesn't translate into a simple dichotomy of aggressive males and peaceful females. The sexes differ both in the amount and kind of aggression they use, so that, while these can be tied to reproductive strategies, doing so requires a more nuanced interpretation, and a consideration of many different levels of explanation. The qualitative differences in aggression are more interesting, and more evolutionarily relevant, than the well-established quantitative difference that has tended to be the

focus of research to date. This is not to say that these strategic sex differences do not exist, but rather to point out, as Voland does, that it is the way these strategic predispositions are fined-tuned to circumstance that makes human behaviour both particularly complex and particularly interesting from an evolutionary perspective.

One thing that makes humans particularly intriguing animals to study is their peculiar life history. This has major implications for the kinds of evolutionary predictions one will make, as Lummaa illustrates. The complete helplessness of human infants means that females require assistance in the raising of offspring, and that males may have been selected to invest more in offspring and less in mating opportunities than is often assumed. The role of kin, particularly grandmothers, in raising offspring successfully is also becoming increasingly prominent, with implications for human life-history evolution. Moreover, as Mace notes, the idea that maximizing the number of surviving offspring is the key to high fitness is also less secure for humans than for other species, due to resource transfers that can occur after the death of parents, and because factors promoting lineage survival in the long term may not be those that promote high reproductive output in the short term. However, we currently know very little about the psychological motivations that underlie reproductive decision-making. While Mace, Voland and Winterhalder all consider the kinds of psychological mechanisms that underlie peoples' reproductive decision-making, and come up with some fascinating suggestions that show clear links to work on cultural evolution, it is also clear that more empirical work is sorely needed.

Mate preferences may also be more complex than originally assumed. Gangestad as well as Rhodes and Simmons provide critical reviews of the corpus of research on mate choice preferences, illustrating the methodological rigour that such studies require, as well as highlighting the need for more detailed, multi-dimensional studies of mate preferences, which would allow the potential synergies between different cues and signals of mate quality to emerge. The pressing need to tie mate preferences to real-life mating decisions is another area where further empirical data would be valuable. Despite the plethora of publications, it is apparent that there is still a lot of mileage in the study of human mate choice, especially given that, as Wedekind indicates, we may have neglected the role played by other sensory modalities.

CHAPTER 22

Body odours and body odour preferences in humans

Claus Wedekind

22.1. Introduction

Most mammals display an enormous interest in olfactory cues of their fellows, while our general reaction to natural body odours is that they are unpleasant and distasteful, and, if we can, we usually put much effort into removing them. Not only do we regularly wash the fatty, scented secretions from our skin and clothes, but many of us routinely shave off the tufts of hair that support bacterial action to produce smells in the most scented regions. Today, modern human communication seems to be based on acoustic, visual and tactile cues, not so much on chemical cues, and the consensus of the current literature suggests that humans do not have a working vomeronal organ of the type found in other mammals (Wysocki and Preti, 2000). But then again, humans have a well developed olfactory system (Wysocki and Preti, 2000) and humans in most cultures use perfumes. They often spend fortunes on them, supporting a billion dollar industry (Van Toller and Dodd, 1991; Ohloff, 1992). Humans have batteries of their own scent-producing glands. We seem to have even more scent glands upon our body than any other ape (Stoddart, 1990), but after we have tried to get rid of our own chemical signals, we use sex attractants of deer, civets and beavers. And even the finest and most expensive perfumes contain notes of a urinary nature which may unconsciously stir our ancient memory of sex attractant pheromones expelled in urine (Van Toller and Dodd, 1991; Ohloff, 1992). We obviously are interested in chemical signals and use them in social contexts. Nevertheless, if we speak about good and bad odours, natural human body odours are in general classified as bad odours, with few context-specific exceptions. Why may that be?

Body odours seem to reveal different kinds of information about us, and we typically behave as if we do not want to give this information away. In the following, I will briefly summarize the kind of information that may be revealed in odours. I will then concentrate on the link between the MHC (major histocompatibility complex, a group of genes) and odours and odour preferences.

22.2. The source of human odours

Even if we were not endowed with scent-producing glands, it seems obvious that a living organism of the size of humans cannot avoid producing some smells. Our metabolism inevitably produces volatile chemicals that may be difficult to hide completely. Therefore, it may not be surprising that our body odours reveal some information about our metabolism, for example about the food we ate (e.g. garlic), what we drank (e.g. alcohol), about some metabolic problems or changes (e.g. stress), and possibly about some of the infectious diseases we carry (Penn and Potts, 1998b).

For many centuries, bad odours were believed to come along with diseases. Malaria, for example, means 'bad air' (Italian: *mal-araia*). Indeed, some diseases come along with changed body odours. Infected mice (Kavaliers and Colwell, 1995) as well as some human disease (Penn and Potts, 1998b) are perceived as such by their odour. However, the kind of knowledge that is used in odour-based diagnosis and treatment seems to be based on traditions, personal experience and intuition rather than on scientific findings. The reason for this lack of scientific knowledge seems obvious: odours are short-lived and difficult to store, hard to describe, and often very difficult to measure in greater detail. Moreover, the connection between body odours and physiology is often a complex one (Penn and Potts, 1998a).

Many odours may be by-products of our general metabolism, but some body odours appear to be produced with a more specific purpose (recent reviews in Hays, 2003; Grammer *et al.*, 2005; McClintock *et al.*, 2005). They seem to have some signalling functions, and they are produced in special glands. Apart from sweat glands, the human skin is endowed with two other types of glands, the sebaceous gland that occurs all over the body and secretes an oily liquid, and apocrine glands that are densest in the armpits and the pubic region (but occur on other parts as well) and secrete a watery fluid. A striking characteristic of sebaceous and apocrine glands is that they become active with puberty and secret only little before (Montagna and Parakkal, 1974). This, and the aggregation of apocrine glands into discrete organs, some of which are close to the sexual organs and provided with springy hair as odour diffusers, already points to their having a function related to sex. The fact that, in humans, the axillary

region appears to be more important as an odour source than the genital region has often been explained as a consequence of bipedalism (Morris, 1967). However, genital odours do not seem to be without importance, as Doty *et al.* (1975) found changes in the intensity and pleasantness of human vaginal odours during the menstrual cycle.

The chemical composition of sebum, the oily product of sebaceous glands, contains many odorous free fatty acids that may contribute largely to our distinctive olfactory signature (Nicolaides, 1974; Singer *et al.*, 1997). However, it is the apocrine glands, especially in the axillae, that may be responsible for most of a healthy adult's body odour. Axillary odours contain a number of often musky-smelling steroids that are produced by microorganisms in hair follicles and on hair. Therefore, shaving the armpits or treatment of the axillary region with antibiotics results in a temporal reduction of axillary odours.

22.3. Odours and sex

There are a huge number of papers on odours and sexual reproduction in animals. Odours are, for example, of primary importance in the sexual life of mice and rats, and certainly not without importance for primate sexual behavior (Keverne, 1983). Compared to the literature on animals, little has been published in the scientific literature on the role of odours in human courtship. Odours are important components of our emotional life, and although the role of odours in human mate choice and sexual behaviour is not as well studied as it is, for example, in rodents, it is clear that such a connection exists and that it may be a complex one. Obviously, the perfume industry would not be that big if there were no connection between odours and sex in our species (Ohloff, 1992). Moreover, women's sensitivity to a range of odours is influenced by their menstrual cycle. Their sensitivity peaks around ovulation (Doty *et al.*, 1981), as does their preference for the scent of symmetrical men (Gangestad and Thornhill, 1998; Rikowski and Grammer, 1999).

Much of the muskiness from human axilla appears to be caused by androstenol, 5α-androstenone, and other steroids (Gower, 1988). Some of them have been shown to be potent pheromones in the sexual biology of other animals (Melrode *et al.*, 1971). They are likely to be one of the main sexual odours in humans, although their attractive force is quite unlike the one observed, for example, in dogs. As Stoddart (1990) puts it nicely: " 'The flower of youth' [the axillary organ] clearly has a fickle odour. As a 'spice box' it has moved poets and writers to plumb the depths of the psyche, but when its odours turn rank and sour it seems no flower." In the unwashed axilla, caprylic and acroic acids are produced that give the armpit its often goaty odour (Stoddart, 1990).

22.4. Odours in other social contexts

Odours seem to play a role in families and in mother–offspring interaction. Babies can recognize their mothers' odours (Chernoch and Porter, 1985), and mothers can correctly recognize their own babies by odour (Porter *et al.*, 1983). This ability could also be shown for fathers, grandmothers and aunts (Porter *et al.*, 1986). However, such kin recognition through odours does not appear to allow for a kind of paternity analysis. Body odours that reveal genetic differences may be produced only later in life.

In rodents, pheromones from adult males can bring forward the onset of sexual maturation, while pheromones of adult females tend in the opposite direction (Vandenbergh, 1983). An analogous effect has been suggested for humans (Burger and Gochfeld, 1985), but strong support for this hypothesis is not available. Also, there is no experimental support for the possibility that some spontaneous terminations of pregnancy in humans are odour-induced, as could be demonstrated in rodents (Yamazaki *et al.*, 1983). In contrast, the observation in rodents that odours and non-volatile pheromones can result in a modification to the oestrous cycle could be confirmed in experiments on humans (McClintock, 1971; Stern and McClintock, 1998).

22.5. Odours and the MHC

A large body of work suggests that a group of genes within the MHC (major histocompatibility complex) is important in the link between

odours and mate preferences in several vertebrates, including humans (reviews in Penn and Potts, 1998a; Penn and Potts, 1999). MHC genes play a central role in controlling immunological self- and non-self recognition. The MHC is also one of the most polymorphic regions of the genome. This extraordinary diversity is thought to be maintained by pathogen interactions (Apanius *et al.*, 1997).

Human noses can distinguish between two congenic inbred mouse strains that differ only in their MHC (Gilbert *et al.*, 1986), and rodents seem to be able to recognize human MHC types (Ferstl *et al.*, 1992). Wedekind *et al.* (1995) found that women's preferences for male odours correlated with the degree of similarity of their own and the men's MHC type. T-shirt odours were judged as more pleasant when they were worn by men whose MHC genotype was different from that of the judging woman. This finding is analogous to findings in mice (Yamazaki *et al.*, 1976; Penn and Potts, 1999; Roberts and Gosling, 2003). The difference in odour assessment was reversed when the women were taking oral contraceptives [studies by Thorne *et al.* (2002) revealed further effects of oral contraceptives on odour perception]. Furthermore, the odours of MHC-dissimilar men were more frequently reminding the women of their own present or former partners than did the odours of MHC-similar men. These memory associations suggested that the MHC or linked genes influence human mate choice. Later experiments (Wedekind and Füri, 1997; Thornhill *et al.*, 2003; Santos *et al.*, 2005) with new combinations of T-shirt wearer and smellers provided further support of a link between MHC and body odours (but see Wedekind, 2002). When men and women sniffed at male and female odours, there was no significant effect of gender in the correlation between pleasantness and MHC similarity (Wedekind and Füri, 1997).

Other research groups provided further support for a link between MHC, odours, and the nose. Carol Ober and her colleagues at the University of Chicago found in a large study on American Hutterites that married couples were less likely to share MHC loci than expected by chance, even after incest taboos were statistically controlled for (Ober *et al.*, 1997). And from a completely different angle: Ehlers *et al.* (2000) and Younger *et al.* (2001) found a gene cluster that contains 36 olfactory receptor genes (OR), of which two belong to the vomeronasal family. This cluster is located at the telomeric end of the MHC complex. It is the largest sequenced olfactory receptor gene cluster in any organism so far. Thirteen of these genes were tested and found to be polymorphic. Although the physiology of MHC-correlated body odours and odour preferences is not at all clear yet (Penn and Potts, 1998a), this polymorphism, and the proximity of such a cluster of olfactory receptor genes to the MHC, suggests that these OR genes could somehow be involved in MHC-related odour preferences.

Not only the physiology, but also the functional, i.e. evolutionary, significance of MHC-correlated body odours and odour preferences is not yet clear. Three non-mutually exclusive hypotheses have been proposed (review in Penn and Potts, 1999). First, MHC-correlated mate preference may have evolved because certain MHC combinations or simply heterozygosity confer a strong advantage to resist pathogens, e.g. by providing a larger range of pathogen epitopes that can be signalled to T-lymphocytes. Second, MHC-correlated mate preference may enable hosts to provide a 'moving target' against rapidly evolving parasites that escape immune recognition. Third, MHC-correlated mate preferences may be a sophisticated mechanism to avoid inbreeding. In the latter case, MHC genes would only serve as markers of the degree of relatedness between two individuals.

In his famous book *Perfume. The Story of a Murderer*, Patrick Süskind (1986) is probably wrong in the assumption that there is a perfect body odour, or the perfect composition of odours. Humans do have highly individualistic body odours that are readily detectable by most people, but preferences for body odours vary enormously, too. In general, 'good' body odours tend to be weak, as ratings of intensity correlate negatively with ratings of pleasantness in our studies (Wedekind *et al.*, 1995; Wedekind and Füri, 1997). Apart from this, the pleasantness score of six different body odours that were presented to 121 male and female smellers each ranged from very unpleasant to very pleasant (Wedekind and Füri, 1997). It seems as if everybody smells nice to someone else, provided that the odour is not too intense. In our laboratory study where we could control for many confounding variables, we could explain up to 23% of the variance in pleasantness by the degree of similarity on the MHC between T-shirt wearer and smeller (Wedekind and Füri, 1997).

All this leads to a hypothesis that could potentially explain another evolutionary puzzle, namely, that there is a great inter-individual variability in preference for fragrances. Milinski and Wedekind (2001) tested whether individual preferences for perfume ingredients correlate with a person's MHC-genotype. A total of 137 male and female students who had been typed for a part of their MHC scored 36 scents in a first test for use on self ('Would you like to smell like that yourself?') and a subset of 18 scents 2 years later either for use on self or for a potential partner ('Would you like your partner to smell like that?'). Overall, MHC genotype and ratings of the scents 'for partner' did not seem to correlate. However, there was a statistically significant correlation between the MHC and the scorings of the scents 'for self' in both tests. In a detailed analysis, presence or absence of the two most common MHC alleles (HLA-A2 and HLA-A1) appeared to correlate best with the rating of the scents in both tests when evaluated for self. This result suggests that persons who share one of these alleles have a similar preference for any of the perfume ingredients. It should be stressed, however, that this effect is weak, i.e. it is probably only detectable with a large sample size. Also, there are obvious further facets of the psychology of fragrance selection besides MHC-correlated odour preferences (Van Toller and Dodd, 1991; Ohloff, 1992).

Acknowledgments

I am supported by a Sarah and Daniel Hrdy Visiting Fellowship and by the Swiss National Science Foundation.

References

Apanius, V., Penn, D., Slev, P. R., Ruff, L. R. and Potts, W. K. (1997) The nature of selection on the major histocompatibility complex. *Critical Reviews in Immunology*, 17: 179–224.

Burger, J. and Gochfield, M. (1985) A hypothesis on the role of pheromones on age of menarche. *Medical Hypotheses*, 17: 39–46.

Chernoch, J. M. and Porter, R. H. (1985) Recognition of maternal axillary odours by infants. *Child Development*, 56: 1593–1598.

Doty, R. L., Ford, M., Preti, G. and Huggins, G. (1975) Human vaginal odours change in pleasantness and intensity during the menstrual cycle. *Science*, 190: 45–60.

Doty, R. L., Snyder, P. J., Huggins, G. R. and Lowry, L. D. (1981) Endocrine, cardiovascular, and psychological correlates of olfactory sensitivity changes during the human menstrual cycle. *Journal of Comparative Physiology and Psychology*, 95: 45–60.

Ehlers, A., Beck, S., Forbes, S. A. *et al.* (2000) MHC-linked olfactory receptor loci exhibit polymorphism and contribute to extended HLA/OR-haplotypes. *Genome Research*, 10: 1968–1978.

Ferstl, R., Eggert, F., Westphal, E., Zavazava, N. and Müller-Ruchholtz, W. (1992) MHC-related odours in human. In R. L. Doty (ed.) *Chemical Signals in Vertebrates VI*, pp. 205–211. Plenum Press, New York.

Gangestad, S. W. and Thornhill, R. (1998) Menstrual cycle variation in women's preference for the scent of symmetrical men. *Proceedings of the Royal Society of London, B*, 265: 927–933.

Gilbert, A. N., Yamazaki, K., Beauchamp, G. K. and Thomas, L. (1986) Olfactory discrimination of mouse strains (*Mus musculus*) and major histocompatibility types by humans (*Homo sapiens*). *Journal of Comparative Psychology*, 100: 262–265.

Gower, D. B. (1988) The significance of odourous steroids in axillary odour. In S. Van Toller and G. H. Dodd (eds) *Perfumery, the Psychology and Biology of Fragrance*, pp. 47–76. Chapman & Hall, London.

Grammer, K., Fink, B. and Neave, N. (2005) Human pheromones and sexual attraction. *Eur. J. Obstetrics, Gynecology and Reproductive Biology*, 118: 135–142.

Hays, W. S. T. (2003) Human pheromones: have they been demonstrated? *Behavioural and Ecological Sociobiology*, 54: 89–97.

Kavaliers, M. and Colwell, D. D. (1995) Discrimination by female mice between the odours of parasitized and non-parasitized males. *Proceedings of the Royal Society of London, B*, 261: 31–35.

Keverne, E. B. (1983) Chemical communication in primate reproduction. In J. G. Vandenbergh (ed.) *Pheromones and Reproduction in Mammals*, pp. 79–92. Academic Press, New York.

McClintock, M. K. (1971) Menstrual synchrony and suppression. *Nature*, 229: 224–245.

McClintock, M. K., Bullivant, S., Jacob, S. *et al.* (2005) Human body scents: conscious perceptions and biological effects. *Chemical Senses*, 30: 1135–1137.

Melrode, D. R., Reed, H. C. B. and Patterson, R. L. S. (1971) Androgen steroids associated with boar odour as an aid to the defection of oestrus in pig artificial insemination. *British Veterinary Journal*, 127: 497–501.

Milinski, M. and Wedekind, C. (2001) Evidence for MHC-correlated perfume preferences in humans. *Behavioural Ecology*, 12: 140–149.

Montagna, W. and Parakkal, P. F. (1974) *The Structure and Function of Skin*. Academic Press, New York.

Morris, D. (1967) *The Naked Ape*. Jonathan Cape, London.

Nicolaides, N. (1974) Skin lipids: their biochemical uniqueness. *Science*, 186: 19–26.

Ober, C., Weitkamp, L. R., Cox, N., Dytch, H., Kostyu, D. *et al.* (1997) HLA and mate choice in humans. *American Journal of Human Genetics*, 61: 497–504.

Ohloff, G. (1992) *Irdische Düfte, himmlische Lust. Eine Kulturgeschichte der Duftstoffe*. Birkhäuser, Basel.

Penn, D. and Potts, W. (1998a) How do major histocompatibility complex genes influence odour and mating preferences? *Advances Immunology*, 69: 411–436.

Penn, D. and Potts, W. K. (1998b) Chemical signals and parasite-mediated sexual selection. *Trends in Ecology and Evolution*, 13: 391–396.

Penn, D. J. and Potts, W. K. (1999) The evolution of mating preferences and major histocompatibility complex genes. *American Naturalist*, 153: 145–164.

Porter, R. H., Chernoch, J. M. and McLaughlin, F. J. (1983) Maternal recognition of neonates through olfactory cues. *Physiology and Behaviour*, 30: 151–154.

Porter, R. H., Balogh, R. D., Chernoch, J. M. and Franchi, C. (1986) Recognition of kin through characteristics body odours. *Chemical Senses*, 11: 389–395.

Rikowski, A. and Grammer, K. (1999) Human body odour, symmetry and attractiveness. *Proceedings of the Royal Society of London, B*, 266: 869–874.

Roberts, S. C. and Gosling, L. M. (2003) Genetic similarity and quality interact in mate choice decisions by female mice. *Nature Genetics*, 35: 103–106.

Santos, P. S. C., Schinemann, J. A., Gabardo, J. and Bicalho, M. D. (2005) New evidence that the MHC influences odour perception in humans: a study with 58 Southern Brazilian students. *Hormones and Behaviour*, 47: 384–388.

Singer, A. G., Beauchamp, G. K. and Yamazaki, K. (1997) Volatile signals of the major histocompatibility complex in male mouse urine. *Proceedings of the National Academy of Sciences of the USA*, 94: 2210–2214.

Stern, K. and McClintock, M. K. (1998) Regulation of ovulation by human pheromones. *Nature*, 392: 177–179.

Stoddart, D. M. (1990) *The Scented Ape. The Biology and Culture of Human Odour*. Cambridge University Press, Cambridge.

Süskind, P. (1986) *Perfume. The Story of a Murderer*. Hamish Hamilton, London.

Thorne, F., Neave, N., Scholey, A., Moss, M. and Fink, B. (2002) Effects of putative male pheromones on female ratings of male attractiveness: Influence of oral contraceptives and the menstrual cycle. *Neuroendocrinology Letters*, 23: 291–297.

Thornhill, R., Gangestad, S. W., Miller, R. *et al.* (2003) Major histocompatibility complex genes, symmetry, and body scent attractiveness in men and women. *Behavioural Ecology*, 14: 668–678.

Van Toller, S. and Dodd G. H. (eds) (1991) *Perfumery: The Psychology and Biology of Fragrance*. Chapman & Hall, London.

Vandenbergh, J. G. (1983) Pheromonal regulation of puberty. In J. G. Vandenbergh (ed.) *Pheromones and Reproduction in Mammals*, pp. 95–112. Academic Press, New York.

Wedekind, C. (2002) The MHC and body odours: arbitrary effects caused by shifts of mean pleasantness. *Nature Genetics*, 31: 237–237.

Wedekind, C. and Füri, S. (1997) Body odour preferences in men and women: do they aim for specific MHC combinations or simply heterozygosity? *Proceedings of the Royal Society of London, B*, 264: 1471–1479.

Wedekind, C., Seebeck, T., Bettens, F. and Paepke, A. J. (1995) MHC-dependent mate preferences in humans. *Proceedings of the Royal Society of London, B*, 260: 245–249.

Wysocki, C. J. and Preti, G. (2000) Human body odours and their perception. Japanese *J. Taste Smell Res.*, 7: 19–42.

Yamazaki, K., Boyse, E. A., Mike, V. *et al.* (1976) Control of mating preference in mice by genes in the major histocompatibility complex. *Journal of Experimental Medicine*, 144: 1324–1335.

Yamazaki, K., Beauchamp, G. K., Wysocki, C. J. *et al.* (1983) Recognition of H-2 types in relation to the blocking of pregnancy in mice. *Science*, 221: 186–188.

Younger, R. M., Amadou, C., Bethel, G. *et al.* (2001) Characterization of clustered MHC-linked olfactory receptor genes in human and mouse. *Genome Res.*, 11: 519–530.

CHAPTER 23

Reproductive strategies and tactics

Steven W. Gangestad

23.1. Games people—and other living things—play

Darwin's theory of natural selection elevates the act of reproduction to the highest level of importance for understanding the evolution of life forms. Individuals differ with respect to the number of offspring they produce, partly because reproduction is not an equal opportunity event. Within each population, some individuals' features promote reproduction more than other people's do. If the developmental systems that give rise to these features contain heritable components (e.g. genetic variants), selection can produce change in the features' representation in the population: favoured features become more common.

In the first half of the twentieth century, evolutionary theorists focused on understanding population genetics and how forces of evolutionary change such as selection affect gene frequencies. When biologists thought about how particular *phenotypic traits* had evolved, they typically considered morphological characters (e.g. the peacock's tail); when they considered behaviour, the focus was often 'instinctive' behaviour (e.g. imprinting of infant ducks to recognize and follow their mothers). A few exceptions were noteworthy. Cole (1954), for instance, asked why an asexual perennial plant

would expend energy on overwintering when, after all, it could replace itself by producing just one seed that survived the winter, which seemingly would require little energy. In so doing, Cole did not ask how the morphology of seeds evolved; he wondered how a particular *behaviour* related to reproduction (overwintering as opposed to producing seeds) had evolved. His question furthermore concerned *strategy*: if there are two ways to play the game, one by overwintering and the other by producing seeds with the energy used to overwinter, why and when does selection favour one way over the other? That is, when does it pay to play one way and when does it pay to play the other way?

Beginning in the 1940s and 1950s, and increasingly in the 1960s and 1970s, many of the most important theoretical developments in evolutionary biology asked and aimed to answer, through rigorous analysis, the kinds of question that Cole posed. What is the optimal number of offspring to produce (e.g. Lack, 1954, 1968)? What is the optimal number of years to grow before reproducing (e.g. Gadgil and Bossert, 1970)? What is the optimal number of sperm to ejaculate (Parker, 1970)? What is the optimal balance of male and female offspring (Hamilton, 1967; Trivers and Willard, 1973; Charnov, 1982)? What is the optimal amount to invest in offspring—and what is the optimal amount of investment to receive from parents (Trivers, 1974)? All of these questions and many more concern *reproductive strategy*.

In general, problems of strategy can be posed as follows. There exists a set of potential strategies that could be executed (e.g. number of offspring to produce, number of sperm to ejaculate); each one has implications for reproductive success (or, more generally, fitness), given how it interacts with an environment imposing constraints on its success (e.g. resources to feed offspring take time and effort to harvest); which one maximizes reproductive success, under those constraints—that is, which one is optimal? In theory, selection should favour that optimum.

Optimality modelling seeks to specify which strategy of a strategy set is optimal under constraints. Broadly speaking, it takes two forms. *Optimization models* are used to predict outcomes when individuals 'play' in the face of fixed constraints (e.g. a constant environment). An example is modelling the optimal number of offspring to produce in light of constraints on the overall amount of investment given to all offspring and the effect of investment on an offspring's probability of surviving. Second, *game theoretical models* are required to model outcomes when two or more players each attempt to optimize their outcomes is response to what the other players do. In a mating market, for instance, each individual competes against others of the same sex and in response to preferences of the other sex—the precise nature of which, in turn, may depend on what members of the first sex do to 'please' their preferences. (For an overview of modelling approaches, see Parker and Maynard Smith, 1991; Dunbar, 2002.)

In sexually reproducing species such as humans, then, the reproductive strategies of each sex *coevolve*. How much each sex should optimally invest in offspring, invest in efforts to seek mates, or compete against other members of the same sex depend on the strategies available to the other sex. Furthermore, precisely what each sex should do to invest in offspring, seek other mates, or compete against members of the same sex depends on what the other sex actually does. A reproductive strategy can be optimal only in the context of the other sex's strategy.

By convention (and despite my looser usage of the term strategy above), the terms strategy and tactic are applied differently. A *tactic* is a specific behavioural act individuals utilize within a strategy. A *strategy* is the full set of tactics utilized. For example, growing a large and extravagant tail is one tactic the peacock uses to attract peahens within a larger reproductive strategy (e.g. Dominey, 1984).

Two other important concepts are those of conditional strategies and alternate strategies (e.g. Gross, 1996). A *conditional strategy* is one in which individuals switch tactics depending on conditions. For instance, an individual who happens to possess features that render him valued in a mating market may be best off engaging in tactics different from the tactics that optimize outcomes of someone who lacks features that members of the other sex value. (Behavioural ecologists refer to decisions to make the best of sub-optimal features as 'making the best of a bad job': Krebs and Davies, 1993.) Conditional strategies are expected to evolve whenever the optimal tactic depends on the conditions an organism finds himself or herself in most often. *Alternate strategies* are ones that different individuals in the population engage in as a result of having different genotypes. The two sexes typically engage in alternate strategies—one for females and one for males. In some species, members of the same sex may engage in alternate strategies due to selection that maintains two (or more) different, viable strategies (most notably, negative frequency-dependent selection). Whereas the strategies of nearly all species are conditional in some ways, within-sex alternate strategies are probably rare.

23.2. Contexts within which tactics evolve

Reproductive strategies have far-ranging implications—from patterns of development (e.g. how fast and long to grow prior to starting reproduction), to how fast to reproduce, to how much to invest in each offspring, just to list a few examples. Other chapters in this volume (notably those by Mace, Lummaa and Voland) broadly address issues of *life-history strategies*, which are variations in reproductive strategy. For the remainder of this chapter, I will focus on tactics that specifically relate to mating—those tactics that constitute *mating strategies* (e.g. Dominey, 1984). (Mating strategies are not separate from life-history strategies and, indeed, I will address life-history tactics within the context of mating. Life-history strategies, however, are typically broader than mating strategies *per se*.)

One categorization of mating tactics partitions them into three categories, as follows.

23.2.1. Tactics of mate competition

Individuals may compete against other individuals of the same sex to gain access to mates. In this category, I consider only 'pure' mate competition—competitive tactics whose success or failure do not hinge on preferences of the other sex based on outcomes of competition. Tactics that intimidate the competition or threaten physical harm, thereby reducing the opportunities the competition have to interact effectively with potential mates, are prime examples.

23.2.2. Tactics that provide or promise a benefit to the other sex

In market economies, individuals who succeed often do so because they offer goods valued by other parties. This truth holds in mating markets. Broadly speaking, mate-seekers are interested in two kinds of 'goods'. First, they can receive *direct benefits*—non-genetic material benefits that increase their reproductive success. This category includes a wide range of specific forms: food provided for mate choosers or their offspring, protection from predators or other group members, direct care of offspring, and merely being disease-free (particularly in circumstances when disease that could be transmitted between mates is prevalent). Second, mates can receive genetic benefits. A sexually reproducing individual combines half of his or her genes with the genes of a mate to produce an offspring. The ultimate fate of an individual's genes—which hinges partly on the offspring's fitness—then, depends partly on the genetic fitness of the complement of genes provided by a mate. Preferences for mates who provide a good complement of genes can therefore evolve because genes promoting them can 'ride' along with that

good complement of genes. Genetic benefits for offspring are therefore referred to as *indirect benefits*. (For a recent review, see Kokko *et al.*, 2003.)

Some benefits may be provided immediately in exchange for mating (e.g. in some insects, males provide nutritional benefits in the spermatophore and females can judge males' ability to provide those benefits by the size of the spermatophore: see Thornhill and Alcock, 1983). In such cases, the individual provides a benefit in exchange for mating. In many other instances, however, mate choosers are not able to directly assess the benefits she or he might garner from potential mateships. In those cases, mate choosers assess 'promises' of benefits. 'Promises' can be broken, of course. The ones that mate choosers are likely to have evolved to 'listen' to are ones that those who promise suffer if they break and hence can be counted on.

Honest signalling of mate quality illustrates how some promises can be counted on. Individuals cannot directly evaluate the value of potential mates' genes for offspring. They cannot, for instance, directly compare DNA copying errors (mutations) in suitors. None the less, they can do so indirectly for precisely the reason choosing mates with 'good genes' is important: they affect their bearers' performance. Selection ensures that mate choosers evolve to be attuned and attracted to those elements of performance sensitive to poorly adapted genes within the species. If the most fit individuals can outcompete same-sex individuals in physical competition, mate choosers should evolve to attend to the outcomes of those competitions. If the most fit individuals can afford to grow larger, mate choosers should evolve to attend to size. In some instances, traits that initially are not correlated with fitness (e.g. a slightly bigger tail) get some advantage on a mating market because they attract attention, and over time evolve to become honest indicators of genetic benefits because only the most fit individuals can afford their costs—the process that, according to some theorists, underlies the evolution of 'arbitrary' indicators of good genes such as the peacock's tail (for a review see Kokko *et al.*, 2003). The honesty of signals is maintained in these instances because individuals who are low in fitness cannot profit from engaging in 'deceit'—exhibiting a signal that advertises good genes—for they actually are worse off for doing so. Honest signals of quality, then, are promises that can be counted on. (See, for instance, Zahavi, 1975; Grafen, 1990; Getty, 1998, 2002.)

Some material benefits are not delivered immediately; they are delivered over time. Consider, for instance, males 'promising' to provision offspring after they are born. When a male could potentially benefit reproductively by mating and then deserting, how can a female extract an honest 'promise' of continued male investment in offspring? The logic of honest advertisements of intent is similar to the logic of honest advertisements of quality: a signal is honest if it doesn't pay for an individual to engage in 'deceit' (e.g. Andrews, 2001). A male who, for instance, engages in costly courtship and forgoes alternative mating opportunities is honestly signalling intent to provide a continuing stream of benefits *if* he couldn't benefit by engaging in this form of signalling and then immediately deserting. One speculation of how passionate love (and attendant infatuation) evolved is that it is an honest signal of intent in this manner: it couldn't pay someone to take on its costs if they were only in the relationship for the very short-term (e.g. Andrews, 2001; see also Gonzaga *et al.*, 2001).

23.2.3. Tactics that increase one's own fitness at the expense of the mate's fitness: sexually antagonistic adaptations

The tactics listed above involve offering or signalling a benefit for another. The tactic succeeds because the individual of the other sex truly benefits. (Indeed, in signalling models described above, for each signal evolved as a tactic by one sex, the other sex correspondingly has evolved a tactic of perceiving and acting upon that signal.) A third class of tactics involves acting in one's own interest *at the expense* of the interests of a mate of the other sex.

Seminal work on *Drosophila melanogaster* by Rice (1996) demonstrates this class of tactics in spectacular fashion. Through ingenious laboratory techniques, Rice prevented females in his population from evolving, whereas males were allowed to evolve. After 30 generations, a series of tests of the relative fitness of these evolved

males with control males from the original stock was performed. Males in the experimental line had increased capacity for remating with females who had previously mated with competitor males taken from the control line. At the same time, competitor males had decreased ability to remate with females previously mated with experimental males, as well as decreased ability to displace sperm inseminated by experimental males. In mixed groups, the reproductive success of experimental males was substantially greater than that of control competitor males. The male traits did not evolve because they benefited females; they evolved at the expense of female fitness. Females that mated with experimental males actually died at a rate greater than females mated to control males, with no compensating increase in fecundity. Previous research had shown that proteins in male *Drosophila melanogaster* seminal fluid are low-level toxins to females (e.g. Fowler and Partridge, 1989; Chapman *et al.*, 1995). The mortality cost to Rice's females was probably due to both an increase in the remating rate (and hence greater exposure to seminal proteins) and enhanced toxicity of male seminal proteins.

The harmful effects of male seminal fluid are probably incidental by-products of beneficial effects on male reproductive success. Its proteins can harm other males' sperm and hence facilitate sperm competition (e.g. Harshman and Prout, 1994). In any case, however, male adaptations evolved at the expense of females; they are sexually antagonistic adaptations.

A key aspect of Rice's work was that he prevented females from evolving. Doing so was crucial. Had he not, he perhaps would not have demonstrated the evolution of sexually antagonistic adaptations in males, for females would have evolved counter-tactics to limit the negative impact of male seminal fluids. This point illustrates a general claim about sexually antagonistic adaptations: they evolve within coevolutionary races between the sexes. A tactic in one sex selects for a counter-tactic in the other sex, and this selects in turn for a counter-counter-tactic in the first sex, and so on. Honest signalling systems like those discussed previously coevolve too, of course; signallers and receivers evolve adaptations together. In theory, however, honest signalling systems often reach stable equilibria, within which each sex is well adapted to the other (though see below). In contrast, antagonistic coevolutionary races may often never reach stable equilibria, as tactics that undermine the other sex's tactics may always be possible.

Antagonistic coevolutionary races are not limited to relationships between individuals that are antagonistic in general. Likewise, mutually beneficial signalling systems are not limited to relationships that are, in general, mutually beneficial. Predators and prey antagonistically coevolve; predator pursuit tactics may be countered by prey escape tactics, which may be undermined by yet other predator tactics, and so on. But potential prey may also signal to predators that they are more difficult to catch than other potential prey (e.g. through handicapping traits; Zahavi, 1975), with predators benefiting from this signal (and hence evolving to attend to it when choosing who to chase). Mating partners who biparentally invest in offspring have common interests in the welfare of the offspring as well as the welfare of each other. But except in the extremely exceptional case of obligate lifetime monogamy (in which case neither partner can possibly remate and hence both partners' reproductive success is perfectly yoked to their partner's), mating partners' interests do not correspond perfectly, and these mismatched interests can fuel antagonistic coevolutionary races. Even in pair-bonded species, mating relationships take shape out of partners' adaptive design for cooperating—often lovingly—with partners in pursuit of shared interests *in conjunction with* each sex's adaptive design for pursuing its own interests (or those of same-sex ancestors) that conflict with partners' interests.

23.2.4. Reproductive strategies are embodied in the adaptations of individuals

Adaptations are features that evolved in their bearers because they enhanced their fitness and were therefore favoured by selection. Adaptations have functions, which are the means by which they enhanced fitness (Williams, 1966). Bird wings have a function of flight. Many details of wings (e.g. their general shape, the properties of flight feathers) were selected because they facilitated this function.

A dictionary definition of a strategy implies a 'plan'. Natural selection, however, does not embody organisms with grand 'plans' to execute and thereby achieve fitness. Rather, organisms' individual features that happen to be associated with greater fitness will be favoured through selection. Because multiple features that work towards common ends often coevolve through selection, constellations of adaptations often promote common functions. For instance, just as bird wings are adapted for flight, so too are aspects of birds' brains, which control wings to enable flight.

Reproductive strategies are abstractions. They are convenient handles used by evolutionary biologists to talk about how specific organisms have been shaped by selection to promote fitness. The concrete embodiments of reproductive strategies are the adaptations that have thereby evolved. To say, then, that an organism has a reproductive strategy of providing biparental care through pair bonding is to say that the organism has physiological (e.g. neural, hormonal, structural) adaptations and behavioural adaptations (with physiological underpinnings) that function to promote fitness through biparental provisioning of offspring, facilitated by male–female pair bonding.

Inference of reproductive strategies entails inference of selection pressures that historically shaped organisms. In turn, the selection pressures that operated on organisms are inferred through the adaptations that those selection pressures yielded. Just as bird wings constitute clear evidence for selection for flight, physiological and behavioral adaptations in humans can constitute evidence that specific ancestral selection pressures operated on human ancestors (e.g. Barrett *et al.*, 2002).

23.3. The evolution of mating tactics in humans: three contemporary debates

I briefly consider three contemporary debates about reproductive tactics and mating strategies in humans as illustrations of how the framework just presented can be applied to an understanding of human evolved psychology.

23.3.1. Did human paternal care and hunting evolve as parenting effort or mating effort?

In most primate species (including our closest relatives), individuals of both sexes are responsible for their own subsistence. Though males may provide physical protection and may sometimes share food in exchange for sex (e.g. Dunbar, 1988), mothers harvest the overwhelming majority of calories consumed by offspring during pregnancy and lactation. In contrast, in the majority of human foraging populations studied to date, the average adult male generates more calories than he consumes. These food resources yield benefits for reproductive women and juveniles by providing extra calories and macronutrients such as protein. Marlowe (2001) estimated that, on average, men produced 64% of the calories in all 95 foraging societies on which sufficient information is available. In Kaplan *et al.*'s (2000) analysis of studies that carefully measured produced foods in nine hunter-gatherer societies, men generated on average about 66%. Women in traditional societies can and do turn the surplus of calories generated by men into production of offspring and thereby reproductively benefit from this surplus generated through male hunting. Across foraging societies, as the surplus of calories generated by men increases, the mean interbirth interval decreases (Marlowe, 2001).

Compared to our close primate relatives, humans consume large amounts of high-quality but difficult-to-extract resources such as animal protein. Whereas chimpanzees obtain about 95% of their calories from collected foods requiring no extraction (e.g. fruits, leaves), only about 8% of calories consumed by modern hunter-gatherers are from foods requiring no extraction. Vertebrate meat in particular accounts for, on average, 30–80% of human hunter-gatherer calorie intake but just 2% of chimpanzee diets (Kaplan *et al.*, 2000). In humans, males' subsidization of female and juvenile diets is largely achieved through male hunting.

Kaplan *et al.* (2000) explain male hunting as the outcome of selection for male parenting effort. Parenting effort is the allocation of time and energy to activities that reproductively pay off because they increase the quality of offspring (Low, 1978). According to Kaplan *et al.* (2000), male hunting functions to harvest nutrients not only for self but also to foster the viability and health of reproductive partners and offspring. Biparental care—fathering as well as mothering—in this view coevolved with other key human features, including long lifespan (and a premium on strategies that reduce mortality), prolonged investment in offspring, a large brain, and investment in learning, which permits reliance on skill-dependent extractive foraging. In theory, biparental care may be selected when male and female investments into offspring synergistically interact to increase offspring fitness, often through a division of labour. In many socially monogamous birds, parents take turns nest guarding and foraging for offspring, tasks one parent cannot simultaneously perform. Men's subsidization of women's diets may have permitted reduction of human birth spacing despite very substantial investment into each offspring.

According to this male-hunting-as-parental-investment theory, the nuclear family is a key economic unit in the evolution of human mating relations. Male hunting surpluses flow to female partners and offspring. Male–female pair-bonding importantly cements the sociopsychological foundations of these resource flows. Though most human societies in the anthropological record allow polygyny, the most common mating arrangement is actually social monogamy.

An alternative view stems from arguments that nuclear families are not potent economic units in foraging societies (Hawkes, 1991, 2004; Hawkes *et al.*, 1991, 2001). In the Hadza of Tanzania and the Aché of Paraguay, for instance, hunters have little control over the distribution of meat generated through their efforts, as meat is shared widely across community members. This pattern particularly characterizes the sharing of meat from large game. At the same time, despite the fact that men generate fewer calories per unit time hunting large game (as well as the fact that, proportionately, they end up with less of the meat from large game), men allocate a substantial portion of their time to hunting large game. Hawkes (2001) argues that male hunting does not effectively or efficiently generate calories for a nuclear family and hence does not function as parenting effort. Instead, men garner prestige and, ultimately, mates through hunting, particularly big-game hunting, precisely because it is a risky and sometimes dangerous activity. According to this view, then, big-game hunting functions as mating effort—effort to gain access to mates. Put otherwise, hunting is a form of 'showing off' (e.g. Hawkes, 1991).

The nuclear family, in this framework, is not an economic unit key to understanding the evolution of human male–female relations. Men and women do have offspring together and form marriages. Furthermore, women prefer better hunters as mates, though not for hunting returns *per se*. Rather, women mated with good hunters may garner indirect material benefits as a result of their mates' status in the community (e.g. protection, deference from others). Women's diets are not subsidized directly by mates but rather through surpluses generated in, and shared throughout, the community in general and by maternal kin (e.g. grandmothers; e.g. Hawkes *et al.*, 2001) in particular. Because men's hunting is invested to gain access to mates in general and not one mating partner in which he invests exclusively, sexual monogamy is less important to either men's or women's fitness outcomes as well.

Though I have laid out the views in polarized forms here, a blended position is possible. Men's hunting may function partly as parenting effort (particularly hunting for smaller game, meat from which hunters appear to control) as well as partly as showing off; historically, men may have benefited reproductively from hunting by improving the viability of offspring as well as access to mates.

One way to decide between these alternative positions is to examine men's psychological make-up for evidence of design shaped for investment in offspring versus mates. One promising line of work examines physiological mechanisms that regulate men's testosterone levels. Across a wide range of taxa, testosterone appears to facilitate male mating effort by diverting energetic resources to features particularly useful in male–male competition (e.g. muscles; see Ellison, 2001). In some species in which males invest in offspring (e.g. marmosets, some birds), male testosterone levels drop after the

birth of the mate's offspring (e.g. Nunes *et al.*, 2000, 2001). These drops may facilitate paternal investment. Indeed, men who have lower testosterone levels respond more prosocially to infant cries (Fleming *et al.*, 2002). Men's testosterone levels too appear to drop when they become mated or have offspring (e.g. Booth and Dabbs, 1993; Mazur and Michalek, 1998; Storey *et al.*, 2000; Berg and Wynne-Edwards, 2001; Gray *et al.*, 2002, 2004; Burnham *et al.*, 2003).

Though these data hint that men have adaptations shaped for the function of parental investment, more research is needed. When polygynously mated, men's testosterone levels remain high (perhaps because maintaining multiple mates requires more sustained mating effort; Gray *et al.*, 2004). And alternatives must be ruled out. For instance, perhaps men simply have lower opportunity to engage in male–male competition when they have offspring as a result of uniquely modern social practices, leading to lower testosterone levels. Or, females may manipulate men's testosterone levels in their own interests and against male interests, such that changes do not reflect male adaptation (e.g. Gray *et al.*, 2002).

23.3.2. Have humans been selected to choose mates for 'good genes'?

Sexually reproducing species, once again, combine half of their genes with half the genes of another individual to create offspring. In theory, individuals should be selected to choose mates who provide better complements of genes with which their own genes are combined; genes facilitating mate choice with individuals possessing 'good genes' are indirectly selected by 'riding along' with good genes. Historically, the issue of whether good genes mate choice is a potent biological phenomenon has been debated vigorously (e.g. Charlesworth, 1988). One key question is whether potential mates differ in their ability to deliver good genes sufficiently to make it worth it for mate choosers to discriminate between mates on this basis. The answer to this question appears to be yes. 'Good genes', in this context, may largely be 'lack of deleterious mutant genes'. Though mutations are rare at any individual locus, most gametes (which, of course, contain many genes) have at least one new mutation and, because slightly deleterious mutations are typically not eliminated for several generations, contain many passed on from the previous generation. By chance, however, individuals inherit and then pass on differing numbers of these mutations and, hence, choosing a mate who has relatively few can enhance fitness by a factor of more than two over choosing a mate who has relatively many. (See e.g. Houle, 1992; Houle and Kondrashov, 2002; Gangestad and Thornhill, 2004. See also Hamilton and Zuk, 1982, on host–parasite coevolution; and Rice and Holland, 1997, on coevolutionary processes in general as alternative sources of genetic differences in fitness.)

Of course, individuals cannot directly 'count' potential mates' deleterious genes. They must discriminate genetic quality based on mates' features. Earlier, I outlined how indicators may come to be associated with 'good genes'. Mate choosers can look to aspects of performance that are affected by good genes. Researchers have attempted to test the idea that women have evolved to prefer men who could, ancestrally, provide genetic benefits to offspring by examining correlations between men's attractiveness or 'mating success' (often simply measured by number of sexual partners, controlled for age) and putative markers of indicators of genetic benefits. One such measure is fluctuating asymmetry (FA): these are departures from perfect symmetry on traits that are bilateral, such as fingers, wrists, and ears. FA is purportedly a measure of developmental instability, imprecise expression of developmental design due to perturbations during development (e.g. those caused by mutations). While the small departures from symmetry in measures of body FA are not themselves 'cues' (as they are generally too small to be reliably detected during normal interaction), they may relate to morphological or behavioural features that are (e.g. facial masculinity, intrasexual competitiveness: see Gangestad and Thornhill, 2004, for a review). Symmetrical men appear to have more sexual partners than do asymmetrical men (see Gangestad and Thornhill, 2004). A recent study showed that men with more masculine faces also appear to have more sexual partners (Rhodes *et al.*, 2005).

These findings do not, by themselves, show that women have evolved to be attracted to indicators of good genes. Although studies hint that symmetry and male facial masculinity may be associated with resistance to some forms of infectious disease (e.g. Rhodes *et al.*, 2003; Thornhill and Gangestad, 2006; see also Waynforth, 1998), the health advantages may not be heritable. Moreover, associations of traits with health status may be quite different in modern environments than in ancestral conditions in which preferences evolved.

Men with low FA and masculine features may also have provided material benefits in ancestral environments, and these benefits, rather than genetic benefits, may have shaped female preferences. In a review of socially monogamous bird species, Møller and Thornhill (1998) found that when females frequently engage in extra-pair copulation (EPC: mating with males other than social partners), attractive males actually tend to perform *less* parental care and hence provide *fewer* material benefits to females. They reasoned that these males put greater effort into seeking EPCs at the expense of parental effort in these species, for females in these species partly choose males for indicators of genetic benefits and hence favour these males. (In species with very low EPC rates, attractive males tend to be better providers, purportedly because there is no 'pool' of EPCs offered by females for males to pursue.) Levels of male mating effort and parental effort in these species are presumably contingent tactics that depend on how females react to males. Human male investment in relationships may be similarly contingent. In one study, symmetrical college men invested less heavily in their romantic relationships than asymmetrical men (see Gangestad and Thornhill, 2004; see also Gangestad and Simpson, 2000).

These ideas assume that males' investment in their romantic relationships is contingent on their own attractiveness to women because attractive men more successfully compete for a 'pool' of short-term relationships offered by women. Ancestrally, most reproductive-aged women purportedly would have been mated and, hence, these short-term relationships would have been female EPCs. This point leads to the next topic.

23.3.3. Have EPCs been a part of women's reproductive strategies?

Many socially monogamous birds are not sexually monogamous: the percentage of offspring sired by extra-pair males averages 10–15% across species (e.g. Petrie and Kempanears, 1998). A number of adaptive hypotheses for EPC in birds have been proposed (e.g. Jennions and Petrie, 2000). One leading theory is that some females can garner genetic benefits to offspring through EPC, particularly when their own social mate does not, relatively speaking, offer genetic benefits to offspring. It predicts that females have an adaptation to engage in EPC conditionally with males who possess indicators of good genes, particularly when their own male does not. These predictions have been supported in some species (e.g. the collared flycatcher of Gotland, Sweden; e.g. Qvarnström, 1997, 1999; Sheldon et al., 1997, 1999; Sheldon and Ellegren, 1999; Michl et al., 2002). (For an explanation of female EPC based on the idea that it results from male manipulation rather than female adaptation, see Arnqvist and Kirkpatrick, 2005.)

Might human females have similarly benefited through EPC ancestrally, their reproductive strategies accordingly shaped by selection? Gangestad and Thornhill (1998) proposed to look for human adaptations that are footprints of these selection forces based on the fact that women are fertile during a brief window of their cycles. If ancestral females benefited from multiple mating to obtain genetic benefits, but at some potential cost of losing social mates, selection may have shaped preferences for indicators of those benefits to depend on fertility status: maximal at peak fertility and less pronounced outside the fertile period. Cycle shifts should furthermore be specific to when women evaluate men as short-term sex partners (i.e. their 'sexiness') rather than as long-term, investing mates (Penton-Voak et al., 1999). The logic is that costs don't pay when benefits can't be reaped.

Over a dozen recent studies show that female preferences clearly do shift. At mid-cycle, normally ovulating, non-pill-using women particularly prefer: (a) the scent of symmetrical men (Gangestad and Thornhill, 1998; Thornhill and Gangestad, 1999; Rikowski and Grammer, 1999;

Thornhill et al., 2003); (b) the scent of dominant men (Havlicek et al., 2005); (c) masculine faces (e.g, Penton-Voak et al., 1999; Johnston et al., 2001); (d) male behavioural displays of social presence and intrasexual competitiveness (Gangestad et al., 2004); (e) vocal masculinity (Puts, 2005); (f) talent in preference to wealth (Haselton and Miller, 2006). Where short-term attractiveness ('sexiness') and long-term attractiveness have been examined separately, effects have been found only for short-term attractiveness (Penton-Voak et al., 1999; Gangestad et al., 2004; Puts, 2005; Haselton and Miller, in press). Symmetry, masculine facial and vocal qualities, intrasexual competitiveness, and various forms of talent may have been indicators of good genes ancestrally (though see caveats noted earlier). Not all valued male traits are sexier to women at mid-cycle, however. Traits particularly valued in long-term mates (e.g. kindness, intelligence, good fathering, and capability to be financially successful) are not especially attractive to fertile women (see Gangestad et al., in press). (For evidence that women's attractiveness judgements do change across the cycle in other ways, however, see deBruine et al., 2005.)

Patterns of women's sexual interests also shift across the cycle. In one study, normally ovulating women reported thoughts and feelings over the past 2 days twice: once when fertile (as confirmed by a luteinizing hormone surge, which normally occurs 1–2 days before ovulation) and once when infertile (during the luteal phase). When fertile, women reported greater sexual attraction to and fantasy about men other than primary partners—but not about primary partners (Gangestad et al., 2002; cf. Pillsworth et al., 2004).

In fact, however, the ovulatory shift hypothesis expects a more finely textured pattern. Though, on average, ancestral women might have garnered genetic benefits through extra-pair mating, it may be the case that women whose primary partners possessed 'good genes' could not. If so, then selection should have shaped interest in extra-pair men mid-cycle in such a way that such selection depends on partner features: only women with men who, relatively speaking, *lack* purported indicators of genetic benefits should be particularly attracted to extra-pair men when fertile. In a replication and extension of Gangestad *et al.* (2002), Gangestad *et al.* (2005) found evidence for this prediction: women with asymmetrical partners expressed greater interest in men when fertile, whereas women with symmetrical partners did not. Similarly, Haselton and Gangestad (2006) and Pillsworth and Haselton (2006) found that women who rated their partners as relatively unattractive were more likely to express greater interest in extra-pair men when fertile. (On selection for 'compatible' genes mid-cycle, see Garver-Apgar *et al.*, 2006; cf. Thornhill *et al.*, 2003.)

If women have been selected to seek 'good genes' mid-cycle, men should have been selected to lessen risks of cuckoldry at this time—and, indeed, men appear to be more vigilant or proprietary of mates when their mates are fertile than when they are infertile (Gangestad *et al.*, 2002; Haselton and Gangestad, in press). Men may use one or more cues to detect partners' fertility status. Men find the scent of ovulating women particularly attractive (e.g. Singh and Bronstad, 2001; Thornhill *et al.*, 2003). One study found that men judge women's faces more attractive when women are mid-cycle (Roberts *et al.*, 2004). And if women's interests change across the cycle, their behaviour might too. Whatever the cues, women are unlikely to have been designed through selection to send them. Rather, men may have evolved to pick up on incidental effects of fertility status. Gangestad *et al.* (2002) found that enhanced male vigilance of partners mid-cycle (as reported by women) was predicted by enhanced female interest in *extra-pair men*, not partners. Similarly, Haselton and Gangestad (in press) and Pillsworth and Haselton (in press) found that men rated as relatively unattractive by their partners showed the greatest increase in jealousy or attentiveness mid-cycle. Men may be particularly vigilant of their partners mid-cycle when their partners least want them to be.

23.4. Conclusions

In the past two decades, evolutionary psychologists have intensively studied adaptations for mating and parenting. Though tremendous progress towards empirically documenting the nature of human mating has been made, fundamental theoretical questions have not yet been fully answered. The next decade or two promises to bring a much fuller understanding of human reproductive strategies.

References

Andrews, P. W. (2001) The psychology of social chess and the evolution of attribution mechanisms: explaining the fundamental attribution error. *Evolution and Human Behavior*, 22: 11–29.

Arnqvist, G. and Kirkpatrick, M. (2005) The evolution of infidelity in socially monogamous passerines: the strength of indirect selection on extrapair copulation behavior in females. *American Naturalist*, 165: S26–S37.

Barrett, L., Dunbar, R. and Lycett, J. (2002) *Human Evolutionary Psychology*. Princeton University Press, Princeton, NJ.

Berg, S. J. and Wynne-Edwards, K. E. (2001) Changes in testosterone, cortisol, and estradiol levels in men becoming fathers. *Mayo Clinic Proceedings*, 76: 582–592.

Booth, A. and Dabbs, J. M. (1993) Testosterone and mens' marriages. *Social Forces*, 72: 463–477.

Burnham, T. C., Chapman, J. F., Gray, P. B., McIntyre, M. H., Lipson, S. F. and Ellison, P. T. (2003) Men in committed, romantic relationships have lower testosterone. *Hormones and Behavior*, 44: 119–122.

Chapman, T., Lindsay, F., Liddle, F., Kalb, J., Wolfner, M. F. and Partridge, L. (1995) Cost of mating in *Drosophila melanogaster* females is mediated by male accessory gland products. *Nature*, 373: 241–244.

Charlesworth, B. (1987) The heritability of fitness. In J. W. Bradbury and M. B. Andersson (eds), *Sexual Selection: Testing the Alternatives*, pp. 21–40. Wiley, New York.

Charnov, E. L. (1982) *The Theory of Sex Allocation*. Princeton University Press, Princeton, NJ.

Cole, L. C. (1954) The population consequences of life history phenomena. *Quarterly Review of Biology*, 29: 103–137.

DeBruine, L. M., Jones, B. C. and Perrett, D. I. (2005) Women's attractiveness judgments for self-resembling faces change across the menstrual cycle. *Hormones and Behavior*, 4: 379–383.

Dominey, W. J. (1984) Alternate mating tactics and evolutionarily stable strategies. *American Zoologist*, 24: 385–96.

Dunbar, R. I. M. (1988) *Primate Social Systems*. Chapman & Hall, London.

Dunbar, R. I. M. (2002) Modelling primate behavioural ecology. *International Journal of Primatology*, 23: 785–819.

Ellison, P. T. (2001) *On Fertile Ground: A Natural History of Reproduction*. Harvard University Press, Cambridge, MA.

Fleming, A. S., Corter, C., Stallings, J. and Steiner, M. (2002) Testosterone and prolactin are associated with emotional responses to infant cries in new fathers. *Hormones and Behavior*, 42: 399–413.

Fowler, K. and Partridge, L. (1989) A cost of mating in female fruitflies. *Nature*, 338: 760–761.

Gadgil, M. and Bossert, W. H. (1970) Life historical consequences of natural selection. *American Naturalist*, 104: 1–24.

Gangestad, S. W. and Simpson, J. A. (2000) The evolution of human mating: The role of trade-offs and strategic pluralism. *Behavioral and Brain Sciences*, 23: 675–687.

Gangestad, S. W. and Thornhill, R. (1998) Menstrual cycle variation in women's preference for the scent of symmetrical men. *Proceedings of the Royal Society of London, B*, 262: 727–733.

Gangestad, S. W. and Thornhill, R. (2004) Female multiple mating and genetic benefits in humans: Investigations of design. In P. M. Kappeler and C. P. van Schaik (eds), *Sexual Selection in Primates: New and Comparative Perspectives*. Cambridge University Press, Cambridge

Gangestad, S. W., Thornhill, R. and Garver, C. E. (2002) Changes in women's sexual interests and their partners' mate retention tactics across the menstrual cycle: evidence for shifting conflicts of interest. *Proceedings of the Royal Society of London, B*, 269: 975–982.

Gangestad, S. W., Simpson, J. A., Cousins, A. J., Garver-Apgar, C. E. and Christensen, P. N. (2004) Women's preferences for male behavioral displays change across the menstrual cycle. *Psychological Science*, 15: 203–207.

Gangestad, S. W., Thornhill, R. and Garver-Apgar, C. E. (2005) Female sexual interests across the ovulatory cycle depend on primary partner developmental instability. *Proceedings of the Royal Society of London, B*, 272: 2023–2027.

Garver-Apgar, C. E., Gangestad, S. W., Thornhill, R., Miller, R. D. and Olp, J. (2006) MHC alleles, sexually responsivity, and unfaithfulness in romantic couples. *Psychological Science*, 17: 830–835.

Getty, T. (1998) Handicap signalling: when fecundity and mortality do not add up. *Animal Behavior*, 56: 127–130.

Getty, T. (2002) Signaling health versus parasites. *American Naturalist*, 159: 363–371.

Gonzaga, G. C., Keltner, D., Londahl, E. A. and Smith, M. D. (2001) Love and the commitment problem in romantic relationships and friendships. *Journal of Personality and Social Psychology*, 81: 246–262.

Grafen, A. (1990) Biological signals as handicaps. *Journal of Theoretical Biology*, 144: 517–546.

Gray, P. B., Kahlenberg, S. M., Barrett, E. S., Lipson, S. F. and Ellison, P. T. (2002) Marriage and fatherhood are associated with lower testosterone in males. *Evolution and Human Behavior*, 23: 193–201.

Gray, P. B., Chapman, J. F., Burnham, T. C., McIntyre, M. H., Lipson, S. F. and Ellison, P. T. (2004) Human male pair bonding and testosterone. *Human Nature—An Interdisciplinary Biosocial Perspective*, 15: 119–131.

Gross, M. R. (1996) Alternative reproductive strategies and tactics: diversity within sexes. *Trends in Ecology and Evolution*, 11: 92–98.

Hamilton, W. D. (1967) Extraordinary sex ratios. *Science*, 156: 477–488.

Hamilton, W. D. and Zuk, M. (1982) Heritable true fitness and bright birds: A role for parasites. *Science*, 218: 384–87.

Harshman, L. G. and Prout, T. (1994) Sperm displacement without sperm transfer in *Drosophila melanogaster*. *Evolution*, 48: 758–756.

Haselton, M. G. and Gangestad, S. W. (2006) Conditional expression of female desires and male mate retention efforts across the human ovulatory cycle. *Hormones and Behavior*, 49: 509–518.

Haselton, M. G. and Miller, G. F. (2006) Evidence for ovulatory shifts in attraction to artistic and entrepreneurial excellence. *Human Nature*, 17: 50–73.

Havlicek, J., Roberts, S. C. and Flegr, J. (2005) Women's preference for dominant male odour: Effects of menstrual cycle and relationship status. *Biology Letters*, 1: 256–259.

Hawkes, K. (1991) Showing off: tests of an hypothesis about men's foraging goals. *Ethology and Sociobiology*, 12: 29–54.

Hawkes, K. (2004) Mating, parenting, and the evolution of human pair bonds. In B. Chapais and C. M. Berman (eds), *Kinship and Behavior in Primates*. Oxford University Press, Oxford, UK.

Hawkes, K., O'Connell, J. F. and Blurton Jones, N. G. (1991) Hunting patterns among the Hadza: Big game, common goals, foraging goals and the evolution of the human diet. *Philosophical Transactions of the Royal Society of London, B*, 334: 243–251.

Hawkes, K., O'Connell, J. F. and Blurton Jones, N. G. (2001) Hunting and nuclear families—some lessons from the Hadza about men's work. *Current Anthropology*, 42: 681–709.

Houle, D. (1992) Comparing evolvability and variability of traits. *Genetics*, 130: 195–204.

Houle, D. and Kondrashov, A. S. (2002) Coevolution of costly mate choice and condition-dependent display of good genes. *Proceedings of the Royal Society of London, B*, 269: 97–104.

Jennions, M. D. and Petrie, M. (2000) Why do females mate multiply?: A review of the genetic benefits. *Biological Reviews*, 75: 21–64.

Johnston, V. S., Hagel, R., Franklin, M., Fink, B. and Grammer, K. (2001) Male facial attractiveness: evidence for hormone mediated adaptive design. *Evolution and Human Behavior*, 23: 251–267.

Kaplan, H., Hill, K., Lancaster, J. and Hurtado, A. M. (2000) A theory of human life history evolution: diet, intelligence, and longevity. *Evolutionary Anthropology*, 9: 156–185.

Kokko, H., Brooks, R., Jennions, M. D. and Morley, J. (2003) The evolution of mate choice and mating biases. *Proceedings of the Royal Society of London, B*, 270: 653–664.

Krebs, J. R. and Davies, N. B. (1993) *An Introduction to Behavioural Ecology*. Blackwell, Oxford.

Lack, D. (1968) *Ecological Adaptations for Breeding in Birds*. Methuen, London.

Low, B. S. (1978) Environmental uncertainty and the parental strategies of marsupials and placentals. *American Naturalist*, 112: 197–213.

Marlowe, F. (2001) Male contribution to diet and female reproductive success among foragers. *Current Anthropology*, 42: 755–760.

Mazur, A. and Michalek, J. (1998) Marriage, divorce, and male testosterone. *Social Forces*, 77: 315–330.

Michl, G., Torok, J., Griffith, S. C. and Sheldon, B. C. (2002) Experimental analysis of sperm competition mechanisms in a wild bird population. *Proceedings of the National Academy of Sciences of the USA*, 99: 5466–5470.

Müller, A. P. and Thornhill, R. (1998) Male parental care, differential parental investment by females and sexual selection. *Animal Behaviour*, 55: 1507–1515.

Nunes, S., Fite, J. E. and French, J. A. (2000) Variation in steroid hormones associated with infant care behaviour and experience in male marmosets (*Callithrix kuhlii*). *Animal Behaviour*, 60: 1–9.

Nunes, S., Fite, J. E., Patera, K. J. and French, J. A. (2001) Interactions among paternal behavior, steroid hormones, and parental experience in male marmosets (*Callithrix kuhlii*). *Hormones and Behavior*, 39: 70–82.

Parker, G. A. (1970) The reproductive behaviour and the nature of sexual selection in *Scatophaga stercoria* L. (Diptera: Scatophagdae). II. The fertilization rate and the spatial and temporal relationships of each sex around the site of mating and oviposition. *Journal of Animal Ecology*, 39: 205–228.

Parker, G. A. and Maynard Smith, J. (1991) Optimality theory in evolutionary biology. *Nature*, 348: 27–33.

Penton-Voak, I. S., Perrett, D. I., Castles, D., Burt, M., Koyabashi, T. and Murray, L. K. (1999) Female preference for male faces changes cyclically. *Nature*, 399: 741–742.

Petrie, M. and Kempenaers, B. (1998) Extra-pair paternity in birds: explaining variation between species and populations. *Trends in Ecology and Evolution*, 13: 52–58.

Pillsworth, E. G. and Haselton, M. G. (2006) Shifts in women's desires and men's mate retention tactics across the ovulatory cycle: further evidence. *Evolution and Human Behavior*, 27: 247–258.

Pillsworth, E. G. Haselton, M. G. and Buss, D. M. (2004) Ovulatory shifts in female sexual desire. *Journal of Sex Research*, 41: 55–65.

Puts, D. A. (2005) Mating context and menstrual phase affect women's preference for male voice pitch. *Evolution and Human Behavior*, 26: 388–397.

Qvarnström, A. (1997) Experimentally increased badge size increases male competition and reduces male parental care in the collared flycatcher. *Proceedings of the Royal Society of London, B*, 264: 1225–1231.

Qvarnström, A. (1999) Different reproductive tactics in male collared flycatchers signalled by size of secondary sexual character. *Proceedings of the Royal Society of London, B*, 266: 2089–2093.

Rhodes, G., Chan, J., Zebrowitz, L. A. and Simmons, L. W. (2003) Does sexual dimorphism in human faces signal health? *Proceedings of the Royal Society of London, B*, 270, S93–S95.

Rhodes, G., Simmons, L. W. and Peters, M. (2005) Attractiveness and sexual behavior: does attractiveness enhance mating success? *Evolution and Human Behavior*, 26: 186–201.

Rice, W. R. (1996) Sexually antagonistic male adaptation triggered by experimental arrest of female evolution. *Nature*, 381: 232–234.

Rice, W. R. and Holland, B. (1997) The enemies within: intragenomic conflict, interlocus contest evolution (ICE), and the intraspecific Red Queen. *Behavioral Ecology and Sociobiology*, 41: 1–10.

Rikowski, A. and Grammer, K. (1999) Human body odour, symmetry and attractiveness *Proceedings of the Royal Society of London* B, 266: 869–874.

Roberts, S. C., Havlicek, J., Flegr, J., Hruskova, M., Little, A. C., Jones, B. C., Perrett, D. I. and Petrie, M. (2004) Female facial attractiveness increases during the fertile phase of the cycle. *Proceedings of the Royal Society of London, B*, 271, S270-S272.

Sheldon, B. C., Davidson, P. and Lindgren, G. (1999) Mate replacement in experimentally widowed collared flycatchers (*Ficedula albicollis*): determinants and outcomes. *Behavioral Ecology and Sociobiology*, 46: 141–148.

Sheldon, B. C. and Ellegren, H. (1999) Sexual selection resulting from extrapair paternity in collared flycatchers. *Animal Behaviour*, 57: 285–298.

Sheldon, B. C. Merila, J., Qvarnström, A., Gustafsson, L. and Ellegren, H. (1997) Paternal genetic contribution to offspring condition predicted by size of male secondary sexual character. *Proceedings of the Royal Society of London, B*, 264: 297–302.

Singh, D. and Bronstad, P. M. (2001) Female body odour is a potential cue to ovulation. *Proceedings of the Royal Society of London, B*, 268: 797–801.

Storey, A. E., Walsh, C. J., Quinton, R. L. and Wynne-Edwards, K. E. (2000) Hormonal correlates of paternal responsiveness in new and expectant fathers. *Evolution and Human Behavior*, 21: 79–95.

Thornhill, R. and Alcock, J. (1983) *The Evolution of Insect Mating Systems*. Harvard University Press, Cambridge, MA.

Thornhill, R. and Gangestad, S. W. (1999) The scent of symmetry: a human pheromone that signals fitness? *Evolution and Human Behavior*, 20: 175–201.

Thornhill, R. and Gangestad, S. W. (2006) Facial sexual dimorphism, developmental stability and parasitic infections in men and women. *Evolution and Human Behavior*, 27: 131–144.

Thornhill, R., Gangestad, S. W., Miller, R., Scheyd, G., McCollough, J. and Franklin, M. (2003) MHC, symmetry and body scent attractiveness in men and women (*Homo sapiens*). *Behavioral Ecology*, 14: 668–678.

Trivers, R. L. (1974) Parent–offspring conflict. *American Zoologist*, 14: 269–264.

Trivers, R. L. and Willard, D. E. (1973) Natural selection of parental ability to vary the sex ratio of offspring. *Science*, 179: 90–92.

Waynforth, D. (1998) Fluctuating asymmetry and human male life history, traits in rural Belize. *Proceedings of the Royal Society of London, B*, 265: 1497–1501.

Williams, G. C. (1966) *Adaptation and Natural Selection*. Princeton University Press, Princeton, NJ.

Zahavi, A. (1975) Mate selection—a selection for a handicap. *Journal of Theoretical Biology*, 53: 205–214.

CHAPTER 24

Symmetry, attractiveness and sexual selection

Gillian Rhodes and Leigh W. Simmons

24.1. Symmetry, attractiveness and sexual selection

Over the last decade, research on the attractiveness of symmetry in humans has been prolific, motivated by the idea that symmetry honestly advertises mate quality and that a preference for symmetry may be an adaptation for mate choice (Palmer and Strobeck, 1986; Parsons, 1990; Gangestad *et al.*, 1994; Watson and Thornhill, 1994; Gangestad and Thornhill, 1997; Thornhill and Møller, 1997; Thornhill and Gangestad, 1999a). *Fluctuating asymmetry* (FA) is a form of asymmetry characterized by random deviations from perfect symmetry in bilaterally paired traits, which arises when stable development is disrupted by environmental stress and/or genetic factors (Mather, 1953; Van Valen, 1962; Zakharov, 1981). FA is therefore recognized as an outward expression of developmental instability and potentially of genetic quality and is of great interest to those studying the evolution of mate preferences via sexual selection (Møller and Swaddle, 1997; Møller and Thornhill, 1998; Polak *et al.*, 2003; Tomkins and Simmons, 2003).

In this chapter we consider whether a human preference for symmetry is an adaptation for mate choice. If it is, then symmetry should be attractive and it should signal mate quality. We begin with a brief introduction to sexual selection and its proposed relation to fluctuating asymmetry, highlighting some important methodological issues about the measurement of symmetry. Next we consider whether symmetry is attractive to humans, using meta-analyses to determine the strength of preferences for symmetric faces and bodies and to examine the effects of potential moderator variables. It will be apparent from this review that FA has not always been measured appropriately. Therefore, we present some new data on the relationship between human FA and mate choice to illustrate some of the appropriate steps required for a robust study. We then consider whether human symmetry honestly signals mate quality and reproductive success. We will argue that although symmetry is attractive, the links to mate quality, and particularly genetic quality, are weak, and that we need more rigorous measurement of FA and mate quality to make progress in this area.

24.2. Sexual selection and fluctuating asymmetry

Darwin (1871) suggested that female mating preferences could act as a selective force generating exaggerated secondary sexual traits in males, and a number of theoretical models have been developed to explain the evolutionary origins and maintenance of such preferences (Kirkpatrick and Ryan, 1991; Andersson, 1994).

These models can be broadly classified into models of direct and indirect selection. Under direct selection, male secondary sexual traits signal their ability to provide material benefits that enhance female fitness (e.g. Price *et al.*, 1993), or male signals arise because of some pre-existing sensory bias (preference) that enhances female fitness outside the context of reproduction (Endler and Basolo, 1998; Ryan, 1998). Under indirect selection, female preferences focus on male traits that honestly reveal an individual's underlying genetic quality. Thus, females that mate with males signalling 'good genes' produce offspring genetically equipped to survive and reproduce (Kokko *et al.*, 2002; Mead and Arnold, 2004).

The left and right sides of the body share the same genome, and all else being equal should undergo the same patterns of growth and development so that the adult organism becomes perfectly symmetrical about its central midline. However, small random perturbations in cell division can arise from the intrinsic stochasticity of developmental processes (Klingenberg, 2003), or can be induced, for example, by environmental stressors such as heat, toxins, pathogens, or dietary limitation (Parsons, 1990; Hoffman and Woods, 2003). Such perturbations can result in changes in the developmental processes that are localized to one or other side of the body. *Developmental instability* refers to an organism's sensitivity to perturbation, or its tendency to produce the morphological changes in response to perturbation that cause differences in morphology between left and right sides of the body (Klingenberg, 2003). Fluctuating asymmetry (FA), small random deviations from bilateral symmetry, can therefore be used as a phenotypic measure of an organism's developmental instability (Klingenberg, 2003; Palmer and Strobeck, 2003; Zakharov, 1981) (Figure 24.1). When we refer to FA in this chapter we mean strictly the random deviations from symmetry that are caused by developmental instability.

Considerable research has focused on the genetic basis of developmental instability. Livshits and Kobyliansky (1989) reported heritability estimates for human body asymmetry to be in the region of 0.25–0.30. A recent review of heritability estimates for a range of species reported median values for developmental instability of 0.017 (range −0.003 to 0.406) and

for FA of 0.020 (range −0.001 to 0.108) (Fuller and Houle, 2003). Although these values might suggest little additive genetic variance, previous studies have lacked the statistical power required to detect additive genetic variance in either developmental instability or FA (Fuller and Houle, 2003). Furthermore, variance in FA might arise, not because of genes that influence FA *per se*, but because of genetic variation at multiple loci that influence condition (Rowe and Houle, 1996) (Figure 24.1). Thus, individuals of intrinsically high condition may be less sensitive to perturbations during development, and exhibit lower levels of FA. If true, we would expect individuals with low levels of FA have greater overall fitness than those with high levels of FA.

There have been several attempts to assess the relationship between FA and fitness in a range of species, using correlates of fitness such as growth, fecundity and survival (Figure 24.1), and direct measures such as survival of offspring (for reviews see Leung and Forbes, 1996; Møller, 1997; Møller and Swaddle, 1997; Møller and Alatalo, 1999; Polak *et al.*, 2003). The results of these analyses do suggest a positive relationship between FA and fitness, but they have been subject to considerable debate (Leung and Forbes, 1996; Clarke, 1998; Møller, 1997, 1999).

A relationship between genetic quality and FA holds important implications for good-gene models of female preference evolution. Because female preferences can be favoured by genetic benefits accruing to offspring, female preferences might be expected to focus on levels of FA. Moreover, because secondary sexual traits can also be condition dependent, FA in these traits should be particularly sensitive to developmental instability, and particularly revealing of a male's genetic quality (Møller, 1993). The 1990s thus saw a surge of research interest into the role of FA in sexual selection. Numerous studies reported associations between secondary sexual trait expression and symmetry (males able to produce more exaggerated traits being found to produce more symmetrical traits) or between symmetry and male competitive success and/or attractiveness to females, and these studies generate an overall significant general effect size of −0.42 (Møller and Thornhill, 1998). Thus, the FA–sexual selection hypothesis was proposed, which states that FA

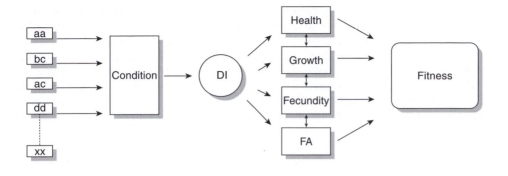

Genotype ⟶ Development ⟶ Phenotype ⟶ Reproductive success

Fig. 24.1 A model of the FA-sexual selection hypothesis. Variation at many loci is thought to influence developmental stability, either directly or via genetic effects on condition. Developmental instability in turn affects a number of correlates phenotypic traits such as health, growth and fluctuating asymmetry (FA), which contribute to fitness.

honestly signals an individual's genetic quality and can be used by females in adaptive mate choice.

Although the FA–sexual selection hypothesis has intuitive appeal, it has also proved controversial, primarily because the measurement of FA is not as simple as might first appear. FAs are extremely small, generally representing 1–2% of trait size, and have statistical properties similar to those of measurement error (Palmer and Strobeck, 2003). FA is measured by subtracting the size of the right side of a bilaterally paired trait from the size of the left side (L–R). Thus measured, FA is characterized by a normal distribution of L–R values about a mean of zero. Errors in the measurement of L–R will also be normally distributed about zero, and will inflate estimates of FA that are caused by developmental instability. An essential component of any study of FA is therefore an assessment of the repeatability of asymmetry measurement, in terms of its magnitude relative to measurement error (Palmer and Strobeck, 2003). This can be done by repeating the measurements and testing whether the variance between subjects is greater than the variance between the repeated measurements.

Moreover, there are three forms of biological asymmetry, directional asymmetry (DA), antisymmetry, and FA, but it is only FA that is caused by developmental instability. DA arises when one side of a trait is systematically larger than the other. In vertebrates for example, a considerable number of genes are known to be expressed on only one side of the body during development and produce dramatic L–R asymmetries in internal organs, and may also play a role in the development of external structures, such as insect wings or mandibles, that superficially appear to be bilaterally symmetrical but in fact exhibit subtle directional asymmetry (Klingenberg, 2003). DA can also arise due to phenotypic plasticity. For example, in human limb bones, differential use due to handedness can generate DA (Malina, 1983; Trinkaus et al., 1994). DA does not represent the morphological outcome of random perturbations during development, is therefore fundamentally different from FA, and not an expression of developmental instability (Klingenberg, 2003). Finally, directional asymmetry can also be a form of measurement error arising from experimenter handedness (Helm and Albrecht, 2000).

Antisymmetry occurs when an organism develops asymmetrically, but the side with the larger trait is determined randomly. In many crustaceans for example, the forelimbs or chaelae are initially symmetrical, but become asymmetrical during development. Asymmetry generally has some functional significance, such as the specialization of one claw for sexual signalling in male fiddler crabs (Backwell et al., 1998) or the specialization of one claw for crushing in lobsters (Govind and Pierce, 1986). The side of specialization is determined during ontogeny but is subject to environmental rather than genetic influence, and so does not reflect developmental instability. Antisymmetry is characterized by a bimodal distribution of L–R values because the side of specialization varies at random (Palmer and Strobeck, 2003). Thus, the second essential component of any study of FA is the assessment of the statistical properties of L–R distributions to confirm that the asymmetries observed are characteristic of FA rather than DA or antisymmetry (Palmer and Strobeck, 2003).

Unfortunately, initial enthusiasm for the FA–sexual selection hypothesis generated many studies that did not adequately assess measured asymmetries, so that in many cases it is not clear to what degree measurement error contributed to reported levels of asymmetry, or whether reported asymmetries were FA, the construct relevant to the FA-sexual selection hypothesis. One might think that if reported measures of asymmetry represented measurement error alone, then there should be no pattern of association between such measures and reproductive success. However, observer expectancy can generate pattern (Rosenthal, 1963). Indeed, meta-analyses of the FA–sexual selection hypothesis have reported general effect sizes that are influenced significantly by use of appropriate statistical methodology; the general effect size for tests of the FA–sexual selection hypothesis is some 30% lower when appropriate methodology is used, and studies that fail to use appropriate methodology have been significantly more likely to support the hypothesis (Simmons et al., 1999; Møller and Cuervo, 2003; Tomkins and Simmons, 2003).

24.3. **FA and human mate preferences**

At the outset we noted that research on the attractiveness of symmetry in humans has been prolific, motivated by the idea that a preference for symmetry may be an adaptation for mate choice. Given the substantial number of studies now available we thought it would be useful to present a meta-analytic review of the strength of the association between symmetry and attractiveness in humans. A meta-analysis allows one to estimate the overall effect size of an association using the effect sizes in published studies. It also offers a powerful tool for assessing the impact of moderator variables that may be of interest. Below we present the results of meta-analyses that assess the attractiveness of face symmetry and body symmetry. We begin with some comments on the measurement of symmetry in humans.

24.3.1. **Symmetry measurement**

Facial symmetry has typically been assessed using ratings. These have been shown to vary systematically with experimental manipulations of symmetry (Rhodes et al., 1999b) and to correlate, albeit modestly, with measured FA (Simmons et al., 2004 and see below; for further discussion see Rhodes, 2006). Body symmetry has usually been assessed using a small set of diverse body traits, although sometimes only dental or dermatoglyphic traits have been used. In Livshits and Kobyliansky's pioneering work (Livshits and Kobyliansky, 1988; Livshits et al., 1998), the following eight traits were measured: ear length, ear breadth, biepicondylar (elbow) breadth, bistyloid (wrist) breadth, hand breadth, bicondylar (knee) breadth, bimaleolar (ankle) breadth and foot breadth. Many subsequent studies have used these traits (except for bicondylar breadth) (e.g. Thornhill and Gangestad, 1994; Gangestad and Thornhill, 1997), although more recent studies have used finger (not thumb) lengths in preference to hands. A composite measure is usually derived by combining the traits because single traits are poor indices of developmental instability (Dufour and Weatherhead, 1996; Gangestad et al., 2001; Polak et al., 2003).

Unfortunately the measurement of human body FA is vulnerable to the methodological problems outlined above. Studies have not always assessed repeatability or inter-rater reliability or excluded DA. Failure to test for DAs is often justified by claiming that the traits used exhibit little DA in a very large sample (e.g. Furlow et al., 1998; Gangestad and Thornhill, 1998; Rikowski and Grammer, 1999; and many others). There is more power to detect

DAs in large samples and large samples provide better estimates of the underlying population distributions. However, the study cited as the primary source for this justification does not provide details about the 'large sample of 700 previous study participants' or any analyses of the data (Furlow *et al.*, 1997, p. 824). Furthermore, both hands and feet are described as showing significant DA (pp. 824 and 826). The large sample appears to be from a single population (University of New Mexico students) and DAs may well vary across populations. Studies with good-sized samples from other populations have certainly found significant DAs in some of these traits (e.g. Livshits *et al.*, 1998; Waynforth, 1998; and see below), and levels of DA can reflect measurement error so that they are unique to a given data set (Helm and Albrecht, 2000). Asymmetry measures with and without DA removed do correlate highly, but it is the non-shared variance that is theoretically important for the FA–sexual selection hypothesis (Gangestad *et al.*, 2001). Thus, a suitable approach would be to use a large sample and to eliminate DAs from the FA measure used. In the meta-analysis we will see how these methodological problems can interfere with effect-size estimates.

24.3.2. Is facial symmetry attractive?

Several early studies found that perfectly symmetric faces were less attractive than normal, slightly asymmetric, faces (Langlois *et al.*, 1994; Kowner, 1996). However, these studies all manipulated symmetry by reflecting each half of the face about the vertical midline to create two symmetric chimeras, which introduces unattractive structural abnormalities and counters any preference for symmetry (see Rhodes, 2006 for discussion). When symmetry is manipulated in other ways (e.g. by blending normal images with their mirror images or by warping normal faces into a symmetric configuration or vice versa) it is attractive (e.g. Rhodes *et al.*, 1998, 1999b; Perrett *et al.*, 1999; but see Swaddle and Cuthill, 1995). Converging evidence from normal, undistorted faces, also confirms the appeal of symmetry (Jones and Hill, 1993, for some ethnic groups; Grammer and Thornhill, 1994; Zebrowitz *et al.*, 1996; Rhodes *et al.*, 1998,

1999a,b; Mealey *et al.*, 1999; Rikowski and Grammer, 1999; Scheib *et al.*, 1999). The appeal of symmetrical faces cannot be explained by any associated increase in averageness (Rhodes *et al.*, 1999b) or change in skin texture (Perrett *et al.*, 1999; Rhodes *et al.*, 1999a).

We conducted a meta-analytic review of studies that have examined the relationship between attractiveness and facial symmetry. The studies were identified by searching literature databases (PsycInfo, MedLine, Biological Abstracts). A summary of the studies included is provided in Table 24.1. This meta-analysis is updated and slightly modified from Rhodes (2006). The main difference is that here we report an overall effect-size estimate based on independent samples. The goals of the meta-analysis were to estimate the strength of association between attractiveness and face symmetry and to assess the importance of some potential moderator variables (see below). Pearson's r was the measure of effect size used, with all calculations carried out using z_r, as recommended by Rosenthal (1991). We report associations with symmetry rather than asymmetry, so that positive relationships are expected if symmetry is attractive.

Estimates of overall effect size were calculated using a single effect size for each independent sample,[1] obtained by averaging across multiple effects where available. Male and female samples were considered independent. In all cases where effect sizes were averaged, size-weighted ($n - 3$) averages were used. We follow Cohen (1988) in interpreting effect sizes of 0.10, 0.30 and 0.50 as small, medium and large, respectively.

The following steps were taken to reduce non-independence when examining the effects of moderator variables (see below for details). Studies were excluded if effect sizes could not be calculated (Friedenberg, 2001), if the sample had been used in a previous paper (Gangestad and Thornhill, 1997; Koehler *et al.*, 2002; Zebrowitz and Rhodes, 2004; Rhodes *et al.*, 2005a), if the data were anecdotal (Baker, 1997), or if symmetric chimeras had been used to

---

[1] Unless explicitly stated to the contrary, we assumed that samples from the same population were independent.

Table 24.1 Summary of studies in faces meta-analysis

Study	Face Type	Face Sex	Face Race	Symmetry	Reliable	Repeatable	DA removed	ES r	n − 3
Jones and Hill (1993)	Normal	f	Brazilian	Measured	n	y	y	0.15	48
	Normal	f	Caucasian	Measured	n	y	y	0.01	49
	Normal	f	Ache	Measured	n	y	y	−0.03	38
	Normal	m	Brazilian	Measured	n	y	y	0.22	20
	Normal	m	Caucasian	Measured	n	y	y	−0.07	28
	Normal	m	Ache	Measured	n	y	y	0.12	39
Grammer and Thornhill (1994)	Normal	f	?	Measured	y	n	n	0.54	13
	Normal	m	?	Measured	y	n	n	0.48	13
Langlois et al. (1994)	Normal	f	?	Rated	na	na	n	0.11	48
Swaddle and Cuthill (1995)	Blend	fm	Caucasian	Manipulated	na	na	n	−0.32	157
Kowner (1996)	Normal	fm	Japanese	Measured	n	n	n	0.07	29
Zebrowitz et al. (1996)	Normal	fm	Caucasian	Rated	na	na	n	0.25	100
Shackelford and Larsen (1997)	Normal	f	?	Measured	y	n	n	−0.10	38
	Normal	m	?	Measured	y	n	n	0.24	13
Shackelford and Larsen (1997)	Normal	f	?	Measured	y	n	n	−0.02	23
	Normal	m	?	Measured	y	n	n	−0.01	15
Rhodes et al. (1998)	Blend	f	?	Rated	na	na	n	0.38	93
	Blend	m	?	Rated	na	na	n	0.23	93
	Normal	f	?	Rated	na	na	n	0.42	21
	Normal	m	?	Rated	na	na	n	0.01	21
Mealey et al. (1999)	Normal	fm	?	Rated	na	na	n	0.67	31
Perrett et al. (1999)	Warp	fm	Caucasian	Manipulated	na	na	n	0.60	27

Study		Sex	Ethnicity					Correlation	n
Perrett et al. (1999)	Warp	f	Caucasian	Manipulated	na	na	n	0.6	29
	Warp	m	Caucasian	Manipulated	na	na	n	0.59	29
Rhodes et al. (1999b)	Blend	f	Caucasian	Rated	na	na	n	0.41	143
	Blend	m	Caucasian	Rated	na	na	n	0.39	143
	Normal	f	Caucasian	Rated	na	na	n	0.41	21
	Normal	m	Caucasian	Rated	na	na	n	0.48	21
Rhodes et al. (1999a)	Normal	fm	Caucasian	Rated	na	na	n	0.69	37
	Blend	fm	Caucasian	Manipulated	na	na	n	0.62	17
	Warp	fm	Caucasian	Manipulated	na	na	n	−0.23	17
Rikowski and Grammer (1999)	Normal	f	?	Measured	y	n	n	−0.14	16
	Normal	m	?	Measured	y	n	n	0.60	13
Scheib et al. (1999)	Normal	m	?	Measured	y	n	n	0.48	37
Fink et al. (2001)	Normal	f	Caucasian	Measured	n	n	n	−0.09	17
Hume and Montgomery (2001)	Normal	f	Various	Measured	n	y	n	0.31	91
	Normal	m	Various	Measured	n	y	n	0.15	92
Jones et al. (2001)	Normal	f	?	Measured	n	n	n	0.41	27
	Normal	m	?	Measured	n	n	n	0.43	27
Penton-Voak et al. (2001)	Normal	m	Caucasian	Measured	n	n	n	0.22	63
	Normal	m	Caucasian	Rated	na	na	n	0.22	63
Rhodes et al. (2001a)	Blend	fm	Japanese	Manipulated	na	na	n	0.72	289
Rhodes et al. (2001b)	Normal	f	Various	Rated	na	na	n	0.24	158
	Normal	m	Various	Rated	na	na	n	0.27	150

Table 24.1 (continued) Summary of studies in faces meta-analysis

Study	Face Type	Face Sex	Face Race	Symmetry	Reliable	Repeatable	DA removed	ES r	n – 3
	Normal	f	Various	Measured	y	n	n	0.22	85
	Normal	m	Various	Measured	y	n	n	0.06	101
Little and Jones (2003)	Warp	fm	?	Manipulated	na	na	n	0.83	11
Baudouin and Tiberghien (2004)	Normal	f	?	Measured	n	n	n	0.34	59
Honekopp et al. (2004)	Normal	f	?	Measured	y	n	n	0.10	74
Jones et al. (2004)	Normal	m	Caucasian	Rated	na	na	n	0.21	110
Simmons et al. (2004)	Normal	f	Various	Measured	y	y	y	0.07	202
	Normal	m	Various	Measured	y	y	y	0.18	169
	Normal	f	Various	Rated	na	na	n	0.54	202
	Normal	m	Various	Rated	na	na	n	0.46	169
Thornhill and Gangestad (2006)	Normal	f	Various	Measured	n	n	n	0.19	200
	Normal	m	Various	Measured	n	n	n	0.05	200
Cardenas and Harris (2006)	Blend	fm	?	Manipulated	na	na	n	0.50	13
	Warp	fm	?	Manipulated	na	na	n	0.67	29

DA, directional asymmetry; ES, effect size; f, female; m, male; y, yes; n, no; na, not applicable.

assess the attractiveness of symmetry (Kowner, 1996; Noor and Evans, 2003).[2]

The overall effect size was 0.30 (SD = 0.30) (Table 24.2). This was estimated from 47 independent samples taken from 28 papers (Table 24.1). It was significantly greater than zero, $t(46) = 6.88$, $P < 0.001$, and the 95% confidence interval (0.22–0.38) clearly excluded zero. The size-weighted mean effect size was 0.28. The number of unpublished studies with null results needed to eliminate the significance of the effect at the 0.05 level, the failsafe number (Rosenthal, 1991), was 3610. Therefore, the result is robust to the file drawer problem (null results unpublished). Possible publication bias against studies that fail to find an association between symmetry and facial attractiveness was assessed by examining the funnel plot which shows effect sizes as a function of sample size (Figure 24.2). In the absence of any publication bias, the distribution will be symmetric about the mean effect for large samples. The obvious symmetry of the distribution, together with the absence of any correlation between effect size and sample size, $r(45) = -0.05$ (not significant), suggests little or no publication bias. All but one study (Jones et al., 2004) used independent measures of attractiveness and symmetry, so the overall estimate of effect size is unlikely to be biased by non-independence of the measures. Clearly, these results indicate a robust association between facial symmetry and facial attractiveness, with a medium effect size (see also Rhodes, 2006).

There was a high degree of heterogeneity across the samples, $\chi^2 (46) = 273.0$, $P < 0.001$, justifying the examination of moderator variables. We examined the effects of sex of face, race of face, and type of symmetry manipulation (none, blending, warping).[3] We also examined several methodological variables: method of assessing symmetry (measurements or ratings) for normal faces, and for measurements, whether inter-rater reliability and repeatability were assessed, and whether DAs were removed (appropriate methodology). To minimize non-independence of the effects included, effect sizes were averaged across rater sex, which does not affect the attractiveness of facial symmetry

---

[2] Rated similarity of left and right chimeric faces can be used as a measure of facial symmetry and studies using that measure were not excluded (Mealey et al., 1999; Jones et al., 2004).

[3] Studies using blending and warping to generate symmetric faces were not distinguished in the Rhodes (2006) meta-analysis. In blending, both texture and shape is affected, whereas in warping, only shape is altered.

Table 24.2 Summary of meta-analysis results for faces and bodies

	Faces	Bodies
Mean effect size (independent samples)	0.30	0.14
SD	0.30	0.14
95% confidence interval	0.22–0.38	0.08–0.20
No. of samples	47	26
No. of papers	28	16
Mean size-weighted ($n - 3$) effect size	0.28	0.11
Heterogeneity	273.0	32.7
Df	46	25
P	<<0.001	0.139
No. of failsafe studies at 0.05	3610	243

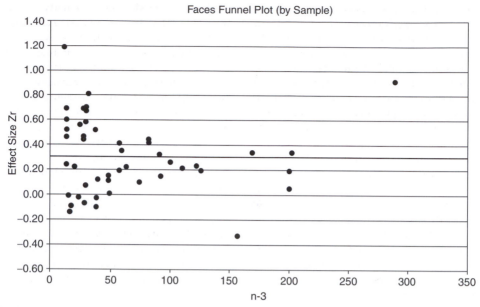

Fig. 24.2 Faces funnel plot. Effect size (Zr) as a function of sample size (N-3). Solid line represents average effect size estimated from all studies.

(Rhodes, 2006) and across different rater age groups where appropriate [excluding data from prepubescent (Zebrowitz et al., 1996) or elderly (Kowner, 1996) raters].

There were no significant effects of sex of face, $F(1,44) = 0.37$, $P = 0.54$ (mean ± SD effect size, 0.23 ± 0.24, $n = 23$, female faces; 0.27 ± 0.21, $n = 23$, male faces) or race of face, $F(2,33) = 0.28$, $P = 0.76$ (0.30 ± 0.34, $n = 18$, Western; 0.24 ± 0.33, $n = 6$, non-Western; 0.24 ± 0.17, $n = 12$, both). There was a significant effect of type of symmetry manipulation, $F(2,55) = 4.40$, $P < 0.02$. Not surprisingly, effect sizes were smaller when normal faces (no symmetry manipulation) were used (0.25 ± 0.24, $n = 44$) than when symmetry was experimentally manipulated by warping (0.54 ± 0.43, $n = 6$) or blending (0.38 ± 0.35, $n = 8$), although only the warping–normal difference was significant on a *post hoc* Scheffé S ($P < 0.03$). Symmetric blends could be more attractive than normal faces because they have smoother skin texture, but this cannot explain the appeal of symmetric warps, which have skin texture identical to the normal configurations. Interestingly, there was no significant difference between blending and warping studies. These results suggest

that stronger effects may occur when symmetry is experimentally manipulated, but importantly that the appeal of facial symmetry is still moderately strong (0.25) for normal faces.

Effect sizes were significantly higher when facial symmetry was rated (0.37 ± 0.24, $n = 14$) than when it was measured (0.18 ± 0.22, $n = 30$), $F(1,42) = 7.95$, $P < 0.008$. Interestingly, symmetry ratings have been shown to reflect facial FA (and not DA) (Simmons et al., 2004), whereas current measurement methods typically do not isolate FA (see Rhodes, 2006 for further discussion). Most measurement studies have not used appropriate methodology. The effect sizes reported in studies that assessed repeatability are about half (0.11 ± 0.12, $n = 10$) that of those that did not (0.22 ± 0.25, $n = 20$), although this difference was not significant, $F(1,28) = 1.60$, $P = 0.22$. There was no significant effect of whether inter-rater reliability was assessed (0.20 ± 0.26, $n = 14$) or not (0.16 ± 0.17, $n = 16$), $F(1,28) = 0.37$, $P = 0.55$.

24.3.3. Is Body symmetry attractive?

As with faces, we addressed this question with a meta-analytic review, following the same general procedures as outlined above. Bodies were considered separately from faces because different measures of attractiveness have been used for the two. Fewer studies have examined the attractiveness of body symmetry than of face symmetry. These are summarized in Table 24.3. The overall effect size was estimated from 26 independent samples taken from 16 papers. It was 0.14 (SD = 0.14), which was significantly greater than zero, $t(24) = 5.10$, $P < 0.001$. The 95% confidence interval (0.08–0.20) excluded zero. The size-weighted estimate of effect size was 0.11. These are small effects. The failsafe number of studies was 243, an order of magnitude lower than for faces. The funnel plot (Figure 24.3) was asymmetric, indicating likely publication bias against studies that failed to find a positive association between body symmetry and attractiveness. This was confirmed by a moderate, albeit non-significant, negative association between effect size and sample size, $r(23)$ = −0.29 (not significant). These results suggest that we should be cautious in concluding that body symmetry is attractive.

There was modest heterogeneity in effect sizes, χ^2 (25) = 32.7, $P = 0.139$. However, in contrast with face symmetry studies, which all examined facial attractiveness, body symmetry has been related to a variety of attractiveness metrics. These include attractiveness of the face, body and scent, and self-reported mating success (e.g. number of sexual partners, number of extra-pair copulations, age of first sex). Although different measures of mating success could potentially have different associations with body symmetry, we collapsed these into a single mating success variable because of the small number of studies available. We therefore examined the effects of the following moderator variables: type of attractiveness (face, body, scent, mating success), sex of body, whether inter-rater reliability and repeatability were assessed and whether DAs were removed.

Several steps were taken to reduce non-independence of effect sizes when examining the effects of moderator variables. We averaged effect sizes across different mating success

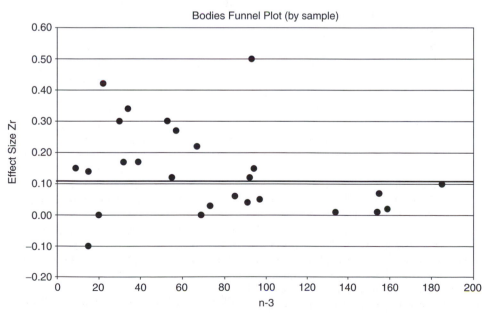

Fig. 24.3 Bodies funnel plot. Effect size (Zr) as a function of sample size (N-3). Solid line represents average effect size estimated from all studies.

Table 24.3 Summary of studies in body meta-analysis

Study	Attractiveness measure	Sex	Race	Symmetry	Reliable	Repeatable	DA removed	ES r	n – 3
Gangestad et al. (1994)	Face	f	Various	Measured	n	n	n	0.17	32
	Face	m	Various	Measured	n	n	n	0.33	34
Thornhill and Gangestad (1994)	Face	f	Various	Measured	n	n	n	-0.01	53
	Face	m	Various	Measured	n	n	n	0.27	57
	Mating success	f	Various	Measured	n	n	n	0.24	57
	Mating success	m	Various	Measured	n	n	n	0.25	56
Singh (1995)	Body	f	Caucasian	Rated	na	na	n	0.15	9
Gangestad and Thornhill (1997)	Face	f	Various	Measured	y	n	n	-0.01	187
	Face	m	Various	Measured	y	n	n	0.00	186
	Mating success	f	Various	Measured	y	n	n	0.03	121
	Mating success	m	Various	Measured	y	n	n	0.17	124
Furlow et al. (1998)	Face	f	?	Measured	n	y	n	0.01	134
	Face	m	?	Measured	n	y	n	0.06	85
Gangestad and Thornhill (1998)	Scent	m	Various	Measured	y	y	y	0.16	39
Waynforth (1998)	Mating success	m	Mayan	Measured	n	n	y	0.00	20
	Mating success	m	Mayan	Measured	n	n	y	0.29	30
Rikowski and Grammer (1999)	Face	f	?	Measured	n	y	y	-0.27	16
	Face	m	?	Measured	n	y	y	0.09	13
	Scent	f	?	Measured	n	y	n	0.08	16
	Scent	m	?	Measured	n	y	y	-0.18	13

Study	Trait	Sex	Population	FA				
Simpson et al. (1999)	Overall	m	?	Measured	y	n	0.00	69
Thornhill and Gangestad (1999b)	Face	f	Various	Measured	y	n	0.04	79
	Face	m	Various	Measured	y	n	0.10	77
	Mating success	f	Various	Measured	y	n	0.00	79
	Mating success	m	Various	Measured	y	n	0.34	77
	Scent	f	Various	Measured	y	n	0.04	62
	Scent	m	Various	Measured	y	n	0.21	46
Waynforth (1999)	Face	m	Mayan	Measured	n	y	0.29	53
Tovée et al. (2000), Expt 1	Body	f	?	Measured	n	n	0.19	22
	Body	f	?	Measured	n	n	0.31	22
Tovée et al. (2000), Expt 2	Body	f	?	Manipulated	na	n	0.65	22
Hume and Montgomerie (2001)	Face	f	Various	Measured	n	y	0.04	91
	Face	m	Various	Measured	n	y	0.12	92
Hughes et al. (2002)	Voice	fm	?	Measured	y	n	0.46	93
Thornhill et al. (2003)	Face	f	Various	Measured	y	y	0.03	97
	Face	m	Various	Measured	y	y	0.09	94
	Scent	f	Various	Measured	y	y	0.06	97
	Scent	m	Various	Measured	y	y	0.20	94
Rhodes et al. (2005)	Body	f	Various	Measured	n	y	0.16	189
	Body	m	Various	Measured	n	y	0.02	161
	Body	f	Various	Rated	na	n	0.19	189
	Body	m	Various	Rated	na	n	0.06	161

Table 24.3. (continued) Summary of studies in body meta-analysis

Study	Attractiveness measure	Sex	Race	Symmetry	Reliable	Repeatable	DA removed	ES r	n − 3
	Mating success	f	Various	Measured	n	y	y	0.03	182
	Mating success	m	Various	Measured	n	y	y	0.00	157
	Mating success	f	Various	Rated	na	na	n	0.00	180
	Mating success	m	Various	Rated	na	na	n	0.00	155

Gangestad et al. (2001) also examined the relationship between body symmetry and number of sex partners ($r = 0.27$, $n = 271$). However, their sample is not independent of Thornhill and Gangestad's (1999b). We include the effect size (ES) from the earlier study here.

DA, directional asymmetry; f, female; m, male; y, yes; n, no; na, not applicable.

measures reported for the same sample. We averaged effect sizes across rater sex because most studies report attractiveness ratings from male and female raters combined, so that the effect of rater sex could not sensibly be examined. We also averaged across female raters with different conception risks, where available. The effect of conception risk was assessed in a separate analysis (see below). Some studies report effect sizes with several different sets of control variables. In these cases, we averaged these effects. When age-controlled effect sizes were reported, these were used in preference to zero-order correlations.

There was no effect of attractiveness metric, $F(3,41) = 1.80$, $P = 0.16$, although the association with body attractiveness (0.23 ± 0.23, $n = 8$) was about double that for the other metrics of attractiveness (face: 0.08 ± 0.14, $n = 17$; scent: 0.12 ± 0.08, $n = 8$; mating success: 0.12 ± 0.14, $n = 12$). There was no significant difference in effect sizes for female (0.10 ± 0.19, $n = 22$) and male (0.14 ± 0.12, $n = 23$) bodies, $F(1,43) = 0.73$, $P = 0.40$.

The results for the methodological variables are particularly interesting. Effect sizes were three times larger when repeatability was not assessed (0.17 ± 0.15, $n = 0.23$) than when it was (0.06 ± 0.11, $n = 17$), $F(1,38) = 5.89$, $P < 0.02$. When repeatability was not assessed the mean effect size was very small (0.06), although still significantly greater than zero, $t(16) = 2.25$, $P < 0.05$. Effect sizes were also small when DAs were removed (0.08 ± 0.17, $n = 10$). These were about half the size of effect sizes when DAs were included (0.15 ± 0.17, $n = 36$), although this difference did not reach significance, $F(1,44) = 1.29$, $P = 0.26$. There was no significant effect of whether inter-rater reliability was assessed (0.12 ± 0.14, $n = 17$) or not (0.13 ± 0.15, $n = 23$), $F(1,38) = 0.04$, $P = 0.84$. These results show that effect sizes are considerably lower when appropriate methodology is used (see Tomkins and Simmons, 2003 for a similar finding from studies of non-human animals).

A few studies have examined menstrual cycle effects on the attractiveness of body symmetry (Table 24.4). A stronger preference at the fertile point of the cycle, when conception risk is high, might be consistent with the preference being an adaptation that targets good genes. We examined the effect of fertility level (high, low, pill-users, unknown) on female preferences for male[4] body symmetry. There was a significant effect of fertility level, $F(3,13) = 8.27$, $P < 0.003$, with a stronger effect size for the high (0.36 ± 0.12, $n = 4$) than the low (0.01 ± 0.13, $n = 4$) and unknown (0.10 ± 0.10, $n = 8$) fertility groups ($P < 0.02$, Scheffé S). The single pill-user group had an intermediate effect size (0.16) which did not differ significantly from any of the other groups. Although based on relatively few studies, these results suggest that body symmetry might be more attractive when conception risk is high, consistent with a good-genes account of symmetry preferences.

24.3.4. Comparing faces and bodies

The estimated overall effect size for bodies (0.14) was based on fewer samples (26) and was significantly smaller than the face effect (0.30), $F(1,91) = 6.74$, $P < 0.02$. Part of the difference in effect size could be due to the greater salience of symmetry in faces. Body symmetry, as typically measured, is extremely subtle, and any associations with attractiveness are probably mediated by associations with other cues (Thornhill and Gangestad, 1993, 1994). The most obvious candidate for such a cue is facial symmetry, but as we shall see below, face and body symmetry do not appear to be correlated. A difference in the design of the face and body symmetry studies may also contribute to the weaker relationship between attractiveness and body symmetry than facial symmetry. Whereas all the face studies assessed facial attractiveness, the body symmetry studies used a variety of attractiveness measures (face, body, scent, mating success). If, as seems likely, body symmetry is more strongly related to body attractiveness than to the other attractiveness measures, inclusion of those other measures would weaken the overall effect size. There is some support for this view, with a stronger average effect size for body attractiveness (0.23) than for the other measures: face (0.08), scent (0.12), or mating success (0.12).

---

[4] The one exception was Tovée et al. (2000), in which female bodies were rated.

Table 24.4 Summary of studies in fertility meta-analysis (all body studies)

Paper	Attractiveness measure	Sex	Symmetry	Reliable	Repeatable	DA removed	Rater fertility	ES r	n − 3
Gangestad and Thornhill (1998)	Scent	m	Measured	y	y	y	High	0.31	39
	Scent	m	Measured	y	y	y	Low	0.02	39
	Scent	m	Measured	y	y	y	Pill	0.16	39
Rikowski and Grammer (1999)	Face	m	Measured	n	y	y	Unknown	0.09	13
	Scent	m	Measured	n	y	n	High	0.50	13
	Scent	m	Measured	n	y	n	Low	−0.18	13
Simpson et al. (1999)	Overall	m	Measured	y	n	n	Unknown	0.00	69
Thornhill and Gangestad (1999)	Face	m	Measured	y	n	n	Unknown	0.10	77
	Scent	m	Measured	y	n	n	High	0.33	46
	Scent	m	Measured	y	n	n	Low	0.09	46
Tovée et al. (2000), Expt 1	Body	f	Measured	n	n	n	Unknown	0.31	22
Hume and Montgomerie (2001)	Face	m	Measured	n	y	n	Unknown	0.12	92
Thornhill et al. (2003)	Face	m	Measured	y	y	n	Unknown	0.09	94
	Scent	m	Measured	y	y	n	High	0.29	94
	Scent	m	Measured	y	y	n	Low	0.11	94
Rhodes et al. (2005)	Body	m	Measured	n	y	y	Unknown	0.02	161
	Body	m	Rated	na	na	n	Unknown	0.06	161

DA, directional asymmetry; ES, effect size; f, female; m, male; y, yes; n, no; na, not applicable.

Although these differences were not significant, this is arguably because of the small sample of studies available. Finally, this body attractiveness effect, which is derived from studies using normal, unmanipulated bodies, is very similar to the face attractiveness effect for normal faces (0.25). Thus, the greater overall effect size for faces may largely reflect the stronger effects obtained in studies that manipulate symmetry.

It is interesting to compare the results of our meta-analysis with those of Møller and Thornhill (1998). Their meta-analysis included studies of birds, insects and fish, as well as mammals, but if we consider just their mammal studies, most of which examined humans, we should have comparable data. Their human samples were almost evenly divided between face and body symmetry measurements, so that we would expect their effect size to be about halfway between those obtained here for faces (0.30) and bodies (0.14), i.e. around 0.22. With species as the unit of analysis, their effect size was 0.22 for mammals[5] and with studies as the unit of analysis it was 0.32. These results are not dissimilar to those obtained here.

24.3.5. Some new results on human FA and mate choice

As already noted, the use of appropriate methodology can substantially reduce effect sizes. For example, the meta-analyses revealed that effect sizes doubled (bodies) or tripled (faces) when repeatability was not assessed. Rigorous measurement of FA is also necessary to infer that a preference for symmetry targets mates of high genetic quality, because only FA is reflective of developmental instability and underlying genetic quality (Figure 24.1). In an attempt to illustrate some of the appropriate methodology, we re-examine the effects of face and body FA on attractiveness and self-reported mating success, in a large sample of 172 male and 205 female subjects for which we have data.

[5] They reported negative associations with asymmetry, which have been reversed here to show the association with symmetry.

We begin by reporting the statistical properties of L–R asymmetries in this sample.

Simmons et al. (2004) conducted a rigorous assessment of these properties for faces in this sample. They used 15 landmarks to generate 35 pairwise distances between points on each side of the face and calculated L–R differences. Measurements were repeated using replicate photographs of each participant's face. All measures were repeatable (Appendix 1 in Simmons et al., 2004). Only 34% of traits in male faces and 20% in female faces had statistical properties characteristic of FA. Conversely, 66% and 80% of traits showed DA, with the right hemiface being significantly larger than the left hemiface. None the less, despite the considerable degree of DA in faces, people's ratings of symmetry were predicted by traits showing FA rather than DA. These results suggest that despite high levels of directional asymmetry in human faces, humans can detect subtle underlying FAs in faces that are revealing of developmental instability. For a more detailed analysis, see Simmons et al. (2004).

Although the statistical properties of facial asymmetries have been examined for this sample, the statistical properties of body asymmetries have not (although some body symmetry data are reported in Rhodes et al., 2005a). We provide this analysis in Box 24.1.

Our analysis shows that for the traits typically measured in studies of human body symmetry, raw values of asymmetry are inappropriate as measures of developmental instability. The use of single traits, such as female foot width or male wrist width that do show FA are unlikely to provide a robust measure of an individual's overall developmental instability (Dufour and Weatherhead, 1996; Gangestad et al., 2001; Polak et al., 2003). Therefore to use information from multiple traits, we need a method whereby FA can be isolated from other forms of trait asymmetry. Previously, we have used Graham et al.'s (1998) major axis technique to calculate estimates of FA for facial traits that have population-wide characteristics of DA (Simmons et al., 2004). We found that for both male and female faces, random deviation from symmetry about the population mean level of DA (FA corrected for DA) was a significant predictor of perceptions of symmetry by human raters, even though DA

Box 24.1 Assessing statistical properties of asymmetry data

We have data available for 166 males and 196 females with which to illustrate some appropriate methodology for the assessement of asymmetry data. Repeated measurements were taken of the left and right foot length, foot width, ankle width, wrist width, elbow width, ear length, and ear width (for detailed methodology see Rhodes *et al.*, 2005a). The asymmetry measurements of all traits were repeatable (see Rhodes *et al.*, 2005a) and the statistical properties of the signed L–R values are provided in Table 24.B1. Male and female bodies are treated separately because of sexual dimorphism in body size and shape. Distributions of traits are frequently leptokurtic, which can arise due to a mixture of individuals with FA and antisymmetry, heterogeneity of L–R variation due to size dependence, or true variation in developmental instability among individuals in the sample (Palmer and Strobeck, 2003). More importantly, however, most traits showed DA. For both male and female bodies, the right ear was larger than the left. This pattern is broadly consistent with the right hemiface dominance reported by Simmons *et al.* (2004), and can be explained by a general tendency for the right side of the head to be larger than the left. For both male and female bodies the elbow was also wider on the left than the right, and for male bodies foot width was on average larger on the right. DA may reflect differences in the functionality of left and right sides of the body, and/or can arise because of handedness of the experimenters measuring the traits (see main text).

The method for determining whether asymmetry in bilateral traits conforms with a population-wide pattern of FA or DA is potentially problematic because it depends on acceptance of the null hypothesis that the mean asymmetry is equal to zero. As such, the tests depend on statistical power. Distinction between FA and DA will therefore depend on sample size, and, with large samples, very small directional asymmetries may be statistically significant even though they have no biological impact. The question of biological significance is therefore relevant here (Colegrave and Ruxton, 2003). Cohen's (1988) standardized effect sizes (d) and their 95% confidence bands are provided in Table 24.B1. For male bodies the effect sizes for traits showing DA range from 0.258 to 0.599 with a mean ± SE of 0.378 ± 0.078. For the smallest effect size, we could reject an effect size <0.103 and >0.413 at the 2.5% level. For female bodies the effect sizes for traits showing DA ranged from 0.159 to 0.320 with a mean of 0.248 ± 0.047. For the smallest effect size, we could reject an effect size smaller than 0.017 and larger than 0.300 at the 2.5% level. These effect sizes show that the traits for which we reject the null hypothesis of FA have biologically relevant levels of DA. The same was true for many facial traits (Simmons *et al.*, 2004).

Finally, asymmetry measures may be influenced by injuries incured during development, so that it is important to obtain such information from participants. In this data set reported injuries did not contribute significantly to asymmetry for males or females (see Rhodes *et al.*, 2005).

Table 24.B1 Statistical properties of left–right measurements of body traits

Trait	Mean	SD	Normality (Shapiro–Wilk)	Skewness	Kurtosis	$H_0 = 0$	P	Effect size, d	95% CI for effect size
Males						t_{165}			
Foot width	-0.70	2.70	0.937***	-0.993	4.649	3.329	0.001	-0.258	-0.413, -0.103
Foot length	0.04	0.31	0.983	-0.192	0.768	1.732	0.085	0.134	-0.019, 0.287
Ankle width	0.34	1.98	0.977**	0.399	1.970	2.207	0.029	0.171	0.018, 0.324
Wrist width	0.12	1.88	0.984*	0.470	0.672	0.787	0.432	0.061	-0.091, 0.213
Elbow width	0.52	1.84	0.935***	-0.736	5.687	3.633	0.000	0.282	0.126, 0.437
Ear length	-1.11	1.85	0.981*	-0.468	0.798	7.718	0.000	0.599	0.433, 0.764
Ear width	-0.56	1.48	0.991	-0.006	-0.559	4.821	0.000	0.374	0.216, 0.531
Females						t_{193}			
Foot width	-0.16	1.89	0.989	0.054	0.331	1.187	0.237	-0.085	-0.226, 0.056
Foot length	0.00	0.24	0.939***	-0.856	2.813	0.205	0.838	0.015	-0.126, 0.155
Ankle width	-0.31	1.60	0.988	0.192	0.873	0.271	0.786	-0.020	-0.160, 0.121
Wrist width	0.08	1.42	0.991	-0.208	0.894	0.820	0.414	0.059	-0.082, 0.200
Elbow width	0.35	1.32	0.978**	0.498	1.687	3.669	0.000	0.263	0.120, 0.406
Ear length	-0.27	1.69	0.994	-0.155	2.856	2.202	0.029	-0.159	-0.300, -0.017
Ear width	-0.60	1.87	0.993	-0.076	0.567	4.449	0.000	-0.320	-0.464, -0.176

$*P < 0.05$; $**P < 0.01$; $***P < 0.001$.

Distributions are skewed to the left or right with negative and positive values respectively. Distributions with positive kurtosis are leptokurtic (an excess of data at the mean and a deficit at the shoulders of the distribution) while those with negative kurtosis are platykurtic (flat or bimodal). Student's t tests the deviation of the mean from zero.

itself was not. Moreover, FA corrected for DA correlated well with asymmetry in facial traits that showed pure FA, suggesting that both metrics extract information relating to developmental instability (Simmons *et al.*, 2004). Correcting for DA is only likely to provide information on developmental instability when asymmetries are small, as in human face and body traits, and it must be recognized that such methods offer best-of-a-bad-job approximations (Klingenberg, 2003; Palmer and Strobeck, 2003). Here we use Graham *et al.*'s (1998) approach on the measures of body asymmetry in our data set of 166 male and 196 female bodies.

Briefly, a principal components analysis (PCA) of the covariance matrix between measures of left and right sides is conducted for each trait. Factor scores on the first principal component represent the sum of the variation in left and right trait sizes. Scores on the second principal component represent estimates of individual asymmetry corrected for the population average difference between sides (Graham *et al.*, 1998). Given that the majority of the seven body traits showed DA (Box 24.1), we conducted a PCA for all traits and calculated a composite measure of FA corrected for DA by summing the absolute PC2 scores across traits and dividing by the number of traits in the composite.

We then asked whether FA influenced perceptions of attractiveness or symmetry. Measured body FA influenced perceptions of symmetry for male but not female bodies (Table 24.5). FA influenced male perceptions of female body attractiveness but did not influence female perceptions of male body attractiveness (Table 24.5). For comparative purposes, in Table 24.5 we also report our previous results for faces. Having extracted body FA scores for these individuals, we then examined whether FA was associated with mating success. Partial correlations between face or body FA and several mating success variables for males and females, controlling for age, are presented in Table 24.6. There is little evidence for any association in men (Table 24.6a) or women (Table 24.6b) in our data set.

In conclusion, we suggest that for faces, our perceptions of symmetry are attuned to the FA that signals underlying developmental instability,

and that FA in men's faces contributes to their attractiveness to women. However, men's (or women's) facial FA did not influence their actual (self-reported) reproductive success. Consistent with the meta-analysis, our data are less clear for bodies. Perceptions of symmetry in men's bodies were dependent upon FA but the same was not true for female bodies. Conversely, FA predicted men's attractiveness judgements of women but not vice versa, and neither men's or women's mating successes were correlated with their face or body FA. The average effect size for attractiveness of our rigorously assessed body FA (0.05) was consistent with the very small overall effect size for rigorous studies in the meta-analysis (0.06), rather than that of studies that failed to adopt appropriate methodology (0.17).

Many studies that have found sexual behaviour to be related to body symmetry have argued that it is unlikely that women (or men) could perceive the subtle deviations from symmetry that characterize FA (e.g. Thornhill and Gangestad, 1994). It is possible that preferences focus on correlated symmetry in faces. However, for our data set there were no significant correlations between FA in faces and FA in bodies (males: body FA in DA traits versus face FA, $r = 0.014$, $n = 161$, $P = 0.860$; and face FA in DA traits, $r = -0.012$, $n = 161$, $P = 0.880$; females: body FA in DA traits versus face FA, $r = -0.028$, $n = 194$, $P = 0.704$; and face FA in DA traits, $r = 0.017$, $n = 194$, $P = 0.820$). The same is true for ratings of face and body symmetry (males: $r = 0.069$, $n = 160$, $P = 0.384$; females: $r = 0.119$, $n = 196$, $P = 0.100$).

24.4. **FA and human mate quality**

Symmetry has been linked with reduced rates of parasitism in a wide range of species, raising the possibility that it might reflect genetic resistance to disease (for reviews see Møller and Swaddle, 1997; Thornhill and Møller, 1997). If it does, then symmetric mates may provide heritable disease resistance to offspring. Alternatively, disease resistance might not be heritable, or causation might go the other way, with infection causing asymmetries. In these cases symmetric mates might provide more direct benefits, such

Table 24.5 Regression coefficients describing the effects of measured fluctuating asymmetry (FA) on perceptions of symmetry and attractiveness

	Male			Female		
	Faces		Bodies	Faces		Bodies
	FA	FA in DA traits	FA in DA traits	FA	FA in DA traits	FA in DA traits
Symmetry	$-0.29 \pm 0.15^*$ (0.07)	$-0.48 \pm 0.19^{**}$ (0.13)	$-0.23 \pm 0.11^*$ (0.08)	$-0.30 \pm 0.13^*$ (0.08)	$-0.61 \pm 0.18^{**}$ (0.12)	-0.08 ± 0.14 (0.02)
Attractiveness	0.39 ± 0.21 (0.07)	$-0.55 \pm 0.19^{***}$ (0.11)	0.00 ± 0.18 (0.00)	0.09 ± 0.16 (0.02)	-0.30 ± 0.22 (0.05)	$-0.46 \pm 0.17^{**}$ (0.10)

$^*P < 0.05$; $^{**}P < 0.01$; $^{***}P < 0.001$.

Effect size r in parentheses. Ratings of symmetry were made by mixed-sex raters, and attractiveness by opposite-sex raters. For faces, two metrics of FA were available, composite FA in traits exhibiting the statistical properties of pure FA, and FA about directionally asymmetrical traits (FA controlling for DA). Thus, for faces, partial coefficients show the relative effects of each metric (taken from Simmons et al., 2004). All asymmetry values were ln(x)-transformed to achieve normality.

Table 24.6a Kendall's partial correlations controlling for age, between men's sexual behaviour and face or body fluctuating asymmetry (FA)

	FA			FA in DA traits		
	Kendall τ	P	n	Kendall τ	P	n
Face						
Age at first sex	0.009	0.879	144	0.035	0.530	144
No. of sexual partners	-0.064	0.220	166	-0.037	0.479	166
Short-term partners	-0.025	0.645	160	-0.063	0.237	160
EPCs (cheating)	-0.045	0.394	165	-0.026	0.616	165
Long-term partners	-0.021	0.698	161	0.020	0.701	161
Body						
Age at first sex				-0.001	0.983	144
No. of sexual partners				0.021	0.683	166
Short-term partners				0.093	0.082	160
EPCs (cheating)				0.005	0.917	165
Long-term partners				0.026	0.621	161

For faces, two metrics of FA were available, composite FA in traits exhibiting the statistical properties of pure FA, and FA about directionally asymmetrical traits (FA controlling for DA). EPCs, extra-pair copulations.

Table 24.6b Kendall's partial correlations controlling for age, between women's sexual behaviour and face or body fluctuating asymmetry (FA)

		FA			FA in DA traits		
		Kendall τ	P	n	Kendall τ	P	n
Face	Age at first sex	−0.075	0.160	158	0.099	0.065	158
	No. of sexual partners	0.051	0.288	196	−0.004	0.930	196
	Short-term partners	−0.033	0.503	192	−0.011	0.827	192
	EPCs (cheating)	−0.036	0.452	194	0.033	0.495	194
	Long-term partners	0.089	0.066	192	−0.007	0.889	192
Body	Age at first sex				−0.037	0.497	156
	No. of sexual partners				−0.037	0.448	194
	Short-term partners				0.015	0.754	190
	EPCs (cheating)				−0.011	0.818	192
	Long-term partners				0.002	0.975	190

For faces, two metrics of FA were available, composite FA in traits exhibiting the statistical properties of pure FA, and FA about directionally asymmetrical traits (FA controlling for DA). EPCs, extra-pair copulations.

as resources or reduced risk of contagion, because they are healthier. In either case symmetry would be an honest indicator of mate quality, and so preferences for symmetry could be adaptations for mate choice. Here we review the evidence for a link between symmetry and mate quality in humans. Most studies have focused on health, as will this review, although health is clearly not the only component of mate quality.[6]

24.4.1. Facial symmetry and mate quality

In a major review of the early literature, Thornhill and Møller (1997) concluded that there were elevated levels of dental asymmetry in major chromosomal disorders, particularly Down's syndrome, in cleft-lip populations, and in other genetic disorders. However, the evidence for elevated facial asymmetry in genetic disorders may be weaker than it first appears, because these studies often focus on single traits (e.g. dental asymmetry) and do not always isolate FA.

The evidence for a link between facial symmetry and health in non-clinical populations is weak (for a recent review, see Rhodes, 2006). There are few studies and all but one (Rhodes et al., 2001b) relied on self-reported health measures (Honekopp et al., 2004; Hume and Montgomerie, 2001; Shackelford and Larsen, 1997), which are vulnerable to forgetting, and to bias. Bias is not a trivial problem. If less symmetric people are less attractive, then their affective state is more likely to be negative as a result of less favourable treatment by others, and negative events will be more likely to be recalled (see Rhodes, 2006 for further discussion). This type of bias could create a spurious correlation between symmetry and self-reported health. Further, the reported correlations were weak (Hume and Montgomery, 2001[7]; Honekopp et al., 2004) or failed to replicate in a second sample (Shackelford and Larsen, 1997). In one case,

more than 1000 correlations were examined, raising the probability of type I statistical errors (Shackelford and Larsen, 1997). The only study that used medically assessed lifetime health data reported no significant correlations between facial symmetry and health at any point during development in a large non-clinical sample (Rhodes et al., 2001b).

Recently, Thornhill and Gangestad (2006) have reported significant correlations of facial asymmetry with number of, and days infected with, self-reported respiratory infections in the last 3 years in a large student sample. However, the correlation with number of infections would not survive Bonferroni correction for multiple correlations ($n = 4$, counting correlations with number of, and days infected with, stomach/intestinal infections). Nor would the correlation with days infected, when age, height, weight and SES are controlled. Correlations with combined respiratory and stomach/intestinal infections did not reach statistical significance.

The non-clinical studies are summarized in Table 24.7. We calculated an effect size for each independent sample in these studies and used these to estimate the mean effect size. The resulting effect size was very small (0.04 ± 0.09, $n = 11$). It did not differ significantly from zero and the 95% confidence interval (-0.01 to 0.09) did not exclude zero. We conclude that there is little evidence that facial symmetry signals health, at least in non-clinical populations.

One possibility is that poor methodology accounts for the largely negative results. These studies have not generally measured true FA or assessed repeatability when asymmetries are measured. However, studies that used ratings of symmetry (Rhodes et al., 2001a; Zebrowitz et al., 2004), which seem to capture facial FA (Simmons et al., 2004), also failed to find an association. Another possibility is that a pre-existing link between facial symmetry and health has been broken by modern medicine. However, no such link was found for participants born in the 1920's before vaccinations and antibiotics were available (Rhodes et al., 2001b). Nor has the link between health and facial averageness or health and masculinity in male faces been broken (Rhodes et al., 2001, 2003), further reducing the plausibility of the broken-link hypothesis.

---

[6] A few studies have examined physiological fitness (e.g. Manning et al., 1997; Tomkinson and Olds, 2000), but these are not reviewed here.

[7] Their symmetry measure combined face and body symmetry.

Table 24.7 Summary of studies examining the relationship between symmetry and health in non-clinical samples

Paper	Health measure	Period	Sex	Race	Reliable	Repeatable	DA removed	ES r	n − 3
Face studies									
Shackelford and Larsen (1997), sample 1	Self-report	4 weeks	f	?	y	n	n	0.02	38
	Self-report	4 weeks	m	?	y	n	n	0.16	13
Shackelford and Larsen (1997), sample 2	Self-report	2 months	f	?	y	n	n	0.13	23
	Self-report	2 months	m	?	y	n	n	−0.14	15
Hume and Montgomerie (2001)	Self-report	Lifetime	f	Various	n	y	n	0	91
	Self-report	Lifetime	m	Various	n	y	n	0	92
Rhodes et al. (2001)	Medical records	Lifetime	f	Various	y	n	n	−0.01	130
	Medical records	Lifetime	m	Various	y	n	n	0.07	71
Honekopp et al. (2004)	Self-report	?	f	?	y	n	n	0.14	74
Thornhill et al. (2006)	Self-report	Last 3 years	f	Various	y	n	n	0.06	200
	Self-report	Last 3 years	m	Various	y	n	n	0.05	200
Body studies									
Waynforth (1998)	Self-report	Adulthood	m	Mayan	n	n	y	0.31	53
Hume and Montgomerie (2001)	Self-report	Lifetime	f	Various	n	y	n	0	91
	Self-report	Lifetime	m	Various	n	y	n	0	92
Milne et al. (2003)	Self-report	Last 5 years	fm	Various	n	?	n	0.06	965
Honekopp et al. (2004)	Self-report	?	f	?	y	y	n	0.17	74
Thornhill et al. (2006)	Self-report	Last 3 years	f	Various	y	n	n	0.06	200
	Self-report	Last 3 years	m	Various	y	n	n	0.03	200

A single size-weighted mean effect size (ES) was calculated for each independent sample.

All ESs are for measured symmetry, except for Rhodes et al. (2001) where effects for measurements and ratings were combined.

DA, directional asymmetry; f, female; m, male; y, yes; n, no.

Another important component of mate quality is intelligence. To our knowledge, only one study has looked for an association between facial symmetry and intelligence. Zebrowitz *et al.* (2002) found a moderate and highly significant correlation between rated facial symmetry and IQ scores in childhood, which was confined to participants who were below the median in symmetry (Zebrowitz and Rhodes, 2004). However, no relationship was found for IQ during puberty, adolescence, middle or late adulthood (these samples overlap with those used in Rhodes *et al.*, 2001b). So far, then, there is no evidence that facial symmetry is a valid cue to the intelligence of potential mates.

24.4.2. Body symmetry and mate quality

Elevated body asymmetry has been reported in a variety of chromosomal and genetic disorders as well as in mental retardation and schizophrenia (for reviews, see Livshits and Kobyliansky, 1991; Thornhill and Møller, 1997). As with the face studies, these studies often focus on single traits (fingerprint asymmetry) and do not isolate FA. However, true FA based on eight morphometric body traits was negatively associated with gestational age (at birth) and positively associated with cardiovascular and respiratory disease in a sample of pre-term and full-term infants (Livshits *et al.*, 1988). More recently, true FA in breast volume (again a single trait) has been reported to be significantly higher in women with breast cancer than in healthy controls (Scutt *et al.*, 1997). The obvious possibility that the asymmetry was directly caused by the tumours was rejected because FA did not correlate with tumour size.

The relationship between body symmetry and health has also been examined in several non-clinical samples. These studies have all used composite measures of FA derived from a small set of body traits, as in the attractiveness studies reviewed above. The strongest association has been reported in a rural sample in Belize with high exposure to pathogens (Waynforth, 1998). Symmetry was assessed based on seven body traits, with DA eliminated. Unfortunately, repeatability could not be demonstrated because the traits could only be measured once. We saw above that

effect sizes for the association between body symmetry and attractiveness were on average three times higher when repeatability was not assessed. If the same relationship holds for the associations between body symmetry and health, then the moderate effect size of 0.31 (calculated from Waynforth's χ^2 result, following Rosenthal, 1991) would reduce to a small effect of 0.10.

Modest associations between symmetry and self-reported number of medical conditions in the last 5 years have also been reported within a very large sample from a Western population (Milne *et al.*, 2003), and with the self-reported number of infections (collapsed across respiratory and stomach/intestinal infections) in the last 3 years in a large student sample (Thornhill and Gangestad, 2006). However, these studies did not measure true FA (DAs were not eliminated), although Milne *et al.* comment that the same results are obtained if they are. Other studies have failed to find such associations. Hume and Montgomerie (2001) failed to find any association with (experimenter-assessed) severity of self-reported diseases in a large student sample. Honekopp *et al.* (2004) also failed to find a significant association with health, assessed using a symptom checklist in a smaller student sample. These non-clinical studies are summarized in Table 24.7. The mean effect size calculated from these studies was 0.09 (SD = 0.12, n = 7). This was only marginally different from zero, $t(6) = 1.98$, $P < 0.10$, and the 95% confidence interval (0.00–0.18) did not exclude zero. Consistent with this result is the finding that chronically undernourished children from a rural population in southern Mexico were no more asymmetric than well-nourished middle class Texans (Little *et al.*, 2002), suggesting that health stress has little impact on human body asymmetry. Elevated asymmetry levels have been found in a foraging population, although it is not clear that this population was under health stress (Gray and Marlowe, 2002). However, neither study measured true FA.

There are problems with the measurement of both health and symmetry in most of these studies. Health is assessed by self-report, which is vulnerable to forgetting and reporting biases, and directional asymmetries have not been eliminated, although repeatability has generally been assessed. Therefore, although there may be some small associations between these symmetry measurements and health, we cannot be confident that FA has been measured, and therefore, that health is dependent upon an individual's underlying genetic quality. Without such an association a preference for symmetry would not identify mates with heritable resistance to disease.

Body symmetry may honestly advertise another important component of mate quality, namely intelligence. Three studies have reported moderate associations between body symmetry and scores on intelligence tests in student samples (Furlow *et al.*, 1998; Prokosch *et al.*, 2005; Thoma *et al.*, 2005). These associations are quite convincing given the relatively restricted range of intelligence expected in a student sample. In Furlow *et al.* (1998), the associations held when true FA was used.

Does symmetry increase reproductive success in humans? The meta-analysis indicated a weak relationship between body symmetry and number of partners, which should translate into greater reproductive success for symmetric men in the absence of contraception. Waynforth (1998) examined whether it does in a community that rarely uses modern contraceptive methods. Body symmetry was a highly significant (regression) predictor of number of children (controlling age and age-squared). However, as noted above, the strong effect (0.41, calculated from his χ^2 data) may overestimate the true association given that repeatability was not assessed. Breast symmetry also predicts number of children in women (Møller *et al.*, 1995; Manning *et al.*, 1997). However, in these studies symmetry was measured after childbearing, and clearly having more children may simply increase asymmetry.

Evidence that sperm quality is higher in men with more symmetric bodies also suggests that reproductive success may be associated with symmetry (in the absence of contraception). Body symmetry (based on four body traits, and without appropriate methodology) predicted the number of sperm in copulatory ejaculations in a small student sample (Baker, 1997). Digit (finger) symmetry (again without appropriate methodology) was correlated with number and motility of sperm in masturbatory samples in a larger fertility clinic sample (Manning *et al.*, 1998), and body FA (rigorously assessed, and based on three traits) predicted sperm number, motility and sperm head length in masturbatory samples in a general population sample (Firman *et al.*, 2003). These results support the view that a preference for body FA could provide direct fertility benefits through mate choice, even though the meta-analysis suggests that preference for body symmetry seems weak at best. The preference for facial symmetry is stronger, and it would be very interesting to know whether facial symmetry is also associated with sperm quality.

There may also be a link between body FA and offspring survival. Livshits and Kobyliansky (1988) found that FA in both mothers and fathers was higher for pre-term (and therefore at-risk) infants, although the difference was only significant for mothers. Waynforth (1998), however, found no link between father's FA and infant mortality in his rural Belize sample. Mother's FA was not measured.

24.5 Conclusions

The last few decades have seen enormous interest in the study of human attractiveness from an evolutionary perspective and much progress has been made. The results of our meta-analytic review clearly show that facial symmetry is attractive, with a moderate effect size and no evidence of publication bias. Our own rigorous analysis of FA shows that it is FA, rather than other forms of asymmetry, that underlies the attractiveness of symmetry in faces. Symmetry is also attractive in bodies, although the meta-analysis yielded a smaller effect size based on fewer studies. There were also indications of possible publication bias against negative effects and evidence that effects were smaller when appropriate methodology is used. Our own analysis of FA revealed a relatively weak link with attractiveness, which was restricted to male bodies, and no link with mating success.

Whereas the link between symmetry and attractiveness was clearer for faces than for bodies, the reverse was true for the proposed link between symmetry and mate quality. For faces, we found little convincing evidence that symmetry is an honest signal of health in the general population, although asymmetry may be elevated in some genetic disorders. For bodies we found a small association with health in non-clinical samples. The strongest evidence came from a rural sample with high exposure to pathogens (Waynforth, 1998), but repeatability was not assessed, which we have seen can be associated with inflated effect sizes. Widespread reliance on self-report measures of health and failure to adopt appropriate methodology, particularly failure to eliminate DA, when measuring FA also weaken these studies. Like facial asymmetry, body asymmetry is elevated in some genetic disorders. However, even this evidence is weak, because studies often focus on single traits, which are poor measures of organism-wide developmental instability, and rigorous assessment of FA is not always used. Associations have been reported between body symmetry and other aspects of mate quality, most notably, intelligence and sperm quality. Again, with few exceptions (Firman *et al.*, 2003) however, FA has not been rigorously measured.

In light of all this, what can we conclude about sexual selection and symmetry preferences in humans? Let's consider faces and bodies separately. For faces, FA is attractive but there is little evidence that it signals mate quality. We cannot, therefore, conclude that a preference for symmetric faces is an adaptation for obtaining indirect genetic benefits from mate choice. Alternatively, it may be a by-product of the way brains process information. That is, our preference for symmetry may conform more to a sensory bias model of direct preference evolution (Endler and Basolo, 1998; Ryan, 1998). The human visual system is very sensitive to bilateral symmetry and symmetry detection facilitates a range of visual processes, including figure–ground segmentation and recognition of objects from novel viewpoints (for discussion see Rhodes *et al.*, 2005b; Scognomillo *et al.*, 2003). Furthermore, symmetry is attractive in a wide range of stimuli other than conspecifics (see Rhodes, 2006 for discussion).

There is also little reason to be confident that a preference for symmetric bodies is an adaptation for obtaining indirect genetic benefits from mate choice. The FA–sexual selection account requires that FA is linked to mate quality and attractiveness, because it is FA that is

theoretically linked to genetic quality (Figure 1). However, as we have seen, many studies have not adequately measured FA, either because they did not distinguish it from measurement error or because they did not eliminate DAs. Nevertheless, reported links between body symmetry and several aspects of mate quality, including health, sperm quality and intelligence, suggest that body symmetry may convey information pertinent to direct benefits. On this account the form of asymmetry is irrelevant, because it does not depend on links with genetic quality or developmental instability. The direct benefits resulting from a preference for symmetric bodies might include the provision of resources or the avoidance of contagion from unhealthy mates.

In this review, we have focused on the FA–sexual selection account. We suggest that future progress in testing this account in humans requires rigorous measurement and analysis of FA. Multiple traits should be used rather than single traits, because they provide better estimates of developmental instability, by better detecting responses to stressors experienced at different points during development and by tapping consistent individual differences in developmental instability (Dufour and Weatherhead, 1996; Gangestad *et al.*, 2001; Polak *et al.*, 2003). More rigorous health measures are also needed, ideally based on medical records over an extended period of development. However, such databases are rarely available, and self-report data will continue to be used. In this case, the data should also cover an extended period and be obtained prospectively, to reduce reliance on memory and the possibility of recall biases.

Acknowledgments

This work was supported by grants from the Australian Research Council to both authors. We thank Louise Ewing for assistance with the literature searches and referencing.

References

Andersson, M. (1994) *Sexual Selection.*: Princeton University Press, Princeton, NJ.

Backwell, P., Jennions, M. and Passmore, N. (1998) Synchronized courtship in fiddler crabs. *Nature*, 391: 31–32.

Baker, R. R. (1997) Copulation, masterbation and infidelity: State-of-the-art. In A. Schmitt, K. Atzwanger, K. Grammer and K. Schäfer (eds) *New Aspects of Human Ethology*. Plenum Press, New York.

Baudouin, J. Y. and Tiberghien, G. (2004) Symmetry, averageness, and feature size in the facial attractiveness of women. *Acta Psychologica*, 117: 313–332.

Cardenas, R. A. and Harris, L. J. (2006) Symmetrical decorations enhance the attractiveness of faces and abstract designs. *Evolution and Human Behavior*, 27: 1–18.

Clarke, G. M. (1998) Developmental stability and fitness: the evidence is not quite so clear. *American Naturalist*, 152: 762–766.

Cohen, J. (1988) *Statistical Power Analysis for the Behavioural Sciences*, 2nd edn. Academic Press, New York.

Colegrave, N. and Ruxton, G. D. (2003) Confidence intervals are a more useful complement to nonsignificant tests than are power calculations. *Behavioral Ecology*, 14: 446–447.

Darwin, C. (1871) *The Descent of Man and Selection in Relation to Sex*. D. Appleton, New York

Dufour, K. W. and Weatherhead, P. J. (1996) Estimation of organism-wide asymmetry in red-winged blackbirds and its relation to studies of mate selection. *Proceedings of the Royal Society of London, B*, 263: 769–775.

Endler, J. A. and Basolo, A. L. (1998) Sensory ecology, receiver biases and sexual selection. *Trends in Ecology and Evolution*, 13: 415–420.

Fink, B., Grammer, K. and Thornhill, R. (2001) Human (Homo sapiens) facial attractiveness in relation to skin texture and color. *Journal of Comparative Psychology*, 115: 92–99.

Firman, R. C., Simmons, L. W., Cummins, J. M. and Matson, P. L. (2003) Are body fluctuating asymmetry and the ratio of 2nd to 4th digit length reliable predictors of ejaculate quality? *Human Reproduction*, 18: 808–812.

Friedenberg, J. (2001) Lateral feature displacement and perceived facial attractiveness. *Psychological Reports*, 88: 295–305.

Fuller, R. C. and Houle, D. (2003) Inheritance of developmental instability. In M. Polak (ed.) *Developmental Instability: Causes and Consequences*, pp. 157–183. Oxford University Press, Oxford.

Furlow, F. B., Armijo-Prewitt, T., Gangestad, S. W. and Thornhill, R. (1997) Fluctuating asymmetry and psychometric intelligence. *Proceedings of the Royal Society of London, B*, 264: 823–829.

Furlow, B., Gangestad, S. W. and Armijo-Prewitt, T. (1998) Developmental stability and human violence. *Proceedings of the Royal Society of London, B*, 256: 1–6.

Gangestad, S. W. and Thornhill, R. (1997) Human sexual selection and developmental stability. In J. A. Simpson and D. T. Kenrick (eds) *Evolutionary Social Psychology*, pp. 169–196. Lawrence Erlbaum, Hillsdale, NJ.

Gangestad, S. W. and Thornhill, R. (1998) The analysis of fluctuating asymmetry redux: the robustness of parametric statistics. *Animal Behaviour*, 55: 497–501.

Gangestad, S. W., Bennett, K. L. and Thornhill, R. (2001) A latent variable model of developmental stability in relation to men's sexual behaviour. *Proceedings of the Royal Society of London, B*, 268: 1677–1684.

Gangestad, S. W., Thornhill, R. and Yeo, R. A. (1994) Facial attractiveness, developmental stability, and fluctuating asymmetry. *Ethology and Sociobiology*, 15: 73–85.

Govind, C. K. and Pierce, J. (1986) Differential reflex activity determines claw and closer muscle asymmetry in developing lobsters. *Science*, 233: 354–356.

Graham, J. H., Emlen, J. M., Freeman, D. C., Leamy, L. J. and Kieser, J. A. (1998) Directional asymmetry and the measurement of developmental instability. *Biological Journal of the Linnean Society*, 64: 1–16.

Grammer, K. and Thornhill, R. (1994) Human (Homo sapiens) facial attractiveness and sexual selection: The role of symmetry and averageness. *Journal of Comparative Psychology*, 108: 233–242.

Gray, P. B. and Marlowe, F. (2002) Fluctuating asymmetry of a foraging population: the Hazda of Tanzania. *Annals of Human Biology*, 29: 495–501.

Helm, B. and Albrecht, H. (2000) Human handedness causes directional asymmetry in avian wing length measurements. *Animal Behaviour*, 60: 899–902.

Hoffman, A. A. and Woods, R. E. (2003) Associating environmental stress with developmental stability: Problems and patterns. In M. Polak (ed.) *Developmental Instability: Causes and Consequences*. Oxford University Press, Oxford.

Honekopp, J., Bartholome, T. and Jansen, G. (2004) Facial attractiveness, symmetry and physical fitness in young women. *Human Nature*, 15: 147–167.

Houle, D. (1998) How should we explain variation in the genetic variance of traits? *Genetica*, 102–103(1–6), 241–253.

Hughes, S. M., Harrison, M. A. and Gallup, G. G. (2002) The sound of symmetry: voice as a marker of developmental instability. *Evolution and Human Behavior*, 23: 173–180.

Hume, D. K. and Montgomerie, R. (2001) Facial attractiveness signals different aspects of "quality" in women and men. *Evolution and Human Behavior*, 22: 93–112.

Jones, B. C., Little, A. C., Penton-Voak, I. S., Tiddeman, B. P., Burt, D. M. and Perrett, D. I. (2001) Facial symmetry and judgements of apparent health: support for a "good genes" explanation of the attractiveness–symmetry relationship. *Evolution and Human Behavior*, 22: 417–429.

Jones, B. C., Little, A. C., Feinberg, D. R., Penton-Voak, I. S., Tiddeman, B. P. and Perrett, D. I. (2004) The relationship between shape symmetry and perceived skin condition in male facial attractiveness. *Evolution and Human Behavior*, 25: 24–30.

Jones, D. and Hill, K. (1993) Criteria of facial attractiveness in five populations. *Human Nature*, 4: 271–296.

Kirkpatrick, M. and Ryan, M. J. (1991) The evolution of mating preferences and the paradox of the lek. *Nature*, 350: 33–38.

Klingenberg, C. P. (2003) A developmental perspective on developmental instability: Theory, models, and mechanisms. In M. Polak (ed.) *Developmental Instability: Causes and Consequences*, pp. 14–34. Oxford University Press, Oxford.

Koehler, N., Rhodes, G. and Simmons, L. W. (2002) Are human female preferences for symmetrical male faces enhanced when conception is likely? *Animal Behaviour*, 64: 233–238.

Kokko, H., Brooks, R., McNamara, J. M. and Houston, A. I. (2002) The sexual selection continuum. *Proceedings of the Royal Society of London B*, 269: 1331–1340.

Kowner, R. (1996) Facial asymmetry and attractiveness judgment in developmental perspective. *Journal of Experimental Psychology: Human Perception and Performance*, 22: 662–675.

Langlois, J. H., Roggman, L. A. and Musselman, L. (1994) What is average and what is not average about attractive faces? *Psychological Science*, 5: 214–220.

Leung, B. and Forbes, M. R. (1996) Fluctuating asymmetry in relation to stress and fitness: effects of trait type as revealed by meta-analysis. *Ecoscience*, 3: 400–413.

Little, A. and Jones, B. (2003) Evidence against perceptual bias views for symmetry preferences in human faces. *Proceedings of the Royal Society of London, B*, 270: 1759–1763.

Little, B. B., Buschang, P. H. and Malina, R. M. (2002) Anthropometric asymmetry in chronically undernourished children from Southern Mexico. *Annals of Human Biology*, 29: 526–537.

Livshits, G. and Kobyliansky, E. (1989) Study of genetic variance in the fluctuating asymmetry of anthropometric traits. *Annual Review of Human Biology*, 16: 121–129.

Livshits, G. and Kobyliansky, E. (1991) Fluctuating asymmetry as a possible measure of developmental homeostasis in humans: a review. *Human Biology*, 63: 441–466.

Livshits, G., Kobyliansky, E., Ben-Amitai, D., Levi, Y. and Merlob, P. (1988) Decreased developmental stability as assessed by fluctuating asymmetry of morphometric traits in preterm infants. *American Journal of Medical Genetics*, 29: 793–805.

Livshits, G., Yakovenko, K., Kletselman, L., Karasik, D. and Kobyliansky, E. (1998) Fluctuating asymmetry and morphometric variation of hand bones. *American Journal of Physical Anthropology*, 107: 125–136.

Malina, R. M. (1983) Human growth, maturation, and regular physical activity. *Acta Medica Auxologica*, 15: 5–27.

Manning, J. T., Koukourakis, K. and Brodie, D. A. (1997) Fluctuating asymmetry, metabolic rate and sexual selection in human males. *Evolution and Human Behavior*, 18: 15–21.

Manning, J. T., Scutt, D. and Lewis-Jones, D. I. (1998) Developmental stability, ejaculate size, and sperm quality in men. *Evolution and Human Behavior*, 19: 273–282.

Mather, K. (1953) Genetic control of stability in development. *Heredity*, 7: 297–336.

Mead, L. S. and Arnold, S. J (2004) Quantitative genetic models of sexual selection. *Trends in Ecology and Evolution*, 19: 264–271.

Mealey, L., Bridgstock, R. and Townsend, G. C. (1999) Symmetry and perceived facial attractiveness: a monozygotic co-twin comparison. *Journal of Personality and Social Psychology*, 76: 151–158.

Milne, B. J., Belsky, J. R., Thomson, W. M. and Caspi, A. (2003) Fluctuating asymmetry and physical health among young adults. *Evolution and Human Behavior*, 24: 53–63.

Møller, A. P. (1993) Developmental stability, sexual selection and speciation. *Journal of Evolutionary Biology*, 6: 493–509.

Møller, A. P. (1997) Developmental stability and fitness: a review. *American Naturalist*, 149: 916–932.

Møller, A. P. (1999) Asymmetry as a predictor of growth, fecundity, and survival. *Ecology Letters*, 2: 149–156.

Møller, A. P. and Alatalo, R. V. (1999) Good genes effects in sexual selection. *Proceedings of the Royal Society of London, B*, 266: 85–91.

Møller, A. P. and Cuervo, J. J. (2003) Asymmetry, size, and sexual selection: factors affecting heterogeneity in relationships between asymmetry and sexual selection. In M. Polak (ed.) *Developmental Instability: Causes and Consequences*, pp. 262–275. Oxford University Press, Oxford.

Møller, A. P. and Swaddle, J. P. (1997) *Asymmetry, Developmental Stability and Evolution*. Oxford University Press, Oxford.

Møller, A. P. and Thornhill, R. (1998) Bilateral symmetry and sexual selection: a meta-analysis. *American Naturalist*, 151: 174–192.

Nijhout, H. F. and G. Davidowitz (2003) Developmental prespectives on phenotypic variation, canalization, and fluctuating asymmetry. In M. Polak (ed.) *Developmental Instability: Causes and Consequences*, pp. 3–13. Oxford University Press, Oxford.

Noor, F. and Evans, D. C. (2003) The effect of facial symmetry on perceptions of personality and attractiveness. *Journal of Research in Personality*, 37: 339–347.

Palmer, A. C. and Strobeck, C. (1986) Fluctuating asymmetry: measurement, analysis, pattern. *Annual Review of Ecology and Systematics*, 17: 391–421.

Palmer, A. R. and Strobeck, C. (2003) Fluctuating asymmetry analyses revisited. In M. Polak (ed.) *Developmental Instability: Causes and Consequences*, pp. 279–319. Oxford University Press, Oxford.

Parsons, P. A. (1990) Fluctuating asymmetry: an epigenetic measure of stress. *Biological Reviews*, 65: 131–145.

Perrett, D. I., Burt, D. M., Penton-Voak, I. S., Lee, K. J., Rowland, D. A. and Edwards, R. (1999) Symmetry and human facial attractiveness. *Evolution and Human Behavior*, 20: 295–307.

Polak, M., Møller, A. P., Gangestad, S. W., Kroeger, D., Manning, J. T. and Thornhill, R. (2003) Does an individual asymmetry parameter exist? A meta-analysis. In M. Polak (ed.) *Developmental Instability: Causes and Consequences*. Oxford University Press, Oxford.

Price, T., Schluter, D. and Heckman, N. E. (1993) Sexual selection when the female directly benefits. *Biological Journal of the Linnean Society*, 48: 187–211.

Prokosch, M. D., Yeo, R. A. and Miller, G. F. (2005) Intelligence tests with higher g-loadings show higher correlations with body symmetry: evidence for a general fitness factor mediated by developmental stability. *Intelligence*, 33: 203–213.

Rhodes, G. (2006) The evolutionary psychology of facial beauty. *Annual Review of Psychology*, 57: 199–226.

Rhodes, G., Proffitt, F., Grady, J. M. and Sumich, A. (1998) Facial symmetry and the perception of beauty. *Psychonomic Bulletin and Review*, 5: 659–669.

Rhodes, G., Roberts, J. and Simmons, L. (1999a) Reflections on symmetry and attractiveness. *Psychology, Evolution and Gender*, 1: 279–295.

Rhodes, G., Sumich, A. and Byatt, G. (1999b) Are average facial configurations attractive only because of their symmetry? *Psychological Science*, 10: 52–58.

Rhodes, G., Yoshikawa, S., Clark, A., Lee, K., McKay, R. and Akamatsu, S. (2001a) Attractiveness of facial averageness and symmetry in non-Western cultures: In search of biologically based standards of beauty. *Perception*, 30: 611–625.

Rhodes, G., Zebrowitz, L. A., Clark, A., Kalick, S., Hightower, A. and McKay, R. (2001b) Do facial averageness and symmetry signal health? *Evolution and Human Behavior*, 22: 31–46.

Rhodes, G., Peters, M., Lee, K., Morrone, C. M. and Burr, D. (2005a) Higher-level mechanisms detect facial symmetry. *Proceedings of the Royal Society of London, B*, 272: 1379–1384.

Rhodes, G., Simmons, L. and Peters, M. (2005b) Attractiveness and sexual behaviour: does attractiveness enhance mating success? *Evolution and Human Behavior*, 26: 186–201.

Rikowski, A. and Grammer, K. (1999) Human body odour, symmetry and attractiveness. *Biological Sciences*, 266(1422): 869–874.

Rosenthal, R. (1963) On the social psychology of the psychological experiment: the experimenter's hypothesis as unintended determinant of experimental results. *American Scientist*, 51: 268–283.

Rosenthal, R. (1991) *Meta-Analytic Procedures for Social Research*, revised edn. Sage, Newbury Park, CA.

Rowe, L. and Houle, D. (1996) The lek paradox and the capture of genetic variance by condition dependent traits. *Proceedings of the Royal Society of London, B*, 263: 1415–1421.

Ryan, M. J. (1998) Sexual selection, receiver biases, and the evolution of sex differences. *Science*, 281: 1999–2003.

Scheib, J. E., Gangestad, S. W. and Thornhill, R. (1999) Facial attractiveness, symmetry and cues of good genes. *Proceedings of the Royal Society of London, B*, 266: 1913–1917.

Scutt, D., Manning, J. T., Whitehouse, G. H., Leinster, S. J. and Massey, C. P. (1997) The relationship between breast asymmetry, breast size and the occurence of breast cancer. *British Journal of Radiology*, 70: 1017–1021.

Scognomillo, R., Rhodes, G., Morrone, C. and Burr, D. (2003) A feature based model of symmetry detection. *Proceedings of the Royal Society of London, B*, 270: 1727–1733.

Shackelford, T. K. and Larsen, R. J. (1997) Facial asymmetry as an indicator of psychological, emotional, and physiological distress. *Journal of Personality and Social Psychology*, 72: 456–466.

Simmons, L. W., Tomkins, J. L., Kotiaho, J. S. and Hunt, J. (1999) Fluctuating paradigm. *Proceedings of the Royal Society of London, B*, 266: 593–595.

Simmons, L. W., Rhodes, G., Peters, M. and Koehler, N. (2004) Are human preferences for facial symmetry focused on signals of developmental instability? *Behavioral Ecology*, 15: 864–871.

Simpson, J. A., Gangestad, S. W., Christensen, P. N. and Leck, K. (1999) Fluctuating asymmetry, sociosexuality and intrasexual competitive tactics. *Journal of Personality and Social Psychology*, 76: 159–172.

Singh, D. (1995) Female health, attractiveness and desirability for relationships: role of breast asymmetry and waist-to-hip ratio. *Ethology and Sociobiology*, 16: 465–481.

Swaddle, J. P. and Cuthill, I. C. (1995) Asymmetry and human facial attractiveness: symmetry may not always be beautiful. *Proceedings of the Royal Society of London, B*, 261: 111–116.

Thoma, R. J., Yoe, R. A., Gangestad, S. W., Halgren, E., Sanchez, N. M. and Lewine, J. D. (2005) Cortical volume and developmental stability are independent predictors of general intellectual ability. *Intelligence*, 33: 27–38.

Thornhill, R. and Gangestad, S. W. (1993) Human facial beauty—averageness, symmetry, and parasite resistance. *Human Nature—An Interdisciplinary Biosocial Perspective*, 4: 237–269.

Thornhill, R. and Gangestad, S. W. (1994) Human fluctuating asymmetry and sexual behavior. *Psychological Science*, 5: 297–302.

Thornhill, R. and Gangestad, S. W. (1999a) Facial attractiveness. *Trends in Cognitive Sciences*, 3: 452–460.

Thornhill, R. and Gangestad, S. W. (1999b) The scent of symmetry: a human sex pheromone that signals fitness. *Evolution and Human Behavior*, 20: 175–201.

Thornhill, R. and Gangestad, S. W. (2006) Facial sexual dimorphism, developmental stability, and susceptibility to disease in men and women. *Evolution and Human Behavior*, 27: 131–144.

Thornhill, R. and Møller, A. P. (1997) Developmental stability, disease and medicine. *Biological Reviews of the Cambridge Philosophical Society*, 72: 497–548.

Thornhill, R., Gangestad, S. W., Miller, R., Scheyd, G., McCollough, J. K. and Franklin, M. (2003) Major histocompatibility complex genes, symmetry, and body scent attractiveness in men and women. *Behavioral Ecology*, 14: 668–678.

Tomkins, J. L. and Simmons, L. W. (2003) Fluctuating asymmetry and sexual selection: paradigm shifts, publication bias and observer expectation. In M. Polak (ed.) *Developmental Instability: Causes and Consequences*, pp. 231–261. Oxford University Press, New York.

Tomkinson, G. R. and Olds, T. S. (2000) Physiological correlates of bilateral symmetry in humans. *International Journal of Sports Medicine*, 21: 545–550.

Tovée, M. J., Tasker, K. and Benson, P. J. (2000) Is symmetry a visual cue to attractiveness in the human female body? *Evolution and Human Behavior*, 21: 191–200.

Trinkaus, E., Churchill, S. E. and Ruff, C. B. (1994) Postcranial robusticity in Homo. II: Humeral bilateral asymmetry and bone plasticity. *American Journal of Physical Anthropology*, 93: 1–34.

Van Valen, L. (1962) A study of fluctuating asymmetry. *Evolution*, 16: 125–142.

Watson, P. M. and Thornhill, R. (1994) Fluctuating asymmetry and sexual selection. *Trends in Ecology and Evolution*, 9: 21–25.

Waynforth, D. (1998) Fluctuating asymmetry and human male life-history traits in rural Belize. *Proceedings of the Royal Society of London, B*, 265: 1497–1501.

Waynforth, D. (1999) Differences in time use for mating and nepotistic effort as a function of male attractiveness in rural Belize. *Evolution and Human Behavior*, 20: 19–28.

Zakharov, V. M. (1981) Fluctuating asymmetry as an index of developmental homeostasis. *Genetika*, 13: 241–256.

Zebrowitz, L. A. and Rhodes, G. (2004) Sensitivity to "bad genes" and the anomalous face overgeneralization effect: cue validity, cue utilization, and accuracy in judging intelligence and health. *Journal of Nonverbal Behavior*, 28: 167–185.

Zebrowitz, L. A., Voinescu, L. and Collins, M. A. (1996) "Wide-eyed" and "crooked-faced": determinants of perceived and real honesty across the life span. *Personality and Social Psychology Bulletin*, 22: 1258–1269.

Zebrowitz, L. A., Hall., J. A., Murphy, N. A. and Rhodes, G. (2002) Looking smart and looking good: facial cues to intelligence and their origins. *Personality and Social Psychology Bulletin*, 28: 238–249.

CHAPTER 25

Sex differences in aggression

Anne Campbell

25.1. Introduction

The sex difference in physical and verbal aggression is one of the most robust (Maccoby and Jacklin, 1974; Archer, 2004), universal (International Criminal Police Organisation, 1994; McCarthy, 1994) and durable (Daly and Wilson, 1988; Davies, 1998). In the USA, men constitute 86% of all violent offenders (Greenfeld and Snell, 1999). The proportionate involvement of men rises with the seriousness of the offence; men commit 82% of simple assaults but 90% of aggravated assaults and homicides. Meta-analyses of psychological studies (Table 25.1) using experimental, observational and self- or other-report methods also find that men are more verbally and physically aggressive than women and that this difference is greater for physical aggression. The ubiquity of this effect, its early developmental onset and its consistency with other primate species suggest the utility of an evolutionary explanation.

25.2. Evolutionary approaches

Daly and Wilson's (1988) account hinges upon the proposal that males have greater incentives to fight than females. In most species, maternal investment exceeds paternal investment, making females a valuable resource and one for which males must compete. In polygynous species,

male fitness variance exceeds that of females, such that some males have the opportunity for extreme reproductive success while others fail to reproduce at all. As the fitness pay-offs for success versus failure become more disparate, there is a greater incentive to compete despite danger to one's life since opting out guarantees reproductive failure. Females in these circumstances have no reason to compete amongst themselves for mating opportunities because, since they bear the brunt of parental investment, males are only too willing to offer copulations. Cross-species comparisons of morphological and physiological traits suggest that humans have a history of mild polygyny consonant with the argument for greater male fitness variance (Daly and Wilson, 1983; Dixson, 1998).

Male same-sex aggression represents a form of competition for dominance over other males and for resources that are attractive to potential mates. In contemporary humans, such goals may be achieved through a variety of means including professional qualifications, highly paid or prestigious jobs or conspicuous material consumption. However, these routes are not open to all and for young men living in economically desperate circumstances, an advertised willingness to engage in direct physical aggression may be a route to dominance and respect in the local community. The peak age of involvement in violence is between the ages of

Table 25.1 Summary of meta-analytic results for the magnitude of effect sizes for sex differences in aggression, weighted d

	Self report or psychometric	Observational	Other report	Experiments	Aggregated methods
Overall aggression	0.30 to 0.42[a]	0.49[a]	0.48 to 0.61[c]	0.29[b]	0.47[c]
	0.33[c]	0.83[c]	0.48[d]	0.30[d]	0.66[d]
	0.46[d]	0.35[d]	0.42 to 0.63[a]	0.24[e]	0.50[f]
	0.28[f]	0.51[f]			
Physical	0.39 to 0.59[a]	0.33 to 0.84[a]		0.40[b]	0.91[c]
				0.36[e]	0.59[d]
					0.60[f]
Verbal	0.19 to 0.30[a]	0.09 to 0.14[a]	0.24 to 0.51[a]	0.18[b]	0.46[c]
				0.30[e]	0.28[d]
					0.43[f]
Indirect	0.03[a]	−0.74[a]	−0.01 to −0.19[a]		−0.07[d]

[a]Archer (in press); [b]Eagly and Steffen (1986); [c]Knight et al. (1996); [d]Knight et al. (2002); [e]Bettencourt and Miller (1996); [f]Hyde (1986).

16 and 24, corresponding to that portion of the lifespan when reputations are made and mates acquired. It is also the age at which muscle strength and aerobic capacity are maximal and during which men show a marked willingness to engage in a variety of risky but reputation-enhancing behaviours including dangerous driving, extreme sports and excessive ingestion of drugs and alcohol. Wilson and Daly (1985, p. 59) have used the term *taste for risk* to capture the psychological instantiation of this young male syndrome.

I have offered a complementary female-centred account that acknowledges that females are as capable of aggression as males but have a higher threshold for employing it as a competitive tactic (Campbell, 1999, 2002). While it is unlikely that ancestral females competed for copulations, there was every reason for females to compete for resources necessary to their offsprings' survival. A female's considerable maternal investment, combined with the relatively few offspring that she could bear in a lifetime, made each child extremely valuable. For example, the loss of a 3-year-old child might cost a woman an irreplaceable 5 years of her life (3 years of lactation and care, 9 months of gestation and a possible further year to achieve another viable pregnancy) and such a loss is not hypothetical—among hunter-gatherer societies the mortality rate for children is estimated to be 50%. This constitutes a strong incentive for competition with regard to resource acquisition. However, this incentive is matched by a strong disincentive; the death of a mother has more lethal consequences for children's survival than the death of a father (Hill and Hurtado, 1996; Sear *et al.*, 2000). In consequence, there was selection not for avoidance of competition but for the use of tactics that would be unlikely to result in personal injury or death. Even in primate species where females show a dominance hierarchy, it is noteworthy that status is inherited through the matrilineal line rather than fought for directly.

A tactic that has been noted in some species of monkeys is stressing competitors by social harassment that falls short of direct attack but that disrupts the oestrous cycle and suppresses pregnancy (Shively *et al.*, 1997; Abbott *et al.*, 1999). Recent studies (Table 25.1) suggest that

an analogous tactic is used by young women: indirect or relational aggression involves social exclusion, reputational attack by gossip and the calculated manipulation of social relationships. Because the identity of the attacker is hidden, the chance of dangerous physical confrontation is reduced. I have suggested that the psychological instantiation of this reluctance to directly expose oneself to physical danger is *fear*. Fear also forms the developmental infrastructure for *behavioural inhibition* so that females are better able to control the behavioural expression of anger when provoked than are men.

Inhibition is also central to Bjorklund and Kipp's (1996) account of sex differences, although the evolutionary rationale differs. They argue that while inhibitory control was important to both sexes in managing complex group living, better *inhibitory abilities* were selected in women than in men as a result of two selection pressures. With respect to sexual behaviour, it would have been advantageous to women to control their sexual arousal in order to make a more studied evaluation of prospective mates and greater inhibition would have allowed them to pursue extramarital relationships without detection and reprisal. With respect to mothering, inhibitory control is hypothesized to be valuable in delaying personal gratification in favour of meeting infants' needs and in suppressing aggression in response to their often anger-provoking behaviour. It is this latter area which qualifies the proposal as relevant to the discussion of sex differences in aggression. They distinguish three forms of inhibition; social (control of emotional expression and arousal, shielding of relationships), behavioural (resistance to temptation, delay of gratification, motor inhibition) and cognitive (e.g. conceptual tempo, Stroop performance, self-regulated and discrimination learning). They conclude that, consonant with their predictions, sex differences favouring women are most consistent for social tasks, less pronounced for behavioural tasks and inconsistent for cognitive tasks.

Based on a similar evolutionary rationale to Campbell, regarding the central importance of maternal survival, Taylor *et al.* (2000) have proposed a biochemical basis for women's avoidance of direct aggression. When under threat (chiefly from predators and males) neither fight nor flight may be an adaptive response for a mother because the former endangers her life and the latter entails abandoning her offspring. They propose that the stress response to threat leads to different behaviours in males and females. Both sexes show the same basic neuroendocrine response: The hypothalamus produces corticotropin-releasing factor (together with oxytocin and vasopressin) which stimulates adrenocorticotropin hormone in the anterior pituitary resulting in the release of corticosteroids from the adrenal cortex. However oxytocin, a peptide hormone associated with parasympathetic functioning, counter-regulates the fear response and has calming and social bonding effects. Oxytocin release in response to stress is greater in female than male rodents and, while androgens inhibit oxytocin release, the anxiolytic effects of oxytocin are enhanced by oestrogen. Under threat, instead of fighting or fleeing, females' stronger oxytocin response triggers 'tending' their young (with beneficial short- and long-term calming effects on the offspring) and 'befriending' other females (with the attendant benefits of maternal stress reduction and group protection from attack). This position addresses women's stronger tendency to affiliate under stress and the greater connectedness and interdependence with same-sex peers but perhaps underplays the role of female competition. Among males, they suggest that testosterone is the link between sympathetic nervous system activation and interpersonal aggression. In Taylor *et al.*'s model, the mediator of the sex difference in aggression is hormonal, and among females stress reduction is both a direct biochemical and indirect behavioural effect of oxytocin. Sex differences in the experience of fear or the efficiency of behavioural inhibition are not centrally implicated.

25.3. **Psychological mediators**

It is not difficult to develop explanations of gender-specific selection pressures on aggression. However, our inability to revisit the vast time periods during which such adaptations arose mean that they largely remain informed speculation. What we can examine are the proximal mediators of the sex difference which may provide clues to its origin and fortunately there is a wealth of data available from psychological studies on which to draw.

Aggression occurs when the rewards of an attack (multiplied by the probability of winning them) outweigh the costs (multiplied by the probability of incurring them). Such calculations rarely if ever take place at a conscious level but emotions can act as a useful guide to strategy selection (Damasio, 1994; Cosmides and Tooby, 2000; Lerner and Keltner, 2000). Anger acts as an impetus to aggression (calibrating rewards) while fear and inhibition act as brakes (calibrating costs). Because provocation, manipulated in laboratory settings, increases the likelihood of aggression it follows that it must either increase anger or reduce fear or inhibition. Provocation also diminishes the magnitude of the sex difference (Bettencourt and Miller, 1996; Knight *et al.*, 2002) and this fact provides a useful tool for examining sex differences. It suggests that in everyday life beyond the laboratory, women either experience lower levels of anger or higher levels of fear or inhibition. Studies and meta-analysis confirm that women do not experience anger less frequently or less intensely than do men (Mirowsky and Ross, 1995; Kring, 2000; Brebner, 2003; Archer, 2004). Below I briefly consider the evidence for the various candidate mediators of sex differences in aggression that have been proposed by different theorists (a full review is given in Campbell, 2006).

25.3.1. **Fear**

The fear system is "designed to detect danger and produce responses that maximise the probability of surviving" (LeDoux, 1996, p. 128). In infancy, girls express fear earlier (Nagy *et al.*, 2001), are more hesitant in approaching novel objects (Martin *et al.*, 1997) and show weaker approach behaviour than boys (Carey and McDevitt, 1978; Hsu *et al.*, 1981; Maziade *et al.*, 1984). Among adults, reviews have generally concluded that women experience fear more intensely than men (Crawford *et al.*, 1992; Brody and Hall, 1993; Fischer, 1993; Gullone, 2000). Three large international surveys of gender and emotion have concluded that women experience fear or anxiety more frequently, more intensely or for longer durations than men (Fischer and

Manstead, 2000; Brebner, 2003; Simon and Nath, 2004). Physiologically, women show greater increases in skin conductance and a more marked startle reflex to physically threatening scenes (Bradley *et al.*, 1999; McManis *et al.*, 2001).

Women also show higher levels of phobic fears (unreasonable, persistent and extreme fear of circumscribed objects or situations), after controlling for gender role, dissimulation, disgust sensitivity and neuroticism (Arrindell *et al.*, 1993, 1999; Gullone and King, 1993). These fears appear to be especially sensitive to the possibility of physical harm or injury. Anxiety sensitivity is fear of anxiety-related sensations that have harmful physical, social and psychological consequences. Women score higher than men only on the physical harm factor (Stewart *et al.*, 1997; Walsh *et al.*, 2004).

Males make riskier decisions than females, especially where the study uses observed rather than hypothetical or self-reported behaviour (Byrnes *et al.*, 1999) and is particularly marked for physical and life-threatening risks (Hersch, 1997). Differences in fear have been implicated in these choices (Lerner and Keltner, 2000, 2001; Loewenstein *et al.*, 2001).

There is also evidence that sex differences in fear directly mediate the magnitude of sex differences in aggression. Female judges rate the danger of aggression displayed in laboratory studies higher than male judges and ratings of danger are the strongest predictor of the magnitude of the sex difference in aggression (Eagly and Steffen, 1986; see also Bettencourt and Miller, 1996). Faced with the same low level of objective danger, women find aggressive situations more dangerous and this predicts their lower level of aggression relative to men.

25.3.2. Inhibition

The term has been used to describe a bewildering range of psychological constructs. For the present purposes, we can broadly distinguish four forms of inhibition; three in which fear is directly or indirectly implicated and a fourth, cognitive inhibition, in which it is not. For each, I examine evidence for its association with aggression and sex differences.

Reactive inhibition, also known as fear-based inhibition, is most closely allied to fear levels.

The relationship has been theorized in terms of the acquisition of conscience as a conditioned response to fear (Mowrer, 1960; Eysenck, 1977; Dienstbier, 1984); the relative strengths of the behavioural inhibition and behavioural activation systems (Gray, 1982); increased attention to environmental threats resulting in 'passive' or 'reactive' control (Rothbart and Bates, 1998); and orbitofrontal and ventromedial modulation of affect and behaviour (Davidson *et al.*, 2000; Blair, 2004). Aggression is associated with poor reactive inhibition, assayed by a variety of measures including: resting heart rate (Lorber, 2004), observer ratings (Eisenberg *et al.*, 2004), the Iowa Gambling Task (Fishbein, 2000) and studies of stimulation, lesion and glucose metabolism in inhibitory prefrontal structures (Grafman *et al.*, 1996; Raine *et al.*, 1997). Sex differences favouring females have been found in almost all these domains. Females show a faster resting heart rate (Raine, 2002), consistently superior control in developmental studies (Kochanska and Knaack, 2003; Eisenberg *et al.*, 2005), larger orbitofrontal regions in the prefrontal cortex (Goldstein *et al.*, 2001; Gur *et al.*, 2002), and the binding potential for serotonin, implicated in the inhibitory control of aggression, is higher in women especially in the prefrontal cortex (Parsey *et al.*, 2002). Although the Iowa Gambling Task does not show a female advantage (Kerr and Zelazo, 2004; Overman, 2004), women appear to systematically avoid the packs that more frequently contain penalties, suggesting a more acute avoidance of anxiety-provoking stimuli.

Effortful control is a second system of conscious attentional control that develops during the toddler period, providing a form of self-regulation that builds upon, but goes beyond, the reactive impact of fear (Derryberry and Rothbart, 1997). Negative relationships, both concurrent and prospective, have been consistently found between effortful control and externalizing behaviours including aggression (Kochanska and Knaack, 2003; Eisenberg *et al.*, 2005). Eleven recent studies have demonstrated girls' superiority in conforming their behaviour to adult proscriptions (Gervai *et al.*, 1993; Kochanska and Aksan, 1995; Kochanska *et al.*, 1996, 1997, 2000, 2001; Olson *et al.*, 1999; Eisenberg *et al.*, 2001, 2004; Kochanska and

Knaack, 2003; Valiente *et al.*, 2003; Liew *et al.*, 2004). Although a quantitative review of resistance-to-temptation studies found a weak effect size favouring females (Silverman, 2003), when studies of examination cheating were excluded (an instrumental act qualitatively different from the immediate suppression of an inherently attractive behaviour), the effect size increased to $d = -0.41$.

Self-control (Gottfredson and Hirschi, 1990) or *impulse control* (Moffitt, 1993) develops during middle childhood and adolescence as the proscriptive social control of adults is internalized. Both are significantly negatively associated with antisocial and aggressive behaviour (Farrington and Loeber, 1999; Pratt and Cullen, 2000; Farrington, 2003; Miller *et al.*, 2003). Young women typically score higher than men on measures of self-control (Tittle *et al.*, 2003) and particularly on the impulsivity and risk-seeking scales (LaGrange and Silverman, 1999). Self-control and impulsivity eliminate or significantly reduce the effect of gender on general and violent offending (Burton *et al.*, 1998; Gibbs *et al.*, 1998; LaGrange and Silverman, 1999; Moffitt *et al.*, 2001).

Executive function (EF). 'Inhibition' is central to effective executive function but the form of inhibition is cognitive (typically maintaining attention on a given dimension of a task and resisting competing stimuli). There is no theoretical link to individual differences in fear. Although studies have reported associations between poor EF task performance and aggression (e.g. Lau *et al.*, 1995; Seguin *et al.*, 1995, 2002; Stanford *et al.*, 1997), the tasks used correlate very highly (> 0.90) with the *g* factor of general intelligence (Kane *et al.*, 2005). It is therefore vital to control for IQ since this is a well-established correlate of antisocial behaviour. Where this has been done, relationships between aggression and at least *one* of a battery of EF tasks have often been found (Giancola and Zeichner, 1994; Seguin *et al.*, 1999; Hoaken *et al.*, 2003) but such control very much attenuates the relationship with aggression (e.g. Seguin *et al.*, 2004). Cognitive inhibition has emerged from factor analytic studies of psychometric impulsivity (White *et al.*, 1994; Whiteside and Lynam, 2001). However the association between this factor and aggression has been non-significant (Lynam and Miller, 2004) or

considerably weaker than behavioural impulsivity measures (White *et al.*, 1994). In this latter study, cognitive impulsivity was unrelated to antisocial behaviour when IQ was controlled (Loeber *et al.*, 2001).

Few studies have examined sex differences in EF performance in the normal population and most have been performed on children. The majority report inconsistent or insignificant gender differences (Kirchner and Kopf, 1974; Levy and Hobbes, 1979; Greenberg and Waldman, 1993; Pascualvaca *et al.*, 1997; Rebok *et al.*, 1997; Navarette *et al.*, 1998; Klenberg *et al.*, 2001). Given the very high correlations with IQ, the absence of gender differences is perhaps not surprising.

In sum, the more the concept of inhibition is rooted in an infrastructure of fear, the greater its negative relationship with aggression and, given the sex differences in inhibition just reviewed, the more promising it looks as a candidate for mediating the magnitude of the sex difference in aggression.

25.3.3. Taste for risk

Wilson and Daly (1985) offer a considerable body of supporting evidence for their contention that a taste for risk underlies young male aggression. However, many of their examples (higher rates of male mortality from external causes, dangerous driving, drug use and gambling) might arise as much from a relative absence of fear or behavioural inhibition as from an appetitive taste for risk. Psychometric measures of sensation seeking (Zuckerman, 1994; Zuckerman *et al.*, 1993) have been widely used and offer more direct access to the proposed psychological mediator. Although sensation seeking has been found to a show significant association with aggression (Zuckerman, 1979, 1994; Zuckerman *et al.*, 1993) negative findings have also been reported (Dahlen *et al.*, 2004) and in other cases, impulsivity items have shown a stronger association than sensation-seeking items (Joireman *et al.*, 2003; Lynam and Miller, 2004).

Sex differences in sensation seeking have been widely reported (Roberti, 2004). Three of Zuckerman's sensation-seeking subscales measure attraction to physically dangerous activities, whereas one—Experience Seeking—measures desire for novel and unusual experiences that do not contain a component of physical risk. In 15 out of 17 cross-cultural studies, no sex differences were found on this scale (Zuckerman, 1994) suggesting that "The lack of difference on ES suggests that while men are high on the more active forms of sensation seeking, women are just as open to novel experiences through the senses and lifestyle as men" (Zuckerman, 1994, p. 101). However, men score higher than women on the three other sensation-seeking scales that measure willingness to take physical risks. Some studies have reported associations between circulating testosterone and sensation seeking (Daitzman *et al.*, 1978; Daitzman and Zuckerman, 1980; Aluja and Torrubia, 2004) although others have not (Rosenblitt *et al.*, 2003; Cohen-Bendahan *et al.*, 2005).

25.3.4. Integration

In addition to correlations between fear and behavioural inhibition reviewed above, significant negative associations have also been found between sensation seeking and both fear (e.g. Lissek and Powers, 2003) and inhibition (Hur and Bouchard, 1997; Roberti, 2004). Factor analyses of 19 different measures of

impulsivity revealed a clear factor of sensation seeking (Whiteside and Lynam, 2001). The association between these three variables is explicable through a well-known law of arousal in relation to subjective pleasantness or hedonic tone (see Figure 25.1). For individuals with characteristically high levels of fear, stimulation or arousal 'turns the corner' from pleasant to aversive at lower levels than among those with low levels of fear (See Zuckerman, 1979). Stimulating activities, such as riding a roller coaster, will be experienced as unpleasant by high-fear individuals but may be actively sought out by those low in fear since they require a higher level of stimulation to achieve maximum hedonic tone. Men enjoy frightening and violent films more than women and such enjoyment is associated with high sensation seeking (Hoffner and Levine, 2005). The same appears to apply in real-life aggressive situations. Even if not actively sought out, low fear individuals will generally find such situations considerably less aversive and may be prepared to tolerate these lower levels of unpleasantness in the service of the benefits that can be accrued (Joireman *et al.*, 2003).

The empirical association between fear, inhibition and sensation seeking combined with evidence of genetic influence on such personality

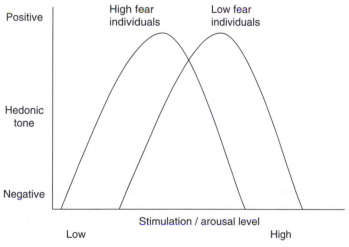

Fig. 25.1 Preference for different levels of stimulation and arousal as a function of fear levels (based on Berlyne, 1960).

traits (Fulker *et al.*, 1980; Tellegen *et al.*, 1988; Koopmans *et al.*, 1995) suggests the possibility that they represent a co-adapted gene complex. Through pleiotropy, linkage disequilibrium or common transcription factors, these traits may 'travel together' as a functional adaptation. In a study of monozygotic twins reared apart, Hur and Bouchard (1997) found that the phenotypic correlation between sensation seeking and impulsivity was mediated almost entirely by genetic factors: "genetic factors which lead to low impulse control overlap with genetic factors important for high sensation seeking" (Hur and Bouchard, 1997, pp. 461–462). In a further link, substantial genetic mediation has been found in two different twin samples for the relationship between impulsivity and aggression, especially irritability (Seroczynski *et al.*, 1999; Vierikko *et al.*, 2004). An important question for future research is the extent to which such a common genetic predisposition is sex-limited (gene expression depends upon hormone levels, such as testosterone) or sex-linked (including non-random X inactivation in females, Craig *et al.*, 2004).

Any finding of a heritable influence on human polymorphic traits inevitably raises questions about its evolutionary source or function. This is a lively debate in itself with genetic difference being viewed as selectively neutral, frequency dependent, the result of rapidly fluctuating environments, or genuine adaptations (Figueredo *et al.*, 2005). Whatever the resolution, it is clear that the phenotypic expression of any genetic predisposition depends intimately on the environment. Specific environmental events may be required for gene activation. Or genetic variability may mediate between environmental events and behavioural response. For example, it is well known that childhood maltreatment is associated with later antisocial behaviour. Yet this relationship is moderated by genetics (Caspi *et al.*, 2002). The gene coding for the enzyme monoamine oxidase A (*MAOA*), which metabolizes neurotransmitters, is polymorphic. It has two alleles: one codes for high and one for low activity. The effect of childhood maltreatment on later antisocial behaviour depends on which gene the individual has. Maltreated individuals with a genotype conferring high levels of *MAOA* expression are less likely to develop antisocial problems than equally maltreated individuals with the alternative allele.

25.4. **Cross-sex aggression**

From an evolutionary perspective, Wilson and Daly (1992a) proposed that male violence towards women was a result of male sexual proprietariness resulting from the combination of male parental investment and the asymmetric possibility of cuckoldry. Years of investment in another man's offspring, the probability of which is enhanced by internal fertilization and concealed ovulation, represent a significant and selective cost. In response, a 'domain-specific masculine psychology' (Daly and Wilson, 1994) evolved by which men became attentive to any sign of possible sexual infidelity from women including, among some men, the use of violence as a response to, and pre-emption of, unfaithfulness. However, there has been debate concerning two empirical issues; the sex of the offender and jealousy as the motive for attack.

In their analysis, Wilson and Daly (1992b) used intimate homicide rates, arguing that they represent a more reliable measure than self-reports of assaults. Data from Canada, Europe and Scandinavia indicate that for every 100 males who killed their spouses, there were between 17 and 40 females who did the same. In the USA, the figure was much closer to equality, which they tentatively attributed to greater male coercion, stronger matrilineal kin networks or defence of children. In a parallel analysis of victims of intimate homicide, Archer (2000) similarly concluded that there was greater equality of victimization between the sexes in the USA (where the proportion of female victims ranged from 0.56 to 0.70) as compared to Africa and India (0.91), European nations (0.79) and Russia (0.86).

However, men have a higher base rate of killing more generally (Harris, 2003). In order to examine whether men are more likely than women to choose *partners* as victims, we can examine the proportionate distribution of victims within sex of offender (see Table 25.2). If calculated as the relative numbers of men and women who kill their spouse, then we would conclude that for every 100 men there are 45 women. However, if we take into account men's greater tendency to

Table 25.2 Offender–victim relationship in homicide as a function of sex

Sex of homicide offender	Victim is an intimate	Victim other	Total
Male	80 000	320 000	400 000
	(20%)	(80%)	(100%)
Female	36 000	24 000	60 000
	(60%)	(40%)	(100%)
Total	116 000	344 000	

Source: Greenfeld and Snell (1999).

kill in general, it is clear that men are very much less likely to kill their spouse (20% of all their victims) than are women (60% of all their victims).

While homicide data may be reliable in the sense that the event is usually detected and a killer is frequently found, the dynamics and correlates of homicide may be qualitatively different from those found in sub-lethal attacks. A meta-analysis of studies which employed the Conflict Tactics Scale or an analogous self- or other-report measure found a small effect size, $d = -0.05$, indicating that women display slightly more aggression than men (Archer, 2000). This female advantage is somewhat stronger for self-report measures, $d = -0.12$, but even when partner reports are analysed, the expected male advantage for aggressive acts is not found, $d = -0.02$. The argument that women are defending themselves from male attack is not supported by studies which have found that women more often admit to initiating the attack (e.g. DeMaris, 1992) and that a substantial proportion of both men and women admit to employing physical aggression even when their partner does not (e.g. Straus and Gelles, 1988).

It appears that either men show comparatively depressed rates of attacks on intimates relative to their level of violence towards strangers or women show enhanced rates of intimate attacks relative to their usual low rates of aggression. There is ample empirical support for the notion that both sexes show greater aggression towards male targets (Archer and Cote, 2005). To decide firmly between these possibilities, we require data from a random sample of men and women on frequencies, within a given time frame, of both their intimate and non-intimate attacks. Acknowledging the problems of criminal justice data (e.g. differential rates of reporting, police attendance, arrest and prosecution), the data in Table 25.3 indicate that whereas men are 8.3 times more likely than women to commit a violent offence against a stranger, they are only 6.6 times more likely than women to commit a

Table 25.3 Offender–victim relationship in violent crime as a function of sex

Sex of offender	Spouse	Stranger	Total
Male offender	1 488 979	12 723 666	14 212 645
	(10%)	(90%)	(100%)
Female offender	224 817	1 538 676	1 763 493
	(13%)	(87%)	(100%)
Total	1 729 360	14 794 960	

Source: Durose et al. (2005).

violent offence against their spouse. This would suggest that men's (relative) restraint from aggression against a spouse may be as interesting a question as women's raised levels of aggression towards their partners.

A second issue is the extent to which male aggression towards spouses stems from a preoccupation with sexual fidelity. Since Daly and Wilson's original proposal, a considerable literature has grown up in this area. Briefly it is proposed that men should find the prospect of sexual infidelity especially upsetting while this is of less concern to women because they cannot be cuckolded. Instead they experience greater jealousy about emotional attachments which threaten a man's commitment to their current relationship. Although there has been debate about methodological issues (Harris, 2003; Sagarin, 2005), recent studies which employ novel methods tend to support the view that men are differentially attentive to signs of sexual infidelity (Schutzhohl and Koch, 2004; Schutzwohl, 2005). However, there is little evidence that men are more upset and angry than women in response to their partner's infidelity (Campbell, 2002) and women report that they are more likely than men to express their anger or attack their spouse (de Weerth and Kalma, 1993; Paul and Galloway, 1994). A meta-analysis of risk factors for male violence concluded that effect sizes for jealousy were small (Stith *et al.*, 2004)

It appears then that men are not the sole perpetrators of intimate violence and that men's violence has not been convincingly linked to concerns with sexual betrayal and resulting non-paternity. One way of reconceptualizing the area is afforded by Johnson's (1995) distinction between intimate terrorism and situational couple violence. In the former, men employ violence as a systematic means of control and their partners are more likely to be injured, to exhibit symptoms of post-traumatic stress, to miss work, to visit the doctor more often, to be in poor health, and to use painkillers and tranquilizers (Leone *et al.*, 2004; Johnson and Leone, 2005). Situational couple violence describes partnerships where mundane disputes occasionally escalate to acts of aggression which may be initiated by either partner. This distinction helps to make sense of the long-standing tension between feminist researchers on one hand, who

typically use shelter and refuge samples of women as their source of data and who attribute the bulk of intimate violence to men, and family conflict researchers, who typically use random samples of couples and conclude that violence is a joint product of interpersonal dynamics. Archer (2000) noted that the effect size for aggressive acts favours men among this first type of study and the injuries sustained by women are higher relative to men. In short, studies of intimate violence may conflate two distinct patterns or syndromes.

Intimate terrorism closely parallels Wilson and Daly's view. Qualitative studies of battered women show a male partner who demonstrates a level of control bordering on house arrest and paranoia about any attempt by the partner to assert independence (Dobash and Dobash, 1983). These women are confined to the home with frequent phone calls throughout the day to ensure their presence, they are denied the right to go out with friends and even shopping trips are timed with sanction if they are late. Sexual jealousy is often extreme; one woman, on being out of her husband's sight for five minutes, was accused of having sex in the kitchen with the host at a neighbourhood party. However bizarre such examples may appear, they are not unusual among women who ultimately seek sanctuary in shelters. Levels of male jealousy in these relationships can appear pathological. Buss (2000) has noted that the threshold for jealousy is likely to be set low where the cost of failure to detect infidelity (false negative) is higher than the cost of a mistaken accusation (false positive). This threshold setting is likely to vary between men with factors such as relative mate value being important; men with few resources and a low probability of finding an alternative mate have a lower threshold for suspicion. To the extent that the woman has few allies (family and friends), the costs of a wrongful accusation are also lowered. This may account for Archer's (2000) finding of a greater sex difference in intimate violence in some non-Western cultures, particularly where women are isolated from their family after marriage.

By contrast, situational couple violence may be more usefully examined not in terms of proprietary sexual jealousy but of long-term reciprocal altruism. Prisoner's Dilemma studies show that mutual cooperation results in net benefits over protracted interactions. However, where defection (failure to offer assistance) occurs, mutual assistance can be restored by punishing some proportion of such defections (Ridley, 1997). More specifically, a failure by the partner to live up to their half of the bargain should eventually evoke retaliation in order to restore equity. (It seems probable also that individuals may not always be 'accurate' in their assessment of the costs of relative effort by both partners. Personal costs may be given a higher weighting than the costs attributed to the partner, as occurs in typical disputes about who is 'contributing more' to the relationship). Divorce, in the USA at least, results from perceived inequities such as suspected infidelity, unequal time commitment to the marriage and money troubles including inequities in earning and spending (Kitson, 1992; Amato and Rogers, 1997). Marital satisfaction declines with the number of children, particularly for mothers of infants (Twenge et al., 2003) and traditional division of gender roles in marriages is associated with higher marital satisfaction among fathers but lower marital satisfaction among mothers (Grote et al., 1996).

The key question then becomes: why are women as willing as men to escalate retaliation about inequities to the point of physical aggression? Since, as already noted, the sexes do not differ in their intensity and frequency of anger, it seems probable that the psychological mediators (fear, inhibition and sensation seeking) may be calibrated differently in intimate relationships than in same-sex encounters. One might expect women to display greater fear of partner violence than men given men's greater physical size and strength. However, a study of at-risk couples in which bidirectional violence was the predominant pattern (Capaldi and Owen, 2001) reported no differences in the extent to which men and women were afraid of their partners and, in both sexes, fear was associated with the frequency of aggression by their partner and reports of injuries sustained. Archer (2000) also notes that a lower level of male aggression predicts higher levels of female aggression, suggesting that women with less to fear in terms of retaliation are more likely to display aggression. Women who initiate partner assaults report that

they feel no fear of retaliation and that men are easily able to defend themselves (Fiebert and Gonzales, 1997). Men perceive greater risks of sanctions for their behaviour than women and both sexes view women's intimate aggression as more trivial than men's (Miller and Simpson, 1991). Just as male attitudes condoning violence are strong predictors of partner assault by men (Stith et al., 2004), normative taboos against such behaviour may inhibit most men from expressing aggression in this context relative to others (Archer, 2004). This in turn may have implications for women's levels of fear and readiness to use aggression. Regarding the role of impulsivity, alcohol abuse is an important correlate of partner violence (Stith et al., 2004) and is also associated with behavioural disinhibition (Lyvers, 2000; Field et al., 2004). Long-term relationships and marriage inevitably result in increased predictability and boredom (Gigy and Kelly, 1992; Aron and Henkemeyer, 1995) and boredom-proneness is associated with physical aggression after controlling for impulsivity and sensation seeking (Dahlen et al., 2004). Future studies might usefully examine fear, impulsivity and sensation seeking in the specific context of cohabiting relationships. Information is needed about sex differences in variables such as these which may contribute to mediating the parity between the sexes in partner violence.

25.5. Conclusions

For many years social science has embraced the view that aggression is a learned behaviour (Reiss and Roth, 1993). Recently this view has been challenged. Aggressive behaviour, rather than showing the expected increase with age and exposure to learning, in fact declines with age (Tremblay and Nagin, 2005). What is acquired during childhood is not aggression but its opposite—behavioural inhibition. This comes as no surprise when we consider the complex interdependent societies in which humans and other primates function. Survival, within the group and as a group, depends on the ability to harmonize relationships in the context of mundane individual competition. For obligately social species, victory at the cost of isolation is a pyrrhic one. Among chimps, de Waal's (2000) work has shown the crucial role of reconciliation following aggressive interchanges. Erstwhile combatants actively seek to behaviourally repair relationships with hugs, kisses and mutual grooming and are encouraged in this by other members of the group.

Yet despite our common dependence on group living for survival, it is males in our own species and in many others who display higher levels of direct aggression. Evolutionary theory can inform us about the distal causes of such a sex difference—in the currency of reproductive success, aggression has benefited some males and cost some females dearly. As evolutionary psychologists, we need to go further to address the proximal and ontogenetic trajectory of this sex difference in humans. The conventional social science viewpoint is that sex differences in aggression, like other sex-differentiated behaviours, result from cognitive development and social learning by which the child tailors its behaviour to gender stereotypes or normative role expectations (Bussey and Bandura, 1999; Martin *et al.*, 2002). However, sex differences in physical aggression are seen by the age of 17 months (Archer and Cote, 2005). This is well below the age at which gender labelling and stereotypes—the proposed mediators of acquired sex differences—are understood. Once grasped by the child, there is no consistent association between the sophistication of the child's understanding of gender and levels of sex-congruent behaviour (Campbell, 1998). Gender stereotypes of aggression, rather than being the cause of sex differences, appear to be a reflection of them.

Although cross-sectional studies indicate that there is no significant change in the magnitude of the sex difference between preschool and puberty (Archer, 2004), longitudinal studies suggest that girls between the ages of 2 and 5 years learn more quickly than boys how to inhibit aggression (Archer and Cote, 2005). While this has traditionally been ascribed to parents' greater proscription of aggressive behaviour in girls, meta-analytic results do not support the view of differential treatment of boys and girls in regard to aggression (Lytton and Romney, 1991). Rather, girls' earlier acquisition of behavioural control may result from a greater sensitivity to parental responses. This in turn may derive from sex differences in fear and thence to earlier and stronger acquisition of the behavioural restraint that is built upon it (Fox *et al.*, 2005). Equally, girls' higher levels of fear may mediate their preferred level of autonomic and cortical stimulation manifested in lower sensation seeking (Zuckerman, 1994) and an unwillingness to escalate conflict to the point of direct aggression.

The ubiquity of the sex difference in our own and other species provides an acid test of any proposed theory of aggression—it should be implicitly predicted by an adequate theory. In social psychology, recent attempts have been made to unify diverse approaches into a general aggression model (Anderson and Bushman, 2002). The model identifies a range of variables including affect, cognition, arousal, appraisal, decision-making, scripts, schema, desensitization, situation and person variables. Sex differences are described in the latter category. But there is no attempt to trace the implication of sex for the host of other variables that are identified as leading to aggression. Rather than infusing the model, sex seems to have been appended in light of the well-established sex differences. By contrast, evolutionary approaches to a range of psychological phenomena consider sex differences *ab initio*. Sexual reproduction by males and females has entailed differential parental investment and, in areas where a behaviour has different implications for reproductive success in the two sexes, we should anticipate different strategies or threshold settings. Aggressive behaviour, in response to environmental cues of threat and competition, is controlled and regulated by the mind and as evolutionary psychologists it is our role to identify the route that the mind has taken. Attitudes, beliefs, expectations, values may all be weigh-stations along the road. But given the phylogeny of sex differences in aggression, it is my guess that the starting point of the route is in the ancient infrastructure of the mind—the emotions.

References

Abbott, D. H., Saltzman, W., Schultz-Darken, N. J. and Smith, T. E. (1999) Specific neuroendocrine mechanisms not involving generalized stress mediate social regulation of female reproduction in cooperatively breeding marmoset monkeys. In C. S. Carter, I. I. Lederhandler and B. Kirkpatrick (ed.) *The Integrative Neurobiology of Affiliation*, pp. 199–220. MIT Press, Cambridge, MA.

Aluja, A. and Torrubia, R. (2004) Hostility–aggressiveness, sensation seeking and sex hormones in men: re-exploring their relationship. *Neuropsychobiology*, 50: 102–107.

Amato, P. R. and Rogers, S. J. (1997) A longitudinal study of marital problems and subsequent divorce. *Journal of Marriage and the Family*, 59: 612–624.

Anderson, C. A. and Bushman, B. J. (2002) Human aggression. *Annual Review of Psychology*, 53: 27–51.

Archer, J. (2000) Sex differences in aggression between heterosexual partners: a meta-analytic review. *Psychological Bulletin*, 126: 651–680.

Archer, J. (2004) Sex differences in aggression in real world settings: a meta-analytic review. *Review of General Psychology*, 8: 291–322.

Archer, J. and Côte, S. (2005) The development of sex differences in aggressive behaviour: an evolutionary perspective. In R. E. Tremblay, W. W. Hartup and J. Archer (eds) *Developmental origins of aggression*. Guilford Press, New York.

Aron, A. and Henkemeyer, L. (1995) Marital satisfaction and passionate love. *Journal of Social and Personal Relationships*, 12: 139–146.

Arrindell, W. A., Kolk, A. M., Pickersgill, M. J. and Hageman, W. J. J. M. (1993) Biological sex, sex role orientation, masculine sex role stress, dissimulation and self-reported fears. *Advances in Behavior Research and Therapy*, 15: 103–146.

Arrindell, W. A., Mulkens, S., Kok, J. and Vollenbroek, J. (1999) Disgust sensitivity and the sex difference in fears to common indigenous animals. *Behavior Research and Therapy*, 37: 273–280.

Berlyne, D. E. (1960) *Conflict, Arousal and Curiosity*. McGraw Hill, New York.

Bettencourt, B. A. and Miller, N. (1996) Gender differences in aggression as a function of provocation: a meta-analysis. *Psychological Bulletin*, 119: 422–447.

Bjorklund, D. F. and Kipp, K. (1996) Parental investment theory and gender differences in the evolution of inhibitory mechanisms. *Psychological Bulletin*, 120: 163–188.

Blair, R. J. R. (2004) The roles of orbital frontal cortex in the modulation of antisocial behaviour. *Brain and Cognition*, 55: 198–208.

Bradley, M. M., Cuthbert, B. N. and Lang, P. N. (1999) Affect and the startle reflex. In M. E. Dawson, A. M. Schnell and A. H. Bohmelt (eds) *Startle Modification: Implications for Neuroscience, Cognitive Science and Clinical Science*, pp. 157–183. Cambridge University Press, New York.

Brebner, J. (2003) Gender and emotions. *Personality and Individual Differences*, 34: 387–394.

Brody, L. R. and Hall, J. A. (1993) Gender and emotion. In M. Lewis and J. M. Haviland (eds) *Handbook of Emotions*, pp. 447–460. Guilford Press, New York.

Burton, V. S., Cullen, F. T., Evans, T. D., Alarid, L. F. and Dunaway, R. G. (1998) Gender, self-control, and crime. *Journal of Research in Crime and Delinquency*, 35: 123–147.

Buss, D. M. (2000) *The Dangerous Passion*. Bloomsbury, London.

Bussey, K. and Bandura, A. (1999) Social–cognitive theory of gender development and differentiation. *Psychological Review*, 106: 676–713.

Byrnes, J. P., Miller, D. C. and Schafer, W. D. (1999) Gender differences in risk taking: a meta-analysis. *Psychological Bulletin*, 125: 367–383.

Campbell, A. (1998) Gender and the development of interpersonal orientation. In A. Campbell and S Muncer (eds) *The Social child*, pp. 325–352. Psychology Press, Hove.

Campbell, A. (1999) Staying alive: evolution, culture and intra-female aggression. *Behavioral and Brain Sciences*, 22: 203–252.

Campbell, A. (2002) *A Mind of Her Own: The Evolutionary Psychology of Women*. Oxford University Press, Oxford.

Campbell, A. (2006) Sex differences in direct aggression: what are the psychological mediators? *Aggression and Violent Behavior*, 11: 237–264.

Capaldi, D. M. and Owen, L. D. (2001) Physical aggression in a community sample of at-risk young couples: gender comparisons for high frequency, injury and fear. *Journal of Family Psychology*, 15: 425–440.

Carey, W. B. and McDevitt, S. C. (1978) Revisions of the infant temperament questionnaire. *Pediatrics*, 61: 735–739.

Caspi, A., McClay, J., Moffitt, T. E., Mill, J., Martin, J., Craig, I. W., Taylor, A. and Poulton, R. (2002) Role of genotype in the cycle of violence in maltreated children. *Science*, 297(5582): 851–854.

Cohen-Bendahan, C. C. C., Buitelaar, J. K., van Goozen, S. H. M., Orlbeke, J. F. and Cohen-Kettenis, P. T. (2005) Is there an effect of prenatal testosterone on aggression and other behavioral traits? A study comparing same-sex and opposite-sex twin girls. *Hormones and Behavior*, 47: 230–237.

Cosmides, L. and Tooby, J. (2000) Evolutionary psychology and the emotions. In M. Lewis and J. M. Haviland (eds) *Handbook of Emotions*, 2nd edn, pp. 91–115. Guilford Press, New York.

Craig, I. W., Harper, E. and Loat, C. S. (2004) The genetic basis for sex differences in human behaviour: role of the sex chromosomes. *Annals of Human Genetics*, 68: 269–284.

Crawford, J., Kippax, S., Onyx, J., Gault, U. and Benton, P. (1992) *Emotion and Gender: Constructing Meaning from Memory*. Sage, London.

Dahlen, E. R., Martin, R. C., Ragan, K. and Kuhlman, M. (2004) Boredom proneness in anger and aggression: Effects of impulsiveness and sensation seeking. *Personality and Individual Differences*, 37: 1615–1627.

Daitzman, R., Zuckerman, M., Sammelwitz, P. and Ganjam, V. (1978) Sensation seeking and gonadal hormones. *Journal of Biosocial Science*, 10: 401–408.

Daitzman, R. and Zuckerman, M. (1980) Disinhibitory sensation seeking, personality and gonadal hormones. *Personality and Individual Differences*, 1: 103–110.

Daly, M. and Wilson, M. (1983) *Sex, Evolution and Behaviour*, 2nd edn. Wadsworth, Belmont.

Daly, M. and Wilson, M. (1988) *Homicide*. Aldine de Gruyter, New York.

Daly, M. and Wilson, M. (1994) Evolutionary psychology of male violence. In J. Archer (ed.) *Male Violence*, pp. 253–288. Routledge, London.

Damasio, A. R. (1994) *Descartes' Error: Emotion, Reason and the Human Brain*. Putnam, New York.

Davidson, R. J., Putnam, K. M. and Larson, C. L. (2000) Dysfunction in the neural circuitry of emotion regulation—a possible prelude to violence. *Science*, 289: 591–594.

Davies, A. (1998) Youth gangs, masculinity and violence in late Victorian Manchester and Salford. *Journal of Social History*, 32: 349–369.

de Waal, F. B. M. (2000) Primates: a natural history of conflict resolution. *Science*, 289(5479): 586–590.

de Weerth, C. and Kalma, A. (1993) Female aggression as a response to sexual jealousy: a sex role reversal? *Aggressive Behavior*, 19: 265–279.

DeMaris, A. (1992) Male versus female initiation of aggression: The case of courtship violence. In C. E. Viano (ed.) *Intimate Violence: Interdisciplinary Perspectives*, pp. 111–120. Hemisphere, Washington DC.

Derryberry, D. and Rothbart, M. K. (1997) Reactive and effortful processes in the organisation of temperament. *Development and Psychopathology*, 9: 633–652.

Dienstbier, R. A. (1984) The role of emotion in moral socialization. In C. E. Izard, J. Kagan and R. B. Zajonc (eds) *Emotions, Cognition and Behaviour*, Vol. 14. *Review of Personality and Social Psychology*, pp. 119–150. Sage, Newbury Park, CA.

Dixson, A. F. (1998) *Primate Sexuality: Comparative Studies of the Prosimians, Monkeys, Apes and Human Beings*. Oxford University Press, New York.

Dobash, R. E. and Dobash, R. (1983) *Violence Against Wives: A Case Against Patriarchy*. Macmillan, New York.

Durose, M. R., Harlow, C. W., Langan, P. A., Motivans, M., Rantala, R. R. and Smith, E. L. (2005) *Family Violence Statistics Including Statistics on Strangers and Acquaintances*. Bureau of Justice Statistics, Washington DC.

Eagly, A. H. and Steffen, V. (1986) Gender and aggressive behaviour: a meta-analytic review of the social psychological literature. *Psychological Bulletin*, 100: 3–22

Eisenberg, N., Cumberland, A., Spinrad, T. L. *et al.* (2001) The relations of regulation and emotionality to children's externalizing and internalizing problem behaviour. *Child Development*, 72: 1112–1134.

Eisenberg, N., Spinrad, T. L., Fabes, R. A. *et al.* (2004) The relations of effortful control and impulsivity to children's resiliency and adjustment. *Child Development*, 75: 25–46.

Eisenberg, N., Sadovsky, T. L., Fabes, R. A., Losoya, S. H., Valiente, C., Reiser, M., Cumberland, A. and Shepard, S. A. (2005) The relations of problem behaviour status to children's negative emotionality, effortful control and impulsivity: Concurrent relations and prediction of change. *Developmental Psychology*, 41: 193–211.

Eysenck, H. J. (1977) *Crime and Personality*, 3rd edn. Routledge & Kegan Paul, London.

Farrington, D. P. (2003) Key results from the first forty years of the Cambridge study of delinquent development. In T. P. Thornberry and M. D. Krohn (eds) *Taking Stock of Delinquency: An Overview of Findings from Contemporary Longitudinal Studies*, pp. 137–183. Kluwer, New York.

Farrington, D. F. and Loeber, R. (1999) Transatlantic replicability of risk factors in the development of delinquency. In P. Cohen, C. Slomkowski and L. N. Robins (eds) *Historical and Geographical Influences on Psychopathology*, pp. 299–329. Lawrence Erlbaum, Hillsdale, NJ.

Fiebert, M. S. and Gonzalez, D. M. (1997) College women who initiate assaults on their male partners and the reasons offered for such behavior. *Psychological Reports*, 80: 583–590.

Field, C. A., Caetano, R. and Nelson, S. (2004) Alcohol and violence related cognitive risk factors associated with the perpetration of intimate partner violence. *Journal of Family Violence*, 19: 249–253.

Figueredo, A. J., Sefcek, J. A., Vasquez, G., Brumbach, B. H., King, J. E. and Jacobs, W. J. (2005) Evolutionary personality psychology. In D. Buss (ed.) *Handbook of Evolutionary Psychology*, pp. 851–877. Wiley, New Jersey.

Fischer, A. H. (1993) Sex differences in emotionality: fact or stereotype? *Feminism and Psychology*, 3: 303–318.

Fischer, A. H. and Manstead, A. S. R. (2000) Gender and emotions in different cultures. In A. H. Fischer (ed.) *Gender and Emotion: Social Psychological Perspectives*, pp. 71–94. Cambridge University Press, Cambridge.

Fishbein, E. (2000) Neuropsychology function, drug use, and violence: a conceptual framework. *Criminal Justice and Behavior*, 27: 139–159.

Fox, N. A., Henderson, H. A., Marshall, P. J., Nichols, K. E. and Ghera, M. M. (2005) Behavioral inhibition: linking biology and behaviour within a developmental framework. *Annual Review of Psychology*, 56: 235–262.

Fulker, D. W., Eysenck, S. B. G. and Zuckerman, M. (1980) A genetic and environmental analysis of sensation seeking. *Journal of Research in Personality*, 14: 261–281.

Gervai, J., Turner, P. J. and Hinde, R. A. (1993) Parents' and teachers' perceptions of personality traits of young children: Sex differences, cross-national comparisons and relations with observed behaviour. *British Journal of Developmental Psychology*, 11: 343–349.

Giancola, P. R. and Zeichner, A. (1994) Neuropsychological performance on tests of frontal-lobe functioning and aggressive behavior in men. *Journal of Abnormal Psychology*, 103: 832–835.

Gibbs, J. J., Giever, D. and Martin, J. S. (1998) Parental management and self-control: an empirical test of Gottfredson and Hirschi's general theory. *Journal of Research in Crime and Delinquency*, 12: 231–235.

Gigy, L. and Kelly, J. B. (1992) Reasons for divorce: perspectives of divorcing men and women. *Journal of Divorce and Remarriage*, 18: 169–187.

Goldstein, J. M., Seidman, L. J., Horton, N. J. *et al.* (2001) Normal sexual dimorphism of the adult human brain assessed by in vivo magnetic resonance imaging. *Cerebral Cortex*, 11: 490–497.

Gottfredson, M. and Hirschi, T. (1990) *A General Theory of Crime*. Stanford University Press, Palo Alto, CA.

Grafman, J., Schwab, K., Warden, D., Pridgen, A., Brown, H. R. and Salazar, A. M. (1996) Frontal lobe injuries, violence, and aggression: a report of the Vietnam Head Injury Study. *Neurology*, 46: 1231–1238.

Gray, J. A. (1982) *The Neuropsychology of Anxiety*. Oxford University Press, Oxford.

Greenberg, L. M. and Waldman, I. D. (1993) Developmental normative data on the test of variables of attention (TOVA). *Journal of Child Psychology, Psychiatry and Allied Disciplines*, 34: 19–30.

Greenfeld, L. A. and Snell, T. L. (1999) *Women Offenders*. Bureau of Justice Statistics, Washington, DC.

Grote, N. K., Frieze, I. H. and Stone, C. A. (1996) Children, traditionalism in the division of family work, and marital satisfaction: "What's love got to do with it?" *Personal Relationships*, 3: 211–228.

Gullone, E. (2000) The development of normal fear: a century of research. *Clinical Psychology Review*, 20: 429–451.

Gullone, E. and King, N. J. (1993) The fears of youth in the 1990s: contemporary normative data. *Journal of Genetic Psychology*, 154: 137–153.

Gur, R. C., Gunning-Dixon, F., Bilker, W. B. and Gur, R. E. (2002) Sex differences in tempero-limbic and frontal brain volumes of healthy adults. *Cerebral Cortex*, 12: 998–1003.

Harris, C. R. (2003) A review of sex differences in sexual jealousy, including self report data, psychophysiological responses, interpersonal violence and morbid jealousy. *Personality and Social Psychology Review*, 7: 102–128.

Hersch, J. (1997) Smoking, seat belts and other risky consumer decisions: differences by gender and race. *Managerial and Decision Economics*, 11: 241–256.

Hill, K. and Hurtado, M. (1996) *Aché Life History: The Ecology and Demography of a Foraging People*. Aldine de Gruyter, New York.

Hoaken, P. N. S., Shaughnessy, V. K. and Pihl, R. O. (2003) Executive cognitive functioning and aggression: is it an issue of impulsivity? *Aggressive Behavior*, 29: 15–30.

Hsu, C., Soong, W., Stigler, J. W., Hong, C. and Liang, C. (1981) The temperamental characteristics of Chinese babies. *Child Development*, 52: 1337–1340.

Hoffner, C. A. and Levine, K. J. (2003). Enjoyment of mediated fright and violence: a meta-analysis. *Media Psychology*, 7: 207–237.

Hur, Y.-M. and Bouchard, T. J. (1997) The genetic correlation between impulsivity and sensation seeking traits. *Behavior Genetics*, 27: 455–463.

Hyde, J. S. (1986). Gender differences in aggression. In J. S. Hyde and M. C. Linn (eds) *The Psychology of Gender: Advances Through Meta-Analysis*, pp. 51–66. Baltimore, MD: Johns Hopkins University Press.

International Criminal Police Organisation (1994) *International Crime Statistics*. ICPO Interpol General Secretariat, Lyons.

Johnson, M. P. (1995) Patriarchal terrorism and common couple violence: two forms of violence against women. *Journal of Marriage and the Family*, 57: 283–294.

Johnson, M. P. and Leone, J. M. (2005) The differential effects of intimate terrorism and situational couple violence: findings from the national violence against women survey. *Journal of Family Issues*, 26: 322–249.

Joireman, J., Anderson, J. and Strathman, A. (2003) The aggression paradox: understanding links among aggression, sensation seeking, and the consideration of future consequences. *Journal of Personality and Social Psychology*, 84: 1287–1302.

Kane, M. J., Hambrick, D. Z. and Conway, A. R. A. (2005) Working memory capacity and fluid intelligence are strongly related constructs: comment on Ackerman, Beier, and Boyle (2005) *Psychological Bulletin*, 131: 66–71.

Kerr, A. and Zelazo, P. D. (2004) Development of "hot" executive function: the children's gambling task. *Brain and Cognition*, 55: 148–157.

Kirchner, G. L. and Kopf, I. J. (1974) Differences in vigilance performance in second-grade children as related to gender and achievement. *Child Development*, 45: 490–495.

Kitson, G. C. (1992) *Portrait of Divorce*. Guilford Press, London.

Klenberg, L., Korkman, M. and Lahti-Nuuttila, P. (2001) Differential development of attention and executive functions in 3- to 12-year-old Finnish children. *Developmental Neuropsychology*, 20: 407–429.

Knight, G. P., Fabes, R. A. and Higgins, D. A. (1996). Concerns about drawing causal inferences from meta-analysis: an example in the study of gender differences in aggression. *Psychological Bulletin*, 119: 410–421.

Knight, G. P., Guthrie, I. K., Page, M. C. and Fabes, R. A. (2002) Emotional arousal and gender differences in aggression: a meta-analysis. *Aggressive Behavior*, 28: 366–393.

Kochanska, G. and Aksan, N. (1995) Mother–child mutually positive affect, the quality of child compliance to requests and prohibitions, and maternal control as correlates of early internalization. *Child Development*, 66: 236–254.

Kochanska, G. and Knaack, A. (2003) Effortful control as a personality characteristic of young children: Antecedents, correlates and consequences. *Journal of Personality*, 71: 1087–1111.

Kochanska, G., Murray, K., Jacques, T. Y., Koenig, A. and Vandegeest, K. A. (1996) Inhibitory control in young children and its role in emerging internalization. *Child Development*, 67: 490–507.

Kochanska, G., Murray, K. T. and Coy, K. C. (1997) Inhibitory control as a contributor to conscience in childhood: From toddler to early school age. *Child Development*, 68: 263–277.

Kochanska, G., Murray, K. T. and Harlan, E. T. (2000) Effortful control in early childhood: Continuity and change, antecedents and implications for social development. *Developmental Psychology*, 36: 220–232.

Kochanska, G., Coy, K. C. and Murray, K. T. (2001) The development of self regulation in the first four years of life. *Child Development*, 72: 1091–1111.

Koopmans, J. R., Boosma, D. I., Heath, A. C. and van Dooren, L. J.P. (1995) A multivariate genetic analysis of sensation seeking. *Behavior Genetics*, 25: 349–356.

Kring, A. M. (2000) Gender and anger. In A. H. Fischer (ed.) *Gender and Emotion: Social Psychological*

Perspectives, pp. 211–231. Cambridge University Press, Cambridge.

LaGrange, T. C. and Silverman, R. A. (1999) Low self-control and opportunity: testing the general theory of crime as an explanation for gender differences in delinquency. *Criminology*, 37: 41–72.

Lau, M. A., Pihl, R. O. and Peterson, J. B. (1995) Provocation, acute alcohol intoxication, cognitive performance and aggression. *Journal of Abnormal Psychology*, 104: 150–155.

LeDoux, J. E. (1996) *The Emotional Brain*. Simon & Schuster, New York.

Leone, J. M., Johnson, M. P., Cohan, C. L. and Lloyd, S. E. (2004) Consequences of male partner violence for low-income minority women. *Journal of Marriage and the Family*, 66: 472–490.

Lerner, J. S. and Keltner, D. (2000) Beyond valence: toward a model of emotion-specific influences on judgement and choice. *Cognition and Emotion*, 14: 473–493.

Lerner, J. S. and Keltner, D. (2001) Fear, anger and risk. *Journal of Personality and Social Psychology*, 81: 146–159.

Levy, F. and Hobbes, G. (1979) The influences of social class and gender on sustained attention (vigilance) and motor inhibition in children. *Australian and New Zealand Journal of Psychiatry*, 13: 231–234.

Liew, J., Eisenberg, N. and Reiser, M. (2004) Preschoolers' effortful control and negative emotionality, immediate reactions to disappointment and quality of social functioning. *Journal of Experimental Child Psychology*, 89: 298–319.

Lissek, S. and Powers, A. S. (2003) Sensation seeking and startle modulation by physically threatening images. *Biological Psychology*, 63: 179–197.

Loeber, R., Farrington, D. P., Stouthamer-Loeber, M., Moffitt, T. E., Caspi, A. and Lynam, D. (2001) Male mental health problems, psychopathy and personality traits: key findings from the first 14 years of the Pittsburgh Youth Study. *Clinical Child and Family Psychology Review*, 4: 273–297.

Loewenstein, G. F., Weber, E. U., Hsee, C. K. and Welch, N. (2001) Risk as feelings. *Psychological Bulletin*, 127: 267–286.

Lorber, M. F. (2004) Psychophysiology of aggression, psychopathy and conduct problems: a meta-analysis. *Psychological Bulletin*, 130: 531–552.

Lynam, D. R. and Miller, J. D. (2004) Personality pathways to impulsive behaviour and their relations to deviance: results from three samples. *Journal of Quantitative Criminology*, 20: 319–341.

Lytton, H. and Romney, D. (1991). Parents' differential treatment of boys and girls: a meta-analysis. *Psychological Bulletin*, 109: 267–296.

Lyvers, M. (2000) 'Loss of control' in alcoholism and drug addiction: a neuroscientific interpretation. *Experimental and Clinical Psychopharmacology*, 8: 225–249.

Maccoby, E. E. and Jacklin, C. N. (1974) *The Psychology of Sex Differences*. Stanford University Press, Palo Alto, CA.

Martin, C. L., Ruble, D. N. and Szkrybalo, J. (2002) Cognitive theories of early gender development. *Psychological Bulletin*, 128: 903–933.

Martin, R. P., Wisenbaker, J., Baker, J. and Huttunen, M. O. (1997) Gender differences in temperament at six months and five years. *Infant Behavior and Development* 20: 339–347.

Maziade, M., Boudreault, M., Thivierge, J., Caperaa, P. and Cote, R. (1984) Infant temperament: SES and gender differences and reliability of measurement in a large Quebec sample. *Merrill-Palmer Quarterly* 30: 213–226.

McCarthy, B. (1994) Warrior values. In J. Archer (ed.) *Male Violence*, pp. 105–120. Routledge, London.

McManis, M. H., Bradley, M. M., Berg, W. K., Cuthbert, B. N. and Lang, P. J. (2001) Emotional reactions in children: verbal, physiological and behavioural responses to affective pictures. *Psychophysiology*, 38: 222–231.

Miller, J. D., Flory, K., Lynam, D. and Leukefeld, C. (2003) A test of the four-factor model of impulsivity-related traits. *Personality and Individual Differences*, 34: 1403–1418.

Miller, S. L. and Simpson, S. S. (1991) Courtship violence and social control: does gender matter? *Law and Society Review*, 25: 335–365.

Mirowsky, J. and Ross, C. E. (1995) Sex differences in distress: real or artefact? *American Sociological Review*, 60: 449–468.

Moffitt, T. E. (1993) Adolescent limited and life course persistent antisocial behaviour: a developmental taxonomy. *Psychological Review*, 100: 674–701.

Moffitt, T. E., Caspi, A., Rutter, M. and Silva, P. A. (2001) *Sex Differences in Antisocial Behaviour: Conduct Disorder, Delinquency and Violence in the Dunedin Longitudinal Study*. Cambridge University Press, Cambrdge.

Mowrer, O. H. (1960) *Learning and Behaviour*. Wiley, New York.

Nagy, E., Loveland, K. A., Kopp, M., Orvos, H., Pal, A. and Molnar, P. (2001) Different emergence of fear expressions in infant boys and girls. *Infant Behavior and Development*, 24: 189–194.

Navarette, M. G., Goulden, L. G. and Silver, C. H. (1998) Children's Executive Functions Scale: Gender and ethnic differences. *Archives of Clinical Neuropsychology*, 13: 80–81.

Olson, S. L., Schilling, E. M. and Bates, J. E. (1999) Measurement of impulsivity: construct coherence, longitudinal stability and relationship with externalizing problems in middle childhood and adolescence. *Journal of Abnormal Child Psychology*, 27: 151–165.

Overman, W. H. (2004) Sex differences in early childhood, adolescence and adulthood on cognitive tasks that rely on orbital prefrontal cortex. *Brain and Cognition*, 55: 134–247.

Parsey, R. V., Oquendo, M. A., Simpson, N. R. *et al.* (2002) Effects of sex, age and aggressive traits in men on brain serotonin 5-HT$_{1A}$ receptor binding potential measured by PET using [C-11]WAY-100635. *Brain Research*, 954: 173–182.

Pascualvaca, D. M., Anthony, B. J., Arnold, L. E. *et al.* (1997) Attention performance in an epidemiological sample of urban children: the role of gender and intelligence. *Child Neuropsychology*, 3: 13–27.

Paul, L. and Galloway, J. (1994) Sexual jealousy: gender differences in response to partner and rival. *Aggressive Behavior*, 20: 203–212.

Pratt, T. C. and Cullen, F. T. (2000) The empirical status of Gottfredson and Hirschi's general theory of crime: a meta-analysis. *Criminology*, 38: 931–964.

Raine, A. (2002) Annotation: The role of prefrontal deficits, low autonomic arousal and early health factors in the development of antisocial and aggressive behaviour in children. *Journal of Child Psychology and Psychiatry*, 43: 417–434.

Raine, A., Buchsbaum, M. and LaCasse, L. (1997) Brain abnormalities in murderers indicated by positron emission tomography. *Biological Psychiatry*, 42: 495–508.

Rebok, G. W., Smith, C. B., Pascualavaca, D. M., Mirsky, A. F., Anthony, B. J. and Kellam, S. G. (1997) Developmental changes in attentional performance in urban children from eight to thirteen years. *Child Neuropsychology*, 3: 28–46.

Reiss, A. J. and Roth, J.A (eds) (1993) *Understanding and Preventing Violence*. National Academy Press, Washington DC.

Ridley, M. (1997) *The Origins of Virtue*. Penguin, London.

Roberti, J. W. (2004) A review of behavioural and biological correlates of sensation seeking. *Journal of Research in Personality*, 38: 256–279.

Rosenblitt, J. C., Soler, H., Johnson, S. E. and Quadagno, D. M. (2003) Sensation seeking and hormones in men and women: exploring the link. *Hormones and Behavior*, 40: 396–402.

Rothbart, M. K. and Bates, J. E. (1998) Temperament. In W. Damon and N. Eisenberg (eds) *Handbook of Child Psychology*, 5th edn, vol. 3, *Social, Emotional and Personality Development*, pp. 105–176. Wiley, Chichester.

Sagarin, B. J. (2005) Reconsidering evolved sex differences in jealousy: comment on Harris (2003). *Personality and Social Psychology Review*, 9: 62–75.

Schutzhohl, A. and Koch, S. (2004) Sex differences in jealousy: the recall of cues to sexual and emotional infidelity in personally more and less threatening context conditions. *Evolution and Human Behavior*, 25: 249–257.

Schutzwohl, A. (2005) Sex differences in jealousy: the processing of cues to infidelity. *Evolution and Human Behavior*, 26: 288–299.

Sear, R., Mace, R. and McGregor, I. A. (2000) Maternal grandmothers improve nutritional status and survival of children in rural Gambia. *Proceedings of the Royal Society of London, B*, 267: 1641–1647.

Seguin, J. R., Pihl, R. O., Harden, P. W., Tremblay, R. E. and Boulerice, B. (1995) Cognitive and neuropsychological characteristics of physically aggressive boys. *Journal of Abnormal Psychology*, 104: 614–624.

Seguin, J. R., Arsenault, L., Boulerice, B., Harden, P. W. and Tremblay, R. E. (2002) Response perseveration in adolescent boys with stable and unstable histories of physical aggression: the role of underlying processes. *Journal of Child Psychology and Psychiatry*, 43: 481–494.

Seguin, J. R., Boulerice, B., Harden, P. W., Tremblay, R. E. and Pihl, R. O. (1999) Executive functions and physical aggression after controlling for attention deficit

hyperactivity disorder, general memory and IQ. *Journal of Child Psychology and Psychiatry*, 40: 1197–1208.

Seguin, J. R., Nagin, D., Assaad, J.-M. and Tremblay, R. E. (2004) Cognitive-neuropsychological function in chronic physical aggression and hyperactivity. *Journal of Abnormal Psychology*, 113: 603–613.

Seroczynski, A. D., Bergman, C. S. and Coccaro, E. F. (1999) Etiology of the impulsivity/aggression relationship: genes or environment? *Psychiatry Research*, 86: 41–57.

Shively, C. A., Laber-Laird, K. and Anton, R. F. (1997) Behavior and physiology of social stress and depression in female Cynomolgus monkeys. *Biological Psychiatry*, 41: 871–882.

Silverman, I. W. (2003) Gender differences in resistance to temptation: theories and evidence. *Developmental Review*, 23: 219–259.

Simon, R. W. and Nath, L. E. (2004) Gender and emotion in the United States: do men and women differ in self-reports of feelings and expressive behaviour? *American Journal of Sociology*, 109: 1137–1176.

Stanford, M. S., Greve, K. W. and Gerstle, J. E. (1997) Neuropsychological correlates of self-reported impulsive aggression in a college sample. *Personality and Individual Differences*, 23: 961–965.

Stewart, S. H., Taylor, S. and Baker, J. M. (1997) Gender differences in dimensions of anxiety sensitivity. *Journal of Anxiety Disorders*, 11: 179–200.

Stith, S. M., Smith, D. B., Penn, C. E., Ward, D. B. and Tritt, D. (2004) Intimate partner physical abuse perpetration and victimization risk factors: a meta-analytic review. *Aggression and Violent Behavior*, 10: 65–98.

Straus, M. A. and Gelles, R. J. (1988) Violence in American families: how much is there and why does it occur? In E. W. Nunnally, C. S. Chilman and F. M. Fox (eds) *Troubled Relationships*, pp. 1410–162. Sage, Newbury Park, CA.

Taylor, S. E., Klein, L. C. Lewis, B. P., Gruenewald, T. L., Gurung, R. A.R. and Updegraff. J. A. (2000) Biobehavioral responses to stress in females: tend-and-befriend, not fight-or-flight. *Psychological Review*, 107: 411–429.

Tellegen, A., Lykken, D. T., Bouchard, T. J., Wilkox, K., Segal, N. L. and Rich, S. (1988) Personality similarity in twins reared apart and together. *Journal of Personality and Social Psychology*, 54: 1031–1039.

Tittle, C. R., Ward, D. A. and Grasmick, H. G. (2003) Gender, age and crime/deviance: a challenge to self-control theory. *Journal of Research in Crime and Delinquency*, 40: 426–453.

Tremblay, R. E. and Nagin, D. S. (2005) The developmental origins of physical aggression in humans. In R. E. Tremblay, W. W. Hartup and J. Archer (eds) *Developmental Origins of Aggression*, pp. 83–106. Guilford, New York.

Twenge, J. M., Campbell, W. K. and Foster, C. A. (2003) Parenthood and marital satisfaction: A meta-analytic review. *Journal of Marriage and the Family*, 65: 574–583.

Valiente, C., Eisenberg, N., Smith, C. L., Fabes, R. A., Losoya, S., Guthrie, I. K. and Murphy, B. C. (2003)

The relations of effortful control and reactive control to children's externalising problems: a longitudinal assessment. *Journal of Personality*, 71: 1171–1195.

Vierikko, E., Pulkkinen, L., Kaprio, J. and Rose, R. J. (2004) Genetic and environmental influences on the relationship between aggression and hyperactivity–impulsivity as rated by teachers and parents. *Twin Research*, 7: 261–274.

Walsh, T. M., Stewart, S. H., McLoughlin, E. and Comeau, N. (2004) Gender differences in childhood anxiety sensitivity index (CASI) dimensions. *Journal of Anxiety Disorders*, 18: 695–706.

White, J. L., Moffitt, T. E., Caspi, A., Bartusch, D. J., Needles, D. J. and Southamer-Loeber, M. (1994) Measuring impulsivity and examining its relationship to delinquency. *Journal of Abnormal Psychology*, 103: 192–205.

Whiteside, S. P. and Lynam, D. R. (2001) The Five Factor Model and impulsivity: using a structural model of personality to understand impulsivity. *Personality and Individual Differences*, 30: 669–689.

Wilson, M. and Daly, M. (1985) Competitiveness, risk taking and violence: the young male syndrome. *Ethology and Sociobiology*, 6: 59–73.

Wilson, M. and Daly, M. (1992a) The man who mistook his wife for a chattel. In J. H. Barkow, L. Cosmides and J. Tooby (eds) *The Adapted Mind*, pp. 289–321. Oxford University Press, New York.

Wilson, M. and Daly, M. (1992b) Who kills whom in spouse killings? On the exceptional sex ratio of spousal homicides in the United States. *Criminology*, 30: 189–215.

Zuckerman, M. (1979) *Sensation Seeking: Beyond the Optimal Level of Arousal*. Lawrence Erlbaum, New Jersey.

Zuckerman, M. (1994) *Behavioral Expressions and Biosocial Bases of Sensation Seeking*. Cambridge University Press, New York.

Zuckerman, M., Kuhlman, D. M., Joireman, J. A., Teta, P. and Kraft, M. (1993) A comparison of three structural models for personality: the Big Three, the Big Five and the Alternative Five. *Journal of Personality and Social Psychology*, 65: 757–768.

CHAPTER 26

The evolutionary ecology of human family size

Ruth Mace

26.1. Introduction to the human life history

Neither human life history nor human social organization resembles that of the other apes. Since the chimpanzees and humans diverged, humans have increased their body and brain sizes, of course, but along with those changes females have increased their lifespans, the size of their offspring and their birth rate (relative to body size), and increased the period of childhood dependence, as well as terminating their reproductive span to end around 20 years before they die (Hill and Kaplan, 1999). This concentration of reproductive effort into the central portion of the lifespan means that motherhood involves the expenditure of a great deal of energy (Mace, 2000). Big babies with big brains are costly to support, and whole families of dependants need more food and care than individual offspring. The most likely explanation for how human females achieve this rapid reproduction is with the help of mates and kin. The early termination of reproduction could be an adaptation either to complete the lengthy, child-rearing process without risking early death through maternal mortality, and/or to help daughters with their reproductive careers (Hawkes et al., 1998; Sear et al., 2000; Shanley and Kirkwood, 2001). There have been a number of formal models of human life history that have highlighted how intergenerational transfers (from both parents and grandparents to offspring) are fundamental to both our life history (Shanley and Kirkwood, 2001; Kaplan and Robson, 2002; Lee, 2003), and even our morphology (particularly brain size, longevity, and our unusual mortality schedules). Kaplan uses the concept of embodied capital as a term for basically everything (skills, body, resources) that parents invest in children to aid their future reproductive success. By assuming that transfers received over the lifetime and given out over the lifetime are the same when populations are in equilibrium, Lee argues that the force of selection is actually strongly related to the remaining transfers to be given out rather than just the number of births—helping to formalize both grandmother hypothesis for the evolution of menopause, as well as providing one possible explanation for the low birth rate/high parental investment scenario now observed in most contemporary human populations. Being human is all about parental investment.

Thus, whereas many male primates expend their energy trying to monopolize large groups of females, and rarely if ever provision other group members, and most primate females raise young without any help, in humans, both parents and even grandparents are more likely to be found provisioning offspring and mates or sharing food amongst the small group of pair-bonded individuals and their families, with whom they live. Mating effort might appear to be the focus of the greater portion of both popular culture and scientific literature; nevertheless it is parental investment that is, quite possibly, the central preoccupation of both men and women for the great majority of their adult lives.

26.2. **Trade-offs between fertility and mortality**

At the heart of evolutionary life-history theory is the notion that energy expended on reproduction cannot be spent on growth and body maintenance (Roff, 1992), and thus an essential trade-off exists between fertility and mortality. As human reproduction is costly, we might expect to see mothers of large families die young, and, with careful statistical analysis, there are some studies that do show that trade-off (Doblhammer and Oeppen, 2003). However, due to phenotypic variation, those reproducing at a faster rate are likely to be those with the capacity to live the longest, so the two effects may cancel each other out. These phenotypic correlations, and the fact that it is impossible to undertake experimental manipulations of the type that have demonstrated costs of reproduction in other species (Gustafsson and Part, 1990), means that this correlation is not always clear to see. Similarly, the cost of a rapid birth interval on the next interval is also masked by phenotypic correlation, as those women capable of rapid reproduction in one birth interval generally go on to show rapid reproduction in subsequent intervals (Sear *et al.*, 2003).

There is also a trade-off between infant survival and mother's fertility, as children compete for her investment. In principle the same problem of phenotypic correlation applies to demonstrating that trade-off; but, presumably because of the asymmetry of the risk between mother and infant, there are numerous studies showing that short birth intervals can endanger the life of the child both opening and closing that interval (Hobcraft *et al.*, 1985); there is also evidence that large families impose costs on older children too (LeGrand and Phillips, 1996). Mothers usually maximize their lifetime reproductive success by having more children than

would maximize offspring survival, a central tenet of parent–offspring conflict (Trivers, 1985).

Blurton Jones (1986) showed that individual hunter-gatherer !Kung mothers with short interbirth intervals experienced higher infant mortality, and the optimal balance between the birth interval and infant survival occurred at around 4 year interbirth intervals. This is a longer interbirth interval than appears to be the current norm for our species, but he argues that this is due to the hunter-gatherer lifestyle and the necessity of carrying both infant and food supply on the back: more closely spaced offspring would be impossible to transport around. It should be noted, however, that in another forager group, the Aché, who also carry their young everywhere (the forest floor is particularly dangerous for infants), manage a 3 year interbirth interval (Hill and Hurtado, 1996). Some authors attribute long !Kung interbirth intervals to the prevalence of sexually transmitted infections in these populations. Further, although Blurton Jones's backload model is plausible, in fact phenotypic correlations yet again make the interpretation of this result unclear.

Figure 26.1 shows data from a natural fertility/natural mortality population of Gambian farmers to illustrate that, on average, high-fertility mothers experience higher infant mortality, but also higher lifetime reproductive success. Whilst it has to be borne in mind that under-reporting of dead babies could be biasing the peak towards a higher optimum, it is none the less clear that only a small proportion (4/400 in this case) of women had more than the apparent 'optimal clutch size' of 10 births, suggesting, as predicted, that almost no one is having 'too many babies' for maximizing their lifetime reproductive success. A similar result was found in a natural fertility population in Mali (Strassmann and Gillespie, 2002). Most mothers in fact achieve reproductive success way below the population maximum, due to phenotypic variation between individuals in the population; some mothers are just better than others at producing viable offspring, and mothers will reproduce only according to their individual optima.

Twinning provides a clear example of the 'supermum' effect. Mothers of twins do experience higher lifetime reproductive success, due to

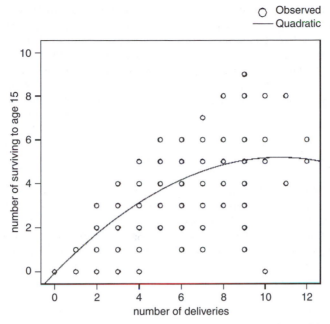

Fig. 26.1 Number of offspring surviving to age 15 years, against number of births (Gambian village sample, births between 1950 and 1975). Women with a larger number of births experience a higher proportion of deaths amongst their offspring, but still end up with a larger number of surviving offspring over most of the range. The quadratic term is highly significant, giving the appearance of an 'optimal clutch size' around at least 10 births. However, only five out of the 401 women who gave birth actually had more than 10 births.

shorter interbirth intervals in general, and longer reproductive spans (Sear *et al.*, 2001). In some studies of natural fertility societies, it has been shown that if both twins are girls the twins can be successful (Lummaa *et al.*, 2001). But overall, there is considerable evidence that twinning may be costly for the twins themselves. In the Gambia, twin mortality is double that of singleton mortality, suggesting that the process is inefficient to the point of maladaptation (Sear *et al.*, 2001). Twinning could be a by-product of polyovulation, which allows these high-quality women to maintain short interbirth intervals; the downside is that twinning sometimes occurs and then infant mortality is high.

Parents may be winning the parent–offspring conflict with respect to birth intervals, but it must not be forgotten that there is also parent–parent conflict. The costs of high infant and maternal mortality has a greater impact on maternal than paternal inclusive fitness. This is because, whilst it benefits no-one when a mother dies, a male and his patrilineal relatives can at least replace that mother through remarriage—whereas that individual is irreplaceable to her matriline, and her children are bound to suffer reduced fitness due to her loss (Sear *et al.*, 2002; Pavard *et al.*, 2005). In natural fertility populations, the costs of reproduction are probably a significant cause of mortality for mothers, which could explain why there is evidence that patrilineal relatives, including grandparents, may favour higher fertility rates than those favoured by matrilineal relatives, who value the survival of existing mothers and children more highly and hence weight the costs of reproduction more heavily in the fertility/mortality trade-off (Mace and Sear, 2005). This conflict is likely to be especially pronounced in the polygynous societies. Strassmann (2000) reviews a situation in Mali (West Africa) where polygynous marriage enhances male reproductive success at the expense of high infant mortality among polygynously married women's offspring.

This presumably represents a scenario in which the matrilineal relatives have somehow lost the ability to bargain effectively on behalf of their daughters, perhaps due to the patrilineal monopolization of resources.

26.3. A culture of low fertility

Over the last century, a major cultural change has occurred, as populations all over the world have moved from natural fertility to low fertility. This fertility decline and the associated mortality decline is known as the demographic transition. The transition started in Europe as early as 200 years ago in some areas, then proceeded (much later) through North America, South America, then more recently in Asia, followed finally by Africa (where fertility decline started only at the end of the twentieth century). Some demographers use the term the 'second demographic transition' to describe a more recent trend, again originating in Europe in the last 30 years, of further reductions in fertility to below replacement levels, accompanied by the weakening of all the traditional institutions of child-bearing such as marriage. The deliberate reduction in birth rates represents something of a challenge to the evolutionary (fitness-maximizing) view of demography. The view that it is adaptive for relatively wealthy parents to choose to have no more than two children is certainly a minority view. There are a number of arguments, mostly rooted in evolutionary psychology and gene–culture coevolutionary theory, arguing that small families could be the outcome of a number of evolutionary processes that could lead to maladaptive outcomes; although it should be stressed that such proximate explanations for low fertility are not necessarily incompatible with more functional interpretations from evolutionary ecology (Borgerhoff Mulder, 1998).

Even those most ardently arguing for the value of intergenerational transfer to enhance quality over quantity believe that contemporary urban humans may have gone too far. Kaplan and others argue that adaptations to hunter-gatherer environments mean that our evolved preferences are causing current levels of investment, in circumstances where contraception is available and wealth is heritable, that are simply leading to maladaptive levels of fertility (Kaplan et al., 2002). Another argument, superficially different but also in effect arguing for a maladaptive decision-making processes, is that prestige bias (a tendency to copy successful individuals) is driving low fertility in conditions where children may now hinder rather than assist our accumulation of status and prestige (Boyd and Richerson, 1985).

Another factor is that increased migration related to education and employment means that the extended family are often not available to help. Further, late reproduction, driven by the need to become educated even after sexual maturity, can reduce the support to be expected from grandmothers as they are simply too old to carry much of a burden, and elder siblings are themselves too busily engaged in gaining education to assist with childcare. Newson et al. (2005) raise the intriguing possibility that your kin are far more likely to encourage reproduction (for reasons of kin selection) than are your 'friends', who at best do not care about your reproductive success or at worst may in fact be in reproductive competition with you. Hence not only do modern parents face a lack of kin support, but a lack of kin encouragement, as well as a wealth of advice to avoid the costs of reproduction. This theory does not address the question of why we have not evolved defence mechanisms against taking advice from unrelated individuals. However, modern levels of exposure to so many non-relatives may be a recent phenomenon in evolutionary terms. Along similar lines, Foster argues that our psychology is as yet unable to resist the temptation of sex without reproduction, as such a choice is an evolutionary novelty, and that selection will now favour a love of parenting as well as a love of sex (Foster, 2000). If these interpretations are correct, modern low fertility should be a relatively short-lived phenomenon in evolutionary time; over the coming generations, we might therefore expect to see the evolution of broody, family-oriented women, who are suspicious of their friends, replacing the gregarious career women whose low reproductive success will confine their high-achieving, outgoing personality traits to oblivion.

That we are strongly influenced by what others say about fertility may sound surprising to a human behavioural ecologist, but to consider fertility decline as a culturally transmitted 'fashion' is currently the most popular theory amongst demographers. There is abundant evidence that, although fertility decline is generally associated with some reduction in mortality, it is hard to associate it with any particular stage of economic development (Cleland and Wilson, 1987), and it is frequently associated with social contact with others that have reduced their fertility. There is evidence that the uptake of modern contraception is more likely if a neighbouring population speaking similar languages (Amin *et al.*, 2002) or individuals in your social network (Valente *et al.*, 1997) or village (Mace *et al.* 2006) are already using contraception. However, just because individuals are influenced by the decisions made by others does not mean that those decisions do not have their basis in maximizing long-term reproductive success. The reason why we copy others might be due to the fact that copying, or social learning (which may include a bit more evaluation of strategies), is actually a useful human trait—possibly even the secret of the prodigious success of our species. Learning about a new environment, or novel innovations within an existing environment, could be done on a trial-and-error basis or by copying others who may appear to be doing the right thing, or even by simply copying the most popular strategy (conformist bias). Clearly, as we have seen, evaluating the long-term pay-offs of different reproductive strategies is a complex task—one that natural selection will usually solve by default, given enough generations, but not when change is rapid. Faced with innovations, or changes in the environments, models show that populations containing some copiers, and some innovators (who use trial and error to evaluate new strategies), do better than populations who only copy (and hence end up chasing their tails) or only learn by trial and error (and hence are slow to catch on). Experimental evidence suggests that some element of copying speeds up the process of reaching an adaptive solution (McElreath *et al.*, 2005; see also this volume, Chapters 38 and 39). Thus decision rules that favour copying at least some of the time, or from some kinds of people, could have been favoured in our evolutionary past, and are, almost certainly, still useful today. As a proximate

means of achieving ultimate, long-term reproductive success, copying may well be the best we can do in many circumstances.

26.4. Optimal reproductive scheduling when resources are inherited

Despite the predominance of explanations of low fertility based on proximate mechanisms of cultural transmission, the acknowledgment of some role of the costs of parental investment in humans remains part of the explanation; and both old and new research in intergenerational transfers has continued to keep open the possibility that reproductive strategies involving high levels of parental investment may in fact be rather successful, and not as maladaptive as is generally assumed.

Parental investment in humans is not just about food. Intergenerational transfers of resources, such as territory, skills or wealth, are key to reproductive success in many social species, including humans. In wealth-inheriting societies, parents may have to show the colour of their money, in the form of bride price or dowry, in order to marry off their children. Bride price is a payment from the groom or his family to the parents of the bride, and is typically associated with polygynous societies (Hartung, 1982), where males use resources to monopolize several females, if they can afford to. Poorer males will loose out in such societies, unable to attract mates. Dowry (where money is paid from the family of the bride either to the newly weds or their family) is associated with the opposite scenario, when it is females that are in competition with each other for mates (Gaulin and Boster, 1990). This female–female competition is most likely to arise in societies with socially imposed monogamy, frequently when societies are stratified. Whereas the benefits of wealth are likely to be diluted among many wives in polygynous societies, in monogamous societies a woman who marries a wealthy man has sole access to his wealth for the benefit of her offspring alone, and hence female–female competition for wealthy men becomes intense. These costs influence parental reproductive scheduling. A father who already has sons does not want too many more in societies where the groom or his family provide the main costs of marriage and setting up home (Mace, 1996a), whereas in dowry societies, female infants with a large number of elder sisters can be at increased risk of infanticide for the same reason (Das Gupta, 1987).

Different strategies for optimal reproductive scheduling, and how they depend on the resources available, can be modelled formally using state-dependent optimality theory. Stochastic dynamic programming is a technique that allows optimal decisions (those that maximize long-term reproductive success) to be modelled as depending on the state (e.g. wealth) of the individual (Houston et al., 1988). It generates an optimal strategy (a set of rules about what to do when in a given state to maximize future reproductive success, given the range of possible outcomes inherent in living in that environment). The observed behaviour in an individual depends on the environment he/she experiences, and includes an element of stochasticity, thus capturing the realistic diversity in observed behaviour (Figure 26.2). Mace used this approach to predict how many sons a camel pastoralist should aspire to in order to maximize number of grandchildren, given that each son needed to be supplied with a herd of camels in order to marry and reproduce (Mace, 1996b; Mace, 1998). The optimal strategy of whether or not to have another baby depends on both number of living sons and the size of the father's camel herd at that time. The value of children (calculated in terms of their ability to produce grandchildren) is thus considered, in addition to just their number. This model predicted the empirically observed facts that birth rates slowed as the number of living sons increased, and that the rate of reproduction correlated positively with wealth. The variation observed in both the number of camels given to each son to start a family, and the size of the families that they then produced, matched those predicted by this model. Whilst this model was specific to one population, it was then generalized to ask what changes in the environment might lead to changes in optimal reproductive scheduling. Mace (1998) was able to show that, if the costs of setting up children with their own household is made higher, then both the optimal wealth at

which to have another baby will go up (causing optimal birth rates to go down) and the optimal allocation of wealth to each child will go up. This has the 'knock-on' effect of increasing the average wealth in the population. The converse of this is that making child-raising less costly would favour increases in birth rate, decreases in the investment in each child, and the total population would become poorer. Thus a rather counter-intuitive relationship is generated: when costs of living are high the population of viable households is wealthier (and the poor fail to marry).

Possible examples of these two scenarios are provided by studies of two other populations that are predominantly of similar ethnic origin to the Gabbra pastoralists described above (i.e. Oromo speakers) but living in different habitats. A study of Oromo agropastoralists in rural Ethiopia examined how the birth spacing changed in response to adding water points in villages that previously had none, thus obliging women to walk many miles, several days of each week, to get water for the family. The response to the provision of water points was that infant mortality went down, and female fertility went up (Gibson and Mace, 2006)—both predictable in a natural fertility, food-limited population in which the energetic costs of living, and hence raising children, has just been reduced. However, as the net food supply had not increased and family sizes had increased, childhood malnutrition also went up. This may be a counter-intuitive result for those in the business of supplying much-needed infrastructural development in such areas, but one that can be understood in the light of optimal reproductive scheduling in a natural fertility population. From a cost-benefit (and life-history) perspective, this can be understood as children becoming less costly, so lifetime reproductive success can be maximized by lower investment in each child. A similar effect may have occurred when treatment for diarrhoea was given to a natural fertility Gambian population, leading to improved child survival but a decline in population averages of child height and weight (Poskitt et al., 1999).

The opposite scenario is unfolding in the capital city of Ethiopia, Addis Ababa. Here the costs of entering into marriage are soaring, not due to

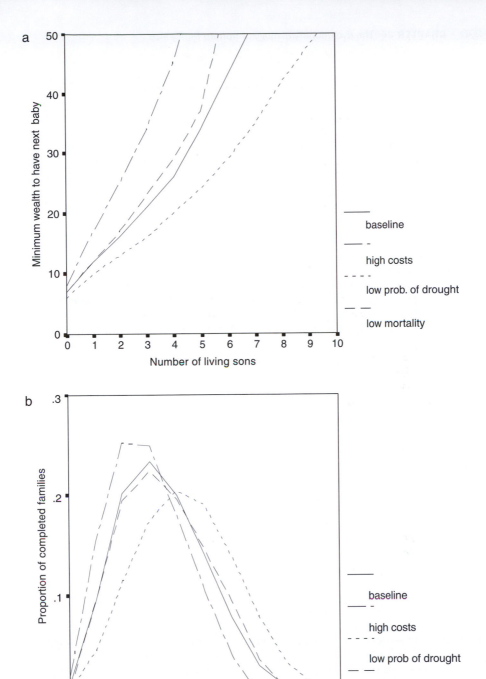

Fig. 26.2 Optimal policies and observed behaviour for four stable populations in different environments (see Mace, 1998). (**a**) Lines represent the minimum wealth at which having another baby would maximize number of grandchildren, given the number of living sons that you already have, for each of these environments, e.g. where marriage costs are high (high cost, dashed and dotted line), then only at very high levels of wealth is it optimal to have more than one or two sons. (**b**) Distribution of observed family sizes, in a stable population following each of the four optimal strategies, subject to stochastic effects in mortality and wealth. Note that family sizes are on average much smaller in the scenario where costs are high.

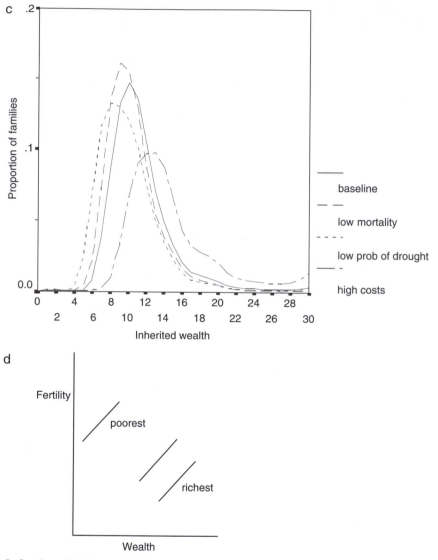

Fig. 26.2 Continued (**c**) The model assumes that parents allocate optimal amounts of wealth to their sons for them to set up households. This shows the distribution of inherited wealth of families in those four populations. Note that the population in which the costs are highest has on average the wealthiest families. (**d**) Schematic representation of how different levels of parental investment in sub-populations can resolve the paradox of why country-level statistics show negative correlations with wealth, whereas within sub-populations, the correlation between wealth and reproductive success is positive, when the richest populations have the highest costs of living and hence the highest levels of parental investment.

bride price, but due to huge competition for housing and jobs, which are considered prerequisites for starting a family. A combination of a stagnant economy and high population growth (fuelled by in-migration to the city from rural areas), without any financial safety-net for the unemployed, means that child-rearing would be almost impossible for the many residents of Addis Ababa, who share crowded accommodation and live without a regular income. Fertility rates have collapsed in recent years, to below replacement level—a phenomenon more commonly associated with European cities. Gurmu and Mace (in press) show that this is a direct response to poverty. Both the probability of getting married, staying married, and having a baby are all correlated positively with wealth. If current conditions continue, more than 50% of current school leavers in Addis Ababa will probably never be able to afford to reproduce— a scenario that appears to be at the root of extremely low fertility in this population. Only through high investment, largely through education, will children be given the opportunity to escape poverty, and hence reduce the risk of total reproductive failure.

This provides an example of a modern, urban setting in which very low human fertility can be attributed to a scarcity of resources for parental investment. Although evolutionary ecologists as early as Lack (1954) have appreciated that a quantity/quality trade-off does mean that there are circumstances where higher investment in fewer offspring can be more successful than low investment in a larger number of offspring, most demographers have largely rejected this explanation on the grounds that it is the wealthiest countries in which birth rates first started to decline. Evidence that within these populations it was the wealthiest individuals who were the first to reduce birth rates is less clear cut [for example in Victorian Britain, there is no evidence that fertility decline started in regions where wealth was concentrated (Bocquet-Appel and Jakobi, 1997)]. However, using cross-country correlations to reject the quantity/ quality trade-off model of low fertility ignores two important caveats. First, country-level data hide population-level differences, as the examples given above from Ethiopia illustrate. Different populations within the same country can have

different levels of optimal and/or actual parental investment (Low, 2000). For example, the returns on investment in education in rural Ethiopia could be much lower than the returns on investment in education in urban Ethiopia. Or, as modelled in Mace (1998), the costs of raising a child into marriage could differ (Figure 26.2). An important conclusion of Mace (1998) was that, if all those scenarios were in the same country, a negative correlation between average population wealth and average family size would emerge across populations within that country, even though within each sub-population the correlation between fertility and wealth would be positive, in line with the evolutionary ecological prediction that family size is ultimately constrained by resources. This is one way of resolving the paradox that wealthy countries generally have lower fertility than poor ones: wealthy countries are those in which the long-term returns on high levels of parental investment are highest, and the very fact that parents are investing highly in offspring is itself increasing the average wealth of households in that population (Figure 26.2).

Kaplan et al. (1995) have tested directly the notion that higher levels of parental investment, achieved by reducing family size, might result in a higher number of grandchildren due to the enhanced competitive abilities of the children that benefited from less sibling competition for parental resources. In a sample of men from New Mexico, they found that individuals from small families did indeed have higher levels of educational attainment, as has been shown in a range of studies (Steelman et al., 2002), and had higher salaries, but this did not translate into more grandchildren—so they rejected the notion of a quantity/quality trade-off as explaining a rational or adaptive fertility decline. However, it is actually not such a surprising result if one considers that, in a stable environment, it would certainly be strange if the long-term strategy that was optimal for generation 1 was not also optimal for generation 2. A strategy that was stable over many generations, or when a population was at equilibrium, would never yield such a prediction. Whilst Mace (1998) derived optimal strategies that are stable over many generations, grandchildren were considered as the quantity to be maximized. However, some have argued that it is necessary to evaluate strategies in terms of descendants after more than two generations (McNamara and Houston, 2006). Fitness of a strategy may be best measured as the growth rate of that strategy, relative to others, far into the future, rather than taking any arbitrary cut-off point.

Given the notion that the number of children or even grandchildren, may actually be less important to long-term reproductive success than the levels of investment, or transfers, to those offspring, then measuring fitness by counting babies, as human evolutionary ecologists are apt to do, becomes suspect, or at least only part of the story (Lee, 2003). McNamara and Houston (2006) show that there are scenarios in which females choosing high-quality males (which in this particular model involves choosing a male that offers lower levels of direct help with child-rearing, thus generating lower fertility—see below) would win, in terms of the rate of growth of that strategy found in the population relative to other strategies; however, the number of individuals following the high-quality strategy would not outnumber those following the other strategy until after five generations. Although empirical testing of such models could be difficult in real human societies, where so many factors might influence the payoffs of different reproductive strategies, the important message is that a strategy that does not maximize reproductive success in the short term, but only over the very long term, can evolve. It is interesting to note that whereas, in traditional societies, transfers of food or other forms of investment have always been down the generations, not up (as predicted by evolutionary theory: Kaplan, 1994; Lee and Kramer, 2002), it is possible now that governments in wealth-owning democracies are, through taxes spent largely on health and social security for the old, forcing wealth transfers in the opposite direction (Lee and Miller, 1994)—so perhaps it is no surprise that the young are finding it increasingly hard to set up home and reproduce in these wealthy countries.

26.5. Runaway parental investment

Whilst cultural trends are favouring ever-declining fertility in most of the world, in my view,

those trends may well be an adaptive response to a perceived or real need to increase parental investment in each child. As children compete with their peers for a small number of advantageous positions, there is almost no limit to the level of parental investment that can be bestowed upon them. A study of Harvard graduates of 1975, whose mean earning ran into millions of dollars, still showed a positive correlation between wealth and reproductive success (Weeden et al. in press). This elite, whose resources appear virtually unlimited in comparison with those available to most of humanity, are in competition with each other for marriage partners that are capable of matching the kind of financial and intellectual investment that they themselves experienced and expect to be able to bestow on their own children. They are in competition for the small number of jobs that can generate enough income to fund those aspirations. Those earning annual incomes in excess of $25 million are more successful in that competition than those earning $1 million (Weeden et al., in press). Are they competing with their college-mates out of mindless folly, or will the massive wealth transfers that their actions enable them to endow upon their children minimize their prospects of long-term reproductive failure?

A psychology that convinces us that the latter is true may have evolved through processes not dissimilar to the psychology that tells us no one can ever be too beautiful. However beautiful you are, if someone else is more beautiful, then they may steal your mate. Theoretical studies of sexual selection show us why you can never be beautiful enough. It may be that we can never stop striving to demonstrate that the quality of genes, perhaps their ability to fight off parasites which keep changing every generation (Hamilton and Zuk, 1982), is better than that of our competitors. We do this through the traits that honestly signal our quality (Zahavi, 1975). Preferences for particular traits can become exaggerated through another process originally described by Fisher (1930), known as 'runaway sexual selection'. If individuals with a preference for a trait mate with individuals who have that trait, then their offspring both have the trait and the preference. This can lead to a runaway process and hence the evolution of evermore exaggerated traits, especially in species where intrasexual competition is most intense. In such species, females gain from choosing males not on the basis of any direct benefits, like parental care or territory, but simply for their appearance, and the fact that that appearance will be inherited by their own offspring, who will themselves be favoured as desirable mates (a scenario dubbed the 'sexy son hypothesis': Weatherhead and Robertson, 1979). No one could argue that a lyre bird's tail, bright blue and shaken repeatedly while the male hangs upside down from a branch, is necessary to the production of viable sperm (which is all the female gets from males in this species), at least not by any normal definition of the word 'necessary'. However, female lyre birds are not interested in males that cannot do this: as such, it is highly adaptive in the sense that it is a major determinant of reproductive success. Cultural attributes are also heritable of course. An annual income of $25 million is not necessary to raise two or three children—even those that stand a good chance of becoming graduates of top universities—but the data on mate choice and parental investment in modern society tell us that $25 million will help you get your children and their children better mates, and a better education, and more money to transfer to future generations, than their competitors. If parental strategies are all about maximizing transfers to future generations, then this is what matters.

If it is worth choosing mates carefully, having high standards can also involve paying the cost of waiting too long to find the right mate, and ending up childless. Child-bearing years may have to be sacrificed in order to gain the qualifications required to earn enough money to attract a suitable mate capable of delivering super-high parental investment, or even to enter into the social environment in which such individuals can be found. Hence these puzzling features of modern fertility patterns, that appear on the face of it maladaptive, could in fact be by-products of an adaptive desire for high-quality offspring.

Anthropologists have long appreciated the benefits of prestige. Wealth is one component of prestige, a very important one, although non-monetary prestige can also have a huge impact on reproductive success (and has the advantage that it is more or less infinitely divisible, unlike wealth which has limits). Josephson (1993) showed that certain family names were highly prestigious in Mormon society during the nineteenth and twentieth centuries, such that women left more grandchildren marrying these prestigious individuals polygynously, even if their wealth was very thinly spread over families sometimes of more than 30 children. Being considered the most prestigious could be enough to secure success. Surely this is why the Y chromosome haplotype of Ghengis Khan is now to be found in one in 200 men in the world (Zerjal et al., 2003) after less than 1000 years since it originated. The material spoils of his exploits were great, but surely not great enough to ensure that level of reproductive success by wealth alone; his cultural inheritance (such as his name or reputation) must have been a major boost to his descendants over many generations and hundreds of years to achieve such a dramatic selective sweep.

Until recently, verbal arguments of this type were largely unsupported by theory. While Fisher's runaway sexual selection has long been widely accepted as operating in nature, it is fair to say that population geneticists have struggled to show how such a genetic system could evolve (Pomiankowski et al., 1991). More recent models that have focused on phenotypic inheritance, including cultural inheritance, have had success in showing that choosing high quality can lead to a runaway process of both genetic and cultural evolution. McNamara and Houston (2006) used state-dependent dynamic modelling to show that strong genetic preferences for males with culturally heritable resources can evolve in females. In their model, males have the culturally heritable trait (that is frequently—although not always—passed on to offspring), and females evolve the genetically heritable preference for that trait. Female preferences evolve towards an optimum, and they show that it is possible for females to evolve strong preferences for high-quality males simply on the basis of the indirect benefit that their own offspring are more likely to inherit those heritable qualities, as in the classic Fisherian case. In humans there is some evidence that females are more interested in badges of status in their mates than are males (Buss, 1989), although the situation is complicated, as females may also be able to confer status, and males can also provide some of the parental investment. However, the basic processes described in McNamara and Houston's model could well be applicable to aspects of the human condition. Their model also shows how, when females have more time in which to make their decisions, the preference for high quality can become even stronger. By analogy, the fact that we live longer and can reproduce later could be intensifying the competition for high-quality mates to an unprecedented level. Boyd and Richerson (1985, Chapter 8) also model a scenario of cultural evolution in which a cultural trait can spread in a runaway process, although they consider the preference for the trait to be an arbitrary product of modes of transmission rather than related to value.

Sexual selection in animals probably proceeds through a combination of honest signalling of good genes and a healthy phenotype capable of returning direct benefits, and runaway selection of genetic and/or phenotypically inherited traits; the balance between the two is likely to depend on the ecology and mating system of the species in question. Those traits that become exaggerated are likely to be based on true signals of quality. In humans, too, there is likely to be a combination of these mechanisms, that may differ in different socio-ecological conditions. In some regions of the world, parents have little power to protect their children from disease or endow them with little more than basic subsistence skills; opportunities to make use of any more technical knowledge are simply not available in their environments. Here, variation in the wealth and status achieved by individuals might be relatively minor. Elsewhere, the returns on high levels of education and skills may be substantial, and the variance in outcomes between successful and unsuccessful individuals could be great. In some countries, elite schools and universities can charge parents well over $30 000 a year to educate their child, and those who can afford this tend strongly to buy such an education. Whilst the models discussed above have not necessarily been applied to real human situations, let alone tested, the theoretical underpinning of evolutionary processes that can lead to excessive parental emphasis on achieving and transferring high status to future generations is beginning to be understood.

All over the world, it is increasingly common to find quite young children spending the evening sitting at a table and doing their homework. From Bejing to Addis Ababa, parents are more or less forcing compliance until the work is done. Ten-year-olds will have forgotten much of what they are learning at school anyway by the time they reach adulthood, but their parents believe they are doing the right thing, and if most parents agree, then they probably are. A norm of favouring high achievers, whose academic or financial success is an honest signal of intelligence, practical ability, parental effort and other skills that could reasonably be passed on to offspring (mainly by cultural means), could have led to levels of parental investment that run on far beyond the range of what is needed to survive and reproduce at a satisfactory level. In the quantity/quality trade-off, if quality is all that matters in the long term, then parental investment knows no bounds.

References

Amin, S., Basu, A. M. *et al.* (2002) Spatial variation in contraceptive use in Bangladesh: looking beyond the borders. *Demography*, 39: 251–267.

Blurton Jones, N. J. (1986) Bushmen birth spacing: a test for optimal interbirth intervals. *Ethology and Sociobiology*, 7: 91–105.

Bocquet-Appel, J. P. and Jakobi, L. (1997) The spatial diffusion of contraception in Great Britain and the origins of the fertility transition. *Population*, 52: 977–1003.

Borgerhoff Mulder, M. (1998) The demographic transition: are we any closer to an evolutionary explanation? *Trends in Ecology and Evolution*, 13: 266–270.

Boyd, R. and Richerson, P. J. (1985) *Culture and the Evolutionary Process.* University of Chicago Press, Chicago.

Buss, D. M. (1989) Sex differences in human mate selection. *Behavioral and Brain Sciences*, 12: 1–49.

Cleland, J. and C. Wilson (1987) Demand theories of the fertility transition: an iconoclastic view. *Population Studies*, 41: 5–30.

Das Gupta, M. (1987) Selective discrimination against female children in India. *Population and Development Review*, 13: 77–101.

Doblhammer, G. and Oeppen, J. (2003) Reproduction and longevity among the British peerage: the effect of frailty and health selection. *Proceedings of the Royal Society of London, B*, 270: 1541–1547.

Fisher, R. A. (1930) *The Genetical Theory of Natural Selection.* Oxford University Press, Oxford.

Foster, C. (2000) The limits to low fertility: a biosocial approach. *Population and Development Review*, 26: 209–234.

Gaulin, S. J. C. and Boster, J. S. (1990) Dowry as female competition. *American Anthropologist* 92: 994–1005.

Gibson, M. and Mace R. (2006) An energy saving development increases birth rate and childhood malnutrition in rural Ethiopia. *PloS Medicine*, 3: e87.

Gurmu, E. and Mace, R. (in press) Fertility decline driver by poverty: the case of Addis Abnba (Ethiopia). *Journal of Biosocial Science.*

Gustafsson, L. and Part T. (1990) Acceleration of senescence in the collared flycatcher, *Ficedula albicollis*, by reproductive costs. *Nature*, 347: 279–281.

Hamilton, W. D. and Zuk M. (1982) Heritable true fitness and bright birds: a role for parasites? *Science*, 218: 384–387.

Hartung, J. (1982) Polygyny and the inheritance of wealth. *Current Anthropology*, 23: 1–12.

Hawkes, K., O'Connell, J. F. *et al.* (1998) Grandmothering, menopause and the evolution of human life histories. *Proceedings of the National Academy of Sciences of the USA*, 95: 1336–1339.

Hill, K. and Hurtado, A. M. (1996) *Aché Life History: The Ecology and Demography of a Foraging People.* Aldine de Gruyter, New York.

Hill, K. and Kaplan, H. (1999) Life history traits in humans: theory and empirical studies. *Annual Review of Anthropology*, 28: 397–430.

Hobcraft, J. N., McDonald, J. W. *et al.* (1985) Demographic determinants of infant and early child mortality: a comparative analysis. *Population Studies*, 39: 363–385.

Houston, A. I., Clark, C. W. *et al.* (1988) Dynamic models in behavioural and evolutionary ecology. *Nature*, 332: 29–34.

Josephson, S. C. (1993) Status, reproductive success and marrying polygynously. *Ethology and Sociobiology*, 14: 391–396.

Kaplan, H. (1994) Evolutionary and wealth flows theories of fertility: empirical tests and new models. *Population and Development Review*, 20: 753–791.

Kaplan, H., Lancaster, J. B. *et al.* (2002) Evolutionary approach to below replacement fertility. *American Journal of Human Biology*, 14: 233–256.

Kaplan, H. S., Lancaster, J. B. *et al.* (1995) Does observed fertility maximize fitness among New Mexican men—a test of an optimality model and a new theory of parental investment in the embodied capital of offspring. *Human Nature*, 6: 325–360.

Kaplan, H. S., and Robson, A. J. (2002) The emergence of humans: the coevolution of intelligence and longevity with intergenerational transfers. *Proceedings of the National Academy of Sciences of the USA*, 99: 10221–10226.

Lack, D. (1954) The evolution of reproductive rates. In J. S. Huxley, A. C. Hardy and E. B. Ford (eds) *Evolution as a Process*, pp. 143–156. Allen & Unwin, London.

Lee, R. D. (2003) Rethinking the evolutionary theory of aging: transfers, not births, shape social species. *Proceedings of the National Academy of Sciences of the USA*, 100: 9637–9642.

Lee, R. D. and Kramer, K. L. (2002) Children's economic roles in the Maya family life cycle: Cain, Caldwell, and Chayanov revisited. *Population and Development Review*, 28: 475–499.

Lee, R. D. and Miller, T. (1994) Population age structure, intergenerational transfer, and wealth—a new approach, with applications to the United-States. *Journal of Human Resources*, 29: 1027–1063.

LeGrand, T. K. and Phillips, J. F. (1996) The effect of fertility reductions on infant and child mortality: evidence from Matlab in rural Bangladesh. *Population Studies*, 50: 51–68.

Low, B. S. (2000) Sex, wealth and fertility: old rules, new environments. In L. Cronk, N. Chagnon and W. Irons (eds) *Adaptation and Human Behaviour: An Anthropological Perspective*, pp. 323–343. Aldine de Gruyter, New York.

Lummaa, V., Jokela, J. *et al.* (2001) Gender difference in benefits of twinning in pre-industrial humans: boys did not pay. *Journal of Animal Ecology*, 70: 739–746.

Mace, R. (1996a) Biased parental investment and reproductive success in Gabbra pastoralists. *Behavioural Ecology and Sociobiology*, B, 38: 75–81.

Mace, R. (1996b) When to have another baby: a dynamic model of reproductive decision-making and evidence from Gabbra pastoralists. *Ethology and Sociobiology*, 17: 263–273.

Mace, R. (1998) The co-evolution of human fertility and wealth inheritance strategies. *Philosophical Transactions of the Royal Society*, B, 353: 389–397.

Mace, R. (2000) The evolutionary ecology of human life history. *Animal Behaviour*, 59: 1–10.

Mace, R., Allal, N. *et al.* (2006) The uptake of modern contraception in a Gambian community: the diffusion of an innovation over 25 years. In J. C. K. Wells, S. Strickland and K. Laland, *Social Information Transmission and Human Biology*, pp. 191–206, CRC Press.

Mace, R. and Sear, R. (2005) Are humans co-operative breeders? In E. Voland, A. Chasiotis and S. W., *Grandmotherhood: The Evolutionary Significance of the Second Half of Female Life*. Rutgers University Press, New Brunswick.

McEalreath, R., Lubell, M., Richerson, P. J., Waring, T. M., Baum, W., Edsten, E., Efferson, C., and Paciotti, B. (2005) Applying evolutionary models to the laboratory study of social learning. *Evolution and Human Behavior*, 26: 483–508.

McNamara, J. M. and Houston, A. I. (2006) State and value: a perspective from behavioural ecology. In J. C. K. Wells, S. Strickland and K. Laland, *Social Information Transmission and Human Biology*, pp. 59–88. CRC Press.

Newson, L., Postmes, T. *et al.* (2005) Why are modern families small? Toward an evolutionary and cultural explanation for the demographic transition. *Personality and Social Psychology Review*, 9: 360–375.

Pavard, S., Gagnon, A. *et al.* (2005) Mother's death and child survival: the case of early Quebec. *Journal of Biosocial Science*, 37: 209–227.

Pomiankowski, A., Iwasa, Y. *et al.* (1991) The evolution of costly mate preferences. 1. Fisher and biased mutation. *Evolution*, 45: 1422–1430.

Poskitt, E. M. E., Cole, T. J. *et al.* (1999) Less diarrhoea but no change in growth: 15 years' data from three Gambian villages. *Archives of Disease in Childhood*, 80: 115–119.

Roff, D. A. (1992) *The Evolution of Life Histories*. Chapman & Hall, New York.

Sear, R., Mace, R. *et al.* (2000) Maternal grandmothers improve the nutritional status and survival of children in rural Gambia. *Proceedings of the Royal Society, B,* 267: 461–467.

Sear, R., Mace, R. *et al.* (2001) The fitness of twin mothers: evidence from rural Gambia. *Journal of Evolutionary Biology,* 14: 433–443.

Sear, R., Steele, F. *et al.* (2002) The effects of kin on child mortality in rural Gambia. *Demography,* 39: 43–63.

Sear, R., Mace, R. *et al.* (2003) A life-history approach to fertility rates in rural Gambia: evidence for trade-offs or phenotypic correlations? In J. L. Rodgers and H. P. Kohler (eds) *The Biodemography of Human Reproduction and Fertility*, pp. 135–160. Kluwer, Boston.

Shanley, D. P. and Kirkwood, T. B. L. (2001) Evolution of the human menopause. *Bioessays,* 23: 282–287.

Steelman, L. C., Powell, B. *et al.* (2002) Reconsidering the effects of sibling configuration: recent advances and challenges. *Annual Review of Sociology,* 28: 243–269.

Strassmann, B. I. (2000) Polygyny, family structure and child mortality: a prospective study among the Dogon of Mali. In L. Cronk, N. Chagnon and W. Irons (eds) *Adaptation and Human Behaviour: An Anthropological Perspective*, pp. 49–67. Aldine de Gruyter, New York.

Strassmann, B. I. and Gillespie, B. (2002) Life-history theory, fertility and reproductive success in humans. *Proceedings of the Royal Society, B,* 269: 553–562.

Trivers, R. (1985) *Social Evolution*. Benjamin/Cummings, Menlo Park, CA.

Valente, T. W., Watkins, S. C. *et al.* (1997) Social network associations with contraceptive use among Cameroonian women in voluntary associations. *Social Science and Medicine,* 45: 677–687.

Weatherhead, P. J. and Robertson, R. J. (1979) Offspring quality and the polygyny threshold—sexy son hypothesis. *American Naturalist,* 113: 201–208.

Weeden, J., Abrams, M. J. *et al.* (in press) Do high status people really have fewer children? Education, income, and fertility in the contemporary U.S. *Human Nature.*

Zerjal, T., Xue, Y. L. *et al.* (2003) The genetic legacy of the mongols. *American Journal of Human Genetics,* 72: 717–721.

CHAPTER 27

Life-history theory, reproduction and longevity in humans

Virpi Lummaa

27.1. Introduction

27.1.1. Life-history theory

Our success, in evolutionary terms, can be measured by the total number of children we produce in our lifetimes which survive to pass our genes on to the following generations. The lifetime reproductive success of individuals depends on two main factors: their reproductive ability and their survival. However, because resources available to individuals are finite and the two body functions, reproduction and self-maintenance, compete for the same pool of energy, increasing the flow of resources to one body function (e.g. reproduction) will necessarily reduce the flow of resources to others (e.g. growth, body condition and maintenance of effective immune defence). This can result in a negative relationship (trade-off) between the two functions, which will constrain an individual's ability to maximize all fitness-related life-history traits at the same time. It is for this reason that increased reproductive effort is predicted to shorten lifespan, and individuals must find the best compromise between these two different components (and others) to be able to maximize their lifetime reproductive success.

The theoretical framework within which we study how individuals optimize trade-offs in life-history traits is called 'life-history theory'. This refers to the scheduling of major events over the lifetime of individuals. For example, how big should one be at the moment of birth? How fast and how long should one grow? At what age and size should maturation take place? How many offspring should be produced, and when, what size and of which sex? How long should one continue reproducing, and when is it time to die? Different solutions to these evolutionary problems ultimately determine an individual's representation in the future generations (i.e. fitness). The basic assumption underlying life-history theory is that natural selection has selected for an optimal combination of life-history traits that maximizes individual fitness (Lessells, 1991; Roff, 1992, 2002; Stearns, 1992). The best studied trade-offs include: (i) investigating how individuals should allocate resources to reproduction versus their own growth and survival; and (ii) when reproducing, how should they divide their effort between current and future reproduction or between the number, sex and quality of offspring (Lack, 1954; Gadgil and Bossert, 1970; Schaffer, 1974,

Charlesworth and Leon, 1976; Charlesworth, 1980; Williams, 1966a,b). Co-ordinated evolution of all these principal life-history traits together determines the life-history strategy of the organism (Stearns, 1976). The environment, in turn, determines the action of natural selection: traits may be adaptive only within reference to a particular environment and few, if any, traits are adaptive in all contexts.

27.1.2. The human life-history trade-offs

All of these trade-offs would be predicted to be pertinent to humans (Hill and Kaplan, 1999). In addition, however, humans have an extra trade-off, that is absent or uncommon in other animals. Life-history theory proposes that, generally, there should be no selection for living beyond one's reproductive capacity. Instead, the 'surplus' energy reserves which would allow post-reproductive survival are predicted to be better off spent earlier in one's life, during reproductive years (Williams, 1957; Hamilton, 1966). In addition, relative levels of investment during reproductive attempts should influence the age at which individuals senesce and die (Kirkwood, 1977; Partridge and Harvey, 1985; Kirkwood and Rose, 1991; Kirkwood and Austad, 2000). In line with this, age-related reductions in fertility rates have been observed in long-lived animals (Ricklefs et al., 2003), and virtually all animals reproduce until they die (or have very short post-reproductive lifespans; Cohen, 2004). However, there is at least one striking exception: women commonly survive long after losing the ability to reproduce themselves (Williams, 1957; Hamilton, 1966), and evidence suggests that this prolonged survival is related to humans allocating more resources to cell maintenance and repair than other animals (Hawkes, 2003). This prolonged lifespan is not an artefact of modern society. The age at which humans terminate reproduction is consistent with the age of termination in other primates when differences in body weight are accounted for (Schultz, 1969). In addition, in both historical and traditional hunter-gatherer populations, about 30% of adult individuals are beyond the age of 45 years (Hawkes, 2004). This large proportion of old, non-reproductive women in human populations also marks a fundamental difference

with other primates. In chimpanzees (*Pan troglodytes*), female fertility declines at the same age as in humans to virtually zero by age 45 years (Nishida et al., 2003), but chimpanzee survival rates, as predicted by life-history theory, follow fertility rates so that less than 3% of adults are over 45 years old (Hill et al., 2001). That women begin a physiological shut-down of reproductive potential around the age of 45 (Peccei, 2001b) but often continue to survive for another 25 years is enigmatic from an evolutionary point of view. Only in short-finned pilot whales (*Globicephala macrorhyncus*) and a few other species of cetaceans is there also good evidence of a menopause and significantly prolonged post-reproductive lifespan (Marsh and Kasuzya, 1984; McAuliffe and Whitelead, 2005).

Importantly, prolonged post-reproductive survival is associated with fitness benefits in human women. Post-reproductive women gain fitness both by increasing the survival and/or reproductive capacity of their own offspring (Lahdenperä et al., 2004; Tymicki, 2004) as well as the survival of their grand-offspring (Hawkes et al., 1997, 1998; Sear et al., 2000; Jamison et al., 2002; Voland and Beise, 2002; Hawkes, 2003; Lahdenperä et al., 2004; Gibson and Mace, 2005; Voland et al., 2005). Whatever the evolutionary origin of this enigmatic life-history trait, that women accrue fitness during both reproductive and post-reproductive phases means that the reproductive success gained prior to menopause represents only a proportion of total fitness in humans. This has fascinating implications regarding optimal fitness-maximizing tactics, rates of senescence and lifespan in humans.

In most animals, individual fitness is maximized by optimizing the trade-off between current and future reproduction, with the amount of selection on early reproduction relative to late reproduction influencing, in part, the rate at which individuals senesce and die. However, research on humans has shown that increasing current reproductive effort may not only reduce future reproductive success (Mace and Sear, 1997; Lummaa, 2001) but also post-reproductive survival rates, for example due to increased susceptibility to infectious disease (Helle et al., 2002, 2004). This suggests that for humans, high investment in a current attempt not only has a negative effect on an individual's ability to invest in future reproductive attempts but also on the ability to help with the reproductive attempts of offspring following menopause. Consequently, fitness in humans is governed by optimization of trade-offs both within the reproductive and between the reproductive and post-reproductive phases. This leads to the intriguing possibility that humans suffer from both reproductive and post-reproductive senescence, with the relative importance of fitness accrued during each phase influencing ultimate lifespan. However, how natural selection ultimately affects the evolution of life-history traits within these trade-offs depends not only on the fitness benefits and costs of variation in such traits, but also on the genetic architecture of the traits, i.e. the amount of heritable, additive genetic variance present in each life history trait and the genetic correlations between them (Kruuk *et al.*, 2000).

The aim of this chapter is threefold. I will illustrate: (i) how increasing reproductive effort has been found to affect future reproductive success and longevity in humans; (ii) what the benefits of long lifespan are, and given the trade-off between current and future reproductive success and survival, how long should one aim to live in order to maximize long-term fitness in the population; and (iii) how this trade-off between reproduction and survival can constrain how natural selection will affect the evolution of both reproductive effort and longevity in humans. In other words, is there significant heritable variation in the life-history traits, senescence rate and fitness, and how do genetic correlations between these traits influence the evolution of life history? I consider all of these trade-offs for the fitness of women only, for measuring reproductive effort in men is difficult and paternity uncertainty often constrains one from making coherent generalizations.

27.2. Trade-offs between current reproduction and future success

27.2.1 Current reproductive effort and future reproduction

It is clear that individual offspring benefit from having greater parental investment directed at them. Offspring from wealthy parents in general have better health, survival and marital prospects than those born in less privileged backgrounds

(Borgerhoff Mulder, 2000). Short inter-birth intervals have negative consequences for the offspring whose parental investment was cut short by the birth of the younger sibling (Blurton Jones, 1986). Babies born with higher birth weight have higher survival probability and can also have superior health and increased reproductive success in adulthood (reviewed in Lummaa and Clutton-Brock, 2002; Lummaa, 2003). However, because high investment in current offspring is predicted to reduce the resources available for both investment in future offspring and self-maintenance, an iteroparous (having >1 reproductive event/lifetime) mother must trade-off current with future reproductive investment to maximize her lifetime reproductive success (Stearns, 1992; Kaplan, 1996; Hill and Kaplan, 1999). Current investment varies with brood/litter size and, if costs of producing males and females differ, the sex ratio of those offspring (reviewed in Charnov, 1982; Clutton-Brock, 1991). In sexually size-dimorphic species, the number and gender of offspring in a current litter are therefore predicted to modify future reproductive investment decisions as well as reproductive success and survival.

Studies on sexually size-dimorphic mammals provide support for the prediction that litters of different sizes and sex ratios can entail differential costs to the mother. In red deer (*Cervus elaphus*), those females that successfully raised a calf the previous season had the lowest survival, fecundity and body condition next year compared to those mothers that either did not reproduce or lost their offspring soon after birth (Clutton-Brock *et al.*, 1989). In addition, females commonly show longer birth intervals (Lee and Moss, 1986; Boesch, 1997; Cameron and Linklater, 2000) and reduced subsequent litter sizes (Clark *et al.*, 1990) after producing offspring of the more expensive gender. For example, in red deer where male calves are born larger, mothers that previously reared a male calf were more likely to die the following winter and, if they survived, less likely to produce a calf the following season compared to mothers that reared females (Clutton-Brock *et al.*, 1983).

Humans are modestly sexually size-dimorphic and, although singletons are typically delivered, 0.6–4.5% of all births (depending on the population) are twins. Twins are usually born smaller than singletons (Bulmer, 1970). In addition, females (twin and singleton) have slower intrauterine growth rates (Marsál *et al.*, 1996) and lighter birth weights (Hoffman *et al.*, 1974; Loos *et al.*, 2001) than males (twin or singleton). Mortality and morbidity following birth are usually male-biased, and foetal growth of males is more retarded than that of females under stressful conditions (reviewed in Stinson, 1985; Wells, 2000). Moreover, giving birth to a son even in modern-day conditions is significantly more laborious than giving birth to a daughter (Eogan *et al.*, 2003). There is also some evidence that maternal energy intake per day is elevated if a mother is carrying a male foetus (Tamimi *et al.*, 2003), and that mothers in good physiological condition might be more likely to give birth to sons than daughters (Cagnacci *et al.*, 2003, 2004; Gibson and Mace, 2003; but see Stein *et al.*, 2003a,b). This evidence indicates that producing a son is physiologically more demanding to the mother than producing a daughter. Hence, the costs of producing offspring appear to be gender-specific in humans and males tend to be the more expensive gender to produce.

There is mixed evidence to suggest that reproductive history in different modern human societies may affect measures of maternal physiological condition (e.g. stature, weight or body mass index; reviewed in Tracer, 2002). Nevertheless, studies on humans living in a range of settings have shown that increased reproductive effort during a given reproductive attempt may reduce later reproductive success. First, in a study on pre-industrial rural Finns, women doubling the number of children produced in a single reproductive event, by giving birth to twins, were more likely to fail to raise their next offspring, or to completely terminate reproduction, as compared with mothers producing a singleton child at the same age and with the same previous birth history (Lummaa, 2001). Moreover, women that did successfully raise offspring after a twin delivery were more likely next to produce a less expensive female offspring as compared with after an unsuccessful twin delivery, and this effect was further influenced by the sex ratio of the twins produced. This is in line with findings showing that the energetic costs of lactation to the mother

may be almost twice as high as those of gestation (Prentice and Whitehead, 1987; Dufour and Sauther, 2002), stressing the importance of including also the survivorship of offspring into the calculations of costs of reproduction. Second, it took a longer time for Gabbra pastoralist mothers who had previously produced a male child to reproduce again, compared to mothers producing a daughter (Mace and Sear, 1997). Finally, in contemporary British mothers, the birth weight of the second-born child was lower if the previous child was a son rather than a daughter (I. J. Rickard, unpublished results).

Taken together, these studies suggest that an increase in the current reproductive effort (producing twins or offspring of the more expensive gender) requires greater maternal investment and can have greater detrimental effects on maternal reproduction in the future. It still remains to be examined whether the gender and survival of the previous offspring affects the subsequent child's reproductive success, but such effects are found in populations of wild mammals (Clutton-Brock, 1991). That such long-term consequences of maternal investment for offspring reproductive success are feasible in humans (reviewed in Lummaa and Clutton-Brock, 2002; Lummaa, 2003) was shown in a study on pregnant women experiencing the Dutch Hunger Winter at the end of Second World War (1944–1945). Female babies exposed to famine *in utero* themselves had offspring of lower birth weight that suffered from higher mortality before and after birth, compared to mothers not exposed to famine as a foetus (Lumey, 1992).

27.2.2. Current reproductive effort and future survival

Increasing current reproductive effort is not only predicted to reduce future reproductive success, but also the future survival rate of mothers. Theories of senescence based on evolutionary trade-offs highlight the adverse effects of high and early reproductive effort on late-life survival (Williams 1957; Kirkwood, 1977; Kirkwood and Rose, 1991). These predictions are upheld in a variety of animals (e.g. Partridge and Barton, 1993; Kirkwood and Austad, 2000; Partridge and Gems, 2002), although they are often difficult to show in nature (Clutton-Brock, 1991).

As discussed in this volume (Mace, Chapter 26 and Voland, Chapter 28), life-history trade-offs are generally difficult to study adequately using natural variation in reproductive output and parental survival because differences in reproductive output may often reflect adaptive tactics made by individuals of different quality ('phenotypic correlations'; Daan and Tinbergen, 1997). For example, women with low resource levels may adaptively adjust their family size or reduce investment in each child, to meet their energetic needs and reduce the costs of reproduction (Sear et al., 2003). Perhaps not surprisingly then, evidence for reproduction-mediated decreases in longevity in humans is at best unequivocal. In historical human populations, only few studies have been able to establish the expected negative effects of high total reproductive effort on post-reproductive longevity (Westendorp and Kirkwood, 1998; Thomas et al., 2000; Doblhammer and Oeppen, 2003; Smith et al., 2003). While there is also some evidence that this trade-off is manifest only among the poorest individuals (Kumle and Lund, 2000; Lycett et al., 2000), most studies find no association between total number of children produced and post-reproductive survival, and some even show a positive correlation between these two traits (Borgerhoff Mulder, 1988; Voland and Engel, 1989; Le Bourg et al., 1993; Wrigley et al., 1997; Korpelainen, 2000, 2003; Müller et al., 2002).

Given the obvious limitations of studies on human life-histories due to an inability to experimentally manipulate family size or reproductive effort, alternative ways of investigating effects of effort on subsequent survivorship need to be used. Moreover, these alternative methods clearly need to be able to control adequately for correlates of maternal quality. One method is to use multivariate statistics that control for differences in maternal condition, resource availability, and environmental conditions, although data that would allow such analyses are relatively rare. Another method is to investigate the effects of increasing reproductive effort in a given reproductive attempt on mortality risk in the same mothers using multivariate statistics with random terms. In the following

paragraphs, I will discuss the evidence for trade-offs between investment and mortality risk by comparing mortality rates of mothers after doubling the number of offspring produced in a reproductive attempt (twins) and producing offspring of the more expensive gender (sons). Of particular note is that significant effects of high investment on maternal mortality appear more detectable when analyses consider high reproductive effort in terms of the production of twins or sons rather than the production of a large family size per se. This is an important point, for most of the studies that have failed to find a negative association between maternal investment and survival have not only failed to consider maternal quality but have considered reproductive investment in terms of family size only.

27.2.2.1. Effects of twinning on maternal survival

Producing twins essentially requires a woman to double her reproductive effort in a given reproductive event. Consequently, twins require mothers to allocate twice as much energy to reproduction and less to somatic maintenance according to the disposable soma theory (Kirkwood and Rose, 1991). It is known that mothers who deliver singletons in quick succession may suffer from maternal depletion syndrome; an inability to restore nutritional reserves after childbirth and breastfeeding (Dewey, 1997). That twin deliveries pose an elevated cost to mothers (particularly if they survive to weaning) is supported by the findings that, after twin births, mothers have longer birth intervals to their subsequent delivery and are more likely to terminate reproduction completely, especially after male–male twins (Lummaa, 2001).

First, mothers who give birth to twins have a higher risk of dying at childbirth (Haukioja et al., 1989; Gabler and Voland, 1994; McDermott et al., 1995). Second, in pre-industrial Finland when rates of fertility and mortality were high and effective healthcare was unavailable, mothers who increased their reproductive effort by delivering twins had 39% higher hazard of death after age 65 years, and consequently reduced post-reproductive lifespan, compared to mothers who produced only singletons during their lifetime (Figure 27.1A; Helle et al., 2004). This was true irrespective of the social class or

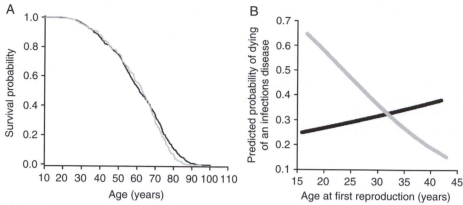

Fig. 27.1 (A) Survival and (**B**) predicted probability of dying from an infectious disease in pre-industrial Finnish mothers as a function of age at first reproduction for mothers of twins (grey line) and singletons (black line). The analyses control for the mothers' total number of offspring, social class and geographic and temporal differences in mortality. Note that mothers of singletons in panel B appeared to have higher risk of dying from infectious disease if they started reproduction after age 32, however this has little impact given that virtually all mothers (>90%) had their first birth before this age. Reproduced with permission from Helle *et al.* (2004).

wealth available to the mothers, and controlling for other reproductive traits such age at first reproduction and total family size and sex ratio. Similarly, rural Gambian mothers delivering twins had a 3.5-fold increase in mortality rates after menopause compared to mothers that had produced singletons only during their lifetimes (R. Sear, unpublished results).

Although the theoretical background for this kind of life-history trade-off between reproductive effort and survival is well established, there is surprisingly little information about the underlying mechanism mediating such costs of reproduction (Zera and Harshman, 2001; Barnes and Partridge, 2003). One prominent hypothesis proposed in animals is that reproductive effort may impair immune function against different pathogens by promoting immunosenescence (reviewed in Sheldon and Verhulst, 1996). The most compelling evidence for this hypothesis comes from the immunological studies in birds, which have demonstrated lowered humoral and cell-mediated responses to antigens as a consequence of experimentally elevated reproductive effort (Gustafsson *et al.*, 1994; Sheldon and Verhulst, 1996; Lochmiller and Deerenberg, 2000; Norris and Evans, 2000; Lozano and Lank, 2003). In addition, increases in reproductive effort can impair immune function

in the long term (Ardia *et al.*, 2003), an effective immune system itself may be costly to maintain (Sheldon and Verhulst, 1996; Lochmiller and Deerenberg, 2000), and may constrain individual reproductive decisions. These kinds of mechanisms may also be in play in humans, but demonstrating that high reproductive effort accelerates immunosenescence would require one to establish a link between reproductive effort and impairment of immune function.

Findings in a study of pre-industrial Finnish twin mothers suggest that their reduced longevity might have been due to accelerated immunosenescence (Helle *et al.*, 2004). Post-reproductive mothers of twins had a seven times higher risk of dying of an infectious disease (mainly tuberculosis) compared to mothers of singletons (Figure 27.1B). In eighteenth- and nineteenth-century Finland, as elsewhere in Europe, tuberculosis was common and many were infected with the disease early in life and carried it dormant for long periods of time before developing acute symptoms if the immune system became compromised (Flynn and Chan, 2001; Rajagopalan, 2001). The risk of dying of an infectious disease for Finnish mothers seemed to be particularly pronounced in mothers of twins after age 65 years (Helle *et al.*, 2004), which corresponds well to the survival curves shown in Figure 27.1A. Young ages at first reproduction seemed to further increase the risk of succumbing to an infectious disease, suggesting that early reproductive effort may also have been relevant for the expression of immunosenescence when mothers produced twins. As mothers of twins did not show higher infection-related mortality during their reproductive ages compared to mothers of singletons, it is possible to exclude the alternative explanation that twinning was more frequent among those women who generally expressed lower levels of immune defence. One possibility is that twin births may be related to elevated maternal stress levels (Salami *et al.*, 2003), which might have a negative bearing on maternal immuno-competence, and thus on their long-term survival (Buchanan, 2000).

27.2.2.2. Effects of producing sons versus daughters on maternal survival

Another way in which the reproductive effort of mothers for a given reproductive event may increase is when the investment is biased into production of offspring of the more expensive sex. In humans, sons are physiologically more demanding to produce than daughters, as indicated by their faster intrauterine growth rate (Marsál *et al.*, 1996), heavier birth weight

(Hoffman *et al.*, 1974; Loos *et al.*, 2001), and the longer time it takes mothers producing sons to reproduce again (Mace and Sear, 1997). The production of large and strongly male-biased families is predicted to be detrimental to maternal longevity in sexually size-dimorphic species in which males are larger (Kirkwood and Rose, 1991), although the resources available may modify such costs.

In line with this prediction, both historical mothers and contemporary mothers who bias their reproductive investment towards sons have reduced longevity compared to those producing a similar bias of daughters (Beise and Voland, 2002; Helle *et al.*, 2002; van de Putte *et al.*, 2004; Hurt *et al.*, 2006). For example, in a study on historical reindeer-herding nomadic Sami of Northern Scandinavia, every son born was found to reduce maternal longevity on average by 34 weeks, whereas having daughters had a positive effect on maternal longevity (Figure 27.2; Helle *et al.*, 2002). These findings suggest that giving birth to sons poses a higher relative long-term survival cost for mothers than giving birth to and raising daughters. This gender bias may be due to the lower direct physiological costs of daughters in conjunction with a family system where daughters help their mothers in their everyday tasks. That males have a negative effect

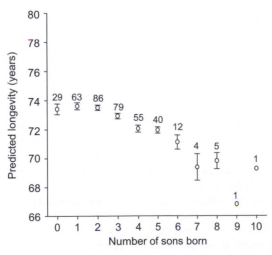

Fig. 27.2 Maternal post-reproductive (beyond age 50) survival in historical Sami mothers as a function of the number of sons produced over a lifetime. Reproduced with permission from Helle *et al.* (2002).

on maternal longevity, whereas daughters have a positive effect, clearly demonstrates why studies can fail to find the predicted negative relationship between investment and survival if only total family size is considered as investment. Therefore, both the direct effects of reproductive investment and the social effects of gender-biased family structure seem to be important determinants of female lifespan in Sami.

Again, consistent with the immunosuppressive idea, one potential mechanism for the negative effects of biasing reproductive investment into production of more expensive sons on lifespan could be the greater loss of resources required to maintain effective immune defences (Sheldon and Verhulst, 1996; Lochmiller and Deerenberg, 2000). One possibility is that interactions between reproductive costs and sex-specific hormones influence maternal immune function and susceptibility to succumbing to infectious diseases. In primates, high concentrations of maternal testosterone can correlate with an excess of male offspring and high concentrations of maternal oestrogens with an excess of female offspring (Meulenberg and Hofman, 1991; Manning *et al.*, 2002; Altmann *et al.*, 2004; Perret, 2005). These hormones also influence maternal immune function: testosterone having negative effects on immunocompetence and estrogens having positive effects (Klein, 2000).

27.3. Benefits of a long life: reproductive and post-reproductive trade-offs

So far we have seen that increasing current reproductive effort may reduce future reproductive success as well as post-reproductive survival rates. Life-history theory would generally predict that negative relations between reproductive effort and post-reproductive survival should be of no evolutionary consequence, since there should be no selection for living beyond one's reproductive years. In addition, given that the selective forces acting on reproductive effort decline with age (Medawar, 1952; Hamilton, 1966), any selection acting on post-reproductive longevity would be predicted to be weak. Despite this, in humans, there is clearly some selection acting on post-reproductive survival,

and this selection appears to be significant enough to allow women to survive for fully one-third of their life as a post-reproductive.

That women experience menopause, a complete and apparently irreversible physiological shut-down of reproductive potential, and then survive for a substantial amount of time thereafter has been the subject of much debate for decades (Pavelka and Fedigan, 1991; Marlowe, 2000; Peccei, 2001a,b; Hawkes, 2003; Lee, 2003). One reason for this debate is that menopause is not only an extreme life-history event, but would appear to be paradoxical from an evolutionary point of view. Another reason is that the selective benefits of menopause cannot be tested, for all women experience it; we will never know whether in our evolutionary past, women experiencing menopause produced significantly more and/or superior offspring than women who continued to reproduce until death.

One possibility is that menopause has itself been under selection (Peccei, 2001a,b). This could arise if the benefits of reproducing late in life are small (Medawar, 1952) while the costs are large (Williams, 1957; Peccei, 2001a). The benefits of reproducing late may be small because pregnancies in old age have an elevated risk of miscarriage, the foetus of older mothers has a higher risk of being born dead (Wood, 1994), having a defect (Gaulden, 1992) or being born small (Jolly *et al.*, 2000). In addition, late reproduction may be costly, for a mother that dies during or shortly after childbirth will not only jeopardize the life of her current child, but also those of earlier children which are still dependent on their mother for sustenance and protection (Williams, 1957; Peccei, 2001). This problem is likely to be more acute in humans than most animals, for human offspring have a long period of dependence and inter-birth intervals are short and so several dependent offspring exist at any one time. Nevertheless, it could be argued that increased probabilities of birth defects late in life are merely a consequence of the onset of menopause rather than the cause.

Other empirical findings would also appear to be at odds with the above idea. First, women reproducing late in life (mid-late 40s) may produce more offspring than those that terminate reproduction early (late 30s–early 40s). For example, in the eighteenth and nineteenth centuries,

Scandinavian Sami, which were reliant on rein-deer herding and fishing and which lacked either medical care or contraceptives, produced more surviving children in their lifetime if they continued childbearing into their late 40s (Helle *et al.*, 2005). Indeed, age at last reproduction explained 28% of the variance in offspring numbers, suggesting a key positive effect of age at last reproduction on evolutionary fitness. One explanation for this may be that in family-living species, the death of a mother may have a lower impact on offspring mortality than is often supposed because other relatives (hus-band, older siblings, grandparents, aunts/uncles, cousins) can subsume the role of a dead mother. Second, there is little evidence to suggest that humans terminate reproduction early in comparison to other primates when differences in body size are accounted for (Schultz, 1969; see Section 27.1).

An alternative explanation is that it has been lifespan that has been under evolutionary selec-tion and that menopause is merely a by-product of more rapid phenotypic changes in lifespan than egg number. If mothers can increase the reproductive success of their offspring by help-ing with child care, then a woman with genes for living beyond her decline in fertility may pro-duce more grandchildren (and hence forward more genes to the following generation) than a woman who died before being able to help her offspring to reproduce. It may be noteworthy to point out that a woman's termination of repro-duction tends to coincide with the onset of her first offspring's reproductive career and so only a small increase in the lifespan of a 'helping' mother would have the potential to lead to fast evolutionary benefits. Nevertheless, that the age of menopause is variable, has a heritable genetic component (Kirk *et al.*, 2001; van Asselt *et al.*, 2004; Murabito *et al.*, 2005; Pettay *et al.*, 2005) and is caused by 'destruction' of eggs rather than a lack of them (Peccei, 2001b), suggests that menopause is unlikely to be a mere by-product of selection on longevity. Consequently, our best guess at present is that both menopause (see above) and longevity (see below) have been (and are) under evolutionary selection.

Whether it has been menopause and/or lifespan that has been under selection, there is now compelling evidence to suggest that post-reproductive women can indeed have a sig-nificant and positive effect on their offspring's reproductive success. In rural Gambia, the pres-ence of a grandmother improves the dietary condition of grandchildren and increases their survival chances (Sear *et al.*, 2000). Among the Hadza hunter-gatherers of Tanzania, variation in child weight is positively correlated with grandmother's foraging time (Hawkes *et al.*, 1997), while in historical populations of Germany (Voland and Beise, 2002) and Japan (Jamison, 2002), the maternal grandmothers improved the survival of grandchildren. Finally, Lahdenperä *et al.*, (2004) showed that mothers gained significant fitness by surviving beyond menopause. They found that in farming/fishing communities of pre-modern (eighteenth and nineteenth centuries) Finnish and Canadian people, women gained two extra grandchildren for every 10 years they survived beyond menopause until their mid-70s, showing that lifespan can be under positive selection at least until this age (Figure 27.3). This effect arose because offspring in the presence of their post-reproductive mothers bred earlier, more frequently, for longer and more successfully. These effects were common to sons and daugh-ters, rich and poor and in predictable and unpredictable food areas, showing that post-reproductive mothers can influence their offspring irrespective of which sex is philopatric and irrespective of habitat quality.

While animals appear to show no identical analogue to human post-reproductive mothers, it is useful to point out that some similarities do exist. First, in eusocial insects, the majority of individuals in a colony are sterile and their sole purpose in life is to increase the reproductive success of their mother. Thus the link between sterility and helping relatives has an equivalent in the animal kingdom, although in this case it is offspring helping mothers rather than the other way around (Foster and Ratnieks, 2005). Second, in cooperatively breeding birds and mammals, although parents are fertile, it is not uncommon for them to help their offspring breed, either because mothers have failed in their own breeding attempt or because offspring and mothers co-breed (Dickinson and Hatchwell, 2004; Russell, 2004). It may not require a major evolutionary leap for ageing

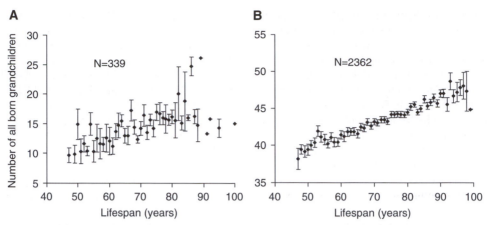

Fig. 27.3 Female post-reproductive lifespan and total number of grandchildren contributed to the following generation in (**A**) pre-industrial Finland and (**B**) pre-industrial Canada. Graphs show predicted means (±1 SE), after controlling for effects of social class, population (Finland) and birth cohort (Finland and Canada). Reproduced with permission from Lahdenperä *et al.* (2004).

mothers to wholly concede reproduction to a daughter (or a son's wife) if competition for resources is intense and the reproductive output/success of younger offspring (aided by the mother) is substantially greater than their own. Nor need it necessarily require a major evolutionary leap for mothers to shut down their reproductive system, if by so doing they can reduce competition with their offspring and prolong their own lifespan.

Thus, because women accrue fitness during both reproductive and post-reproductive phases, this means that the reproductive success gained prior to menopause represents only a proportion of total fitness. This has implications regarding optimal fitness-maximizing tactics, rates of senescence and lifespan in humans. In most animals, individual fitness is maximized by optimizing the trade-off between current and future reproduction, with the amount of selection on early reproduction relative to late reproduction influencing, in part, the rate at which individuals senesce and die. However, increasing current reproductive effort by humans not only reduces future reproductive success but also their post-reproductive survival rates (see above), suggesting that high investment in a reproductive attempt not only has a negative effect on the ability to invest in future reproductive attempts but also on the ability to invest following menopause. Consequently, fitness in humans may be maximized by optimization of

trade-offs both within the reproductive and between the reproductive and post-reproductive phases. This leads to the intriguing likelihood that humans suffer from both reproductive and post-reproductive senescence with the relative importance of fitness accrued during each phase influencing ultimate lifespan.

However, it is currently largely unknown how early reproductive effort influences rates of reproductive senescence, or how reproductive effort overall affects rates of post-reproductive senescence. Previous research has typically identified the factors that influence 'fitness' either before or after menopause and has generally failed to combine the two or to consider how fitness gained during reproduction influences fitness gained after reproduction. In addition, it is currently unknown how reproductive tactics interact with ecology and demography to influence overall fitness and rates or types of reproductive and post-reproductive senescence. Investigations along some of these avenues are likely to be an exciting and fruitful direction for future research.

27.4. Heritability, genetic constraints and evolutionary trade-offs

We have seen that increase in reproductive effort may be beneficial as it leads to the production of more and/or better quality offspring, but that such increases in investment into current reproduction may be detrimental for maternal future reproductive success and longevity. We have also seen how, in humans, high investment during reproduction attempts may compromise a woman's ability to invest in the reproductive attempts of her offspring following menopause. Finally, we have seen that women can accrue fitness during both reproductive and post-reproductive phases, and hence fitness in humans is maximised by optimization of trade-offs both within the reproductive and between the reproductive and post-reproductive phases. The questions are: are life-history traits under genetic control, and what constrains the evolution of both high reproductive effort and long lifespan?

Because the premises of organic evolution involve genetic variability and heritability in different life-history traits, the most fruitful way to investigate associations among life-history traits is by estimating genetic correlations between traits from sibling analysis, or from selection experiments, and not from phenotypic correlations (Reznick, 1985, 1992). However, conclusions of most human life-history studies to date have been based on the phenotypic correlations without information on the underlying genetic components or correlations. Such studies are unable to determine the evolutionary response to selection on the traits studied. Yet from an evolutionary point of view, phenotypic correlations are particularly interesting only if they have a genetic basis, since natural selection can only lead to an evolutionary response when it acts on a heritable character. Unfortunately, estimating heritability of human life-history traits is problematic. First, obtaining data from humans that allows an estimation of heritabilities and genetic correlations for life-history traits is difficult. Second, effects of a common environment shared by close relatives and cultural transmission can inflate estimates of heritability. A lack of information on the heritability and genetic constraints of reproductive traits in human populations has resulted in a limited understanding of whether the phenotypic selection documented could lead to evolutionary changes over time.

There are some recent exceptions that provide interesting insights into the evolution of life-history traits. First, Kirk *et al.* (2001) used a twin-study design to calculate heritabilities for a set of life-history traits in a contemporary Australian population. Second, Pettay *et al.* (2005) used pedigree records of pre-industrial Finns using a maximum-likelihood (REML)-based technique and an 'animal model'. This latter methodology controls for common environmental effects and considers the similarity between pairs of individuals that vary in their degree of relatedness and for whom shared environments are less problematic (Falconer and Mackay, 1996; Lynch and Walsh, 1998; Kruuk, 2004).

In both contemporary Australian and rural historical Finnish women, the key female life-history traits, such as age at menarche and menopause, reproductive rate and longevity, had significant additive genetic heritability, potentially permitting rapid evolutionary responses to selection (Kirk *et al.*, 2001; Pettay *et al.*, 2005). Furthermore, in both populations, there was also substantial heritable variation in fitness itself: in Finns 47% and in Australians 39% of the variance in fitness was attributable to additive genetic effects (the remainder of the variation in the Australians, for example, consisting of unique environmental effects and small effects from education and religion). However, there were also considerable genetic constraints between reproductive traits and longevity (negative genetic trade-offs), which are usually considered fundamental for life-history trait optimization by natural selection. For example, in the Finns, there were significant negative genetic correlations between age at first reproduction and longevity, and the mean inter-birth interval and longevity (Pettay *et al.*, 2005). Their existence implies that females who started reproducing early, or had short inter-birth intervals, had relatively shorter lifespans too, supporting the hypothesis that rate of reproduction should trade-off with longevity (Williams, 1957; Kirkwood, 1977; Kirkwood and Rose, 1991). This type of negative additive genetic correlation, or antagonistic pleiotropy, is often expected for fitness components, and may be one force maintaining additive genetic variation in nature (Falconer and Mackay, 1996), although it may generally be rare in natural populations (Kruuk, 2004).

These trade-offs may have had important implications for the evolution of human life-history, given that human females may gain fitness benefits through outliving their own reproductive capacity by improving the reproductive success of their offspring and the survival of their grand-offspring. Such positive fitness effects of post-reproductive survival would intensify selection for genes increasing longevity, but the negative genetic correlations between measures of reproductive rate and longevity set constrains on any response to such selection imposed by countervailing selection favouring early or frequent breeding (Käär et al., 1996). The correlations are also interesting since they suggest some underlying genetic mechanism affecting the starting age of reproduction and longevity, and rate of reproduction and longevity. The relatively large additive genetic variance and genetic constraints between key life-history traits that both studies found suggest that in these populations, human life-history certainly has had the potential to evolve by optimizing natural selection, as classical life-history theory predicts. The significance of the maternal effects, e.g. for female age at first reproduction in Finns (Pettay et al., 2005), further emphasizes that social aspects, like wealth of the family, also play an important role in human life-history evolution. Studies showing how phenotypic selection gradients translate into genetic responses to selection in different human populations are an essential and much-needed direction for future research.

27.5. Synthesis and future directions

Human life-history evolution is a fascinating subject and substantial advancements to our understanding of how our life-history compares and contrasts with that of animals have been made over the past decades. Humans are a problematic study species for many life-history questions because manipulative experiments, which have been highly illuminating in similar studies of animals, are out of the question and because culture has a strong influence on reproductive patterns. Nevertheless, humans have some substantial advantages, too. First, not surprisingly,

findings of human studies are of broad interest to scientists and lay-peoples alike. Second, the medical literature on humans, although often under-used by those interested in life-history evolution, allows significant insights into the mechanism driving life-history trade-offs. Third, the ability to follow the fate of virtually all dispersing individuals in some human populations over several generations allows a better estimation of the effects of life-history strategies on evolutionary fitness than for most wild vertebrates.

Life-history theory was developed for animals. The available evidence clearly demonstrates that such theory is highly applicable to humans. For example, offspring quality/quantity trade-offs and trade-offs between current and future reproduction have been documented in humans (Mace and Sear, 1997; Lummaa et al., 1998, 2001). In addition, in both animals and humans, demonstrating a trade-off between reproductive investment and longevity has proved to be inherently difficult, presumably because mothers of high quality are both more able to invest heavily in reproduction and to survive for a long time (Clutton-Brock, 1991). While animal studies can often reduce this problem by manipulating reproductive effort, the inability to manipulate reproductive investment in humans further reduces our ability to test for trade-offs between reproductive investment and longevity. That most studies in humans actually report a positive correlation between investment and longevity is testament to the problem of confounding influences of maternal quality. Future studies investigating such relationships must be acutely aware of this and would benefit substantially by endeavouring to circumvent the obvious problems. The use of multivariate statistics, which allow one to control for the many potential confounding influences, is essential. Potentially confounding influences include: maternal age, previous investment (e.g. number, delivery type, sex, survival, inter-birth interval of previous offspring) and resource availability. Furthermore, an appreciation of the difference between producing offspring at the same time versus at different times and the potentially contrasting effects of producing sons versus daughters on maternal survival are also potentially of critical importance.

An area of human life-history evolution that has been almost wholly devoid of attention is the unified area of heritability and selection, despite being at the core of the whole field. For selection to influence the life-history trait of an individual, that trait must have a heritable genetic component. Moreover, for variation in the trait to be potentially receptive to selection, one must be able to demonstrate additive genetic variance associated with the trait. The majority of the few attempts made to investigate such possibilities have used phenotypic correlations. Estimating heritabilities and genetic correlations for life-history traits is complicated by the fact that our estimations of heritability can be inflated by shared family effects and cultural transmission within genetic lineages. While comparisons of twins have some advantages (Kirk *et al.*, 2001), an alternative method, and that which is most commonly adopted in animal studies, is to use residual maximum likelihood methods and an 'animal model' which can control for shared family effects (Kruuk, 2004).

In conclusion, theoretical models developed to explain life histories in animals and previous empirical tests in humans have led to a significant advancement in our understanding of the evolution of human life histories. However, we are far from a complete understanding. Armed with the findings over the past few decades and recent analytical advancements for estimating fitness, heritability, selection and rates of senescence, the field of human life-history evolution is at an enthralling stage of its own evolution.

Acknowledgments

I thank Andy Russell, Charlotte Faurie and Ian Rickard for constructive comments and suggestions made on earlier drafts of this chapter; Samuli Helle, Mirkka Lahdenperä and Jenni Pettay for collaboration on the Finnish and Sami people; Terho Koira for continuous help; and the Royal Society of London for financial support.

References

Altmann, J., Lynch, J. W., Nguyen, N., Alberts, S. C. and Gesquiere, L. R. (2004) Life-history correlates of steroid concentrations in wild peripartum baboons. *American Journal of Primatol*, 64: 95–106.

Ardia, D. R., Schat, K. A. and Winkler, D. W. (2003) Reproductive effort reduces long-term immune function in breeding tree swallows. *Proceedings of the Royal Society of London, B*, 270: 1679–1683.

Barnes, A. I. and Partridge, L. (2003) Costing reproduction. *Animal Behaviour*, 66: 199–204.

Beise, J. and Voland, E. (2002) Effect of producing sons in maternal longevity in premodern populations. *Science*, 298: 5592.

Blurton Jones, N. (1986) Bushman birth-spacing: a test of optimal interbirth intervals. *Ethology and Sociobiology*, 7: 91–105.

Boesch, C. (1997) Evidence for dominant wild female chimpanzees investing more in sons. *Animal Behaviour*, 54: 811–815.

Borgerhoff Mulder, M. (1988) Reproductive success in three Kipsigis cohorts. In T. Clutton-Brock (ed.) *Reproductive Success*, pp. 419–435. Cambridge University Press, Cambridge.

Borgerhoff Mulder, M. (2000) Optimizing offspring: the quantity–quality tradeoff in agropastoral Kipsigis. *Evolution and Human Behavior*, 21: 391–410.

Buchanan, K. L. (2000) Stress and the evolution of condition-dependent signals. *Trends in Ecology and Evolution*, 15: 156–160.

Bulmer, M. G. (1970) *The Biology of Twinning in Man*. Clarendon Press, Oxford.

Cagnacci, A., Renzi, A., Arangino, S., Alessandrini, C. and Volpe, A. (2003) The male disadvantage and the seasonal rhythm of sex ratio at the conception. *Human Reproduction*, 18: 885–887.

Cagnacci, A., Renzi, A., Arangino, S., Alessandrini, C. and Volpe, A. (2004) Influences of maternal weight on the secondary sex ratio of human offspring. *Human Reproduction*, 19: 442–444.

Cameron, E. Z. and Linklater, W. L. (2000) Individual mares bias investment in sons and daughters in relation to their condition. *Animal Behaviour*, 60: 359–367.

Charlesworth, B. (1980) *Evolution in Age-structured Populations*. Cambridge University Press, Cambridge.

Charlesworth, B. and Leon, J. A. (1976) The relation of reproductive effort to age. *American Naturalist*, 110: 449–459.

Charnov, E. L. (1982) *The Theory of Sex Allocation*. Princeton University Press, Princeton.

Clark, M. M., Bone, S. and Galef, B. G. (1990) Evidence of sex-biased postnatal maternal investment by Mongolian gerbils. *Animal Behaviour*, 29: 735–744.

Clutton-Brock, T. H. (1991) *The Evolution of Parental Care*. Princeton University Press, Princeton.

Clutton-Brock, T. H., Guinness, F. E. and Albon, S. D. (1983) The costs of reproduction to red deer hinds. *Journal of Animal Ecology*, 52: 367–383.

Clutton-Brock, T. H., Albon, S. D. and Guinness, F. E. (1989) Fitness costs of gestation and lactation in wild mammals. *Nature*, 337: 260–262.

Cohen, A. A. (2004) Female post-reproductive lifespan: a general mammalian trait. *Biological Reviews*, 79: 733–750.

Daan, S. and Tinbergen, J. M. (1997) Adaptations of life histories. In J. R. Krebs and N. B. Davies (eds) *Behavioural Ecology. An Evolutionary Approach*, pp. 311–333. Blackwell, Oxford.

Dewey, K. G. (1997) Energy and protein requirements during lactation. *Annual Review of Nutrition*, 17: 19–36.

Dickinson, J. D. and Hatchwell, B. J. (2004) Fitness consequences of helping. In W. D. Koenig and J. L. Dickinson (eds) *Ecology and Evolution of Cooperative Breeding Birds*, pp. 48–66. Cambridge University Press, Cambridge.

Doblhammer, G. and Oeppen, J. (2003) Reproduction and longevity among the British peerage: the effect of frailty and health selection. *Proceedings of the Royal Society of London, B*, 270: 1541–1547.

Dufour, D. L. and Sauther, M. L. (2002) Comparative and evolutionary dimensions of the energetics of human pregnancy and lactation. *American Journal of Human Biology*, 14: 584–602.

Eogan, M. A., Geary, M. P., O'Connell, M. P. and Keane, D. P. (2003) Effect of fetal sex on labour and delivery: retrospective review. *British Medical Journal*, 326: 137.

Falconer, D. S. and Mackay, T. F.C. (1996) *Introduction to Quantitative Genetics*. Longman, Essex.

Flynn, J. L. and Chan, J. (2001) Tuberculosis: latency and reactivation. *Infection and Immunity*, 69: 4195–4201.

Foster, K. R. and Ratnieks, F. L. W. (2005) A new eusocial vertebrate? *Trends in Ecology and Evolution*, 20: 363–364.

Gabler, S. and Voland, E. (1994) Fitness of twinning. *Human Biology*, 66: 699–713.

Gadgil, M. and Bossert, W. (1970) Life history consequences of natural selection. *American Naturalist*, 104: 1–24.

Gaulden, M. E. (1992) Maternal age effect: the enigma of Down syndrome and other trisomic conditions. *Mutation Research*, 296: 69–88.

Gibson, M. A., Mace, R. (2003) Strong mothers bear more sons in rural Ethiopia. *Proceedings of the Royal Society of London, B*, 270: S108–S109.

Gibson, M. A., Mace, R. (2005) Helpful grandmothers in rural Ethiopia: A study of the effect of kin on child survival and growth. *Evolution and Human Behavior*, 26: 469–482.

Gustafsson, L., Nordling, D., Andersson, M. S., Sheldon, B. C. and Qvarnström, A. (1994) Infectious diseases, reproductive effort and the cost of reproduction in birds. *Philosophical Transactions of the Royal Society of London, B*, 346: 323–331.

Hamilton, W. D. (1966) The moulding of senescence by natural selection. *Journal of Theoretical Biology*, 12: 12–45.

Haukioja, E., Lemmetyinen, R. and Pikkola, M. (1989) Why are twins so rare in *Homo sapiens*? *American Naturalist*, 133: 572–577.

Hawkes, K. (2003) Grandmother and the evolution of human longevity. *American Journal of Human Biology*, 15: 380–400.

Hawkes, K. (2004) Human longevity—the grandmother effect. *Nature*, 428: 128–129.

Hawkes, K., O'Connell, J. F., Blurton Jones, N. G. (1997) Hadza Women's time allocation, offspring provisioning, and the evolution of long postmenopausal life spans. *Current Anthropology*, 38: 551–577.

Hawkes, K., O'Connell, J. F., Jones, N. G., Alvarez, H. and Charnov, E. L. (1998) Grandmothering, menopause, and the evolution of human life histories. *Proceedings of the National Academy of Sciences of the USA*, 95: 1336–1339.

Helle, S., Lummaa, V. and Jokela, J. (2002) Sons reduced maternal lifespan in pre-modern humans. *Science*, 296: 1085.

Helle, S, Lummaa, V. and Jokela J (2004) Accelerated immunosenescence in pre-industrial twin mothers. *Proceedings of the National Academy of Sciences of the USA*, 101: 12391–12396.

Helle, S., Lummaa, V. and Jokela, J. (2005) Late, but not early, reproduction correlated with longevity in historical Sami women. *Proceedings of the Royal Society of London, B*, 272: 29–37.

Hill, K. and Kaplan, H. (1999) Life history traits in humans: theory and empirical studies. *Annual Review of Anthropology*, 28: 397–430.

Hill, K., Boesch, C., Goodall, J., Pusey, A., Williams, J. and Wrangham, R. (2001) Mortality rates among wild chimpanzees. *Journal of Human Evolution*, 40: 437–450.

Hoffman, H. J., Stark, C. R., Lundin, F. E. and Ashbrook, I. D. (1974) Analysis of birth weight, gestational age, and fetal viability, U. S. births, 1968. *Obstetrical and Gynecological Survey*, 29: 651–681.

Hurt, L. S., Ronsmans, C. and Quigley, M. (2006) Does the number of sons born affect long-term mortality of parents? A cohort study in rural Bangladesh. *Proceedings of the Royal Society of London, B*, 273: 149–155.

Jamison, C. S., Cornell, L. L., Jamison, P. L. and Nakazato, H. (2002) Are all grandmothers equal? A review and a preliminary test of the "grandmother hypothesis" in Tokugawa Japan. *American Journal of Physical Anthropology*, 119: 67–76.

Jolly, M., Sebire, N., Harris, J., Robinson, S. and Regan, L. (2000) The risks associated with pregnancy in women aged 35 years or older. *Human Reproduction*, 15: 2433–2437.

Kään, P., Jokela, J., Helle, T. and Kojola, I. (1996) Direct and correlative phenotypic selection on life-history traits in three pre-industrial human populations. *Proceedings of the Royal Society of London, B*, 263: 1475–1480.

Kaplan, H. K. (1996) A theory of fertility and parental investment in traditional and modern human societies. *Yearbook of Physical Anthropology*, 39: 91–136.

Kirk, K. M., Blomberg, S. P., Duffy, D. L., Heath, A. C., Owens, I. P. F. and Martin, N. G. (2001) Natural selection and quantitative genetics of life-history traits in western women: a twin study. *Evolution*, 55: 423–435.

Kirkwood, T. B. L. (1977) Evolution of ageing. *Nature*, 270: 301–304.

Kirkwood, T. B. L. and Austad, S. N. (2000) Why do we age? *Nature*, 408: 233–238.

Kirkwood, T. B. L. and Rose, M. R. (1991) Evolution of senescence: late survival sacrificed for reproduction. *Philosophical Transactions of the Royal Society of London, B*, 332: 15–24.

Klein, J. L. (2000) The effects of hormones on sex differences in infection: from genes to behaviour. *Neuroscience and Biobehavior Reviews*, 24: 627–638.

Korpelainen, H. (2000) Fitness, reproduction and longevity among European aristocratic and rural Finnish families in the 1700s and 1800s. *Proceedings of the Royal Society of London, B*, 267: 1765–1770.

Korpelainen, H. (2003) Human life histories and the demographic transition: a case study from Finland, 1870–1949. *American Journal of Physical Anthropology*, 120: 384–390.

Kruuk, L. E. B. (2004) Estimating genetic parameters in natural populations using the 'Animal Model'. *Philosophical Transactions of the Royal Society of London, B*, 359: 873–890.

Kruuk, L. E. B., Clutton-Brock, T. H., Slate, J., Pemberton, J. M., Brotherstone, S. and Guinness, F. E. (2000) Heritability of fitness in a wild mammal population. *Proceedings of the National Academy of Sciences of the USA*, 97: 698–703.

Kumle, M. and Lund, E. (2000) Patterns of childbearing and mortality in Norwegian women. A 20-year follow-up of women aged 40–96 in the 1970 Norwegian census. In J.-M. Robine, T. B. L. Kirkwood and M. Allard (eds) *Sex and Longevity: Sexuality, Gender, Reproduction, Parenthood*, pp. 117–128. Springer, Berlin.

Lack, D. (1954) *The Natural Regulation of Animal Numbers*. Clarendon Press, Oxford.

Lahdenperä, M., Lummaa, V., Helle, S., Tremblay, M. and Russell, A. F. (2004) Fitness benefits of prolonged post-reproductive life span in women. *Nature*, 428: 178–181.

Le Bourg, E., Thon, B., Légaré, J., Desjardinds, B. and Charbonneau, H. (1993) Reproductive life of French-Canadians in the 17–18th centuries: a search for a trade-off between early fecundity and longevity. *Experimental Gerontology*, 28: 217–232.

Lee, R. (2003) Rethinking the evolutionary theory of aging: transfers, not births, shape senescence in social species. *Proceedings of the National Academy of Sciences of the USA*, 100: 9637–9642.

Lee, P. C. and Moss, C. J. (1986) Early maternal investment in male and female African elephants. *Behavioral Ecology and Sociobiology*, 18: 353–361.

Lessells, C. M. (1991) The evolution of life histories. In J. R. Krebs and N. B. Davies (eds) *Behavioural Ecology: An Evolutionary Approach*, pp. 32–68. Blackwell, Oxford.

Lumey, L. H. (1992) Decreased birthweights in infants after maternal *in utero* exposure to the Dutch famine of 1944–1945. *Paediatrics and Perinatal Epidemiology*, 6: 240–253.

Lummaa, V. (2001) Reproductive investment in pre-industrial humans: the consequences of offspring number, gender and survival. *Proceedings of the Royal Society of London, B*, 268: 1977–1983.

Lummaa, V. (2003) Reproductive success and early developmental conditions in humans: downstream effects of prenatal famine, birth weight and timing of birth. *American Journal of Human Biology*, 15: 170–179.

Lummaa, V. and Clutton-Brock, T. H. (2002) Early development, survival and reproduction in humans. *Trends in Ecology and Evolution*, 17: 141–147.

Lummaa, V., Haukioja, E., Lemmetyinen, R. and Pikkola, M. (1998) Natural selection on human twinning. *Nature*, 394: 533–534.

Lummaa, V., Jokela, J. and Haukioja, E. (2001) Gender difference in benefits of twinning in pre-industrial humans: boys did not pay. *Journal of Animal Ecology*, 70: 739–746.

Lochmiller, R. L. and Deerenberg, C. (2000) Trade-offs in evolutionary immunology: just what is the cost of immunity? *Oikos*, 88: 87–98.

Loos, R. J.F., Derom, C., Eeckels, R., Derom, R. and Vlietinck, R. (2001) Length of gestation and birthweight in dizygotic twins. *Lancet*, 358: 560–561.

Lozano, G. A. and Lank, D. B. (2003) Seasonal trade-offs in cell-mediated immunosenescence in ruffs (*Philomachus pugnax*). *Proceedings of the Royal Society of London, B*, 270: 1203–1208.

Lycett, J. E., Dunbar, R. I. M. and Voland, E. (2000) Longevity and the costs of reproduction in a historical human population. *Proceedings of the Royal Society of London, B*, 267: 31–35.

Lynch, M. and Walsh, B. (1998) *Genetics and Analysis of Quantitative Traits*. Sinauer, Sunderland, MA.

Mace, R. and Sear, R. (1997) Birth interval and the sex of children in a traditional African population: an evolutionary analysis. *Journal of Biosocial Science*, 29: 499–507.

Manning, J. T., Martin, S., Trivers, R. L. and Soler, M. (2002) 2nd to 4th digit ratio and offspring sex ratio. *Journal of Theoretical Biology*, 217: 93–95.

Marlowe, F. (2000) The patriarch hypothesis—an alternative explanation of menopause. *Human Nature*, 11: 27–42.

Marsál, K., Persson, P. H., Larsen, T., Lilja, H., Selbing, A. and Sultan, B. (1996) Intrauterine growth curves based on ultrasonically estimated foetal weights. *Acta Paediatrica*, 85: 843–848.

Marsh, H. and Kasuzya, T. (1984) Changes in the ovaries of the short-finned pilot whale, *Globicephala macrorhynchus*, with age and reproductive activity. In W. F. Perrin, R. L. Brownell and D. P. DeMaster (eds) *Reproduction in Whales, Dolphins and Porpoises*, pp. 311–335. Report of the International Whaling Commission, Cambridge.

McAuliffe, K.,and Whitelead, H. (2005) Eusociality, menopause and information in matrilineal whales. *Trends in Ecology and Evolution*, 20: 650.

McDermott, J. M., Steketee, R. and Wirima, J. (1995) Mortality associated with multiple gestation in Malawi. *International Journal of Epidemiology*, 24: 413–419.

Medawar, P. B. (1952) *The Unsolved Problem of Biology*. H. K. Lewis, London.

Meulenberg, P. M. M. and Hofman, J. A. (1991) Maternal testosterone and fetal sex. *Journal of Steroid Biochemistry and Molecular Biology*, 39: 51–54.

Müller, H., Chiou, J., Carey, J. R. and Wang, J. (2002) Fertility and lifespan: late children enhance female longevity. *Journal of Gerontology, Biological Sciences and Medical Sciences*, 57: B202–B206.

Murabito, J. M., Yang, Q., Fox, C., Wilson, P. W. F. and Cupples, L. A. (2005) Heritability of age at natural menopause in the Framingham Heart Study. *Journal of Clinical Endocrinology and Metabolism*, 90: 3427–3430.

Nishida, T., Corp, N., Hamai, M. *et al.* (2003) Demography, female life history, and reproductive profiles among the chimpanzees of Mahale. *American Journal of Primatology*, 59: 99–121.

Norris, K. and Evans, M. R. (2000) Ecological immunology: life history trade-offs and immune defense in birds. *Behavioral Ecology*, 11: 19–26.

Partridge, L. and Barton, N. H. (1993) Optimality, mutation and the evolution of ageing. *Nature*, 362: 305–311.

Partridge, L. and Gems, D. (2002) Mechanism of ageing: public or private. *Nature Reviews Genetics*, 3: 165–175.

Partridge, L. and Harvey, P. H. (1985) Costs of reproduction. *Nature*, 316: 20.

Pavelka, M. S. M., Fedigan, L. M. (1991) Menopause: a comparative life history perspective. *Yearbook of Physical Anthropology*, 34: 13–38.

Peccei, J. S. (2001a) A critique of the grandmother hypotheses: old and new. *American Journal of Human Biology*, 13: 434–452.

Peccei, J. S. (2001b) Menopause: adaptation or epiphenomenon? *Evolutionary Anthropology*, 10: 43–57.

Perret, M. (2005) Relationship between urinary estrogen levels before conception and sex ratio at birth in a primate, the gray mouse lemur. *Human Reproduction*, 20: 1504–1510.

Pettay, J. E., Kruuk, L. E. B., Jokela, J. and Lummaa, V. (2005) Heritability and genetic constraints of life-history trait evolution in pre-industrial humans. *Proceedings of the National Academy of Sciences of the USA*, 102: 2838–2843.

Prentice, A. M. and Whitehead, R. G. (1987) The energetics of human reproduction. *Symposium of the Zoological Society of London*, 57: 275–304.

Rajagopalan, S. (2001) Tuberculosis and aging: a global health problem. *Clinical and Infectious Diseases*, 33: 1034–1039.

Reznick, D. (1985) Cost of reproduction: an evolution of empirical evidence. *Oikos*, 44: 257–267.

Reznick, D. (1992) Measuring the costs of reproduction. *Trends in Ecology and Evolution*, 7: 42–45.

Ricklefs, R. E., Scheuerlein, A. and Cohen, A. (2003) Age-related patterns of fertility in captive populations of birds and mammals. *Experimental Gerontology*, 38: 741–745.

Roff, D. A. (1992) *The Evolution of Life Histories: Theory and Analysis*. Chapman & Hall, New York.

Roff, D. A. (2002) *Life History Evolution*. Sinauer Associates, Sunderland, MA.

Russell, A. F. (2004) Mammalian contrasts and comparisons. In W. D. Koenig and J. Dickinson (eds) *Ecology and Evolution of Cooperative Breeding in Birds*, chap. 13. Cambridge University Press, Cambridge.

Salami, K. K., Brieger, W. R. and Olutayo, L. (2003) Stress and coping among mothers of twins in rural Southwestern Nigeria. *Twin Research*, 6: 55–61.

Schaffer, W. M. (1974) Selection for optimal life histories: the effects of age structure. *Ecology*, 5: 291–303.

Schultz, A. H. (1969) *The Life of Primates*. Universe Books, New York.

Sear, R., Mace, R. and McGregor, I. A. (2000) Maternal grandmothers improve nutritional status and survival of children in rural Gambia. *Proceedings of the Royal Society of London, B*, 267: 1641–1647.

Sear, R., Mace, R. and McGregor, I. A. (2003) A life history approach to fertility rates in rural Gambia: evidence for trade-offs or phenotypic correlations? In J. Lee and H.-P. Kohler (eds) *The Biodemography of Human Reproduction and Fertility Rodgers*, pp. 135–159. Kluwer, Boston.

Sheldon, B. C. and Verhulst, S. (1996) Ecological immunology: costly parasite defences and trade-offs in evolutionary ecology. *Trends in Ecology and Evolution*, 11: 317–321.

Smith, K. R., Mineau, G. P. and Bean, L. L. (2003) Fertility and post-reproductive longevity. *Social Biology*, 49: 55–75.

Stearns, S. C. (1976) Life-history tactics: a review of the ideas. *Quarterly Review of Biology*, 51: 3–47.

Stearns, S. C. (1992) *Evolution of Life Histories*. Oxford University Press, New York.

Stein, A. D., Barnett, P. G. and Sellen, D. W. (2003a) Maternal undernutrition and the sex ratio at birth in Ethiopia: evidence from national sample. *Proceedings of the Royal Society of London, B*, 271: S37–S39.

Stein, A. D., Zybert, P. A. and Lumey, L. H. (2003b) Acute undernutrition is not associated with excess of females at birth: the Dutch Hunger Winter. *Proceedings of the Royal Society of London, B*, 271: S138–S141.

Stinson, S. (1985) Sex differences in environmental sensitivity during growth and development. *Journal of Physical Anthropology*, 28: 123–147.

Tamimi, R. M., Lagiou, P., Mucci, L. A., Hsieh, C. C., Adami, H. O. and Trichopoulos, D. (2003) Average energy intake among pregnant women carrying a boy compared with a girl. *British Medical Journal*, 326: 1245–1246.

Thomas, F., Teriokhin, A. T., Renaud, F., De Meeûs, T. and Guégan, J. F. (2000) Human longevity at the cost of reproductive success: evidence from global data. *Journal of Evolutionary Biology*, 13: 409–414.

Tracer, D. P. (2002) Somatic versus reproductive energy allocation in Papua New Guinea: life history theory and public health policy. *American Journal Human Biology*, 14: 621–626.

Tymicki, K. (2004) Kin influence on female reproductive behavior: the evidence from reconstitution of the Bejsce parish registers, 18th to 20th centuries, Poland. *American Journal of Human Biology*, 16: 508–522.

van de Putte, B., Matthijs, K., Vlietinck, R. (2004) A social component in the negative effect of sons on maternal longevity in pre-industrial humans. *Journal of Biosocial Science*, 36: 289–297.

van Asselt, K. M., Kok, H. S., Pearson, P. L., Dubas, J. S., Peeters, P. H. M., Velde, E. R. T. and van Noord, P. A. H. (2004) Heritability of menopausal age in mothers and daughters. *Fertility and Sterility*, 82: 1348–1351.

Voland, E. and Beise, J. (2002) Opposite effects of maternal and paternal grandmothers on infant survival in historical Krummhörn. *Behavioral Ecology and Sociobiology*, 52: 435–443.

Voland, E. and Engel, C. (1989) Women's reproduction and longevity in a premodern population (Ostfriesland, Germany, 18th century). In A. E. Rasa, C. Vogel and E. Voland (eds) *The Sociobiology of Sexual and Reproductive Strategies*, pp. 194–205. Chapman & Hall, London.

Voland, E., Chasiotis, A. and Schiefenhövel, W. (eds) (2005) *Grandmotherhood—The Evolutionary Significance of the Second Half of Female Life*. Rutgers University Press, New Brunswick and London.

Wells, J. C. K. (2000) Natural selection and sex differences in morbidity and mortality in early life. *Journal of Theoretical Biology*, 202: 65–76.

Westendorp, R. G. J. and Kirkwood, T. B. L. (1998) Human longevity at the cost of reproductive success. *Nature*, 396: 743–746.

Williams, G. C. (1957) Pleiotropy, natural selection and the evolution of senescence. *Evolution*, 11: 398–411.

Williams, G. C. (1966a) *Adaptation and Natural Selection*. Princeton University Press, Princeton.

Williams, G. C. (1966b) Natural selection, the cost of reproduction, and a refinement of Lack's principle. *American Naturalist*, 100: 687–690.

Wood, J. W. (1994) *Dynamics of Human Reproduction: Biology, Biometry, Demography*. Aldine de Gruyter, New York.

Wrigley, E. A., Davies, R. S., Oeppen, J. E. and Schofield, R. S. (1997) *English Population History from Family Reconstitution 1580–1837*. Cambridge University Press, Cambridge.

Zera, A. J. and Harshman, L. G. (2001) The physiology of life history trade-offs in *Animals*. *Annual Review of Ecology and Systematics*, 32: 95–126.

CHAPTER 28

Evolutionary psychology meets history: insights into human nature through family reconstitution studies

Eckart Voland

28.1. Introduction

There are various methodological approaches for studying the evolved nature of the human psyche. In addition to the classic techniques of data collection, such as surveys, observation and experiments, there is one, which, although developed outside of psychology, can nevertheless be utilized for exploring evolutionary issues, namely the method of family reconstitution. This method uses historical archives with personal data in order to trace (or 'reconstitute') individual life histories, and even whole family histories, across several generations. This allows us to determine reproductive performance within a social group, a community or, with favourable databases, within a whole region of neighbouring communities. The reasons for the establishment of such archives vary greatly. Personal and dynastic interests in lineages of descent have contributed to these collections of data, and so has the desire of the authorities to document the compositions of households or the performance of church ceremonies for reasons of regulatory policy. In European history, the church registers, which were introduced more or less with the start of the 18th century, contain more or less reliable data on vital statistics, the compilation of which generate life and reproductive histories. A family reconstitution based on the church registers can be augmented by other data, such as census lists and tax lists. The latter are particularly valuable, because the data on the property and assets of families contained therein permit a reconstitution of the socio-economic differentiation of the communities according to objective criteria.

The genealogical data of family reconstitution studies is of interest to research inspired by Darwinian theory primarily for two reasons. First, they contain personal data and not highly aggregated statistics, such as are typically analysed in demography. Therefore, the individual- and family-oriented structure of the records permits analysis of the variation within populations. This fits the basic assumption of evolutionary theory—that, for various reasons, there may be a variety of optimal solutions to the life history and reproductive decisions that individuals within a given population can take. This possibility has hitherto not been taken into consideration in conventional historical demography, with its focus on the analysis of aggregated data at the population level (Clarke and Low, 2001). Second, family reconstitution studies achieve a temporal depth with overlapping generations that cannot usually be attained in anthropological demography studies of recent populations, most of which lack reliable historical records. This temporal dimension makes it possible for us to study differential reproduction, with its social, cultural, psychological and biographical correlates. This is important because differential reproduction is a key phenomenon of biological evolution. The analysis of differential reproduction is, thus, the most important heuristic tool available to the adaptationist programme of evolutionary anthropology and evolutionary psychology. Indeed, family reconstitutions make it possible to study two other evolutionarily important aspects of human behaviour. One is the analysis of behavioural and reproductive strategies within the constraints of the evolved human life history. The other is the study of kin selection and intergenerational transfers. These make it possible for us to assess the 'strategic rationality' of the observed phenomena (e.g. the degree of optimality), and they make possible population and sub-group comparisons with regard to the parameters of reproductive performance. These comparisons are guided by questions about the role of transmitted culture (mentality, religion) as opposed to ecology or economy in population differentiation.

In this paper, I explore these issues in more depth and raise the question of the growth of knowledge that family reconstitution studies have contributed to research on the evolved human psyche. General background information on family reconstitution studies, their history and academic dissemination, as well as their techniques and problems of reliability, are to be found elsewhere (Voland, 2000).

28.2. **Trade-offs in human reproductive decision-making**

As reproduction requires resources and resources are always limited, natural selection optimizes the manner in which organisms accumulate and invest resources in reproduction. Therefore, humans, like all other organisms, are evolutionarily shaped as reproductive strategists who constantly have to make decisions on the best possible use of their limited investment possibilities. Some of these allocation decisions have been genetically fixed during phylogeny, but others require spontaneous adjustments to the prevailing living conditions. As organisms can only spend (invest) their time, energy and other resources once, allocation conflicts arise. This is automatically the case if two different tactics are limited by the same resource—or to put it differently, if the benefits from one tactic are paid for by the costs of another. In the evolutionary analysis of reproductive strategies, the issue is how organisms distribute the accumulation versus the investment of their reproductive value across their lifespan, and with what reproductive consequences this is associated.

Among the most important allocation decisions is the issue of whether to continue to invest in oneself in order to reinforce one's quality and competitiveness (to develop, to grow, and to repair oneself, and to accumulate resources, including those of an extrasomatic kind, such as education or property) or whether instead to commence reproduction? This is the issue of the conflict between current and later reproduction. Should one even reproduce at all, and instead attempt to support the reproductive efforts of one's kin by assuming the role of 'helper at the nest'? How many offspring should one produce? How long should the intervals between the individual reproductive phases be? Should children be protected and cared for as long as possible, or be allowed to become independent as quickly as possible? What should the parents' personal commitment be like? Should they 'give their all' and thus reproduce less frequently, or should they invest less in each offspring and so have more children? Should they, indeed, invest equally in all offspring?

Family reconstitution studies have allowed us to explore a number of these allocation problems, in particular: the trade-off between mating and parenting; that between wealth and health of the offspring; that between the quantity and the quality of the offspring; and allocation decisions during the course of differential parental investment. Most such decisions come about as a result of the individual's emotional responses and are implemented at the behavioural level. However, the regulation of some trade-off problems are not emotionally instantiated: in this case, the solution tends to be purely physiological rather than psychological. These include, for example, the issue of the trade-off between fertility and longevity, and the trade-off between early and later survival. While life-history issues of this kind have been dealt with by Lummaa (this volume, Chapter 28), I review what is known from family reconstitution studies about life-history trade-offs that tend to operate on a more psychological level.

28.2.1. Mating versus parenting

Those reproductive decisions which tend to be regulated emotionally and thus are psychologically perceptible include, for example, deciding whether to give priority to mating or to parenting. The evolutionary background of this conflict has to do with evolved sex-specific strategic interests. In the historical milieux of hominization, male reproductive success was primarily limited by the availability of female fecundity, whereas female reproductive success depended particularly on resources required to conceive, successfully give birth to and subsequently raise the offspring to adulthood. Corresponding sex-typical mate-selection preferences evolved, which are supposed to push these limits as far as possible. When selecting a mate, men therefore initially tend to attach importance to indicators of fertility (i.e. a woman's age and her physical appearance as cues of fecundity and health), whereas women also tend to attach importance to indicators of social success, such as wealth, social status, power, prestige, clan affiliation etc. Depending on whether they are pursuing a short- or a long-term mate selection strategy, men and women can be expected to weigh the individual components of their sex-typical preferences differently (Buss, 1999).

In a socially and ecologically limited world, individuals are inevitably forced to compromise on their evolved mate-selection preferences. Women that men dream about and men that women dream about tend to be rare and, when they do appear, they ensure lots of competition among members of the opposite sex. Instead, when the implementation of evolved mate-selection preferences is limited by local opportunities, a mating market arises in which supply and demand find a dynamic balance. The question arises as to what personal or socio-ecological factors have an influence on actual mate-selection behaviour. What trade-offs do men and women see themselves exposed to in the mate-selection market?

For men, the trade-off problem lies in the question of whether they are able to enhance their fitness more by trying to maximize the number of their matings or by making paternal investments, or some mix of these two extremes. Since polygamy was permitted, Mormons in nineteenth-century Utah could enhance their fitness either through additional marriages or through increased paternal effort in a monogamous marriage. Because the probability of marriage (and thus the size of the harem) depended on the husband's prosperity, men whose wealth was above average selected the marriage option and thus acquired a disproportionate share of the community's available female fecundity. Relatively poorer men, who made less attractive husbands, increased their paternal effort instead, with the consequence that their wives were more successful in raising their children (Heath and Hadley, 1998).

For women, on the other hand, there is a trade-off in the question of whether they should invest more time in selecting a mate in the expectation of finding a mate with better quality, or instead should reproduce with any man that happens to be available. Thus, Voland and Engel (1990) were able to demonstrate for the Krummhörn population (Ostfriesland, Germany, 1720–1874) that the more prosperous the available suitors are, the younger are the women willing to enter into marriage with them. This correlation is the outcome of that typical trade-off problem which arises due to the fact that men utilize their resources to increase their reproductive success, while women are able to transform their youth into reproductive success (Low, 1990; Røskaft et al., 1992; Klindworth and Voland, 1995).

The longer women wait for an above-average man, the longer is the delay in the onset of reproduction, and the more fecund lifetime they lose; conversely, the more quickly they enter into marriage, the higher are the costs of sub-optimal mate selection. Therefore, for women, the question arises as to when is the optimal switch-point between continuing to search for a husband who is as attractive as possible and commencing their own reproduction. The average duration of mate selection will depend on (i) how strongly male reproductive success depends on their social position and (ii) whether the population is expanding or stagnating.

The trade-off problem between mating and parenting was particularly life-determining for single mothers in historical times. Should they increase their parental effort, in order to ensure the survival and upbringing of their illegitimate child to the best possible degree, even if this made marriage to a man other than the child's father difficult, or should they instead increase their mating effort and strive for marriage with another man, which under historical conditions could typically only be achieved by giving up their illegitimate child? Data from both the little German rural town of Ditfurt and the Krummhörn region document the fact that in the eighteenth and nineteenth (and even in the early twentieth) centuries, this allocation conflict was frequently resolved at the expense of the illegitimate children (Voland and Stephan, 2000). The mortality risk of illegitimate children often depended to a crucial degree on whether the single mother remained permanently single (or married the alleged father of the child) or whether she later married a man other than the one who officially acknowledged his status as the child's biological father. In the latter case, infant mortality rose to approximately six times the average. The death of the child increased the mother's chances of marriage by about 75%; in effect, child neglect increased mating success.

Similarly, evidence from many very different cultures demonstrates that, when a father dies or abandons the mother, his children have an increased risk of being killed or neglected (Daly and Wilson, 1984; Hill and Hurtado, 1996; Bhuiya and Chowdhury, 1997; Gaudino *et al*.,,

1999). However, there are two possible functional backgrounds for this phenomenon, which must be distinguished for analytical purposes. On the one hand, the loss of paternal investment inevitably means a drastic reduction of the child's reproductive value in many societies, because mothers (or their kin) are often unable to compensate for the missing paternal investment. Similarly, if the reproductive value of a child is reduced for extrinsic reasons, parental investment theory tells us that the benefit of continued reproductive investment by the mother is reduced if further maternal investment promises little chance of success and, therefore, is expensive.

On the other hand, quite apart from the question of the extent to which the lack of a father actually lowers the child's reproductive value, continued investment could lead to opportunity costs for the mothers. It is conceivable that in societies such as those in Ditfurt or in the Krummhörn, which are partially buffered ecologically, support from grandparents, for example, would improve the survival chances of illegitimate children. The neglect of these children, even though their reproductive value is not perceptibly reduced by extrinsic factors, can nevertheless be understood as an adaptive reaction, if by this means high opportunity costs—namely the factual exclusion of the mother from the marriage market—can be avoided.

Maternal underinvestment can, therefore, be adaptive for two reasons as a consequence of the lack of male support: either against the background of natural selection, which favours a reduction of parental investment in offspring with reduced reproductive value, or against the background of sexual selection, which favours a reduction of investment in offspring even if they have an average reproductive value, if by this means the mother's chances of marriage/remarriage are increased. Whereas underinvestment in offspring with reduced reproductive value is a strategy that can also be observed in the animal kingdom, the underinvestment of mothers in their own children appears to be an exclusively human affair, being an outcome of the unusual but characteristically human mating versus parenting conflict (Voland and Stephan, 2000).

28.2.2. Wealth of offspring versus health of offspring

Inbreeding leads to fewer vigorous offspring on average. This is why natural selection has produced a psychological mechanism which makes mating among close relatives (e.g. sibling incest) difficult. Mating among more distant relatives, such as between cousins, is genetically less risky and, correspondingly, is far less objectionable. This raises the question of when marriages within one's own family or clan are considered acceptable, even if they are associated with reproductive risks. Economic opportunities form part of the answer, because kin marriages can frequently prevent the fragmentation of family wealth and the dilution of political influence, i.e. the erosion of important components of familial competitiveness. Against this background, marriage between family members is possible as a strategy for acquiring social (and ultimately genetic) competitiveness at the expense of momentary fitness, because strengthening one's own lineage through wealth concentration by inbreeding coincides with drawbacks for the vitality of the offspring through inbreeding depression. Kin marriages are all the more probable when the cultural (and thus, the biological) success of a family depends on inheritable property. As this is more likely to be the case under conditions of displacement competition than under conditions of expansion competition, it cannot come as a surprise to learn that family reconstitution studies reveal high inbreeding coefficients, especially in populations under ecologically or economically saturated conditions (e.g. Rabino-Massa *et al.*, 2005). Even though the antagonism between the wealth and health of offspring is well known from both anthropological and historical research, no one has yet attempted to model this trade-off systematically. So it is unclear to what degree wealth really is maximized at the expense of health under more or less saturated conditions.

28.2.3. Quantity versus quality of offspring

Natural selection cannot favour both maximum fertility and at the same time maximum offspring fitness. The consequence is a trade-off between the quantity and the quality of offspring. In the end, success in the upbringing, and in the social placement, of one's offspring decides lifetime reproductive success, which is why fertility and genetic fitness only correlate highly to each other in certain ecological situations, whereas in other situations they may be linked together only very loosely. Fertility decisions are influenced by a series of factors with impacts on the cost/benefit matrix of parental investment (see Voland, 1998 for details and references). The question of whether or not the observed fertility rates allow a quantity-versus-quality trade-off to be recognized are of considerable theoretical significance. The pioneering analysis of Blurton Jones and Sibley (1978) concerning the demographic data of the !Kung San disclosed a correlation between fertility and fitness (estimated through lifetime reproductive success) which is inversely U-shaped—just as the well-known ecological principle enunciated by Lack (1966) would lead us to expect. Lack showed, with data from songbirds, that producing more offspring than the habitat could support was counterproductive, since it invariably resulted in the death of more offspring, as well as taxing the parents who were forced to work harder finding food. In the case of the !Kung San, producing more than the average number of children reduced the lifetime reproductive success of their mothers. However, doubts have since been voiced as to how valid and generalizable this finding is (Blurton Jones, 1997). Studies of Aché women, for example, have found a linear correlation between fertility and lifetime reproductive success, suggesting that these women would have been able to increase their lifetime reproductive success if they had been successful in increasing their fertility (Hill and Hurtado, 1996). The same applies to Mennonite women of the eighteenth and nineteenth centuries (Stevenson *et al.*, 2004). In this community, too, there is a linear correlation between fertility and the number of surviving children, without any suggestion of a point of optimal balance. In this case, fertility is regulated primarily through maternal depletion, so that, on the psychological level, a quantity-versus-quality trade-off obviously does not appear to play a role.

This changes if heritable resources start to play a bigger role in subsistence strategies.

The physiological regulation of fertility is augmented and covered up by more cognitive mechanisms of fertility regulation. Although, in land- and livestock-based economies, resources would be available for postponing the physiological limits of fertility, yet precisely the opposite can happen and optimal fertility rates become apparent (Borgerhoff Mulder, 2000; Strassman and Gillespie, 2002). A spectacular highlight of this paradox is the demographic transition which commenced in France at the beginning of the nineteenth century, and which is only now becoming visible in developing countries. This paradox bundles two sets of observations. First, in industrialized and post-industrial societies, the relative wealth of resources is not invested in one's reproduction to the extent that this would be possible physiologically. Secondly, the correlation of wealth and reproductive success that is so typical for pre-transitory societies obviously disappears. Interestingly enough, it was the property-owning elite in European demographic history which first began to show a reduction in fertility.

Even though a number of Darwinian-inspired explanations have been proposed to account for this phenomenon (Borgerhoff Mulder, 1998, 2000; Mace, 1998, 2000, and this volume, Chapter 26; Boone and Kessler, 1999; Kaplan and Lancaster, 2000; Low, 2000; Kaplan et al., 2002), it still remains rather unclear which functional logic the cognitive modules of our evolved human psyche obey, or even whether they have a fertility-regulating impact at all. According to the 'embodied capital theory of life-history evolution' proposed by Kaplan and co-workers (e.g. Kaplan, 1996; Kaplan and Lancaster, 2000; Kaplan et al., 2002), parents are able to estimate the impact of their investment on the competitiveness of their children. Fertility and investment decisions are designed on average so that they maximize the income of children once they are adults—even under the modern conditions of a capital-oriented economy with a competitive labour market. Accordingly, fertility reduction would be a functional measure regulated by biologically evolved cognitive mechanisms, and the demographic transition—even the below-replacement fertility regimes of a few high-income countries—would be the plausible outcome of the quantity-versus-quality trade-offs in socio-economic milieux in which reproductive success depends to a crucial degree on the quality of the children (i.e. their competitiveness and social placement). This hypothesis is founded on the assumption that the evolved human psyche has adaptive tools on hand to functionally handle and to allocate extra-somatic wealth. It is important to note, nevertheless, that even though human psychology obviously makes calculations of the type discussed, the result of these calculations may not enhance genetic fitness under the currently prevailing conditions, but rather enhances the prospects of education and income (Kaplan et al., 1995). It may be, however, that the utility function is not maximizing capital per se, but maximizing the investment needed to place children in the most advantageous position possible so as to maximize lineage survival (Mace, 2000; Barrett et al., 2002). This would imply a much more phenotypically flexible cognition whose genetic focus is placed into a slightly deeper historical frame, i.e. the production of grandchildren.

Alternatively, it could be that the reduction in fertility can only partly be described as the result of a quantity-versus-quality of offspring trade-off problem. In addition, it could also reflect the result of a cost/benefit problem of the mothers. Social science studies make it clear that the decision in favour of or against a child is frequently perceived by the mother as a conflict in opportunity structures (e.g. Conrad et al., 1996). Generative (i.e. reproductive) and economic impulses are noticeably in conflict with each other and it could be that the evolved psyche often gives in to economic impulses because, in the environment of evolutionary adaptedness (EEA), complying with economic interests in the event of a conflict increased lifetime reproductive success more than did compliance with generative interests. Conceiving children was probably not a bottleneck of personal reproduction to the same degree as actually bringing them up, which requires resources. The biologically evolved preference of economic benefit maximization could lead to dysfunctional results in modern and affluent milieux, because adaptive material motivations no longer have fitness-enhancing consequences under the conditions of a modern economy. Through the repeated postponement of the desire for children, there is a risk, due to the economic stimuli, that ultimately both fewer children than desired will be born and also that fewer children will be born than predicted by the fitness optimality model. If this were the case and the demographic transition is to be understood as the result of the functional decoupling of evolved preferences and modern economic milieux, this would argue in favour of one of the key assumptions of evolutionary psychology: humans are adaptation executors, and are only fitness enhancers to the extent that their psyche, which evolved in the EEA, is suitable for solving the adaptive problems under modern conditions (Tooby and Cosmides, 1992).

28.2.4. Differential parental investment

Individual children within one family often have completely different status in terms of the parents' reproductive strategies: it is widely recognized that there are preferred and less-preferred children within the same family (for details and references see Voland, 1998). Family reconstitution studies can help to discover the complexity and conditionality of these reproductive strategy decisions. The basic idea is that differential parental investment should also be reflected in differential infant and child mortality. In the Krummhörn population from Ostfriesland, for example, relatively more boys than girls died in farmers' families during the eighteenth and nineteenth centuries, i.e. more than would have been expected given the general overmortality of male infants (Voland and Dunbar, 1995). As the Krummhörn is bordered in the west by the North Sea and is surrounded by a belt of moor towards the interior, the fertile marshland was cultivated to its limits and divided into properties rather quickly. From an economic standpoint, this is a 'saturated habitat'.

These situations, which are also known from the animal kingdom in a form that is definitely comparable with humans, are described as 'local resource competition' scenarios. Many species, especially among birds but also among mammals (and, in particular, among primates: Van Schaik and Hrdy, 1991), react to such ecologically limited conditions with differential parental investment,

in order to achieve a reduction of competition within their own progeny. And this is precisely what the Krummhörn marsh farmers did. By limiting the number of male heirs, they defused the competition among their children in the interests of concentrating resources and a bundling of reproductive opportunities. The investment in male offspring by farmers (but not, however, by labourers!) was subject to the law of diminishing returns: with every surviving son in addition to the heir, the reproduction costs increased (not least because of the additional share in the inheritance to which they were entitled), but the benefit of every additional son (measured in units of reproductive fitness) did not rise to the same degree. A reduced probability of marriage and an increased rate of emigration reduced the fitness expectations which farmer parents were able to associate with every additional son; and, accordingly, the reproductive interest in these children steadily declined.

The question of which offspring to invest in more, and which less, depends on the costs which the parents assume if they invest in a child and the benefits promised by an investment in a particular child. Offsetting these two accounts results in a net balance which decides the adaptive value of a possible investment. Accordingly, parents should be more willing to assume costs (i.e. be more willing to waive part of their remaining reproductive potential to the benefit of their current offspring) the greater the fitness outcome from this reproductive effort promises to be (Trivers' Principle). On the other hand, the more expensive their parental effort, the more parents should hesitate in making investments, given the same expectations of benefits (Lack's Principle).

28.2.5. The gap between theory and evidence

The study of reproductive decisions and life-history trade-offs makes an epistemic problem visible. Regardless of whether it is the trade-off between the quantity versus quality of offspring, or even other trade-offs, one finds often only marginal effects where strong effects are expected on theoretical grounds. There are four possible reasons for this.

1. *The intrinsic heterogeneity of the individuals.* For genetic and/or developmental reasons, the individuals in a population differ, which can lead to a covariation of individual life-history traits, even if they are in an antagonistic relationship with each other. Whoever is constitutionally robust can have both many children and grow old, so that the costs of reproduction simply remain hidden due to this covariation (Sear *et al.*, 2003). At the same time, phenotypic covariation ensures reproductive differentials. Maternal heterogeneity, for example, proves to be the main predictor for infant and child mortality (Stevenson *et al.*, 2004) and thus threatens to mask age, parity and social status effects.

2. *The heterogeneity of the individuals' life circumstances.* Human populations are not infrequently stratified and segregated, so that within populations there can be parallel stages for Darwinian competition. These various socio-cultural scenarios possibly provide very different opportunity structures and cost/benefit matrices for behavioural and reproductive decisions. If this form of heterogeneity is ignored, it can easily lead to the disappearance of the expected correlations between life-history traits (Mace, 2000). In contrast, homogeneous samples frequently show the predicted correlations: a positive correlation between social status and the number of children is found, for example, among many pre-modern societies (Low, 2000). Sometimes these effects can become quite complex: a positive correlation was found between social status and number of children among the male employees of the University of Vienna, for example, but not among the female employees (Fieder *et al.*, 2005). The theoretically predicted correlation can thus often remain undetected, in analyses of highly aggregated samples. It seems that the more the samples are socio-culturally homogeneous, the more the results conform to the theory.

3. *The functional logic of the trade-offs.* It cannot be ruled out that a only few trade-offs can be presented as linear functions, whereas others have the effect of being threshold phenomena (Borgerhoff Mulder, 2000). It is conceivable, for example, that the costs of child-bearing (as reflected in terms of reduced life expectancy) only come into play after there is a certain number of children. Evidence suggests that the human uterus is designed to carry up to seven pregnancies to term. Higher fertility would be beyond the physiological optimum, so that the fertility-versus-longevity trade-off will only kick in among women with extremely high fertility (as suggested, in fact, by the data collected by Voland and Engel, 1989).

4. *The social intermeshing of the costs and the benefits of reproductive decisions.* Humans are cooperative breeders (Hrdy, 2005; Mace and Sear, 2005), which means that the costs of reproductive investment might be spread across several persons. Grandmothers, other kin and fathers can often be integrated into the reproductive process, so that the reproductive costs of the mother may be lower than expected because of compensation by social support from the helpers. But effects in the opposite direction are also conceivable. In families in which resources are divided, the early commencement of reproduction can mean extra costs for the elderly, if there is a shortage of resources (Helle *et al.*, 2005). What this reminds us is that calculating the cost/benefit ratio of reproductive decisions without taking kin effects into account is a risky enterprise.

28.3. Kin strategies

When studying kin effects on reproduction, methodological rigorousness requires a perfect knowledge of the benefits and costs (including the opportunity costs) of nepotism, namely both for the nepotists but also for the recipients. A quantification of these parameters is, however, not easy to achieve. Even if reproductive consequences of kin support can be measured, the costs side of nepotism often may remain unknown. It may, therefore, be difficult to mask unequivocal claims about the benefits of kin support: although the helpers may have helped their kin to have more offspring, they may have had to pay a high price in direct fitness in order to do so. Due to their genealogical structure, family reconstitutions are particularly suited to taking this problem into consideration and to studying the functional logic of 'helpers-at-the-nest' systems because they can examine the long-term effects of kin strategies.

Three types of human helper-at-the-nest systems can be described, depending on which reproductive status the helpers assume. If they are adults and basically capable of reproduction, but live celibate lives so that their kin support coincides with their own childlessness, we are dealing with non-reproductive helpers. Such systems occur under specific ecological conditions: either there is a lack of productive breeding places (or suitable mating partners) or leaving home incurs ruinous dispersion costs (Strassmann and Clarke, 1998). Non-reproductive helpers are to be distinguished from pre-reproductive helpers: these are typically the offspring (occasionally grandchildren) of a woman, who during their youth (i.e. while they themselves are not yet physiologically capable of their own reproduction) support their (grand-)mothers with her reproduction either directly with childcare or indirectly by making an economic contribution. And finally there are post-reproductive helpers, which are probably uniquely typical of humans: these, of course, normally involve grandmothers who invest their vitality in the support of their adult children (mostly their adult daughters and the latter's descendants) after the end of their own fertile phase.

28.3.1. Non-reproductive helpers-at-the-nest

On the Greek island of Karpathos, the agricultural utility of the land is so limited that resident farmers have no possibility of increasing their net yield, either by the use of capital or by enlarging the area of land under cultivation. As a result, economic growth is practically impossible. The combination of ecological limitations on making a living and high dispersion costs means that farmers' children who do not inherit the land remain unmarried (Vernier, 1984). Under these conditions, the farmers have developed social reproduction strategies that help them to preserve (and, in some cases, even increase) their economic positions. The core of these strategies is a bilateral right of the firstborn: the firstborn daughter inherits the assets of her mother, while the firstborn son inherits the assets of his father.

The continued social and biological existence of farmer families is made possible because later-born siblings altruistically withdraw from competing with the inheriting siblings. Younger daughters remain unmarried and childless, and eke out an existence as maids on the farms of their older sisters. These sister-maids do not receive any wages and are also often excluded from the lavish consumption habits of the farmer couple. From an economic, social and psychological standpoint, their living circumstances can be characterized as a slave-like dependence on the big sister who receives an inheritance. By this means, the dominating group of firstborns create the 'helpers at the nest' required to ensure their own biological reproduction, as well as implementing the correspondingly different upbringing of their own children.

But why do these female helpers accept their social and reproductive subordination to the interests of their sisters? The answer is: because very high dispersion costs are associated with alternative possibilities for making a living (see Strassmann and Clarke, 1998 for a similar scenario in historical Ireland). Leaving the family and marrying a man without property is a risky strategy, because the low demand for workers on the island rules out almost completely the possibility of securing one's existence by working as a farm labourer for someone else. On the other hand, marriage with a propertied man (that is, a farmer's son who will inherit a farm) would actually enhance fitness and be superior to the helper strategy. This is rarely possible, however, because the property-owning older daughters out-compete their non-inheriting sisters on the marriage market. Emigration is also associated with very high costs: due to the situation of the island, migration automatically means long-distance migration with all of the risks associated therewith. Hence, despite the high price of celibacy there is no real strategy available to laterborn women which would allow them to enhance their fitness more than they can achieve by self-sacrificing help. A similar argument can be made for the laterborn brothers in the male line of descent, although long-distance migration plays a much greater role in their life strategies.

European history is rich in examples similar to the Karpathos scenario, but two different types of reason for the emergence of such scenarios are apparent. On the one hand, we have the economic constraints in saturated habitats (usually in mountainous or insular habitats) as in the Karpathos case. In addition, however, non-reproductive helpers can sometimes also be found in certain segments of society, though usually as a result of social constraints. In aristocratic and elite bourgeois families, the reproductive neutralization of daughters (and, to a lesser degree, also of sons) by sending them to cloisters and convents commonly serves dynastic interests. This was primarily due to the concentration of property and power without the helpers literally having to help (Boone, 1986; Hill, 1999; Qirko, 2002).

28.3.2. **Pre-reproductive helpers-at-the-nest**

The Karpathos scenario is an extreme case, because it produces reproductive and non-reproductive offspring within one family practically without any transition. This fixture of roles is rigid and lifelong. Of course, less rigid systems have also been observed in which younger offspring (usually girls) assist with the care of their younger siblings while they are too young to be married; in these cases, women are usually able to produce more children when they have early-born daughters than when they have early-born sons (Turke, 1988; Hill and Hurtado, 1996; Strassmann and Clarke, 1998; Crognier et al., 2001, 2002; Bereczkei and Dunbar, 2002; Kramer, 2002; Sear et al., 2002). In this case, the positive kin effects on familial reproduction are likely to be an expression of conditional and strategic flexibility with the option of being able to switch between being a helper to reproducing oneself within one lifespan. Children help their mothers to bring up their siblings or in the family economy, but do not hesitate to commence their own reproduction once they have reached the appropriate age. In such cases, it remains questionable whether kin support necessarily has to coincide with a sacrifice of direct fitness. There are intermediate cases, of course, and the commencement of one's own reproduction may be postponed for some time, but without the need to commit oneself to lifelong celibacy.

Depending on the nature of the ecological and social constraints, it can happen, of course, that helper structures do not even arise. For reasons which are discussed in detail by Hames and Draper (2004), pre-reproductive helpers are less efficient in forager economies. Agricultural societies too, in which there are various possibilities for efficient use of child labour, do not automatically generate helper effects. Thus, for example, Tymicki (2004) was able to demonstrate for the Polish community of Bejsce that older children tend to lower the parity progression ratio of their mothers rather than to increase it. For reasons which still have to be examined in more detail, cooperative breeding does not arise here, even though the familial prerequisites exist.

This negative finding warns us against uncritical interpretations of correlative findings, because it could also be that what looks like a kin effect at first glance will turn out to have been caused by something other than by familial support after more detailed analysis. Since fertility differentials have a genetic component (Rodgers et al., 2001), women with above-average fertility have parents with above-average fertility, and the correlation between the size of the kin group and one's own family size may thus have nothing to do with kin support, but could merely be an expression of genetic inheritance. Analysing family reconstitution data from four villages in the Ludwigshafen district (Rhineland-Palatine, Germany), A. Kemkes-Grottenthaler (unpublished manuscript) does not find any positive effects of pre-reproductive helpers (i.e. older children, especially older girls) on four measures of the mothers' reproductive performance: completed fertility, laterborn sibling survival, birth spacing and reproductive span. If it is nevertheless observed that women with many daughters have a higher probability of having another child after birth order six (i.e. of becoming 'grandmultiparous'), then this is simply the effect of a strong sex preference in favour of sons and has nothing to do with the helper-at-the-nest behaviour of the older children.

If kin support arises, it can either benefit both parties or the beneficiary manipulates the helper's cost/benefit matrix, by making the helper's own reproduction more expensive, thereby exploiting the helper. Such helpers have no other choice but to make the best of a bad job. A special form of expensive nepotism was found by Pavard *et al.* (2005) among the French settlers in Quebec. After the death of their mothers, girls as young as 3 years of age were exposed to a much higher mortality risk than boys. The authors see this as an outcome of the fact that the daughters, but not the sons, had to take over the role of the mother in their families.

There is anecdotal evidence for how helpers are recruited. In their social-history study of the southwest German community of Hausen, Illien and Jeggle (1978, p. 76, my translation) describe the process as follows.

> In many families children are systematically kept dumb and crippled. Not only was the competition [for other siblings] reduced, but for example, one daughter was tied to the house in order to be able to care for the elderly. A dumb daughter could still do the housework and did not make any demands. There were such simple-minded persons in many families. The historical sources do not reveal the way in which they produced this effect, but many residents of Hausen remained aware of the fact that this process was not as natural as it often appears to be; they don't say 'So-and-so is dumb', but there is always talk of So-and-so having been 'made dumb' or more clearly as 'being kept dumb'.

We must ask, therefore, whose interests are being served when we observe nepotistic behaviour—those of the nepotist or those of the recipient. In other words, what causes nepotistic altruism? Is this an adaptive choice by the nepotist or social manipulation by the recipient? Trivers (1974) was the first to recognize that genetic parent/offspring conflicts can arise, especially about different expectations concerning altruistic services within families. Hence, 'helpers-at-the-nest' may by no means increase their inclusive fitness but instead submit to parental manipulation. Possibly this structural conflict between parents and their offspring explains the evolution of the conscience as an extended phenotype of the parents' 'selfish gene' to exploit their offsprings' reproductive effort (Voland and Voland, 1995). Briefly: kin strategies can be, but do not have to be, cooperative.

28.3.3. Post-reproductive helpers-at-the-nest

In striking contrast to the life history of other primates (including the great apes), human life history has a considerable post-reproductive lifespan. In traditional populations, there are approximately 20 years of life on average between menopause and the end of life, during which women—who have been robbed of the possibility of their own reproduction—support the life and reproductive efforts of their adult children (preferably the adult daughters) (see the contributions in Voland *et al.*, 2005 for more details; also the family reconstitution studies of Ragsdale, 2004; Tymicki, 2004; Lahdenperä *et al.*, 2004; Gibson and Mace, 2005; Kemkes-Grottenthaler, 2005). In part at least, the evolution of human life history must have been shaped by the reproductive contributions of post-reproductive women, and there are good arguments for saying that this contribution ultimately was the primary driver of the evolution of human life history (Hawkes and Blurton Jones, 2005). At any rate, the role of the post-reproductive helper is an indispensable constituent of human life history, which is why there are good reasons for classifying humans as cooperative breeders (Hrdy, 2005, Mace and Sear, 2005).

More recent studies point out an interesting difference in the behaviour of grandmothers that depends on whether their sons' or their daughters' families form the focus of their strategies. Despite wide variances in the power of these effects, the following generalization seems to be indicated: in pre-modern societies, the support of maternal grandmothers manifests itself in the increased survival chances of their grandchildren, but not in increased fertility of their daughters, whereas the influence of paternal grandmothers is not reflected in improved survival chances for their grandchildren, but is more likely to result in the increased fertility of their daughters-in-law (Mace and Sear, 2005). Post-reproductive helpers obviously pursue two distinguishable strategies, probably because the evolved interest of a grandmother in her adult daughters is different from her interest in her daughters-in-law. Whereas the reproductive interests of post-menopausal mothers and their adult daughters overlap for the most part and can only conflict if a mother wants to distribute her support among several adult daughters, the reproductive interests of mothers and the female partners of their adult sons are basically different and only run in parallel under certain conditions. According to the assumptions of Darwinian theory, mothers have been shaped by natural selection to support the reproductive interests of their sons, whereas it is to be expected that the female partners of these sons will pursue their own reproductive interests. The interest of a mother-in-law in her daughter-in-law is limited to the extent that the daughter-in-law works towards the reproductive interests of her mother-in-law. Any difference in interests on the part of the daughter-in-law will not find any support.

The mother-in-law's ultimate interest in a daughter-in-law is initially restricted to that phase of life in which the daughter-in-law is married to her son. In pre-modern demographic regimes with significant mortality rates in all age classes, marriages only existed for a comparatively short time on average. Accordingly, second marriages or phases of widowhood were likely. For this reason, the interests of mothers-in-law in their daughters-in-law were restricted to a more or less limited period of time and did not comprise their whole lifespan.

These genetic conflicts of interest can lead to open, stress-inducing behavioural conflicts. Voland and Beise (2005) demonstrated for the Krummhörn population in the eighteenth and nineteenth centuries that mothers-in-law who lived nearby increased considerably the risk of a daughter-in-law having a stillbirth, and did so more often than mothers-in-law who lived further away—not only at the beginning of a marriage, but throughout the whole duration of the marriage. Mothers-in-law also increased endogenously caused neonatal mortality. It is quite obvious that the mother-in-law/daughter-in-law conflict led to so much stress that the young daughters-in-law experienced real difficulty giving birth to vigorous children. There are at least three fields of conflict in which the different strategic interests of mothers-in-law and daughters-in-law meet and become manifest in behaviour. These have to do with sexual monopolization versus autonomy for the

women, with increasing versus decreasing mating success of the men and with issues of the utilization of economic yields.

Sexual monopolization ('mate guarding'). In order to reduce the uncertainty of paternity, mothers should be selected to support the sexual monopolization attempts of their sons. This is why it would be conceivable that mothers-in-law exert pressure on daughters-in-law in the interest of their sons—and thus ultimately also in their own interest—to compel marital faithfulness and virtuousness, and whenever doubts arise, to increase the pressure.

Increase in the sons' mating success ('mating enhancement'). Furthermore, mothers-in-law could have an interest in enhancing the mating success of their sons, whereas daughters-in-law want to continue the reproductive cooperation with their husbands. The hostility of the mothers-in-law would then have the strategic goal of weakening the emotional bonds between their sons and daughters-in-law, perhaps even excluding the daughters-in-law from the family completely, or at least marginalizing her socially, so that new, extramarital mating opportunities could open up for the sons/husbands. Such a strategy would, of course, only succeed under very special socio-cultural conditions: a certain degree of promiscuity would be necessary, as would a lack of paternal investment possibilities (such that there is no adaptive reason for fathers to develop a lasting interest in their children).

Economic exploitation. Another conflict arises with regard to the issue of how much the daughter-in-law is supposed to contribute to the family economy. Insofar as her social standing in the family is strong enough, a mother-in-law could be motivated to drive her daughter-in-law to work excessively, in order to allow the surplus thus earned to flow to her own (i.e. the mother-in-law's) descendants. This could mean that mother-in-law pushes her daughters-in-law to work harder in the household, the garden or in the business than she does her own daughters. The fact that the workload of pregnant women influences the risks of stillbirth and of neonatal mortality is well documented (e.g. Reid, 2001). Ultimately, it might not have been worthwhile to look after daughters-in-law, even during pregnancy or after they have given birth. Even if the economic exploitation of daughters-in-law occasionally costs a newborn grandchild, the strategy might be successful in the long run under certain socio-economic conditions because dead grandchildren can usually be replaced quite quickly. Even a dead daughter-in-law would not be irreplaceable. Here we are dealing with a system of exploitation in which the work output of the daughter-in-law is demanded just as matter of factly as her fertility.

Of course, the market for reproductive resources can also be completely different and daughters-in-law could become a commodity that is in short supply—for example, in founding populations, such as the population of the Saint Laurent Valley in Quebec in the seventeenth and eighteenth centuries, when male-dominated migration led to a local shortage of women. The consequence of this was a very low marriage age for the women and a high remarriage rate for widows. In this kind of situation, wives were hard to replace. In addition, lost reproductive opportunities could hardly be compensated for in view of the high fertility within an expanding demographic system. An analysis of the mortality in Quebec disclosed that, in contrast to the stagnating system in the Krummhörn, mothers-in-law had a very positive and protective influence on their daughters-in-law during pregnancy (Beise, 2005). Post-reproductive helpers are obviously extremely flexible, strategically speaking, as managers of their own interests.

Even if kin groups are more likely to be places of cooperation and solidarity than of overt competition, family reconstitution studies also show intrafamilial conflicts, quite in keeping with 'selfish-gene' theory, which ultimately can be understood as genetic conflicts of interest. We have already mentioned parent/child conflicts concerning the amount of intrafamilial altruism, and also mother-in-law/daughter-in-law conflicts. Another area of conflict is visible in the reconstitution of the families of seven Slavonic communities (Croatia, 1750–1898). Hammel and Gullickson (2004) show how, in this strong patrilineal society with agnatic corporacy and joint household organization, the risk of maternal mortality decreases with the size of patriarchal kin group of the women (i.e. both with the size of the natal patriarchal kin group and also with the size of the patriarchal kin group into which the women have married). Interestingly enough, however, the risk of maternal mortality is increased by both the presence of the wives of the husband's brothers and by being married to a husband junior among his brothers. The authors attribute the lower chances of women's survival to the rivalry between such women and to the ability of more senior men to insist on better care for their wives.

28.4. Do we need culture as an explanation for differences in reproductive decision-making?

Family reconstitution studies impressively illustrate how humans have organized their lives and their reproduction in the past, as well as the strategic cunning that is frequently involved. On the basis of the results of these studies, the human psyche can be understood as a behaviour-control device, which perceives constraints and opportunities with great sensitivity and conditionally reacts to these. However, the question arises of how optimal the reproductive decisions of our historical ancestors really were. Opinions on this issue cover a wide range. On the one hand, some want to emphasize the historic break between the environment of evolutionary adaptedness (EEA) and modern milieux (and, in these terms, even the historical data from the family reconstitution studies stem from evolutionarily modern milieux, of course). In view of the ecological, social and cultural contrasts between the milieu of hominization and current times, the assumption is that functional solutions to adaptive problems can hardly be expected. It is claimed that the genetically fixed Darwinian algorithms of human behavioural control are not flexible enough to optimally process modern information. Even if the information stems from novel contexts, the processing of this information occurs in accordance with the old pattern that preserves selection but is blind to the present. Hence, suboptimal solutions to contemporary adaptive problems are more likely to be expected than are optimal solutions. In this way, there is a structural break between adaptive behaviour and current fitness.

On the other hand, there are grounds for advocating the hypothesis that the strategic flexibility of human behavioural regulation comprises a bandwidth, which also produces functional results in modern milieux. Accordingly, the human psyche is as much 'on track' in modern milieux as it was in past ones, and thus produces behaviour which on average is likely to be fitness-enhancing. The null hypothesis is that modern behaviour also falls under the assumption of optimality. In this context, the demographic transition (see above) offers an especially interesting case study. Was the reduction in fertility in the historical situation of Europe more fitness enhancing than the continuation of the demographic *ancien régime* would have been? Or is the demographic transition a non-optimal outcome of Pleistocene preferences in historically new cost/benefit structures? There is no generally accepted answer to this question. It reminds us, however, that the issue of the degree of optimality of individual journeys through life is simply an open question. Note that this applies not only to issues of fertility reduction, but as a matter of principle to every reproductive decision—regardless of whether it belongs in the area of mating strategies, differential parental investment or to any other of the components of human life history discussed above.

The existing uncertainty in this matter is more than just a trivial issue of arcane interest. A gain in understanding would also have an impact on the manner in which the human condition could be interpreted from the Darwinian point of view. Humans are 'adaptation executors' (Tooby and Cosmides, 1992), but are they also fitness enhancers? In which areas are they, and under what circumstances? Or if they are not, when and why would adaptation executing no longer lead to fitness maximization? Here, of course, the question of the role of cultural contingencies comes in.

The question of the role of culture in explaining human life and reproduction strategies is repeatedly raised in anthropology and demography (see the illuminating survey by Roth, 2004). Opinions diverge widely. On the one hand, positions that consider culture to be the crucial determinant of differences in human behaviour can be found, and, on the other hand, there are exceedingly sceptical positions, such as that taken by Betzig (1997), when she writes: "I, personally, find 'culture' unnecessary."

To be analytically manageable for family reconstitution studies, this megaproblem must be reduced to the specific analytical level of inter- and intra-population differences in reproductive performance and the causes of these differences. Differences are, of course, not unfamiliar to family reconstitution studies: they occur both in comparisons between populations across regions and also in comparisons of local sub-groups. The problem comes to a head with the question of whether cultural differences are biologically functional or not. It is quite conceivable that every demographic system investigated corresponds to a plausible Darwinian functional logic. But the question to ask is why there are so many different 'systems', with each being plausible and logical in and of themselves but quite different from each other? Why does the population of the Krummhörn reproduce differently from the population of the neighbouring sandy uplands and moor regions? Why do people of different faiths reproduce differently in same city, in the same cultural, ecological and historic setting (Heller-Karneth, 1996; McQuillan, 1999; Kemkes-Grottenthaler, 2003)?

There are only two possible answers: either these differences are biologically functional or they are not. They would be functional, if, in the final analysis, they were to prove to be different adaptive responses to different underlying socio-ecological conditions. The differences have—perhaps very subtle—causes which it should be possible to reconstruct using evolutionary theory. Or the differences are not functional, but instead are arbitrary and idiosyncratic. A cultural system maintains itself through the various mechanisms of social learning and the formation of traditions without a biologically relevant reason being recognizable for the difference from a neighbouring culture. Cultural differences and, with them, the differences in reproductive strategies would ultimately be due to stochastic contingencies, which have established themselves historically. The fact that Catholics and Jews pursue different reproductive strategies may be based on a coincidence which goes back 2000 years, and not to reasons which were of biological significance in the time horizon under investigation.

Family reconstitution studies document the coexistence of both possibilities. For example,

Hammel (1995) was able to demonstrate how, in eighteenth- and nineteenth-century Slavonia, the differences in fertility among the ethnic groups can be better explained by economic and socio-structural background variables than by affiliation with a certain cultural group. He summarizes as follows: "Where distinctly different ethnic groups are allocated to similar structural positions, or where the same ethnic group is allocated to different structural positions, ethnicity will not proxy the structural factors well, with the consequent loss of its explanatory power in the elucidation of demographic behaviour." (Hammel, 1995, p. 225.)

Studies of this type make plain the risk of over-hastily accepting culture as the explanation for population and sub-group differences if possible co-existing ecological or economic correlations cannot be definitively ruled out. Nevertheless, it is clearly the case that we cannot completely reduce cultural differences to differences in the underlying socio-ecological conditions. On the basis of a family reconstitution of Alzey, a German city with residents of three faiths (Catholics, Lutherans and Calvinists), Heller-Karneth (1996) was able to show that differences in faith ultimately hide differences in social class affiliation, as was to be expected. But even after taking this into consideration, a residual difference remains that cannot be broken down any further (see also Van Poppel et al., 2002). Heller-Karneth argues that a collective difference in mentality is responsible (i.e., a cultural difference) which is deeply rooted in history but does not seem to have any recognizable current biological significance. Cultural differences—which have occurred in history at some point in time for whatever reason—can very obviously persist as something that keeps going, even though the causes for their emergence have long since disappeared. Imhof (1983), referring to German history, points out that the differences in mentality, such as denominationally different attitudes to the body and to life, have their origins in the historical experience of the Late Middle Ages and Early Modern Times. Some parts of the population were more strongly and collectively traumatized by epidemics, wars and famines during this period than others. The consequence is a different appreciation of life itself and of the investment in children (as well as in the elderly and pregnant women) which persisted as a culturally fundamental conviction well into the late nineteenth century and which has left a noticeable mark on contemporary reproductive behaviour. In other words, collective experiences during the Thirty Years' War still determine attitudes to life 200 years later. If Imhof's (1983) analysis is correct, it would be a strong empirical argument for the point of view that not every cultural difference is to be understood as making adaptive sense in the time horizon studied. Instead, a historical dimension needs to be incorporated into the examination which allows for the possibility of long-term consequences of past events, and thus also for the possibility of a historically generated non-functional variability in the life courses of humans. In any case, one should take into account that it may simply be a matter of speed of adaptation (i.e. the 'stickiness' of the system). What look like cultural effects may simply be the period of adjustment before the biological system reasserts itself. We can refer to these as cultural effects, but the claim that they oppose Darwinian processes is really an empty claim.

References

Barrett, L., Dunbar, R. and Lycett, J. (2002) *Human Evolutionary Psychology*. Palgrave, Basingstoke and New York.

Beise, J. (2005) The helping and the helpful grandmother—the role of maternal and paternal grandmothers in child mortality in the seventeenth- and eighteenth-century population of French settlers in Québec, Canada. In E. Voland, A. Chasiotis and W. Schiefenhövel (eds) *Grandmotherhood—The Evolutionary Significance of the Second Half of Female Life*, pp. 215–238. Rutgers University Press, New Brunswick and London.

Bereczkei, T. and Dunbar, R. I. M. (2002) Helping-at-the-nest and sex-biased parental investment in a Hungarian gypsy population. *Current Anthropology*, 43: 804–909.

Betzig, L. (1997) People are animals. In L. Betzig (ed.) *Human Nature—A Critical Reader*, pp. 1–17. Oxford University Press, New York and Oxford.

Bhuiya, A. and Chowdhury, M. (1997) The effect of divorce on child survival in a rural area of Bangladesh. *Population Studies*, 51: 57–61.

Blurton Jones, N. (1997) Too good to be true? Is there really a trade-off between number and care of offspring in human reproduction? In L. Betzig (ed.) *Human Nature—A Critical Reader*, pp. 83–86. Oxford University Press, New York and Oxford.

Blurton Jones, N. and Sibley, R. M. (1978) Testing adaptiveness of culturally determined behaviour: Do bushman women maximize their reproductive success by spacing births widely and foraging seldom? In N. Blurton Jones and V. Reynolds (eds) *Human Behaviour and Adaptation*, pp. 135–157. Taylor & Francis, London.

Boone, III, J. L. (1986) Parental investment and elite family structure in preindustrial states: a case study of late medieval-early modern Portuguese genealogies. *American Anthropologist*, 88: 859–878.

Boone, J. L. and Kessler, K. L. (1999) More status or more children? Social status, fertility reduction, and long-term fitness. *Evolution and Human Behaviour*, 20: 257–277.

Borgerhoff Mulder, M. (1998) The demographic transition: are we any closer to an evolutionary explanation? *Trends in Ecology and Evolution*, 13: 266–270.

Borgerhoff Mulder, M. (2000) Optimizing offspring: the quantity–quality tradeoff in agropastoral Kipsigis. *Evolution and Human Behaviour*, 21: 391–410.

Buss, D. M. (1999) *Evolutionary Psychology—The New Science of the Mind*. Allyn & Bacon, Boston.

Conrad, C., Lechner, M. and Wolf, W. (1996) East German fertility after unification: crisis or adaptation? *Population and Development Review*, 22: 331–358.

Crognier, E., Baali, A. and Hilali, M.-K. (2001) Do "helpers at the nest" increase their parents reproductive success? *American Journal of Human Biology*, 13: 365–373.

Crognier, E., Villena, M. and Vargas, E. (2002) Helping patterns and reproductive success in Aymara communities. *American Journal of Human Biology*, 14: 372–379.

Daly, M. and Wilson, M. (1984) A sociobiological analysis of human infanticide. In G. Hausfater and S. B. Hrdy (eds) *Infanticide—Comparative and Evolutionary Perspectives*, pp. 487–502. Aldine de Gruyter, Hawthorne.

Fieder, M., Huber, S., Bookstein, F. L., Iber, K., Schäfer, K., Winckler, G. and Wallner, B. (2005) Status and reproduction in humans: new evidence for the validity of evolutionary explanations on basis of a university sample. *Ethology*, 111: 940–950.

Gaudino, Jr, J. A., Jenkins, B. and Rochat, R. W. (1999) No fathers' names. A risk factor for infant mortality in the State of Georgia, USA. *Social Science and Medicine*, 48: 253–65.

Gibson, M. A. and Mace, R. (2005) Helpful grandmothers in rural Ethiopia: a study of the effect of kin on child survival and growth. *Evolution and Human Behaviour*, 26: 469–482.

Hames, R. and Draper, P. (2004) Women's work, child care, and helpers-at-the nest in a hunter-gatherer society. *Human Nature*, 15: 319–341.

Hammel, E. A. (1995) Economics 1, culture 0: Fertility change and differences in the northwest Balkans, 1700–1900. In S. Greenhalgh (ed.) *Situating Fertility—Anthropology and Demographic Inquiry*, pp. 225–258. Cambridge University Press, Cambridge.

Hammel, E. A. and Gullickson, A. (2004) Kinship structures and survival: maternal mortality on the Croatian–Bosnian border 1750–1898. *Population Studies*, 58: 145–159.

Hawkes, K. and Blurton Jones, N. (2005) Human age structures, paleodemography, and the grandmother hypothesis. In E. Voland, A. Chasiotis and W. Schiefenhövel (eds) *Grandmotherhood—The Evolutionary Significance of the Second Half of Female Life*, pp. 118–140. Rutgers University Press, New Brunswick and London.

Heath, K. M. and Hadley, C. (1998) Dichotomous male reproductive strategies in a polygynous human society: Mating versus parental effort. *Current Anthropology*, 39: 369–374.

Helle, S., Lummaa, V. and Jokela, J. (2005) Are reproductive and somatic senescence coupled in humans? Late, but not early, reproduction correlated with longevity in historical Sami women. *Proceedings of the Royal Society of London, B*, 272: 29–37.

Heller-Karneth, E. (1996) *Drei Konfessionen in einer Stadt—Zur Bedeutung des konfessionellen Faktors im Alzey des Ancien Régime*. Bayerische Blätter für Volkskunde, W¸rzburg.

Hill, E. (1999) Lineage interests and nonreproductive strategies: an evolutionary approach to medieval religious women. *Human Nature*, 10: 109–134.

Hill, K. and Hurtado, A. M. (1996) *Aché Life History—The Ecology and Demography of a Foraging People*. Aldine de Gruyter, Hawthorne, NY.

Hrdy, S. B. (2005) Cooperative breeders with an ace in the hole. In E. Voland, A. Chasiotis and W. Schiefenhövel (eds) *Grandmotherhood—The Evolutionary Significance of the Second Half of Female Life*, pp. 295–317. Rutgers University Press, New Brunswick and London.

Illien, A. and Jeggle, U. (1978) *Leben auf dem Dorf: Zur Sozialgeschichte des Dorfes und zur Sozialgeschichte seiner Bewohner*. Westdeutscher Verlag, Opladen.

Imhof, A. E. (1983) Unterschiedliche Einstellungen zu Leib und Leben in der Neuzeit. In A. E. Imhof (ed.) *Der Mensch und sein Körper—Von der Antike bis heute*, pp. 65–81. Beck, München.

Kaplan, H. (1996) A theory of fertility and parental investment in traditional and modern human societies. *Yearbook of Physical Anthropology*, 39: 91–135.

Kaplan, H. S. and Lancaster, J. B. (2000) The evolutionary economics and psychology of the demographic transition to low fertility. In L. Cronk, N. Chagnon and W. Irons (eds) *Adaptation and Human Behaviour—An Anthropological Perspective*, pp. 283–322. Aldine De Gruyter, Hawthorne, NY.

Kaplan, H. S., Lancaster, J. B., Bock, J. A. and Johnson, S. E. (1995) Does observed fertility maximize fitness among New Mexican men? *Human Nature*, 6: 325–360.

Kaplan, H. S., Lancaster, J. B., Tucker, W. T. and Anderson, K. G. (2002) Evolutionary approach to below replacement fertility. *American Journal of Human Biology*, 14: 233–256.

Kemkes-Grottenthaler, A. (2003) More than a leap of faith: the impact of biological and religious correlates on reproductive behaviour. *Human Biology*, 75: 705–727.

Kemkes-Grottenthaler, A. (2005) Of grandmothers, grandfathers and wicked step-grandparents. Differential impact of paternal grandparents on grandoffspring survival. *Historical Social Research*, 30: 219–239.

Klindworth, H. and Voland, E. (1995) How did the Krummhörn elite males achieve above-average reproductive success? *Human Nature*, 6: 221–240.

Kramer, K. L. (2002) Variation in juvenile dependence: helping behaviour among Maya children. *Human Nature*, 13: 299–325.

Lack, D. (1966) *Population Studies of Birds*. Clarendon Press, Oxford.

Lahdenperä, M., Lummaa, V., Helle, S., Tremblay, M. and Russell, A. F. (2004) Fitness benefits of prolonged post-reproductive lifespan in women. *Nature*, 428: 178–181.

Low, B. S. (1990) Occupational status, landownership, and reproductive behaviour in 19th-century Sweden: Tuna parish. *American Anthropologist*, 92: 457–468.

Low, B. S. (2000) Sex, wealth, and fertility: old rules, new environments. In L. Cronk, N. Chagnon and W. Irons (eds) *Adaptation and Human Behaviour—An Anthropological Perspective*, pp. 323–344. Aldine de Gruyter, Hawthorne, NY.

Mace, R. (1998) The coevolution of human fertility and wealth inheritance strategies. *Philosophical Transactions of the Royal Society*, London, 353B: 389–397.

Mace, R. (2000) Evolutionary ecology of human life history. *Animal Behaviour*, 59: 1–10.

Mace, R. and Sear, R. (2005) Are humans cooperative breeders? In E Voland, A Chasiotis and W Schiefenhövel (eds) *Grandmotherhood—The Evolutionary Significance of the Second Half of Female Life*, pp. 143–159. Rutgers University Press, New Brunswick and London.

McQuillan, K. (1999) *Culture, Religion, and Demographic Behaviour—Catholocs and Lutherans in Alsace, 1750–1870*. Liverpool University Press, Liverpool.

Pavard, S., Gagnon, A., Desjardins, B. and Heyer, E. (2005) Mothers death and child survival: The case of early Quebec. *Journal of Biosocial Science*, 37: 209–227.

Qirko, H. (2002) The institutional maintenance of celibacy. *Current Anthropology*, 43: 321–329.

Rabino-Massa, E., Prost, M. and Boetsch, G. (2005) Social structure and consanguinity in a French Mountain population (1550–1849). *Human Biology*, 77: 201–212.

Ragsdale, G. (2004) Grandmothering in Cambridgeshire, 1770–1861. *Human Nature*, 15: 301–317.

Reid, A. (2001) Neonatal mortality and stillbirths in early twentieth century Derbyshire, England. *Population Studies*, 55: 213–232.

Rodgers, J. L., Hughes, K., Kohler, H.-P., Christensen, K., Doughty, D., Rowe, D. C. and Miller, W. B. (2001) Genetic influence helps explain variation in human fertility: evidence from recent behavioural and molecular genetic studies. *Current Directions in Psychological Science*, 10: 184–188.

Røskaft, E., Wara, A. and Viken, Å. (1992) Reproductive success in relation to resource-access and parental age in a small Norwegian farming parish during the period 1700–1900. *Ethology and Sociobiology*, 13: 443–461.

Roth, E. A. (2004) *Culture, Biology, and Anthropological Demography*. Cambridge University Press, Cambridge.

Sear, R., Mace, R. and McGregor, I. A. (2003) A life history approach to fertility rates in rural Gambia: evidents for trade-offs or phenotypic correlations? In J. L. Rodgers and H.-P. Kohler (eds) *The Biodemography of Human Reproduction and Fertility*, pp. 135–159. Kluwer, Boston.

Sear, R., Steele, F., McGregor, I. A. and Mace, R. (2002) The effects of kin on child mortality in rural Gambia. *Demography*, 39: 43–63.

Stevenson, J. C., Everson, P. M. and Grimes, M. (2004) Reproductive measures, fitness, and migrating Mennonites: an evolutionary analysis. *Human Biology*, 76: 667–687.

Strassmann, B. I. and Clarke, A. L. (1998) Ecological constraints on marriage in rural Ireland. *Evolution and Human Behaviour*, 19: 33–55.

Strassmann, B. I. and Gillespie, B. (2001) Life-history theory, fertility and reproductive success in humans. *Proceedings of the Royal Society of London, B*, 269: 553–562.

Tooby, J. and Cosmides, L. (1992) The psychological foundations of culture. In J. H. Barkow, L. Cosmides and J. Tooby (eds) *The Adapted Mind—Evolutionary Psychology and the Generation of Culture*, pp. 19–136. Oxford University Press, New York and Oxford.

Trivers, R. L. (1974) Parent–offspring conflict. *American Zoologist*, 14: 249–264.

Turke, P. W. (1988) Helpers at the nest: childcare networks on Ifaluk. In L. Betzig, M. Borgerhoff Mulder and P. Turke (eds) *Human Reproductive Behaviour—A Darwinian Perspective*, pp. 173–188. Cambridge University Press, Cambridge.

Tymicki, K. (2004) Kin influence on female reproductive behaviour: the evidence from reconstitution of the Bejsce parish registers, 18th to 20th centuries, Poland. *American Journal of Human Biology*, 16: 508–522.

Van Poppel, F., Schellekens, J. and Liefbroer, A. C. (2002) Religious differentials in infant and child mortality in Holland, 1855–1912. *Population Studies*, 56: 277–289.

Van Schaik, C. P. and Hrdy, S. B. (1991) Intensity of local resource competition shapes the relationship between maternal rank and sex ratios at birth in cercopithecine primates. *American Naturalist*, 138: 1555–1562.

Vernier, B. (1984) Putting kin and kinship to good use: the circulation of goods, labour, and names on Karpathos (Greece) In H. Medick and D. W. Sabean (eds) *Interest and Emotion. Essays on the Study of Family and Kinship*, pp. 28–76. Cambridge University Press, Cambridge.

Voland, E. (1998) Evolutionary ecology of human reproduction. *Annual Review of Anthropology*, 27: 347–374.

Voland, E. (2000) Contributions of family reconstitution studies to evolutionary reproductive ecology. *Evolutionary Anthropology*, 9: 134–146.

Voland, E. and Beise, J. (2005) "The husband's mother is the devil in house"—Data on the impact of the mother-in-law on stillbirth mortality in historical Krummhörn (1750–1874) and some thoughts on the evolution of postgenerative female life. In E. Voland, A. Chasiotis and W. Schiefenhövel (eds) *Grandmotherhood—The Evolutionary Significance of the Second Half of Female Life*. Rutgers University Press, New Brunswick & London.

Voland, E. and Dunbar, R. I. M. (1995) Resource competition and reproduction—the relationship between economic and parental strategies in the Krummhörn population (1720–1874). *Human Nature*, 6: 33–49.

Voland, E. and Engel, C. (1989) Women's reproduction and longevity in a premodern population (Ostfriesland, Germany, 18th century). In A. E. Rasa, C. Vogel and E. Voland (eds) *The Sociobiology of Sexual and Reproductive Strategies*, pp. 194–205. Chapman & Hall, London and New York.

Voland, E. and Engel, C. (1990) Female choice in humans: a conditional mate selection strategy of the Krummhörn women (Germany, 1720–1874). *Ethology*, 84: 144–154.

Voland, E. and Stephan, P. (2000) "The hate that love generated"—sexually selected neglect of one's own offspring in humans. In C. P. Van Schaik and C. H. Janson (eds) *Infanticide by Males and its Implications*, pp. 447–465. Cambridge University Press, Cambridge.

Voland, E. and Voland, R. (1995) Parent-offspring conflict, the extended phenotype, and the evolution of conscience. *Journal of Social and Evolutionary Systems*, 18: 397–412.

Voland, E., Chasiotis, A. and Schiefenhövel, W. (eds) (2005) *Grandmotherhood—The Evolutionary Significance of the Second Half of Female Life*. Rutgers University Press, New Brunswick & London.

CHAPTER 29

Risk and decision-making

Bruce Winterhalder

29.1. Introduction

Risk is about unpredictable outcomes of behaviour and decisions, and their consequences for fitness or utility. We are interested particularly in decisions, conscious or not, which lead to actions based on the expectation of a certain result. We presume the outcome is unpredictable to some degree and, for simplicity, characterize it by a probability distribution, such as the normal distribution. This formalizes the outcome expectation as the mean value and alerts us to the chance that the actual result may fall significantly above or below it, with ascertainable odds but without surety. In subsistence studies, outcome risk is usually evaluated as a shortfall, the one-tailed chance of falling below a minimum outcome. There is no reason, however, that it might not instead or also be evaluated as an attempt to avoid a surfeit, say of a toxin found at varying levels in an otherwise essential food source.

Risk, then, is unpredictable variation in an outcome with consequences that matter. Because colloquial use of the term confounds several definitions, we must distinguish outcome risk from exposure to danger or hazards (He engages in risky—read hazardous—behaviour) and from simple chance or odds (He has some risk—read chance or odds—of catching the flu). Risk is distinct from uncertainty or incomplete knowledge, which by definition can be overcome by gathering information. Thus I can alleviate uncertainty about the day's weather forecast by reading the meteorology section of the newspaper, but there is no escaping the unpredictability implied in the statement that there is a 40% chance of rain. The outcome—precipitation—can be assigned odds, but otherwise is not known in advance. These distinctions and the narrowing of the meaning of risk may be somewhat artificial, something to overcome with a more mature and integrated theory (Daly and Wilson, 2002), but for the moment they are essential.

Outcome risk is ubiquitous. It may be present in any behaviour in which choice can result in more than one outcome, unpredictable to some degree, and for which the outcomes have non-linear effects on a measure of value such as fitness or utility. Its importance will vary by the range of possible outcomes and the degree of their unpredictability, along with the extent to which they affect welfare. Where outcome risk is significant we expect that organisms will evolve to avoid harmful outcomes, whether shortfalls or surfeits, minimizing their occurrence to the extent that they can; we expect organisms to have risk-sensitive adaptations. In making this assumption we invoke various conceptual tools of behavioural ecology (Winterhalder and Smith, 2000), microeconomics (Landa and Wang, 2002) and cultural evolution (Henrich and McElreath, 2003).

This essay provides a brief survey of the analysis of outcome risk: what it is, in what circumstance it is important, what analytical tools we have for describing and analysing it, what examples demonstrate the utility of these tools, and what inferences we can draw from a risk-sensitive approach to behaviour. Because risk analysis is based on well-developed mathematical theory, it is necessary to sketch in the first two sections some of technical details. The final sections summarize empirical evidence bearing on these ideas. Those who find the mathematics daunting may wish to begin with the examples in Section 29.4.

29.2. **Risk in concurrent outcomes**

A risk-sensitive analysis of a particular behaviour entails two steps: first, each possible option for the behaviour must be associated with a frequency distribution of its odds. A particular choice of cultivars for one particular field will result in a certain frequency distribution of yields, say of barley. Then each outcome, or in this case each yield, must be assigned a value which might be measured as fitness, utility or some other currency of relevance. Each yield of barley has a certain fitness value to the peasant family engaged in subsistence endeavour. The summed product of the distribution of outcomes times their individual values gives the overall or expected value of the option. We might find, for instance, that inter-cropping two varieties of barley yields more expected value than one or three varieties.

The algorithm that distinguishes between a probability distribution of outcomes and a matched distribution of values has its roots in Pascal's Wager. About 1660 the French mathematician, Blaise Pascal, reasoned that the probability of there being or not being a Christian God as described in the Old Testament was 50:50. He then decided that the eternal reward of heaven set against the damnation of hell, should God exist, tipped the equation decidedly in favour of belief. In Pascal's view, the value function established a decisive rebuttal to agnosticism even though the outcome distribution was inconclusive. Bernoulli (1954; first published 1738) and much later Friedman and Savage (1948) developed the mathematical formalities of this insight through the instrument of concave and convex utility functions.

Risk assessment entails sums over the product of frequency-weighted outcomes and their associated values. Mathematically, for the continuous case:

$$E_i[V(x)] = \int f_i(x)V(x)dx$$

This reads: the expected value of option i, $E_i[V(x)]$, equals the integral (continuous summation) of the product of the outcome distribution for i, $f_i(x)$, and the value function for each outcome, $V(x)$, summed of all possible outcomes, x. In the discontinuous case we replace the integral form, $\int dx$, with simple summation, $\sum$.

Value here is a gloss for fitness and utility, the central metrics of neo-Darwinian and microeconomic theory, respectively. A value function might take many forms, but in the general case it can be visualized as a sigmoid, or convex–concave, curve (Figure 29.1). This formulation is prized for its versatility. Value accelerates with quantity when the outcome resource is in short supply; it decelerates with quantity as the outcome resource grows abundant. This non-linear form represents the changing marginal value of the resource as a function of its abundance.

In the convex portion of this curve, if an organism is given a choice between a fixed reward and even odds of that fixed reward plus or minus a small increment, it should opt for the even odds. Because the curve is accelerating in slope, the weighted upside gain more than offsets the weighted downside loss to beat the sure average. The organism should elect to be risk-prone in the sense of seeking the less predictable option. In the concave portion, the reverse is true: the sure average beats the weighted probability of the odds multiplied by their values. The organism is said to be risk-averse. The formal statement of this result is known as Jensen's inequality; refinements can be found in Kuznar *et al.* (2002).

Because the designations *risk-prone* and *risk-averse* run somewhat counter to common usage, it is important to emphasize that they mean only variance-prone or variance-averse. Note also that this example carries out the two-step procedure introduced earlier: sum over outcome frequency times value. It demonstrates that it may be in the organism's best interests— that is, may maximize its expected reward—to elect the less certain choice.

The example just given is a highly simplified comparison of two outcomes of equal probability,

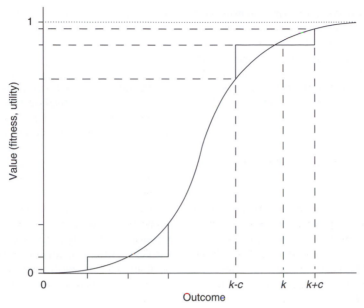

Fig. 29.1 The sigmoid value function. The curve shows the relationship between outcome and value, expressed as fitness or utility. In the concave portion of the curve, downward marginal returns are decreasing and the organism will prefer a constant return k to an equal probability of a variable outcome, $(k + c, k - c)$. The value associated with k is above the mid-point or average value for $k + c$ and $k - c$; the organism is risk-averse. In the convex portion of the curve, the segment with increasing marginal returns, the average of the unpredictable, variable outcomes is higher and the organism is predicted to be risk-prone.

equally distant from the fixed case, against the certain reward of that fixed case. Each possibility is confined to a limited portion of the value function falling on either the convex or concave segments. All other kinds of risk-sensitive analysis are variations on this procedure which complicate the outcome distribution, the value function, or both.

A risk-sensitive analysis requires certain assumptions. We assume the organism is capable of assessing and acting on the outcome distribution and value function, a premise that entails its having acquired significant information about the environment. The organism's choices need not be conscious, rational enactments of college mathematics. They might be entirely unconscious, coded by evolution in cognitive mechanisms, cultural decision heuristics or rules of thumb (Henrich and McElreath, 2002). We assume the environment is well behaved, at least to the degree that the parameters of the

outcome distribution are stable over time periods encompassing action and result. We assume that there is a single, unique value function guiding choice and that it is similarly well-behaved. Finally, we assume that the resource in question is divisible in increments small enough to make comparison of sigmoid positions meaningful (Henrich and McElreath, 2002).

While this list may appear to be highly restrictive, and perhaps decidedly unrealistic, evolutionary ecology studies show a variety of non-human organisms to be capable of risk-sensitive, adaptive behaviour (citations in Winterhalder *et al.*, 1999). Experiments have shown, for instance, that yellow-eyed juncos (*Junco phaeonotus*) have a sigmoid value function for food (Caraco *et al.*, 1980). Small, temperate-zone endotherms which generally are solitary feeding specialists, with low endogenous food reserves and high metabolic requirements, appear to be more risk sensitive than tropical omnivores with more forgiving environments and metabolic characteristics (Winterhalder *et al.*, 1999, pp. 316–25). The taxonomic diversity of risk sensitivity highlights its general evolutionary significance.

The *z*-score model (Figure 29.2) for risk-sensitive analysis has proved to be particularly useful (Stephens and Charnov, 1982). It adopts a normal distribution for characterizing outcomes and a step function to represent value. A step function is a limiting form of the sigmoid curve: below the threshold, R_{min} (defined as a resource minimum) value is zero; above the threshold, its value is one. A risk-sensitive organism will do its best to minimize the one-tail chance of falling below R_{min}, equivalent to maximizing the odds of being above it.

If μ and σ represent the mean and standard deviation of the normal distribution, respectively,

we can express these relationships using the equation for the standard normal deviate, $z = (\mu - R_{min})/\sigma$ rearranged as the slope-intercept equation, $\mu = (R_{min} + \sigma z)$. This positions μ as the *y*-axis coordinate, σ as the *x*-axis coordinate, and R_{min} as the intercept. z is the slope of the line segment extending from R_{min}. Each possible behavioural option is associated with an outcome which has a unique mean (μ) and standard deviation (σ). The best option is that intersected by the intercept line of maximum slope (or maximum z).

The *z*-score model produces two simple rules and a more complex graphical or mathematical solution. The *expected energy-budget rule* says that organisms whose expected or average outcome is below R_{min} will always prefer a variable (unpredictable) to a constant (certain) reward, if their means are equal. The reverse is true of organisms

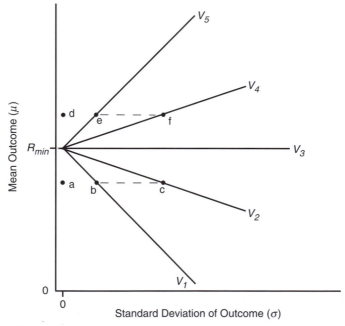

Fig. 29.2 *z*-Score model. σ is the standard deviation and μ is the mean of the normal distribution of outcomes. R_{min} is defined by using a step-function for assessing the values of these outcomes; it is the minimum threshold the organism must meet. The best risk-minimizing option is found via the highest slope line connecting R_{min} and a (σ, μ) pair. The option associated with that particular combination of mean and standard deviation of outcome is optimal. Options along the line have the same value, making the set of such lines (e.g. v_1 through v_5) a risk indifference or iso-value map. The expected energy-budget rule is illustrated by comparing points a–b to d–e; the extreme variance rule by comparing b–c to e–f (see text).

whose expected outcome is above R_{min}. The *extreme variance rule* says that organisms whose expected outcome is below R_{min} will elect outcomes with greater over lesser unpredictable variance at the same mean, whereas those above the R_{min} threshold will do the reverse. More generally, the *z*-score model allows us to compare the expected value of any set options, each characterized by a mean and standard deviation, as a function of R_{min} (Figure 29.2).

Winterhalder *et al.* (1999, pp. 310–13) show that the *z*-score model and an alternative risk-sensitive formulation, the linear discounting function, are specific instances of the general sigmoid model of Figure 29.1, drawing attention again to its versatility. They describe the circumstances in which the more specific conceptualization should give robust results.

We also can treat R_{min} or the sigmoid inflection point not as a starvation threshold but rather as an aspiration level. In a stratified society, we might predict that individuals will be alternately risk-prone and, then risk-averse, followed by another such cycle as they advance up the class-differentiated income scale (Friedman and Savage, 1948). Those who have moved solidly into the next higher class will be intent on consolidating their gains and not slipping backward, hence risk-averse. Those who may be positioned to make a socially attractive leap into the next higher class may, by contrast, adopt more risk-prone options. Kuznar (2002) provides a mathematical function to represent stacked sigmoid-shaped curves, along with an interpretation of its parameters and description of how to apply and test it with field data.

29.3. Temporal discounting and risk

So far we have been examining coincident outcomes, those occurring in the same time frame. Neither the frequency distribution of outcomes nor the value function incorporates the effects of delay. However, it is possible that outcome rewards are spread unpredictably over time and, if the reward for a decision is delayed, it may be subject to temporal discounting. Discounting is evident when an organism decides for a small reward immediately rather than a larger one at a later time; it assesses the effect of time delay on preference. For instance, pigeons that are risk-averse to variably sized outcome rewards delivered after the same short delay may shift to a risk-prone tactic when the rewards are delivered at unpredictable intervals of time (Hamm and Shettleworth, 1987). They appear to discount delayed rewards, favouring a chance at immediacy. Humans also may discount the utility of options with delayed rewards (Samuelson, 1937; citations in Tucker, 2006).

Rogers (1994) combines (i) kin selection (specifically the decay in relatedness from parents to children to grandchildren), (ii) demography (male and female fertility and survivorship schedules through their lifespan) and (iii) population ecology (the rate of population growth or decline) to formulate a model of the 'natural' discount rate. Using data from extant natural fertility populations and the assumption that population growth was zero over the long term, he calculates a natural discount rate of 2% per year. Rogers's model correctly predicts that young adults have a higher discount rate than their elders and, while it focuses on the discount rate for delayed investment in fitness, if preferences are in equilibrium that estimate must equal the discount rate for utility.

Discounting is usually represented either by an exponential or hyperbolic model. Both can be shown to fit experimental data sets, the latter achieving somewhat higher levels of significance (Tucker, 2006). Mathematically, a hyperbolic discount function is represented as:

$$V = A/(1+kD)$$

where V is the discounted value, D is the delay, A is the reward value when D is zero (the return is immediate) and k is the discount rate. Both the exponential and hyperbolic models are, of course, abstractions that entail considerable smoothing. For instance, the discounted value of a crop will jump as it successfully concludes an especially sensitive period of development.

In a risk-sensitive analysis, temporal delay may affect the outcome distribution, the value function, R_{min}, or all three. We also can divide factors potentially affecting discount rates into those that are exogenous and those that are endogenous to the individual decision-maker.

There have been few attempts to assess the determinants of human discount rates in naturalistic settings. By experimentally titrating toward indifference between various hypothetical comparisons—Would you prefer x sacks of maize immediately or $x + k$ sacks 6 months from now?—Tucker (2006) was able to determine that the discount rate of individuals who primarily are foragers is significantly greater than those who depend primarily on farming, for populations living in rural Madagascar.

Discounting is linked to risk because time to reward may be unpredictable, with consequences for its value and likelihood. In terms of procedure, this means that a risk-sensitive analysis of behaviours incorporating significant delay must consider separately the effect of delay on the outcome distribution and the value function. But discounting may also occur without any risk. Comparing a small but certain meal now to a large certain meal after several days of hunger is a discounting problem, but not one that has anything to do with risk. That is, discounting may be evident even if the timing and size of each specific outcome is perfectly predictable.

Kacelnik and Bateson (1997) suggest that cognitive constraints related to Weber's Law may help to explain the prevalence of risk-proneness when variability concerns delay to reward. They argue that scalar impacts on the cognitive processing of time intervals introduce positive skew into the organism's perception of the outcome distribution, with the result that more than half of the outcomes fall below the fixed, average reward.

In summary, quantitative models of risk-sensitive adaptations lead us to conclusions that are counter-intuitive. Humour or despair are not our only means of dealing with the unpredictable. There are effective ('ecologically rational', see Landa and Wang, 2002), patterned responses to outcome risk arising from stochastic factors affecting organisms and their environments. The best risk-sensitive behaviour may require that organisms either embrace or avoid options with higher outcome variance. The sure bet is not always the best bet. The conditions that determine this choice can be specified quite precisely, the key analytical elements being the outcome distribution and the associated value function. In cases of delayed outcomes, both elements must be adjusted for discounting.

29.4. **Examples of risk-sensitive adaptation as behaviour**

The literature on subsistence risk is large but it is generally qualitative and intuitive, whether focused on prehistory and archaeological analyses (Halstead and O'Shea, 1989; Tainter and Tainter, 1996) or the ethnographic present (de Garine and Harrison, 1988; Cashdan, 1990). Use of formal models is rare. The following examples are exceptions to this generalization. They are described in order to highlight various features of a more rigorous approach to questions of risk-sensitive adaptations, as described in previous sections.

29.4.1. **Agricultural field scattering (Cuyo Cuyo, Peru)**

The peasant agricultural community of Cuyo Cuyo, Department of Puno, southern Peru, rests high in one of many drainages flowing down the eastern escarpment of the Andes. Families here cultivate land on steep, terraced slopes located between 2700 and 4100 m in altitude. Potatoes and other Andean tubers and cereals are major crops, with potatoes making up the bulk of the diet.

In a test of McCloskey's (1976) proposal that field scattering is an effective mechanism of risk reduction, Goland (1993) examined data on more than 600 field plots representing cultivation by 18 families over two annual cropping cycles. Her information allowed her to determine what portion of yield variance among plots was explained by fixed landscape features such as altitude, slope and exposure, and by input factors under the control of the farmers: seeding density, fertilizer, weeding. After statistically removing effects of these variables, the residual variance—a substantial 70% of the total—was presumed to be unpredictable variability due to stochastic environmental features.

Goland then performed an analysis in which she used the empirical experience of each family each year to examine the range of yields they would have experienced had all of their production been located at any one of the spots they planted. She continued this exercise by looking at all possible combinations of investing their production opportunities in any two plots, any combination of three plots, etc., up to and including the actual number of fields they planted. This gave her a mean and range (standard deviation) of outcomes representing all potential degrees of field scattering, from one consolidated field to the dozen or so scattered plots typical of Cuyo Cuyo practice. In a procedure inspired by the z-score model, she was then able to calculate the odds a family would fall below their minimum need for potatoes, as a function of their degree of field scattering. Figure 29.3 shows the results for one of the 12 families who effectively eliminated the chance of a shortfall through field scattering.

A GIS-based, topographic analysis of the trail network connecting these fields allowed Goland to conduct a time and energy analysis of moving among them with tools and loads. It showed the total cost of scattering to be a 7% decrement to net production, a small value relative to the risk-minimizing gains achieved by scattering. McCloskey's hypothesis was supported.

Goland's work highlights three important methodological issues. First, she isolated the portion of outcome variability that can be attributed to stochastic factors. Not all variation in outcomes is outcome risk. Second, she found a way to quantify the counter-factual elements of her analysis—the consequences of lesser degrees of field scattering than were observed empirically. Counter-factuals usually are left implicit in behavioural study. And finally, she focused on quantifying the costs as well as the

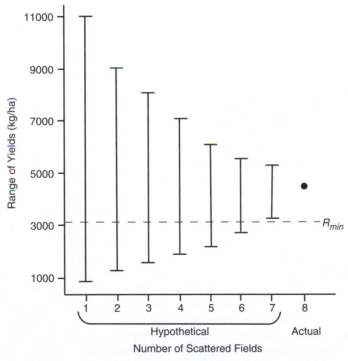

Fig. 29.3 Potential range of yields, compared to the family minimum requirement (R_{min}), as a function of the number of independent (scattered) plots they plant. This household planted eight different fields, obtaining a pooled (average) yield of 4477 kg/ha, comfortably above their requirement of 3100 kg/ha. Had they planted all of their potatoes in just one of the locations of their fields, they would have faced a one-in-eight chance of a catastrophic return of 958 kg/ha.

benefits of the practice, whereas studies of adaptation often rest after showing a benefit.

29.4.2. Pastoralism (east Africa)

Mace and Houston (1989) used the method of stochastic dynamic programming models and empirical evidence to predict the mix of small-stock (goats, sheep) and large-stock (camels) that minimizes the chance of household failure in a drought-prone, pastoralist environment. Small stock have high reproductive rates and recover population size quickly, but they are drought-susceptible. They are a high-mean, high-variance resource. Camels reproduce and recover more slowly, but are drought-resistant, making them a low-mean but low-variance resource. Mace shows that optimal investment patterns depend on household wealth. Impoverished households should—and evidence shows they do (Mace, 1990)—invest in small stock and then, as their wealth grows, they trade up, exchanging sheep and goats for camels. This is consistent with the energy-budget rule: engage in more risk-prone management practices when reserves are below the household minimum needs and switch to risk-averse tactics when above.

In a second analysis using the same methodology, Mace (1993) shows that the nomadic pastoralist Gabbra manipulate the breeding of sheep according to the same risk-sensitive principles and long-term goals. Poor households do not restrict male access to ewes, whereas relatively wealthy households impose such restrictions in order to slow breeding rates of females and thus increase their longevity. Both are adopting the tactic that best serves their long-term survival.

29.4.3. Social exchange (prehistoric south west USA)

Precipitation signatures read from tree rings and a wealth of environmental data on soil moisture balance and early maize yields in south west USA are the basis for a risk-sensitive analysis of prehistoric agriculture by the archaeologists Kohler and Van West (1996). They focus on the Mesa Verde region over a period of about 400 years (AD 901–1300) and a society known as the northern Anasazi. Kohler and Van West hypothesize that in periods of fair to relatively

good precipitation (propitious conditions for agriculture), Anasazi households achieved risk-averse outcomes by forming communities and exchanging corn amongst themselves to minimize the likelihood that individual households would suffer debilitating shortfalls. A string of drought years, in contrast, compromised this mechanism and would shift households into a more risk-prone state, which they achieved by dissolving community ties and dispersing. In particularly bad times, each household did best by attempting to make it on its own, the high-variance option.

In fact, the archaeological record of aggregation and dispersion over the four centuries correlates with environmental patterns in the expected manner. Stretches of adequate-to-abundant rainfall are characterized by village formation, whereas periods of extended or closely spaced droughts signal dispersion of households and the disappearance of villages. Community-level social arrangements apparently were adjusted to achieve risk-averse or risk-prone adaptive outcomes, depending on need.

These results echo Hegmon's (1989) simulation of household survival among the early twentieth-century Hopi engaged in corn agriculture. The Hopi practised field scattering and they further reduced yield variation via obligatory inter-household exchange. In a computer simulation of this practice, Hegmon showed that predicted survival over a 20 year period was 46% for completely independent households (no exchange); 73% for unrestricted sharing (pool the total harvest and divide equally); and 92% for a pattern in which households met their own needs and then pooled and divided only the surplus. The most successful tactic for the Hopi recognizes that unrestricted sharing to cover the losses of the least successful may compromise the survival of many who otherwise would have been marginally above their minimum requirements. Hegmon notes that a sharing ethic which acknowledges this limitation will do better over the long term than one which is unconditional.

29.4.4. Fertility

Completed family size also has been analysed from the perspective of risk (Winterhalder and

Leslie, 2002). In pre-modern populations, sub-adult mortality is high and largely unpredictable. A binomial distribution for childhood survival establishes the outcome distribution for number of surviving adult children achieved by a couple. Winterhalder and Leslie argue that the socio-economic conditions in pre-modern populations entailed a non-linear value function for adult children. For instance, a minimum number of adult offspring may have been required to secure inheritance or defence of fixed property assets. Similarly, because children provided old age insurance for their parents, foresight required that young couples allow for mortality and plan for the minimal set needed to provision them. Desertion by the occasional wayward child, varying capacities and uncertain sex ratios would have further complicated achieving the desired size and composition of the set of adult children.

Thus, falling below one's target adult sibling group might have been a disaster; overreaching it might have imposed rather more modest costs. If this is the case, the value function will be non-linear and risk-sensitive family planning would be constrained to overproduce children relative to the optimum, in order to avoid the very high costs of falling short.

Winterhalder and Leslie term this the 'variance compensation hypothesis' (VCH) and they develop mathematical scenarios to show how the direction and magnitude of the effect depends on differing assumptions about the outcome distribution and value function. The VCH is potentially relevant to various population issues: the rate of growth in natural fertility populations, demographic transitions, and processes of agricultural intensification among them. Unfortunately, most demographic work has treated stochastic features of life history as noise and thus without adaptive significance. There are almost no data at present that would allow us to assess this model.

29.4.5. Subsistence diversification (Mikea, central Madagascar)

The Mikea of south central Madagascar are former agriculturalists who fled into forest regions and took up hunting and gathering to avoid the slavery and tribute demands of Andrevola kings and later the taxes imposed on them by French colonial officials. Presently they mix foraging with low-intensity horticulture, craft production, fishing and marketing in a highly diversified economy. Tucker (2006) argues that discounting can help to explain this mixed portfolio of subsistence activities. Although the average return rate for agriculture makes it highly profitable compared to foraging, cultivation also represents investment in a long-delayed reward with high risk. As a consequence, throughout the early months of the agricultural cycle, the opportunity costs of immediate return foraging compete with investment in a highly discounted agriculture. Three days of field clearing puts no food on the table and Mikea must interrupt cultivation to forage. Likewise the discounted return to weeding is well below that of gathering. As a consequence, foraging and cultivation alternate, the former offering low-level but reliable immediate returns, the latter the potential of a windfall with low reliability. The continued mix of these activities and the desultory level of investment in food production result from an ecologically rational balancing of risk and discounted values.

29.4.6. Late Paleolithic microlithic technology

In an application that is admittedly more speculative, Elston and Brantingham (2002) argue that paleolithic stone tool production may have reflected risk-sensitive choices. They compare the costs and functional advantages of blade stone tools which are lethal but brittle and subject to a high failure rate, to organic, bone and wood tools, which are less lethal but more durable and reliable, to tools made of micro-blade stone set into organics which are lethal and durable but have high production costs. In the argot of Paleolithic technology, wedge-shaped cores are associated with greater uniformity of micro-blade output, making them a risk-averse choice. By contrast, boat-shaped cores imply greater variability and they represent a more risk-prone choice expected only in the dire circumstance of greater need for raw materials than are likely to be available. Neither the experimental nor archaeological data are yet sufficient to test these propositions, although there is a general association of micro-blade technology with the increasingly variable environment following the Late Glacial Maximum.

This analysis is supported by a second and likewise somewhat provisional study. In a stepwise, multiple regression analysis using data from 20 hunter-gatherer populations, Collard *et al.* (2005) show that the diversity and complexity of their toolkits is highly correlated with environmental variables thought to be reasonable proxies for risk. The same analysis allows them provisionally to reject three other hypothesized predictors of toolkit diversity and complexity: the nature of the resources, residential mobility, and the population size of the foragers. If archaeologists are able to test this proposition as conclusively as they can establish sharing from prehistoric sites (Enloe and David, 1992; Waguespack, 2002)—intra-group transfers of food and other materials also being explicable in part by risk reduction advantages (Winterhalder, 1900)—it will go a long way to establishing the prominence of risk-sensitive behaviour in human prehistory.

29.5. **Examples of risk-sensitive adaptations as psychology and decision**

Although still limited, ethnographic evidence on adaptive responses to outcome risk is consistent: humans, in a variety of socio-economic systems and for a variety of behaviours, are able to act as if capable of assessing outcome distributions, value functions and needs or aspiration levels, and of implementing effective, risk-sensitive actions. They are sometimes risk-averse and sometimes risk-prone. In this, they continue the evolved capacities found in other species.

However, the careful qualification of this assertion ('able to act as if ...') brings us to the admission that we know very little about how this is accomplished at the level of psychology and cognition, individual choices, social context and learning; little about how it works as decision-making, conscious or not.

By the standards of probability and statistics, humans in experimental settings prove to be quite fallible in their judgments (Tversky and Kahneman, 1974). Were it otherwise, university classes in these subjects would be more intuitive

and less necessary. Our choices regularly deviate from those ascertained through the formalities of probability and utility theory, and much has been made in psychology of our shortcomings and susceptibilities when making decisions in uncertain or unpredictable circumstances. But this evaluation of human rationality makes sense only if the adaptive demands on evolving human beings have had the same structure as is represented in probability theory. Two examples of the cognition of risk-sensitive decisions make this point.

Rhode *et al.* (1999) argue that we have inherited from our foraging past a specific cognitive mechanism for solving risk-sensitive, adaptive problems. They explicitly address the claim, based on standard expected-utility theory, that humans exhibit an irrational ambiguity avoidance, that is, they tend to avoid options with unknown distributions due to missing or imprecise information, even if those options have the same or greater expected value than a fixed reward.

Rhode *et al.* (1999) assume that people quite reasonably equate an ambiguous outcome distribution with an unpredictable one, and, having evolved as a risk-sensitive hunter-gatherer, assess not only their personal value function but the outcome distribution and R_{min}. Re-cast as a risk-sensitive choice, we sometimes quite reasonably reject the higher-mean/high-variability option. Using experimental protocols, these authors show that people prefer ambiguity to transparent but greater unpredictability; they also elect ambiguity over certainty in situations in which the reward structure predicts a risk-prone choice. Both results point to a single conclusion: ambiguity avoidance is not an indiscriminate matter of avoiding uncertainty. Rather it is tactical, and rational. They also show how their interpretation provides a more consistent and parsimonious explanation of the Ellsberg two-colour problem and other results from experimental psychology.

Rhode *et al.* (1999) infer from their work a domain-specific cognitive module designed by evolution in the context of our foraging past. It gives us the capacity to assess outcome distributions, value functions and R_{min} or aspiration levels. While such a capacity could be related to hunter-gatherer subsistence, similar adaptive problems arise in technological and fertility choices. If a cognitive module exists for comparing the three variables of a risk-sensitive adaptation, it probably has more general sources and applications.

A second case is framing effects, an example of a cognitive heuristic approach which emphasizes the way in which human cognition can go wrong via irrational preference reversals. Tversky and Kahneman (1974) presented subjects with treatment options for a population of 600 hypothetical patients facing a fatal illness. A deterministic-outcome treatment plan resulted in sure survival for 33% of the patients and death for the remainder; a probabilistic-outcome plan resulted in a 33% chance all individuals would survive. When the question was phrased as the number of patients who would be saved, the majority of test subjects made the deterministic choice. When phrased as the number who would perish, subjects elected the probabilistic option. Strictly speaking, this shift due to a rephrasing is irrational as the expected utilities of the treatments are the same.

An evolutionary approach to this experiment would direct attention to the size and nature of the groups found in human prehistory: 15–30 individuals in the immediate band, many of them kin. Wang (1996) repeated the treatment-selection experiments but included group sizes of six and 60, finding that the framing effect disappeared. Further, subjects tended towards the probabilistic treatment option, a result consistent with a risk-sensitive approach if we make the reasonable assumption that the value function is convex for small groups typical of hunter-gatherers. Saving four (0.33 × 12) members of your small band only to have them starve is a poor choice if you have a 33% chance of saving a viable economic unit. Wang argues that we are designed to reason effectively when the experimental set-up is attuned to the context in which such capacities evolved. As the decision shrinks to the family domain and concerns relatives, subjects become more probabilistic and risk-prone; more rational.

In both examples cited, human reasoning in the face of unpredictable outcomes proves to be quite fallible when assessed by the normative canons of formal probability theory and economic rationality. By contrast, risk-sensitive decisions prove to be more robust when the test of what is rational is framed by the 'ecological rationality' (Landa and Wang, 2001) we would expect from the settings and adaptive problems actually faced by our ancestors. These decision studies, far from undermining the assumptions of behavioural ecology, appear to support them.

29.6. Pressing analytical issues

Much about risk-sensitive behaviour is only nascently and imperfectly understood. For instance, we know little about the actual structure of environmental variation and how it affects outcome distributions. This severely limits our ability to make conjectures about ecological rationality. For instance, experimental psychologists have made much of the failure of human cognition to readily appreciate the statistics of independent samples. However, if the environments of human adaptation are significantly autocorrelated (M. W. Grote and B. Winterhalder, unpublished data), such conclusions will need to be reassessed. Obvious and attractive proxy metrics of patterning in an environmental feature, like rainfall, may not correspond to a metric of more immediate interest, like yield (Lee *et al.*, in press). Human behaviour and, by implication, human cognitive mechanisms have been designed to solve the problems of living in actual socio-ecological environments, not the abstractions of a statistics textbook (Barrett and Fiddick, 2000).

Likewise, we have far too few studies of value functions (Henrich and McElreath, 2002; Kuznar, 2002). As a consequence it is not possible to be empirically precise about their shape, or to say with confidence how they respond to such basic variables as age, sex, socio-economic status and security, health, number of descendants, population growth or decline, social history, or other relevant factors.

Continuing with the components of a basic risk-sensitive analysis, there has been little work on R_{min} or the related concept of aspiration level. For instance, in a stratified society there may be multiple aspiration levels across the full range of socio-economic statuses or class (Friedman and Savage, 1948; Kuznar, 2002). The study of how discounting affects these parameters is just beginning, as is analysis of the assumptions that underlie risk-sensitive models.

29.7. Conclusion

The analysis of risk-sensitive behaviour and decisions faces two hurdles: (i) there is a tendency in some social sciences to see environmental stochasticity as noise, thus not as an element of environment for which there can be effective, patterned responses; and (ii) those who seek to analyse risk often rely on intuitive, qualitative assessments of what are and are not appropriate behavioural responses. In fact, there are adaptive responses to outcome risk that can be studied effectively using formal concepts and models.

I see three conclusions in this brief summary:

1. The behavioural ecology of risk-sensitive adaptations and the evolutionary psychology of risk-sensitive cognition and decision-making are necessary complements. Kacelnik and Bateson (1997) recommend 'theoretical plurality' for this topic, with a reminder that it will be most successful if the various theories pay attention to one another. Evolutionists acknowledge a distinction between ultimate analysis focused on the explanation of evolutionary or adaptive advantage, and proximate analysis focused on explanation of mechanisms (Mayr, 1976). This is roughly the distinction between the behavioural ecological study of adaptation—How did it come about?—and the evolutionary psychology study of cognition and decision—How does it function? The former is showing risk-sensitive behaviour in a variety of settings; the latter is beginning to reveal the linkage between these settings and the 'ecological rationality' of cognition and decision. Neither is complete without the other.

2. Evolutionary psychology has sometimes entailed the premise that the human mind is made up of specific modules, each designed to solve a particular problem in a particular context. These modules can be inferred by reverse-engineering observations of contemporary behaviour in terms of their Pleistocene, evolutionary context, also known as the EEA

or environment of evolutionary adaptedness (critical review in Buller, 2005).

If risk-sensitivity is such a module, it would appear that it is better described as a quite general capacity, not limited to a particular task or context. The bases for this claim are: first, the logically sufficient conditions for hypothesizing a risk-sensitive element to any adaptation—unpredictable outcomes and non-linear adaptive consequences—are themselves likely to be ubiquitous; and second, we now have suggestive empirical evidence from behavioural ecology that humans exhibit risk sensitivity across a wide variety of behaviours and contexts: subsistence production and distribution in hunter-gatherer, pastoralist and agricultural societies, choice and design of technological implements, and reproductive behaviour. Also in favour of this argument is the fact that the cognitive capacity to act in a risk-sensitive manner long antedates hominids and the evolution of the neural features unique to our species.

3. Finally, and drawing somewhat more speculatively on the previous two observations, synthesis of insights from behavioural ecology and evolutionary psychology may help us to predict which of our capacities are domain general and which are domain specific, and in what circumstances. Among the basic adaptive tools likely to be domain general are the ability to make marginal assessments, to appraise opportunity costs, and to discount delayed outcomes, along with the capacity to assess and respond to risk.

References

Barrett, H. C. and Fiddick, L. (2000) Evolution and risky decisions. *Trends in Cognitive Sciences*, 4: 251–252.

Bernoulli, D. (1954; first published 1738) Exposition of a new theory on the measurement of risk. *Econometrica*, 22: 23–36.

Buller, D. J. (2005) Evolutionary psychology: the emperor's new paradigm. *Trends in Cognitive Sciences*, 9: 277–283.

Caraco, T., Martindale, S. and Whittam, T. S. (1980) An empirical demonstration of risk-sensitive foraging preferences. *Animal Behaviour*, 28: 820–830.

Cashdan, E. (ed.) (1990) *Risk and Uncertainty in Tribal and Peasant Economies*. Westview Press, Boulder, CO.

Collard, M., Kemery, M. and Banks, S. (2005) Causes of toolkit variation among hunter-gatherers: a test of four competing hypotheses. *Canadian Journal of Archaeology*, 29: 1–19.

Daly, M. and Wilson, M. (2002) Editorial introduction: two special issues on risk. *Evolution and Human Behavior*, 23: 1–2.

de Garine, I. and Harrison, G. A. (eds) (1988) *Coping with Uncertainty in Food Supply*. Clarendon Press, Oxford.

Elston, R. G. and Brantingham, P. J. (2002) Microlithic technology in Northern Asia: a risk-minimizing strategy of the Late Paleolithic and Early Holocene. In R. G. Elston and S. L. Kuhn (eds) *Thinking Small: Global Perspectives on Microlithization*, pp. 103–116. American Anthropological Association, Washington, DC.

Enloe, J. G. and David, F. (1992) Food sharing in the Paleolithic: carcass refitting at Pincevent. In J. L. Hofman and J. G. Enloe (eds) *Piecing Together the Past: Applications of Refitting Studies in Archaeology*, pp. 296–315. Tempvs Reparatvm, Oxford.

Friedman, M. and Savage, L. J. (1948) The utility analysis of choices involving risk. *Journal of Political Economy*, LVI: 279–304.

Goland, C. (1993) Field scattering as agricultural risk management: a case study form Cuyo Cuyo, Department of Puno, Peru. *Mountain Research and Development*, 13: 317–338.

Grote, M. W. and Winterhalder, B. (2006) Robust search path characteristics of a spatially explicit forager (manuscript).

Halstead, P. and O'Shea, J. (eds) (1989) *Bad Year Economics: Cultural Responses to Risk and Uncertainty*. Cambridge University Press, Cambridge.

Hamm, S. L. and Shettleworth, S. J. (1987) Risk aversion in pigeons. *Journal of Experimental Psychology: Animal Behavior Processes*, 13: 376–383.

Hegmon, M. (1989) Risk reduction and variation in agricultural economies: a computer simulation of Hopi agriculture. *Research in Economic Anthropology*, 11: 89–121.

Henrich, J. and McElreath, R. (2002) Are peasants risk-averse decision makers? *Current Anthropology*, 43: 172–181.

Henrich, J. and McElreath, R. (2003) The evolution of cultural evolution. *Evolutionary Anthropology*, 12: 123–35.

Kacelnik, A. and Bateson, M. (1997) Risk-sensitivity: crossroads for theories of decision-making. *Trends in Cognitive Sciences*, 1: 304–309.

Kohler, T. A. and Van West, C. R. (1996) The calculus of self-interest in the development of cooperation: sociopolitical development and risk among the Northern Anasazi. In J. A. Tainter and B. B. Tainter (eds) *Evolving Complexity and Environmental Risk in the Prehistoric Southwest*, pp. 169–196. Addison-Wesley, Reading, MA.

Kuznar, L. A. (2002) Evolutionary applications of risk sensitivity models to socially stratified species: comparison of sigmoid, concave, and linear functions. *Evolution and Human Behavior*, 23: 265–280.

Kuznar, L. A., Henrich, J. and McElreath, R. (2002) On risk-prone peasants: cultural transmission or sigmoid utility maximization? and Reply. *Current Anthropology*, 43: 787–789.

Landa, J. T. and Wang, X. T. (2001) Bounded rationality of economic man: decision making under ecological, social, and institutional constraints. *Journal of Bioeconomics*, 3: 217–235.

Lee, C. T., Tuljapurkar, S. and Vitousek, P. M. (in press) Risky business: temporal and spatial variation in preindustrial dryland agriculture. *Human Ecology*.

Mace, R. (1990) Pastoralist herd compositions in unpredictable environments: a comparison of model predictions and data from camel-keeping groups. *Agricultural Systems*, 33: 1–11.

Mace, R. (1993) Nomadic pastoralists adopt subsistence strategies that maximise long-term household survival. *Behavioral Ecology and Sociobiology*, 33: 329–334.

Mace, R. and Houston, A. (1989) Pastoralist strategies for survival in unpredictable environments: a model of herd composition that maximises household viability. *Agricultural Systems*, 31: 185–204.

Mayr, E. (1961) Cause and effect in biology. *Science*, 134: 1501–1506.

McCloskey, D. N. (1976) English open fields as behavior towards risk. In P. Uselding (ed.) *Research in Economic History vol. 1*, pp. 124–170, JAI Press, Greenwich, CT.

Rhode, C., Cosmides, L., Hell, W. and Tooby, J. (1999) When and why do people avoid unknown probabilities in decisions under uncertainty? Testing some predictions from optimal foraging theory. *Cognition*, 72: 269–304.

Rogers, A. R. (1994) Evolution of time preference by natural selection. *American Economic Review*, 84: 460–81.

Samuelson, P. A. (1937) A note on measurement of utility. *Review of Economic Studies*, 4: 155–161.

Stephens, D. W. and Charnov, E. L. (1982) Optimal foraging: some simple stochastic models. *Behavioral Ecology and Sociobiology*, 10:251–263.

Tainter, J. A. and Tainter, B. B. (eds) (1996) *Evolving Complexity and Environmental Risk in the Prehistoric Southwest*. Addison-Wesley, Reading, MA.

Tucker, B. (2006) A future discounting explanation for the persistence of a mixed foraging-horticulture strategy among the Mikea of Madagascar. In D. J. Kennett and B. Winterhalder (eds) *Behavioral Ecology and the Transition to Agriculture*, pp. 22–40, University of California Press, Berkeley, CA.

Tversky, A. and Kahneman, D. (1974) Judgment under uncertainty: heuristics and biases. *Science*, 185: 1124–1131.

Waguespack, N. M. (2002) Caribou sharing and storage: refitting the Palangana site. *Journal of Anthropological Archaeology*, 21: 396–417.

Wang, X. T. (1996) Domain-specific rationality in human choices: violations of utility axioms and social contexts. *Cognition*, 60: 31–63.

Winterhalder, B. (1990) Open field, common pot: harvest variability and risk avoidance in agricultural and foraging societies. In E. A. Cashdan (ed.) *Risk and Uncertainty in Tribal and Peasant Economies*, pp. 67–87. Westview Press, Boulder, CO.

Winterhalder, B. and Leslie, P. (2002) Risk-sensitive fertility: the variance compensation hypothesis. *Evolution and Human Behavior*, 23: 59–82.

Winterhalder, B. and Smith, E. A. (2000) Analyzing adaptive strategies: human behavioral ecology at twenty-five. *Evolutionary Anthropology*, 9: 51–72.

Winterhalder, B., Lu, F. and Tucker, B. (1999) Risk-sensitive adaptive tactics: models and evidence from subsistence studies in biology and anthropology. *Journal of Archaeological Research*, 7: 301–348.

SECTION VI

The self and the social world

Humans are, above all, social. As with all primates, we owe our success as a species in large measure to our ability to cooperate in finding solutions to the problems of everyday survival and reproduction. We can do that mainly because we can call upon the willing commitment of moderately large numbers of individuals. In effect, we live in societies that are implicit—and sometimes explicit—social contracts. It is here that the issue of multi-level selection that was discussed in Section I comes to the fore. However, that kind of sociality presents serious conflicts for the individual, because the continued existence of a social group depends on individuals being willing to sink at least some of their personal interests for the benefit of the larger community in order to maintain the coherence of the coalition. There will inevitably be tensions that ultimately have to resolved. We return to this particular issue again in Section VII. Our concern here, however, lies with the more immediate questions of individual psychology, on the one hand, and, on the other hand, the larger-scale influences and tensions that affect the structure of societies within which every individual is embedded.

Although evolutionary ideas first gained currency within psychology mainly in the context of cognitive psychology, recent years have witnessed a particular upsurge of interest among social psychologists. This is in some ways not so surprising. Indeed, it is surprising only in that it has taken so long to do so: social psychology would seem to be a natural arena for evolutionary ideas in that social psychology's interests focus on overt behaviour and its psychological underpinnings. Both the strategic approach offered by behavioural ecology and the more cognitive approach offered by evolutionary psychology *sensu stricto* add new dimensions to the social psychologist's toolkit. Of course, intellectual evolution is necessarily a two-way process, and social psychology opens up topics (and hence challenges) for an evolutionary approach that have yet to be explored in any detail. Among these are the nature of the 'self' (an issue explored here from both anthropological and psychological perspectives by Crook, and Skronowski and Sekidides, respectively), the importance of individual differences (Nettle) and aspects of social cognition such as disgust and social rejection (Schaller and colleagues). It is worth remarking here that the term 'social cognition' is used in the social psychology literature in a somewhat different sense to that in comparative (and developmental) psychology. In the latter, it refers to a handful of high-level capacities like theory of mind; in the former, it has a much wider usage that includes both basic cognitive processes (memory, perception) and larger-scale processes like the way reputations can be influenced by the presence of onlookers.

The conflict between the individual and societal levels has spawned a considerable literature in both social psychology and economics, where the main workhorse has been the public goods problem. Any social contract, as Salter shows, involves the risk of exploitation (the freerider or freeloader problem, sometimes also known as the public goods dilemma), and humans have a wide range of mechanisms for reducing the intrusiveness of freeriding. In traditional societies, for example, kinship often plays a central role in mitigating these risks, and badges of kinship and group membership (which may include dialects and shared knowledge, as well as more conventional badges like hair or clothing styles) are an important mechanism for enforcing conformity. Other mechanisms, as van Vugt and colleagues point out, include both punishment of 'social loafers' (altruistic punishment whereby the punisher of a backslider pays a cost for doing so, but society as a whole benefits) and prosociality (the strong predisposition to behave altruistically).

Many of the topics of more traditional anthropological interest continue to remain central to this debate. These include the nature of kinship and the way kinship terms are used to partition members of the community into classes (Cronk and Gerkey) and the influence that both ecology and culture have on marriage and inheritance patterns (Low). Classificatory kinship (as socio-cultural anthropologists term it) can cut across genetic kinship. This has sometimes been interpreted as disproving any claim that genetic kinship is relevant to human social behaviour, but such claims are based on a misunderstanding and are, at best, premature. To be sure, the relationship between classificatory and genetic kinship is not always straightforward, but that is because classificatory kinship represents the intersection of conflicting genetic and social interests (a point stressed both by Hamilton's (1964) conception of inclusive fitness and by Hughes (1988) in an important but little-appreciated book). Elucidating this remains a central, and genuinely interesting, problem for evolutionary psychology.

Finally, by being embedded within a society—whether traditional or modern—we inherit a specific culture or world view, a set of intellectual rules that define how the world is seen and how to travel through both the physical and the social state spaces created by it. So far, the evolutionary approach has given scant attention to this topic and its psychological roots. It remains an important problem for the future, and one that provides the potential for a better articulation between evolutionary psychology and socio-cultural anthropology. Crook offers us a glimpse of that world and its possibilities through his analysis of shamanism.

References

Hamilton, W. D. (1964) The genetical evolution of social behaviour. I, II. *Journal of Theoretical Biology*, 7: 1–52.

Hughes, A. L. (1988) *Evolution and Human Kinship*. Oxford University Press, Oxford.

CHAPTER 30

Ecological and socio-cultural impacts on mating and marriage systems

Bobbi S. Low

30.1. Introduction

Among vertebrates, humans have some of the most diverse arrays of behaviours known. Consider mating systems: in most vertebrates, a species is characterized by a single mating system (although, if it is something other than polygyny, 'extra-pair copulations' or EPCs are likely to exist alongside the dominant pattern). Our mating arrangements, in contrast, are extremely diverse. Non-marital mating arrangements may be relatively open, and children acknowledged, or may be entirely clandestine. In most societies, arrangements are not simply the outcome of one man's and one woman's desires, but rather the culmination of negotiations by members of the older generation; an individual might be betrothed before birth to another not yet born, for example. Marriage itself typically involves the giving or exchange of goods (in some societies from the bride's family to the groom's; in others vice versa), and sometimes of women or of services. Perhaps only the Dunnock (*Prunella modularis*), a British little brown bird, exhibits within a single species

(sometimes within a single population) mating diversity comparable to that of humans: there are monogamous pairs, polyandrous females with their mates, polygynous males with their mates, and polygynandrous groups of males and females, each of whom has multiple mates (Davies, 1992).

None the less, mating systems in other species tend to have not only ecological influences, but also more phylogenetic constraints than is typical of human reproduction. For example: among mammals, because females are specialized for postnatal infant nutrition, some form of polygyny is the default mating system; in many birds, because males may be able to assist in feeding, social monogamy (usually with EPCs; e.g. Reichard and Boesch, 2003) is relatively common. Further, we must distinguish between genetic mating systems (actual genetic maternity and paternity), and social mating systems (who feeds, protects, etc.). The genetic mating system may not (indeed probably seldom does) match the social mating system (e.g. Reichard and Boesch, 2003). That is why, in many socially monogamous systems, there are EPCs, and thus extra-pair paternity.

30.1.2. **Marriage *and* mating**

Not only do humans exhibit many mating arrangements, but we are also more complex than all other species in another aspect of our reproduction. We complicate matters: we have not only mating systems, but marriage systems, in which more than the simple reproductive interests of male and female may be important. Human marriage is a social institution involving societal rules about how many spouses are allowed at any one time, allowable consanguinity in pair-bonds, allowable ages of mates, and so on.

This distinction between marriage versus mating highlights an extraordinary feature of our cultural life. Compared to other mammals, we are probably not unique in the ways we might expect. Social transmission—learning from others—is not even a peculiarly human phenomenon, although its importance to us is extreme. We have more complex social rules than other species (see Dunbar, 2003, Hill and Dunbar, 2003), and we have elaborated culture to such an extraordinary degree that cultural and genetic evolution are almost certainly linked in most human cultures (e.g. see Richerson and Boyd, 2005). But there are predecessors in other species: other organisms exhibit complex and multilayered behaviours such as alliance formation in intra- and intergroup conflict; moreover, other species can have reciprocal and rather complex 'political'—coalitional—behaviour. Humans have developed many such phenomena to new extremes, but it is rare to find unique human phenomena, without parallels or predecessors in other species (Alexander, 1979). Yet though we may have few truly new or unique behaviours, we often exhibit behaviours that are unusual in their extremity.

In a few cases, we do appear to be unique in ways that are important to marriage patterns: namely, the complexity of 'third-party' interests. Other species, for example, exhibit territoriality; but an absent 'owner' loses the territory. We go further and define property rights, in which the holdings of absent owners are supported and protected by (disinterested) third parties; our legal systems, in fact, are specifically concerned with third-party decisions that are accepted by a group as fair. With regard to mating and marriage patterns, third-party roles are well-defined in most societies (see below; also Plotkin, this volume, Chapter 2).

Here I wish to explore how human mating and marriage systems are affected by ecological conditions (e.g. the distribution, abundance, and defensibility of resources), by cultural practices, and by the interactions of these two forces. Given the great diversity in marriage rules and rules about association and sexual conduct across societies, it would be easy to throw up one's hands and regard these patterns as somehow 'purely cultural'. There are, however, often (sometimes non-obvious) influences of the distribution, abundance and predictability of resources that shift the likelihood of success and persistence for different cultural systems.

Thus, cultural and genetic changes over time seem to be inevitably linked, and marriage rules lie at the heart of this phenomenon. But defining 'culture' in a way useful to hypothesis testing is difficult, and culture and genetics change in different ways. Under natural selection, genes are passed from parents to children, and may be passed intact, lost (failure to pass), or passed in a mutated form. Cultural beliefs and behaviours may be passed, lost, or changed as well—but they may be passed not only 'down' but 'up' (as parents acquire beliefs from their children, for example), transversely (as siblings learn from each other), and obliquely (as children learn from non-related teachers, or adults learn from younger non-relatives; Cavalli-Sforza and Feldman, 1981; Boyd and Richerson, 1985; Richerson and Boyd, 2005). Our cultural practices are so deeply intertwined with all aspects of our lives and sociality that Richerson and Boyd (2005) argue that rather than culture being an emergent property of our evolution as a smart social ape (as was once thought), it is an intrinsic force helping shape human evolution.

Certainly it is true that cultural inventions feed back into social actions. Here, without attempting to define where things start and stop, I explore the mutual influences of essential resources and cultural practice in testing hypotheses: What influences marital residence? Are dowry and bride price randomly distributed?

What about infanticide, and discriminatory parental solicitude? In the face of such complexity, how resource conditions correlate with particular cultural aspects of mating and marriage systems is of interest. The underlying hypothesis is that the cultural institutions we see are those that, given the particulars of resource abundance, distribution, and economic defensibility, allow individuals in at least some lineages to profit both reproductively and (at least sometimes) in terms of physical resources.

30.1.3. Why polygyny is common

It is important to understand why polygyny is the default—likeliest, *ceteris paribus*—mating system among species that have gametic sexual reproduction, including humans. The 'male–female phenomenon'—a consistent pattern of differences between males and females in behaviour—is pervasive. There are two non-alternative reasons for this pattern, both resulting in profitability to making *either* large or small gametes (Parker *et al.*, 1972; Hurst, 1992, 1995; Hurst and Hamilton, 1992; Epelman *et al.*, 2005)—but not both. The evolution of anisogamy changes the costs and benefits for possessors of large versus small gametes, and means that small-gamete-makers ('males'), barring unusual ecological circumstances, profit most by specializing in high-risk, high-gain mating effort. If they spend parental effort (Low, 1978) it is likely to be of the generalizable sort (e.g. watching for predators). In contrast, large-gamete-makers ('females') have more to lose if an offspring is lost, and will specialize, *ceteris paribus*, in parental behaviour, which tends to have more linear returns for effort, and is often offspring-specific true parental investment (Trivers, 1972).

Whenever females can raise offspring successfully without male assistance, the mating system is likely to be polygynous; males will concentrate their effort on seeking matings. A female and her dependent offspring will comprise the ecologically independent unit. Females will be able to raise offspring alone when the offspring are precocial (as in chickens and many other bird species), or when she can provide for an altricial (helpless) child by herself. The first is common in many birds, and the second is true

of many primates (the mother nurses, carries and protects the infant, and although the father is often nearby and may occasionally play with the infant, he is primarily concerned with his own status and rank among males). When these conditions are met, by far the most common result is *female specialization in parental effort and male specialization in mating effort.*

For mammals, these biases are exacerbated, because females are physically and physiologically specialized for carrying the fetus internally, and for nourishing the offspring after birth. For both sexes in many mammals, five traits seem to contribute to reproductive success: age, body size, dominance rank, early development patterns (high early growth rate), and quality of mates chosen. For females, these typically contribute to getting good nutrition and converting it into healthy and successful offspring. For males, the pay-off is typically greater mating success.

When males take risks in direct mating competition, they are likely to die sooner than females. Thus, for males, lifetime breeding success is most variable in species with direct conflict over mating access, whether by prolonged defence of territories (as in elephant seals) or in competition over single females (e.g. some butterflies). Male lifetime breeding success tends to be least variable in species in which males compete indirectly, as in many human societies (more below).

30.2. The resource ecology of primate mating systems

30.2.1. Polygyny

Underneath all the complex 'add-ons' of our culture, we are primates; as Strier (2003) noted, primate studies can enrich our understanding of human systems. It is important to understand that ecological conditions (distribution of resources, safe cover, presence of predators, etc.) set the stage for the particulars of solitary-versus-group living, and that they interact with phylogenetic constraints to yield different mating systems (e.g. Strier, 2003). The result is richly patterned variation in the kind (e.g. all-female, all-male, mixed; kin, non-kin, mixed) and stability of groups. As noted above, within mammals, including primates, the fact that females are specialized to give postnatal nutritional care (nursing) means that there is a bias toward polygynous systems, but even within polygynous systems, resource distribution affects the type of polygyny. If reproductively useful resources are predictably abundant and economically defensible, there will be resource-defence polygyny (e.g. territoriality), as in the defence of birthing beaches by male elephant seals (e.g. Le Boeuf and Reiter, 1988). Among primates, however, moving groups of either a single male with multiple females, or multi-male/multi-female groups are more common than resource-defence polygyny.

In most primates, then, because females and their young comprise an independent ecological/economic unit (see Strier, 2003; Low, 2000, Chapter 4 for an overview), polygyny is the likeliest mating system. But the *kind* of polygyny is ecologically influenced. When the terrain is open, with little safe cover, predation risk is likely to be high—and groups will be larger than others that live in heavy cover.

About half of primate species live in multi-female groups. Females tend to distribute themselves in response to predation and food pressures and males, in turn, tend to distribute themselves around females (Ridley, 1986; Altmann, 1990; see also Strier, 2003, Chapter 5; Shuster and Wade, 2003). Two major hypotheses for the formation of primate groups are: (i) avoiding predation through 'selfish herd' groups (e.g. Hamilton, 1971; Cheney and Wrangham, 1987), and (ii) defence of food by multi-female groups (e.g. Wrangham, 1980; van Schaik and Hrdy, 1991; Barton *et al.*, 1996; van Schaik, 1989, 1996). It is not clear that these are true alternative hypotheses; both may operate.

Whether one or several males join a group of females depends, again, on ecological conditions. When predation pressure is high and food is rich, the likeliest result is multi-male/multi-female groups, as in savannah baboons. When predation is a risk, females are likely to forage in groups (e.g. Alexander, 1974) and the number of males in a group shifts with the number of females (e.g. Altmann, 1990; Mitani *et al.*, 1996). Female group size (the number of females available) appears to be the primary determinant of the number of males in a multi-male group (van Schaik and Hörstermann, 1994; Mitani *et al.*,

1996). In mountain populations of savannah baboons, males distribute themselves in an ideal free distribution in response to female availability (Henzi *et al.*, 1998); further, they 'herd' females when this will increase the distance between troops (and the likelihood of outsiders trying to join). Within multi-male groups, there is a strong correlation between male rank and reproductive success (e.g. review by Strier, 2003, pp. 168–170), but there are some clear costs to male reproductive striving: males who are mate-guarding feed less, and may suffer reduced energy intake (Alberts *et al.*, 1996) When female groups are small, a single male may succeed in monopolizing the group (e.g. Mitani *et al.*, 1996), although again, if predation risk is high, even small groups of females may have multiple male consorts (van Schaik and Hörstermann, 1994).

30.2.2. Monogamy and polyandry

Monogamous, single-pair primates are rare. There are three hypotheses about the evolution of monogamy in primates. One simply argues that when two-parent care is markedly more effective than maternal care alone, monogamy will evolve (e.g. Kurland and Gaulin, 1984; Wright, 1984). The second suggests that monogamy evolves when mated males are able to protect their infants from infanticide by other males in the group (e.g. van Schaik and Dunbar, 1990; van Schaik, 1996; van Schaik and Paul, 1996). The third suggests that for primates, as for many other species, ecological factors influence a male's ability to monopolize more than one female (e.g. Mitani, 1984). There are clear ecological implications for each hypothesis; sadly, there have been few tests.

Polyandry is even rarer than monogamy. Some tamarins are polyandrous: females give birth to large twins (about 25% of the mother's weight), who also grow rapidly. Soon after birth they are so large that the mother cannot carry both. The reproductive unit most commonly comprises a female and two males; both males help care for the offspring, carrying it, playing with it, and protecting it. The 'extra' male may be an unrelated male (in which case the female mates with both males) or a non-reproductive son who remains with his parents (Terborgh and Goldizen, 1985; Sussman and Garber, 1987; Goldizen and Terborgh, 1989).

30.2.3. Ecological and social interactions affect individual traits

These mating arrangements, created by the ecology of resources, have a further impact on individual traits (Harvey and Harcourt, 1984): individuals in pair-living monogamous, single-male polygynous, and multi-male polygynous species differ in extraordinary ways. Testis size, canine size, and male body size relative to female body size are all smallest in males living in monogamous arrangements. Males in single-male group species face high-risk, high-gain challenges from other males to fight for control of the females; they are physically much larger than females and have very large canines, as in gorillas.

Males in multi-male group-living species have a more subtle problem as well: other males are always about, sometimes in shifting coalitions. Sneak matings by other males in the group are, like overt fights, a serious problem. Males in such species are bigger than females (though not so strikingly as in single-male group species), have large canines, but also have extremely large testes. Here competition exists not only among individuals, but devolves to the level of sperm competition (e.g. see Dixson, 1983; Dixson and Anderson, 2004; Simmons *et al.*, 2004; Maestripieri and Roney, 2005). Males in socially monogamous pair-living species are not much larger than females and have, relative to body size, the smallest canines and the smallest testes. The ecology of group living thus influences male–male competition—and secondarily body size, canine size, and testis size (Harvey and Harcourt, 1984). Humans fit in the 'multi-male polygynous group' portion of the continuum (male body size moderately larger than female, testes relatively large), consistent with reports of 2–22% EPCs in socially monogamous as well as polygynous societies (Simmons *et al.*, 2004).

30.3. Human ecology, mating, and marriage

As noted above, humans have elaborated on these basic ecological patterns: we have not only the complexity of genetic versus social mating systems, but we have *marriage* systems as well as *mating* systems, and these are not identical (e.g. Betzig, 1997; Reichard and Boesch, 2003).

Thus, various relatives and even non-related third parties, can influence marriage arrangements (more below), with social impacts, although not necessarily any genetic influence. Far more than the self-interest of potential mates is involved; in fact, in most societies, the prospective bride and groom may not make the choice of mate—others, usually male relatives, do. Some basic patterns in human mating and marriage systems reflect social solutions to ecological problems. Other patterns reflect: (i) intensification of human sociality and intergroup conflict; (ii) elaboration of non-parental (mostly nepotistic) care and associated shifts in human life history; and (iii) extraordinary elaboration of non-kin 'third-party' influences in human social patterns (Low, 2003a). Each of these has important impacts on human mating and marriage systems.

30.3.1. Polygyny

For the reasons outlined above, under most ecological conditions, polygyny will be sought by males of most species. Humans are no exception: broad data about the prevalence of different marriage arrangements are found in Murdock's *Ethnographic Atlas* (1967), *Atlas of World Cultures* (1981), and Murdock and White's *Standard Cross-Cultural Sample* (1969). They suggest that about 83% of societies are polygynous, almost none (0.05%) are polyandrous, and those societies coded as 'monogamous' are mostly 'monogamous or mildly polygynous,' and thus genetically polygynous. In part this may be because human males, for a variety of reasons, appear to have solved many problems that lead to monogamy in other primates without relinquishing polygyny. A man need not guard his wife if he has family (or eunuchs) to do so; mate guarding is clearly present and effective in many polygynous societies. Human residence patterns mean that men are able to monopolize multiple females under most conditions. Most societies are patrilocal, so that a man lives among his kin and a woman comes to live among her husband's kin. Groups of related males can effectively defend resources, including wives.

Environmental conditions correlate in interesting ways with marriage systems. In theory, one would expect fluctuations in major environmental variables (those that, like rainfall, may strongly influence certain resource availabilities) to be associated with increased variance in men's abilities to compete for resources, and thus polygyny. Further, when resources can be effectively garnered by women, the possibility of polygyny should be enhanced; that is, when women can provide the resources necessary for healthy children, men can concentrate their efforts into acquiring more wives (and the subsequent reproductive success thus generated). In contrast, when a father must contribute true parental investment to his offspring, he has less available for mating effort. And indeed there appear to be some associations. As rainfall becomes more constant, the degree of polygyny decreases, and the more that women contribute to the subsistence base, the more polygynous the society is likely to be (Low, 1990a).

30.3.1.1. Pathogens, disease, and the distribution of polygyny

In a curious interaction, the ecology of pathogen and disease transmission interacts with mating (and subsequently, marriage) systems. Hamilton and colleagues (Hamilton, 1980, 1982; Hamilton and Zuk; 1982; Hamilton et al., 1990) argued that pathogens might provide the kind of environmental unpredictability that would foster the evolution of sex; subsequent work (Low, 1988, 1990b) suggested that pathogens might also influence sexual selection. Indeed, if one examines the distribution of pathogens with the characteristics specified by Hamilton (life threatening, leaving a mark), there is an association with marriage rules. The pattern is not linear, because men are likely to seek polygyny whenever possible: it is simply that monogamy disappears in high-pathogen stress areas (Low, 1990b).

Polygyny, no matter how it is measured, increases with the level of exposure to pathogens meeting Hamilton's criteria. Level of pathogen stress alone accounts for 28% of the variation in the degree of polygyny around the world, independent of geographic region or any other factor (Low, 1988, 1990b, 2003a). Under high pathogen stress, a woman's best strategy may be to become the second or subsequent wife of a healthy man (a form of Orians' polygyny

threshold; Orians, 1969). For men the situation is more complex. A successfully polygynous man has more children than a monogamous one. Across societies, non-sororal polygyny is somewhat more common than sororal polygyny, but in areas of high pathogen stress, not only does monogamy disappear, but the sororal-non-sororal difference is exaggerated. Men may profit genetically from this shift: their children will not be more numerous, but genetically more variable (Low, 1990). Here it is worth noting that, in several mammalian species, including humans, some male-female 'matches' in the major histocompatibility complex (MHC), result in improved offspring immunocompetence. That is, rather than a uniform preference for 'good genes' in this highly polymorphic region, there may be mate preferences (by both males and females) for mates who will produce more heterozygous offspring (e.g. Potts et al., 1991; Jordan and Bruford, 1998; Penn and Potts, 1999; Tregenza and Wedell, 2000; Roberts et al., 2006).

However, there are potential costs to polygyny in terms of other kinds of diseases and pathogens, principally from sexually transmitted diseases. Nunn et al. (2000, 2003) found, in both primates and carnivores, that the prevalence of multiple matings correlated with heightened white blood cell counts (a reflection of increased disease exposure). They concluded that the risk of sexually transmitted diseases may well be a major factor leading to systematic differences in immune system. Comparative population analyses within humans are in their infancy (Goncalves et al., 2003, 2004), and this is a fruitful avenue to explore.

30.3.2. Monogamy and polyandry

The ecological conditions that favour greater male expenditure on offspring-specific true parental investment include: (i) relatively safe adult life (low mortality), combined with conditions that (ii) allow adults to extend that safety to their offspring (e.g. species like geese), resulting in (iii) greatly enhanced offspring success with care by more than one parent. As noted above, men have often circumvented these culturally under many conditions, allowing them to invest without the constraints of true genetic monogamy.

Fewer than 16% of traditional human societies are socially monogamous. What this means is unclear, because social monogamy seldom reflects genetic monogamy (Reichard and Boesch, 2003). Many socially monogamous societies—societies with one-spouse-at-a-time rules—would be polygynous in a biological definition: more men than women fail to marry, and more men than women remarry after death or divorce, producing families in these later unions. The most reproductive men have many more children than the most fertile women. These things mean that the variance of men's reproductive success is high compared to women's. However, we seldom have the data to calculate the biologically important relationships from anthropological data.

Social monogamy is unevenly distributed geographically. Almost 45% of living arrangements in 'circum-Mediterranean' societies are coded as some form of monogamy, and four forms are described. In contrast, only 2.7% of African societies are considered monogamous, and these three societies are all independent nuclear families (Low 2003a). Many ethnographies suggest that monogamy is more common in relatively harsh ecological conditions (e.g. very dry, very cold, low plant productivity), which perhaps might make monogamous two-parent care reproductively advantageous (also true for polyandry, see below). Although the examples are suggestive, there are no clear statistical patterns, probably for two reasons: (i) there are few 'monogamous' societies with sufficient data to test; and (ii) the use of the term 'monogamy' is anthropological—it means monogamous-to-mildly polygynous. There are some statistically significant associations between social monogamy and certain environmental conditions (Low 1989, 2003a). Within monogamous societies, it could be rewarding to explore the strength of ecological influences on family organization, which might be more responsive to ecological constraints than monogamy itself. Social monogamy in humans includes many forms, and some of these seem likely to have quite different biological impacts.

Polyandry, even rarer than monogamy in human marriage arrangements, is almost always fraternal (brothers marry a single woman), and appears to result from brother–brother coalitions in order to combat resource scarcity or from attempts to control the distribution of a resource like land, which is immobile and loses its value when too finely divided. Polyandry is rare for several reasons, including the fact that men who share sexual access to one woman will have fewer descendants under most circumstances than men who have either sole access to one woman or access to more than one woman. However, as Mace (1997) points out, such men may fare no worse than younger brothers in systems with primogeniture, in which the oldest son inherits but younger sons do not. Polyandry simply throws these conflicts into sharp relief.

Resource constrictions clearly affect these costs and benefits. Among the Nyimba of northwestern Nepal, brothers marry a single woman, but if there are more than two brothers in the marriage, the likelihood of 'conjoint' marriage (adding another wife) or 'partitioning' (in which one or more brothers leaves the household and forms a new household) is greatly increased (Levine and Silk, 1997).

30.4. Social correlates in human systems

Human social conventions, just like canine size and testis size in primates in general, might be expected to vary with mating system. Hartung (1982, 1983, 1997) found that inheritance tends to be male-biased in polygynous systems; in such systems, resources influence male reproductive success more than female reproductive success. In bride-price systems, for example, young, high-reproductive-value women may cost more than older women (Borgerhoff Mulder, 1988, 1995)—which means that wealthier men can have more, and younger, wives than other men. Cowlishaw and Mace (1996), using a phylogenetic approach, confirmed this pattern, and Mace's further work (Mace, 1998, 2000) has modelled the ways in which such systems are likely to succeed.

Although polygyny is the commonest marriage system across human societies, it is also true that human males are extraordinarily paternal. None the less, patterns of paternal investment vary greatly across societies, apparently independent of the marriage system. In polygynous societies with low confidence of paternity (e.g. where men and women live apart), it is common for children's maternal uncles to invest in them, rather than their (putative or nominal) father, for example. In traditional societies with few heritable resources, stepfathers may invest as much time and training in stepchildren as in their genetic children (e.g. Hewlett, 1992; Hewlett *et al.*, 2000). In modern socially monogamous (but genetically polygynous) societies with remarriage, there exist both high resource stakes and considerable step-parenting. In these conditions, stepchildren are, in many societies, more vulnerable than genetic children to lowered investment (Anderson *et al.*, 1999a,b; Lancaster and Kaplan, 2000; Hofferth and Anderson, 2003), child abuse, and infanticide (Daly and Wilson, 1984, 1985, 1987, 1988; see review in Low, 2000, Chapter 6).

Dowry, a marriage system in which the bride's family gives resources to the groom or groom's family, is 50 times more common in monogamous, stratified societies than in polygynous or non-stratified monogamous ones (Gaulin and Boster, 1990, 1997; Lang, 1993); in these societies males typically vary greatly in their status and wealth. Women married to wealthy, high-status men benefit reproductively, so it pays would-be brides (usually, the brides' fathers) to compete, bargaining for wealthier men as mates. In many of these societies, poorer women's families must pay more dowry than wealthy women's families; dowry becomes a form of mate competition among women (Gaulin and Boster, 1990, 1997; Srinivasan, 2005). Such mate competition may have costs, as in modern rural India. Since about 1950, demographic shifts have resulted in declining numbers of potential grooms for potential brides of marriageable ages—and dowries have risen steadily. By 1990, a dowry was likely to be over 50% of a household's assets. Wives from poor families, able to pay less in dowry, are less likely to marry; if they marry, they have a high risk of being abused by their husbands. Further, domestic violence and spousal abuse have correlated with increases in dowry worth; 'insufficient dowry' is an important recorded cause of spousal abuse (Rao, 1993a, 1993b, 1997).

30.4.1. **Further social rules and ecological influences**

A number of social rules surround marriage. Some of these, like rules of marital residence, appear to arise from the ecology of resource distribution. Fully two-thirds of the 862 societies in Murdock (1967) mandate living with the husband's kin. There are, of course, complexities: the rule may involve either patrilocality or virilocality (these are equivalent except for the details of how the man's kin are distributed spatially), and may also have a minor pattern, or different rules, for the first years of marriage. Matrilocality, living with the wife's kin, is relatively rare and is associated with external warfare combined with women contributing greatly to subsistence (Ember and Ember, 1971).

Consider marriage arrangements as alliance formation: in terms both of getting and protecting resources from others, and in terms of resource impact on reproductive success, men typically profit more from alliances than do women. It does appear than many arrangements cross-culturally favour men's interests over women's when there is a conflict. In Whyte's (1978, 1979) examination of women's status in pre-industrial societies (using the 93 odd-numbered societies of the Standard Cross-Cultural Sample), the most common patterns favoured men's interests. In terms of the older generation's rule in arranging marriages, men (fathers, uncles) monopolize arrangements or have more say than women in 55% of societies. With regard to the influence of the potential bride and groom, men had more ability to initiate or refuse arrangements in 34% of societies; women in 4%. Women moved farther away from their natal localities than did men in 69% of societies. Mild-to-strong institutionalized deference of wife to husband exists in 66% of societies. We typically think of such norms as 'simply cultural' but I suggest that although the 'resource connection' to these norms may be hidden, it helps generate the patterns we see.

The relative importance of resource control for men's versus women's reproductive success plays out further in an interesting and widespread set of patterns: prohibitions and preferences in cousin marriages. In many societies, first cousins are the preferred or mandated mates. Genealogically, a man might marry any of four types of first cousin:

1. His father's brother's daughter (FBD).

2. His mother's brother's daughter (MBD).

3. His father's sister's daughter (FZD).

4. His mother's sister's daughter (MZD).

The first and fourth of these are called 'parallel cousin' marriages (the parent and his/her sibling are the same sex); the second and third are called 'cross-cousin' marriages. For some time, anthropologists considered the choice of type of cousin to be purely a cultural phenomenon. For example, Murdock (1949, p. 287) argued that "Since the daughters of the father's brother, father's sister, mother's brother, and mother's sister are consanguineally related to male Ego in exactly the same degree, all intercultural differences in marriage regulations applying to the several types of cousins represent divergences from biological expectations."

However, as Flinn and Low (1986) pointed out, this is an incomplete idea of the concept of 'biological expectations'. The ecology of resource concentration—who gets how much of what—leads to a far more complex set of predictions; part of the underlying hypothesis is that marriage rules and preferences will be manipulated in the reproductive interests of those who control them. For example, societies with symmetrical cross-cousin marriage rules (either FZD or MBD allowed) also tend to exchange women (rather than goods or resources): these societies are also characterized by poor resource bases and the absence of inheritance rules (Flinn and Low, 1986). In richer resource areas, asymmetrical cousin-marriage rules also show relationships to resource distribution and men's coalitions around resource control. The most striking, perhaps, is that MZD, which would enhance nepotism and reciprocity among *female* kin, is virtually unknown, regardless of other factors. The other asymmetrical rules (FBD, MBD, FZD) all enhance the power of coalitions among male relatives, and are associated with residency patterns that enhance the particular kind of male coalition (e.g. FBD is associated with patrilocal residency, while MBD is associated with avunculocal residency; see Cronk and Gerkey, this volume, Chapter 31).

30.5. Conflicts between the sexes and third-party interests

Marriage is about far more than simple mating. The partitioning of polyandrous households among the Nyimba (above) resulted from conflicts of interests among brothers. Such reproductive conflicts of interests—not only between polyandrous brothers, but between co-wives and the two sexes—add, along with third-party interests, further complexity and variation to the mating and marriage arrangements of humans.

Women seldom fully share men's reproductive interests, and each partner has kin who may act to shift the balance of reproductive costs and benefits. In socially monogamous systems, the reproductive interests of parents typically converge to some degree, but this does not necessarily protect women's reproductive interests. Women's interests seldom converge completely with their husbands' even in socially monogamous situations. Consider socially monogamous modern Thailand: studies of men's and women's attitudes about sexual matters (Knodel *et al.*, 1997) highlight this sexual conflict of interests. There is a long tradition of men, married as well as single, visiting sex workers in the context of men's social evenings out. In addition, some men have 'minor wives' whom they support at least partially. Thai wives have historically had little ability to constrain these behaviours, and have held a long-standing preference that their husbands, if sexually active outside marriage, visit sex workers, because the transaction is brief, and represents only a minor diversion of resources from the wife and children. In contrast, a minor wife can represent a real drain of resources. However, with the spread of HIV, an increasing proportion of women prefer the husband to have a minor wife; while the resource conflict is heightened, the health risks are reduced.

When marriage systems concern not only male and female reproductive interests, but the interests of third parties, those third parties (particularly kin) can influence social patterns. Third-party interests are particularly elaborated in humans: there can be legal and political arrangements that enforce marriage arrangements in the interests of third parties, even when those parties are not present. Specific areas of the law (e.g. family law and part of criminal law) deal in particular with third-party interests in sexual behaviour, reproduction (and the avoidance of reproduction), and conflict resolution within families (e.g. see Jones and Goldsmith, 2005).

In many societies, parents may use children's marriages to form alliances with wealthy and powerful families. In some societies, children are betrothed well before puberty; in a few societies, they are promised even before birth. Among the Arunta of central Australia, for example, a couple may be betrothed even before birth, and the marriage will take place even if the parents who made those arrangements have died.

In most societies, social and cultural inventions such as marriage, divorce, inheritance, involve the interests of other individuals— sometimes individuals with no apparent interest in the particular decision (caliphs, ministers, shamans, etc.). Such human-invented conventions, like physical resource conditions, affect the costs and benefits of marriage for individuals. Thus, marriage patterns in humans follow a variety of rules, as ecological and socio-cultural complexities interact.

30.6. When culture and ecology interact

Most of the cultural rules about mating and marriage discussed above have clear ecological influences. In theory we can invent *any* sort of cultural innovation. We can invent cultural innovations that are, in fact, deleterious to the persistence of our lineage—nothing prohibits that. In fact, because we did not evolve to consider issues like reproductive success as conscious goals, perhaps biologically deleterious practices should arise frequently. Whether such innovations spread and persist is another issue (e.g. see Richerson and Boyd, 2005, pp. 235–236).

Consider celibacy. Individual decisions to become celibate probably have little effect on lineage persistence (unless, of course, it is your only child who becomes celibate). Institutionalized celibacy can present another situation. In the Catholic Church, celibacy was not always required of the religious, but it has been mandated now for several hundred years (priestly

marriage was forbidden in 1139, but effective enforcement appears to date from the Council of Trent in 1545–1563). When Catholic families were large, the designation of a younger son for a celibate life in the Church resulted in lowered competition among brothers (for example, land inheritance), some elevation of status from having a priest in the family, and possibly some resource improvement also. Celibacy did not spell the death of lineages; in fact, it could be profitable to a lineage. In contrast, today's Catholic Church is having difficulty in the wealthier parts of the world in recruiting people for the celibate religious life. A devout family faces a difficult decision if there is only one son and he is being urged into the priesthood (e.g. Rice, 1990; Sipe, 1990). The Shakers, too, required celibacy in relatively modern times; few of them remain alive today. Nothing prohibits our invention of rules that might be reproductively deleterious, even ridiculous—but such rules will not become and remain the common rules.

Similarly, the strong son-preference of several modern Asian nations, within the context of large-scale cultural rules (e.g. China's One Child Policy during the 1980s) and modern technology, has created an interesting ecological problem for many lineages (see review in Low, 2000, Chapter 10). Even before the One Child Policy, large-scale rules—rules not even aimed at reproduction—resulted in frequent dramatic increases in mortality and decreases in fertility. The social and political upheavals of state interventions such as the Cultural Revolution and the Great Leap Forward created high birth deficits, and high mortality, particularly in rural areas (Ting, 2004a,b). These rules were not intended to affect fertility and mortality, but were principally aimed at compressing income and educational opportunities across social classes (Ting, 2004a). In response, white-collar parents appear to have made a quantity–quality trade-off, having fewer children but educating them better than lower-status parents; the disruption of families (e.g. sending educational elites to work in rural areas) also heightened mortality rates. In an analysis of three Chinese provinces over 50 years (Ting, 2004a,b), only one natural event (an earthquake in Hebei Province) created a shift in mortality that could even be detected at the scale of the effects of the political rules. The unintended impact of these rules on overall population parameters was, in fact, far greater (through impacts on birth and death rates) than the One Child Policy (Ting, 2004a,b).

Although the One Child Policy had little effect on population numbers, the proportion of families with just one child did increase, and family sex ratios shifted—principally in third and fourth births. The sex ratio for first births was 105.6 (the same as the world average). The sex ratio of third births when there were already two daughters was 224.5; when there were already two sons, it was 74.1 (Peng, 1991; Wen, 1993). The result has been a change in what biologists call the 'operational sex ratio'—the sex ratio of potential mates in the adult population. Now, men born in the 1980s are having trouble finding brides. In parts of Korea, Japan, and India, a similar situation obtains. It will be interesting to see, as brides become rare and valuable, whether the value of daughters will increase, as some theoretical studies suggest (Kumm and Feldman, 1997).

Women in the Western developed nations of the world also face a conflict between social goals and reproductive success. Seeking hard-won social gains like equal pay is laudable, but it is also clear by now that women face harsh trade-offs when it comes to having children, gaining resources, and allocating those resources to them. Below-replacement fertility is now common in several Western European nations, and in the USA fertility is just above replacement levels. It is clear that, whether the demographic transition made ecological sense in terms of switching from high fertility to high investment in competitive circumstances (Becker 1991; Becker and Lewis 1974; Easterlin, 1978; Low, 1993, 2003b), Western women's current reproductive patterns no longer make any ecological sense (Borgerhoff Mulder, 1998; Low *et al.*, 2002, 2003; Richerson and Boyd, 2005).

The more we examine the connections between cultural practices and human reproduction, the clearer it becomes that most really persistent cultural practices, perhaps especially those of mating and marriage, usually make ecological sense. Examples of cultural institutions and/or practices that run counter to our evolution are instructive. In a sense, we are our own experiment.

References

Alberts, S. C., Altmann, J. and Wilson, M. L. (1996) Mate guarding constrains foraging activity of male baboons. *Animal Behaviour*, 51: 1269–1277.

Alexander, R. D. (1974) The evolution of social behavior. *Annual Review of Ecology and Systematics*, 5: 325–383.

Alexander, R. D. (1979) *Darwinism and Human Affairs*. University of Washington Press, Seattle.

Altmann, J. (1990) Primate males go where the females are. *Animal Behaviour*, 39: 193–195.

Anderson, K. G., Kaplan, H., Lam, D. and Lancaster, J. B. (1999a) Paternal care by genetic and step fathers II: Reports by Xhosa high school students. *Evolution and Human Behavior*, 20: 433–51

Anderson, K. G., Kaplan, H. and Lancaster, J. B. (1999b) Paternal care by genetic fathers and stepfathers. I: Reports by Albuquerque men. *Evolution and Human Behavior*, 20: 405–431.

Barton, R. A., Byrne, R. W. and Whiten, A. (1996) Ecology, feeding competition, and social structure in baboons. *Behavioral Ecology and Sociobiology*, 38: 3211–329.

Becker, G. S. (1991) A treatise on the family. Harvard University Press, Cambridge MA.

Becker, G. and Lewis, H. G. (1974) Interaction between quantity and quality of children. In: T. Schultz *Economics of the family: marriage, children and human capital*, pp. 81–90. University of Chicago Press, Chicago.

Betzig, L. (1997) People are animals. In: L. Betzig (ed) *Human Nature: a critical reader* pp. 1–11. Oxford University Press, Oxford.

Borgerhoff Mulder, M. (1988) Kipsigis bridewealth payments. In M. Betzig, M. Borgerhoff Mulder and P. Turke (ed.) *Human Reproductive Behavior: A Darwinian Perspective*, pp. 65–82. Cambridge University Press, Cambridge.

Borgerhoff Mulder, M. (1995) Bridewealth and its correlates. *Current Anthropology*, 36: 573–603.

Borgerhoff Mulder, M. (1998) The demographic transition: are we any closer to an evolutionary explanation? *Trends in Ecology and Evolution*, 13: 266–270.

Boyd, R. and Richerson, P. J. (1985) *Culture and the Evolutionary Process*. University of Chicago Press, Chicago.

Cavalli-Sforza, L. L. and Feldman, M. W. (1981) *Cultural Transmission and Evolution*. Princeton University Press, Princeton, NJ.

Cheney, D. and Wrangham, R. (1987) Predation. In B. Smuts, D. Cheney, R. Seyfarth, R. Wrangham and T. Struhsaker (ed.) *Primate Societies*, pp. 227–239. University of Chicago Press, Chicago.

Cowlishaw, G. and Mace, R. (1996) Cross-cultural patterns of marriage and inheritance: a phylogenetic approach. *Ethology and Sociobiology*, 17: 87–97.

Daly, M. and Wilson, M. (1984) A sociobiological analysis of human infanticide. In G. Hausfater and S. B. Hrdy (ed.) *Infanticide: Comparative and Evolutionary Perspectives*, pp. 1271–1274. Aldine de Gruyter, New York.

Daly, M. and Wilson, M. (1985) Child abuse and other risks of not living with both parents. *Ethology and Sociobiology*, 6: 197–210.

Daly, M. and Wilson, M. (1987) Children as homicide victims. In R. J. Gelles and J. Lancaster (eds) *Child Abuse and Neglect: Biosocial Dimensions*, pp. 201–14. Aldine de Gruyter, New York.

Daly, M. and Wilson, M. (1988) Evolutionary social-psychology and family homicide. *Science*, 242: 519–524.

Davies, N. (1992) *Dunnock Behaviour and Social Evolution*. Oxford University Press, Oxford.

Dixson, A. F. (1983) Observations on the evolution and behavioral significance of "sexual skin" in female primates. *Advances in the Study of Behavior*, 13: 63–106.

Dixson, A. F. and Anderson, M. J. (2004) Sexual behavior, reproductive physiology and sperm competition in male mammals. *Physiology and Behavior*, 83: 361–371.

Dunbar, R. (2003) The social brain: mind, language, and society in evolutionary perspective. *Annual Review of Anthropology* 32: 163–181.

Easterlin, R. (1978) The economics and sociology of fertility: a synthesis. In C. Tilly (ed.) *Historical Studies of Changing Fertility*, pp. 57–134. Princeton University Press, Princeton, NJ.

Ember, M. and Ember, C. R. (1971) The conditions favoring matrilocal versus patrilocal residence. *American Anthropologist*, 73: 571–194.

Epelman, M. A., Pollack, S., Netter, B. and Low, B. (2005) Anisogamy, expenditure of reproductive effort, and the optimality of having two sexes. *Operations Research*, 53: 560–567.

Flinn, M. V. and Low, B. S. (1986) Resource distribution, social competition, and mating patterns in human societies. In *Ecological Aspects of Social Evolution* (ed.) D. Rubenstein, R. Wrangham, pp. 217–43. Princeton University Press, Princeton, NJ.

Gaulin, S. J.C. and Boster, J. (1990) Dowry as female competition. *American Anthropologist*, 92: 994–1005.

Gaulin, S. J.C. and Boster, J. (1997) When are husbands worth fighting for? In *Human Nature: A Critical Reader* (ed.) L. Betzig, pp. 372–374. Oxford University Press, Oxford, UK.

Goldizer, A. W. & Terborgh, J. (1989) Demography and dispersal patterns of a tamarin population: possible causes of delayed breeding. *American Naturalist*, 134: 208–224.

Goncalves, S., Kuperman, M. and Ferreira da Costa Gomes, M. (2003) Promiscuity and the evolution of sexual transmitted diseases. *Physica A: Statistical Mechanics and its Applications*, 327: 6–11.

Goncalves, S., Kuperman, M. and Ferreira da Costa Gomes, M. (2004) A social model for the evolution of sexually transmitted diseases. *Physica A: Statistical Mechanics and its Applications*, 342: 256–262.

Hamilton, W. D. (1971) Geometry for the selfish herd. *Theoretical Biology*, 31: 295–311.

Hamilton, W. D. (1980) Sex versus non-sex versus parasite. *Oikos*, 35: 282–290.

Hamilton, W. D. (1982) Pathogens as causes of genetic diversity in their host populations. In R. M. Anderson,

R. M. May (ed.) *Population Biology of Infectious Diseases*, pp. 269–296. Springer, New York.

Hamilton, W. D., Axelrod, R. and Tanese, R. (1990) Sexual reproduction as an adaptation to resist parasites (a review). *Proceedings of the National Academy of Sciences of the USA*, 87: 3566–3573.

Hamilton, W. D. and Zuk, M. (1982) Heritable true fitness and bright birds: a role for parasites? *Science*, 218: 384–387.

Hartung, J. (1982) Polygyny and the inheritance of wealth. *Current Anthropology*, 23: 1–12.

Hartung, J. (1983) In defense of Murdock: a reply to Dickemann. *Current Anthropology*, 24: 125–126.

Hartung, J. (1997) If I had it to do over. In L. Betzig (ed.) *Human Nature: A Critical Reader*, pp. 344–348. Oxford University Press, Oxford.

Harvey, P. and Harcourt, A. H. (1984) Sperm competition, testis size and breeding systems in primates. In R. L. Smith (ed.) *Sperm Competition and the Evolution of Animal Mating Systems*, pp. 589–600. Academic Press, New York.

Henzi, S. P., Lycett, J. E. and Weingrill, T. (1998) Mate guarding and risk assessment by male mountain baboons during inter-troop encounters. *Animal Behaviour*, 55: 1421–1428.

Hewlett, B. S. (ed.) (1992) *Father–Child Relations: Cultural and Biosocial Contexts*. Aldine, Chicago.

Hewlett, B. S., Lamb, M. E., Leyendecker, B. and Scholmerich, A. (2000) Parental strategies among Aka foragers, Ngandu farmers, and Euro-American urban-industrialists. In L. Cronk, N. Chagnon and W. Irons (ed.) *Adaptation and Human Behavior: An Anthropological Perspective*, pp. 155–178. Aldine de Gruyter, New York.

Hill, R. A. and Dunbar, R. I. M. (2003) Social network size in humans. *Human Nature*, 14: 53–72.

Hofferth, S., Anderson, K. G. (2003) Are all dads equal? Biology versus marriage as basis for paternal investment. *Journal of Marriage and Family*, 65: 213–232.

Hurst, L. (1992) Intragenomic conflict as an evolutionary force. *Proceedings of the Royal Society of London, B*, 244: 91–99.

Hurst, L. (1995) Selfish genetic elements and their role in evolution: the evolution of sex and some of what that entails. *Philosophical Transactions of the Royal Society of London, B*, 349: 321–332.

Hurst, L. and Hamilton, W. D. (1992) Cytoplasmic fusion and the nature of sexes. *Proceedings of the Royal Society of London, B*, 247: 189–207.

Jones, O. D. and Goldsmith, T. H. (2005) Law and behavioral biology. *Columbia Law Review*, 105: 405–502.

Jordan, W. C. and Bruford, M. W. (1998) New perspectives on mate choice and the MHC. *Heredity*, 81: 239–245.

Knodel, J., Low, B., Saengtienschai, C. and Lucas, R. (1997) An evolutionary perspective on Thai sexual attitudes and behavior. *Journal of Sex Research*, 34: 292–303.

Kumm, J. and Feldman, M. W. (1997) Gene-culture coevolution and sex ratios: II. Sex-chromosomal distorters and cultural preferences for offspring sex. *Theoretical Population Biology*, 52: 1–15.

Kurland, J. and Gaulin, S. J. C. (1984) The evolution of male parental investment: effects of genetic relatedness and feeding ecology on the allocation of reproductive effort. In D. M. Taub (ed.) *Primate Paternalism*, pp. 259–306. Van Nostrand Reinhold, New York.

Lancaster, J. B. and Kaplan, H. S. (2000) Parenting other men's children: costs, benefits and consequences. In L. Cronk, N. Chagnon and W. Irons (ed.) *Human Behavior and Adaptation: An Anthropological Perspective*. Aldine de Gruyter, New York. PAGES

Lang, H. (1993) Dowry and female competition: A boolean reanalysis. *Current Anthropology* 34: 775–778.

Le Boeuf, B. and Reiter, J. (1988) Lifetime reproductive success in Northern elephant seals. In T. H. Clutton-Brock (ed.) *Reproductive Success: Studies of Individual Variation in Contrasting Breeding Systems*, pp. 344–383. University of Chicago Press, Chicago.

Levine, N. E. and Silk, J. B. (1997) Why polyandry fails. *Current Anthropology*, 38: 375–388.

Low, B. S. (1978) Environmental uncertainty and the parental strategies of marsupials and placentals. *American Naturalist*, 112: 197–213.

Low, B. S. (1988) Pathogen stress and polygyny in humans. In L. Betzig, M. Borgerhoff Mulder and P. Turke (ed.) *Human Reproductive Behaviour: A Darwinian Perspective*, pp. 115–128. Cambridge University Press, Cambridge.

Low, B. S. (1989) Human responses to environmental extremeness and uncertainty: a cross-cultural perspective. In *Risk and Uncertainty in Tribal and Peasant Economies* (ed.) E. Cashdan, pp. 229–255. Westview Press, Boulder, CO.

Low, B. S. (1990a) Human responses to environmental extremeness and uncertainty: a cross-cultural perspective. In E. Cashdan (ed.) *Risk and Uncertainty in Tribal and Peasant Economies*, pp. 229–255. Westview Press, Boulder, CO.

Low, B. S. (1990b) Marriage systems and pathogen stress in human societies. *American Zoologist*, 30: 325–339.

Low, B. S. (2000) *Why Sex Matters*. Princeton University Press, Princeton, NJ.

Low, B. S. (1993) Ecological demography: a synthetic focus in evolutionary anthropology. *Evolutionary Anthropology*, 2: 176–187.

Low, B. S. (2003a) Ecological and social complexities in human monogamy. In U. H. Reichard and C. Boesch (ed.) *Monogamy: Mating Strategies and Partnerships in Birds, Humans, and Other Mammals*, pp. 161–176. Cambridge University Press, Cambridge.

Low, B. S. (2003b) *Sex, Wealth, and Fertility—Old Rules, New Environments*, pp. 323–344.

Low, B. S., Simon, C. P. and Anderson, K. G. (2002) An evolutionary ecological perspective on demographic transitions: modeling multiple currencies. *American Journal of Human Biology* 14: 149–67.

Low, B. S., Simon, C. P. and Anderson, K. G. (2003) The biodemography of modern women: tradeoffs when resources become limiting. In J. L. Rodgers and H. P. Kohler (ed.) *The Biodemography of Human Reproduction and Fertility*, pp. 105–134. Kluwer Academic Publishers, Boston.

Mace, R. (1997) Commentary on Levine and Silk. *Current Anthropology*, 38: 396.

Mace, R. (1998) The coevolution of human fertility and wealth inheritance strategies. *Philosophical Transactions of the Royal Society of London, B*, 353: 389–397.

Mace, R. (2000) An adaptive model of human reproductive rate where wealth is inherited. In L. Cronk, N. Chagnon and W. Irons (ed.) *Adaptation and Human Behavior: An Anthropological Perspective*, pp. 261–281. Aldine de Gruyter, Hawthorne, NY.

Maestripieri, D. and Roney, J.R. (2005) Primate copulation calls and postcopulatory female choice. *Behavioral Ecology*, 16: 106–113.

Mitani J. (1984) The behavioral regulation of monogamy in gibbons (*Hylobates muelleri*). *Behavioral Ecology and Sociobiology*, 15: 225–229.

Mitani, J., GrosLouis, J. and Manson, J. (1996) Number of males in primate groups: comparative tests of competing hypotheses. *American Journal of Primatology*, 38: 315–332.

Murdock, G. P. (1967) *Ethnographic Atlas*. University of Pittsburgh Press, Pittsburgh.

Murdock, G. P. (1981) *Atlas of World Cultures*. University of Pittsburgh Press, Pittsburgh.

Murdock, G.P and White D. (1969) Standard cross-cultural sample. *Ethnology*, 8: 329–369.

Nunn, C. L., Gittleman, J. and Antonovics, J. (2000) Promiscuity and the primate immune system. *Science*, 290: 1168–1170.

Nunn, C. L., Gittleman, J. and Antonovics, J. (2003) A comparative study of white blood cell counts and disease risk in carnivores. *Proceedings of the Royal Society of London, B*, 270: 347–356.

Orians, G. (1969) On the evolution of mating systems in birds and mammals. *American Naturalist*, 103: 589–603.

Parker, G. A., Baker, R. R. and Smith, V. G. F. (1972) The origin and evolution of gamete dimorphism and the male–female phenomenon. *Journal Theoretical Biology*, 36: 529–553.

Peng, X. (1991) *Demographic Transition in China*. Clarendon Press, Oxford.

Penn, D. J. and Potts, W. K. (1999) The evolution of mating preferences and major histocompatibility complex genes. *American Naturalist*, 153: 145–164.

Potts, W. K., Manning, C. J. and Wakeland, E. K. (1991) Mating patterns in seminatural populations of mice influenced by MHC genotype. *Nature*, 352: 619–621.

Rao, V. (1993a) Dowry "inflation" in rural India: a statistical investigation. *Population Studies*, 47: 283–293.

Rao V. (1993b) The rising price of husbands: a hedonic analysis of dowry increases in rural India. *Journal of Political Economics*, 101: 666–677.

Rao, V. (1997) Wife-beating in rural south India: a qualitative and econometric analysis. *Social Science and Medicine*, 44: 1169–1180.

Reichard, U. and Boesch, C. (2003) *Monogamy: Mating Strategies and Partnerships in Birds, Humans, and Other Mammals*. Cambridge University Press, Cambridge.

Rice, D. (1990) *Shattered Vows: Priests Who Leave*. Triumph, New York.

Richerson, P. J. and Boyd, R. (2005) *Not by Genes Alone: How Culture Transformed Human Evolution*. University of Chicago Press, Chicago.

Ridley, M. (1986) The number of males in a primate troup. *Animal Behaviour*, 34: 1848–1858.

Roberts, S. C., Hale, M. L. and Petrie, M. (2006) Correlations between heterozygosity and measures of genetic similarity: implications for understanding mate choice. *Journal of Evolutionary Biology*, 19: 558–569.

Shuster, S. M. and Wade, M. J. (2003) *Mating Systems and Strategies*. Princeton University Press, Princeton, NJ.

Simmons, L. W., Firman, R. C., Rhodes, G. and Peters, M. (2004) Human sperm competition: testis size, sperm production and rates of extrapair copulations. *Animal Behaviour*, 68: 297–302.

Sipe, A. (1990) *A Secret World: Sexuality and the Search for Celibacy*. Brunner Mazel, New York.

Srinivasan, S. (2005) Daughters or dowries? The changing nature of dowry practices in south India. *World Development*, 33: 593–615.

Strier, K. (2003) Primate behavioral ecology: from ethnography to ethology and back. *American Anthropologist*, 105: 16–27.

Sussman, R. W. & Garber, P. A. (1987) A new interpretation of the social organisation of the callitrichidae. *International Journal of Primatology*, 8: 73–92.

Terborgh, J. and Goldizen, A. W. (1985) On the Mating System of the cooperatively breeding saddle-backed tamarin (*saguinus fuscicollis*) *Behavioral Ecology & Sociobiology*, 16: 293–300.

Ting, T. F. (2004a) Resources, fertility, and parental investment in Mao's China. *Population and Environment*, 25: 281–297.

Ting, T. F. (2004b) Shifts in reproductive patterns in China. *Population and Environment*, 25: 299–317.

Trivers, R. L. (1972) Parental investment and sexual selection. In B. G. Campbell (ed.) *Sexual Selection and the Descent of Man 1871–1971*, pp. 136–179. Aldine, Chicago.

Tregenza, T. and Wedell, N. (2000) Genetic compatibility, mate choice and patterns of parentage: Invited review. *Molecular Ecology*, 9: 1013–1027.

van Schaik, C. P. (1989) The ecology of social relationships among female primates. In V. Standen and R. Foley (ed.) *Comparative Socioecology: The Behavioural Ecology of Humans and Other Mammals*, pp. 195–218. Blackwell, Oxford.

van Schaik, C. P. (1996) Social evolution in primates: the role of ecological factors and male behaviour. *Proceedings of British Academy*, 88: 9–31.

van Schaik, C. P. and Dunbar, R. (1990) The evolution of monogamy in large primates: a new hypothesis and some crucial tests. *Behaviour*, 115: 30–61.

van Schaik, C. P. and Hörstermann, M. (1994) Predation risk and the number of adult males in a primate group: a comparative test. *Behavioral Ecology and Sociobiology*, 35: 261–272.

van Schaik, C. P. and Hrdy, S. B. (1991) Intensity of local resource competition shapes the relationship between maternal rank and sex-ratios at birth in cercopithecine primates. *American Naturalist*, 138: 1552–1562.

van Schaik, C. P. and Paul, A. (1996) Male care in primates: does it ever reflect paternity? *Evolutionary Anthropology*, 5: 152–156.

Wen, X. (1993) Effect of son preference and population policy on sex ratios at birth in two provinces of China. *Journal of Biosocial Science*, 25: 509–521.

Whyte, M. K. (1978) Cross-cultural codes dealing with the relative status of women. *Ethology*, 17: 211–237.

Whyte, M. K. (1979) *The Status of Women in Pre-industrial Society*. Princeton University Press, Princeton, NJ.

Wrangham, R. (1980) An ecological model of female-bonded primate groups. *Behaviour*, 75: 262–300.

Wright, P. (1984) Biparental care in *Aotus trivirgatus* and *Callicebus moloch*. In M. Small (ed.) *Female Primates*, pp. 59–75. Alan Liss, New York.

CHAPTER 31

Kinship and descent

Lee Cronk and Drew Gerkey

31.1. Hamilton's Rule and Sahlins' Fallacy

The evolutionary biological study of interactions among kin begins with Hamilton's Rule, $C < Br$, where C is the cost to the actor in terms of lost future reproduction of an altruistic act and B is the benefit to the recipient of the altruism in terms of its future reproduction, devalued by r, the degree of relatedness between the two individuals (Hamilton, 1964). If the conditions of Hamilton's Rule are met, natural selection will favour genes in the actor that lead to the altruistic act because, with a probability equal to r, they may also be carried by the recipient. This simple but powerful idea transformed the way that ethologists and evolutionary biologists thought, not only about interactions among kin but about evolution more broadly. Thus, Hamilton's Rule has been a foundational principle leading to the approach represented by this volume.

Before Hamilton, human kinship was already the intellectual territory of another discipline: social anthropology. While kinship is recognized in all human societies, it is a particularly important organizing principle in the non-Western, non-urban societies traditionally studied solely by anthropologists. It is no wonder, then, that the application of Hamilton's Rule to humans met with resistance from many social anthropologists. The most prominent anthropological critic, Marshall Sahlins, argued that Hamilton's

Rule was flawed because few humans and certainly no members of any other species could do the mental calculations necessary for it to guide their behavior (Sahlins, 1976). Evolutionary biologists soon labelled this 'Sahlins' Fallacy' (Dawkins, 1979, 1989, pp. 291–292), and it is now a standard cautionary tale in evolutionary psychology classes. As a social scientist, Sahlins assumed that behaviour must be the result of conscious deliberation informed by culture. Evolutionary biologists make no such assumptions. Indeed, many evolved mechanisms, perhaps including some that lead organisms to favour kin, may work better because they remain at a subconscious level.

Sahlins' Fallacy also demonstrates the depth of misunderstanding between Darwinian and non-Darwinian approaches to human behaviour, particularly when it comes to kinship. Social anthropology and evolutionary biology approach kinship in such different ways that they usually talk past each other. One purpose of this chapter is to highlight ways in which the two fields converge and complement each other. This is made easier by recognizing that each discipline focuses on different but related phenomena. The evolutionary biology of kinship is about the behaviour of organisms towards their kin and the evolved psychology underlying such behaviour. The anthropology of kinship is about the socially transmitted information—in a word, culture—in which behaviour towards kin is embedded. While evolutionary biologists document and analyse nepotistic behaviour, social anthropologists seek to understand and interpret the language, values, and symbols that often distinguish the collective behavioural patterns of one society from another. The evolutionary biologist's position follows logically from the fact that most organisms cannot talk. When dealing with organisms that do have language, this position needs to be supplemented by the anthropological focus on kinship terminology, descent, and alliance. The social anthropologist's position, though taken to an extreme by some who claim that human kinship has nothing whatsoever to do with biology or even behaviour (e.g. Schneider, 1984), needs to be supplemented by the evolutionary biological focus on behavioural patterns, mental representations, and the selection pressures that help to shape them. Thus, the study of human kinship is an example of a broader need to reconcile the study of culture as an ideational phenomenon with the evolutionary study of human behaviour (Cronk, 1995, 1999).

31.2. **Nepotism and human behaviour**

Applications of Hamilton's Rule go by several different names, each one emphasizing a different aspect of the theory. *Kin selection* focuses attention on the theory's relevance to behaviour among kin. *Inclusive-fitness theory* focuses attention on a calculation of fitness that includes not only an individual's reproduction but also how that individual's behaviours impact the reproductive success of kin. *Indirect reproduction* draws attention to the way that individuals are able to ensure that their genes appear in future generations not only by reproducing themselves but also by helping relatives to reproduce. *Nepotism* emphasizes the link between Hamilton's theory and the broader phenomenon of kin-biased behaviours.

Full tests of Hamilton's Rule require that all of its elements—cost to self, benefit to other, and degree of relatedness—are clearly operationalized and accurately measured. In short-lived species (e.g. pied kingfishers; Reyer, 1990), this is sometimes feasible because the impact of routine behaviours on reproductive success can be assessed over several generations. In species with long generation times, such as human and non-human primates, this is much more difficult. A comparative approach to human and non-human primate kinship, often referred to as the 'primatology of human kinship' (Fox, 1975; Rodseth *et al.*, 1991; Rodseth and Wrangham, 2004) highlights many of the difficulties in applying Hamilton's Rule to these species, while also suggesting a number of methodological approaches to overcoming them (Chapais and Berman, 2004). Despite the difficulties, Hamilton's Rule has been successfully applied to human groups throughout the world, inspiring a resurgence in the study of kinship among human behavioural ecologists, evolutionary psychologists, and biologists (Cronk *et al.*, 2000). Most applications of Hamilton's Rule to humans settle for relatively rough estimates of costs, benefits and relatedness while demonstrating a broad behavioural tendency to favour kin over non-kin and close kin over more distant kin. A classic of this literature is Chagnon and Bugos's (1979) analysis of a fight in a Yanomamö village, which showed a tendency for participants to take sides according to their degrees of relatedness to one another. Similarly, Chagnon (1975) demonstrated a tendency for close kin to remain together when Yanomamö villages fission; Berté (1988) demonstrated the importance of relatedness to the organization of farm labour among the K'ekchi' Maya; Smith (1991) explored the role of relatedness in the formation of Inuit hunting parties; and Daly and Wilson (1988) showed that murderers are more likely to collaborate with kin and kill non-kin.

Such demonstrations of a broad nepotistic tendency, while interesting, neither test whether organisms behave according to Hamilton's Rule nor demonstrate predictions that are novel in comparison to existing social science models or even folk psychology. More useful are studies that closely examine the costs, benefits and limits of nepotism. Taking a step in that direction, Turke (1988) showed that child care provided by daughters and grandparents on the Pacific atoll of Ifaluk has reproductive benefits for parents and costs for daughters. Crognier *et al.* (2001, 2002) have shown similar positive effects of 'helpers-at-the-nest' on women's reproductive success in Morocco and Bolivia. Some have argued that prevalence of adoption shows that Hamilton's Rule is inapplicable to humans (Sahlins 1976; cf. Silk, 1980, 1987). Challenging that view, Silk (1987) found evidence that adoption is most common among closely related kin. More recently, Case *et al.* (2000) found evidence that in the USA and South Africa household spending on food was lower when a child was being raised by a non-biological mother (see also Anderson, 2005). Most interesting is the fact that this effect was present regardless of whether the non-biological relationship was one of adoption, fosterage, or step-parenthood despite differences in the ways these relationships are generally conceived.

31.3. Kinship versus descent

Kinship and *descent* are closely related but distinct principles of social organization that are easily confused with each other (Keesing, 1975, p. 21). Kinship is recognized and considered important in all human societies; descent is recognized in some but not all societies. Kinship is reckoned with reference to a focal individual, commonly referred to as 'ego', from whom it radiates symmetrically, forming ego's *kindred* or circle of relatives. Descent is reckoned with reference to a single ancestor. Kinship links all of an individual's relatives, while descent links only a subset of them. Kinship relationships are relative (no pun intended) in the sense that one is a 'son' or 'niece' in relation to certain individuals, not everyone. Descent, in contrast, is absolute: one is either a member or not a member of any particular descent group. Both kinship and descent are expressed in *kinship terminologies*, which vary in significant but limited ways across human societies.

Kinship as studied by social anthropologists is not so different from kinship as studied by evolutionary biologists. Both conceive of the individual as the centre with circles of relatedness radiating out like ripples in a pond. Social anthropologists focus on the labels given to those ripples by the people they study, while evolutionary biologists quantify them with *r*. Descent, on the other hand, has no equivalent in evolutionary biological theories of social

behaviour. Indeed, because descent systems emphasize some kin over others, they may generate behaviours contrary to the predictions of Hamilton's Rule. For this reason, descent is often seen as a challenge to the application of Hamilton's Rule to human kinship, and more generally to the evolutionary study of human behaviour. Recent research, however, indicates that the situation is both more complex and more interesting than a simple cultural challenge to biological principles.

31.4. Defining descent

Descent systems can be classified according to the sex of the founding ancestor and the mix of male and female links traced back to him or her that qualify an individual for membership in a descent group. *Patrilineal* descent refers to a system in which one is a member of a descent group because one has all male links back to the male founding ancestor. Patrilineality is the most common descent system in the ethnographic record, and is well documented in classic works of social anthropology, such as Fortes' research on Tallensi kinship in West Africa (1945, 1949) and Evans-Pritchard's studies of the Nuer of East Africa (1940, 1951). *Matrilineal* descent refers to a system in which one is a member of a descent group because one has all female links back to the female founding ancestor. Though numerically less common and theoretically underrepresented (Schneider and Gough, 1961), these descent systems are also the subject of classic works in social anthropology, such as Malinowski's study of the Trobriand Islanders of Melanesia (1922) and Morgan's study of the Iroquois of North America (1904; first published 1851). In *double descent* systems, one is a member of both a patrilineal and a matrilineal group simultaneously (e.g. the Yakö of Nigeria; Forde, 1950). In *cognatic* or *ambilineal* descent systems, both males and females may be used to link an individual to the group's founder (e.g. the Kwaio of the Solomon Islands; Keesing, 1970)

Anthropologists also make distinctions among descent groups according to the number of members they claim and the genealogical depth of the ancestors that link them. Smaller descent groups with well-known ties to a relatively recent founding ancestor are called *lineages*. Larger groups with less certain links to a more distant founding ancestor are usually referred to as *clans* or, if they are larger still, *phratries*. If descent groups in a society come in matched pairs, effectively dividing the society in two, they are known as *moieties*. Large and small groups are often arranged in nested hierarchies (e.g. several lineages per clan and several clans per phratry), which is known as a *segmentary descent system*. When segmentary descent systems become very complex, the standard terminology is modified to accommodate the extra levels (e.g. sub-clans, sub-phratries, minimal and maximal lineages). It is usually at this point that most people throw their hands up and renounce any further involvement in the study of descent. Though the terminology can quickly become confusing, these basic organizational principles are useful when documenting and comparing patterns of descent (for a lesson in descent system basics, see Fox, 1967, Keesing, 1975; Schusky, 1983; or Schwimmer, 2003).

Labels like 'patrilineal' and 'matrilineal', though essential, may create an incorrect impression of uniformity both within societies and between them. Even if people in a particular society take their rule of descent very seriously, some flexibility regarding descent group membership may be common. Among the patrilineal Mukogodo of Kenya, for example, some individuals with no male links to a lineage are accepted as members because their paternity is either uncertain or not publicly acknowledged and their mothers were either born into or married into the lineage (Cronk, 2004). Similarly, societies that fall in the same category regarding their overall descent system may vary a great deal. Some patrilineal societies have formal and elaborate descent-group organizations with roots long in the past, influencing many aspects of their members' lives (e.g. Samburu: Spencer, 1965). Others have recently founded relatively informal organizations that have less impact on their members' lives (e.g. Yanomamö: Chagnon, 1996). In some matrilineal societies, men control most property and hold most political offices despite the importance of female links in the formation of descent groups (e.g. Trobriand Island: Malinowski, 1922; cf. Weiner, 1988), while in others, women control most property

and dominate public life (e.g. Khasi: Leonetti *et al.*, 2005). These levels of variation observed in descent systems throughout the world have led to considerable debate among social anthropologists about the utility of descent as a descriptive and analytical category (Kuper, 1982). In the case of patrilineal descent, British anthropologists emphasized the segmented lineage structures commonly found in African groups, obscuring important differences within this category of descent found elsewhere (e.g. see Barnes, 1962 on New Guinea and Murphy, 1979 on South America). Efforts to reconcile the tension between describing shared patterns of descent while appreciating unique variations have been left unresolved, coinciding with a broader shift in the focus of social anthropology away from questions of kinship and descent. However, the ethnographic research generated through this debate documented important aspects of kinship and descent that also articulate with the political, religious, and economic behaviours of individuals and groups throughout the world. Whether or not principles of descent operate in similar ways cross-culturally, studying descent systems can provide an entry point for understanding a diverse array of social phenomena.

31.5. **What descent groups do**

What descent groups do for their members varies a great deal across societies, but it is common for them to own and manage property together, organize religious observances and rituals, mediate their members' relations with members of other groups, and play a role in their members' choices of marriage partners. What these activities have in common is that they all use ties among kin to overcome collective action dilemmas, i.e. situations where people are reluctant to contribute to the provision of a public good for fear of freeriders (Olson, 1965). Why have so many societies found descent groups especially useful for this purpose despite the fact that they do not sort kin according to degrees of relatedness (r)? After all, if humans have an evolved tendency to favour kin, would it not be easier to get them to behave cooperatively by emphasizing relatedness rather than descent? Why is it not more common for kindreds, which do radiate from focal individuals in a manner analogous to calculations of r, to organize collective action?

In some societies, kindreds are indeed used to provide public goods. Among the Tareumiut of the north Alaskan coast, for example, men who own large boats rally their kindreds to join their whaling crews (Sheenan, 1985). In the interior of Alaska, Nunamiut organize large-scale hunts of migrating caribou in a similar way (Pospisil, 1964). But because kindreds overlap and do not have clear boundaries, their usefulness for organizing group activities requires the constant diligence of the focal individual. It is far more common in the ethnographic record for descent groups, which overlap either not at all (in patrilineal and matrilineal systems) or less than kindreds (in ambilineal and double descent systems) and which do not depend on the attention of any one individual for their continuation, to organize the provision of public goods. Because descent groups have relatively unambiguous membership, they allow the rights and duties of their members to be specified with precision, making freeriders more easy to identify (Alvard, 2003; Smith, 2003)

In the ethnographic literature, examples abound of descent group involvement in the provision of public goods. Before Mukogodo began to herd livestock in the early twentieth century, patrilineages held and defended territories for hunting and beehive placement (Cronk, 2004). On Ifaluk, matrilines own large sailing canoes used for fishing (Sosis, 2000). Hopi matrilineages owned both land and the right to organize certain ceremonies (Eggan, 1950). Turkish patrilineages play a role in their members' choice of marriage partners, encouraging both lineage and village endogamy (Stirling, 1965; Schwimmer, 2003), while ancient Hebrew patrilineages organized political life, including warfare (Schwimmer, 2003)

Anthropologists working more recently in the evolutionary biological tradition have documented the role descent groups play in overcoming a wide variety of collective action dilemmas. Inspired by the example of the Yanomamö (Chagnon, 1996), Irons (1981) focused on the common phenomenon of lineage exogamy, i.e. the requirement that members of a descent group find marriage partners from outside that group. At first glance, an exogamous lineage would seem to reduce its members' numbers of potential marriage partners by removing people from that category. However, a broader perspective shows that such a rule actually increases the chance that all members of a group will find partners. In populations where polygynous marriages are common, men may often have difficulties finding marriage partners. In the case of the Yanomamö, a man's kin play an important role in negotiating marriage partnerships by providing implicit support in case conflicts arise. If groups of men who are close kin form mutual support networks, each individual can negotiate more effectively. Moreover, by pledging not to marry each other, the members of a lineage give people in other lineages reason to believe that a reciprocal exchange arrangement with them will not be plagued by freeriders. The seriousness of such pledges is reflected in the fact that they are usually expressed through kinship terminologies that equate same-generation lineage members with siblings and marriage among them with incest. Once reciprocal marriage exchanges are established, they can provide the basis for building economic, political and religious alliances that benefit both groups (Van den Berghe, 1979; see Fox, 1967 for a discussion of exogamy and reciprocal exchange)

Alvard (2003) has applied similar reasoning to the organization of whale hunting by descent groups in the Indonesian community of Lamalera. Whale hunting is a relatively difficult subsistence strategy that requires the combined resources, skill and effort of multiple individuals. Yet, successful whale hunts also provide greater average returns than alternative solitary strategies, such as fishing. Because these returns are shared among the members of the crew according to precise rules of distribution, a simple application of Hamilton's rule might predict that average levels of relatedness would be higher among crew members than between crews. However, because whale hunting is primarily organized by patrilineal descent groups, an individual choosing which whaling crew to join should feel tension between the pull of kindred (and his or her benefits through inclusive fitness) and the collective interests of the descent group. Alvard found that lineage identity was a better predictor of crew membership than degrees of relatedness, suggesting that the

Lamaleran descent system offers benefits to individual crew members beyond those achieved through inclusive fitness. Alvard suggests that these benefits include a relatively stable and consistent group with access to the necessary skills and resources that enable whale hunting, thus minimizing the potential risks of adopting low-success/high-reward strategies and maximizing long-term economic returns. In this way, principles of kinship and descent make important contributions to the evolutionary approach to understanding nepotistic behaviour and inclusive fitness.

31.6. Understanding differences in descent

Given that descent groups help to solve important social problems, why are there different descent rules? Why, for example, are some societies matrilineal and others patrilineal? More specifically, why is the most important intergenerational relationship among males in some societies that found between a man and his sister's son rather than between a man and his own son? Indeed, the former pattern is so common in the ethnographic record that it has its own name: the avunculate. This contrast is often seen as having something to do with paternity certainty. This notion probably circulated as folk wisdom for millennia before it was first written down nearly a thousand years ago. The Arab chronicler Al-Bakri explained the matrilineal system in the ancient West African kingdom of Ghana by pointing out that the king "has no doubt that his successor is a son of his sister, while he is not certain that his son is in fact his own" (Al-Bakri, 1981, p. 79; see also Bloch and Sperber, 2002).

The idea that matriliny and the avunculate are associated with low paternity certainty was rediscovered and formalized by evolutionary-minded anthropologists in the 1970s and 1980s (Alexander, 1974, 1977, 1979; Greene, 1978; Kurland, 1979; Flinn, 1981; Hartung, 1985). Flinn (1981) examined a sample of 288 societies, coding each one for inheritance patterns and for behaviours, such as high rates of extramarital sex, that might lead to low paternity confidence. He found that there are no matrilineal societies in which average paternity confidence is at least moderate and no patrilineal ones in which paternity confidence is low. Hartung (1985) presented similar findings, pointing out that paternity confidence must be very low indeed for a man's investment in his sisters' sons to be a better nepotistic strategy than investment in his wives' sons. Hartung's solution argued that matriliny may be better understood through an examination of its benefits for women and their relatives rather than for individual men. Matriliny is the best strategy for women (and, by extension, their consanguineal kin) any time paternity confidence is less than 100%. A mother can be certain that she is related to all of her daughter's children, whereas the paternity of her son's children is never certain. However, matriliny becomes the best strategy for men only when paternity confidence is less than 46%, even if benefits over several generations are included in the calculation.

The fact remains, however, that matriliny is far less common than patriliny. Ellison (1994) offered one possible explanation, pointing out that the persistence of any lineage over time depends upon the reproductive success of the gender that is the focal point of the system—females in matriliny, males in patriliny. When there is a higher variance in reproductive success among males than among females, perhaps caused by polygyny or a high rate of male deaths in warfare, patrilineages are less stable over time than matrilineages. In these cases, more males than females will fail to reproduce and thus fail to extend the descent group another generation. This creates a situation in which patrilineages are likely to be shallower than matrilineages. In that case, any two individuals are likely to have a more recent common male than female ancestor, and focusing on the common male ancestor will produce a more accurate estimate of r than focusing on the common female ancestor. Following Chagnon (1979), Ellison also points out that patrilineages, though shallower than matrilineages, are also more likely to be broader, i.e. to contain more living members of any particular degree of relatedness. One is related to more people through one's polygynous father and other male relatives than through one's monogamous mother and other female relatives. These dynamics may make patriliny more effective than matriliny in coordinating large numbers of people for the provision of public goods, such as group defence.

Polygyny may also lead to situations where property is best inherited by males, whether sons or sisters' sons, because it enhances their reproductive success more than that of females. Polygyny comes in two non-exclusive forms, female (or harem) defence, in which males monopolize sexual access to multiple females directly, and resource defence, in which males control sexual access to multiple females by controlling resources that the females need for reproduction (Emlen and Oring, 1977). Resource control can also be important to male reproductive success because of its usefulness in paying bridewealth. Hartung (1982) showed that there is a correlation across cultures between polygyny and inheritance of wealth by males. Cowlishaw and Mace (1996) replicated Hartung's study, applying a recently developed and more sophisticated method using cultural phylogenies to control for the lack of independence of different cultures in the data set (Mace and Pagel, 1994; cf. Borgerhoff Mulder, 2001; Borgerhoff Mulder et al. 2001).

Three polygynous societies in Kenya exemplify this pattern. The Gabbra are camel-keepers living in northern Kenya. Livestock have a much greater impact on the reproductive success of Gabbra males than females, and, accordingly, inheritance rules favour sons over daughters (Mace, 1996). Similar patterns hold among the agropastoralist Kipsigis (Borgerhoff Mulder, 1989) of western Kenya and pastoralist Mukogodo of north central Kenya (Cronk, 2004). The Mukogodo case is particularly interesting because inheritance of livestock by sons runs counter to a pattern of daughter favouritism shown towards young children. While Mukogodo daughter favouritism makes evolutionary sense because females generally have better reproductive prospects than males (Trivers and Willard, 1974), inheritance by sons also makes sense because livestock, if available at all, can help sons more than daughters by giving them the chance to marry, perhaps even polygynously.

However, because livestock can help a man's sister's sons as well as his wives' sons to become polygynous, the relationship between polygyny and the inheritance of wealth by males alone does not explain why some societies are matrilineal and some patrilineal. To untie this knot, Holden et al. (2003) suggest thinking of matriliny not in terms of inheritance by a man's sisters' sons, but rather in terms of inheritance by daughters. They point out that daughter inheritance is a common pattern in many places, including parts of Africa and the New World. Whether daughter inheritance is adaptive depends on the types of resources being passed and their effect on the reproductive success of males and females and on the prevalent rate of paternity uncertainty. Inheritance by daughters is adaptive if the benefits of inheritance to sons do not outweigh the possibility that a son's wives' offspring are not also his. If there is little difference between the benefits of the resource to sons and daughters, these conditions can be met even when paternity confidence is high. These conditions are often met in horticultural societies, which are often matrilineal (Aberle, 1961) and in which agricultural land has about the same effect on male and female reproductive success. In pastoralist societies, in contrast, patriliny is the norm, a pattern that makes sense given the greater impact of livestock on male than on female reproductive success. Again using Mace and Pagel's (1994) phylogenetic method for cross-cultural analysis, Holden and Mace (2003) showed that the acquisition of cattle in sub-Saharan Africa frequently led to a shift from matriliny to patriliny. Interestingly, though coincidentally, the idea that matriliny preceded patriliny is in keeping with certain nineteenth century models of societal change (e.g. Morgan, 1877). Unlike those models, the Darwinian approach does not preclude change in the opposite direction or make any value judgements about such changes.

31.7. Classifying kin: relatedness and rhetoric

"... there is not a single system of marriage, post-marital residence, family organization, interpersonal kinship, or common descent in human societies that does not set up a different calculus of relationship and social action than is indicated by the principles of kin selection."

Marshall Sahlins (1976, p. 26)

In this case, Sahlins is not stating another fallacy. He is correct that nowhere on Earth does any human group classify kin in a way that conforms to *r*. Kin recognition in our species is mediated not solely by the biological mechanisms spelled out elsewhere in this volume (see Wedekind, this volume, Chapter 22), but also by culturally constructed categories of kin: brothers, sisters, cousins, and so on. Sahlins' error is thinking that this dooms to irrelevance the evolutionary biological study of human kinship and descent (Hawkes, 1983).

To be sure, kinship terminologies do create some special challenges not faced by those who study non-humans. While most people assume that the kinship terminology with which they were raised is uniquely logical and therefore universal, there is actually considerable diversity in how human groups classify kin. That diversity, however, can be reduced to just a handful of basic patterns repeated among widely separated groups. This fact is one of the great discoveries of nineteenth-century anthropology (Morgan, 1871), and kin term systems are still known by the ethnic labels given to them at that time. The system in use among most English speakers is known as *Eskimo*. It makes distinctions between members and non-members of the nuclear family and between lineal kin (direct ancestors and direct descendants) and collateral kin (those to the side) while lumping together same-generation relatives within those categories. For example, one's mother's brothers' offspring and one's father's sisters' offspring are both put in the *cousin* category. The result is a kin-term system that, like a kindred, radiates symmetrically from the focal individual. In the *Hawaiian* or generational system, distinctions are drawn between males and females and between generations, but otherwise kin are lumped in the same categories as nuclear family members. Thus, male and female cousins are referred to as 'brothers and sisters', respectively. None of this should be taken to indicate any confusion about biological relationships. People who use the same word to refer to both their father and their father's brother, for example, are aware of which is which. It is helpful to remember that kin terms, like other classification schemes (e.g. colour terms: Berlin and Kay, 1969; Kay and Reiger, 2003), have *focal referents*, i.e. the types of relatives to which they primarily

and most importantly refer, from which they are extended to other types of relatives (Shapiro, 2005; see also Scheffler, 1978; D'Andrade, 1995).

In some ways, the reasons societies have particular kin-term systems are not very mysterious. For example, the *Omaha* and *Crow* systems are associated with patrilineal and matrilineal descent, respectively. In the Omaha system, one makes fine distinctions among kin in one's own patrilineage while lumping kin in one's mother's patrilineage (in anthropological jargon, the lineage of 'complementary filiation': Fortes, 1953) into broad categories distinguished only by gender. The Crow system is the Omaha system's mirror image: one makes fine distinctions among members of one's mother's matrilineage while lumping kin in one's father's matrilineage together. As explained above, low paternity confidence is associated with matriliny while high paternity confidence is associated with patriliny. Not surprisingly, the Omaha system produces a set of kin terms that correspond more closely to *r* than those produced by the Crow system when paternity confidence is high, whereas the Crow system produces a terminology that corresponds more closely to *r* when paternity confidence is low (Hughes, 1988).

Recently, Jones (2003a,b, 2004) has attempted to cut through the confusion surrounding kin terminologies with a tool called 'optimality theory'. Borrowed from linguistics, this theory should not to be confused with optimization approaches used by behavioural ecologists and economists. Linguistic optimality theory (Prince and Smolensky, 1993) posits that a speaker of a language, faced with options regarding how to produce statements considered appropriate by other speakers of the language (e.g. the correct plural of a noun), will do so by filtering possibilities through a series of ranked constraints. Even a small number of constraints can produce a wide range of outputs if applied in different orders. Jones suggests that most of the observed variation in kin terminologies can be generated by varying the ranking of only a few dozen constraints derived from four broad schemas: (i) genealogical distance, such as the distinction between lineal and collateral kin; (ii) social rank; (iii) group membership; (iv) exchange or reciprocity. The fourth is necessary only if affinal (in-law) relationships are included.

The improvement this represents over existing approaches to kin terminologies is shown by the fact that optimality theory can explain things that other approaches cannot. It has been known for a long time that kin terminologies can be thought of as a series of sorting rules. People make distinctions among kin based on gender, generation, lineality/collaterality, and so on. But if we treat these rules as binary switches, we can generate kin terminologies and specific kin terms that do not exist in any known society. For example, societies are known in which father's brother and mother's brother are referred to by the same term as father. In others, father's brother and mother's brother are referred to by the same term, but that term is different from the one used for father. In others, father and father's brother are terminologically equivalent to each other but different from mother's brother. In no society, however, is father equated terminologically with mother's brother but not also with father's brother (Hage, 1997; Jones, 2004). The existing patterns for 'uncle' terms can be generated by activating rules for lineal/collateral distinctions and maternal/paternal distinctions in different orders, but no ordering of those rules can generate a system in which father is equated with mother's brother but not also with father's brother.

Echoing and elaborating upon earlier claims that kin terms are natural categories (Fox, 1979, 1989; Bloch and Sperber, 2002), Jones further suggests that the kin-term schemes identified through optimality theory are not arbitrary but rather represent a universal underlying cognitive architecture of kinship and social life (see also Schaller et al., this volume, Chapter 33). Such a psychology of kinship, while essential to human social life, may also leave us vulnerable to manipulation through the creative use of kin terms. Political rhetoric, for example, is often imbued with kinship metaphors: 'Fatherland', 'Motherland', 'brothers and sisters', George Washington and other 'founding fathers', and so on (Johnson 1986, 1987, 1989; Daly et al., 1997). Such usage may be best understood in light of animal signalling theory (Maynard Smith and Harper, 2003). Particularly relevant is that aspect of signalling theory that focuses on the importance of receiver psychology and the manipulation of receivers by signallers

(Dawkins and Krebs, 1978; Dawkins, 1982; Krebs and Dawkins, 1984; Guilford and Dawkins, 1991; Cronk, 1994, 1995, 1999, 2005a,b). Salmon (1998) has shown that political rhetoric using kin terms such as 'brothers' and 'sisters' is more persuasive than political rhetoric using either friend terms or no endearing terms. Qirko (2002, 2004a,b) has shown that institutionalized celibacy is associated across cultures with the use of kin terms in contexts, such as monasteries, in which biological kinship is absent. In addition to documenting our vulnerability to the rhetorical exploitation of kin terms, such studies also provide strong indirect support for the idea that the way we understand and talk about kinship is a manifestation of a cognitive architecture that evolved for this purpose.

The use of kin terms in political rhetoric may ultimately have reproductive consequences (Betzig, 1986), but Chagnon (1988, 2000) provides an example of how kin terms can be manipulated for more immediate reproductive gains. Chagnon studies the Yanomamö of South America, who use a kin terminology known as *Iroquois-Dravidian* that is often associated with a rule of lineage exogamy and a preference for cross-cousin marriage. *Cross-cousins* are those connected to a person through a pair of different-sex siblings, such as mothers' brothers' offspring and fathers' sisters' offspring. Mothers' sisters' offspring and fathers' brothers' offspring are *parallel cousins*. In the Iroquois-Dravidian terminology, parallel cousins are terminologically equated with siblings, making marriage with them both incestuous and a violation of the rule of lineage exogamy. An individual in such a system does not necessarily need to have detailed genealogical knowledge in order to find an eligible member of the opposite sex. Rather, all one needs to know is what term is associated with eligibility. For a Yanomamö man, that term is suaböya, which means 'potential wife', 'wife', 'potential sister-in-law', 'sister-in-law', and 'female cross-cousin', all wrapped into one.

The problem for Yanomamö men is that there are often few or no suaböya who are both unmarried and old enough to be married. Such mismatches between terminological generations and chronological ages are commonplace, occurring, for example, in societies with the Eskimo terminology when a nephew is older than his uncle. In the Yanomamö case, an opportunity for kin term manipulation is created by the fact that most people are related in multiple ways. Although the convention is that one should call a relative by the term associated with one's closest relationship with him or her, sometimes people violate that rule by emphasizing a more distant tie. Chagnon hypothesized that men would tend to use the term suaböya for women for whom it is not technically appropriate more often than they would call women who are legitimately in that category something else. This tendency would have the effect of increasing their numbers of potential marriage partners. To test this hypothesis, he showed photos of members of the local population to Yanomamö of both sexes within a wide age range. Adult males displayed the predicted tendency to put younger women in the suaböya category. They also had a tendency to move older women into the mother-in-law (*yaya*) category, a move that makes sense as a way of claiming that those women's daughters would, by implication, be suaböya. Juvenile males, in contrast, tended to move women into the mother (*naya*) category, a move that may make sense as a way of improving their chances of receiving aid from those women. All of this relates to the preceding discussion of Irons' model of lineage exogamy. If the rule of lineage exogamy and associated Iroquois kin terminology provide a public good for members of the lineage, men who violate the rules by putting parallel cousins and other ineligible relatives in the suaböya category are attempting to freeride on the system. In that light, it is worth noting both that such rule violations are exceptional and that they do occasionally inspire accusations of incest and physical conflict (Fredlund, 1985)

31.8. **Future directions**

The complementary of evolutionary and anthropological approaches to kinship and descent is shown by recent research applying the conceptual framework of collective action (e.g. Alvard, 2003). Collective-action theory unites the study of individual nepotistic behaviours with the study of shared cultural norms and values of kinship. Indeed, some of the more interesting and puzzling aspects of human kinship emerge from this tension between individual actors and the contexts of their social groups. Understanding the dynamic tensions between individual and collective interests remains a fundamental challenge for research on human kinship.

Though descent systems clearly play an important role in overcoming political, economic, and religious collective action dilemmas among kin, the relationship between shared patterns of descent and individual long-term reproductive success remains poorly understood. Quinlan and Flinn (2005) have sought to address this question, studying the impact of kinship and descent on reproductive rates on the Caribbean island of Dominica. Because the people of Dominica trace descent in a variety of ways and circumstances, Quinlan and Flinn examined the relative influence of kindreds, locally recognized patrilineages, and informal matrilineages on individuals' long-term reproductive success, measured in numbers of grandchildren. As in Alvard's (2003) research on Lamaleran whaling, lineage had a substantially greater influence than kindred on Dominica, better accounting for individual variations in reproductive success. Interestingly, reproductive success peaked at apparently optimal sizes for both patrilineages and matrilineages. Locally recognized patrilineages showed a larger optimal size than the informal matrilineages, providing suggestive evidence that established norms and values of descent may enable lineages to maintain individual and collective benefits on a larger scale than less formalized patterns of descent. Though the exact relationship between lineal descent and reproductive success on Dominica remains unclear, these results do suggest that the collectively held norms and values of lineage membership are important factors in understanding the reproductive success of individual men and women.

If descent groups enhance their members' reproductive success by solving collective action dilemmas, how do these solutions arise in the first place? Cultural norms and values are certainly important to the maintenance of descent patterns, but how do these traditions emerge from individual action? Using mathematical models that expand Hamilton's equation from a dyadic exchange between two related individuals to the more complex interactions found within groups, Jones (2000) suggests the theory of 'group nepotism' as a solution. By sharing the costs of an altruistic act, two related individuals can improve their inclusive fitness by providing a benefit to a shared relative who is more distantly related to them than if either one were to bear the costs of the altruistic act alone. However, a collective action dilemma remains in that kin who do not share in paying the costs of Hamilton's equation can none the less reap the benefits of nepotistic behaviour in terms of inclusive fitness. If individuals coordinate their actions towards kin around shared norms, values and expectations, sanctioning those who violate them, kin-based collective action can emerge. In this way, Jones argues, the logic of Hamilton's Rule can be extended to analysing a number of aspects of kinship that were previously considered challenges to biological principles, including the varying sizes of kin groups, the socially imposed rules of reciprocity among kin, and the asymmetrical patterns of relatedness defined by descent group membership and kin terminologies.

For Jones' abstract model to provide benefits to the evolutionary study of behaviour, it will need to generate testable predictions regarding actual human behaviour and culture. How exactly to take that next step is not entirely clear (Smith, 2000). Jones suggests that group nepotism might shed light on a variety of widespread patterns in human societies. For example, anthropologists working in many societies have noted an ethic of obligatory aid among kin. This widespread ethic has been given such labels as 'the axiom of amity' (Fortes, 1969), 'communal sharing' (Fiske, 1991), and Sahlins' (1965) misleading phrase, 'generalized reciprocity' (which is not reciprocity at all). Such ethics are usually not expected to work by themselves to shape behaviour or to rely upon warmth and goodwill among kin to have the desired affect. Rather, they are usually coupled with a sense of duty and a list of sanctions to be applied to those who fail to live up to their duty. Jones suggests that this pattern of social pressure being brought to bear to increase altruism among kin and reduce the problem of freeriders may have emerged through a process of group nepotism. By building theoretical suggestions like these into rigorously

testable hypotheses, many questions that have puzzled social anthropologists for years may find answers.

When kinship still occupied a central place in the discipline of anthropology, social anthropologists debated whether patterns of descent or patterns of alliance were more important to understanding human kinship (Parkin and Stone, 2004). Though we have no interest in reviving this debate, the precise relationships between descent and alliance remain poorly understood. With few exceptions, we have chosen to focus our discussion on research examining principles of descent, yet research suggesting the importance of marital alliances in kin-based collective action deserves mention. If patterns of lineal descent emerge from the converging interests of individuals seeking to overcome collective-action dilemmas and enhance their long-term reproductive success, what role do marital alliances play in this process? Although Hamilton's Rule applies to relationships between consanguines (relatives by 'blood'), Dow (1984) has extended its logic to relationships among affines (relatives by marriage). While affines may not share any ancestors, they have an incentive to cooperate because they share descendants. This principle is clearly at work when mates cooperate to raise offspring, but it may also apply to cooperation among more distant affines, such as parents-in-law and siblings-in-law. Dow applied this idea to Hawkes' (1983) data from the Binumarien of New Guinea, arguing that the importance of shared descendants (alliance) provided a more complete explanation of Binumarien helping behaviours than the importance of shared ancestors (descent).

The importance of shared descendants may seem obvious to evolutionary biologists, yet social anthropologists have more often directed their gaze backwards, stretching the memories of their informants in attempts to reconstruct genealogies and discover shared ancestors that would help explain observed patterns of descent and alliance. Evolutionary approaches invite us to reckon kinship forward, particularly in those cases where individuals coordinate their actions around shared descendants. Hughes (1988) has provided a quantitative evolutionary approach to understanding the importance of shared descendents, arguing that principles of descent and alliance converge around 'focal offspring', or children with high reproductive value (Fisher, 1930) that may enhance the inclusive fitness of other members of the group. Using Evans-Pritchard's research on Nuer kinship to illustrate the importance of focal offspring, Hughes shows that small groups of shared descendants serve as nexus points for Nuer communities, forging important alliances and residential patterns among members of different lineages that were previously considered 'paradoxical' (Hughes, 1988, p. 73). Focusing on shared descendants and focal offspring may also provide important insights into the ways that individual actors reproduce cultural norms and values of kinship as a means of enhancing their reproductive success over time. As these norms and values are transmitted from one generation to the next, tensions are likely to emerge between the interests of ancestors and the interests of their descendants. Indeed, a number of researchers have suggested that principles of descent and alliance may actually provide benefits to ancestors while inflicting costs on descendants (Palmer and Steadman, 1997; Quinlan and Flinn, 2005). Though intriguing, these dynamics remain poorly understood and in need of further research designed to disentangle the varying interests of ancestors and descendants as individuals and collective groups.

Further research in these directions may proceed within a broader approach to human cooperation, incorporating kin selection, reciprocity, and collective action as distinct but related phenomena of interdependence between individuals (Roberts, 2005). In Roberts' model, cooperation depends on the extent to which individuals have a stake in each other's welfare. In kin selection, individuals have a stake in one another because they share genes by common descent; when either individual reproduces, both benefit. However, when individuals coordinate their actions to achieve a shared goal, whether hunting a whale or producing offspring, they also have a stake in each other's welfare. In this view, kin selection, reciprocity, group nepotism, descent, and alliance all become special cases of a broader theory of sociality.

Evolutionary biologists, equipped with theoretical and methodological approaches that are effective in documenting and explaining individual nepotistic behaviours, highlight the competing interests between individuals that can undermine collective action. Social anthropologists, with an appreciation for the importance of shared norms and values, describe the emergent benefits of kin-based collective action. Both perspectives are useful in answering the important questions facing the contemporary study of kinship. We see the framework of collective action providing an effective means for synthesizing advances in one with advances in the other.

31.9. **Conclusion**

The study of kinship and descent was once the heart of social anthropology. Today, this topic is studied by relatively few anthropologists, others considering it to be quaint, out of vogue, or irrelevant to matters of more current concern. In contrast, evolutionary social scientists, including many who consider themselves still to be social and cultural anthropologists, have not only embraced kinship, but have even shed light on this important topic in exciting new ways. Many of these developments have been described here. One result is that the complexities of kinship and descent among humans have forced evolutionary scientists to develop new models and insights that go beyond existing evolutionary biological models of behaviour among kin. Another result is that evolutionary scientists have gained a new appreciation of the work of previous generations of social anthropologists, without whose detailed ethnographies and thoughtful analyses we would often become lost among the varying patterns of descent and alliance. Perhaps, at some time in the future, social anthropology will once again turn its attention to kinship, and evolutionary psychology will be able to return the favour.

Acknowledgments

We would like to thank the editors for inviting us to contribute to this volume. We also thank Michael Alvard, Robin Fox, Martha Gerkey, William Irons, Doug Jones, Warren Shapiro, and the editors for helpful comments on the manuscript. We retain all responsibility for any errors or shortcomings that may remain.

References

Aberle, D. F. (1961) Matrilineal descent in cross-cultural perspective. In D. M. Schneider and K. Gough (eds) *Matrilineal Kinship*, pp. 655–727. University of California Press, Berkeley.

Al-Bakri (1981) Ghana and the customs of its inhabitants. In N. Levtzion and J. F. P. Hopkins (eds) *Corpus of Early Arabic Sources for West African History*, pp. 79–87. Cambridge University Press, Cambridge.

Alexander, R. D. (1974) The evolution of social behavior. *Annual Review of Ecology and Systematics*, 5: 325–383.

Alexander, R. D. (1977) Natural selection and the analysis of human sociality. In C. E. Goulden (ed.) *Changing Scenes in Natural Sciences*. Bicentennial Monograph, Philadelphia Academy of Natural Sciences, Philadelphia.

Alexander, R. D. (1979) *Darwinism and Human Affairs*. University of Washington Press, Seattle.

Alvard, M. (2003) Kinship, lineage identity, and an evolutionary perspective on the structure of cooperative big game hunting groups in Indonesia. *Human Nature*, 14: 129–163.

Anderson, K. G. (2005) Relatedness and investment in children in South Africa. *Human Nature*, 16: 1–31.

Barnes, J. (1962) African models in the New Guinea highlands. *Man*, 62: 2–9.

Berlin, B. and Kay P. (1969) *Basic Color Terms. Their Universality and Evolution*. University of California Press, Berkeley.

Berté, N. A. (1988) K'ekchi' horticultural labor exchange: productive and reproductive implications. In L. Betzig, M. Borgerhoff Mulder and P. Turke (eds) *Human Reproductive Behaviour: A Darwinian Perspective*, pp. 83–96. Cambridge University Press, Cambridge.

Betzig, L. (1986) *Despotism and Differential Reproduction*. Aldine de Gruyter, Hawthorne, NY.

Bloch, M. and Sperber D. (2002) Kinship and evolved psychological dispositions: the mother's brother controversy reconsidered. *Current Anthropology*, 43: 732–748.

Borgerhoff Mulder, M. (1989) Reproductive consequences of sex-biased inheritance for the Kipsigis. In V. Standen and R. A. Foley (eds) *Comparative Socioecology*, pp. 405–427. Blackwell, Oxford.

Borgerhoff Mulder, M. (2001) Using phylogenetically based comparative methods in anthropology: more questions than answers. *Evolutionary Anthropology*, 10: 99–111

Borgerhoff Mulder, M., George-Cramer, M., Eshelman, J. and Ortolani A. (2001) A study of East African kinship and marriage using a phylogenetically-based comparative method. *American Anthropologist*, 103: 1059–1082.

Case, A., Lin, I. and McLanahan, S. (2000) How hungry is the selfish gene? *Economic Journal*, 110: 781–804.

Chagnon, N. A. (1975) Genealogy, solidarity, and relatedness: limits to local group size and patterns of fissioning in an expanding population. *Yearbook of Physical Anthropology*, 19: 95–110.

Chagnon, N. A. (1979) Is reproductive success equal in egalitarian societies? In N. A. Chagnon and W. Irons (eds) *Evolutionary Biology and Human Social Behavior: An Anthropological Perspective*, pp. 374–401. Duxbury Press, North Scituate.

Chagnon, N. A. (1988) Male Yanomamö manipulations of kinship classifications of female kin for reproductive advantage.. In L. Betzig, M. Borgerhoff Mulder and P. Turke (eds) *Human Reproductive Behaviour: A Darwinian Perspective*, pp. 83–96. Cambridge University Press, Cambridge.

Chagnon, N. A. (1996) *Yanomamö*. Wadsworth, London.

Chagnon, N. A. (2000) Manipulating kinship rules: a form of male Yanomamö reproductive competition. In L. Cronk, N. A. Chagnon and W. Irons (eds) *Adaptation and Human Behavior: An Anthropological Perspective*, pp. 115–31. Aldine de Gruyter, Hawthorne.

Chagnon, N. A. and Bugos, P. (1979) Kin selection and conflict: an analysis of a Yanomamö ax fight. In N. A. Chagnon and W. Irons (eds) *Evolutionary Biology and Human Social Behavior: An Anthropological Perspective*, pp. 374–401. Duxbury Press, North Scituate.

Chapais, B. and Berman, C. M. (eds) (2004) *Kinship and Behavior in Primates*. Oxford University Press, Oxford.

Cowlishaw, G. and Mace, R. (1996) Cross-cultural patterns of marriage and inheritance: a phylogenetic approach. *Ethology and Sociobiology*, 17: 87–97.

Crognier, E., Baali, A. and Hilali, M. K. (2001) Do "helpers at the nest" increase their parents' reproductive success? *American Journal of Human Biology*, 13: 365–373.

Crognier, E., Villena, M. and Vargas, E. (2002) Helping patterns and reproductive success in Aymara communities. *American Journal of Human Biology*, 14: 372–379.

Cronk, L. (1994) Evolutionary theories of morality and the manipulative use of signals. *Zygon: Journal of Religion and Science*, 29: 81–101.

Cronk, L. (1995) Is there a role for culture in human behavioral ecology? *Evolution and Human Behavior*, 16: 181–205.

Cronk, L. (1999) *That Complex Whole: Culture and the Evolution of Human Behavior*. Westview Press, Boulder.

Cronk, L. (2004) *From Mukogodo to Maasai: ethnicity and cultural change in Kenya*. Westview Press, Boulder.

Cronk, L. (2005a) The application of animal signaling theory to human phenomena: some thoughts and clarifications. *Social Science Information/Information sur les Sciences Sociales*, 44: 603–620.

Cronk, L. (2005b) Comment on "Signaling Theory, Strategic Interaction, and Symbolic Capital" by R. Bliege Bird and E. A. Smith. *Current Anthropology*, 46: 239–240.

Cronk, L., Chagnon, N. A. and Irons W. (eds) (2000) *Adaptation and Human Behavior: An Anthropological Perspective*. Aldine de Gruyter, Hawthorne.

D'Andrade, R. (1995) *Development of Cognitive Anthropology*. Cambridge University Press, Cambridge.

Daly, M. and Wilson, M. (1988) *Homicide*. Aldine de Gruyter, Hawthorne.

Daly, M., Salmon, C. and Wilson, M. (1997) Kinship: the conceptual hole in psychological studies of social cognition and close relationships. In J. A. Simpson and D. T. Kenrick (eds) *Evolutionary Social Psychology*, pp. 265–296. Lawrence Erlbaum, Mahwah.

Dawkins, R. (1979) Twelve misunderstandings of kin selection. *Zeitschrift für Tierpsychologie*, 51: 184–200.

Dawkins, R. (1982) *The Extended Phenotype*. Oxford University Press, Oxford.

Dawkins, R. (1989) *The Selfish Gene*, 2nd edn. Oxford University Press, Oxford.

Dawkins, R. and Krebs, J. (1978) Animal signals: information or manipulation? In J. Krebs and N. Davies (eds) *Behavioural Ecology: An Evolutionary Approach*. Blackwell, Oxford.

Dow, J. (1984) The genetic basis for affinal cooperation. *American Ethnologist*, 11: 380–383.

Eggan, F. R. (1950) *Social Organization of the Western Pueblos*. University of Chicago Press, Chicago.

Ellison, P. T. (1994) Extinction and descent. *Human Nature*, 5: 155–165.

Emlen, S. T. and Oring, L. W. (1977) Ecology, sexual selection, and the evolution of mating systems. *Science*, 197: 215–223.

Evans-Pritchard, E. E. (1940) *The Nuer*. Clarendon Press, Oxford.

Evans-Pritchard, E. E. (1951) *Kinship and Marriage Among the Nuer*. Oxford University Press, Oxford.

Fisher, R. A. (1930) *Genetical Theory of Natural Selection*. Clarendon: Oxford.

Fiske, A. P. (1991) *Structures of Social Life: The Four Elementary Forms of Human Relations—Communal Sharing, Authority Ranking, Equality Matching, Market Pricing*. Free Press, New York.

Flinn, M. V. (1981) Uterine and agnatic kinship variability. In R. D. Alexander and D. W. Tinkle (eds) *Natural Selection and Social Behavior: Recent Research and New Theory*, pp. 439–475. Chiron, New York.

Forde, D. (1950) Double Descent among the Yakö. In A. R. Radcliffe-Brown and D. Forde (eds) *African Systems of Kinship and Marriage*, pp. 285–332. Oxford University Press for the International African Institute, London.

Fortes, M. (1945) *The Dynamics of Clanship Among the Tallensi*. Oxford University Press, Oxford.

Fortes, M. (1949) *The Web of Kinship Among the Tallensi*. Oxford University Press for the International African Institute, London.

Fortes, M. (1953) The structure of unilineal descent groups. *American Anthropologist*, 55: 17–41.

Fortes, M. (1969) *Kinship and the Social Order: The Legacy of Lewis Henry Morgan*. Aldine, Chicago.

Fox, R. (1967) *Kinship and Marriage*. Penguin Books, London.

Fox, R. (1975) Primate kin and human kinship. In R. Fox (ed.) *Biosocial Anthropology*, pp. 9–35. Malaby Press, London.

Fox, R. (1979) Kinship categories as natural categories. In N. A. Chagnon and W. Irons (eds) *Evolutionary Biology and Human Social Behavior: An Anthropological Perspective*, pp. 374–401. Duxbury Press, North Scituate.

Fox, R. (1989) *The Search for Society: Quest for a Biosocial Science and Morality*. Rutgers University Press, New Brunswick.

Fredlund, E. V. (1985) The use and abuse of kinship when classifying marriages: a Shitari Yanomamö case study. *Ethology and Sociobiology*, 6: 17–25.

Greene, P. (1978) Promiscuity, paternity, and culture. *American Ethnologist*, 5: 151–159.

Guilford, T. and Dawkins, M. S. (1991) Receiver psychology and the evolution of animal signals. *Animal Behaviour*, 42: 1–14.

Hamilton, W. D. (1964) The genetical evolution of social behaviour I and II. *Journal of Theoretical Biology*, 7: 1–16 and 17–52.

Hartung, J. (1982) Polygyny and inheritance of wealth. *Current Anthropology*, 23: 1–12.

Hartung, J. (1985) Matrilineal inheritance: new theory and analysis. *Behavioral and Brain Sciences*, 8: 661–688.

Hawkes, K. (1983) Kin selection and culture. *American Ethnologist*, 10: 345–363.

Holden, C. J., Sear, R. and Mace, R. (2003) Matriliny as daughter-biased investment. *Evolution and Human Behavior*, 24: 99–112.

Hughes, A. L. (1988) *Evolution and Human Kinship*. Oxford University Press, Oxford.

Irons, W. (1981) Why lineage exogamy? In R. D. Alexander and D. W. Tinkle (eds) *Natural Selection and Social Behavior: Recent Research and New Theory*, pp. 476–489. Chiron, New York.

Johnson, G. R. (1986) Kin selection, socialization, and patriotism: an integrating theory. *Politics and the Life Sciences*, 4: 127–54.

Johnson, G. R. (1987) In the name of the fatherland: an analysis of kin term usage in patriotic speech and literature. *International Political Science Review*, 8: 165–74.

Johnson, G. R. (1989) The role of kin recognition mechanisms in patriotic socialization: further reflections. *Politics and the Life Sciences*, 8: 62–9.

Jones, D. (2000) Group nepotism and human kinship. *Current Anthropology*, 41: 779–809.

Jones, D. (2003a) The generative psychology of kinship, part I: cognitive universals and evolutionary psychology. *Evolution and Human Behavior*, 24: 303–319.

Jones, D. (2003b) The generative psychology of kinship, part II: generating variation from universal building blocks with Optimality Theory. *Evolution and Human Behavior*, 24: 320–350.

Jones, D. (2004) The universal psychology of kinship: evidence from language. *Trends in Cognitive Sciences*, 8: 211–15.

Kay, P. and Regier, T. (2003) Resolving the question of color naming universals. *Proceedings of the National Academy of Sciences*, 100: 9085–9089.

Keesing, R. M. (1970) Shrines, ancestors, and cognatic descent: the Kwaio and Tallensi. *American Anthropologist*, 72: 755–775.

Keesing, R. M. (1975) *Kin Groups and Social Structure*. Holt, Rinehart & Winston, New York.

Krebs, J. R. and Dawkins, R. (1984) Animal signals: mind-reading and manipulation. In J. R. Krebs and N. B. Davies (eds) *Behavioural Ecology: An Evolutionary Approach*, 2nd edn, pp. 380–40. Blackwell Scientific, Oxford.

Kuper, A. (1982) Lineage theory: a critical retrospective. *Annual Review of Anthropology*, 11: 71–95.

Kurland, J. A. (1979) Paternity, mother's brother, and human sociality. In N. A. Chagnon and W. Irons (eds) *Evolutionary Biology and Human Social Behavior: An Anthropological perspective*, pp. 145–180. Duxbury Press, North Scituate, MA.

Leonetti, D. L., Nath, D. C., Hemam, N. S. and Neill, D. B. (2005) Kinship organization and the impact of grandmothers on reproductive success among the matrilineal Khasi and patrilineal Bengali of northeast India. In E. Voland, A. Chasiotis and W. Schiefenhövel (eds) *Grandmotherhood: The Evolutionary Significance of the Second Half of Female Life*, pp. 194–214. Rutgers University Press, New Brunswick, NJ.

Mace, R. (1996) Biased parental investment and reproductive success in Gabbra pastoralists. *Behavioral Ecology and Sociobiology*, 38: 75–81.

Mace, R. and Pagel, M. (1994) The comparative method in anthropology. *Current Anthropology*, 35: 549–564.

Malinowski, B. (1922) *Argonauts of the Western Pacific*. Routledge, London.

Maynard Smith, J. and Harper, D. (2003) *Animal Signals*. Oxford University Press, Oxford.

Morgan, L. H. (1871) *Systems of Consanguinity and Affinity of the Human Family*. The Smithsonian Institute, Washington, DC.

Morgan, L. H. (1877) *Ancient Society*. Macmillan, London.

Morgan, L. H. (1904; first published 1851) *League of the Ho-De-No-Sau-Nee or Iroquois*. Dodd, Mead, New York.

Murphy, R. F. (1979) Lineage and lineality in lowland South America. In M. L. Margolis and W. E. Carter (eds) *Brazil: Anthropological Perspectives*, pp. 217–24. Columbia University Press, New York.

Olson, M. (1965) *Logic of Collective Action: Public Goods and the Theory of Groups*. Harvard University Press, Cambridge, MA.

Palmer, C. T. and Steadman, L. B. (1997) Human kinship as a descendant-leaving strategy: a solution to an evolutionary puzzle. *Journal of Social and Evolutionary Systems*, 20: 39–51.

Parkin, R. and Stone, L. (2004) *Kinship and Family: An Anthropological Reader*. Blackwell, Oxford.

Pospisil, L. (1964) Law and societal structure among the Nunamiut Eskimo. In W. H. Goodenough (ed.) *Explorations in Cultural Anthropology: Essays in Honor of G.P. Murdock*, pp. 395–431. McGraw-Hill, New York.

Prince, A. and Smolensky, P. (1993) Optimality: from neural networks to universal grammar. *Science*, 275: 1604–1610.

Qirko, H. N. (2002) The institutional maintenance of celibacy. *Current Anthropology*, 43: 321–328.

Qirko, H. N. (2004a) Altruistic celibacy, kin-cue manipulation, and the development of religious institutions. *Zygon*, 39: 681–706.

Qirko, H. N. (2004b) 'Fictive kin' and suicide terrorism. *Science*, 304: 49–51.

Quinlan, R. J. and Flinn, M. V. (2005) Kinship, sex, and fitness in a Caribbean community. *Human Nature*, 16: 32–57.

Reyer, H.-U. (1990) The pied kingfisher: ecological causes and reproductive consequences of cooperative breeding. In P. Stacey and W. Koenig (eds) *Cooperative Breeding in Birds: Long-term Studies of Ecology and Behavior*, pp. 529–557. Cambridge University Press, Cambridge.

Rodseth, L. and Wrangham, R. W. (2004) Human kinship: a continuation of politics by other means? In B. Chapais and C. H. Berman (eds) *Kinship and Behavior in Primates*, pp. 389–419. Oxford University Press, Oxford.

Rodseth, L., Wrangham, R. W., Harrigan, A. M. and Smuts, B. B. (1991) The human community as a primate society. *Current Anthropology*, 32: 221–54.

Sahlins, M. (1965) On the sociology of primitive exchange. In M. Banton (ed.) *The Relevance of Models for Social Anthropology*, pp. 139–236. Tavistock, London.

Sahlins, M. (1976) *The Use and Abuse of Biology: An Anthropological Critique of Sociobiology*. University of Michigan Press, Ann Arbor.

Salmon, C. (1998) The evocative nature of kin terminology in political rhetoric. *Politics and the Life Sciences*, 17: 51–57.

Schneider, D. M. (1984) *A Critique of the Study of Kinship*. University of Michigan Press, Ann Arbor.

Schneider, D. M. and Gough, K. (eds) (1961) *Matrilineal Kinship*. University of California Press, Berkeley.

Schusky, E. L. (1983) *Manual for Kinship Analysis*, 2nd edn. University Press of America, Lanham, MD.

Schwimmer, B. (2003) *Kinship and Social Organization: An Interactive Tutorial*. Available at: http://www.umanitoba.ca/faculties/arts/anthropology/kintitle.html.

Shapiro, W. (2005) Universal systems of kin categorisation as primitivist projects. *Anthropological Forum*, 15: 45–59.

Sheenan, G. W. (1985) Whaling as an organizing focus in northwestern Alaskan Eskimo society. In T. D. Price and J. A. Brown (eds) *Prehistoric Hunter-gatherers: The Emergence of Cultural Complexity*, pp. 123–153. Academic Press, New York.

Scheffler, H. W. (1978) *Australian Kin Classification*. Cambridge University Press, Cambridge.

Silk, J. B. (1980) Adoption and kinship in Oceania. *American Anthropologist*, 82: 799–820.

Silk, J. B. (1987) Adoption and fosterage in human societies: adaptations or enigmas? *Cultural Anthropology*, 2: 39–49.

Smith, E. A. (1991) *Inujjuamiut Foraging Strategies: Evolutionary Ecology of an Arctic Hunting Economy*. Aldine de Gruyter, Hawthorne, NY.

Smith, E. A. (2000) Comment on Jones' "Group nepotism and human kinship." *Current Anthropology*, 41: 802.

Smith, E. A. (2003) Human cooperation: perspectives from behavioral ecology. In P. Hammerstein (ed.) *The Genetic and Cultural Evolution of Cooperation*, pp. 401–427. MIT Press, Cambridge, MA.

Sosis, R. (2000) The emergence and stability of cooperative fishing on Ifaluk atoll. In L. Cronk, N. A. Chagnon and W. Irons (eds) *Adaptation and*

Human Behavior: An Anthropological perspective,
pp. 437–472. Aldine de Gruyter, Hawthorne, NY.

Spencer, P. (1965) *The Samburu: A Study of Gerontocracy in a Nomadic Tribe.* Routledge & Kegan Paul, London.

Stirling, A. P. (1965) *Turkish Village.* Weidenfeld & Nicolson, London.

Trivers, R. L. and Willard, D. E. (1973) Natural selection of parental ability to vary the sex ratio of offspring. *Science,* 179: 90–92.

Turke, P. W. (1988) Helpers at the nest: childcare networks on Ifaluk. In L. Betzig, M. Borgerhoff Mulder and P. Turke (eds) *Human Reproductive Behaviour: A Darwinian Perspective,* pp. 173–188. Cambridge University Press, Cambridge.

Van den Berghe, P. L. (1979) *Human Family Systems: An Evolutionary View.* Elsevier, New York.

Weiner, A. B. (1988) *Trobrianders of Papua New Guinea.* Thomson-Wadsworth, Belmont, CA.

CHAPTER 32

Individual differences

Daniel Nettle

32.1. Introduction

The enduring differences between individuals have been one of psychology's central concerns over the past 100 years or more. In the last 25 years, evolutionary thinking has begun to make a huge impact on psychological explanation, particularly in social and cognitive psychology. However, the integration of evolutionary thinking into the study of individual differences has been more uneven (for some of the few major reviews, see Buss, 1991; MacDonald, 1995; Buss and Greiling, 1999). Evolutionary psychologists were initially more concerned with explaining central tendencies, and species-typical or sex-typical patterns of cognition, than they were with the individual variation. Nonetheless, a wave of recent work on humans and other species, including both theory and empirical study, has shed considerable light on how evolution shapes inter-individual variation. This chapter outlines the key frameworks that we have for explaining distributions of individual differences from an adaptive perspective. The focus is primarily on heritable individual differences, that is, differences underlain by population polymorphisms of particular genes. Individual differences which are temporally stable but non-heritable are considered briefly in Section 32.4.

32.1.1. Background

Variation is a pervasive feature of biological populations, and indeed, it was the observation of variation that allowed Darwin to formulate his theory of natural selection. Despite this, some evolutionary psychologists have given the impression that variation is only to be found in functionally unimportant characteristics, and that those traits for which an adaptive explanation is appropriate are precisely those that show no variation. Tooby and Cosmides (1992) argue, for example that "selection interacting with sexual recombination ... tends to impose near uniformity" in psychological mechanisms (p. 79). Variability, they argue "is so often limited in its scope to micro-level biochemical variation, instead of introducing design differences." They will concede at most a "thin film" of inter-individual variation of any functional significance (p. 80). Thus, in summary, they assert that:

> Human genetic variation ... is overwhelmingly sequestered into functionally superficial biochemical differences, leaving our complex functional design universal and species typical. (Tooby and Cosmides, 1992, p. 25)

The logic of this position is that natural selection uses up genetic variation, by increasing the frequency of the variant with highest fitness until it reaches fixation, whilst removing others from the gene pool. Selection then becomes stabilizing in character, constantly winnowing out mutations, which are usually deleterious, or have the additional disadvantage of disrupting developmentally coordinated suites of genes. Thus, traits or mechanisms with a history of selection will, according to this view, tend to display little or no heritable variation. This position has been referred to as 'Fisher's fundamental theorem' (Fisher, 1930).

It is true that genes coding for basic structures, such as body plans, generally reach fixation, and are thereafter conserved by stabilizing selection. However, the assertion that heritable variation is absent from all important characteristics is certainly not correct. The 'thin film' may not be nearly as thin as Tooby and Cosmides imply. The effect of many genetic variants, especially on behaviour, is to produce a large or small increment of change in the calibration or timing of a characteristic, and variation of this kind is very common in natural populations. Indeed, Lynch and Walsh (1998), in their textbook of evolutionary genetics, state that "almost every character in every species that has been studied intensively exhibits nonzero heritability." Such genetic variation sometimes produces a phenotypic continuum, such as that of size in many animals, or the propensity to call in male crickets (*Gryllus integer*; Cade, 1981), and sometimes gives rise to a number of discrete morphs or strategies underlain by one or a few genetic switches (an example is independent versus satellite mating in the ruff, *Philomachus pugnax*; Lank *et al.*, 1995). Many heritable traits have been demonstrated to be relevant to fitness. Indeed, Houle (1992, 1998) has shown that coefficients of genetic variation are often *higher* in those traits that are fitness-relevant than those

which are likely to be neutral. Fitness itself can even be substantially heritable (for further discussion of this paradox, see Sections 32.1.2 and 32.1.3).

Genetic variation is just as common in humans as would be expected from the study of other species. For example, the genes coding for the serotonin and dopamine transmitter–receptor systems in humans are massively and ubiquitously polymorphic in the human population (Cravchik and Goldman, 2000). Given that these systems seem to be intimately involved in emotional responsiveness to the environment, it is likely that such variation is highly relevant to fitness (see Section 32.2, below). A few of the traits which have been established to be significantly heritable are listed in Table 32.1, along with, where known, their relationships to fitness-relevant outcomes. After an overview of this table, it cannot possibly be argued that the only traits which display genetic variation are those which are functionally superficial.

How does variation persist, when some of the variants can clearly reduce fitness? Two main classes of mechanism have been identified, and the next two sections briefly review them in turn. Both rest on the axiom that variation in a biological population is the product of two forces: mutation, which introduces polymorphism, and selection, which removes it. In the case of a trait affected by a single gene where one allele has consistently higher fitness than all others, and mutations are rare, Fisher's fundamental

Table 32.1 A selection of characteristics in humans that display heritable variation, and effects on fitness where known

Trait	Fitness effects
Stature	Positive for men, may be sexually disruptive
Personality	Various effects on life expectancy, morbidity, mating success
Vulnerability to schizophrenia	Reduced life expectancy and reproductive success
Vulnerability to depression	Morbidity and effect on relationships
Intelligence	Increases marriage probability for men, but in modern populations decreases family size
Attitudes	Unknown
Handedness	Left-handedness reduces life expectancy, possible frequency-dependent combat advantage

theorem means that heritability will indeed drop to zero. However, if many genes, and thus many possible targets for mutation, are involved, or if the relative fitness of different alleles fluctuates, then considerable standing heritability can be maintained (Maynard Smith, 1998).

32.1.2. Fluctuating selection

Biological changes that have fitness benefits will very often have costs too. This is because organisms are generally engaged in compromising between different goals that are all relevant to fitness, but involve zero-sum trade offs. To give a classic example, growing large may lead to success in intra-specific competition, but it delays the onset of reproduction (for many other examples of trade-offs, see Roff, 1992). Where a genetic variant increases or prolongs the expression of a mechanism, such as growth, it will produce both the benefits of increased size and the costs of delayed maturity. Thus, alleles, if they have benefits, will often have costs too.

The fitness of a particular copy of an allele is a function of its immediate environment. Relatively small ecological changes are sufficient to affect allelic fitness, by either favouring the benefits of some allele, or disfavouring its costs. Nowhere has this been more clearly demonstrated than by Peter Grant and colleagues, in a long series of investigations of Darwin's finches (*Geospiza* spp.) in the Galapagos (Grant, 1986; Grant and Grant, 1989). Not only do different islands, by subtle ecological variations, produce different relationships of beak size to fitness, but the fitness optimum on any given island fluctuates dramatically over time. For example, a dry year in 1977 reduced food availability on the island of Daphne, favouring larger birds with deeper beaks who could open large hard seeds. Selection was so strong that by 1978, the average body size of a young finch on Daphne was 0.31 standard deviations higher than it had been in 1976, and beak depth had increased by 4% (Grant, 1986). However, with the return of the rains in 1978, smaller, soft seeds would have become abundant once more and this selection possibly reversed. Change on this order is far too rapid for Fisher's fundamental theorem to operate and drive a particular beak genotype to fixation. Instead,

finch populations maintain high levels of genetic diversity, as alleles that one year were becoming rarer flourish in the next. In general, the more ecological conditions fluctuate, the more diversity is retained (MacKay, 1981).

Trade-offs and fluctuating selection also affect behavioural dispositions. To give one example, in the Trinidadian guppy (*Poecilia reticulata*), there is heritable variation in behavioural traits that affect the probability of survival in the presence of a piscivorous fish (Dugatkin, 1992; O'Steen *et al.*, 2002). Guppies that come from populations living upstream of waterfalls, where there are no such predators, are bolder and less likely to survive in the presence of a pike, whereas those downstream show enhanced ability to do so. These effects are heritable, and thus not based on individual experience with predators. When predators are introduced into previously predator-free streams, change in the population distribution of behaviour in the presence of predators is rapid. However, when predators are removed, circumspection in the presence of predators is very rapidly lost, and within 20 years or so, the populations are like those with no history of predation at all (O'Steen *et al.*, 2002). This suggests that anti-predator vigilance is imposing costs—in terms, for example, of lost foraging or mating time—as well as providing benefits, so selection will move the population distribution around in response to local predation intensity. There is gene flow between different guppy populations, and so, if the population of guppies is considered *in toto*, there is a normal distribution, underlain by genetic polymorphism, of anti-predator vigilance, even though for any specific guppy, there may be a unimodal optimum.

Such interactions can be even more complex, as Dingemanse *et al.* (2002, 2003, 2004) have shown in a series of exquisite recent experiments on the great tit, *Parus major*. Individuals of this species differ on a behavioural dimension called exploration, with high scorers being aggressive and bold in exploring the environment, and low scorers exploring less freely and showing low levels of aggression. Exploration is consistent within individuals and substantially heritable ($h^2 = 0.3$–0.6). Dingemanse *et al.* (2004) show that in poor years, when food resources are scarce, there is a linear positive relationship between exploration score and the probability of survival for females. This is because the bolder individuals are more successful at locating and competing for what resources there are. However, in years of abundance, when there is mast seeding of beech trees, there is a strongly negative linear relationship between female survival and exploration score. The authors suggest this may be because high-scoring individuals become involved in dangerous and costly aggressive encounters which, with resources limitless, have no benefit. For males, the patterns are diametrically opposite. Males are generally dominant in this species, and much of their effort is directed to defending territories. In poor years, males lower in boldness do well. This is because, with higher overall mortality, competition for territories is relaxed, and thus aggressive interactions with other males are less important. However, in good years, more fledglings survive and compete for territories, and so there is increased male–male aggression. Here, males with a high exploration score fare better.

The great tit experiments show that levels of exploration have both costs and benefits: costs in terms of getting into aggressive encounters, with all the harm that can bring, and benefits in terms of holding resources or territories when these are limited. The optimal balance between these costs and benefits depends on exact local conditions and the sex of the individual. As these vary, the overall population maintains a normal distribution of exploratory tendencies, and genetic polymorphism underlying it.

Another mechanism that is often discussed as a possible reason for the maintenance of variation is negative frequency-dependent selection (e.g. in Buss and Greiling, 1999). This is the situation where the fitness advantage of an allele declines as it becomes more common in the population. However, because conspecifics are part of the environment, negative frequency-dependent selection is just a sub-case of fluctuating selection, where the relevant parameter is the distribution of surrounding individuals. It has long been recognized that negative frequency-dependent selection can in theory lead to the maintenance of polymorphism (Maynard-Smith, 1982), though it has been harder to demonstrate empirically that such a

mechanism is in operation. One such demonstration comes from the bluegill sunfish, *Lepomis macrochirus* (Gross, 1991). Males of this species can either be 'parental' or 'cuckolding', with the former delaying reproduction and building nests, and the latter maturing small and early, and sneaking into nests built by other males. Gross (1991) shows that the reproductive success of the cuckolding males is high when they are rare in a colony, but declines steeply as they become more common. Thus, selection must produce a dynamic equilibrium between the frequency of cuckolds and parentals.

In summary, then, fluctuating selection can maintain genetic diversity wherever there are costs and benefits to the phenotype associated with a particular allele, and varying local conditions (including the distribution of competitors) favour different balances between the costs and benefits. Possible human examples are discussed in Section 32.2.

32.1.3. Fitness indicators

Fitness itself can display heritable variation. This appears paradoxical given Fisher's fundamental theorem, since selection might be expected to winnow low fitness alleles. A related phenomenon is the so-called 'Lek paradox' (Rowe and Houle, 1996). Females of many species select the mates of highest phenotypic quality, which might be expected to quickly use up heritable variation in male quality, yet such variation is observed to persist. For example, male peacocks (*Pavo cristatus*) with elaborate trains have increased reproductive success, and their offspring have better physical condition (Petrie *et al.*, 1991; Petrie, 1994). Since train elaboration is heritable, non-elaborate trains might be expected to disappear very rapidly. Yet this does not happen.

A solution to this paradox is that variation in many genes—perhaps most of the genome—affects general condition, as expressed in characteristics like train elaboration. There are thus numerous targets for mutations affecting condition, and condition becomes an index of the mutational load that the individual is carrying. General condition related traits affected by numerous genes are known as 'fitness-indicator' traits. The most widely discussed non-human example is physical symmetry (see Moller and Swaddle, 1997). To reiterate the difference between fluctuating-selection traits and fitness-indicator traits, in the former case there are trade-offs, whereas in the latter, there are no disadvantages associated with increasing the trait. Selection is directional and uniformly positive. However, mutation affecting multiple genes is constantly introducing variation, which selection takes time to remove. The trait thus serves as an index of mutational load, and may consequently be used in mate choice. Examples of possible fitness-indicator traits are discussed in Section 32.3.

32.2. **Fluctuating selection models**

An explicit application of fluctuating selection and trade-off ideas to human personality variation is advanced by Nettle (2005, 2006). Nettle argues, drawing comparisons with animal research, that the variation in the major personality continua described by psychologists such as Costa and McCrae (1992) has both positive and negative effects on different components of fitness. For example, extraversion represents sensitivity to rewards available in the environment.

Increasing extraversion increases the number of sexual partners, including extra-pair copulations. On the other hand, those scoring highly in extraversion, since they are drawn to risky activities, have an elevated probability of hospitalization through accidents (Nettle, 2005).

Similar hypotheses can be advanced for the other 'Big Five' personality domains (Table 32.2). The argument is that varying levels of the traits produce particular behavioural strengths and weakness, and the optimal combination of these in terms of fitness depends on very precise characteristics of the local environment, including the surrounding population. Thus, the human population considered *in toto* retains a normal distribution. For the cases other than extraversion, many of the behavioural costs or benefits have already been demonstrated empirically by psychologists not working within an explicitly evolutionary framework, and so the adaptive significance of the trade-offs has not been spelled out. Agreeableness, for example, is positively associated with harmonious interpersonal relationships, but negatively associated with status gain amongst male executives (Caprara *et al.*, 1996; Suls *et al.*, 1998; Boudreau *et al.*, 2001). Agreeableness is sexually dimorphic, with females having a higher level than males on average (Budaev, 1999; Heaven *et al.*, 2000). This finding

Table 32.2 The 'Big Five' personality domains, along with possible advantages and disadvantages of increasing levels, and relevant references

Domain	Benefits	Costs
Extraversion	Mating success; social allies; exploration of environment	Physical risks; reduced family stability
Neuroticism	Vigilance to dangers; striving and competitiveness	Stress and depression, with interpersonal and health consequences
Openness	Creativity, with effect on attractiveness	Unusual beliefs, depression, psychosis
Conscientiousness	Attention to long-term fitness benefits; enhanced life expectancy	Missing of immediate fitness gains; obsessionality; rigidity
Agreeableness	Harmonious interpersonal relationships; valued coalitional partner	Failure to maximize selfish advantage; disadvantageous in status competition

From Nettle (2006). For references see text.

is robust across several cultures, and might be argued to reflect differing influences of status and social connection on fitness in the two sexes over evolutionary history. Perhaps an extreme case of the low-agreeableness life-history strategy is sociopathy. Mealey (1995) argues that sociopathy is maintained as a frequency-dependent variant, since sociopaths require a majority of trusting individuals to exploit.

Conscientiousness is associated with increased life expectancy (Friedman *et al.*, 1995), probably through more careful and hygienic behaviours, but negatively associated with taking short-term mating opportunities (Schmitt, 2004), and may even be associated with obsessive–compulsive type traits (Austin and Deary, 2000). Openness to experience is associated with artistic creativity (McCrae, 1987), and this in turn has been argued to be linked to attractiveness (Miller, 2000a). For example, in a vignette study, women find men described as creative attractive, especially at the most fertile phase of the ovulatory cycle (Haselton and Miller, 2006). Poets and visual artists of both sexes also have more sexual partners than non-producers in these domains (Nettle and Clegg, 2006). However, artistic groups are also distinguished by high rates of mental illness (Andreasen, 1987; Jamison, 1989), and reduced life expectancy, especially through suicide (Kaufman, 2003). Openness to experience is elevated in groups of patients with affective disorder (Nowakowska *et al.*, 2004), and the Unusual Experiences schizotypy scale, which is elevated in schizophrenia patients as well as poets and artists (Nettle, in press), is correlated with Openness to Experiences (Rawlings and Freeman, 1997). Nettle (2001) thus argues that the openness to experience spectrum is subject to trade-offs. Increasing it increases the probability of socially valued, sexually attractive creative output, but also increases the risk of damaging psychopathology.

Finally, neuroticism, which relates to the ease of elicitation of negative emotions, has clear negative effects on psychological and physical health, probably due to the chronic activation of stress mechanisms (Neeleman *et al.*, 2002). However, those high in neuroticism are also more achievement-striving and competitive than those lower in the dimension (McKenzie *et al.*, 2000;

Ross *et al.*, 2001). If animal analogies are any guide (e.g. Dugatkin, 1992), they may also have been better at avoiding physical dangers such as predators in the ancestral environment. Thus it is not obvious that even this most personally damaging of characteristics has a uniformly negative effect on fitness.

Another trait that has been given a fluctuating-selection explanation is handedness (Billiard *et al.*, 2005). Right-handedness is the modal pattern across all cultures, but there is a minority of variable size that shows a left-hand advantage. Left-handedness is associated with health costs, leading to reduced life expectancy among left-handers (Coren and Halpern, 1991). On the other hand, there is strong evidence that left-handers, as long as they are rare, have an advantage in adversarial sports (Raymond *et al.*, 1996). It has thus been argued that left-handed individuals under ancestral conditions would have a frequency-dependent advantage in hand-to-hand combat. Billiard *et al.* (2005) produce a model with a fixed fitness cost to left-handedness, through health disadvantages, and a frequency-dependent benefit expressed in combat. The model predicts, at equilibrium, a level of left-handedness that is less than 50% and proportional to the rate of violent combat in the society. In keeping with this prediction, Faurie and Raymond (2005) find that the rate of left-handedness across a sample of traditional societies is proportional to estimates of the homicide rate. This intriguing work awaits further replication.

A final example of a fluctuating-selection explanation of heritable variation comes from work on stature. Pawlowski *et al.* (2000) and Mueller and Mazur (2001) had shown that taller-than-average men have increased reproductive success, apparently due to the enhanced ability to attract mates. This would appear to constitute directional selection. However, Nettle (2002) shows that amongst British women, those with the highest probability of marriage and children are actually below average height. It may be that relatively tall women are found less attractive, or that women growing less tall develop more feminine body shapes. It is certainly the case that growing tall delays puberty (Nettle, 2002). Thus, for stature, selection can be sexually disruptive, tending to increase it in men and decrease it in women. Since the mechanisms of inheritance of height are not sex-linked, the result is the maintenance of variation.

32.3. Fitness-indicator models

The most obvious example of a fitness-indicator trait is physical symmetry. The achievement of symmetry during development reflects a good genotype and benign developmental conditions. Symmetry in humans is associated with physical attractiveness (Hume and Montgomery, 2001; Simmons et al., 2004) and mating success (Gangestad et al., 2001). It is likely that the psychology of attraction has become responsive to cues of symmetry precisely because symmetry is condition-dependent in the manner required. As physical symmetry is such a clear example of a fitness-indicator trait, one way of identifying other such traits is finding that they correlate with physical symmetry.

Geoffrey Miller has argued, for example, that general intelligence is a fitness-indicator trait (Miller, 2000a,b). The basis of variation in general intelligence is not well understood, though it is significantly heritable (Bouchard and McGue, 1981) and probably reflects a number of systemic properties of the central nervous system (MacKintosh, 1998). Not only is IQ positively correlated with physical symmetry (Furlow et al., 1997), but those measures of IQ which load most heavily on the general factor of intelligence, g, are precisely those with the highest physical symmetry correlations (Prokosch et al., 2005). Intelligence is also correlated with perceived attractiveness (MacIntyre and West, 1991).

There are relatively few studies of achieved fitness and general intelligence. Increasing intelligence increases probability of marriage for men in modern populations (Taylor et al., 2005), at least partly because it is associated with gain in social status. However, for women, both intelligence and social status actually decrease probability of marriage (Taylor et al., 2005). Moreover, because higher socio-economic groups have smaller family sizes, the effect of intelligence on overall reproductive success tends to be negative (see MacKintosh, 1998). It seems likely, though, that these patterns are a specific product of highly developed, post-demographic transition societies. It has plausibly been more common in

human history for there to be a manifold of positive relationships between intelligence, status and reproductive success.

Miller also extends his fitness-indicator argument to the cover verbal and artistic creativity more generally (Miller, 2000a). He notes that creative output in artistic domains tends to peak during the years of highest reproductive competition [Miller, 1999; this is also true of output in the fields of science and criminal endeavour (Kanazawa, 2000, 2003), and output is generally diminished by marriage]. As discussed above, creative activity appears to increase attractiveness and mating success (Nettle and Clegg, 2006; Haselton and Miller, 2006). Furthermore, Clegg (2006) has shown, in a sample of non-artists, that female raters are able to judge with some accuracy the IQ of a man from an artwork that he has made under experimental conditions. These considerations all suggest that creative activity is functioning to display an underlying fitness-indicator trait of mental ability.

Note, however, that in the case of artistic creativity, there is an overlap of fluctuating selection and fitness-indicator accounts. Nettle (2001) argues that the artistically creative temperament is subject to trade-offs, since increasing creativity is associated with increased mating success on the one hand, but increased risk of psychiatric disorder and reduced life expectancy on the other (see Section 32.2). Miller, on the other hand, sees creativity as a fitness-indicator trait. It is possible to reconcile these two perspectives. Increasing levels of creative temperament does indeed have the costs and benefits proposed by Nettle, but what determines whether an individual reaps the benefits of successful creative activity, or the costs of psychopathology, is general condition. In support of this view, schizophrenia patients and poets score in very similar ways on measures of unusual thought and experience, but differ drastically on measures of social withdrawal and negative affect (Nettle, in press b). Schizophrenia patients have decreased physical symmetry (Yeo et al., 1999), and increased rates of perinatal and developmental disturbances (Kunugi et al., 2001). This suggests that where general condition is poor, a schizotypal temperament is converted into psychopathology, whereas where it is good, it is converted into creativity and mating success (Shaner *et al.*, 2004).

32.4. **Non-heritable variation**

This chapter has focused on the maintenance of genetically based heritable variation relevant to phenotypic traits. However, stable individual differences are by no means wholly attributable to genetic polymorphisms. Behaviour genetic studies of a wide variety of traits, mainly in developed, Western populations, produce heritabilities of around 0.5, which means that 50% of the variance in the trait is not associated with genetic variation in these populations.

The design of behaviour genetic studies generally allows variation to be partitioned into three categories: that due to heredity, that due to the shared environment, and that due to the unique environment. Shared environmental factors are those parameters which are constant within a given family environment, such as general parenting practices and socio-economic background. Both biological and adoptive siblings have the same shared environment as each other. The unique environment is those factors that differ—or whose effects differ—across individuals in the same household. For example, a child might have an early illness, or premature birth, or obstetric complications, that obviously would not characterize his or her siblings.

One of the most striking findings has been that the shared environment seems relatively unimportant in many cases, whereas unique aspects of the environment can be very influential (Plomin and Daniels, 1987). One interpretation of these findings is that our developing nervous systems have evolved to be sensitive to certain kinds of early cues which lead to the calibration of development. Such effects are very common in other species. For example, in rats, administering glucocorticoid stress hormones to pregnant females has a suite of effects on the offspring. This includes lower birthweight, metabolic differences, and, crucially, an apparently permanent up-rating of the glucocorticoid response to environmental stressors (see Weinstock, 2005, for a review). Although the effects of these phenotypic shifts lead to pathologies such as Type II diabetes in the long term, they can none the less be interpreted as

adaptive (Worthman and Kuzara, 2005). The foetus may be detecting cues that the local environment is hostile, and calibrating the trade-off of investment between immediate and long-term survival appropriately. The stress system in general is an allocation mechanism for switching effort from long- to short-term somatic maintenance, and thus making it more reactive would favour immediate survival. The long-term costs in terms of impaired growth, reduced immune competence and excessive anxiety may simply be irrelevant in a local context where the rate of mortality is very high.

Theory predicts that such developmental calibration mechanisms can evolve where the environment fluctuates, such that selection cannot fix the optimal genotype, but where these fluctuations are not so fast as to require radical recalibration many times during an individual's life. If environmental change were too rapid, then early-life conditions would be no guide to the conditions to be faced later, and a permanent calibration would be maladaptive.

There are a few human phenomena which are suggestive of early-life calibration effects. For example, birth weight is related to basal salivary cortisol levels in human adults, and is also predictor of the amplitude of the cortisol response to an experimental stressor (Wust *et al.*, 2005). Several studies have linked self-reported maternal anxiety or stress during pregnancy with later anxiety, emotional disorders or hyperactivity in the child (see O'Connor *et al.*, 2002; Weinstock, 2005). The effect is found even when controlling for post-natal maternal depression, which suggests that a direct endocrine mechanism is at work rather than genetic transmission or post-birth learning. There is also evidence that early-life sexual abuse can permanently affect the regulation of the stress hormone system (Heim *et al.*, 2000).

One area where there appears to be strong evidence of perinatal programming effects is season of birth. In high-latitude environments, season of birth is related to birth weight, and historically at least, it has been related to long-term survival and reproductive success (Doblhammer and Vaupel, 2001; Lummaa and Tremblay, 2003). It is likely that winter-gestated babies experience cues of environmental hostility such as lowered energy availability from the mother, or maternal hormonal or immune changes. Several studies have found that people gestated in winter in temperate latitudes display, as adults, higher levels of sensation or novelty seeking (Chotai et al., 2003; Joinson and Nettle, 2005). These are personality dimensions similar to extraversion and characterized by elevated risk-taking. Season of birth is also a risk factor for several psychiatric disorders, which suggests that it might be associated with elevated neuroticism or stress susceptibility (Castrogiovanni et al., 1998). Thus, it would not be implausible to speculate that winter gestation, by introducing cues of environmental hostility, calibrates the developing offspring towards a shorter-term survival strategy of increased risk-taking and greater harm-avoidance. This calibration would appear to be lifelong.

Such effects may be quite numerous, and their study is just beginning. It is not yet clear what the relevant critical periods and cues are. It is, however, clear that they can be post-birth as well as perinatal. One post-birth calibration effect that is well-studied in humans is that of either father absence, family conflict or childhood stress on sexual maturation in women. Girls who have been abused, stressed or have no father figure present reach puberty more quickly, begin sexual behaviour earlier, become pregnant earlier, and have greater interest in infants, than controls (Belsky et al., 1991; Hoier, 2003; Maestripieri et al., 2004; Vigil et al., 2005). This is consistent with a calibration model in which stress or father absence is a cue of an environment in which survival may be curtailed, and so reproduction should be brought forward (Belsky et al., 1991; Belsky, this volume, Chapter 18; Bereczkei, this volume, Chapter 19). A recent extension of this model links relatively hostile early conditions to reduced agreeableness and conscientiousness in adulthood as well as to sexual behaviour changes (Figueredo et al., 2005).

Many of these calibrational cues, such as season of birth, or father absence, will not be shared by siblings, and so their effects on long-term individual differences such as personality would show up in the unique environment rather than the shared environment in behaviour genetic studies. Thus, a suite of developmental calibration effects may well explain the bulk of the non-heritable variation in individual difference traits.

32.5. Conclusions

In conclusion, we have seen that there is abundant evidence that the 'film' of individual differences that overlays our shared psychological architecture is not really that thin. In fact, the enduring differences between individuals are quite marked, and relevant to fitness. This situation is not unique to humans; it is the norm in all animal populations.

Differential traits tend to exhibit non-zero heritabilities in all the human populations that have been studied so far. I have argued that there are two classes of explanation which may account for the maintenance of such genetic variation. On the one hand, there are trade-offs between different classes of response, and the optimum fluctuates with local conditions, such that a spectrum of different strategies is maintained in the population. Trade-off accounts seem particularly relevant to personality traits, which represent continua of adaptive strategies.

On the other hand, there are fitness-indicator traits, where selection is directional, but such a large number of genes contribute to the trait that a level of variation is maintained. It was suggested that variation in intelligence might be maintained this way.

Finally, there is abundant evidence of non-genetic effects, mostly from unique early-life factors. In at least some cases, such calibration may represent the functioning of adaptive mechanisms designed to optimize the phenotype to its local setting.

Empirical research in the evolutionary psychology of individual differences is still in its infancy, and it is yet to be seen how developmental calibration, fluctuating selection, fitness-indicator traits, and other mechanisms all interact in maintaining the levels of individual differences that we observe in the human population.

References

Andreasen, N. C. (1987) Creativity and mental illness: prevalence rates in writers and their first degree relatives. *American Journal of Psychiatry*, 151: 1650–1656.

Austin, E. J. and Deary, I. J. (2000) The four 'A's: a common framework for normal and abnormal personality? *Personality and Individual Differences*, 28: 977–995.

Belsky, J., Steinberg, L. and Draper, P. (1991) Childhood experience, interpersonal development, and reproductive strategy—an evolutionary theory of socialization. *Child Development*, 62: 647–670.

Billiard, S., Faurie, C. and Raymond, M. (2005) Maintenance of handedness polymorphism in humans: a frequency-dependent selection model. *Journal of Theoretical Biology*, 235: 85–93.

Bouchard, T. J. and McGue, M. (1981) Familial studies of intelligence: a review. *Science*, 212: 1055–1059.

Boudreau, J. W., Boswell, W. R. and Judge, T. A. (2001) Effects of personality on executive career success in the United States and Europe. *Journal of Vocational Behavior*, 58: 53–58.

Budaev, S. V. (1999) Sex differences in the Big Five personality factors: testing an evolutionary hypothesis. *Personality and Individual Differences*, 26: 801–813.

Buss, D. M. (1991) Evolutionary personality psychology. *Annual Review of Psychology*, 42: 459–491.

Buss, D. M. and Greiling, H. (1999) Adaptive individual differences. *Journal of Personality*, 67: 209–243.

Cade, W. H. (1981) Alternative male strategies: genetic differences in crickets. *Science*, 212: 563–564.

Caprara, G. V., Barbaranelli, C. and Zimbardo, P. (1996) Understanding the complexity of human aggression: affective, cognitive and social dimensions of individual differences. *European Journal of Personality*, 10: 133–155.

Castrogiovanni, P., Iapichono, S., Paccherotti, C. and Pieraccinni, F. (1998) Season of birth in psychiatry. *Neuropsychobiology*, 37: 175–181.

Chotai, J., Lundberg, M. and Adolfsson, R. (2003) Variations in personality traits among adolescents and adults according to their season of birth in the general population: further evidence. *Personality and Individual Differences*, 35: 897–908.

Clegg, H. (2006) Testing the sexual selection model of creativity. PhD thesis, Open University.

Coren, S. and Halpern, D. F. (1991) Left-handedness: a marker for reduced survival fitness. *Psychological Bulletin*, 109: 90–106.

Costa, R. and McCrae, R. (1992) Four ways five factors are basic. *Personality and Individual Differences*, 135: 653–665.

Cravchik, A. and Goldman, D. (2000) Neurochemical individuality—genetic diversity among human dopamine and serotonin receptors and transporters. *Archives of General Psychiatry*, 57: 1105–1114.

Dingemanse, N. J., Both, C., Drent, P. J., Van Oers, K. and Van Noordwijk, A. J. (2002) Repeatability and heritability of exploratory behaviour in great tits from the wild. *Animal Behaviour*, 64: 929–938.

Dingemanse, N. J., Both, C., van Noordwijk, A. J., Rutten, A. L. and Drent, P. J. (2003) Natal dispersal and personalities in great tits (Parus major). *Proceedings of the Royal Society of London, B*, 270: 741–747.

Dingemanse, N. J., Both, C., Drent, P. J. and Tinbergen, J. M. (2004) Fitness consequences of avian personalities in a fluctuating environment. *Proceedings of the Royal Society of London, B*, 271: 847–852.

Doblhammer, G. and Vaupel, J. W. (2001) Length of life depends on month of birth. *Proceedings of the National Academy of Sciences of the USA*, 5: 2934–2939.

Dugatkin, L. A. (1992) Tendency to inspect predators predicts mortality risk in the guppy (Poecilia reticulata) *Behavioral Ecology*, 3: 124–127.

Faurie, C. and Raymond, M. (2005) Handedness, homicide and negative frequency-dependent selection. *Proceedings of the Royal Society of London, B*, 272: 25–28.

Figueredo, A. J., Sefcek, J. A., Vasquez, G., Brumbach, B. H., King, J. E. and Jacobs, W. J. (2005) Evolutionary personality psychology. In D. M. Buss (ed.) *Handbook of Evolutionary Psychology*, pp. 851–877. Wiley, Hoboken, NJ.

Fisher, R. A. (1930) *The Genetical Theory of Natural Selection*. Clarendon Press, Oxford.

Friedman, H. S., Tucker, J. S., Schwartz, J. E., Martin, L. R., Tomlinsonkeasey, C., Wingard, D. L. and Criqui, M. H. (1995) Childhood conscientiousness and longevity—health behaviors and cause of death. *Journal of Personality and Social Psychology*, 68: 696–703.

Furlow, B. F., Armijo-Prewitt, T., Gangestad, S. W. and Thornhill, R. (1997) Fluctuating asymmetry and psychometric intelligence. *Proceedings of the Royal Society of London, B*, 264: 823–829.

Gangestad, S. W., Bennett, K. L. and Thornhill, R. (2001) A latent variable model of developmental instability in relation to men's sexual behaviour. *Proceedings of the Royal Society of London, B*, 268: 1677–1684.

Grant, B. R. and Grant, P. R. (1989) *Evolutionary Dynamics of a Natural Population: The Large Cactus Finch of the Galapagos*. University of Chicago Press, Chicago.

Grant, P. R. (1986) *Ecology and Evolution of Darwin's Finches*. Princeton University Press, Princeton.

Gross, M. R. (1991) Evolution of alternative reproductive strategies: frequency-dependent sexual selection in male bluegill sunfish. *Philosophical Transactions of the Royal Society of London, B*, 332: 59–66.

Haselton, M. G. and Miller, G. F. (2006) Fertility favors creative intelligence. *Human Nature*, 17: 50–73.

Heaven, P. L., Fitzpatrick, J., Craig, F. L., Kelly, P. and Sebar, G. (2000) Five personality factors and sex: preliminary findings. *Personality and Individual Differences*, 28: 1133–1141.

Heim, C., Newport, D. J., Heit, S., Graham, Y. P., Wilcox, M., Bonsall, R., Miller, A. H. and Nemeroff, C. B. (2000) Pituitary–adrenal and autonomic responses to stress in women after sexual and physical abuse in childhood. *Journal of the American Medical Association*, 284: 595–597.

Hoier, S. (2003) Father absence and age at menarche—a test of four evolutionary models. *Human Nature*, 14: 209–233.

Houle, D. (1992) Comparing evolvability and variability of quantitative traits. *Genetics*, 130: 195–204.

Houle, D. (1998) How should we explain variation in the genetic variance of traits? *Genetica*, 102/3: 241–253.

Hume, D. K. and Montgomery, R. (2001) Facial attractiveness signals different aspects of "quality" in women and men. *Evolution and Human Behavior*, 22: 93–112.

Jamison, K. R. (1989) Mood disorders and patterns of creativity in British writers and artists. *Psychiatry*, 52: 125–134.

Joinson, C. and Nettle, D. (2005) Season of birth variation in sensation seeking in an adult population. *Personality and Individual Differences*, 38: 859–870.

Kanazawa, S. (2000) Scientific discoveries as cultural displays: a further test of Miller's courtship model. *Evolution and Human Behavior*, 21: 317–321.

Kanazawa, S. (2003) Why productivity fades with age: the crime–genius connection. *Journal of Research in Personality*, 37: 257–272.

Kaufman, J. C. (2003) The cost of the muse: poets die young. *Death Studies*, 27: 813–831.

Kunugi, H., Nanko, S. and Murray, R. M. (2001) Obstetric complications and schizophrenia: Prenatal underdevelopment and subsequent neurodevelopmental impairment. *British Journal of Psychiatry*, 40, S24–29.

Lank, D. B., Smith, C. M., Hanotte, O., Burke, T. and Cooke, F. (1995) Genetic polymorphism for alternative mating behaviour in lekking male ruff Philomachus pugnax. *Nature*, 378: 59–60.

Lummaa, V. and Tremblay, P. (2003) Month of birth predicted reproductive success and fitness in pre-modern Canadian women. *Proceedings of the Royal Society of London Series B-Biological Sciences*, 270: 2355–2361.

Lynch, M. and Walsh, B. (1998) *Genetics and Analysis of Quantitative Traits*. Sinauer, Sunderland, MA.

MacDonald, K. (1995) Evolution, the 5-factor model, and levels of personality. *Journal of Personality*, 63: 525–567.

MacIntyre, S. and West, P. (1991) Social, developmental, and health correlates of 'attractiveness' in adolescence. *Sociology of Health and Illness*, 13: 152–167.

MacKay, T. (1981) Genetic variation in varying environments. *Genetical Research*, 37: 79–93.

MacKintosh, N. J. (1998) *IQ and Human Intelligence*. Oxford University Press, Oxford.

Maestripieri, D., Roney, J. R., De Bias, N., Durante, K. M. and Spaepen, G. M. (2004) Father absence, menarche and interest in infants among adolescent girls. *Developmental Science*, 7: 560–566.

Maynard-Smith, J. (1982) *Evolution and the Theory of Games*. Cambridge University Press, Cambridge.

Maynard Smith, J. (1998) *Evolutionary Genetics*, 2nd edn. Oxford University Press, Oxford.

McCrae, R. (1987) Creativity, divergent thinking and openness to experience. *Journal of Personality and Social Psychology*, 52: 1258–1265.

McKenzie, J., Taghavi-Knosary, M. and Tindell, G. (2000) Neuroticism and academic achievement; the Furneaux factor as a measure of academic rigour. *Personality and Individual Differences*, 29: 3–11.

Mealey, L. (1995) The sociobiology of sociopathy—an integrated evolutionary model. *Behavioral and Brain Sciences*, 18: 523–541.

Miller, G. F. (1999) Sexual selection for cultural displays. In C. Power (ed.), *The Evolution of Culture*, pp. 71–91. Edinburgh University Press, Edinburgh.

Miller, G. F. (2000a) *The Mating Mind: How Mate Choice Shaped the Evolution of Human Nature*. Doubleday, New York.

Miller, G. F. (2000b) Mental traits as fitness indicators: expanding evolutionary psychology's adaptationism.

In P. Moller (ed.), *Evolutionary Approaches to Human Reproductive Behavior*. New York Academy of Sciences, New York.

Moller, A. P. and Swaddle, J. P. (1997) *Asymmetry, Developmental Stability, and Evolution*. Oxford University Press, Oxford.

Mueller, U. and Mazur, A. (2001) Evidence of unconstrained selection for male tallness. *Behavioral Ecology and Sociobiology*, 50: 302–311.

Neeleman, J., Sytema, S. and Wadsworth, M. (2002) Propensity to psychiatric and somatic ill-health: evidence from a birth cohort. *Psychological Medicine*, 32: 793–803.

Nettle, D. (2001) *Strong Imagination: Madness, Creativity and Human Nature*. Oxford University Press, Oxford.

Nettle, D. (2002) Women's height, reproductive success, and the evolution of sexual dimorphism in modern humans. *Proceedings of the Royal Society of London, B*, 269: 1919–1923.

Nettle, D. (2005) An evolutionary approach to the extraversion continuum. *Evolution and Human Behavior*, 26: 363–373.

Nettle, D. (2006) The evolution of personality variation in humans and other animals. *American Psychologist*, 61: 622–631.

Nettle, D. (in press) Schizotypy and mental health amongst poets, artists and mathematicians, *Journal of Research in Personality*.

Nettle, D. and Clegg, H. (2006) Schizotypy, creativity and mating success in humans. *Proceedings of the Royal Society of London, B*, 273: 611–615.

Nowakowska, C., Strong, C. M., Santosa, S., Wang, P. W. and Ketter, T. A. (2004) Temperamental commonalities and differences in euthymic mood disorder patients, creative controls, and healthy controls. *Journal of Affective Disorders*, 85: 207–215.

O'Connor, T. G., Heron, J. and Glover, V. (2002) Antenatal anxiety predicts child behavioural/emotional problems independently of postnatal depression. *Journal of the American Academy of Child and Adolescent Psychiatry*, 41: 1470–1477.

O'Steen, S., Cullum, A. J. and Bennett, A. F. (2002) Rapid evolution of escape ability in Trinidadian guppies (Poecilia reticulata). *Evolution*, 56: 776–784.

Pawlowski, B., Dunbar, R. I. M. and Lipowicz, A. (2000) Tall men have more reproductive success. *Nature*, 403: 156.

Petrie, M. (1994) Improved growth and survival of offspring of peacocks with more elaborate trains. *Nature*, 371: 598–599.

Petrie, M., Halliday, T. and Sanders, C. (1991) Peahens prefer peacocks with elaborate trains. *Animal Behaviour*, 41: 323–332.

Plomin, R. and Daniels, D. (1987) Why are children in the same family so different from each other? *Behavioral and Brain Sciences*, 10: 44–55.

Prokosch, M. D., Yeo, R. A. and Miller, G. F. (2005) Intelligence tests with higher g-loadings show higher correlations with body symmetry: evidence for a general fitness factor mediated by developmental stability. *Intelligence*, 33: 203–213.

Rawlings, D. and Freeman, J. L. (1997) Measuring paranoia/suspiciousness. In G. Claridge (ed.),

Schizotypy: Implications for Illness and Health, pp. 38–60. Oxford University Press, Oxford.

Raymond, M., Pontier, D., Dufour, A. B. and Moller, A. P. (1996) Frequency-dependent maintenance of left handedness in humans. *Proceedings of the Royal Society of London, B*, 263: 1627–1633.

Roff, D. A. (1992) *The Evolution of Life Histories: Theory and Analysis*. Chapman & Hall, New York.

Ross, S. R., Stewart, J., Mugge, M. and Fultz, B. (2001) The imposter phenomenon, achievement dispositions, and the five factor model. *Personality and Individual Differences*, 31: 1347–1355.

Rowe, L. and Houle, D. (1996) The lek paradox and the capture of genetic variance by condition-dependent traits. *Proceedings of the Royal Society of London, B*, 263: 1415–1421.

Schmitt, D. P. (2004) The big five related to risky sexual behavior across 10 world regions: Differential personality associations of sexual promiscuity and relationship infidelity. *European Journal of Personality*, 18: 301–319.

Shaner, A., Miller, G. F. and Mintz, J. (2004) Schizophrenia as one extreme of a sexually selected fitness indicator. *Schizophrenia Research*, 70: 101–109.

Simmons, L. W., Rhodes, G., Peters, M. and Koehler, N. (2004) Are human preferences for facial symmetry focused on signals of developmental instability? *Behavioral Ecology*, 15: 864–871.

Suls, J., Martin, R. and David, J. P. (1998) Person-environment fit and its limits: agreeableness, neuroticism, and emotional reactivity to interpersonal conflicts. *Personality and Social Psychology Bulletin*, 24: 88–98.

Taylor, M. D., Hart, C. L., Smith, G. D., Whalley, L. J., Hole, D. J., Wilson, V. and Deary, I. J. (2005) Childhood IQ and marriage by mid-life: the Scottish mental survey 1932 and the Midspan studies. *Personality and Individual Differences*, 38: 1621–1630.

Tooby, J. and Cosmides, L. (1992) The psychological foundations of culture. In J. H. Barkow and L. Cosmides and J. Tooby (eds) *The Adapted Mind: Evolutionary Psychology and the Generation of Culture*, pp. 19–136. Oxford University Press, New York.

Vigil, J. M., Geary, D. C. and Byrd-Craven, J. (2005) A life history assessment of early childhood sexual abuse in women. *Developmental Psychology*, 41: 553–561.

Weinstock, M. (2005) The potential influence of maternal stress hormones on development and mental health of the the offspring. *Brain Behavior and Immunity*, 19: 296–308.

Worthman, C. M. and Kuzara, J. (2005) Life history and the early origins of health differentials. *American Journal of Human Biology*, 17: 95–112.

Wust, S., Entringer, S., Federenko, I. S., Schlotz, W. and Hellhammer, D. H. (2005) Birth weight is associated with salivary cortisol responses to psychosocial stress in adult life. *Psychoneuroendocrinology*, 30: 591–598.

Yeo, R. A., Gangestad, S. W., Edgar, C. and Thoma, R. (1999) The evolutionary genetic underpinnings of schizophrenia: the developmental instability model. *Schizophrenia Research*, 39: 197–206.

CHAPTER 33

Human evolution and social cognition

Mark Schaller, Justin H. Park and Douglas T. Kenrick

33.1. Introduction

The massive and complex information-crunching capacities of the human brain were designed to help our ancestors make functional decisions in an environment that included other people as a prominent feature. Some of those people were relatives; some were strangers. Some were socially dominant; some were meek. Some were potential allies; others were potential enemies. Some were potential mates; others were potential competitors for those mates. Many aspects of human cognition—especially the processes that define the conceptual territory of social cognition—are adapted to the recurrent problems and opportunities posed by these other members of ancestral human populations.

So, if we are to understand social cognition fully and deeply, it is useful—perhaps even essential—to employ the following scientific strategy. First, identify the set of fitness-relevant 'problems' recurrently posed by human social environments (what opportunities and dangers have other people traditionally posed?). Second, employ an evolutionary cost-benefit analysis to deduce plausible cognitive adaptations that would have helped 'solve' those problems. Third, deduce the specific implications of these adaptations for human cognition in contemporary social environments. And, fourth, test those hypothesized implications rigorously with empirical data.

This evolutionarily informed approach to the study of human social cognition produces at least two substantial scientific benefits. First, this approach can yield a deeper understanding of many well-documented social cognitive phenomena—an appreciation not only for the proximate triggers of those phenomena in the contemporary workings of the human mind, but also for the ultimate causes of these phenomena within the history of the species. When considered in an evolutionary light, human social cognition is not merely one domain of inquiry within the small scientific province of social psychology; it is instead a topic of relevance to any scientist who cares about the evolution and behavioural ecology of mammalian species in general. Beyond connecting social cognition to these broader questions, the other benefit is its powerful heuristic potential. To those whose primary goal is simply to predict human social cognition and behaviour, the evolutionary approach to social cognition yields novel and important discoveries about the contemporary workings of the human mind.

33.2. The problem set: perils and prospects of social life

So just what were the enduring social problems that imposed selection pressures on ancestral populations? A number of different social scientists have attempted to answer this question. Some answers focus on fundamental domains of sociality—whether defined in terms of elementary forms of social relationships (A. P. Fiske, 1992), algorithms of social life (Bugental, 2000), or social geometries that govern interpersonal interactions (Kenrick et al., 2002, 2003). Other answers focus on fundamental human motives that are aroused by and govern behaviour within different kinds of social interactions (Kenrick et al., 1999; S. T. Fiske, 2004). Across these various conceptualizations, there emerges a set of enduring problems that likely exerted substantial influence on the evolution of human populations. This set of problems can be broken down into two subsets: (i) a set of social prospects or opportunities, the successful obtainment of which would have had a positive impact on inclusive fitness; and (ii) a set of social perils, the successful avoidance of which would have had a positive impact on inclusive fitness.

Table 33.1 lists some examples of specific prospects and perils pertaining to specific domains of social life. We will illustrative several of them.

Consider first the positive impact of other people. Affiliating with others offers the potential for interpersonal bonds and social support, and the successful attainment and maintenance of these interpersonal relationships can have important positive consequences for fitness (Dunbar, 1997; Taylor and Gonzaga, 2006). Social interactions also provide the necessary means for selectively distributing resources to one's offspring and other kin, and more generally provide the opportunity to help ensure the reproductive success of those kin. And, of course, it is the act of reproduction itself that is the pre-eminent prospect offered by social interaction. Mammals do not reproduce alone; reproductive fitness has depended crucially on successful mating. This requires that individuals not only successfully solve the problem of

Table 33.1 Examples of evolutionarily relevant opportunities and dangers that emerge in different domains of social life

Domain of interaction	Goal	Social opportunities	Social dangers
Alliance formation	Develop and maintain cooperative alliances	Shared resources Material support Emotional support	Exposure to disease Cheating Incompetence Excessive demands Rejection
Status	Gain and maintain prestige within group	Status-enhancing alliances	Loss of respect Loss of power
Self-protection	Protect oneself from others who desire one's resources	Strength in numbers	Violence from outgroup Violence within group
Finding mates	Locate mates with features indicating fitness	Sexual access to desirable mates	Intrasexual competition
Maintaining mates	Preserve alliances with fit partners	Long-term parental alliances	Sexual infidelity Mate-poaching
Kin care	Successfully raise children and care for other relatives	Enhanced fitness Account-free resource sharing	Especially high costs imposed by close kin

attracting a mate, but also the problem of selecting a mate (or mates) bearing characteristics optimal to one's own inclusive fitness. Of course, given differences in parental investment that have characterized so much of human evolutionary history, different mating tendencies have had different fitness-relevant costs and benefits for males and females. Thus, when faced with the prospect of selecting a mate who optimizes one's own inclusive fitness, one expects to witness sex differences in the behavioural strategies employed by men and women, and in the goals that they look to satisfy (Kenrick *et al.*, 1990; Buss and Schmitt, 1993).

Social interactions are not only a source of potential benefits; they are the source of many fitness-relevant perils as well. The set of perils includes threats to health and well-being (e.g. Kurzban and Leary, 2001; Schaller *et al.*, 2003; Neuberg and Cottrell, 2006). Such threats may result from another's intention to do harm, or they may be unintentional, such as the threat of contracting parasites or pathogens from someone who is already infected. A rather different sort of peril arises in the guise of cheating, stealing, or other forms of social contract violation, such as when another individual fails to reciprocate a resource-consuming prosocial act (Cosmides and Tooby, 1992). Even if one's own health or welfare is not at stake, any such threat to one's kin would also have consequences on inclusive fitness. The set of perils is not merely limited to other individuals who engage in behaviour that affects oneself (or one's kin) directly. To the extent that one's fitness outcomes are dependent on the presence of a social group and the efficient functioning of that group, then any individual who engages in behaviour detrimental to the functioning of the group can also be viewed as a source of peril. In addition, given that many fitness outcomes have historically depended upon group living, a fundamental form of social peril lies in the potential to be cast out or rejected from one's social group (Baumeister and Leary, 1995).

These and other social problems—prospects to be achieved and perils to be avoided—have endured for countless generations in human evolutionary history. These problems are likely to have exerted non-trivial selection pressures on the evolution of human social cognition.

33.3. The solution set: evolved features of social cognition

With this quick review of fitness-relevant problems in mind, we can now address the central question: just what evolutionarily plausible cognitive adaptations might have arisen to help solve one or more of these problems? Table 33.2 provides examples, most of which pertain to specific attentional hypersensitivities or information-processing biases. To understand the evolutionary origins of these cognitive adaptations, it is useful to first deconstruct each fitness-relevant problem into a set of smaller sub-problems. After all, although each problem is defined in terms of behavioural outcomes, the solution may require a cascade of cognitive events that precede and promote specific kinds of behaviour.

At the very least, there are two kinds of cognitive steps implicated in any functionally useful behavioural response to social stimuli. One must first attend to any set of social stimuli so as to identify and differentiate between individuals with different implications for one's inclusive fitness. And, after fitness-diagnostic clues have been perceived, one must have some means for efficiently facilitating a functionally beneficial behavioural response. Therefore, in discussing the evolved features of social cognition, we begin with these two sub-problems—one that implicates attentional processes and the other that implicates a variety of higher-order cognitive processes—and review possible cognitive adaptations that help to solve them.

33.3.1. Hypervigilance and selective allocation of attentional resources

In order to solve any of the fitness-relevant problems of social life, one must identify those individuals who pose specific kinds of perils or prospects. In order to avoid contracting contagious diseases, for instance, one must identify individuals who are already infected and discriminate them from those who are not. In order to choose an optimal mate, one must identify those individuals who have desirable characteristics and discriminate them from those who do not. Successful social identification and discrimination requires the allocation of attention

Table 33.2 Examples of adaptive social cognitive sensitivities and biases

Domain of interaction	Examples of adaptive cognitive biases
Alliance formation	Hypersensitivity to disease-linked cues in others Hypersensitivity to unfair exchanges Hypersensitivity to rejection cues Dampening of such sensitivities for close relatives
Status	Sensitivity to cues indicating one's own position in hierarchy Heightened sensitivity among males
Self-protection	Attention to cues indicating ingroup versus outgroup membership Sensitivity to local ratio of ingroup versus outgroup members False-positive bias regarding signs of potential threat in outgroup males
Finding mates	Attention to fitness-linked features Attention to age-linked fertility cues by men Attention to men's status by women Attention to competitor attractiveness by women Attention to competitor status by men Overinterpretation of sexual interest by men Conservative bias in evaluating signs of men's commitment by women
Maintaining mates	Diminished concern with equity between mates Enhanced concern with behavioural cues to infidelity Hypervigilance for cues that other members of one's own sex might be mate-poachers
Kin care	Concern over equity between siblings (amplified for step-siblings) Diminished concern over self–other equity when dealing with offspring (excepted for step-parents)

to features that are actually diagnostic of those specific dangers or opportunities.

Attention is a limited resource. To the extent that attention is allocated to specific kinds of features or to specific individuals in the social environment, one is less able to allocate attention to other features or individuals. It would have been adaptive for individual animals to selectively allocate attentional resources to particular pieces of information in the social environment that are especially relevant to recurrent problems of social life and that most readily compel fitness-optimizing solutions to those problems.

Plenty of evidence in the behavioural ecology literature indicates that animals selectively acquire information that is relevant to survival and reproduction (Dukas, 2002). Conceptually similar findings are well documented in the literature on human perception and cognition. Most of this research focuses on visual attention. For instance, compared with other less threatening kinds of visual stimuli, people are especially quick to visually detect the presence of snakes and spiders (Öhman *et al.*, 2001). This finding is buttressed by neural correlates of attention: studies assessing event-related potentials (ERPs) in the human brain indicate a faster response to emotionally negative stimuli than to either emotionally positive or neutral stimuli (Carretié *et al.*, 2004). It appears that visual attention is selectively allocated to the detection of threats in the natural environment.

Does this conclusion apply also to threats unique to the social environment? Yes. There is a burgeoning literature on the effects of human faces and facial features on visual attention.

People are uniquely attentive to the features of human faces, especially those features—such as the eyes, eyebrows, and mouth—that are most strongly diagnostic of facial emotions (e.g. Ristic *et al.*, 2002; Lunqvist and Öhman, 2005). People seem to be particularly attentive to facial expressions that connote threat. Compared with other kinds of social stimuli—including more emotionally positive facial expressions—angry faces are especially quick to grab and/or hold attention (Fox *et al.*, 2001). As with non-social stimuli, these effects are buttressed by ERP results indicating a more immediate neural response to angry faces (Schupp *et al.*, 2004).

People selectively allocate attention not only to potential sources of threat, but also to potential sources of reproductive reward. In a study that assessed the temporal duration of eye-fixations on male and female faces of varying physical attractiveness, Maner *et al.* (2003) found that men allocated substantially more time looking at attractive (relative to unattractive) female faces. Given that facial attractiveness serves as a cue indicating fitness and fertility (Thornhill and Gangestad, 1999; Fink and Penton-Voak, 2002), this finding is consistent with the hypothesis that men selectively allocate attention to individuals who offer the greatest promise of reproductive reward. (Men did not show any such attentional bias toward attractive male faces—a context in which physical attractiveness would not serve as a cue to reproductive fitness. Further, women showed a qualitatively different pattern of results—consistent with logic derived from the theory of differential parental investment, indicating that physical attractiveness serves a somewhat different function in the mating strategies of men and women.)

In many circumstances, there is a positive relationship between the attention allocated to a target individual and later memory for that individual's identifying features. Consequently, allocation of attention can sometimes be indicated indirectly by memory measures. Using such an approach, various lines of research suggest that attentional resources are selectively allocated to those individuals who appear to be potential sources of reproductive prospect or peril. For instance, several studies have examined whether 'cheaters'—individuals who violate social contracts—are especially memorable. It appears that they are (Mealey *et al.*, 1996; Oda, 1997; Yamagishi *et al.*, 2003).

In sum, the human mind seems to be hyper-vigilant to cues connoting fitness-relevant perils and prospects. The evolutionarily enduring problems of social life have left their mark on the highly automatized processes of social attention.

33.3.2. Activation and manipulation of social knowledge structures

Selective attention alone is insufficient to solve the recurrent problems of social life. Animals must not only gather fitness-relevant information about the world around them; their minds must do something with that information. Therefore, animals likely evolved specific kinds of higher-order cognitive processes that provide quick, efficient means of facilitating adaptive behavioural responses whenever fitness-relevant information is detected.

Theory and research in this broad domain of inquiry can be loosely lumped into two categories: (i) research that focuses on reasoning and human decision processes, and (ii) research that focuses more simply on the activation of knowledge structures into working memory.

Within the realm of reasoning, it has been argued that there evolved cognitive algorithms of information integration that facilitated accurate diagnosis of those individuals who violate social contracts (Cosmides and Tooby, 1992). The plausibility of a special 'cheater-detection' mode of reasoning has been the focus of an extensive line of research. Abundant evidence suggests that people show enhanced facility for a specific form of propositional reasoning under conditions in which the reasoning task is clearly relevant to social contract violations (e.g. Cosmides, 1989; Fiddick *et al.*, 2000; Sugiyama *et al.*, 2002). Indeed, neuroscience data have indicated that a somewhat different set of brain structures is involved in fitness-relevant versus fitness-irrelevant forms of the same logical reasoning task (Adolphs, 1999; Stone *et al.*, 2002).

Other lines of research on reasoning and decision-making have focused on the evolutionary implications of other kinds of social problems, including problems related to the allocation of resources to kin versus non-kin (Burnstein *et al.*, 1994) and problems pertaining to the navigation of social hierarchies (Cummins, 1999). There are several lines of research that focus specifically on predictable biases in social judgement and social decision-making (e.g. Nesse, 2005; Haselton and Nettle, 2006). For instance, within the realm of mating, there is a predictable bias such that men misjudge women to be more desirous of sexual relations than they actually are—a bias that can be readily predicted from an evolutionarily informed cost-benefit analysis indicating that for men (compared with women), ignoring a willing mate incurs heavier fitness costs than approaching an unwilling one (Haselton and Buss, 2000). Conceptually similar analyses have been applied to many other domains of social interaction, yielding hypotheses specifying adaptive 'errors' and biases across a broad range of judgement and decision-making. The empirical database supports these evolutionarily informed hypotheses (Haselton and Funder, 2006; Haselton and Nettle, 2006).

Research on reasoning yields conclusions that pertain primarily to processes through which information, already in working memory, is manipulated and integrated. But how does that information get into working memory in the first place? In some cases, the information is perceived directly and concurrently from the external environment—thanks in part to the selective allocation of attentional resources, discussed above. In addition, other potentially useful information may have been acquired previously (e.g. learned associations) and archived in long-term memory. It would have been adaptive for individuals to have selective access to whatever archived information is especially pertinent to the adaptive problems of social life—information that most readily compels fitness-optimizing solutions to those problems. Thus, there is another class of evolved cognitive algorithms. These are simple stimulus–response algorithms in which some perceived cue acts as a stimulus, automatically activating into working memory specific cognitions that dispose individuals to respond in ways that confer fitness benefits.

When one perceives a potentially threatening individual, for instance, adaptive behaviour (e.g. avoidance or the adoption of a defensive posture) is facilitated by the automatic activation of cognitions characterizing the individual as a threat. This stimulus–response algorithm not only influences cognitive responses to obvious sources of social peril (e.g. individuals with angry facial expressions), it also leads to predictable biases in the stereotypes that are activated when people encounter members of racial or ethnic outgroups. Ethnic group membership represents a contemporary analogue to the sorts of coalitional group memberships that have played a substantial role in social life throughout human evolutionary history (Kurzban *et al.*, 2001). Throughout that history, coalitional ingroups were sources of support and safety, whereas encounters with outgroup members (perhaps especially unexpected encounters with outgroup males) represented potential threats to personal welfare. Consequently, perceptual encounters with unknown outgroup members may automatically activate cognitions connoting threat. This is evident not only in the semantic contents of cognitively accessible stereotypes about ethnic outgroups (Schaller *et al.*, 2003), but also in the fearful emotional responses to these outgroups (e.g. Cottrell and Neuberg, 2005). These patterns of cognitive response are bolstered by data indicating that the perception of ethnic outgroup members stimulates greater activity in brain structures associated with fear and triggers a physiological threat response (Phelps *et al.*, 2000; Blascovich *et al.*, 2001).

Other perceptual cues—associated with other kinds of potential peril—automatically activate qualitatively different kinds of threat-relevant cognitions into working memory. Morphological anomalies, such as physical disabilities and facial disfigurements, are likely to have historically served as heuristic cues indicating parasitic infection; consequently, humans and other primates respond aversively to individuals bearing such anomalies (Goodall, 1986; Kurzban and Leary, 2001; Park *et al.*, 2003). Underlying these behavioural reactions, it appears that the very perception of these morphological anomalies automatically activates disease-relevant cognitions into working memory—even under conditions in which perceivers explicitly know that the disfigured individual poses no health risk at all (Park *et al.*, 2003).

Cues connoting potential fitness-relevant opportunities have similar algorithmic consequences, activating specific kinds of cognitions that promote adaptive behaviour. In the realm of mating, men erroneously detect exaggerated levels of sexual arousal from the objectively neutral facial expressions of physically attractive women, compared with unattractive women or with attractive men; no such effect occurs among women (Maner *et al.*, 2005). These results suggest that when men perceptually encounter physically attractive opposite-sex others (a constellation of cues that connotes a fitness-enhancing opportunity), this activates a set of optimistic attributions about additional characteristics of those women. It is exactly this sort of attribution that increases the likelihood of actually pursuing a mating opportunity.

Finally, there is plenty of evidence indicating that the perception of kinship cues triggers highly automatized cognitive responses. Animals rely on crude heuristic cues to infer the extent to which a conspecific is genetically related; and like many other animal species, humans use cues pertaining to familiarity and phenotypic similarity (Hepper, 1991; Lieberman *et al.*, 2003; Rendall, 2004). If indeed these cues serve as stimuli triggering an evolved stimulus–response mechanism, then the perception of such cues in another person—even if that other person is known to be genetically unrelated—should immediately trigger emotional and cognitive responses that (i) inhibit sexual intercourse and (ii) facilitate prosocial allocation of resources. Empirical evidence is consistent with these predictions. For instance, perceived facial similarity triggers attributions indicating both greater trustworthiness and decreased sexual attractiveness (DeBruine, 2002, 2005). Greater attitudinal similarity—even in a total stranger—automatically activates semantic cognitions connoting kinship and is associated with a variety of prosocial intentions (Park and Schaller, 2005).

In sum, just as the enduring problems of social life have left their mark on low-level attentional processes, they have left their mark on a variety of higher-order cognitive processes as well. And in doing so, they exert a predictable influence on social cognition in contemporary environments.

33.3.3. Costs, benefits, and the functional flexibility of evolved social cognition

Evolved psychological mechanisms may operate automatically, but that does not mean that they are invariant in their operation. Quite the contrary: these mechanisms are highly flexible and predictably influenced by regulatory cues in the immediate environment. This point—easily deduced from an evolutionary cost-benefit analysis—has enormous implications for social cognitive phenomena.

Evolved psychological mechanisms are associated with specific benefits (animals that had these capacities had greater reproductive fitness than those that did not) but their actual operation typically entails some potential costs as well. Attentional hypervigilance consumes metabolic resources (or reduces the time available for acquiring those resources), as does the activation of knowledge structures. This is the case especially when these cognitive processes are accompanied by specific affective responses as well, as they often are. Moreover, because of the finite metabolic resources available to an organism at any moment, the engagement of any one specific adaptive mechanism limits the extent to which other adaptive mechanisms might be engaged. Thus, to be more optimally adaptive, these evolved cognitive mechanisms should have evolved in such a way to be functionally flexible; they are especially likely to be engaged when additional information in the immediate environment indicates that the functional benefits are especially likely to outweigh the functional costs (but are less likely to be engaged when additional information indicates either lower benefits or higher costs). For example, the perception of a sudden loud noise automatically triggers a startle response. This acoustic startle reflex is surely adaptive in the promotion of self-protection. But it is also variable: the response is stronger under conditions—such as ambient darkness—in which people feel especially vulnerable to harm (Grillon *et al.*, 1997).

Information signalling potential costs and benefits, and thus potentially moderating the engagement of evolved social cognition processes, may lie not only in individuals' external environments (physical and social contexts that may change from moment to moment), but also in the cognitive environments that individuals carry with them chronically (acquired attitudes, personality traits, and other dispositions). Thus, for instance, attentional hypervigilance to spiders occurs more strongly among arachnophobes, and hypervigilance to snakes occurs more strongly among individuals who are more chronically fearful of snakes (Öhman *et al.*, 2001).

The same point applies to social cognition, too. Regardless of whether cost-benefit information is implied by chronic individual differences (e.g. individual differences in mating motives; Simpson and Gangestad, 1991) or by transitory aspects of one's immediate social context, this information leads the human mind to prioritize implicitly the adaptive problems that need to be solved at any given moment. Because of this adaptive functional flexibility, evolved social cognitive phenomena vary predictably across individuals and in response to specific kinds of contextual cues.

In the realm of social attention, hypervigilance to social threat varies as a function of the perceiver's chronic feelings of vulnerability: angry faces capture attention more quickly—and hold attention for longer periods of time—among more highly anxious individuals (Bradley *et al.*, 2000; Fox *et al.*, 2001). Conceptually similar effects have been found in the domain of mating. People who chronically adopt an 'unrestrictive' approach to mating (and who thus chronically seek mates) are especially likely to allocate visual attention to physically attractive members of the opposite sex (Maner *et al.*, 2003).

Evolved mechanisms of reasoning, judgement and decision-making are also engaged flexibly in response to heuristic cost-benefit information. For instance, in altruistic judgement tasks, people predictably discriminate in favour of closer kin; but this effect itself shows up more strongly in life-and-death situations than in other situations in which the costs of not helping are less profound (Burnstein *et al.*, 1994). Even the paradigmatic example of an evolved reasoning algorithm—the form of propositional reasoning that serves a 'cheater-detection' goal—is moderated by the perceiver's social status (Cummins, 1999). Compared with low-ranking individuals, high-ranking individuals (who have more resources and so are more likely to suffer costs

from the presence of undetected cheaters) are more likely to demonstrate error-free propositional logic when reasoning about social contracts.

There is also abundant evidence of functional flexibility in the activation of adaptive knowledge structures into working memory. People who are chronically worried about the dangers posed by other people or have been made to feel temporarily vulnerable to harm are especially prone to the automatic activation of threat-relevant stereotypes when they perceive members of an ethnic outgroup (Schaller *et al.*, 2003). This phenomenon not only affects stereotypic judgements about the entire outgroup, but also shapes inferences about the characteristics of individuals. For instance, people who are in a temporarily fearful state are especially likely to erroneously perceive anger—but not fear or other negative emotions—in the face of an outgroup member (Maner *et al.*, 2005). These effects occur even if the actual outgroup poses no realistic threat whatsoever, and even if the sense of vulnerability is the result of a blatantly artificial manipulation (e.g. a temporary lack of ambient light in a psychology laboratory or a few minutes' viewing of a Hollywood movie). Conceptually similar evidence of functional flexibility emerges in the automatic responses to cues that connote parasite infection and transmission (Park *et al.*, 2003; Faulkner *et al.*, 2004). For example, Faulkner *et al.* (2004) hypothesized that the subjective foreignness of an ethnic group might serve as a heuristic cue connoting the threat of parasite transmission. Consistent with this hypothesis, xenophobic attitudes toward foreign peoples was especially pronounced among individuals who felt chronically vulnerable to disease and among individuals for whom the risk of parasite transmission was temporarily salient. Further support is provided by evidence that newly pregnant women (e.g. in the first 10 weeks of pregnancy, a time during which the developing fetus is especially vulnerable) show an enhanced sensitivity to disgust and stronger xenophobic attitudes toward subjectively foreign groups (Navarrete *et al.*, unpublished manuscript).

Finally, in the domain of mating, the tendency for men to optimistically perceive sexual arousal in the faces of attractive women is stronger among men for whom a mating motive has been artificially induced, and it is also stronger among men who are sexually unrestricted and thus have a chronically more active mating motive (Maner *et al.*, 2005). Meanwhile, among women, the menstrual cycle moderates the strength of adaptive sexual responses to specific stimulus features in men. During the most fertile phase of the cycle, women are especially likely to respond positively to men who are symmetrical, masculine, and have various other characteristics indicative of high reproductive fitness (Gangestad and Thornhill, 1998; Penton-Voak and Perrett, 2000; Gangestad *et al.*, 2004).

Emerging from these and other results is a portrait of a human mind that evolved in response not only to the perils and prospects of the social environment, but also to the fact that specific perils and prospects matter more under some circumstances than others. Functional flexibility is an adaptation of profound importance, and implications of this adaptive functional flexibility can be found everywhere within the social cognition literature.

33.4. **Thinking ahead: perils and prospects of evolutionary social cognition**

Inquiries into evolutionary processes, particularly when applied to contemporary human social cognition and behaviour, attract an unusually high number of detractors. Some of these criticisms appear to be motivated by personal ideologies that have little to do with science. Others, however, implicate epistemological challenges that are unique to—or at least unusually acute for—the enterprise of evolutionary psychology.

Any hypothesis about the evolutionary bases of contemporary cognition implicates several very different kinds of causal processes, operating at very different levels of analysis—evolutionary processes operating on ancestral populations over very long stretches of historical time, ontogenetic and developmental processes operating on individuals across the lifespan, cognitive processes operating within individuals' neural structures over the course of mere microseconds. Evidence regarding all the presumed

levels underlying a given hypothesis can rarely be provided, even by the most perfect results obtained with the typical tools of psychological research (Conway and Schaller, 2002; Schmitt and Pilcher, 2004). Thus, despite their consistency with evolutionary arguments, controversy and criticism often attend evolutionary conclusions based on empirical results of the sort summarized above.

How does one respond? The most productive responses rise to the epistemological challenge by attempting to directly engage some of the thorniest issues that emerge in the study of evolution and social cognition. We close with a brief discussion of three issues and their implications for new directions in the study of evolutionary social cognition.

33.4.1. **Neuroscience**

Evolutionary psychologists speak of cognitive adaptations in much the same way that behavioural ecologists speak of behavioural adaptations—with the tacit assumption that these observed phenomena are the product of some set of more specific adaptations that exist at more purely biological (e.g. neurophysiology) levels of analysis. Explicit attention to these deeper levels of analysis is not a necessary condition for meaningful progress in evolutionary psychology. Nevertheless, just as an evolutionary perspective may be useful tool toward accurately articulating the functional physiology of the human brain (Duchaine *et al.*, 2001), attention to the functional physiology of the brain may usefully inform the theory and research in evolutionary psychology (Panksepp and Panksepp, 2000). As the tools of neuroscience become more advanced and integrated into the psychological sciences, they provide a potentially valuable means of addressing important questions that are often raised in the realm of evolutionary social cognition.

One question is this: what is to be considered a cognitive adaptation? A particular cognitive phenomenon may be functional in the sense of solving some fitness-relevant problem, but that may not necessarily mean that the phenomenon evolved as a direct consequence of that particular enduring fitness-relevant problem. It is possible that the phenomenon is simply one application of cognitive mechanisms that evolved for entirely different reasons altogether. How is one to distinguish between a problem-specific adaptation and some generally useful set of cognitive operations? Just as some researchers have argued that domain specificity is a diagnostic hallmark of cognitive adaptations (e.g. extraordinary prowess at propositional reasoning should be specific to the domain of cheater detection; Cosmides and Tooby, 1992), others have argued that true cognitive adaptations are implicated by the presence of neural circuitry dedicated specifically to their operation (Öhman and Mineka, 2001; Schmitt and Pilcher, 2004). The only way to address that latter criterion is through rigorous application of the methods of cognitive neuroscience.

There is now abundant neuroscientific evidence indicating that there do appear to be specialized neural structures devoted to such social perceptual tasks as face perception and the detection of eye gaze (e.g. Hoffman and Haxby, 2000; Kanwisher, 2000). Other neurological evidence is consistent with additional speculations about the adaptive basis of other prominent social cognitive capacities, hypersensitivities, and biases (e.g. Adolphs, 1999; Duchaine et al., 2001). Much of this evidence is very preliminary, however. Moreover, there remain difficulties in relating neuroscientific evidence to social psychological phenomena, and there are differing opinions about the kinds of neuroscientific evidence that are most relevant to hypotheses in evolutionary psychology (Panksepp and Panksepp, 2000; Willingham and Dunn, 2003). The field of cognitive neuroscience is maturing rapidly, however, and our knowledge of the functional physiology of the brain is accumulating quickly. As this evidentiary database becomes more sophisticated, we will have an increasingly useful source of information to inform and constrain hypotheses connecting human evolution to social cognition. And as the methodological tools become more sensitive, we will have increasingly rigorous means of testing those hypotheses.

33.4.2. Learning

Critical appraisals of evolutionary psychology sometimes proceed from the misperception that an evolutionary approach ignores the important role of learning and other developmental processes (e.g. Lickliter and Honeycutt, 2003). Responses to these criticisms often remind readers that, in fact, development and learning are fundamental components of evolutionary inquiry (e.g. Tooby et al., 2003).

The developmental psychological literature suggests that there are innate constraints and predispositions that allow infants to learn about specific kinds of recurrent features of the social world quickly and efficiently (Springer, 1992; Hirschfeld, 1996; Gergely and Csibra, 2003). The concept of an innate preparedness to learn also figures prominently in research on the evolved basis of fear. When Öhman and Mineka (2001) argue that there is an evolved basis for the common human tendency to fear snakes, they do not suggest that there is an innate fear of snakes. Rather, they suggest that there is an innate predisposition to learn to fear snakes—a specialized adaptation that manifests in the extraordinarily efficient acquisition of a specific stimulus–response algorithm through which the perception of a snake triggers a fear response. Does fear of snakes truly result from the operation of this hypothesized problem-specific learning module? Or might the rapidly acquired fear of snakes result from the flexible application of some other, more general learning mechanism (of which there are many; Moore, 2004) that might have evolved for different reasons altogether? If we really want to know what evolved mechanisms underlie psychological phenomena, these are non-trivial questions. There now exist data that bear on these questions (Öhman and Mineka, 2001).

The same logical template may be productively applied to a broad range of topics in social cognition. As we reviewed above, people respond to angry faces and other danger-connoting features in others in ways that are conceptually similar to the way they respond to snakes. We might assume that people learn those danger-connoting features at a young age. But just what is the nature of that learning process? Is it a highly specialized domain-specific associative learning process, of the kind that underlies taste aversions and—as Öhman and Mineka (2001) suggest—snake phobias? Or is it a more domain-general associative learning process that is applied broadly across any domain of perception and cognition? Or is it some other learning process entirely? Similar questions can be raised in areas of social cognitive inquiry. How exactly do people acquire the set of cues that we use to distinguish kin from non-kin? The role of learning processes—imprinting, associative learning—in kin recognition is implicated across many animal species within the behavioural ecology literature (e.g. Hepper and Cleland, 1999; Sharp et al., 2005), but it has yet to receive more than cursory attention within the literature on human kin recognition. How exactly do people acquire the set of cues that they use to distinguish those who might be carriers of contagious pathogens? How exactly do men and women acquire the set of cues that they use to functionally distinguish desirable from undesirable mates?

These are not easy questions to answer, and there are many different evolved learning processes to consider (Moore, 2004). Nevertheless, by raising questions like this—and attempting to address them empirically—we will eventually be in a position to draw more accurate inferences about what specific psychological mechanisms did evolve, and why, and how they contribute to observed social cognitive phenomena.

33.4.3. Culture

Not only did people evolve to learn specific things about other people, we also evolved to learn *from* other people (Henrich and Boyd, 1998; Henrich and Gil-White, 2001). In part because of the power of imitation, modelling, and other social learning mechanisms, we are cultural animals. Individual-level cognitions and social interactions are importantly influenced by the specific cultural context within which individuals develop (for a review, see Lehman et al., 2004). And, of course, the reverse is also true: cultures—and the social norms that define them—are importantly influenced by the cognitions of and interactions between the people who make up those cultural populations (Lehman et al., 2004; Schaller and Crandall, 2004). An evolutionary analysis of social cognitive processes, and their interpersonal implications, can help us more fully understand the specific beliefs, myths, and other norms that define a culture.

Many cultural norms are socially constructed. They are sculpted and maintained, often unintentionally, through processes of interpersonal communication (Latané, 1996; Harton and Bourgeois, 2004). Communication isn't random. People are motivated to communicate about some kinds of information more than others, and these more highly communicable knowledge structures are more likely to become culturally popular (Schaller et al., 2002). The social construction of culture is, therefore, constrained by individual-level cognitive processes. As we have seen, many cognitive processes may be adaptations designed to solve specific problems of social life. Thus, just as some cognitive adaptations may contribute to cultural norms independent of social transmission (Tooby and Cosmides, 1992), cognitive adaptations may also influence the transmission processes through which cultures are socially constructed.

Many aspects of culture show evidence of these evolved constraints on the transmission and spread of socially shared knowledge structures. One set of studies (Heath et al., 2001) revealed that individuals are more inclined to transmit an urban legend if it more strongly elicits the evolutionarily adaptive self-protective emotion of disgust; consequently, more highly disgust-arousing urban legends are more likely to become and remain a part of popular culture. Other research documents the popularity of erroneous belief in the so-called 'Mozart effect' (the alleged, but actually non-existent, effect whereby children who listen to classical music become more intelligent; Bangerter and Heath, 2004). The unusual success of this false belief may be attributable to the presumably adaptive parental desire to produce children with qualities—such as intelligence—that will help them to eventually compete successfully for mates. Consistent with this reasoning, Bangerter and Heath (2004) reported that the Mozart effect was especially popular within populations in which there was greater collective anxiety about the quality of early childhood education. Other research implicates the role of cognitive adaptations in the interpersonal transmission and eventual popularity of folktales, stereotypes, and other kinds of cultural knowledge (e.g. Schaller et al., 2004; Norenzayan et al., 2006).

These lines of empirical research complement many other lines of inquiry that explore the influence of evolutionary processes on human culture (e.g. Boyd and Richerson, 1985; Tooby and Cosmides 1992; Dunbar *et al.*, 1999; Kenrick *et al.*, 2003; Krebs and Janicki, 2004). Inquiry into the evolutionary underpinnings of social cognition helps to illuminate not only the complex nature of the human mind, but also the nature of the social worlds that human minds create.

Acknowledgments

Preparation of this chapter was supported by research funds provided by the United States National Institutes of Health (Grant # 1RO1MH64734-01A1) and the Social Sciences and Humanities Research Council of Canada (Grant # 41020052224).

References

Adolphs, R. (1999) Social cognition and the human brain. *Trends in Cognitive Sciences*, 3: 469–479.

Bangerter, A. and Heath, C. (2004) The Mozart effect: tracking the evolution of a scientific legend. *British Journal of Social Psychology*, 43: 605–623.

Baumeister, R. F. and Leary, M. R. (1995) The need to belong: desire for interpersonal attachments as a fundamental human motivation. *Psychological Bulletin*, 117: 497–529.

Blascovich, J., Mendes, W. B., Hunter, S. B., Lickel, B. and Kowai-Bell, N. (2001) Perceiver threat in social interactions with stigmatized others. *Journal of Personality and Social Psychology*, 80: 253–267.

Boyd, R. and Richerson, P. J. (1985) *Culture and the Evolutionary Process*. University of Chicago Press, Chicago.

Bradley, B. P., Mogg, K. and Millar, N. H. (2000) Covert and overt orienting of attention in anxiety. *Cognition and Emotion*, 14: 789–808.

Bugental, D. B. (2000) Acquisition of the algorithms of social life: a domain-based approach. *Psychological Bulletin*, 126: 187–219.

Burnstein, E., Crandall, C. and Kitayama, S. (1994) Some neo-Darwinian decision rules for altruism: weighing cues for inclusive fitness as a function of the biological importance of the decision. *Journal of Personality and Social Psychology*, 67: 773–789.

Buss, D. M. and Schmitt, D. P. (1993) Sexual strategies theory: an evolutionary perspective on human mating. *Psychological Review*, 100: 204–232.

Carretié, L., Hinojosa, J. A., Martín-Loeches, M., Mercado, F. and Tapia, M. (2004) Automatic attention to emotional stimuli: neural correlates. *Human Brain Mapping*, 22: 290–299.

Conway, L. G. III and Schaller, M. (2002) On the verifiability of evolutionary psychological theories: an analysis of the psychology of scientific persuasion. *Personality and Social Psychology Review*, 6: 152–166.

Cosmides, L. (1989) The logic of social exchange: has natural selection shaped how humans reason? *Cognition*, 31: 187–276.

Cosmides, L. and Tooby, J. (1992) Cognitive adaptations for social exchange. In J. H. Barkow, L. Cosmides and J. Tooby (eds) *The Adapted Mind*, pp. 163–228. Oxford University Press, Oxford.

Cottrell, C. A. and Neuberg, S. L. (2005) Different emotional reactions to different groups: a sociofuntional threat-based approach to "prejudice." *Journal of Personality and Social Psychology*, 88: 770–789.

Cummins, D. D. (1999) Cheater detection is modified by social rank: the impact of dominance on the evolution of cognitive functions. *Evolution and Human Behavior*, 20: 229–248.

DeBruine, L. M. (2002) Facial resemblance enhances trust. *Proceedings of the Royal Society of London, B*, 269: 1307–1312.

DeBruine, L. M. (2005) Trustworthy but not lust-worthy: context-specific effects of facial resemblance. *Proceedings of the Royal Society of London, B*, 272: 919–922.

Duchaine, B., Cosmides, L. and Tooby, J. (2001) Evolutionary psychology and the brain. *Current Opinion in Neurobiology*, 11: 225–230.

Dukas, R. (2002) Behavioural and ecological consequences of limited attention. *Philosophical Transactions of the Royal Society of London, B*, 357: 1539–1547.

Dunbar, R. (1997) *Grooming, Gossip, and the Evolution of Language*. Harvard University Press, Cambridge Massachusetts, USA.

Dunbar, R., Knight, C. and Power, C. (1999) *The Evolution of Culture: An Interdisciplinary View*. Edinburgh University Press, Edinburgh.

Faulkner, J., Schaller, M., Park, J. H. and Duncan, L. A. (2004) Evolved disease-avoidance mechanisms and contemporary xenophobic attitudes. *Group Processes and Intergroup Behavior*, 7: 333–353.

Fiddick, L., Cosmides, L. and Tooby, J. (2000) No interpretation without representation: the role of domain-specific representations and inferences in the Wason selection task. *Cognition*, 77: 1–79.

Fink, B. and Penton-Voak, I. (2002) Evolutionary psychology of facial attractiveness. *Current Directions in Psychological Science*, 11: 154–158.

Fiske, A. P. (1992) The four elementary forms of sociality: framework for a unified theory of social relations. *Psychological Review*, 99: 689–723.

Fiske, S. T. (2004) *Social Beings: A Core Motives Approach to Social Psychology*. Wiley, Hoboken, NJ.

Fox, E., Russo, R., Bowles, R. and Dutton, K. (2001) Do threatening stimuli draw or hold visual attention in subclinical anxiety? *Journal of Experimental Psychology: General*, 130: 681–700.

Gangestad, S. W. and Thornhill, R. (1998) Menstrual cycle variation in women's preference for the scent of symmetrical men. *Proceedings of the Royal Society of London, B*, 262: 727–733.

Gangestad, S. W., Simpson, J. A., Cousins, A. J., Garver-Apgar, C. E. and Christensen, P. N. (2004) Women's preferences for male behavioral displays change across the menstrual cycle. *Psychological Science*, 15: 203–207.

Gergely, G. and Csibra, G. (2003) Teleological reasoning in infancy: the naïve theory of rational action. *Trends in Cognitive Sciences*, 7: 287–292.

Goodall, J. (1986) Social rejection, exclusion, and shunning among the Gombe chimpanzees. *Ethology and Sociobiology*, 7: 227–239.

Grillon, C., Pellowski, M., Merikangas, K. R. and Davis, M. (1997) Darkness facilitates acoustic startle reflex in humans. *Biological Psychiatry*, 42: 453–460.

Harton, H. C. and Bourgeois, M. J. (2004) Cultural elements emerge from dynamic social impact. In M. Schaller and C. S. Crandall (eds) *The Psychological Foundations of Culture*, pp. 41–75. Lawrence Erlbaum, Mahwah, NJ.

Haselton, M. G. and Buss, D. M. (2000) Error management theory: a new perspective on biases in cross-sex mind reading. *Journal of Personality and Social Psychology*, 78: 81–91.

Haselton, M. G. and Funder, D. (2006) The evolution of accuracy and bias in social judgment. In M. Schaller, J. A. Simpson and D. T. Kenrick (eds) *Evolution and Social Psychology*, pp. 15–37. Psychology Press, New York.

Haselton, M. G. and Nettle, D. (2006) The paranoid optimist: an integrative evolutionary model of cognitive biases. *Personality and Social Psychology Review*, 10: 47–66.

Heath, C., Bell, C. and Sternberg, E. (2001) Emotional selection in memes: the case of urban legends. *Journal of Personality and Social Psychology*, 81: 1028–1041.

Henrich, J. and Boyd, R. (1998) The evolution of conformist transmission and between-group differences. *Evolution and Human Behavior*, 19: 215–242.

Henrich, J. and Gil-White, F. J. (2001) The evolution of prestige: freely conferred status as a mechanism for enhancing the benefits of cultural transmission. *Evolution and Human Behavior*, 22: 165–196.

Hepper, P. G. (1991) *Kin Recognition*. Cambridge University Press, Cambridge.

Hepper, P. G. and Cleland, J. (1999) Developmental aspects of kin recognition. *Genetica*, 104: 199–205.

Hirschfeld, L. A. (1996) *Race in the Making: Cognition, Culture, and the Child's Construction of Human Kinds*. The MIT Press, Cambridge MA.

Hoffman, E. and Haxby, J. (2000) Distinct representations of eye gaze and identity in the distributed human neural system for face perception. *Nature Neuroscience*, 3: 80–84.

Kanwisher, N. (2000) Domain specificity in face perception. *Nature Neuroscience*, 3: 759–763.

Kenrick, D. T., Sadalla, E. K., Groth, G. and Trost, M. R. (1990) Evolution, traits, and the stages of human courtship: qualifying the parental investment model. *Journal of Personality*, 58: 97–116.

Kenrick, D. T., Neuberg, S. L. and Cialdini, R. B. (1999) *Social Psychology: Unraveling the Mystery*. Allyn & Bacon, Boston.

Kenrick, D. T., Maner, J. K., Butner, J., Li, N. P., Becker, V. and Schaller, M. (2002) Dynamical evolutionary psychology: mapping the domains of the new interactionist paradigm. *Personality and Social Psychology Review*, 6: 347–356.

Kenrick, D. T., Li, N. P. and Butner, J. (2003) Dynamical evolutionary psychology: individual decision-rules and emergent social norms. *Psychological Review*, 110: 3–28.

Krebs, D. and Janicki, M. (2004) Biological foundations of moral norms. In M. Schaller and C. S. Crandall (eds) *The Psychological Foundations of Culture*, pp. 125–148. Lawrence Erlbaum, Mahwah NJ.

Kurzban, R. and Leary, M. R. (2001) Evolutionary origins of stigmatization: the functions of social exclusion. *Psychological Bulletin*, 127: 187–208.

Kurzban, R., Tooby, J. and Cosmides, L. (2001) Can race be erased? Coalitional computation and social categorization. *Proceedings of the National Academy of Sciences of the USA*, 98: 15387–15392.

Latané, B. (1996) Dynamic social impact: the creation of culture by communication. *Journal of Communication*, 6: 13–25.

Lehman, D. R., Chiu, C.-Y. and Schaller, M. (2004) Psychology and culture. *Annual Review of Psychology*, 55: 689–714.

Lickliter, R. and Honeycutt, H. (2003) Developmental dynamics: toward a biologically plausible evolutionary psychology. *Psychological Bulletin*, 129: 819–835.

Lieberman, D., Tooby, J. and Cosmides, L. (2003) Does morality have a biological basis? An empirical test of the factors governing moral sentiments regarding incest. *Proceedings of the Royal Society of London, B*, 270: 819–826.

Lunqvist, D. and Öhman, A. (2005) Emotion regulates attention: the relation between facial configurations, facial emotion, and visual attention. *Visual Cognition*, 12: 51–84.

Maner, J. K., Kenrick, D. T., Becker, D. V. et al. (2003) Sexually selective cognition: beauty captures the mind of the beholder. *Journal of Personality and Social Psychology*, 85: 1107–1120.

Maner, J. K., Kenrick, D. T., Becker, D. V. et al. (2005) Functional projection: how fundamental social motives can bias interpersonal perception. *Journal of Personality and Social Psychology*, 88: 63–78.

Mealey, L., Daood, C. and Krage, M. (1996) Enhanced memory for faces of cheaters. *Ethology and Sociobiology*, 17: 119–128.

Moore, B. R. (2004) The evolution of learning. *Biological Reviews*, 79: 301–335.

Navarre, C. D., Fessler, D. M. T. and Eng, S. J. (unpublished manuscript) Elevated ethnoantrism across pregnancy. (Harvard University).

Nesse, R. M. (2005) Natural selection and the regulation of defenses: a signal detection analysis of the smoke detector principle. *Evolution and Human Behavior*, 26: 88–105.

Neuberg, S. L. and Cottrell, C. A. (2006) Evolutionary bases of prejudices. In M. Schaller, J. A. Simpson and D. T. Kenrick (eds) *Evolution and Social Psychology*, pp. 163–187. Psychology Press, New York.

Norenzayan, A., Atran, S., Faulkner, J. and Schaller, M. (2006) Memory and mystery: the cultural selection of minimally counterintuitive narratives. *Cognitive Science*, 30: 531–553.

Oda, R. (1997) Biased face recognition in the prisoner's dilemma games. *Evolution and Human Behavior*, 18: 309–315.

Öhman, A. and Mineka, S. (2001) Fear, phobia, and preparedness: toward an evolved module of fear and fear learning. *Psychological Review*, 108: 483–522.

Öhman, A., Flykt, A. and Esteves, F. (2001) Emotion drives attention: detecting the snake in the grass. *Journal of Experimental Psychology: General*, 130: 466–478.

Panksepp, J. and Panksepp, J. B. (2000) The seven sins of evolutionary psychology. *Evolution and Cognition*, 6: 108–131.

Park, J. H. and Schaller, M. (2005) Does attitude similarity serve as a heuristic cue for kinship? evidence of an implicit cognitive association. *Evolution and Human Behavior*, 26: 158–170.

Park, J. H., Faulkner, J. and Schaller, M. (2003) Evolved disease-avoidance processes and contemporary anti-social behavior: prejudicial attitudes and avoidance of people with physical disabilities. *Journal of Nonverbal Behavior*, 27: 65–87.

Penton-Voak, I. S. and Perrett, D. I. (2000) Female preference for male faces changes cyclically: Further evidence. *Evolution and Human Behavior*, 21: 39–48.

Phelps, E. A., O'Conner, K. J., Cunningham, W. A. *et al.* (2000) Performance on indirect measures of race evaluation predicts amygdala activation. *Journal of Cognitive Neuroscience*, 12: 729–738.

Rendall, D. (2004) "Recognizing" kin: mechanisms, media, minds, modules, and muddles. In B. Chapais and C. M. Berman (eds) *Kinship and Behavior in Primates*, pp. 295–316. Oxford University Press, Oxford.

Ristic, J., Friesen, C. K. and Kingstone, A. (2002) Are eyes special? It depends on how you look at it. *Psychonomic Bulletin and Review*, 9: 507–513.

Schaller, M. and Crandall, C. S. (2004) *The Psychological Foundations of Culture*. Lawrence Erlbaum, Mahwah, NJ.

Schaller, M., Conway, L. G. III and Tanchuk, T. L. (2002) Selective pressures on the once and future contents of ethnic stereotypes: effects of the communicability of traits. *Journal of Personality and Social Psychology*, 82: 861–877.

Schaller, M., Faulkner, J., Park, J. H., Neuberg, S. L. and Kenrick, D. T. (2004) Impressions of danger influence impressions of people: an evolutionary perspective on individual and collective cognition. *Journal of Cultural and Evolutionary Psychology*, 2: 231–247.

Schaller, M., Park, J. H. and Faulkner, J. (2003) Prehistoric dangers and contemporary prejudices. *European Review of Social Psychology*, 14: 105–137.

Schmitt, D. P. and Pilcher, J. J. (2004) Evaluating evidence of psychological adaptation: how do we know one when we see one? *Psychological Science*, 15: 643–649.

Schupp, H. T., Öhman, A., Junghofer, M., Weike, A. I., Stockburger, J. and Hamm, A. O. (2004) The facilitated processing of threatening faces: an ERP analysis. *Emotion*, 4: 189–200.

Sharp, S. P., McGowan, A., Wood, M. J. and Hatchwell, B. J. (2005) Learned kin recognition cues in a social bird. *Nature*, 434: 1127–1130.

Simpson, J. A. and Gangestad, S. W. (1991) Individual differences in sociosexuality: evidence for convergent and discriminant validity. *Journal of Personality and Social Psychology*, 60: 870–883.

Springer, K. (1992) Children's awareness of the biological implications of kinship. *Child Development*, 63: 950–959.

Stone, V. E., Cosmides, L., Tooby, J., Kroll, N. and Knight, R. T. (2002) Selective impairment of reasoning about social exchange in a patient with bilateral limbic system damage. *Proceedings of the National Academy of Sciences*, 99: 11531–11536.

Sugiyama, L. S., Tooby, J. and Cosmides, L. (2002) Cross-cultural evidence of cognitive adaptations for social exchange among the Shiwiar of Ecuadorian Amazonia. *Proceedings of the National Academy of Sciences*, 99: 11537–11542.

Taylor, S. E. and Gonzaga, G. C. (2006) Evolution, relationships, and health: the social shaping hypothesis. In M. Schaller, J. A. Simpson and D. T. Kenrick (eds) *Evolution and Social Psychology*, pp. 211–236. Psychology Press, New York.

Thornhill, R. and Gangestad, S. W. (1999) Facial attractiveness. *Trends in Cognitive Sciences*, 3: 452–460.

Tooby, J. and Cosmides, L. (1992) The psychological foundations of culture. In J. H. Barkow, L. Cosmides and J. Tooby (eds) *The Adapted Mind*, pp. 19–136. Oxford University Press, Oxford.

Tooby, J., Cosmides, L. and Barrett, H. C. (2003) The second law of thermodynamics is the first law of psychology: evolutionary developmental psychology and the theory of tandem, coordinated inheritances. *Psychological Bulletin*, 129: 858–865.

Willingham, D. T. and Dunn, E. W. (2003) What neuroimaging and brain localization can do, cannot do, and should not do for social psychology. *Journal of Personality and Social Psychology*, 85: 662–671.

Yamagishi, T., Tanida, S., Mashima, R., Shimoma, E. and Kanazawa, S. (2003) You can judge a book by its cover: evidence that cheaters may look different from cooperators. *Evolution and Human Behavior*, 24: 290–301.

CHAPTER 34

Temporal knowledge and autobiographical memory: an evolutionary perspective

John J. Skowronski and Constantine Sedikides

34.1. Introduction

One characteristic of humans is that they have a sense of self. Exactly what does this mean? Examination of research and theory exploring the psychology of the self suggests that it has at least three important aspects.

The first of these aspects is *representation*: the memory system contains mental structures that store and organize different kinds of self-relevant knowledge. Some of this knowledge is affective, reflecting the feelings that people have about themselves. Also, some of the knowledge is behavioural, reflecting mental procedures that contain memories of how to carry out various routines (e.g. riding a bicycle). This procedural information is often stored in non-verbal form. In addition, some of the knowledge reflects episodic memories of specific life events. These memories contain perceptual details of events, as well as information about event contexts (e.g. the time at which an event occurred). Furthermore, some of the knowledge is semantic, reflecting memories of self-judgements or the judgements that others have made of, and

conveyed to, the self. These self-judgements can be global (e.g. I am an uncoordinated person) or situationally constrained (e.g. I am good at cooking Indian food). These semantic representations can also contain memories of meta-cognitions (e.g. ideas about how others perceive one's behaviour), information referring to dyadic relationships, information about one's position within a group, and information about intra-group dynamics and inter-group relations. Moreover, these semantic representations might contain information about how one compares to others or to the groups to which one belongs. Such information highlights those attributes that make one unique and distinct from attributes that characterize others (*personal self*), those attributes that are shared with others with whom one has interpersonal relations (*relational self*), or those attributes that one shares with the groups to which one belongs (*collective self*) (Sedikides and Brewer, 2001).

The second attribute of the human self is that it maintains an *executive* function, regulating an individual's relation with the social and physical environment. Three classes of motives likely guide this capacity (Sedikides and Skowronski, 2000; Sedikides *et al.*, 2004): *valuation* (i.e. protecting and enhancing the self), *learning* (i.e. pursing a relatively accurate image of the self, improving skills and abilities), and *homeostasis* (i.e. seeking and endorsing information that is consistent with the self).

The third attribute of the self is *reflexivity*. This term can be defined as the organism's ability to depict itself in its ongoing relation with other objects. Reflexivity is manifested in the interplay between the representational and executive capacities. For example, reflexivity allows the organism to alter long-term goals and render them congruent with anticipated environmental changes. This ability to reflect on the self also involves the capacity for humans to engage in *mental time travel*. That is, humans can remember (or, more accurately, use their knowledge to reconstruct) specific events in the past, and can have some knowledge of the time and the place at which those events occurred. Humans can also reflect on their role in future events and engage in alternative mental simulations of future events in which the nature of those events, an individual's role in those events, and each event's outcome can be manipulated.

In previous writings (Sedikides and Skowronski, 1997, 2000, 2003; Sedikides *et al.*, 2004; Skowronski and Sedikides, 1999; Sedikides *et al.*, in press), we discussed these aspects of the self in the context of evolution. Our argument has been that these self-aspects developed in response to the environmental challenges that were encountered by the ancestors of the human species and by early humans. These environmental challenges included not only the pressures imposed by the physical environment (e.g. food procurement, climate, predation), but also the pressures imposed by the social and cultural context of human behaviour.

34.2. Temporal knowledge in the context of evolution

The present chapter will recapitulate some of these themes in the context of the ability of humans to remember events in their lives at specific points in time. We do so with some

trepidation, for the study of time and memory has a long intellectual history. For example, in his *Confessiones*, penned early in the fourth century, Saint Augustine (Book XI, see Haddan's 1872 translation) derived the then-radical conclusion that perceptions of time itself (or, at least, perceptions of the past and of the future) are things that are contained in the mind. Augustine was largely concerned with the estimation of durations; the length of time events happened or the length of time between events. This interest in event durations significantly influenced early scientific psychological theorizing (James, 1890) and is reflected in the modern discipline of mental chronobiology (Bradshaw and Szabadi, 1997).

However, the ability to make these duration judgements presupposes the ability to know how long ago the beginning of an event (or when a prior event) occurred. Thus, in order to understand duration estimates, psychologists need to know how an individual knows the age of events. Whereas event-specific temporal knowledge has not been studied as thoroughly as duration perceptions, it too has a long intellectual history (Hoffding, 1892; James, 1890; Sturt, 1925) and has recently been the subject of intense empirical scrutiny (Hoerl and McCormack, 2001; Friedman, 2004).

Why might the ability to know the time at which an event occurred, or the event's age, be important to humans? One reason lies in the fact that humans have a self-concept, and many elements of this self-concept incorporate, or require the use of, at least some event-specific temporal knowledge. For example, an individual's sense of growth and change comes from their ability to know when events occurred in their lives. How can one draw any conclusions about progress in one's ability in a given domain if one cannot properly order recollections of the early episodes of struggle and the later episodes of accomplishment? More generally, just imagine how incomplete one's sense of self might be without the ability to temporally locate autobiographical events. Given this line of argument, it seems reasonable to argue that, to understand the self, one must understand the nature of one's ability to remember events in their temporal context.

The evolutionary twist to this idea is the argument that the capacity to develop a self-concept may have been a product of evolution (Sedikides and Skowronski, 1997, 2000, 2003; Sedikides *et al.*, in press). That is, the capacity to think about the self in an abstract manner was likely an adaptive response to the environmental pressures faced by both the species that were ancestors to modern humans and the early members of the human species. The possession of a self-concept can endow the possessor with several rewards, ranging from advantages in food procurement, predation avoidance, and interpersonal relations with other group members. We extend this line of reasoning by taking an evolutionary perspective on an organism's ability to remember when an event or behaviour occurred. We argue that being able to store temporally relevant information and being able to retrieve and use that information to determine the time at which an event occurred has adaptive value to a species.

What might that adaptive value be? Being sensitive to temporal information can improve the fit between an organism and the environmental niche that the organism occupies. For example, many organisms have the ability to remember the time of day at which given sources of food are available (Gallistel, 1990). Similar kinds of temporal sensitivity may guide the instigation of migratory behaviours, as well as times in which an individual chooses to be relatively inactive. Such inactivity minimizes energy use at low-payoff times or helps to protect an organism from predation. In short, in many circumstances time is one of the discriminative cues that an organism uses to optimize its behaviour in a given environment. It matters for an organism to be sensitive to, and use, temporal information.

One element of this sensitivity to time is the ability to store temporal information in, and retrieve it from, memory. This can be accomplished in several ways. One might build temporal sensitivity into an organism in such a way that the temporal stimulus is a relatively automatic trigger for behaviour. One hypothetical example is activity level. For some organisms, when light levels fall below a given threshold, the neural system may automatically instigate behaviour inactivity. A second way in which an organism can be sensitive to temporal information is via some sort of conceptual or rule-based knowledge. For example, an individual organism

may have developed abstract concepts allowing differentiation among different types of flowers, and might come to learn that a given type of flower is good to visit when the sun goes down because that is when the flowers open and make the flowers' sweet-tasting nectar available. This does not require memory for specific flower visits. It requires only the realization that a given flower type, visited at a given time, is likely to yield a food reward. A third way in which an organism can be sensitive to temporal information occurs when temporal information is stored as a part of memories for specific episodes. For example, an organism might remember that a given river contained many fish when the river was visited at a particular time of day and in a particular season. Such event-based recollections might induce the organism to visit that river again at that same time during that same season.

These sources of temporal knowledge correspond to the three different types of knowledge (*anoetic, noetic* and *autonoetic*) that can be stored in memory and that may comprise different memory subsystems (Tulving, 1985). This distinction, too, is of potential evolutionary importance. Some scholars have argued that not all organisms share these different knowledge systems, and that some systems are more characteristic of organisms that have particularly large and differentiated brains that can perform numerous specialized and complex thinking tasks. For example, Suddendorf and Corballis (1997) suggest that the ability to remember single specific episodes from one's past is a relatively recent evolutionary development, relying on the ability to think about oneself in abstract terms. In their view, the fact that the self has the property of reflexivity is what allows humans so easily to think about past behaviours and events that occur at a particular time and in a particular place. The product of this reflexive thinking can then be stored in memory. Hence, in the view of Suddendorf and Corballis, the ability to have episodic memories can only occur once an organism has acquired the capacity to think about oneself abstractly (e.g. as a symbolic self; Sedikides and Skowronski, 1997). Their thesis, then, is that there can be no memory for individual events without a functional self-concept.

We disagree with this thesis. Both reason and data suggest to us that the ability to represent and use recalled event-specific information (including temporal information) evolved independently of the capacity to form and use a symbolic self. Instead, we propose that the evolution of a symbolic self depends, in part, on the prior ability to mentally represent the details of specific life events. Hence, we would expect to observe evidence that the ability to know the time at which events occurred emerged earlier in evolution and was a more widespread adaptation compared to the ability to form a symbolic self.

In evaluating this proposal, one must first consider whether the ability to recall the temporal context of specific life episodes itself could be an adaptation driven by evolution. Friedman (2001) argues that the ability to remember the temporal context of specific episodes may not have much adaptive potential. Instead, he argues that the ability to remember information relevant to the typical time cycles that are important to an organism's environmental niche is a more likely candidate for the action of natural selection. We disagree. Rather, we maintain that, in many circumstances, it can be very adaptive for an organism to have even approximate knowledge of when a past event occurred or when a prior action was performed.

Consider, for example, animals who engage in food-caching behaviour. Some cached foods are relatively impervious to decay (e.g. nuts). Other types of food are relatively decay-prone. If an organism is to make efficient use of time in retrieving food from multiple caches, then it would be useful if the organism could remember how long ago a given food item was cached—especially if the animal has the ability to learn that some foods spoil when stored for long periods of time.

This is not a hypothetical example. Griffiths *et al.* (1999; also see de Kort *et al.*, 2005) trained jays in a task in which the jays cached either worms or peanuts in two separate sand-filled trays. The birds were given the opportunity to learn that the worms decayed and were inedible 124 h after caching, but that the peanuts were still edible. After training, the jays were later presented with a task in which one food was cached in one side of a tray and, 120 h later, the other food was cached on the other side of the tray. Four hours later, the jays were allowed to forage in the tray. When the worms were the first food cached

(124 h ago), the jays preferentially searched for peanuts. This did not occur when the worms were the second food cached (4 h ago). Such behaviour required that the jays remembered what they had hidden, where they had hidden it, and how long ago it was hidden. The jays' use of all of these kinds of information would seem to be hallmarks of memories for specific episodes.

However, as we will note later in this chapter, the behaviour of the jays does not necessarily imply that they had specific memories for each of the caching events. Several theorists (Roberts, 2002; Suddendorf and Corballis, 1997) have claimed that other, non-event specific memory information might be responsible for the jays' ability to remember how long ago a food was cached. At the moment, more important for our purposes is the idea that memory for an event's age can sometimes have adaptive value for an organism, and hence, is potentially an attribute that can be evolutionarily selected.

The ability to locate events in time is not solely restricted to jays. For example, Schwartz *et al.* (2005) have conducted studies with King, an adult male western lowland gorilla. The results of these studies showed that King's behaviour reflected episodic-like memory properties, in that King could remember the order of past events (Experiment 1) and could remember where events occurred (Experiment 2).

In our view, the generality of such findings across species is an important fact favouring an evolutionary genesis of the ability to locate events in time. In fact, we would be quite surprised if this ability were solely the purview of humans. It has often been said that evolution is a tinkerer, and works by taking old characteristics and modifying them. Hence, it seems sensible that one would find the precursors of temporal knowledge abilities, or simple versions of a temporal knowledge system, in those species that are relatively close to humans on the bush of evolution. Moreover, because nature often re-uses solutions, when species confront similar environmental pressures, evolution often comes up with similar responses to those pressures. Hence, even species that are distantly related may come to share similar traits because of the extent to which those traits aid adaptiveness to the similar environments shared by those species. This suggests that, if the ability to remember temporal knowledge is an adaptation, then it may be shared by many species that inhabit similar environments.

Obviously, the adaptive value of temporal knowledge will be particularly high for species whose environments continually present problems that can be best solved if one has access to the temporal context of past events and behaviours. Humans are one of these species. For example, a crucial motive that drives human behaviour is self-enhancement (Sedikides and Gregg, 2003; Sedikides and Strube, 1997). One of the hallmarks of self-enhancement is the perception of personal growth—that one has improved one's status or abilities from where one was in the past. Development and maintenance of veridicality in such self-judgements relies on the ability to remember what one was like at various points in the past. We do not claim that humans are perfect in this regard—people's recollections of what they were like at various points in the past can be biased in many ways (Cameron *et al.*, 2004). Instead, our main point is that pursuit of self-enhancement is promoted by the ability to perceive improvement from one's prior state. In order to do that, one will need to have at least an approximate sense of the point in time at which that prior state existed.

The ability to remember the temporal context of events may be particularly critical to knowledge in the social domain. In previous work (Sedikides and Skowronski, 1997, 2003), we have argued that the line of evolution that yielded modern humans was likely to have occurred in a relatively unstructured social context. This unstructured social context resembles modern human behaviour, in which alliances form, shift, disengage, and reform with a relatively high frequency. Optimal functioning in such an environment would seem to be facilitated if organisms were able to keep track of who had done what with whom (or to whom) at different specific times in the past. Such knowledge would likely help individuals to make better decisions about interpersonal behaviour. For example, if you recall that one group member was a cheater (e.g. hoarded provisions) in his early days, but has not engaged in such behaviour recently, you might be more likely to trust that individual than when you could not remember the times at which that individual had cheated or had been honest.

Another example might concern decisions about paternity in a species (e.g. humans) that does not maintain exclusivity in sexual partners. For example, if a female had sex with one individual 15 months ago, with a second individual 8 months ago, and with a third individual 2 months ago, the female needs to recall the age of those encounters reliably to infer the paternity of the infant to whom she just gave birth. Evolution-driven paternity concerns are paramount for females who invest large amounts of time and effort in their young (Sagarin, 2005). Hence, it would seem beneficial if the new mother could accurately recall the time at which intercourse with each partner was initiated so that paternity could be definitively established.

34.3. On humans' ability to remember when

Up to this point in the chapter, we have discussed humans' ability to place personal life events in time in an abstract manner. However, we believe that it would be beneficial if some time were spent reviewing a few specific findings pertaining to this ability. These findings can be particularly enlightening with respect to the kinds of information that are used when individuals attempt to place events in time, and can help clarify some important questions with respect to the possible evolution of the capacity to store and retrieve temporal knowledge.

Results of a good deal of temporal judgement research suggest that temporal knowledge becomes less accurate with increases in time from the target event. For example, in several studies conducted in the laboratory of one of this chapter's co-authors (Thompson *et al.*, 1988a; Skowronski *et al.*, 1995), participants entered events in a dated diary, then later attempted to reproduce the date when cued with each event (Thompson *et al.*, 1996). Participants could report an autobiographical event's exact date often (70% of the time) if an event was a week old. However, by the time an autobiographical event was 10 weeks old, the exact accuracy rate of event dating dropped substantially (e.g. 20% accuracy rate). Another way to illustrate increasing inaccuracy across time is to calculate the extent to which the average amount of error associated with event date estimates increases over time. In studies reported by Thompson *et al.* (1996), that amount was approximately 1 day per week of event age. That is, estimates of event dates that were 10 weeks old evinced an approximate average of 10 days of error; events that were 20 weeks old evinced an approximate average of 20 days of error, etc.

A second consistent pattern, also illustrated by the above-mentioned findings, is that participants do not often recall the exact time at which an event occurred. In the Thompson *et al.* (1996) investigation, even when events were only 10 weeks old, and even when participants had the advantage of writing the events in a dated diary, participants could still date only one in five events with exact accuracy. Friedman (1987) reported that this paucity of event-specific temporal memory was evidenced across multiple time frames: participants in his study infrequently reported exact temporal knowledge about events, regardless of whether one asked about the month in which an event occurred, the day of the month, the day of the week, or the hour of the day.

The accumulating data also suggest a relationship between memory for an event's content and the accuracy of event dating: the better an event is remembered, the more accurate the temporal estimate provided for the event. For example, in several studies (Skowronski *et al.*, 1991; Betz and Skowronski, 1997), participants provided ratings of how well they remembered autobiographical events, as well as providing event dates. Self-rated memory strength was significantly related to the accuracy of the temporal estimates that were provided by participants. That this should occur is obvious—if one recalls that an event occurred when snow was on the ground, one would probably suspect that the event occurred in winter. Participants' self-reports of the process by which they obtained event dates fit with this notion. They indicated that they did sometimes use their ability to remember event details to reconstruct the time at which an event occurred.

The notion that event dates are reconstructed leaves open the possibility that those reconstructions can be biased. Indeed, many such biases have been identified. These biases often reflect the influence of abstract real-world knowledge on temporal judgements. For example, one bias occurs due to the presence of a bounded time period specifying the starting and ending points between which events must have occurred. Many of the studies conducted in this line of research used such bounded periods—typically the beginning and end of academic terms. The presence of such boundaries produced *telescoping effects* in the date estimates (Thompson *et al.*, 1988b). When the events were recent, the events were misdated in the direction of being older than they were (*backward telescoping*); when the events were old, the events were misdated in the direction of being younger then they were (*forward telescoping*). The telescoping effects reflect the impact of landmark boundaries on those guesses: dating errors drift toward the middle of the period defined by the boundaries (Rubin and Baddeley, 1989).

Errors in dating observed by Thompson *et al.* (1993) provided additional evidence for the use of landmarks to construct date estimates. One typical landmark event is the start of a connected event sequence, such as the start of a vacation. To estimate the dates of all the same-vacation events listed in one's diary, one simply has to establish the date of the initial event and subsequently date all the vacation events relative to that initially dated landmark. However, if the first event is misdated, then the remaining events would be misdated by exactly the same amount of time. Thompson *et al.* (1993) showed that there were frequent 'error runs' in the date estimates: clusters of similarly misdated events (e.g. a series of events on 5 consecutive days, all of which were misdated by 7 days) occurred at a rate greater than that expected by chance.

One other consistently observed finding is that, when temporal information is reconstructed, the reconstructions often use available information that can operate on relatively independent multiple time scales. For example, Skowronski *et al.* (1991) first showed that error frequencies in date estimates showed a peculiar 'scalloping' pattern: the most frequent errors in date estimates were at multiples of 7 days (7, 14, 21, etc.). Such error patterns reflect the fact that a standard blank calendar that included day of the week was used to cue participants' date estimates (Gibbons and Thompson, 2001), and that participants had day-of-week knowledge available to them that was cued by these day-of-week labels.

Hence, the calendar might prompt people to recall that an event happened on a Tuesday, but not *which* Tuesday.

Betz and Skowronski (1997) elaborated on this finding. They showed that participants were more likely to make dating errors within particular day-of-week segments than between day-of-week segments. For example, it was relatively likely that a person would misdate a Saturday event (e.g. attending a nephew's soccer match) as occurring on a Sunday; but it was relatively less likely that the person would misdate that event as occurring on a Tuesday. They argued that these findings followed from top-down knowledge about the nature of events that occur within a given week. That is, for many people, weeks are temporally segmented into subunits: a typical segmentation is weekend versus weekday. Hence, when trying to reconstruct the date on which an event occurred, people may be able to place it in a week sub-segment (e.g. a weekend event), but not the exact day within that sub-segment. Thus, misdating errors are likely to occur for days within a given sub-segment, but not between sub-segments.

Many of the findings described in the preceding paragraphs point to the notion that substantial reconstruction is needed to establish the time at which an event occurred. The effortful nature of such reconstructions seemed to be confirmed by the subjective responses of participants in the Thompson–Skowronski event dating studies. The process of determining event dates was subjectively difficult for many of these individuals (e.g. they often complained about the difficulty of the task), and it typically took participants a long time to complete the dating task.

However, not all temporal knowledge needs to be so painstakingly reconstructed. For example, some studies exploring temporal knowledge ask participants to judge the order in which two events occurred. Response accuracy and latency are commonly recorded in such studies (Skowronski *et al.*, 2003, and in press). One outcome of such studies is *a temporal distance effect*: Controlling for the ages of the events that are involved, the farther apart in age the two events are, the easier (faster, more accurate) the judgement becomes. This temporal distance effect is inconsistent with the notion that event age

estimates are obtained with great difficulty. Instead, for events that are far apart in age, event-order judgements are made with great speed and accuracy. This suggests that there is some characteristic of event representations that allows rapid identification of rudimentary forms of temporal knowledge.

In fact, when viewed through a different lens, many of the studies in the Thompson–Skowronski programme of research can also be viewed as supportive of such mechanisms. For example, even though the error magnitudes associated with event date estimates increased substantially with an event's age, it was none the less the case that the average of the date estimates across participants often approximated an event's real age. Thus, though erroneous, the event dates were not random guesses—participants' responses often reflected some temporal knowledge. This rough level of accuracy emerged even when participants indicated that the event date that they provided was not a product of reconstruction, but was it was just a guess.

On the basis of his research with children, Friedman (2001) came to a similar conclusion about the fact that some temporal knowledge may not come from elaborate temporal reconstructions. He reviewed the results of several studies suggesting that young children have the ability to know approximate event ages (at least up to a point), despite being unable to engage in relatively sophisticated temporal reconstructive strategies.

Possible sources of rough information about an event's age come from the characteristics of a memory: its accessibility or its vividness, for example. The stronger the memory, or the more easily it comes to mind, the more recent the event. In fact, although not voluminous, the literature already provides some evidence for the operation of such mechanisms (Bradburn *et al.*, 1987).

A second possibility is that autobiographical events are linked to semantic information that has temporal implications (Conway and Pleydell-Pearce, 2000). That is, there may be a 'header' or 'tag' linked to an event that identifies the broad period in which the event occurred. This tag could be 'graduate school' or 'my first job' or 'when I was a kid.' When events are separated by long periods of time, temporal discriminations may be easy because the temporal orderings are specified by the tags ('when I was a kid' comes before 'graduate school'). When events are relatively close in time, such time-discriminating event tags may not be present and people may need repeatedly to access fine-grained event knowledge in their attempt to determine event orders. Such repeated access is difficult, which would be indicated by responses that take a long time and are often incorrect. Recent research (Skowronski *et al.*, in press) has confirmed this prediction.

Another possibility lies in the fact that the self-concept can serve as a context for memory (Skowronski *et al.*, in press). When recalling an autobiographical event, one's recollection might include memories about self—both external characteristics and abilities as well as internal states and traits. For example, when reminded about scoring a game-winning goal, one might bring to mind that she or he was insecure because or a recent move to a new town, was small in physical stature in comparison to other players on the team, and had just mastered a new bicycle kick that allowed the goal to be scored. This activated self-image can serve as a 'rough and ready' cue that helps to place an event in temporal context. Thus, one might be able roughly to place an event in time by comparing the self-image activated by the event recall to one's current self-image. Self-images that are highly discrepant imply old events; self-images that are congruent imply recent events. Similarly, when trying to decide which of two events is more recent, the event that prompts recall of a self-image that is more discrepant from the current self is the event that will be judged to be older.

One final possibility is that some form of temporal information is encoded when events are stored in memory. For example, Brown *et al.* (2000) suggest the presence of an array of neural-array oscillators that work at different frequencies. The state of the array at any given moment is a learning context that can become a part of the stored memory for a given experience. Generally speaking, the greater the temporal distance between two events, the greater the difference in the values output by the oscillator array. Hence, one should theoretically be able to determine how long ago events occurred by examining the state of the oscillator information that was encoded with a given memory and comparing it to the current oscillator state. Likewise, the oscillator states of two retrieved memories could be used to determine the relative recency of two recalled events. Such knowledge need not be explicitly accessed, but can instead be an implicit part of the memory system (Brown and Chater, 2001). Hence, when this mechanism is operative people may simply 'know' the relative times of events without the need for extensive reconstruction.

These oscillator models of temporal knowledge have several advantages. One is that they can be mathematically modelled, as Brown *et al.* (2000) have done for their OSCAR model. A second advantage is that, because such models do not involve the operation of higher-order cognitive processes, they can also be applied to the data derived from non-humans. Indeed, as noted earlier in this chapter, a large corpus of knowledge suggests that animals are sensitive to time and often behave as though they had access to event-specific temporal knowledge associated with specific event memories. For example, after being fed at different locations at different times of day, pigeons learn to anticipate where they will get fed (Saksida and Wilke, 1994). Also, animals can make recency judgements between two events: to obtain a reward in a conditional discrimination task, animals can respond to a stimulus array by choosing the stimulus that was presented most recently (Zentall, 2005).

However, the application of the Brown *et al.* (2000) oscillator model mechanisms to animal temporal judgements would seem to assume that animals possess an episodic memory (see McCormack, 2001, p. 292 for a similar argument). Whether or not non-human animals possess this type of memory system has been the subject of much recent debate. The nature of various memory systems, their potential contributions to temporal knowledge, and the potential existence of these memory systems across species are topics that are treated in the next section.

34.4. The types of memory that contribute to knowledge of an event's age

Obviously, attempts at establishing the time at which an event occurred require that an individual have some form of memory. But what kind of memory? We mentioned previously the distinction among three levels of knowing: anoetic (non-knowing), noetic (knowing) and autonoetic (self-knowing) (Tulving, 1985). Anoetic knowledge reflects the traces of experience that are unknowable to the knower. Psychology abounds with demonstrations of this kind of knowledge. For example, studies of subliminal priming show that individuals' responses to the world around them can be influenced by stimuli presented outside the level of conscious awareness (Stapel and Koomen, 2005). In comparison, noetic knowledge reflects one's knowledge about the world. For example, people know that babies are small in size and that dogs are often kept as pets. Finally, autonoetic knowledge reflects memory for one's own personal experiences, such as the time one of this chapter's co-authors was stuck in the airport in Rome.

The empirical evidence indicates that these three types of knowledge reflect different memory systems with different neural substrates (Buckner and Schacter, 2004). Some of the more exotic findings involve patients with various forms of amnesia. These often take the form of dissociations in which only one of the three memory systems seems to show impairment. The distinction between anoetic knowledge and the other two forms of knowledge is indicated by the fact that some patients, such as the famous H.M., lost the ability to remember past experiences but were clearly influenced by those experiences (Ogden and Corkin, 1991). Other patients show seeming dissociations in their ability to remember information about the world in general and in their ability to recall specific events. For example, semantic dementia is primarily a disease in which semantic memory is compromised (Hodges et al., 1992). Patients who show evidence of this dementia have adequate memory for personal events, but are unable to name previously familiar objects, people, and places. They show poor language comprehension and experience deficits on verbally-based semantic memory tests such as category fluency and picture naming, as well as on non-verbal tests of semantic memory. The opposite can also occur: individuals may show evidence of impaired memory for personal episodes while retaining much of their general knowledge about the world (Wheeler and McMillan, 2001; Klein et al., 2002).

The existence of these distinct memory systems implies to some that they have evolved via mechanisms of evolution. This argument is plausible. Each of the memory systems captures a different type of information, and retention of each type of information appears to be beneficial to a species.

In humans, these memory systems seem to emerge at different times in an infant's development. Research on infants' early ability to make sensory discriminations suggests that anoetic forms of memory emerge early in individual human development (DeCasper and Fifer, 1980). Similarly, conceptual knowledge in infants emerges quite early in individual development (Mandler, 2003).

In comparison, it is currently believed that the capacity for episodic memory does not emerge until the beginning of second year of life, at the earliest (Knopf et al., 2005). The phenomenon of childhood amnesia, in which individuals fail to recall events in their early childhood (Loftus, 1993), is also seen by many as evidence for the late emergence of autonoetic memory. According to Perner and Ruffman (1995), this amnesia is caused by children's inability to represent the experiential origins of one's knowledge. That is, children only gradually attain the mental ability to represent events as things that actually happened to them (as opposed to things that are known). According to Howe and Courage (1993), the construction of such representations can occur only when one has developed a personal identity.

Due to the notion that episodic memory contains specific information about the time and place at which events and behaviours occurred, one might be tempted to link the ability to place events in time exclusively to this memory system. We maintain, however, that this inference would be a mistake. Instead, each of the memory systems can make a contribution to the extent to which an individual knows when an event occurred. Consider how general (noetic) knowledge might aid temporal estimation. Even though an adult individual may not be able to recall specifically the time when she fell out of her high chair, she might reasonably make an inference that the event is old. This can occur because of the general knowledge that babies sit in high chairs. Individuals may also use anoetic knowledge in their quest for information. They are likely unaware that they sometimes use the strength or vividness of their memory to judge the age of an event, but they seem to do it, none the less (Bradburn et al., 1987).

To the extent that the ideas underlying the use of these techniques are valid predictors of an event's age, they can help place events in time. However, they are not infallible. Adults may sometimes sit in high chairs, as when being part of a theatrical performance. The strength or vividness of memories can vary for reasons other than an event's age; one such reason is poorly encoded events.

Such reasoning might suggest that a high level of accuracy in temporal knowledge requires autonoetic knowledge. For example, one of this chapter's co-authors vividly remembers skiing in the Rocky Mountains. When remembering the event, he has visual images of the ski slopes, re-experiences the feeling of a brisk wind in the face, and re-experiences feeling the cold of the snow when a tumble was taken (and when a crown fell off a tooth). These sensations are clues as to when the event occurred: sometime in winter. Moreover, in an attempt to narrow down the range of winters in which the event occurred, the co-author can recall his companions, the purpose of the trip, and how he felt after skiing. This implies that there ought to be a relation between how well one recalls an event and the accuracy with which one can place the event in time—a relation that we have already noted has been oft-supported in the literature.

This line of thought can be extended from the level of the individual to the level of the species. If individuals who possess an autonoetic memory system (containing episodic memories) are better at placing events in time than those who do not possess such memories, then those species that possess autonoetic memory systems ought to be better at placing events in time than those that do not. Do any species possess autonoetic memory systems? Which ones? Can these species use these systems to locate specific events in time?

These questions are currently provoking a fair amount of debate. Some theorists (Suddendorf and Corballis, 1997; Roberts, 2002) have claimed that only humans possess an autonoetic memory system. As evidence for this claim, they note that there is not solid and unequivocal evidence pointing to the idea that non-human species can recall individual and specific events. However, others look at this claim with some scepticism (Olton, 1984; Eichenbaum *et al.*, 2005; Zentall,

2005), pointing out that animals often respond as if they had memories for specific events in their lives.

Supporters of the thesis that only humans possess episodic memories would correctly counter by pointing out that temporally sensitive behaviour does not necessarily require the presence of an episodic memory system. For example, the behaviour of the jays in the Griffiths *et al.* (1999) research can be explained by a trace-strength mechanism. The jays may have learned that a weak memory trace of meal-worm locations implied decayed worms, but a stronger memory trace of meal-worm locations implied non-decayed worms. Similar non-episodic mechanisms can be applied to explain the temporal discrimination ability of non-human animals. Such explanations are especially attractive to some because they rely on anoetic knowledge. That is, they can explain the use of prior knowledge without the necessity of resorting to higher-order conceptual knowledge (noetic) or episodic knowledge (autonoetic).

However, several recent behavioural experiments suggest the presence of autonoetic knowledge in non-human animals. For example, Mercado *et al.* (1998) trained dolphins to perform a number of complex responses when given arm-gesture commands. Among the commands was one that indicated that the dolphin was to repeat the most recent response. Another command was for the dolphin to execute a novel response (i.e. not something recently done). On probe trials, the dolphins were signalled to execute a novel response, then to repeat the most recent response. To respond correctly, the dolphin must have used its memory for its own prior behaviour for the subsequent response—that is, the dolphin must have had the capacity to recall the specific episode encompassed by the initial novel response.

Ultimately, the debate about whether animals have autonoetic knowledge may not be settled by behavioural evidence alone. Neurological analyses are especially relevant to the debate's outcome. Along these lines, Rolls et al. (2005) made recordings from single hippocampal formation neurons while macaques performed an object–place memory task. This task required the monkeys to learn associations between objects and where they were shown in a room. The recordings revealed that some neurons responded differently to different objects independently of location; other neurons responded to the spatial view independently of which object was present at the location; while still other neurons responded to a combination of a particular object and the place where it was shown in the room. These results suggest that, in the primate hippocampus, there are separate as well as combined representations of objects and their locations in space. Rolls *et al.* argue that such results are consistent with the presence of an episodic memory system, in which the formation of associations between objects and the places where they are seen is required.

Another study looking at whether episodic memory is neurologically plausible in animals similarly implicated the hippocampus in episodic memory. Ergorul and Eichenbaum (2004) trained rats to remember single training episodes. Each episode consisted of a series of odours presented in different places on an open field. The test task examined whether the rats could recall the order of the presented events. The researchers examined the individual contributions of odour and spatial cues to the rats' order judgements. Normal rats used a combination of spatial ('where') and olfactory ('what') cues to distinguish when events occurred. Moreover, rats with lesions of the hippocampus failed to use combinations of spatial and olfactory cues in these judgements. These data suggest that rats integrate 'what', 'where', and 'when' information in memory for single experiences, and that the hippocampus is critical to this capacity.

While acknowledging that the debate about episodic memory in non-humans is not yet resolved, we admit favouring a hypothesis that is grounded in principles of evolution. As noted earlier, we think that it could be advantageous to a species to have at least some memory for specific life episodes. Hence, given the presence of appropriate genetic material and selection pressures, it strikes us as plausible that such a memory system could have developed in non-humans. None the less, given that the self-concept is much more evolved in humans than in non-humans, and that the evolutionary pressures of human environments may favour those who possess temporal knowledge, it also strikes us as reasonable that the human episodic memory system should be more advanced than any similar systems that evolved in non-human animals.

34.5. Summary

In this chapter, we argued that the capacity to retain temporal knowledge about specific events in an individual's life was a trait subjected to the pressures of evolution. Those pressures may have been: (i) environmental, resulting from the need to respond adaptively to the need for optimally regulating activities such as food procurement; (ii) social, resulting from the need to establish interpersonal facts, such as infant paternity; and (iii) internal, resulting from the needs and requirements of a mental system capable of symbolically representing and manipulating information about the self.

We supported this argument by pointing out that the capacity to possess event-specific temporal knowledge was not unique to humans, and that some of the same mental mechanisms available for the establishment of temporal knowledge in humans are also available to non-human species. In addition, however, we noted that existing evidence suggests that the capacity to represent and use temporal knowledge is better evolved in humans than in other species. A case in point is the presence of an autonoetic memory system, giving humans especially good access to event-related information that could aid in establishing the time at which an event occurred. A review of the human literature pointed to the use of this information in the reconstruction of temporal knowledge, as well as to the operation of other mental mechanisms involving both anoetic and noetic forms of information.

References

Betz, A. L. and Skowronski, J. J. (1997) Self-events and other-events: temporal dating and event memory. *Memory and Cognition*, 25: 701–714.

Bradburn, N. M., Rips, L. J. and Shevell, S. K. (1987) Answering autobiographical questions: the impact of memory and inference on surveys. *Science*, 236: 151–167.

Bradshaw, C. M. and Szabadi, E. (eds) (1997) *Time and Behaviour: Psychological and Neurobehavioural Analyses.* In G. E. Stelmach and P. A. Vroon (eds) *Advances in Psychology*, vol. 120. Elsevier, Amsterdam.

Brown, G. D. A. and Chater, N. (2001) The chronological organization of memory: Common psychological foundations for remembering and timing. In C. Hoerl and T. McCormack, *Time and Memory: Issues in Philosophy and Psychology*, pp 77–110. Clarendon Press, Oxford.

Brown, G. D. A., Preece, T. and Hulme, C. (2000) Oscillator-based memory for serial order. *Psychological Review*, 107: 127–181.

Buckner, R. L. and Schacter, D. L. (2004) Neural correlates of memory's successes and sins. In M. S. Gazzaniga (ed.), *The Cognitive Neurosciences*, 3rd edn, pp. 739–752. MIT Press, Cambridge, MA.

Cameron, J. J., Wilson, A. E. and Ross, M. (2004) Autobiographical Memory and Self-Assessment. In D. R. Beike, J. M. Lampinen and D. A. Behrend (eds) *The Self and Memory*, pp. 207–226. Psychology Press, New York.

Conway, M. A. and Pleydell-Pearce, C. W. (2000) The construction of autobiographical memories in the self-memory system. *Psychological Review*, 107: 261–288.

DeCasper, A. J. and Fifer, W. P. (1980) Of human bonding: newborns prefer their mother's voices. *Science*, 208: 1174–1176.

de Kort, S. R., Dickinson, A. and Clayton, N. S. (2005) Retrospective cognition by food-caching western scrub-jays. *Learning and Motivation*, 36: 159–176.

Eichenbaum, H., Fortin, N. J., Ergorul, C., Wright, S. P. and Agster, K. L. (2005) Episodic recollection in animals: "If it walks like a duck and quacks like a duck …". *Learning and Motivation*, 36: 190–207.

Ergorul, C. and Eichenbaum, H. (2004) The hippocampus and memory for "what," "where," and "when". *Learning and Memory*, 11: 397–405.

Friedman, W. J. (1987) A follow-up to "Scale effects in memory for the time of events": the earthquake study. *Memory and Cognition*, 15: 518–520.

Friedman, W. J. (2001) Memory processes underlying humans' chronological sense of the past. In C. Hoerl and T. McCormack, *Time and Memory: Issues in Philosophy and Psychology*, pp. 139–168. Clarendon Press, Oxford.

Friedman, W. J. (2004) Time in autobiographical memory. *Social Cognition*, 22: 591–605.

Gallistel, C. R. (1990) *The Organization of Learning.* MIT Press, Cambridge, MA

Gibbons, J. A. and Thompson, C. P. (2001) Using a calendar in event dating. *Applied Cognitive Psychology*, 15: 33–44.

Griffiths, D., Dickinson, A. and Clayton, N. (1999) Episodic memory: what can animals remember about their past? *Trends in Cognitive Sciences*, 3: 74–80.

Haddan, A. W. (1872) *The Works of Aurelius Augustine. A New Translation*, ed. Rev. M. Dods. T. & T. Clark, Edinburgh.

Hodges, J. R., Patterson, K., Oxbury, S. and Funnell, E. (1992) Semantic dementia: progressive fluent aphasia with temporal lobe atrophy. *Brain*, 115: 1783–1806.

Hoffding, H. (1892) *Outlines of Psychology.* (M. E. Lowndes translation) Macmillan, London.

Hoerl, C. and McCormack, T. (2001) *Time and Memory: Issues in Philosophy and Psychology.* Clarendon Press, Oxford.

Howe, M. L. and Courage, M. L. (1993) On resolving the enigma of infantile amnesia. *Psychological Bulletin*, 113: 305–326.

James, W. (1890) The Principles of Psychology. Henry Holt, New York.

Klein, S. B., Loftus, J. and Kihlstrom, K. F. (2002) Memory and temporal experience: the effects of episodic memory loss on an amnesic patient's ability to remember the past and imagine the future. *Social Cognition*, 20: 353–379.

Knopf, M., Mack, W. and Kressley-Mba, R. (2005) Knowing and remembering: on episodic memory in infants and preverbal children. *Psychologische Rundschau*, 56: 113–122.

Loftus, E. F. (1993) Desperately seeking memories of the first few years of childhood: the reality of early memories. *Journal of Experimental Psychology: General*, 122: 274–277.

Mandler, J. M. (2003) Conceptual categorization. In D. H. Rakison and L. M. Oakes (eds) *Early Category and Concept Development: Making Sense of the Blooming, Buzzing Confusion*, pp. 103–131. Oxford University Press, New York.

McCormack, T. (2001) Attributing episodic memory to animals and children. In C. Hoerl and T. McCormack (eds) *Time and Memory: Issues in Philosophy and Psychology*, pp. 285–313. Clarendon Press, Oxford.

Mercado, E., III, Murray, S. O., Uyeyama, R. K., Pack, A. A. and Herman, L. M. (1998) Memory for recent actions in the bottlenosed dolphin (*Tursiops truncatus*): repetition of arbitrary behaviors using an abstract rule. *Animal Learning and Behavior*, 26: 210–218.

Ogden, J. A. and Corkin, S. (1991) Memories of H.M. In W. C. Abraham, M. C. Corballis and K. G. White (eds) *Memory Mechanisms: A Tribute to G.V. Goddard*, pp. 195–215. Lawrence Erlbaum, Hillsdale, NJ.

Olton, D. S. (1984) Comparative analysis of episodic memory. *The Behavioral and Brain Sciences*, 7: 250–251.

Perner, J. and Ruffman, T. (1995) Episodic memory and autonoetic consciousness: developmental evidence and a theory of childhood amnesia. *Journal of Experimental Child Psychology*, 59: 516–548.

Roberts, W. A. (2002) Are animals stuck in time? *Psychological Bulletin*, 128: 473–489.

Rolls, E. T., Xiang, J. and Franco, L. (2005) Object, space, and object–space representations in the primate hippocampus. *Journal of Neurophysiology*, 94: 833–844.

Rubin, D. E. and Baddeley, A. (1989) Telescoping is not time compression: a model of the dating of autobiographical events. *Memory and Cognition*, 17: 653–661.

Sagarin, B. J. (2005) Reconsidering evolved sex differences in jealousy: comment on Harris (2003). *Personality and Social Psychology Review*, 9: 62–75.

Saksida, L. M. and Wilke, D. M. (1994) Time-of-day discrimination by pigeons. *Animal Learning and Behavior*, 22: 143–154.

Schwartz, B. L., Hoffman, M. L. and Evans, S. (2005) Episodic-like memory in a gorilla: a review and new findings. *Learning and Motivation*, 36: 226–244.

Sedikides, C. and Brewer, M. B. (2001) *Individual Self, Relational Self, Collective Self.* Psychology Press, Philadelphia, PA.

Sedikides, C. and Gregg, A. P. (2003) Portraits of the self. In M. A. Hogg and J. Cooper (eds) *Sage Handbook of Social Psychology*, pp. 110–138. Sage, London.

Sedikides, C. and Skowronski, J. A. (1997) The symbolic self in evolutionary context. *Personality and Social Psychology Review*, 1: 80–102.

Sedikides, C. and Skowronski, J. J. (2000) On the evolutionary functions of the symbolic self: the emergence of self-evaluation motives. In A. Tesser, R. Felson and J. Suls (eds) *Psychological Perspectives on Self and Identity*, pp. 91–117. APA Books, Washington, DC.

Sedikides, C. and Skowronski, J. J. (2003) Evolution of the self: issues and prospects. In M. R. Leary and J. P. Tangney (eds) *Handbook of Self and Identity*, pp. 594–609. Guilford, Press, New York.

Sedikides, C. and Strube, M. J. (1997) Self-evaluation: to thine own self be good, to thine own self be sure, to thine own self be true, and to thine own self be better. *Advances in Experimental Social Psychology*, 29: 209–269.

Sedikides, C., Skowronski, J. J. and Gaertner, L. (2004) Self-enhancement and self-protection motivations: from the laboratory to an evolutionary context. *Journal of Cultural and Evolutionary Psychology*, 2: 61–79.

Sedikides, C., Skowronski, J. J. and Dunbar, R. I. M. (in press) When and why did the self evolve? In M. Schaller, J. A. Simpson and D. T. Kenrick (eds) *Frontiers in Social Psychology: Evolution and Social Psychology*. Psychology Press, Philadelphia.

Skowronski, J. J. and Sedikides, C. (1999) Evolution of the symbolic self. In D. H. Rosen and M. C. Luebbert (eds) *Evolution of the Psyche*, pp. 78–94. Greenwood, Westport, CT.

Skowronski, J. J., Betz, A. L., Thompson, C. P. and Shannon, L. (1991) Social memory in everyday life: the recall of self-events and other-events. *Journal of Personality and Social Psychology*, 60: 831–843.

Skowronski, J. J., Betz, A. L., Thompson, C. P. and Larsen, S. F. (1995) Long-term performance in autobiographical event dating: patterns of accuracy and error across a two-and-a-half year time span. In A. L. Healy and L. B. Bourne (eds) *Learning and Memory of Knowledge and skills: Durability and Specificity*, pp. 206–233. Sage Publications, Thousand Oaks, CA.

Skowronski, J. J., Walker, W. R. and Betz, A. L. (2003) Ordering our world: An examination of time in autobiographical memory. *Memory*, 11: 247–260.

Skowronski, J. J., Walker, W. R. and Edlund, J. E. (in press) How do you feel about it now and when did it happen? Judgments of emotion and judgments of time in autobiographical memory. In L. J. Sanna and E. C. Chang (eds) *Judgments Over Time: The Interplay of Thoughts, Feelings, and Behaviors*. Oxford University Press, Oxford.

Skowronski, J. J., Ritchie, T. R., Walker, W.R., Betz, A. L., Sedikides, C., Bethencourt, L. A. and Martin, A. L. (in press) *Ordering Our World: The Quest for Traces of Temporal Organization in Autobiographical Memory*.

Stapel, D. A. and Koomen, W. (2005) When less is more: the consequences of affective primacy for subliminal priming effects. *Personality and Social Psychology Bulletin* , 31: 1286–1295.

Sturt, M. (1925) *The Psychology of Time*. Harcourt, Brace & Co. New York.

Suddendorf, T. and Corballis, M. C. (1997) Mental time travel and the evolution of the human mind. *Genetic, Social and General Psychology Monographs*, 123: 33–167.

Thompson, C. P., Skowronski, J. J. and Lee, D. J. (1988a) Reconstructing the date of a personal event. In M. M. Gruneberg, P. E. Morris and N. Sykes (eds) *Practical Aspects of Memory: Current Research and Issues*, pp. 241–246. Academic Press, New York.

Thompson, C. P., Skowronski, J. J. and Lee, D. J. (1988b) Telescoping in dating naturally-occurring events. *Memory and Cognition*, 16: 461–468.

Thompson, C. P., Skowronski, J. J. and Betz, A. L. (1993) The use of partial temporal information in dating personal events. *Memory and Cognition*, 21: 352–360.

Thompson, C. P., Skowronski, J. J., Larsen, S. F. and Betz, A. L. (1996) *Autobiographical Memory: Remembering What and Remembering When*. Lawrence Erlbaum, Hillsdale, NJ.

Tulving, E. (1985) How many memory systems are there? *American Psychologist*, 40: 385–398.

Wheeler, M. A. and McMillan, C. T. (2001) Focal retrograde amnesia and the episodic–semantic distinction. *Cognitive, Affective, and Behavioral Neuroscience*, 1: 22–36.

Zentall, T.R. (2005) Animals may not be stuck in time. *Learning and Motivation*, 36: 208–225.

CHAPTER 35

Shamans, yogins and indigenous psychologies

John H. Crook

35.1. How should we examine culture?

Scattered around the globe on each and every continent are ancient societies of native peoples who in their behaviour, ecological adaptation and world-view still remain largely outside the modern world. In their difference from and resistance to missionary Christianity they were, in the Western colonial period, regarded as 'primitive', often treated abusively, exploited for their resources, and even subjected to periodic genocide, dispossession of their lands, forcible conversions and resettlements. Since their remaining territories may stand in the way of commercial forestry, the expansion of ranging land or cultivation, many of these people still suffer social and cultural breakdown under intense economic and cultural pressure with a resultant loss of an intimate knowledge of their own worlds. Yet, as is becoming increasingly realized, such peoples are the repositories of ways of being of immense antiquity, often extreme social complexity and the bearers of world-views that relate very successfully to their environments. Furthermore, there is reason to suppose that their ways of life echo those of archaic peoples of prehistoric times (Lewis-Williams, 2002). They have thus gradually become of the greatest interest to anthropology, particularly perhaps to evolutionary psychologists

concerned with the interface between biology and culture, evolution and history.

What then is an appropriate way to approach world-views within evolutionary psychology? Several starting points are important; holism, multi-level selection theory and historical context. First, we need to recall Susan Oyama's (2000) stress on a holistic approach to the development of systems as complex as the organism or culture. She argues (p. 39):

> What we are moving towards is a conception of a developmental system, not as the reading off of a pre-existing code, but as a complex of interacting influences, some inside the organism's skin, some external to it, and including its ecological niche in all its spatial and temporal aspects. — It is in this ontogenetic crucible that form appears and is transformed, not because it is immanent in some interactants and nourished by others but because any form is created by the precise activity of the system.

If we accept this approach then it is through a systems analytical orientation rather than any form of reductionism that we must proceed.

The Russian interpreter of culture, Michail Bakhtin (1981), would certainly agree, arguing that cultural meaning is not contained within social groups, persons or linguistic terms but rather co-emerges between them. A relational rather than a reductionist psychology is implied in such views. In his view, the history of cultural evolution can be seen as falling into three phases.

1. The 'ancient matrix' in which personal identity is relational, structured in terms of the immediate social world and environment of exploitation. The self is deeply participatory, involved within and pervaded by the unified life of the world system as perceived; time is felt as cyclic based on a harmony within nature, the relationship with which is governed by detailed rules regulated by shamanic discourse including means for restoration when broken. The social vehicle is mytho-poetic discourse, often revealed in trance states wherein fantasy reflects themes in both social and environmental relationships.

2. Individualism is enhanced through an awareness of time as a personal becoming moving towards destinies distinct from the world matrix. This phase coincides with the appearance of class systems and religions of personal salvation emphasizing a separation between identity and the cosmos. Thought is here anchored in reified usages of terms expressing self, identity, ethics and the linear process descriptive of commercial advance and personal salvation.

3. There is an emerging awareness of personal belief and world-view as contingent upon their context rather than as being in some sense 'absolute'. Such awareness is necessarily associated with a sense of the relativity of faith and opinion in which the monologic discourses of previous religions/philosophies are opened up to questioning through reflexive awareness.

The second point of departure is the emergence of 'multi-level selection theory' based in a reappraisal of the importance of group selection (Sober and Wilson, 1998; Wilson, 2002). Whenever organisms come together in a collective that begins to function as a unit and becomes subject to selection as such, we can perceive group selection in action; the evolution of multicellular organisms from independent single cells is the basic example. We can see that groups possessing traits that prove to have increased fitness will increase in a population of groups. An evolutionary transition shifts the emphasis to a new composite unit. Within-unit selection will enhance their cohesion

and internal functioning while inter-unit selection sustains continuing adaptive radiation of such newly integrated groups. In advanced birds and mammals, the mechanisms being selected may or may not have a genetic base; some are clearly cultural. Selection of 'selfish genes' does not cease but happens within the context where group selection for altruism may be occurring. Evolution proceeds through operating on contrasting mechanisms at several levels (Plotkin and Odling-Smee, 1981; Odling-Smee, 1995). Among human beings the role of culture in adaptation is presumed to be predominant although explanation in terms of genetics and the operation of evolved cognitive modules (Barkow *et al.*, 1992) may remain important in some contexts. What is needed, however, is an integrative developmental theory of how culture arises.

An important aspect of any such theory must focus on the unique emergence in *Homo sapiens* of four and in some persons five levels of intentionality. This crucial outcome of primate cognitive evolution allows individuals to assess the motivations of others and to infer others' beliefs about their companion's intentions or purposes. Without these preadaptations, Dunbar (2004) argues, culture based in the communal holding of world-views simply could not exist. This must be especially true when the higher levels are used in the context of elaborate metaphorical symbolism. Such symbolism is made possible through the human ability to fantasize emotional relating. It seems that this is not only an effect of imaginative ability but also due to unconscious processes operating to create representations of everyday events, both present and derived from memory, that come to symbolize social process. This seems to be the reason why dreams are often sufficiently interpretable to make personal and social sense. Dunbar calculates that such abilities underlying communally shared beliefs probably only emerged well after the evolution of language at the time of Cro-Magnon man 200 000 years ago.

The third essential in an examination of the origins of world-views is necessarily the study of the history of ideas through archaeological research related to interpretative readings in depth of ancient texts. Such work indeed provides the material evidence with which we may assess the sequencing of socio-cultural developments that underlies the passage through the phases of change abstracted by Bakhtin as especially significant. This chapter offers a brief account of the processes of world-viewing, particularly in selected representatives of the 'ancient matrix', and indicates how they may change as the second and third of Bakhtin's phases impact upon them.

35.2. Shamanic society

The forms of religion found in hunter-gatherer societies of the 'ancient matrix' (Bakhtin, 1981) are commonly described as 'shamanic'. Although they vary considerably in form and function, such cultures share several key attributes in common.

Members of the society participate in a common understanding or world-view from which they draw an understanding of themselves in relation to their perception of the universe. Each society in question may have its own metaphysical picture of reality but all are essentially holistic with individuals deeply involved in a universal process.

The world-view is expressed publicly through a relationship between individuals and those who specialize in its presentation. These individuals are known as 'shamans' after the name of such specialists among the Tungus, a Siberian tribe. There is considerable variation in the social functioning of shamans and related specialists in contrasting types of healing (Hitchcock and Jones, 1976; Jacobs, 1990; Winkelman, 2000).

The shaman commonly interprets the world-view through psychological dissociation in trance wherein he travels to spiritual realms, meets spirit beings, retrieves lost souls, speaks with the gods and returns with oracular predictions or announcements. Alternatively the shaman may be possessed by such entities who speak through him when in trance. Psychologically the nature of mental dissociation in trance is still poorly understood. Inconsistent parenting may play a role in contemporary Western cases (Main and Hesse, 1992) and Winkelman (2000) has initiated extensive work on the neurophysiological bases of such states.

The shaman often acquires his status after an illness involving apparent possession by spirits or the psychological force of others. His/her training involves strict discipline under supervision of an older expert until controlled trance can be used in the service of individuals or the community as a whole.

The shamanic world-view is a fantasized image of the natural world symbolized by personifications of natural and psychological forces as sentient spirits. Shamans may travel to their abodes or become possessed by these entities. In lucid dreaming and under the influence of hallucinogens, some shamans go travelling within a complex representation of their natural environment and/or of the belief system of the people. Shamans usually have a deep knowledge of natural history and/or a sensitive appreciation of their social system and the personal tendencies of community members. Interpretation of social conflict on a 'cosmological' level removed from actual social process amounts to an appeal to a neutral world transcending actual interpersonal conflict or sickness (Riches, 1994). This enables the shaman to suggest or enforce rules of behaviour that may tend to produce environmental stability through the control of exploitation and the psychotherapeutic healing of disturbed or deviant individuals.

Shamanism is associated with art, music, dance, social, sexual and personal discipline and tends towards community health in the broadest sense. These disciplined societies are none the less commonly highly egalitarian and institutional complexity is absent.

Shamanism is characteristic of hunter-gatherer societies but may not be completely lost when the transition to Bakhtin's second phase occurs. Although the personal definition of the self changes with the increased social stratification associated with agriculture, the appearance of the market, institutionalized religion and government, participation in residual shamanic cults often with healing functions may still occur—even, for example, within so strict a religious environment as Islam (Boddy, 1989). Rationalized theologies, professional clergy and liturgical rituals none the less progressively replace the shaman. Mystical ecstasy and trance become exceptional and increasingly poorly understood, indeed commonly perceived as threatening to the collective power of a priesthood. In the fascinating case of Tibet, shamanic themes have become deeply enmeshed within the complexities of tantric Buddhism to form a unique system of psychological practice with soteriological functions leading to the 'salvation' of the self (Samuel, 1993).

In hunter-gatherer and other tribal societies the structure attributed to the self often differs greatly from the individualism apparent in more advanced cultures (Neisser and Jopling, 1997). As we shall see there is commonly a strong identification with the natural world and the group/clan so that the dualism between self and other, self and environment, is far less marked than in modern societies. Attributions to self form part of a world-view just as a world-view is shaped by attributions to self.

Many Africans in their traditional worlds are said to have little conception of a person separate from community. Community and person may be so closely conflated that in a legal conflict in Lower Congo senior members of the matrilineage will argue for the defendant, but the clan as a whole wins or loses a case. Membership of an African community may depend on the presence of certain social properties, positions in a hierarchy or membership of an age class, for examples. Parenthood is often vital because an individual who is not reproductive is not connected to the past or future and therefore not a 'member' of the group. Personhood, in contrast, is conferred as a result of participation in the collective world.

Another common feature in such worlds is a failure to distinguish clearly between the spiritual and material, the mind and body. The feeling for communality may extend even to dead ancestors who are perceived as potentially present, playing active parts in the life of the group and to whom various obligations are due. The person exists within a spiritual world and the boundaries of a person may extend beyond the physical self. People may take care not to step on someone's shadow or have their own stepped upon since personal power is lost to the other under such circumstances.

Yet, Africans are also aware of individual idiosyncrasies that are described in folk tales and appear in self-expression, for example in dance. None the less, Lienhardt (1985) argues that, while degrees of individuality are appreciated, the self of a person is seen as hidden or undiscoverable, perhaps because it is not envisaged as an entity separable from society. We may suggest, following La Fontaine (1985), that the notions characterizing a person in a society are closely linked to the nature of authority and kinship in that society as well as its economic functioning. Above all, self-understanding and self-conceptualization arise within the social representations by which an individual's world is conceived. It is within the communal attributions to selfhood that a shaman will play his/her healing roles.

35.2.1. Amazonian shamanism

One of the finest accounts of the world-view of a shamanic society prior to any major impact of the modern world comes from the researches among the Tukano Indians of the upper Amazon by Gerardo Reichel-Dolmatoff (1997). The Tukano are hunter-gatherers who also create gardens for manioc cultivation within the forest. Their world-view is a profoundly elaborate symbolic representation of the natural history and ecological process of their environment based in a conception of energy flow emanating from the sun. There are however two suns, the visible and the invisible. The visible sun is the representative of the invisible 'sun father' and fills the cosmos with a spermatic life force, which, however, often manifests irregularly and with destructive as well as creative force. The energy from the invisible sun is always beneficial, it is androgynous in character and underlies the visible energy. The shaman is able to influence this energy to correct any harmful effects arising in visible manifestations. Strangely, this world is in a sense seen as inert because its life is only given in the presence of human interpretation.

Energy is perceived by shamans as present in sensorial phenomena (colour, odour, sound, visions) which in a highly complex discourse are given abstract meanings used in interpreting events that may then be visualized in many forms. Energy is perceived as a flow through phenomena. A key concept is derived from the flickering of light in the heart of a hexagonal crystal, hexagonal shapes appearing again and again in their mythologies. Many of the symbolizations are derived from sexual narratives. A particular term, for a 'handle', say, may appear metaphorically on several overlapping and interlacing levels of discourse from the sexual to the ecological.

A key symbolization is that of the 'master of animals', commonly an anthropomorphic figure carrying a hunter's spoils that vary seasonally in relation to the reproductive cycles of particular species. When a shaman, or perhaps an individual temporarily lost in forest, 'meets' the 'master of animals' this is commonly perceived as a warning that too much hunting of specific types is being carried out either by an individual or a group. This personal experience is then utilized by the shaman to adjust behaviour within rules that may have been broken. These rules entail very elaborate constraints, for example specific modes and times of celibacy, dietary restriction and taboos on certain activities.

In order to go hunting a man has to undergo complex ritual preparation. These may include several days of abstinence from sex with his wife and indeed all dreams of an erotic nature. He eats only unseasoned cooked food. On the morning of the hunt he purifies himself by drinking a large quantity of liquid pepper, some of which is absorbed through the nostrils. Tucking special aromatic plants in his belt he paints his body with designs indicating potency and fertility in order to attract animals. A hunt is conceived as a form of courtship and animal behaviour is interpreted through human parallels.

Hunters may spend hours watching animals, for example from a perch in a tree near a salt-lick. The somnolent hunter may see animals as if in a dream taking human form, their sound, appearance and odour may trigger images of another world in which patterns of experience from hallucinogenic séances may recur. Places such as salt-licks are seen as thresholds. Shamans say that some hunters may cross the threshold and enter another world, become transformed into tapirs and never return. Reichel-Dolmatoff argues that the elaborate and sometimes threatening interpretation of events symbolizes the natural world and that the taboos and restrictions that shamans may impose have the effect of regulating their exploitation of that world. Groups of Indians practice self-sufficiency largely through the specific coercions on deviance from rules that shamans can impose.

In the largely flat terrain occupied by the Tukano, certain hilly areas with flat tops are regarded as the special preserve of the 'master of animals'. These are dangerous places to visit. One may for example get lost in the forest for ever and be transformed into another creature. Avoidance of hunting near such areas creates natural reserves for wildlife. Needless to say, the arrival of Western missionaries, together with entrepreneurs, intent on exploiting the Amazonian forest leads to a breakdown of ecological balance through the decadence of unrestricted agricultural capitalism. In other studies, however, whether traditional hunter-gatherers are always good conservationists has been questioned (Cowlishaw and Dunbar, 2000).

On ceremonial occasions, the *Banisteriopsis* hallucinogen is consumed by adult men, who are led by shamans and attended by encouraging women. The men dance, sing and play musical instruments but these are not frenzied sessions, rather an atmosphere of seriousness prevails. As the evening progresses the dancing becomes more coordinated so that the group appears more and more like a single organism. The drug takes effect in two stages. In the first, dots and squiggles, star shapes etc. (known as phosphenes) appear, weaving complex patterns which are often used in art, for example in house decoration. In the second stage, when the drug may have been reinforced with tobacco, complex hallucinations of living creatures appear that are then interpreted according to the world-view of the people. Finally the images disappear and the men sit silently in a state of serene bliss. Reichel-Dolmatoff remarks: "These trances, then, are of social-ecological importance. The shaman-controlled drug experience is a technique of behavioural modification, and its latent phosphenes continue to influence behaviour in normal states of awareness." Other studies have suggested that such episodes of social bonding may allow things experienced in such states to be more effectively learnt than when such intense experiences are absent.

The visions are interpreted as a return to the womb, a reversal of time. The ancestors may appear, plants and animals may complain of ill treatment, events from the personal past may be re-lived and re-ordered. The images seen in these states become the topics of discussion led by shamans. The experiences are not private but freely shared and interpreted in a group led by a shaman. Detailed questions about the precise form of experiences may be asked and interpreted in complex, many-layered discussions. Individuals come to understand their experience in the light of the communal worldview in which the authority of the shaman is confirmed.

In sum, Reichel-Dolmatoff has suggested the manner in which these societies maintain a self-regulation in relation to their resources and social cohesion through a world-view of great complexity essential for their welfare. Personal and social disaster commonly follows its loss.

35.2.2. Asian Shamanism in relation to Buddhism

Research on Asian shamanism is extensive (Hitchcock and Jones, 1976) and is particularly interesting for evolutionary psychology in that it reveals the manner in which shamanism of the 'ancient matrix' gradually became incorporated within the relatively more rationalized schemata of Bakhtin's second phase. Originally the largely nomadic societies of central Asia found meaning in world-views focused on mediation in a spirit world by shamans whose speciality was journeys in trance to mystical lands to obtain prophecies or advice (oracles), assist the final journey of the dead or to retrieve lost souls. In his pioneering work, Marcel Eliade (1989, first published 1964) considered this to be the fundamental shamanic type. However, a major variation is the Tibetan *lha.pa* who becomes possessed by gods, spirits or other spiritual agents while in trance. Here the 'gods' come to the shaman rather than vice versa. Such *lus.gyer*, 'vehicles for the gods', have been particularly studied in Ladakh where they have psychological functions in healing states of ill-health often resulting from possession by witches or spirits of place, etc. (Brauen, 1980; Kuhn, 1988; Day, 1989; Phylactou, 1989; Kaplanian [undated]; Crook, 1997, 1998; Rösing, 2003). Asian shamanism appears more directly concerned with personal, social or ethical issues than with the environment. The shaman is commonly concerned with tensions, quarrels or even crimes. By interpreting events on the level of the noumenal he is not involved in judgements that may immediately shame. He provides a symbolic interpretation upon which communal discussion

develops and a tension-relieving outcome may arise without direct accusations (Riches, 1994).

The occurrence of shamanic trance is not quite universal. In eastern Nepal, the shaman tells long stories concerning his travels, which may sometimes appear more as dream-like fantasies or lucid dreaming than full trance. These stories are subsequently discussed and interpreted communally to provide meaning (Sagant, 1996). In Ladakh too, the depth of trance may vary, some consultations or social events giving more the impression of wilful drama than possession. It may be that oracles are not always able to enter a deep trance and then 'ham it up' to sustain their reputations (Rösing, 2003). In contemporary Ladakh the number of shamans appears to be increasing together with modern forms of stress, but with less meticulous training it may be that the ability to go into full trance may not always be present or only arise fully in matured adepts. In full trance it appears that no memory of what transpires in the entranced session is retained. Extraordinary, even death-defying, feats may be performed and these are often completely convincing.

Possession by spirits or witches is extremely common in Ladakh, especially among young women whose hysterical behaviour is most distressing to the households in which they occur. These psychological disturbances seem closely linked to stress arising within the family on marriage. Although women are generally freer and of higher status than in many comparable societies, young wives leave their homes to enter those of their husbands and find this a formidable challenge. Until recently in this traditionally polyandrous society, two or three brothers may marry the same wife in a system sustaining the subsistence value of the undivided estate, while at the same time maintaining sufficient labour to work it and a low birth rate (Crook and Crook, 1988; Crook 1995). Men are the key figures in the maintenance of the agricultural family. Women are essentially involved only in procreation and have little status until becoming mature mothers of children (Day, 1989; Phylactou, 1989).

Incoming wives are subordinate to powerful mothers-in-law, have to relate to a new household deity and new domestic rituals to avoid pollution, and have to supply high-quality food and drink on social occasions while showing behaviour entailing exaggerated humility (*zangs*). Prestige in Ladakh is expressed through systems of deference whereby everyone endeavours to present others as higher in rank than themselves. The complex negotiations between this practice and the actual influence of an individual in a community become subtle, requiring tact and interpersonal skill. The system is part of the means whereby the necessary reciprocity between subsistence families in a village is peacefully maintained.

The period after marriage is thus stressful for young women who come to depend on intimate relations with women in similar positions. These dependencies can become fraught through jealousies, paranoid reactions and distrust, none of which is easily expressed in a household of strangers with high expectations of a young wife and concerned to avoid shame. It is in such contexts that women fall foul of witches who are normally projections of their own imaginations, quite often upon a good friend. The actual women privately accused will normally be blameless of any sort of witchcraft as such. The symptoms of possession involve hysterical outbursts damaging to family pride, speaking in another voice and falling into dissociative trance. After some conventional remedies have failed the afflicted is taken to a *lha.pa*, the local shaman. Men are less troubled by witches but may fall foul of demons of place etc. in the course of sustaining family well-being.

The *lha.pa* will have been authorized to practice by a reincarnating lama (*rinpoche*) of a nearby Buddhist monastery and will have gone through similar episodes of affliction of a more severe nature in which gods and demons have appeared. There is an extraordinary pantheon of spirits that may cause possession, spirits of the dead, wandering ghosts, harmful last thoughts of the dying, spirits of ancestors, the gods of local shrines and, more rarely, high gods of mountains and passes. The *lha.pa*'s task is to interview the possessing agent when in trance. The whole negotiation thus occurs between two entranced individuals, demons and benevolent gods are manifested, sorted out, the former being expelled. The *lha.pa*'s knowledge of community conditions leads her or him to suggest forms of recompense whereby broken relationships may be healed or laid aside. Persistent

cases are sent to the *rinpoche* who may force the spirits to appear only when called upon under vow to help others. If this happens, the possessed is then usually sent for training with a senior *lha.pa* and thus to become one himself or herself. Once again the social negotiations on the plane of trance enable the participants to avoid any taint of direct responsibility. Everything has been lifted onto the table of the gods and resolved there.

Lewis (1971) has argued that becoming a shaman, especially in women, is an attempt to promote oneself from a lowly 'peripheral' status to a more 'central' one. Further he has argued that becoming a shaman is for a woman an escape from the dominance of men and indeed a means for manipulating them. While there is some truth in this view, more recent studies suggest it to be over-precise. What is certainly involved for both genders is a move from low self-esteem and depression to one in which a degree of sometimes fearful respect has been achieved. A maturing woman recovering from possession may either become a respected matron who is no longer afflicted or indeed take up the path of a shaman, receiving ample attention (Crook, 1997, 1998).

A key figure in Ladakhi communities is the oracle who may be a lay person but more usually an accomplished monk. Their roles may be considered to be 'central' to the social process in that they participate in the meta-narrative whereby Tibetan Buddhism controls the 'peripheral' activities of the lay *lha.pas*. Some of these monastic *lus.gyers* can produce the most extraordinary performance in deep trance while uttering advice on local ethics, harvest forecasts and healing the sick. The monk as a trained meditator is reckoned to be above ordinary possession. At the monastery of Mattro two monks are randomly selected every few years to train to become monastic oracles at the major annual festival of the monastery (*chams*). They do not experience any initiatory illness but are confined to their cells for 9 months visualizing a text while vigorously playing a small drum and bell. They sit in a small box, which, apart from visits to the toilet, they are not allowed to leave. They receive ritual washing from the head of the monastery and are attended by a small boy (usually a relative). The text depicts the spirits of the gorges, the *Rong bTsan*, who comprise two of five brothers brought from Tibet by a lama many centuries before as personal protectors. At first housed in the monastery, they are now said to spend most of the year in shrines at the head of the valley whence water for irrigation descends. They are thus considered to be protectors of the whole area. As the weeks go by the monks gradually enter trance from time to time. Finally during the festival they emerge in full force, chiding the villagers for their ethical omissions, powering up the whole Buddhist community, and even receiving respectful visits from high officers of the Indian army. Their words are broadcast on the radio locally and are still felt as powerful, although the rulers they formerly advised no longer function politically.

In trance they cut their tongues with swords without harm and run blindfolded along the monastery parapets from which a fall would be instantly fatal. Prior to the festival, they have been strictly confined for months without exercise and have had no prior practice in handling swords, roof-running or any other athletic training. Such undoubted feats certainly raise questions about the nature of enhanced skills while under trance. Other major Tibetan oracles show similar powers.

A clue to the significance of these festivals and the appearance of such powerful oracular protectors at such times lies in the 'miracle' plays that form a key aspect of the event. These depict the subjugation of ancient demons and spirits of Tibet by the great tantric master Padmasambhava (Guru Rinpoche to the Tibetans). These stories tell of the overcoming of the old shamanic Bon religion of Tibet by powerful charismatic Buddhist missionaries from India. Their skill lay in not destroying these noumenal forces but in putting them under vow to appear only when called upon to support the Buddha Dharma or as protectors of the community. By accepting these conditions almost the entire shamanic pantheon of Tibet was preserved but now under vow to Buddhism. The repetitions of such plays annually supported by the appearance in entranced monks of some of these spirits thus acts as a reinforcer of the presence of Buddhism and a reminder of its communal power. The meta-narrative of Buddhism over-rules the narrative of the shaman. It is in this relationship that we can trace the transition from the undiluted 'ancient matrix' to a more complex secondary

development dominated now by the philosophies of Buddhism (Crook, 1997, 1998).

The competition between shamanism and Buddhism did not cease centuries ago but still persists. Stan Mumford (1990) found a community of villages in Gyasumdo, eastern Nepal, where, in a remote region, one village was occupied by Tibetan Buddhists and the other by Gurung shamanic believers. Although at the time of his research the Buddhists were becoming increasingly influential and modern ideas had hardly appeared, many of the ideas of shamanism had penetrated Buddhism to create an ongoing dialogue between the two world-views manifesting in an unstable balance between them. The key contrast between the two was that in shamanism the emphasis was on the cycle of nature and the need to relate oneself to that cosmic reality. The person was to express himself in relation to the seasonality and cyclic changes apparent in the world. By contrast Buddhism offered a precise path whereby a clearly defined individual might progress towards a better life in repeated incarnations ending in a blissful escape from the whole painful process. The implicit individualism and the Buddhist attempt to transcend it along a linear path contrasts markedly from the holistic cycles of shamanism and suggests a very different appreciation of what it is to be a self. This local dialogue between two communities probably depicts what was a long-drawn-out historical dialogue throughout the Tibetan world. That the three-way dialogue continues is probably due to a balancing act that Tibetan religion is able to maintain between the attractions of linear logical progression as the business of life, on the one hand, and more ancient intuitions rooted in the cyclicity of the natural world on the other hand.

35.3. **Yogins and the reflexive mind**

The Tibetan monk or nun may, given the appropriate inclination, choose an especially arduous path of practice in which it is no longer the journey towards enlightenment that is significant but the discovery of a freedom from all views through the realization that all ideas concerning paths and becoming are no more than expressions of thought based in metaphysical assumptions of the sort the Buddha himself actually refused to discuss. Any one viewpoint is perceived as having no more validity than another since all are contingent upon personal aspirations and relative to systems of belief. In effect, monks following this path (the practices associated with *prajnaparamita, madhyamaka* and *cittamatra* philosophies: Snelgrove, 1987) have moved across the boundary between Bakhtin's second and third phases of cultural development and, as a result of acutely accurate inspection of mental process, have understood the whole process of logical reification.

Reification is the process whereby abstract ideas are presented as if they were locatable, precise things, entities or persons. Social or religious abstractions 'reified' in this way allow individuals to find security for their equally imputed selves in fictional entities derived from metaphysical abstraction. Such concepts then appear to exist independently from their creators and to possess power to control thought and values. Personal understanding of this process and the entrapment of self that it can entail requires a 'de-reification' of the mind that Berger and Luckmann (1967) consider to be a late development in both history and an individual's life.

The Buddhist monk's insight shows that a capacity for 'de-reification' is by no means simply a post-modern development based in post-Christian existentialism but goes back at least to the origins of Buddhism itself. The Buddhist world-view developed as the old Vedic economy of India moved from pastoralism to agriculture with concomitant production of surplus, local trade, banking and the shift to social hierarchies based in wealth rather than rooted in religion and caste (Collins, 1982). Political structures were becoming more centralized, requiring leadership by individuals of a much more modern character, thinking in linear rather than cyclic themes. In an extraordinary, scholarly *tour de force*, Thomas McEvilley (2002) demonstrates how sociocultural changes paralleling the emergence of urban economies throughout the ancient world (Egypt, Mesopotamia, India and Greece) stimulated shifts in the meanings by which individuals understood their lives. Moral authority became vested in governing institutions of priesthoods derived in part from older shamanic roles in society. Economies based in cities with imperial governance led to the replacement of shamanism by a range of authoritative thought systems of personal transcendence in which rebirth through reincarnation took beneficial or negative forms depending on the ethical quality of an individual's previous life.

Increasingly the explanations and meanings put forward by such religious authorities came to be questioned. The basic syllogisms upon which their metaphysical reifications were based were confronted by the emergence of dialectical questioning that undermined the reasoning upon which the priestly control relied. India appears to have influenced Greece with reincarnational ideas in the pre-Socratic period but philosophically strong forms of deconstructive dialectic appear to have originated in Greece and came to underlie Buddhist philosophy following Alexander's conquests in the later Hellenistic period. The conflict between metaphysical arguments for monotheism apparent in Zoroastrianism, Judaism, Christianity and Islam and the deconstructive dialectic of Indian, particularly Buddhist, thought has therefore an ancient origin.

The Buddhist monk/nun practitioners of deconstruction are known as yogins because their practice involves an extensive use of mental yogas of advanced meditation (Crook and Low, 1997). Yogins are the commandos of the Buddhist view who have dispensed with attachment to linear, rational thinking to allow a fuller imaginative picture of mental life to arise, clearly perceived as relative to mental states. The understanding of that very relativity is seen by them as the way to escape attachments to any rigid formula whatsoever. Here too we find the paradoxes of Chinese Zen, which has followed a closely similar path based in the same philosophical analyses of language and thought and the experiential practices that are associated with them (McRae, 2004).

The yogin's practice also involves extensive visualizations of Buddhas and Bodhisattvas with whom he or she identifies in such a way that the psychological principle they embody is realized. Thus the visualization of Avalokiteshvara is associated with compassion, Manjusri with insightful wisdom. In this way the self is slowly transformed from, say, an egotistical personality to someone considerate to others. At the same time, any 'good' or any 'not good' is perceived as a relative position contingent upon a reifying dualism. Persistent investigation of relativity leads towards a freedom from all relative positions. It is this rather than a linear path towards 'enlightenment' that is then seen as the way to freedom and compassion within Buddhist insight.

Yogins do not normally teach this viewpoint, considering it beyond what most villagers would comprehend, but they use its insights in taking up their roles as spiritual consultants at whatever level a troubled soul may approach them. One might risk a comparison with Wittgenstein, who used philosophical investigation to get 'the fly out of the fly bottle'. A yogin's discourse is pitched at the level of the respondent but has exactly this ultimate aim.

The final development of this understanding of relativity within Buddhism appears in the Hua-yen philosophy of China in which discourse is seen as multi-layered (Chang, 1972). Water can be conceived as wet, as a vapour, as solid like ice, as flowing or rigid, as H_2O or the ocean. All such views are equally true and usable, and entwine and envelop with one another. The concept is relative to the context in which it is thought, and development in dialogue may cut across levels. The root of such a view is the 'law of co-dependent arising', a prime principle of the Buddha closely resembling modern systems thinking (Macy, 1991; Loy, 1998; Kurak, 2003). Here indeed is an example of Bakhtin's third phase, not as a modern development resulting from the breakdown of Cartesian dualisms, but as a condition of insightful thought that may have arisen more than once through the contemplation of self in relation to confinement by concepts. Indeed, the dialogue between all three levels goes on today. The leading translator of these texts, Thomas Cleary (1983), explains:

> The Hua-yen doctrine shows the entire cosmos as one single nexus of conditions in which everything simultaneously depends on, and is depended on by, everything else. Seen in this light, then, everything affects and is affected by, more or less immediately or remotely, everything else; just as this is true of every system of relationships, so it is true of the totality of existence. In seeking to understand individuals and groups, therefore, Hua-yen thought considers the manifold as an integral part of the unit and the unit as an integral part of the manifold; one individual is considered in terms of relationships to

other individuals as well as to the whole nexus, while the whole nexus is considered in terms of its relation to each individual as well as to all individuals. The accord of this view with the experience of modern science is obvious, and it seems to be an appropriate basis upon which the question of the relation of science and bioethics ... may be resolved.

35.4. Conclusions

The indigenous psychologies of shamans, priesthoods and yogins have emerged through shifts between the three phases in cultural change usefully suggested by Michail Bakhtin. The problems of individuals and communities are approached by shamanic, priestly or yogic practitioners through world-views that may be placed on one or other of these three levels. We have seen, all too briefly, how in our Asian example the ancient shamanic matrix was replaced by the more linear style of thinking of the Buddhist path to salvation but that it never entirely disappeared. Indeed Tibetan Buddhism may be read as a continuing dialogue between themes stemming from both levels.

The emergence of Bakhtin's third phase with its awareness of the paradoxical relativity of concept to mental contingency and allowing a return to a tolerance of mytho-poetic intuitions, has come about through an understanding that personal expression need not be confined by rigidities in patterns of thought. Although such a perception is indeed characteristic of the post-modern world, the Greek and Indian philosophers had already opened its puzzling character to investigation many centuries ago. It seems clear that certain cultural conditions involving profound yogic practices of mind examination, initially at least through retreats well outside the contexts of normal daily life, allow a 'de-reification' of thought in a context of hope and healing far from the nihilism of post-modernism. Such perspectives may be of great significance to a world beset by conflict resulting from persistent beliefs in arbitrary metaphysical entities.

References

Bakhtin, M. (1981) *The Dialogic Imagination*. University of Texas, Austin.

Barkow, J. H., Cosmides, L. and Tooby, J. (1992) *The Adapted Mind: Evolutionary Psychology and the Generation of Culture*. Oxford University Press, Oxford.

Berger, P. and Luckmann T. (1967) *The Social Construction of Reality. A Treatise in the Sociology of Knowledge.* Penguin, London.

Boddy, J. (1989) *Wombs and Alien Spirits: Women, Men and the Zar Cult in Northern Sudan.* University of Wisconsin Press, Madison.

Brauen, M. (1980) *Feste in Ladakh.* Academische Druk und Verlaganstalt, Graz.

Chang, G. C. C. (1972) *The Buddhist Teaching of Totality, The Philosophy of Hwa Yen Buddhism.* Allen & Unwin, London.

Cleary, T. (1983) *Entry into the Inconceivable: An Introduction to Hua-Yen Buddhism.* University of Hawai Press, Honolulu.

Collins, S. (1982) *Selfless Persons. Imagery and Thought in Theravada Buddhism.* Cambridge University Press, Cambridge.

Cowlishaw, G. C. and Dunbar, R. I. M. (2000) *Primate Conservation Biology.* Chicago University Press, Chicago.

Crook, J. H. (1995) Psychological processes in cultural and genetic co-evolution. In E. Jones and V. Reynolds (eds) *Survival and Religion. Biological Evolution and Cultural Change.* Wiley, London.

Crook, J. H. (1997) The indigenous psychiatry of Ladakh, Part 1. *Anthropology and Medicine*, 4, 289–307.

Crook, J. H. (1998) The indigenous psychiatry of Ladakh, Part II. *Anthropology and Medicine*, 5, 23–43.

Crook, J. H. and Crook, S. (1988) Tibetan polyandry: problems of adaptation and fitness. In L. M. Betzig, M. Borgerhoff Mulder and P. Turke (eds) *Human Reproductive Behaviour: a Darwinian perspective.* Cambridge University Press, Cambridge.

Crook, J. H. and Low, J. (1997) *The Yogins of Ladakh.* Motilal Banarsidas, Delhi.

Day, S. (1989) Embodying spirits, oracles and possession ritual in Ladakh, North India. PhD thesis, London School of Economics.

Dunbar, R. I. M. (2004) *The Human Story.* Faber & Faber, London.

Eliade, M. (1989; first published 1964) *Shamanism. Archaic Techniques of Ecstasy.* Arkana, London.

Hitchcock, J. T. and Jones, R. L. (1976) *Spirit Possession in the Nepal Himalayas.* Vikas, New Delhi.

Jacobs, J. (ed) (1990) *The Nagas: Hill peoples of Northeast India.* Thomas and Hudson, London.

Kaplanian, P. (n.d.) *Ladakh de la transe a l'extase. Peuples du monde.* Hachette, Paris.

Kuhn, A. S. (1988) *Heiler und ihre patienten auf dem Dach der Welt: Ladakh aus ethnomedizinischer Sicht.* Peter Lang, Frankfurt am Main.

Kurak, M. (2003) The relevance of the Buddhist theory of dependent co-origination to cognitive science. *Brain and Mind*, 4, 431–351.

La Fontaine, J. S. (1985) Person and individual: some anthropological reflections. In M. Carrithers, S. Collins and S. Lukes (eds) *The Category of the Person: Anthropology, Philosophy, History.* Cambridge University Press, Cambridge.

Leinhardt, G. (1985) Self: public, private. Some African representations. In M. Carrithers, S. Collins and S. Lukes (eds) *The Category of the Person: Anthropology, Philosophy, History.* Cambridge University Press, Cambridge.

Lewis, I. M. (1971) *Ecstatic Religion: An Anthropological Study of Spirit possession and Shamanism.* Penguin, Baltimore.

Lewis-Williams, D. (2002) *The Mind in the Cave.* Thames & Hudson, London.

Loy, D. (1998) *Nonduality: A Study in Comparative Philosophy.* Humanity Books, New York.

Main, M. and Hesse, E. (1992) Disorganised/disoriented infant behavior in the Strange Situation, lapses in monitoring and discourse during the parent's Adult Attachment Interview and dissociative states. In M. Ammaniti and D. Stern (eds) *Attachment and Psychoanalysis.* Gius, Laterza & Figli, Rome.

Macy, J. (1991) *Mutual Causality in Buddhism and General Systems Theory.* SUNY Press, New York.

McEvilley, T. (2002) *The Shape of Ancient Thought.* Allworth Press, New York.

McRae, J. R. (2004) *Seeing Through Zen: Encounter, Transformation and Genealogy in Chinese Chan Buddhism.* University of California Press, Berkeley.

Mumford, S. (1990) *Himalayan Dialogue: Tibetan Lamas and Gurung Shamans in Nepal.* Tiwari, Kathmandu.

Neisser, U. and Jopling, D. A. (eds) (1997) *The Conceptual Self in Context.* Cambridge University Press, Cambridge.

Odling-Smee, J. (1995) Biological evolution and cultural change. In W. E. Jones and V. Reynolds (eds) *Survival and Religion.* Wiley, New York.

Oyama, S. (2000) *The Ontogeny of Information: Developmental Systems and Evolution.* Duke University Press.

Phylactou, M. (1989) Household organisation and marriage in Ladakh, Indian Himalaya. PhD thesis, London School of Economics.

Plotkin, H. C. and Odling-Smee, F. J. (1981) A multiple level model of evolution and its implications for sociobiology. *Behavioral and Brain Sciences*, 4, 225–268.

Reichel-Dolmatoff, G. (1997) *Rainforest Shamans: Essays on the Turkano Indians of the Northwest Amazon.* Themis Books, Dartington.

Riches, D. (1994) Shamanism: The Key to Religion. *Man*, 29: 381–406.

Rösing, I. (2003) *Trance, Besessenheit und Amnesie bei den Schamanen der Changpa-nomaden im ladakhischen Changthang.* Weishaupt Verlag, Gnas.

Sagant, P. (1996) *The Dozing Shaman: The Limbus of Eastern Nepal.* Oxford University Press, Bombay.

Samuel, G. (1993) *Civilized Shamans: Buddhism in Tibetan Societies.* Smithsonian, Washington.

Snelgrove, D. (1987) *Indo-Tibetan Buddhism: Indian buddhists and their Tibetan Successors.* Serindia, London.

Sober, E. and Wilson, D. S. (1998) *Unto Others: The Evolution and Psychology of Unselfish Behavior.* Harvard University Press, Cambridge, MA.

Winkelman, M. (2000) Shamanism: *The Neural Ecology of Consciousness and Healing.* Bergin and Garvey, Westport (conn).

Wilson, D. S. (2002) *Darwin's Cathedral: Evolution, Religion and the Nature of Society.* University of Chicago Press, Chicago.

CHAPTER 36

Competitive altruism: a theory of reputation-based cooperation in groups

Mark Van Vugt, Gilbert Roberts and Charlie Hardy

"I have lost my reputation! I have lost the immortal part, sir, of myself, and what remains is bestial, …"

Cassio, in *The Tragedy of Othello*, by William Shakespeare

36.1. Introduction

Humans are a remarkably moral social species. Humans engage in heroic acts to save the lives of complete strangers in emergencies, sometimes at substantial risk to themselves (Becker and Eagly, 2004). They cooperate with each other to help needy others, for example, spending time doing volunteer work, donating money to charitable causes, paying taxes, and contributing to a better environment (Penner *et al.*, 2005; Van Vugt *et al.*, 2000). Furthermore, human societies often reward people for their altruistic contributions through medals for bravery in wars, statues for political and military leaders, and awards for nurses and teachers. At the same time, they punish those who fail to consider the interests of others, for example, public condemnation of cheaters, imprisonment of criminals, and

execution of army deserters in wars (Levine and Moreland, 2002; Van Vugt and Chang, 2006).

The moral altruistic disposition of humans is also demonstrated in research on the 'prisoner's dilemma', a game involving a conflict between private and collective interests (Dawes, 1980). When this game is played in the laboratory among anonymous strangers in single interactions, there being no incentive for altruism, between 40% and 60% of people still cooperate (De Cremer and Van Vugt, 1999). Furthermore, many players are keen to punish non-cooperators even when punishing is costly and they will have no further interaction with them (Fehr and Gaechter, 2002). It seems that humans are distinctively moral. They readily empathize and cooperate with strangers, and harm those who fail to do so (Boyd and Richerson, in press).

How can we explain this moral altruistic tendency of our species? First, we must be clear about what we mean by altruism and morality. We define altruism in terms of a design to benefit others at a cost to oneself (Tooby and Cosmides, 1996; Van Vugt and Van Lange, 2006).

In psychology, altruism is defined in terms of a *motivation* to help (Batson, 1998; Sober and Wilson, 1998). It is often assumed that this motivation is conscious, although this is by no means necessary. Research suggests that humans are often not aware of why they behave as they do (Bargh and Chartrand, 1999).

Moral altruism is defined as a design to reward altruists and punish non-altruists. Moral altruists go one step further. Not only do they offer help, they also reward helpers by making resources available to them while punishing non-altruists by taking resources away from them (Alexander, 1987). This is consistent with Alexander's (1987) views on morality: "To establish moral rules is to impose rewards and punishments (typically assistance and ostracism, respectively) to control social acts that, respectively, help or hurt others." (p. 77).[1] Moral altruism is akin to the notion of strong reciprocity as coined by Fehr and Gaechter (2002), and moralistic aggression as coined by Trivers (1971). What then is the evolutionary basis for human moral altruism?

36.2. Kin explanations of moral altruism: the 'big-mistake' hypothesis

Humans are unique in their propensity to cooperate with non-relatives, sometimes in very large groups. In other ultrasocial species, like the social insects, highly cooperative societies are based exclusively on kinship (Wilson, 1975). The reason for this is derived from the logic of inclusive fitness, which was first developed by Hamilton (1964). According to this logic, natural selection favours traits and behaviours that benefit an individual's direct fitness or the fitness of genetically related individuals—the theory of inclusive fitness or kin selection. This is not the place for a detailed treatment of kin-selection theory. For more information on

the condi-tions under which altruism towards relatives evolves, see any evolutionary biology text (e.g. Alcock, 1998).

Kin helping accounts for a substantial part of altruism in human society today. Especially when the costs of helping are substantial, humans turn to their families for practical, financial and emotional assistance regardless of whether they live together in a village in the Amazon (Hames, 1978) or are dispersed over a large country such as the USA (Amato, 1993). We literally travel the world to see our relatives and when we die we leave our possessions to our descendants whether or not we like them (Smith *et al.*, 1987). There is no doubt that kin selection is a major force in the evolution of altruism but to what extent can it account for the unique aspects of human sociality and morality?

Some researchers have argued that cooperation with strangers is a relatively recent cultural phenomenon. The genus *Homo* is about 2 million years old and during most of that time humans probably lived in relatively small groups of kin rather like their non-human primate cousins (Barrett *et al.*, 2002). The social dispositions of humans evolved in a very different environment than today's world where social groups consist of a mixture of kin and non-kin. If humans behave altruistically towards others, it is because they erroneously believe they are dealing with kin, according to the 'big-mistake' hypothesis (Boyd and Richerson, in press). The mistake hypothesis argues that kin-detection systems are imperfect because, being around kin for much of human history, there was no need to improve them. Instead humans use cues, which are sometimes fallible, to distinguish between kin and non-kin such as physical cues like facial similarity, behavioural cues like habits, and cultural cues like language (Rushton, 1989; Park and Schaller, 2005). These cues are important in deciding who to help. For example, people are more likely help a stranger in an e-mail study if they happen to share the same surname (Oates and Wilson, 2002). And, students entrusted more money to strangers with whom they shared facial resemblance (DeBruine, 2002).

It remains to be seen whether or not such cues activate a kin-detection system, and exactly how this could be empirically verified (for a promising procedure see Park and Schaller, 2005).

---

[1] This is not to imply that morality and altruism are the same. Some forms of altruism may not be guided by moral principles, for example, helping one's own child. Furthermore, sometimes moral principles might lead to selfish rather than altruistic behaviour, for example, when a person feels entitled to take money from others (for a discussion of the relationship between altruism and morality, see Sober and Wilson, 1998).

Furthermore, the fact that most cultures have detailed kin-classification systems suggests that humans are well aware of who is kin or not. Finally, a misfired kin system cannot really account for the moral aspects of human altruism, because there does not seem to be any inclusive benefit associated with rewarding altruistic or punishing non-altruistic relatives, especially in interactions with strangers.

36.3. Direct reciprocity: from small to large scale cooperation

A different version of the big-mistake hypothesis is that altruistic behaviours in large groups are derived from adaptations for small-group cooperation. The theory of reciprocal altruism (Trivers, 1971) suggests that cooperation between two individuals develops if they are able to "enlarge the shadow of the future" (Axelrod, 1984, p. 126). Once people are locked in a relationship together, they can achieve mutual cooperation by adopting a 'tit-for-tat' strategy whereby after an initial cooperative move, each partner mimics the action of the other. Evidence shows that direct reciprocity leads to a stable level of cooperation in both humans (Axelrod and Hamilton, 1981; Van Lange and Semin-Goosens, 1998) and other animals that live in small stable groups such as vampire bats (Wilkinson, 1984).

Some theorists have argued that adaptations for direct reciprocity could account for the evolution of cooperation in large groups (e.g. Trivers, 1971). The main argument against this idea is that it does not address the problem of freeriding. Statistically, large groups are more likely to suffer from freeriders than small groups (Kerr, 1989). In small groups, freeriders can be identified and kept in place through a tit-for-tat strategy. Yet, in large groups, if people respond to a non-altruist by withholding their contributions then others will follow suit, pushing the group towards a non-cooperative equilibrium (Boyd and Richerson, 1988). Further, direct reciprocity cannot explain why humans act morally by altruistically rewarding and punishing others (Fehr and Gaechter, 2002). So the question about the origins of human moral altruism remains.

36.4. Group size, indirect reciprocity and reputation concerns

To understand the evolution of moral altruism, we must first understand why humans formed alliances with non-relatives in ever larger groups. Extrapolating from data on the relative neocortex size of modern humans, compared to early humans, monkeys and apes, suggests that there has been a steady increase in average group size in human evolution (Dunbar, 1992). There are different hypotheses regarding selection pressures for an increased group size. One theory suggests that ecological pressures forced humans onto the savannah where they were at risk from attacks by predators (Dunbar, 2004). Furthermore, resources like food and water-holes would have been distributed over larger areas, which forced kin groups to form alliances with other groups. These ecological conditions consequently lead to the formation of larger groups operating in so-called fission-fusion societies (like the Aboriginals in Australia). Another scenario is that competition between groups drove group size, resulting in an arms race between groups to grow larger and larger (Alexander, 1987; Diamond, 1997).

Engaging in coalitions with other individuals, kin and non-kin, would have been paramount to cope with the pressures of living in large groups. For example, male coalitions would be able to keep in place any single, aggressive individual, and female alliances could protect women from sexual harassment by men—much like in modern hunter-gatherer societies (Chagnon, 1997). Pressures on groups to expand therefore created new adaptive problems in terms of finding reliable and resourceful coalition partners and advertising oneself as an attractive partner. Large groups effectively became a market-place in which individuals would trade as buyers and sellers of cooperation in order to form the most successful coalitions (cf. Noe and Hammerstein, 1994).

This dynamic group context might have created new opportunities for the development of cooperation. To behave altruistically could now bring benefits, even if it was not reciprocated directly, as long as there were observers who used this information to form coalitions, leading to the formation of indirect reciprocity networks (Alexander, 1987). Although in reality it is a little more complex than this (Nowak and Sigmund, 2005), here is how it might work. If A is generous to B, and C is observing this, C expects A to also be generous to him, and will therefore pick A in a future coalition. Equally, if A is being nasty to B, observer C would want to avoid dealing with A in the future. Reputations matter a great deal in these social exchange networks, and it might pay to develop an altruistic reputation because being seen as an altruist would create opportunities unavailable to non-cooperators. It thus became possible for cooperators to team up in a 'conspiracy of doves' (Dawkins, 1976) and exclude non-cooperators from groups.

Moral altruism could have spread via the same mechanism. Acting morally, for example, punishing repeat offenders or rewarding heroes would be costly. Yet, it might be viewed by others as something desirable, perhaps a sign of leadership, which would increase opportunities for this person to engage in coalitions with others (Hardy and Van Vugt, 2006).

In sum, pressures to form large, flexible groups of both kin and non-kin kick-started a competition for the most cooperative, valuable and resourceful allies. In turn, this created selective advantages for individuals with (moral) altruistic tendencies. We refer to this process as competitive altruism (Hawkes, 1993; Roberts, 1998; Miller, 2001). Unlike kin altruism and reciprocal altruism, competitive altruism provides a more promising account of the unique moral and altruistic attributes of humans. It has no problems in explaining why people cooperate in large groups of strangers—in fact, the larger the group the greater the audience. Further, it explains why people help when there is very little chance of reciprocation such as volunteering to work with a terminally ill patient, or, like judges, police officers, or traffic wardens, they punish someone who has not harmed them personally (Van Vugt et al., 2000).

36.5. Competitive altruism: theory and conditions

Competitive-altruism theory is based on two simple premises. First it assumes that there are individual differences in altruism (for reasons that we outline below). Second, in forming alliances there is competition for the most moral and cooperative partners (Hardy and Van Vugt, 2006). As a consequence, people compete to behave more altruistically than others and establish an altruistic reputation. Competitive altruism is just one of several pathways to the development of cooperation in human groups. It is therefore important to recognize the kind of altruism that is most likely to be explained by competitive-altruism theory. We therefore need to specify conditions under which competitive altruism is likely to evolve and be phenotypically expressed.

Altruism as costly signal. First, if altruism is to act as a signal that makes the receiver behave preferentially towards the altruist, then it must be a reliable indicator of a person's resources, motivations, and/or intentions. If it is cost-free and easy to perform by anyone then observers would not be able to discriminate between people who are genuinely altruistic and cheaters, thus making the signal unreliable. Because altruism is by definition costly, altruism is particularly likely to have evolved into an honest signal (Hardy and Van Vugt, 2006). According to costly-signalling theory (Zahavi and Zahavi, 1997), organisms sometimes engage in self-handicapping acts as a way of signalling honest information about themselves. The peacock's tail is often cited as an example, because having a long and colourful tail is extremely costly for the animal as it makes it difficult to move around an escape predation. Imitation is therefore impossible for other animals lacking the 'good' genes to grow such an ornament. Models have shown that the same logic can apply in the case of altruism (Gintis et al., 2001).

So what does altruism signal? The most obvious answer is resources. By engaging in costly altruism, people signal that they can afford to help others rather than themselves. Hence, altruism conveys both resource potential and generosity, an ideal combination in an exchange partner. In addition, it might signal kindness, trustworthiness, honesty, self-control, strength of character, or even intelligence. For example, people who cooperate in a prisoner's dilemma are seen as more intelligent (Van Lange and Liebrand, 1991), presumably because it takes brainpower to appreciate the long-term benefits of cooperation. Moral forms of altruism could signal leadership potential, a desirable trait in groups (Van Vugt, in press).

Attracting an audience. For a particular act to be classified as a signal, it must be readily observable to others. Hence, there must be an audience which interprets the act (or the intention behind it) as altruistic, and uses this information to form a judgement about the giver. Ideally, they would pass on this information to multiple others in the form a reputation. From this, we predict that people will be more generous in public than in private situations, which happens to be true. People are, for example, more likely to give to street beggars in the company of a friend than when alone (Goldberg, 1995). Charity donations go up when donors are named publicly (Harbaugh, 1998). Finally, reputation concerns might explain why many people cooperate on the first trial of a prisoner's dilemma game (De Cremer and Van Vugt, 1999).

There should be a preference for performing altruistic acts in large crowds, but the evidence from bystander intervention experiments suggests the opposite: people are less inclined to help in large groups than in small groups. One explanation is that in these experiments helpers were non-identifiable (Latanè and Darley, 1970). Competitive altruism predicts that people are more likely to aid someone if they can be identified as helpers. Consistent with this, the social-loafing literature suggests that cheating is more prevalent in large groups unless cheaters can be identified (Van Vugt et al., 2000). Large groups create opportunities for both altruists and cheaters, and it probably depends upon the vigilance of the crowd whether it pays to be generous and helpful.

The audience should also be interested in the act to pay attention. For acts of altruism there is likely to be an audience, because there are benefits to be gained from being in the presence of an altruist. A look around the modern media confirms this. Heroic acts of strangers helping in emergencies, soldiers saving the lives of comrades, and philanthropic events like Comic Relief and Live Aid attract large crowds. People also spend a great deal of their conversations gossiping about the moral aspects of others' behaviour (Dunbar, 2004).

Long-term benefits of altruism. Third, there must be a long-term benefit for the altruist.

An evolutionary analysis delineates that competitive altruism only evolves if there are long-term benefits for the altruist (or their close relatives). We have already suggested that access to coalitions is one such benefit. While cheaters and non-reciprocators are at risk of being increasingly ostracized from groups, altruists are in huge demand as coalition partners in future social exchanges like sharing food. But benefits may be more subtle. For example, altruists may recoup the costs of their actions by increasing their attractiveness as a mate, thus being able to attract more and better sexual partners (Roberts, 1998; Miller, 2001). Perhaps this is the reason why males tend to be especially kind and generous in the presence of females (Goldberg, 1995; Campbell et al., 2002). It is also possible that altruists profit indirectly: being in a group with altruists, their group would fare better in competitions with groups containing fewer altruists (Darwin, 1871; Alexander, 1987; Sober and Wilson, 1998).

Individual differences in altruism. Competitive altruism theory may explain why moral altruism is widespread in humans, but it does not explain why there are substantial individual differences (Van Vugt et al., 1995; Van Lange et al., 1997; Kurzban and Houser, 2005). One explanation is the cost of altruism. Only people with substantial resources could afford to be generous, as costly-signalling theory suggests, and many people simply cannot afford to forego a golden opportunity to cheat (Frank, 1988). Another reason is that in some societies, it is easier to get away with cheating, for example, because the society is large and mobile, putting limits on the importance of reputations. A third reason is that a society might be so small that cooperation occurs primarily within family networks, and cooperating with strangers is too rare for people to invest in an altruistic reputation (cf. Yamagishi, 1986).

36.5.1. Competitive altruism: anthropological and non-human evidence

Because of the novelty of the competitive-altruism theory, there have not been many tests on its core predictions. Earlier we presented some anecdotal results as well as results from research designed for a different purpose. We now turn to evidence from studies carried out specifically to test predictions derived from competitive-altruism theory. We start with the anthropological and non-human literatures.

There are various examples of costly displays of altruism found in this literature (see Hardy and Van Vugt, 2006). For example, among the Aché of Paraquay, individuals who share more than average with others in good times tend to receive more food from people when they are sick or injured than those who have been less generous in the past (Gurven *et al.*, 2000). Thus, sharing food in good times serves as an insurance policy to cover for bad times. Among the Shuar, individuals who take on voluntary administration jobs are rewarded with status and prestige (Price, 2003). Such social benefits might be the main reason for killing large game in hunter-gatherer societies (Hawkes, 1993).

On various Melanesian islands, a few years after someone's death, the family of the deceased puts on an elaborate feast to commemorate the dead person. All the guests receive a bounty of food and gifts, with no expectation of reciprocation. One of the dishes is turtle meat, which is very difficult to obtain. Giving out as much turtle meat as possible serves as an honest signal of the physical quality of the family members, increasing the family's reputation and esteem (Smith and Bliege-Bird, 2000). Similarly, among Native American clans in the North-West Pacific, it is common for chiefs to organize large feasts—a 'potlatch'—to which members of neighbouring clans were invited to indulge in a bonanza of delicacies such as salmon. This public display of generosity possibly serves to build and strengthen coalitions between neighbouring clans in the face of threats from rivals (Bliege-Bird and Smith, 2005).

36.5.2. Evidence from non-humans

These displays of generosity are paralleled by activities in non-human primates, particularly chimpanzees. After killing a small animal, like a colobus monkey, chimpanzees sometimes share their meat with other members in their troop, particularly females and possibly in exchange for sex (De Waal, 1996). There is also evidence that individuals select grooming partners based on their reputation as a reciprocator (Barrett

et al., 2000). Furthermore, captive chimpanzees only solicit food from humans that have reputations as food sharers (Russell and Dunbar, 2005). Finally, there is anecdotal evidence that in babblers, a highly social bird species, individuals compete for prestige through being altruistic in allofeeding and nest guarding (Zahavi and Zahavi, 1997; but see Wright, 1997).

These are just some non-human examples of behaviour that may be shaped ultimately by competitive-altruism tendencies. Humans have probably built on this primordial tendency by extending the scale, variety and intensity of these competitive-altruism displays in human societies.

36.5.3. Competitive altruism: laboratory evidence

In recent years, researchers have tested various predictions derived from competitive-altruism theory in the laboratory, using data from computer simulations and small-group experiments. Although this research is ongoing, it is encouraging that many of the predictions from competitive altruism theory have been supported so far. If the conditions outlined by competitive-altruism theory are met, cooperation among strangers is sustained in even large groups.

Computer-simulation studies have revealed, for example, that when agents can assess the altruistic 'reputation' of other agents, and can use this information to decide whether or not to cooperate with a given interaction partner, then cooperation can evolve. One reputation method, called image scoring, gives a score to individuals based on their previous interaction history (Nowak and Sigmund, 1998). If an individual aids someone in a round, a point is added to his reputation score, whereas if he fails to give aid, he loses a point. In image scoring, building up a reputation as an altruist is beneficial, because other agents use the image scores of other agents to decide whether to cooperate or defect. There are other types of reputation strategies, for example a 'good-standing' strategy (Sugden, 1986) which takes into account the context of a partner's previous behaviour. This has been shown to be superior to image scoring (Leimar and Hammerstein, 2001). Undoubtedly, there are other kinds of reputation systems that could give an edge to altruists, but they still await further investigation (Nowak and Sigmund, 2005; but see Panchanathan and Boyd, 2004).

Small-group experiments have also provided support for various aspects of competitive-altruism theory. Such experiments are usually conducted with small groups of students that are given a prisoner's dilemma type task to study the development of cooperation in groups. In one study, cooperation was achieved when participants played against a stooge (a preprogrammed computer strategy) that matched the investment of the participants, leading effectively to an escalation of cooperation, as competitive altruism theory would predict (Roberts and Renwick, 2003). In another study, members of four-person groups were more likely to contribute to a public good if they knew that afterwards they could be selected to participate in a dyadic cooperative game with one of the other group members (Barclay, 2004).

Essentially the same result was obtained in a set of studies by Hardy and Van Vugt (2006). These researchers also found that public good contributions increased when group members' contributions were made public, which is entirely consistent with the competitive altruism idea. A recent study shows that even a pair of artificial eyes on a computer screen enhances people's cooperation more in an otherwise entirely anonymous situation (Haley and Fessler, 2005). Thus, there is abundant evidence that reputational concerns lie at the basis of many altruistic activities even in largely (but not exclusively) anonymous laboratory settings.

Some experiments have also shown clear benefits for the altruists. For example, members who contributed more to the public good were given more status and prestige than other group members, and were more likely to be selected as group leaders and representatives (M. Van Vugt, unpublished data). In addition, altruists in the public goods game were chosen more often as coalition partners in a subsequent game. This resembles the results of a study by Milinski *et al.* (2002) who found that when individuals were involved in two games at the same time, a public goods game and a reciprocity game (Wedekind and Milinski, 2000), people in the latter game donated more to people who acted altruistically in the public goods game.

Taken together, these findings suggest that altruism is influenced by reputational needs and that having an altruistic reputation brings benefits to individuals.

36.6. Conclusions and implications

Competitive-altruism theory proposes that altruism evolves once there are selection pressures to form coalitions with other individuals, non-kin, in large groups. In human evolution, coalition formation appears to be a major force in dealing with group size, resource unpredictability, and intergroup competition (Alexander, 1987; Dunbar, 2004). A general preference for more cooperative partners then creates a competitive market in which people with prosocial traits are more likely to be chosen as coalition partners, friends, or mates. Because having an altruistic reputation pays off in such an environment, it is paramount for people to invest in it, which is best achieved through public displays of morality and altruism. Could this theory explain the peculiar moral aspects of human nature?

Several core predictions of competitive altruism theory are supported so far in empirical research. For example, people are more generous in public than in private settings (Hardy and Van Vugt, 2006). Altruistic individuals are selectively rewarded by observers and non-altruists are selectively punished. Computer simulations show that if reputational information is available, altruism becomes an evolutionary stable strategy. Finally, anthropologists have documented numerous public displays of generosity, like funeral parties, pot-latches, charity and philanthropy, which could be accounted for by competitive-altruism theory.

Many aspects of competitive-altruism theory remain to be tested. For example, do altruists recoup the costs of their activities by entering into productive, cooperative alliances, or do they benefit in other ways, for example, by attracting mates? Some have suggested that altruism is an honest signal to convey one's qualities as a sexual partner (Zahavi and Zahavi, 1997), but there is no empirical evidence for this yet. Furthermore, exactly what does altruism signal? Does it primarily signal resource potential or also virtues like trust and benevolence, and possibly even intelligence. Finally, does moral altruism have a distinctive signalling quality, and, if so, what does it signal—leadership potential perhaps (Van Vugt, in press)? Also, competitive altruism predicts that people should sometimes act altruistically to people who do not need it, and that potential recipients should sometimes refuse help when they need it. This needs to be examined in further research.

There are several theoretical issues to be resolved. First, we acknowledge that competitive altruism is just one of the evolutionary routes to human cooperation. Kin helping, direct reciprocity, and group-selected altruism probably account for a large proportion of altruism in human society (Amato, 1993; Sober and Wilson, 1998). Competitive altruism explains the more public displays of helping, like philanthropy, heroism, bystander intervention, charity work, and volunteering. A clear strength of the theory is that it has no problem in accounting for unreciprocated altruism because it presupposes that there will be compensating long-term benefits. Equally, this kind of altruism does not have to be enforced by groups because they can simply avoid interactions with non-altruists; hence there is no second-order freerider problem, unlike with altruistic punishment (Fehr and Gaechter, 2002).

Is altruism always a desirable trait? Being seen as an indiscriminate altruist, for example, helping members of antagonistic out-groups may not be regarded as a desirable quality in some coalitions, for example, in groups in conflict. Also, someone who consistently helps defectors might develop a bad reputation (Nowak and Sigmund, 2005). Finally, could people not easily fake altruism in order to get access to desirable groups or mates? If people could easily obtain an altruistic reputation it would be a serious problem for the theory because it would make altruism a meaningless signal. There are two arguments against this. First, altruism is by definition a costly activity, and so it automatically excludes people who cannot afford to be altruistic (e.g. a poor individual cannot spend too much on charity). Second, across all human societies, people work extremely hard to invest in their reputations, and there are reputation systems in place to constantly monitor whether people's status and esteem matches their contributions to the group.

There are several unique features of human societies facilitating competitive altruism and reputation-based cooperation in groups. For example, language is a unique human capacity that is believed to have evolved to build alliances in large, dispersed groups (Dunbar, 2004). One of the most frequent conversation topics is gossip about others not present, and the gossip tends to revolve around the status, achievements and failures of other people. So it is perhaps not too far-fetched to assume a relationship between language and the spread of competitive altruism in humans.

Finally, there are other unique aspects of human culture that might have a basis in competitive altruism, such as philanthropy, religion, the military, architecture, science, artistry and entertainment. In all of these domains, there are individuals 'showing off' their resourcefulness by contributing to public goods that, once they are available, are free for all to use and consume. For example, once the nineteenth century British engineer Brunel had created a design to build steam boats, they could be built and used by anyone. In this regard, it is perhaps not surprising to find that the highest-status members in human society are scientists, doctors, military and political leaders, artists and entertainers, whose contributions benefit all (Hardy and Van Vugt, 2006). Competitive altruism may explain why social hierarchies in human groups are built on status and prestige rather than dominance and coercion as in many other social species (Henrich and Gil-White, 2001). We should be pleased about this.

Acknowledgments

Writing this chapter was made possible by grants from the Economic and Social Research Council to the first and third authors. The authors would like to thank Rob Kurzban and the members of the Evolution and Social Sciences group at the University of Kent for their comments on an earlier version.

References

Alcock, J. (1998) *Animal Behaviour: An Evolutionary Approach*, 6th edn. Sinauer, Sunderland, MA.

Alexander, R. D. (1987) *The Biology of Moral Systems*. Aldine de Gruyter, New York.

Amato, P. R. (1993) Urban–rural differences in helping friends and family members. *Social Psychology Quarterly*, 56: 249–262.

Axelrod, R. (1984) *The Evolution of Cooperation*. Basic Books, New York.

Axelrod, R. and Hamilton, W. D. (1981) The evolution of cooperation. *Science*, 21: 1390–1396.

Barclay, P. (2004) Trustworthiness and competitive altruism can also solve the "tragedy of the commons". *Evolution and Human Behaviour*, 25: 209–220.

Bargh, J. A. and Chartrand, T. L. (1999) The unbearable automaticity of being. *American Psychologist*, 54: 462–479.

Barrett, L., Dunbar, R. and Lycett, J. (2002) *Human Evolutionary Psychology*. Palgrave, London.

Barrett, L., Henzi, S. P., Weingrill, T., Lycett, J. E. and Hill, R. A. (2000) Female baboons give as good as they get, but they do not raise the stakes. *Animal Behaviour*, 59: 763–770.

Batson, C. D. (1998) Altruism and prosocial behaviour. In D. Gilbert, S. Fiske and G. Lindzey (eds) *Handbook of Social Psychology*, pp. 282–316. McGraw-Hill, New York.

Becker, S. and Eagly, A. H. (2004) The heroism of women and men. *American Psychologist*, 59: 163–178.

Bliege-Bird, R. and Smith, E. A. (2005) Signalling theory, strategic interaction, and symbolic capital. *Current Anthropology*, 46: 221–248.

Boyd, R. and Richerson, P. J. (1988) The evolution of reciprocity in sizable groups. *Journal of Theoretical Biology*, 132: 337–356.

Boyd, R and Richerson, P. J. (in press) Culture and the evolution of the human social instincts. In S. Levinson and N. Enfield (eds) *Roots of Human Sociality*. Berg, Oxford.

Campbell, L., Simpson, J. A., Stewart, M. and Manning, J. T. (2002) Men's waist-to-hip ratio, intrasexual competition, and interpersonal perception in leaderless groups. *Human Nature*, 13: 345–362.

Chagnon, N. A. (1997) *Yanomamo*. Wadsworth, London.

Darwin, C. (1871) *The Descent of Man*. Murray, London.

Dawes, R. M. (1980) Social dilemmas. *Annual Review of Psychology*, 31: 169–193.

Dawkins, R. (1976) *The Selfish Gene*. Oxford University Press, Oxford.

DeBruine, L. M. (2002) Facial resemblance enhances trust. *Proceedings of the Royal Society of London, B*, 269: 1307–1312.

De Cremer, D. and Van Vugt, M. (1999) Social identification effects in social dilemmas: a transformation of motives. *European Journal of Social Psychology*, 29: 871–893.

De Waal, F. (1996) *Good Natured: The Origins of Right and Wrong in Humans and Other Animals*. Harvard University Press, Cambridge, MA.

Diamond, J. (1997) *Guns, Germs and Steel*. Vintage, London.

Dunbar, R. I. M. (1992) Neocortex size as a constraint on group size in primates. *Journal of Human Evolution*, 20: 469–493.

Dunbar, R. I. M. (2004) Gossip in evolutionary perspective. *General Review of Psychology*, 8: 100–110.

Fehr, E. and Gaechter, S. (2002) Altruistic punishment in humans. *Nature*, 415: 137–140.

Frank, R. (1988) *Passions Within Reason*. Norton, New York.

Gintis, H., Smith, E. A. and Bowles, S. (2001) Costly signalling and cooperation. *Journal of Theoretical Biology*, 213: 103–119.

Goldberg, T. L. (1995) Altruism towards panhandlers: who gives? *Human Nature*, 6: 79–89.

Gurven, M., Allen-Arave, W., Hill, K. and Hurtado, M. (2000) "It's a Wonderful Life": signalling generosity among the Ache of Paraguay. *Evolution and Human Behaviour*, 21: 263–282.

Haley, K. J. and Fessler, D. M. T. (2005) Nobody's watching? Subtle cues affect generosity in an anonymous economic game. *Evolution and Human Behaviour*, 26: 245–256.

Hames, R. (1978) A behavioural account of the division of labour among the Ye'kwana. Doctoral dissertation, University of Santa Barbara.

Hamilton, W. D. (1964) The genetical evolution of social behavior, I, II. *Journal of Theoretical Biology*, 7: 1–52.

Harbaugh, W. T. (1998) The prestige motive for making charitable transfers. *American Economic Review*, 88: 27–282.

Hardy, C., and Van Vugt, M. (2006) Nice guys finish first: the competitive altruism hypothesis. *Personality and Social Psychology Bulletin*, 32: 1402–1413.

Hawkes, K. (1993) Why hunter-gatherers work—an ancient version of the problem of public goods. *Current Anthropology*, 34: 341–361.

Henrich, J. and Gil-White, F. J. (2001) The evolution of prestige. Freely conferred deference as a mechanism for enhancing the benefits of cultural transmission. *Evolution and Human Behaviour*, 22: 165–196.

Kerr, N. (1989) Illusions of efficacy: the effects of group size on perceived efficacy in social dilemmas. *Journal of Experimental Social Psychology*, 25: 287–313.

Kurzban, R. and Houser, D. (2005) An experimental investigation of cooperative types in human groups: A complement to evolutionary theory and simulations. *Proceedings of the National Academy of Sciences of the USA*, 102: 1803–1807.

Latanè, B. and Darley, J. M. (1970) *The Unresponsive Bystander: Why Doesn't He Help?* Appleton-Century-Crofts, New York.

Leimar, O. and Hammerstein, P. (2001) Evolution of cooperation through indirect reciprocity. *Proceedings of the Royal Society of London, B*, 268: 745–753.

Levine, J. L. and Moreland, R. (2002) Group reactions to loyalty and disloyalty. In E. Lawler and S. Thye (eds) *Group Cohesion, Trust, and Solidarity* (*Advances in Group Processes*, vol. 19, pp. 203–228). Elsevier Science, Amsterdam.

Miller, G. (2001) *The Mating Mind*. Vintage, London.

Milinski, M., Semmann, D. and Krambeck, H.-J. (2002) Reputation helps solve the 'tragedy of the commons'. *Nature*, 415: 424–426.

Noe, R. and Hammerstein, P. (1994) Biological markets: supply and demand determine the effect of partner choice in cooperation, mutualism and mating. *Behavioural Ecology and Sociobiology*, 35: 1–11.

Nowak, M. and Sigmund, K. (1998) Evolution of indirect reciprocity by image scoring. *Nature*, 393: 573–577.

Nowak, M. and Sigmund, K. (2005) Evolution of indirect reciprocity. *Nature*, 437: 1291–1298.

Oates, K. and Wilson, M. (2002) Nominal kinship cues facilitate altruism. *Proceedings of the Royal Society of London, B*, 269: 105–109.

Panchanathan, K. and Boyd, R. (2004) Indirect reciprocity can stabilize cooperation without the second-order freerider problem. *Nature*, 432: 499–502.

Park, J. H. and Schaller, M. (2005) Does attitude similarity serve as a heuristic cue for kinship? Evidence of an implicit cognitive association. *Evolution and Human Behaviour*, 26: 158–170.

Penner, L. A., Dovidio, J. F., Schroeder, D. A. and Piliavin, J. A. (in press) Altruism and prosocial behaviour. *Annual Review of Psychology*.

Price, M. (2003) Pro-community altruism and social status in a Shuar village. *Human Nature*, 14: 191–208.

Roberts, G. (1998) Competitive altruism: from reciprocity to the handicap principle. *Proceedings of the Royal Society of London, B*, 265: 427–431.

Roberts, G. and Renwick, J. (2003) The development of cooperative relationships: an experiment. *Proceedings of the Royal Society of London, B*, 270: 2279–2284.

Rushton, J. P. (1989) Genetic similarity, human altruism, and group selection. *Behavioral and Brain Sciences*, 12: 503–559.

Russell, Y. and Dunbar, R. I. M. (2005) Image scoring in great apes. Paper presented at the meeting 'Understanding human altruism', October 2005, Brighton, UK (organised by Joel Peck).

Smith, E. A. and Bleige-Bird, R. L. (2000) Turtle hunting and tombstone opening: public generosity as costly signalling. *Evolution and Human Behaviour*, 21: 245–261.

Smith, M. S., Kish, B. L. and Crawford, C. B. (1987) Inheritance of wealth as human kin investment. *Ethology and Sociobiology*, 8: 171–182.

Sober, E. and Wilson, D. S. (1998) *Unto Others: The Evolution and Psychology of Unselfish Behaviour*. Harvard University Press, Cambridge, MA.

Sugden, R. (1986) *The Economics of Rights, Cooperation and Welfare*. Blackwell, Oxford.

Tooby, J. and Cosmides, L. (1996) Friendship and the banker's paradox: other pathways to the evolution of adaptations for altruism. In W. G. Runciman, J. Maynard Smith and R. I. M. Dunbar (eds), *Evolution of Social Behaviour Patterns in Primates and Man. Proceedings of the British Academy*, 88: 119–143.

Trivers, R. (1971) The evolution of reciprocal altruism. *Quarterly Review of Biology*, 46: 35–57.

Van Lange, P. A. M. and Liebrand, W. B. (1991) The influence of others' morality and own social value orientation on cooperation in the Netherlands and the U.S.A. *International Journal of Psychology*, 26: 429–449.

Van Lange, P. A. M. and Semin-Goossens, A. (1998) The boundaries of reciprocal cooperation. *European Journal of Social Psychology*, 28: 847–854.

Van Lange, P. A. M., Otten, W., De Bruin, E. M. N. and Joireman, J. A. (1997) Development of prosocial, individualistic, and competitive orientations: theory and preliminary evidence. *Journal of Personality and Social Psychology*, 73: 733–746.

Van Vugt, M. (in press) The evolutionary origins of leadership and followership. *Personality and Social Psychology Review*.

Van Vugt, M. and Van Lange, P. A. M. (in press) Psychological adaptations for prosocial behaviour. In M. Schaller, D. Kenrick and J. Simpson (eds), *Evolution and Social Psychology*. Psychology Press, New York.

Van Vugt, M., Meertens, R. M. and Van Lange, P. A. M. (1995) Car versus public transportation? The role of social value orientations in a real-life social dilemma. *Journal of Applied Social Psychology*, 25: 258–278.

Van Vugt, M., Snyder, M., Tyler, T. and Biel, A. (2000) *Cooperation in Modern Society: Promoting the Welfare of Communities, States, and Organizations*. Routledge, London.

Wedekind, C. and Milinski, M. (2000) Cooperation through image scoring in humans. *Science*, 88: 850–852.

Wilkinson, G. S. (1984) Reciprocal food sharing in the vampire bat. *Nature*, 308: 181–184.

Wilson, E. O. (1975) *Sociobiology: The New Synthesis*. Harvard University Press, Cambridge, MA.

Wright, J. (1997) Helping-at-the-nest in Arabian babblers: signalling social status or sensible investment in chicks? *Animal Behaviour*, 54: 1439–1448.

Yamagishi, T. (1986) The structural goal/expectation theory of cooperation in social dilemmas. In E. Lawler (ed.) *Advances in Group Processes*, vol. 3, pp. 51–87. JAI Press, Greenwich, CT.

Zahavi, A. and Zahavi, A. (1997) *The Handicap Principle: The Missing Piece of Darwin's Puzzle*. Oxford University Press, Oxford.

CHAPTER 37

Ethnic nepotism as heuristic: risky transactions and public altruism

Frank Salter

37.1. Introduction: ethnic-nepotism theory

Kin selection, the popular name given to Hamilton's (1964) theory of inclusive fitness, has been successful in predicting variation in human altruism shown towards kin of different proximity (e.g. Silk, 1980; Dunbar, 1995; Daly and Wilson, 1999; Case *et al.*, 2001; Burnstein *et al.*, 2002). By the early 1970s, Hamilton had reworked his theory to make it applicable to interactions between random members of whole populations (1971, p. 89). Hamilton argued that altruism could be adaptive between genetically similar non-kin, such as co-ethnics, when fitness costs and benefits obeyed Hamilton's Rule for adaptive altruism. Hamilton suggested, and Harpending (2002) confirmed, that ethnic kinship is equivalent to the genetic variation between populations, allowing ethnic kinship to be quantified and compared to family kinships. Ethnic kinship is small when the comparison is between closely related ethnic groups, but can be surprisingly high when comparing ethnic

groups that evolved on different continents. This can be illustrated by considering different hypothetical societies formed by drawing borders around various combinations of populations. In a society consisting solely of Danes, two randomly chosen individuals have zero kinship. In a society consisting of the Danish and English populations, two randomly chosen Danes have a slight kinship. But in a society consisting of Danes and, say, Chinese, two randomly chosen Danes have kinship equivalent to that between grandparent and grandchild (as do two randomly chosen Chinese). Co-ethnics can be as closely related as full siblings. In global comparison, ethnic kinship is typically equivalent to that between grandparent and grandchild (Salter, 2002a). This quantification of ethnic kinship adds plausibility to the theory of ethnic nepotism, developed by I. Eibl-Eibesfeldt, P. van den Berghe, J. P. Rushton and others.

Kin-selection theory interprets the behavioural universal of nepotism to be a product of evolutionary history. In that theory, the rigors of natural selection meant that altruism—including the unreciprocated giving of resources to another individual—was only viable when practised between close kin (Hamilton, 1964).

According to Eibl-Eibesfeldt (1982, 1998) and van den Berghe (1978, 1981), ethnic groups develop some degree of solidarity because their members think of themselves as extended kin groups. Indeed, among the definitions of ethnicity, the common denominator is putative common descent (Connor, 1994). This makes sense from van den Berghe's kin-selection perspective, but also fits with classical ethological theory as expounded by Eibl-Eibesfeldt (1972, first published 1970), who observed that national solidarity is based on family feeling. A similar point is made by Horowitz (1985) in his major treatment of ethnic conflict. Horowitz concurs with van den Berghe and Eibl-Eibesfeldt (though without referencing them) that ethnicity is based on 'family resemblance', that kinship is crucial to understanding the central role of family structure in determining ethnic identity and in explaining the intensity of ethnic conflict.

Of course the genetic relatedness of co-ethnics is less than that within families. Nevertheless, two randomly chosen members of the same ethnic group usually share, on average, more genes than they do with members of other groups. Depending on circumstances, it might be adaptive for an individual to make sacrifices for a numb.. of co-ethnics, if the result is an increase in the altruist's genetic representation in the metapopulation (Hamilton, 1971, p. 89; Harpending, 1979, 2002). Ethnic kinship is too weak to justify (in terms of pay-off in genetic fitness) significant altruism between individuals. However, contributing to public goods such as big-game hunting, group defence, and the assertion of group status allows an individual to benefit a large population (Goetze, 1998). Under these conditions, even small average relatedness between an actor and the population benefited can result in a fitness pay-off (Salter, 2002a).

Ethnic solidarity is most likely to become a strong determinant of interpersonal relationships following indoctrination and manipulation by rituals, symbols and ideologies that generalize familial loyalties to larger populations (Connor, 1993; Eibl-Eibesfeldt, 1998). Ethnic identification is more stable than is intensity of investment in the ethnic group, or mobilization

in sociological terminology. The magnifying role of culture does not alter our species' basic motivational repertoire, and ethnic-nepotism theory proposes that the motivational basis of ethnic loyalty is nepotism, a phylogenetically old adaptation. This is consistent with the role of cultural 'recognition markers' such as language, religion, and physiognomic differences in demarcating groups. Due to this group-level nepotism, individuals are more willing to invest resources and emotions in the whole ethnic group. Cultural factors have a major role in defining group boundaries and intensity of solidarity. Thus, evolutionary thinking about ethnic relations and social behaviour is thoroughly interactionist, and might be thought of as a type of constructionism, albeit a non-relativistic and biologically informed version. One name that differentiates it as such is 'social technology' (Caton, 1988; Geiger, 1988; Salter, 1995).

Evolutionary theory underlying ethnic nepotism is not well developed. There are two main approaches. The first is to portray ethnic nepotism as a literal extension of the family variety, with shared homologies in emotions, psychological mechanisms, and releasers (such as perceived attacks on the group). This view assumes no special psychological structures beyond those evolved for managing family relationships. This is the thinking behind the use of kinship terms in patriotic speech (Johnson, 1987; Connor, 1993; Holper, 1996). Eibl-Eibesfeldt's (1972) core argument is that ethnic solidarity is an extension of kinship motivation. Although van den Berghe is not explicit about evolutionary mechanisms, his analysis seems to fit into this literalist approach. Rushton's (1989b) theory, based on genetic similarity, also extrapolates from small-group dynamics to the mass-population level, though the family is only one domain in which resemblance operates to allow detection of genetically similar individuals.

The second approach is to allow for ethnic and kin motivation to be different. The emotions and psychological structures they engage are evolved specifically to manage investment in identity groups beyond the family, namely the hunter-gatherer band and the tribe. This approach allows for overlap, for example in releasing conditions, but claims that identity processes go beyond kin, and are the outcome of an evolutionary history different to kin selection. One well-known example is Richerson and Boyd's (2001) dual evolutionary model of the evolution of patriotism. The label 'ethnic nepotism' applies somewhat tenuously to this theory because family and nepotistic feeling are not part of it. However, it does deal with altruism directed towards ethnic groups. An earlier, genetically rather naïve, group-selectionist theory was offered by Keith (1968, first published 1947) to explain the cluster of related motivations: patriotism, nationalism, tribalism. But the theory offered no mechanisms for resisting free riders, a fatal flaw in early group-selection theories (Maynard Smith, 1976). Eibl-Eibesfeldt (1982) augments literal ethnic nepotism with a group-selection model that generates a predisposition to ethnocentrism. The model is based on tight familial bonding and, like Richardson and Boyd's model, includes punishment of freeriders. This fully deserves to be called a theory of 'nepotism' because it predicts some engagement of kinship motivation, and the continuing importance of kinship symbols.

Social-technology theory can accommodate both evolutionary scenarios, though conceivably some phenomena will be better explained by one or the other. For example, the expectation from literalist theory is that ethnic identities should not readily include more than one racial group, while the dual evolutionary model puts greater weight on cultural similarity. Most studies, however, do not differentiate between these evolutionary mechanisms, instead being directed to testing the efficacy of ethnic nepotism defined as altruism directed at the ethnic group, in contemporary and recent societies. Vanhanen (1991), for example, treated his study of conflict in India as a case study in the politics of ethnic nepotism. More than 90% of violent social conflicts occurred between different ethnic groups. Rushton (1989a) used blood tests to measure the genetic similarity of male friends in England, and found that friends were more similar than a random sample.

In the following sections, I review two sets of recent empirical findings that are generally confirmatory of ethnic-nepotism theory, although there are some disconfirming results. At its present stage of development, the theory is best viewed as a useful heuristic. As the case studies described below indicate, developing the theory as explanation will necessitate incorporating psychological, cultural, economic and political factors.

37.2. Ethnic nepotism and risky transactions

One set of studies concerns partner choice for conducting risky transactions (Salter, 2002b). The first type considered was criminal business. Transacting business without the protection of contract law is subject to the risk of defection by one of the parties. Illicit activities are also risky because of police and competition from other criminals. A major risk is that of defectors who inform the police or competitors. This risk makes trust a valuable resource for partners in crime. In economic terminology, trust lowers transaction costs. Evolutionary theories of kin and ethnic nepotism offer some insights into the nature of trust, and hence might help explain and even predict a role for families and ethnically bonded networks in risky enterprises. Clearly families figure prominently in conducting transactions that require mutual trust but are not protected by contract law.

Inquiry can be broadened beyond illicit business to the question of whether evolved kin and ethnic altruism mitigate the risk of other kinds of transactions. Where else is kinship or ethnicity an important organizing principle? Does kin altruism help explain the workings of that principle? Are kin and ethnic relationships favoured when the relationship itself poses a serious risk?

A number of studies have tested the hypothesis that family members and co-ethnics are more trusted, and trustworthy, in situations where contracts are not enforced by the wider social system. These include studies of exchange networks in hunter-gatherer societies such as the !Kung Bushmen of Southern Africa, psychological experiments concerning social cognition of joint risk, of organized crime, of middleman trading networks such as the ethnic Chinese in Malaysia, persecuted minorities, US Supreme Court proceedings, and tourist behaviour, all of which confirmed the hypothesis. However, the hypothesis was disconfirmed in a case study of male homosexual partnering behaviour.

37.2.1. **Risk mitigation in Bushman exchange networks**

An empirical test of an evolutionary theory should begin by describing the species in question in its natural condition. No human population remains in its pristine Pleistocene state but approximations are offered by societies that presently live or until recently lived by hunting and gathering, the means of subsistence pursued by *Homo sapiens* for most of its evolutionary history. This mode of existence forces groups to remain small and mobile, and retain social ties able to mitigate risks from the environment and the predations of other groups.

Wiessner (2002) reports on how the social ties of the !Kung Bushmen of the Kalahari have fared under the impact of rapid social change occasioned by the Namibian Government's provision of stable water points allowing a sedentary lifestyle. Wiessner has been documenting !Kung exchange networks for more than 20 years. Her original studies confirmed the importance of kin ties in mitigating risk of defection from exchange relationships, allowing the !Kung's 'social security' net to extend over large distances. The longitudinal extension of her research traced the development of these ties, whose *raison d'être* of providing security against famine and conflict was undermined by an era of relative plenty and stability. Exchange ties are valuable and difficult to replicate once lost. In a process analogous to bequeathing land, elderly Bushmen also pass on their exchange ties to children. Thus, low-risk exchange ties are inherited from parents and grandparents.

Wiessner's research also contributes to the debate over 'fictive' versus 'socially constructed' kinship. The debate hinges on the question of how easy it is to manipulate humans into treating non-kin like real kin. Some theorists such as van den Berghe (1981) argue that ethnic groups have a genealogical component to their identity, and that despite some exceptions people usually direct altruism towards groups with which they are the most closely related. Others argue in the opposite direction, that ethnic groups are social constructs with little or no genetic reality (e.g. Reynolds, 1980). Wiessner shows that in Bushman society, fictive kinship based on shared names has some influence on patterns of exchange, but that delayed reciprocal arrangements—a riskier type

of transaction than that yielding immediate returns—are made with closer genetic kin.

37.2.2. **Ethnic groups and domain-specific decision-making**

Wang (2002) argues for the importance of 'domain specific' cognitive mechanisms as the agents responsible for making decisions regarding risks to different kinds of groups. The human brain is not rational in the normative sense of generally giving equivalent answers to equivalent problems. Individuals respond differently to logically identical problems that are put to them in different words—the framing effect. Wang pays special attention to framing effects generated by perceived kinship and non-kinship. Respondents show greater concern for groups of kin than for groups of non-kin. As Wang puts it, his findings suggest that decision making rationality is kinship specific: "[The result] argues against an all-purpose viewpoint and indicates that human choice mechanisms automatically distinguish kinship from pseudo-kinship or quasi-kinship." Wang also finds cultural differences: compared to American subjects, mainland Chinese subjects treat much larger hypothetical groups as kith and kin.

37.2.3. **Blood symbolism and the Sicilian Mafia**

Blok's research on the Sicilian Mafia shows how biological kinship and metaphorical 'shared blood' serve to bind together members of crime 'families' and 'brotherhoods': "Given its pre-eminence in Mafia coalitions, agnatic kinship in Sicily, as in other Indo-European kinship systems, provides for relationships of 'diffuse, enduring solidarity' [citation]. If, in the absence of effective state control, trust can be found anywhere, it is primarily in the bonds between agnatic kinsmen (that is, paternal "blood" relatives)." (Blok, 2002, p. 110–111.) While biological kinship forms the core of Mafia families, alliances between intermarried families are also important, with sets of brothers-in-law often forming the core of groups of Mafia families. The bond is cemented with rituals that establish metaphorical brotherhood. The resulting relationships are more trusting than contracts. Kinship, both real and socially defined, is an economic and political asset because it facilitates both the taxing of local businesses and trading in drugs. These practices are risky because of competition from other Mafia clans and because they are illicit and thus vulnerable to police informers.

37.2.4. Ethnically homogeneous middleman groups

One clear example of kinship acting to reduce the risk of transactions is ethnically homogeneous middleman groups. Landa (1981) wrote one of the earliest analyses of this world-wide phenomenon, describing how ethnic-Chinese business people in Malaysia preferentially extend credit to family and ethnic members, rather than to ethnic Malays. Such is the trust that exists between family and ethnic members that credit is extended on the basis of a handshake. Landa (2002) has reformulated the theoretical basis for her analysis. The new theory is grounded in the New Institutional Economics (NIE; see Landa, 1994) and incorporates the cognitive anthropology of Mary Douglas. The NIE has largely ignored the cognitive and classificatory foundations of social institutions. Yet Landa argues convincingly that classification is such a central aspect of human social cognition that our species might be renamed 'Homo classificus'. Humans are compulsive classifiers, sorting other individuals into demographic and behavioural categories. Prominent among these social categories are kinship and ethnicity, the latter corresponding to the linguistic–tribal identities in the evolutionary milieu. When a person categorizes someone as close kin or fellow-ethnic, that person becomes a candidate recipient of greater altruism and trust, as Landa illustrates with her remarkable ethnographic data on Chinese middleman groups in Malaysia. These successful business men and women categorize their social worlds into seven nested circles of kinship and ethnicity, beginning with the nuclear family. Trust and loyalty then go to more distant kinsmen from the extended family and lineage, then to clansmen, fellow villagers, dialect group from the same province in China, Chinese speaking a different dialect; and finally to non-Chinese. A broader phenomenon in need of Landa's theory is that of the ethnic economic networks which dominate many developing economies (Chua, 2003) and play important roles in even the most developed economies, such as the United States (Light and Karageorgis, 1994).

37.2.5. Strategies for mitigating risk among diaspora Jewish groups

Jews, perhaps more than any other religious or ethnic group, have had to face persecution for maintaining their traditions, including distinctive communal associations and economic roles. Merely belonging to a Jewish community has often constituted a risky transaction, as has Jews' frequent middleman status. The Jewish diaspora has survived intermittent persecution for two millennia, more than sufficient time to develop cultural patterns adapted to mitigation-associated risks. MacDonald (2002) describes Jewish organizational and cultural responses to anti-Semitism. The resulting analysis is a testament to our species' ability as 'flexible strategizers' (Alexander, 1979). Jewish communities have adopted strategies ranging from defensive assimilation to assertive legal and cultural manoeuvres as means for disarming their critics and persecutors in attempting to render their communal transactions less risky.

37.2.6. Supreme Court justices' risky interactions with counsel: dialect and sex effects

Schubert et al. (2002) find ethnic bias in the speech behaviour of Supreme Court justices during oral argument. The bias is not in the Court's judgments but in the justices' paralinguistic behaviour during the important oral argument phase of proceedings, although the authors do not rule out indirect effects on rulings. When Supreme Court judges hear weighty cases, namely those that require interpretation of the Constitution, a risk is posed to the reputation of the Court as well as to the reputation of individual judges. The hypothesis was that during these higher-risk proceedings judges would show greater anxiety in their questioning of lawyers who exhibited differently accented English, and be more relaxed in questioning lawyers who shared their own accent. Anxiety was operationalized as reduced questioning of lawyers during oral argument. The logic is that judges must concentrate more on lawyer's words when they are spoken in a novel accent.

Greater concentration means greater cognitive effort, itself anxiety-producing in the adversarial context of court hearings. All this places a premium on detecting any attempts at deception in evaluating communications. But cues to veracity are more opaque when presented by speakers using an unfamiliar accent or dialect, creating a degree of uncertainty and hence anxiety. For the purposes of their study the authors compared judges' behaviour towards lawyers with standard American idiom and those with a Southern idiom. Eighteen cases of the Southern accent were observed out of 160 randomly sampled cases. They also compared judges' behaviour towards women and men, to control for the possibility that other than linguistic differences were causing the changes in speech behaviour. The results confirmed the hypothesis. Justices spoke less in questioning lawyers who had a Southern accent, but their volubility actually increased when questioning female lawyers, indicating less anxiety with female than with male lawyers.

37.2.7. Ethnicity and tourists' risky transactions

Van den Berghe (2002) studied the role of ethnicity in the real and imagined risks of tourism. Tourism in strange cultural settings is a microcosm of the global village, in which jumbo jets bring people together across contents in unprecedented numbers. The quest for foreign looks, tastes and smells is countered by the feelings of security that come from the company of co-ethnics and familiar environments. Most tourists prefer to sample foreign experiences rather than undergo prolonged immersion. Sallying forth for several hours at a time from the ethnic redoubt of a five-star hotel or vetted hostel is more the rule than is 'going native'. And expeditions are usually conducted with kith and kin from the home country.

37.2.8. Disconfirmation: homosexual partner choices in the face of AIDS

Schubert and Curran (2002) tested the hypothesis that people show preference for physiognomic similarity in choosing a partner with whom to conduct risky relationships, specifically that there was reduced cross-ethnic homosexual partnering in the face of the AIDS epidemic. Schubert and Curran focused on the

incidence of HIV infection between the time that information about 'gay-related immunodeficiency disease' was publicized and the time that the HIV virus and its modes of transmission and prevention were discovered. They examined time-series data on AIDS incidence rates in the USA for Whites, Blacks and Hispanics, broken down by geographic region. It is well established that the AIDS epidemic initially took off within the White population. On this basis, Schubert and Curran operationalize the hypothesis as a slow down in the spread of HIV to minority populations. But no such effect was found. The disconfirmation provided by Schubert and Curran stands as an exception to the pattern of ethnic trust that began with the observation of ethnic mafias. Schubert and Curran also report an intriguing and tragic difference between White and minority incidents of AIDS. White homosexuals appear to have reduced multiple partnering behaviour prior to knowledge about HIV transmission, while Black and Hispanic homosexuals evidently did not for approximately a 2 year period. Instead of a lag in the spread of the disease, this resulted in a 2 year rapid spread of the disease in these minority groups, probably due to less access to information about risk. This delayed risk-avoiding behaviour might have obviated the perceived need for ethnic trust.

Taken together, these case studies point to a hierarchy of tie strengths, stronger and more focused between close kin, weaker and more diffuse between co-ethnics, and weakest or non-existent between different ethnic groups. In situations where transactions are not protected by contract law, interpersonal trust reduces transaction costs, and kin and fellow ethnics are favoured as partners. However, kin and ethnic bonds vary in strength, and cultural and ritual enhancements are typically used to increase those bonds and the resulting trust.

37.3. Ethnic nepotism and public altruism

The second set of studies concerns the interaction of ethnicity and public altruism. According to ethnic-nepotism theory, altruism should be stronger within ethnic groups than between them. The hypothesis, extrapolated from ethnic-nepotism theory, that more public altruism will be shown towards strangers who appear to be of similar ethnicity than towards strangers who have a different ethnic appearance, was confirmed by an observational study of street begging in Moscow, two separate studies of the world's welfare states, a study of regional differences in collections by a large US charity, and a study of Canadian welfare arrangements concerning the province of Quebec. Another study found that foreign-aid-giving by relatively homogeneous countries is substantially more generous than that by more heterogeneous societies. However, a study of the provision of US local council infrastructure disconfirmed the hypothesis in a comparison of White and Hispanic neighbourhoods, while confirming it in the case of Black neighbourhoods.

37.3.1. Moscow beggars

A field study of street beggars in Moscow conducted by Butovskaya *et al.* (2004) found that passers-by, mostly ethnic Russians, give more to beggars from their own ethnic group. The effect is strong enough that Gypsies, a recognizable outgroup, resort to more extreme and less dignified methods of begging than are typically employed by ethnic Russians. Nevertheless, they receive less charity.

37.3.2. Two studies of welfare and ethnic diversity

There are two cross-national studies of welfare and heterogeneity. Sanderson's (2004) cross-national study of redistributive welfare and ethnic heterogeneity covers 42 countries distributed across all continents. He finds that ethnic

diversity is a major correlate of low redistributive welfare. Only organized labour, democracy, and national wealth explain more or comparable between-country variance. Vanhanen's (2004) multi-national study looks at all welfare taken together, including redistributive and non-redistributive. He finds a low but statistically significant negative effect of diversity on welfare payment. By combining their measures of diversity and welfare expenditure to produce four analyses, Sanderson and Vanhanen (2004) were able to explain how differences arose between their independent earlier studies. In three analyses, ethnic diversity was a good (negative) predictor of welfare spending, and in one it was a weak predictor. The correlations are set out in Table 37.1.

37.3.3. US charity and ethnic diversity

Schubert and Tweed (2004) found a low correlation between ethnic diversity and donations to the large US charity, the United Way. Community size was a much larger factor, smaller towns donating more. Interestingly, donations did not decline in linear manner as diversity increased. There was a threshold of about 10% minority representation below which diversity had no effect. Above that level donations slowly declined. Interpreting their results, they suggested that the fall-off in charity would have been much larger if rising minority donations had not compensated for falling majority donations. In this interpretation, ethnic nepotism suppressed White charity as diversity increased, because it is generally known that charity goes disproportionately to poor minority ethnic groups. But ethnic nepotism boosted minority-giving for the same

Table 37.1 Sanderson and Vanhanen's (2004) reconciled correlations between ethnic diversity and welfare expenditure in the world's welfare states

Welfare measures	Correlation	Significance	Variance explained
WD-93[1]	−0.535	0.002	0.286
HD-95[2]	−0.492	0.011	0.242
SS-TGE[3]	−0.564	0.000	0.318
PE-GDP[4]	−0.286	0.283	0.082

[1]WD-93   Central government expenditure an social security and welfare, 1993.
[2]HD-95   Percentage of central government expenditure on social security & welfare, 1980, 1992–5.
[3]SS-TGE   Social Security spending as percentage of total government expenditure, 1996.
[4]PE-GDP   Public expenditure on social security as percentage of GDP 1980–85. 1989–1994.

reason, since minorities realize that their charity goes differentially to their own communities. Schubert and Tweed concluded that their study concurred with the study by Alesina *et al.* (1999) that more racially diverse cities spend a smaller proportion of their budgets and less per capita on public goods than do more homogeneous cities.

37.3.4. Canadian welfare for Quebec

A study by James (2004) documents higher welfare payments sent to the province of Quebec than to other Canadian provinces. This appears to disconfirm ethnic nepotism, since Quebec has a large French-speaking minority while most of Canada is English-speaking. However, James points out that a minority's geographical concentration creates a special condition because such minorities are better able to seek and secure independence. Schiff (1998) makes the same point regarding the Ivory Coast, which pays special benefits to an independence-minded province. Both James and Schiff argue that the special payments to secessionist minorities amount to an attempt by the majority group, or its elites, to buy territorial unity. Minority leaders can be aware of the terms of this arrangement and exploit it to maximize revenues for their people. As Parizeau, the Quebec leader in 1998, declared: "As long as we're in Canada, we'll go get our booty … And sovereigntist premiers have better success than federalist premiers in grabbing money from Ottawa." (*Ottawa Citizen*, November 26, 1998, p. A1.)

37.3.5. Council infrastructure for US neighbourhoods

Masters' (2004) paper is important because it offers the only empirical disconfirmation of the ethnic-nepotism hypothesis with regard to public goods of which I am aware. Masters compared the provision of some public goods at the county level in the USA with the proportion of the local population comprised of Blacks and Hispanics. He found that the number of public sewers per capita is not negatively correlated with the proportion of Hispanics, and takes this as disconfirmation of the ethnic-nepotism hypothesis. However, he did find a negative correlation with the proportion of Blacks, supposedly in agreement with the hypothesis. More importantly, however, the

proportion of both Blacks and Hispanics in counties did correlate with lower per caput welfare payments, which offers some confirmation to the hypothesis.

There is a good reason to treat the welfare correlations as more telling for the hypothesis than the number of sewers per caput. Sanderson (2004) found that redistributive welfare, such as cash payments to single mothers, is more sensitive to ethnic diversity than are genuine public goods such as sewers and water supply, which are difficult to subdivide and which prevent disease, thus benefiting all taxpayers. Provision of police, which Masters also analysed, is especially problematic in this respect, because police are simultaneously a public good for one part of society—those with property, for example—and a means of social control against other segments—such as the poor, especially those who supplement income with illegal activity. Hama's (1998) comparison of 77 US cities found that expenditure on police increases with an increasing proportion of Black population, contradicting Masters' finding. This is unlikely to be an expression of growing public altruism. Rather, it is probably a response to relatively high Black crime rates. Police expenditures can be seen as pure public goods within multiethnic societies where all groups have approximately the same levels of wealth and criminality and police do not discriminate. Otherwise, care should be taken to distinguish this motive from that of social control by one group over another. The hypothesis would be disconfirmed if ethnic diversity was found not to depress contributions to a public good that redistributed net resources between ethnic groups. Such a disconfirmation is yet to be presented.

37.3.6. Foreign aid

Masters and McMillan (2004) offered a fascinating cross-national analysis of foreign aid payments for the period 1962–1992, finding that ethnic diversity has a depressing effect. One measure of ethnic diversity alone accounts for 80% of the between-country variance in foreign aid during that period, controlling for income and government size. Ethnic diversity may impede cooperation for all national goals requiring broad consensus.

These findings are confirmed by recent research in economics, political science and sociology.

Already mentioned is the study by Alesina *et al.* (1999) on the depressing effect of ethnic diversity on US city spending on public goods. In addition, Gilens (1999) has found that in the US, cross-racial transfers are a major point of resistance to taxation to support means-tested welfare payments. Gilen's survey-based analysis confirms the thesis advanced by political theorists that racial divisions in the USA have distorted and subverted attempts to construct a European-style welfare state (Skocpol, 1988; Quadagno, 1994). Extensive welfare rights emerged from political struggles and decisions made within ethnically homogeneous states such as France, Germany and Sweden. Given the shifting ethnic and racial balance in Western societies, a relevant question now is whether the decline of homogeneity will spell the curtailment of those rights. Emerging research findings indicate this to be a likely outcome. A comparison by Faist (1995) of US and German welfare politics found that nationalist–populist reaction to large-scale immigration was leading to the polarization of views towards welfare along ethnic and racial lines, and had contributed to the decline of welfare expenditure in both countries. Ethnic and racial diversity present opportunities for nationalist–populist politicians who advocate reserving welfare rights for the native population. The same diversity appears to be an obstacle for cosmopolitan–liberal politicians who seek a more inclusive welfare system, Faist argues. This analysis was foreshadowed by Freeman (1986), who interpreted the process as the 'Americanization of European welfare' due to large-scale immigration. Further evidence in this direction comes from economic research. Poterba (1997) found that public spending on education is particularly low in districts where the elderly residents are from a different racial group to the school age population. Similarly, Alesina *et al.* (1999) found that the more ethnically or racially diverse cities spent a smaller proportion of their budgets, as well as less per caput, on public goods than did the more homogeneous cities. These results parallel the findings of Brown (1995) and Hero and Tolbert (1996) that states' per caput expenditure on Medicaid generally declines as racial diversity increases. Hero and Tolbert also analysed voting patterns by race and ethnicity in the 1994 referendum in which Californians voted on Proposition 187 (that social services to illegal immigrants be restricted). They found that minority diversity accounted for about 40% of the between-county variation in support for the proposition, such that support increased in tandem with the degree of racial diversity.

The negative relation between racial diversity and public contributions to public goods with a redistributive component might be a more tenacious version of the problem faced by emerging polities, that of inducing families and clans to extend their loyalty to the civic sphere. Indeed, Easterly and Levine (1997) found that, in Africa, ethnic diversity is a major predictor of low public investment in such public goods as schooling and infrastructure.

These results and others (Salter, 2004a,b,c) contribute to knowledge of how ethnicity affects modern mass society in the political and economic realms. It is important to know that persistent ethnic diversity generates costs as well as the benefit of increasing cultural variety. Those costs are considerable. They include a tendency to lower redistributive welfare and charity, increased collective violence, lower economic growth in economies most in need of it, and lower foreign aid. Ethnic diversity also tends to reduce the efficiency of government and the fairness of policing, damages social capital in the form of public trust and commitment to the community, and raises levels of inequality and corruption.

37.4. Conclusion

While broadly confirmatory, the studies reviewed above also show that ethnic-nepotism theory alone is an incomplete explanation of fluctuations in ethnic investment or mobilization. A complete theory will need to incorporate psychological, cultural, economic, and political factors. The incorporation of evolutionary theory should thus be seen as an augmentation of previous approaches to ethnicity, rather than a break with them.

References

Alesina, A., Baqir, R. and Easterly, W. (1999) Public goods and ethnic divisions. *Quarterly Journal of Economics*, 114: 1243–1284.

Alexander, R. D. (1979) *Darwinism and Human Affairs*. University of Washington Press, Seattle.

Blok, A. (2002) Mafia and blood symbolism. In F. K. Salter (ed.) *Risky Transactions. Kinship, Ethnicity, and Trust*, pp. 109–128. Berghahn, Oxford and New York.

Brown, R. D. (1995) Party cleavages and welfare effort in the American states. *American Political Science Review*, 89: 23–33.

Burnstein, E., Branigan, C. and Wieczorkowska-Nejtardt, G. (2002) Altruism begins at home: evidence for a kin selection heuristic sensitive to the costs and benefits of helping. In F. K. Salter (ed.) *Risky Transactions. Kinship, Ethnicity, and Trust*, pp. 71–106. Berghahn, Oxford and New York.

Butovskaya, M., Salter, F. *et al.* (2004) Urban begging and ethnic nepotism in Russia: An ethological pilot study. In F. K. Salter (ed.) *Welfare, Ethnicity, and Altruism. New Data and Evolutionary Theory*, pp. 27–52. Cass, London.

Case, A., Lin, I.-F. *et al.* (2001) Educational attainment of siblings in stepfamilies. *Evolution and Human Behavior*, 22: 269–89.

Caton, H. P. (1988) *Introduction. The Politics of Progress: The Origins and Development of the Commercial Republic, 1600–1835*. University of Florida Press, Gainesville.

Chua, A. (2003) *World on Fire: How Exporting Free Market Democracy Breeds Ethnic Hatred and Global Instability*. Doubleday, New York.

Connor, W. (1993) Beyond reason: the nature of the ethnonational bond. *Ethnic and Racial Studies* 16: 373–389.

Connor, W. (1994) *Ethnonationalism. The Quest for Understanding*. Princeton University Press, Princeton, NJ

Daly, M. and Wilson, M. (eds) (1999) *Stepparental Investment*. Special issue of *Evolution and Human Behavior*, 20(6).

Dunbar, R. I. M., Clark, A. Hurst, N. L. (1995) Conflict and cooperation among the Vikings: contingent behavioral decisions. *Ethology and Sociobiology*, 16: 233–246.

Easterly, W. and Levine R. (1997) Africa's growth tragedy: policies and ethnic divisions. *Quarterly Journal of Economics* 112: 1203–1250.

Eibl-Eibesfeldt, I. (1972) *Love and Hate: The Natural History of Behavior Patterns*. Holt, Rinehart & Winston, New York. [Original German edition, 1970; R. Piper, Munich.]

Eibl-Eibesfeldt, I. (1982) Warfare, man's indoctrinability and group selection. *Ethology (Zeitschrift für Tierpsychologie)*, 60: 177–198.

Eibl-Eibesfeldt, I. (1998) Us and the others: the familial roots of ethnonationalism. In I. Eibl-Eibesfeldt and F. K. Salter (eds), *Indoctrinability, Ideology, and Warfare: Evolutionary Perspectives*, pp. 21–53. Berghahn, Oxford and New York.

Faist, T. (1995) Ethnicization and racialization of welfare-state politics in Germany and the USA. *Ethnic and Racial Studies*, 18: 219–250.

Freeman, G. P. (1986) Migration and the political economy of the welfare state, *The Annals of the American Academy (AAPSS)*, 485: 51–63.

Geiger, G. (1988) On the evolutionary origins and function of political power. *Journal of Social and Biological Structures* 11: 235–250.

Gilens, M. (1999) *Why Americans Hate Welfare: Race, Media, and the Politics of Antipoverty Policy*. University of Chicago Press, Chicago.

Goetze, D. (1998) Evolution, mobility, and ethnic group formation. *Politics and the Life Sciences*, 17: 59–71.

Hama, A. (1998) Demographic change and social breakdown in U.S. cities. *Mankind Quarterly*, 38: 299–309.

Hamilton, W. D. (1964) The genetic evolution of social behavior, parts 1 and 2. *Journal of Theoretical Biology*, 7: 1–51.

Hamilton, W. D. (1971) Selection of selfish and altruistic behavior in some extreme models. In J. F. Eisenberg and W. S. Dillon (eds) *Man and Beast: Comparative Social Behavior*, pp. 59–91. Smithsonian Institute Press, Washington, DC.

Harpending, H. (1979) The population genetics of interactions. *American Naturalist*, 113: 622–630.

Harpending, H. (2002) Kinship and population subdivision. *Population and Environment*, 24: 141–147.

Hero, R. E. and Tolbert C. J. (1996) A racial/ethnic diversity interpretation of politics and policy in the states of the U.S. *American Journal of Political Science*, 40: 851–871.

Holper, J. J. (1996) Kin term usage in *The Federalist*: evolutionary foundations of Publius's rhetoric. *Politics and the Life Sciences*, 15: 265–272.

Horowitz, D. L. (1985) *Ethnic Groups in Conflict*. Berkeley, University of California Press.

James, P. (2004) Canadian welfare policy and ethnopolitics: towards an evolutionary model. In F. K. Salter (ed.) *Welfare, Ethnicity, and Altruism. New Data and Evolutionary Theory*, pp. 232–247. Cass, London.

Johnson, G. R. (1987) In the name of the fatherland: an analysis of kin terms usage in patriotic speech and literature. *International Political Science Review*, 8: 165–174.

Keith, A. (1968, first published 1947) *A New Theory of Human Evolution*. Philosophical Library, New York.

Landa, J. T. (1981) A theory of the ethnically homogeneous middleman group: an institutional alternative to contract law. *Journal of Legal Studies*, 10: 349–362.

Landa, J. T. (1994) *Trust, Ethnicity, and Identity. Beyond Trading Networks, Contract Law, and Gift-exchange*. Ann Arbor, Michigan University Press.

Landa, J. T. (2002) Cognitive foundations of trust and informal institutions: a new and expanded theory of ethnic trading networks. In F. K. Salter (ed.) *Risky Transactions. Kinship, Ethnicity, and Trust*, pp. 129–142. Berghahn, Oxford and New York.

Light, I. and S. Karageorgis (1994) The ethnic economy. In N. J. Smelser and R. Swedberg (ed.) *The Handbook of Economic Sociology*, pp. 647–671. Princeton University Press, Princeton.

MacDonald, K. (2002) Strategies for mitigating risk among Jewish groups. In F. K. Salter (ed.) *Risky Transactions. Kinship, Ethnicity, and Trust*, pp. 151–71. Berghahn, Oxford and New York.

Masters, R. D. (2004) Why welfare states rise–and fall: ethnicity, belief systems, and environmental influences on the support for public goods. In F. K. Salter (ed.) *Welfare, Ethnicity, and Altruism. New Data and Evolutionary Theory*, pp. 248–280. Frank Cass, London.

Masters, W. and McMillan M. (2004) Ethnolinguistic diversity, government, and growth. In F. K. Salter (ed.) *Welfare, Ethnicity, and Altruism. New Data and Evolutionary Theory*, pp. 123–147. Cass, London.

Maynard Smith, J. (1976) Group selection. *Quarterly Review of Biology*, 51: 277–83.

Quadagno, J. (1994) *The Color of Welfare: How Racism Undermined the War on Poverty*. Oxford University Press, New York.

Poterba, J. M. (1997) Demographic structure and the political economy of public education. *Journal of Public Policy and Management* 16: 48–66.

Reynolds, V. (1980) Sociobiology and the idea of primordial discrimination. *Ethnic and Racial Studies*, 3: 303–315.

Richerson, P. J. and R. Boyd (2001) The evolution of subjective commitment to groups: A tribal instincts hypothesis. In R. M. Nesse (ed.) *The Evolution and the Capacity for Subjective Commitment*, pp. 186–220. Russell Sage Foundation, New York.

Rushton, J. P. (1989a) Genetic similarity in male friends. *Ethology and Sociobiology* 10: 361–373.

Rushton, J. P. (1989b) Genetic similarity, human altruism, and group selection. *Behavioral and Brain Sciences*, 12: 503–559.

Salter, F. K. (1995) *Emotions in Command. A Naturalistic Study of Institutional Dominance*. Oxford University Press, Oxford.

Salter, F. K. (2002a) Estimating ethnic genetic interests: is it adaptive to resist replacement migration? *Population and Environment*, 24: 111–140.

Salter, F. K., Ed. (2002b) *Risky Transactions. Kinship, Ethnicity, and Trust*. Berghahn, Oxford and New York.

Salter, F. K. (ed.) (2004a) *Welfare, Ethnicity, and Altruism: New Data and Evolutionary Theory*. Cass, London.

Salter, F. K. (2004b) Introduction: the symposium target paper in broader context. In F. K. Salter (ed.) *Welfare, Ethnicity, and Altruism. New Data and Evolutionary Theory*, pp. 3–24. Cass, London.

Salter, F. K. (2004c) Ethnic diversity, foreign aid, economic growth, social stability, and population policy: a perspective on W. Masters and M. McMillan's findings. In F. K. Salter (ed.) *Welfare, Ethnicity, and Altruism. New Data and Evolutionary Theory*, pp. 148–171. Cass, London.

Sanderson, S. (2004) Ethnic heterogeneity and public spending: testing the evolutionary theory of ethnicity with cross-national data. In F. K. Salter (ed.) *Welfare, Ethnicity, and Altruism. New Data and Evolutionary Theory*, pp. 74–87. Cass, London.

Sanderson, S. and Vanhanen, T. (2004) Reconciling the differences between Sanderson's and Vanhanen's results. In F. K. Salter (ed.) *Welfare, Ethnicity, and Altruism. New Data and Evolutionary Theory*, pp. 119–120. Cass, London.

Schiff, M. (1998) Ethnic divisions and economic reform in Sub-Sahara Africa. *Journal of African Economies*, 7: 348–362.

Schubert, J. and Curran, M. (2002) Ethnicity, transactional risk of HIV, and male homosexual partnering behaviour. In F. K. Salter (ed.) *Risky Transactions. Kinship, Ethnicity, and Trust*, pp. 175–187. Berghahn, Oxford and New York.

Schubert, J., Peterson, S. *et al.* (2002) Dialect, sex and risk effects on judges' questioning of counsel in Supreme Court oral argument. In F. K. Salter (ed.) *Risky Transactions. Kinship, Ethnicity, and Trust*, pp. 189–203. Berghahn, Oxford and New York.

Schubert, J. and Tweed, M. (2004) Ethnic diversity, population size, and charitable giving at the local level in the United States. In: F. Salter (ed) *Welfare, ethnicity and altruism: New data and evolutionary theory*, pp 53–73. Cass, London.

Shaw, R. P. and Wong, Y. (1989) *Genetic Seeds of Warfare: Evolution, Nationalism, and Patriotism*. Unwin Hyman, London.

Silk, J. (1980) Adoption and kinship in Oceania. *American Journal of Sociology*, 80: 799–820.

Skocpol, T. (1988) The Limits of the New Deal System and the Roots of Contemporary Welfare Dilemmas. In M. Weir, A. S. Orloff and T. Skocpol (eds) *The Politics of Social Policy in the United States*, pp. 293–311. Princeton University Press, Princeton.

van den Berghe, P. L. (1978) Race and ethnicity: a sociobiological perspective. *Ethnic and Racial Studies*, 1: 401–411.

van den Berghe, P. L. (1981) *The Ethnic Phenomenon*. Elsevier, New York.

van den Berghe, P. (2002) Risk and deceit in transient, non-repeated interactions. The case of tourism. In F. K. Salter (ed.) *Risky Transactions. Kinship, Ethnicity, and Trust*, pp. 205–215. Berghahn, Oxford and New York.

Vanhanen, T. (1991) *Politics of Ethnic Nepotism: India as an Example*. Sterling, New Delhi.

Vanhanen, T. (2004) An exploratory comparative study of the relationship between ethnic heterogeneity and welfare politics. In F. K. Salter (ed.) *Welfare, Ethnicity, and Altruism. New Data and Evolutionary Theory*, pp. 88–118. Cass, London.

Wang, X. T. (2002) Kith-and-kin rationality in risky choices: theoretical modeling and cross-cultural empirical testing. In F. K. Salter (ed.) *Risky Transactions. Kinship, Ethnicity, and Trust*, pp. 47–70. Berghahn, Oxford and New York.

Wiessner, P. (2002) Taking the risk out of risky transactions: a forager's dilemma. In F. K. Salter (ed.) *Risky Transactions. Kinship, Ethnicity, and Trust*, pp. 21–43. Berghahn, Oxford and New York.

Cultural evolution

If there is anything that sets humans apart from other animals, it has to be culture. Although we can point to behaviour that meets the definition of culture in many other species (see Plotkin, Section I; van Schaik, Section II), none the less the reality is that no animal comes close to producing the kinds of 'higher culture'—literature, art, music, religion, philosophy or even science—that we find in modern humans. Studies of animal culture allow us to point to the origins of this unique human capacity, its phylogenetic history, but we are still left with the puzzle of explaining why it should have developed to such a remarkable extent in just one lineage of primates.

There are several separate issues here. First, it is perhaps obvious that most cultural activities are based on social learning (imitation of those with whom one lives or comes into contact, as well as that learned through instruction). The human capacity for imitation (and, in particular, the human *child's* capacity for imitation) is really quite extraordinary by the standards of more conventional animals. So we have a cognitive capacity to explain. But imitation on that scale can result in the imitator giving up his/her own interests in order to copy someone else's behaviour—in effect, behaving altruistically. Hence, there is a substantive question about why such high levels of behavioural altruism should be so common. Most of the literature on cultural evolution probably implicitly assumes that imitation is good for you (and hence your fitness)

because it allows you to acquire knowledge more quickly about how to behave than could be done by individual trial and error. It need not always be so, of course. Henrich and McElreath explore this issue.

Second, there are questions to be asked about the processes involved and how they work in a Darwinian world dominated by genetic mechanisms of inheritance. It is clear that the dynamics of gene–culture evolution can be very complex, as McElreath and Henrich show. But there have been questions about just what is involved in the processes of cultural learning. Dawkins (1975) famously coined the term *meme* to refer to the cultural equivalent of *gene* in the processes of cultural transmission—a term that has not been without its problems, as Aunger points out. However, while recognizing that the term does have problems, we do need a generic label for whatever it is that is being culturally transmitted. For the moment, *meme* is probably the best we have.

Third, given that culture has a general function, we still need to ask how some of the more peculiar forms of culture maximize fitness. Just what functions do music or literature serve? Are they, as Pinker (1997) famously asserted, mere cheesecake—froth on the evolutionary seascape? The answer simply has to be "no". As a rule of thumb, evolutionary biologists would insist that anything on which individuals lavish so much time, energy and (in our case) money *must* have a function. The mistake has probably been to think in terms of fitness as it reflects an individual's immediate abilities to survive or reproduce. It probably *is* true to say that song and dance has little effect on anyone's ability to survive, though one might argue with Miller (2000) that the abilities to sing or dance do have genuinely beneficial effects on one's opportunities to mate (with obvious and very real consequences for fitness). But there are other reasons why culture might be important, and these hark back to the ideas about multi-level selection that Wilson discusses in his contribution to this volume (see also Dunbar *et al.*, 2005). When a species is as dependent on cooperation in social groups as humans are, forces that bond the individuals in those groups and enhance their cooperativeness become essential. Many aspects of 'high' culture, from story-telling to dance to religion, may be as important in creating that sense of groupishness as more conventional mechanisms like altruistic punishment (discussed by Gintis *et al.*) and cheat detection mechanisms (Cosmides, 1989). And, of course, all of these are dependent on another recent human trait—language (which Kirby addresses).

Fourth, we can ask when culture in this advanced form first evolved. Archaeologists have, of course, concerned themselves a great deal with just this question, though they have largely confined themselves to what is termed 'material culture', the physical forms that human cultural activity can take (stone or bone, occasionally wooden tools and other functional objects, artwork like Venus statues, and cave paintings). While there are important issues of timing that obviously bear on whether culture is uniquely human or shared with other animals, the archaeological record can, as Shennan points out, tell us a great deal more about the pace and process of cultural evolution than will ever be possible from observing living human populations. A closer integration between archaeologists and evolutionary psychologists (in the broad sense we use here) is long overdue.

We have mentioned music and literature in passing in this discussion, but it is worth highlighting the fact that these are two areas of human culture that are (i) of immense social importance, (ii) virtually unstudied from an evolutionary perspective and (iii) fascinating in their own right in terms of the cognitive capacities on which they depend. Carroll and Cross provide comprehensive reviews of these two topics, but it is clear that there are many layers of explanation that have not yet been tapped. The capacity to deal with imagined worlds is not merely cognitively very demanding (Barrett *et al.*, 2000; Dunbar *et al.*, 2005), but clearly fundamentally important to many aspects of human social life. Much the same can be said of religion, another important force for binding social groups. None the less, despite the centrality of religion as a topic in socio-cultural anthropology, evolutionary anthropologists and evolutionary psychologists have been very slow indeed to give it any attention. Bulbulia takes up this particular challenge in a very comprehensive review of recent work. Culture, and the capacity for culture, is in many ways the single most important problem in human evolutionary psychology.

References

Barrett, L., Dunbar, R. I. M. and Lycett, J. E. (2000) *Human Evolutionary Psychology*. Palgrave/Macmillan, Basingstoke and Princeton University Press, Princeton.

Cosmides, L. (1989) The logic of social exchange: has natural selection shaped how humans reason? Studies with the Wason selection task. *Cognition*, 31: 187–276.

Dawkins, R. (1975) *The Selfish Gene*. Oxford University Press, Oxford.

Dunbar, R. I. M., Barrett, L. and Lycett, J. E. (2005) *Evolutionary Psychology: a beginner's guide*. OneWorld, Oxford.

Miller, G. (2000) *The Mating Mind*. Heinemann, London.

Pinker, S. (1997) *How the Mind Works*. Penguin, Harmondsworth.

CHAPTER 38

Dual-inheritance theory: the evolution of human cultural capacities and cultural evolution

Joseph Henrich and Richard McElreath

38.1. Introduction

In the early 1930's Wintrop and Luella Kellogg (1933) began co-rearing their 10.5-month-old son, Donald, with a 7.5-month-old female chimpanzee named Gua. The Kelloggs expected that Gua, with the chimpanzee's popular reputation for aping, would acquire numerous behaviors and practices via imitation from both Donald and themselves. Unexpectedly, however, while Gua did finally acquire a few human patterns (e.g. combing his hair), Donald was the one who began to imitate the chimpanzee in some dramatic ways. Following Gua, Donald acquired the habits of knuckle walking (which he continued well after achieving full bipedality), chewing on shoes, scraping his teeth against interior walls, and hard biting. Donald even adopted some stereotypical chimpanzee food grunts, barks and hoots, using a particular bark as the word for orange. Thus, it was the human who did most of the aping.

People in many small-scale societies believe that a human fetus is formed by many repeated ejaculations of sperm into the womb. This belief means that a child can have multiple fathers, who share paternity according to the number of times they had sex with the mother prior to birth (in anthropological parlance, 'partible paternity'). In response to this cultural belief, women in many of these societies actively seek out extramarital copulations, often to provide their child with extra fathers. And, while male jealously from the husband is sometimes a problem, it is regarded as socially inappropriate and thus suppressed. Detailed statistical analyses from two such societies, the Barí of Venezuela (Beckerman et al., 2002) and Aché of Paraguay (Hill and Hurtado, 1996), show that the optimal number of fathers for a child's survival is more than one. These 'other fathers' (non-husbands of mom) provide resources, in the form of fish and meat, to their offspring and the mothers, both during pregnancy and while the child is growing up. Interestingly, since much of the sex associated with 'extra fathers' occurs after conception, many of these social fathers cannot be the genetic fathers. Culturally transmitted beliefs in partible paternity have been recorded in various linguistically unrelated societies across lowland

South America, as well as in New Guinea, by multiple researchers over the last 75 years (Beckerman and Valentine, 2002).

These examples illustrate two key points about humans. First, while chimpanzees do show some capacities for imitative learning (Horner and Whiten, 2005; Whiten *et al.*, 2005), their cultural transmission shows substantially lower degrees of fidelity, frequency and internal motivation. Compared to chimpanzees, humans are "imitation machines" (Tomasello, 1999). More generally, while only limited social learning abilities are found elsewhere in nature, social learning in our species is high fidelity, frequent, internally motivated, often unconscious, and broadly applicable. Humans learn, via observation of others, everything from motor patterns to goals and affective responses, in domains ranging from tool-making and food preferences to altruism and suicide. We will refer to this form of social learning, which may be particular to humans, as cultural learning.

The combination of both the high fidelity and frequency of social learning in our lineage has generated *cumulative cultural evolution*, which may exist to any significant degree only in our lineage: this is the process through which learning builds a body of culturally transmitted information (behaviour, practices, beliefs, etc.) in a population in such a way that locally adaptive aspects aggregate over time, with the accumulation of successful additions and modifications. Cumulative cultural evolution builds adaptive practices, tools, technique, and bodies of knowledge (about animal behaviour, medicinal plants, etc.) that *no single individual could figure out* in their lifetime, and that can only be understood as products of cultural evolutionary processes. Paleoarchaeology suggests that substantial cumulative cultural evolution has likely been occurring for at least the last 280 000 years (McBrearty and Brooks, 2000), and is thus a key element in understanding human genetic evolution.

Our second point is illustrated by societies with partible paternity: culturally acquired beliefs can shape how we understand the world in ways that influence decisions, including decisions arising from essential aspects of our evolved cognition. To invest in their offspring, for example, males need to figure out which offspring are theirs. Evidence indicates that we use a variety of cues to identify our kin, including phenotypic similarity and scent (DeBruine, 2002; Thornhill *et al.*, 2003), but humans also apparently use their culturally transmitted beliefs about kinship and reproduction. More generally, there is also evidence that culture influences our spatial cognition, perception of visual illusions (Segall *et al.*, 1966), judgement (Nisbett, 2003), risk preferences (Henrich and McElreath, 2002), and notions of fairness or preferences for equity (Henrich *et al.*, 2004).

Given all this, we think that a proper evolutionary framework for studying human psychology and behaviour needs to reckon with our species' heavy reliance on cultural learning and cultural evolved adaptations. In providing such a framework, *dual-inheritance theory* (Cavalli-Sforza and Feldman, 1981; Boyd and Richerson, 1985; for similar approaches also see Durham, 1991; Laland *et al.*, 2000) aims to incorporate these and other aspects of human culture under the Darwinian umbrella by focusing on three key concepts:

1. *Cultural capacities as adaptations.* Culture, cultural learning and cultural evolution arise from genetically evolved psychological adaptations for acquiring ideas, beliefs, values, practices, mental models, and strategies from other individuals by observation and inference. Thus, the first step is to use the logic of natural selection to theorize about the evolution and operation of our cultural learning capacities.

2. *Cultural evolution.* Our cultural learning mechanisms give rise to a robust second system of inheritance (cultural evolution) that operates by different transmission rules than genetic inheritance, and can thus produce phenomena not observed in other, less cultural, species. Theorizing about this process requires taking what we know about human cultural learning and human cognition, embedding these into evolutionary models that included social interaction, and studying the emergent properties of these models. This approach allows researchers to cobble up from psychology and individual decision-making to sociology and population-level phenomena.

3. *Culture–gene coevolution.* The second system of inheritance created by cultural evolution can alter both the social and physical environments faced by evolving genes, leading to a process termed *culture–gene coevolution*. For example, suppose that the practice of cooking meat spread by social learning in ancestral human populations. In an environment of 'cooked meat', natural selection may favour genes that shorten our energetically costly intestines and alter our digestive chemistry. Such a reduction of digestive tissue may have freed up energy for more 'brain building'. In this way, human biology is adapting to culturally transmitted behaviour.

38.2. Concept 1: evolved psychological mechanisms for cultural learning

Our approach to understanding culture begins by considering what kinds of cognitive learning abilities would have allowed individuals to efficiently and effectively extract adaptive ideas, beliefs, and practices from their social worlds in the changing environments of our hunter-gatherer ancestors. This approach diverges from mainstream evolutionary psychology in its emphasis on the *costly information hypothesis* and on the evolution of specialized *social* learning mechanisms. The costly information hypothesis focuses on the evolutionary trade-offs between acquiring accurate behavioural information at high cost and gleaning less accurate information at low cost. By formally exploring how the costly information hypothesis generates trade-offs in the evolution of our social learning capacities, we can generate predictive theories about the details of human cultural psychology. When acquiring information by individual learning is costly, natural selection will favour cultural learning mechanisms that allow individuals to extract adaptive information—strategies, practices, heuristics and beliefs—from other members of their social group at a lower cost than through alternative individual mechanisms (like trial-and-error learning). Human cognition probably contains numerous heuristics, directed attentional biases, and inferential tendencies that facilitate the acquisition of useful traits from other people.

Such cultural learning mechanisms can be categorized into (i) *content biases* and (ii) *context biases*. Content biases, or what Boyd and Richerson (1985) have called *direct biases*, cause us to more readily acquire certain beliefs, ideas or behaviours *because* some aspect of their content makes them more appealing (or more likely to be inferred from observation). For example, imagine three practices involving different additives to popcorn: the first involves putting salt on popcorn, the second favours adding sugar, and the third involves sprinkling chalk dust on the kernels. Innate content biases that affect cultural transmission will guarantee that chalk dust will likely not be a popular popcorn additive in any human society. Both salt and sugar have positive innate content biases for sensible evolutionary reasons: foods with salty or sugary flavours were important sources of scarce nutrients and calories in ancestral human environments. Thus, natural selection favoured a bias to acquire a taste for salty and sweet foods so that we would be motivated to acquire and eat them. Of course, if you grew up in a society that only salts its popcorn, you may steadfastly adhere to your salting preference even when you find that sugar is the standard popcorn seasoning in other societies. Thus, human food preferences are simultaneously culturally learned and influenced by innate content biases.

Content biases may be either reliably developing products of our species-shared genetic heritage (i.e. innate) or they may be culture specific. In considering the influences of innate biases (such as those for salty or fatty foods), keep in mind that evolutionary products like human minds are likely to contain accidental by-products and latent structures that create biases for fitness-neutral behaviours, ideas, beliefs and values. Boyer (2001) details one kind of by-product content bias in his explanation for the universality of certain religious concepts (like ghosts).

On the cultural side, people may acquire beliefs, values and/or mental models that then act as content biases for other aspects of culture. That is, having acquired a particular idea via cultural transmission, a learner may be more likely to acquire another idea, because the two 'fit together' in some cognitive or psychological sense. For example, believing that a certain ritual in the spring will increase the crop harvest in the summer might favour the acquisition of a belief that a similar ritual will increase a woman's odds of conception, a healthy pregnancy, and/or of successfully delivering a robust infant.

Context biases, on the other hand, exploit cues from the 'individuals who are being learned from' (we term these individuals 'models'), rather than features of the 'thing being learned', to guide social learning. There is a great deal of adaptive information embodied in both *who* holds ideas and how *common* the ideas or practices are. For example, because information is costly to acquire, individuals will do better if they preferentially pay attention to, and learn from, people who are highly successful, particularly skilled, and/or well-respected. Social learners who selectively learn from those more likely to have adaptive skills (that lead to success) can outcompete those who do not. A large amount of mathematical modelling effort has been expended in exploring the conditions under which different context biases will evolve, how they should be constructed psychologically, and what population patterns will emerge from individuals using such learning mechanisms. Moreover, a vast amount of field and laboratory data confirms that these learning biases are indeed an important part of our cognition, that they are used by both children and adults, and that they influence economic decisions, opinions, judgements, values, and eating behaviour. Our remaining discussion of psychological mechanisms focuses on the theory and evidence for two categories of context biases in cultural learning: (i) success and prestige biases and (ii) conformity bias.

38.2.1. Selecting good cultural models: success and prestige biases

Once an individual is learning from others, she would be wise—in an adaptive evolutionary sense—to be selective about who she pays attention to for the purposes of learning (Henrich and Gil-White, 2001). The idea is that a learner should use cues from, or characteristics of, the individuals in their social world to figure out who is most likely to have useful ideas, beliefs, values, preferences, or strategies that might be

gleaned, at least partially, through observation. For example, an aspiring farmer might imitate the strategies and practices of the most skilful, successful or prestigious farmers who live around him. Simply figuring out who obtains the biggest yields per hectare and copying them is a lot easier than doing all the trial-and-error learning for the immense variety of decisions a farmer (or anyone else) has to make. A purely individual learner would have to experiment with many types of crops, seeds, fertilizers, planting schedules, and various plowing techniques. The variety of combinations creates a combinatorial explosion of possibilities, making it virtually impossible for an individual to figure out the best farming strategy by relying entirely on experimentation. This is true of many, if not most, real-world decisions. However, along with figuring out who is the most successful or most skilled, learners should also be concerned about how the things they might learn will fit with their own abilities, the expectations of their role or gender, and their personal context. Learners should assess *certain kinds* of 'similarity'—between themselves and potential models—and weigh this alongside their assessments of 'skill' and 'success'. Following this logic, we argue below that learners might preferentially learn social norms from individuals who share their ethnic markers (e.g. their dialect, language, or dress, see McElreath *et al.*, 2003).

Figuring out who possesses the adaptive skills, strategies, preferences, and beliefs is often not straightforward. To achieve this, people rely on a range of cues related to *skill* (or *competence*), *success*, and *prestige*. For rhetorical purposes, this tripartite distinction is helpful because it captures the continuum of cues from direct observation by the learner (of skill or competence) to completely indirect assessments based on prestige (defined below). Noting someone's skill or competence, for our purposes, means that one has *directly* observed and judged their technique or performance. An apprentice might watch two craftsmen working side by side, one hitting all of his marks and gliding right along to a perfect final product (say a handmade chair) while another struggles, cuts himself twice, curses a bit, and produces something that only the bravest of his friends would venture to sit on. Direct observation indicates who the learner should pay attention to for learning to make chairs.

Cues of success are less direct and take advantage of easily observable correlates of competence (especially those that are difficult to fake), as we have defined it. Depending on the domain and society, such cues might be measured by house size, family size, number of wives and/or children, number of peer-reviewed publications, costliness of their car, number of tapirs killed, number of heads taken in raids, the size of their biggest yam, etc., each of which, in particular social contexts, is related to some domain of skill. While these cues provide only an indirect measure, they are sometimes superior to cues of competence. If performances are noisy, the observations of a small sample may lead a learner to misperceive competence. Cues of success, in contrast, often average over many performances, which can help to reduce the error in the learner's assessment of who to learn from.

The evolutionary theory underpinning this form of model-based cultural learning proposes that once the psychological machinery that makes use of competence- and success-based cues for targeted cultural learning has spread through the population, highly skilled and successful individuals will be in high demand, and social learners will need to compete for access to the most skilled and successful. This creates a new selection pressure for such learners to pay deference to those they assess as most valuable (those judged most likely to possess adaptive information) in exchange for *preferred access* and assistance in learning. Deference benefits may take many forms, including coalitional support, general assistance (helping with laborious projects), public praise, caring for the offspring of the skilled, and gifts (Gurven, 2001).

With the spread of deference for highly skilled individuals, natural selection can take advantage of the observable patterns of deference to further save on information-gathering costs. Naïve entrants (say immigrants or children), lacking detailed information about the relative skill or success of potential cultural models, may take advantage of the existing pattern of deference by using the amounts and kinds of deference different models receive as cues of underlying skill. Assessing differences in deference-received provides a best guess to the skill ranking until more information can be accumulated. Figuring out who to learn from, using the distribution of deference, is merely a way of aggregating the information (opinions) that others have already gleaned about who is a good person to learn from.

As part of these deference patterns, people unconsciously cue who they think is a good model through a series of ethological and behavioural phenomena that arise directly from efforts to imitate these individuals. These patterns relate to attention, eye gaze, verbal tones and rhythms, and behavioural postures. As learners seem keenly attuned to these subtle patterns, it appears that natural selection has favoured attention to these patterns of deference, as a means of assessing whom to pay attention to for cultural learning. As we discuss below, a mechanism like 'copy the majority' (conformist transmission) provides an effective way to aggregate the information gathered by observing and listening to others. In this case, conformist transmission can be used to figure out who to pay attention to for cultural learning.

To understand the difference between cues of *prestige, success* and *skill*, consider the following stylized example of an academic department. A new PhD entering a department and aiming at tenure might assess his senior colleagues in order to figure out who to learn from (with the goal of getting tenure). Initially, he can glean a measure of people's *prestige-deference* by listening to and observing how people act towards each other. If he's really serious, he might pull up everyone's CVs and count their publications (and divide by their 'years since PhD'). This would give a measure of *success*. Finally, if our fresh PhD still has not given up all hope of finding a good model, he might read everyone's papers (or at least those who rank high in 'success' and 'prestige') and watch them teach. This would give our learner a measure of skill or competence. Aggregating all these measures, he'd have a decent estimate of who to learn from.

Interestingly, the indirect nature of assessing another person's utility as a cultural model (i.e. their possession of adaptive information that could be useful to the learner) creates an important phenomenon. In a complex world, such indirect measures do not tell the learner which of the model's behaviours, ideas, practices and strategies causally contribute to his success or competence. For example, are people successful in farming because of what they plant, when they plant, how they plant, or how they make sacrifices to the spirits—or all four? Because of this ambiguity, humans may have evolved the propensity to copy successful individuals across a wide range of cultural traits, only some of which may actually relate to the individuals' success. When information is costly it turns out that this strategy will be favoured by natural selection even though it may allow neutral and even somewhat maladaptive traits to hitch-hike along with adaptive cultural traits.

38.2.1.1. Evidence of selective model-based cultural learning

Evidence for these learning mechanisms is plentiful, and comes from across the social sciences. A broad spectrum of work shows that both kids and adults will preferentially learn all kinds of things from other individuals demonstrating particular cues of competence, success and/or prestige—and there need not be any particular relationship between domains of prestige or competence and the things being learned. Unfortunately, the details don't go much beyond that. For example, we would like to know how different kinds of information are integrated. How important is observed competence compared to prestige? How important is individual information when it contradicts the behaviour of highly successful people? Having looked at a wide range of social learning evidence, it is clear that the tendency to imitate prestigious and successful people is one of the most powerful aspects of cultural learning.

In providing a taste of the evidence for success and prestige-biased cultural learning, we emphasize six main points. (i) These imitative patterns spontaneously appear in incentivized (where individual's choices influence monetary payoffs or other kinds of returns) and non-incentivized circumstances, in both non-social and social situations, including situations that involve direct competition among the learners. 'Social situations' are those in which a person's pay-offs and those of others are *jointly* influenced by their choices. (ii) The effects repeatedly emerge across a broad range of contexts, including economic decisions, opinions, food preferences and

consumption, beliefs, and dialects. (iii) Consistent with theory, the amount of cultural learning observed depends critically on the degree of uncertainty found in the environment. As uncertainty increases, so does cultural learning. (iv) These learning patterns emerge even when the model's domain of competence, success or prestige is apparently unrelated to the behavioural domain in question. (v) Diverse findings from laboratory experiments in both economics and psychology, using very different experimental paradigms, consistently converge—giving us confidence in the findings' robusticity across experimental contexts. (vi) The patterns of cultural learning observed in the laboratories fit closely with field data—giving us confidence that the effects observed in the artificial context of experiments actually matter in the real world. Below, we summarize some of the laboratory findings to illustrate points (i)–(v), and then describe a few key field studies that illustrate point (vi).

Experimental evidence from Pingle (1995) confirms that people (well, university students) imitate the strategies of successful individuals when pay-offs are on the line. Using a series of computerized decision situations, participants had to repeatedly select the amount of three different inputs (e.g. 'fertilizer', 'seed' and 'labour') into a production problem for either 21 or 31 rounds, depending on the treatment. Before each decision, i.e. before setting the final amounts $(x_1, x_2$ and $x_3)$ of the three inputs for a given round, subjects could pay to find out what profit they would get if they used different sets of inputs (a 'costly experiment'). In the baseline treatment, subjects could only learn from their own analyses and direct experience (i.e. what they earned each round from their chosen inputs). To calculate profit in each round, the subject's inputs were run through a pre-set production function. This function, which was unknown to players, had only one set of optima inputs (x_1^*, x_2^*, x_3^*); these inputs would make the most money. In four other treatments, opportunities for imitation were introduced in varying ways and with different costs. Participants in all treatments faced the same environment (the same production function) for rounds 1 to 11 (Block 1). At round 12, the environment shifted and again remained constant through round 21. For treatments 2–4 and the control, there was also a 'competitive' environment that commenced in round 22 with an environmental shift that lasted through 31 (Block 3). During this Block, the optimal set of inputs shifted dynamically and depended on what other players had done. This means that participants faced a new environment beginning in rounds 1, 12 and 22. Blocks 1 and 2 are non-social decisions, while Block 3 provides one type of social interaction.

The different treatments manipulated the information available for imitation: in treatment 1, during each round (starting in round 2) participants could, at a cost, look at the inputs and output of *one* other subject who had previously played *that* round. In treatment 2, participants could, at a cost, look at a list of inputs and outputs for that round for all the subjects who had gone before them. In treatment 3, before the play for each Block commenced, subjects were given the best outputs and inputs of previous players for that Block. In treatment 4, each subject watched two other subjects complete all 31 rounds before playing themselves. Each treatment used different subjects, who were paid real money according to the profit they earned, which was determined by their choices of inputs.

A comparison of the findings from across the treatments highlights several important points about imitation, all of which have been anticipated by cultural evolutionary models (Boyd and Richerson, 1985, 1988, 1995; Weibull, 1995):

1. In non-social situations, participants use imitation, often to a substantial degree, even when decisions are financially motivated and cost-benefit analysis is possible (but costly). The pattern of results across all four experiments, *vis-à-vis* the non-imitation control, shows the strength of our propensity for imitation: in round 2 of treatments 1 and 2, which can be compared directly to round 2 in the no-imitation control, people imitated 87% and 57% of the time, respectively.

2. Imitation tendencies remain strong even in competitive social environments. About 43% of subjects imitated in round 22 of treatment 2.

3. People tended to imitate (the inputs) of more successful players (those who got higher outputs). The patterns in the data are only explicable if people are looking at the difference in performance and using that as a cue about who and when to imitate.

4. Uncertainty causes a substantial increase in the reliance on imitation. In rounds 2, 12, 22, when a new environment is first encountered, rates of imitation are highest.

5. The availability of imitative opportunities, even costly ones, improves the average performance of the group. As a group, subjects in imitation treatments outperformed those of the control.

6. The 'imitation environment' (treatment) affects the average performance of the group. Average performance in treatments 3 and 4 exceeds that of treatments 1 and 2. Only the informational environment of treatment 3 avoids a substantial degradation in group performance during the Block 3.

Other work by economists confirms these findings. Kroll and Levy (1992) show that individuals readily imitate the investments of successful players, and that adding the possibility of imitation improves the overall performance of the group. Offerman and Sonnemans (1998) show that, not only will people copy economic choices and investment strategies, but they will also preferentially imitate beliefs about the state of the world from successful people. Work studying competitive Cournot markets demonstrates the power of this form as imitation (Alpesteguia *et al.*, 2003).

Recent studies exemplified by the above experiment are important because the decision-making is incentivized and the available information is rigorously controlled. Qualitatively however, these findings from economics merely confirm older empirical insights from psychology. Research elsewhere in psychology has shown that individuals preferentially acquire opinions from prestigious sources, especially in ambiguous, uncertain, or difficult situations, and even when these opinions are not connected to the model's domain of expertise. See Henrich and Gil-White (2001) for a review of this evidence. Not only do these cultural learning mechanisms operate in incentivized decision-making, but they also appear in non-incentivized situations in which behaviour, opinions and preferences shift spontaneously and unconsciously.

The same evolved cultural learning mechanisms emerge outside the laboratory, across a wide range of behavioural domains, including two areas that we mention here: (i) the diffusion of innovation and (ii) the epidemiology of suicide. In his massive review of the literature on the *Diffusion of Innovations*, Rogers (1995, p. 18) summarizes some of the lessons from 50 years of research as follows:

> Instead, most people depend mainly upon a subjective evaluation of an innovation that is conveyed to them from other individuals like themselves who have previously adopted the innovation. This dependence on the experience of near peers suggests that the heart of the diffusion process consists of the modelling and imitation by potential adopters of their network partners who have adopted previously.

Rogers devotes an entire chapter to explaining how the diffusion of new ideas, technologies, and practices is strongly influenced by 'local opinion leaders'. Compiling findings from many diffusion studies, Rogers describes these individuals as: (i) locally high in social status (e.g. high status within the village or village cluster); (ii) well respected (indicating prestige); (iii) widely connected; and (iv) effective social models for others. Rogers' insights are particularly important here because they confirm that success and prestige-biased cultural learning are important for the spread of novel technologies and practices.

The theory derived from the logic of selective model-based cultural learning even illuminates some of the robust patterns observed in studies of suicide. Data from industrialized societies show that committing suicide, including the methods (poisoning, gun, hanging, burning, etc.), are imitated according to prestige and self-similarity (Wasserman *et al.*, 1994; Stack, 1996). For prestige, many studies in the USA, Japan and Germany show that suicide rates spike more after celebrity suicides than non-celebrity suicides (Stack, 1987; Kessler *et al.*, 1988), even once media coverage is controlled for (Stack, 1990, 1996; Jonas, 1992). For similarity, the results show that the individuals who kill themselves after celebrity suicides tend to match their models on age, sex and ethnicity. Finally, the time trends of these suicides do not show regression to the mean during the subsequent month, indicating that these were not individuals who would have committed suicide in the near future.

Because suicide is strongly influenced by imitation, it can spread in epidemic fashion, showing patterns similar to those observed for diseases, novel cultural practices, and innovations. In Micronesia (Rubinstein, 1983), beginning in 1960 and lasting for at least 25 years, a suicide epidemic spread through certain island populations. This case is particularly stark because the suicides are geographically patterned and distinctively stereotyped. The typical victim was a young male between 15 and 24 (modal age of 18) years who still lived at home with his parents. After a disagreement with his parents or girlfriend, the victim was visited in a vision by past suicide victims who 'called him to them' (we know this from parasuicides). Heeding the call, the victim performed a 'lean hanging' from either a standing or sitting position, usually in an abandoned house, until he died of anoxia, or was accidentally discovered. In 75% of the cases there was no prior hint of suicide or depression. These suicides occur sporadically in local outbreaks among socially interconnected male adolescents who ethnically identify as from Truk or the Marshals (matching on sex and ethnicity), and can sometimes be traced to the precipitating suicides of prominent sons from wealthy families (associated with prestige).

Prestige bias also appears in studies of linguistic change (Labov, 1972, 1980), the transmission of managerial styles (Weiss, 1977; Weiss *et al.*, 1999) and in naturalistic studies of jaywalking manipulation (Mullen *et al.*, 1990). It also been repeatedly observed by ethnographers in an immense variety of contexts (Berreman, 1972, p. 141; Dove, 1993; Boyd, 2001; Rao, 2001).

38.2.3. Conformist transmission

As an adaptive learner, what do you do when any observable differences in skill, success, and prestige among individuals do not covary with the observable differences in behaviour, beliefs, practices, or values? For example, suppose everyone in your village uses blowguns for hunting, except one regular guy who uses a bow and arrow, and obtains fairly average hunting returns. Do you adopt the bow or the blowgun? One solution for dealing with such information-poor dilemmas is to copy the behaviours, beliefs and strategies of the majority (Boyd and Richerson, 1985; Henrich and Boyd, 1998). Termed *conformist transmission*, this mechanism allows individuals to aggregate information over the behaviour of many individuals. Because these behaviours implicitly contain the effects of each individual's own experience and learning efforts, conformist transmission can be the best route to adaptation in information-poor environments. To see this, suppose every individual is given a noisy signal (a piece of information) from the environment about what the best practice is in the current circumstances. This information, for any one individual, might give them a 60% chance of noticing that blowguns bring back slightly larger returns than bows. Thus, using individual learning alone, learners will adopt the more efficient hunting practice with probability 0.60. But, if an individual samples the behaviour of 10 other individuals, and simply adopts the majority behaviour, his chances of adopting the superior blowgun technology increase to 75%.

The same logic can be applied to aggregate and improve the imperfect information about the relative success of others, who may be useful as cultural models. Some individuals may obtain accurate information that allows them effectively to select and copy the most successful individuals, while others may receive noisy (inaccurate) information about relative success, which prevents them from effectively distinguishing differences. This second group can still take advantage of the more accurate information received by the first group by adopting the traits adopted by the majority. To see this more clearly, imagine a group of 200 individuals, wherein 100 are experienced hunters and 100 are novices who need to figure out which technology to invest in learning. Of the 100 experienced individuals, suppose that 40 used bows and 60 use blowguns for hunting. In their current environment (which recently changed), however, bows obtain a more efficient return, although the difference is small and hunting returns in general are highly variable. Nevertheless, using the returns of the experienced hunters, 40 of the 100 novices selected a bow hunter to learn from, 50 were left confused, and 10 picked a blowgun hunter to learn from (they got bad information due to the noise in hunting returns). In their confusion, the 50 decide to use conformist transmission, where now 80 hunters use bows (40 + 40) and 70 use blowguns. This will result in *more than*

53.3% of the 'confused' individuals adopting bows. For example, of the confused 50, 40 might adopt bows, while 10 still decide to go with blowguns. After all of the transmission this generation, 120 hunters will use the more adaptive bow, while only 80 use blowguns. If the older ('experienced') generation dies, 80% of the new generation will use bows (compared to only 40% of the now dead cohort).

This kind of verbal reasoning has been rigorously tested in both analytical models (Boyd and Richerson 1985, Chapter 7) and extended to more complex environments using evolutionary simulations (Henrich and Boyd, 1998; Kameda and Nakanishi, 2002). In their computer simulation, Henrich and Boyd investigated the interaction and coevolution of vertical transmission (parent–offspring transmission), individual learning, and conformist transmission in spatially and temporally varying environments. The results confirm that conformist transmission is likely to evolve under a very wide range of conditions. In fact, these results show that the range of conditions that favour conformist transmission are *broader* than those for vertical transmission alone—suggesting that if true imitation (via parent–child transmission) evolves at all, we should also expect to observe a substantial conformist component. Taken together, this work leads to several specific predictions about human psychology. First, this model predicts that learners will prefer conformist transmission over vertical transmission, assuming it is possible to access a range of cultural models at low cost (which is often but not always the case). While a direct test of this prediction is lacking, we note that a substantial amount of research in behavioural genetics indicates that parents actually transmit very little culturally to their offspring—once genetic transmission is accounted for, vertical cultural transmission often accounts for less than 5% of the variation among individuals (Harris, 1995, 1998; Plomin et al., 2000). Those familiar with earlier work on cultural transmission might recall high correlations between parents and offspring, suggesting an important role for vertical cultural transmission (e.g. Cavalli-Sforza et al., 1982). This work neglected the similarity between parents and offspring created by genetic transmission. Once the influence of genetic transmission is accounted for, the effect of vertical cultural transmission in creating parent–offspring correlations largely evaporates. Certainly there may be cases in which parents are the only viable models, and so have a large role, such as in early language acquisition or family recipes. But that does not indicate that people prefer to imitate their parents, nor that parents have a large effect in general. Second, the model predicts that as the accuracy of information acquired through individual learning decreases, a learner's reliance on conformist transmission (over individual learning) will increase. Third, as the proportion of models—in the learner's sample of models—displaying a trait increases, the strength of the conformist effect should increase non-linearly as well. We address the second and third predictions below.

A substantial amount of empirical research from psychology shows that people conform in a wide range of circumstances, particularly when problems are complex or difficult to solve on one's own. This work reveals that humans have two different types of conformity that operate in different contexts (Baron *et al.*, 1996). The first, often called *informational conformity*, matches the theoretical expectations from models of conformist transmission and is used to figure out difficult or ambiguous problems. Informational conformity results in people actually altering their private opinions and beliefs about something. The second, often called *normative conformity*, is conformity for the purposes of going along with the group to avoid appearing deviant. Under this type of conformity, people alter their superficial behaviour, but often do not change their underlying opinions, preferences or beliefs.

Experimental work shows that conformist transmission is important in individual decision-making situations (non-social circumstances). In an experimental design that parallels the aforementioned simulation constructed by Henrich *et al.* (2004), McElreath *et al.* (2005) had undergraduate subjects repeatedly face an economic choice between two options, A or B, for 20 rounds. This was posed as a 'farming decision' in which A and B were different crops with different yields and yield variances. Players did not know the mean yields or yield variances for the two crops, but were told that the local environment might fluctuate such that the mean yields of the

crops change. After each round, each farmer learned the yield realized in that year for his field, and could choose to look at the decisions (crop A or B, but not the yields) of other farmers in the past year. At the end of the 20 rounds players were paid according to their total yield over the 20 seasons, making between $4 and $8. Consistent with theoretical predictions, McElreath *et al.*'s analysis confirms that (i) people increase their appetite for social information when crop variance is high and decrease it in temporally fluctuating environments, and (ii) a simple conformist learning rule (copy the majority) seems to capture an important part of decision-making in this problem, although there is quite a bit of individual heterogeneity.

A naturalistic experiment using non-incentivized behaviour further confirms these conformist effects by showing the non-linear influence of the frequency of a behaviour (Coultas, 2004) on its adoption. Here, subjects entered a computer laboratory one-by-one, not realizing they were in an experiment, and observed a 'rare behaviour' that involved placing the keyboard cover on top of the monitor. In pre-testing, the experimenters confirmed that no one, without modelling, ever put the cover on top of the monitor—so without modelling the expected frequency of placing the cover on the monitor is zero. The experimenters were able to manipulate the number of individuals placing the cover on the monitor by silently giving explicit instructions to some few through their computer monitors. Others, not receiving these instructions, were observed to see if they placed the cover on top of the monitor. Figure 38.1 summarizes the results by showing how the frequency of models performing the cover placement affected a subject's likelihood of making the same placement. The horizontal axis gives the percentage of individuals already present in the room who had their keyboard covers on top of their monitor as the subject entered. The vertical axis gives the probability that the subject would then place his keyboard cover on top of his monitor. As predicted, the likelihood of performing this behaviour, which is not otherwise performed, increases non-linearly as the percentage of models performing the behaviour rises above 50%. One problem with this experiment is that it does not carefully

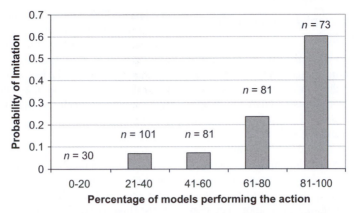

Fig. 38.1 The figure shows how the percentage of models performing the 'covers on the monitor' behavior influences the likelihood of others performing the same behavior. The *n* values above each bar gives the number of individuals observed for that bar—e.g., 73 subjects entered a room in which between 81 and 100 percent of the people in the room had their keyboard covers on their monitors; about 60% of these subjects then put their covers on the monitor.

distinguish informational from normative conformity.

As with prestige-biased transmission, conformist transmission is also important in social situations, including cooperative interactions. Conformity effects have also been observed in experimental situations involving opportunities for cooperation and punishment. Players in these games were willing to use conformist learning for acquiring cooperative behaviour, selfish behaviour, the costly punishment of non-cooperators, and even the costly punishment of those who refuse to punish non-cooperators (Carpenter, 2004; Denant-Boemont *et al.*, 2005). In general, the powerful effects of cultural learning on cooperation and altruism are empirically well-established (for summary see Henrich and Henrich in press, Chapter 2).

38.3. Concepts 2 and 3: cultural evolution and culture–gene coevolution

By combining these kinds of working hypotheses about the nature of our evolved individual-level adaptive learning mechanisms (e.g. prestige-biased and conformist-biased transmission) with formal models of *population processes* (see McElreath and Henrich, this volume, Chapter 39)

dual-inheritance theory can generate a wide range of higher-level theories about the cultural evolutionary and culture-gene coevolutionary origins of sociological phenomena (e.g. ethnic groups). Instead of arguing that unidirectional causation exists at either the individual or society level, dual-inheritance theory *explicitly* models individuals with evolved or evolving psychologies in interactions with other individuals to understand more precisely how cultural learning mechanisms give rise to cultural evolution, and how this might feed back on genetic evolution (Cavalli-Sforza and Feldman, 1981; Boyd and Richerson, 1985). Here we discuss theory, rooted in formal modelling efforts, applied to the following questions: (i) why do cultural evolutionary rates and degrees of adaptation vary among populations (Shennan, 2001; Henrich, 2004) and how might this have influenced the basic cognitive abilities of different human groups and (ii) why do ethnically-marked groups emerge and how did our 'ethnic psychology' develop (Gil-White, 2001; McElreath *et al.*, 2003). Other work in this area examines how adaptive cultural learning can sometimes give rise to the otherwise puzzling patterns of maladaptive cultural practices, such as the demographic transition (Richerson and Boyd, 2005), cooperation as well as uniquely human forms psychology (McElreath and Henrich, this volume, Chapter 39).

38.3.1. Demography and cultural evolutionary rates

In the last 10 000 years, the rate of cumulative cultural adaptation has accelerated many times over, but the distribution in rates has been very uneven across the continents (Diamond, 1997). While much of this variation is likely to be explained by historical particulars, we suspect several important general processes are also at work (Turchin, 2003). While difference between continents is probably the most significant pattern in human history, evolutionary approaches, at least those devoid of an explicit appreciation of cultural transmission, have remarkably little to say about it. To illustrate, we briefly discuss one cultural evolutionary model that explores the interaction between demographic conditions and cultural evolutionary rates of adaptation (e.g. in technology, skills, knowledge) that may help explain *both* variable rates of cultural adaptation in different places and peculiar cases of maladaptive cultural and technological losses.

As the most extreme and archaeologically best-documented case of maladaptive techno-logical loss, Tasmania provides an intriguing puzzle, and good point of departure for an inquiry. Humans first arrived in Tasmania about 34 000 years ago and were subsequently cut off from mainland Australia between 12 000 and 10 000 years ago by rising seas that filled the 200 km stretch of land linking Tasmania to Victoria. At the time of European discovery, Tasmania had the simplest technology of any population ever encountered. A combination of ethno-historical and archaeological data suggests that, over the 10 000 year period after being cut off from mainland Australia, Tasmanians likely lost, or never evolved, the ability to make bone tools, fitted cold-weather clothing, hafted tools, fishing spears, barbed spears, nets, and boomerangs. Bone sewing needles, of the kind used ethnographically by Australian aboriginals to make fitted clothing, are clearly present in Tasmania before the seas rose. To hunt and fight, Tasmanian men used only one-piece spears, rocks and throwing clubs. In all, the entire Tasmanian toolkit consisted of only about 24 items, and contrasts starkly with both their contemporary aboriginal cousins just across the Bass Strait in southern Australia and other cold-climate foragers such as the Ona and Yahgan of Tierra del Fuego. The Australian mainlanders pos-sessed the entire Tasmanian toolkit plus hun-dreds of additional specialized tools including multi-pronged fish spears, spear throwers, boomerangs, mounted adzes, sewn bark canoes, ground edge axes, string bags, composite tools, and a variety of nets for birds, fish and wallabies (Henrich, 2004).

With this puzzle in mind, Henrich (2004) constructed a model in which individuals pref-erentially imitate highly skilled individuals. Unlike previous models, however, Henrich's model left open the possibility that transmission was both noisy (highly variable) and negatively biased (copies are usually worse than the originals)—both plausible assumptions, especially for com-plex technological skills and areas of knowledge. The analytical results show two things worthy of note: (i) the rate of adaptive evolution depends on the natural logarithm of the *effective* popula-tion size (effective population size incorporates absolute size and degree of interconnectedness: the size of the pool of interacting social learners); and (ii) if a well-adapted large population suddenly shrank, it could enter a regime of gradual maladaptive deterioration, as it moved towards a new, less-well-adapted, *equilibrium*. Empirically, the intervening time-period between the two equilibria would show a gradual loss of complex skills and knowledge (easy-to-learn skills would not be affected). Effective population size influences the evolutionary rate by making 'positive' errors—those that result in a more adaptive practice—more likely. This, along with a few other nuances in the archaeological record, indicates that the Tasmania pattern of deterioration may have been ignited by the interaction between the dynamics of cultural transmission and the sudden drop in effective population size created when rising oceans sev-ered the link to the social learning networks of southern Australia. Overall, besides revealing the possibility of maladaptive deteriorations when networked populations are cut off, this simple model also shows that larger, more inter-connected, populations can evolve both more rapidly and to a better-adapted equilibrium than smaller, or less well interconnected, populations. This may provide an evolutionary explanation why Diamond's observation that rates of technological evolution proceeded at different rates on different continents.

With the adaptive nature of cultural evolution in mind, it is important not to underestimate the degree to which culture, and cumulative cultural evolution, can influence basic facets of human cognition. Consider two aspects of our psychology: (i) spatial cognition and (ii) numerical conceptions of quantity.

Spatial cognition. At most, human languages possess three different systems for describing spatial position: (a) absolute: the ball is north of the tree; (b) object-centered: the ball is on Richard's left [as an object, Richard inherently has a (culturally defined) left, right, front, etc.]; and (c) relative: the ball is to the left of the tree (here an imaginary line is drawn from the speaker or other reference point to the tree, thus creating a 'left' for the tree). However, not all languages have evolved all three systems, with some cultures and languages lacking the relative system, and relying heavily on the absolute system. Cognitively, speakers of these languages (i) possess incredible dead-reckoning abilities and seem to have a constantly running mental compass, and (ii) perform very differently in non-linguistic tests of spatial memory (Levinson, 2003). It seems that the cultural evolution of linguistic system, and associated cultural routines, for discussing and dealing with space and orientation influences our non-linguistic spatial cognition.

Numerical conceptions of quantity. Number systems are an aspect of culture and language that varies substantially among societies. Many societies, for example, only have ordinal numbers up to 3. Recent work using experiments from cognitive science among two Amazonian groups demonstrates that growing up with such number systems greatly influences people's abilities in non-linguistic tasks that involve memory and matching, in dealing with quantity and number (Pierre *et al.*, 2004; Gordon, 2005). Thus, the cultural evolution of a number system influences the brains of those who grow up using it.

38.3.3. The coevolution of ethnically marked groups and ethnic psychology

A curious feature of human societies is their subdivision into self-ascribed arbitrarily marked groups, sometimes called 'ethnic groups' (Barth, 1969). These groups are sometimes the loci of cooperation and collective action (Henrich and Henrich, in press, Chapter 9), as well as outgroup hatred (LeVine and Campbell, 1972). Many social scientists hold the opinion that these groups and their markings form out of collective interest alone, or that they are the result of strategic switching and signalling on the part of political actors. While we think this is partly true, the existence of strategic ethnic manipulation makes the maintenance of these arbitrarily marked groups problematic. If individuals can merely choose their ethnicity at any time, then why should anyone pay attention to the cheap labels at all? Models of ethnic markers as signals of cooperative intentions in fact show that the process is unlikely to work (Nettle and Dunbar, 1997; Roberts and Sherratt, 2002; see McElreath *et al.*, 2003 for more discussion of analogous biological models).

To explore the relation between social norms, symbolic markers, and cultural learning, McElreath *et al.* (2003) constructed a mathematical model to study the claim that arbitrary and easily acquired 'ethnic markers' (e.g. dialect, dress, hairstyle) may function to signal hidden, important norms of behaviour that differ among population subdivisions.

The model assumes that the population is subdivided spatially into 'groups' linked by migration. Groups are large and each individual is characterized by one of two norms. Norm differences arise in the model because the authors assumed that the norms solve coordination problems, such that individuals with locally common behaviours are at an advantage in terms of individual success (locally if everyone pays bride price, not dowry, one should also pay bride price, to coordinate with others). The model assumes that these behaviours are not observable, because many norms are unconscious and not easy to anticipate (Nave, 2000; Gil-White, 2001). Each individual also adopts one of two visible markers. These markers are costless, but may be observed prior to interacting based upon the hidden norms. Individuals may preferentially interact with those with the same markers as themselves, but this tendency is allowed to evolve within the model.

Naïve individuals acquire both norms and markers by imitating successful individuals (as discussed above). With some chance, they acquire both from the same individual, which may generate covariance between markers and behaviours. This bundled imitation is also allowed to evolve in the model.

The central question addressed by the model is not whether stable norm differences can evolve, but rather whether, given stable norm differences, stable regions of ethnic marking will arise that covary with norm boundaries. That is, do adaptive cultural learning mechanisms sometimes give rise to ethnic groups, as an emergent by-product? And, if they do, how does this emergent social environment influence the genetic evolutionary processes that shaped human psychology? It is important to realize that in a purely genetic model ethnic groups would be unlikely to emerge, as migration between subdivisions would normally swamp selection. Yet, empirically we know that ethnic groups manage to maintain apparent norm differences despite migration rates of one sex approaching 1: along the Vaupes river linguistic exogamy means that people must marry someone from a group who does not speak their language (Jackson, 1983). Only extreme selection could maintain genetically based behaviour differences under such migration. However, as mentioned in the preceding sections, both social interactions and mechanisms like conformist transmission can maintain differences between social groups, even when interaction and the physical movement of bodies is common. Likewise, selective cultural-learning processes can be strong even when the direct pay-off differences among behaviours are small (see McElreath and Henrich, this volume, Chapter 39).

A feedback loop generates and maintains ethnic marking, as long as migration exists but is not too strong relative to the selective processes created by success-biased cultural learning (that arise from the need to coordinate social interactions). The model works as follows.

1. Migration creates small amounts of covariance between specific markers and behaviours within each local group. This occurs even if there is initially no covariance within each group. The reason is subtle. If local groups differ at all in their frequencies of markers and behaviours, then there is covariance at the population level. Population structure is represented by the covariance across groups. Migration among local groups transfers this population covariance into within-group covariance.

2. Direct selective processes favouring common behaviours create indirect selection on markers, proportional to the covariance between behaviours and markers. This increases markers associated with common behaviours, within each local group.

3. Natural selection favours a psychological bias for interacting with those with the same marker as oneself, because there is always some covariance between markers and behaviours, due to migration. As this interaction bias increases, selection increases the covariance further, because then makers and behaviours form co-adapted pairs.

4. While migration may be needed to get the process going, if it is too strong, it swamps the selective forces above, leading to unmarked groups, sometimes even if behavioural (norm) differences remain. This is where the plausibility of weak migration relative to the strong forces of our cultural learning psychology is crucial to the model. If individuals are not strongly disposed to learn from group members with higher pay-offs, then mixing will erode differences between neighbouring groups.

Once regions of norms and ethnic markers exist, selection on genes favours an increased predisposition to interact with those who look like oneself (share one's markers). It also favours acquiring bundles of traits, norms and markers together, from the same individual during social learning (this may further enhance the tendency of individuals to learn things from successful models that do not directly relate to their domain of success or expertise). Importantly, the cultural evolution of behaviourally distinct groups and their markers leads to natural selection on aspects of psychology. This is the kind of culture–gene coevolution that we think is common in human evolution.

In conclusion, if we are right, then constraining ourselves to purely genetic models of human evolution will handicap our attempts to understand important domains of human behaviour, because the crucial selective forces that may account for some of our psychological adaptations arose first through the evolution of culture.

This is not to say that humans may have in any sense 'transcended' natural selection, any more than domesticated animals have. Rather, the sources of our selection pressures may often be different in important respects from those of closely related species, because of our evolved capacities for cultural transmission. Our bet, bolstered now by more than two decades of formal models of culture–gene coevolution and substantial evidence from laboratory and field sciences, is that it will prove very hard in the long run to understand the structure of human psychology without reference to the dynamic population processes that help to construct our selection pressures.

References

Baron, R., Vandello, J. and Brunsman, B. (1996) The forgotten variable in conformity research: impact of task importance on social influence. *Journal of Personality and Social Psychology*, 71: 915–927.

Barth, F. (1969) Introduction. In *Ethnic Groups and Boundaries*, pp. 9–38. Little, Brown & Co., Boston.

Beckerman, S., Lizarralde, R., Lizarralde, M. *et al.* (2002) The Bari Partible Paternity Project, Phase One. In S. Beckerman and P. Valentine (eds) *Cultures of Multiple Fathers: The Theory and Practice of Partible Paternity in Lowland South America*, pp. 27–41. The University Press of Florida, Gainesville.

Beckerman, S. and Valentine, P. (2002) Introduction: the concept of partible paternity among native South Americans. In S. Beckerman and P. Valentine (eds) *Cultures of Multiple Fathers: The Theory and Practice of Partible Paternity in Lowland South America*, pp. 1–13. University of Florida, Gainesville.

Berreman, G. D. (1972) *Hindus of the Himalayas: Ethnography and Change*. University of California Press, Berkeley.

Boyd, D. (2001) Life without pigs: recent subsistence changes among the Irakia Awa, Papua New Guinea. *Human Ecology*, 29: 259–281.

Boyd, R. and Richerson, P. J. (1985) *Culture and the Evolutionary Process*. University of Chicago Press, Chicago.

Boyd, R. and Richerson, P. J. (1988) An evolutionary model of social learning: the effects of spatial and temporal variation. In T. R. Zentall and B. G. Galef (eds) *Social Learning: Psychological and Biological Perspectives*, pp. 29–48. Lawrence Erlbaum, Hillsdale, NJ.

Boyd, R. and Richerson, P. J. (1995) Why does culture increase adaptability? *Ethology and Sociobiology*, 16: 125–143.

Boyer, P. (2001) *Religion Explained: The Evolutionary Origins of Religious Thought*. New York, Basic Books.

Carpenter, J. (2004) When in Rome: conformity and the provision of public goods. *Journal of Socio-Economics*, 4: 395–408.

Cavalli-Sforza, L. L. and Feldman, M. (1981) *Cultural Transmission and Evolution*. Princeton University Press, Princeton.

Cavalli-Sforza, L. L., Feldman, M. W., Chen, K. H. and Dornbusch, S. M. (1982) Theory and observation in cultural transmission. *Science*, 218 (4567): 19–27.

Coultas, J. (2004) When in Rome … an evolutionary perspective on conformity. *Group Processes and Intergroup Relations*, 7: 317–331.

DeBruine, L. (2002) Facial resemblance enhances trust. *Proceedings of the Royal Society of London, B*, 269: 1307–1312.

Denant-Boemont, L., Masclet, D. and Noussair, C. (2005) *Anonymity in Punishment, Revenge and Cooperation: A Public Goods Experiment*. Atlanta.

Diamond, J. M. (1997) *Guns, Germs, and Steel: The Fates of Human Societies*. Norton, New York.

Dove, M. (1993) Uncertainty, humility and adaptation in the tropical forest: the agricultural augury of the Kantu. *Ethnology*, 32: 145–167.

Durham, W. H. (1991) *Coevolution: Genes, Culture, and Human Diversity*. Stanford University Press, Stanford, CA.

Gil-White, F. (2001) Are ethnic groups biological 'species' to the human brain? Essentialism in our cognition of some social categories. *Current Anthropology*, 42: 515–554.

Gordon, P. (2005) Numerical cognition without words: evidence from Amazonia. *Science*, 306: 496–499.

Gurven, M. (2001) Does market exposure affect economic game behavior? the ultimatum game and the public goods game among the Tsimane' of Bolivia. In J. Henrich, R. Boyd, S. Bowler, C. Camerer, E. Fehr and H. Gintis (eds.) *Cooperation, Reciprocity and Punishment: Experiments in Fifteen Small-scale Societies*, pp. 194–231, Oxford University Press, Oxford.

Harris, J. R. (1995) Where is the child's environment? A group socialization theory of development. *Psychological Review*, 102: 458–489.

Harris, J. R. (1998) *The Nurture Assumption: Why Children Turn Out the Way They Do*. Touchstone, New York.

Henrich, J. (2004) Demography and cultural evolution: why adaptive cultural processes produced maladaptive losses in Tasmania. *American Antiquity*, 69: 197–214.

Henrich, J. and Boyd, R. (1998) The evolution of conformist transmission and the emergence of between-group differences. *Evolution and Human Behavior*, 19: 215–242.

Henrich, J. and Gil-White, F. (2001) The evolution of prestige: freely conferred deference as a mechanism for enhancing the benefits of cultural transmission. *Evolution and Human Behavior*, 22: 165–196.

Henrich, N. S. and Henrich, J. (in press) *Why Humans Cooperate: A Cultural and Evolutionary Explanation*. Oxford University Press, Oxford.

Henrich, J. and McElreath, R. (2002) Are peasants risk-averse decision makers? *Current Anthropology*, 43: 172–181.

Henrich, J., Boyd, R., Bowles, S., Camerer, C., Fehr, E. and Gintis, H. (eds) (2004) *Foundations of Human Sociality: Economic Experiments and Ethnographic Evidence From Fifteen Small-Scale Societies*. Oxford, Oxford University Press.

Hill, K. and Hurtado, A. M. (1996) *Ache Life History*. Aldine de Gruyter, New York.

Horner, V. and Whiten, A. (2005) Causal knowledge and imitation/emulation switching in chimpanzees (Pan trogiodytes) and children (Homo sapiens). *Animal Cognition*, 8: 164–181.

Jackson, J. E. (1983) *The Fish People: Linguistic Exogamy and Tukanoan Identity in Northwest Amazonia.* Cambridge University Press, Cambridge.

Jonas, K. (1992) Modeling and suicide: a test of the Werther effect. *British Journal of Social Psychology*, 31: 295–306.

Kameda, T. and Nakanishi, D. (2002) Cost-benefit analysis of social/cultural learning in a non-stationary uncertain environment: an evolutionary simulation and an experiment with human subjects. *Evolution and Human Behavior*, 23: 373–393.

Kellogg, W. and Kellogg, L. (1933) *The Ape and the Child: A Study of Environmental Influence Upon Early Behavior.* McGraw-Hill, New York.

Kessler, R. C., Downey, G. and Stipp, H. (1988) Clustering of teenage suicides after television news stories about suicide: a reconsideration. *American Journal of Psychiatry*, 145: 1379–83.

Kroll, Y, and Levy, H. (1992) Further tests of the separation theorem and the capital asset pricing model. *American Economic Review*, 82: 664–670.

Labov, W. (1972) *Sociolinguistic Patterns.* Philadelphia, University of Pennsylvania Press.

Labov, W. (1980) The social origins of sound change. In W. Labov (ed.) *Locating Language in Time and Space*, pp. 251–265. Academic Press, New York.

Laland, K. N., Odling-Smee, J., and Feldman, M.W. (2000) Niche construction, biological evolution, and cultural change. *Behavioral and Brain Sciences*, 23: 131–175.

LeVine, R. A. and Campbell, D. T. (1972) *Ethnocentrism.* Wiley, New York.

Levinson, S. C. (2003) *Space in Language and Cognition.* Cambridge University Press, Cambridge.

McBrearty, S. and Brooks, A. (2000) The revolution that wasn't: a new interpretation of the origin of modern human behavior. *Journal of Human Evolution*, 39: 453–563.

McElreath, R., Boyd, R. and Richerson, P. J. (2003) Shared norms and the evolution of ethnic markers. *Current Anthropology*, 44: 122–129.

McElreath, R., Lubell, M., Richerson, P. et al. (2005) Applying evolutionary models to the laboratory study of social learning. *Evolution and Human Behavior*, 26: 483–508.

Mullen, B., Cooper, C. and Driskell, J. E. (1990) Jaywalking as a function of model behavior. *Personality and Social Psychology Bulletin*, 16: 320–330.

Nave, A. (2000) Marriage and the maintenance of ethnic group boundaries: the case of Mauritius. *Ethnic and Racial Studies*, 23: 329–52.

Nettle, D. and Dunbar, R. (1997) Social markers and the evolution of reciprocal exchange. *Current Anthropology*, 38: 93–99.

Nisbett, R. E. (2003) *The Geography of Thought: How Asians and Westerners Think Differently … and Why.* Free Press, New York.

Offerman, T. and Sonnemans, J. (1998) Learning by experience and learning by imitating others. *Journal of Economic Behavior and Organization*, 34: 559–575.

Pierre, P., Lemer, C., Izard, V. and Dehaene, S. (2004) Exact and approximate arithmetic in an Amazonian Indigene group. *Science*, 306: 499–503.

Pingle, M. (1995) Imitation vs. rationality: an experimental perspective on decision-making. *Journal of Socio-Economics*, 24: 281–315.

Plomin, R., Defries, J. and McLearn, G. E. (2000) *Behavioral Genetics.* W. H. Freeman, New York.

Rao, V. (2001) Poverty and public celebrations in rural India. *Annals of the American Academy of Political and Social Science*, 573: 85–104.

Richerson, P. and Boyd, R. (2005) *Not by Genes Alone: How Culture Transformed Human Evolution.* University of Chicago Press, Chicago.

Roberts, G. and Sherratt, T. (2002) Does similarity breed cooperation? *Nature*, 418: 499–500.

Rogers, E. M. (1995) *Diffusion of Innovations.* Free Press, New York.

Rubinstein, D. H. (1983) Epidemic suicide among Micronesian adolescents. *Social Science Medicine*, 17: 657–665.

Segall, M., Campbell, D. and Herskovits, M. J. (1966) *The Influence of Culture on Visual Perception.* Bobbs-Merrill, New York.

Shennan, S. (2001) Demography and cultural innovation: a model and its implications for the emergence of modern human culture. *Cambridge Archaeology Journal*, 11: 5–16.

Stack, S. (1987) Celebrities and suicide: a taxonomy and analysis, 1948–1983. *American Sociological Review*, 52: 401–412.

Stack, S. (1990) Divorce, suicide, and the mass media: an analysis of differential identification, 1948–1980. *Journal of Marriage and the Family*, 52: 553–560.

Stack, S. (1996) The effect of the media on suicide: evidence from Japan, 1955–1985. *Suicide and Life-Threatening Behavior*, 26: 132–142.

Thornhill, R., Gangestad, S. W., Miller, R., Scheyd, G., McCollough, G. and Franklin, M. (2003) Major histocompatibility complex genes, symmetry, and body scent attractiveness in men and women. *Behavioral Ecology*, 15: 668–678.

Tomasello, M. (1999) *The Cultural Origins of Human Cognition.* Harvard University Press, Cambridge, MA.

Turchin, P. (2003) *Historical Dynamics: Why States Rise and Fall.* Princeton University Press, Princeton, NJ.

Wasserman, I. M., Stack, S. and Reeves, J. L. (1994) Suicide and the media: The New York Times's presentation of front-page suicide stories between 1910 and 1920. *Journal of Communication*, 44: 64–83.

Weibull, J. W. (1995) *Evolutionary Game Theory.* MIT Press, Cambridge, MA.

Weiss, H. (1977) Subordinate imitation of supervisor behavior: the role of modeling in organizational socialization. *Organizational Behavior and Human Decision Processes*, 19: 89–105.

Weiss, H. M., Suckow, K. and Rakestraw, T. L. (1999) Influence of modeling on self-set goals: direct and mediated effects. *Human Performance*, 12: 89–114.

Whiten, A., Horner, V. and de Waal, F. B. M. (2005) Conformity to cultural norms of tool use in chimpanzees. *Nature*, 437(7059): 737–740.

CHAPTER 39

Modelling cultural evolution

Richard McElreath and Joseph Henrich

39.1. Introduction

When Darwin left for his voyage around the world on the Beagle, he took with him the first volume of Charles Lyell's *Principles of Geology*. Later in the voyage he received the second volume by post somewhere in South America. Lyell never accepted Darwin's account of evolution by natural selection, presumably because of his religious beliefs. It is ironic then that Lyell's work played a crucial role in the development of Darwin's thinking. In some ways Lyell's principle of uniformitarianism is as central to Darwinism as is natural selection.

Before Lyell, it was common to explain the features of the earth's geology in terms of past catastrophes: floods, earthquakes and other cataclysms. In contrast, Lyell tried to explain what he observed in terms of the cumulative action of processes that we could observe every day in the world around us—the sinking of lands and the build-up of sediments. By appreciating the accumulated small effects of such processes over long time spans, great changes could be explained.

Darwin took the idea of small changes over long time spans and applied it to populations of organisms. Darwin was a good naturalist and knew a lot about the everyday lives of plants and animals. They mate, they reproduce, they move from one place to another, and they die.

Darwin's insight was to see that organisms vary, and the processes of their lives affect which types spread and which diminish. The key to explaining long-run change in nature, to explaining the origin of new species, of whole new types of organisms, and of life itself was to apply Lyell's principle of uniformitarianism to populations. By keeping track of how the small events of every-day life change the composition of populations, we can explain great events over long time scales.

Biologists have been thinking this way ever since Darwin, but it is still news in most parts of the social sciences. Are people products of their societies or are societies products of people? The answer must be 'both', but theory in the social sciences has tended to take one side or the other (Marx's dialectic being an obvious exception). In evolutionary models, this classical conflict between explanations at the level of the society (think Durkheimian social facts) and explanations at the level of individuals (think microeconomics) simply disappears. Population models allow explanation and real causation at both levels (and more than two levels) to exist seamlessly and meaningfully in one theory. We don't have to choose between atomistic and group-level explanations. Instead, one can build models about how individuals can create population-level effects which then change individuals in powerful ways. Cultural evolutionary models are much the same as better-known genetic ones: events in the lives of individuals interact at the scale of populations to produce feedback and powerful long-term effects on behaviour. There are three basic steps.

1. One begins by specifying the structure of the population. How large is it? Is it sub-divided? How do sub-divisions affect one another? How does migration work? How is the population size regulated?

2. Then one defines the life cycle of the organism. How does mating work? When is learning possible? What states do individuals pass through from birth to death?

3. Finally, one defines the different heritable variants possible in the model. What is the range of strategies or mutations over which evolution operates? How do these variants affect events in the life cycle of the organism, such as death or development, including learning, attention, and inference?

Since cultural evolutionary models can contain two interacting biological systems of inheritance, culture and genes, the answers to these questions can be different for each system. For example, individuals may be able to acquire many different socially learned behaviours, but the range of possible genetically inherited learning strategies may be very small. The number of genetic parents has an upper limit of two (for most vertebrates at least), but cultural parents can be many and the contributions among them can be very unequal. In some cultural evolutionary models, the contribution of each parent is typically non-additive in ways most people consider impossible in genetics.

After the structure of the model is completely specified, the objective is to transform these assumptions into mathematical expressions that tell us how the frequencies of each cultural and genetic variant (and the covariance among them, if necessary) change during each stage of the life cycle. These expressions, called recursions, do the work of integrating events in the lives of individuals into micro-evolutionary consequences—changes observable over short time spans. The next goal is to deduce the long-term macro-evolutionary consequences of the assumptions. This is done by finding any combinations of cultural and genetic variants that lead to steady states, equilibria, and what combinations

of environmental conditions and life-cycle variables make different equilibria possible. Some of these equilibria will be stable, meaning the population will be attracted to them, while others will be unstable, meaning the population will move away from them. Stable equilibria are candidates for long-term evolutionary outcomes, and unstable ones are important because they often inform us as to how likely the population is to reach any of the stable equilibria or how much time it may spend at each.

Thus by writing down formal expressions that capture assumptions about how tiny events in the lives of individuals affect survival, reproduction, and the probabilities of being a cultural parent, evolutionary models allow one to deduce the population-level evolutionary consequences of individual-level psychologies, decision rules, and behaviour. At the same time, since these expressions simultaneously define how events in the life cycle affect the population and how the population affects individuals, it is a two-way street. The mass action arising from individuals integrates up at the population level to have potentially powerful effects on the fates of individuals with different cultural and genetic variants. These different fates in turn lead to further changes in the population, which lead to yet more consequences for individuals.

It is not easy to keep all of these balls in the air simultaneously. The slipperiness of verbal reasoning is famous, and that is perhaps the reason why so many fields, from philosophy to economics to physics, use formalism to make deductions about complex systems. The steady stream of interesting and counter-intuitive results that emerge from these formalisms has demonstrated their value and made them centrepieces of theory development.

Many social scientists and biologists work on how individuals make decisions and how behaviour is acquired. Fewer ask how those decisions and mechanisms of learning aggregate at the population level. Our position is that both are inherently interesting and crucial for understanding evolving systems, including culture. In the remainder of this paper, we explore three key, and sometimes controversial, issues in the evolution of culture which arise by examining the population processes cultural inheritance may generate. We invite the reader to join us in a tour of this biological frontier and see how formal population models of cultural systems may clarify and address questions about human behaviour, psychology, and society.

39.2. Why bother with cultural evolution?

Some phenotypes need more than genes and environment, to be represented in a formal model.

Sometimes people ask us why we should even bother with modelling cultural evolution? Why are genetic models not sufficient? What scientific pay-off is there in the added complexity? These are fine questions, and they have fine answers. The basic issue is to identify the minimal requirements for representing evolution of phenotype in a species. For example, we could construct a very simple genetic model in which the change (Δ) in the frequency of an allele, p, is a function of environmental state, E. This system would have a single recursion:

$$\Delta p = F(p,E),$$

where the function $F(p,E)$ is to be specified depending upon what model of adaptation to the environment we might choose. It might be that E has little effect on individuals with different alleles, or it might be that E favours one over the others. It might be that E is fluctuating, so that selection favours different alleles at different times. The change might depend upon p itself, as it does in the example of sickle-cell anaemia and other cases of overdominance. But nowhere do we allow in such a system for E itself to evolve in response to p.

The scientific question is whether such models are sufficient to model the evolution of a given human phenotype. If we only knew genotypes and the state of the environment, could we predict the behaviour of organisms in the next time period? When the answer to this question is 'no', we need at least one more equation:

$$\Delta p = F(p, q, E),$$
$$\Delta q = G(p, q, E),$$

where q is the frequency of some cultural variant (a dialect, say), and $G(p, q, E)$ a function telling us how dialect responds to environment, E, and

its own previous state, q, and the frequency of an allele, p.

This all sounds rather complex. And it can be. However, when important parts of phenotype are acquired during development and depend upon previous phenotypes, some system like this is useful for understanding how the organism evolves. Unless we think that existing behaviours could be predicted solely from knowing the environment and the distribution of genes, at some point evolutionary models must incorporate the dynamics of behavioural inheritance. No heroic assumptions are required for behavioural inheritance to exist: if portions of phenotype depend upon the phenotypes of other individuals, then weak or strong inheritance of behaviour can exist. In the long run, in a given model, it might turn out that behavioural dynamics have little effect on the outcome. In others, it will make a huge difference.

Cultural evolutionary models (as well as niche construction models; see Odling-Smee *et al.*, 2003) can model just the non-genetic behavioural dynamics, as if q above did not depend upon p, as well as joint dynamics of a coupled gene–culture system (Sforza and Feldman, 1981; Boyd and Richerson, 1985; Durham, 1991). In each case, however, the structure of the model is decided by the question of interest. In the rest of this review, we show how cultural evolution models have been used to address questions about human behaviour.

39.3. Transmission in noisy systems

The imperfection of the analogy between genetic and cultural evolution does not mean culture does not evolve. While evolutionary principles are equally applicable to almost any dynamical system, many researchers approach models of cultural transmission and evolution via an analogy with genetic evolution. This has led some to be concerned about the strength of this analogy (Sperber, 2000).

If cultural variants are not discrete, are prone to 'mutation', and are strongly affected by learning biases, then is it appropriate to speak of 'transmission' of culture at all? While we have no particular attachment to the term 'transmission', we think the answer is definitively 'yes'. Even if all the above is true, culture can still be an evolving system that leads to cumulative adaptation. This does not mean that evolved psychology has no role to play in how culture evolves (we think psychology has a huge role to play in understanding culture), but we think it does mean that dismissing cultural evolution on the basis of imperfection of the genetic analogy is unwarranted.

Many people—enthusiasts of the 'meme' approach and critics alike—seem to have been persuaded by Richard Dawkins' abstract statements on what is required for adaptive evolution to occur. In *The Extended Phenotype* (1982), he argued that any successfully replicating entity must exhibit (i) longevity, (ii) fecundity, and (iii) fidelity. The entity must last long enough (longevity) to make copies of itself (fecundity) that are reasonably similar to it (fidelity). Some have interpreted this to mean that anything with high mutation rates cannot be a successful replicator. Thus if cultural ideas change in the process of social learning, the conclusion is that they do not constitute an evolving system at all (see citations in Henrich and Boyd, 2002). Similarly, if cultural variants are continuous and blended entities, then they never exactly replicate, and again cannot produce adaptive evolution.

These conclusions are unfounded. Read very generally, Dawkins' conditions are necessary and sufficient: there must be some heritability for adaptive evolution to occur. However, there are many ways to produce heritable variation. So in the strict sense in which many people have read them, while Dawkins' conditions are sufficient, they are definitely not necessary. Reverse-engineering DNA may tell us how inheritance can work, but it does not tell us how it must work. Henrich *et al.* (in press) examines the problems with this reverse-engineering in greater depth.

In this section, we address concerns arising from the gene–culture analogy by demonstrating ways that transmission can deviate substantially from the genetic analogy but nevertheless produce both heritable variation and adaptive evolution. Our broader message is that biologists and social scientists alike have tended to think too narrowly in terms of the genes metaphor.

Many other systems of inheritance are possible in principle, and culture is only one. We believe that it is more productive to drop the genetic analogy and instead study cultural transmission and evolution on its own.

39.3.1. Noisy learning can maintain heritable cultural variation

Before the union of genetics and Darwinism, most biologists, including Darwin, thought that inheritance was a blending process: offspring were a mix of parental phenotypes. Darwin was troubled by Fleeming Jenkin's (1864) argument that natural selection could not produce adaptations, because inheritance would quickly deplete the variation natural selection relies upon. Fisher's (1918) argument reconciling genetics with continuous phenotypic variation purportedly rescued Darwin, but in reality both Jenkin's argument and those who think that Fisher saved Darwin are simply wrong: blending inheritance can preserve variation, and particulate inheritance is neither necessary nor sufficient to preserve variation (Maynard Smith, 1998, has a chapter that examines this problem).

Boyd and Richerson (1985) presented a simple model to prove this point. The model assumes that (i) cultural variants are continuous (non-discrete), and (ii) naïve individuals sample n cultural parents and adopt a weighted average of their observed behaviour–blending inheritance. Observations and reconstructions are prone to an arbitrary amount of error, however, and therefore inheritance here involves continuous traits, blending, and noise/error. They derive a recursion for the variation in cultural behaviour after one generation of learning. To simplify their presentation, assume that there are only two cultural parents and that each contributes equally to socialization. Let ε be the variance in error in cultural learning. When ε is large, learning is noisy. When $\varepsilon = 0$, cultural variants replicate perfectly. After some calculus, the variation in cultural behaviour, V, after learning is (see Boyd and Richerson, 1985, pp. 73–74):

$$V' = \tfrac{1}{2}(V + \varepsilon).$$

If $\varepsilon = 0$, then the above has only one stable value, $V' = V = 0$. Blending reduces variation each generation until it is all gone. In this case,

Jenkin was correct. However, if $\varepsilon > 0$, the equilibrium amount of variation (found where $V' = V$) is:

$$\hat{V} = \varepsilon.$$

Thus if there is substantial noise, there will be substantial variation at equilibrium. This variation can be subject to selective forces and produce adaptive change, just as in the genetic case.

The population comes to rest at the amount of variation above, because while blending inheritance does deplete variation, error in learning replenishes it. In the long run, the balance between these two forces results in the expected amount of variation in the population being equal to the average amount of error individuals commit when learning. Blending can never reduce variation below this amount, because as soon as it does, more mistakes are made, and more variation is pumped into the system. Variation cannot stay forever above this amount, because learning averages out any 'error' that exceeds that inherent in the learning itself.

Boyd and Richerson also showed that if cultural parents assort by phenotype, then assortment can help to maintain variation. This might occur if similar types inhabit similar environments or if similar types are more likely to mate and jointly socialize their offspring. When this happens, the parents being blended together are more similar to one another and therefore the loss of variation due to blending is less than in the case above. If parents are weighted unequally (mom is more important than dad), this will also tend to slow the rate at which blending reduces variation, because unequal weighting reduces the effective number of cultural parents.

How cultural learning actually works is a good empirical question, but models like this one prove that the argument that cultural variants cannot evolve in a meaningful way, because they are (i) not discrete entities like genes and (ii) prone to error, is simply not a valid deduction. Likewise, the observation that culture does evolve does not imply that there are any units analogous to genes nor that imitation and other forms of social learning are highly accurate.

We also think that the empirical evidence is quite strong that many aspects of human behaviour (including technology) evolve in a Darwinian fashion (Richerson and Boyd, 2005). Many of these are not plausibly genetic, in any immediate sense. Thus non-deductive philosophical arguments that culture cannot evolve seem very suspicious, especially when there are existing deductive arguments to the contrary.

39.3.2. Noisy learning can produce adaptive evolution

Some authors (Sperber and Hirschfeld, 2004) have made a lot out of the results of experiments that resemble games of 'telephone' (as it is called in North America) or 'Chinese whispers' (as it is called in Britain). When pairs of individuals pass a signal along a chain, the message tends to be corrupted. Thus, we might conclude, social learning is too error-prone to maintain variation or content in and of itself. Strong, innate inferential mechanisms may be needed to stabilize cultural differences, and these cognitive attractors may swamp any evolutionary dynamics possible in culture.

We do not doubt that psychological biases for learning exist, and their importance has long been a part of cultural evolutionary modelling [see Boyd and Richerson's (1985) direct bias]. However, Henrich and Boyd (2002) have addressed whether strong innate inferential mechanisms swamp adaptive cultural evolution—influenced by selective forces like imitating successful people—by deriving a model of cultural transmission that assumes continuously varying representations under the influence of weak selective transmission and strong cognitive attractors. This model addresses the complaint that culturally transmitted ideas are rarely if ever discrete, but instead blend, as well as the complaint that cognitive influences on social learning swamp transmission effects such that cultural variation is not heritable. Using a very general model, they show that these complaints are deductively invalid. In fact, they derive a non-intuitive conclusion: if inferential biases are sufficiently strong relative to selective forces, a continuous representation (quantitative blending) model reduces to the discrete-trait replicator dynamic commonly used in population models of both culture and genes. Thus, powerful and biased inferential mechanisms actually mean that even a weak selective component will eventually determine the final equilibrium of the system, in true Darwinian fashion. The important assumption here is that learners' psychology has multiple inferential systems—that is, there are multiple cognitive attractors. Strong cognitive biases do not swamp selective effects, but rather make discrete models better estimates of the actual dynamics.

In two other models in the paper, Henrich and Boyd (2002) construct systems with large amounts of transmission error to show that accurate individual-level replication of cultural variants is not necessary for selective forces to generate either cultural inertia or cumulative cultural adaptation. Their second model shows that if learners aggregate information from multiple cultural parents using a conformist bias (see Henrich and McElreath, this volume, Chapter 38) they can dramatically reduce the average noise/error in their inferences, suggesting that our psychology may have genetically evolved a conformist bias, in part, to reduce transmission error (see Henrich and Boyd, 1998, for discussion of other adaptive advantages of conformist transmission). In the aggregate, this bias creates heritability at population level, and can lead to cultural inertia. In the third model, Henrich and Boyd combine all the potential problems with models of cultural evolution, assuming continuous (non-discrete) cultural representations, incomplete transmission, and substantial inferential transformations. Despite these assumptions, they construct a model which produces adaptive cultural evolution.

39.3.3. **Other inheritance systems**

In many baboons, females inherit dominance rank from their mothers and sisters (Silk and Boyd, 1983). In these species, fitness is strongly affected by this extragenetic inheritance: any female adopted at birth into a high-ranking matriline would be better off than if she were adopted into a low-ranking matriline. And this female will have her dominance rank before she fights a single member of her social group. Dominance is heritable, has important effects on fitness, and yet the mechanism of inheritance is at least partly non-genetic. The rules of how this inheritance works are complicated and very unlike genes. It probably depends upon the composition of one's own matriline, the composition of the entire social group, and

local resource density and feeding competition. And yet no primatologist could completely understand baboon biology without taking this complicated extragenetic pedigree into account. Its existence may lead females to strive for rank because of its downstream consequences, in addition to its immediate resource access effects (Boyd, 1982; Leimar, 1996).

Extra- or 'epigenetic' (Maynard Smith, 1990) systems like this are increasingly recognized: everywhere biologists look, they find hints of inheritance systems either built on top of genes or built from entirely different mechanisms. If the key question is what mechanisms account for heritable phenotypic differences among organisms, then the answer appears to be 'many'. Jablonka and Lamb's *Evolution in Four Dimensions* (2005) mounts the empirically rich argument that heritable differences in many species are due to the action of several inheritance systems (genetic, epigenetic, behavioural and symbolic), sometimes interacting, sometimes acting in parallel.

If one thinks about cell division for a moment, it is obvious that processes other than the replication of DNA are needed to explain how it works. Organelles need to be copied (Sheahan *et al.*, 2004), and the genetic code itself needs to be copied (and this is not contained in the DNA, nor could it be). Beyond cell division, adult phenotypes depend upon imprinting and other forms of learning that may channel the environments to which offspring are exposed (a kind of niche construction; Odling-Smee *et al.*, 2003). And finally, most biologists believe that DNA was certainly not the first form of hereditary biological material (Szathmáry and Maynard Smith, 1995). Thus some inheritance systems must be able sometimes to create complementary and even usurping inheritance systems.

In light of these plausible 'inheritance systems', it appears that human culture may not be so special or surprising at all, in the sense of being a non-genetic system of inheritance. Organisms as diverse as arabidopsis (a small plant related to mustard that is a favourite of geneticists), common fruit flies and single-celled microscopic animals such as paramecia exhibit heritable differences due at least in part to mechanisms other than the sequence of nucleotides in their DNA. The existence of social learning as a system of inheritance and adaptation that functions in complement to DNA may turn out to be unremarkable.

To someone who makes formal models of evolutionary systems, the question that we must answer is whether it will be sufficient to represent human (or any other organism's) evolution with just state variables for its alleles. If we require state variables for early childhood experience, imprinting, or behaviours acquired via social learning, to make useful models of our own evolution, then attempts to construct culture-free models are simply scientifically inadequate. As with each of the possible systems above (e.g. Maynard Smith, 1990; Jablonka and Lamb, 1991; Pál and Miklós, 1999), the specific dynamics and consequences of cultural learning may be rather unique and very important for understanding both micro- and macro-evolution.

In the next two sections, we explore models of the possible dynamic consequences of cultural inheritance. While such models do not tell us how human evolution actually works, they direct our attention to possibilities we are unlikely to consider, if we consider DNA to be the only important source of heritable variation in our species.

39.4. The relative strength of forces of cultural evolution

Cultural evolution may be most different in the relative difference in strength of evolutionary forces, rather than the absolute speed of its evolution.

It is commonly observed that cultural evolution may be much faster than genetic evolution. Styles of dress and speech, technological innovations, and reorganizations of human societies happen much faster than the average tempo of genetic evolution. Despite the massive differences in behaviour and social organization among human societies, there is little genetic variation among groups within our species (Pääbo, 2001), leading most social scientists to infer that differences among human groups are due to rapid cultural evolution, not selection on genes.

While we agree that cultural evolution is typically absolutely faster than genetic evolution, at least in the short term, this is only part of the story. The danger with the summary we just gave is that it encourages the view that cultural and genetic evolution lead to similar outcomes, only on different time scales. The *relative* rates of competing evolutionary forces are very different in the two systems. Population geneticists tend to think of evolution as the result of the balance of forces acting on alleles. Migration, mutation and selection all act to alter allele frequencies, but appreciating the balance of these forces is what makes population genetics predictive. Because the balance is likely quite different in cultural models (and presumably the real systems the models caricature), quite different outcomes are possible.

39.4.1. The balance of selective forces and migration

For our discussion, we focus on the relative strengths of two forces, migration and selection. Selection in the cultural case refers to learning forces that favour some behavioural variants over others. For example, people probably prefer to imitate the successful (see Henrich and McElreath, this volume, Chapter 38), and this favours behaviours that lead to success.

An ounce of mixing is a pound of effect, in most models of genetic evolution. In large animals like ourselves, migration among sub-populations is typically a very strong force. This strong force of migration tends to unify sub-populations of alleles with respect to selection. However, this is only true because measured selection coefficients tend to be small, relative to the force of mixing (Endler, 1986). If selection were stronger (and it sometimes is—see again Endler, 1986), then more differences could be maintained among sub-groups.

But in a cultural model, the strength of learning biases that, for example, favour behaviours with higher pay-offs over behaviours with lower pay-offs can be arbitrarily strong. Natural selection of ideas does occur, such as when different fertility ideologies influence the differential growth of religious groups (Stark, 2005). A school of American archaeology used to argue that most important cultural and technological change came about through natural selection of this kind (see Boone and Smith, 1998, for references). It would therefore be useful to consider how strong such selection is, relative to what we might consider fairly fast genetic evolution—such as the 4% increase in the depth of finch beaks Peter and Rosemary Grant recorded on Daphne Major, an island in the Galapagos, during a 2 year drought in 1976 and 1977. This strength of selection is sufficient to produce beaks substantially deeper in less than a decade, assuming that selection would continue at the same rate (Grant and Grant, 1993).

An extrapolation from an empirical example of cultural evolution will help to make clear how much stronger 'selective' forces—by which we mean forces that favour different variants in a non-random way—can be in cultural systems. The classic study of the diffusion of technological innovations is that by Ryan and Gross (1943) on the diffusion of hybrid corn in Iowa farmers. Hybrid corn became available in Iowa in 1928 and was eventually adopted by nearly all farmers by 1941, over a period of 13 years. For those completing and reviewing the study, the shock was how long it took hybrid corn, which had a 20% increase in yield over then-existing varieties, to spread. We want to make something of the opposite point: hybrid corn diffused much more quickly than we might expect, based upon

its pay-off difference with existing strategies and how natural selection would respond. If we take the genetic replicator model and use it to model the diffusion of hybrid corn, we can get a feeling for how much stronger selective forces can be in cultural evolution. This thought experiment violates many truths. We are assuming that a year is the generation time, and that there is no individual decision-making beyond imitation of successful strategies. However, the ordinary population genetic-replicator dynamic and that for simple imitation models is very similar (Gintis, 2000, provides a general derivation). The most basic model, in which individuals compare their own pay-off against that of a random individual and preferentially copy the strategy with the higher pay-off, yields:

$$\Delta p = p(1 - p)\beta(w_1 \, \overline{w}),$$

where p is the frequency of the cultural variant (hybrid corn), a rate parameter, and w_1 and w have similar meanings to the genetic model, pay-off to the behaviour of interest and the average pay-off, respectively.

Figure 39.1 shows these models with two strengths of 'selection', compared to the actual

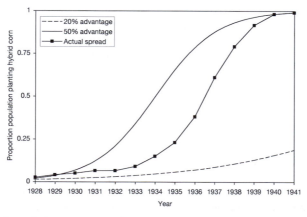

Fig. 39.1 The diffusion of hybrid corn, modelled with the simple replicator dynamic presented in the text, for two strengths of 'selection'. The dashed curve shows the predicted spread using the actual pay-off difference between hybrid corn and then-existing varieties (20%). If this were natural selection, a 20% difference in fitness from one generation to the next would be tremendous and rare. At this strength, the curve falls far short of predicting a spread in about 13 years. The solid curve shows the predicted spread for a 50% advantage, which is capable of predicting a spread in the approximately 13 years it took for hybrid corn to diffuse. See Henrich (2001)

spread of hybrid corn. At the actual pay-off difference between hybrid corn and then-existing varieties, the spread would have been far slower than observed. A difference as large as 50% is needed to predict the diffusion of hybrid corn in 13 years. The actual spread lagged behind this prediction for as much as half of the diffusion period, but then accelerated, so clearly other forces were at work in this example (Henrich, 2001). For current purposes, note that whatever social learning mechanisms are at work here must magnify observed pay-off differences. Consider also that a 20% difference in yield is unlikely to result in a 20% difference in reproduction or survivorship important to natural selection on genes. Many other behaviours matter for aggregate fitness of an individual. Thus the magnitude of 'selection' in this case of cultural diffusion seems even larger in comparison to typical genetic estimates.

Because selective forces, arising from human psychology, that favour some variants over others may be strong, and especially strong relative to mixing, cultural evolution may produce outcomes that are very unlikely in genetic evolution. In this section, we explain one important case in which cultural evolutionary models produce equilibrium results that are possible, but highly unlikely, in analogous genetical models. As discussed in Henrich and McElreath (this volume, Chapter 38), other examples may include ethnic marking (McElreath et al., 2003) and ethnocentrism (Boyd and Richerson, 1985; Gil-White, 2001).

39.4.2. Group selection for altruistic behaviour

By focusing on competition among cultural groups (cultural group selection), several modelling efforts have demonstrated how the cultural transmission of behaviours related to cooperation and punishment may explain some otherwise puzzling patterns of human prosociality (Boyd and Richerson, 1985; Boyd et al., 2003). See Henrich (2004) and Henrich and Henrich (2006) for reviews. The reason these models can result in stable cooperative equilibria, while analogous genetical models cannot, is due to the plausibility of strong imitation forces opposing forces of mixing (Boyd et al., 2003).

Mixing is an enemy of altruism because selective forces can only produce altruism when the between-group variance in behaviour is large enough to overcome within-group selection opposing altruism. Price (1972) and later Hamilton (1975) showed that selection favours altruism when:

$$\text{var}(p_i)(w_i, p_i) > \text{E}(\text{var}(p_{ij})(w_{ij}, p_{ij})),$$

where p_i is the frequency of an altruism gene in population subdivision i, w_i is the average fitness in group i, and p_{ij} and w_{ij} are the frequency of altruism and fitness of individual j in group i, respectively. (x, y) indicates the slope of the linear regression of x on y $((\partial x/(\partial y))$. Thus the beta coefficients above are selection gradients for different components of fitness. In plain language, this condition can be read as:

> The product of the variance in altruism among groups and the rate of change in the average fitness of individuals in a group as a function of the number of altruists in the group
>
> **must exceed**
>
> the average product of the variance within each group and the rate of change in individuals' fitness as a function of the amount of altruism the individuals exhibit.

'Groups' here are defined by the scale at which helping behaviour benefits other individuals. Behaviours that aid brothers and behaviours that aid entire ethnic groups are both governed by this fact. However, common descent maintains genetic variation among kin groups, while variation among large groups is much harder to sustain. Mixing is very strong in animals like ourselves, leading to either very little equilibrium variance among large groups of individuals or the steady leaching away of variation (see the model by Rogers, 1990). If learning forces such as conformity effectively reduce mixing of cultural variants, then variation among groups can remain high enough to support group selection. There is nothing heretical about this statement. W. D. Hamilton himself saw kin selection as a special case of this general condition (see Hamilton, 1975). The key issue in any model of the evolution of altruism is what forces are available to maintain variation among groups.

In the cultural case, it is plausible, although hardly yet proven empirically, that strong learning dynamics combined with weak effective migration can result in more variance than analogous genetical models (Boyd *et al.*, 2003, models this process). This in turn might produce selection on culturally transmitted ideas that lead to self-sacrifice. Groups with such ideas may either defeat their neighbours in open conflict, because they can muster more fighters to the field of battle, or defend themselves better from aggression, because they can recruit more people to dig trenches, build walls, or mount a defence of arms.

We must caution the reader to avoid a mistake others have made in understanding this hypothesis. Cultural group selection trades off the very fact that human ethnic groups are well-mixed genetically, but still maintain appreciable cultural distinctiveness. Alleles for group-oriented self-sacrifice are unlikely to spread, because genes move among ethnic and other cultural groups quite often. However, this mixing does not always destroy cultural variation. Immigrants do not necessarily erode the variation in such ideas among groups, because immigrants may quickly conform to local beliefs, even though they cannot change their alleles. The group selection is on culturally transmitted beliefs, not on physical bodies. It is possible to construct a working cultural group selection model (Boyd and Richerson, 2002) in which comparison across groups generates the equilibrium shifts, not differential reproduction or survival of groups. In this case, the group selection may involve no differential death or birth of human bodies at all.

An effect like this might seem initially implausible. Would a system of phenotypic transmission like social learning, created by genetical evolution, actually lead to qualitatively different outcomes for an organism? But the evolution of sexual reproduction transformed how traits are inherited and created equally (if not more) novel evolutionary dynamics. Models of sexual selection of animal signals have no problem producing situations in which males produce and females prefer costly ornaments that lower the overall fitness of the population (Fisher, 1930; Lande, 1981). Few people have a problem calling such equilibria fundamentally Darwinian, even though evolution sometimes proceeds quite differently in sexual than asexual species. Similarly, we should not balk at noticing

that a genetically evolved system for acquiring behaviour via social learning might end up producing equilibria that are not the self-same ones the genes themselves would be selected to arrive at.

39.5. Gene–culture coevolution

Gullibility may be an adaptation, because critical thinking is costly.

Over the very long run, cultural dynamics cannot continue always to outrun genetics. Genes must have an eventual influence. One reason could be that, as variation among cultural variants diminishes, the rate of evolution will slow, and then lagging changes in genetic variants will become more important. Also, the cultural system should eventually reach some stationary distribution, even if it is stochastic. Then selection on genes, however slow, may determine how this equilibrium shifts. Even rates of change in classic organic evolution appear to vary on different scales (Penny, 2005). Thus it seems that ignoring genes in the long run is probably a mistake.

In this final section we present a very simple model of gene–culture coevolution. It helps to explain one way to model the joint evolution of transmission systems with very different rates of change. Also, this model allows us the opportunity to explain a few important predictions about behaviour that arise from gene–culture models.

39.5.1. When culture is much faster than genes

One way to deal with the difference in rates is to assume that the distribution of cultural variants reaches an equilibrium instantaneously, with respect to genetic evolution. The distribution of alleles then responds to this stationary distribution of cultural variants. Provided cultural dynamics are sufficiently faster than genetic ones, then this method yields a good approximation of the joint system dynamics. Boyd and Richerson (1985) and Rogers (1988) have used this tactic to derive joint evolutionary equilibria for simultaneous cultural and genetic recursions, without resorting to more-complex multi-dimensional techniques. Numerical analysis of the recursions shows that the infinitely-fast-culture assumption does not result in misleading results.

The basic problem is that the change in frequency of a single cultural variant can be represented in a one-dimensional system by the abstract function:

$$\Delta p = F(p).$$

This means we can compute the change in the frequency, if we know the current frequency. But if we add a simultaneous second recursion for genes that specify how culture is acquired, then we have a two-dimensional system with two functions:

$$\Delta p = F(p, q),$$
$$\Delta q = G(p, q).$$

Now we must know both the frequency of the cultural variant and the genes influencing social learning in order to find the change in either. The trick is to determine stability in such systems. In principle, stability in these two-dimensional systems can be solved with matrix techniques. However, if the cultural dynamics are fast enough relative to the genetic dynamics, the cultural dimension p will come to rest at its steady state, $\hat{p}$, very quickly. This can be true either because there are many opportunities to learn and update behaviour per selection event or because selection coefficients are weak, compared to the rate of change due to learning (see the previous section). If either is true, then the system arrives at a cultural equilibrium quickly, and q will respond to this value. As q changes under selection on genes, of course, $\hat{p}$ will also change. But now since p instantly reaches its steady state for any given value of q, we have a one-dimensional system again:

$$\Delta \hat{p} = F(q),$$
$$\Delta q = G(\hat{p}, q).$$

With such a system, all we have to worry about is the stability of the genetic equilibria. The cultural equilibrium just responds to it. You might think that this means the genes run the show, and that such a model produces the same outcomes as a culture-free model. But as we will demonstrate, not even the simplest models back up that intuition.

Here is a model in the spirit of Rogers (1988). We think this very simple model demonstrates the vulnerability of some commonly held beliefs about what kinds of behaviour we expect natural selection to produce. Imagine a simple organism capable of imitating the behaviour of older individuals, in addition to investing effort in updating behaviour through individual trial and error. We use the discrete formulation, but as with all models of this type, there is an equivalent continuous formulation (in which individuals do some imitation and some individual learning). Each generation, individuals learn according to an inherited allele (individual or social) and then receive pay-offs determined by whether what they have learned is adaptive under current circumstances.

First, a caveat. People sometimes complain that it is unrealistic to consider a pure 'social learning' strategy, because real people always make inferences while being influenced by the behaviour of others. We agree. All social learning depends upon individual psychology and how that process works. If we expressed this model in its completely equivalent continuous form, with a family of mixed strategies that rely upon a mix of individual and social influence, fewer people would complain. The version we present here is better for illustrating the insights we wish to draw from it. Models are like cartoons: there is an optimal amount of detail, and often that amount is very small. We caution readers of such models not to get hung up on vague words like 'social learning' that have different meanings in different sub-disciplines, but instead to attend to the structure of the assumptions. As others have shown, equivalent models can be derived under the assumption that individuals are entirely Bayesian updaters, but able to observe what other people do (Bikhchandani et al., 1992; Boyd and Richerson, 2005).

Suppose an infinite number of behaviours are possible, but only one is adaptive for current environmental circumstances and yields a pay-off B. All others yield a pay-off of zero. This assumption just sets the scale of pay-offs, so we lose no generality with it. The environment itself changes state, making a new behaviour optimal, with probability u each generation. When this happens, since there exists a very large number of possible behaviours, we assume that all existing behaviour in the population is rendered maladaptive. Individual learners pay a cost for experimentation and mistakes (C), but they always arrive at the currently adaptive behaviour. In contrast, social learners pay no upfront costs, but they just copy a random adult from the previous generation, so they have no guarantee of acquiring the *currently* adaptive behaviour.

With the above assumptions, we can write fitness expressions for each allele, I for individual learners and S for social learners. Let a be the frequency of currently adaptive behaviour among adults of the previous generation. Then:

$$W(I) = B - C,$$
$$W(S) = Ba.$$

The variable a is the frequency of adaptive behaviour at any one moment, but it changes over time. This implies a recursion for how a changes, and this process will depend upon how the population learns. Let L be the frequency of individual learners in the population. Then the frequency in the next generation is:

$$a' = u(0) + (1 - u)(L(1) + (1 - L)a)$$

The parameter u is the fraction of the time that the environment changes, rendering all past behaviour maladaptive, each generation. The rest of the time, L of the population learned for themselves and arrived at adaptive behaviour with certainty. The remaining $1 - L$ of the population imitates and transmits the previously adaptive frequency a.

Now we apply the assumption that cultural dynamics are much faster than genetic dynamics. This allows us to find the steady-state value of a, call this $\bar{a}$, for any given L. This exists where $a' = a$ and is:

$$\bar{a} = \frac{L(1 - u)}{1 - (1 - L)(1 - u)}.$$

Over the long run, the fitness of social learners will depend upon this value. We plug $\bar{a}$ into the expression for $W(S)$ and find the value of L that yields a genetic equilibrium, the end-point of the long-term selection on genes. The equilibrium frequency of individual learning, $\hat{L}$, turns out to be:

$$\hat{L} = \frac{B/C - 1}{1/u - 1}.$$

This expression tells us how the stable frequency of individual learning responds to the costs

of learning and the unpredictability of the environment. The quantity B/C is the ratio of the benefits of acquiring adaptive behaviour to the costs of learning it. As this goes down, learning is more costly, and the frequency of individual learning declines. The second effect is that as the environment becomes less predictable (u increases), the denominator decreases and the equilibrium frequency of individual learning increases. If the world is unstable, what your parents did may no longer be adaptive, so it pays more to think for yourself.

The most obvious result of this model is that natural selection can easily favour substantial amounts of social learning. Unless u is very large or B/C is very small, there will be a substantial frequency of social learners at equilibrium.

39.5.2. Gullibility as an adaptation

An interesting further deduction from the above model is the frequency of adaptive behaviour once genes also reach equilibrium. Call this $\hat{a}$. This is found by substituting the value of $\hat{L}$ for L in the expression for $\bar{a}$. After simplification:

$$\hat{a} = 1 - \frac{C}{B}.$$

This result is very interesting. Notice that it does not depend upon u. Natural selection adjusts learning in response to u so that, at equilibrium, the value of socially acquired behaviour, $\hat{a}$, is governed only by the cost of information. When the world is relatively stable from one generation to the next, there are more social learners at equilibrium, which reduces the expected value of socially acquired behaviour. However, the countervailing effect is that, in a more-stable world, adaptive behaviour has a better chance to accumulate, so a smaller number of individual learners can provide the same expected accuracy of behaviour as a large number, in an unstable world.

Richerson and Boyd (2005) call this effect the 'costly information hypothesis': when information about the world is costly to acquire, it pays to rely upon cheaper ways of learning. Consider what proportion of behaviour is adaptive to current circumstances, when C/B is very small, perhaps 1/100. In this case, because information is very cheap to acquire, most individuals (if not all) will be individual learners, and the expected accuracy of behaviour, $\hat{a}$, will be nearly 100%. But when information is costly, because it is dangerous, time consuming, or difficult to acquire and process, then the expected accuracy will be much smaller.

When we look at a population of animals and ask why they behave as they do, this model (and many others like it, see Boyd and Richerson, 1995) suggests it will be risky to assume that development (in this case, learning) is irrelevant to our explanations of what behaviour we will see. If the costs of information are high, then substantial portions of the population will be practising maladaptive behaviour.

Moreover, this will be the optimal strategy, from the point of view of the genes. Any more individual learning would not be an equilibrium, even though it would lead to more accurate behaviour. What is happening is that social learning saves fitness costs at one point in the life cycle, only to pay other fitness costs later. Even models of cumulative culture (Boyd and Richerson, 1996) show the same trade-off. When we sample behaviours, we might not notice the information-gathering costs paid by individual learners and conclude that individual learning has higher fitness, because on average individual learners practice more-accurate behaviour.

The social learners in this very stylized model are gullible. They believe whatever the previous generation demonstrates. In this case, gullibility is an adaptation, because the costs one would have to pay to verify all the suggested behaviour in the world would be too great. Some individual learning is always favoured, because otherwise the population cannot track the environment at all. But large doses of gullibility can be adaptive, because information is costly.

Our impression of real human societies is that many people will believe nearly anything you tell them, at least at first. Many readers of this chapter will be successful students or professional scholars, who have substantial experience with teaching. Isn't it amazing that students are willing to take our word on so many abstruse topics? We think models like this one suggest an answer: being gullible when a problem is abstruse is adaptive, because it is often beyond the individual's means alone to verify the accuracy of it. If we insisted on learning everything for ourselves, we would miss out on many very adaptive solutions. Given how hard it is for agricultural scientists to decide what crops in what proportions to plant, it seems implausible that many real agriculturists, who have to live off their produce, can afford to experiment and analyse their year-to-year yields (Henrich, 2002).

The cost of being adaptively gullible may be that we are sometimes, perhaps often, led astray. The universal existence of magical thinking might be a symptom of this trade-off. After all, if you cannot disprove that there are dangerous spirits in the forest, it may be best to just trust that there are. We think this possibility is provocative, because it suggests that behavioural maladaptation in some domains may be a standard feature of human societies, even in our proper evolutionary niche. Clearly some of the non-adaptive things humans do, like gorge on fatty foods, are probably products of our minds being adapted to a world in which fatty foods were rare. But this kind of out-of-equilibrium explanation of maladaptive behaviour is not the only possibility. If the above model captures the texture of human cultural adaptations, then even in Pleistocene environments, human societies probably showed widespread non-adaptive and maladaptive behaviours, because such behaviours are a side-effect of relying upon social learning as an adaptation. Thus we suspect that even Pleistocene foragers did a lot of 'silly' things, from the perspective of genetic fitness. This would not mean that culture, as a system of behavioural evolution, is a maladaptation, any more than that the cost of producing sons means that sexual reproduction is a maladaptation. But it would unfortunately mean that predicting behaviour is harder than simply applying optimality criteria. It would mean that both development and population dynamics are central to Darwinian explanations of individual behaviour.

References

Bikhchandani, S., Hirshleifer, D. and Welch, I. (1992) A theory of fads, fashion, custom, and cultural change as informational cascades. *Journal of Political Economy*, 100: 992–1026.

Boone, J. and Smith, E. (1998) Is it evolution yet? A critique of evolutionary archaeology. *Current Anthropology*, 39: 141–173.

Boyd, R. (1982) Density-dependent mortality and the evolution of social interactions. *Animal Behaviour*, 30: 972–982.

Boyd, R. and Richerson, P. J. (1985) *Culture and the Evolutionary Process*. University of Chicago Press, Chicago.

Boyd, R. and Richerson, P. J. (1995) Why does culture increase human adaptability? *Ethology and Sociobiology*, 16: 125–143.

Boyd, R. and Richerson, P. (1996) Why culture is common, but cultural evolution is rare. *Proceedings of the British Academy*, 88: 77–93.

Boyd, R. and Richerson, P. J. (2002) Group beneficial norms spread rapidly in a structured population. *Journal of Theoretical Biology*, 215: 287–296.

Boyd, R. and Richerson, P. J. (2005) Rationality, imitation, and tradition. In *The Origin and Evolution of Cultures*, chapter 18, pp. 379–396. Oxford University Press, Oxford.

Boyd, R., Gintis, H., Bowles, S. and Richerson, P. J. (2003) The evolution of altruistic punishment. *Proceedings of the National Academy of Sciences of the USA*, 100: 3531–3535.

Cavalli-Sforza, L. L. and Feldman, M. W. (1981) *Cultural Transmission and Evolution: A Quantitative Approach*. Princeton University Press, Princeton.

Dawkins, R. (1982) *The Extended Phenotype: The Long Reach of the Gene*. Oxford University Press, Oxford.

Durham, W. H. (1991) *Coevolution: Genes, Culture, and Human Diversity*. Stanford University Press, Stanford.

Endler, J. (1986) *Natural Selection in the Wild*. Princeton University Press, Princeton.

Fisher, R. A. (1918) The correlation between relatives on the supposition of Mendelian inheritance. *Transactions of the Royal Society of Edinburgh*, 52: 399–433.

Fisher, R. A. (1930) *The Genetical Theory of Natural Selection*. Dover, New York.

Gil-White, F. J. (2001) Are ethnic groups biological 'species' to the human brain?: Essentialism in our cognition of some social categories. *Current Anthropology*, 42: 515–554.

Gintis, H. (2000) *Game Theory Evolving*. Princeton University Press, Princeton.

Grant, B. R. and Grant, P. R. (1993) Evolution of Darwin's finches caused by a rare climatic event. *Proceedings of the Royal Society London, B*, 251: 111–117.

Hamilton, W. D. (1975) Innate social aptitudes of man: an approach from evolutionary genetics. In R. Fox (ed.) *Biosocial Anthropology*, pp. 133–153. Malaby Press, London.

Henrich, J. (2001) Cultural transmission and the diffusion of innovations: adoption dynamics indicate that biased cultural transmission is the predominate force in behavioral change and much of sociocultural evolution. *American Anthropologist*, 103: 992–1013.

Henrich, J. (2002) Decision-making, cultural transmission and adaptation in economic anthropology. In J. Ensminger (ed.) *Theory in Economic Anthropology*, pp. 251–295. AltaMira Press.

Henrich, J. (2004) Cultural group selection, coevolutionary processes and large-scale cooperation. *Journal of Economic Behavior and Organization*, 53: 3–35.

Henrich, J. and Boyd, R. (2002) On modeling cognition and culture: why replicators are not necessary for cultural evolution. *Journal of Cognition and Culture*, 2: 87–112.

Henrich, N. and Henrich, J. (2006) *The Origins of Cooperation: A Cultural and Evolutionary Exploration Among the Iraqi Chaldeans of Metro-Detroit*. Oxford University Press, New York.

Henrich, J., Boyd, R. and Richerson, P. J. (in press) Five common mistakes in cultural evolution. In D. Sperber (ed.) *Epidemiology of Ideas*. Open Court Publishing.

Jablonka, E. and Lamb, M. (2005) *Evolution in Four Dimensions*. MIT Press, Cambridge, MA.

Jablonka, E. and Lamb, R. M. (1991) Sex chromosomes and speciation. *Proceedings of the Royal Society of London, B*, 243: 203–208.

Jenkin, F. (1864) The origin of species. *North British Review*, 46: 277–318.

Lande, R. (1981) Models of speciation by sexual selection on polygenic traits. *Proceedings of the National Academy of Sciences USA*, 78: 3721–3725.

Leimar, O. (1996) Life history analysis of the Trivers–Willard sex-ratio problem. *Behavioral Ecology*, 7: 316–325.

Maynard Smith, J. (1990) Models of a dual inheritance system. *Journal of Theoretical Biology*, 143: 41–53.

Maynard Smith, J. (1998) *Evolutionary Genetics*. Oxford University Press, Oxford.

McElreath, R., Boyd, R. and Richerson, P. J. (2003) Shared norms and the evolution of ethnic markers. *Current Anthropology*, 44: 122–129.

Odling-Smee, F. J., Laland, K. N. and Feldman, M. W. (2003) *Niche Construction: The Neglected Process in Evolution. Monographs in Population Biology*, No. 37. Princeton University Press, Princeton.

Pääbo, S. (2001) The human genome and our view of ourselves. *Science*, 16: 1219–1220.

PáC. and Miklós, I. (1999) Epigenetic inheritance, genetic assimilation and speciation. *Journal of Theoretical Biology*, 200: 19–37.

Penny, D. (2005) Relativity for molecular clocks. *Nature*, 436: 183–184.

Price, G. R. (1972) Extension of covariance selection mathematics. *Annals of Human Genetics*, 35: 485–490.

Richerson, P. J. and Boyd, R. (2005) *Not by Genes Alone: How Culture Transformed Human Evolution*. University of Chicago Press, Chicago.

Rogers, A. R. (1988) Does biology constrain culture? *American Anthropologist*, 90: 819–831.

Rogers, A. R. (1990) Group selection by selective emigration: the effects of migration and kin structure. *American Naturalist*, 135: 398–413.

Ryan, B. and Gross, N. (1943) The diffusion of hybrid seed corn in two Iowa communities. *Rural Sociology*, 8: 15–24.

Sheahan, M. B., Rose, R. J. and McCurdy, D. W. (2004) Organelle inheritance in plant cell division: the actin cytoskeleton is required for unbiased inheritance of chloroplasts, mitochondria and endoplasmic reticulum in dividing protoplasts. *Plant Journal*, 37: 379–390.

Silk, J. B. and Boyd, R. (1983) Female cooperation, competition, and mate choice in matrilineal macaque groups. In S. K. Wasser (ed.) *Social Behavior of Female Vertebrates*, pp. 315–347. Academic Press, New York.

Sperber, D. (2000) An objection to the memetic approach to culture. In R. Aunger (ed.) *Darwinizing Culture: The Status of Memetics as a Science*, pp. 163–173. Oxford University Press, Oxford.

Sperber, D. and Hirschfeld, L. A. (2004) The cognitive foundations of cultural stability and diversity. *Trends in Cognitive Sciences*, 8: 40–46.

Stark, R. (2005) *The Rise of Mormonism*. Columbia University Press, New York.

Szathmáry, E. and Maynard Smith, J. (1995) The major evolutionary transitions. *Nature*, 374: 227–232.

CHAPTER 40

Evolutionary perspectives in archaeology: from culture history to cultural evolution

Stephen Shennan

40.1. Introduction

When prehistoric archaeology began as a discipline in Europe in the late nineteenth century it was in a climate of nationalism. It had became apparent to nationalist intellectuals that the increasing quantities of archaeological material that were being found as a result of expanding industrialization could potentially be used to trace a history of 'peoples' into the remote past. This depended on establishing a relationship between records of such peoples in ancient sources and sets of material remains whose origins could then be traced still further back into pre-literate antiquity. It was soon clear that this involved two main descriptive tasks: identifying patterns of similarity and difference in space and placing them in time. This was archaeology as culture history: identifying prehistoric cultures and putting them in order. It implied tracing histories of social information transmission and identifying breaks in transmission, spatial and chronological. The factors that were believed to produce the continuities and discontinuities in traditions were migration and diffusion.

This concern with culture history was more or less universal in the first half of the twentieth century and continues to be significant today. However, in the 1960s the main emphasis in Anglo-American archaeology shifted from a concern with the tracing of traditions, migration and diffusion to a new interest in adaptation: explaining changes in material culture as the result of new social and economic patterns, from the emergence of social hierarchies to the adoption of new subsistence systems such as agriculture. The motor for change came from the environment: new conditions produced appropriate adaptive reactions. This new approach had little time for history. The task of this New Archaeology was to come up with 'laws of culture process'.

The adaptationist perspective did not so much solve the problems that the culture historians were interested in; by and large it simply ignored them. The emerging recognition in the 1980s that this was the case, together with a growing awareness of the sociology of knowledge and the impact of political interests on interpretation, led many archaeologists to a rejection of scientifically based empirical methods for making inferences about the prehistoric past and to the adoption of an 'anything goes' approach to the production of 'stories about the past'.

A different perspective began to be taken by a much smaller group of archaeologists and anthropologists. They took the view that a scientific approach to the past remained possible and that evolutionary biology provided a model for how studies of adaptation and the history of cultural traditions could actually be integrated with one another in a way that did justice to both. Further than that, they argued, since the study of human culture from an evolutionary perspective is so new and underdeveloped, anthropological and archaeological case-studies can contribute to the development of the necessary new cultural evolutionary theory.

The use of Darwinian evolutionary models to understand patterns of social, economic and cultural change in the prehistoric past is now becoming increasingly well established (e.g. Neiman, 1997; O'Brien and Lyman, 2000; Dominguez, 2002; Nagaoka, 2002; Shennan, 2002; Stiner and Munro, 2002). This paper will demonstrate the role of evolutionary approaches in archaeology by focusing on four different topics that have long been of interest to archaeologists of virtually all theoretical persuasions. It will examine how evolutionary theory can be used to illuminate them by presenting specific concrete examples. The four topics concern different but interrelated histories: of foraging adaptations, human populations, social institutions and cultural patterns. Addressing these topics on the basis of archaeological data from an evolutionary point of view involves making use of several different strands from the range of complementary and sometimes conflicting evolutionary approaches to understanding human behaviour (Smith, 2000).

Clearly, if we think of archaeology as a field for developing cultural evolutionary theory or testing evolutionary models, as opposed to merely interpreting archaeological data in the light of evolutionary theory, then it has serious disadvantages: there is no possibility of experimentally manipulating relevant variables nor is it possible to observe mechanisms and processes directly. On the other hand, archaeology provides unique quantitative information on population-level distributions of cultural attributes over long periods of time. This information concerns not only socially transmitted cultural traditions but also the ongoing process of niche construction. In many cases we actually know far more about the day-to-day material life of communities living thousands of years ago whose settlements have been excavated than we do about modern ones. Moreover, the archaeological data capture variation, essential to evolutionary analysis, as opposed to the generalized normative accounts provided by most sociologists and ethnographers. The value of this information is now being greatly enhanced by the increasing quantities of data that are becoming available on potential external selective factors operating over long periods of time, for example climate change. Nowhere are these points clearer than in the study of past foraging adaptations.

40.2. **Foraging adaptations**

There is a major distinction within evolutionary approaches to human behaviour between human behavioural ecology (HBE) and those viewpoints that attach a significant role to culture, in particular, dual-inheritance theory. Such a distinction has also long been present within archaeology, and indeed goes back to the adaptationist 'New Archaeology' of the 1960s referred to above. On the adaptationist view, now superseded by human behavioural ecology, the motor of change comes from the environment; humans have the behavioural plasticity, and the capacities honed by millions of years of natural selection, to respond to changes in ways that tend to maximize their survival and reproductive success. When new technologies are helpful to exploit new situations, necessity is the mother of invention. Thus, culture is largely an irrelevance and everything comes down to individual cost–benefit decision-making. From the dual-inheritance perspective, in contrast, history matters. What solutions, if any, are found to new subsistence problems is likely to depend, for example, on patterns and processes of information diffusion and will not arise simply as a response to environmental stimuli. Unsurprisingly perhaps, the main framework for studies of the history of past foraging adaptations in archaeology has been

HBE, and specifically the application of optimal-foraging theory.

The archaeological application of optimal-foraging theory is different from its use in an ethnographic context in two major respects. First, there is the matter of methodology. It is obviously impossible for archaeologists to go out with the foragers they are studying, time how long they are hunting or collecting, and then calculate the calorific value of the food they have obtained. Archaeologists must find a way of obtaining equivalent information from the residues surviving on archaeological sites. Since plant remains tend to survive less well than animal remains and are also more problematical to quantify, the majority of such archaeological studies have looked at animal bones. Key predictions derived from the assumptions of optimal-foraging theory are incorporated in the diet breadth model, which proposes that the highest-return diet will only include the small number of resources that provide the best return for a given amount of effort. When these are scarce, foragers do not have the option of passing up those giving lower returns; they have to include these as well, so the number of species taken increases. Accordingly, one of the ways in which archaeologists can explore optimal-foraging theory ideas is by finding a way of using assemblages of animal bones to measure diet breadth or alternative indicators of the exploitation of high-return versus low-return resources.

Important though these methodological issues are when it comes to actually operationalizing the ideas of optimal-foraging theory in an archaeological context, they would be irrelevant if archaeology did not differ from conventional ethnographic human behavioural ecology in another important respect: the window it offers on human environmental exploitation in the past, and the extent to which it followed optimal-foraging principles. Nobody ever systematically wrote down such things and the pictures the ethnographers provide are no more than static snapshots of a single moment in time. By ethnographic observation it is possible to establish whether people's behaviour at a particular moment corresponds to optimal-foraging predictions, but that does not tell us about the long-term history of resource exploitation—for example, what people actually did when their highest-return resources became too rare to produce a living, or indeed what happens to the human population when such resources decline. Over the long term that archaeologists are interested in, people do not just have an impact on resources; the availability of resources has an impact on people.

Finally, archaeology is the only source of information that can help to resolve a specific issue which is often raised in critiques of ethnographic optimal-foraging analyses. This is the suggestion that insofar as modern people living traditional lives follow optimal-foraging principles, it is because they have been 'contaminated' by capitalist values as result of their involvement on the periphery of the modern world-system over the last 500 years. Archaeology can tell us whether or not people behaved as optimal foragers even in the Palaeolithic.

Archaeological examples of the application of HBE principles, optimal-foraging theory in particular, are now legion, but an excellent illustration is provided by the work of Stiner and Munro (2002) on changing patterns of small-game exploitation in the Levant between c.50 and 10 KYA, based on an assessment of the amount of work involved in the capture of different species. By c.50–40 KYA there is evidence for predation pressure on tortoises, with a decrease in the size of specimens taken. Not only are these easy to catch but their reproductive rates are low. What happens in the later Palaeolithic is an increasing trend towards the exploitation of fast-moving small game, such as hare, rabbits and partridges, which are much more resilient to exploitation but more difficult to obtain. Stiner and Munro's analysis focused in particular on the Natufian period (c.13–10 KYA), and the faunal remains from the site of Hayonim cave. For the first three Natufian phases, the proportion of fast-moving small game is high and of slow-moving game low, but, contrary to what might be expected, in the last two phases the situation is reversed, with slow-moving game now in the majority. It appears that these slow-moving game populations were able to recover and that exploitation was now not sufficiently intense to reduce them again. What we know independently from regional data on site sizes and occupation intensities is that, in the Early Natufian phase, sites were large and occupation intensity was high. In the Later Natufian, occupation was more sporadic and sites were smaller. The beginning of this phase corresponds with the onset of the Younger Dryas cold and dry climatic phase *c.*11 KYA, which seems to have resulted in lower carrying capacities and a human response of decreasing population (through emigration) and decreased completed family sizes, or a combination of the two. Only at the end of the Younger Dryas did populations start to rise again, at the same time as the beginnings of cereal agriculture.

Cases such as this demonstrate the power of the optimal-foraging approach in generating convincing explanations of patterning in the archaeological record, the long-standing importance of evolutionarily based optimality principles to the behaviour of human groups, and the capacity of the archaeological record to provide information on this topic. It has even been suggested (Kelly, 1995, p. 90) that archaeological data may be better than ethnographic records in this respect because the time-averaging processes that create the archaeological record will smooth out random short-term variations and reveal robust patterns more clearly. Of course, optimality predictions will not always be fulfilled, but when they are not the reasons are bound to be interesting and only the application of the theory makes it possible to recognize anomalies that need explaining.

Optimal-foraging theory and the associated calculus of costs and benefits thus seems to be the obvious starting point for any archaeological study of past economies. But it is essentially acultural and involves no more than assuming that humans, like other animals, are good at picking up relevant environmental cues and acting appropriately on them in ways that are likely to maximize their survival and reproductive success. However, it is reasonable to ask whether these optimal decisions are based on individual trial-and-error learning or some sort of biased cultural transmission process (for example copying the most successful foragers in the community). For the human behavioural ecologist, as opposed to the dual-inheritance theorist, this is really an irrelevance, but the archaeological record may in some circumstances be able to throw light on it.

The data from prehistoric-lake village sites in Switzerland (*c.*6000–4500 KYA) offer great possibilities in this respect because sites can be extremely accurately dated through the use of dendrochronology. A study by Schibler *et al.* (1997) of through-time fluctuations in the proportional and absolute frequencies of wild and domestic animal bones, reflecting the changing importance of hunting versus livestock keeping, showed that they were often quite sharp and sudden. It was demonstrated that they related to climatic fluctuations and also to the increase in forest clearance over time, both independently evidenced, rather than to socially transmitted traditions of what absolute or proportional amount of the diet should come from eating hunted as opposed to domestic animals. Moreover, the patterns cross-cut the contemporary cultural patterns identified on the basis of pottery-making traditions, which certainly are socially transmitted. When cultural transmission is the predominating force in determining the form and prevalence of a tradition we do not expect to see radical changes from one short time-step to the next. If we put pottery assemblages in chronological order, for example, we expect chronologically adjacent ones to be similar to one another and thus to show a relatively smooth pattern of changes through time (O'Brien and Lyman, 2000, Chapter 6). If adjacent assemblages do not tend to be similar then we have to doubt whether we have evidence of a socially learned tradition. Equally, a sudden very marked alteration in what appears to be such a tradition is an indication that the tradition has been broken.

In the Swiss case the chronological resolution is so good that for much of the record only 10 years separates successive observations. Thus, even if biased transmission processes, such as copying the most successful, were instrumental in converging onto a given degree of reliance on hunting, they must have been so fast as to be archaeologically invisible since the resulting pattern seems to have been determined by the costs and benefits. This stands out all the more strongly against the pattern of change in the ceramic styles associated with the faunal assemblages, which, as noted above, are known to be determined largely by social learning.

40.3. Population history and natural selection on cultural traditions: the spread of cereal agriculture into Europe, c.11.5–7KYA

As pointed out already, optimal-foraging theory is completely acultural and assumes no more than the behavioural plasticity characteristic of all complex animals. For a Darwinian theory of culture, such as dual-inheritance theory, to be relevant to archaeology we need to entertain the possibility that culture is subject to natural selection—or rather that cultural traditions, like genes, are relevant to variations between individuals in their survival and reproductive success, and that these differences affect the prevalence of the traditions in the next generation. This is by no means easy for archaeology to achieve. We may be able to show, for example, that a particular type of stone tool increases in frequency through time, but it is virtually impossible to relate this to survival or reproductive rates in the population, which is what is required to infer that its frequency is affected by natural selection. One case where it is possible—where we can show that a particular practice leads to greater reproductive success and that the cultural transmission of the practices associated with that success also occurs—concerns the origin and spread of farming in the Near East and Europe.

Farming in western Eurasia began in the so-called Fertile Crescent of the Near East c.12 KYA. This is now clear both from archaeological evidence and from recent genetic studies which show that sheep and goat, cattle and the key cereals were domesticated only once, or in some cases perhaps twice, in this region (Zohary, 1999; Bollongino *et al.*, 2005). Already by 11.5 KYA, early farming groups had colonized the island of Cyprus (Peltenburg *et al.*, 2001) and this was only the beginning of an expansion which within 4 K years had reached the Atlantic coast of Portugal and the Low Countries of north-west Europe, not to mention areas far to the east of the Fertile Crescent (for an overview see Harris, 1996). How this new adaptation emerged, and the factors affecting its emergence, remain unclear (see e.g. Richerson *et al.*,

2001; Colledge *et al.*, 2004). However, once it did emerge it had the potential to sustain higher population densities than previous adaptations, meaning that for a time people locally had the chance to achieve greater reproductive success than previously, until a new ceiling was reached. New adaptations will be especially successful if dispersal opportunities are available to the populations practising them (Voland, 1998), so that when a local ceiling has been reached expansion can continue elsewhere. The spread of farming into Europe can be regarded as a classic example of a dispersal opportunity.

In large parts of Europe, away from coastal and riverine areas with rich aquatic resources, Mesolithic hunter-gatherer population densities were very low. However, the areas with low population densities included zones that were very suitable for growing cereal crops and could thus sustain much higher densities of farmers than hunter-gatherers. Moreover, the combination of annual cereals and domestic animals, in addition to supporting higher population densities and therefore greater reproductive success before a new higher ceiling was reached, was extremely portable, far more so than many other agricultural systems. The result was a process of demic diffusion, which would have subsumed the small hunter-gatherer populations existing in the areas initially occupied by early farmers. In other words, this is a classic example of natural selection acting on people through an inherited cultural tradition, which gave a selective advantage to those who adopted it and passed it on to their children. In fact, the process involved not simply the inheritance of a tradition but also the transmission of a new niche, since the actual descendants of the cereal crops and animals that had originally been domesticated were being carried along as part of the dispersal.

The visible evidence of the success of the agriculturally based dispersal process in natural selection terms for the human population is seen not only in the greatly increased density of human settlement in those areas where farming arrived, but also in the demographic profiles of prehistoric cemeteries in Europe and western Asia, as Bocquet-Appel (2002) has shown. Prior to the arrival of farming, population growth rates inferred from cemetery populations were at or just below replacement level; afterwards they were growing, albeit at varying rates. On the basis of studies of the number, size and density of settlements of the first farmers in Central Europe, Petrasch (2001, 2005) has calculated population growth rates of between 0.9% and 2.7% for the first farming societies in this area. In detail, the expansion process seems to have involved the colonization of patches favourable to the new economy, rather than uniform expansion (van Andel and Runnels, 1995), hence the rapidity with which it occurred in many areas.

Underlying the above account is evolutionary life-history theory. The archaeological record can, if approached in the right way, provide us with the evidence for macro-scale population outcomes arising from individual decision-making over time in individual regions, and therefore of reproductive success histories. Through life-history theory we can postulate well-founded models. These make sense of many patterns in population history and their relation to such processes as the spread of agriculture which are inexplicable in terms of traditional frameworks. Furthermore, the population patterns have major implications in the cultural domain. The adaptive processes associated with reproductive decisions in particular times and places produce specific population histories which can carry cultural traditions with them, and also lead to their demise. This is certainly not the only process through which cultural patterns are propagated and disappear, but it is an important one.

40.4. **Social institutions**

The use of archaeological evidence to provide an evolutionary history of social institutions can be illustrated by focusing on the consequences of this same agricultural expansion at a more localized scale and making use of the principle of the 'ideal despotic distribution' from population ecology (Sutherland, 1996) as a basis for understanding the consequences of the patch colonization process that the spread of farming into Europe involved (van Andel and Runnels, 1995). The 'ideal free distribution' proposes that individuals occupy the resource patch which gives them the best returns. As more individuals occupy the patch, the returns to each individual

decline, to the point that the returns to an individual from the best patch are no better than those from the next best patch which has no occupants. Once the returns from both patches are equal, they will be occupied indiscriminately until such time as the population grows to the point at which there is an equal benefit to be gained by occupying a still worse patch, and the process is repeated. When there is territoriality, however, the situation is different. Here the 'ideal despotic distribution' applies. The first individual occupying the area is able to select the best territory in the best patch. Subsequent individuals settling there do not affect the first arrival, but have to take the next best territory, and so on, until there comes a point where the next settler will do just as well by taking the best territory in the next best patch. Subsequent individuals will then take territories in either patch where the territories are equally suitable. In contrast to the ideal free distribution, where new settlers decrease the mean return for everybody, including those who arrived first, in the case of the ideal despotic distribution the returns depend on the order of settlement, so that the initial settlers of the best territory in the patch will do best, so long as they can defend the territory against anyone who might seek to take it from them.

It is apparent in those areas where detailed archaeological work has been carried out, particularly in Central Europe, that over time these local early farming societies became more unequal. The evidence for this comes from both their settlements and their cemeteries. In the settlements, some houses were larger than others and had granaries (van der Velde, 1990). In some cases, these houses also had more stone artefacts made of exotic raw materials that would have had to be obtained by exchange; in others, there is evidence of higher proportions of domestic animal bones being associated with large houses and more remains of hunted animals with smaller ones (Hachem, 2000). It also seems that, within settlements, particular households and groups of households continued through time, with continuing inheritance of status witnessed by the rebuilding of houses of the same type in the same places. Over time, the proportional frequency of small houses as opposed to large ones increased, suggesting growing inequality. As far as burials are concerned, it is clear that the earliest cemeteries present a picture of relatively egalitarian societies, with indications of achieved status for older men, while the later ones tend to have a small group of graves, including child burials, clearly distinguished from the rest by the presence of markedly richer grave-goods and probable symbols of power (Jeunesse, 1997).

These developments are best accounted for in terms of the logic of the ideal despotic distribution. The first-comers to favourable settlement patches were able to settle in the best locations; indeed, the founding settlements invariably remained the most important ones. Despite the high population growth rate there was initially no competition between different groups because, as new households were formed, they were able to move to favourable locations in adjacent patches—indeed, this is what made the population growth possible. However, individual micro-regions began to fill up relatively rapidly. This did not affect the suitability of the area for those who had already established themselves there, because success depended on having a territory and they controlled the best ones. Cemeteries would have come into existence to represent an ancestral claim to territory (van der Velde, 2000, cited in Zimmermann, 2002) in the face of increasing competition as local carrying capacities began to be reached.

Strontium and oxygen isotope analyses of human skeletons make it possible to infer whether people spent the early part of their lives in the same region as they were buried. Analyses of the skeletons of the first farmers in Central Europe (Bentley et al., 2002) suggest that, when farmers first arrived, there was fairly general mobility but that in the later phases it was mainly women that moved. This would point to the emergence of patrilineal corporate groups. One can postulate that over time the senior line of the lineage in a given patch would have maintained control of the prime location and its territory and is represented archaeologically by the larger houses in the founding settlements. The junior branches, on the other hand, would be in increasingly inferior positions and would have relatively little option to go elsewhere because the same process was going on everywhere around them, hence the increasing number of smaller houses in the settlements.

One can further speculate that once local patches became full, contest competition between lineages would have become increasingly important and members of the senior line would increasingly have had to assert their position in order to maintain it. In such a context the deposition of rich grave-goods in some burials in the later phases of the first farmer occupation, referred to above, should probably be seen as a form of costly signalling (Bliege Bird and Smith, 2005). In this case, the number of rich burials would not simply be a reflection of the size of the senior lineage but of the competitive pressure it was under in particular places and times.

At the local level, then, the requirements of the agricultural economy, as mediated through the population processes characterized by the ideal despotic distribution, created new social institutions as a result of new selection pressures. These redefined the form and nature of social competition and by implication would also have had natural selection consequences leading to differential reproductive success among the descendants of particular lineage founders. Unfortunately, the data and methodologies currently available do not enable us to test this latter idea. To that extent, it may be argued that what has been presented is no more than a plausible scenario described in evolutionary terms. The example certainly does not provide a test of the ideal despotic distribution model or of the extent to which it might apply to humans. Nevertheless, the model provides a strong set of natural-selection-based predictions about the kinds of things that happen during colonization processes; more importantly, perhaps, the available archaeological evidence, which has been interpreted in similar ways to those above by others who have not adopted this framework, corresponds very closely to what the model predicts.

40.5. Cultural drift

The previous example of the spread of farming showed how a set of culturally transmitted practices, and the constructed niches that went along with them, had a profound effect in giving a reproductive advantage, in comparison with hunting and gathering, to people who adopted those practices and passed them on to their children.

However, just as gene frequencies are subject to the effects of drift as well as selection, so it is possible to entertain the possibility that cultural attributes, in addition to the various selection and biased transmission processes which may affect them, may also be subject to the process of drift, random variation in the replicative success of particular cultural practices, dependent on the sampling effects of copying in finite populations. Even if no other processes are operating, some variants will be copied more frequently and some less frequently than others. This idea has been current for a long time in archaeology and anthropology in various guises but it was Neiman (1995) who showed how genetic drift models could be used as a basis for generating quantitative predictions about the neutrality or otherwise of the processes affecting distributions of cultural variants through time. In effect, they provide the basis for a null hypothesis. If a particular distribution fails to depart from neutrality, there is no reason to postulate anything other than drift as the process producing it (Bentley et al., 2004). If there is a departure, then something further needs to be invoked to account for it (see Shennan and Wilkinson, 2001). It is important to note that drift as a process can only exist in the context of an evolutionary model which includes transmission. It has no role in HBE, nor in any other approach which lacks an inheritance concept.

If neutrality holds, then the diversity of an assemblage, θ, will be a function of the innovation rate and the effective population size. Since, for any given assemblage, we will know the number of different decorative variants present and the assemblage size, we can insert the relevant numerical values into an equation produced by Ewens (1972) to obtain the value of θ_{pre}, the predicted diversity if drift is the only process operating (Neiman, 1995):

$$E(k) = \sum_{i=0}^{n=1} \frac{\theta_{pre}}{\theta_{pre} + i}$$

where $E(k)$ is the expected number of different variants and n corresponds to the assemblage size.

This may be compared with the actual diversity value, θ_{obs} obtained from the data by squaring the proportional frequencies of each variant and summing the resulting values:

$$\theta_{obs} = \frac{1}{\sum_i p_i^2} - 1$$

where p_i represents the proportional frequency of the ith decorative variant.

Predicted and observed values were obtained for the decorative motifs from a series of pottery assemblages from early farming sites in southwest Germany, where each assemblage came from a single phase at a single site (Shennan and Bentley, in press). Some phases were represented at several sites, others at only one. The correlation between the predicted and observed values was high ($r = 0.75$, $P < 0.000$, $v = 26$). In addition, the mean of the pairwise differences between the two was not significantly different from zero ($t = 1.025$, $P = 0.315$). Plots of the predicted and actual diversity values for each of the successive phases of this early farming culture showed the same pattern of increasing diversity with a decrease at the end (Figure 40.1).

It appears that in this case the patterns in the frequency and diversity distributions of the decorative motifs from each site-phase assemblage are neutral and therefore solely a function of the rate of innovation of new decorative motifs and of the effective population size. Looked at from the perspective of any single site, both the innovation rate and the effective population size depend to some extent on the amount of inter-site interaction. If there is more interaction between pottery makers at different sites, then the effective population size will be greater. In addition though, under neutrality greater interaction will also mean that motifs currently not existing locally will be copied from other places and will thus represent local innovations (this corresponds to migration in genetic models). It appears that in the case of the pottery of the early farmers from south-west Germany we have evidence for a trend of gradually increasing then decreasing interaction, and a corresponding trend in absolute population size (with actual diversity as dependent and inter-site similarity and a proxy population

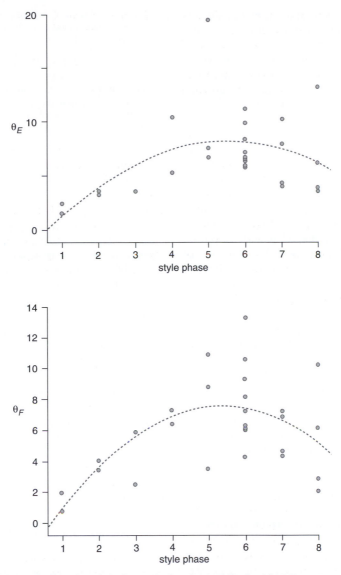

Fig. 40.1 (a) The neutral diversity values for each site phase plotted against the sequence of phases. A least-squares regression line has been fitted to the data. $r = 0.52$. Both the linear and quadratic component are significant ($P < 0.05$). **(b)** The actual diversity values for each site phase plotted against the sequence of phases. A least-squares regression line has been fitted to the data. $r = 0.62$. Both the linear and quadratic component are significant ($P < 0.005$).

measure as independents: $R = 0.6$; partial r between diversity and inter-site similarity controlling for the population proxy $= 0.43$, $P = 0.046$; between diversity and population proxy controlling for inter-site similarity $r = 0.36$, $P = 0.1$, $n = 23$).

It is important to emphasize, however, that such analyses do not always fail to reject the null hypothesis of neutrality. Kohler *et al.*'s (2004) study of diversity in pottery styles in prehistoric New Mexico showed that the assemblages were less diverse than predicted by the model, despite increased local population size. The authors concluded that conformist transmission was operating as one element in a process of enhancing cooperation within larger groups. Shennan and Wilkinson's (2001) study in contrast showed an emerging pattern of excess diversity, pointing to a bias in favour of novelty.

40.6. Conclusion

It would be idle to pretend that disentangling the histories of foraging strategies, cultural traditions, social institutions and human populations is straightforward. However, the examples presented in this paper show that a variety of different archaeological phenomena, from changing animal bone frequencies, through burial patterns to pottery decoration distributions are explicable in terms of various evolutionary processes. The fact that these explanations are based on a set of well-founded theoretical premises that have already received a lot of support from other disciplines and the subjects they study, as opposed to being an *ad hoc* set of accommodative inferences, greatly strengthens the probability that they contain some truth. Archaeology does have some unique advantages as a domain of cultural evolutionary study through the access it gives us to the long term, and because archaeological data are inherently suited to providing quantitative information on diachronic variation, in contrast to most other sources of information about the history of human societies. An enormous range of sophisticated theoretical cultural evolutionary models now exists, but it is not at all clear which of them represent processes that have actually been important in human history. To the extent that archaeologists succeed in offering satisfactory explanations for the patterns they observe they are contributing to the justification and development of cultural evolutionary theory.

References

Bentley, R. A., Price, T. D., Lüning, J., Gronenborn, D., Wahl, J. and Fullagar, P. D. (2002) Human migration in Early Neolithic Europe. *Current Anthropology*, 43: 799–804.

Bentley, R.A, Hahn, M. W. and Shennan, S. J. (2004) Random drift and culture change. *Proceedings of the Royal Society of London, B*, 271: 1443–1450.

Bliege Bird, R. and Smith, E. A. (2005) Signaling theory, strategic interaction, and symbolic capital. *Current Anthropology*, 46: 221–248.

Bocquet-Appel, J. P. (2002) Paleoanthropological traces of a neolithic demographic transition. *Current Anthropology*, 43: 637–647.

Bollongino, R., Edwards, C. J., Bradley, D., Alt, K. W. and Burger, J. (2005) Phylogenie und Populationsgenetik neolithischer Haus- und Wildrinder. Paper presented at the conference *Die Neolithisierung Mitteleuropas*, Mainz, Germany, June 2005.

Colledge, S., Conolly, J. and Shennan, S. (2004) Archaeobotanical evidence for the spread of farming in the East Mediterranean. *Current Anthropology*, 45(Suppl 4): S35–S58.

Dominguez, S. (2002) Optimal gardening strategies: maximizing the input and retention of water in prehistoric gridded fields in North Central New Mexico. *World Archaeology*, 34: 131–163.

Ewens, W. J. (1972) The sampling theory of selectively neutral alleles. *Theoretical Population Biology*, 3: 87–112.

Hachem, L. (2000) New observations on the Bandkeramik house and social organisation. *Antiquity*, 74: 308–312.

Harris, D. (ed.) (1996) The origins and spread of agriculture and pastoralism in Eurasia. UCL Press, London.

Jeunesse, C. (1997) *Pratiques funéraires au néolithique ancien: sépultures et nécropoles Danubiennes 5500–4900 av. J.-C.* Errance, Paris.

Kelly, R. L. (1995) *The Foraging Spectrum: Diversity in Hunter-Gatherer Lifeways*. Smithsonian Institution Press, Washington DC.

Kohler, T. A., VanBuskirk, S. and Ruscavage-Barz, S. (2004) Vessels and villages: evidence for conformist transmission in early village aggregations on the Pajarito Plateau, New Mexico. *Journal of Anthropological Archaeology*, 23: 100–118.

Nagaoka, L. (2002) Explaining subsistence change in Southern New Zealand using foraging theory models. *World Archaeology*, 34: 84–102.

Neiman, F. D. (1995) Stylistic variation in evolutionary perspective: inferences from decorative diversity and inter-assemblage distance in Illinois Woodland ceramic assemblages. *American Antiquity*, 60: 7–36.

Neiman, F. (1997) Conspicuous consumption as wasteful advertising: a Darwinian perspective on spatial patterns in classic Maya terminal monument dates. In C. M. Barton and G. A. Clark (eds) *Rediscovering Darwin: Evolutionary Theory in Archaeological Explanation*, pp. 267–290. American Anthropological Association, Arlington, Virginia.

O'Brien, M. J. and Lyman, R. L. (2000) *Applying Evolutionary Archaeology*. Plenum Press, New York.

Peltenburg, E., Colledge, S., Croft, P., Jackson, A., McCartney, C. and Murray, M. A. (2001) Neolithic dispersals from the Levantine corridor: a Mediterranean perspective. *Levant*, 33: 35–64.

Petrasch, J. (2001) 'Seid fruchtbar und mehret euch und fullet die Erde und.machet sie euch untertan'. … *Archaeologisches Korrespondenzblatt*, 31: 13–25.

Petrasch, J. (2005) Demografischer Wandel am Beginn der Bandkeramik. Paper presented at the conference *Die Neolithisierung Mitteleuropas*, Mainz, Germany, June 24–26, 2005.

Richerson, P. J., Boyd, R. and Bettinger, R. L. (2001) Was agriculture impossible during the Pleistocene but mandatory during the Holocene? A climate change hypothesis. *American Antiquity*, 66: 387–412.

Schibler, J., Jacomet, S., Hüster-Plogmann, H. and Brombacher, C. (1997) Economic crash in the 37th and 36th centuries cal. BC in Neolithic lake shore sites in Switzerland. *Anthropozoologica*, 25–26: 553–570.

Shennan, S. J. (2002) *Genes, Memes and Human History: Darwinian Archaeology and Cultural Evolution*. Thames & Hudson, London.

Shennan, S. J. and Bentley, R. A. (in press) Style, interaction and demography among the earliest farmers of Central Europe. In M. J. O'Brien (ed.) *Case Studies in Evolutionary Archaeology*. Society for American Archaeology, Washington DC.

Shennan, S. J. and Wilkinson, J. R. (2001) Ceramic style change and neutral evolution: a case study from Neolithic Europe. *American Antiquity*, 66: 577–593.

Smith, E. A. (2000) Three styles in the evolutionary analysis of human behaviour. In L. Cronk, N. Chagnon and W. Irons (eds) *Adaptation and Human Behaviour*, pp. 27–46. Aldine de Gruyter, New York.

Stiner, M. C. and Munro, N. D. (2002) Approaches to prehistoric diet breadth, demography, and prey ranking systems in time and space. *Journal of Archaeological Method and Theory*, 9: 181–214.

Sutherland, W. J. (1996) *From Individual Behaviour to Population Ecology*. Oxford University Press, Oxford.

van Andel, T. H. and Runnels, C. N. (1995) The earliest farmers in Europe. *Antiquity*, 69: 481–500.

van der Velde, P. (1990) Banderamik social inequality—a case study. *Germania*, 68: 19–38.

van der Velde, P. (2000) Dust and ashes: the two neolithic cemeteries of Elsloo and Niedermerz compared. *Analecta Praehistorica Leidensia*, 25: 173–188.

Voland, E. (1998) Evolutionary ecology of human reproduction. *Annual Review of Anthropology*, 27: 347–374.

Zimmermann, A. (2002) Landschaftsarchäologie I. Die Bandkeramik auf der Aldenhovener Platte. *Bericht der Römisch-Germanischen Kommission*, 2002: 17–38.

Zohary, D. (1999) Monophyletic vs. polyphyletic origin of the crops on which agriculture was founded in the Near East. *Genetic Resources and Crop Evolution*, 46: 133–142.

CHAPTER 41

Memes

Robert Aunger

'**M**eme' is a recently coined name (Dawkins, 1976) for an old idea: that culture evolves through a process of inheritance involving bits of information (e.g. Tarde, 1903). A meme is thus considered to be analogous to a gene as the unit of cultural, as opposed to genetic, evolution. Dawkins' (1976) original definition of memes as "tunes, catch-phrases, clothes fashions, ways of making pots or of building arches" has been seen as insufficiently precise, in particular concerning their physical nature (Aunger, 2002; Distin, 2004)—are memes beliefs, behaviour or artefacts? This lack of precision has not been rectified by the major contemporary proponents of memes (Dennett, 1995; Blackmore, 1999; Distin, 2004): the definition remains vague.

Of course, memes could simply be defined as whatever underlies the process of cultural change, just as genes were at first defined by their functional role in biological change, prior to being found to be instantiated in DNA. Some memeticists have taken this route, being content to call memetic whatever information is socially learned (e.g. Gil-White, 2004). However, while this appears to be a legitimate position to take, due to the analogy to biology, it is not particularly helpful because it is potentially vacuous: it could be the case that memes have nothing to explain. Some evolutionary psychologists, for instance, argue that transmission is not the important phenomenon behind culture; instead, environmental contingency, combined with genetic predispositions, serve to cause what appear to be cultural behaviours—behaviours in fact determined by information inherited through genes, thanks to a prior history of adaptive responses to similar conditions (Tooby and Cosmides, 1992). The gene analogy is not a good one in the end because genes and brains could be enough to explain culture, whereas biological phenomena could never have been explained without something like a gene (Aunger, 2002).

Nevertheless, what makes memetics distinct from other formulations in the 'market' to explain cultural evolution (e.g. sociobiology/evolutionary ecology, evolutionary psychology, gene–culture coevolutionary theory) is the idea that cultural change is underpinned by the replication of particulate information packets, just like genes (Aunger, 2002; Distin, 2004). Most memeticists therefore would want to call memes replicators, if only to distinguish memetics from other evolutionary theories of cultural change (Aunger, 2002), or because, for historiographic reasons, they feel it is necessary to keep to Dawkins' original definition of a meme as analogous to the biological replicator, genes (Dennett, 1995; Blackmore, 1999).

But what does replication mean? Some memeticists believe that inheritance is enough to define replication. For example, Blackmore (2000, p. 25) argues that "as long as we accept that ... information of some kind is passed on ... then, by definition, memes exist." Following Dawkins, Blackmore also argues that imitation is the replication mechanism which memes use: "Dawkins [1976, p. 192] said that memes jump from 'brain to brain via a process which, in the broad sense, can be called imitation'. I will also use the term 'imitation' in the broad sense" (Blackmore, 1999, p. 6)—by which she means to include processes like reading. However, this is not a definition of imitation which social psychologists would accept (see Plotkin, 2000). For most psychologists, imitation involves observation of a behavioural model—a figure conspicuously absent when reading a text.

Further, involving artefacts like books in social learning creates problems for the notion of inheritance. A typical story about meme replication through artefacts would be as follows (see e.g. Dennett, 1991 or Blackmore, 1999 for stories of the following type). Ms X creates a new innovation, a wadjet; Mr Y comes along and, simply by observing the wadjet in operation, infers its function and recreates a copy of the device, even though Mr Y has never met or spoken to Ms X. The wadjet idea or meme has been recreated in the mind of Mr Y from information contained solely in a sample wadjet. Mr Y can even build a second wadjet through a process of reverse engineering, based on inferred knowledge from the sample wadjet.

This story implies an evolutionary lineage of events as follows: Ms X → wadjet → Mr Y → wadjet. Crucially, the story depends on memes passing from one person to the next through an artefact: in effect, memes must exist in artefacts. However, artefacts do not contain representations of themselves; instead, human minds construct such representations based on signals of the form and function of the artefacts (Distin, 2004). Nothing in the form or action of an artefact necessarily expresses its function. The fact that a wheel rolls along (when pushed on its side) does not tell the world that its function is transportation. Artefacts, of themselves, belong to a dead physical world without meaning. Determining functionality is an act of interpretation by an appropriately prepared mind, depending on prior experience and knowledge about the general category to which an artefact belongs. But without knowledge of function, it is impossible to determine which features are crucial and which are incidental, when attempting to copy the artefact. For example, Mr Y could make a wadjet out of wood, but it might not do the job for which wadjets were intended. If a copy of an artefact such as a wadjet *is* successfully made, it is thanks to the fact that Mr Y has brought specialized knowledge to the situation (such as the fact that wadgets need to be made of materials with significant tensile strength like metal), rather than having acquired that knowledge from the object under study. The wadjet-making information does not derive from Ms X, nor from instructions symbolically embedded in the wadjet; rather, it originates with Mr Y, thus violating the principle quality of replication being discussed: information inheritance (Distin, 2004). Reverse engineering owes more to the skill and knowledge of the engineer than to the information contained in the wadjet. Crucially, the information that makes one wadjet similar to another is based in the engineer's concept of what a wadjet is; the artefact itself has no sense of identity.

Of course a 'wadjet construction manual' could be written, but that would be a separate artefact, not a wadjet. In the case of other acknowledged replicators—genes, prions and computer viruses—the information that makes the copy similar to the source comes directly from the source: DNA uncoils to expose one strand so that its complement can be created; a protein unfolds to be reshaped into the form that makes it a prion (proteins that convert normal proteins into copies of themselves merely through contact); computer memory registers are flipped on the instructions of a computer virus. A similar model would have artefacts playing an equally active role in instructing people how to make them. But there is nothing intrinsic to an artefact that provides such knowledge. Instead, Mr Y must bring this knowledge to the duplication process—or infer it using background knowledge he already possesses about how the world works. Even a 'wadjet construction manual' would tell Mr Y nothing about where to find the components, much less how to make them, nor which tools he might need, nor where to find *them*, nor in which manner to hit component A so that it fits into a slot on component B. Now imagine the manual is written in a language Mr Y doesn't understand! All of this crucial information is implicit and must be supplied—in highly variant ways—by the wadjet-maker.

So even if we allow artefacts to contain symbolic information—if the manual could be inscribed on the surface of the wadjet itself—the same story holds: the manual must still be interpreted by a device (like a human being) that understands those symbols.

Thus, artefacts can be the *phenotypic effects* of memes (i.e. a consequence of their action, typically in the environment), but cannot be considered memetic *interactors* (the equivalent of organisms, as the phenotypic product of genes) because they do not carry memes around inside them (Aunger, 2002, in press; Distin, 2004). Artefacts are thus incapable of housing memes.

This analysis demonstrates that replication must be something more than just the inheritance of information. Replication can be more precisely defined as a special relationship between a source and a copy such that four conditions hold:

(i) causation (the source must play some role in bringing about the conditions that lead to a copy being made);

(ii) similarity (the source and copy must resemble each other in relevant respects);

(iii) information transfer (what makes the copy similar to the source must be derived from the source); and

(iv) duplication (the source and copy must coexist for some time) (Aunger, 2002; Hull and Wilkins, 2001; Sperber, 2000; Godfrey-Smith, 2000).

The question then is whether cultural reproduction of any type fulfils the criteria for replication. The classic example of the face-to-face transmission of information, as in conversation, may work, as it avoids the complications of artefacts as cultural vectors. However, a further problem for the meme concept is that empirical studies of communication are not particularly sanguine about the likelihood of information replicating in the process. As the unit of inheritance, a meme should vary, so that evolution can occur, but not too much; it must be able to replicate reliably, and thus serve as the foundation for a chain or lineage of cultural inheritance (Dawkins, 1976). But if results from laboratory-based studies of cultural transmission are to be believed, then cultural transmission is a weak replicator of information at best. The progenitor of this line of studies was Bartlett (1932), who invented

a protocol much like the parlour game of Chinese whispers in which messages are passed from one person to the next to observe how message content changes along this social chain (see Mesoudi, 2005, for review). A general result from these studies is that the content of social messages rapidly decays to a kind of lowest common denominator. For example, complex everyday narratives tend to be simplified by 'chunking' events into simple, stereotypical scripts (Mesoudi and Whiten, 2004). What these studies suggest is that information is manipulated considerably during communication rather than being a mechanical process of replication.

From a theoretical perspective, it also seems unlikely that minds work like copying machines, given the constraints of the need to communicate information via messages (Sperber, 2000; Richerson and Boyd, 2004). The message receiver may be able to reconstruct the information in the meme hosts' mind, but it is currently unknown whether there is sufficiently robust mental machinery to cause significant similarity of the reconstructed information based on the 'impoverished' signal that is transmitted.

The difficulties of thinking of communication as the duplication of mental representations leads others to a position in which the roles of phenotype and genotype are reversed: behaviours are considered replicators, and mental representations their phenotypes (Benzon, 1996; Gatherer, 1998). This appears to be sensible, because it is quite easy to observe behaviours which are duplicated: people are expert at mimicry. Further, the imitation of behaviour need *not* entail duplication of information in the brain: the behavioural phenotype can be duplicated through any number of mental processes. In fact, one might argue that brains are just very complex machines for replicating behaviours and artefacts: just think of people on the factory floor, repeating behaviour sequences over and over, thereby making copies of machines. In this view, there are no memes in minds, only out in the world. We are not cultural interactors, just the equivalent of RNA that enables behaviours and artefacts to reproduce time and again.

The difficulty with this position is that complex culture, and the kind of rapid cultural accumulation seen in humans simply cannot be based on behaviour copying; if it was enough to watch each other's behaviour and then mimic it, then chimpanzees and other species would have developed cumulative culture (Tomasello *et al.*, 1993). Presumably the design of complex technology also requires something more than fixing simple elements together in clever combinations. So technology itself counts against minds being merely the servants of machinery.

Memes thus appear to be in minds, if they exist anywhere. But what is their role in minds? Dawkins suggested that memes are 'mind viruses' in the sense that they invade minds to use them for their own purposes, regardless of whether they cause behaviour beneficial to the meme's 'host'. To the extent that a virus is defined as a (proto) life-form which appropriates existing machinery for its own purposes, then memes can only be called mind viruses if they appropriate machinery developed to replicate other kinds of information (Distin, 2004, p. 76). That is, for memes to be mind viruses, there must be mind 'genes', the bits of information which the brain was *designed* to replicate. But the brain has not evolved primarily to replicate information; in fact, most organisms are not social and cannot learn from social interaction. Rather, brains evolved to guide the production of adaptive, flexible behavioural responses to evolutionarily significant problems (Tooby and Cosmides, 1992; Plotkin, 1994; Llinas, 1999).

Still, parts of the human brain *are* devoted to communication, a process in which one person attempts to infer what is in the mind of others. Arguably, then, in those species which can learn socially, something like words might be 'mind genes'. So either memes do more work than biological viruses to replicate themselves, because the mind was not designed to replicate bits of information like them, or memes piggyback on the linguistic system. Either way, Distin (2004) points out that Blackmore (1999) and Dennett (1995) tend to conflate memes-as-thoughts with memes-as-things-to-think-with. She uses the philosophical notion of a propositional attitude to clarify the distinction: memes are just information like propositions, but thoughts can reflect on this information, such that we form attitudes towards that information, like beliefs or fears or desires. Blackmore and Dennett thus fail to distinguish between memes and attitudes towards memes, which leads them

to believe that that there is nothing to the mind but a collection of memes (e.g. Dennett 1991, p. 210). From this false proposition, Blackmore and Dennett draw the incorrect inference that all of culture is composed of memes, since memes are just socially communicated ideas. However, if memes are mind parasites, they must be thoughts that use independent psychological machinery to get themselves replicated; by definition, they cannot be all there is inside one's head. The epidemiological view of memes is thus inconsistent with the claim that the mind is a complex of memes and nothing more. In such a case, we can only think with memes, and not 'rise above' them, through meta-representational thought which represents our own thoughts to ourselves. There must be innate structure in the mind prior to social learning which influences which information will be accepted through social learning; mental filters exist which are not made of memes that keep out 'mind viruses' (Aunger, 2002).

This perspective limits the role of memes in culture. They cannot be all of culture, much less all thoughts (some of which must be internally created rather than socially learned). If memes must be parasitic on thinking, then memes are unlikely to be the fundamental explanation of cultural evolution. Further, if most forms of communication do not qualify as a replication process, then some other kind of process is responsible for most of what we commonly call cultural learning. Memetics must be buttressed by another kind of explanation for cultural change which accounts for the process which memes parasitize.

These difficulties have meant that memetics has not yet generated a distinctive body of research. Without a more precise definition of meme, it is difficult to develop claims which are specific enough to be contestable with alternative theories of social learning. Why can't the voluminous literature on public opinion, based on social surveys, qualify as memetics, for example? Just calling whatever we learn from others a 'meme' does not distinguish memetics from other brands of social psychology; indeed, calling what we learn a 'cultural trait' would have greater authority and cause less controversy because that term does not make a claim about exactly *how* social information was learned.

If we knew that social learning typically involved information replication, a case could be made; however, even though a lot of work concerning how social learning occurs has been done, it is limited to showing how one mechanism of learning (e.g. imitation) differs from another in terms of the speed and accuracy with which new things can be learned from modelled behaviour in various contexts (e.g. Whiten and Byrne, 1988; Heyes and Galef, 1996; Laland and Bateson, 2001; Hurley and Chater, 2005). Similarly, the diffusion of innovations literature (e.g. Rogers, 1995), or the investigations into information transmission through social networks (e.g. Rosnow *et al.*, 1986; Marsden and Friedkin, 1993; Strang and Soule, 1998), or the relatively few field-based studies of cultural transmission (e.g. Hewlett and Cavalli-Sforza, 1986; Aunger, 2000), might be argued to qualify as examples of empirical memetics, even though none of them claims to be investigating memes *per se*. Cultural transmission studies have even been conducted using readily available databases documenting human communication patterns: electronic chat groups and e-mail lists (e.g. Best and Pocklington, 1999). While all of these literatures are interesting, they remain tangential in that they do not establish that their subject matter is information chunks replicated via transmission between people.

The primary difficulty with calling any of these literatures memetics is that no one has yet observed information replication happening directly, inside people's heads. What is needed to confirm that social learning involves information replication is information about brain mechanisms for information acquisition, storage and management. Only in this way can we determine whether any instance of imitation is an act of information replication, as defined above. Even brain scanning techniques are not currently able to achieve that goal. As a result, no study has been able to address directly the central question of whether information replicates in the process of cultural transmission. Meanwhile, the use of proxies—phenotypes of various kinds—seems inevitable (although there is the possibility of testing meme-based hypotheses using computer simulation models of populations of artificial agents, which some have taken up with some enthusiasm, particularly to investigate the

role of imitation and intentionality in communication, e.g. Hales, 2002; Conte, in press).

The concept of a meme as a unit of cultural transmission has thus proven very popular. But despite considerable enthusiasm for the meme idea in a variety of fields, much of the literature on memes continues to be given over to arguing about which particular theoretical conception of memes is most useful; the field of memetics is marked by a startling absence of empirical research. This is because, as we have seen, there are many difficulties with the meme concept. While it is likely that the term 'meme' will continue to be widely used, it may simply become an everyday term for socially learned ideas and values, rather than the foundation of a new social science—a role the 'culture' concept served for anthropology or 'power' for political science.

References

Aunger, R. (2000) The life history of culture learning in a face-to-face society. *Ethos*, 28: 1–38.

Aunger, R. (2002) *The Electric Meme*. Simon & Schuster, New York.

Aunger, R. (2006) What's the matter with memes? In A. Grafen and M. Ridley (eds) *Richard Dawkins: How a Scientist Changed the Way We Think*, pp. 176–188. Oxford University Press, Oxford.

Bartlett, F. C. (1932) *Remembering*. Macmillan, Oxford.

Benzon, W. (1996) Culture as an evolutionary arena. *Journal of Social and Evolutionary Systems*, 19: 321–62.

Best, M. L. and Pocklington, R. (1999) Meaning as use: transmission fidelity and evolution in NetNews. *Journal of Theoretical Biology*, 196: 278–284.

Blackmore, S. (1999) *The Meme Machine*. Oxford University Press, Oxford.

Blackmore, S. (2000) The meme's eye view. In R. A. Aunger (ed.) *Darwinizing Culture: The Status of Mimetics as a Science*, pp. 25–42. Oxford University Press, Oxford.

Boyd, R. and Richerson, P. J. (1985) *Culture and the Evolutionary Process*. University of Chicago Press, Chicago.

Boyd, R. and Richerson, P. J. (2000) Memes: universal acid or a better mouse trap? In R. Aunger (ed.) *Darwinizing Culture: The Status of Memetics as a Science*, pp. 143–162. Oxford University Press, Oxford.

Conte, R. (in press) A cognitive memetic analysis of reputation. *Cognitive Science Quarterly*.

Dawkins, R. (1976) *The Selfish Gene*. Oxford University Press, Oxford.

Dennett, D. C. (1995) *Darwin's Dangerous Idea*. Simon & Schuster, New York.

Dennett, D. C. (1991) *Consciousness Explained*. Little, Brown & Co., New York.

Distin, K. (2004) *The Selfish Meme: A Critical Reassessment.* Cambridge University Press, Cambridge.

Gatherer, D. (1998) Why the 'thought contagion' metaphor is retarding the progress of memetics. *Journal of Memetics—Evolutionary Models of Information Transmission* 2. Available at: http://www.cpm/mmu.ac.uk/jom-emit/1998/vo12/gatherer_d.html

Gil-White, F. J. (2004) Common misunderstandings of memes (and genes): the promise and the limits of the genetic analogy to cultural transmission processes. In S. Hurley and N. Chater (eds) *Perspectives on Imitation: From Mirror Neurons to Memes.* MIT Press, Cambridge, MA.

Godfrey-Smith, P. (2000) The replicator in retrospect. *Biology and Philosophy,* 15: 403–423.

Hales, D. (2002) Memetic engineering and cultural evolution. *UNESCO Encyclopedia of Life Support Systems.* UNESCO, London.

Hewlett, B. and Cavalli-Sforza, L. L. (1986) Cultural transmission among Aka pygmies. *American Anthropologist,* 88: 922–934.

Heyes, C. M. and Galef, B. G., Jr (1996) *Social Learning in Animals: The Roots of Culture.* Academic Press, San Diego.

Hull, D. and Wilkins, JS. (2001) Replication. *Stanford Encyclopedia of Philosophy.* Available at: http://plato.stanford.edu/entries/replication/

Hurley, S. and Chater, N. (eds) (2005) *Perspectives on Imitation.* MIT Press, Cambridge, MA.

Laland, K. N. and Bateson, P. (2001) The mechanisms of imitation. *Cybernetics and System,* 32: 195–224.

Llinas, R. (1999) *I of the Vortex: From Neurons to Self.* MIT Press, Cambridge, MA.

Marsden, P. V. and Friedkin, N. E. (1993) Network studies of social influence. *Sociological Methods and Research,* 22: 127–151.

Mesoudi, A. (2005) The transmission and evolution of culture. PhD thesis, Department of Psychology, St Andrews University.

Mesoudi, A. and Whiten, A. (2004) The hierarchical transformation of event knowledge in human cultural transmission. *Journal of Cognition and Culture,* 4: 1–24.

Plotkin, H. (1994) *Darwin Machines and the Nature of Knowledge.* Harvard University Press, Cambridge, MA.

Plotkin, H. C. (2000) Culture and psychological mechanisms. In R.Aunger (ed.) *Darwinizing Culture: The Status of Memetics as a Science,* pp. 69–82. Oxford University Press, Oxford.

Rosnow, R. L., Yost, J. H. and Esposito, J. L. (1986) Belief in rumor and likelihood of rumor transmission. *Language and Communication,* 6: 189–194.

Richerson, P. J. and Boyd, R. (2004) *Not By Genes Alone.* University of Chicago Press, Chicago.

Rogers, E. M. (1995) *Diffusion of Innovations,* 4th edn. Free Press, New York.

Sperber, D. (2000) An objection to the memetic approach to culture. In R. Aunger (ed.) *Darwinizing Culture: The Status of Memetics as a Science,* pp. 163–174. Oxford University Press, Oxford.

Strang, D. and Soule, S. A. (1998) Diffusion in organizations and social movements: from hybrid corn to poison pills. *Annual Review of Sociology,* 24: 265–290.

Tarde, G. (1903, first published 1890) *The Laws of Imitation.* Henry Holt, New York.

Tomasello, M., Kruger, A. C. and Ratner, H. H. (1993) Cultural learning. *Behavioural and Brain Sciences,* 16: 495–552.

Tooby, J. and Cosmides, L. (1992) The psychological foundations of culture. In J. H. Barkow, L. Cosmides and J. Tooby (eds) *The Adapted Mind,* pp. 19–136. Oxford University Press, Oxford.

Whiten, A. and Byrne, R. (eds) (1988) *Machiavellian Intelligence: Social Expertise and the Evolution of Intellect in Monkeys, Apes, and Humans.* Oxford University Press, Oxford

CHAPTER 42

Explaining altruistic behaviour in humans

Herbert Gintis, Samuel Bowles, Robert Boyd and Ernst Fehr

42.1. Introduction

The explanatory power of inclusive-fitness theory and reciprocal altruism (Hamilton, 1964; Williams, 1966; Trivers, 1971) convinced a generation of researchers that what appears to be altruism—personal sacrifice on behalf of others—is really just long-run self-interest. Richard Dawkins, for instance, struck a responsive chord when, in *The Selfish Gene* (1979, p. vii), he confidently asserted: "We are survival machines—robot vehicles blindly programmed to preserve the selfish molecules known as genes. ... This gene selfishness will usually give rise to selfishness in individual behaviour." Dawkins allows for morality in social life, but it must be socially imposed on a fundamentally selfish agent. "Let us try to teach generosity and altruism," he advises, "because we are born selfish" (Dawkins, *The selfish Gene*, p. 3). Yet even social morality, according to R. D. Alexander, the most influential ethicist working in the Williams– Hamilton tradition, can only superficially transcend selfishness. In *The Biology of Moral Systems* (1987), Alexander asserts (p. 3): "ethics, morality, human conduct, and the human psyche are to be understood only if societies are seen as collections of individuals seeking their own self-interest." In a similar state of explanatory euphoria, Ghiselin (1974) claims (p. 247): "No hint of genuine charity ameliorates our vision of society, once sentimentalism has been laid aside. What passes

for cooperation turns out to be a mixture of opportunism and exploitation ... Scratch an altruist, and watch a hypocrite bleed."

However, recent experimental research has revealed forms of human behaviour involving interaction among unrelated individuals that cannot be explained in terms of self-regarding preferences. One such trait, which we call strong reciprocity (Gintis, 2000b; Henrich *et al.*, 2001), is *a predisposition to cooperate with others, and to punish those who violate the norms of cooperation, at personal cost, even when it is implausible to expect that these costs will be repaid either by others or at a later date.*

In this chapter, we present evidence supporting strong reciprocity. We then explain why, under conditions plausibly characteristic of the early stages of human evolution, a small fraction of strong reciprocators could invade a population of self-regarding types, and why strong reciprocity is an evolutionarily stable strategy. Throughout this chapter, we use the term 'self-regarding' rather than the more common term 'self-interested' to avoid the (uninteresting, we believe) question as to whether it is selfish to help others if that is how one 'maximizes utility'. Although most of the evidence we report is based on behavioural experiments, the same behaviours are regularly observed in everyday life, and of great relevance for social policy (Gintis *et al.*, 2005).

Despite the fact that strong reciprocity is altruistic, our results do not contradict traditional evolutionary theory. A gene that promotes self-sacrifice will die out unless those who are helped carry the mutant gene, or its spread is otherwise promoted. In a population without structured social interactions of individuals, behaviours of the type found in our experiments and illustrated in our models could not have evolved. However, multi-level selection and gene–culture coevolutionary models support cooperative behaviour among non-kin (Feldman *et al.*, 1985; Sober and Wilson, 1998; Gintis, 2000b, 2003; Henrich and Boyd, 2001; Bowles *et al.*, 2003). These models, some of which are discussed below, are not vulnerable to the classic critiques of group selection by Williams (1966), Dawkins (1976), Maynard Smith (1976), Rogers (1990), and others.

An alternative account of strong reciprocity is that in our hunter-gatherer ancestral environment, strong reciprocity was not altruistic, but rather was individually fitness-maximizing, as it allowed individuals to develop a reputation for being both willing to cooperate, yet committed to retaliating against those who betray their trust. In the contemporary environment, so the argument goes, strongly reciprocal behaviour persists in situations where it is altruistic, but these situations would rarely have arisen in our hunter-gatherer past, where anonymous, one-shot interactions were supposedly extremely rare. We think this alternative is unlikely, and address the issue in Section 42.7. Indeed, we argue in Section 42.6 that through gene–culture coevolution, our species developed a whole range of social emotions, including shame, guilt, pride and honour, that both promoted individual well-being and a high level of social cooperation. The remainder of the chapter is devoted to a deeper analysis of social emotions.

42.2. Experimental evidence: strong reciprocity in the labour market

Strong reciprocity is most clearly exhibited in laboratory experiments. In one such experiment (Fehr *et al.*, 1997) the experimenters divided a group of 141 subjects (college students who had agreed to participate in order to earn money) into a set of 'employers' and a larger set

of 'employees'. The rules of the game are as follows. If an employer hires an employee who provides effort e and receives a wage w, the employer's pay-off p is 100 times the effort e, minus the wage w that he must pay the employee ($p = 100e - w$), where the wage is between zero and 100 ($0 = w = 100$), and the effort between 0.1 and 1 ($0.1 = e = 1$). The pay-off u to the employee is then the wage he receives, minus a 'cost of effort', $c(e)$ ($u = w - c(e)$). The cost-of-effort schedule $c(e)$ is constructed by the experimenters such that supplying effort $e = 0.1, 0.2, 0.3, 0.4, 0.5, 0.6, 0.7, 0.8, 0.9$ and 1.0 costs the employee $c(e) = 0, 1, 2, 4, 6, 8, 10, 12, 15$ and 18, respectively. All pay-offs are converted into real money that the subjects are paid at the end of the experimental session.

The sequence of actions is as follows. The employer first offers a 'contract' specifying a wage w and a desired amount of effort e^*. A contract is made with the first employee who agrees to these terms. An employer can make a contract (w, e^*) with at most one employee. The employee who agrees to these terms receives the wage w and supplies an effort level e, which *need not equal the contracted effort*, e^*. In effect, there is no penalty if the employee does not keep his promise, so the employee can choose any effort level, $e \in [0.1, 1]$, with impunity. Although subjects may play this game several times with different partners, each employer–employee interaction is a one-shot (non-repeated) event. Moreover, the identity of the interacting partners is never revealed. This experiment is especially relevant because it models a situation that could have resulted in one-shot interactions among acquaintances in small-scale societies. An individual makes a promise, and then, because monitoring is not possible, fails to keep it.

If employees are self-regarding, they will choose the zero-cost effort level, $e = 0.1$, no matter what wage is offered them. Knowing this, employers will never pay more than the minimum necessary to get the employee to accept a contract, which is 1 (assuming only integral wage offers are permitted). The employee will accept this offer, and will set $e = 0.1$. Since $c(0.1) = 0$, the employee's pay-off is $u = 1$. The employer's pay-off is $p = 0.1 \times 100 - 1 = 9$.

In fact, however, this self-regarding outcome rarely occurred in this experiment. The average

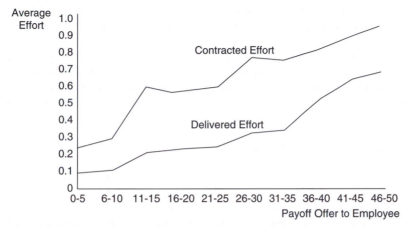

Fig. 42.1 Relation of contracted and delivered effort to worker pay-off (141 subjects). From Fehr et al. (1997).

net pay-off to employees was $u = 35$, and the more generous the employer's wage offer to the employee, the higher the effort provided. In effect, employers presumed the strong reciprocity predispositions of the employees, making quite generous wage offers and receiving higher effort, as a means to increase both their own and the employee's pay-off, as shown in Figure 1. Similar results have been observed in Fehr *et al.* (1993, 1998).

Figure 40.1 also shows that, though most employees are strong reciprocators, at any wage rate there still is a significant gap between the amount of effort agreed upon and the amount actually delivered. This is not because there are a few 'bad apples' among the set of employees, but because only 26% of employees delivered the level of effort they promised! We conclude that strong reciprocators are inclined to compromise their morality to some extent, just as we might expect from daily experience.

The above evidence is compatible with the notion that the employers are purely self-regarding, since their beneficent behaviour *vis-à-vis* their employees was effective in increasing employer profits. To see if employers are also strong reciprocators, following this round of experiments, the authors extended the game by allowing the employers to respond reciprocally to the actual effort choices of their workers. At a cost of 1, an employer could increase or decrease his employee's pay-off by 2.5. If employers were self-regarding, they would of course do neither,

since they would not interact with the same worker a second time. However, 68% of the time, employers punished employees who did not fulfil their contracts, and 70% of the time, employers rewarded employees who overfulfilled their contracts. Indeed, employers rewarded 41% of employees who exactly fulfilled their contracts. Moreover, employees expected this behaviour on the part of their employers, as shown by the fact that their effort levels increased significantly when their bosses gained the power to punish and reward them. Underfulfilling contracts dropped from 83% to 26% of the exchanges, and overfulfilled contracts rose from 3% to 38% of the total. Finally, allowing employers to reward and punish led to a 40% increase in the net pay-offs to all subjects, even when the pay-off reductions resulting from employer punishment of employees are taken into account. Several researchers have predicted this general behaviour on the basis of general real-life social observation and field studies, including Homans (1961), Blau (1964) and Akerlof (1982). The laboratory results show that this behaviour has a motivational basis in strong reciprocity and not simply long-term material self-interest.

We conclude from this study that the subjects who assume the role of 'employee' conform to internalized standards of reciprocity, even when they know that there are no material repercussions from behaving in a self-regarding manner. Moreover, subjects who assume the role of 'employer' expect this behaviour and are rewarded for acting accordingly. Finally, 'employers' draw upon the internalized norm of rewarding good and punishing bad behaviour when they are permitted to punish, and 'employees' expect this behaviour and adjust their own effort levels accordingly.

42.3. **Experimental evidence: the ultimatum game**

In the ultimatum game, under conditions of anonymity, two players are shown a sum of money, say $10. One of the players, called the 'proposer,' is instructed to offer any number of dollars, from $1 to $10, to the second player, who is called the 'responder'. The proposer can make only one offer. The responder, again under conditions of anonymity, can either accept or reject this offer. If the responder accepts the offer, the money is shared accordingly. If the responder rejects the offer, both players receive nothing.

Since the game is played only once and the players do not know each other's identity, a self-regarding responder will accept any positive amount of money. Knowing this, a self-regarding proposer will offer the minimum possible amount, $1, and this will be accepted. However, when actually played, *the self-regarding outcome is never attained and never even approximated.* In fact, as many replications of this experiment have documented, under varying conditions and with varying amounts of money, proposers routinely offer respondents very substantial amounts (50% of the total generally being the modal offer), and respondents frequently reject offers below 30% (Güth and Tietz, 1990; Roth *et al.*, 1991; Camerer and Thaler, 1995).

The ultimatum game has been played around the world, but mostly with university students. We find a great deal of individual variability. For instance, in all of the above experiments a significant fraction of subjects (about a quarter, typically) behave in a self-regarding manner. But, among student subjects, average performance is strikingly uniform from country to country.

To expand the diversity of cultural and economic circumstances of experimental subjects, Henrich *et al.* (2004) undertook large

cross-cultural study of behaviour in various games including the ultimatum game and the public goods game. Twelve experienced field researchers, working in 12 countries on four continents, recruited subjects from 15 small-scale societies exhibiting a wide variety of economic and cultural conditions. These societies consisted of three foraging groups (the Hadza of East Africa, the Au and Gnau of Papua New Guinea, and the Lamalera of Indonesia), six slash-and-burn horticulturists (the Aché, Machiguenga, Quichua, and Achuar of South America, and the Tsimané and Orma of East Africa), four nomadic herding groups (the Turguud, Mongols, and Kazakhs of Central Asia, and the Sangu of East Africa) and two sedentary, small-scale agricultural societies (the Mapuche of South America and Zimbabwe farmers in Africa). We can summarize our results as follows.

1. The canonical model of self-regarding behaviour is not supported in any society studied. In the ultimatum game, for example, in all societies either respondents, or proposers, or both, behaved in a reciprocal manner.

2. There is considerably more behavioural variability across groups than had been found in previous cross-cultural research. While mean ultimatum game offers in experiments with student subjects are typically between 43% and 48%, the mean offers from proposers in our sample ranged from 26% to 58%. While modal ultimatum game offers are consistently 50% among university students, sample modes with these data ranged from 15% to 50%. In some groups rejections were extremely rare, even in the presence of very low offers, while in others, rejection rates were substantial, including frequent rejections of hyper-fair offers (i.e. offers above 50%). By contrast, the most common behaviour for the Machiguenga was to offer zero. The mean offer was 22%. The Aché and Tsimané distributions resemble American distributions, but with very low rejection rates. The Orma and Huinca (non-Mapuche Chileans living among the Mapuche) have modal offers near the centre of the distribution.

3. Differences among societies in 'market integration' and 'cooperation in production' explain a substantial portion of the behavioural

variation between groups: the higher the degree of market integration and the higher the pay-offs to cooperation, the greater the level of cooperation and sharing in experimental games. The societies were rank-ordered in five categories: 'market integration' (how often do people buy and sell, or work for a wage), 'cooperation in production' (is production collective or individual), plus 'anonymity' (how prevalent are anonymous roles and transactions), 'privacy' (how easily can people keep their activities secret), and 'complexity' (how much centralized decision-making occurs above the level of the household). Using statistical regression analysis, only the first two characteristics, market integration and cooperation in production, were significant, and they together accounted for 66% of the variation among societies in mean ultimatum game offers.

4. Individual-level economic and demographic variables did not explain behaviour either within or across groups.

5. The nature and degree of cooperation and punishment in the experiments was generally consistent with economic patterns of everyday life in these societies. In a number of cases the parallels between experimental game play and the structure of daily life were quite striking.

Nor was this relationship lost on the subjects themselves. Here are some examples.

- The Orma immediately recognized that the public goods game was similar to the harambee, a locally initiated contribution that households make when a community decides to construct a road or school. They dubbed the experiment 'the harambee game' and gave generously (mean 58% with 25% maximal contributors).

- Among the Au and Gnau, many proposers offered more than half the pie, and many of these 'hyper-fair' offers were rejected! This reflects the Melanesian culture of status-seeking through gift-giving. Making a large gift is a bid for social dominance in everyday life in these societies, and rejecting the gift is a rejection of being subordinate.

- Among the whale hunting Lamalera, 63% of the proposers in the ultimatum game divided the pie equally, and most of those who did not offered more than 50% (the mean offer was 57%). In real life, a large catch, always the product of cooperation among many individual whalers, is meticulously divided into pre-designated parts and carefully distributed among the members of the community.

- Among the Aché, 79% of proposers offered either 40% or 50%, and 16% offered more than 50%, with no rejected offers. In daily life, the Aché regularly share meat, which is distributed equally among all other households, irrespective of which hunter made the kill. The Hadza, unlike the Aché, made low offers and had high rejection rates in the ultimatum game. This reflects the tendency of these small-scale foragers to share meat, but with a high level of conflict and frequent attempts of hunters to hide their catch from the group.

- Both the Machiguenga and Tsimané made low ultimatum game offers, and there were virtually no rejections. These groups exhibit little cooperation, exchange or sharing beyond the family unit. Ethnographically, both show little fear of social sanctions and care little about 'public opinion'.

- The Mapuche's social relations are character-ized by mutual suspicion, envy, and fear of being envied. This pattern is consistent with the Mapuche's post-game interviews in the ultimatum game. Mapuche proposers rarely claimed that their offers were influenced by fairness, but rather by a fear of rejection. Even proposers who made hyper-fair offers claimed that they feared rare spiteful responders, who would be willing to reject even 50/50 offers.

42.4. Experimental evidence: the public goods game

The public goods game has been analysed in a series of papers by the social psychologist Toshio Yamagishi (1986a,b, 1988), by the political scientist Elinor Ostrom *et al.* (1992), and by economist Ernst Fehr and his coworkers (Gächter and Fehr, 1999; Fehr and Gächter, 2000, 2002). These researchers uniformly found that, although they rarely attained efficiency, *groups exhibit a much higher rate of cooperation than can be expected assuming the standard economic model of the self-interested actor*, and this is especially the case when subjects are given the option of incurring a cost to themselves in order to punish freeriders.

A typical public goods game consists of a number of rounds, say 10. The subjects are told the total number of rounds, as well as all other aspects of the game. The subjects are paid their winnings in real money at the end of the session. In each round, each subject is grouped with several other subjects, for example three others, under conditions of strict anonymity. Each subject is then given a certain number of 'points', say 20, redeemable at the end of the experimental session for real money. Each subject then places some fraction of his points in a 'common account,' and the remainder in the subject's 'private account'. The experimenter then tells the subjects how many points were contributed to the common account, and adds to the private account of each subject some fraction, say 40%, of the total amount in the common account. So if a subject contributes his whole 20 points to the common account, each of the four group members will receive 8 points at the end of the round. In effect, by putting the whole endowment into the common account, a player loses 12 points but the other three group members gain in total 24 (= 8 × 3) points. The players keep whatever is in their private account at the end of the round.

A self-regarding player will contribute nothing to the common account. However, only a fraction of subjects actually conform to the self-regarding model. Subjects begin by contributing on average about half of their endowment to the public account. The level of contributions decays over the course of the 10 rounds, until in the final rounds most players are behaving in a self-regarding manner (Dawes and Thaler, 1988; Ledyard, 1995). In a meta-study of 12 public goods experiments Fehr and Schmidt (1999) found that in the early rounds, average and median contribution levels ranged from 40% to 60% of the endowment, but in the final period 73% of all individuals ($n = 1042$) contributed nothing, and many of the remaining players contributed close to zero. These results are not compatible with the self-interested actor model, which predicts zero contribution on all rounds, though they might be predicted by a reciprocal altruism model, since the chance to reciprocate

declines as the end of the experiment approaches. However, this is not in fact the explanation of moderate but deteriorating levels of cooperation in the public goods game.

The explanation of the decay of cooperation offered by subjects when debriefed after the experiment is that cooperative subjects became angry at others who contributed less than themselves, and retaliated against free-riding low contributors in the only way available to them—by lowering their own contributions (Ostrom et al., 1994; Andreoni, 1995).

Experimental evidence supports this interpretation. When subjects are allowed to punish non-contributors, they do so at a cost to themselves (Orbell et al., 1986; Sato, 1987; Yamagishi, 1988a,b, 1992). For instance, in Ostrom et al. (1992) subjects interacted for 25 periods in a public goods game, and by paying a 'fee,' subjects could impose costs on other subjects by 'fining' them. Since fining costs the individual who uses it, but the benefits of increased compliance accrue to the group as a whole, we might expect a self-regarding player to refrain from punishing. However, even a self-regarding player might engage in *strategic punishment*, expecting that by punishing in early rounds, the level of cooperation would rise enough in later rounds to render the punishing profitable. The experimenters found a significant level of punishing behaviour, but their experimental protocols made it impossible to say whether this was due to strategic punishment or strong reciprocity, since subjects were not told in advance how many periods of play they would undergo, precisely to avoid 'endgame effects'.

This shortcoming was addressed by Fehr and Gächter (2000), who set up an experimental situation in which *the possibility of strategic punishment was removed*. They used six and ten round public goods games with groups of size four, and with costly punishment allowed at the end of each round, employing three different methods of assigning members to groups. There were sufficient subjects to run between 10 and 18 groups simultaneously. Under the 'Partner' treatment, the four subjects remained in the same group for all 10 periods. Under the 'Stranger' treatment, the subjects were randomly reassigned after each round. Finally, under the 'Perfect Stranger' treatment the subjects were randomly reassigned and assured that they would never meet the same subject more than once. Subjects earned an average of about $35 for an experimental session.

Fehr and Gächter (2000) performed their experiment for 10 rounds with punishment and 10 rounds without [for additional experimental results and their analysis, see Bowles and Gintis (2002) and Fehr and Gächter (2002).] Their results are illustrated in Figure 42.2. We see that when costly punishment is permitted, cooperation does not deteriorate, and in the Partner game, despite strict anonymity, cooperation increases almost to full cooperation, even on the final round. When punishment is not permitted, however, the same subjects experience the deterioration of cooperation found in previous public goods games. The contrast in cooperation rates between the Partner and the two Stranger treatments is worth noting, because the strength of punishment is roughly the same across all treatments. This suggests that the credibility of the punishment threat is greater in the Partner treatment because in this treatment the punished subjects are certain that, once they have been punished in previous rounds, the punishing subjects are in their group. The prosociality impact of strong reciprocity on cooperation is thus more strongly manifested, the more coherent and permanent the group in question.

42.5. The evolutionary stability of strong reciprocity

Gintis (2000b) developed an analytical model showing that under plausible conditions strong reciprocity can emerge from reciprocal altruism, through group selection. The paper models cooperation as a repeated n-person public goods game (see Section 42.4) in which, under normal conditions, if agents are sufficiently forward-looking, cooperation can be sustained by the threat of ostracism (Fudenberg and Maskin, 1986; Gintis, 2000a). However, when the group is threatened with extinction or dispersal, say through war, pestilence, or famine, cooperation is most needed for survival. During such critical periods, which were common in the evolutionary history of our species, future gains from cooperation become very uncertain, since the probability that the group will dissolve becomes high. The threat of ostracism then carries little weight, and cooperation cannot be maintained if agents are self-regarding. Thus, *precisely when a group is most in need of prosocial behaviour,*

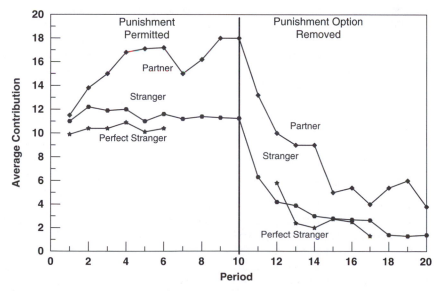

Fig. 42.2 Average contributions over time in the Partner, Stranger, and Perfect Stranger treatments when the punishment condition is played first. Adapted from Fehr and Gächter (2000).

cooperation based on reciprocal altruism will collapse.

But a small number of strong reciprocators, who punish defectors *whether or not it is in their long-term interest*, can dramatically improve the survival chances of human groups. Moreover, among species that live in groups and recognize individuals, humans are unique in their capacity to formulate and communicate rules of behaviour and to inflict heavy punishment at low cost to the punisher (Bingham, 1999), as a result of their superior tool-making and hunting ability (Goodall, 1964; Darlington, 1975; Plooij, 1978; Fifer, 1987; Isaac, 1987). Under these conditions strong reciprocators can invade a population of self-regarding types. This is because even if strong reciprocators form a small fraction of the population, at least occasionally they will form a sufficient fraction of a group such that cooperation can be maintained in bad times. Such a group will then outcompete other self-interested groups, and the fraction of strong reciprocators will grow. This will continue until an equilibrium fraction of strong reciprocators is attained.

While the above results can be obtained analytically, there is no easily interpretable mathematical expression for the equilibrium fraction of strong reciprocators. A computer simulation, however, is quite revealing. For instance, suppose in good times a group has a 95% chance of surviving one period, while in bad times (which occur one period out of 10), the group only has a 25% chance of surviving. Then the lower curve in Figure 42.3 shows the equilibrium fraction f^* of strong reciprocators as the cost of retaliation (c_r) varies and there are 40 members per group. The upper curve shows the

same relationship when there are eight members per group. The latter curve would be relevant if groups are composed of a small number of 'families', and the strong reciprocity characteristic is highly transmittable within families. Note that a very small fraction of strong reciprocators can ensure cooperation, but the lower the cost of retaliation, the larger the equilibrium frequency of strong reciprocators.

This model highlights a key adaptive feature of strong reciprocity—its independence from the probability of future interactions—but it presumes that reciprocal altruism explains cooperation in normal times, when the probability of future interactions is high. However, reciprocal altruism does not work well in large groups (Taylor, 1976; Joshi, 1987; Boyd and Richerson, 1988). This is because when one withdraws cooperation in retaliation for the defection of a single group member, one inflicts punishment on all members, defector and cooperators alike. The only evolutionarily stable strategy in the *n*-person public goods game is to cooperate as long as all others cooperate and to defect otherwise. For any pay-off–monotonic dynamic, the basin of attraction of this equilibrium becomes very small as group size increases, so the formation of groups with a sufficient number of conditional cooperators is very unlikely, and, as a result, such an outcome may be easily disrupted by idiosyncratic play, imperfect information about the play of others, or other stochastic events. As a result, if group size is large, such an equilibrium is unlikely to be arrived at over reasonable historical time scales. Moreover, the only equilibrium is a 'knife-edge' that collapses if just one member deviates.

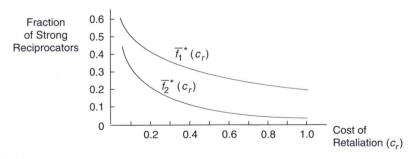

Fig. 42.3 The equilibrium fraction of strong reciprocating families: a computer simulation.

Another influential model of cooperation among self-regarding agents relies upon *reputation* effects in a repeated game setting. For instance, in *standing models* (Sugden, 1986; Boyd, 1989; Panchanathan and Boyd, 2003) individuals who are 'in good standing' in the community cooperate with others who are in good standing. If an individual fails to cooperate with someone who is in good standing, he falls into 'bad standing', and individuals in good standing will not cooperate with him. Such models are less sensitive to errors, but require that each individual know the standing of each other individual, updating with a high degree of accuracy in each period. This is plausible for small groups, but not for larger groups in which each individual observes only a small fraction of the total number of interactions among group members in each period.

In sum, strategies supporting contingent cooperation in large groups have to achieve two competing desiderata. To be stable when common, they must be intolerant of defection. But, to increase when rare there must be a substantial chance that groups with enough reciprocators can form, otherwise they cannot be evolutionarily stable, as defectors will prosper. As groups increase in size, this becomes geometrically more difficult.

To inject more realism in an evolutionary model of strong reciprocity, Henrich and Boyd (2001) developed a model in which norms for cooperation and punishment are acquired via pay-off-biased transmission (imitate the successful) and conformist transmission (imitate high-frequency behaviour). They show that if two stages of punishment are permitted, then an arbitrarily small amount of conformist transmission will stabilize cooperative behaviour by stabilizing punishment. They then explain how, once cooperation is stabilized in one group, it may spread through a multi-group population via cultural group selection. Once cooperation is prevalent, they show how prosocial genes favouring cooperation and punishment may invade in the wake of cultural group selection, for instance, because such genes decrease an individual's chance of suffering costly punishment.

This analysis reveals a deep asymmetry between altruistic cooperation and altruistic punishment, explored further in Boyd et al. (2003), who show that altruistic punishment allows cooperation in quite larger groups because the pay-off disadvantage of altruistic cooperators relative to defectors is independent of the frequency of defectors in the population, while the cost disadvantage of those engaged in altruistic punishment declines as defectors become rare. Thus, when altruistic punishers are common, selection pressures operating against them are weak. The fact that punishers experience only a small disadvantage when defectors are rare means that weak within-group evolutionary forces, such as conformist transmission, can stabilize punishment and allow cooperation to persist. Computer simulations show that selection among groups leads to the evolution of altruistic punishment when it could not maintain altruistic cooperation.

42.6. Gene–culture coevolution

If group selection is part of the explanation of the evolutionary success of cooperative individual behaviours, then it is likely that group-level characteristics, such as relatively small group size, limited migration, or frequent inter-group conflicts, that enhance group selection pressures coevolved with cooperative behaviours. Thus, group-level characteristics and individual behaviours may have synergistic effects. This being the case, cooperation is based in part on the distinctive capacities of humans to construct cultural forms that reduce phenotypic variation within groups, thus heightening the relative importance of between-group competition, and hence allowing individually costly but within-group-beneficial behaviours to coevolve with these supporting environments through a process of inter-demic group selection. The idea that the suppression of within-group competition may be a strong influence on evolutionary dynamics has been widely recognized in eusocial insects and other species. Boehm (1982) and Eibl-Eibesfeldt (1982) first applied this reasoning to human evolution, exploring the role of culturally transmitted practices that reduce phenotypic variation within groups. Examples of such practices are levelling institutions, such as monogamy and food sharing among non-kin, namely those which reduce within-group differences in reproductive fitness or material well-being. By reducing within-group differences in individual success, such structures may have attenuated within-group genetic or cultural selection operating against individually costly but group-beneficial practices, thus giving the groups adopting them advantages in inter-group contests. Group-level institutions thus are constructed environments capable of imparting distinctive direction and pace to the process of biological evolution and cultural change. Hence, the evolutionary success of social institutions that reduce phenotypic variation within groups may be explained by the fact that they retard selection pressures working against in-group beneficial individual traits and the fact that high frequencies of bearers of these traits reduce the likelihood of group extinctions. We have modelled an evolutionary dynamic along these lines, exploring the possibility that inter-group contests play a decisive role in group-level selection. Our models assume that genetically and culturally transmitted individual behaviours, as well as culturally transmitted group-level characteristics, are subject to selection (Bowles, 2001; Bowles et al., 2003). We show that inter-group conflicts may explain the evolutionary success of both: (a) altruistic forms of human sociality towards non-kin; and (b) group-level institutional structures such as food sharing and monogamy which have emerged and diffused repeatedly in a wide variety of ecologies during the course of human history. In-group-beneficial behaviours may evolve if (i) they inflict sufficient costs on out-group individuals and (ii) group-level institutions limit the individual costs of these behaviours and thereby attenuate within-group selection against these behaviours.

Our simulations show that if group-level institutions implementing resource sharing or non-random pairing among group members are permitted to evolve, group-beneficial individual traits co-evolve along with these institutions, even where the latter impose significant costs on the groups adopting them. These results hold for specifications in which cooperative individual behaviours and social institutions are initially absent in the population. In the absence of these group-level institutions, however, group-beneficial traits evolve only when inter-group conflicts are very frequent, groups are small, and migration rates are low. Thus the evolutionary success of cooperative behaviours during the last few hundred thousand years of human

evolution may have been a consequence of distinctive human capacities in social-institution-building (Boyd and Richerson, 2004).

42.7. **Is strong reciprocity an adaptation?**

Some behavioural scientists have suggested that the behaviour we have described in this chapter was individually fitness-maximizing in our hunter-gatherer past, when anonymity and one-shot interactions were, so they say, virtually non-existent (Johnson et al., 2003; Trivers, 2004). The human brain, they note, is not a general-purpose information processor, but rather a set of interacting modular systems adapted to solving the particular problems faced by our species in its evolutionary history. Since the anonymous, non-repeated interactions characteristic of experimental games were not a significant part of our evolutionary history, we could not expect subjects in experimental games to behave in a fitness-maximizing manner when confronted with them. Rather, we would expect subjects to confuse the experimental environment in more evolutionarily familiar terms as a non-anonymous, repeated interaction, and to maximize fitness with respect to this reinterpreted environment. This critique, even if correct, would not lessen the importance of strong reciprocity in contemporary societies, to the extent that modern life leads individuals to face the frequent anonymous, non-repeated interactions that are characteristic of modern societies with advanced trade, communication and transportation technologies. Thus, even if strong reciprocity were not an adaptation, it could nevertheless be an important factor in explaining human cooperation today.

But we do not believe that this critique is correct. In fact, humans are well capable of distinguishing individuals with whom they are likely to have many future interactions, from others, with whom future interactions are less likely. Indeed, human subjects cooperate much more if they expect frequent future interactions than if future interactions are rare (Gächter and Falk, 2002; Keser and vanWinden, 2000). Humans with fine-tuned behavioural repertoires depending on whether they face kin or non-kin, repeated or one-time interactors, and whether they can or cannot gain an individual reputation probably had an evolutionary advantage in our ancestral environment. The likely reason for this advantage is that humans faced many interactions where the probability of future interactions was sufficiently low to make defection worthwhile (Manson and Wrangham, 1991; Gintis, 2000b). Humans are similarly capable of recognizing when their actions are hidden from view and profiting from such situations.

42.8. Psychological and behavioural aspects of altruism: prosocial emotions and strong reciprocity

Prosocial emotions are physiological and psychological reactions that induce agents to engage in cooperative behaviours as we have defined them above. The prosocial emotions include some, such as shame, guilt, empathy, and sensitivity to social sanction, that induce agents to undertake constructive social interactions, and others, such as the desire to punish norm violators, that reduce freeriding when the prosocial emotions fail to induce sufficiently cooperative behaviour in some fraction of members of the social group (Frank, 1987; Hirshleifer, 1987).

Without the prosocial emotions, we would all be sociopaths, and human society would not exist, however strong the institutions of contract, governmental law enforcement, and reputation. Sociopaths have no mental deficit except that their capacity to experience shame, guilt, empathy, and remorse is severely attenuated or absent. They comprise 3–4% of the male population in the USA (Mealey 1995), but account for approximately 20% of the US prison population and between 33% and 80% of the population of chronic criminal offenders.

Prosocial emotions are responsible for the host of civil and caring acts that enrich our daily lives and render living, working, shopping, and travelling among strangers feasible and pleasant. Moreover, representative government, civil liberties, due process, women's rights, respect for minorities, to name a few of the key institutions without which human dignity would be impossible in the modern world, were brought about by people involved in collective action, pursuing not only their personal ends, but also a vision for all of humanity. Our freedoms and our comforts alike are based on the emotional dispositions of generations past. While we think the evidence is strong that prosocial emotions account for important forms of human cooperation, there is no universally accepted model of how emotions combine with more cognitive processes to affect behaviours. Nor is there much agreement on how best to represent the prosocial emotions that support cooperative behaviours, although Bowles and Gintis (2002) is one attempt in this direction.

42.9. The coevolution of institutions and behaviours

If group selection is part of the explanation of the evolutionary success of cooperative individual behaviours, then it is likely that group level-characteristics—such as relatively small group size, limited migration, or frequent inter-group conflicts—that enhance group selection pressures co-evolved with cooperative behaviours. Thus group-level characteristics and individual behaviours may have synergistic effects. This being the case, cooperation is based in part on the distinctive capacities of humans to construct institutional environments that limit within-group competition and reduce phenotypic variation within groups, thus heightening the relative importance of between-group competition, and hence allowing individually costly but in-group-beneficial behaviours to coevolve with these supporting environments through a process of inter-demic group selection.

The idea that the suppression of within-group competition may be a strong influence on evolutionary dynamics has been widely recognized in eusocial insects and other species. Alexander (1979), Boehm (1982) and Eibl-Eibesfeldt (1982) first applied this reasoning to human evolution, exploring the role of culturally transmitted practices that reduce phenotypic variation within groups. Examples of such practices are levelling institutions, such as resource sharing among non-kin, namely those which reduce within-group differences in reproductive fitness or material well-being. These practices are levelling to the extent that they result in less pronounced within-group differences in material well-being or fitness than would have obtained in their absence. Thus, the fact that good hunters who are generous towards other group members may experience higher fitness than other hunters and enjoy improved nutrition (as a result of consumption smoothing) does not indicate a lack of levelling unless these practices also result in lesser fitness and worse nutrition among less successful hunters (which seems highly unlikely).

By reducing within-group differences in individual success, such practices may have attenuated within-group genetic or cultural selection operating against individually costly but group-beneficial practices, thus giving the groups adopting them advantages in inter-group contests. Group-level institutions thus are constructed environments capable of imparting distinctive direction and pace to the process of biological evolution and cultural change. Hence, the evolutionary success of social institutions that reduce phenotypic variation within groups may be explained by the fact that they retard selection pressures working against in-group-beneficial individual traits and the fact that high frequencies of bearers of these traits reduce the likelihood of group extinctions.

We have modelled an evolutionary dynamic along these lines with the novel features that genetically and culturally transmitted individual behaviours as well as culturally transmitted group-level institutional characteristics are subject to selection, with inter-group contests playing a decisive role in group-level selection (Bowles, 2001; Bowles *et al.*, 2003).

Our simulations show that if group-level institutions implementing resource sharing or non-random pairing among group members are permitted to evolve, group-beneficial individual traits coevolve along with these institutions, even where the latter impose significant costs on the groups adopting them. These results hold for specifications in which cooperative individual behaviours and social institutions are initially absent in the population. In the absence of these group-level institutions, however, group-beneficial traits evolve only when inter-group

conflicts are very frequent, groups are small, and migration rates are low. Thus the evolutionary success of cooperative behaviours in the relevant environments during the first 90 000 years of anatomically modern human existence may have been a consequence of distinctive human capacities in social-institution-building.

42.10. **The internalization of norms**

An internal norm is a pattern of behaviour enforced in part by internal sanctions, including shame and guilt as outlined in the previous section. People follow internal norms when they value certain behaviours for their own sake, in addition to, or despite, the effects these behaviours have on personal fitness and/or perceived well-being. The ability to internalize norms is nearly universal among humans. Although widely studied in the sociology and social psychology literature (socialization theory), it has been virtually ignored outside these fields [but see Caporael *et al.* (1989) and Simon (1990)].

Socialization models have been strongly criticized for suggesting that people adopt norms independent of their perceived pay-offs. In fact, people do not always blindly follow the norms that have been inculcated in them, but at least at times treat compliance as a strategic choice (Gintis, 1975). The 'oversocialized' model of the individual presented in the sociology literature can be counteracted by adding a phenotypic copying process reflecting the fact that agents shift from lower to higher pay-off strategies (Gintis, 2003).

All successful cultures foster internal norms that enhance personal fitness, such as future-orientation, good personal hygiene, positive work habits, and control of emotions. Cultures also universally promote altruistic norms that subordinate the individual to group welfare, fostering such behaviours as bravery, honesty, fairness, willingness to cooperate, and empathy with the distress of others.

Given that most cultures promote cooperative behaviours, and if we accept the sociological notion that individuals internalize the norms that are passed to them by parents and other influential elders, it becomes easy to explain human cooperation. If even a fraction of society internalizes the norms of cooperation and punishes freeriders and other norm violators, a high degree of cooperation can be maintained in the long run. The puzzles are two: why do we internalize norms, and why do cultures promote cooperative behaviours?

In Gintis (2003), we provide an evolutionary model in which the capacity to internalize norms develops because this capacity enhances individual fitness in a world in which social behaviour has become too complex and multifaceted to be fruitfully evaluated piecemeal through individual rational assessment. Internalization moves norms from constraints that one can treat instrumentally towards maximizing well-being, to norms that are then valued as ends rather than means. It is not difficult to show that if an internal norm is fitness enhancing, then for plausible patterns of socialization, the allele for internalization of norms is evolutionarily stable. We may then use this framework to model Herbert Simon's (1990) explanation of altruism. Simon suggested that altruistic norms could 'hitchhike' on the general tendency of internal norms to be fitness-enhancing. However, Simon provided no formal model of this process and his ideas have been widely ignored. This paper shows that Simon's insight can be analytically modelled and is valid under plausible conditions. A straightforward gene–culture coevolution argument then explains why fitness-reducing internal norms are likely to be prosocial as opposed to socially harmful: groups with prosocial internal norms will outcompete groups with antisocial, or socially neutral, internal norms.

42.11. Conclusion

Contemporary behavioural theory is the legacy of several major contributions (Hamilton, 1964; Williams, 1966; Trivers, 1971; Wilson, 1975; Maynard Smith, 1982; Dawkins, 1989; Tooby and Cosmides, 1992), all of which assumed that the relations between non-kin could be modelled using self-regarding actors. It is not surprising, then, that the most successful research in behavioural theory has been in the area of the family, kinship, and sexual relations, while the attempts to deal with the more complex interactions characteristic of social group behaviour have

been less persuasive. To address this situation, we believe that more attention should be paid to: (i) the origin and nature of social emotions (including guilt, shame, empathy, ethnic identity, and ethnic hatred); (ii) the coevolution of genes and culture in human social history; (iii) the role of group structure and group conflict in human evolution; and (iv) integrating sociobiological insights into mainstream social sciences.

Acknowledgments

We would like to thank Martin Daly, Steve Frank and Margo Wilson for helpful comments, and the Santa Fe Institute and John D. and Catherine T. MacArthur Foundation for financial support.

References

Akerlof, G. A. (1982) Labor contracts as partial gift exchange. *Quarterly Journal of Economics*, 97: 543–569.

Alexander, R. D. (1979) *Biology and Human Affairs*. University of Washington Press, Seattle.

Andreoni, J. (1995) Cooperation in public goods experiments: kindness or confusion. *American Economic Review*, 85: 891–904.

Bingham, P. M. (1999) Human uniqueness: a general theory. *Quarterly Review of Biology*, 74: 133–169.

Blau, P. (1964) *Exchange and Power in Social Life*. Wiley, New York.

Boehm, C. (1982) The evolutionary development of morality as an effect of dominance behavior and conflict interference. *Journal of Social and Biological Structures*, 5: 413–421.

Bowles, S. (2001) Individual interactions, group conflicts, and the evolution of preferences. In S. N. Durlauf and H. P. Young (eds) *Social Dynamics*, pp. 155–190. MIT Press, Cambridge, MA.

Bowles, S. and Gintis, H. (2002) Homo reciprocans. *Nature*, 415: 125–128.

Bowles, S., Choi, J. and Hopfensitz, A. (2003) The co-evolution of individual behaviors and social institutions. *Journal of Theoretical Biology*, 223: 135–147.

Boyd, R. (1989) Mistakes allow evolutionary stability in the repeated prisoner's dilemma game. *Journal of Theoretical Biology*, 136: 47–56.

Boyd, R. and Richerson, P. J. (1988) The evolution of reciprocity in sizable groups. *Journal of Theoretical Biology*, 132: 337–356.

Boyd, R. and Richerson, P. J. (2004) *The Nature of Cultures*. University of Chicago Press, Chicago.

Boyd, R., Gintis, H., Bowles, S. and Richerson, P. J. (2003) Evolution of altruistic punishment, *Proceedings of the National Academy of Sciences of the USA*, 100: 3531–3535.

Camerer, C. and Thaler, R. (1995) Ultimatums, dictators, and manners. *Journal of Economic Perspectives*, 9: 209–219.

Caporael, L., Dawes, R., Orbell, J. and van de Kragt, J. C. (1989) Selfishness examined: Cooperation in the absence of egoistic incentives. *Behavioral and Brain Science*, 12: 683–738.

Darlington, P. J. (1975) Group selection, altruism, reinforcement and throwing in human evolution. *Proceedings of the National Academy of Sciences of the USA*, 72: 3748–3752.

Dawes, R. M. and Thaler, R. (1988) Cooperation. *Journal of Economic Perspectives*, 2: 187–197.

Dawkins, R. (1976, 2nd edition 1989) *The Selfish Gene*. Oxford University Press, Oxford.

Eibl-Eibesfeldt, I. (1982) Warfare, man's indoctrinability and group selection. *Journal of Comparative Ethnology*, 60: 177–198.

Fehr, E. and Gächter, S. (2000) Cooperation and punishment. *American Economic Review*, 90: 980–994.

Fehr, E. and Gächter, S. (2002) Altruistic punishment in humans. *Nature*, 415: 137–140.

Fehr, E. and Schmidt, K. M. (1999) A theory of fairness, competition, and cooperation. *Quarterly Journal of Economics*, 114: 817–868.

Fehr, E., Kirchsteiger, G. and Riedl, A. (1993) Does fairness prevent market clearing? *Quarterly Journal of Economics*, 108: 437–459.

Fehr, E., Gächter, S. and Kirchsteiger, G. (1997) Reciprocity as a contract enforcement device: experimental evidence. *Econometrica*, 65: 833–860.

Fehr, E., Kirchsteiger, G. and Riedl, A. (1998) Gift exchange and reciprocity in competitive experimental markets. *European Economic Review*, 42: 1–34.

Feldman, M. W., Cavalli-Sforza, L. L. and Peck, J. R. (1985) Gene–culture coevolution: models for the evolution of altruism with cultural transmission. *Proceedings of the National Academy of Sciences of the USA*, 82: 5814–5818.

Fifer, F. C. (1987) The adoption of bipedalism by the hominids: a new hypothesis. *Human Evolution*, 2: 135–147.

Frank, R. H. (1987) If Homo Economicus could choose his own utility function, would he want one with a conscience? *American Economic Review*, 77: 593–604.

Fudenberg, D. and Maskin, E. (1986) The folk theorem in repeated games with discounting or with incomplete information. *Econometrica*, 54: 533–554.

Gächter, S. and Falk, A. (2002) Reputation and reciprocity: consequences for the labour relation. *Scandinavian Journal of Economics*, 104: 1–26.

Gächter, S. and Fehr, E. (1999) Collective action as a social exchange. *Journal of Economic Behavior and Organization*, 39: 341–369.

Ghiselin, M. T. (1974) *The Economy of Nature and the Evolution of Sex*. University of California Press, Berkeley.

Gintis, H. (1975) Welfare economics and individual development: a reply to Talcott Parsons. *Quarterly Journal of Economics*, 89: 291–302.

Gintis, H. (2000a) *Game Theory Evolving*. Princeton University Press, Princeton, NJ.

Gintis, H. (2000b) Strong reciprocity and human sociality. *Journal of Theoretical Biology*, 206: 169–179.

Gintis, H. (2003) The hitchhiker's guide to altruism: genes, culture, and the internalization of norms. *Journal of Theoretical Biology*, 220: 407–418.

Gintis, H., Bowles, S., Boyd, R. and Fehr, E. (2005) *Moral Sentiments and Material Interests: On the Foundations of Cooperation in Economic Life*. MIT Press, Cambridge, MA.

Goodall, J. (1964) Tool-using and aimed throwing in a community of free-living chimpanzees. *Nature*, 201: 1264–1266.

Güth, W. and Tietz, R. (1990) Ultimatum bargaining behavior: a survey and comparison of experimental results. *Journal of Economic Psychology*, 11: 417–449.

Hamilton, W. D. (1964) The genetical evolution of social behavior i & ii. *Journal of Theoretical Biology*, 7: 1–16, 17–52.

Henrich, J. and Boyd, R. (2001) Why people punish defectors: weak conformist transmission can stabilize costly enforcement of norms in cooperative dilemmas. *Journal of Theoretical Biology*, 208: 79–89.

Henrich, J., Boyd, R., Bowles, S., Camerer, C., Fehr, E., Gintis, H. and McElreath, R. (2001) Cooperation, reciprocity and punishment in fifteen small-scale societies. *American Economic Review*, 91: 73–78.

Henrich, J., Boyd, R., Bowles, S., Camerer, C., Fehr, E. and Gintis, H. (2005) Economic man' in cross-cultural perspective: behavioral experiments in 15 small-scale societies. *Behavioral and Brain Sciences*.

Hirshleifer, J. (1987) Economics from a biological viewpoint. In Barney, J. B. and Ouchi, W. G. (eds) *Organizational Economics*, pp. 319–371. Jossey-Bass, San Francisco.

Homans, G. (1961) *Social Behavior: Its Elementary Forms*. Harcourt Brace, New York.

Isaac, B. (1987) Throwing and human evolution. *African Archeological Review*, 5: 3–17.

Johnson, D. P., Stopka, P. and Knights, S. (2003) The puzzle of human cooperation. *Nature*, 421: 911–912.

Joshi, N. V. (1987) Evolution of cooperation by reciprocation within structured demes. *Journal of Genetics*, 66: 69–84.

Keser, C. and van Winden, F. (2000) Conditional cooperation and voluntary contributions to public goods. *Scandinavian Journal of Economics*, 102: 23–39.

Ledyard, J. O. (1995) Public goods: a survey of experimental research. In Kagel, J. H. and Roth, A. E. (eds) *The Handbook of Experimental Economics*, pp. 111–194. Princeton University Press, Princeton, NJ.

Manson, J. H. and Wrangham, R. W. (1991) Intergroup aggression in chimpanzees. *Current Anthropology*, 32: 369–390.

Maynard Smith, J. (1976) Sexual selection and the handicap principle. *Journal of Theoretical Biology*, 57: 239–242.

Maynard Smith, J. (1982) *Evolution and the Theory of Games*. Cambridge University Press, Cambridge, UK.

Mealey, L. (1995) The sociobiology of sociopathy. *Behavioral and Brain Sciences*, 18: 523–541.

Orbell, J. M., Dawes, R. M. and Van de Kragt, J. C. (1986) Organizing groups for collective action. *American Political Science Review*, 80: 1171–1185.

Ostrom, E., Gardner, R. and Walker, J. (1994) *Rules, Games, and Common-Pool Resources*. University of Michigan Press, Ann Arbor.

Ostrom, E., Walker, J. and Gardner, R. (1992) Covenants with and without a sword: self governance is possible. *American Political Science Review*, 86: 404–417.

Panchanathan, K. and Boyd, R. (2003) A tale of two defectors: the importance of standing for evolution of indirect reciprocity. *Journal of Theoretical Biology*, 224: 115–126.

Plooij, F. X. (1978) Tool-using during chimpanzees' bushpig hunt. *Carnivore*, 1: 103–106.

Rogers, A. R. (1990) Group selection by selective emigration: the effects of migration and kin structure. *American Naturalist*, 135: 398–413.

Roth, A. E., Prasnikar, V., Okuno-Fujiwara, M. and Zamir, S. (1991) Bargaining and market behavior in Jerusalem, Ljubljana, Pittsburgh, and Tokyo: an experimental study. *American Economic Review*, 81: 1068–1095.

Sato, K. (1987) Distribution and the cost of maintaining common property resources. *Journal of Experimental Social Psychology*, 23: 19–31.

Simon, H. (1990) A mechanism for social selection and successful altruism. *Science*, 250: 1665–1668.

Sober, E. and Wilson, D. S. (1998) *Unto Others: The Evolution and Psychology of Unselfish Behavior*. Harvard University Press, Cambridge, MA.

Sugden, R. (1986) *The Economics of Rights, Co-operation and Welfare*. Blackwell, Oxford.

Taylor, M. (1976) *Anarchy and Cooperation*. Wiley, London.

Tooby, J. and Cosmides, L. (1992) The psychological foundations of culture. In J. H. Barkow, L. Cosmides and J. Tooby (eds) *The Adapted Mind: Evolutionary Psychology and the Generation of Culture*, pp. 19–136. Oxford University Press, New York.

Trivers, R. L. (1971) Mutual benefits at all levels of life. *Science*, 304: 964–965.

Trivers, R. L. (2004) The evolution of reciprocal altruism. *Quarterly Review of Biology*, 46: 35–57.

Williams, G. C. (1966) *Adaptation and Natural Selection: A Critique of Some Current Evolutionary Thought*. Princeton University Press, Princeton, NJ.

Wilson, E. O. (1975) *Sociobiology: The New Synthesis*. Harvard University Press, Cambridge, MA.

Yamagishi, T. (1986) The provision of a sanctioning system as a public good. *Journal of Personality and Social Psychology*, 51: 110–116.

Yamagishi, T. (1988a) The provision of a sanctioning system in the United States and Japan. *Social Psychology Quarterly*, 51: 265–271.

Yamagishi, T. (1988b) Seriousness of social dilemmas and the provision of a sanctioning system. *Social Psychology Quarterly*, 51: 32–42.

Yamagishi, T. (1992) Group size and the provision of a sanctioning system in a social dilemma. In W. Liebrand, D. M. Messick and H. Wilke (eds) *Social Dilemmas: Theoretical Issues and Research Findings*, pp. 267–287. Pergamon Press, Oxford.

CHAPTER 43

The evolution of religion

Joseph A. Bulbulia

43.1. Introduction

In this chapter, I review recent theoretical and experimental work in the cognitive and evolutionary psychology of religion, and motivate an adaptationist stance. By 'religious cognition' and 'religiosity' I mean belief and practice relative to the supernatural beings and powers—call them 'gods'.

Much of the work in the naturalistic study of religion views religiosity as an after-effect or spandrel of a mind not designed for religion. Some theorists explain religion as the product of viral-like ideas working for their own success; on this view, religion is an adaptation but not ours (Dawkins, 1976; Blackmore, 2000; Dennett, 2006). Other researchers urge that religion's adaptive features emerge at the level of religious groups; these features (where they exist) are best studied in virtue of cultural evolution. We inherit religious ideas and practices (some maladaptive) from our parents through a flow of ideas, not genes (Boyd and Richerson, 1985; Richerson and Boyd, 1989; Wilson, 2002; Richerson and Boyd, 2005). Here religion may be adaptive without being an adaptation, a *species* trait. Others maintain that genetic resources predispose some individuals to spirituality but there is individual variation in these dispositions. The relevant traits do not describe god commitment but rather describe 'spirituality' (Hamer, 2004). Presumably, selection maintains variation in these dispositions through frequency-dependent selection on the relevant alleles. It is not yet clear how to integrate the inchoate studies on spirituality genes with the separate (though perhaps related) phenomena of belief and practices relative to the supernatural powers and agents; for spirituality genes are not god genes.

Below I suggest that religiosity—god commitment and the behaviour it prompts and that motivate it—bears the hallmark of adaptive design. Religious cognition solves functionally useful and enduring problems that would have confronted ancestral hominids, and there is evidence that we possess a very specific and otherwise improbable mental architecture to do its business. Adaptive (indeed non-lethal) religiosity is more like an achievement than a harmless mistake, as spandrelists urge, or catching a cold, as meme theorists urge. And the cognitive demands on the intergenerational flow of religious ideas are substantial, allowing selection to target and amplify dedicated cognitive architecture to facilitate the transmission and improvement of religious ideas and practices. So I will contend.

Let's begin with a serious obstacle to any evolutionary treatment of religion. Science assumes methodological naturalism. We do not stipulate the gods out of existence. But we begin with the idea that nature is secular and see how far this assumption takes us. For all we know naturalists of the distant future will appeal to gods in their explanations for our belief in them. But for now, our aim is to produce a good explanation from minimal assumptions about the complexity of the world.

From the naturalistic stance religiosity is striking. If the gods do not exist then religious persons systematically err in their judgements about the world. This is puzzling because cognition evolved to enable agents to get the world right. For misunderstanding the world typically comes at a cost to an organism's inclusive fitness. Given the fitness costs of error, it seems that selection should have weeded out cognitive features that allow us to produce religious mistakes (Godfrey-Smith, 1996; Sterelny, 2003).

Yet religious commitment is rampant. It appears in all cultures, is nearly universal among foragers (whose life-ways resembles those of our distant ancestors), and even remains popular in scientifically advanced societies. Where ancient religious traditions are losing their hold, new-age spiritualities, astrologies, and spiritualist fusions are rushing in (e.g. Reader and Tanabe, 1998). Whatever one's position on the spandrel/adaptation question, we know natural selection did not substantially cull the psychological structures that allow for supernatural commitment. Religion remains persuasive.

More puzzling, religious commitment stimulates reproductively costly behaviour. Some of these costs are substantial. Ritual participants subject themselves to fatigue, exposure, injury, disease, bodily discomfort, and impairment. At the extreme, practices of suicide bombing, genital mutilation and celibacy are straightforwardly devastating to gene lineages prone to them. Yet even mundane religious practices come with opportunity costs: sitting in silence, bowing before statues, flattering priests, defers the commerce of life. Religion saddles the committed with *practical costs*. And if you are a religious eunuch, self-immolator, suicide soldier, or celibataire, these saddles can be heavy indeed.

It is easy to imagine that selection permitted religiosity because its benefits outweigh these harms. Naturalists have discerned important functionality: religion enhances solidarity, provides existential purpose, explains our origins and fates, and activates placebo healing (Preus, 1987; Sosis and Alcorta, 2003). Some question the adequacy of these functional interpretations (Boyer, 2001; Dennett, 2006). Yet even conceding this functionality, naturalists have underrated the explanatory problem. For there appear to be less costly, evolvable designs.

It remains mysterious why functions related to health would hinge on priestcraft: our interests do not converge perfectly. Similarly baffling is how trials by fire or witch hunts or celibate lifestyles feed the need for scientific explanation. Selection should prefer no science to bad science because the costs of bad science are manifold (e.g. arsenic as a treatment for hysteria, etc.: Shapiro and Shapiro, 1997). Likewise it is hard to understand how fellow feeling and solidarity might benefit from silent meditation, walking over coals, or livestock sacrifice. The strong bonds of friendship, for example, require no extraneous theology, trials by fire, or slaughter. Whether religion provides meaning and solace is debatable. For the gods can be capricious, arbitrary, and terrifying (Berger, 1990). More problematically, existential worries themselves need to be explained, for philosophical anxiety distracts us from the tasks of life.

The epistemic and practical costs of religion leave us with *the cost problem*. Organisms shouldn't think and act as we do (Atran, 2002, 2004; Bulbulia, 2004a; see also Dennett, 2006, for thorough discussion). Why then, did natural selection not reduce or eliminate religious tendencies?

43.2. **Spandrel theories**

The standard picture of cognitive evolution presents selection as incrementally assembling ever more intricate and discerning cognitive designs. Gradually, lineages get better at appreciating and responding to stable features of their environments relevant to survival. Perceptual systems become more resolved, reflexes more finely attuned, and behavioural responses more elaborate, flexible, and precise. Selection gradually makes animals more god-like.

Much of our cognitive complexity comports to this picture, but the picture needs to be revised. Selection must factor the evolutionary costs and accessibility of accurate registration against alternative designs. Getting the world right is no easy task. Our evolutionary interests frequently diverge from those around us. Indeed, large chunks of the world are hostile to our interests. Organisms pollute the epistemic environments of their rivals; the signals an agent receives are often noisy. Filtering the noise to accurately represent the world is computationally intensive, and there may not be enough time, information, or cognitive resource to get it right. Frequently error will satisifice a fitness function. Assigning cost and benefits to response strategies is difficult, for not all parameters are known; yet abstractly we know that where:

Average reproductive costs of perfection of accuracy < Average costs of inaccuracy,

then,

All things being equal, selection will favour inaccuracy.

We have assumed that there are no gods in nature. This is true of the gods we worship, and it is also true of ourselves. The first wave of cognitive research on religion began with an appreciation of human imperfection. The field's vanguards understood natural selection's power to build intricate psychological architecture, but they also understood that this power is constrained. In an early work in the field, Stewart Guthrie argued that religious experience emerges from dispositions to overgeneralize agency (Guthrie, 1993). We believe the world is filled with human agents because hair-trigger perceptual-response strategies animate the world around us. Our tendency to anthropomorphism optimizes a tough problem; the world is ambiguous. When sighting persons, false positives bring little cost. Yet false negatives can be disastrous. Other persons are critical to our existence and progress in life; they also provide the most significant threats. Hence, we need to find other agents when they are there. Given the benefits of agent detection, the low costs of false positives when compared with false negatives, and the stability of this equation over phylogenic time, a 'Hyperactive Agent Detection Device' (HADD) looks evolvable ('HADD' is a term coined by Justin Barrett, 2000).

This conjecture is amenable to empirical testing, and Guthrie (1993, 2001) marshals much evidence that we anthropomorphize. We see faces in the clouds, dramas in inkblots, night shadows as villains; and we see the supernatural everywhere.

Yet clearly this story cannot explain all religious thought and behaviour. In response to ambiguous person sightings, we do not typically tattoo our faces, or spend decades building Gothic cathedrals, or give up sex for life. At best, HADD explains an aspect of a more elaborate

causal process. Furthermore, HADD mischaracterizes the perceptual aspects of religious cognition. If religion were simply based on fast and dirty perceptual heuristics, we could easily correct religious errors. You leap, note it was only the wind, and cease worrying. Yet we generally don't correct for supernatural mistakes in this way. A Hindu won't give up Shiva worship when you tell her it was only the wind. Guthrie's book did not ignite a worldwide movement to atheism—'Alas God was only a face in the cloud.' Instead, religious judgement becomes easily entrenched. It resists fast and substantial revision (Berger and Luckmann, 1972). Yet such entrenchment usually does not hold off inferences to the best explanation in other domains, certainly not in most perceptual domains.

Perhaps a more significant problem here is that the gods are never experienced as human agents. We do not, strictly speaking, project humanity into the world. We project *super-humanity*. And why we do so remains mysterious on Guthrie's account. For if religious experience happens because it is important to find people, why does religious understanding never turn on people-sightings?

About the time Guthrie was developing his HADD account, the cognitive anthropologist Pascal Boyer was developing an alternative that addresses this explanatory lacuna (Boyer, 1992, 1994; for similar accounts see also Pyysiainen, 2001; Atran, 2004). The central theme running throughout Boyer's work is that religious ideas are conceptually configured to activate multiple features of the intuitive inference systems that govern our ordinary understandings of the world. For Boyer, religious ideas are memorable precisely because they violate our intuitive expectations— that is, *because they are supernatural*.

Notice: culture matters to how we understand and engage with the world and each other. Yet psychologists have discovered that many features of cognitive processing and development closely resemble the function and growth of biological organs. Children know more than they learn. The perception and inference engines that guide us through hostile reality need to operate quickly. And for invariant aspects of our world, richly structured and rapid cognitive processing can emerge in a lineage without strong external scaffolding. Large parts of our tracking and response systems function implicitly. Children appear to acquire folk physics, much of language and agent-psychology, and basic biological reasoning without explicit or heavily structured learning environments (Gelman and Markman, 1987; Gelman and Kremer, 1991; Spelke *et al.*, 1995) though see (Sterelny, 2003, 2006).

Boyer has shown experimentally that 'supernatural' concepts are intrinsically memorable (Boyer and Ramble, 2001). He conjectures that because supernatural concepts violate our intuitive expectations for the relevant natural kinds, they are both striking and present fewer memory demands. The gods are unusual and uncanny agents. We heed them precisely because they are so counter-intuitive and strange. Boyer further observes there are constraints on the degree to which intuition-violating concepts are memorable. For counter-intuitive concepts are subject to threshold effects. Minimally counter-intuitive concepts come with low memory demands: intuitive psychology dictates how we think about them, save the striking, attention-grabbing difference. God thinks like a man, and is in most respects like a man, but unlike a man created everything and can destroy everything. The notion that there is such a being is interesting and thus memorable. However, the architectonic multiple-intuition-violating gods of the philosophers—those superconfigurations of properties described in lengthy theological tomes—are not memorable. For we cannot rely on folk psychology to guide our intuitions about all the relevant properties of these matrix gods. Once supernatural concepts become too unusual and extraordinary, we are neither interested nor influenced (Boyer and Ramble, 2001).

It is crucial to Boyer's (2001) story that no single cognitive mechanism is responsible for religious thought. 'Religiosity' is not a natural kind. Nor has religiosity evolved to benefit religious agents or groups (p. 330): "There is no religious instinct, no specific inclination in the mind, no particular disposition for these concepts, no special religion center in the brain, and religious persons are not different from nonreligious ones in essential cognitive functions." Instead, many different systems grinding through the same conceptual information produces

behaviour we in ordinary language loosely describe under a common adjective 'religious'. But this language is inadequate to science (p. 330): "Instead of a religious mind, what we have found is a whole frustration of invisible hands."

There is much experimental evidence to support Boyer's account (reviewed by Boyer, 2003). The theory predicts that religious persons will not process religious commitments as elaborate theological doctrines of the kind religious elites promote, and in which, during reflective moments, religious persons claim to believe. Instead the theory predicts that religious agents will think of their gods as persons, save for a few extraordinary properties. In an important experiment, Justin Barrett and Frank Keil (1996, 1998) confirmed that religious devotees in America and India represent their gods anthropomorphically. Indeed, Barrett and Keil found that such representations conflict with believers' expressed theological commitments. For example, participants in these experiments assent to the theological proposition that their god is all knowing, but nevertheless believe that prayer is sometimes necessary to communicate thoughts to the divine. So it appears Guthrie was almost right: *minimally adjusted* anthropomorphic thought is religiosity's universal mode (see Barrett, 2004).

Does Boyer's spandrel theory adequately explain why we believe in the gods, and commit passionately to them? Spandrel theory manifests the theoretical virtue of parsimony. It is better if religion can be explained without reference to a special-purpose mind design, for we should not look for complexity beyond necessity. Yet I am among a growing number of naturalists who are not satisfied that religion is an evolutionary accident (Irons, 1996, 2001; Sosis, 2003, 2004; Bering, 2004; Bulbulia, 2004a,b; Dunbar, 2005; Johnson, 2005). In our view, spandrel explanations fail to explain why religious agents strongly commit to supernatural reality in a natural world lacking supernatural inputs. Memory of a concept is one thing. Giving over your life is another. Adaptationists do not believe that spandrelizing religion solves the cost problem. In our view, it is nearly miraculous (if you will) that agents come to identify so strongly with gods. The poverty of stimulus here is almost complete. There are no dragon-tongued gods to generate dragon-tongue god beliefs. Moreover selection is highly conservative. Were religious cost maladaptive, selection should have reduced and eliminated religious inclinations as it compared alternative designs over hundreds of generations. Indeed there are at least three evolutionary pathways bypassing costly religious cognition. (i) Any gradual *improvement in epistemic accuracy* would have displaced religious errors, with flow-on effects to practical costs. And so were religion maladaptive, selection would have targeted dispositions to meet counter-intuitive information with scoffing incredulity rather than pious commitment. Furthermore, (ii) by holding accuracy fixed but *minimizing the error rate*, selection would have reduced epistemic costs, thereby undercutting the basis for religious practice. If we only thought to believe in Zeus twice in our lives etc., we'd have saved much sacrificial cattle. Finally, (iii) *severing the motivational connections* linking belief to practice would have rendered religious beliefs, however common, inert and nearly harmless. If religious belief were dislodged from motivational processing it would cause less maladaptive harm. Without religious passion there would be no heavy reproductive cross to drag. Yet selection did not nudge religious cognition in any of these three directions. If anything, the motivational knobs of religious conviction and emotion are set too high.

To shed light on religion's adaptive functionality, I urge viewing the costs surrounding religion as adaptive signals. Religiosity may be adaptive in other ways (for example, see an account of healing functions in McClenon, 2002). Here I will focus only on the signalling dimension. To motivate this adaptationist stance I need to introduce two conceptual tools: (i) elementary game theory, from economics, and (ii) costly signalling theory, from behavioural ecology.

43.3. Game theory and the evolutionary dynamics of cooperation

An important factor in the biological success of our lineage has been our capacity to secure reliable cooperation among non-kin (Sterelny, 2003). Working together, agents can pool their resources to achieve more than going it alone.

For many organisms it makes sense to team up with others, and many lineages exhibit powerful social tendencies. Fish school to reduce the risks of predation and to increase vigilance. A large cohort brings lower odds that the local predator will eat you; lots of eyes are better than two. Gray wolves coordinate their attacks on large prey; lots of jaws bring down the beast, and a shared kill is better than none at all.

We are an impressively cooperative primate. Indeed, our encephalization appears to have been driven by the demands of social life (Dunbar, 1998). We think well to cooperate well. By co-coordinating our plans, and anchoring individual fates to collective outcomes, agents are able to promote their interests more effectively than by going it alone. Yet our alliances are notoriously unstable. Defectors benefit by stealing the advantages of collective life without sacrifice. Exchange usually pays better than it costs. But defecting from exchange, taking its spoils without paying a price, often pays better still. And where many defect, the benefits of cooperation are lost (Skyrms, 1996).

To understand the issues, consider an exchange problem among a pair of unrelated individuals. This problem is called a 'generalized prisoner's dilemma' (PD; there are many types of cooperation problem but PDs are probably the easiest to understand). Assume that P is the fitness pay-off (the relevant utility) of non-cooperative individual action. Call R, the reward for cooperative action (give and take). Let T = the temptation (i.e. the pay-off) to cheat (to take but not give), and let S = the pay-off for cooperating when an exchange partner cheats (to give but not take).

Though the prisoner's dilemma is not an a priori given in nature, a large class of interactions will conform to the following pay-off matrix:

T (cheating) > R (reciprocity) > P (solitary action) > S (getting cheated).

Where an exchange is structured in this way, an agent built to optimize self-interest will choose to defect. No matter what other agents do, prisoner dilemma exchange is structured so that a defector maximizes utility by cheating. 'Defection' strongly dominates cooperation. It is what economists call the 'Nash equilibrium' for this exchange (Nash, 1951; Schelling, 1960). The tragedy of such interactions is that that cooperation is 'strictly efficient'. If agents were simply to opt for reciprocal exchange, they would be better off than by going it alone (Skyrms, 1996).

Nevertheless cooperation is not lost. The problem is solved when defection is made too costly, too risky, or too difficult to arrange. There are numerous means by which agents can alter pay-off schedules so that R > T. In iterated dilemmas agents with memories can punish defectors by avoiding them in future encounters (Axelrod, 1990). Moreover agents can develop various commitment devices and technologies for securing exchange. By empowering Bob to cut my arm off should I not keep to the arrangement bargain, I've ensured that I will. Yet how do I grant and maintain these powers? The policing of exchange can be costly and unreliable in ever so many ways (Axelrod, 1997; Bulbulia, 2004a; Johnson, 2005).

Moralizing religious understandings can solve cooperative problems cheaply. They do so by altering the expected returns of cooperative action. Consider self-interested agents who believe that cooperation always pays better than defection. Assuming their belief–desire psychology remains in tact, such agents will have motivations to exchange cooperatively. This remains true whatever the actual (i.e. natural) pay-off matrix. Suppose the reward for a cooperative response is perceived to be eternal bliss and the punishment for defection is perceived to be reincarnation as a dung beetle. Such belief is at odds with nature, for it inaccurately depicts probable outcomes. We assume you won't come back as anything. Here the relevant causal processes are supernatural. Yet *because* cognition errs in precisely this way, it cheaply motivates reciprocity. The belief that what goes around comes around polices behaviour without police.

Perceived supernatural pay-off matrix: R > P > S > T

If you believe in karma, or that infidels are punished, or that religion is its own best reward (for religious motivations need not be extrinsic), then your religiosity when shared can solve prisoner's dilemmas. The key word here is 'shared'. Selection will equip agents for moralizing religion only where it is possible to reliably recognize the presence of common moralizing religious understanding. Thus, solving the *recognition constraint* is critical to the evolution of religious cognition. For discerning and

signalling religious commitments would have been an essential precondition to establishing moralizing religious dispositions in our lineage. The supernatural reward hypothesis therefore predicts that reliable signalling mechanisms will emerge to solve the recognition constraint. For in the absence of such mechanisms tendencies to moralizing religion would be quickly eliminated.

43.4. **Costly signalling theory**

Cooperators seek to exchange only with other cooperators. In order to do this, cooperators must identify each other. But how? An arbitrary signal of cooperative intention will not work. For it is always in a defector's interest to mimic such a signal, only to defect when favourable (Zahavi, 1993). In an evolutionary arms race, defectors will always match the arbitrary signals of religious cooperators. Selection therefore needs to equip religious agents with the capacity to produce signals that *only* religious persons can reliably produce. Note that the recognition constraint is far from trivial. For what could count as such a signal? In answering this question, we can begin to understand how the many of the *practical* costs of religion have adaptive value (Irons, 2001; Sosis, 2003; Sosis and Alcorta, 2003; Sosis and Ruffle, 2003). For these costs identify cognitive and motivational resources that religious persons possess, but which non-religious persons do not possess.

The study of animal signalling systems has shed much light on how selection outfits organisms with biological devices capable of indicating and measuring cooperative commitment (Zahavi and Zahavi, 1997). Organisms use 'handicaps' to authentically signal their properties and intentions (Zahavi, 1975). A reliable signal will be structured so that only a signaller that actually possesses the relevant property or intention will be able to afford producing the signal. Suppose I want to know if you're rich. You can say you're rich—anyone can—but the Ferrari provides real evidence.

Costly signals of intention and worth are rampant in nature. The songs of male bulbuls (*Pycnonotidae*) are carefully arranged to signal strength and fitness. The musical ornamentation correlates with fitness, so is able to attract mates and frighten rivals. The whistling of skylarks when chased by predatory merlins is also a costly signal of aerobic fitness, one that generally forestalls the chase. Skylarks able to sing as predators stalk are unlikely to be caught, so merlins generally do not bother them. The stotting of springbok gazelle in the presence of lions is another hard-to-fake signal of fitness and speed. The gazelle would like the lions to starve; the lions would prefer gazelle to lie down without a chase. Stotting allows for a cooperative compromise, one that averts constant chasing (the option in this PD of 'going it alone'; for discussion see Bulbulia, 2004b).

With respect to religious signals, consider how *religious emotions* function as hard-to-fake signals of religious commitment. Emotions are not private affairs of the heart locked away from view, not even in England. They can be detected in facial expressions, intonations, trembling, perspiration, blushing, violent outbursts and other perceptual traces. Furthermore emotions are difficult to manage. They are processed in the limbic system, outside of the executive control centres of the cerebral cortex (Frank, 1988; Ramachandran and Blakeslee, 1998). It is precisely because emotions are difficult to manipulate that they function as reliable signals. We can lie with words but faking tears is harder. I conjecture that religious emotions function as signals that identify the presence of moralizing motivations and commitments (Bulbulia, 2004a). Weeping before a statue of Shiva suggests commitment to a cosmos in which Shiva reigns. Arm waving and ecstatic grimacing at a Christian rock concert are hard-to-fake markers of Christian commitment. It may well be that such emotional signals modulate to assess the degree to which a believer is committed. For informally, it seems we can distinguish between powerful and weak religious displays. Lots of tears and arm waving suggests strong commitments; moderate half-hearted flinching, perhaps, less. If there is a link between motivations and expressions, it would appear that the magnitude of a devotion signal is inversely proportional to the odds for defection (Bulbulia, 2004a). This conjecture can be tested by assessing how religious persons factor emotional signals into their exchange forecasts and plans. (Below I will come back to empirical results that bear on these conjectures.)

Emotional signals predict future behaviour. But for a display to be effective, there must be an audience. A significant facilitator of religious display is public religious ritual, occasions that both elicit and enable the scrutinizing of hard-to-fake religious emotions. Rituals appear to have many functions—to conventionally communicate intentions, inculcate doctrines, promulgate laws, forge alliances, build hope and solace, mark transitions, calm, excite, or entertain participants—and these functions vary with contexts and individuals. Evolutionary researchers also suggest that ritual functions to provide forums in which religious emotions, and other costly signals of commitment, can be produced and evaluated (Sosis, 2003). Though no theorist, I am aware of suggestions that ritual behaviour emerges from genetic endowment (as does the exquisite dance of male peacocks or the display propensities of bowerbirds). Our love for ritual activity and the disposition to scan and process the information we acquire from them may well be guided by internally structured design. While the jury is out on how far biological endowment shapes and constrains ritual design, even if rituals are construed as fully technological artefacts (invented, and transmitted in the flow of cultural ideas), their presence and improvement would have greatly enhanced the evolution of tendencies to form supernatural convictions and commitments. For I repeat, such tendencies will not be selected in the absence of a solution to the recognition constraint. (For non-adaptationist accounts that posit strong psychological constraints on the design of religious rituals see: Whitehouse, 1992, 2000, 2004; McCauley and Lawson, 2002.)

A second means by which the religious can reliably signal supernatural commitment is by undertaking *practical costs*. Turning up at a ritual or hazarding a religious practice minimally involves an opportunity cost. And beyond such costs, rituals demand sacrifices of attention and resource, and some religious practices are exhausting, dangerous, painful, and supremely boring to the undevout. Again, were religious practice not adaptive, it is hard to understand why selection would tolerate religious costs. Adaptationists urge that such practices are generally adaptive. Participation, under the scrutinizing eye of an audience, serves to signal religious, and so cooperative, commitment. Adaptationists predict that ritual trials will be fashioned so that only those committed to moralizing super-nature will be willing to endure them frequently. The practical costs of ritual participation will render expected utilities explicit in ways directly related to supernatural belief. This condition is especially important where groups compete against each other for resources, and so where defection incentives are especially high.

Consider Bob a religious believer in a moralizing supernatural order. Bob faces a decision whether to partake of a strenuous or tedious ritual. Bob must weigh the costs of ritual participation times their frequency against the conditional probability the gods will bring about an outcome whose benefit outweighs the expected total practical cost of participation. If Bob thinks that participation brings (intrinsic or extrinsic) supernatural reward then:

The cost of religious practice × frequency < conditional probability of value through supernatural reward.

Now consider Roz the unbeliever. Roz wants to fake religious commitment and defect. Roz doesn't think the gods will give her anything for her time, energy, and resource outlay. She anticipates only further rituals everlastingly with no supernatural commission. Beyond ongoing practical costs, Roz must factor the conditional risk of getting caught, and, in the relevant setting, punished. Hence Roz's expected utility from costly religious practice may well exceed her perceived utility in cheating the devout. For she has no supernatural surplus weighting the religious option. Hence for Roz:

The conditional probability of value from cheating the devout < costs of ritual participation × frequency

So the practical costs of religion are neither arbitrary nor maladaptive. While verbal expressions of religious conviction are cheap; religious practice assesses whether the religious are willing to back locutions with deeds (for further discussion see Sosis and Alcorta, 2003; Bulbulia, 2004a).

Notice that where the pay-offs from defection are high, religious imposters can nevertheless invade religious communities. The expectation, therefore, is for the costs surrounding religious practice to modulate to assess the strength of religious devotion. Adaptationists hypothesize that ritual costs and frequency will correlate with defection incentives. This leads to a surprising prediction. When facing crisis, religious individuals will tend to devote *more* time and material resources to costly ritual participation than they normally do. At first glance such outlays are puzzling, for with adversity we would ordinarily predict a tendency to conserve. Daniel Chen observed precisely this correlation in his analysis of the Indonesian financial crises of the late 1990s (Johnson, 2003; D. Chen, unpublished data). As money and resources dried up, Muslim Indonesian families devoted a greater share of their dwindling reserves to religious observance. Though apparently maladaptive, Chen observes that religious institutions provide social insurance. They minimize the risks by collectively supporting the most needy. Costly observance in insurance societies makes the join–defect–leave strategy more expensive.

There is further experimental support for the ritual adaptationist hypothesis. Bill Irons and his colleagues Lee Cronk and Shannon Steadman found that among the people of Utila (a Bay Island of Honduras), men prefer to marry women who frequently attend church. However, this preference is not reversed: women are less interested in the religious piety of husbands. Why the difference? Irons notes that the men of Utila spend much time away from home in maritime work. Given frequent separation, the risk of infidelity is especially high. The risks of false parenting fall disproportionately on men. (Women know when they are biological mothers. The signs are unmistakable). Irons explains the data by conjecturing that religious signalling is favoured among Utilan women as a signal of sexual virtue (Irons, 2001).

In a comparative study of 200 religious and secular communes in the nineteenth century, Rich Sosis determined that the religious communities were far more likely to outlast their non-religious counterparts—four times as likely in any given year (Sosis, 2000). In a subsequent study, Sosis and Bressler showed that religious communes imposed over twice as many costly requirements on their members than did secular communes, and further that the number of costly requirements was positively correlated with group lifespan. Interestingly a similar effect did not hold for secular communes, where costly requirements did not correlate with secular commune lifespan (Sosis and Bressler, 2003). Sosis and Ruffle have further shown that religious ritual influences cooperation in contemporary religious kibbutzim. Using common-pool resource games, the authors found that religious males were significantly more altruistic in their play than were religious and secular females, and secular males. The authors discovered no sex differences in cooperation among the secular kibbutz members, eliminating the possibility that there were broader differences in the ways males and females play the game. Noting that only orthodox men are expected to participate in communal prayer three times a day, the authors conclude that costly ritual participation (rather than any inherent differences between the sexes) accounts for the discrepancy (Sosis and Ruffle, 2003).

43.5. Religiosity as a cognitive adaptation

Religious behaviour may be adaptive; even so, it does not follow that dedicated mental architecture produces it. It may well be that religious thought is a commonly discovered invention, shaped for specific tasks, and passed down as future generations use their culturally inherited religion as a platform for further improvements. We do not require dedicated architecture for reading, fire cognition, and water extraction. Yet these skills are probably more widespread in the hominid lineage than religion, and arguably they are more adaptive. Moreover, when we consider the substance of religious life, we see the trail of the cultural serpent everywhere; children are not born knowing what to do with chalices and menorahs, how to meditate, how Ganesh got his elephant head. Indeed the conventionality of religion—its cultural dependence—facilitates costly theological signalling by insulating religious communities from religious imposters who don't know all the dogmas and rules. The more elaborate and esoteric are theological and ritual conventions, the harder are they to counterfeit. Local theologies and folklores serve as encryption technologies.

Thus religiosity's functionality *benefits* from cultural variation. Given that dependency, why should we think that religious cognition emerges from a cognitive design selected for it?

Undeniably substantial aspects of an individual's religiosity come by way of contingent social involvements. We cannot fully understand an individual's religiosity without understanding how these cultural settings bear on psychological development. The nature/nurture dualism has no place in the cognitive study of religion (indeed the dualism misleads nearly everywhere in the cognitive study of mind). Furthermore, whether religiosity is a psychological adaptation is itself of little theoretical interest (Atran, 2004). For the goal is to produce a better theory of religious minds, not to speculate about ancestral history. The adaptationist stance is interesting because, if correct, then reverse-engineering techniques likely will prove fruitful.

These provisos aside, four considerations suggest the presence of dedicated religiosity architecture that serves the adaptive functions just described.

43.5.1. Encapsulation

First, religious cognition must be encapsulated, and it is hard and risky to rely on teaching for the monitoring of information flow. Notice that though religiosity relies on error, we cannot become globally impoverished at assessing the contents of distal reality. Cognitive adaptationism predicts that god belief will not inform inferences to explanation in all domains. Nor will supernatural error impinge on practical task solving and priority assessment. For unconstrained religious error is an evolutionary death sentence. An organism that allows error to corrupt all empirical inferences about the world will be quickly absorbed by its hostile elements. So over time, selection will eliminate unconstrained error-prone designs. Functional religiosity must be insulated from unrelated problem domains. Thus religiosity demands specific meta-representational structuring to curtail inferential haemorrhaging. It requires a scope-syntactic architecture of the kind that enables us to consider fictional worlds, engage in counterfactual reasoning and planning, and remember the past without confusing these imagined worlds with reality (for an excellent general discussion of the architecture required for meta-representational thought see Cosmides and Tooby, 2000).

The encapsulation constraint leads to specific, testable predictions. For example, functional religious representations need to be tagged with high degrees of subjective confidence—for we have seen how such confidence when shared solves generalized prisoner's dilemmas. Yet such representations must not factor into decisions that mediate a religious agent's practical involvements with the world, except to meet signalling demands. The theory therefore predicts that we will believe with our hearts that the gods will provide, while striving with our hearts to provide for ourselves. You may believe in karma—that moral causality guarantees just outcomes in this life or the next. Yet unless punishment is also viewed as a karmic duty, an unbounded architecture might well permit the inference: *do not punish enemies (... for they shall get theirs anyway, as the wheel turns)*. Or it may warrant complacency about death among the well-behaved. However, to give up caring about punishment or life is a bad idea for survival.

While I am unaware of studies that assess the scope, magnitude, and variation to which religiosity is encapsulated, there is evidence that religiosity is not too reproductively damaging. Religious persons are generally not less successful, healthy and fertile than their secular counterparts; indeed religious persons in North America frequently score higher on measures of physical and mental health (Koenig *et al.*, 2001; Pargament, 2002; Bulbulia, 2006). We know that erroneous religious understandings do not impair individuals as they would if these understandings were inferentially robust. However, we need better meta-representational analyses to show how (Bulbulia, 2006; but see Pyysiainen, 2003).

43.5.2. Integration

Second, religious representations need to be precisely integrated to other cognitive systems. Though inferentially encapsulated, cognitive adaptationism predicts that religiosity will not be inferentially inert. For religious representations are functional precisely because they strategically mediate an agent's engagement with her world in a few domains. Religiosity cannot be insulated to the degree that it is thought free-spinning in a void. Its rubber must meet the road at strategic moments, for example, by the production of costly signs to mark and verify religious motivations. Again, at present we do not have a clear picture of the scope-grammars that structure religious cognition. Informally, we know that religious concepts are linked to emotional and motivational processing. Unlike esoteric false beliefs (in the reality of possible worlds or that colours are intrinsic properties) agents form motivational commitments to their gods, and these motivations powerfully affect behaviour. We know further that religious beliefs strongly motivate social norms. Understanding this moral functionality enables us to hazard more precise predictions about the religiosity's design.

For example, the theory predicts that religious representations will not merely consist of minimally violating anthropomorphic concepts. Rather, supernatural concepts will be arrayed to police behaviour, either through their perceived intrinsic or extrinsic properties. Indeed, there is much anecdotal evidence that religious concepts are moralizing (Malinowski, 1935). And there is some recent quantitative evidence as well. In a study of 186 cultures, Dominic Johnson (2005) found that the salience of 'high gods' correlates positively with enhanced reciprocity. While Johnson notes that the category of high gods and punishing gods do not perfectly overlap (the relevant ethnographic data contain gaps) nevertheless the study yields an intriguing result. In societies where gods are imagined as powerful there appears to be less selfish behaviour. However, if religious cognition is a cognitive adaptation then Johnson needs to explain how the cultural variant 'weak gods' becomes popular in some populations. ("non-moralizing" gods may be artefacts of informal description; one virtue of cognitive adaptationism is that it enables more precise descriptive practices: see Bulbulia, 2004b).

Cognitive adaptationism further predicts that evidence of supernatural commitment will factor into exchange decisions. We have already reviewed Sosis's studies showing that ritual participation correlates positively with altruism and group longevity. In a recent study, Bulbulia and

Mahoney found that enhanced altruism strategies were more common in cooperation games among Christian New Zealanders ($n = 61$) when compared to New Zealand 'citizen' controls ($n = 55$). Out of a possible $5 'gift' (enough to buy lunch) we found mean gifting by Christians was $2.84 (SD = $1.56) whereas in the control group it was only $0.73 (SD = $1.34). There is, however, a dark side to the religious altruism of Christian New Zealanders. The games were structured so that the altruistic gifting was always to an anonymous group member observed to incur a financial cost by punishing an out-group member, merely for having an out-group status. We know of no explicit Christian teaching that reinforces rewarding fellow religionists for such punishing behaviours, so the behaviour is probably not learned from Christian sources (at least not directly). Such behaviours appear less anomalous if core structural features of religious morality are features of biological endowment, for such punishing is another instance (and signal) of reciprocity: a giving to one who has given to the group. We believe more empirical work is needed before we can be confident that religious morality is special; the causally important differences between the dominant exchange strategies differentiating individuals in these groups may lie elsewhere. (For discussion of non-religious factors that influence strategic norms see Henrich *et al.*, 2004.) Nevertheless the data so far strongly indicate that religiosity is especially morally motivating.

43.5.3. Self-deception

Thirdly, cognitive adaptationism conjectures that religious commitment is supported through a cognitive architecture that biases and distorts information flow to bolster subjective confidence in the relevant group-organizing religious concepts. Remember, nothing in our experience should make the prospect of supernatural existence a live question, any more than our experience should lead us to suppose unicorns exist or that Mickey Mouse is real. To repeat: the poverty of supernatural stimulus is nearly complete. Getting agents to believe in super-nature presents a significant design problem. Even a very careful structuring of a cultural environment by religious

elites (for example, see Roes and Raymond, 2003) could not easily do the trick, for the requisite stimuli—projecting an eight-armed goddess, or Hermes—are substantial.

A prediction of the conjecture that biasing and distortion machines underlie religious commitment is that people genuinely believe in the supernatural. [This prediction may sound odd, yet Dennett (2006) and Palmer and Steadman (2004) challenge it; for these theorists, religionists only 'believe in belief'.] It seems to me, however, a good bet that incredulity is fairly rare, perhaps itself only a cognitive prospect in very recent cultures—and even in these, still fairly rare. How to test this prediction? We hardly need to. Costly emotional signals and dispositions to participate in religious trials assess these beliefs for us, naturally; for we have seen how such signals are hard to fake absent the relevant supernatural commitments. Of course, to convince the sceptics we require quantitative measures. These remain on the horizon of inquiry.

Another prediction of the theory is that religionists will be disinclined to accept functional explanations for their commitments. For it would appear that the functional utility of religious representations is optimized through self-deception about the nature of that functionality. There are good reasons for thinking that the architecture supporting religious commitment yields this obscurantism. It is not merely that religious agents have no need to be aware of the functionalist nature of their commitments (as language speakers have no need for explicit access to universal grammar), the functionality of the system may be threatened by self-conscious knowledge of its design; such knowledge can lead to a failure of confidence in religious morality. If we can explain moralizing supernatural commitment without appeal to moralizing forces, then altruists require non-religious reasons to motivate cooperative behaviour. If the gods are perceived to motivate exchange then disenchantment with the gods, all things being equal, will threaten those motivations.

Moreover, because moralistic condemnation of ulterior motives is a hard-to-fake signal of genuine supernatural (and so moral) commitment, cognitive adaptationists predict that such condemnation will form part of religiosity's functional design. In particular, we predict that whatever its merits, cognitive-adaptationist theory will have few adherents among fundamentalistically committed religionists. We furthermore observe that it is within their power to refute cognitive adaptationism by embracing and praising it (for discussion see Bulbulia, 2006).

Of course, exchange partners may possess a raft of motivations apart from religion to moderate selfishness, including a powerful distaste for cheating, natural affection, sensitivity to reputation, and worry over natural policing or retribution. We claim only that religiosity supplements these ordinary moral motivations, but to do so, we must believe in non-natural rewards.

43.5.4. Development

Fourth, religious commitments appear to come on-line early in childhood development, before robust and explicit religious education directs these commitments in cultural-specific directions. This emergence is consistent with religiosity's internal structuring. Barrett and colleagues have shown that children reason about God as different from other persons (Barrett and Richert, 2003). After the age of 5 years children begin to understand that human agents do not know everything, but children do not give up that assumption about God. God belief is resilient to theory-of-mind correction. Conversely before the age of 5 years, children credit all agents with omniscience. The authors suggest that children are better prepared to conceptualize god properties than they are human properties. Children appear born to believe. [Knight *et al.* (2004) have replicated this result in a cross-cultural study.]

The developmental psychologist Deb Keleman has taken this line further by showing that American children before the age of 5 years are biased to reason about the natural world in terms of intention and purpose; they are 'intuitive theists' who prefer explanations of designing intention everywhere (for a review see Kelemen, 2004). Children see clouds as "for raining" and mountains as "pointy so that animals won't sit on them and smash them" or "so that animals could scratch on them when they got itchy" (Kelemen, 1999b). These biases endure into late childhood, a pattern also observed in British children (Kelemen, 2003). Children also prefer

to explain items in the world as being caused by supernatural agents, a bias that endures into early adolescence, *even in children from non-religious households* (so they're not straightforwardly getting this bias from their parents; Evans, 2000, 2001). Keleman and DiYanni moreover have recently shown that rampant teleology and preference for supernatural explanation is connected. Not only do children prefer to find purpose in nature, they prefer explanations in which agents are responsible for providing these purposes (DiYanni and Kelemen, 2005; Kelemen and DiYanni, 2005).

It may be that this intuitive theism has moral dimensions. Bering (2004) has shown that after being primed to believe in a supernatural agent (an invisible 'Princess Alice'), children display inhibitive responses when tempted to cheat in reward games. Children strongly police their behaviour when natural anomalies (for example, a picture falling off the wall) suggest the presence of a supernatural being. "Even the youngest children behave as if they've been caught red-handed."

In sum, while there remain significant gaps in our understanding of how children and adolescents come to commit to gods, the data so far are consistent with the view that all children possess a religiosity faculty with entrenched features. The data suggest that this faculty emerges naturally in the course of childhood development, without the need for a robustly scaffolded religious education (for discussion see Bulbulia, 2005).

43.6. Conclusion

Time to briefly summarize the state of play. First, I used game theory and the prisoner's dilemma to illustrate how the epistemic costs of religious belief may facilitate cooperation where there are incentives for individuals to defect. I observed that because religious cooperators perceive the world as strongly discouraging cooperation, religious commitment when shared and recognized helps to build stronger coalitions. In short, *because the gods police social contracts, the epistemic costs of religious consciousness have adaptive value*. Second, I used costly signalling theory to show how religious cooperators satisfy the recognition constraint. In order for religious cooperation to work, religious agents need to find each other. Because defectors will always have incentives to mimic religious signals, such signals must incur costs that only genuine religionists will bear. Emotional displays provide hard-to-fake signals of authentic commitment to the gods, because emotions are difficult to control consciously. Moreover, rituals provide venues for the committed to advertise conviction. The various practical costs of religious ritual are, for the committed, understood as investments: for by their lights, ritual brings supernatural rewards. Cost is here perceived to be an investment. Defectors, on the other hand, will perceive no such investment incentive. Therefore they generally will not be willing to expend as much as those genuinely committed to the gods. Ritual costs thus act as a social filter. Generalizing, *because the practical costs of religion signal religious commitment, they have adaptive value*. I then noted that religiosity may be adaptive without relying on a dedicated cognitive architecture, but examined four separate data streams converging to the view that religiosity is at least partially controlled by internal cognitive resources we do not explicitly learn.

My focus in this chapter has been on internal psychological architecture, one I believe underlies our capacity for religion. I think that one of the most important horizons of future inquiry lies in developing a more precise and detailed account of that architecture. Yet I also believe that progress will be impaired unless we integrate this evolutionary psychological approach with the growing psychological literature on religious development in children, with archaeological studies, experimental economics, and with the vast and expanding ethnographies that record variation in religious cultural groups. For fruitful integration to occur, we need to begin thinking about our religious traditions not as snake trails of mistakes and costly maladaptations—'barking mad' as one researcher puts it—but as practices for human flourishing, sculpted by psychological adaptations, and every bit as intricate and functional as a forager's spear or an Eskimo's canoe.

References

Atran, S. (2002) *In Gods We Trust: The Evolutionary Landscape of Religion.* Oxford University Press, New York.

Atran, S. (2004) Religion's evolutionary landscape: counterintuition, commitment, compassion, communion. *Behavioral and Brain Sciences,* 27: 713–730.

Axelrod, R. (1990) *The Evolution of Co-operation.* Penguin, London.

Axelrod, R. (1997) *The Complexity of Cooperation.* Princeton University Press, Princeton, NJ.

Barrett, J. L. (2000) Exploring the natural foundations of religion. *Trends in Cognitive Sciences,* 4(1): 29–34.

Barrett, J. L. (2004) *Why Would Anyone Believe in God?* AltaMira Press, Lanham, MD.

Barrett, J. L. and Keil, F. (1996) Conceptualizing a nonnatural entity. *Cognitive Psychology,* 31: 219–247.

Barrett, J. L. and Keil, F. C. (1998) Cognitive constraints on Hindu concepts of the divine. *Journal for the Scientific Study of Religion,* 37: 608–619.

Barrett, J. L. and Richert, R. A. (2003) Anthropomorphism or preparedness? Exploring children's God concepts. *Review of Religious Research,* 44: 300–312.

Berger, P. (1990) *The Sacred Canopy: Elements of a Sociological Theory of Religion.* New York, Doubleday.

Berger, P. and Luckmann, T. (1972) *The Social Construction of Reality: A Treatise in the Sociology of Knowledge.* Doubleday, New York.

Bering, J. M. (2004) The evolutionary history of an illusion: religious causal beliefs in children and adults. In B. Ellis and D. F. Bjorklund (eds) *Origins of the Social Mind: Evolutionary Psychology and Child Development.* Guilford Press, New York.

Blackmore, S. (2000) *The Meme Machine.* Oxford University Press, New York.

Boyd, R. and Richerson, P.J. (1985) *Culture and the Evolutionary Process.* University of Chicago Press, Chicago.

Boyer, P. (1992) Explaining religious ideas: elements of a cognitive approach. *Numen,* XXXIX: 27–57.

Boyer, P. (1994) *The Naturalness of Religious Ideas: A Cognitive Theory of Religion.* University of California Press, Berkeley.

Boyer, P. (2001) *Religion Explained: The Evolutionary Origins of Religious Thought.* Basic Books, New York.

Boyer, P. (2003) Religious thought and behaviour as by-products of brain function. *Trends in Cognitive Sciences,* 7: 119–124.

Boyer, P. and Ramble, C. (2001) Cognitive templates for religious concepts: cross-cultural evidence for recall of counter-intuitive representations. *Cognitive Science,* 25: 535–564.

Bulbulia, J. (2004a) Religious costs as adaptations that signal altruistic intention. *Evolution and Cognition,* 10: 19–38.

Bulbulia, J. (2004b) The cognitive and evolutionary psychology of religion. *Biology and Philosophy,* 18: 655–686.

Bulbulia, J. (2005) Are there any religions? *Method and Theory in the Study of Religion,* 17: 71–100.

Bulbulia, J. (2006) A scope syntax for religious representations. *In Preparation.*

Bulbulia, J. A. (2006) Nature's Medicine: empirical constraint and the evolution of religious healing.

In P. MacNamara (ed.) *Where Man and God Meet: The New Sciences of Religion and Brain.* Greenwood Publishers, Westwood, CT.

Chen, D. Economic Distress and Religious Intensity: Evidence from Islamic Resurgence During the Indonesian Financial Crisis. Submitted 2005. American Economic Review.

Cosmides, L. and Tooby, J. (2000) Consider the source: the evolution of adaptations for decoupling and metarepresentation. In D. Sperber (ed.) *Metarepresentation.* Oxford University Press, New York, pp. 53–116.

Dawkins, R. (1976) *The Selfish Gene.* Oxford University Press, New York.

Dennett, D. C. (2006) *Breaking the Spell: Religion as a Natural Phenomenon.* Viking, New York.

DiYanni, C. and Kelemen, D. (2005) Time to get a new mountain? The role of function in children's conception of natural kinds. *Cognition,* 97: 327–335.

Dunbar, R. I. (1998) The social brain hypothesis. *Evolutionary Anthropology,* 6: 178–190.

Dunbar, R. I. (2005) *The Human Story: A New History of Mankind's Evolution.* Faber & Faber, London.

Evans, E. M. (2000) The emergence of beliefs about the origin of species in school-age children. *Merrill Palmer Quarterly,* 46: 221–254.

Evans, E. M. (2001) Cognitive and contextual factors in the emergence of diverse belief systems: Creation versus evolution. *Cognitive Psychology,* 42: 217–266.

Frank, R. (1988) *Passions Within Reason: The Strategic Role of The Emotions.* Norton, New York.

Gelman, S. and Kremer, K. (1991) Understanding natural cause: children's explanations of how objects and their properties originate. *Child Development,* 62: 396–414.

Gelman, S. A. and Markman, E. (1987) Young children's inductions from natural kinds: the role of categories and appearances. *Child Development,* 58: 1532–1540.

Godfrey-Smith, P. (1996) *Complexity and the Function of Mind in Nature.* Cambridge, Cambridge University Press.

Guthrie, S. (1993) *Faces in the Clouds: A New Theory of Religion.* New York, Oxford University Press.

Hamer, D. (2004) *The God Gene: How Faith is Hardwired into our Genes.* New York, Doubleday.

Henrich, J., Boyd, R. et al. (eds) (2004) *Foundations of Human Sociality: Economic Experiments and Ethnographic Evidence from Fifteen Small-Scall Societies.* New York, Oxford University Press.

Irons, W. (1996) Morality, religion, and evolution. In W. M. Richardson (ed.) *Religion and Science: History, Method, and Dialogue,* pp. 375–399. Routledge, New York.

Irons, W. (2001) Religion as hard-to-fake sign of commitment. In R. Nesse (ed.) *Evolution and the Capacity for Commitment.* Russell Sage Foundation, New York.

Johnson, C. (2003) During economic turmoil, religion is 'insurance'. *Science and Theology News,* 4.

Johnson, D. D. P. (2005) God's punishment and public goods: a test of the supernatural punishment hypothesis in 186 world cultures. *Human Nature,* 16: 410–446.

Kelemen, D. (1999b) Why are rocks pointy? Children's preference for teleological explanations of the natural world. *Developmental Psychology,* 35: 1440–1453.

Kelemen, D. (2003) British and American children's preference for teleo-functional explanations of the natural world. *Cognition,* 88: 201–222.

Kelemen, D. (2004) Are children intuitive theists?: Reasoning about purpose and design in nature. *Psychological Science,* 15: 295–230.

Kelemen, D. and DiYanni, C. (2005) Intuitions about origins: purpose and intelligent design in children's reason about nature. *Journal of Cognition and Development,* 6: 3–31.

Knight, N., Sousa, P. et al. (2004) Children's attributions of beliefs to humans and God: cross-cultural evidence. *Cognitive Science,* 28: 117.

Koenig, H. G., McCullough, M. E. et al. (2001) *Handbook of Religion and Health.* Oxford University Press, New York.

Malinowski, B. (1935) *The Foundations of Faith and Morals: An Anthropological Analysis of Primitive Beliefs and Conduct with Special Reference to the Fundamental Problem of Religion and Ethics.* Oxford University Press, London.

McCauley, R. N. and Lawson, E. T. (2002) *Bringing Ritual to Mind.* Cambridge University Press, New York.

McClenon, J. (2002) *Wondrous Healing: Shamanism, Human Evolution, and the Origin of Religion.* Northern Illinois University Press, DeKalb, IL.

Nash, J. (1951) Noncooperative Games. *Annals of Mathematics,* 54: 289–295.

Palmer, C. T. and Steadman, L. B. (2004) With or without belief: a new approach to the definition and explanation of religion. *Evolution and Cognition,* 10: 138–147.

Pargament, K. I. (2002) The bitter and the sweet: an evaluation of the costs and benefits of religiousness. *Psychological Inquiry,* 13: 168–189.

Preus, J. S. (1987) *Explaining Religion: Criticism and Theory from Bodin to Freud.* Yale University Press, New Haven.

Pyysiainen, I. (2001) *How Religion Works: Towards a New Cognitive Science of Religion.* Brill, Leiden.

Pyysiainen, I. (2003) True fiction: philosophy and psychology of religious belief. *Philosophical Psychology,* 16: 109–125.

Ramachandran, V. S. and Blakeslee, S. (1998) *Phantoms in the Brain: Probing the Mysteries of the Human Mind.* Quill William Morrow, New York.

Reader, I. and Tanabe, G. J. J. (1998) *Practically Religious: Worldly Benefits and the Common Religion of Japan.* University of Hawaii Press, Honolulu.

Richerson, P. and Boyd, R. (1989) The role of evolved predispositions in cultural evolution. Or, human sociobiology meet Pascal's Wager. *Ethology and Sociobiology,* 10: 195–219.

Richerson, R. and Boyd, R. (2005) *Not by genes alone: how culture transformed human evolution* University of Chicago Press, Chicago.

Roes, F. L. and Raymond, M. (2003) Belief in moralizing gods. *Evolution and Human Behavior,* 24: 126–135.

Schelling, T. (1960) *The Strategy of Conflict.* New York, Oxford University Press.

Shapiro, A. and Shapiro, E. (1997) The placebo: is it much ado about nothing? In A. Harrington (ed.) *The Placebo Effect,* pp. 12–36. Harvard University Press, Cambridge, MA.

Skyrms, B. (1996) *Evolution of the Social Contract.* Cambridge University Press, New York.

Sosis, R. (2000) Religion and intragroup cooperation: preliminary results of a comparative analysis of utopian communities. *Cross-Cultural Research,* 34: 77–88.

Sosis, R. (2003) Why aren't we all Hutterites? *Human Nature,* 14: 91–127.

Sosis, R. (2004) The adaptive value of religious ritual. *American Scientist,* 92: 166–172.

Sosis, R. and Alcorta, C. (2003) Signalling, solidarity, and the sacred: the evolution of religious behavior. *Evolutionary Anthropology,* 12: 264–274.

Sosis, R. and Bressler, E. (2003) Co-operation and commune longevity: a test of the costly signaling theory of religion. *Cross-Cultural Research,* 37: 11–39.

Sosis, R. and Ruffle, B. (2003) Religious ritual and cooperation: testing for a relationship on Israeli religious and secular kibbutzim. *Current Anthropology,* 44: 713–722.

Spelke, E., Phillips, A. *et al.* (1995) Infants knowledge of object motion and human action. In D. Sperber, D. Premack and A. Premack (eds) *Causal Cognition.* Clarendon Press, Oxford.

Sterelny, K. (2003) *Thought in a Hostile World: The Evolution of Human Cognition.* Blackwell, Oxford.

Sterelny, K. (2006) The evolution and evolvability of culture. Mind and Language, 21: 137–165.

Whitehouse, H. (1992) Memorable religions. *Man,* 27: 777–797.

Whitehouse, H. (2000) *Arguments and Icons.* Oxford, Oxford University Press.

Whitehouse, H. (2004) *Modes of Religiosity: A Cognitive Theory of Religious Transmission.* AltaMira Press, Lanham, MD.

Wilson, D. S. (2002) *Darwin's Cathedral: Evolution, Religion, and the Nature of Society.* University of Chicago Press, Chicago.

Zahavi, A. (1975) Mate selection: a selection for a handicap. *Journal of Theoretical Biology,* 67: 603–605.

Zahavi, A. (1993) The fallacy of conventional signalling. *Philosophical Transactions of the Royal Society of London,* B, 338: 227–230.

Zahavi, A. and Zahavi, A. (1997) *The Handicap Principle: A Missing Piece of Darwin's Puzzle.* Oxford University Press, New York.

CHAPTER 44

Evolutionary approaches to literature and drama

Joseph Carroll

44.1. The philosophical orientation of adaptationist literary study

Adaptationist literary study has emerged as a distinct movement only in the past 15 years. Contributors include both literary scholars who have assimilated the ideas of evolutionary psychology and also evolutionary social scientists who have taken literary works as a subject of study. Contributors from both disciplinary fields have appeared together in symposia, conference panels, special issues of journals, and edited books, and they have also entered together into collaborative research projects. This blurring and crossing of disciplinary boundaries points to the largest philosophical principle that distinguishes Darwinian literary study—the idea of 'consilience'. Reintroduced into philosophical parlance by Edward O. Wilson (1998), the term 'consilience' denotes that nature forms a unified field of determinate causal relations and that all fields of knowledge are thus integrally connected. Within the consilient world view, physics constrains chemistry; chemistry constrains biology; biology constrains psychology, anthropology, and the other human sciences, and all these sciences constrain the study of human cultural production, including literature, drama, and the other arts.

Adaptationist literary scholars identify evolution as a crucial link in a causal chain that produces literary artefacts. They accept the argument that over evolutionary time the human mind has evolved in an adaptive relationship with its environment, and they affirm that the 'adapted mind' has a definite structure—a distinctly configured set of species-typical behavioural dispositions. The common designation for that species-typical configuration—both in literary tradition and in evolutionary psychology—is 'human nature'. Like most traditional literary theorists, adaptationist literary scholars argue that literary works are produced and consumed to fulfil the needs of human nature, that they depict human nature, and that they are constrained, in their formal organization, by the species-typical dynamics of human social interaction.

In the following three sections I shall describe the historical context of adaptationist literary study, survey the work that has already been published in adaptationist literary studies, and then consider some of the directions further research might take.

44.2. The historical context of adaptationist literary study

Literature did not become the subject of an academic discipline until the last two decades of the nineteenth century, and until the 1940s, it consisted in two main forms: (i) philological and historical scholarship; and (ii) moralized aesthetic commentary of a very general, impressionistic character (see Graff, 1987; Abrams, 1997). In the 1930s, a new methodology arose, a form of 'close reading' or formal analysis of theme, tone, and style. 'The New Criticism', as this school is still called, dominated academic literary study in England and America until the late 1970s. By focusing on formal analysis, the school provided a methodology admirably suited to classroom study and to the mass production of scholarly publication in the burgeoning industry of higher education.

Between the middle of the 1970s and the middle of the 1980s, a revolution took place in literary studies. 'Poststructuralism' or 'postmodernism', spearheaded by the 'deconstructive' philosophy of Jacques Derrida, swept across the landscape of literature departments and infiltrated all the departments of the humanities. The fundamental tenets of poststructuralism are 'textualism' and 'indeterminacy'. Textualism is the belief that language or 'discourse' is the elemental stuff of existence, that it constitutes or at least fundamentally determines all forms of reality. Indeterminacy is the belief that all meaning contradicts itself and that no determinate meaning is possible. If all meaning is indeterminate, all texts are open to perpetual reinterpretation. In postmodern essays, this particular inference, though it sounds fairly determinate, has itself been explicitly reiterated with the monotonous regularity of a monastic liturgy. Given that literary scholars deal with a finite body of texts, the motivating force that attaches to this industrial academic rationale can hardly be overestimated.

New Criticism was fundamentally conservative in orientation. Its practitioners were often politically or ideologically conservative, and it shared with Victorian humanism a reverential attitude towards the canonical texts of Western culture—and by extension, towards Western culture itself. The ideological impulses that animated the postmodern revolution were, in contrast, radical and subversive. Under the aegis of Michel Foucault, the postmodernists adopted a stance of suspicion and hostility to all established forms of 'power': bourgeois, patriarchal, heterosexist, Western, colonial, white, rational,

and scientific. In the past decade, 'deep ecology' has added one more item to this list of suspect epithets, the anthropocentric emphasis on the specifically 'human' (see Carroll, 2004, Part 1, Chapter 8). Since the middle of the 1980s, the bulk of postmodern criticism has had a political slant, and much of it has been predominantly political. Feminism emerged in the 1970s, independently of postmodernism, as a highly politicized literary movement driven by the transformation of women's social roles and by the changing demographics of the university itself. By the middle of the 1980s, literary feminism had assimilated itself to the larger postmodern creed, and almost all literary feminism now adopts one or another of the postmodern idioms as the medium for its preoccupation with the concerns of women. In the postmodern political arena, textualism and indeterminacy serve as means for deprecating the legitimacy of dominant social, psychological, or sexual norms. Postmodern science theory treats of science itself as merely a political and cultural construct that reflects and supports these dominant norms (Gross and Levitt, 1994; Sokal, 1996; Gross *et al.*, 1997; Koertge, 1998; Sokal and Bricmont, 1998; Parsons, 2003).

Until the advent of postmodernism, academic literary study and standard social science ran on separate but parallel tracks. Darwinian influences on anthropology, psychology and sociology died out in the first two decades of the twentieth century and were replaced by the doctrines of cultural autonomy and behaviourist conditioning (see Brown, 1991, pp. 1–38; Buss, 1999, Part 1; Degler, 1991; Fox, 1989, Chapters 3 and 4; Freeman, 1992, 1999, pp. 17–27; Tooby and Cosmides, 1992, p. 28). From the 1940s to the middle of the 1970s, the New Critical orthodoxy held that literary meaning is itself autonomous and fully intelligible without reference to any contextual influence. The social scientists wished to protect culture from any suspicion of biological influence, and the literary critics wished to protect literature from any suspicion not only of biological influence but also of social influence. Postmodernism expanded the notion of textual autonomy to include not just the isolated literary text but the whole textual universe—the world constituted by 'discourse'. The idea of cultural autonomy brought the postmodernists into alignment with important aspects of standard social science, and in the 1990s postmodernism began to seep over into anthropology. Much standard social science remains distinct from postmodernism in that standard social scientists, though they reject the idea of human nature and deny that biology influences culture, none the less continue to regard scientific methodology as a medium of objective knowledge about a real world that exists independently of cultural and linguistic constructs.

Adaptationist literary theorists have rejected both the irrationalism of postmodernism and the blank-slate model of human behaviour that informs standard social science. They affirm the ideas of 'truth' and 'reality', and they think that in studying the products of the human imagination, truth and reality can be most adequately served by an adaptationist understanding of human nature.

44.3. **Contributions to adaptationist literary study**

Literary study inspired by adaptationist social science can be grouped into six large, partially overlapping categories: (i) general programmatic expositions, manifestos and prolegomena; (ii) commentaries on the relation of adaptationist literary study to the bordering fields of ecological literary criticism and cognitive rhetoric; (iii) discussions of the adaptive function of literature; (iv) essays on topics of literary theory (genre, evaluation, and point of view); (v) critiques of specific literary works; and (vi) studies that not only assimilate concepts from the social sciences but also incorporate empirical methodology in the study of literature.

Programmatic expositions rehearse the basic logic of an adaptationist understanding of human nature, affirm that literary production falls within the scope of that logic, and suggest ways in which literary scholars can use evolutionary psychology as a theoretical foundation for literary study (Easterlin, 1993, 1999b, 2001b; Storey, 1993, 1996; Barrow, 1995; Carroll, 1995, 2004, Part 2, Chapters 1 and 6; Carroll, 2005; Boyd, 1998, 2005a; Evans, 1998; Cooke, 1999b; Nieves, 2001; Barash and Barash, 2002, 2005; Fromm 2003a,b; Gottschall and Wilson, 2005; Headlam Wells and

McFadden, in press; McEwan, 2005). Some programmatic expositions have focused on the 'consilient' or comprehensively interdisciplinary nature of adaptationist literary study (Carroll, 2004, Part 1, Chapter 7; Gottschall, 2003c; Love, 1999a,b; Nordlund, 2002). Other expositions have used evolutionary psychology as a framework within which to criticize the poststructuralist conceptions that currently dominate academic literary study (Carroll, 1995, 2004, Part 1, Chapters 2 and 3, and in press d; Storey, 1996; D. S. Wilson, 2005). Within the literary poststructuralist paradigm, psychology is still predominantly Freudian, and some adaptationist scholars have used evolutionary psychology— and especially findings on incest avoidance— to criticize Freudian literary theory (Storey, 1996; Easterlin, 2000; Scalise Sugiyama, 2001c; Evans, 2005).

Over the past two decades or so, in roughly the same period that adaptationist literary study has been developing, literary study has also extended itself into the bordering areas of cognitive science and ecology. 'Cognitive rhetoric' and 'ecocriticism' share little in the way of concepts or concerns with one another, but both overlap in some measure, at different points, with adaptationist literary study.

In its broadest reaches, cognitive rhetoric concerns itself with brain functions and with the emotions involved in literary production and response, but as a distinct school of literary theory it affiliates itself primarily with the linguistic theories of Mark Johnson and George Lakoff. Johnson and Lakoff argue that language is based on metaphor and that metaphors often derive from 'the body', but unlike adaptationist critics, cognitive rhetoricians do not attempt to identify a species-typical structure of behavioural dispositions. Cognitive rhetoricians are generally hostile to evolutionary psychology, and some adaptationist critics have criticized cognitive rhetoric for the limitations in its conceptual scope (Carroll, 2004, Part 1, Chapter 5, pp. 57–58; Part 2, Chapter 1, pp. 104–106; Carroll, 2005, p. 938; Gottschall, 2004). Other adaptationist critics have sought to identify common ground between cognitive rhetoric and adaptationist criticism (Boyd, 1999; Easterlin, 2002).

Ecocriticism is not so much a distinct body of theory or method as, rather, a subject matter.

Ecocritics have for the most part been animated by environmentalist concerns and sympathies. As specifically literary critics, they have concentrated heavily on a distinct tradition of 'nature' writing, most often American writing. In their theoretical orientation, ecocritics range from postmodernism to a strongly naturalistic and Darwinian outlook. Two prominent ecocritics, Glen Love and Harold Fromm, have sought to assimilate the topics and concerns of ecology to an adaptationist framework (Fromm, 1996, 1998, 2001; Love 1999a,b, 2003). Carroll and Easterlin criticize ecocriticism from an adaptationist perspective and argue that a concept of human nature must take the central place in any theory about the relations of human beings to their physical environment (Carroll, 2004, Part 1, Chapter 8; Part 2, Chapter 4; Easterlin, 2004).

Arguments about the adaptive function of literature fall into three main groups: (i) that literature and the other arts are not adaptive but are, rather, non-adaptive side-effects of cognitive capacities that have developed for adaptive reasons; (ii) that literature and the other arts are indirectly adaptive in that they can be made to contribute to one or another adaptively useful activity; and (iii) that literature and the other arts fulfil adaptive functions that are peculiar to themselves and that could be fulfilled by no other means. Pinker (1997, 2002) argues that the arts, like pornography and rich foods, are means for exploiting psychological mechanisms that evolved for other purposes. He also argues that literature can be adaptively useful in presenting models of situations in which its readers might at some point find themselves. Scalise Sugiyama (2001a) argues that literature can convey adaptively useful information about the environment—specific, concrete information about material resources and physical conditions. Coe (2003) argues that in ancestral environments visual art conveyed information about kin relations. Miller (1999, 2000), Power (1999) and Voland (2003) argue that literature and the other arts, like all other forms of mental activity, subserve the purposes of sexual display. From this perspective, art has no intrinsic adaptive functions but is indirectly adaptive in that, like the peacock's tail, it contributes to processes of sexual selection. Dissanayake, Cooke, and Boyd argue that art evolved as a means of focusing attention on adaptively salient concerns, and Dissanayake, Boyd, and Dunbar emphasize the utility of literature and the other arts in creating and reinforcing social bonds (Boyd, 2005b; Cooke, 1999a; Dissanayake, 1995a,b, 2000, 2001; Dunbar, 2004, 2005). Dissanayake, Cooke, and Boyd emphasize the adaptively relevant content of art. Dunbar concentrates attention on theory of mind or perspective-taking as central mechanisms of human social interaction. E. O. Wilson, Carroll, and Tooby and Cosmides argue that the arts serve a unique adaptive function in that they provide an emotionally saturated cognitive order that mediates between innate dispositions and the complexities of contingent circumstances (Carroll, 2004, Part 1, Chapters 6 and 7; Part 2, Chapter 6, and in press a and c; Tooby and Cosmides, 2001; E. O. Wilson, 1998, pp. 225–26). Tooby and Cosmides converge with Pinker and Scalise Sugiyama in arguing that in listening to stories people rehearse adaptively relevant scenarios. Carroll acknowledges this practical function but also stipulates that the larger adaptive function is not merely practical. Literature and its oral antecedents create models or images of people acting in the world; those models are imbued with emotion and moral value; and they thus provide general psychological maps or guides through which people assess motives and behaviour and evaluate alternatives. In comparison with that of other animals, even other primates, the human cognitive universe is exceptionally complex, and so far as we know humans are unique in creating an imaginative universe and in regulating their behaviour in relation to the imaginative models they construct.

Genre is a composite concept in literary theory, consisting of various proportions of three chief elements: emotional quality, subject matter, and formal organization. The primary emotional component is a polarity between sadness or grief (tragedy) and joy or mirth (comedy). This polarity is compounded by the kind of mirth that involves ridicule or mockery and that produces satire. Storey (1996) and Nettle (2005a,b) have explored the polarity of tragedy and comedy in adaptationist terms, and Storey and Boyd have explored the theory of humour (Boyd, in press b; Storey, 2001, 2003). Storey locates the source of tragedy in struggles over power, and he locates a primate source for comedy in 'the relaxed open mouth display'. Nettle associates tragedy with conflicts over status, and he associates comedy with mate selection. Carroll (2004, pp. 127, 158) correlates tragedy, comedy, and satire with the 'basic emotions' of Ekman 2003, who correlates tragedy with sadness, fear, and anger, comedy with joy and surprise, and satire with anger, disgust, and contempt. Cooke (2002) has examined a specific form of satire, that of the dystopian political novel, and he argues that the satire depends crucially on contrasting the social conditions of a totalitarian state with the evolved needs of a universal human nature. Cooke (1994, 1996) has also examined a generic category, science fiction, that is based more on subject matter than on emotional quality, and he locates the central themes of science fiction in the core issues of survival and reproductive success. Evolutionary psychologists have used mate selection theory to explain the generic features of pornography and romance fiction, paired off, respectively, as male and female forms of fantasy (Ellis and Symons, 1990; Whissel, 1996; Salmon and Symons, 2001; Salmon, 2005). The largest formal distinctions are those between drama, narrative fiction, and poetic verse. Turner (1992, pp. 61–108) has examined the biological basis of poetic meter; he argues for a biologically based three-second metric. Scalise Sugiyama (1996, 2001b, 2005) and Steen (2005) both identify the core elements of narrative as those of goal-oriented agents coping with the adaptive problems of resources and social life. Nettle (2005b) creates a typology of drama through the intersection of two central conflicts (status and mating) and two possible outcomes (negative and positive). Three studies have examined the correlation between the sizes of human social groups and the formal organization of dramas (Stiller et al., 2004; Matthews and Barrett, 2005; Stiller and Hudson, 2005). These studies are oriented to a model for the evolution of the human brain that is driven by social group size, and they use anthropological data on social group size to analyse the organization of social groups in the populations of specific plays and genres.

Adaptationist discussions of literary value, like adaptationist critiques of literary depictions, have tended to focus on the issue of human universals. Turner (1992, p. 26) identifies literary merit with the sheer number of universal themes in any given work. Cooke (1999b, p. 55) associates literary merit with the presence of conflict among biologically based dispositions. Easterlin (1999a, 2005) counters the emphasis on universals by drawing attention to the way elements of literary tradition and other culturally conditioned factors enter into judgements of literary value. Carroll (2004, p. 145) argues that judgements of value typically depend on a combination of factors: elemental motives linked with basic emotions, coherent thematic structures, stylistic felicity, and the quality of mind and heart in the writer. He also invokes a principle of 'integrity' in the conception of a subject and in the formal organization of a literary work (Carroll, 2004, Part 2, Chapter 5).

Point of view is a standard technical term in literary narrative and involves distinctions like those between 'first-person narrator', 'third-person omniscient narrator', 'third-person limited narrator', and so on. In its broader signification, the concept of 'point of view' opens into the anthropological and psychological theory of literature as a social and communicative act. Dunbar, Barrett and Lycett argue that the evolution of specifically human sociality is crucially dependent both on language and on the capacity for empathy or 'theory of mind', that is, the capacity to envision the world from someone else's point of view—to intuit another person's perceptions, thoughts, and beliefs (Barrett et al., 2002, Chapters 11, 12 and 13; Dunbar, 2004, 2005; Dunbar et al., 2005, Chapters 8, 9 and 10). Scalise Sugiyama (1996) examines the way oral narratives are shaped to manipulate audiences in the interest of the narrator. Carroll argues that literary meaning emerges through the negotiation among three distinct sets of point of view: that of the author, of the characters, and of the audience. Since point of view involves individual identity, Carroll argues that literary theory needs to make use of an empirically derived set of categories, including those of personality theory, for analysing individual differences (Carroll, 2004, Part 2, Chapters 3 and 6; 2005, and in press d).

A large portion of the work done in adaptationist literary study has consisted in interpretive commentary on specific literary texts. Most characteristically, these commentaries identify behaviours in the texts that correspond (or fail to correspond) to species-typical patterns of behaviour. Topics have included all the standard categories in which evolutionary psychologists tend to divide human life-history effort: survival, resource acquisition, mate selection, parenting, childhood development, kin relations, and social life, including status seeking, coalition building, cheater detection, and in-groups and out-groups. The most sophisticated of these interpretive commentaries have analysed the interplay between elemental dispositions and particular social and cultural ecologies, and they have also incorporated the concepts of traditional literary analysis: the analysis of style and tone, symbolism, figures of speech, point of view, narrative and dramatic structure, the interplay with audience expectations, and the problems of literary value.

The curricula of departments of literature are commonly organized by period and genre, and those categories will serve here as a framework for outlining adaptationist contributions to interpretive criticism.

One distinct generic group consists in studies of folk tales, fairy tales, fantasies, and works of science fiction. Cooke (1995) and Easterlin (2001a) have examined specific fairy tales. Jobling (2001b) gives a generalized account of ogre stories. (Gottschall has compared large numbers of fairy tales from different cultures; these studies will be cited below under the category of empirical literary analysis.) In all of these studies, emphasis is given to the way in which the stories embody universal themes grounded in evolved psychology. Other critics have examined works in which symbols of human universals are lodged within highly specific cultural or ecological conditions. Boyd (2001) gives an extensive critique of a fantasy tale by Dr Seuss and takes it as a critique of American xenophobia. Cooke has delved into futuristic science fiction (1987, 2002) and has also given a book-length critique of a single literary work, Zamyatin's dystopian futuristic fantasy *We* (Cooke, 2002). He locates this novel within the larger contexts of dystopian fiction and Soviet literature and takes evolutionary psychology as an implicit satiric frame for Soviet totalitarianism. Carroll critiques three works of paleo-fiction (2004, Part 2, Chapter 5) in which Neanderthals and Cro-Magnons encounter one another, and he uses the specific conditions of Palaeolithic life as a touchstone for assessing the imaginative quality of the novels.

Epics have received a good deal of attention. Nesse (1995) examines three poetic versions of the Guinevere myth, assessing differences in the sexual ethos of different cultural moments. Thiessen and Umezawa (1998) give a sociobiological reading of a medieval Japanese novel and see in it an exemplification of universal human mating dispositions. Fox (1995, 2005) has used evolutionary findings on mate selection to examine male mating conflict in a number of epics. Gottschall (2001, 2003a) examines the Homeric poems within their anthropological context, using sociobiology as a conceptual frame for understanding the sexual ecology of the poems. Barash and Barash (2002, 2005) comment on Virgil's *Aeneid* in the light of evolved sexual psychology. [Barash and Barash (2005) give brief commentaries on adaptationist themes in dozens of works in world literature from the time of Homer to the twentieth century.]

Shakespeare has been a frequent subject of adaptationist criticism. Stiller, Hudson, Nettle, and Dunbar have taken Shakespeare as a focal point for analysing the correlation between human social-group size and the organization of characters within drama (Stiller *et al.*, 2004; Stiller and Hudson, 2005). (See the comments above on the form of drama.) Nettle's (2005a) analysis of tragedy and comedy illustrates its theory with commentary on *Richard III* and *Twelfth Night*. Boyd (in press a) uses kin selection as a chief category for the analysis of dramatic conflict in *Titus Andronicus*. Nordlund (2005) and Headlam Wells (in press) integrate concepts of an evolved human nature with knowledge of Shakespeare's specific historical environment. Nordlund argues that the romantic love is grounded in evolved psychology, and he takes romantic love as a basis of comparison between *Troilus and Cressida* and *All's Well That Ends Well*. Headlam Wells concentrates on the humanist moral vision in *Twelfth Night*, *The Merchant of Venice*, *Measure for Measure*, *The Winter's Tale*, *Romeo and Juliet*, *Julius Caesar* and *King Lear*. Boyd (1999, 2005a) and Nettle (2005b) take *Hamlet* as the basis for exploring the psychological foundations of drama. Scalise Sugiyama (2003) examines a native African people's response to *Hamlet* and draws important conclusions about the relations between human universals and culturally specific values and beliefs.

Lyric poetry has received some attention from adaptationist critics. Jobling (2002) discusses Byron as a figure who exemplifies the 'cad' mating strategy. (This study was extended as an empirical study by Kruger *et al.*, 2003.) Easterlin (2000) examines the pervading theme of mother–infant relations in the poetry of Wordsworth, correlates Wordsworth's insights with those of modern attachment theory, and sets both in contrast with an extensive body of Freudian feminist criticism. Evans (in press) has examined poems about sports in the light of evolutionary psychology.

A number of adaptationist critics have given interpretive accounts of narrative fiction of the nineteenth and twentieth centuries. Cooke (1999c, 2002) has studied Slavic subjects, but most contributors have studied topics in British and American fiction. Boyd and Carroll have interpreted works of Jane Austen (Boyd, 1998; Carroll, 2004, Part 2, Chapters 3 and 6), and Carroll has also critiqued works by Dickens, Charlotte Brontë, Cather, Bennett, Hardy, Wilde, and others (2004, Part 1, Chapters 6 and 8, Part 2, Chapters 1 and 3; in press b). Carroll (2004, Part 2, Chapter 3) uses five novels to exemplify different kinds of relations among human universals, culturally specific contexts, and individual identities in authors, and he also invokes human universals as a touchstone for canonical status. Jobling (2001a) and Kruger *et al.* (2003) have studied the novels of Sir Walter Scott from a specifically adaptationist perspective. Jobling uses sociobiological mating and ethical theory to explain the pattern of dark and light heroes in Scott's novels, and Kruger *et al.* use characters from Scott and Byron to test hypotheses about differences in cad/dad mating strategies. Easterlin (2005) gives an account of meta-fictional reworkings of *Jane Eyre* and *David Copperfield*, examining the way universals are altered by the self-reflexive contexts of a literary tradition. Love (2003) comments on novels by Howells, Cather, and Hemingway, locating all these commentaries in relation to ecological constraints within the physical environment. Saunders (2005, and in press) comments on a novel by Wharton and a story by Anderson, in both cases

assessing the way the narrative is shaped by the underlying, not fully conscious, force of an evolved sexual psychology. Storey (1996) analyses a novel by Iris Murdoch and argues that Murdoch's conscious Freudian psychology is tacitly subverted by her intuitive apprehension of evolved sexual psychology. Perchan (2004) examines a novel by Graham Greene in order to assess the way in which evolved sexual psychology shapes interpersonal relations in exotic conditions. Carroll and Gottschall (in press) have used an evolutionary understanding of motives, mate selection, and personality to produce a content analysis of the motives, mate preferences, and personality characteristics of 170 characters in 44 British novels of the nineteenth century.

All the theoretical and critical works I have cited make use of information derived from evolutionary psychology—information that is itself derived at least in part from empirical research. Another distinct body of work not only makes use of empirically derived information but conducts empirical research into literature. Miall and Dissanayake (2003) perform metric, phonetic, and foregrounding analyses of 'motherese' and situate their analysis within an adaptationist theory of mother–infant interaction. Scalise Sugiyama (2001a) analyses the incidence of adaptively relevant information about resources in the narratives of native peoples. D. S. Wilson *et al.* (1998) conducted an experiment to assess the relation of Machiavellianism to the fictional stories produced by experimental subjects. Kruger *et al.* (2003) use literary texts to assess differences in short and long-term mating strategies in respondents. The studies of pornography and romance fiction, cited above in the paragraph on genre, all make use of quantitative analysis and work with predictions about sex differences in mating psychology (Ellis and Symons, 1990; Whissel, 1996; Salmon and Symons, 2001; Salmon, 2005). The studies that examine the relation between social group size and dramatic structure, also cited above in the paragraph on genre, begin with an empirical analysis of correlations between social group size and the evolution of the brain, and they bring these findings to bear on analyses of group sizes in dramatic representations (Stiller *et al.*, 2004; Matthews and Barrett, 2005; Stiller and

Hudson, 2005). Gottschall and his colleagues have conducted a series of studies analysing the correlation of species-typical behaviours with representations of behaviour in large numbers of folk tales, fairy tales, and literary works (Gottschall, 2003b, 2005; Carroll and Gottschall, in press; Gottschall *et al.*, 2004, 2005, in press a and b).

44.4. Directions for further research

Most of the research areas outlined above have been explored in only a preliminary fashion. Up to the present time, the only area that has been fully developed is that of programmatic expositions. As both evolutionary psychology and adaptationist literary study develop further, and as the institutional context of literary study changes, it will be necessary periodically to reassess the whole field. For the time being, the most productive efforts could probably be devoted to the other areas under review.

Theories about the adaptive function of literature and the other arts remain in a highly speculative state. The background knowledge for this area—knowledge about the last few hundred thousand years of human evolution, the development of language, the evolution of social life, and the emergence of symbolic culture within the past 100 000 years or so—is itself still speculative and controversial (see Carroll, in press c). Further understanding of this issue will depend in part on developments in the primary field of anthropological research into human evolution and in part on psychological studies of the actual functions that are currently fulfilled by the production and consumption of imaginative artefacts.

Major topics in literary theory have been broached but by no means fully explored by adaptationist scholars. A better understanding of tone and genre will depend in part on a more precise and adequate knowledge of the nature of emotion. Research into 'basic emotions' and affective neuroscience provide chief points of departure for this research. Knowledge of the way 'point of view' enters into literary meaning can be advanced by new findings in theory of mind, in the evolution and nature of human sociality, and in personality. Literary value, like all value, is subjective, but subjective mental events are themselves susceptible to empirical research, and the same kinds of research that illuminate an understanding of emotion, point of view, and social dynamics will further illuminate our understanding of literary values.

The interpretive critique of individual literary works, and of works grouped by author, genre and period, provide a main field for further development in adaptationist literary study. Current studies have made only an occasional lodgement on the coast of a continent in which the interior remains largely unexplored. Vast tracts of world literature, and whole phases even of English and American literature, remain virgin forest. The medieval period has barely been touched, and virtually nothing has been written about seventeenth- and eighteenth-century literature. Scarcely more has been written about modern literature. Most poetry remains to be explored. Apart from the works of Shakespeare, most drama has not yet been brought under scrutiny.

The social sciences are in general not strongly oriented to the study of cultural history. Evolutionary psychology grounds itself in deep history—in evolutionary history—and it is preoccupied with the human universals that emerge from that history, but it has made only rudimentary progress in understanding how universal human dispositions vary in the varying cultural ecologies of the past 10 000 years—the period for the emergence of agriculture, mass societies, and literacy. One of the chief challenges to adaptationist scholars, and one of the chief ways in which they can contribute to the larger project of an adaptationist understanding of human nature, is to integrate a knowledge of species-typical behavioural dispositions with a scholarly knowledge of specific cultural ecologies.

Most literary scholars have not been trained in empirical methodology, and few social scientists have taken literature as a source for data. That disciplinary barrier is now being surmounted, and the new methodologies that are being developed should fundamentally influence every area of literary study. New knowledge produces new concepts, and new concepts alter the terms in which we formulate literary theories and analyse individual texts. By developing quantitative methods of analysis and by using data to test specific hypotheses, literary scholars can produce knowledge that is both falsifiable and genuinely progressive. They can link their own work ever more closely with the continuously developing knowledge in the empirical sciences, and they can produce new knowledge.

A truly adequate form of adaptationist literary study would combine at least four areas of expertise: (i) a thorough knowledge of evolutionary psychology—including a knowledge of its current limitations and its chief topics of controversy; (ii) a deep and broad humanistic training, with specialized knowledge of one or more historical periods, including the demographics, economics, politics, cultural forms, and literary traditions of those periods; (iii) expertise in the methods of 'close reading'— a knowledge of the inner workings of tone, imagery, style, figures of speech, and the formal organization of narrative, drama, and verse; and (iv) a practical acquaintance with empirical methodology and a readiness to incorporate empirical analysis into literary research. Literary scholars will need both to develop new forms of expertise and also to imitate the sciences in the practice of working collaboratively, in research teams, so as to pool different forms of expertise. The demands are heavy, but the rewards great. We have opportunities of discovery that are, in the humanities, unprecedented.

References

Abrams, M. H. (1997) The transformation of English studies: 1930–1995. *Daedalus*, 126: 105–132.

Barash, D. and Barash, N. (2002, October 18) Biology as a lens: evolution and literary criticism. *Chronicle of Higher Education*, 49, B7–B9.

Barash, D. and Barash, N. (2005) *Madame Bovary's Ovaries: A Darwinian Look at Literature*. Delacorte, New York.

Barrett, L., Dunbar, R. I. M. and Lycett, J. (2002) *Human Evolutionary Psychology*. Princeton University Press, Princeton.

Barrow, J. D. (1995) *The Artful Universe*. Oxford: Clarendon Press.

Boyd, B. (1998) "Jane, meet Charles": literature, evolution, and human nature. *Philosophy and Literature*, 22: 1–30.

Boyd, B. (1999) Literature and discovery. *Philosophy and Literature*, 23: 313–333.

Boyd, B. (2001) The origin of stories: *Horton Hears a Who*. *Philosophy and Literature*, 25: 197–214.

Boyd, B. (2005a) Literature and evolution: a bio-cultural approach. *Philosophy and Literature*, 29: 1–23.

Boyd, B. (2005b) Evolutionary theories of art. In J. Gottschall and D. S. Wilson (eds) *Literature and the human animal*, pp. 147–176. Northwestern University Press, Evanston, IL.

Boyd, B. (in press a) Kind and unkindness: Aaron in *Titus Andronicus*. In B. Boyd (ed.) *Words that Count: Essays on Early Modern Authorship in Honor of MacDonald P. Jackson*. University of Delaware Press, Newark, NJ.

Boyd, B. (in press b) Laughter and literature: a play theory of humor. *Philosophy and Literature*.

Carroll, J. (1995) *Evolution and Literary Theory*. University of Missouri Press, Columbia.

Carroll, J. (2004) *Literary Darwinism: Evolution, Human Nature, and Literature*. Routledge, New York.

Carroll, J. (2005) Literature and evolutionary psychology. In D. Buss (ed.) *The Handbook of Evolutionary Psychology*, pp. 931–952. Wiley, Hoboken, NJ.

Carroll, J. (in press a) The adaptive function of literature. In C. Martindale, P. Locher and V. Petrov (eds) *Evolutionary and Neurocognitive Approaches to Creativity and the Arts*. Baywood, Amityville, NY.

Carroll, J. (in press b) Aestheticism, homoeroticism, and Christian guilt in *The Picture of Dorian Gray*: a Darwinian critique. *Philosophy and Literature*.

Carroll, J. (in press c) The human revolution and the adaptive function of literature. *Philosophy and Literature*.

Carroll, J. (in press d) Literature and evolution. In R. Headlam Wells and J. McFadden (eds) *Human Nature: Fact and fiction*. Continuum, London.

Carroll, J. and Gottschall, J. (in press) Human nature and agonistic structure in canonical British novels of the nineteenth and early twentieth centuries: a content analysis. In U. Klein, K. Mellmann and S. Metzger (eds) *Anthropologie und Sozialgeschichte der Literatur Heuristiken der Literaturwissenschaft*. Mentis, Paderborn, Germany.

Coe, K. (2003) *The Ancestress Hypothesis: Visual Art as Adaptation*. Rutgers University Press, New Brunswick.

Cooke, B. (1987) The human alien: in-groups and out-breeding in *Enemy Mine*. In G. Slusser and E. Rabkin (eds) *Aliens: The Anthropology of Science Fiction*, pp. 179–198. Southern Illinois University Press, Carbondale.

Cooke, B. (1994) Sociobiology, science fiction and the future. *Foundation: The Review of Science Fiction*, 60: 42–51.

Cooke, B. (1995) Microplots: the case of *Swan Lake*. *Human Nature*, 2: 183–196.

Cooke, B. (1996) The biology of immortality: a Darwinist perspective on science fiction. In G. Slusser, G. Westfahl and E. Rabkin (eds) *Immortal engines: Immortality and Life Extension in Science Fiction*, pp. 90–101. University of Georgia Press, Athens, GA.

Cooke, B. (1999a) On the evolution of interest: cases in serpent art. In D. H. Rosen and M. Luebbert (eds) *Evolution of the Psyche*, pp. 150–168. Praeger, Westport, CT.

Cooke, B. (1999b) The promise of a biothematics. In J. B. Bedaux and B. Cooke (eds) *Sociobiology and the Arts*, pp. 43–62. Editions Rodopi, Amsterdam.

Cooke, B. (1999c) Sexual property in Pushkin's "The Snowstorm": a Darwinist perspective. In B. Cooke and F. Turner (eds) *Biopoetics: Evolutionary Explorations in the Arts*, pp. 175–204. ICUS, Lexington, KY.

Cooke, B. (2002) *Human Nature in Utopia: Zamyatin's We*. Northwestern University Press, Evanston, IL.

Degler, C. (1991) *In Search of Human Nature: The Decline and Revival of Darwinism in American Social Thought*. Oxford University Press, Oxford.

Dissanayake, E. (1995a) Chimera, spandrel, or adaptation: conceptualizing art in human evolution. *Human Nature*, 6: 99–117.

Dissanayake, E. (1995b, first published 1992) *Homo Aestheticus: Where Art Comes From and Why*. University of Washington Press, Seattle.

Dissanayake, E. (2000) *Art and Intimacy: How the Arts Began*. University of Washington Press, Seattle.

Dissanayake, E. (2001) Aesthetic incunabula. *Philosophy and Literature*, 25: 335–346.

Dunbar, R. I. M. (2004) *The Human Story: A Brief History of Mankind's Evolution*. Faber & Faber, London.

Dunbar, R. I. M. (2005) Why are good writers so rare? An evolutionary perspective on literature. *Journal of Cultural and Evolutionary Psychology*, 3: 7–22.

Dunbar, R. I. M., Barrett, L. and Lycett, J. (2005) *Evolutionary Psychology: A Beginner's Guide*. One World, Oxford.

Easterlin, N. (1993) Play, mutation, and reality acceptance: toward a theory of literary experience. In N. Easterlin and B. Riebling (eds) *After Poststructuralism: Interdisciplinarity and Literary Theory*, pp. 105–125. Northwestern University Press, Evanston, IL.

Easterlin, N. (1999a) Do cognitive predispositions predict or determine literary value judgments? Narrativity, plot, and aesthetics. In B. Cooke and F. Turner (eds) *Biopoetics: Evolutionary Explorations in the Arts*, pp. 241–262. ICUS, Lexington, KY.

Easterlin, N. (1999b) Making knowledge: bioepistemology and the foundations of literary theory. *Mosaic*, 32: 131–147.

Easterlin, N. (2000) Psychoanalysis and the "discipline of love". *Philosophy and Literature*, 24: 261–279.

Easterlin, N. (2001a) Hans Christian Andersen's fish out of water. *Philosophy and Literature*, 25: 251–277.

Easterlin, N. (2001b) Voyages in the verbal universe: the role of speculation in Darwinian literary criticism. *Interdisciplinary Literary Studies*, 2: 59–73.

Easterlin, N. (2002) Romanticism's gray matter. *Philosophy and Literature*, 443–455.

Easterlin, N. (2004) "Loving ourselves best of all": ecocriticism and the adapted mind. *Mosaic*, 37: 1–18.

Easterlin, N. (2005) How to write the great Darwinian novel: cognitive predispositions, cultural complexity, and aesthetic evaluation. *Journal of Cultural and Evolutionary Psychology*, 3: 23–38.

Eckman, P. (2003) Emotions Revealed: Recognizing faces and feelings to Improve Communication and Emotional Life. Henry Holt, New York.

Ellis, B. and Symons, D. (1990) Sex differences in sexual fantasy: an evolutionary psychological approach. *The Journal of Sex Research*, 27: 527–555.

Evans, D. (1998) Evolution and literature. *South Dakota Review*, 36: 33–45.

Evans, D. (in press) The flash and dazzle of sports poetry. *Aethlon: The Journal of Sports Literature*.

Evans, D. (2005) From Lacan to Darwin. In J. Gottschall and D. S. Wilson (eds) *Literature and the human animal*, pp. 38–55. Northwestern University Press, Evanston, IL.

Fox, R. (1989) *The Search for Society: Quest for a Biosocial Science and Morality*. Rutgers University Press, New Brunswick.

Fox, R. (1995) Sexual conflict in the epics. *Human Nature*, 6: 135–144.

Fox, R. (2005) Male bonding in the epics and romances. In J. Gottschall and D. S. Wilson (eds) *Literature and the human animal*, pp. 126–144. Northwestern University Press, Evanston, IL.

Freeman, D. (1992) Paradigms in collision. *Academic Questions*, 5: 23–33.

Freeman, D. (1999) *The fateful hoaxing of Margaret Mead: A Historical Analysis of her Samoan Research*. Westview, Boulder, CO.

Fromm, H. (1996) From transcendence to obsolescence: a route map. In C. Glotfelty and H. Fromm (eds) *The Ecocriticism Reader: Landmarks in Literary Ecology*, pp. 30–39. University of Georgia Press, Athens.

Fromm, H. (1998) Ecology and ecstasy on Interstate 80. *Hudson Review*, 51: 65–78.

Fromm, H. (2001) A crucifix for Dracula: Wendell Berry meets Edward O. Wilson. *Hudson Review*, 53: 657–664.

Fromm, H. (2003a) The new Darwinism in the humanities: from Plato to Pinker. *Hudson Review*, 56: 89–99.

Fromm, H. (2003b) The new Darwinism in the humanities, part two: back to nature again. *Hudson Review*, 56: 315–327.

Gottschall, J. (2001) Homer's human animal: ritual combat in the *Iliad*. *Philosophy and Literature*, 25: 278–294.

Gottschall, J. (2003a) An evolutionary perspective on Homer's invisible daughters. *Interdisciplinary Literary Studies*, 4: 36–55.

Gottschall, J. (2003b) Patterns of characterization in folk tales across geographic regions and levels of cultural complexity: literature as a neglected source of quantitative data. *Human Nature*, 14: 365–382.

Gottschall, J. (2003c) The tree of knowledge and Darwinian literary study. *Philosophy and Literature*, 27: 255–268.

Gottschall, J. (2004) Literary universals and the sciences of the mind. *Philosophy and Literature*, 28: 202–217.

Gottschall, J. (2005) Quantitative literary study: a modest manifesto and testing the hypotheses of feminist fairy tale studies. In J. Gottschall and D. S. Wilson (eds) *Literature and the Human Animal*, pp. 199–224. Northwestern University Press, Evanston, IL.

Gottschall, J. and Wilson, D. S. (2005) Introduction: Literature—a last frontier in human evolutionary studies. In J. Gottschall and D. S. Wilson (eds) *Literature and the human animal*, pp. xvii–xxvi. Northwestern University Press, Evanston, IL.

Gottschall, J., Martin, J., Quish, H. and Rea, J. (2004) Sex differences in mate choice criteria are reflected in folktales from around the world and in historical European literature. *Evolution and Human Behavior*, 25: 102–112.

Gottschall, J. *et al.* (2005) The heroine with a thousand faces: universal trends in the characterization of female folk tale protagonists. *Evolutionary Psychology*, 3: 85–103.

Gottschall, J., Allison, E., De Rosa, J. and Klockeman, K. (in press a) Can literary study be scientific? Results of an empirical search for the virgin/whore dichotomy. *Interdisciplinary Literary Studies*.

Gottschall, J *et al.* (in press b) A census of the Western canon: literary studies and quantification. *Interdisciplinary Literary Studies*.

Graff, G. (1987) *Professing Literature: An Institutional History*. University of Chicago Press, Chicago.

Gross, P. R. and Levitt, N. (1994) *Higher Superstition: The Academic Left and its Quarrels with Science*. Johns Hopkins University Press, Baltimore.

Gross, P. R., Levitt, N. and Lewis, M. W. (eds) (1997) *The Flight from Science and Reason*. Johns Hopkins University Press, Baltimore.

Headlam Wells, R. (in press) *Shakespeare's Humanism*. Cambridge University Press, Cambridge.

Headlam Wells, R. and McFadden, J. (in press) Introduction. In R. Headlam Wells and J. McFadden (eds) *Human Nature: Fact and Fiction*. Continuum, London.

Jobling, I. (2001a) Personal justice and homicide in Scott's *Ivanhoe*: an evolutionary psychological perspective. *Interdisciplinary Literary Studies*, 2: 29–43.

Jobling, I. (2001b) The psychological foundations of the hero-ogre story: a cross-cultural study. *Human Nature*, 12: 247–272.

Jobling, I. (2002) Byron as cad. *Philosophy and Literature*, 26: 296–311.

Kruger, D., Fisher, M. and Jobling, I. (2003) Proper and dark heroes as dads and cads: alternative mating strategies in British and romantic literature. *Human Nature*, 14: 305–317.

Love, G. A. (1999a) Ecocriticism and science: toward consilience? *New Literary History*, 30: 561–576.

Love, G. A. (1999b) Science, anti-science, and ecocriticism. *Interdisciplinary Studies in Literature and the Environment*, 6: 65–81.

Love, G. A. (2003) *Practical Ecocriticism: Literature, Biology, and the Environment*. University of Virginia Press, Charlottesville.

McEwan, I. (2005) Literature, science, and human nature. In J. Gottschall and D. S. Wilson (eds) *Literature and the Human Animal*, pp. 5–19. Northwestern University Press, Evanston, IL.

Matthews, P. and Barrett, L. (2005) Small-screen social groups: soap operas and social networks. *Journal of Cultural and Evolutionary Psychology*, 3: 75–86.

Miall, D. and Dissanayake, E. (2003) The poetics of babytalk. *Human Nature*, 14: 337–364.

Miller, G (1999) Sexual selection for cultural displays. In R. Dunbar, C. Knight and C. Power (eds) *The Evolution of Culture*, pp. 71–91. Rutgers University Press, New Brunswick.

Miller, G. (2000) *The Mating Mind: How Sexual Choice Shaped the Evolution of Human Nature*. Doubleday, New York.

Nesse, M. (1995) Guinevere's choice. *Human Nature*, 6: 145–163.

Nettle, D. (2005a) The wheel of fire and the mating game: explaining the origins of tragedy and comedy. *Journal of Cultural and Evolutionary Psychology*, 3: 39–56.

Nettle, D. (2005b) What happens in *Hamlet*? Exploring the psychological foundations of drama. In J. Gottschall and D. S. Wilson (eds) *Literature and the Human Animal*, pp. 56–75. Northwestern University Press, Evanston, IL.

Nieves, E. (2001) The new (r)evolutionary criticism and the American literary academy: interdisciplinary insurrections 2000. In J.-P. Barbiche (ed.) *Devolutions et federalismes: Des faits et des idées*, pp. 111–119. Lharmattan, Paris.

Nordlund, M. (2002) Consilient literary interpretation. *Philosophy and Literature*, 26: 312–333.

Nordlund, M. (2005) The problem of romantic love: Shakespeare and evolutionary psychology. In J. Gottschall and D. S. Wilson (eds) *Literature and the Human Animal*, pp. 107–125. Northwestern University Press, Evanston, IL.

Perchan, R. (2004) The Darwinian world of Graham Greene's The Quiet American. *New Korean Journal of English Language and Literature*, 46: 155–172.

Pinker, S. (1997) *How the Mind Works*. W. W. Norton, New York.

Pinker, S. (2002) *The Blank Slate: The Modern Denial of Human Nature*. Viking, New York.

Power, C. (1999) "Beauty Magic": The origins of art. In R. Dunbar, C. Knight and C. Power (eds) *The Evolution of Culture*, pp. 92–112. Rutgers University Press, New Brunswick.

Salmon, C. (2005) Crossing the abyss: erotica and the intersection of evolutionary psychology and literary studies. In J. Gottschall and D. S. Wilson (eds) *Literature and the human animal*, pp. 244–257. Northwestern University Press, Evanston, IL.

Salmon, C. and Symons, D. (2001) *Warrior Lovers: Erotic Fiction, Evolution, and Female Sexuality*. Weidenfeld & Nicolson, London.

Saunders, J. (2005) Evolutionary biological issues in Edith Wharton's *The Children*. *College Literature*, 32: 83–102.

Saunders, J. (in press) Male reproductive strategies in Sherwood Anderson's "The Untold Lie." *Philosophy and Literature*.

Scalise Sugiyama, M. (1996) On the origins of narrative: storyteller bias as a fitness enhancing strategy. *Human Nature*, 7: 403–425.

Scalise Sugiyama, M. (2001a) Food, foragers, and folklore: the role of narrative in human subsistence. *Evolution and Human Behavior*, 22: 221–240.

Scalise Sugiyama, M. (2001b) Narrative theory and function: why evolution matters. *Philosophy and Literature*, 25: 233–250.

Scalise Sugiyama, M. (2001c) New science, old myth: an evolutionary critique of the Oedipal paradigm. *Mosaic*, 34: 121–136.

Scalise Sugiyama, M. (2003) Cultural relativism in the bush: toward a theory of narrative universals. *Human Nature*, 14: 383–396.

Scalise Sugiyama, M. (2005) Reverse-engineering narrative: evidence of special design. In J. Gottschall and D. S. Wilson (eds) *Literature and the Human Animal*, pp. 177–196. Northwestern University Press, Evanston, IL.

Sokal, A. D. (1996) Transgressing the boundaries: toward a transformative hermeneutics of quantum gravity. *Social Text*, 14: 217–252.

Sokal, A. D. and Bricmont, J. (1998) *Fashionable Nonsense: Postmodern Intellectuals' Abuse of Science*. Picador, New York.

Steen, F. (2005) The paradox of narrative thinking. *Journal of Cultural and Evolutionary Psychology*, 3: 87–105.

Stiller, J. and Hudson, M. (2005) Weak links and scene cliques within the small world of Shakespeare. *Journal of Cultural and Evolutionary Psychology*, 3: 57–73.

Stiller, J., Nettle, D. and Dunbar, R. I. M. (2004) The small world of Shakespeare's plays. *Human Nature* 14: 397–408.

Storey, R. (1993) "I am I because my little dog knows me": prolegomenon to a theory of mimesis. In N. Easterlin and B. Riebling (eds) *After Poststructuralism: Interdisciplinarity and Literary Theory*, pp. 45–70. Northwestern University Press, Evanston, IL.

Storey, R. (1996) *Mimesis and the Human Animal: on the Biogenetic Foundations of Literary Representation*. Northwestern University Press, Evanston, IL.

Storey, R. (2001) A critique of recent theories of laughter and humor, with special reference to the comedy of *Seinfeld*. *Interdisciplinary Literary Studies*, 2: 75–92.

Storey, R. (2003) Humor and sexual selection. *Human Nature*, 14: 319–336.

Thiessen, D. and Umezawa, Y. (1998) The sociobiology of everyday life: a new look at a very old novel. *Human Nature*, 9: 293–320.

Tooby, J. and Cosmides, L. (1992) The psychological foundations of culture. In J. H. Barkow, L. Cosmides and J. Tooby (eds) *The Adapted Mind: Evolutionary Psychology and the Generation of Culture*, pp. 19–136. Oxford University Press, New York.

Tooby, J. and Cosmides, L. (2001) Does beauty build adapted minds? Toward an evolutionary theory of aesthetics, fiction, and the arts. *SubStance* 30: 6–27.

Turner, F. (1992, first published 1985) *Natural classicism: Essays on literature and science*. University of Virginia Press, Charlottesville.

Voland, E. (2003) Aesthetic preferences in the world of artifacts—adaptations for the evaluation of honest signals? In E. Voland and K. Grammer (eds) *Evolutionary Aesthetics*, pp. 239–260. Springer, Berlin.

Whissel, C. (1996) Mate selection in popular women's fiction. *Human Nature*, 7: 427–447.

Wilson, D. S. (2005) Evolutionary social constructivism. In J. Gottschall and D. S. Wilson (eds) *Literature and the Human Animal*, pp. 20–37. Northwestern University Press, Evanston, IL.

Wilson, D. S., Near, D. and Miller, R. (1998) Individual differences in Machiavellianism as a mix of cooperative and exploitative strategies. *Evolution and Human Behavior*, 19: 203–211.

Wilson, E. O. (1998) *Consilience: The Unity of Knowledge*. Alfred A. Knopf, New York

CHAPTER 45

Music and cognitive evolution

Ian Cross

45.1. Introduction and historical background

In 1858 Herbert Spencer sent Charles Darwin a collection of essays which set out Spencer's thinking on a range of issues (Spencer, 1858), including the "origin and function of music". Darwin responded, thanking Spencer for the present; he congratulated him on the "admirable" nature of his "remarks on the so-called Development Theory", admitting that he himself was presently engaged on "an abstract of a larger work on the change of species", though treating the subject "simply as a naturalist & not from a general point of view; otherwise, in my opinion, your argument could not have been improved on & might have been quoted by me with great advantage". Darwin continued, declaring that "Your article on Music has also interested me much, for I had often thought on the subject & had come to nearly the same conclusion with you, though unable to support the notion in any detail" (Darwin, 1858).

By the time Darwin came to set out his thoughts on music in *The Descent of Man and Selection in Relation to Sex* of 1871 (Darwin, 2004), however, something of a divergence of view had emerged, perhaps partly accelerated by Darwin's increasing exasperation with the extent to which his concept of evolution as founded in natural selection had been confounded in the public mind with the teleological theories propounded by Spencer. In *The Descent*, Darwin suggests that music arose as a functional component of processes of sexual selection; it should be regarded as having been analogous in its utility to the sounds produced by the males of a wide variety of species to attract mates (Darwin instances, *inter alia*, insects, fish, birds, mice and apes). While music is incapable of functioning in the ways that "articulate speech" may do, its powers of representation being vague, it has great powers to arouse in us "various emotions". Music's affective powers arise through its association with processes of sexual selection, being employed "during the season of courtship, when animals of all kinds are excited not only by love, but by the strong passions of jealousy, rivalry, and triumph". Indeed, impassioned speech exhibits profoundly musical characteristics; as Darwin puts it, the powers of music are reflected in the "cadences of oratory". Music constitutes a basis for the emergence of language, being a capacity widely shared with other animals and constituting a medium ideally suited for the communication of affect rather than representation. Darwin thus viewed music as a precursor of language, its ultimate roots lying in its adaptive value in sexual selection.

Darwin contrasted his views with the position of Spencer that he had praised in 1858.

Spencer had proposed that the prosodic features of emotional speech constituted the basis for music; Darwin claimed that in asserting this basis for the origin of music Spencer is largely following Diderot (an intellectual predecessor certainly not acknowledged in Spencer's essay). Darwin felt that while he had defensible reasons for claiming that music preceded language in evolutionary terms, Spencer had no good grounds to argue for a genesis of music in "the cadences used in emotional speech"; Spencer, for Darwin, is unable to offer "any satisfactory explanation ... why high or deep notes should be expressive, both with man and the lower animals, of certain emotions." In other words, Darwin claimed that Spencer had not put forward a cogent rationale for the emergence of music from speech; he simply observed that it appears to have done so but without providing an account of the mechanism that motivated it, which for Darwin lies in the utility of music in sexual selection processes and its concomitant association with contexts of high arousal.

Notwithstanding their differences, for both Spencer and Darwin music was conceived of as integrally expressive of affect. In *The Expression of the Emotions in Man and Animals* of 1872, Darwin expands somewhat on the notion that music's affective potency reflects an ancient lineage for musical capacities and fits it for a role as the foundation of language. (The second, revised edition of *The Expression* appeared in 1889, and the psychologist Paul Ekman edited a third edition, incorporating a commentary on Darwin's text, which appeared in 1998; page numbers given in subsequent citations refer to this last edition.) Music mirrors or captures the relationships between affective state and sound that are found across a wide range of species, particularly in respect of vocal music, which Darwin (1998, p. 94) suggests "must be taken as the primary type of all music." Interestingly, Darwin suggests that the effects of music do not lie in its sounds alone but also in the actions which produce these. He notes that a melody transposed from one pitch range to another may lose much of its effectiveness, and suggests (ibid.) that "The effect is thus seen to depend not merely on the actual sounds but also in part on the nature of the actions which produces the sounds." As will be seen, this hint concerning an

association between the powers of musical sound and action is one which resurfaces in evolutionary thinking about music only in recent years.

For Darwin, then, music was explicable in evolutionary terms; it arose as an integral component in processes of sexual selection, its affective powers explained by the context in which it had originated. But while the scientific prestige of Darwin's theory certainly helped to secure a place for evolution in thinking about music for the next 40 years or so, it was Spencer's ideas, and particularly the governing principle that he had adduced in explaining the emergence of music from articulate speech, that shaped the ways in which a role for evolution was conceived in the study of music around end of the nineteenth century. This governing principle was likely to have been one of the principal factors underlying Darwin's dismissal of Spencer's ideas on music. For Spencer (1858) "certain general law[s] of progress" could account for the development of human civilizations, and indeed, Spencer imbued his own writings on evolution with just such a teleological bias. Evolution was, for Spencer, a scientific manifestation of such laws and in 1893 he published an essay entitled "The inadequacy of natural selection", propounding a sort of 'folk-Lamarckian' notion of evolution as guided development. Such views would have been anathema to Darwin; they harked back to the immanent principles of design that his theory of natural selection with random variation had expressly sought to refute.

Nevertheless, the Spencerian view prevailed within evolutionary thinking about music across the transition between the nineteenth and twentieth centuries and beyond. For those involved in exploring music in its own right or as an adjunct to the study of culture or of mind, Spencerian teleological evolutionism appeared to provide a helpful framework within which to formulate an understanding of two of the most evident features of music: its cultural diversity and historical mutability. Particularly in continental Europe, historical and comparative musicologists both exploited this framework in exploring and explaining the ways in which music differed from culture to culture and over historical time within Western culture (see Rehding, 2000).

For historical musicologists such as Guido Adler and music theorists such as Hugo Riemann,

Spencer's evolutionary teleology pervaded their preferred narratives of directed historical change in Western musical practice and theory. Adler could claim that contemporary harmonic usages could be traced to a 'natural' predisposition to sing in harmony, a practice that was subject to a process of increasing refinement through to the present day. Riemann, the most influential music theorist of his day, could claim that a principal difference between the 'Celto-Germanic-Slavic' peoples and other races was that the former were more naturally predisposed to employ harmony in their music, hence more likely to give rise, over historical time, to music that conformed to the highest, most developed, principles of organization (i.e. that conformed to his theoretical prescriptions).

The teleological thinking of Spencer combined with a reification of racial difference in much of the work of both historical and comparative musicologists of the time. The egregious Willi Pastor is noted by Rehding (2000, p. 358) as claiming in respect of 'primitive' peoples (*Naturvölker*) that "When shown melodic instruments, for example, *Naturvölker* did not learn what melody is from using them but rather misunderstood their function and degraded them to produce mere sounds, the only form of music that they were capable of understanding". In 1893 Richard Wallaschek published *Primitive Music* (published in Germany in 1902 as *The Origins of Music*), an attempt to make sense of what was then known about non-literate musical cultures from the perspective of their inevitable evolutionary endpoint: late-nineteenth century Western music based on complex harmonic structures and relationships.

Wallaschek's work was followed by others such as Alexander Ellis (the English translator of Helmholtz), Carl Stumpf, and Erich von Hornbostel, a student of Stumpf (see Nettl, 1956). While the principal focus of these comparative musicologists was on the ways in which different types of pitch systems could be regarded as underlying the melodic practices of different cultures, much of their thinking subscribed to the notion that racial differences determined ways in which music manifested itself in different cultures. In particular, it was held that a member of a 'primitive' culture was likely to privilege an acuity of sensory faculties over the use of reason.

The consequences of such views can be seen in the statement of Charles Myers (1905), in his study of rhythm in the music of Sarawak, when he notes that while "the Malays enjoy the faculty of combining successive dissimilar [rhythmic] periods and of regarding them as members of a complex unity", these were "carried to such lengths ... that their aesthetic effect may neither be appreciated nor reproducible by more advanced peoples". An unbridgeable gulf appeared to exist between the musics—indeed, the mentality of the members—of different cultures, and teleological evolutionary thinking appeared to underpin these cultural differences (for a review of the relationships between evolutionary and anthropological thinking in the early twentieth century see (Shore, 1996, Chapter 1). Myers continued to speculate about music from an evolutionary perspective, suggesting in an essay of 1913 that "We may be disposed to conclude that the beginnings of music have been derived from speech. It would be safer, however, to conclude that both have been evolved from a mechanism designed for the vocal 'expression of meaning.'"

This essay, however, represents not a beginning but an end. Several different factors converged to suggest that evolutionary thinking about music was likely to be unfruitful. Over much of the twentieth century consideration of origins in the study of music moved away from any exploration of music's relationship to biology to re-focus on the historical relationships between contemporary Western musical theory and practice, and Western musical history (see, e.g., Kerman, 1985), or on music's relationships with abstract domains such as mathematics (the latter exemplified in works such as Schillinger (1941) and Forte (1973). For both strands of thought, evolution was simply irrelevant to their concerns which were viewed as primarily musicological, focused on the explication of the historical and ontological roots of Western music.

Within anthropology, the increasing tendency to focus on the cultural specificities of societies rather than on pan-cultural universalities diminished the apparent explanatory role of any biological foundation for culture and mind (see, e.g., Plotkin, 1997, Chapter 2). This anthropological tendency increasingly to focus on cultural diversity seems likely to have arisen partly through a change in the relative importance accorded to the notion of psychic unity (see Shore, 1996), and partly through a change in explanatory focus within the discipline away from mind towards culture or society. From early in the twentieth century, exploration of music beyond the bounds of Western societies came to concentrate on detailed ethnographic description and on attempts to understand the structures and functions of music in terms derived from the societies' own understandings of their music—in other words, in emic rather than etic terms (see, e.g., Nettl, 1956). While lip service is occasionally paid to evolution in this literature (see, e.g., Kunst, 1955, pp. 46–48), there is little evidence of evolutionary thinking as having had any significant impact on understanding music within societies or across cultures. Nevertheless, a vital feature of these ethnomusicological studies is the evidence they provide concerning the heterogeneity of music across different societies, a heterogeneity that has come to cast the Western conception of music in a new light and to problematize the very notion of 'music' (see Blacking, 1976; Titon and Slobin, 1996; Clayton *et al.*, 2003; Nettl, 2005). And any evolutionary approach to understanding music requires at least an operational definition of what might constitute 'music'.

45.2. **Issues in the definition of music**

Music varies from society to society to the extent that one culture's music may not be recognizable as music by members of another culture. This applies both to the structural features of the music and to the functions that it may fulfil. What any non-Western culture conceives of and practices as music may have features that do not map onto Western musical practices in any straightforward way. For example, Western music exploits a dynamic and binary perceptual distinction between sounds that are consonant and those that are dissonant so as to articulate musical structures in time. This usage may have no evident relation to practices in other cultures that conceptualize and exploit the consonance–dissonance distinction in other ways, as in the music of the *campesino* culture of Northern

Potosí (Stobart, 1996; Cross, in press), or which do not appear to employ or even exploit the binary distinction in the first place (as in Indonesian gamelan music, see Perlman, 2004). And societies may severely circumscribe the functions of music in ways that would seem extraordinary in Western cultures, as has been the case in certain Islamic societies (Nettl, 2005), or they may use music to fulfil functions that, in contemporary Western cultures, would be fulfilled by means of formal linguistic interaction within institutionalized frameworks of legal process (as appears to be the case in at least some traditional Australian aboriginal societies, see Marrett, 2005). At the same time, one might find oneself responding to another culture's music in terms that would be appropriate in respect of the music of one's own society. The criteria that determine what is experienced as music evidently vary between cultures. This can be the case even within a society that thinks of itself as sharing a common culture (as witness the periodic rejection by older generations of the preferred 'music' of younger people in recent Western society—a rejection that tends to be mutual).

Nevertheless, ethnomusicologists insist that this cultural diversity exists in conjunction with what appears to be a universal musicality. Nettl (2005, p. 23) states that "All cultures regard music as at least minimally valuable"; Titon and Slobin, (1996, p. 1) assert that "So far as we know, every human society has music" but append the caveat that "Music is universal, but its meaning is not." And John Blacking (1995, p. 224) states that "Although every known human society has what trained musicologists would recognize as 'music', there are some that have no word for music or whose concept of music has a significance quite different from that generally associated with the word 'music'." Indeed, there are many societies whose languages do not distinguish a set of phenomena that are cognate with those identified by the English word 'music'. The notion of 'music' itself is problematized by such findings, and the issue of its relationship to evolutionary thinking cannot be addressed unless attention is paid to defining what is intended by the term 'music'.

On the whole, ethnomusicologists have given surprisingly little consideration to this question. Amongst the few significant exceptions are Bruno

Nettl, Alan Merriam and John Blacking, who adopt somewhat different perspectives. Nettl (2005) takes a pragmatic approach, suggesting that etic (Western) and emic accounts should each feed in to determine what it is that ethnomusicologists should focus on as 'music'. Merriam (1964) suggests that 'music' can best be explored in terms of a tripartite model that embraces music as *sound* (what might conventionally be thought of as constituting music from a Western perspective), as *behaviour* (which embraces the musical—and 'non-musical'—acts of musicians, and the activities in which the production of music is embedded) and as *concept* (how people think about music in terms of its powers and its relations to other domains of human life). Blacking (1995, p. 223), on the basis of his extensive field-work with the Venda peoples of southern Africa, and in particular, on his study of Venda children's music (Blacking, 1967) claims that " 'Music' is a primary modelling system of human thought and a part of the infrastructure of human life. 'Music'-making is a special kind of social action which can have important consequences for other kinds of social action."

Blacking's claims appear to locate music as central to, and in some ways indissociable from, other domains of human behaviour. While the claim for music's centrality is not widely echoed in the ethnomusicological literature, the conception of music as embedded in broader suites of behaviour is more general; as Bohlman (2000, p. 293) puts it, "... expressive practices do not divide into those that produce music and those that produce something else, say ritual or dance. Music accumulates its identities ... from the ways in which it participates in other activities ...." For those engaged in understanding music as it manifests itself across different cultures and historical times, 'music' appears to be protean, and its identification in any consistent manner seems to be particularly intractable.

Certainly, music cannot be defined in the terms in which it is conventionally conceived of in contemporary Western societies, as a consumable commodity constituted of complexly patterned sound that is produced by a class of specialists and engaged with through listening for primarily hedonic reasons. In many, perhaps most, non-Western cultures it involves overt action and active group engagement (see Arom, 1991). It is often indistinguishable from dance in emic conceptions (see, e.g., Gbeho, quoted in Merriam, 1964, p. 273; Gourlay, 1984). The specialized roles of performer and audience are by no means universal, and in some respects might almost be considered a minority practice, music being something that is collectively performed rather than passively consumed. In almost all known cultures music is employed not only in caregiver–infant interaction (see Trehub *et al.*, 1993; Trehub, 2003), entertainment and courtship but also in ritual, particularly at times of significant life transitions (such as the passage from adolescence to adulthood, from season to season, or from life to death). And more often than not, music is frequently bound up with individual and group identity and is an integral part of a wider range of everyday activities. If a category of behaviours that can be termed 'music' has any generality across cultures, it seems that it can best be characterized as active, as founded in interaction, and as permeating most other aspects of social life.

Given that, in the ethnomusicological view, music and other human activities are interfused, are there any features that would serve to distinguish 'music' as a discrete category of human thought and behaviour? At first sight, music seems to possess few characteristics that are not shared with other domains of behaviour, notably dance and language. Music involves patterned action in time, as does dance. Music appears communicative, complex, generative and representational, as does language.

The concept of music is amalgamated with that of dance in many—perhaps the majority of—cultures (see Arom, 1991). This fact, together with the stress on music as action in much of the ethnomusicological literature (Merriam, 1964; Blacking, 1976) suggests that it would be parsimonious to treat music and dance either as intrinsically related or simply as different manifestations of the same phenomenon. Relationships between music and language are more difficult to disentangle, but perhaps the most significant factors that differentiate them are the types of structured interactions that they allow and their contexts of use. While ethnomusicologists might debate whether or not a particular cultural phenomenon is or is not music, it is unlikely that such a difficulty would be encountered by comparative linguists. Linguistic interactions are typically structured in time so as to co-ordinate the temporal succession of participants' contributions (Condon, 1982; Kendon, 2004). Language possesses a generative complexity that allows for the production and reception of a potentially unlimited set of utterances (Hauser *et al.*, 2002). And language—whether verbal, gestural, signed or written—is evidently directed towards the communication of ideas, states of affairs, attitudes and affects that have relevance (see Sperber and Wilson, 1986) to their contexts of production and reception.

While music seems to share some of these characteristics with language, at least three significant differences are apparent:

1. Music may allow participants to act simultaneously rather than asynchronously as in language; for music, this property appears to have positive effects, while for language the effect would be to reduce its communicative functionality.

2. Music can certainly be conceptualized as possessing generativity (Lerdahl and Jackendoff, 1983; Jackendoff, 1987; Temperley, 2001); however, that generativity has been postulated principally in respect of Western tonal music and its generality remains to be rigorously tested.

3. Music may be experienced as having quite specific meanings (see, e.g., Koelsch *et al.*, 2004); however, the extent to which those meanings are necessarily stable or shared with other participants in a musical act is much less specifiable than is the case for language (Langer, 1942; Meyer, 1956).

Music's capacity to enable participants to act and to contribute to music-making simultaneously exploits the capacity of entrainment (see Clayton *et al.*, 2004), a capacity that may be unique within the hominid lineage. Entrainment has received minimal attention in the ethological literature, particularly that concerned with primates; while several species of arthropods and aneurans do appear to entrain (Merker, 2000, provides an overview), they do so in ways that appear different from those implicated in human entrainment and the issue of the origins of entrainment in the hominid or

hominin lineage remain to be explored (Bispham, in press).

Entrainment here refers to the co-ordination in time of one participant's behaviours with those of another and involves the organization of the perception and behaviour of participants around temporal regularities that are inferred (generally non-consciously) from musical sounds and actions in the form of a periodic pulse or beat that is sensed by all participants. It is evidenced in continual processes of correction of errors in both period and phase by participants and appears to be more or less automatic, not seeming to require conscious intervention (see Thaut, 2005). Even engagement with music in apparently passive listening appears to rely on such entrainment processes, evidenced in periodic modulation of attentional load (Jones, 1976; Jones and Boltz, 1989). [It should be noted that Condon (1982) suggests that processes that appear similar to entrainment underpin linguistic interaction, though his claim remains to be validated empirically.]

The issue of the extent to which music exhibits generativity of a type similar to that of language remains at present unclear. A generative foundation for musical structures has often been claimed but has not as yet been demonstrated, even for Western tonal music. While music certainly can possess considerable structural complexity, it may be more appropriate to conceive of this complexity as operating on a local level, perhaps in a manner analogous to phonological grammar (Peperkamp, 2003), rather than as possessing the complex combinatoriality of linguistic syntax.

Language has an indisputable efficacy in human interaction in the achievement of immediate and deferred goals, in large part by virtue of its capacities to mean. It is often supposed that music's meanings can be reduced to the emotions it represents, expresses or elicits, which would suggest that meaning in music is a poor or natural cousin of meaning in language (which certainly incorporates affective values in its semantic content). However, while it is undoubtedly the case that music is valued for its affective powers in all societies, often being used to regulate and co-regulate individual and group moods and emotional states (see Juslin and Sloboda, 2001), music's meanings extend beyond its affective value; as Tolbert (2001) notes, music's meanings are equally embodied, natural or affective, and artificial or symbolic. Indeed, studies indicate that music can elicit meanings quite as precise as those of language, seemingly based on a common neural substrate (Koelsch *et al.*, 2004); in general, however, meaning in music appears to be less susceptible to consensual determination than is meaning in language. Music certainly bears meaning, but the meanings that it can bear are more impenetrable and susceptible to change according to the context in which they are experienced than are those of language. As Blacking (1995, p. 237) notes, "Not only can the 'same' patterns of sound have different meanings in different societies; they can also have different meanings within the same society because of different social contexts." This is an attribute of music characterized by Cross, 2003a, 2005) as 'floating intentionality'. Cross goes further in suggesting (after Langer, 1942), that the meanings of any particular musical act or event are susceptible to different, and perhaps even conflicting, interpretations, by participants (a feature that certainly characterizes the critical literature on music).

So music is differentiable from language in its exploitation of the human capacity to entrain, in the probable scope of its generativity and in ways in which it can mean. In some ways, this comparison could appear to objectify music as an impoverished version of language. However, music and language coexist in all societies and fulfil different (though perhaps complementary) functions in those societies. While language is capable of expressing semantically decomposable propositions that have unambiguous reference, music cannot. Nevertheless, there are numerous social situations in which unambiguous reference in communicative acts is not a desideratum as it may precipitate conflict in attitudes or actions. Music's exploitation of the human capacity for entrainment allows participants to experience a sense of 'shared intentionality' (Tomasello *et al.*, 2005) whilst under-specifying goals in ways that permit individuals to interact even while holding to personal interpretations of goals and meanings that may actually be in conflict, in particular, in situations that are on the edge, situations in respect of which outcomes

are neither clear beforehand nor retrospectively identifiable by reference to particular outputs or products (Cross, in press). Music appears to have a profoundly social efficacy, and it appears possible to delineate music as a medium that is interactive, entraining, and that exhibits floating intentionality. Such a definition seems almost to exclude Western listening, which may often be passive and solitary rather than social. However, the object of listening—the music—can be conceived of as constituting a trace of human activity with which a listener 'virtually' interacts (as indeed can the musical score, which provides prescriptions for activity and is itself a trace of human musical activity).

45.3. Music in evolutionary thinking since 1984

Over the last decade a revival of evolutionary thinking about music has taken place, at least partly in the light of the ethnomusicological reconceptualizations of music outlined above but largely motivated by the generic applicability to every aspect of human life of ideas emerging from evolutionary psychology. However, two slightly earlier contributions to the debate appear to have arisen from somewhat different roots: a paper published in 1984 by Juan Roederer, a physicist and psychoacoustician, and one of 1992 by Bryan Levman, published in the journal *Ethnomusicology*.

Roederer's brief paper (1984) makes a number of suggestions which were to resurface in more recent literature. He focuses mainly on the complex structures of pitch and timbre characteristic of musical sound, suggesting that learning to deal with—to perceive and to produce—these complex structures could play a significant role in the development of infant linguistic capacities. Roederer is effectively following Spencer's notion that language preceded the emergence of music, and appears to be conceiving of music as a purely sonic phenomenon (perhaps unsurprising given his psychoacoustical background). Roederer suggests that the competences acquired by the infant in 'proto-musical' exchanges with the mother are crucial in learning to deal with the prosodic aspects of language that are sometimes described as musical [interestingly, a recent study (Schön *et al.*, 2004) appears to support some such link, finding evidence linking an enhanced capacity to make judgments about prosodic structure in language to early musical training]. However, he also lays stress on the apparent utility of these early musical interactions between mother and infant in strengthening affective bonds. He expands on this notion in suggesting that the affective dimension of music could serve important functions in group bonding, as participants in a musical act would be more likely than not to be influenced in similar ways by music's affective powers. Roederer's paper had little immediate impact; it is only with the efflorescence of interest in music from an evolutionary perspective over the last few years that certain of his ideas have come to be reappraised and their innovativeness acknowledged.

Levman's (1992) paper adopts a quite specific perspective on the evolution of music, summarized in his opening sentence (p. 146) which states that "This article proposes to evince evidence in support of the hypothesis that language and music evolved out of a common 'proto-faculty' which was primarily musical in nature." In pursuit of this aim, Levman aligns himself with Darwin rather than Spencer in suggesting that music preceded language in evolutionary terms. He draws on a range of literatures, including ethology, phonology and ethnomusicology, in claiming a primacy for 'musical' features of speech—essentially, pitch and timbre—over other linguistic features in the development of linguistic competence and in the evolution of language. While many of the ethnomusicological sources that he adduces appear to uphold his argument, it is undermined by the narrowness of the linguistic references that he employs as well as a failure to acknowledge the provisional status of many of the empirical findings that he cites. Moreover, in spite of relying heavily on ethnomusicological evidence, Levman appears to view the communicative use of sound in non-human animals as continuous with the human faculty for music. This view is highlighted in his assertions that (p. 158) "most ethologists would agree that they [animals] have a form of song or music" and that (p. 164) "the music faculty is ... non-symbolic". In respect of the first claim, song is certainly a capacity of non-human species, according the

criteria given in Holy and Guo (2005, citing Broughton, 1963); but most ethologists (see, e.g., the chapters by Slater and by Marler in Wallin *et al.*, 2000) concur in claiming that non-human animals do *not* produce music. In respect of the second claim, ethnomusicologists (see, e.g., Tolbert, 1992, 2001; Feld and Fox, 1994) have suggested that the notion of music as 'natural' and hence non-symbolic, as Levman's thesis would suggest, is itself a cultural construct (though found in many different cultures); music is as symbolic as it is natural. In addition, Levman undermines his arguments by the vagueness of his account of the selection mechanisms that may have precipitated the emergence of a musical communication system, as well as by his reliance on the notion that ontogeny recapitulates phylogeny to substantiate his claims. Nevertheless, this paper, together with that of Roederer, identifies and rehearses many points that have proven to be central in the more recent debates over music and evolution.

At the beginning of the 1990s (around the time Levman's article was published), evolutionary psychology was coalescing as an identifiable and significant strand of thinking within both psychology and evolutionary theory. Little attention was devoted to music within the discipline at first, but by 1996 and 1997 two of its main protagonists, Dan Sperber and Steven Pinker, had produced distinctly different evolutionary treatments of music which nevertheless both relegated music to the status of evolutionary by-product.

Sperber, in his 1996 book *Explaining Culture*, uses music to exemplify a particular feature of his modular model of mind, the capacity of a mental module to have both *proper* and *actual* (in the case he describes, *cultural*) domains. He hypothesizes that in hominin evolution a mental module arose to deal with the types of complex sound patterns varying in pitch and rhythm that were producible by early hominin vocal systems and were employed in communication. He suggests (p. 141) that "The proper domain of the module we are imagining is the acoustic properties of early human vocal communication", and that individuals would have been strongly motivated to develop its acuity (i.e. its development would have had hedonic value) so as to ensure that they were detecting appropriate signals. Over evolutionary time another module arises to deal with more finely structured and generative characteristics of hominin vocal signals, but the earlier module is still extant; it is no longer central to hominin communication but persists as a feature of the hominin mind because its use is associated with pleasure. Hence, music: or rather, a mental module that allows modern humans to experience pleasure in the complex patterns of pitch and rhythm that, for Sperber, characterize music. The module has changed its functionality; its proper domain has been displaced, but it has gained a cultural (actual) domain of application. He suggests (p. 142) that "humans have created a cultural domain, music, which is parasitic on a cognitive module, the proper domain of which pre-existed music and had nothing to do with it." He does note (p. 141), however, that the hypothesis that he outlines is intended as "an example of a way of thinking suggested by the epidemiological approach [to the exploration of the relationships between mind and culture] rather than a serious scientific hypothesis, which I would not have the competence to develop."

Notwithstanding this disclaimer, Sperber's conclusions concerning the role of music in the evolutionary model of mind were echoed the following year in Steven Pinker's book *How the Mind Works*. Pinker devotes 10 pages of his final chapter, entitled The Meaning of Life, to considering music, because, in his words, he wishes to consider a mental faculty which "shows the clearest signs of not being" [an evolutionary adaptation] to set against examples of mental faculties that are self-evidently adaptive, such as language. Pinker starts from the premise that (p. 528) "as far as biological cause and effect are concerned, music is useless", noting that music is variable in its complexity from culture to culture, that while all tend to enjoy listening to music only a small subset of the population are practitioners, and that music communicates nothing but formless emotion. Hence, he concludes, music shows clear signs of being a 'technology', a human capacity developed and exploited for its own sake and at best evolutionarily neutral, rather than an adaptation. He suggests that this technology developed to exploit capacities that had arisen for largely adaptive reasons, claiming (p. 534) that "music is auditory

cheesecake, an exquisite confection crafted to tickle the sensitive spots of at least six of our mental faculties", these being language, auditory scene analysis, emotional calls, habitat selection, motor control and "something else".

Irrespective of whether or not music is non-adaptive, the significance of Pinker's discussion of music is severely diminished by the lack of fit between his conception of music and that outlined in the first part of this chapter. In effect, Pinker appears to be subscribing to an over-simplistic notion of music as it tends to be overtly manifested within late-twentieth-century Western culture, as a commodified set of complex sound patterns produced by the few and consumed by the many, rather than as the complexly and integrally social (and individual) actions and structures that it is and has been both in the West (see, e.g., Finnegan, 1989) and in other cultures, places and times. The conception of music that is treated here from the perspective of evolutionary psychology is fundamentally ethnocentric, and is not representative of music's range of manifestations and significances. It can also be suggested that Pinker's focus on traits as adaptive in wholly individualistic terms (less than two pages of a 600 page text are allotted to discussing—and dismissing—issues of selection at the group level) limits the potential of his chosen approach to deal with traits of which the principal impact may be on individual capacities to manage intra- and inter-group interaction (see, e.g., Boyd and Richerson, 1985; Sober and Wilson, 1998), and musicality can be regarded as one such trait. Overall, while Pinker's view of music has been widely disseminated, its ethnocentricity significantly limits its explanatory adequacy, as does its commitment to the seductive simplicities of 'self-interest'.

A similar focus on the effects of music at the level of individual fitness is evident in the work of Geoffrey Miller, though here the conclusions reached are startlingly at variance with those of Pinker. Miller (1997, 2000, 2001) harks back to Darwin in suggesting that music's primary role is located in processes of sexual selection. For Miller, music constitutes a medium that is well-suited to demonstrate the 'protean', unpredictable and creative, properties of an individual, properties that are selectively advantageous (their exercise constitutes an evolutionarily stable strategy for achieving or maintaining social dominance) and hence desirable in the determination of mate choice. Music is well-suited to make manifest such properties as it combines (1997, p. 322) "ritualised rules of tonality, rhythmicity, melody and harmony and protean intentions and variations". Hence protean individuals might well advertise their creative assets in musical display; for such individuals, music constitutes an excellent medium in which to exploit the impact of ritual and the power of innovation. Miller (2000) seeks to support this argument by reference to a range of Western musical practices; for example, he refers to Jimi Hendrix, claiming that the sexual opportunities afforded by rock-star status are in line with the predictions of his theory.

While Miller's theory that "tunes help you breed more easily" may have held for the post-contraceptive, pre-AIDS, world of 1970s rock, it seems likely that its scope is now more limited. Although music is certainly used for courtship in most, if not all, societies, the ethnomusicological evidence indicates that its roles are always more multifarious. Moreover, Miller's theory would predict that musical ability should exhibit, or at least should have exhibited, a significant sexual dimorphism. While this would be difficult to ascertain in our predecessor species, it does not appear to be the case with modern humans; while musical roles are often sexually differentiated, in most cultures musicality appears to be equally exhibited by both males and females; if anything, the manifestation of musicality that is perhaps most culturally widespread, in the form of the use of proto-musical and musical forms of interaction between caregiver and infant, is primarily evidenced by females. Moreover, as Fitch (2006) points out, the precocious capacities of human infants in music perception would suggest that musicality is a trait that is unlikely to have been sexually selected for, given that such traits tend to emerge only in sexual maturity in other species.

A different rationale for music playing an evolutionary role through its effects on individual fitness is proposed in Cross (1999). This chapter draws on the developmental theory of Karmiloff-Smith (1992) and Mithen's (1996) account of later hominin evolution as being marked by a shift from domain-specific to domain-general competences, suggesting a role for music in motivating this shift. Cross proposes that music's floating intentionality might have been a factor in the emergence of domain-general competence by virtue of the capacity of musical behaviours simultaneously to be embedded in, and to signify differently within, different domains of human mental life. Music is conceived of here as underpinning a capacity to integrate information across different cognitive domains by offering a means of bridging the gap between these domains by means of its semantic openness and its ability to be integrated into other activities. The implications of this proposal appear to agree with findings that musical training can influence children's IQ positively (see Schellenberg, 2003, 2004). However, it has to be noted that musical training in Western cultures (where all experimental studies of the effect of music on other domains in development have been conducted) involves procedures that are directly analogous to school tuition; hence, an impact on IQ is unsurprising. Indeed, before a claim for music as central to the establishment of domain-general competence can be made securely, much remains to be uncovered about the relations between musical and general (enculturative) development and training in cultures other than those of the West, ideally employing a more generalizable measure of integrative cognitive competence than IQ. As matters stand, only one significant study has explored in depth the dynamics of the development of musicality in a non-Western context, that reported in Blacking (1967).

Blacking found that the principal effects of childhood engagement with music lay in the domain of sociality; as he states (1967, p. 31): "Knowledge of the children's songs is a social asset and in some cases a social necessity for a child who wishes to be an accepted member of his own age group." It seems likely that any evolutionary account of music might be more appropriately rooted in consideration of music's role in managing social relations and in the formation of social skills than in its putative effects on individual fitness. As noted above, there is certainly evidence that music is embedded in social activities and can be considered to have a proximate efficacy in managing social interactions. Early approaches to understanding evolution in terms of group selection (such as that of Wynne-Edwards, 1962) have been discarded on the grounds that any effects of selection for benefits at the level of the group would be far weaker than, and would effectively be over-written by, the powerful effects of selection for individual fitness. However, more recent theories such as those proposed by Sober and Wilson (1998) and surveyed by Shennan (2002) have tended to substantiate a role for relationships between social environment and individual fitness in profoundly social species such as humans. In a social species, the behaviours of conspecifics are likely to constitute a highly significant component of the environment that governs the viability of any individual's behaviours. In such species behaviours that contribute towards survival and reproductive success may be determined as much by relations between conspecifics (and by individual capacities to manage such relations) as by relations between individuals and their physical environments.

The majority of recent evolutionary treatments of music have focused on its effects at the level of the group, approaches tending to fall into one of two categories. In general, those in the first stress music's possible effects on *inter-group* interaction, regarding music as strengthening or as signalling within-group collaboration so as to benefit musical groups (who will appear strongly bonded and effective as a social unit) as against less musical groups (who will appear weakly bonded and hence less effective in inter-group interactions and conflicts). Those in the second adopt a focus on music's role in *intra-group* relations, highlighting music's possible effects within groups either in terms of its role in the formation of group identity (and hence the reinforcement of within-group cooperativity) or on its efficacy as a means of managing, and of learning to manage, social relations (and hence its positive impact on individual fitness, and on conflict minimization, within groups).

Merker (2000) proposes a role for music in managing inter-group relations that has its origins in chimpanzee 'fruit-tree carnivalling', unsynchronized group calling and display that is characteristic of groups of (male) chimps on discovery of abundant fruit sources. He suggests that chimp carnivalling constitutes an index of chimpanzee within-territorial male cooperativity

and of number of fruit-trees, and acts as audible markers of these for—and hence as potential attractors of—migrating (exogamous) females. He points out that were chimp carnivalling to involve *synchronous* cries the range over which they would be audible would be greatly increased and their efficacy as indexes of group resources would be enhanced. He hypothesizes that a hominin descendant of the common hominin-chimp ancestor acquired the capacity to carnival synchronously (in effect, to entrain), this contributing positively to their evolutionary fitness and constituting an origin for music. Merker's theory does provide an evolutionary basis for the significance within musical behaviour of the capacity to entrain, but is perhaps too conjectural; moreover, the narrowly constrained (and sexually differentiated) bases for the origins of music that it proposes are difficult to square with the broad scope of musical behaviours evident in contemporary societies.

Hagen and Bryant (2003) adopt a similar evaluation of music's likely role in evolution as a signifier of group resources. They suggest, however, that those resources that are being exhibited in group musical display consist of the *appearance* of group cohesion and efficacy, music acting as an excellent indicator of group stability and of the capacity to engage in complex, collective and coordinated, action. They reach their position by claiming that, as musical behaviours are not a good indicator of an individual's capacity to contribute to group survival, coalition signalling constitutes the only possible rationale for the utilization of musical behaviours. However, this focus on the immediate instrumental utility of actions in social contexts as the sole criteria for evaluating their potential fitness benefits under-values the extent to which such actions may have affective and inter-subjective consequences that are not presently and overtly evident, but that contribute positively to individual fitness within the group. It is certainly possible that the coalition-signalling function proposed by Hagen and Bryant played some role in instantiating music into the modern human repertoire, but one could equally well find other potential rationales that are founded in consideration of inter-group relationships; for example, it could by hypothesized that music emerged to function somewhat as does language in Nettle

(1999), as a means of securing a group against infiltration by freeriders by virtue of inter-group variation in musical style. In general, however, approaches that seek to ground music in inter-group relations seem to focus too narrowly on the notion of music as display while neglecting the significance of music as a participatory behaviour.

Brown's (2000a,b) treatment of music in evolution acknowledges its prospective role in inter-group relations but emphasizes its functionality within groups. Brown (2000a) presents an account of structural similarities between music and language in terms of combinatorial syntax and into national phrasing, positing a common evolutionary origin for both music and language. The extent to which music possesses the syntactic combinatoriality of language notwithstanding, Brown makes a cogent case for language and music to be conceived of as rooted in common mechanisms at the phonological level, a proposal that seems more parsimonious than the suggestion of Pinker and Jackendoff (2005) that these mechanisms are homologous but distinct for language and for music. Brown (2000b) develops the notion of music as efficacious at the level of the group, suggesting that music typically acts to influence behaviours at the group level. He suggests that music acts to reinforce cooperative behaviour within the group by means of group ritual activities, promoting a sense of 'groupishness' that is likely to enhance prospects of group survival in addition to being effective in situations of inter-group conflict.

This focus on music's significance in promoting cooperative, within-group behaviours, is mirrored by others. Kogan (1997) and Vaneechoutte and Skoyles (1998) view music as significant in human evolution by virtue of its embeddedness in social interaction and its effect of the formation of group identity, as does Dunbar (2004), who suggests that its primary effect is in the consolidation of group bonds. Mithen's (2005) extensive treatment echoes Brown in presenting a view of music and language as having common origins and in suggesting that music had an evolutionary efficacy in the formation of social bonds (after McNeill, 1995).

Cross (2001, 2003a,b, 2005, in press) also subscribes to the notion that music has a bonding effect, but suggests in addition that music, through its polyvalent significances, can contribute positively to individual fitness within the group by facilitating communicative interactions that, were they to be conducted linguistically, might give rise to conflict, a view also presented in Morley (2002, 2003) and Cross and Morley (in press). Whilst maintaining that music may have an impact on individual fitness outwith social contexts by virtue of its 'metaphorizing' powers (see above), Cross suggests that music's powers of entrainment, together with its 'floating intentionality', fit it for use as a medium for communicative interactions in which meanings are under-determined to the extent that participants are free to develop their own interpretations of the significance of their own, and others', contributions to the collective musical behaviour. At the same time its potential for group entrainment provides a framework for coordinated action that guarantees the integrity and continuity of that collective musical behaviour. In effect, it allows participants to explore the prospective consequences of their actions and attitudes towards other participants within a framework that is likely to align participants' sense of goals. Hence music can be regarded as possessing attributes that complement those of language—music and language here being viewed as different components of the human communicative toolkit that differ primarily in the degree to which they are capable of specifying meaning unambiguously.

Most of the preceding accounts view music's efficacy in shaping individual or group fitness as deriving from its proximate effects; however, they do not, in general, offer clear rationales for music's assimilation into the human repertoire of behaviours. That is, they tend either to avoid considerations of the ultimate factors that would have led to the emergence of music or to conflate proximate effects with ultimate causes (see also Fitch, 2005). One approach that does explicitly consider ultimate causes is that of Dissanayake (2000), who suggests that the use of music, or para-musical behaviours in the form of 'motherese', in affect regulation and co-regulation in mother-infant interactions provides a rationale for music's roles in (p. 398) "social regulation and emotional conjoinment" (see also Trehub, 2003). She suggests (p. 399) that "dyadic behaviors of mothers and infants [are] a biologically endowed ritualized behavior" which is predicated on the exploitation of musical features in human communication, suggesting (p. 390) that these behaviours are precipitated by a need to accommodate to increasing altriciality in the hominin lineage, leading to longer periods of infant dependency and mother–infant interaction and hence to the consolidation of musical behaviours into the adult repertoire. Cross (2003b) adopts a similar position, starting from the premise that altriciality and social complexity appear directly related in primates; the more complex the social organization of a species the longer the juvenile period (Joffe, 1997). This lengthened juvenile period assists acquisition of the skills required by the need to interact flexibly with conspecifics. It is evident that our predecessor species exhibited shorter juvenile periods that were less differentiable into discrete stages of maturation than is the case for modern humans (Bogin, 1999), and it can be hypothesized that with increases in hominin altriciality there would have been increasing selection pressures to accommodate to an increased prevalence of juvenile modes of thought and behaviour within populations. Music can be thought of as a way of extending into the adult repertoire of thought and behaviour the benefits of juvenile exploratory behaviours and cognitions and of regulating their expression, and hence viewed as an adaptive consequence—an exaptation—which arises from processes of progressive altricialization and stage-differentiation in the later hominin lineage.

45.4. Ethological, cognitive scientific and archaeological evidence

Dissanayake's argument is echoed in that of Falk (2004) for the importance of infant-directed speech in the evolution of human communication systems, including music. Falk claims that the continuous, positively valenced, affective vocalizations that characterize mother–infant interactions in modern humans are absent in our nearest extant relatives, chimps and bonobos, and suggests that these features arose in part to 'substitute' for the mother's proximity as hominin infants became more altricial and less able to cling

to the mother. While Falk is here postulating a discontinuity between the behaviours of humans and of other species to account for the emergence of music-like behaviours in humans, others have explored the prospects of identifying behavioural continuities. Indeed, Darwin's (2004) suggestion that music originated as a mechanism for sexual selection was motivated in part by the correspondences that he felt existed between human music and bird song.

Several contributors to the volume by Wallin et al. (2000) explore the possibility that aspects of animal communication constitute evolutionary precursors of human musicality. Marler, Geissmann and Ujhelyi consider that music may be related to, respectively, bird song, the duetting calls of gibbons and the vocalizations of bonobos. Each author takes a somewhat different approach to delineating the nature of the relationship between the animal behaviours in question and music; however, all appear to conceive of human music as a complex sonic pattern related to the expression of affect rather than as a socially situated complex of communicative and intentional sounds and actions with symbolic potential, which limits the explanatory significance in respect of music of the features of animal vocal signals that they explore. Moreover, pace the suggestion of Hauser (2000, p. 97) that animal vocal communication may share significant features with human vocal communication (such as, at least social, referentiality), most current theories (see, e.g., Owings and Morton, 1998; Seyfarth and Cheney, 2003) suggest that non-human animal vocal signals are in general more limited in function, serving principally to manage behaviours of conspecifics—and of other species in the immediate environment—through direct expression of affective state.

A recent overview of comparative perspectives on music in evolution (Fitch, in press a) suggests that whether or not animal vocal signals are considered synapomorphic or pleisiomorphic in respect of music (or indeed any form of human communication), human musicality can be considered to be constituted of a suite of discrete behavioural capacities, each having prospectively different evolutionary roots. He notes that studies of avian song learning are beginning to disentangle their functional, behavioural, neural and developmental bases in ways that allow helpful parallels to be drawn with human vocal learning and behaviour. Moreover, he points out that key components of musicality such as entrainment, the use of periodic sounds and gestures in social interaction, have barely begun to be studied in non-human species. A few studies have been conducted (e.g. McDermott and Hauser, 2005) which seek to explore continuities and discontinuities between the capacities of non-human species and human musicality; however, these have tended to treat music solely as sonic pattern and have so far demonstrated only that non-human primates seem insensitive to types of distinctions that appear structurally significant in music from Western cultural contexts.

From the perspective of cognitive psychology and neuroscience, over the last fifty years significant advances have been made in our understanding of processes of music perception and production (see, e.g. Deutsch, 1999; Zatorre and Peretz, 2003). For example, several large-scale research programmes have demonstrated that many important features of music cognition can be accounted for in terms of generic cognitive processes. Associationistic processes of feature abstraction and schematicization appear to explain aspects of our experience of pattern in musical pitch (see Krumhansl, 1990; Krumhansl and Toiviainen, 2003), while processes of auditory scene analysis (Bregman, 1990) have been shown to underlie many features of our experience of local form in musical structures (see Huron, 2001a). Both of these types of process appear likely to have a degree of phylogenetic generality (see Plotkin, 1997, Chapter 4) which would suggest that aspects of human musicality are grounded on perceptual and neural processes that may be continuous with those of at least some other species.

However, many of these cognitive scientific advances are largely in respect of Western musical systems and perceptions. There are, to date, few studies that have explicitly sought to investigate cognitive or neural processes that might be common in engagements with music across a range of cultural contexts, or in engagement with music outside the confines of the Western 'concert hall simulation' that serves as the paradigm for most laboratory-based research in the

cognition and neuroscience of music. There are, of course, significant exceptions, including papers by Castellano *et al.* (1984), Drake and El Heni (2003), Hannon and Trehub (2005) and Sloboda *et al.* (2001). Several commentators have noted the urgent need to extend the range of experimental methods and cultural contexts that should be explored (Stobart and Cross, 2000; Huron, 2001b; Stevens, 2004).

Nevertheless, certain features that are of prospective significance for an understanding of music in evolutionary terms have been clarified in addition to those mentioned above. The experience of music has been shown to be bound to periodic modulations of attention (Jones, 1976; Jones and Boltz, 1989) that appear to reflect constraints on, or at least common processes in, the timing of human action (Pöppel and Wittmann, 1999; Thaut, 2005). Several studies have demonstrated unequivocally that music is capable of eliciting affect (e.g. McCoy *et al.*, 1996; Blood and Zatorre, 2001). Others have reinforced a view of music as necessarily involving action or the experience of action; a meta-review by Janata and Grafton (2003) indicates that ostensibly passive listening to music involves activation of brain areas associated with motor planning, while a study by Koelsch *et al.* (2006) found that listening to pleasant music implicates brain circuitry associated with pre-motor representations for vocal sound production. Notwithstanding these advances, research in the cognitive neurosciences of music has a tendency to reflect, in the models that it produces, the constraints imposed by experimental methodology and by a focus on musical structures and modes of engagement with music that are bound to Western cultural contexts, pointing up the need for creative collaboration across disciplines in exploring human musicality.

This need for collaboration across disciplines is also evident in respect of other potentially significant sources of evidence about the relationships between music and processes of human evolution, in particular the theories and findings of archaeology and of biological anthropology. When Darwin considered material evidence for music in prehistory in *The Descent* (2004, p. 636), he could only adduce the findings of Lartet, who had "described two flutes made out of the bones and horns of the reindeer, found in caves together with flint tools and the remains of extinct animals." In some respects the situation has not advanced greatly since Darwin's time, as the issue of music—and indeed, of sound—in prehistory has received little attention in the archaeological literature (see Scarre and Lawson, 2006). However, a recent paper (D'Errico *et al.*, 2003) summarizes what is known in the context of a re-evaluation of current archaeological approaches, particularly in the light of recent finds in southern Africa (Henshilwood *et al.*, 2002). It notes that the earliest unequivocally musical artefact found to date is a bone pipe from Geissenklösterle in southern Germany, dating to *c.*36 000 BP. A further sequence of bone pipes has been found at Isturitz in southern France (in contexts rich in parietal art), with dates ranging from 20 000 to 35 000 BP. The earliest of these dates more or less coincides with the arrival of modern humans in Europe and suggests that something like music was of high significance to those peoples. As D'Errico *et al.* (2003) comment, these artefacts are extremely sophisticated, exhibiting subtle design features that are analogous to those found in historic wind instruments; the time, effort and expertise devoted to their manufacture must have been considerable and suggests that music was probably of great importance to a people who had just come to inhabit a new and potentially threatening environment.

In this context it should be stressed that the 'Neandertal flute' found at Divje Babe in Slovenia, a femur of a juvenile cave bear that has been interpreted as a musical artefact, is shown in D'Errico and Villa (1997) and in D'Errico *et al.* (2003) to have arisen as a result of carnivore action. As D'Errico *et al.* (2003, p. 38) state, "Of course, this does not mean that Neandertals were unable to manufacture and play musical instruments. It simply means that we cannot use *this* object to support that hypothesis ...." The status of the artefact is somewhat complicated by the ways in which representations of it have been employed since its discovery (for instance, a silver 'replica' was presented to the Pope); however, the evidence would suggest strongly that this is not a musical artefact.

It has been suggested that the use of musical instruments, and the use of the voice, derive from distinct and different evolutionary roots (Nettl, 2005; Fitch, in press b). While contemporary societies often differentiate between vocal and instrumental musics in quite rigid ways (for example, in assigning specific gender roles to singers and to instrumentalists), there are perhaps as many instances where, in the pedagogical tradition of a culture, the sound of an instrument is taught as constituting an analogue of the human voice (as is the case in both Western and North Indian cultures). It is perhaps more parsimonious to consider the use of instruments as extending the sound-producing capacities of the human body (in terms of frequency range, intensity and timbre), instruments in effect functioning as prosthetic devices. In any case, the use of musical artefacts will have been preceded by the expression of musical capacities by voice and body, and would appear likely to have an ancient provenance. The ubiquity of music in native American and Australian societies in forms that are not directly relatable to historic Eurasian or African musics strongly suggests that modern humans brought musicality with them out of Africa. Indeed, vocal and auditory capacity characteristics of modern humans appear to have emerged around 500 000 BP; intriguingly, the findings of Martinez *et al.* (2004) in respect of the auditory capacities of *heidelbergensis* would suggest that by this point in hominin evolution, a coadaptation of vocal and auditory systems had occurred that privileged human vocal, social information over other environmental sounds. In other words, the vocal and auditory capacities that subserve the experience of music today were present in hominins half a million years ago; whatever its precursors, modern musicality is likely to have very ancient roots.

45.5. Conclusion

Music has had an intermittently audible, yet long-standing, resonance in thinking about human origins. It was viewed as functional by Darwin, as an offshoot of language by Spencer, as exemplifying (in the forms that it took in late-nineteenth-century Europe) the culmination of a process of guided development in human history and prehistory, and more recently as parasite, 'cheesecake', and as central to the consolidation of the human capacity for culture. However, many of the views adopted in evolutionary thinking about music have misread music's cultural specificities as universal attributes. The notion of music as expressing 'pure emotion' disregards the extent to which music is self-evidently embedded in, and expressive of, symbolic systems, while the notion that the paradigmatic mode of engagement with music is listening neglects the extent to which music is manifested in active interaction. Nevertheless, conceptions of music are emerging from ethnomusicological, cognitive, neuroscientific and philosophical contexts (for this last, see Robinson, 2005) which enable music's locations and functions within the modern human repertoire of thought and behaviour to be fixed with an increasing degree of certainty. Music appears to be a human universal in the form of communicative behaviour that under-specifies goals yet facilitates a sense of joint action, enabling participants to sustain interaction while holding to potentially conflicting personal interpretations of goals and meanings. The ways in which it achieves this remain to be identified in detail, but music seems likely to be central in any attempt to specify the dynamics of human minds in cultures and the evolutionary processes that set the parameters for those dynamics.

In some ways it appears that thinking about the origins of music has not developed greatly since the *philosophes* were discussing the question in the context of the origins of language, and of the relative merits of French and Italian music, in the eighteenth century, contributors to the debate including the composer Rameau and the philosopher (and composer) Rousseau. As Downing Thomas (1995) notes, "For Rousseau, vocal sounds are not so much expressions of ideas as they are moments of identification and social bonding" (p. 105), leading him to the conclusion that "the focus of the verbal [and, by implication, musical] paradigm in Rousseau has shifted from representation as reproduction to representation as a form of communion" (ibid., p. 143). Such ideas seem to prefigure the conceptions of music as a medium for, and motivator of, social interaction that have emerged through the twentieth century. Indeed, Thomas's suggestion that, in the eighteenth-century debates, music was conceived of as

"the anthropological 'missing link' in the eighteenth-century attempt ... to pinpoint the semiotic moment which separates culture from nature, and human beings from animals" (ibid., p. 9) seems increasingly applicable in present-day debates about the evolutionary roots of language, music, and the capacity for culture.

References

Arom, S. (1991) *African Polyphony and Polyrhythm*. Cambridge University Press, Cambridge.

Bispham, J. (in press) Rhythm in Music: What is it? Who has it? And Why? *Music Perception*.

Blacking, J. (1967) *Venda Children's Songs: a study in ethnomusicological analysis*. Witwatersrand University Press, Johannesburg.

Blacking, J. (1976) *How Musical is Man?* Faber, London.

Blacking, J. (1995) *Music, Culture and Experience*. University of Chicago Press, London.

Blood, A. J. and Zatorre, R. J. (2001) Intensely pleasurable responses to music correlate with activity in brain regions implicated in reward and emotion. *Proceedings of the National Academy of Sciences*, 98: 11818–11823.

Bogin, B. (1999) *Patterns of Human Growth*. Cambridge University Press, Cambridge.

Bohlman, P. (2000) Ethnomusicology and music sociology. In D. Greer (ed.) *Musicology and Sister Disciplines*, pp. 288–298. Oxford University Press, Oxford.

Boyd, R. and Richerson, P. (1985) *Culture and the Evolutionary Process*. University of Chicago Press, Chicago.

Bregman, A. S. (1990) *Auditory Scene Analysis: the Perceptual Organisation of Sound*. MIT Press, Cambridge, MA.

Brown, S. (2000a) The 'musilanguage' model of music evolution. In N. Wallin, B. Merker and S. Brown (eds) *The Origins of Music*, pp. 271–300. MIT Press, Cambridge, MA.

Brown, S. (2000b) Evolutionary models of music: from sexual selection to group selection. In F. Tonneau and N.S. Thompson (eds) *Perspectives in Ethology*, vol. 13, *Behavior, Evolution and Culture*, pp. 231–281. Plenum Press, New York.

Castellano, M. A., Krumhansl, C. L. and Bharucha, J. J. (1984) Tonal Hierarchies in the Music of North India. *Journal of Experimental Psychology—General*, 113: 394–412.

Clayton, M., Herbert, T. and Middleton, R. (eds) (2003) *The Cultural Study of Music: A Critical Introduction*. London, Routledge.

Clayton, M., Sager, R. and Will, U. (2004) In time with the music: the concept of entrainment and its significance for ethnomusicology. *ESEM Counterpoint*, 1: 1–82.

Condon, W. S. (1982) Cultural microrhythms. In M. Davis (ed.) *Interaction Rhythms: Periodicity in Communicative Behavior*, pp. 77–102. Human Science Press, New York.

Cross, I. (1999) Is music the most important thing we ever did? Music, development and evolution. In Suk Won Yi (ed.) *Music, Mind and Science*, pp. 10–39. Seoul National University Press, Seoul.

Cross, I. (2001) Music, cognition, culture and evolution. *Annals of the New York Academy of Sciences*, 930: 28–42.

Cross, I. (2003a) Music and biocultural evolution. In M. Clayton, T. Herbert and R. Middleton (eds) *The Cultural Study of Music: A Critical Introduction*, pp. 19–30. Routledge, London.

Cross, I. (2003b) Music and evolution: causes and consequences. *Contemporary Music Review*, 22: 79–89.

Cross, I. (2005) Music and meaning, ambiguity and evolution. In D. Miell, R. MacDonald and D. Hargreaves (eds) *Musical Communication*, pp. 27–43. Oxford University Press, Oxford.

Cross, I. (in press) Music and social being. *Musicology Australia*.

Cross, I. and Morley, I. (in press) Music in evolution and evolutionary theory: the nature of the evidence. In S. Malloch and C. Trevarthen (eds) *Communicative Musicality: Narratives of Expressive Gesture and Being human*. Oxford University Press, Oxford.

Darwin, C. (1858) Calendar number 2373. The Darwin Correspondence Online Database. Available at: http://darwin.lib.cam.ac.uk/

Darwin, C. (1998) *The Expression of the Emotions in Man and Animals*. HarperCollins, London.

Darwin, C. (2004) *The Descent of Man and Selection in Relation to Sex*. Penguin, London.

D'Errico, F. and Villa, P. (1997) Holes and grooves: the contribution of microscopy and taphonomy to the problem of art origins. *Journal of Human Evolution*, 33: 1–31.

D'Errico, F., Henshilwood, C., Lawson, G. *et al.* (2003) Archaeological evidence for the emergence of language, symbolism, and music—an alternative multidisciplinary perspective. *Journal of World Prehistory*, 17: 1–70.

Deutsch, D. (ed.) (1999) *The Psychology of Music*. Academic Press, London.

Dissanayake, E. (2000) Antecedents of the temporal arts in early mother–infant interactions. In N. Wallin, B. Merker and S. Brown (eds) *The Origins of Music*, pp. 389–407. MIT Press, Cambridge, MA.

Drake, C. and El Heni, J. B. (2003) Synchronizing with music: intercultural differences. *Annals of the New York Academy of Sciences: Neurosciences and Music*, 999: 429–437.

Dunbar, R. I. M. (2004) *The Human Story*. Faber & Faber, London.

Falk, D. (2004) Prelinguistic evolution in early hominins: whence motherese? *Behavioral and Brain Sciences*, 27: 491–541.

Feld, S. and Fox, A. A. (1994) Music and language. *Annual Review of Anthropology*, 23: 25–53.

Finnegan, R. (1989) *The Hidden Musicians: Music-making in an English Town*. Cambridge University Press, Cambridge.

Fitch, W. T. (2005) The evolution of music in comparative perspective. *Annals of the New York Academy of Sciences*, 1060: 29–49.

Fitch, W. T. (2006) The biology and evolution of music: a comparative perspective. *Cognition*, 100: 173–215.

Forte, A. (1973) *The Structure of Atonal Music*. Yale University Press, New Haven, CT.

Gourlay, K. A. (1984) The non-universality of music and the universality of non-music. *The World of Music*, 26: 25–36.

Hagen, E. H. and Bryant, G. A. (2003) Music and dance as a coalition signaling system. *Human Nature*, 14: 21–51.

Hannon, E. E. and Trehub, S. E. (2005) Metrical categories in infancy and adulthood. *Psychological Science*, 16: 48–55.

Hauser, M. (2000) The sound and the fury: primate vocalizations as reflations of emotion and thought. In N. Wallin, B. Merker and S. Brown (eds) *The Origins of Music*, pp. 77–102. MIT Press, Cambridge, MA.

Hauser, M. D., Chomsky, N. and Fitch, W. T. (2002) The faculty of language: what is it, who has it and how did it evolve? *Science*, 298: 1569–1579.

Henshilwood, C. S., d'Errico, F., Yates, R. *et al.* (2002) Emergence of modern human behavior: middle Stone Age engravings from South Africa. *Science*, 295: 1278–1280.

Holy, T. E. and Guo, Z. (2005) Ultrasonic songs of male mice. *PLoS Biology*, 3: 1–10. Available at: e386, http//www.plosbiology.org

Huron, D. (2001a) Tone and voice: a derivation of the rules of voice-leading from perceptual principles. *Music Perception*, 19: 1–64.

Huron, D. (2001b) Is music an evolutionary adaptation? *Annals of the New York Academy of Sciences*, 930: 43–61.

Jackendoff, R. (1987) *Consciousness and the Computational Mind*. MIT Press, Cambridge, MA.

Janata, P. and Grafton, S. T. (2003) Swinging in the brain: shared neural substrates for behaviors related to sequencing and music. *Nature Neuroscience*, 6: 682–687.

Joffe, T. H. (1997) Social pressures have selected for an extended juvenile period in primates. *Journal of Human Evolution*, 32: 593–605.

Jones, M. R. (1976) Time, our lost dimension: towards a new theory of perception, attention and memory. *Psychological Review*, 83: 323–355.

Jones, M. R. and Boltz, M. (1989) Dynamic attending and responses to time. *Psychological Review*, 96: 459–491.

Juslin, P. and Sloboda, J. A. (eds) (2001) *Music & Emotion: Theory and Research*. Oxford University Press, Oxford.

Karmiloff-Smith, A. (1992) *Beyond modularity*. MIT Press, London.

Kendon, A. (2004) *Gesture: Visible Action as Utterance*. Cambridge University Press, Cambridge.

Kerman, J. (1985) *Musicology*. Fontana, London.

Koelsch, S., Kasper, E., Sammler, D., Schultze, K., Gunter, T. and Frederici, A. (2004) Music, language and meaning: brain signatures of semantic processing. *Nature Neuroscience*, 7: 302–307.

Koelsch, S., Fritz, T., von Cramon, D. Y., Müller, K. and Friederici, A. D. (2006) Investigating emotion with music: an fMRI study. *Human Brain Mapping*, 27: 239–250.

Kogan, N. (1997) Reflections on aesthetics and evolution. *Critical Review*, 11: 193–210.

Krumhansl, C. L. (1990) *Cognitive Foundations of Musical Pitch*. Oxford University Press, Oxford.

Krumhansl, C. L. and Toiviainen, P. (2003) Tonal cognition. In I. Peretz and R. Zatorre (eds) *The Cognitive Neuroscience of Music*, pp. 95–108. Oxford University Press, Oxford.

Kunst, J. (1955) *Ethno-musicology*. Martinus Nijhoff, The Hague.

Langer, S. (1942) *Philosophy in a New Key*. Harvard University Press, Cambridge, MA.

Lerdahl, F. and Jackendoff, R. (1983) *A Generative Theory of Tonal Music*. MIT Press, Cambridge, MA.

Levman, B. (1992) The genesis of music and language. *Ethnomusicology*, 36: 147–170.

Marrett, A. (2005) *Songs, Dreamings, and Ghosts: The Wangga of North Australia*. Wesleyan University Press, Hanover, CT.

Martinez, I., Rosa, M., Arsuaga, J.-L. *et al.* (2004) Auditory capacities in Middle Pleistocene humans from the Sierra de Atapuerca in Spain. *Proceedings of the National Academy of Sciences*, 101: 9976–9981.

McCoy, K. A., Levenson, R. W. and Krumhansl, C. L. (1996) Physiological responses to the emotional qualities of music. *Psychophysiology*, 33: S60–S60.

McDermott, J. and Hauser, M. (2005) The origins of music: innateness, uniqueness, and evolution. *Music Perception*, 23: 29–59.

McNeill, W. H. (1995) *Keeping Together in Time*. Harvard University Press, London.

Merker, B. (2000) Synchronous chorusing and human origins. In N. Wallin, B. Merker and S. Brown (eds) *The Origins of Music*, 315–328. MIT Press, Cambridge, MA.

Merriam, A. P. (1964) *The Anthropology of Music*. Northwestern University Press, Chicago.

Meyer, L. B. (1956) *Emotion and Meaning in Music*. University of Chicago Press, London.

Miller, G. F. (1997) Protean primates: the evolution of adaptive unpredictability in competition and courtship. In A. Whiten and R. W. Byrne (eds) *Machiavellian Intelligence II: Extensions and Evaluations*, pp. 312–340. Cambridge University Press, Cambridge.

Miller, G. F. (2000) Evolution of human music through sexual selection. In N. Wallin, B. Merker and S. Brown (eds) *The Origins of Music*, pp. 329–360. MIT Press, Cambridge, MA.

Miller, G. F. (2001) *The Mating Mind: How Sexual Choice Shaped the Evolution of Human Nature*. Vintage/Ebury, London.

Mithen, S. (1996) *Prehistory of the Mind*. Thames & Hudson, London.

Mithen, S. (2005) *The Singing Neanderthals*. Weidenfeld & Nicholson, London.

Morley, I. (2002) Evolution of the physiological and neurological capacities for music. *Cambridge Archaeological Journal*, 12: 195–216.

Morley, I. (2003) The evolutionary origins and archaeology of music: an investigation into the prehistory of human musical capacities and behaviours. PhD dissertation, University of Cambridge, Cambridge.

Myers, C. S. (1905) A study of rhythm in primitive peoples. *British Journal of Psychology*, 1: 397.

Myers, C. S. (1913) The beginnings of music. In *Essays and Studies Presented to William Ridgway*. Cambridge University Press, Cambridge.

Nettl, B. (1956) *Music in Primitive Culture*. Harvard University Press, Cambridge, MA.

Nettl, B. (2005) *The Study of Ethnomusicology: Thirty-one Issues and Concepts*. University of Illinois Press, Urbana & Chicago.

Nettle, D. (1999) Language variation and the evolution of societies. In R. Dunbar, C. Knight and C. Power (eds) *The Evolution of Culture*, pp. 214–227. Edinburgh University Press, Edinburgh.

Owings, D. H. and Morton, E. S. (1998) *Animal Vocal Communication: A New Approach*. Cambridge University Press, Cambridge.

Peperkamp, S. (2003) Phonological acquisition: recent attainments and new challenges. *Language and Speech*, 46: 87–113.

Perlman, M. (2004) *Unplayed Melodies: Javanese Gamelan and the Genesis of Music Theory*. University of California Press, London.

Pinker, S. (1997) *How the Mind Works*. Allen Lane, London.

Pinker, S. and Jackendoff, R. (2005) The faculty of language: what's special about it? *Cognition*, 95: 201–236.

Plotkin, H. (1997) *Evolution in Mind*. Allen Lane, London.

Pöppel, E. and Wittmann, M. (1999) Time in the mind. In R. A. Wilson and F. C. Keil (eds) *The MIT Encyclopedia of Cognitive Sciences*, pp. 841–843. MIT Press, Cambridge, MA.

Rehding, A. (2000) The quest for the origins of music in Germany circa 1900. *Journal of the American Musicological Society*, 53: 345–385.

Robinson, J. (2005) *Deeper than Reason: Emotion and its Roles in Literature, Music and the Arts*. Oxford University Press, Oxford.

Roederer, J. G. (1984) The search for a survival value of music. *Music Perception*, 1: 350–356.

Scarre, C. and Lawson, G. (eds) (2006) *Acoustics, Space and Intentionality: Identifying Intentionality in the Ancient Use of Acoustic Spaces and Structures*. McDonald Institute for Archaeological Research, Cambridge.

Schellenberg, E. G. (2003) Does exposure to music have beneficial side effects? In I. Peretz and R. Zatorre (ed.) *The Cognitive Neuroscience of Music*, pp. 430–448. Oxford University Press, Oxford.

Schellenberg, E. G. (2004) Music lessons enhance IQ. *Psychological Science*, 15: 511–514.

Schillinger, J. (1941) *The Schillinger System of Musical Composition*. C. Fischer, New York.

Schön, D., Magne, C. and Besson, M. (2004) The music of speech: Music training facilitates pitch processing in both music and language. *Psychophysiology*, 41: 341–349.

Seyfarth, R. M. and Cheney, D. L. (2003) Signalers and receivers in animal communication. *Annual Review of Psychology*, 54: 145–73.

Shennan, S. (2002) *Genes, Memes and Human History*. Thames & Hudson, London.

Shore, B. (1996) *Culture in Mind: Cognition, Culture, and the Problem of Meaning.* Oxford University Press, Oxford.

Sober, E. and Wilson, D. (1998) *Unto Others: The Evolution and Psychology of Unselfish Behavior.* Harvard University Press, London.

Sloboda, J. A., O Neill, S. A. and Ivaldi, A. (2001) Functions of music in everyday life: an exploratory study using the Experience Sampling Method. *Musicae Scientiae,* 5: 9–32.

Spencer, H. (1858) *Essays, Scientific, Political and Speculative,* Vol. 1 Williams and Norgate, London. http//www.gutenberg.net

Sperber, D. (1996) *Explaining Culture.* Blackwell, Oxford.

Sperber, D. and Wilson, D. (1986) *Relevance: Communication and Cognition.* Blackwell, Oxford.

Stevens, C. (2004) Cross-cultural studies of musical pitch and time. *Acoustics, Science and Technology,* 25: 433–438.

Stobart, H. F. (1996) The Llama's flute: musical misunderstandings in the Andes. *Early Music,* 24: 470–482.

Stobart, H. F. and Cross, I. (2000) The Andean Anacrusis? rhythmic structure and perception in Easter songs of Northern Potosí, Bolivia. *British Journal of Ethnomusicology,* 9: 63–94.

Temperley, D. (2001) *The Cognition of Basic Musical Structures.* MIT Press, Cambridge, Mass.

Thaut, M. H. (2005) Rhythm, human temporality, and brain function. In D. Miell, R. MacDonald and D. Hargreaves (eds) *Musical Communication,* pp. 171–191. Oxford University Press, Oxford.

Thomas, D. A. (1995) *Music and the Origins of Language: Theories from the French Enlightenment.* Cambridge University Press, Cambridge.

Titon, J. T. and Slobin, M. (1996) The music-culture as a world of music. In J. T. Titon (ed.) *Worlds of Music: An Introduction to the Music of the World's peoples,* pp. 1–16. Schirmer Books, New York.

Tolbert, E. (1992) Theories of meaning and music cognition: an ethnomusicological approach. *The World of Music,* 34: 7–21.

Tolbert, E. (2001) Music and meaning: an evolutionary story. *Psychology of Music,* 29: 84–94.

Tomasello, T., Carpenter, M., Call, J., Behne, T. and Moll, H. (2005) Understanding and sharing intentions: the origins of cultural cognition. *Behavioral and Brain Sciences,* 28: 675–691.

Trehub, S. E. (2003) Musical predispositions in infancy: an update. I. Peretz and R. Zatorre (eds) *The Cognitive Neuroscience of Music,* pp. 3–20. Oxford University Press, Oxford.

Trehub, S. E., Unyk, A. M. and Trainor, L. J. (1993) Adults identify infant-directed music across cultures. *Infant Behavior and Development,* 16: 193–211.

Vaneechoutte, M. and Skoyles, J. R. (1998) The memetic origin of language: modern humans as musical primates. In *Journal of Memetics—Evolutionary Models of Information Transmission 2.* [available at: http://efpm.org/jonn.ernit/1998/vol2/vaneechoutte_m& skoyles_jr.html]

Wallin, N., Merker, B. and Brown, S. (eds) (2000) *The Origins of Music.* MIT Press, Cambridge, MA.

Wynne-Edwards, V. C. (1962) *Animal Dispersion in Relation to Social Behaviour.* Oliver & Boyd, Edinburgh.

Zatorre, R. and Peretz, I. (eds) (2003) *The Cognitive Neuroscience of Music.* Oxford University Press, Oxford.

CHAPTER 46

The evolution of language

Simon Kirby

46.1. Introduction: language and the evolution of life

Maynard Smith and Szathmáry (1997) set out eight 'major transitions' in the evolution of life. These are events in the history of our planet that signal radical changes in the way evolution works. They start with a change in the way molecules replicate in the very earliest stages of the origins of life, through the emergence of DNA, and go on to include larger-scale later phenomena like the evolution of colonies where once there were only solitary individuals (see Figure 46.1). What makes the work of these two eminent evolutionary biologists so interesting for us is their inclusion of the most recent evolutionary transition: the emergence of language.

Why is the emergence of language such a significant event? One of Maynard Smith and Szathmáry's observations is that, despite their diversity, these transitions have some features in common. In particular, many of the transitions give rise to a new mechanism for the transmission of information. Language, they argue, provides just such a novel mechanism—essentially enabling a system of cultural transmission with unlimited heredity.

It is clearly true that language enables the transmission and storage of very complex cultural information. Arguably, it is this aspect of

our biological heritage that makes our species' impact so great, and so unusual. But how does human language achieve this? To answer this question, it is worth briefly surveying the structural features of language, and the characteristics of language as a biological endowment.

46.1.1. The structure of language

One way of thinking about language (although by no means the only way, e.g. Origgi and Sperber, 2000) is as a coding system that maps between two spaces: the space of concepts and intentions on the one hand, and of articulation and perception on the other (see Figure 46.2). Traditionally, the study of the structure of language has been divided into a number of sub-disciplines, each of which tackles a different aspect of this mapping system:

(i) *Phonetics*: the production and perception of sounds/manual gestures.

(ii) *Phonology*: the systematic behaviour of the sounds of language.

(iii) *Morphosyntax*: the system for combining the basic meaningful units of language into words and sentences. (Note that sometimes this is divided into morphology and syntax, dealing with the below-word and above-word level respectively. Equally, linguists

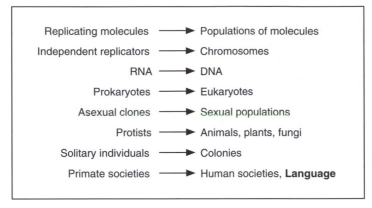

Fig. 46.1 Maynard Smith and Szathmáry's (1997) eight major transitions in the evolution of life.

sometimes use 'syntax' to refer to morphosyntax as I will do in this chapter.)

(iv) *Semantics*: the meaning of words and sentences in isolation.

(v) *Pragmatics*: the system for relating word/-sentence meaning to communicative intention in the context of communication.

The first two and last two sub-disciplines on this list deal in the main with the two ends of the mapping in Figure 46.2, whereas morphosyntax is most clearly the study of the aspects of language that govern how these two are connected. In one influential view of how language works, syntax is the study of the computational system that accesses our mental lexicon and bridges the gap between the conceptual–intentional and articulatory–perceptual 'interfaces' (Chomsky, 1995).

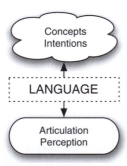

Fig. 46.2 Language as a system mapping between concepts/intentions and perception/articulation.

What is extraordinary about this system, and what makes it particularly important for Maynard Smith and Szathmáry, is that it is constructed in such a way as to allow unbounded yet faithful transmission of information (sometimes termed 'digital infinity'). This combination of an infinite range of messages with a high-fidelity mechanism for transmitting those messages is almost unique in nature. Arguably the only other example is the genetic code itself.

It is easy to see why human language is in principle unbounded. If we were to try to find the longest sentence of English, we would fail. This is because the syntactic system delivers us mechanisms that will allow us to elaborate on sentences in an unlimited fashion (e.g. by adding subordinate clauses, adverbial phrases, prepositional phrases etc.). This kind of infinity is 'digital' because it does not rely on continuous changes in the signal to convey changes in meaning but rather the addition of discrete elements. In contrast, we could imagine a different signalling system where the pitch of a signal conveyed differences in meaning (say, the severity of a particular threat). This system would be infinite, since there are infinitely many different pitches, but it would not be digital.

Another unusual aspect of human language is that the lexicon is flexible. New words can be added, and the meanings of words can change. Although this feature of language is not discussed as much as digital infinity, it is actually the combination of these two that really set human language apart as a uniquely powerful tool for the unbounded transmission of cultural information. In summary, language structure allows high-fidelity, unbounded and flexible communication.

46.1.2. Language as a biological endowment

Language structure is unusual and unusually powerful, so how do we come to have this system? Obviously, language is at least in part a learned behaviour. Languages differ from each other, and these differences have no obvious correlations with genetic differences in their speakers. Language variation is primarily a hallmark of those aspects of language that are learned. This is most obvious in the lexicon, which varies in a largely arbitrary way from language to language (although historically related languages will have more or less similar lexica, and this can be used to trace language history). Indeed, the fact that the words of a language are learned is what enables the flexibility of expression mentioned in the previous paragraph.

The lexicon is not the sole locus of variation in language, however. The phonological structure of languages varies, as does their syntax. That said, this variation seems to be constrained in various ways. In other words, there exist certain language universals that become obvious when a large number of languages are examined, or when historically distant languages are compared in detail. It is a matter of controversy what these constraints on variation indicate—for example, they could reflect those aspects of language that are not learned (i.e. that are innate), or they could result from universal properties of the way language is used (Newmeyer, 1998; Kirby, 1999).

In any case, however much of language is learned it is clear that language is both enabled and constrained by our biology, and much research in linguistics is aimed at characterizing what this biological endowment is. Whatever the final definitive account of this is (and we are some way off anything approaching consensus), we can expect it to include neurological systems for the acquisition of language, the representation of linguistic knowledge, and the rapid on-line processing of language, as well as physical apparatus for the production of speech.

46.1.3. Evolutionary questions

The emergence of language is an important evolutionary event, and arguably our species' defining characteristic, but how exactly did it evolve? Questions surrounding the origins and evolution of language have, since the early 1990s, seen a huge explosion of interest in the scientific community, across a very wide range of disciplines. In the remainder of this chapter, I will try to give a flavour of the work that is going on by surveying three different areas of interest. It is important to realize that this is very far indeed from being an exhaustive summary of a subject that draws on evidence from archaeology to computer science, from genetics to philosophy. The interested reader is encouraged to look at a survey of the field such as that by Christiansen and Kirby (2004) or the series of books arising from the biennial conference series on Language Evolution (Hurford et al., 1998; Knight et al., 2000; Wray, 2002; Tallerman, 2005).

Before diving into the subject, however, it is worth reflecting on the sorts of questions that researchers are, often implicitly, trying to answer. It may be that some confusion in debates in the field actually arises from the fact that different questions are being asked. These can be roughly characterized as follows.

(i) *Structure*: Why is language the way it is and not some other way? How can an evolutionary approach explain the particular language universals we observe?

(ii) *Uniqueness*: Why are we unique in possessing language? What is so special about humans?

(iii) *Function*: How could language evolve? What were the selective pressures involved?

(iv) *History*: What is the evolutionary story for language? When did it evolve? Were there intermediate stages?

It is tempting to compare these questions with Tinbergen's (1963) four famous evolutionary 'why' questions. However, in contrast, I mean these to reflect the kinds of questions that get posed in the literature on language evolution, some of these being clearly specific to language evolution (e.g. the *uniqueness* question).

46.2. **Language and human uniqueness: the comparative approach**

The first area to be surveyed is in some sense a methodological one, although it relates to the *structure* and *uniqueness* questions above. It is surprisingly controversial and it goes to the heart of what we mean when we talk about human language and human uniqueness.

It is probably fair to say that linguists have traditionally stressed the distinctiveness of human language as compared to other communication systems in the natural world. Communication is very much the norm among almost all species on the planet, whether it be between animals, insects, plants or bacteria, but language is normally considered to be something very different. Indeed, humans also have communication systems that are not language, that seem to share many similarities with communication in other species. So, for example, we do not consider the various vocalizations like screaming, laughter or crying to be linguistic, but they are arguably communicative.

It is natural, and reasonable, for linguistics as a field to see language as a unique phenomenon and set out the properties of human language that make it special (see, for example, Hockett, 1960, for an early attempt to set out language's *design features*). The problem with this stance

from an evolutionary point of view is that it downplays what we can learn about language by looking at other species. If language is a one-off phenomenon—an *autapomorphy*—then how can we apply the standard methodologies from evolutionary biology?

46.2.1. **Dividing the language faculty**

A fairly recent development in the field suggests that we are moving beyond this point of view. In a paper in *Science* in 2002, two biologists joined forces with one of the architects of modern linguistic theory to focus on the relevance of data from other species to our understanding of human language and its evolution (Hauser *et al.*, 2002). They argue that many of the problems in discussions of language in its evolutionary context may arise from treating the language faculty as a unitary whole. As an alternative, they propose two different senses of the term biological language faculty: the faculty of language in the broad sense (FLB), and the faculty of language in the narrow sense (FLN). The former includes all aspects of the language faculty, including conceptual–intentional apparatus, perceptual–articulatory apparatus and so on. The latter includes only the core computational systems that govern the system of mapping in Figure 46.2. More specifically, Hauser *et al.* (2002) put forward the strong hypothesis that FLN is essentially limited to a mechanism implementing *recursion*, which gives rise to the digital infinity mentioned earlier (see Figure 46.3).

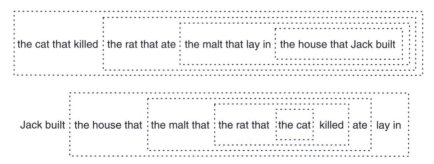

Fig. 46.3 Recursion in English. Noun-phrases can be recursively embedded within one another using the relative clause construction in English (boxes mark the boundaries of each noun-phrase). Recursion allows us to create sentences of potentially unlimited complexity, although in some cases the result can be difficult for us to process, such as when centre-embedding is over-used (as in the lower of the two examples).

Having made this distinction between a broad and narrow sense of the term, Hauser *et al.* (2002) set out three logically possible hypotheses about the evolution of the faculty of language:

1. FLB is homologous to animal communication. All aspects of FLB (including FLN) can be found relatively unchanged in animals.

2. FLB is a derived, uniquely human adaptation to language.

3. Only FLN is uniquely human.

Discovering which of these hypotheses is correct requires a collaboration between linguists and comparative biologists to determine how the language faculty (in the broad sense) can be divided up, and which aspects of the language faculty are shared with other species.

Hauser *et al.* (2002) argue that the comparative data point only to FLN being uniquely human. In other words, all aspects of the language faculty excepting the recursive system of mapping can be found in other species. For example, consider the system we have for acquiring complex signals—a crucial aspect of FLB. It turns out that there are analogues of this in a number of other species who have a capacity for vocal learning: song birds, parrots, hummingbirds, bats, cetaceans (Jarvis, 2004), a list to which have recently been added seals (Van Parijs *et al.*, 2003), elephants (Poole *et al.*, 2005) and possibly even mice (Holy, 2005).

What about recursion—how can we test if other species have this computational ability? One approach is to use *artificial grammar learning* to probe the ability of different species to learn and process languages with different computational properties. Fitch and Hauser (2004) compare cotton-top tamarins and humans on a task with languages that differ in their requirement for recursion. Their results suggest that the difference between these two species does indeed hinge on a recursive capacity.

This approach, which puts forward a minimal account of human uniqueness, is not without its critics. For example, Pinker and Jackendoff (2005) argue that there is much more that is special to language and to humans than merely the capacity for recursion. Their arguments are of two main types. First, they suggest that there are non-syntactic aspects of language that are uniquely human. For example, for them the

huge size and rapid acquisition of the lexicon strongly suggests that this is a uniquely human adaptation. There is little evidence that any other species can acquire words in the same way children do, sometimes with only a single exposure. Having said that, there is intriguing experimental evidence that domestic dogs actually may be able to learn a few hundreds of words by employing a mutual exclusivity bias that is argued to have very close parallels in child language acquisition (Kaminski *et al.*, 2004).

A second criticism by Pinker and Jackendoff (2005) is that treating FLN as containing simply a mechanism for recursive computation oversimplifies the syntactic aspects of human language. Their view treats the syntactic system as a complex adaptation to the problem of "communicating propositional structures through a serial interface" (Pinker and Bloom, 1990)— an adaptation consisting of many interacting sub-systems. The arguments for and against a *minimalist* view of syntax are well beyond the scope of this chapter (see Parker, 2006, for an extended discussion), but what is interesting is how these specifically linguistic arguments are increasingly being informed by evolutionary thinking and comparative data.

The debate over the nature and uniqueness of FLN continues, and interested readers can also look at Fitch *et al.*'s (2005) reply to Pinker and Jackendoff (2005), and even Jackendoff and Pinker's (2005) further response to this reply.

46.2.2. The descended larynx

One area where the comparative approach has had a substantial impact is in our understanding of the evolution of the vocal tract. Lieberman *et al.* (1969) note an unusual feature of the human vocal tract that appears to set it apart from the primate norm. Our larynx is positioned rather low in the throat (if you are a man, you will be able to find its position by feeling on your neck for your Adam's apple). This is puzzling because it means that we must coordinate breathing and swallowing carefully to avoid choking. If our larynx were higher, as it is in other mammals and in human infants, then it could be projected into the nasal cavity, allowing us to breathe and swallow at the same time.

Lieberman (1969) suggests that this apparently counter-functional trait in humans is actually the result of an adaptation to communication. The descent of the larynx over our evolutionary history radically changed the shape of the vocal tract from one which essentially had the acoustic properties of a straight tube to one in which that tube has a bend in the middle (where the oral cavity meets the pharynx). What this does is to increase the diversity of vowel sounds that we can produce, which in turn increases the informational carrying capacity of the vocal channel.

More recently, Fitch and Reby (2001) have shown that there are other possible adaptive advantages to a descended larynx by looking carefully at the comparative data. It turns out that other mammals *do* lower their larynxes during vocalization, and indeed some species (such as red deer) have a permanently lowered larynx in the male of the species. These animals certainly do not have complex vocal communication that requires the enhanced carrying capacity of a vocal tract with a bend in it, so what is going on?

What lowering the larynx does in addition to creating a bend in the vocal tract is to increase the total length of the tract. This changes the acoustic properties of vocalizations in such a way as to *increase the perceived size of the animal making the sound*. Fitch (2000) suggests that it is this perceived-size enhancement that is the driving force behind the descent of the larynx in species without complex vocalizations. Animals, particularly males, that appear to be large may be more successful in competition for mates, and in avoiding predation. If this is the case, then might it not also be a factor in the evolution of the human vocal tract? Certainly, even in humans there is some sexual dimorphism, with the male larynx undergoing a second descent around puberty.

What this example demonstrates is the role that evidence from other species can play in understanding the evolution of language, even if those species do not necessarily possess anything like a capacity for complex communication.

46.3. **Protolanguage: living fossils and intermediate stages**

Setting aside for a moment the language *faculty* and looking at the structure of language itself, it is clear that there is a huge gulf between the communication systems of our nearest primate relatives and human language. How was that gulf bridged by evolution? Did we move in one step from a largely innate, limited and fixed repertoire of unstructured signals to the open-ended syntactic system that we have now? Or can we envisage a gradual process involving intermediate stages? The question 'what good is half an eye?' is a familiar sceptical response to adaptationism, suggesting that something as complex as an eye could not have evolved gradually. A similar question might be 'what good is half a language?' A gradual story for the evolution of the eye is possible because it turns out that there are 'intermediate' eyes that are indeed useful and that there is a plausible evolutionary trajectory from these intermediate forms to the modern eye. The study of *protolanguage* aims to demonstrate that the same is true for language.

Of course, it may be true that language *did* emerge in one step, that a *saltational* view is a possible alternative to *gradualism*. This is only really plausible if language isn't as complex as it appears. (The appearance of eyes fully formed in evolution in one step is implausible precisely because the eye is a complex organ.) One of the consequences of Chomsky's minimalist approach to language is that there may be no need to posit intermediate stages (Berwick, 1998). However, as noted in the previous section, this whole issue is a matter of considerable ongoing debate.

46.3.1. **Bickerton's protolanguage**

One of the difficulties for evolutionary linguists is that language does not fossilize. Although we are able to infer some things from the skeletal remains of our hominid ancestors it is hard to find *direct* evidence of the form of evolutionarily primitive language. Instead, Bickerton (1990, 1995) proposes that we look for *living fossils*. These are types of communication used by modern humans that are close to, but do not share all the features of, fully modern language. Finding such living fossils demonstrates that there are possible intermediate stages, and provided that we can find a plausible evolutionary trajectory that will take us from this protolanguage to full human language gives us a potential answer to the *history* question posed in Section 46.1.

Bickerton (1995, Appendix A) gives examples of three kinds of linguistic behaviour that, he says, constitute living fossils of protolanguage:

(i) *Pidgin communication.* This is the type of communication system, typically formed in slave plantations, where adults with diverse linguistic backgrounds are brought together and must negotiate a *lingua franca*. These examples are from Pidgin Hawaiian in the late-eighteenth and early nineteenth centuries:

Nuinui pool. Make kanaka. (Much-much gun. Kill men.)

Maitai, nana Amerita. (Good, see America.)

Apopo tabu. Aole hanahana. (Tomorrow forbidden. Not work.)

Maitai, nuinui maitai. (Good, much-much good.)

(ii) *Child language.* These examples are from one 23-month-old boy:

Fix it.

Tear up.

More doggie.

Door shut.

(iii) *Language of trained apes.* These examples are from Koko, a language-trained Gorilla:

That cat.

More pour.

Me good.

Koko purse.

What do these have in common? They all have some minimal structure in that sentences are made of words which have distinct meanings and the meaning of the whole sentence is in some way composed of those word-meanings. However, this is very far from the systematic syntactic structure of 'full human language'. Note the following features of language that are missing: recursive embedding leading to indefinitely long sentences; propositional structure based on a verb and arguments which are optional only if their meaning is recoverable; grammatical elements (such as agreement markers, conjunctions, case-endings etc.) that do not directly correspond to aspects of the meaning of a sentence, but rather have purely structural roles.

Could this type of protolanguage constitute an evolutionarily early stage in the evolution of full human language? If so, then we are at least one step towards bridging the gulf between no-language and the syntactically structured linguistic system that is our species' defining characteristic. Note that protolanguage, like an intermediate eye, is *functional*. It can be used to communicate. An adaptationist programme for human language, such as Pinker and Bloom's (1990) which stresses communication as the adaptive function of language, is strengthened if such functional intermediates can be found.

46.3.2. Holistic protolanguage

Bickerton's is not the only proposal, however. Jackendoff (1999), for example, has suggested a greatly elaborated sequence of potential intermediate stages each of which implies a different protolanguage (although one of these is Bickerton's). A rather different perspective is set out by Wray (1998) as an alternative to the multi-word syntax-free intermediate stage. Like Bickerton, Wray seeks a living fossil—a qualitatively different kind of language that lacks the complexity normally associated with human syntax. She focuses on certain sequences in normal discourse whose structure appears to be essentially unanalysed in language production and perception: *holistic* language.

Whereas we normally think of the meanings of utterances being composed by combination of meaningful words, this is not always the case. Holistic *formulae* can be found in everyday language use, most obviously in idiomatic expressions such as *bought the farm* (whose meaning, *died*, appears to be arbitrarily related to its form). Wray (1998) suggests that other holistically processed expressions include adjuncts (*by and large*), collocations (*pure coincidence*, but never *true coincidence*), sentence frames (*NP be-TENSE sorry to keep-TENSE you waiting*), and standard situational utterances (*Was there anything else?*).

The existence of these formulae, which form a large proportion of our day-to-day language use, demonstrates that we are predisposed to store and manipulate unanalysed chunks of language despite also possessing syntactic mechanisms that could deliver purely compositional expressions by rule whenever needed. For Wray, it is reasonable to suppose that there existed a stage where we spoke a purely holistic protolanguage. Rather than building utterances through the combination of small numbers of referential words as Bickerton's protolanguage does, this holistic communication system would simply consist of a store of expressions each with a conventionalized meaning and stood alone as a complete utterance.

Note that formulae in modern language are rather different since they appear to contain individual words. Of course, this is only possible once a fully modern human language with separate words already exists. Despite this difference, the argument is that the function and processing of these expressions in modern language and protolanguage is essentially the same.

46.3.3. **The process of transition**

One crucial difference that separates these two views of what protolanguage was like is the different process of transition proposed that takes us from protolanguage to full human language.

For Bickerton, the transition between these two forms of language was a biological one. Some genetic change or changes led to a novel language faculty that enabled individual language users to go beyond their cultural heritage (a syntax-free protolanguage) and innovate a modern language. Exactly how this change in the linguistic system would progress cannot be known for sure, but we might see parallels in the process of *creolization* whereby children innovate a full human language after exposure to a pidgin.

Wray on the other hand sketches in some detail exactly how a holistic proto-language might be transformed into full human language through a process of *fractionation* of the language by generations of language users. Correspondences between signals and meanings that arise by chance in the repertoire of holistic expressions are analysed by language learners who eventually generalize these analyses systematically to novel utterances. Kirby (2000) has shown that this analytic route is actually the inevitable outcome of applying the same mechanisms needed to acquire compositional expressions to randomly created holistic ones. The point here is that Wray focuses on a cultural process of transition rather than a biological one.

This difference in emphasis does not mean that accepting a holistic protolanguage commits us to a view that our protolanguage-speaking ancestors were genetically identical to us. Similarly a Bickertonian view of protolanguage is compatible with the notion that the first generations of anatomically modern humans had languages that were not identical in structure to our own. As I will discuss in the next section, the processes of cultural and biological evolution are both likely to be involved in the emergence of human language.

This brief overview has only scratched the surface of the debate on what constitutes a viable theory of protolanguage (or indeed whether we need assume protolanguage at all). Readers interested in other authors' views on the debate between Wray and Bickerton are referred to: Hurford (2000) who proposes a distinction between analytic and synthetic routes to complex language; Arbib (2005) and Kirby (2001), for example, who discuss the plausibility of the analytic process; Tallerman (in press) who sets out a series of problems for holistic protolanguage; and Smith (2006) who challenges the validity of Tallerman's arguments.

46.4. **Evolutionary mechanisms: the complex adaptive systems view**

This chapter started with the view that the emergence of language constituted a major evolutionary transition because it introduced a new system for transmitting information, a feature shared by many other major transitions. When Maynard Smith and Szathmáry talk about the information that language is transmitting, they are referring to the unbounded semantic information that we can convey with linguistic expressions.

There is, however, another sense in which language is a novel system of information transmission. Because language is not completely innately coded, much of its structure must be learned. Most researchers (see, e.g., Pinker, 1995, for review) agree that language learning can proceed normally with little, if any, reliable feedback in the way of reinforcement or negative evidence (i.e. the explicit labelling of children's incorrect output as errors by parents). In other words, language can be reliably acquired purely through the observation of instances of its use. In a very real sense, language not only transmits semantic information, but also *information about its own construction*.

This process of information transmission has been termed *iterated learning* to reflect the fact that linguistic behaviour is learned through observation of that behaviour in others who themselves learned that behaviour using the same mechanism (e.g. Kirby *et al.*, 2004). Language is therefore repeatedly transformed from external linguistic behaviour to internal linguistic representation to external linguistic behaviour and so on. What implications does this have for an evolutionary approach to language? A number of authors have argued that it means language is itself an evolutionary system, but one that operates on a cultural, rather than biological, timescale (e.g. Christiansen, 1994; Deacon, 1997; Kirby, 1999; Croft, 2000). As noted in the previous section, this does not rule out biological evolution as an explanatory mechanism, rather it is only part of the picture.

Biological evolution and cultural evolution (of which the transmission of information about the construction of language is a particular type) are both *dynamical systems* in that the transmission of information over time results in change of that information. In fact, they are not the only dynamical systems involved in language—individual learning is another one, operating at an even shorter timescale to that of culture and biological evolution.

What is particularly interesting about language as a natural system is that these three dynamical systems interact in non-trivial ways (see Figure 46.4). The mechanisms for learning language are part of our biological inheritance, and are thus subject to biological evolution. It is these learning mechanisms that underpin the cultural process of linguistic transmission through iterated learning. Finally, the languages that emerge from the dynamics of the cultural evolution will in part determine the biological fitness of the individuals possessing them and ultimately impact on the evolutionary trajectory of the learning mechanisms for language. There is, therefore, a complex circle of interactions between these dynamical systems acting on three different timescales.

Understanding the implications of this view of language is a significant theoretical challenge. A growing area of research into the evolution of language employs the methodology of *complex adaptive systems* research to tackle this challenge (see, e.g., Kirby, 2002, for a review). This approach uses computational or mathematical models of populations of individuals (usually referred to as *agents*) each embodying the basic learning mechanisms under study. Models of agents vary greatly from simple mathematical idealizations (Komarova and Nowak, 2003) through abstract computational simulations (Brighton *et al.*, 2005) to physical instantiations in real robots (Steels, 2003). However they are modelled, these agents interact, producing linguistic behaviour, and in so doing transmit their linguistic knowledge through iterated learning. In some models, there may be variation in the

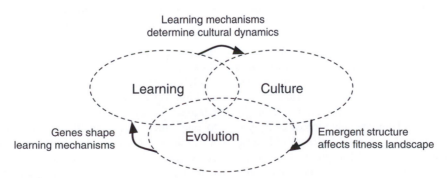

Fig. 46.4 Language emerges from the non-trivial interactions of three dynamical systems operating on three different timescales: individual learning, cultural transmission and biological evolution

agents' learning mechanisms and this variation is inherited by agents' 'offspring'. Combined with some mechanism to measure the fitness of agents, this implements biological evolution in addition to cultural transmission and individual learning.

This multiple dynamical systems approach to language evolution is still in its infancy, but it has already yielded the following interesting insights, particularly into the *structure* and *function* questions posed in the introduction.

46.4.1. Language and adaptation

The adaptationist approach to explaining complex structure in human language appeals to an apparent fit of this structure to the function of communication (see, e.g., Pinker and Bloom, 1990). This fit is assumed to be explained by adaptation of the innate language faculty by natural selection. This basic approach is familiar to many aspects of evolutionary psychology. The complex adaptive systems perspective, however, demonstrates that there are other potential explanations for adaptive complexity. Kirby (1999) shows how the process of cultural transmission itself can lead to adaptation of language to the needs of language users. The challenge therefore is to determine for each feature of language that we wish to explain whether natural selection or iterated learning is the right explanatory mechanism.

46.4.2. Bottlenecks and linguistic generalization

It is a widely recognized fact that the data available to the language-learning child is at best a noisy and limited reflection of the linguistic system that must be acquired (which is, after all, infinitely expressive). This 'poverty of the stimulus' is often taken to be an argument for strong innate constraints on the language acquisition process (Chomsky, 1965). Work on iterated learning (e.g. Zuidema, 2003) points to a different consequence, however. We can think of the knowledge of language being forced every generation through a narrow bottleneck of linguistic experience. In models of iterated learning it has been found that it is this bottleneck that acts as the primary pressure to which the culturally evolving language must adapt. At the risk of

oversimplifying, languages (or more correctly systems within languages) can only survive through iterated learning if they can be acquired from an impoverished sample of their output. It turns out that in computational models the sorts of languages (or structures within languages) that emerge out of iterated learning when a bottleneck is in place are exactly those that we find in real language. More specifically, the presence of a transmission bottleneck eventually leads to the evolution of regularity in language, since a regular pattern can be learned even if not all the instances of that pattern are observed. As Hurford (2000) puts it, social transmission favours linguistic generalization.

46.4.3. The 'Baldwin effect'

It is a common misconception that adaptation occurring within an individual organism's lifetime cannot affect genetic evolution unless we take a Lamarckian view of inheritance (i.e. that an individual's acquired characteristics are transmitted to its offspring). In a linguistic context, this quite reasonably implies that the fact that I have acquired English (as opposed to some other language) cannot influence the evolution of the language faculty.

Perhaps surprisingly, very early in the history of evolutionary thinking (Baldwin, 1896) it was pointed out that although acquired characters are not inherited this does not mean that they cannot influence evolution. In fact, complex adaptive systems research has shown that if generations of agents are faced with some environmental problem that involves learning, if this problem is relatively constant, and if learning involves some cost, then natural selection can lead to learned knowledge becoming innate knowledge over time. Several researchers (e.g. Briscoe, 2000; Turkel, 2002) have suggested that the Baldwin effect has a natural application in the case of language evolution. Computational models provide support for the idea that this evolutionary mechanism could take us from a relatively domain-general learning mechanism to one which is specialized for language and which allows for just the kind of semi-constrained cross-linguistic variation that we find in real language. This is an area of ongoing research, and the Baldwin effect is not without its problems (see, e.g., Yamauchi, 2004). In fact, this may be only one of a number of evolutionary principles that come into play when multiple adaptive systems are brought together (see, e.g., Deacon, 2003; Ritchie and Kirby, 2007). Previous work in the complex adaptive systems literature looked mainly at the interaction between learning and genetic evolution, but with language we must also take cultural evolution into account (Kirby and Hurford, 1997; Smith, 2002). It is likely to be some time before we have the solid theoretical grounding that will allow us to make straightforward predictions about the behaviour of the system shown in Figure 46.4.

46.5. Conclusion

In the Introduction, we saw that there are many questions about the evolution of human language, each of which suggests a different approach to research drawing upon very different sorts of evidence.

In this brief survey of three areas of current controversy, the *function* question has not been treated in detail. For example, it is very much a matter for debate whether communication is the function of language that drove its evolution; and, if so, how the consequent problems of the evolution of altruistic behaviour are solved; and how such a cheap signalling system could nevertheless be trusted (Knight, 1998). Other possible functions that have been discussed are internal 'speech' (mentioned by Chomsky, 2002), social grooming (Dunbar, 1993), sexual display (Miller, 2000), and alliance forming (Dessalles, 2000) among others.

Nor have we considered fully the types of evidence available to constrain our theories of language evolution. Of course, the primary source of evidence should be language itself, and it is crucial that those researching language evolution pay attention to developments in linguistics, a discipline which aims to provide the best account of the phenomenon we are trying to understand. In addition, ongoing work in neuroscience, archaeology and genetics should further narrow down the set of plausible accounts of the evolution of language.

Finally, one of the biggest challenges ahead will be to establish whether the different answers to the four evolutionary questions in Section 46.1 are actually compatible with each other.

For example, is a particular view of protolanguage that proposes multiple stages with intermediate forms compatible with a view of language with a minimal FLN? Do the adaptive mechanisms surveyed in Section 46.3 constrain the kinds of protolanguage that are possible?

It is a perfectly acceptable research strategy to focus solely on one of the four questions, or a combination of them. However, ultimately we should be careful that our answers to any one of them do not preclude finding an answer to the others. This highlights an important and difficult challenge facing the study of language evolution: the need for cooperation between different disciplines and between researchers working on different aspects of the problem. Without this cooperation a satisfactory account of the evolution of human language, and therefore of human language itself, is likely to be elusive.

References

Arbib, M. (2005) From monkey-like action recognition to human language: an evolutionary framework for neurolinguistics. *Behavioral and Brain Sciences*, 28: 105–167.

Baldwin, J. (1896) A new factor in evolution. *American Naturalist*, 30: 441–451.

Berwick, R. (1998) Language evolution and the minimalist program: the origins of syntax. In J. Hurford, M. Studdert-Kennedy and C. Knight (eds) *Approaches to the Evolution of Language: Social and Cognitive Bases.* Cambridge University Press, Cambridge.

Bickerton, D. (1990) *Language and Species.* University of Chicago Press, Chicago.

Bickerton, D. (1995) *Language and Human Behavior.* University College London Press, London.

Brighton, H., Smith, K. and Kirby, S. (2005) Language as evolutionary system. *Physics of Life Reviews*, 2: 177–226.

Briscoe, E. J. (2000) Grammatical acquisition: Inductive bias and coevolution of language and the language acquisition device. *Language*, 76: 245–296.

Chomsky, N. (1965) *Aspects of the Theory of Syntax.* MIT Press, Cambridge, MA.

Chomsky, N. (1995) Bare phrase structure. In G. Webelhuth (ed.) *Government and Binding and the Minimalist Program.* Blackwell, Oxford.

Chomsky, N. (2002) *On Nature and Language.* Cambridge University Press, Cambridge.

Christiansen, M. H. (1994) Infinite languages, finite minds: connectionism, learning and linguistic structure. PhD thesis, University of Edinburgh.

Christiansen, M. H. and Kirby, S. (eds) (2004). *Language Evolution.* Oxford University Press, Oxford.

Croft, W. (2000) *Explaining Language Change: An Evolutionary Approach.* Longman, London.

Deacon, T. W. (1997) *The Symbolic Species: The Co-evolution of Language and the Brain.* Norton, New York.

Deacon, T. W. (2003) Multilevel selection in a complex adaptive system: the problem of language origins. In B. Weber and D. Depew (eds) *Evolution and Learning: The Baldwin Effect Reconsidered.* MIT Press, Cambridge, MA.

Dessalles, J.-L. (2000) Language and hominid politics. In C. Knight, J. Hurford and M. Studdert-Kennedy (eds) *The Evolutionary Emergence of Language: Social Function and the Origins of Linguistic Form.* Cambridge University Press, Cambridge, MA.

Dunbar, R. (1993) Co-evolution of neocortex size, group size and language in humans. *Behavioral and Brain Sciences,* 16: 681–735.

Fitch, W. T. (2000) The evolution of speech: a comparative review. *Trends in Cognitive Sciences,* 4: 258–267.

Fitch, W. T. and Hauser, M. (2004) Computational constraints on syntactic processing in a nonhuman primate. *Science,* 303: 377–380.

Fitch, W. T., Hauser, M. and Chomsky, N. (2005) The evolution of the language faculty: clarifications and implications. *Cognition,* 97: 179–210.

Hauser, M., Chomsky, N. and Fitch, W. T. (2002) The faculty of language: what is it, who has it, and how did it evolve? *Science,* 298:1569–1579.

Hockett, C. (1960) The origin of speech. *Scientific American,* 203: 88–96.

Holy, T. E. and Guo, Z. (2005) Ultrasonic songs of male mice. *PLOS Biology,* 3: e386.

Hurford, J. (2000) Social transmission favours linguistic generalization. In C. Knight, J. R. Hurford and M. Studdert-Kennedy (eds) *The Evolutionary Emergence of Language: Social Function and the Origins of Linguistic Form,* pp. 324–352. Cambridge University Press, Cambridge.

Hurford, J., Studdert-Kennedy, M. and Knight, C. (eds) (1998) *Approaches to the Evolution of Language: Social and Cognitive Bases.* Cambridge University Press, Cambridge.

Jackendoff, R. (1999) Possible stages in the evolution of the language capacity. *Trends in Cognitive Sciences,* 3: 272–279.

Jackendoff, R. and Pinker, S. (2005) The nature of the language faculty and its implications for evolution of language (reply to Fitch, Hauser and Chomsky, 2005). *Cognition,* 97: 211–225.

Jarvis, E. (2004) Learned birdsong and the neurobiology of human language. *Annals of the New York Academy of Sciences,* 1016: 749–777.

Kaminski, J., Call, J. and Fischer, J. (2004) Word learning in a domestic dog: Evidence for fast mapping. *Science,* 304: 1682–1683.

Kirby, S. (1999) *Function, Selection and Innateness: the Emergence of Language Universals.* Oxford University Press, Oxford.

Kirby, S. (2000) Syntax without natural selection: how compositionality emerges from vocabulary in a population of learners. In C. Knight, J. R. Hurford and M. Studdert-Kennedy (eds) *The Evolutionary Emergence of Language: Social Function and the Origins of Linguistic Form,* pp. 303–323. Cambridge University Press, Cambridge.

Kirby, S. (2001) Spontaneous evolution of linguistic structure: an iterated learning model of the emergence of regularity and irregularity. *IEEE Transactions on Evolutionary Computation,* 5: 102–110.

Kirby, S. (2002) Natural language from artificial life. *Artificial Life,* 8: 185–215.

Kirby, S. and Hurford, J. (1997) Learning, culture and evolution in the origin of linguistic constraints. In P. Husbands and I. Harvey (eds) *ECAL97,* pp. 493–502. MIT Press, Cambridge, MA.

Kirby, S., Smith, K. and Brighton, H. (2004) From UG to universals: linguistic adaptation through iterated learning. *Studies in Language,* 28: 587–607.

Knight, C. (1998) Ritual/speech coevolution: a solution to the problem of deception. In J. Hurford, M. Studdert-Kennedy and C. Knight (eds) *Approaches to the Evolution of Language: Social and Cognitive Bases.* Cambridge University Press, Cambridge.

Knight, C., Hurford, J. and Studdert-Kennedy, M. (eds) (2000) *The Evolutionary Emergence of Language: Social Function and the Origins of Linguistic Form.* Cambridge University Press, Cambridge.

Komarova, N. L. and Nowak, M. A. (2003) Language, learning, and evolution. In M. Christiansen and S. Kirby (eds) *Language Evolution: The States of the Art.* Oxford University Press, Oxford.

Lieberman, P., Klatt, D. and Wilson, W. (1969) Vocal tract limitations on the vowel repertoires of rhesus monkey and other nonhuman primates. *Science,* 164(3884): 1185–1187.

Maynard Smith, J. and Szathmáry, E. (1997) *The Major Transitions in Evolution.* Oxford University Press, New York.

Miller, G. (2000) *The Mating Mind: How Sexual Choice Shaped the Evolution of Human Nature.* Doubleday, New York.

Newmeyer, F. (1998) *Language Form and Language Function.* MIT Press, Cambridge, MA.

Origgi, G. and Sperber, D. (2000) Evolution, communication and the proper function of language. In P. Carruthers and A. Chamberlain (eds) *Evolution and the Human Mind: Modularity, Language and Meta-Cognition,* pp. 140–169. Cambridge University Press, Cambridge.

Parker, A. (2006) Evolution as a constraint on theories of syntax: the case against minimalism. PhD thesis, University of Edinburgh.

Pinker, S. (1995) Language acquisition. In L. Gleitman and M. Liberman (eds) *An Invitation to Cognitive Science,* 2nd edn, vol. 1, pp. 135–182. MIT Press, Cambridge, MA.

Pinker, S. and Bloom, P. (1990) Natural language and natural selection. *Behavioral and Brain Sciences,* 13: 707–784.

Pinker, S. and Jackendoff, R. (2005) The faculty of language: what's special about it? *Cognition,* 95: 201–236.

Poole, J. H., Tyack, P. L., Stoeger-Horwath, A. S. and Watwood, S. (2005) Elephants are capable of vocal learning. *Nature*, 434: 455–456.

Ritchie, G. and Kirby, S. (2007) A possible role for selective masking in the evolution of complex learned communication systems. In C. Lyon, C. Nehaniv and A. Cangelosi (eds.) *Emergence of Communication and Language*, pp. 387–402. Springer, London.

Smith, K. (2002) Natural selection and cultural selection in the evolution of communication. *Adaptive Behavior*, 10: 25–44.

Smith, K. (2006) The protolanguage debate: bridging the gap? In A. Cangelosi, A. Smith and K. Smith (eds) *The Evolution of Language: Proceedings of the 6th International Conference on the Evolution of Language*, pp. 315–322. World Scientific, Singapore.

Steels, L. (2003) Evolving grounded communication for robots. *Trends in Cognitive Sciences*, 7: 308–312.

Tallerman, M. (ed.) (2005) *Language Origins: Perspectives on Evolution*. Oxford University Press, Oxford.

Tallerman, M. (in press) Did our ancestors speak a holistic protolanguage? *Lingua*.

Turkel, W. J. (2002) The learning guided evolution of natural language. In T. Briscoe (ed.) *Linguistic Evolution through Language Acquisition: Formal and Computational Models*, Chapter 8. Cambridge University Press, Cambridge.

Van Parijs, S. M., Corkeron, P. J., Harvey, J., Hayes, S. A., Mellinger, D. K., Rouget, P. A., Thompson, P. M., Wahlberg, M. and Kovacs, K. M. (2003) Patterns in the vocalizations of male harbour seals. *Journal of the Acoustical Society of America*, 113: 3403–3410.

Wray, A. (1998) Protolanguage as a holistic system for social interaction. *Language and Communication*, 18: 47–67.

Wray, A. (ed.) (2002) *The Transition to Language*. Oxford University Press, Oxford.

Yamauchi, H. (2004) *Baldwinian Accounts of Language Evolution*. PhD thesis, University of Edinburgh.

Zuidema, W. (2003) How the poverty of the stimulus solves the poverty of the stimulus. In S. Becker and K. Obermayer (eds) *Advances in Neural Information Processing Systems 15* (*Proceedings of NIPS'02*). MIT Press, Cambridge, MA.

Index

Note: page numbers in *italics* refer to Figures and Tables.